THE FUTURE OF CITIES
AND URBAN REDEVELOPMENT

Urban Redevelopment Study

(1948-1951)

1313 EAST 60TH STREET · CHICAGO

ADMINISTRATIVE COMMITTEE

HERBERT EMMERICH
Chairman
Director, Public Administration Clearing House, Chicago

CHARLES B. BENNETT
Director of Planning, City Planning Department, Los Angeles

WALTER H. BLUCHER
Executive Director, American Society of Planning Officials, Chicago

ROBERT D. SIPPRELL *(to January 1949)* AND
JOHN M. DUCEY *(1949–51)*
Executive Directors, National Association of Housing Officials, Chicago

ERNEST J. BOHN
Director, Cleveland Metropolitan Housing Authority, and
Chairman, City Planning Commission, Cleveland

DIRECTOR

COLEMAN WOODBURY

THE FUTURE OF CITIES AND URBAN REDEVELOPMENT

By

CATHERINE BAUER

HENRY S. CHURCHILL

FRANK CLIFFE

VERNON DE MARS

RICHARD DEWEY

ARTHUR B. GALLION

VICTOR JONES

G. HOLMES PERKINS

WILLIAM L. SLAYTON

ROBERT C. WEINBERG

COLEMAN WOODBURY

Edited by

COLEMAN WOODBURY

THE UNIVERSITY OF CHICAGO PRESS

CHICAGO & LONDON

URS was made possible by a grant of $100,000 authorized in June 1948 by The Spelman Fund of New York to Public Administration Clearing House as trustee. Under the terms of the grant the study was ". . . to be conducted under the supervision of the Director of the Public Administration Clearing House, the Executive Directors of the American Society of Planning Officials and the National Association of Housing Officials, and two additional persons who shall be selected by the three above named and who shall not be employed by any of the organizations at '1313' . . ."

The University of Chicago Press, Chicago 60637
The University of Chicago Press. Ltd., London

International Standard Book Number: 0-226-90650-7

THIS VOLUME IS DEDICATED TO

CHARLES E. MERRIAM

IN GRATITUDE FOR HIS FRIENDSHIP AND

COUNSEL AND IN RECOGNITION OF HIS DISTINGUISHED

CONTRIBUTIONS, BOTH IN THOUGHT AND ACTION,

TO THE LIFE OF CITIES IN THE

UNITED STATES

PREFACE

THIS volume and its companion—*Urban Redevelopment: Problems and Practices* are the chief products of the Urban Redevelopment Study.

Quite early in its existence, the Study defined urban redevelopment rather broadly—as those policies, measures, and activities that would do away with the major forms of physical blight in cities and bring about changes in urban structure and institutions contributing to a favorable environment for a healthy civic, economic, and social life for all urban dwellers.

With this definition as a guide, the Study identified a number of subjects, problems, and issues for investigation, analysis, and discussion. These fall into three broad categories: (*a*) major operating problems and practices in local redevelopment programs, (*b*) underlying factors in urban growth and development that, more or less directly, have helped to produce the problems now faced by redevelopment agencies and on which some substantial changes in public understanding and policy would seem to be required if the long-term objectives of redevelopment are to be realized, and (*c*) certain questions of objectives and values that underlie many of the actual program and policy issues. As their titles indicate, this volume deals primarily with the second and third of these divisions of subject matter; its companion with the first. For all sections of its program, whatever their complexities, the Study has tried to define clearly the problems and issues, to show their relations to the long-term goals of redevelopment, to analyze available experience and published materials, at some points to recommend policies and procedures and, at others, to suggest further inquiries and research.

Throughout the Study, the emphasis has been on conditions, problems, issues, and possibilities primarily in urban communities of this country. Although many of the issues and potentialities of urban redevelopment cannot be confined to municipal or even metropolitan areas, relatively little attention has been given here to policies and programs of federal or state governments. Of course, federal and state responsibilities in urban redevelopment are substantial and their programs deserve analysis and review. It seems quite likely, however, that these matters will not be ignored. Besides, URS' agenda was put together before most of the federal and state programs of grants and other aids had been in operation long enough to be studied effectively.

These reasons as well as the complex and urgent nature of many of the local questions in redevelopment seemed to justify this orientation of the Study at this time.

In general, the Study has tried to reach four groups: (1) Public officials, elected and appointed, who are in positions to influence public policies and administrative action in urban redevelopment; (2) Civic leaders and other private citizens who also are concerned with substantive issues of policy and method; (3) Prospective investors in redevelopment projects—both individuals and institutions; and (4) Professional students of urban life and institutions, in universities and elsewhere, who may be expected to contribute to the further understanding of many issues and questions in this and allied fields. Quite probably, the different parts of the Study's output will vary in interest among the members of these groups. We hope, however, that most sections will prove useful to at least many persons in all four. To this end, those chiefly responsible for the investigation and writing have tried to put their findings and conclusions in reasonably clear, nontechnical English.

When the Study was started, urban redevelopment as an organized activity in this country was in its early infancy. The major proposal for federal aid was still before the Congress and was not to be passed until about a year later. A few states and major cities had made funds available for a start. In most urban localities, however, redevelopment was only a subject of exploration and discussion among relatively small groups of officials and private citizens.

Although its start almost at the beginning of public activity in urban redevelopment gave the Study an unusual opportunity, it also posed some problems of program and procedure in addition to those that are common to all studies of urban life and affairs. The absence of any considerable body of accumulated experience that could be analyzed and compared from locality to locality aggravated the difficulties of research in some sub-areas and made it impossible in others. Several persons who could have made important contributions to the Study could not be spared from administrative and advisory jobs with federal or local agencies. Inflation also played its usual part in such matters. In these circumstances it has not been possible to cover all phases of so wide and complex a public-private undertaking nor to treat definitely any segment of it.

The division of work and responsibility in URS can be stated briefly. The Administrative Committee passed upon the major objectives and formulations of the program from time to time. It reviewed and established budgets submitted by the Director. Its members also read and criticized drafts of most of the sections but are not responsible for them—either as to content or organization. The Director, with the advice of members of the Administrative Committee and others, formulated the Study's program, made preliminary outlines of the subjects for study, made arrangements with the researchers and writers, advised with them during their work, and edited their products.

For considerable periods of time, Mr. William L. Slayton as Assistant Director of the Study and Mr. Frank Cliffe as Research Assistant were members of the full-time staff. The other contributors worked primarily on their special subjects. Several of them came to the Study's headquarters in Chicago for part of their research and writing; others worked in their own offices elsewhere. Their training, backgrounds and experience in the urban scene vary widely. Neither the Administrative Committee nor the Director, however, attempted to force conformity as to interpretation of facts or the expression of opinions and recommendations. Editorial forewords to the major divisions of this volume point out their relations to other parts of the Study, state why these subjects were thought to be significant, identify those who have written on them for URS, and emphasize any special difficulties in the inquiries undertaken.

Any sizable study carried forward in this way in a wide and ever-changing field raises the question of what to do, if anything, to keep up-to-date the descriptive parts of those sections that are completed first. Several courses of action and the pros and cons of each are fairly obvious. URS decided to make additions or revisions of this kind only for those changes that were clearly of first-rate significance to the analysis or recommendations of their sections. Any other policy would have made for delay and additional expense. Some of the sections even if revised to the day copy went to the printers might be somewhat "behind the times" when made available to readers. Finally and most importantly, the Study has tried to choose subjects of more or less enduring concern. It is not a news service about redevelopment but rather, we hope, a contribution to an understanding of some of the major issues in urban life and growth as well as a partial guide to wise public and private policy on them.

COLEMAN WOODBURY
Director, URS

CONTENTS

PART I

ESSAYS ON REDEVELOPMENT: GOALS, DESIGN, AND STRATEGY

PART II

INDUSTRIAL LOCATION AND URBAN REDEVELOPMENT

COLEMAN WOODBURY WITH THE ASSISTANCE OF FRANK CLIFFE

Contents

PART III

URBAN REDEVELOPMENT AND THE URBANITE

WILLIAM L. SLAYTON AND RICHARD DEWEY

TABLES

PART IV

LOCAL GOVERNMENT ORGANIZATION IN METROPOLITAN AREAS: ITS RELATION TO URBAN REDEVELOPMENT

VICTOR JONES

Contents

TABLES

PART V

THE BACKGROUND AND PROSPECTS OF URBAN REDEVELOPMENT IN THE UNITED STATES

COLEMAN WOODBURY

Contents

PART I

ESSAYS ON REDEVELOPMENT: GOALS, DESIGN,
AND STRATEGY

BY
CATHERINE BAUER
G. HOLMES PERKINS
HENRY S. CHURCHILL
ROBERT C. WEINBERG
ARTHUR B. GALLION
VERNON DE MARS

EDITOR'S FOREWORD

NEARLY all public issues and movements can be studied and discussed in several ways. For instance, the conditions that have led to or "produced" a recognized problem can be studied systematically, i.e., they can be carefully analyzed; earlier studies of them can be thoroughly reviewed; hypotheses on their origin and evolution (or on parts of them) can be formulated, tested, revised, rejected, or perfected; these early explanations can be used as starting points for further careful, critical work. Also, after a body of experience has accumulated on ways and means of handling the issues or problems, it, *in toto,* or more likely, in part, can be similarly dealt with. In rough, general terms this is the scientific method or attack. Beyond this, proposals for new or revised policy and action can be devised, criticized, and reshaped. These proposals may be based wholly or largely upon scientific work plus direct experience in the same or related areas. In essence, this is what is sometimes called social invention or social engineering.

Urban redevelopment certainly needs more studies and policy recommendations of these kinds. It is, however, one of many movements and problems that also need other and supplementary kinds of treatment.

Many of its difficulties and perplexities stem, partly at least, from vagueness and muddy thinking on the elusive but highly significant matters of objectives and values. Why should public authorities take a major part in the remaking of our cities? What should be the objectives or the end results of the process? Is there any basic agreement on them behind the confusion of tongues in which they usually are discussed? How can these objectives be reduced to their most simple or basic forms? Once this is done or approached, what does it mean in planning the essential methods and strategy of redevelopment programs, and the specific rebuilding projects that are important parts of them? What direct bearing, if any, do these objectives or values have on the actual procedures or processes of the work? What are the conflicts, if any, between the end values of redevelopment as a public activity and the accepted values of architects, mortgage lenders, public officials, and others who take part in the work?

Many, though not all, of these matters are outside the scope of scientific approach and method as they are usually defined. They call for other and supplementary ways of looking at and thinking about human beings and social relationships. They place a high premium on a keen but sympathetic understanding of men and their ways of life. No less do they require the insights, sensitiveness and imagination of the artist —whatever his medium or form of expression.

Finally, redevelopment sorely needs perspective, a philosophy if you will, in the sense of a deliberate continuous attempt to see things steadily and to see them whole.

Quite early in the Study, therefore, we decided to set aside one part of our undertaking for a consideration of matters and questions of these kinds. This collection of six essays is the major result of this decision and, even more importantly, of the good-will, thoughtfulness, patience, and perception of Miss Bauer and Messrs. Churchill, De Mars, Gallion, Perkins, and Weinberg. We are indeed grateful to each of them for his contribution to the common cause.

URS' good fortune in this part of its program is shown both by the essays themselves and by a quick glance at the background and experience of those who wrote them:

Catherine Bauer, in private life Mrs. William W. Wurster, is one of America's best known and most influential critics of urban housing, planning, and development. Her *Modern Housing* is one of the most widely read works in the field both here and abroad. She is vice-president of the National Housing Conference and a member of the advisory committee of the Division of Slum Clearance and Urban Redevelopment, HHFA. She has taught at Harvard and the University of California.

G. Holmes Perkins is dean of the School of Fine Arts at the University of Pennsylvania. For some years before taking this position he was Norton Professor of Regional Planning at Harvard. He also has practiced architecture, taught it at Harvard, served on the staff of the National Housing Agency during World War II, and was a consultant on city planning to the British Ministry of Town and Country Planning.

Henry S. Churchill has an active and varied practice in architecture and city planning with offices in New York City. He has lectured at several universities and has written *The City Is the People* as well as many articles. He is a Fellow of the American Institute of Architects and a member of the American Institute of Planners.

Robert C. Weinberg also is a New York architect and city planner. Besides this practice he has been a staff member of the official city planning commissions of New York and Cleveland and of the New England office of the National Housing Agency. He is a lecturer in public administration at New York University, instructor in city planning in the New School for Social Research, and book review editor of the *Journal of American Institute of Planners*.

Arthur B. Gallion is dean of the School of Architecture at the University of Southern California. He has practiced architecture in Oakland and Berkeley, California, and has served as planner and regional director of development for the Housing Division of PWA, the United States Housing Authority, and the Federal Public Housing Authority. He is a commissioner of the Housing Authority of the County of Los Angeles. He has written *The Urban Pattern* (with Simon Eisner) and various articles for architectural journals.

Vernon De Mars is an architect now practicing in California where he is also a lecturer in architecture at the University of California and a consultant to the Redevelopment Agency of the City and County of San Francisco. He was an architect for the Farm Security Administration in the West, chief of the Housing Standards Section of the National Housing Agency, and a visiting professor in architecture at the Massachusetts Institute of Technology.

Each of the writers of these essays worked almost entirely on his own. The essays were written in the individuals' homes or offices with only rather general written suggestions from URS as to their character and none as to their specific content. None of the essayists saw any of the other pieces in the section before sending in his own. Naturally on several points they differ among themselves and with other parts of the Study.

After the proposal for these essays was in outline form, Holmes Perkins undertook to arrange for and to edit the series. When he had lined up most of the essayists, his new position as dean of the School of Fine Arts at the University of Pennsylvania prevented him from carrying through on the assignment. He did, however, help materially in shaping this section and found time from his administrative duties to turn out his essay on "The Regional City." We are particularly grateful to him.

C. W.

CHAPTER I

REDEVELOPMENT: A MISFIT IN THE FIFTIES[1]

CATHERINE BAUER

THIS article reflects a viewpoint that I have argued for some years past, and which seems today more than ever to represent mere common sense deduction from the obvious facts of the times. But it is not my nature to enjoy the lonely role of Isaiah crying in the wilderness forever, and if my opinions are still shared by so few then I am ready to admit that there may be something wrong with my logic, and certainly with my persuasive powers. But I'll try once more.

There are, of course, all kinds of exceptions to the trends and attitudes here attacked: perhaps the argument would have been more convincing had they been included. But this is simply a kind of general outline, and there is a great deal of additional and impressive documentation on *my* side that was likewise omitted. Moreover, an unpopular viewpoint must be somewhat cartooned to be heard at all.

THE CURRENT OBSTACLE RACE

Why is it so hard to get the program going?—The fact that redevelopment progress is exceedingly slow need hardly be documented. Fifteen years ago when the Housing Act of 1937 was taking shape it was already clear that broader machinery for dealing with slums would ultimately be necessary. The private redevelopment corporation idea was rapidly succeeded by a wave of state enabling legislation granting broad public powers for the acquisition and redevelopment of blighted areas. The Taft report of 1945 recognized the need for federal subsidy, and after a succession of hearings and professional and congressional disputes the general Housing Act was finally passed in July, 1949, including Title I with its generous aids to facilitate proper civic development and redevelopment.

But this was more than two years ago. And today (September, 1951), although "capital grant reservations" have been made for some two hundred-odd localities, of whom forty-three have been approved for "planning advances," there is only one project actually under way.

1. Certain sections of this article have been adapted from a speech made at Vancouver, B.C., and printed in the *Community Planning Review* for August, 1951.

Why so slow? After all, there is a long background of public concern and study in a great many cities and real consciousness of the slum problem. There has never been any organized national opposition to redevelopment, as there has been to public housing and almost every other domestic reform throughout the postwar period. And the kind of pioneering zeal that once attached to public housing is now much more evident in the redevelopment field, a fact that markedly distinguishes HHFA's Division of Slums and Urban Redevelopment from its other branches and many local redevelopment agencies from some of the housing authorities.

But to many of those concerned the program has become a kind of combination obstacle race and maze, a tortuous process of finding some feasible route in a vast dim wilderness full of uncharted hobgoblins, stumbling blocks, and divergent paths, all the time wondering if the next impediment won't be the final death-blow.

The removal and rehousing of blighted area residents, plus the question of who should live in the area after reconstruction, plunges most redevelopers into a hornet's nest of housing problems and controversies, including the over-all shortage, the resistance of families to be displaced, the public housing rows, the question of housing for middle-income and special groups, the hydra-headed issue of density and dwelling types, the quixotic complexity of private building incentives, and the mounting obstacles of high costs and emergency restrictions.

Where the housing shortage has finally forced consideration of vacant or near-vacant sites, whether for public housing or for Title I operations, there is likely to be a rather apologetic sense of failure after all the emphasis on dramatic "slum clearance" in explaining the program to prominent citizens and officials. And in any case the Washington people may be opposed. Or it may turn out that all suitable vacant sites are outside the jurisdiction of the agency concerned.

And finally, looming above all else in many local redevelopment difficulties, is the race relations question, sharpening most of the housing issues to a razor edge and forcing basic, community-wide decisions on the matter of discrimination and segregation.

It is not surprising that a great many citizens earnestly concerned about the reconstruction of blighted areas are either impatient or discouraged—impatient that so many vast and seemingly extraneous problems have to be solved along the way, or discouraged about effectuating long-term civic improvement in a period of such varied and unpredictable emergencies. There is a feeling that "if they'd only let us alone," or "if we could just get back to normal times," the program would move ahead as originally anticipated.

Well, perhaps. But there may be certain fallacies behind this view that are worth a little exploration.

THE INHERENT DIFFICULTY

Redevelopment for whom and for what?—In the first place there would have been some extremely complex problems to be resolved in connection with most local redevelopment programs under any conditions due to the varied and often conflicting interests actively concerned. One reason Title I and the state enabling acts had so little opposition is the fact that different groups of people, like the blind men feeling the elephant, made entirely different assumptions as to the essential nature and purpose of this legislation.

To the housers and social welfare groups it simply extended our power to get rid of bad living conditions and provide everyone with a decent home in a decent neighborhood. To most of those who started the "urban redevelopment" movement, however, and coined the term back in the thirties, the goals were quite different, namely, to bolster up waning property values in central areas and to devise a substitute for the Housing Act of 1937 that would facilitate slum clearance, but *without* public housing. Closely akin to the concern for central property values has been the desire of certain business interests and local officials to use redevelopment as a tool to stop decentralization and to bring back some of the substantial consumers, voters, and taxpayers who have fled to the suburbs; also the interest of big private builders in securing valuable central sites otherwise impossible to acquire and dead to profitable enterprise.

The leaders of the city planning profession had still a different idea. They saw redevelopment as the means toward more rational and efficient organization of central areas, by removing wasteful or inappropriate land uses and facilitating new development in conformance with some kind of plan for the area. For various reasons, including the desire to keep redevelopment uncontaminated by the raucous housing controversies, they too sought a program that would be set up and administered entirely apart from housing agencies and housing considerations.

All in all, quite an array of purposes for a single piece of legislation to fulfil! Seldom has such a variegated crew of would-be angels tried to sit on the same pin at the same time. As it turned out, the legislative framework reflects mainly a kind of shotgun marriage between the housers and the planners, with enough concessions to other interests to keep them reasonably hopeful and friendly. Obviously such a program is likely to be a kind of Tower of Babel in its early stages, incapable of concrete result until its inner conflicts have somehow been resolved. And this takes time and trouble.

Moreover, I think it could now fairly be claimed that all of the parties concerned tended to underestimate the full responsibilities and implications of the job. To remove by force the people, buildings, homes, and businesses from a large, long-established area, and to decide what should be put there instead, is no casual undertaking. Spot treatment won't take care of it, however earnestly applied. For it is a major social-economic operation, which affects not only the people who use the neighborhood before and after, but ultimately the whole pattern of population distribution and functional organization of an urban region. And to perform this operation successfully it is not sufficient merely to have proved the existence of slums and blight statistically, figured out some more attractive or profitable use for the area, and devised some reasonably humanitarian solution for displaced families. Basic and far-reaching decisions are involved at every step, decisions that few cities have faced up to as yet. These decisions require some defensible hypotheses, at least, on such large questions as the way people want to live, the proper relation between homes and work places, whether a "neighborhood" plan should promote or combat segregation, the future function of the city center *in re* the surrounding region, and all the other issues that arise from the trend toward urban decentralization.

But even the planners, with all their demand for "flexibility" and "master plans," were on the whole as blind as any other group to the larger issues bound to be raised by a redevelopment program. And a large part of the delay is because some of these questions *have* come up, inescapably, and have had to be answered one way or another, however inadequate the guiding philosophy and the administrative machinery. In some ways the laggard production statistics are a healthy sign. Had we moved as fast as we thought we could, the next generation might have inherited a whole flock of Stuyvesant Towns.

In addition to the inherent reasons for slow progress in redevelopment, however, there are certainly a number of obvious and serious obstacles resulting directly from special present-day conditions. And the question is: Should we continue to try to ignore these obstacles, or battle them head-on? Or must redevelopment wait on the sidelines for better days? Or do the peculiar conditions created by the current emergency, e.g., the chronic housing shortage, and the emphasis on decentralization, merely dramatize the basic limitations of the Title I program and force, at long last, a broader approach to the problems of civic planning, development, and redevelopment?

CIVIC PROGRESS AND "EMERGENCIES"

The responsibility of leadership.—Doubtless the housers, planners, redevelopers, and other reformers of all ages have longed for peace and quiet and orderly progress toward the Good Life. But the fact is that their major opportunities have often come during hectic periods of crisis.

More than a century ago it was mainly the international epidemics of cholera and revolution in the Hungry Forties that induced the British to adopt the great Public Health Act of 1848, certainly one of the foundation stones of modern social and civic planning, and as a corollary the first piece of national housing legislation in 1851. In some ways these "emergency" measures were actually in advance of the scientific developments that later proved how essential they were, yet they laid the basis for one of the fundamental planning concepts of modern democracies: that it is in the public interest to insure minimum standards of social welfare for all citizens.

And from that time to this any history of the housing movement would unavoidably focus itself around the achievements called forth by successive crises of one sort or another. Within our own era the chapter heads might well read: World War I, Postwar Shortage I, The Crash, The Depression, World War II, and Postwar Crisis II. For even our long-term gains in housing policy and practice have almost invariably resulted from some particular set of emergency needs and conditions.

Perhaps a history of city planning would show a more rational and orderly development, less subject to the whim of fate and extraneous emergency, but I doubt it. Such catastrophes as fire, earthquake, and war devastation probably played a major role in city planning progress from the beginning of time, while the planning function in American city government was transformed and strengthened by the depression, as Walker pointed out, and the vast population shifts called forth by the war added another chapter.

This is not to suggest, however, that the "challenge of adversity" makes progress either automatic or easy. But a crisis that affects the conditions of living and social-economic organization is likely to do two things that have great potential significance for those who are concerned with improving the civic environment. It forces change, whether for better or worse, and often requires unprecedented action. And it may dramatize certain basic, long-standing problems in a way that clarifies them in the public mind and gives them here-and-now urgency.

As John Gaus pointed out about public policy in general: "Catastrophe, especially when leadership and knowledge are prepared with long-time programs into which the immediate hurried relief action can be fitted, has its place in the ecology of administration. It not only is destructive, so that relief and repair are required on a scale so large that collective action is necessary, but it also disrupts, jostles or challenges views and attitudes, and affords the inner self as well as others a respectable face-saving reason for changing one's views as to policy. The atomic bomb gave to many, perhaps, a determining reason for a change of attitude toward international organization."[2] Might it not also help us to face the facts of life about one of the basic questions that confront planners and housers, and redevelopers, namely decentralization?

But, of course, all such opportunities are double-edged. The atomic bomb also intensified hysterical isolationism in some quarters. The misery and social unrest that induced the British a century ago to attack sanitation and housing produced only a refinement of suppressive military measures in some other countries. And the bombing of London during the last war *might* have called forth mainly a crop of congested skyscrapers back of St. Paul's instead of the most enlightened urban planning policy extant.

Whether or not the opportunities for civic progress presented by a crisis are effectively grasped depends on a great many subtle factors and forces. Probably indispensable, however, is a combination of political and professional leadership qualities among those who set themselves up as the responsible experts in this complicated field. On the one hand they must be extremely sensitive to immediate needs, hopes, attitudes, and possibilities, and adaptable to changing conditions. But on the other hand they must have the sureness that comes from basic knowledge and compelling goals, and persuasive awareness of how immediate action to fit the emergency can produce permanent benefit.

Are American planners and housers providing this kind of leadership as the country faces the peculiarly critical conditions of the 1950's?

SLUM CLEARANCE

The wrong handle for this emergency.—Some may feel that this suggests a rather ignominious and opportunist role for the experts on human environment, trimming their sails to whatever storms may brew and often making some entirely different port from that originally charted. And they may feel very sincerely that the prime responsibility of those concerned with the redevelopment and public housing pro-

2. John Gaus, *Reflections on Public Administration* (University of Alabama Press, 1947), pp. 16–17.

grams is not to swerve with the times, but to stick by the original goal through thick and thin, in order to keep alive the real spark of civic hope for ultimate slum riddance that the movement has managed to kindle.

This viewpoint must be respected: certainly we must do what we can about the slums under any and all conditions. The case would be stronger, however, if the "redevelopment" idea had ever really reflected a coherent positive program for civic improvement, or even just for better living conditions. But as a matter of fact the philosophy expressed in the present program is hardly more than a collection of varied (and often inconsistent) arguments for negative action, "clearance," and most of these arguments were so directly geared to the particular depression conditions from which they sprang that they have lost much of their validity in the opposite conditions of today.

During most of the 1930's, the vacancy rate in slum areas and elsewhere was quite high, property prices were extraordinarily low as were building costs, and any and all forms of building activity were desirable to counter unemployment. It would have been the ideal time to engage in wholesale clearance and reconstruction.

But now—and indeed, ever since wartime—every one of these conditions is reversed, with the result that any former argument for a vast program of civic betterment geared almost exclusively to clearance operations is immeasurably weakened. No wonder it is so difficult! And no wonder it tends to produce some strange results.

For now we have a housing shortage that bids fair to be chronic, and automatically cancels most of the social arguments for slum clearance until the supply of low-rent homes available elsewhere has been enormously increased. Slums are full and profitable, which means that they are expensive and difficult to acquire. High building costs and mounting restrictions due to defense requirements are serious obstacles, particularly for the type of construction usually required in central areas. And finally there is the added push toward decentralization and dispersal which, even at this tentative stage in defense policy, certainly renders questionable any program that tends mainly to result in high-density construction in the middle of the most congested urban areas.

Meanwhile, the "emergency" need and the big opportunity lay elsewhere. Throughout the postwar period, with its vast inevitable suburban building boom, the key issue for long-term civic progress was the proper planning of *outlying* development, bound to go ahead anyway for better or worse, rather than central clearance. It was the chance of our lifetime to tackle the vast, vague issues of metropolitan and regional organization, to preserve open spaces before they were gobbled up forever, and to guide the standardized speculative sprawl into properly planned communities serving varied needs and functions. It would have meant transforming the "redevelopment" idea from a limited, confused, and negative concept, focused solely on central districts, into a positive over-all philosophy and guiding mechanism for urban and regional development, in which clearance and *re*construction would be an essential tool, to be employed in relation to broader goals and other measures. But we didn't do it. And now that the "postwar period" has passed into another "defense emergency," the new set of conditions merely makes our failure the more tragic and the need for basic changes in our viewpoint and strategy the more urgent.

The notion that such a transformation might actually have been made is no mere *post facto* theorizing. For after all, it *was* done in Britain. Of course, every country and even every community has its own peculiar dynamics in such matters, and there are some historic factors in the English scene that may have favored the sudden emergence of a mature and integrated policy for housing, planning, development, and redevelopment. Up to the war, however, they had proceeded no further than we had with city and regional planning, except for longer experience with public housing and a handful of private community experiments. In the latter thirties they were equally concentrated on slum clearance and central redevelopment. And the natural emotional reaction to wartime devastation in these same central areas would have given them a much better excuse than we had to focus their postwar energies on reconstruction at the expense of the larger urban issues. Moreover, while they did the planning we did the building that needed the planning, because they could not devote anything like the volume of labor and materials to new construction that we have, who tossed some five million dwellings helter-skelter into the suburbs in little more than five years.

The postwar political climate in Britain, it will be said, is very different from that in America. But as far as land and city planning policy are concerned, it seems pretty clear from the legislative record that the Tories would have adopted much the same principles and program as Labour, had they been in power. And even here in these conservative United States, we have persuaded the people to give us substantial powers and funds in order, we promised, to improve cities and living conditions. If the legislation was too narrow to fit current needs and conditions, or is not being used in the most effective way, should we blame those whom we ourselves persuaded that it would do the job?

THE FAILURE TO BROADEN THE PROGRAM

A little history for the record.—The fact that we find ourselves, like Epaminondas in the old story, trying to attack current problems with the methods designed for an entirely different situation, is perhaps worth delving into some not too ancient history. In the first place, the movement for housing reform in America, in any effective political sense, was a creature of the depression. On the one hand, the building industry had to be stimulated somehow, and on the other, the WPA surveys shocked the country into recognizing the extent and degredation of our slums and the impossibility of dealing with them without drastic public action. Thus was born the Housing Act of 1937.

By emphasizing the civic and economic as well as the social aspects of "blight," the city planners broadened the concept of the slum problem and laid the basis for "redevelopment." But still the economic arguments of the depression were paramount. It would "save" the bankrupt cities, provide employment, stimulate private as well as public investment.

Then came the war, and along with the succession of wartime housing crises, there was almost immediately a great deal of earnest concern about "postwar planning"—perhaps almost as much as there was in England. But the best of us, from economists and politicians to housers and city planners, were still thoroughly imbued with a depression viewpoint. The Senate hearings and reports of 1945 and 1946, which laid the basis for the policy that was finally enacted in the Housing Act of 1949, faithfully reflect the viewpoint of the time: that housing and redevelopment were essentially a means of achieving certain permanent social and civic benefits via national policy to promote employment and stable prosperity. In other words, they were among the various worthy tails attached to the kite of a particular set of emergency conditions which, as it turned out, were not the conditions we actually confronted.

This is no Jovian critique of the failings of others: I shared the general views. Moreover, we might well have had a depression and in any case no one could possibly have predicted the exact situation we now find ourselves in. But there may be some lesson here for future planners nonetheless. Perhaps long-term plans for civic or other improvement, and the machinery for executing such plans, should be designed so broadly and flexibly that they can achieve progress under varying future conditions.

And we can be blamed for failing to take the inevitable postwar housing shortage fully into account. By our own statistics it was bound to be extremely acute as soon as the veterans began to return, irrespective of economic conditions, and we should have been able to foresee some of its implications for housing policy and civic development. It was this failure that explained (if it did not justify) the shelving of the General Housing Bill during the Wyatt era, in favor of hastily concocted "emergency" measures of doubtful long-term value, to say the least. And it is the possibility of a similar situation today that suggests the danger of losing our slum clearance program entirely, unless we can manage to adapt it to current needs . . . in time.

There were, of course, some sporadic efforts to broaden postwar purpose and policy, but on the whole they made little dent in the prevailing slum-mindedness of housing and planning leadership. Back in 1942, the Urban Land Institute's initial "Outline for a Legislative Program to Rebuild our Cities" was in some ways an exceedingly bold proposal. The liberals might well have borrowed some of its ideas on the scope of the problem. In the same year Frederick Babcock, reflecting the viewpoint of certain business interests, was making speeches complaining that "the objectives of urban redevelopment" were too limited, weak, and nostalgic, and that instead of exclusive emphasis on *re*building we should be planning for decentralization and a dynamic pattern of new communities. And the California Housing and Planning Association was saying that *"Re*-development absolutely requires on the other side of the coin, coordinated control of the development of vacant land on the outskirts."

By 1946, when the shortage had struck in full force, there were a few more of us. And the great nation-wide wave of interest in co-operative community development, initially sparked by the CIO and swelled by unified veteran and labor support, provided spontaneous popular evidence of the needs and possibilities of the times—alas, almost wholly frustrated for the lack of a policy framework to aid and guide such projects.

Early in 1948, the President's Economic Report to Congress recognized in general terms the needs for integrating new community development and broader planning with central reconstruction, and the "Housing Program for Now and Later," issued by a joint committee of the National Association of Housing Officials and the National Housing Conference, spelled out the necessity for such a policy in more detail. Later in the same year a joint committee representing the American Institute of Architects, American Institute of Planners, American Society of Civil Engineers, American Society of Landscape Architects, and the American Society of Planning Officials, drafted a bill to set up an Urban Land Administration, which would have aided and encouraged local public agencies to acquire necessary vacant as well as blighted sites on an equal basis, and promoted unified regional plans for development and redevelopment. This bill was never actively indorsed or pushed by the professional organizations, however, and no effort was made to co-operate with the housers who were doing the serious legislative work and had powerful public support.

The Federal Works Agency, in its unsuccessful effort to outbid the

Housing Agency for jurisdiction over urban redevelopment, experimented with the idea of promoting federal aid for satellite communities. The housers were properly suspicious of any FWA proposal, but this undoubtedly contributed to the revision of Title I.

And finally in the 81st Congress, following the recommendation of the Senate Banking and Currency Committee and in recognition of shortage conditions and possible defense needs, the scope and language of Title I were somewhat broadened. "Redevelopment" became "development and redevelopment"; "open" and "predominantly open" sites were recognized as eligible for certain types of aid, as well as deteriorated areas; an admirably positive "Declaration of National Policy" was included; and some rather vague instructions to encourage planning on a unified metropolitan or regional basis were tacked on. This move was largely the result of effort and testimony from the National Housing Conference, the Regional Plan Association of New York, the Westchester County Planning Commission, and the city of Milwaukee, the only city in the country with positive public plans and policy for satellite community development.

In actual administrative practice, however, this broader language has largely been ignored. The Agency's lawyers have consistently interpreted Title I as narrowly as possible, and the "Manual of Policies and Requirements" recognizes open and predominantly open sites only when they can be proved to be absolutely necessary adjuncts to a specific slum clearance program. And even in such cases, local agencies are actively discouraged from leaving the straight and narrow path, although a few cities like San Francisco, with inlying vacant areas of arrested development, have managed to persist. But perhaps the most inexcusable failure of the Agency has been the lack of any effort whatever to aid or encourage the broadening of state-enabling legislation to conform to Title I, and thus permit local agencies to take full advantage of its provisions.

It would doubtless be argued by the Agency that this line has been followed solely in order to protect the program, on the grounds that Congress and the public expect slum clearance and only slum clearance, from Title I. To the extent that this is true, however, it is solely because 99 per cent of our promotional and educative efforts have been devoted to selling slum clearance, and only slum clearance, and incidentally promising a great many benefits that such a program cannot possibly deliver, particularly today. If we had spent even *half* of our time and energy explaining why present-day conditions necessitate a more flexible and comprehensive approach to community improvement, I think we would have won more interest and support than we lost. And there would be far less danger of losing the hard-won gains of the Housing Act of 1949 altogether, while adopting a new series of hasty, half-baked "emergency" measures.

SOME STRANGE RESULTS

The price of pushing against the times.—Trying to do the right thing at the wrong time is likely to result in a long chain of rationalizations which, after infinite trouble to all concerned, may only produce the wrong thing after all. And pushing demolition in the midst of a housing shortage has tended all too frequently to follow this pattern.

A severe shortage of homes is a many-sided evil. It harms family life, restricts freedom and mobility, puts people at the mercy of exploitive landlords and builders, hits low-income families the hardest and those with children hardest of all, prevents the enforcement of standards, and necessitates controls that disrupt the economy and are almost impossible to administer justly. The only way to overcome a shortage is to increase the total supply of dwellings available in all price ranges as rapidly as possible. To justify a demolition policy under such conditions is difficult, but it was argued that the program was so small in relation to quantitative housing needs, or to the demolition caused by highways and public works, that it would not really make much difference; that clearance would start slowly in any case; and that the shortage would be solved pretty soon anyway.

But it has not been so simple in practice. The families scheduled for removal were not interested in long-term statistical logic; they simply wanted to be sure of a place to live here and now, and often they were deeply attached to the area. If they belonged to a minority group they naturally were even more fearful. And the immediate reaction to redevelopment plans in many localities was a wave of hostility and resistance that alienated much popular and political support.

These difficulties had some good results. They demonstrated that the redevelopment program was dealing first and foremost with people— their likes, dislikes, needs, and the pattern of their daily lives—and not just with old buildings and "nonconforming uses." They also forced public recognition of the extent and effect of racial discrimination. But these achievements were made at a heavy price.

To meet public pressures as well as to conform with the law, complicated machinery has been set up to uncover vacancies and "relocate" people elsewhere, often in public housing to whatever extent may be feasible. And this has had the salutary effect of converting many redevelopment supporters to the need for public housing. But at the same time it must be pointed out that when a local housing authority systematically reserves all vacancies for families displaced by clearance operations, the public housing program is contributing nothing whatever to solving the basic shortage of low-rent homes, nor is it serving in-migrants who may be necessary to defense activities. Although of course the problem of rehousing minority families satisfactorily has special ramifications, including the whole segregation question, that are not so readily solved even in a superficial sense.

And now the defense restrictions on building probably mean a chronic housing shortage for an indefinite period to come in most urban areas, particularly for lower-income families. How then is clearance justified?

The answer is, "Demonstrations," ltmited examples of what must be done on a much larger scale when conditions permit. And this might be a very good answer indeed. Some tangible, enduring models of really pleasant, well-planned neighborhoods in the middle of our cities—of opening up congested central areas to provide the kind of living conditions that most American families want—would make up for a great many difficulties and inconsistencies along the way. But alas, despite the substantial subsidies made available for both public housing and redevelopment, in large part for the purpose of reducing congestion, present conditions seem all too often to promote densities and dwelling types difficult to justify in terms of any responsible urban land-use plan.

Why such a strange result? For one thing, slums are full and profitable today and few owners have the enthusiasm for being bailed out that they had fifteen years ago, with the result that central property is abnormally expensive. Q.E.D., either exorbitant subsidy, *or* less land per home. Then there is that bright idea conceived and applied with such monumental enterprise in New York that it has been grasped with gratitude and enthusiasm all across the country, namely, that the way to do central clearance and redevelopment today, and at the same time help solve the housing shortage, is to double or treble the densities in blighted areas.

The ultimate effects of such a policy might have been more seriously questioned, however, had it not been for a widespread delusion fostered by the times. Back in the thirties a great many cities were beginning to recognize, however painfully, the drastic implications of metropolitan expansion and decentralization for old congested areas. But today, although the long-term trends are as strong as ever, the facts of life are obscured by the housing shortage. The cities are overcrowded and booming, property values and tax income are high, and property owners, builders, investors, and city officials have drowned their healthy fears in a new wave of optimism. Even many planners and housers seem to have forgotten that, sooner or later, central districts must be able to compete successfully with outlying communities in the quality of living they offer.

As a result of the high densities favored by these combined influences (aided and abetted by the surprisingly numerous architects with a curious technocratic mania for skyscrapers à la Corbusier), there has been a sudden transcontinental rash of elevator apartments. This is particularly evident today in public housing, which is somewhat farther along than the Title I program, and the trend is particularly indefensible in the case of projects destined primarily for low-income families with children, who would probably live more happily and healthily in the most modest shacks than in the fanciest skyscrapers. But there is no reason to suppose that similar conditions will not produce similar results in the private redevelopment program. And while there is undoubtedly a case for some high apartment buildings to serve certain special groups, particularly single workers and adult families, this demand is probably quite limited particularly at the prices likely to be asked.

For one thing we cannot possibly demonstrate in such a program under present conditions is low costs or low "economic" rents. All building costs are high, but the price of the first-class fireproof construction required in "high rise" buildings is relatively far greater than that of small frame houses, a fact that is beginning to cause the Public Housing Administration and some local authorities considerable trouble as they try to justify high buildings that, to simpler minds, seem eminently unsuited to their purpose in any case. And the gap will only be widened by restrictions on critical materials. The small home builders have been managing (with extra favors from the federal government it is true) to serve a certain proportion of middle-income families, but there is little evidence that apartment developers can reach this group except perhaps through some special form of encouragement for co-operatives not now available.

Have I cartooned this unhappy chain of cause and effect? At least there are enough concrete examples in support of my argument to point the dangers of the present course. But the ultimate price of sticking to a narrow formula that does not fit the times is not only the danger of losing, or compromising, the very thing we are trying so desperately to save, namely the hopes and machinery embodied in the 1949 Act. Like the timid brother who hid his talent, we may at the same time be losing out on much greater opportunities.

THE CHALLENGE OF PRESENT-DAY CONDITIONS

The peculiar quality of the present emergency, by comparison with the long succession of varied crises our generation has already managed to survive, is the practical certainty that it will continue in one form or another for a long time to come. There may or may not be a sudden all-out conflict, but there is very little chance of any sudden all-out peace within the visible future.

And the shifting uncertainties of chronic half-war create new problems on the domestic front that are just now becoming rather painfully apparent. We have to be ready to confront extreme emergency at any time, but we do not want to subject ourselves unnecessarily to the rigid controls of a military economy, above all for a period of indefinite duration. And it is therefore current national policy to endeavor to increase production to a point where military and foreign requirements, and most civilian needs, can *both* be served.

But this takes planning: planning to keep the basic economy and social morale healthy despite unavoidable strain; planning to meet potential emergencies without all the waste and disruption that usually accompany emergency programs, because we simply cannot afford such waste in a defense period that might continue for decades; planning, wherever possible, to solve immediate problems in such a way that long-term progress is enhanced rather than hindered. Indeed, perhaps the basic problem for our entire civilization in a period of successive and mounting emergencies is whether or not we can manage to do more than merely survive from one to the next.

Here is a major test for the whole principle of democratic planning: can common sense, enlightened co-operation, and trained foresight actually do a job that otherwise requires total control from the top down? And there is no aspect of domestic policy for which this challenge has more positive implications than for the network of acivities that deal with physical environment: housing, city and regional planning, community and resource development, transportation and public works. This important segment of our national economy not only directs the utilization of a major share of the available supply of labor, materials, and credit. It is also largely subject to public control or guidance already through an established machinery for federal and local, and public and private, collaboration. And this should make it much more readily "plannable," at least in theory, than many other aspects of our social economy.

Moreover most of the decisions about land use, building, communication, and functional organization that are the province of public and private agencies in this field are inherently double-edged in their effect. They not only have direct here-and-now significance for productive efficiency, civilian morale, and defense strategy: they also produce permanent material results that will affect our daily lives, and the structure of our communities for years to come. Once made, these decisions cannot easily be undone; they are part of our environment.

Whatever we can do, therefore, to make building and civic development serve both immediate and long-term ends satisfactorily, will be a major contribution to the national welfare. As the Board of the National Housing Conference recently put it, this "doesn't mean killing off normal home production, and then suddenly jumping into some kind of planless, wasteful, last-minute 'emergency' program of direct Federal construction. It means adapting the normal home building machinery to present requirements." And it does not mean tossing "slum clearance" on the scrap heap, but expanding and adapting the redevelopment program to serve current needs and broader ends, while continuing to clear blighted areas wherever such projects can be fitted in successfully.

Important lessons were learned in the last war that provide some useful ABC's for today. These include the fact that speculative builders can supply only part of the housing needs of industrial workers; that any necessary public housing should be built and managed by local agencies in so far as possible; that "temporary" home construction is wasteful; that adequate community facilities are essential to worker and family morale; and that long-distance commuting makes for high turnover and inefficiency. Some of these lessons, despite their axiomatic nature, have been forgotten in the flood of the postwar boom; perhaps now we can begin to profit by them once more. If we used these principles to assure well-planned, well-equipped permanent communities located in some sensible relationship to places of employment, and including homes built by private builders, co-ops, and public agencies to meet a wide range of needs, we would make a more enduring contribution to long-term civic improvement than was achieved by the entire postwar boom.

But there are also some issues of new and crucial significance in the housing and planning field today. They are all old problems, long awaiting solution, but they have never before been posed with such urgency, or with such a real chance for effective solution.

Race relations: a chance for planners to help save democracy.—To some future historian the most significant fact about housing and city planning policy in the United States in our time may be the extent to which it promoted racial integration or, conversely, strengthened the pattern of discrimination and segregation.

A number of forces have combined to make race relations an inescapable issue in our field of activities and responsibility. For some time there has been rapid movement of Negroes from rural areas to industrial cities, and from South to North. This migration has tended to result in certain marked improvements in their economic condition and educational opportunities and in their political status and acumen. But it brought no such progress in their housing situation, which was frequently worse than ever. In a severe housing shortage they were the latest comers, which meant doubling up in the cast-offs. Moreover fear and prejudice were greatly sharpened by the shortage, with the result that all the barriers to normal movement were enormously strengthened. And Negroes began to look to political action as the only possible solution of their housing problem and the only insurance of improved social status.

Meanwhile it became apparent that there was no neutral course, no "safe" middle ground, for housing and planning policy, particularly for public housing and redevelopment in northern cities. When a large area is cleared or developed by public action, with public subsidy and according to a public plan, there is clear-cut public responsibility for the social effects. The displaced minority families are either better off or worse off afterward. And the new housing is either segregated or nonsegregated.

The political trend in the North seems to point inevitably toward nonsegregation as a firm public policy. The successful experience with "open" public housing in such pioneering cities as New York, Seattle, and Pittsburgh is rapidly inducing other localities to follow their example. The current battle-line centers around private redevelopment projects, where New York has already pointed the way and San Francisco may soon follow. And federal court decisions are raising the question for private housing in general.

In the South there is increasingly conscious use of housing policy to improve race relation per se as well as physical living conditions. Indeed, if "progress" means improvement from a former situation, there is probably far greater net progress in the housing condition of Negroes in the South than in the North.

This nation-wide trend is by no means solely the result of the rising demand by minority racial groups for first-class citizenship. Nor will its effects be felt solely in our domestic race relations. It is the international situation that has sharpened our conscience and made us more willing to listen to the demands. And it is in our crucial relationship to the colored peoples of the world that the results of our domestic policies will ultimately be tested.

Public housing experience has already punctured some hoary fallacies. Documented by unimpeachable research, it has proved that for low-income families in northern cities, at least, living together tends to improve interracial attitudes rather than otherwise, particularly if the pattern is entirely free, totally disregarding color or race distinctions. And if the current difficulties do not stop the redevelopment program entirely, it may produce some extremely valuable demonstrations of racial integration in private developments as well. But such progress would probably be far less difficult, on the whole, if we were focusing our attention on entirely *new* communities, instead of clearance projects.

Decentralization: a key planning issue posed at last.—"Dispersal" has been a front-page defense issue for some time, but it would be much less confused and controversial if those who handle housing and planning policy had taken a more active and responsible part in the arguments.

The military and scientific authorities apparently all agree that space and decongestion are major defense weapons in modern warfare. But how to achieve such a pattern is quite another matter. Some demand the most drastic and expensive kind of all-out federal initiative. Some think it cannot be done in time or at all or without paying too great a price. And in between there are limited programs like the National Security Resources Board's active effort to promote the "deployment" of new industries to open areas, or the General Services Administration's proposal to locate vast new federal office buildings outside Washington proper, in both cases without serious attention to related matters such as housing, communications, protective open space, etc.

A number of private individuals have expounded the problem and the possibilities with real knowledge and vision, and much more fully than I can here. But it comes down to the following ABC's: that forces promoting urban decentralization are extremely powerful anyway, quite apart from military necessity; that they reflect healthy trends at base but now mainly result in sprawling chaos and insoluble traffic problems, inimical alike to military and civic efficiency; that they could be guided without great difficulty, however, into a pattern of balanced, reasonably self-sufficient communities with open space between, and that this is what we ought to be doing anyway; that congested central areas could be thinned out by the same process, and large open spaces introduced, which would likewise bring permanent benefit as well as immediate protection; and that our ordinary rate of residential and industrial development, highway construction, and population mobility is so high that considerable change could be effected in the land-use pattern within a very few years without using additional resources.

It is a strong case, and it would be a big job. But it would not require any formidable degree of direct federal initiative or ruthless "emergency" powers (as has sometimes too readily been assumed) if we set out to adapt all our existing machinery for housing, planning, and civic development to this end as thoroughly as possible. The "open land" provisions of Title I could be a key tool, as soon as suitable state, metropolitan, or county agencies were available to initiate the development of new communities on open land in suitable locations. And this would certainly be done very promptly in a great many localities if the national defense authorities asked it, and the Housing Agency helped show the way.

But no such effort is being made, least of all by the federal officials who would have to provide the necessary bridge between national defense policy and local action. Instead, what do we have? More skyscrapers than ever out of PHA, and the ultimate irony of the Agency's administration of Title I. All policy statements are now studded with pious instructions to adapt the program to defense needs, but meanwhile policy itself excludes more rigidly than ever the very kind of project most likely to fit defense conditions and requirements. While on the other hand, despite all we learned so painfully in the last war, the new Defense Housing Act contains the threat, however small as yet, or another federal "emergency" program, entirely divorced from the responsible, experienced framework for housing, planning, and community development.

Local initiative: now is the time.—As long as federal leadership is so weak, the responsibility for shaping a program suited to the needs and opportunities of the times is wholly with private and professional groups, and perhaps most of all with local agencies. But this is not too much to expect: after all, the planning commission, the housing authority, the redevelopment agency, and significant regional bodies like the port authority, were all invented at the local level. And what is needed today is little more than an extension of the jurisdiction of such agencies to permit them to deal effectively with regional land-use problems related to defense needs, including land-acquisition for new communities. And there are a great many current local efforts that point the way: in Milwaukee's program to purchase and annex land for a complete satellite community; in the New York State proposal to establish a state agency for community development in outlying areas; and in the numerous revitalized efforts, in Washington, D.C., and elsewhere, to achieve effective regional or metropolitan planning.

The all-important factor in planning progress is obvious, concrete, immediate needs that clarify larger problems and issues in the public mind. And if we grasp the right handles today, the 1950's can provide the essential milieu for transforming the urban redevelopment movement from a narrow and largely frustrated reform effort into a positive philosophy and effective machinery for long-term community and regional development—including redevelopment.

CHAPTER II

THE REGIONAL CITY

G. Holmes Perkins

Neither fire, nor earthquake, nor the V-1 bomb has deterred man in his urge to build. Cities thrive upon adversity and after each catastrophe rise Phoenix-like from the ashes with ever gayer plumage. Nor has the prospect of worse to come cut down the stream of immigrants headed for the metropolis. Each successive census hurls the lie in the teeth of those prophets of doom who have for generations predicted the decline and twilight of our cities.

There continue to be such overpowering attractions in the city life that we are willing though reluctant to pay the pyramiding costs of public services and fantastic expenditures for roads and subways. To taste its pleasures we endure years of discomfort and exhaustion in commuting and put up with the social maladjustments of our conurbations. But irritations however small at first can, if unguarded against, become diseases that can lead to tragedy. If we are to reverse the trend which makes the city constantly more expensive to operate, more parasitic and ever more destructive of the family we must identify with utmost clarity those elements of the city which are healthy and attractive. These virtues must be preserved. In contrast the dirt, confusion, delays, the nervous tensions, the social decay, the lack of open space and recreation, and the mounting costs of government that add nothing to the security or richness of life must be eliminated. To identify the shortcomings will not of itself give us the cure. Only creative vision can produce a better city which, once conceived, can perhaps with some measure of success be tested by personal experience or, even before construction, by the techniques the social scientists already have at hand.

No longer can we reasonably doubt the city's survival as a social institution. The city will not be abandoned to the jungle despite the nostalgic sighs of those who advocate a return to the soil or to the quaint village of colonial times, forgetful of its inconveniences, its lack of plumbing, its limited horizon, or the decline in living standards that would inevitably follow. I trust therefore I shall not be misunderstood if I suggest that the metamorphosis of the city as we know it is long overdue.

26

The problem that confronts us is not the question of survival but of the form that we want the city of the future to assume. Never before in history has man been so free to create a city in the image of his desires. In America no compromises are needed for economic reasons. We could double, if we wished, the number of cities over 50,000 (about 200) in ten years by putting less than one quarter of our new housing in them should we continue to build at the 1950 rate. Nor would the total ten-year cost approach the bill for this year's armaments. It may appear a paradox, therefore, that this relative freedom from economic restraints will doubtless make our choices more difficult. Yet surely this will be the case.

ADAPTABILITY AND VARIETY

The danger all designers and advocates of new forms of cities have faced is that by the very nature of things they are bound to describe a vision of utopia as seen through their own eyes. Prophetic as these visions have often been they at best recognize only a transitory moment of history. A frozen image full of the promise of perfection beguiles the reader into a world of unreality. For nothing could be more remote from actuality or nature than to suppose it possible to attain such perfectability and to maintain it through the centuries. We must therefore preface all suggestions with the warning that the first ingredient of any future plan is the provision of simple and effective machinery to encourage constant renewal of the fabric of the city. The guiding principle of its design must be adaptability to change. The second must be the principle of variety within the unity of concept to provide for freedom of choice of individuals and families as to jobs, homes, recreation, schooling, or any of those myriad activities that give richness, contrast, and life to a community.

Now it is obvious that neither change nor variety is in itself a virtue. But each successive plan is valuable only to the same degree that it is sensitive to the subtle barometric changes in the social climate and to the diversity of wants of all. It might be thought from such a statement that our highest aspiration as planners is to be a weathervane recording uncritically the changes of the wind. Nothing could be farther from the truth. Instead our mission is to build a city not based exclusively on efficiency, economy, and safety but one whose very form will promote happiness, a sense of decency, neighborliness, and those other Christian virtues that we hold most dear.

The social climate has undergone a revolution in the last century and a half. At times the changes have verged on chaos and it is little wonder that our cities have reflected this indecision. During this period men's ancient roots in the soil have been uprooted. At a time when more families than ever before were seeking something they sensed the large city alone could give, an almost equal number fled the city for the suburbs. But as men rushed into the arms of the all-devouring city there arose in the 1880's a persistent and successful drive to preserve the wilderness, to create national parks, to reserve for public use many of the natural wonders of our nation, and on a more modest metropolitan scale, to build forest preserves and continuous park systems along streams and hills. Taken together, these movements suggest that men were seeking a renewal of that balanced life which was snatched away by the industrialization of our society.

Perhaps because we placed so high a value on the machine we have been prone to forget the family in favor of the economic man. If in our system of values we were to elevate man rather than money or machines to a position of dominance our whole concept of the city would undergo a revolutionary change. A balanced life would become the goal combining manual and intellectual, rural and urban pursuits, communion with nature, and contact with the metropolitan world of art and music. Surely this points to the necessity of dealing with these problems on a regional basis.

Balance in the Urban Region

The concept of the region implies a balance between cultivated farmland, the city and unravaged nature. Each offers its unique contribution to man, each complements the other, and through such variety man's whole existence is enriched. The region thus conceived can become the healthy basis for our future plans whereas the continued conflict between the city and the country life robs each. The very existence of the words "urban" and "rural" point out the grievous losses that man suffers from overspecialization of function in each area. No matter where he chooses to live he has lost something which the city dweller attempts to recapture artifically by summers in the country or the farmer by weekends in the city.

It is the metamorphosis of the present metropolis into the balanced region to which I look forward. This new metropolitan region will embrace many towns and counties, will cross state lines, and will bear only a faint resemblance to the conurbations of yesterday. A principal ingredient of each new region will be a galaxy of new towns. A second is the full-fledged redevelopment of the old city with congestion eliminated and light and life let into the old stagnating areas.

New towns as the keystones of a region are the best hope we have of creating a better environment capable of constant renewal and improvement. They are economically and technically possible today.

Yet it will be argued that the cost will be prohibitive. Let us examine for a moment this fallacy. How will the building of new towns rather than extending the present sprawl add a dollar to the cost of homes, to the cost of schools, of roads, of water and sewer lines, to fire and police protection or to the cost of doing business? Although the decisive reasons for new towns lie in the possibility of an incomparably better social environment rather than in the comparative costs, I am convinced that real savings are possible even at vastly higher physical standards.

Homes in a new town would be built over a relatively short period of time. Under such a large and efficient organization it has been proved over and over again by such builders as Levitt, Burns, and Bohannon that such methods can and do produce better and cheaper houses (as well as greater profits to the builder). To compare the rent for the same space in the cliff dwellings of Manhattan (or any large city) with that of single family houses on new land is quickly to convince one's self that economically the advantage is all with the family homes in open land.

But even so it will be asked whether it would not be cheaper to build on land already served by sewers and water. The fact is no such choice is possible. Fifteen years ago, following that fantastic orgy of subdividing in the 1920's, large tracts could have been found in tax-delinquent areas for new communities, neighborhoods, or housing projects. Chicago and Detroit each had a half-million empty lots in 1935. Today, relatively little land remains with sewers and water available. A second argument, that it would be cheaper to extend existing lines, assumes that major mains, whether water or sewer, are capable of taking the enormously increased loads that would result. Rarely would this be the case. But what is more important is that the major cost of utilities lies in the local distributing and collection systems, which would have to be built in either case. Certainly the design of a system for a new town where the demand may be accurately calculated would produce far greater economies than the piecemeal extension of roads and utilities.

As for schools, most of our cities are already financially hard pressed to provide for their war and postwar babies. State aid is being lavishly offered. Federal aid is advocated and tomorrow will be given. This is only a pragmatic recognition of realities, since local revenues cannot stand the strain. No more schools are required in a new town than for a similar number of pupils living elsewhere. Land, on the other hand, would be cheaper and more plentiful—removing two major headaches of every school board in its search for a solution of this pressing problem. Savings, not added costs, would result here if state (and federal) aid were available on equal terms to old cities and new towns.

In a planned community the shopping centers, while offering immeasurably greater convenience to the shopper, could be built more cheaply because of a lower land cost. On no other point have we more convincing evidence from private developers of the advantages of planning. From the Country Club District of Kansas City to Hancock Village, and the myriad developments of California the testimony is unanimous.

In addition, there are the clear advantages to the manufacturer in locating on inexpensive land where room for expansion can be reserved at little or no cost. Too little advantage has been taken of the possibilities of planned industrial districts in aiding manufacturers in their constant effort to reduce costs in a highly competitive economy.

The prospect that new towns may cost no more is not evidence that they offer a better life. But since they will cost no more, our decisions need not be prejudiced by any uncomfortable qualms that we are talking of an unattainable utopia.

New Towns—Groupings of Families

The new town fitting into the complex of the metropolitan region might take any one of many forms. Any thoughtful examination of its future shape must start from the needs of the smaller social units. As a basic premise I would assume that one of our most urgent tasks is to strengthen family ties, to bring harmony and happiness to each individual within the family, and to allow each one the chance to make friends readily. Now families differ radically in size, in age, in income, and in tastes and this calls for a wide variety of houses and apartments. We need not be overly concerned here with the details of arrangement within the apartment or the home. Our attention instead must focus on the relation of homes to one another and to those community spaces whose arrangement may well have a decisive effect upon the formation of social habits and patterns.

Seen through the eyes of the preschool child the city hardly exists beyond the few blocks nearest home. A few key points such as the movie, perhaps his brother's school, the neighborhood shops, a playground if he is fortunate, are known. To this young explorer the rest is *terra incognita*. His world is that of his friends and neighbors whom he can visit on foot. This small world of the pedestrian is, as sociologists are finding, an extremely real one that is not confined to the youngest members of the family.

Walking distances and the patterns followed in the daily routine play an important and sometimes decisive role in molding the social intercourse of families. Here contacts are most easily made and friendships cultivated. How different the cordial behavior of one pedestrian to another from that of the speeding motorist. How quickly there develops a pride of place; how warmly one defends his neighbors once they are met and understood. Yet how sadly most cities provide for youngsters or their mothers. This civic neglect seems particularly tragic since so many of the activities of the family, perhaps a majority of their collective time, are carried on within walking distance of the home. Surveys of the habits of individuals and families from different income, occupational or regional groups are becoming plentiful enough to make us fully aware how vital the physical layout of a neighborhood is in making friends. Proximity is perhaps the dominant factor but is modified by the actual arrangement of the homes and particularly the habits of preschool age children. For the latter the irresistible appeal of pavements where bicycles can be raced has upset many of the best-laid plans of architects who visualized the children romping carefree on the lawn and among the trees behind the houses. In rental or in sales projects alike the smoothly paved cul-de-sac with its dozen to sixteen houses tightly grouped around it proves invariably the meeting place for children and, of course, the mothers, while the large, safe, attractive (apparently to adults only) park areas remain deserted.

The future city must recognize clearly the function of these small groupings of families as part of the social organization of the larger neighborhood. There is a crying need for units intermediate in size between the family and the large group needed to support an elementary school. Sir Charles Reilly has attempted for English conditions a solution to this problem. Many of his ideas could bear fruit in this country though in two aspects his proposals would prove unacceptable here. The first is the inadequate provision for cars; the second the rather universal insistence on the row house. The latter is, in this country, a much maligned form of housing largely because of its rather unscrupulous exploitation in the gridiron plan complete with alleys. Reilly, however, makes an asset of its architectural form and private gardens by grouping thirty to fifty houses around a village green whose oval form suggests a neighborly spirit.

In this country solutions to this problem have been sought which recognize the universal use of the automobile. The experiments at Radburn, Greenbelt, and Baldwin Hills Village demonstrated with a growing measure of success that groupings could be designed which gave primacy to the pedestrian—and yet took fullest advantage of the automobile. But these designs did far more than create safe islands in a sea of traffic. The social fabric was closely knit with opportunity for the widest variety of activity. At Baldwin Hills the small patio with its family privacy is complemented by the smaller play areas for groups of youngsters, and finally there is provided a community center with resources that can be enjoyed by all members of the family. These distinct levels of social activity recognize the fact that though many functions are native to the home, many others are best shared with others. In almost every category of activity, whether it be recreation or laundering, part is carried on within the home and part outside. We join others not only to share expenses in an enterprise we could not afford alone, as in the case of the golf or swimming club, but also because we want the company of friends outside our immediate family. The need of small and intimate groupings becomes critical if we would prevent the city from tragically becoming still more inhuman and impersonal. It is largely through good site design that individual dignity can be regained and a friendly atmosphere created. Yet our official agencies have been prone to approve and even foster those very designs that place a premium on anonymity, that grant the children sidewalks and street for play and place every obstacle in the way of friendly intercourse and neighborly contact.

THE NEIGHBORHOOD

The small social groupings of fifteen to thirty families around the green have been almost universally neglected in our plans, yet they are essential elements of the community. As we achieve through our designs some measure of success in making it easy for children and their parents to meet without effort, we may find the problems of the larger neighborhood simplified and clarified. But especially here we need an even clearer statement of our objectives for the concept of the neighborhood has gained such classic currency that it is almost immune to criticism. The idea that it should be safe and easy to walk to school, to local shops, the clinic, library, and the park can hardly be refuted. No less convincing is its corollary of grouping these facilities so that they may reinforce each other by making their use easier and the daily contact of their patrons more frequent and we may hope thereby more friendly. Yet there are difficulties in this concept.

There are several unwarranted assumptions hidden in these two ideas. The first is that each of these public services will draw from identical areas and numbers of families, secondly that these areas can be precisely determined ahead of time, and finally the unstated but almost universally repeated magic number of 5,000 persons in each neighborhood. Now I am not unaware that other figures have been proposed but each bears evidence of the same black magic. In every analysis which I have seen of existing, new, or proposed neighborhoods the curve of the school population projected over the life of the school (perhaps thirty years) has not resolved but created insoluble dilemmas for the school building program. Every new subdivision imposes financially back-breaking burdens upon the community for new schools to serve a sharp peak of enrolment. To build for the peak is financial suicide yet to build for anything less is to cheat our children educationally. Only by a real mixture of younger and older families, couples and single people can community facilities, especially schools, be designed to operate efficiently over the lifetime of the building.

Although the decisive asset of the mixed development is the promotion of a wholesome social atmosphere, there are architectural possibilities inherent in it which deserve more study than they have yet had. This very variety will at the same time promote a greater stability of tenure and will thereby reduce materially the speed of obsolescence of the neighborhood. An indiscriminate scattering of architectural types, however, will fail to take advantage of the social opportunities afforded by good design where it is made easy rather than difficult for neighbors to become friends.

In terms of schools it will be possible to plan and to schedule construction that can keep pace with needs without producing white elephants for another generation to pay for since the varied family sizes, ages, and conditions insures considerable stability in the school population. Because the classic neighborhood of planning literature assumes the school to be the focus, its proper size fixes conclusively the number of families served. Today, largely for economic reasons there is a tendency to build elementary schools of six grades for 500–700 children. Yet at best the economies are small while two disadvantages lend great weight to the argument for smaller plants of 300 at most; perhaps at times an even stronger case could be made for ones of 150–200 pupils. A school of 600 is socially out of scale with the child and does nothing that the smaller one could not do in a more intimate and human way, and the smaller unit would preserve the dignity of the individual. Secondly, in new developments where the density of population is most likely to be low the walking distances to school are stretched beyond the breaking point for the younger pupils. To be sure a bus can be provided but such devices are the mechanical and expensive crutches upon which only poor designs need lean. And in their way, they destroy some of the values of the pedestrian community.

For such simple reasons I would advocate neighborhoods of fewer families in keeping with smaller and more human schools while retaining the parks, shops, playgrounds, library, and clinic as reinforcing social magnets.

MIXED DEVELOPMENT

Mixed development presupposes sale and rental housing built cheek by jowl. An increasing portion of our housing will be built by large developers that will in many cases retain an interest in the rental portions or the shopping centers. The large operator is usually more knowing and aware of new ideas than his small competitor whose annual output is a dozen houses or so. By the same token he can afford to do many things denied to the builder who only works both sides of a single block. Yet it is significant that the most progressive builders are relying upon ideas propounded at least two decades ago and first experimented with by pioneer companies not primarily concerned with profits. Because of their very size, it is particularly essential to get a mixture of families of all sizes and circumstances. For social reasons we cannot tolerate in a democracy the continued building of the "homogeneous" subdivision, which in reality is merely an officially blessed form of social snobbery. In the past such neighborhoods were thought more stable and therefore safer investments for the mortgage lender particularly when apparently protected by zoning. Yet despite such caution it is the rare neighborhood that survives the changes of a generation. The mixed community will in this respect prove an even more stable investment because it provides for movement as the family cycles unfold, permitting one to move from apartment to house and back again while keeping close contact with one's lifetime friends. Still further stability will stem from the continuing interest of large investors in the rental portions of the community where examples of good maintenance can prove contagious.

Under present zoning and subdivision regulations it is virtually impossible to build such communities. Though unsuccessful, the courageous attempt in Washington to build with real imagination has had some happy repercussions. New zoning methods and districts have been proposed which may overcome the handicaps imposed by traditional regulations. The use, height and density controls as now enacted are peculiarly inflexible. At the same time their form creates large tracts of land where only subdivisions that are rigidly segregated by type and cost can flourish. And only with difficulty can shops to serve the new families be properly placed in relation to an over-all plan. In fact it is this rigidity in zoning as practiced by local officials and blessed by federal lending and insurance policies that is one of the major obstacles to good design. New types of districts that leave some discretion in the hands of planning officials could go far to improve the situation. Unless some such progressive move is soon made we are likely to find that zoning will create more problems than it solves.

Four Criteria

Out of this discussion of the neighborhood there appear to emerge four criteria by which the quality of design of these smaller social units may be measured. The first is that the social values to the individual and to the community shall, in case of conflict, outweigh any temporary financial advantage. And to my mind enough variety in homes, jobs, and play to give a freedom of choice to all persons regardless of age, temperament, or purse is an essential ingredient of every design. Secondly, the plan must foster family life with widely diverse opportunities for wholesome outdoor as well as indoor social activities. But gregariousness also breeds a demand for privacy. The plan that fails to give asylum to the individual who wishes at times to escape the most friendly crowd is guilty of as grievous a shortcoming as that which neglects the public parks and playgrounds.

The third of the criteria is the effectiveness of the scheme in promoting friendliness among neighbors. This involves an ability to recognize or to create those physical arrangements which bring preschool-age children and their mothers together almost daily in natural and informal play and talk. Doubtless these same greens may also, if properly designed, become the rallying point for groups of older children and their parents after work or school is over. On a larger scale the neighborhood park, the playground, school, the clinic, library, and shops by their mutual support may act as catalysts in promoting a community sense of participation among the larger group. The Peckham Health Center in London demonstrated the enormous appeal that grows out of such a collective enterprise where families may come and where each one can find activities of interest to his age and temperament. Adult programs must become an inherent part of every school and not something added on and tolerated with reluctance by the staff. Nor must the school be a nine-month affair where, as in so many cities, the doors are locked throughout the summer and even playgrounds forbidden the children because of inadequate staff to keep them safely open. To some extent our failure to achieve the utmost with our resources stems from that creeping disease of overspecialization that even divides responsibility for schools, recreation, public clinics, and libraries between departments with little knowledge and less curiosity about each other's objectives and ambitions. Even in the relatively simple problems of site selection there rarely appears any sincere attempt at co-operation.

The fourth criterion is the recognition of the rightful dominance of the pedestrian within the social unit centering on the smaller elementary school. This does not mean exclusion of the automobile since it has become second nature for the American to expect door-to-door transportation in his daily activities and he is happiest when this ideal is most closely approached. The super-block of Baldwin Hills comes near to achieving this goal at no real inconvenience to the driver. It must be recognized, however, that where individual homes are mixed with apartments the ingenuity of the designer is doubly taxed.

INDUSTRIES IN URBAN PATTERNS

When thinking of homes and neighborhoods it has become almost second nature for us to exclude industry or jobs other than local services and shops. This concept is a false legacy from the nineteenth century. Segregation of factories and homes was then a healthy reaction to the blighting influence of smoke-belching factories on workers' homes. Today there are numerous plants that anyone would be glad to claim as neighbors, whose lawns are green, whose walls gleam, where quiet reigns. In fact I am certain that there are times, and mostly inconvenient ones, when my neighbor's and my own children make more irritating noises than many a modern factory. Of course all industries have not yet, and perhaps because of the nature of their processes, cannot ever attain the stature of good neighbors in a residential area. But certainly many have and this fact alone should make us reconsider our hidebound attitude toward industrial quarantine.

Industries are peculiarly diverse by nature. Their space requirements range from one to sixty acres for each two hundred employees; some need vast docks for unloading ore or sugar from overseas while others are quite content with a good connection with the highway for light trucks; some store mountains of coal, raw materials, or waste upon their land, yet many need little in the way of bulk; and still others must get rid of great volumes of industrial waste whose improper disposal has polluted so many of our rivers.

Within the general framework of the metropolis I would suggest that there should be encouraged three general types of industrial groupings. The smallest, cleanest, least noisy, and lightest industries could to advantage be grouped near homes providing a nucleus of local employment within walking distance of the home. I do not suggest that we can return to the medieval workshop in the home or to Borsodi's utopian escape but rather that a small segment of industry (perhaps not more than 10–20 per cent of the employment) could be located side by side with homes to their mutual advantage. The grouping of these workplaces, primarily because of trucking of supplies and finished products, should be on the highways bordering the residential areas to avoid the dangers and inconveniences of the resulting traffic.

The second type of manufacturing district would provide jobs for the majority of the industrial workers. Such districts adjacent to each town of 30,000–50,000 would offer men and women an unusual choice of jobs within a few minutes of home and the manufacturer a more efficient place of doing business than any but the largest concerns can now afford. Each district, served by rail and express highway, would be planned, maintained, and operated as a public utility where space might be leased by individual concerns. As space requirements change, provision can be made far more easily, flexibly, and infinitely more economically than would be the case were each firm forced to anticipate its own needs unaided. In a period when capital for plants is scarce the provision of rental space could have a decisive effect in encouraging new business ventures.

From the worker's viewpoint there would result a spectacular and welcome reduction in the cruel waste of time now spent in commuting. Even in towns with such low residential densities as three to four families to the acre the maximum distance should not be greater than three miles or ten minutes by bus and less by car. But these are maximum distances and there will be many who will still be within walking distance of work. Such districts because of the diversity of work available would offer a most welcome choice of jobs to sons and daughters as well as to the main wage-earners of each family. To maintain such breadth of opportunity it may be necessary to impose some limits on the size of plant quite apart from any question of undesirability because of noise, odors, smoke, or other similar nuisances. It would certainly be desirable for social reasons to avoid the proved handicaps imposed by the domination of a single concern as in our company towns of an earlier generation. This would suggest that an upper employment limit for a single plant should probably not exceed one quarter of the expected payroll in the given industrial district; in the case of the smaller ones this might be 1,000, in the larger perhaps 2,000.

The third type of industrial grouping would include those plants with rather special requirements. Some will need harbor or river frontage for transportation or water, some because they create major nuisances will need to be more isolated from homes than would be possible in the usual industrial district, and still others merely because of their size will require special consideration. In a sense each plant will offer a unique problem. Yet certain relatively simple principles should permit suitable sites to be found.

Along the waterfronts there are especially strong competitive claims for land with industry, shipping, highways, and public recreation the principal contenders. Too often commercial interests have overbuilt along the water. In Boston more than half the wharves are liabilities that slowly rot away, for nearly all the coastwise and transatlantic shipping could be handled at a dozen modern piers at enormous savings over the present chaotic methods. The same picture holds in London where long reaches of the lower Thames are in the process of recapture for riverside parks. Nor do I believe we should in the name of expediency sacrifice all such dearly reclaimed land to expressways as has been done in New York's east and west side or more recently along the lower basin of the Charles River in Boston. Yet each of these uses has a valid claim.

In terms of priority, industry and shipping still deserve first call, but with this a most important reservation: first, that only industries requiring water transportation be permitted to locate on the water and, secondly, that areas for industry should be designed in depth to usurp the minimum of actual frontage on the harbor. If these two principles were followed vast areas would be left for other uses. The second claim upon this space would be that of recreation. And in almost no case would it seem advisable to use such land for expressways, since highways thus located will seldom serve the areas they are intended to as efficiently as roads placed on more direct routes. At the same time they tend to cut off pedestrian access to the parks. This is not to suggest that where such green areas are deep it would not be feasible and pleasant to have driveways well back from the water permitting safe and pleasant use of the river or harborside but we must guard against the expressway that cuts to ribbons miles of narrow park.

Now there will be oversized plants and those that must be quarantined but that still need accommodation. These will tend to draw upon a labor market far wider than a single town primarily because of size but also because they will often require rather special skills. Therefore, large and custom-designed industrial districts should be built on railroad and expressways yet sufficiently remote from any single town to prevent the spread of blight. Located in the interstices between the new towns they can draw on several for workers without imposing unduly heavy commuting burdens.

Each of these three industrial groupings takes its natural place in the evolving molecular structure of the region.

A New Attack on Congestion

In discussing residential neighborhoods and their related work-places we have been forced to assume a radically changed pattern of movement of men and goods. To be sure all cities are studying these problems and most are prepared to spend millions to speed more people and more goods to the already choked centers of the cities. This vicious spiral must be broken. The time has already come when we are wasting our substance by attempting to squeeze more cars, goods, and people into smaller and smaller areas. The simple geometry of the plan will surely defeat us no matter how long we postpone the day by ingenious engineering and expensive stopgaps, which almost without exception are outmoded and inadequate before they can be finished. The area available as we approach a center shrinks as the square of the distance, yet lanes needed to carry the traffic multiply; the parking areas needed get entirely out of hand at the same time that business demands remain unsatisfied even as story after story is piled skywards. There can be no resolution to this dilemma until many of the traffic generators are removed to outlying sites. Space, not more mechanical gadgets, is the only sound solution. The same logic applies to the railroads whose attempts to get downtown have backfired. Terminals and yards waste valuable close-in land yet do not provide economical or rapid transfer of goods between roads or different parts of a metropolis. Yards farther out with good interchange on some circumferential line would speed service and provide natural industrial sites for the new towns. Such a new highway and rail net would provide the healthy sinews to a mature economy.

Size and Spacing of New Towns

When speaking of the new growth we assumed the creation of towns which, though dependent on the larger organism, have some degree of independence and local pride of place. In a sense they will by public control of intervening land be limited in their ability to expand. In fact it appears that the extent of this land to remain open may become the key to our cities' and towns' ability to survive an atomic attack or the even surer and more relentless attacks of obsolescence. The competition of more open and efficient towns cannot fail to put the older cities more and more at a disadvantage if their future growth is not more imaginatively guided. Therefore large areas several miles in width should separate the new towns. This land is not intended to lie fallow and unused but instead could well become the greatest social asset. Several uses quickly suggest themselves: first, truck gardening for local consumption; secondly, active recreation where streams or natural features suggest boating, swimming, riding, climbing, or winter sports, and finally, the preservation of a natural wilderness that can be reached by all.

It will, of course, be suggested that we cannot afford to reserve such large areas between settlements and that all that is needed is a 400-foot expressway for the fast traffic which should bypass the local centers. Yet the additional cost in land acquisition if done ahead of need is almost negligible though fantastically high if bought too late. Foresight, not millions, are needed. Nor would such green wedges and parks increase travel distances by more than a few miles and would reduce these distances in time immensely over present conditions. But the important measure of the value of these new farms and parks is the social gain for the community. Mumford has long and rightly pointed out the impact of the man-made desert of asphalt upon family life as reflected in the lowered birth rate. Surely the new setting first of home, of neighboring families around the common green, the school, and playground with its many related and adjacent services of library, clinics, and shops, and, finally, the regional parks and farms will do much to make children welcome and happy.

In many ways control of the large open breathing spaces between developments becomes the most crucial issue in the continued growth and even existence of our cities. I would far rather stress the social advantages and the economic gains of such an arrangement rather than the obvious reasons of defense, which I am inclined to think are already overstressed and which bear the stamp of opportunism when used in support of a national policy of federal aid for the building of new towns. It is a foregone conclusion that distances that are safe today will not be enough by the time the town is built; certainly it is a historical truism that new offensive weapons will constantly outrun any static defense. Yet federal support will be needed if new towns grouped in metropolitan regions are to be built, for local municipal responsibilities run counter to the larger objectives and lay insuperable obstacles in the way of such far-sighted schemes. Land acquisition, tax-assessment practices, speculative values, and competitive local government make a shambles of any attempt at co-operative local action. Our cities have significantly failed since 1900–10 to extend on a metropolitan scale holdings of land comparable to those planned and acquired before that time in Philadelphia, Boston, or Chicago. In fact, the small increase has in no way kept pace with the population growth and in no instance has there been any real attempt through regulation by zoning to preserve agricultural land or blocks of park land truly adequate to the growing demands.

This enlarged concept of open space is not merely on a larger scale the revival of the drive for parks that characterized the early decades of the planning movement in this country. For though its form may resemble the metropolitan park dreams of Eliot it really stems instead from the concept of the region as an organic planning unit. Here there is a basic sense of interrelation of city and country, of different ways of life each of which gains significance and richness from its contact with, and understanding of, the other. As the clouds part there is revealed below us no longer a city but a region. It is a region whose molecular structure becomes instantly clear, whose ordered hierarchy of neighborhoods studded with green, of industrial groupings, of local civic and business centers lead successively to higher levels that culminate in the major focus of the region embodying civic and business enterprise. The new center by its architectural form becomes the symbol of unity for the citizens of the whole region.

THE REGIONAL CENTER

The new towns, the industrial estates, and the decentralization of business and shopping will have usurped many of the most lucrative and vital functions of the old centers. What is left for the former center of the metropolis?

The departure of many factories, the decentralization of shopping by the forced sharing of the department store trade between the mother store and its suburban offspring, the movement of insurance offices and research institutes to smaller towns or open land are all symptoms of a changed technology that permits new physical arrangements. Individual movement by car has come to dominate our present and future development as overpoweringly as the suburban railroad and the subway with their cheap mass transportation did the city building of forty years ago. Such developments can lead only to an unprecedented opening up of the city and to its accelerated decentralization. The redevelopment of the old areas may be expected to follow in somewhat blurred form the lead of the new towns. An open character will replace today's congestion; large pedestrian islands free of shrieking cabs and lumbering trucks will replace the traffic conflicts of the man on foot and the auto; and these islands will be connected by bridges so that, as in Venice, we may walk in peace and safety from one end to the other of the center.

Although its form may undergo a transformation, there will remain the functional and symbolic need for the center. For it will crown the hierarchy of functions of government, of business, of education, and of culture exemplified by the nursery and kindergarten, elementary school, the high school, and the junior college or that commercial hierarchy of the corner store, the neighborhood shop, suburban center, and the central department store. Each social grouping from the smallest to the all-embracing region will, if history and human nature are any guide, develop a justifiable pride of place that asks some tangible expression as its symbol. The center will become more than a functional expression of the commerical, governmental, and social activities of the community, for by its design it must express as well the spiritual aspirations of its citizens. A hill, a commons, or a historic site have often had solemn significance as rallying points for a community, and as molders of character they are not to be dismissed summarily.

In the center will still be located the cultural magnets of the region —the symphony, the great library, the science and art museums, and the theater. Nor do I see the glamor of the center reduced because it is more comfortably reached and freer of jostling crowds. Although some writers profess a nostalgic feeling for such confusion, I am prepared to forego such dubious and falsely sentimental joys.

In Conclusion

The regional city will assume a special character growing out of a changed emphasis on social values. It will be distinguished by contrasts of vast open and productive land with closely knit social units, of safely speeding traffic with the peaceful calm of pedestrian parkways, and of the simple world of the preschool-age child with the vast opportunities of the regional city.

But to return to our original premises, let us remind ourselves again that neither the new towns nor the redeveloped center will long remain new. And a generation later we will hear all too clearly nostalgic sighs when our sons begin to redevelop their new town. Nor would I ask them to pause a single moment in their efforts to improve our old-fashioned designs. In fact I am convinced that before we are finished with our first job the rebuilding will have to begin again. The process will be continuous.

Perhaps, therefore, only a few points deserve repetition here. The first is that in making judgments of the value of each proposal we give decisive weight to the promotion of social values. The second stems directly from the first: that variety and contrast are essential if the individual is to have true freedom in its deepest sense. And may I emphasize that this cannot be achieved through the directives of a single designer; variety will only be achieved through the democratic process of many gifted men working as free agents within the flexible framework of an over-all plan. The third is that we must plan for constant change leading to the development of a finer way of life.

If we build in a spirit that encourages exploration and experiment, we may achieve that variety and freedom so dear to Americans. But constant care must be taken to avoid the strait jacket of dogma or any narrowing of choice. From the stream of ideas will come a constant evolution leading to designs of towns that will serve men better. Each town will, in its special way, contribute to this 'betterment and will in turn serve as a laboratory in which designers may learn how to improve the next model.

We are not kept from having our regional cities by any lack of technological know-how or by lack of means. But until now we have lacked the will to face the basic policy decisions that must be made.

CHAPTER III

WHAT KIND OF CITIES DO WE WANT?

HENRY S. CHURCHILL

THE immediate possibility of large-scale redevelopment finds the planner without any satisfactory philosophical basis from which to start planning. He is, therefore, subject to forces that he can neither control nor direct. Whether the dominant ones happen in any particular city to be radical or reactionary, the planner finds he can make progress only by bowing to whichever element of political action or mercenary desire happens to be in power. Since he has no ideology of his own to establish conviction, even his "long-range" plans are merely projections of the least objectional features of today into inconsequential changes for the future.

It can be argued that this is not wholly bad. In such a time of flux and uncertainty as that in which we live, no one is able to see very clearly; and besides the essence of getting something done, of earning a living, is that of enlightened opportunism. The swiftly changing technology which almost overnight revolutionizes not only processes of industry and communication but of scientific thought, the gradual devolution of our economic structure, the continuation of what Henry Adams called the degradation of democratic dogma, the growing lack of faith not just in religion or even materialism but in humanity itself, are all against the formation of any sound policy in any field. The city-planner can hardly be expected to do better.

The techniques of physical planning, based as they are on architectural concepts, are reasonably well defined and can be well carried out. The city-planner, in gratuitously taking over the social and economic aspects of city development has plunged himself into a trackless jungle through which he is trying desperately to cut a path—to where? It is bad enough that he has no compass to guide him, but the sun and the stars are still making their appointed rounds if he is willing to be aware of them as directional guides. What is lacking is an inner determination to go north, south, east, or west. Without a direction in which to go, one is likely to go in a circle and come back to the same place. And that, I am afraid, is where our urban redevelopment is going.

WHAT IS A CITY?

What kind of a city do we want? An answer to that requires an answer to "what kind of people are going to live in them?" Are they going to be frightened, frustrated people, or "people" abstracted from the census, or human beings living a full life? The answer lies somewhere in the realm of technology, for people are becoming—or are in danger of becoming—creatures of technological function. I do not pretend to know the answer, but every planner should read Norbert Wiener's *The Human Use of Human Beings*[1] and Lancelot L. Whyte's *The Next Development in Man*[2] for some idea of where we may be heading.

What is a city, anyway? It is, of course, a place where people congregate to earn a living. It is also a place in which people are interdependent because of an extreme degree of occupational specialization. It is also a place in which there is an enormous variety of things and people among which to pick and choose. Its essence is gregariousness and anonymity. The small town is the opposite of the city. Its essence is propinquity and nosiness. The suburb is just the bastard of the two.

They should not be confused; they are not just different physically, they are two different ways of life. That has been so ever since there were cities, town, and country, the slick and the hick. They don't mix, except as each serves as a vacation-land escape for the other.

City-planners are generally pretty well agreed about certain things they consider desirable to take the place of blight and slums. More light, although, alas! not in the Goethean sense, more air, more quiet, stabilized land values. Most of them envisage a community of like-minded souls dwelling in well-ordered harmony amid neat community facilities. Most of them, of course, would die if they had to live in one of their own dull Utopias, but they keep talking about them. I believe they do their cause considerable harm, even though it may be the natural reaction to the noise, confusion, and frustration of the cities with which they deal. They forget that what makes them queasy is to many the only reason the city has for its existence, a vast confusion in the midst of which opportunity, honorable or other, offers its golden charms, and where melting away among other unknown failures is the solace for those who muff their chance. The great novelists, from Balzac to Joyce, better sociologists than the professors of that solemn discipline, have described what the fascination is that brings men and women from the provinces to the city, what it is that makes the city the lure it is, for both good and evil. Any effort to recreate the small

1. Boston: Houghton Mifflin Co., 1950.
2. New York: The New American Library, 1950.

town in the city—*rus in urbe*—is foredoomed, since it is a contradiction in purpose.[3]

The city therefore should remain the city, and I say this in spite of the fact that hordes of people are getting out of the cities, turning alleged green pastures into the asphalt corrals of the suburbs. They are looking for sunlight, air, quiet, decent schooling for their children, a place to park their cars—the very things the planners want to give them. But at the same time they try to keep the opportunities and pleasures of the city. They commute. Suggest that they desert the city altogether, find them a home and work in a small town or in the frightening country, there would be small response. Nor would their children be content to stay in such places after they grew up. Indeed it remains to be seen what will happen to the chicken-coop garnishings of the suburban fringe when the present generation attains the age of indiscretion.

PEOPLE ARE DIFFERENT

So the problem becomes one of making the city tolerable and still keeping it the City. For our big cities have indeed become intolerable, not because they are not like villages but because technological devices have been used to exploit land without any regard for either human needs or human values. If people are deserting them, even for the pseudo-satisfactions of the suburb and the subdivision, it is because of a purely biological will to survive.

It is basically fruitless to think about future city patterns in terms of the present economics that have made them what they are. New patterns, more suited to the use of human beings cannot be evolved under the system of city finances based on *ad valorem* taxes, on the accrual of unearned increment solely to the land-owner, and on the speculative theory of unimpeded growth. There is plenty of evidence that these economic devices are already becoming subject to readjustment. Title I of the Housing Act of 1949 itself is the most notable exhibit.

It should be clear, I think, that if we replan our cities so as to "make them pay" we will only make the most superficial improvements. To overcrowd the land vertically instead of horizontally is no solution at all, since density is a function of total population and not of coverage. There is more open space in the vertical City of Towers, but it is less accessible, and the problems of circulation have merely been trans-

3. Some sociologists, Svend Riemer, for instance, are coming to the conclusion that the "village in the city" is not socially possible even if desirable—and the desirability has never been sociologically proved.

formed, not solved. The social problems likewise: Percival and Paul Goodman have given a most acute analysis of the vertical city in *Communitas*[4]—the only American book on planning I know of that even tries to give an analysis of human use and sees use in the urban sense as not necessarily the equivalent of either Corbusier's totalitarianism or Ebenezer Howard's provincialism.

It seems to me also that certain important segments of people and certain aspects of their livelihood are being overlooked in much of our planning, devoted as it is to the housing ghetto and to industry. There are notable exceptions, but in general little thought is given on how to fit those whom Shaw called "the undeserving poor" into the picture. Public housing is not the answer. Public housing is for the deserving poor, and not for all of them because public housing must not, by any fell circumstance, have a vacancy. There must be a long waiting list of deservers, so that management—and the politician too, perhaps—can have a threat for the recalcitrant tenant. And the undeserving poor do not want to live in a "project" anyway, if they can scratch together enough to go their own unregenerate way. There are people—not counting the "unsocially minded"—who just do not like to live in rabbit warrens. Where, in the bright City of Eniak, are they going to live?

What is also overlooked is that industrial employment is not the only form of work. "Service workers," those who do not work in the basic industries, at least equal the industrial workers in number. And there are a very great many people who live with their work. They are proprietors of small stores, various kinds of small industries such as repair shops, and so on. They don't make much money, but they are independent and they get by. They line the side streets and secondary avenues of every city. Some have come down in the world and are just hanging on; some are on their way up. Our present brand of redevelopment destroys them. Our new plans make no provision for these people, none whatever. They do not belong either to the skyscrapers or the nice little "residential" communities. Where are they to go, what are they to do?

PLANNING IS NOT STATISTICS

There are many other human problems that must receive thoughtful consideration before any sound pattern for the future can be determined. Is our cultural future going to be wholly one of mass production? For the moment it looks that way, but art is long. Civic art and architecture are arts that traditionally spoke to the masses of people.

4. Chicago: University of Chicago Press, 1947.

The city planners who know nothing of architecture and the architects who care nothing for civic art (except the single civic "monument") are doing a grave disservice to our culture.

Will our school systems continue to waste our children's potential by routine mass methods that fail to stir the dull and dull the intelligent? One of the principal reasons for the flight to the suburbs is because there it seemed possible to influence schools and teaching; in any case the smaller classes and better plant seemed to offer better education and care than was possible in the ancient city schools. Will our redeveloped cities go in for smaller schools, scaled to the children both physically and educationally, or will they continue to be "efficient"?

Planners cannot decide these things, but they must know.

What kind of a people are we going to be? Is George Orwell right? Will Wiener's fears be justified? Too much planning thinking leans in the direction of acquiescence. Or perhaps it is planning thoughtlessness, the too ready acceptance of the cliché and "scientific method" in a sphere that is neither scientific nor in possession of a sound methodology. The substitution of number for the specific, the curious belief that the statistical average is a reality, make for an easy process of planning, but the easy way may be wrong. The hard way is to take a good look at the statistical process itself and judge whether it is a method of evaluating something in terms of use and human need or a device for eliminating consideration of the individual. It is going to be hard to do this, because we have gotten a quasi-religious faith that statistics "prove" something. This is not so, as any player of the Wall Street averages—or the racing forms—can tell you. Statistics can indicate a probable result based on past performance of a limited number of factors, but can tell nothing about the rightness or wrongness, in terms of human value, of such a result should it by chance come about.

The dilemma of course is that we have to plan now for something and we cannot plan for everyone. But the way out is not—if we wish to keep away from authoritarianism—to plan for averages. We must, I believe, make little plans for little people, lots and lots of plans to human scale. It may mean doing a lot of wrong things and some right ones, but that is better than to do just one thing wrong and no chance for anything right. We need variety and the experience variety brings, not formulas.

I admire the New York Life Insurance Company because it has had the courage to try two totally different concepts of housing. (That is more than either FHA or PHA has ever had.) Fresh Meadows is a highly successful development, yet in Chicago New York Life is going to build its absolute opposite: twenty-three story slab apartments with open corridors, and, even so, a density of only about 20 families per gross acre. The two structures are spaced widely apart, there will be two-story apartments surrounding the vast court. It would have been easy to repeat the Fresh Meadows idea; to go to the Chicago extreme takes guts. I happen to prefer Fresh Meadows; for one thing it provides a greater variety of living, for another it is more human in scale. Nevertheless, the Chicago project may prove the better. It will certainly suit many people and it opens up new possibilities for congested living. But I cannot help wondering, if the example is successful and is widely followed, what will happen when the buildings become old and decrepit and the area is again obsolete, and the cost of operation and repair exceeds a "fair return" and they become vast vertical slums; what then? These wonderful elevators, these glass walls, these complicated heating systems and miles of pipe and miles of dirt-swept "sidewalks in the sky," who will maintain them? Well, it is a long time off, fifty years or twenty, and the investor will be paid out. It is no concern of ours—now. And, as I said, it may be a step toward a solution of the problem of how to reconcile compacted living to satisfy the gregarious instinct with the space needed for the mobility of the machine. The principal present objection I see is that in order to escape one's neighbors even for a moment one must depend on a machine—the elevator—or else jump.

Large-Scale vs. Human Values

There is a very serious danger in the continued emphasis on, and desire for, "large-scale" action in rebuilding our cities, and in the general belief that only by large-scale financing and construction can a satisfactory and "permanent" result be brought about. Large-scale building means mass production for mass consumption, i.e., further steps toward a lowering of standards to the level of the lowest common denominator. It may be a long first step towards the establishment of an urban feudalism similar in many ways to the rural feudalism of medieval times. It took a great many hundreds of years to break down the feudalism that was rooted in the vast holdings of agricultural land; in many countries, notably South America and China, the system still persists. Urban feudalism would be different, of course; but the ownership and control of shelter gives tremendous political power, and what begins as well-intentioned paternalism easily turns to despotism —perhaps benevolent, perhaps not. The individual must be encouraged to retain his individuality, if democracy is to survive. For the planner that means the individual's right to his choice of a way of life must not be circumscribed by arbitrary physical limitations imposed in the name of "order" or "efficiency." Within the broadest possible frame-work of the general good, disorder must be allowed for, lest the people perish. Any form of initiative is disordering of the status quo and so needs encouragement, not suppression, if democracy is to retain vitality.

I believe we can get the carbon dioxide out of our cities, that we can create islands of quiet and beauty in them, that we can channel our cars so there will be less congestion and more safety, that the insanity rate can be lowered (unless the psychiatrists set up new standards of "normal" still more exclusive of themselves). We need to give fresh thought to the cliché of the "neighborhood," to the fetish of "stability." The first may turn out to be a sociological absurdity and the latter an economic impossibility. We need to reappraise the use of automotive transportation. We still have two legs and perhaps the private car should only take us *nearly* to where we want to go, like the street car or the subway does. The places in which we live, work, shop might be thought of as pedestrian islands rather than as interferences to a moving vehicle. After all, is not that the basic idea behind the new suburban shopping centers and of the properly designed super-block? It needs to be carried to its logical conclusion, a complete separation of traffic and people. Within some islands there can be as much congestion of people, confusion, life, and noise as is characteristic and necessary for the gregarious anonymity of the city. Within others there can be peace and quiet, and ordered beauty of architecture, the unordered interest of the picturesque. Within a broad frame there is space for community needs, for ample schools, for recreation for the aged. The human scale could be restored, and the human pace, the chance to look and to comprehend. The traffic ways would be designed for a different order of speed, a different kind of receptivity.

Only the public works would need large capital. In other kinds of development large capital investment would be welcome, small capital would have opportunity.

The new technology—Wiener's "second industrial revolution"—can be used for such good purposes if it is not allowed to become the power of the new feudalism, i.e., become the exclusive property of vast capital. The need for physical presence at many functions can be reduced, and traffic thereby reduced. Automatic controls, conferences by television, duplication of documents in several places simultaneously, can reduce the need of people to rush themselves through the streets.

We are at the commencement of a crucial period in city development, and the technician is an important, if not a decisive, factor in the turn of events. It is his responsibility to be aware of where he will arrive once he makes a choice of his road. I have suggested some of the things he should consider, the terms of the alternatives.

I have very little sympathy for those who cry that unless we do things in a Big Way it will all have to be done over again in fifty years or so. I should hope it will be, and with more human understanding than we have now, and with better means for accomplishment. Is not our trouble today that we must undo the work of our grandfathers? What makes us think we are any more prescient than they? Of course, our cities must be rebuilt again in the future, and again thereafter. Our choice now in so far as we can choose, is between the roads that lead to the City of Man or the City of Eniak.

CHAPTER IV

NOT BY BREAD ALONE: AN EVALUATION OF THE DESIGN ELEMENT IN LARGE-SCALE PLANNING

ROBERT C. WEINBERG

INTRODUCTION

WHAT sort of cities do we want to build? What type of urban environment should the next generation grow up in? Is a solution of the sanitary, legal, economic, engineering, and social problems involved the whole answer to the question? If not, what is the missing element and how do we go about supplying it? And how does this all tie up with the redevelopment program that the federal government is now committed to? The following paragraphs try to answer some of these questions from the viewpoint of an architect-planner who has long felt that the pendulum has swung too far in the opposite direction from the City Beautiful ideal of half a century ago, and that the whole planning movement, and with it the preponderance of those who are in a position to establish policies under the redevelopment program, are missing the boat if they think that the mere provision, in increasingly greater quantities, of more sun and air, better plumbing, adequate recreation spaces, fireproof construction, and the maximum provision for motor cars—parked or in motion—can alone create communities that will be truly satisfying to the needs of man.

I shall try to show, by quotation and example, that the incorporation of the design element as an integral part of the plan of the new community, and not its exterior application as an afterthought, is basically essential. Further, I would point out that the key to the process lies in designing from the point of view of the human being and not from that of the statistic, the financial statement, or the arbitrary pattern of the drafting room. And if the British have, by political circumstance or economic necessity, been prevented up to now from realizing most of their current plans, they have, at least, in their officially adopted reconstruction schemes and in their scholarly publications, shown that humanism—expressed in terms of architecture, site planning, and community building—is not incompatible with mid-twentieth century technological processes.

Finally, there is the question of whether negative controls—not to build this or that, to be limited to such and such a maximum bulk or coverage, to provide these or those minima in respect to various facilities—will ever achieve any lasting results in the way of desirable new cities to live and work in. With the passage of Title I of the Housing Act of 1949, the time has come for positive, qualitative directives, outlined by those who have given thought to what we want our cities to be, in appearance as well as in function, rather than resting satisfied with the spectacular, large-scale elimination of the worst of what we are getting rid of. To say this is not to belittle the fine beginning that has been made in replacing our urban slums with bright new towers and shining superhighways. But the individual man craves something more than that, and he needs to see it around him in forms that he can measure against himself, in scale with his day-to-day movements, his natural pleasures, and his spontaneous emotional reactions.

The Human Being in the Urban Scene

We are considering, here, the physical-planning aspects of urban redevelopment. Only indirectly affected by what I have to say are legal and economic problems, such as land acquisition, ownership, financing, and taxation. Similarly, the social questions of tenant selection, rehousing displaced slum dwellers, management of the completed projects, the decisions confronting engineer and contractor as to foundations, structural strength, and choice of mechanical equipment raise problems which, while of interest, are not primarily involved in redesigning the physical aspects of our cities. Yet, this job seems often left, in current writing and discussion as well as in actual practice, to citizens and officials whose background and claim to fame lie in the realms of law, sociology, engineering, economics, and large-scale public works contracting. Let us assume that all these people are well qualified and that, with the aid of their respective technical staffs they solve the problems they are concerned with (and which are the ones they understand) with utmost ability and superhuman perfection—an unthinkable hypothesis, but let us use it for the sake of argument. The resulting agglomeration of physical undertakings—clearance of slums and the mass creation of new buildings and open spaces of every sort— can and will still be lacking something that is needed to fuse them into a living new environment, an urban pattern that is meaningful and satisfying to those who are to dwell and work in it.

A number of observers of the planning scene have been commenting on this situation. For example, Charles F. Fuller, long active in federal housing activity, writes:

While a huge amount is known and tabulated about the evils of megalopolitan life, there has been very little study of what urban life should be like. This may sound strange to a public already familiar with the bold plans for rebuilding London, but it is true that the basic assumptions as to what urban man needs and should have are just that—assumptions. Planners have advised with doctors, particularly those engaged in public health work, jurists, social workers, economists and other specialists. As a result, planners tend to be chiefly aware of evils to be corrected: evils of overcrowding, unsanitary houses, lack of sunlight, smoke, noise, dirt. They abide too much with statistics, neglecting man, the individual, in favor of the more easily charted averages of man's behavior. The ideals of practicing planners of today can be summed up as medical-missionary bourgeois. . . . It is an attractive picture in a tidy way: a safe, healthy, laboratory-tested life, with a balanced diet of work, sleep, fresh air, amusement, and presumably, spiritual instruction.

Wherever serious replanning is being undertaken today . . . the work follows, pretty generally, this picture. If the U.S. were to become so realistic tomorrow as to put the democratic ideal of the greatest good for the greatest number to work, the redevelopment of its cities would undoubtedly follow this same pattern of minimum standards, which, while it provides the essential skeleton, does almost nothing to give life to the subject.[1]

Of course, the element of conscious design is absent in all parts of our modern cities and its provision is not necessarily or exclusively the problem of those concerned with redevelopment areas. However, to make good civic design effective, it does imply the laying out—under simultaneous control—of large-scale undertakings involving more than a few buildings or even "projects."[2] Thus with the exception of such special situations as a university, medical or civic center, or the establishment in the heart of the city of a new United Nations headquarters, we must look to Title I of the 1949 Housing Act for the opportunity for the large-scale *redesigning* as well as the rebuilding of our cities. We all hope, moreover, that while the redevelopment undertakings will in themselves be laid out well, they will also spread their influence to the city as a whole. Since the general principles of "civic design" (I put it in quotes because I have still not found a substitute for this somewhat unsatisfactory phrase) are applicable to all new large-scale replanning of our cities, they are immediately of interest to those concerned with "urban redevelopment" as that term is currently and perhaps narrowly employed. The discussion of these principles, then, in the following paragraphs, need not specifically mention urban redevelopment any further.

The current emphasis on social and economic progress, to the ex-

1. "Man against the Skyline," *The Commonweal* (August, 1948).

2. I use this term in its strict sense of applying to a single group of housing units, an industrial plant of more than one building, or any other major undertaking actually constructed as one operation by a single owner or agency—public or private—at one time and designed by one architect. I deliberately reject the meaning incorrectly given, I think, in the 1949 Housing Act, and in some state legislation, where it is used to denote the complete redevelopment program of a large urban area, which by its very nature must include a number of "projects" in the true sense of this word, as well as a variety of other improvements such as streets, schools, parks, and shopping centers.

clusion of human and spiritual values, is becoming the subject of thoughtful comment in wider fields than that of city planning. In a recent article the British philosopher-naturalist, Julian Huxley, says that the only antidote to "creeping totalitarianism" and eventual "mass man" is a renewed recognition of that essential element which he optimistically expects "to rouse us from our internal lethargy and confusion," and which he identifies as beauty, the "necessary ingredient of full living."

Once we really grasp that our duty and our destiny is to provide and to live a richer life, we shall regard it as socially immoral to build ugly factories, to plan a drab and lifeless housing estate, or to spend money on vulgar public building.

. . . Beauty is part of the necessary emotional cement of society. Thus, every industry should have headquarters which worthily symbolizes it and its value, both to its workers and to the nation at large; and its regional and local buildings should also canalize the emotions in their appropriate ways.

. . . At present our approach is concerned almost entirely with economics, social security, and physical health. This material approach is frankly not enough; however adequately it deals with the foundations of life, it leaves out all its upper stories. Our new view of human destiny insists that emotional and intellectual and spiritual satisfactions must also be taken into account.[3]

This, then, applied to the urban scene as a whole, is the theme of my argument. It is far from being, as one might suppose, a plea for recapturing for the architect the place in the city-planning picture he may have forfeited a generation ago by a narrow insistence on the City Beautiful thesis. While the architect still is and must be the leader and over-all impresario of the urban planning team, the general run of architects who concern themselves with the design of individual buildings and projects only are as much in need of a new viewpoint as are those who call themselves city-planners because of their activity in this wider sphere. But it is particularly the *non*-architectural members of the planning fraternity who must become aware of the essential nature of this missing ingredient and who must clearly comprehend its basic relationship to planning as opposed to tolerating it as an applied gadget. Only then can the *architect*-planner, in turn, receive his assignment with the fullest confidence and responsibility, and see his job in the right light—as something a great deal more than turning out a sketch plan on his drafting board or lining up a few cornice heights here and there.

Design Must Be Intrinsic

In 1947, shortly after our recent ambassador to Mexico was first elected mayor of New York, he was guest of honor at a dinner meeting

3. "Population and Human Destiny," *Harper's Magazine* (September, 1950), p. 37.

arranged by a group of earnest liberals who had supported him for election. An outstanding person in each of a dozen or so fields of city affairs was asked to present the pressing problems confronting the city in this field and Mr. O'Dwyer answered each in turn, telling how he intended to handle the problems. The executive vice-president of the Regional Plan Association presented the case for city planning, giving as an example of the need for comprehensive handling of important problems, the case of the Second Avenue subway. He said that plans for the subway should not be left to the Board of Transportation alone when so many other questions have to be considered simultaneously, such as combining it with a needed express highway, the location of stations and connecting transportation, the density of population as governed by new zoning of surrounding areas and many other aspects obviously involving long-range planning. Hizzoner was most affable. "Don't worry about your city planning, Kim," he said, patronizingly, "we probably won't get around to building the Second Avenue subway for a number of years. But before construction begins, we will let your boys have a look at the plans and make any suggestions you want to."

More recently, at a meeting of the New York chapter of the American Institute of Planners at which a number of foreign visitors were present, the question came up as to what extent we were bringing to bear upon our current redevelopment plans a conscious recognition of the need for creating surroundings which would be aesthetically in harmony with the spirit of this modern age. It appeared that the planners from Europe, skilfully trained to relate modern construction to traditional backdrops, sensed the great opportunities for celebrating these values in current USAnian city plans. "Don't worry about that," said the then president of the chapter (an engineer) in his most mellifluous tone of voice, "I am sure that city planners are always glad to have the architects come in and add their particular touches to the plans our commissions are making—if . . . er,—if there is time to do it and funds are available to add such flourishes." Perhaps I am not quoting my esteemed colleague quite precisely, but the point of view I ascribe to him is a common one in the planning fraternity.

I deliberately juxtapose these two episodes, for while every *planner* at the O'Dwyer dinner was fully aware of the shallowness and misconception of the mayor's reaction to the implications of the Second Avenue subway situation—a complete failure to understand the place of over-all planning in relation to the day-to-day administration of modern city government—the planning profession itself seems to be blissfully unconscious of the true relation of the design factor to city planning. In the words of Sir Patrick Abercrombie:

The quality of design is not limited to buildings; it should interpenetrate every aspect and *enter into every stage of the plan;* the direction or curve of a road, the treatment of an intersection, the conformity to, or contrast between, natural features and human additions, the siting of a group of houses, all these and many more are matters requiring, in addition to engineering skill, design, in which the claims of natural and artificial promptings are duly respected.[4]

If I have spoken so far in generalities, it is because I took for granted that the reader of these essays would know what I mean when I talk of the quality of design in our urban planning procedures. But as the episode at the New York AIP meeting indicates, even the most well intentioned of planners still thinks of "civic design" as something that is not only applied externally to solutions previously arrived at on the basis of other techniques and values, but also as being somehow esoteric, peculiar to classroom aesthetics and of interest to a rare few. They fail to see it as a matter of satisfying the natural but unrealized desire on the part of the general public for legitimate, attainable pleasures and emotional responses. It is just this misconception that has made difficult the establishment in this country of any of the procedures that go under the general heading of architectural control. It is generally not a question of arranging buildings and open spaces in an abstract pattern, pleasing perhaps to the *cognoscenti* but unnoticed by the mass of men, although a carefully studied effect often affects the beholder in a subtle, subconscious way of which he may not be immediately aware. It is, rather, to create in the physical environment something so obviously striking, appropriate, and pleasure-giving to everyone that a certain inner satisfaction results which makes a man say, "Here is a city that is great and is beautiful and this is where I want to live and work."

Amenity Reconciled with Mass Production

Inquiring into the nature of this element we find an apparent paradox. There is, on the one hand, the recognition of the integral character of beauty which is indivisible, whether in a single work of art or in a whole city; yet, on the other hand, in the urban scene, this very overall beauty is made up of an infinite number of aspects, both small and large, into each of which must have gone some skill, some imagination, some taste, and a great deal of thought given to human values, sentiments, habits, and traditions. For examples of this latter aspect we need go no further than the British who have, after all, a word for it,

4. *Town and Country Planning* (London: Thornton Butterworth, Ltd. 1933), p. 165. Italics added.

"amenity," the modest, unassuming label they attach to a large number
of these rather important things. Further on I will attempt to describe
a few of them in detail and indicate how we might apply them to our
own urban design problems.

The over-all beauty of a city, or of any part of it, moreover, is never
an applied *pastiche,* figuratively or literally speaking, but a deliberate
dramatization of its most significant features with a concomitant placing of its recognized and realized minor amenities in their proper relationship to each other and to the larger, more striking features. It implies a conscious use of physical symbolism wherever possible, often
achieved not so much by specific, monumental structures as by the relationship between buildings and open spaces (of which the traditional
village green is the simplest example) thought of as an arrangement of
the physical environment in which we live and work so as to give it
that character and individuality which can make each community as
distinctive and as different from the next and from other communities
in other USAnian cities as one man's home is from his neighbor's. The
man whose house is laid out identically to the one next door may enjoy,
perhaps, initial pride in ownership but soon loses it because he no
longer can differentiate his own "castle" from his neighbor's—similarly
with the citizen of a community consisting of one or more projects almost identical to each other in tedious uniformity as to height of building and color of brick.

If the very nature of our modern techniques seem to imply repetitive
mass production it must be borne in mind that this applies to the part,
the unit of the building, and not to the whole. Even a well-thought-out
set of standardized building units, of different shapes, heights, and sizes
can be selected and arranged to create an effective composition, in-
stinctively pleasing in its harmony and balance—as Whittlesey and
Mayer have proved with their James Weldon Johnson Houses in Harlem.

Some architects and planners are beginning to realize that the pendulum may have swung too far in the direction of the theoretic and the
mechanistic. It is from the drawing boards of those who recognize this
danger, who may not necessarily operate successful "plan-factories"
but who at least study the site in advance, that we must look for this
consideration of the people who now live, and those who will in future
live, in our redevelopment areas, and how to give them direct *pleasure*
by exercising, in Mumford's phrase, "the little acts of aesthetic grace
and insight making the universal forms of the machine both regional
and personal." And again Mumford puts his finger on the spot when he
remarks, apropos of some of the newer designs by Brazil's Niemeyer,

that "it is a confirmation of my thesis that the restoration of the personal and symbolic is the new mark of modern architecture."

How to plan new or rebuilt areas of our great cities so as to make them something more than the correct financial and engineering solutions of economic and social problems is something that depends on the skill and imagination of the city planner in charge of the operation. The last phrase of this sentence must be taken very literally indeed. The city planner must be consulted at the very outset in the selection of what is to be kept and what demolished, as well as in making decisions of general policy as to the type of thing that is to be created, and this city planner must be one who is trained in the discipline of design as that term has been known throughout the ages. He must, besides, be able to apply his training with courage, imagination, and an unquestioned flair for understanding individual human feeling as well as the material needs of masses of men. As Sir Raymond Unwin wrote of Werner Hegemann: "He had, moreover, the essential equipment for a planner, in that his interest and appreciation tended to be most strongly aroused by the relations between men and things, and the new values which might be created by securing more appropriate relations and more accurate proportions."[5]

I cannot here proceed to give a course in city-planning design; even the barest outline would require graphic illustration beyond the confines of a short paper. What I can do is to list a few of the elements that go into imaginative city planning as it is now being practiced in other countries, and to show how some of these might be applied to our current USAnian scene. The order in which the following observations are given should not be taken as an indication of their relative importance, nor do I claim that they cover all or nearly all that might be said on the subject. But a listing of some neglected design opportunities in connection with recent large-scale undertakings will have served its purpose if the attention of the nondesign-conscious houser and planner, and of those architects who still think only in terms of single buildings or "projects," can be aroused.

MAN, THE MEASURE

Many of the redevelopment plans we see these days look well as plans on paper; and perhaps they are good as workable site plans. But since they so often involve buildings of great height, areas of great extent and streets of great length, the relation of them to the human being

5. In Werner, Hegemann, *City Planning: Housing*, Vol. III (New York: Architectural Book Publishing Co., 1938), Foreword.

is quite forgotten. As a result the contemplated development is inhuman, overpowering, even when the plan has been further studied in the form of a three-dimensional model. It is difficult for most members of the planning team, to say nothing of the political and financial partners in the enterprise, to visualize in advance just what effect the whole business is going to have on the people who will inhabit, work, or move about in it. Yet it is for these people and for those who follow—since our redevelopment undertakings are intended to last for at least two generations, if not longer—that they are being built.

The sudden acceptance of Le Corbusier's thesis of La Ville Radieuse by some of our spectacular redevelopment designers is fraught with danger. Lesser lights among contemporary continental European writers have looked lovingly, and with remarkable naïveté, on vast skyscrapers, widely spaced, as the universal panacea for all our urban ills, and as the one and only antidote to crowded cities. While the application of the Le Corbusier system may be quite appropriate in the case of office buildings, e.g., the plan for Pittsburgh's Triangle Point development, it must be used sparingly, if at all, in creating the environment where people are to live. Even the combination of a few tall buildings with many low and medium-sized ones, as at Fresh Meadows, has not prevented adverse criticism of the tall buildings there as keeping people too far from the ground, figuratively as well as literally. And the European intellectuals' romantic acceptance of the infinite standardization of units, added to their adulation of the widely spaced skyscraper, is one that seems to be accepted too unquestioningly here and may be overdone by those given the responsibility of designing redevelopment areas if we don't watch out.

We make much of the fact that we are clearing away something that has been bad for human beings over several generations. Yet we are seldom certain that we are providing something better, unless light, air, fire-safety, and sanitation are the only things that count. That our new large-scale construction must provide more than these becomes obvious when we visit any of the housing projects built in the last decade. As Dean Hudnut says: "Our housing authorities and those agencies associated with them are destroying an environment which is the outcome of one way of life in order to substitute an environment which will be, no doubt, the cause of another way of life. . . ."[6] This "other way of life" means—if we read correctly recent projects and current plans—families living in tall elevator buildings, the space between which consist of parking lots and clipped lawns, an environment in which the individual has little or no opportunity to move around and do as he

6. Joseph Hudnut, "Housing and the Democratic Process," *The Architectural Record* (June, 1943).

pleases on foot except within his own tiny flat, as compared with the old slum where, however dilapidated the building, he could at least go in and out of the house with comparative ease and plunk a chair on the sidewalk on a hot summer evening. Have our planners thought this through—a day in the life of the average man, in this new environment?

Consider for a moment, the point of view from which the average man will look at his bright new world when he emerges from the front door of his home or, more usually, his flat. What does he see? A corridor? A lawn with a "Keep Off!" sign? A street clogged with cars? At street level, what does he see on line with his eye? What does he see when he looks out of his window at whatever floor he lives on? Did the designers of recent large-scale undertakings put themselves in the place of the proverbial man in the street or of his wife leaning on her elbows looking out of a ninth-story window? The view from the office or factory window is just as important, of course, and the impression given the man on the street is not limited by any means to what he sees around his home. It is part of my thesis that *all features of the physical environment should be thought of from the point of view of the people who will most frequently look at them*. For instance, the location and arrangement of major buildings; the provision of openings to sky, to views of water or greenery beyond; the use and placing of frankly decorative elements such as varieties in the color and shape of structures as well as occasional ornaments in the form of sculpture or abstract surface pattern on a building; the location of directional signs, house numbers, placards, and all outdoor devices including, especially, those which, like lampposts, are installed by a different city department; street names, traffic control signals, television antennae, water tanks, elevator penthouses, fire escapes, vent flues, and the designs of all other obvious and necessary accessories to modern construction should all be considered as dramatic design potentials. Heretofore these factors have been generally left to chance or at best been detailed and specified by underlings in a huge impersonal "plan factory" as a minor part of an abstract pattern previously sketched, hurriedly, and at small-scale on the drafting board of an absentee architect. Yet these factors in a "townscape" are the most frequently noticed in the daily life of a citizen. The average designer of large-scale projects often gives as little thought to how an individual man is going to see the product of his pencil as Gulliver did to what his shoelaces looked like to the Lilliputians.

The result of this careless attitude has been—as for example in many of the Metropolitan Life's projects from Parkfairfax to Parkchester—that a great deal of wasted effort and expense went into giving the public what the builders thought were "attractive" elements, which actually are unappreciated because they are inappropriate and unnecessary, due largely to this failure to think them out from the point of view of the individual human being.

If the designer's first consideration must be the man in the street or the woman in the window (or vice versa, and not forgetting the children in both places!) we must also remember that people see cities from moving vehicles on the ground, in the air, and on water. It is seldom that the modern planner thinks of the street as a composition in itself and when he does, he too often goes back to eighteenth-century models—out of date already even when Haussmann mass-produced them with vulgar banality in the mid-nineteenth century. The old street was designed for the observer moving slowly in a horsedrawn vehicle; the modern street must be conceived of at a wider angle and a more consciously horizontal line if any sort of total effect is to be produced on the eye that moves at forty miles or more per hour.

From the air, still a different concept must emerge; while the plane goes faster than the car its very distance from the view causes the latter to be seen more as a unit and the opportunity for dramatizing new forms in the redevelopment areas of our cities have been wasted. Flying over Chicago, Cleveland, Philadelphia, and New York these days, the recent housing and redevelopment groupings are seen as nothing but enormous splotches of unrelieved monotone, even less dramatic—if that were possible—than when seen from the ground. What a missed opportunity! Some of the older streets, parks, and avenues where regular patterns of pavement and planted foliage make contrasts of line and shape, and formal, accentuated axes provide the air-borne observer with at least the pleasure of identity, if nothing more.

It is from the water—in those cities that are flanked by lake or sea or river—that the total aspect of an urban scene may best be observed; and here the effect is often entirely accidental. Even the most dramatic view of Manhattan Island is a product of chance and not of design. While sailing up the Hudson or in a boat offshore on Lake Michigan one sees lines of buildings whose picayune, fussy details are gratefully lost in the haze but even then, unfortunately, do not merge into a rational pattern. They simply become a messy set of objects against the sky, just as the newly rebuilt areas seen from the air fail to create any view at all. These lost opportunities of making our great cities look the exciting things they are can be recaptured by the simple expedient of imaginative application of simple design principles in the basic planning of the large-scale undertakings which are currently challenging us all over the land. To think not only in plan but from the point of view of the beholder on foot, in the window, in a car, plane, or ship is only one of the primary skills that need to be applied by the planner.

THE ART OF TOWNSCAPE

The conscious arrangement of physical things for man's convenience, safety and pleasure rings in my mind as Charles Eliot's definition of the planner's art. It derives, perhaps, from the classic Wotton phrase, "commodity, firmness, and delight." Convenience and safety are given plenty of attention in our plans today, but if man's pleasure and delight are ever achieved it is by accident or afterthought. It need not be. Nor is it necessarily a matter of expense, other than a modicum of time and effort on the part of the designer. And as Dean Hudnut has said in criticizing some recent housing projects, "the strict economies noticeable in the purchase of brains . . . account for the wholesale nature of our enterprises, its machine-like processes, its tedious uniformity." It takes so little expenditure for the right brains to do the job as it should be done.

The missed opportunities are constantly at hand. The other day I drove past a vast new project, Ravenswood Houses, in Queens. Not too bad, as a whole—what one could see of it in its unfinished state. But there, at one side, loosely attached to a building that differed in no particular way from a dozen others as to size, shape, and position, stood a huge cylindrical smokestack, throwing the whole composition off balance. A little thought and care might have relocated or redesigned such a functional element making it the dramatic focus of the whole group of buildings instead of the eyesore it is. One recalls how successfully Perkins, Wheeler and Will, in collaboration with Eliel and Eero Saarinen, accentuated the smokestack in their Crow Island School at Winnetka, making it the crowning feature of their design. This failure to realize the potentialities of the countless "service" aspects of modern buildings and of groups of buildings seems to haunt contemporary designers who strive, usually in vain, to "apply" meaningless decorative elements, while ignoring the lively possibilities that are there for the taking, before their very eyes, in the form of smokestacks, watertanks, elevator shafts, pump houses, garages, and other elements considered unworthy, apparently, of "architectural" treatment.

The art of capturing these potentialities of design in making a group of urban structures a delight to the eye has been given much more attention in Britain than in the U.S.A. There, they have worked up a whole branch of city-planning that they sometimes refer to by the term "townscape," an ingenious name for the art of urban design. The *Ar-*

chitectural Review, which is probably the most sophisticated and spirited as well as the most scholarly of periodicals in the field, carries in almost every issue an article dealing with one or another phase of this art. For example, special study is given to "hazards," by which term they mean the artificially created buffers to traffic—pedestrian or vehicular; to such problems as "intricacies," "multiple use," "changes of level," "floorscape," and the careful design of "street furniture" and "significant obstacles." The whole problem of trees and the question of "paving versus planting of open spaces" are considered as integral parts of the "townscape" from the beginning, not as a problem in horticulture or "landscaping," in the way that our redevelopment planners so often handle it as an applied afterthought, treating the landscape architect as a sort of "exterior decorator." This is, of course, self-evident to some of our better-informed planning agencies and housing authorities who have worked with enlightened architects, site planners and landscape architects, and it would be presumptuous for me to hold that there is not, occasionally, collaboration at the very outset among these groups in some of our own large-scale undertakings. But it is the exception rather than the rule, and its necessity must become recognized and accepted among the administrators at the federal and state level and by the sociologists, the engineers, the run-of-the-mill "housing" architects, to say nothing of the lay members of municipal councils, commissions, and authorities who select and engage professional talent.

(Come to think of it, probably the best concrete suggestion I could offer for improving the design quality of our large-scale undertakings would be for the government to provide every member of a local redevelopment commission and housing authority, as well as every architect, landscape architect, and site-planner involved, with a subscription to the *Architectural Review,* which perhaps could be written off against some future "aid to Britain"!)

Among recent articles in the *Architectural Review,* whose very titles seem curious to us until we see what they have in mind, is, for example, a piece entitled "Truncation," which describes the psychological effect of the view obtained by the *gradual* revelation of a background by the intervening foreground as opposed by a view that is seen all at once. The author gives two examples, first, a scene in a Dutch town where only the gabled roofs are seen until one crosses a bridge and the lower parts of the houses are revealed; and, secondly the famous Lutyens-Baker controversy over the truncation of the main axial view of the great Viceroy's house at New Delhi. Here, as always, the British planner, in the main tradition of great planning through the ages, thinks in terms of the human observer and usually not in terms of grandiose vistas—making the exception where these are as clearly called for in such specific instances as New York's United Nations Capitol, just as they are by India's government buildings and Washington's Mall.

Too often the argument for "civic design" is taken as a plea for the grand effect everywhere, at all costs. And if some of its protagonists have held to this view it is all the more important that the terminology be clarified. For, admitting that impressive vistas and axes have their place as important symbols in the world's great capitols—if sparingly used—it is the more intimate aspects and local features of cities that need the most conscious, careful attention and design. Small squares, as free of athletic activity as of vehicular traffic, for pedestrians to wander through and get a sense of inclosure and peace, are sadly missing in our ambitious schemes for high towers, widely spaced in vast, windy expanses of playing and parking fields. The reaction against closed courtyards, just because many of them were too narrow, has gone far enough. We need more of them: the hollow square or rectangle has its place and should reappear in our site plans. The use of arched passageways cut through building blocks, of continuous planting and paved walks extending through and under buildings raised on piers above the average ground level; the introduction of occasional setbacks in the façade of a row of street level walls—whether of shops or houses—to relieve the eye and provide occasional shelter from sun or wind; the creation of subtle differences in level, accented by retaining walls, flights of steps or ramps, and bits of small-scale sculpture at eye level; the placing of benches where the weary walker really wants to find them; the encouragement of outdoor eating and drinking places, intimate, inexpensive, and sheltered from the extremes of climate and close enough to where people live and work; or of open store fronts, similarly sheltered, inviting leisurely shopping safe from dangers of street and playground; colorful planting, selected judiciously for long-term durability as well as for direct enjoyment; paving that, like granite-block-and-grass, can make a pattern on the ground, costs little and yet discourages fast motion on wheels of every sort.

All these and more are the common language of our planners, true enough, but usually thought of in their social aspects, less often as being the vocabulary from which the designer, in building up an effect makes his conscious selections and placements to delight the eye and the spirit. Giving to each and to all of these the sensitive attention needed to fuse them into a harmonious whole, while always remembering that each must serve to give direct enjoyment to people if they are to be worth including at all, requires that they be considered from the very beginning of the planning process and not fitted in at the end of it, when and if there is place for them. And to combine these small-scale pleasures with the large-scale outlook—to tie in the intimate, interior of the neighborhood with what lies outside it, the surrounding presence of the great city of which the neighborhood is but a part—calls for the designer's skill at its highest level.

A splendidly successful example of such all-around, conscious design (involving "truncation," incidentally, among other things) is Valley View Homes, a public housing project in Cleveland designed by J. Byers Hays and others. Here an arrangement of residential and community structures, beautifully in scale with the human occupant and sensitively following every contour of an irregular site, takes advantage of the opportunity of contrasting foregrounds skilfully planted with colorful perennials, and pointed up with occasional sculpture, all placed in masses that partially conceal yet partly let in the spectacular view of the industrial valley below and beyond. Turning around, the spectator looks uphill, through a foreground of other small buildings, suitably subordinated, to a many domed Greek orthodox cathedral, symbol of the faith of many in the neighborhood, which is fittingly allowed to dominate the scene. Such examples are all too rare in our cities but opportunities to create them can be found in every redevelopment area and made much of if the will is there to do it and the imagination and skill available to turn the raw materials of site and structure into a well-composed whole that has the direct effect of providing the eye with exhilaration and the mind with satisfaction.

British Planners Lead the Way

In Britain, today, almost every plan that we see is an example of the generous use of this technique; it can be recognized at a glance by the intricacy of a small-scale reproduction of a planning scheme which, when examined carefully, reveals hundreds of distinct, individual groupings, of new and retained buildings, small open spaces, varieties of footways and other means of circulation, winding ways and countless other evidences of the painstaking care that went into every phase of the work. By contrast, our plans look as if they had been done by the fist of a giant, indiscriminately stamping an identical pattern of spots representing spaced towers over square mile after square mile of what had once been, and what might have become again, a living neighborhood.

The recently available schemes for the Lansbury-Stepney-Poplar reconstruction area in London are a case in point. Here, a series of eleven neighborhoods are being planned so as to "maintain and recreate" the three communities involved, with all their "amenities." If, in London, one can still use the power of selection as to what is to be retained where so much demolition occurred haphazardly through the blitz, surely we could apply this method to our blighted areas where demolition will fortunately, we hope, be strictly under control. These British plans show a sensitivity to local color and tradition that would not permit the ruthless, wholesale wiping out of an entire thriving neighborhood as is being proposed by some of the USAnian redevelopment schemes now in the works, including that for Greenwich Village in New York. Where there is the slightest possibility of retaining, restoring, or improving any building, group of buildings, open spaces, row of trees or blooming meadow, monument or even ruin in blitzed London these are skilfully, economically, gratefully, even lovingly, worked into the new layout. The only added expense is for the brains and care hired to do the selection and the planning.

Moreover, these plans in almost every case provide for gradual reconstruction rather than doing it in one fell swoop. The careful timing of various stages of a redevelopment scheme is one of the noteworthy features of the British system, seldom used in the U.S.A.

Adjusting the style of new buildings to that of some of the old ones retained within the area is another facet of the skill whose application I am calling for. So often our large-scale undertakings seem to have been conceived in a vacuum, at a distance, on a drawing board mounted in the proverbial tower—not of ivory but of the brass that characterizes some of our more affluent "plan factories." What results looks as if it were surrounded by a solid wall—as New York's Stuyvesant Town almost literally is—so little relation does it bear to the existing, growing city all around it of which it can and should be a living part. But the redevelopment of whole communities is often intrusted to absentee designing-firms who know little and care less about the spirit and customs of the locality they are changing so drastically, even when some proportion of the present residents are theoretically, according to law, to be rehoused or given new places of business in the same area. Is it any wonder, then, that so little thought is given to the "amenities," the chance to give pleasure to the individual who is to live and work there?

What so strongly characterizes the British schemes is this accent on the intimate, the small-scale, and the human. Instead of La Ville Radieuse, imitated unconsciously, perhaps, but repeated *ad nauseam* and decked out in tedious red brick and limestone trim—in strange, perverted deference, presumably, to some vague "colonial" ideal—the new London neighborhoods will recreate the beauties of the small town, the college close, and the village square, but in the structural vernacular, wherever a new building is called for, of clear, honest, contemporary design.

While the planner need not, necessarily, be concerned with the actual design of individual buildings, his over-all control and selection of the style, character, and general type of every building to be part of his whole scheme should not be questioned.

So far as civic design is concerned, it is the association of one building with its fellows and a building in relation to its setting that is important, not the actual design of the individual building, which is the concern of pure Architecture. However perfectly a building may fulfil its function, it is like matter in the wrong place, if it does not suit its surroundings. And in the properly planned city there should be a clear distinction made in situation and treatment between buildings of a public character and business premises and private dwellings.[7]

I would go Sir Patrick one better and say that so far as civic design is concerned it is the relation of each individual project to the others within a redevelopment area and of the latter to the surrounding, existing city that is important, and not only the relation of one building to the others, or of these to the scheme of one individual project in the area.

There is nothing new in this idea, of course: commenting on recent public housing projects in NAHO's *Journal of Housing,* Samuel Ratensky puts it, "no project should be designed as an island unto itself." It is obvious that this approach is needed if we are to attain what Dean Hudnut calls the "general improvement of the product as a *living environment* and as a part of the larger city pattern by way of more thoughtful and skilful designs."

Positive Directives, Not Negative Controls

Many of our architects are trying to insert some degree of legal architectural control into our new or revised zoning ordinances and perhaps this is all to the good if they can work it out. I am inclined to think that by coercive means the best one can achieve is a mere perfunctory adherence to dry, academic standards. Our official art commissions are not distinguished by their creative imagination, and aesthetic zoning would, of necessity, be pegged to the "acceptable" taste of some board of review. I would rather stress here, in connection with redevelopment design, a somewhat broader, yet more practicably achievable form of control.

So far, most cities, like New York, have simply indicated on their master plan—"in so far as adopted"—areas that are "suitable for clearance, replanning and redevelopment," with, in some cases, quantitative specifications as to densities that are not to be exceeded within them. The local *use-* and *bulk*-zoning of the customary sort, as on the books at the time, is also applied as a natural part of the procedure.

7. Abercrombie, *op. cit.,* p. 162.

These are all negative controls. Could there not be added to the official designation of clearance areas something in the way of a positive directive on the part of the city—presumably acting through an intelligent planning agency—as to what sort of new community is to be created, and to state this in qualitative terms? Dean Hudnut in one of his speeches pointed out the danger of allowing a public agency to create entirely new environments not only undirected by any general policy concerned with human enjoyment but actually dictated by the same old urge of obtaining the maximum financial return, ignoring the fact that the entire machinery of the redevelopment act, providing government grants in writing down the cost of land, is aimed at making such a necessity no longer the bugbear it has previously been to planners. The designs of the majority of recent large-scale redevelopment projects says Mr. Hudnut, "have been shaped by intentions which have sometimes only an incidental relation to more permanent social objectives; and these intentions, wholly financial and material, are stamped on their character."

Some indication could be given, in the planning agency's designation of a redevelopment area, as to the character of the new environment that is to be created. In many cases, it might not be entirely new, but in part an improvement and rehabilitation of some existing section that may be only partially deteriorated, due to economic conditions, yet containing social and aesthetic elements clearly worth retaining or even reviving. This is especially true in our large cities where foreign groups have settled in colonies, with their own local color. I would not go so far as to say with New York's Housing Commissioner Stichman that the rebuilding of Chinatown should be replete with fake pagodas and jingle bells, nor do I want to fall into the trap of appearing to encourage the continuance of racial ghettoes. But harmonized and perhaps derivative, rather than imitative, design has its lawful place, and it would not be unreasonable for our city-planning agencies to be responsible for directing the retention, by the designers of projects within a redevelopment area, of certain social, historic, and aesthetic characteristics valued by the existing community. Within larger areas designated for development, special sections could be selected and designated in advance by the planning agency for preservation or rehabilitation as opposed to outright demolition. In so doing much will be salvaged and handed on to the future that may be as important as mere sanitation and sunlight—one or more buildings of historic or architectural value that can easily be renovated, a narrow street of shops that has become a neighborhood market place, a small park, or group of old trees, a church or a settlement house of special significance whose removal would violate feelings even though a straighter street or some other advantage to modern speed and traffic might have to be sacrificed in leaving it where it is and building to and around it.

The British are already providing for such control outside as well as inside redevelopment areas by the workings of the Town Planning Act. To quote from Charles Haar:

> Certain sections of the Act are concerned primarily with the preservation of the aesthetic aspects of the physical environment. . . .
> Provision is made for the permanent preservation of trees and woodland by means of Tree Preservation Orders, to be issued by local planning authorities and confirmed by the Minister of Town and Country Planning. . . . Provision may be made for the payment of compensation for damages resulting from an order. Contravention of a tree conservation order is punishable by a fine not exceeding £50. . . .
> A local planning authority can make an order for the preservation of a building of special architectural or historic interest in its area, in order to restrict the demolition, alteration, or extension of the building. This order, which requires confirmation by the Minister, cannot be made unless the authority (or Minister) is satisfied that the execution of the works prohibited in the order would seriously affect the character of the building. . . . Compensation is payable for damages or expenditures. Contravention is punishable by a penalty not exceeding £100, and the local planning authority may require the reinstatement of the building.
> As a guide for local authorities in the making of building preservation orders, the Minister is under an obligation to compile a list of buildings which would be appropriate for such protection. There is no appeal against the inclusion of a building in a list. . . .
> Where a building preservation order is in force the Minister, or the Minister of Works, can authorize local authorities to purchase the building, if proper steps for its preservation are not being taken.[8]

But over and above the retaining of the good and the old there remains the directing of the new; and while here again we tread upon the dangerous ground of trying to control taste and deciding who is to make the choices, I feel strongly that something can and must be done in the way of conscious direction given by the planning agency to the designers of individual projects as parts of redevelopment undertakings if any sort of order and beauty is to result. Here again Sir Patrick Abercrombie has stated the case better than I could:

> In re-modelling the central areas, therefore, it is impossible to stop at the plan only; some general indications of the architectural treatment must be given, there must be *positive* direction. The regrettable absence of such positive direction can be seen in the new Kingsway and the rebuilt Regent Street; in both cases the direction would have been easy through the existence of a single landowner (the Crown and the L.C.C.). The original Regent Street had been subject to this direction, showing that the beginning of the nineteenth century was more advanced than the beginning of the twentieth in this aspect of town planning. Building under the direction of a

8. *Land Planning Law in a Free Society* (Cambridge: Harvard University Press, 1951), pp. 89–90.

general design (though not necessarily in uniformity) produces a finer effect and costs less than allowing each building complete license.

Improved architecture, both civic and individual, depends of course upon education of the general public and of the architects, the one to desire and the other to provide good building; in the meantime, however, it is necessary to have some machinery to prevent outrage, which is the modest role of the architectural control that may be and should be exercised under planning schemes.[9]

Much might be accomplished simply by the general recognition and understanding of what we really want our cities to look like by those responsible for guiding the course of major public and private construction. Lewis Mumford, in commenting on the rather appalling implications of some of the Skidmore, Owings, and Merrill models currently on display, says, "these developments fulfill the major physical requirements—sunlight, open space, view—but they lack the intimate mediating architectural touches that bring it down to the human scale. The architectural means are skilfully applied but the view of man's needs implicit in these forms is obsolete. . . . This sort of clean, crystallized order has its own kind of beauty . . . but human measure and feeling are absent." And he looks with hope away from these USAnian adaptations of Le Corbusier's doctrine to the work of some lesser known contemporary designers who think in the more intimate scale of the old world and perhaps are indebted to the teachings of Camillo Sitte ". . . not for buildings as such, but for the quality of space and human relationship."

SOME MISSED OPPORTUNITIES

The application of architectural control to planning schemes in Britain, as Sir Patrick conceives it, is something that is usually lost sight of in the more spectacular redevelopment proposals that have been under discussion in our own cities since the war. As a New Yorker, I can speak most easily of those in my home town, but a few that I have seen in Chicago and elsewhere lead me to assume that the situation is a pretty general one.

A carefully worked out redevelopment of Brooklyn's Civic Center some years back appeared, at first glance, to be an excellent solution *as a site plan*. But even overlooking, for our purposes, the fact that it wholly fails to solve the traffic and parking problems involved, the Planning Commission's master plan left the design of each major public building and housing project that was assigned a space in the scheme completely to the whim of the separate department or agency concerned with building it. Thus we are to have a courthouse, a jail, a

9. Abercrombie, *op. cit.*, pp. 162–63.

library, a high school, several administrative buildings, two or three different housing projects, a park, and a war memorial, each going ahead under different auspices, with different architects, out of touch with each other and with no over-all control whatsoever. The total effect will only be revealed as time goes on, and it will be a miracle if it hangs together in any way. A great opportunity missed.

In spite of the attention that was called to this by local architects, the Commission has gone ahead with a similar master plan for a city-wide civic center in Manhattan, which also involves demolition of some substandard areas between the present City Hall Park and the East River. Again neither directives nor controls—merely the assigning of sites, and another opportunity missed to create something of character and distinction. The situation in the area surrounding the United Nations Buildings is another case in point and much has been written about this, many meetings held by interested architectural and civic groups, but to no avail, except for the somewhat ineffective designation of the whole area as "suitable for redevelopment"—a weak and tardy action which, having no teeth in it by way of legal means to prevent inappropriate interim construction by either private or public interests, is of little practical effect. Thus one of the most important of all locations for large-scale controlled planning may go by default, and the U.N. group itself be lost in a confusion of miscellaneous loft buildings and clogged traffic arteries.

In East Harlem a half-dozen sizeable housing projects, each designed by a different architect, have been erected in ill-assorted locations and another half dozen are in prospect which, when all are completed, would rebuild perhaps one-third of this community of several hundred thousand underprivileged citizens of Italian, Puerto Rican, and Spanish origin. Several excellent privately sponsored studies are in existence, with complete and detailed plans, both sociological and physical, showing the way to make of East Harlem a complete, integrated community consisting of several clear-cut residential neighborhoods related to each other and to new and existing public thoroughfares, and with open spaces arranged so as to create a series of vistas open to the river. But these plans are being ignored by the city's "Construction Coordinator" and no effort is being made to relate the existing housing projects with each other or with the various new projects contemplated, some of these to be built with Title I federal aid, or of relating these latter to each other, although all of them lie within the same community, one that has long cried out for replanning. There is still a chance of fusing them together if those now in the works are added to a comprehensive plan for all East Harlem—perhaps by creating a new community center on the site of the ancient Dutch village of "New Haerlem" and connecting it with the broad water-front areas and spectacular bridges to the east. In some such way this very much alive community (and the same holds true of its neighboring, predominantly Negro-populated West Harlem) could become a section of the city of striking personality and unique character rather than a series of haphazardly placed twentieth-century super-blocks, as drab and colorless as the preceding nineteenth-century blocks of the tenements had been.

These examples from the New York scene are being repeated across the land in every large metropolitan area. The application of the design principle to the whole undertaking, before too many detailed plans are fixed, and as a matter of policy, is the only way to save the situation, in each case, if it still can be saved.

Conclusion

I have referred above to Wotton's famous phrase, "commodity, firmness, and delight" which he gave to guide master-builders. What I have been saying here is an attempt to find an equivalent for master planners. Abercrombie paraphrases it by speaking of "sanitation, convenience and amenity," which may be a somewhat clearer statement of the planners' objective than Geddes' trinity, "environment, function and organism." But the label we use does not matter. It is the time that the element of amenity, delight, pleasure, joy, or whatever we call it, becomes once more a living part of the pattern of our cities. The redevelopment program, if it takes this into account, offers the greatest single opportunity for making it a reality. It can do so, however, only if the nature of its relationship to the comprehensive planning process is fully recognized by all who are concerned with redevelopment undertakings at the high-policy level and at their inception. We cannot continue to be satisfied with negative controls to prevent this or that abuse, limiting, quantitatively, the mere mass of building. Positive direction toward clearly conceived qualitative goals of amenity in all its aspects can and must be given at the very outset of any undertaking. To quote Dean Hudnut once more: "The visible pattern of our cities has power to shape the society which inhabits them. . . . Whoever determines the form of our cities determines also the temper of our lives."

Postscript

Since the foregoing was written there has appeared, in the July, 1951, issue of the *Architectural Record*, the text of an address before the annual convention of the American Institute of Architects delivered by John Ely Burchard, dean of humanities and social studies, Massachusetts Institute of Technology. In this paper Mr. Burchard expresses, for architects, the same thesis that I have attempted to express here for planners and for nonplanners involved in policy-making affecting the redevelopment of our cities. Among the many well-chosen quotations Mr. Burchard has used there is one, from Ruskin, which, if the words "architecture" and "edifices" were replaced by the words "planning" and "communities," respectively, would sum up, as no other single sentence could do, what I have tried to say here:

Architecture is the art which so disposes and adorns the edifices raised by man for whatsoever uses, that the *sight* of them contributes to his mental health, power and pleasure.[10]

10. John Ruskin, *Seven Lamps of Architecture* (undated Crowell ed.), p. 15.

CHAPTER V

CIVIC DESIGN AND DEMOCRACY

Arthur B. Gallion

CIVIC design has been associated with affairs so far outside the orbit of our ordinary urban experience since the industrial revolution that the words have a strange ring. Visions of great renaissance squares and baroque plazas loom before us. We visualize patrons of art and their designers lavishing skill and fortune upon the arrangement of buildings and the spaces they surround. Or perhaps we recall the City Beautiful movement and the civic center designs proposed for our home towns but never quite completed. Done up in the finest classic embroidery, civic design implies a monumental splendor with which old cities were adorned and which new cities were promised. We wonder how it all vanished and why those civic center designs fared no better than storage in the municipal archives. The struggle of eclecticism to simulate the effects with pedigreed façades draped along the city streets could not quite recapture civic design as we interpreted it.

Design is not alone a matter of what we see, it is also a matter of what we know. It requires no lengthy proof to substantiate the proposition that cities are for people and that civic design implies some comprehension of human affairs. It is not some abstract form in stone and space; it has a relation to its time and place. Civic art is a social art; this is its beginning and its reason for being. We can admire a handsome façade or a well-modeled building mass but civic design is essentially the form and arrangement of the whole urban environment. This definition covers a lot of ground but so does the future prospect for redevelopment of our worn-out city pattern.

The Key Is Democratic Action

The city is a paradox. Glutted with indispensable mechanical contrivances, the living and working environment is deteriorating in inverse ratio to the progress of technology. A machinery for rehabilitation of the decaying city is now being devised but how are we to achieve civic art in the new design?

Diverted by the everyday task of making a living precious little

75

time is wasted on this question, but most of us are aware that ugliness pervades our surroundings. We are justly proud of our technical prowess but find the city an unsatisfactory place in which to live. Discontent festers, we quarrel among ourselves and with others, and wonder why. We have plenty of gadgets and when others are needed they are promptly invented. But we are unhappy with our lot. It is a puzzling predicament.

The search for good civic design has followed devious paths in vain. The City Beautiful promised much and then vanished. "Architectural control" harnessed the license of too much freedom and froze up. Now salvation appears in the guise of large-scale planning. This new formula captures the scale of the City Beautiful and assures control without the bother of enforcing architectural restrictions. Our redevelopment wagon is hitched to the star of large-scale planning and fervor is at high pitch.

The meanness of the urban environment is intolerable. Block upon block of slums and blight broken into a multitude of ownerships, the obsolete street system, congestion and traffic hazards, inadequate parks and open space, mixed land uses, schools and tiny playgrounds swallowed up by commerce and industry, all fit the large-scale formula so logically. Redevelopment of the city on a large scale is so plausible. It piques our imaginations. The prospects for wiping clean the evil mess and rebuilding in great broad strokes is fascinating; the opportunity to replace blight with fine new communities cannot be lightly dismissed.

These flights are exhilarating but when one views the whole city from such lofty heights a sensation of vertigo wells up. Just how does large-scale replanning offer the solution to our urban ills and produce the design of a city we seek? It might be well to examine this proposition and I should like to begin some two hundred years ago.

The industrial revolution, accompanied by political revolutions in the latter part of the eighteenth and the early nineteenth centuries combined to produce a new social and economic order. This new order brought with it on a sweeping scale a concept of human behavior that we call democracy. It established a framework for human enterprise that was never present in the past. The philosophical substance was present in the Golden Age of Athens and in the great religious teachings before and since, but the political organization of society and the manifold instruments with which to realize the freedom it created are something quite new.

This is the foundation of my thesis and I know it is hackneyed. Much lip-service is given the cause of democracy these days and profuse compliments are paid it. Well-modulated testimonials of faith lull us, though we are conscious of the disonant and sometimes raucous accompaniment of greed and corruption. Skepticism is not uncommon and one is sometimes reminded of a time in history when the Athenians found freedom and then lost it by default.

Perhaps a superior foundation for the freedom of humankind may be cultivated for this world in the future but none now looms on the horizon. Until the arrival of that millennium it is by way of democracy as a way of life and of government, by which the design of cities must improve. This implies more rigorous attention to the quality of civic development than has been our custom and it calls for some changes in our urban conduct.

Most of our swift trip through the first half of this century has been spent in building up to wars and depressions or recovering from them, and present prospects suggest that we may finish the trip, or much of it, in similar state. This is not fertile soil for the cultivation of civic art; it thrives best in an active cultural climate, a culture defined by the dictionary as "the training, improvement and refinement of mind, morals and taste." We have sufficient evidence to conclude that this era has not reached its peak of civilization so, unless we blow ourselves to kingdom come in an orgy of human and material spoliation unprecedented in history, we can anticipate yet unconceived heights of cultural progress. Acknowledging some apprehension, I nevertheless assume that our concern for civic design implies the more hopeful of these prospects even though our preparation may be destined for realization in the twenty-first century.

THE ILLUSION OF TRADITION

I believe that the root of the urban dilemma is one of confusion between cause and effect. We are generally disposed to observe an effect and diagnose it as the cause. This is apparent in practically all of the steps currently taken to solve the traffic problem or to overcome high land costs or to recover a degree of order in the city. To cope with traffic the number of impediments is increased; to cope with high land costs density of population is intensified; and now large-scale planning is the means proposed to obtain a more orderly use of land and a greater harmony in physical appearance.

A curious illusion about the tradition of civic design has conditioned our attitude toward the visual character expected in our surroundings; it has created a state of mind that is thoroughly inconsistent with the nature of our economy, our technical achievement, and our social concepts. Our notion of what an orderly arrangement of buildings and spaces should look like subconsciously stems from times, places, and conditions for which we share no affinity whatsoever. Our image of civic design is invariably projected from conditions when civic art was the property of Pharoahs, kings, or merchant princes; when rulers, desiring the acclaim of their people or goaded by their personal vanity, adorned their cities with palaces and plazas; when great projects were initiated to secure more firmly the prestige of their builders rather than to enhance the environment of the people; when impressive projects, executed with consummate skill and craftsmanship, were grafted upon the city as symbols of the power and might of rulers.

We identify the frontispieces of fine façades as civic design, but forget the streets and slums where the people dwelt. Significance is attributed to the immaculate beauty of the Greek temples in the fifth century B.C., while the attention by city-builders of that time to the amenities of the urban population, the arrangement of dwelling blocks for appropriate orientation and the design of the *agora* for the circulation of the people and the transaction of affairs goes unnoticed. The medieval town contributes its picturesque effects to our tradition rather than the appropriate arrangement of the various parts of the city. Our concept of the tradition of civic art is rooted in a past when rulers established the axis of their authority and ordered the design of space to center upon it; when a grandeur of space was matched by a monumental scale of building forms.

This is the tradition of civic art that has passed along from generation to generation. The City Beautiful movement embraced it and the schools attached pedigree to it. It was a fabulous catalogue of dehydrated forms to be selected and ingeniously assembled upon the loose frame of the metropolis. Monumental symmetry was interpreted as the guaranty of harmony in future city building.

The formula did not come off and civic art was dealt a severe blow. The disillusionment turned into eclecticism; the complete inconsistency between tradition and the new forces of freedom unleashed by the industrial revolution escaped notice or was ignored. Voices were raised in explanation or exhortation but they fell upon deaf ears. Louis Sullivan wove the philosophy of democracy into his works and writings, but the energies of society were absorbed in enterprises that created more immediate fortunes than the spiritual welfare of the people offered. The contradiction between the prefrozen tradition of civic art and the plastic qualities of free and creative minds is slowly dawning, but the tradition lingers on. It has a "new look" and the patrons are different people in a different time, but the tradition is that of their ancestors. Open space is not so broad because land cost is high, but the buildings are higher; the scale is not so monumental because it does not pay dividends, but the bulk is greater. The appearance is different, but the great projects of our cities today are symbolic of the same tradition in civic design.

The impact of the industrial revolution undermined the older tradition but we have not recovered from the shock, and adjustment to the new order is not complete. It is little wonder, therefore, that the prospect for improving the physical environment of cities through redevelopment reverts to projects of large and impressive scale. The meanness of city development and the disease of physical blight is diagnosed as a cause, and we prescribe the large-scale formula as the antidote. The tradition of the big project returns and we seek masters to take the helm and guide us through the morass of our blight to the glorious city of tomorrow. Shades of plutocracy continue to roll across the urban scene.

This is not the purpose of the large-scale formula to be sure. The democratic processes are the fountainhead of the new program for redevelopment, and the rebuilding of our cities is essential to the restoration of decent standards of physical form and arrangement for living. Rehabilitation is essential to the full productive use of our creative powers and the fulfilment of human desires in a peaceful world. These objectives, we contend, may be reached through large-scale redevelopment.

So saying, do we forget that democracy means opportunities for all, not just a few; that many people in our democracy can participate only at the humble scale of individuals in their society? Do we overlook the human scale in democratic processes and that this means the affairs of all men? Are we aware that the large-scale formula is a current in all enterprise that is pressing outward from the center, and that the pressure is drifting more and more people to the periphery of daily enterprise in all walks of life? Is this center to become again the sanctuary for those who are favored with the affluence or influence to receive the honor of responsibility for the great projects of civic design? The curse of blight and the physical deterioration of the city are distracting, but they cannot blind us to these questions as we contemplate the hopeful prospect of recovering a decent urban environment.

LOOK TO THE STANDARDS

To repeat: when the freedom of democracy was substituted for the autocracy from whence came our tradition of civic design, an entirely new concept of human conduct emerged. Democracy is a government of men established upon a foundation of law. The laws are the rules by which people are guided in their conduct. Democracy replaced the age when people were directed by decree, when rulers or otherwise privileged individuals dictated the design of cities. In our time the acts of representative government guide our destiny in more or less direct response to the demands of the people. All may participate in building the city; all may exercise their initiative and skill within the climate of free enterprise, but all are expected to perform within the limits prescribed by law.

Control of the urban environment is through the rules and regulations established by representative government. We have neither faith in, nor desire for, personal power to order the shape of our cities; we accept the rules and regulations adopted through the democratic process as the guides for city-building. Individual competence, skill, and imagination thus assume ever greater importance. The quality of our cities is what the people make it; it is the measure of the collective competence of the individuals who build it.

We are compelled to seek improvement in civic design through the standards of city building that the laws prescribe. The plea for increased competence of people, more imagination on the part of designers, a greater social awareness on the part of builders, financiers, and all the others, is not diminished by this fact, but the laws that apply to city building set the standards for the minimum quality we can expect in civic design.

It is by way of this process that cities have been built. It is by way of this process that they are now in need of rehabilitation, and the diagnosis of this malady should get at the cause, rather than the effect, in order to determine the appropriate cure.

Urban building approaches a state of anarchy. It would seem that the conscience of righteous men alone would restrain them from the rank exploitation of our urban resources but our cities are glaring evidence that modern man retains the instincts of the primitive, when lust was unrestrained by social responsibility.

All this urban mayhem has been committed in accordance with the law; in varying degrees it reflects the standards prescribed in times past and currently by the rules and regulations governing the building of cities. It has come about through the very processes we support for the freedom and welfare of mankind and, perceiving dissatisfaction with the effects, we mistake them for the cause. The cause for the physical deterioration of the city is the inadequacy of standards for urban land use and development. The outrageous density of population permitted in our zoning ordinances is one chief reason for overcrowding of land and buildings; the mixture of land uses permitted to continue by current zoning practice is the cause of blight, community deterioration, and retarded growth. The impotency of police powers to enforce decent standards of physical maintenance is the reason that decay and slums fester in the city. Our laws include provisions that apply to all these conditions, but the standards they establish are so deficient they cannot produce a decent urban environment. This condition is not due to the absence of large-scale planning and building, it is the result of inadequate standards for urban development.

This may have a ring of the old argument that proper standards properly enforced will result in good cities. In a sense this is true but the weakness of that argument is the fact that the question of proper standards has seldom been detached from the strange affection for land values as the basis for arriving at the standards. When the difficulty of high land values is acknowledged, public ownership of land is frequently assumed as the last desperate answer. The issue of public ownership is outside the scope of this essay but there is hardly sufficient evidence to support a proposition that ownership of the land is the single thread upon which the prospect for good city development hangs. Pressure to crowd the land with buildings and indiscriminately mix the uses would persist regardless of who owned the land and it is apparent that our concept of decent standards of land *use* is still vague.

The economic pressure of the low-income group in our society has also impaired the argument for effective enforcement of proper standards. The public housing program, however, was adopted to relieve this pressure and it provides an instrument with which to cope with this vexing deterrent to enforcement of adequate housing standards.

The production of good design in our civic environment is the subject of every building and the space it occupies whether the venture is large or small. Good design is not a matter of size, it is a matter of the relation between all the projects, big and little, that make the city, and this relationship is in large measure determined by the rules by which all are governed in their individual enterprise. It is in the nature of these standards that we will find the prospect for improvement of civic design and it behooves us to address our attention to them before the foundations of democracy are infested with termites.

The Standards Are Deficient

When the industrial revolution exploded the tradition of civic design in our faces, city growth accelerated at such a tempo that regulations for the control of city building could not keep pace. Freedom and license were frequently confused in the mad rush to accommodate the growing urban population and city building turned into land exploitation. Space was crushed beneath a great pile of buildings, congestion was taken for granted and it became the foundation for the currently accepted "economics" of land improvement. Concentration was rationalized to support the spiraling land values; the desirability of proximity to employment and the saving in transportation time were featured as the advantages of congestion.

This sequence reached its logical conclusion in a building bulk so huge that every advantage assigned to it was nullified and we are now obliged to reverse the trend, through redevelopment, by invoking public powers of condemnation and financial assistance from the public treasury. The talent for ingenious design of space inclosed within buildings induced by our concept of land economics is now needed for the design of open space. The accommodation of human activities within open space, the circulation of vehicles and pedestrians, the space for vehicles to travel and to stop, the space for people to move about with some degree of comfort, convenience, and safety, and the space in which human sensibilities may find some measure of psychological repose is the direction that civic design must now turn.

Civic design involves all the dimensions that affect our vision, including motion, and all that affects our other senses of smell, sound, and touch. When we contemplate the beauty of ancient civic art we subconsciously associate, as an integral part of it, the rumble of cart wheels over cobblestone streets, the costumes of the people, the fragrance of landscaped gardens in plaza and courtyard, and the cooling spray of fountains. Civic design is for the purpose of fulfilling the deep human satisfactions that result from the favorable effects upon all the senses. The scream of traffic and the fumes of thousands of exhaust pipes, the sea of asphalt and grease, the distraction of trolley cars, automobiles, busses, and trucks, the steaming heat and glaring reflections from concrete pavements and canyons of masonry walls, are all elements of civic design and they must be reckoned with. It is not enough to manipulate building forms, façades, and masses within the restricted area of inadequate lots; the problem of civic design is the arrangement and allocation of open space. Proof of this is not alone the higher costs to which land is soaring within the city, but the exodus of the people escaping to the suburbs where they may find enough room to live.

This problem requires a new attitude toward the standards of space prevailing in regulations that control urban improvements. It requires a modification in the proportion of building floor space to ground space now permitted in zoning ordinances and building codes. It is not enough to depend upon large-scale projects as the only device for a restoration of balance between buildings and open space; the balance must be prescribed in the legal standards that apply to all city building.

It is a curious characteristic of our current zoning practices that, with the exception of single-family zones, the classifications of land uses do not mean what their names imply. It seems quite natural to assume that the use for which land is zoned would be the use for which it is intended. This suggests, for example, that an industrial zone would be restricted to industrial uses. Paradoxically, however, this is not the case; rather than being restricted to industrial uses, an industrial zone simply means that any use is permitted therein. Similarly, a commercial zone means that any type of development is permitted except industries.

This practice dissipates the advantage of zoning in city development; it is another of the standards that has produced the anarchy of urban building and made the city a game of speculation. Zoning is a negative system of mixed land uses that stands in complete opposition to the principle of planned land uses implied by city planning. Large-scale redevelopment may contribute to the long-range execution of plans for an orderly use of land but it is not a remedy for the sordid effect of mixed land uses. Civic design will improve when zoning itself is designed for the purpose of establishing by law the specific uses for which land is reserved; this marks the difference between planning and gambling in city building.

The quality of our environment is not measured alone by the new improvements that enhance it but by the standard of maintenance we expect of all improvements through the years. Blight is the result of inattention to these standards, and civic design will improve when the people of a city determine that their community shall be maintained at decent standards and that physical deterioration shall be removed by those who are responsible for it. The necessity for such a program is emphasized by the obvious inability of police powers currently vested in local agencies to insist upon adequate standards of urban housekeeping. Slums and blight are admittedly not new phenomena but there is some slight justification for assuming that the experience of some 5,000 years of city building should have taught us some of the ways and means to bring obsolescence under social control. Is it not time to require blighted property in our midst to pay its share of the cost it imposes for community services? Our ad valorem system of taxation on real estate presumes that the cost of community services is in proportion to the capital value of the land and improvements. The natural physical deterioration of cities demonstrates that quite the reverse is the rule. As buildings grow older, receive little or no maintenance or improvement, and contribute to the decay of neighborhoods, the cost to the community increases while taxation decreases. Would it not make sense to reverse our ad valorem taxation and increase rather than decrease the taxation on buildings as they grow older to bring their share of taxes into more direct ratio to their burden of cost to the community. Is it not reasonable to stop penalizing productive enterprise by the uncontrolled competition of old and worn-out facilities privileged as they are with lower and lower taxes and physical maintenance?[1]

CITY BUILDING IS A PROCESS

These views on civic design do not promise an early transformation of the urban scene, and it is strong temptation to substitute devices that offer more immediate results, or the hope for them. We shall undoubtedly proceed with the current redevelopment program; we shall schedule projects and time them for completion, and we shall see some of them built. We shall see in the design of these projects some striking demonstrations of the talent with which many are endowed and we shall also see some sadly mediocre results. The large-scale formula will produce big projects and they will be impressive. They will give us cause to boast of our technical prowess and the vast financial resources at our command.

As we gaze upon these masterpieces of construction, however, and beat our chests with the fervent pride of great constructors, let us realize that we are viewing a return of the old tradition. Dressed in the new look they may appear very up to date but they will not contribute to the strength of democracy in city-building. They will be parts of the city, but they will not be counted among those parts that generate the climate of freedom in our society.

Cities will continue to be rebuilt over the years as they have been built to this day and they will grow as they are being rebuilt. But where, amidst the boundless enthusiasm for large-scale enterprise, has our concept of city planning disappeared? It would seem that, of a sudden, the scale of planning has diminished rather than expanded; that the process of city planning has been diverted to the task of sponsoring big projects for replanning and rebuilding relatively small pieces of the city structure. The words in the planning vocabulary are applied to this process but they do not describe the acts that seem to prompt the redevelopment program.

Large-scale planning is necessary to the future development of the urban environment, but the scale of this planning must embrace the entire area of the city, that area which, despite its geographical and social limitations, presents a political unit for the application of democratic action. Within this unit—the city—it is not the size of the proj-

1. This subject is further developed in Arthur B. Gallion, *The Urban Pattern* (New York: D. Van Nostrand & Co., 1950).

ects that really matters; it is the degree to which each and every project, be it large or small, actually contributes to the welfare of the people who live and work within the total environment. In our burning ambition for bigness let us expand the scale of our planning to the boundaries of the city and restore our concept of city planning that really harmonizes with the democratic processes. Let us establish, by this process adequate standards of urban development within our rules of conduct—the laws—which will reopen the rebuilding and the expansion of our cities to all who seek opportunities for investment in proportion to their means. This is the process by which our cities have been built and it is this process, not big projects reserved for the few to share, that civic design is stamped upon the living and working environment. *Rebuilding, like the building of our cities, is a process rather than a program.*

A Contemporary Aesthetic

The disturbing agglomeration of structures and crowded spaces in our cities will not be boldly swept away when we accept this premise for redevelopment, but there is little prospect for essential improvement in civic design, by whatever path we may elect, until society is adjusted to the new aesthetic perceptions of our time. Technology has outstripped our cultural development and our aesthetic concepts are lagging. The grind toward cultural maturity is sporadic, and many blind alleys have been explored on the way. The industrial revolution shattered all precedents to guide us, and science and invention set a course of unparalleled achievement and tempo.

The machine and mass production altered all previous conceptions about the quality, quantity, and the distribution of goods in society. More and still more amenities for urban living flow into the stream of social activity. Floundering in this sea of production, physical development of cities is turned topsy-turvy. The city is expected to accommodate these changes and it does after a fashion. But the conventional aesthetic assumptions associated with the romance of civic design are disrupted. They cannot be reconciled with the nature of the new facilities in the city, and a curious caution pervades civic design. An imitation of a classic plaza converted to a parking lot is an anachronism, and the presence of a filling station where an ancient fountain ought to be requires not a little adjustment in one's aesthetic perception of civic design.

Our technology and social concepts are geared to the democracy of the industrial age but our aesthetic postulates are not reconciled to the new forms this emancipation portends. Traditional aesthetic assumptions resist acceptance of forms that issue from the solution of contemporary building arrangement and construction. Ages of construction in stone through the long history of city building firmly established an aesthetic conditioned by structural forces in compression. Then the age of steel introduced forces in tension as a new structural principle and the form and arrangement of space was liberated from the traditional limitations of structure. The new forms seem strange and violate entrenched aesthetic assumptions so civic art, whether in modern or traditional dress, is adorned with an excess of architectural trappings to retain an appearance of aesthetic stability. Where two vertical columns provide adequate supports for a building the appearance of three seems necessary, and when traditional forms are discarded unnecessarily odd shapes are substituted to satisfy a conventional visual expectation. Mechanical power and the increase of competitive enterprise changes the requirements for space in our cities, but our traditional concept of urban space is difficult to shake off. Ugliness is attributed to the automobile and electric signs rather than the restricted space that our traditional sense of scale accepts as appropriate. Only recently has the freeway begun to alter this concept of space in civic design.

Overburdened with a building bulk created by the orgy of land exploitation and glutted with the phenomenal flow of products from our industry, it will take time to recover our balance in city design and building. Perception is sharpening and natural forms are emerging, but progress will not come with the mere passing of time. It will take a more highly cultivated moral sense and the identification of man as a creative entity, free to be himself rather than a cultural mimic. It will take a more active city-planning movement to establish appropriate land uses, the circulation system, and the allocation of open space for recreation, schools, parking, and shopping centers. It will take a revision of zoning ordinances and building regulations to require a decent standard of land improvement. It will take maturity in aesthetic perception and judgment to integrate the variety of facilities that make the city. Civic design will then begin to acquire that organic quality we associate with cities of the past and the talents of men will be released to produce a natural habitat for twentieth- (or perhaps twenty-first-) century man.

Then small-scale enterprise need not be suspect of inadequate capacity to produce its share of city building and rebuilding; it will be accommodated in harmony with whatever large-scale development may be necessary. Projects of human scale can be assimilated within the pattern of city development, and projects of rare size and resources will not be requisites to participation in a program of redevelopment. It is conceivable that large-scale redevelopment will be planned and executed as a series of small projects integrated within a master plan and thus may benefit from the creative approach of a number of designers. A human scale will be restored and the variety of solutions will spark the urban environment.

Some predilection for the standardization that is typical of our industrial system may inspire a resistance to variety as an aim in civic design. It is popular to draw the analogy between the house and the automobile, to compare their methods of production, and to conclude that variety is not a characteristic of our age and, therefore, should not be striven for in design. I know the chaos that much wilful variety has produced, the monotony in the application of traditional forms and the façadism produced in the name of diversity. But this knowledge does not alter the fact that the repetition of row upon row of buildings, typical of current large-scale housing projects, impress their inhabitants as "barracks" just as forcibly as the monotonous repetition of quaint speculative subdivisions impress many of us as a hodgepodge of "dingbats."

The industrial system has improved the production of shelter, and more progress will come. But civic design is the relation of all parts that make the urban scene, and it is the juxtaposition of all the parts, regardless of the means by which they are produced, that makes the difference between monotony, chaos, and order. The automobile is not analogous to building construction. It is a moving object and its movement produces its own kind of variety in the visual sense. Buildings are stationary objects permanently attached to the land; they are forms of inclosed space with a fixed relation to the open space they occupy. Imagine a row of Fords (or Cadillacs if you prefer) stationed permanently along a street; the effect would be more montonous than the rows of typical jerry-built houses in a subdivision.

The monotony of repetition occurs less from the application of standardized industrial processes to building construction than from the invariable effort to achieve that traditional unity of form and character expected of large-scale development. A designer does not change his personality each time he rounds the corner of a building; he does not change his spots because a project is big rather than little. Perhaps the quality of design in large-scale projects would be improved if participation were limited to those endowed with the rare skill of genius, but it is hardly such an élite upon which we wish to rely for improvement in the whole living environment.

The most deadly effect of standardization results, not through the rational employment of machine techniques in building design, but from the delusion about the "economics" of land development. In the name of economy population density intensifies to cope with high land cost, only to have land values further increase because of the greater density. The giant piles of brick and concrete skyscrapers and the drab monotony of vault-like row houses in private and public housing projects are the result. Overpowering their inhabitants, devoid of human scale and violating human sensibilities, the permanent burden of these formidable projects upon the living environment is unpleasant to contemplate. The search for that fugitive thing called the "economics" of city building is an occupational disease that afflicts the officialdom of public and corporate agencies alike.

The formula for redevelopment offered in federal and local legislation comes to grips with this dilemma and provides for the liquidation of excess values that have accumulated through the practice of land "economics." It is important, therefore, that rehabilitation set as its first and foremost goal the restoration of human scale in the physical form of the living environment. The huge behemoths of masonry walls punched with holes for windows and stripped of embellishment bear no more resemblance to contemporary civic design than the barbered classic, shorn of its cornices, its pediments, caps, and bases trimmed and its flutes flattened, by which traditional design of monumental edifices bowed to modernity. They are remnants of a lingering feudalism and represent no connection with democratic behavior nor have they contributed one whit to the solution of our real economic problem of urban disintegration.

There Is No Formula

With room for all to play their parts in city building, civic design will not freeze into a mold; it will be responsive to the senses of the people and the variety of forms will be harmonized through the common pursuit of solutions in terms of contemporary methods, materials, and social ideals of democracy. This optimistic moment will not arrive quickly nor will we perceive it as a moment. There will be abuses along the path; exploitation by men of greed, and obstruction and confusion by irresponsible persons will undoubtedly persist, but the preservation of democratic processes, the establishment of decent standards of land use in the laws that govern urban development, and a mature philosophy of our contemporary aesthetics are the steps toward the improvement of civic design.

There is no formula suggested here, no prescription with a label to shake well before using. There are no remedies of architectural control, no art juries, no substitution of one man's taste for another's, that will produce the appropriate design of our civic environment. There is no recipe of large-scale rebuilding to substitute for deficient standards in the rules and regulations that govern city building. There are no statistics and calculations that can be substituted for the creative energy of people intent upon discharging the responsibility demanded of them in a democratic society. Civic design is a social art that has as its purpose the appropriate arrangement of the facilities that form our urban environment. It is an art that requires the expanding freedom and enthusiasm of creative people adjusted to the conditions of their age.

CHAPTER VI

TOWNSCAPE AND THE ARCHITECT: SOME PROBLEMS OF THE URBAN SCENE[1]

VERNON DE MARS

NEW TOWNS

THE English, as part of a national program of decentralizing the urban congestion of London and other large cities, are actually embarked on the planning and building of some twenty new towns, designed to avoid the evils that have come elsewhere in the wake of industrialism.

Now it has been proposed that a similar activity in new town building be undertaken in this country as part of the program of dispersal and decentralization for national defense. And however deplorable and distressing the reasons for taking such measures, there is an understandable excitement on the part of architects and planners in contemplating the opportunities offered by such a program.

The very idea of planning and building new towns has never failed to fire the imagination. It is in many ways the highest art, one time the pleasure of kings. Every age has had its thoughtful men who aspired to, and sometimes did, lay out the urban scene more closely to the heart's desire. And it is so today. What architect would not leap at the chance to do a new town. I have purposely said "to do a new town" as one would say: "to do a school, or a home or an office building"—because this is the popular picture. Both professional and layman would say that, ideally, you would design what you want, then set about and build it according to your designs.

But should any man or any group, for that matter, be allowed to impress their likes and dislikes on a whole community? No, I should say, unless they can approach their task with great humility. For the urban community is a most sensitive organism. It throbs with life and vitality, sometimes under the most adverse physical conditions. Again, it dies or never comes to life in surroundings which would be thought ideal. Is this a plea for generalized planning instead of detailed designing, that is, setting the broad framework of development and leaving

1. A condensation of this paper was presented at the Convention of the American Institute of Architects in Chicago May 9, 1951.

90

the details to a kind of laissez faire? The answer is both yes and no.

I think we put too much faith in planning, that is, planning as such. Men have always planned, but only recently have a complex set of techniques been assembled into a fascinating new profession—"planning as a process," something to be applied to any problem or situation like a poultice. It is not so much that planners on any specific undertaking feel themselves infallible. A great part of the activity of modern planning consists of the assembling and presentation of facts, and the more thoroughly this is done the sounder the judgments may be that are based on them. But it is these judgments that are the meat of the planning activity. They are necessarily human judgments, subject to human fallibility. The soundness of the planners' judgments derive from other less tangible skills than the techniques of assembling pertinent data. The danger here is that faith in these techniques can well become a substitute for thinking.

Familiarity with some of the techniques or even the mere jargon of any human activity can make one appear to be an "expert" in that field. During a stage of my service with the government we were plagued with a succession of "experts." And someone happily found an apt description of them as the men who could avoid all the minor pitfalls as they swept on to the grand fallacy. This description fits too often both planners and architects who set about to "tinker" with our environment.

Not only the urban community but the urban scene is also a sensitive affair. Have you not often seen situations of the greatest charm that were patently unplanned, and others of complete sterility, if not ugliness, which must have been the result of conscious design?

This is not said to prove you cannot plan. It is a plea for greater knowledge of people's needs and desires on the part of planners and architects. It is certainly a subject worthy of greater study but there is one safe conclusion to be made without further study: People desire a great many different things and they need above all, in any planning scheme, a range of choice in where and how they may work, play, and live. This last means choice of dwelling type to suit their temperament, family composition, and pocketbook. And, by way of example, I do not consider an elevator apartment in the middle of town, with the only alternative a house and garden two hours in the suburbs, a range of choice, if neither of them really suits your needs.

There should be, roughly within a neighborhood area, detached houses, rows, flats, and elevator apartments. The new towns could provide this range of choice if the designers set about purposely to plan for it.

THE CITY CENTER

But what about the central areas of the present city? One school of thought says: "Let 'em rot." And so they do in many spots.

But let us be realistic. It won't happen fast enough and completely enough to lower values to the point where redevelopment will be automatic. In the meantime there is undoubted economic waste in the ever growing congestion and inefficiency of most urban centers. And there still remains in most cases all the valid reasons for the city being where it is, and if the original reasons for its location have disappeared, new ones have likely evolved or it would be making no bid for survival. In spite of trends toward great new suburban shopping centers, the central urban core is still the greatest magnet for shopping, business, and cultural activities. This same drawing power is the cause of near strangulation in many cities.

It is interesting to observe, in passing, the extremes of this process: Los Angeles, where no one would dream of going anywhere without his automobile; New York City, where no one would dream of going anywhere with one. Clarence Stein and Aalvar Aalto have both observed that Venice is perhaps the only completely modern city, for here alone is there complete separation of the pedestrian from all other traffic. Merchandising policy in most urban centers is now again based on the shopper as a pedestrian. Are there not implications here for newer patterns? Such proposals as George Nelson has made for Syracuse and New York City, where Main Street or the equivalent is transformed into a planted mall, and cross streets for the most part dead ended as parking bays. This is a planning and functional concept. Aesthetically the removal of traffic from Main Street could hardly fail to seem an improvement. There is a danger though that unless this liberated area is put to imaginative use, the aspect may be one of Wall Street on Sunday—completely "dead." The merchants won't like it— things don't look busy. The shopper may shun it as one does a restaurant with no patrons. The former street area could contain a variety of activities, not excluding outdoor restaurants, refreshment kiosks, benches, kiddie parking for shoppers, etc.

This transformation of Main Street has not, to my knowledge, taken place in any existing city, but a considerable number of new shopping centers, mostly outlying, have been planned on this principle and many of them actually built. One which comes close to embodying all of the current, advanced architectural and planning thought is the shopping center at Park Forest, a suburban housing development some twenty miles south of Chicago. The sidewalks are covered—no need for awnings. There is a lawn where the street would be and vast areas of parking are tucked around out of sight. Cinema, super market, clock tower are all interesting examples of contemporary design, yet the whole thing does not seem to quite come off—does not quite add up to one's expectations considering that so much of progressive planning has gone into it.

It is partly a matter of scale. The sidewalk roofs, at a practical height functionally, are none the less low enough to give a subway concourse affect, and speciality shops are therefore seen only as an entrance door and show windows. Signs are controlled to the extent of being mere indicators of a standard size comparable to street names or "Men" and "Women." One definitely misses the visual interest of flamboyant competitive advertising. This comes as a surprise, for the bane of Main Street is that the cacophony of signs cancel each other out in a kind of visual din. One suspects that this and many other considerations in the urban scene are matters of degree rather than of kind, yet the reformer in all of us, architects or planners, will seldom brook compromise, and our cures for existing evils are usually somewhat overstated. Thus, in this same development, the customary lack of sufficient recreational open space in the average city residential pattern has led the designers (and the management) to provide nothing but open space. Not only are private yards, private planting and gardens not provided—they are not allowed.

The complete removal of Main Street's signs might leave a sorry sight behind. The possibility of course is purely academic, but something is wrong here that might yield to improvement. The English would gather all these considerations under the heading of "Townscape"—the total visual impact of the urban scene. It is a term that does not allow compartmentalization. The building façade, seen for the most part at a sharp angle, is a small part of the visual image of the street, in fact the street surface itself in many cases presents a larger area to the eye than the buildings lining it. Could it not be given more consideration even if we might seldom afford the marble paving of a St. Marks Plaza or the terrazzo zebra stripes of the sidewalks in Buenos Aires? Asphalt and cement are not the only practical covering for horizontal surfaces. Brick and cobblestones can add texture and visual interest in areas of specialized use. "Townscape" includes also the furniture of the street: the lamp posts, trolley poles, fire hydrants, street signs, refuse containers, mail boxes, benches, phone booths, and plant boxes. There are quite enough of these impedimenta to cause some distraction as one seeks to indulge in the pure aesthetic line of a new façade. All that is asked for the street furniture is that as much consideration as possible be given to its design and placement.

In view of the foregoing, it is obvious that shop signs and advertising become almost a dominant element in any townscape. I would not have them abolished if I could. They are a delight by night, particularly since the advent of neon lights (some years now). At night the exclamation "a veritable fairyland" is applied to such places as Times Square and the main street of Reno, Nevada, no things of beauty by day. Can it be that the lettering itself, the work of trained and capable sign artists, is well designed for the most part and coupled with the inherent grace of a thin glass tube, and the glowing spectrum colors, contains all the elements of a pleasant aesthetic experience. By day the tubes are invisible and the sign must compete for interest, not only with all the other signs but with all the things to be seen in the light of day, people's clothes, buildings and their materials, the bright colored objects of transportation, even the sky and clouds. Backgrounds and mountings are thus understandably made large, but it is exceptional when the sign composes with or enhances the building of which it is often so large a part. In color it will blatantly ignore its background. In design it will not have advanced beyond Refrigerator Regency or Juke Box Modern.

Signs are an interesting, colorful, and legitimate part of the street scene. Their designers must be taken into the sphere of the planner and architect. Could they not be made a little more conscious of a certain civic responsibility and even of the art form which they are exercising? The architect, on his part, should give greater consideration to sign design and location, bearing in mind that if he is overly discreet, the adjustment will be made later and not at all to his liking. There have been examples where whole shop façades have been treated as a huge two- or three-dimensional poster lending a change of pace and scale to the street when well done.

It is not this centermost part of the existing city, however, that most concerns us here, but rather that first or second ring of growth which now, for reasons known to all of you, has earned the epithet of "blighted." It is convenient, yet no one would build there; it is slowly sinking economically, yet it is considered so valuable by everyone that nothing at all can be done to change it. Here is one place where redevelopment under the federal Act of 1949 is meant to operate.

The Aesthetics of Housing

Many cities are well along in the planning stages of their redevelopment programs and sooner or later their proposals must take three-dimensional form. The question of *what* form—what *patterns* are to be created, *how* redeveloped is the same as for new towns and is the province of anyone qualified to deal with or even to think about the matter: the sociologist, the historian, the planner—yes, even the architect. The architect should, of course, have some of the qualifications of these others, but whether he has or not, it will be the architect who gives the finite architectural form to these proposals. It is not a small responsibility.

The reasons for providing a range of choice, both cost-wise and in dwelling type, seem as valid to me here as in the new towns with their likely lower densities. The proportion of types might be different but the principle holds. And the architect will find this one principle his greatest weapon in combating the seemingly inevitable deadliness and sterility of so many large planning or housing schemes. This is an aesthetic or, at any rate, a visual consideration, a question again of townscape. It will also be found a factor of stability from the point of view of both sociology and economics.

It is, however, these very aesthetic considerations that I should like to pursue further, for who else is to deal with them if not the architect.

First, let me say, the aesthetics of the urban scene are far from pure. Architects and planners should thus question all generalized or mass solutions to the city pattern, whether "builders' suburbia," Corbusier's "towers in the park," or insurance companies' "towers surrounded by more towers." These may be dramatic, impressive, even aesthetically exciting in an abstract way, but they are not human and they cannot be appraised visually without the observer sensing the false premises on which the design is based. They cannot possibly express the way that more than a minority of the occupants would prefer to live if they had any other choice.

Should we not perhaps recognize certain real values of the old city. Why do architects who plan housing projects for others prefer to live in Georgetown, Telegraph Hill, and the East Side? These are symbols, but many other slum areas will do. I think it was Catherine Bauer who said that any sensible city planner doing a new town would always include a good slum where the architects and planners could remodel themselves interesting places to live. Corbusier, you know, in his new plan for Algiers proposed to tear down the whole city, all except, of course, "The Casbah," the great magnificent slum, teeming with life and "human scale."

But the appeal of such areas cannot be brushed aside as mere snobbery (or antisnob snobbery). There are almost always real values and certain amenities, usually in convenience of location, small gardens or remnants of them, a corner grocery close by, a restaurant and a pub or two. The streets, no doubt, are narrower than FHA would have it, and lend much of the charm, and result besides in more room for private gardens. With off-street parking the pattern still would work. The whole thing may be cheek-by-jowl with apartments, studios, and shops, and none the worse for it. If there is a name for all of this it *is* human scale.

These areas all just happened. Why not plan some that way! Not that you can be quite literal about it. But would it not be worth some study? The sociology, economics, and aesthetics of such areas might give some valuable clues to the design of new areas. Just think of the possibilities: a kind of "planned chaos."

I have taken Corbusier's great living slabs somewhat to task but I am not against the high-rise dwelling structure as such. I think it is particularly appropriate to certain types of family—obviously the family with no children or only one or two small ones—traditionally the landlord's preference. But what I want to discuss here about the high-rise is: how high? No higher than the dome of the Capitol, they say in Washington, D.C. A nice height, I say, comes to about eight stories— neither too high or too low. And if you do have children you can recognize them on the ground, even from the eighth floor. Eight stories just clears the treetops in Washington, lends a vertical note in the landscape and still has human scale. And not being allowed to go higher— they somehow, strangely enough, are able to make the economics of it all work out. I do not believe I would like to see apartments twenty stories high in Washington, D.C.

And while on apartments, I think that every dwelling off the ground should be required to provide some private, outdoor, open space adjacent to the dwelling unit. Of course, it will cost something to do it. But private bathrooms are costly too and they have not always been provided either in housing for rent. The private balcony is provided to a far greater extent abroad than it is here even in housing for the lowest-income groups. It is inconceivable that we cannot somehow afford to do it here as well.

I hope I have convinced you that I am not an anti-apartmentite—at least not to the extent of the British planner F. J. Osborn, of Welwyn Garden City, and the New Towns movement. He claims the ten-story "block of flats" has been foisted on the British public by a bunch of upstart young architects, purely for the dramatic effect in the landscape, and there is likely a grain of truth in his statement. I had the opportunity of asking Mr. Osborn just how high a block of flats should be. "Two stories" says he. "No—on second thought—one!"

Aesthetically speaking again, the medium high apartment block has been handled with great distinction in recent years, particularly abroad. I might mention the really beautiful project of Lucio Costa in Rio de Janeiro and the recent flats by the Tecton firm, whose High-point Apartment group in London is now a classic in this field. One should, in all fairness, mention Meyer and Whittlesey's and Skidmore Owens and Merrill's New York Manhattan House apartments, which resolve their particular problem with more than usual distinction, even though they rise twelve stories beyond the particular brand that I have been stumping for here.

It is in another area, however, where I feel that the contemporary architect meets his greatest aesthetic challenge and has so far performed least ably. This is in the collective architecture of the street or group of houses.

The architect who does a single house gives most detailed consideration to the exact site and all conditions surrounding it—trees, slopes, and other houses. If he does a group of three houses, they are likely still to be entities and will receive a quite thoroughly individual treatment and subtle adjustment to each other's presence. But if the group is ten—or worse yet, fifty—we have a "project." Now subtlety goes out the window. We have a broader canvas and must paint in bolder strokes. It is assumed, as a tenet of good design, that "unity" is always a desired quality. Yet it is "unity" that makes "projects" out of housing. The builder may well be more nearly right, were his "variety" not so naïve, with his superficial parade of styles all in one city block. But it is presumptuous on the part of the designer to state that people do not really need variety; that it is a bourgeois conception. In this context it is something deeper than that. There is no use comparing houses with automobiles off the assembly line. ("You don't mind owning a car just like your neighbor, do you?") How often do you find a group of cars lined up, of the same make, off the same assembly line, as you often see a group of houses. Only at the plants, or in delivery, or showroom, or army compound, none of these situations the normal environment of the car.

Nor will a reference to the Italian hill town or Mexican village serve but to prove that *their* harmony, through repetition of form and materials, is of a quite different order from the soulless repetition of the speculative builder or assembly line project planner. The element of chance and imperfection and the human touch is present in the first case though the materials are the same. These are all lacking in the second case through the very processes that make the buildings possible at the present time. The totality of the effect is the difference between a garden wall of field stone and another wall of precast blocks.

We must not labor these analogies, we should not wish to make modern production processes any *less* efficient. A question: Can the planner find for us a way to permit a certain scrambling of builders' activities in any one area so that no more than a few of his current products are contiguous? There might ensue less false variety in each of the latter, but the total texture of the urban pattern would be improved. I know of a building type—a small group of flats which has appeared in scattered spots throughout a western city. It is immediately recognizable—sometimes the treatment varies from site to site, but one does not mind seeing this same scheme repeated, decentralized in this manner. I should have quite other feelings about seeing them all collected in one vast "project."

Repetition of elements is a basic device in architectural design. Columns, windows, beam ends are often used to create pattern or rhythm through repetition. There are occasions where repetition of an architectural entity has been employed with heightened aesthetic effect. There seem to have been twin temples, twin towers, and twin pavilions at various periods. Alfred Roth's and Marcel Breuer's Doldertal Apartments in Zurich gain immeasurably through being twins in a series, set at an angle to the street. The proposed third repetition was never built and though it might possibly—not necessarily—have made the whole a third more effective; I feel definitely that the composition could not have stood a fourth. Each entity in itself was too complete, perhaps too unique. This does not seem to be so much a matter of scale. Repetitions of much larger, though less assertive blocks of flats, have been carried to the number of eight or more with apparent success. This is perhaps because the *large* block of flats is rather of necessity a formal composition and its entity can take further formal composing.

All this I feel is in marked contrast with the problem of the detached or row house. I class these together for they share no facilities or activities (such as elevators, entrances, corridors, etc.) with other dwellings. The row house's party wall does not have the same functional implications in design. Then what is the design expression of these. In both cases we have a complete living unit, including a portion of street or garden frontage. Each unit should have a life of its own, expressive of the lives within. The gardens will vary with each family's desires. Some will paint their trim a different color. Some will add a porch—why not? The typical housing-project row house today could not take this treatment. It has been designed as an entity for six or perhaps eight families. There is no expression of the separate units and change in trim color on the fifth and sixth windows from the left end would look silly.

What is needed in the design approach to the row house is a grouping of no particular length, breaking where needed with the topography and with some aesthetically satisfactory demarcation of each unit so that changes may take place there that will add subtly to the interest of the group. This might be called noncomposition, or even unity-through-variety or again "planned chaos." I'd like to call it organic, but William Lescaze has said that organic is the term that Frank Lloyd Wright uses to describe his architecture, and that Mr. Wright incidentally will not concede that any one else's work is either organic or architecture.

SOME RECOMMENDATIONS

I have tried in the foregoing to pose some problems for the student of the urban scene. These are problems that do need study. And there are new techniques in sociology to tackle some of them—those dealing with families' needs, desires, and the way they live in the things we build for them.

Schools of architecture and planning could render valuable service by undertaking problems of research testing densities and patterns possible for central urban areas, and carrying such studies to an advanced design stage such as the studies of the London County Council made during the last war. City-planning and architecture students at M.I.T. prepared alternate schemes for the East Boston area, at a wide range of densities. The models of these schemes gave striking evidence of what was possible and what was impossible under the various population densities chosen.

If we are to break down the pattern of endless uniformity often forced on architect or builder by outmoded zoning concepts, planners must tackle the problem of flexible zoning to allow diversification of land uses within comparatively small areas.

Architects on their part must go after the builders who are still doing most of the new housing of the country and without their help. But the architect should seriously consider revision of his services and fees to suit the builder's problem. This may have to be a "marriage of convenience." Love can come later.

Finally, architects, planners, and students of human behavior should all give greater consideration to the design of the "micro-environment" —that area bigger than the dwelling, smaller than the neighborhood or even the block, the area where all the details controllable as design add up to poor, or better, living.

PART II

INDUSTRIAL LOCATION AND URBAN REDEVELOPMENT

BY
COLEMAN WOODBURY
with the assistance of
FRANK CLIFFE

EDITOR'S FOREWORD

CHAPTER I outlines the case for including this subject in URS. May I here, therefore, offer only a few additional comments.

In broad terms, I believe that one of the weakest points in the theory and practice of urban planning is the insufficient attention given to processes of growth, development, decline, and decay in cities. This is no new idea, but it will bear restatement. For instance, we take a snapshot of the buildings and facilities of a city—a land-use map. We put together a "plan for its future"—a series of drawings and descriptions of what the city pattern might be. We do not entirely neglect the evolution that has resulted in the present pattern nor the forces at work that will help shape the future one, but, a few generalities aside, what do we actually know about the changes, evolution, processes, dynamics —call them what you will—that might help and might hinder the realization of our objectives? We have a weak sense of time and process in urban planning and, in my opinion, this accounts for more of our failures and inadequacies than is generally recognized.

Of course exceptions to this generalization could be noted. I would like to believe that this part of URS may amount to one small addition to this list and that it may encourage others to lengthen it much further.

Second, this part of the Study is an attempt to analyze and even to explain some aspects of urban growth and change. Except incidentally at a few points and in some parts of chapter iv, it does not deal with objectives—what we should plan for—or with methods—the tools and devices urban communities have at their command today to guide the ongoing processes of change so that they will move in the direction of the objectives.

Even as an analysis and partial explanation, however, this section does not go far. It is concerned to clear the ground, to review what is now known, and to add a little understanding of the broad drifts and trends in industrial location. No planner or redeveloper should expect to find here information of direct application to his particular locality with its own particular industrial make-up. In other words, this section of URS will be useful to planners only or, at least, primarily as they or others supplement it by specific locality studies and with analyses of industrial location trends in specific industries and industry groups. In these studies other units of measurement and other methods of analysis may be advisable. We in URS do hope, however, that some uniformity or similarity will be maintained so that the results may be meaningfully compared.

Next, we have tried to report our methods and findings in ways that will mean something both to planners and redevelopers, on the one hand, and to professional and prospective students of city growth and industrial location, on the other. We have done this in the conviction that the contributions of both groups are needed if urban planning is to advance as it should. The background and interests of these groups vary notably. We ask that each recognize the other's needs. If some parts of this report seem old stuff to planners, maybe they do not to industrial location specialists, and vice versa.

Frank Cliffe did much of the preliminary exploration of this subject and was responsible for the statistical work. Under his supervision, most of the computations were made by Donald Alan Newton and Janet McGovern.

Finally, nearly all of chapter iv was written before President Truman's statement, in early August, 1951, on a policy for industrial dispersal as a defense measure. If this chapter had been written after his statement, it would have been organized somewhat differently but would not have been much changed in substance.

C. W.

CHAPTER I

INTRODUCTION—WHY STUDY INDUSTRIAL LOCATION?

CERTAINLY no elaborate argument is needed to support the statement that urban redevelopment programs, particularly those in large urban or metropolitan areas, make heavy demands on the intellectual capacity and judgment of those persons primarily responsible for them. Not only is this true of redevelopment officials, but it also holds for their collaborators in other official positions as well as for interested civic leaders and for actual and prospective investors.

At the outset of this discussion of industrial location and urban redevelopment, it is only fair, therefore, to ask: Why should redevelopment officials and their associates be concerned with industrial location? Are the relations between industrial location and the essentials of redevelopment clear, direct, and significant?

It is our opinion that several of the connections between industrial location and redevelopment of urban areas are important. We also believe that these relations will become increasingly significant as time goes on and as the redevelopment of American cities gains in stature and momentum. We propose, therefore, in the remainder of this chapter to point out briefly the main ties, influences, or relationships—call them what you will—between the facts, processes, and changes in industrial location and the redevelopment of urban and metropolitan areas.

Some of these connections, to be sure, may be quite apparent not to say obvious. Others may be rather more obscure or even elusive. It seems to us, however, that listing them here and outlining them very briefly should provide a useful background or foundation for the parts of this discussion that follow.

INDUSTRIES AS REDEVELOPERS

First of all, in many urban localities industries of one kind or another may be prospective redevelopers of land acquired and made available for private reuse. What kinds and sizes of industrial plants, if any, are likely to be interested in coming into cleared sites in near-in locations in different kinds of urban or metropolitan areas? Into dead subdivision areas? Into open land essential for sound community growth? Although federal aid under Title I of the Housing Act of 1949 is available for dead subdivision and open land projects only if the new use is predominantly residential, some local redevelopment agencies may wish to undertake projects in these areas for industrial reuse with other kinds of financing. Also, it is not impossible that at some future date the terms of federal aid might be liberalized in this respect.

These questions suggest others. Assuming that some industries will be interested in certain redevelopment sites, which ones would seem to be properly located there in the light of adjacent land uses and of a rational land use pattern for the urban or metropolitan locality as a whole? What sizes of areas would be required to serve these industries satisfactorily? Can local redevelopment agencies provide adequate sites not only for industrial plants, storage, parking, and other ancillary purposes, but also land for possible future expansion of plants and other facilities?

In many localities these and similar questions about industries as prospective reusers of land are aggravated by more or less unsatisfactory conditions as to the present supply of areas for industrial use. Although many zoning ordinances have marked out rather substantial areas as industrial districts, in many urban centers, for one reason or another, substantial parts of these areas have not been attractive to many industries. Also, the trend in many industries in recent years toward one-story plant buildings has increased substantially their land requirements. Some attention has been given recently to the fact that orthodox zoning practice has not excluded residential and other non-industrial uses from industrial zones. As a result, quite considerable parts of some areas zoned for industry have been absorbed by other uses and the supply of good industrial land has been correspondingly reduced. In one sense these are separable problems, but as a matter of practical fact they are closely tied in with the position of many industries as prospective users of land in redevelopment programs.

DISPLACED INDUSTRIES

Quite surely the clearance of some project areas will displace industrial plants and operations of one kind or another. Where will they wish to go? Where in terms of their needs and as parts of an intelligent over-all land use pattern for the urban or metropolitan area should they be encouraged to go? Is there substance in the often expressed fear that once displaced from their present quarters many of these industries would pick up and leave their present urban areas altogether? If so, in what circumstances would such moves seem to be in the interests of the general welfare? In what circumstances would they not be? What responsibility, if any, should redevelopment or other official agencies have to assist displaced industries to find desirable sites for their future operations?

One fact about many of these displaced industrial plants should not be overlooked. Quite often they will be not only small but new or marginal enterprises that have located in blighted industrial or mixed areas primarily because they could find there low rentals in old and rather obsolete buildings. Industries of this kind also are often attracted by the large and diversified labor supply on which they can draw in a more or less central location of a populous urban center. Some of their managers may feel that they would be handicapped in a smaller center or in an outlying location because, in these locations, they would suffer in competition with larger, more stable employers in a more restricted labor market.

In short, then, the first clear, direct relations between urban redevelopment and industrial location are found in industries as potential re-users of redevelopment sites and also in industries displaced by clearance of blighted areas.

INDUSTRIES AS FACTORS IN URBAN PATTERNS

In most urban and nearly all metropolitan areas, industrial uses, not only by their own land requirements but also through their linkages to and effects upon other kinds of uses, are powerful factors in determining the physical structure or land use pattern of the localities. From this it follows that any substantial changes in industrial location in urban areas might well affect, sharply and directly, the structure of these areas in the future. Clearly any changes of this kind should not only be known in general but also should be understood as clearly as possible by planners and redevelopment officials, one of whose major objectives is to help shape intelligent land use patterns for their communities. Some students of the urban scene believe that important changes in industrial location within urban areas are either now under way or imminent. We shall take up this question in some detail later in our discussion. Here the point is that the facts and trends of industrial location, whether or not they may be changing or about to change markedly, do influence the physical urban structure and pattern of growth.

Because this seems to us a consideration of real importance, we wish to emphasize it by outlining in summary form what seem to us to be major factors and forces determining urban structure or land use patterns. From this outline we will try to point out the influences that industrial uses exert.

Although no one can claim to have a complete or satisfactory explanation of what land uses go where in urban areas, several major forces, factors, or influences on urban structure have been identified. They operate in various combinations and in some fairly clear and in other more complex ways. With no attention to refinements or nice points of definition or elaboration, these major factors are:

1. *Topography.*—For example, retail business, most industries, and rail transportation lines ordinarily seek fairly level sites. High income residential districts often are found on heights, in rolling land adjacent to pleasant bodies of water or other physiographic features that provide amenities or attractiveness.

2. *Competition of uses.*—The various major categories of land use differ markedly in their location needs as well as in their ability to pay land rents or purchase prices. A "hierarchy of rent-paying ability" has been recognized.[1] In general, a common order of ability to command sites in competition with other uses is: (*a*) office buildings for financial, advertising, and similar tenants are more or less tied with higher cost and volume retail uses; (*b*) highest-income residence; (*c*) secondary retail uses—neighborhood stores; (*d*) wholesaling and some light, loft-type industries; (*e*) moderate-income housing; (*f*) other industries; (*g*) low-income housing. Although no listing of this kind will hold without qualifications for all urban areas because of their differences in size, aggregate income, and economic composition, the order given here illustrates the principle.

Obviously not all of these or even most of these types of uses will be in direct competition for any large number of sites. Often, however, two or more of them are in direct competition and each of these may be in competition with others in other parts of the urban area. Thus, by a kind of link-chain effect competition of uses for sites does operate. Also it is obvious that this competition takes place not only among the various categories of land use but also within each of them. Further, the land or space requirements of a corporation, industry, or other unit may be split up. Thus the central offices of a large insurance company may compete for space in the most expensive part of the central business district while its voluminous records and many of its clerical employees may be in a building in a district of much lower land cost.

It has been suggested that, within the requirements of each land use, competition for space operates to reduce to a minimum the "costs of friction": i.e., transportation costs plus site rentals or costs of owning.[2]

1. See, for example. *Regional Survey of New York and Its Environs,* Vol. I B, monograph on "The Retail Shopping and Financial Districts" (Regional Plan of New York, 1928), p. 13 ff.

2. Robert Murray Haig and Roswell C. McCrea, *Regional Survey of New York and Its Environs,* Vol. I, "Major Economic Factors in Metropolitan Growth and Arrangement," chap. ii.

This is an interesting hypothesis, but it has not yet been verified. Measuring site costs is not too difficult, but what or whose costs of transportation?

3. *Limiting or retarding influences on competition for sites.*—These include (*a*) direct measures of public control, such as zoning; (*b*) high asking prices for sites based on more or less speculative holding in anticipation of future higher-income uses; and (*c*) zoning and assessment practices that recognize and indirectly support these speculative elements. Operating against speculative holding are the various carrying charges incurred by the owner. These, in turn, are often offset wholly or in part by taxpayer uses so-called—either buildings or other uses devised for this purpose—or the "mining" of existing structures to the same end.

The working of competition in this field is also complicated by the fact that most urban land improvements have long physical lives. Old buildings that by any rational system of accounting would have been entirely depreciated through one or more ownerships still continue in the market and in competition with other property. Also, some uses of land clearly are able to push off many of the costs that they entail onto other uses or the community at large. Probably the chief offenders in this respect are the highest density uses in the central business district. Many of them produce large incomes, but the municipality struggles with the costs of parking, long-haul transit, traffic congestion, and control that they help to produce. To be sure, they meet some of these costs through the substantial taxes they pay, but it seems very probable that often a substantial part of these costs are paid by others.

All in all, these retarding and complicating factors in various combinations exercise a very considerable influence on land-use competition. Unless they are at least recognized and partly understood, competition of uses as a force in urban land structure may become almost a meaningless or even misleading phrase.

4. *Transit and transportation facilities and costs.*—Although their effects on urban structure are also complex, their importance in determining land use patterns is unquestioned. Accessibility for persons and goods is an essential quality of nearly all urban land. Easy, frequent, and relatively inexpensive access for both people and materials is one of the distinguishing characteristics of most retail districts and only to a lesser degree, of most types of industrial areas.

5. *Complementary and opposed uses.*—Not only do land uses compete but many of them supplement each other. This fact largely accounts for certain affinities or linkages among uses. Thus wholesale, storage, and similar uses cluster around major retail districts. High cost shops often pull out of the main retail districts in the direction of

the highest purchasing power residence. Job printing and other service activities are often located outside of but very near to the major financial and office center. Although we do not know much about the journey to work of urban dwellers, a fair amount of evidence points to the probability that industrial workers, as distinguished from people employed in central business districts, sooner or later seek housing fairly close to their places of employment.[3] Thus industrial location, at least that in sizable districts, may be a major force in determining certain kinds of residential land use.

, Also, it is quite clear that some uses repel or drive away others. Industries that produce noise, fumes, smoke, heavy truck and rail traffic are the prime examples of this fact. From it has come almost unexamined the common idea that all industry or at least most of it should be segregated from other types of development. More recently this idea has been questioned in many quarters. It is now contended that many kinds of industries are quite satisfactory neighbors for residential, secondary shopping, and even some kinds of recreational land use. If this notion should be generally accepted and zoning and other public measures adapted to it, the result would be another substantial modification in land use patterns.

6. *Social-psychological factors.*—Although this complex of forces is little explored, examples of its influence are on every hand. The prestige of certain residential and business addresses is reflected in the rentals they command. The widespread and apparently growing segregation of residential uses by income, race, tenancy or ownership, size, and social position of families is discussed elsewhere in URS. At one time it was said that every skyscraper office building was a monument, an advertisement, or a failure. This may not be strictly true, but it points to the far from simple motivation responsible for many of these structures. The differing social values (in the noneconomic sense) attached to land speculation accounts for some substantial differences between the land use and planning problems of American and British cities. One or two recent investigations of the location of new industrial plants indicate that the officers responsible for the decisions have not been blind to the quality of schools, parks, hospitals, and other public and civic services in different localities. Also it seems evident that the exactions of rackets and of elective and other local officials who take "honest graft" in the form of payments for permits, licenses, and other services have an effect on industrial location out of all proportion to the amounts of money involved.

Even a quick examination of this or any similar list of factors de-

3. For example, J. Douglas Carroll, Jr., "Some Aspects of the Home-Work Relationships of Industrial Workers," *Land Economics* (November, 1949), pp. 414–22.

termining urban land use patterns should substantiate the opinion that industrial uses have important influences on the over-all structure of urban areas. Industrial uses, themselves, account for some 5 to 15 per cent of the privately owned, built-up area of many cities of different sizes and composition. In the future these proportions seem almost certain to increase because of the trend toward one-story plant buildings, off-street parking, and other ancillary uses of land. Thus, industries are important competitors for and users of urban space. Not only are they highly dependent on various forms of transport and transit, but often their needs, actual or prospective, have helped to determine the location or extension of these facilities. Various industrial uses not only have important linkages among themselves—e.g., suppliers and warehousers to industrial customers, and users of semifinished products or by-products to primary producers—but they also help to determine the location of substantial amounts of housing. Some but not all industries repel other uses and attract still others.

Certainly even this rapid and generalized analysis goes far enough to indicate that industrial location as a factor in urban land use patterns deserves the careful attention of redevelopment officials and their collaborators in most urban and nearly all metropolitan areas.

INDUSTRIALIZATION AND POPULATION GROWTH

In still another way industrial location bears upon local redevelopment. In recent years and particularly since World War II, much has been said and written about broad inter-regional or intersectional shifts or migrations of industries in this country. Economic and industrial publications have frequent articles on one or another aspect of this phenomenon. Even popular magazines run highly colored accounts of the industrial booms in such relatively young metropolitan areas as Houston and Los Angeles.

As we shall point out in more detail later, the common phrases of industrial shifts and industrial migrations are rather misleading. With relatively minor exceptions, industries have not been moving out of one section or geographic region of the country into others. Rather what has been happening is a marked difference in the rates of industrial growth among the different major sections. Some of the less thoroughly industrialized regions have been attracting new industries and branch plants of larger companies at a much more rapid rate than they did previously and at a relatively higher rate than some of the more highly industrialized sections. Growing markets in these less industrialized regions, new supplies of labor tapped and developed during World War II, newly developed or augmented sources of relatively cheap power or raw materials, and hitherto neglected advantages of climate and other resources are among the factors in these shifts in the rates of industrialization. It also should be noted that rates of industrial growth vary not only by regions, but also among the various major groups of industries.

Here we wish only to point to the fact that these differences in rates of industrialization often affect materially the rates of population growth in urban and metropolitan areas. Both the rates of growth and the economic and social composition of population increases have to be reckoned with by urban redevelopers and their associates in several ways.

The implications of this statement probably need little elaboration. We might assume, for example, two urban localities of substantially the same size and population. One might be in a section of the country in which the rate of industrial expansion is high and increasing; the other in a more or less stationary or slowly growing region. In the first, a redevelopment program would have to be planned in the light of the requirements for private and public capital investment to serve the needs of additional industry and population. Its prospects for a continuing housing shortage across the board would be higher than in the second city. Simply because the first locality would see its industry and population growing more or less under the impetus of forces outside the city itself, its redevelopment officials might find the public response to their program more apathetic than in the second urban center where many people might be somewhat apprehensive of the future and, therefore, might be looking for ways and means of improving the attractiveness of their city by doing away with its worst areas of blight and congestion. Even more clearly the relative emphasis on redevelopment of built-up areas on the one hand and on dead subdivision and open land undertakings on the other would differ substantially between the two cities. Land speculation as an obstacle in redevelopment operations probably also would differ markedly from one of these areas to the other.[4]

In short, not only directly as redevelopers and as determinants of urban structure and pattern but indirectly as factors in population growth and composition, industrial undertakings will help to shape

4. Because most urban centers in this country have had, so far, records of fairly steady to spectacular population growth, most of their citizens and many of their officials are inclined to assume this to be a continuing phenomenon. Much of the common arguments for urban planning and redevelopment is based on expectations that all or nearly all cities will continue to grow more or less as they have in the past. This, of course, is by no means assured nor is it essential to the case for planning and redevelopment. A good example of competent urban planning based on an expected decline in population is the *City of Manchester Plan* (England) by R. Nicolas (Norwich and London: Jarrold and Sons, Ltd., 1945).

both redevelopment programs and problems. It would seem only common sense, therefore for those primarily responsible for redevelopment to know more than a little about the industrial prospects of their localities in light of these broad differentials in industrial growth.

Industrialization, of course, is by no means the only or even, in some urban areas, the main factor in population growth. As an economy matures the proportion of industrial workers usually declines somewhat. Distribution, including retail business, professional, governmental, personal and commercial services—e.g., recreation, finance, and real estate—increase relatively. Furthermore, urban centers vary considerably in their reliance on industry for their economic life and growth.[5] With full recognition of these facts, however, industry is a mainstay of most urban centers, and therefore, its broad patterns of distribution and change are significant considerations in urban growth, planning, and redevelopment.

It might be argued that local redevelopment officials and other reasonably wide-awake persons will know well enough whether their locality is booming in population and industry or merely holding its own or actually declining. This may well be, but it does not seem to us an adequate reason for brushing aside available information on trends in industrial expansion. Some of these differentials in rates of growth have been in the making for some time. Others have developed relatively rapidly. Planners and redevelopers not only should know what is happening in their localities now but also, and more significantly, what lies behind these happenings and whether or not they are likely to continue. Certainly no urban planning or redevelopment agency has so much information and knowledge that it can afford to neglect any of the background facts and trends that might help it to make out a little more clearly the probable future growth of its area and the character of its probable needs for development and redevelopment.

THE ECONOMIC BASES OF URBAN AREAS

The final point in our case for suggesting that industrial location is a subject of first-rate importance for urban redevelopment programs is rather closely related to the one we have just sketched. It also rests on what we take to be the demonstrated fact that satisfactory redevelopment requires not only good urban planning but also a close and effective relationship between the officials primarily responsible for these two activities of urban government.

As the scope of urban planning has grown over the past fifteen or

5. See William H. Ludlow, *Urban Redevelopment: Problems and Practices,* Part II, "Urban Densities and Their Costs," chap. iv, footnote 11.

twenty years, more and more local planning agencies have begun to look more carefully into what is often called the economic base of their communities. In other words, urban planners are trying to identify the economic activities that are the primary support of their urban communities, that account in large part for its existence and its economic and physical characteristics, that may influence directly the growth in population and the amount and distribution of its aggregate income in the future. A somewhat similar objective has been recognized and similar techniques have been developed by federal and local housing agencies over the past several years. They constitute one part of what has come to be called housing market analysis.

Not only are planning agencies analyzing local economic factors and experimenting with methods of using them in estimates of future urban growth and composition, but at least a few of them have suggested what they take to be desirable additions to the economic base of their communities. Almost always these suggestions are for a diversification of economic activity, including industry in its usual sense of manufacturing or fabricating operations.

All of this work is in its earlier stages of evolution. Clearly it presents some difficult problems in procedure and method as well as equally difficult questions of interpretation and policy recommendations. An example of the latter is this issue or objective of industrial diversification. Certainly it seems sensible for urban centers, particularly those that have a large part of their economic base in heavy or producer-goods industries normally subject to wide swings in volume of output and employment, to try to attract other industries with more stable records of economic activity.[6] On the other hand, not all localities are suitable locations for all kinds of industrial activity. Query: How far should local planning agencies go, with or without the help of state

6. At least for the very large metropolitan areas, this proposal may need considerable further examination and qualification. Philip Neff and Annette Weifenbach in their *Business Cycles in Selected Industrial Areas* (Berkeley: University of California Press, 1949) undertook a fairly thorough analysis of cyclical movements in Chicago, Cleveland, Detroit, Pittsburgh, San Francisco, and Los Angeles. In their chapter on "Conclusions:" "The relative amplitude of area cycles cannot be foreseen from knowledge of the industrial pattern of the area involved, of its resource base, of the region it serves, or its rate of growth or decline. Simple rules for prejudging cyclical variation are not possible because the factors conditioning cyclical response are too diverse. Pittsburgh, relatively constant in size and in concentration in producers' durable goods, does not generally have abnormally severe cyclical swings. Los Angeles, growing rapidly, and like Chicago in its diversity, failed to show evidence of comparative stability and resembled Pittsburgh in its response to cycles more than any other area. Cleveland likewise differs from Los Angeles in nearly every respect except the intensity of its business cycles. Only in Detroit did industrial pattern invariably reflect itself in measurably different cycles, and here the influence of its one great industry, automobiles, is sufficient to affect noticeably not only the real series but also debits and store sales. Economic life in Detroit may be said to be dominated in all phrases by this industry . . ." (p. 193).

industrial or development agencies, in planning for and offering inducements to types of industry not now located in them? How can they
avoid planning for industries that in fact will not come into their localities? Conversely, perhaps they will be able to attract certain industries that will be improperly located in their areas and, therefore, may
find the going hard or even impossible. How can urban agencies estimate the balance of gains and costs to their communities from various
kinds of industrial growth? Increasingly this is being recognized as a
problem. The old assumption, more or less explicit, that for most communities any and all kinds of industrial expansion are beneficial has
been seriously questioned or actually given up as false.

Questions of this kind are clearly outside the range of this discussion.
This relatively new phase of present-day urban planning, however,
should be understood by redevelopment officials. Few, if any, parts of
urban planning are foreign to their interests and concern. In addition,
redevelopment operations that help to provide good sites for industry
and attractive living conditions for industrial workers may well prove
to be factors in attracting new industries as well as making possible
the expansion of those already in the locality.

Summary and Warnings

What then does the discussion in this chapter add up to? We have
tried to analyze in fairly general terms the major relations between
industrial location and urban redevelopment. We believe that these
relations are fairly direct. Furthermore, they are important to the
preparation and administration of effective redevelopment programs.
Industries of various kinds may be desirable redevelopers of some
sites acquired and cleared by redevelopment agencies. Other industries
will be displaced by the clearance of blighted areas and, therefore,
will have to find new quarters in the locality or elsewhere. The location
of industries within an urban metropolitan area is one of the chief
factors in determining its over-all structure and land use pattern.
Changing needs as to location or shifting preferences among parts of
large urban areas or between them and small cities may help to bring
about substantial changes in these over-all patterns. Through their
effects on urban population growth and composition, broad intersectional shifts in the rates of industrialization will be factors in determining the scope and nature of local redevelopment programs. Finally,
the increasing concern of urban planners with the economic base of
their communities also raises questions and issues that bear directly
upon the work of redevelopment officials.

Two comments of a different kind seem to deserve a place in this introductory chapter. Both are more or less in the form of warnings.

The word industry and its derivatives are used frequently in these pages. Often, they may seem to imply that there is an entity known as industry, the parts of which have the same characteristics in about the same proportions. This, of course, is true only in a very limited sense. The Census of Manufactures recognizes some 450 industries, which it classifies into twenty major industry groups. Among these major groups and among many industries in each of them, wide differences are found in the relative weights of various factors that determine their location. Kind and weight of raw materials and products, the nature of the processes performed, principal markets, capital investment per worker, wages as a percentage of cost of product, dependence on various kinds of transportation, linkages with other plants, and floor area or site area per worker are only some of the more obvious characteristics in which industries differ—sometimes markedly. These and other differences have important effects upon the broad, country-wide patterns of their location as well as on their most appropriate positions within urban and metropolitan areas.

These differences should never be forgotten in reading these pages or in work directly on the industrial aspects of redevelopment. In later parts of our discussion we shall note some points at which differences among industries are significant. To try to point out all such instances, however, would make this discussion more wordy and labored than it may otherwise be. We therefore offer this general warning now.

Also, in this chapter and elsewhere we have put down a number of questions. We have tried to limit these to queries that seem to us of real importance to urban planning and redevelopment. A few of them are rhetorical questions that more or less indicate their own answers. Most of them are not of this kind.

Although most of our readers may not need this warning, we do wish to say that we make no claim that all of these questions are answered in what we can now write. Many of them, as a matter of fact, can be answered usefully not in general terms but only in the light of the particular conditions and circumstances that obtain in individual localities. Others are questions that cannot be answered definitely and flatly even in these terms. In respect to these, however, we hope that posing the questions may serve at least to indicate points to which attention should be given and in which some dangers may lie if they are ignored or brushed over lightly. And, of course, we hope that some parts of the discussion may give background and perspective on concrete local questions and thus enable local officials and others to deal with them as wisely as current information and understanding make possible.

In the chapters to come we propose to take up four more or less re-lated subjects: (1) the main outlines of current theory on industrial location and the major findings of a few recent studies of the consid-erations and factors that influence actual decisions in locating industrial plants; (2) the broad regional pattern of industrial distribution and change to which we have referred above; (3) national security or defense issues in industrial location, particularly as these affect urban structure and patterns; and (4) the major facts and tendencies of actual plant location within various classes of localities, including the major subdivisions of the larger urban and metropolitan areas—the old question of decentralization.

As in other parts of URS, on none of these topics will the analysis or discussion be definitive. The subjects are too broad and complex; the facts and forms of analysis at our command are too weak. Nor do we intend to give equal space to these various subjects. On the first three we simply will bring together what seem to us significant findings and suggestions from the work of others and add a few comments of our own. Most of the items covered have been selected for their probable value to urban planners and redevelopers—not to professional students or researchers in these fields. On the fourth we shall supplement this treatment with the results of some direct investigation and analysis made in URS.

CHAPTER II

LOCATION THEORY AND PRACTICE

THE literature of industrial location is not very impressive. On the whole the subject has received relatively little study from economists or others in English speaking countries. Although this neglect may be understandable in a relatively small, rather homogeneous country such as Great Britain, it is curious that American economists have given so little attention to the supply of material afforded by industrialization in the United States with its vast geographic area and its inequalities in the distribution of raw materials, sources of industrial power, transportation facilities, the supply and character of manpower, and in markets. Most of the scholarly work on this subject has been done by Germans, and relatively little of it has been translated into English.[1] In recent years, however, economists and other professional men in both Britain and the United States have begun to redress this balance a little.

Recent Interest in the Subjects

In Britain in the 1930's conditions in certain depressed industrial areas forced themselves on official and public attention. Under the label of *special areas* they were investigated from various points of view and several more or less thorough analyses led to a number of proposals on what should be done about them. Later the investigations of the Barlow Commission and its well-known report dealt not only with these problems but also notably with many questions of direct interest to urban planners that had arisen from or had been aggravated by the rapid industrial growth of the London metropolitan area, particularly during the 1930's. After World War II, the New Towns program and the policies of the central government in directing and controlling both the amount and location of industrial expansion have kept this question in the public and scholarly eye.[2]

1. For example: August Lösch, *Die Räumliche Ordnung der Wirtschaft* (2d ed.; Jena: Gustaf Fischer Verlag, 1944) ; and *Alfred Weber's Theory of the Location of Industries*, Carl J. Friedrich (trans.) (Chicago: University of Chicago Press, 1928). Lösch's work is reported to be in translation into English but the translation has not been published.

2. The Barlow report is officially *Report, Royal Commission on the Distribution of the Industrial Population*, Cmd. 6153 (London: His Majesty's Stationery Office, 1940). Re-

In the United States much of the pioneering research and exploratory work of the National Resources Planning Board and its predecessors touched directly or indirectly on this subject. During World War II the enormous increase in industrial capacity made location a matter of real concern to many groups in different parts of the country. This interest has been kept alive by the postwar production boom, the recurrent controversy about the capacity of steel and other basic industries, the basing-point decision of the United States Supreme Court, the announced intention of the Office of Defense Mobilization to increase industrial capacity to the point where the nation can have both guns and butter, the atomic bomb as a military weapon, and the prospect that sooner or later atomic power may become an important source for industrial and other civilian uses. Undoubtedly influenced in part by these developments, an increasing number of American scholars and research men in the social sciences have begun to turn their attention to various aspects of industrial location.[3]

A Good Summary of the Theory

In our opinion the best single summary of current location theory for the urban redeveloper and planner is in Mr. Edgar M. Hoover's *The Location of Economic Activity*.[4] Most of its merits for our purposes probably stem from two sets of facts.

First, it was written for an audience that certainly includes profes-

lated in some ways is *Report of the Committee on Land Utilization in Rural Areas* Cmd. 6378 (London: His Majesty's Stationery Office, 1942). This Committee was established by the Ministry of Works and Buildings and its report is commonly referred to as the Scott Report—after its chairman Lord Justice Scott. Other official reports of interest include *First Report of the Commissioner for the Special Areas* (*England and Wales*) Cmd. 4957 (London: His Majesty's Stationery Office, 1935) and *Distribution of Industry* Cmd. 7540 (London: His Majesty's Stationery Office, 1948).

Useful nonofficial discussions include *Report on the Location of Industry in Great Britain* (London: Political and Economic Planning [PEP], 1939); S. R. Dennison, *The Location of Industry and the Depressed Areas* (London: Oxford University Press, 1939); M. P. Fogarty, *Plan Your Own Industries* (Oxford: Basil Blackwell, 1947); P. Sargant Florence, *Investment, Location, and Size of Plant* (London: Cambridge University Press, 1948); and Wilfred Smith, "The Location of Manufacturing Industry in Great Britain," *Town Planning Review* (April, 1950).

Writings on the New Towns program already are so many and varied that even a fair sample of them cannot be listed here. For general background and rationale a good introduction is in *Garden Cities and Satellite Towns* (Report of Departmental Committee, [London: His Majesty's Stationery Office, 1935]); and *Final Report of the New Towns Committee* Cmd. 6876 (London: His Majesty's Stationery Office, 1946).

3. Several products of university men and government agencies are referred to elsewhere in this discussion—some of them at considerable length. Edgar M. Hoover's *The Location of Economic Activity* (see footnote 4) has a selected bibliography.

4. New York: McGraw-Hill Book Co., 1948. A critical and capable review of Mr. Hoover's book by Rutledge Vining of the University of Virginia is in the *American Economic Review* (June, 1951), pp. 502–10.

sional men in these fields. It is one of an "Economic Handbook Series" edited by Seymour E. Harris of Harvard University. The volumes in this series have been prepared not only for classroom use but for adult readers who are not specialists in the subject matter. In the words of Professor Harris' introduction:

> . . . they give the essentials of the subject matter within the limits of a few hundred pages; they present a distillate of accepted theory and practice, without the detailed approach of the technical treatise. . . . The time has come to redress the balance between the energies spent on the creation of new ideas and on their dissemination. Economic ideas are unproductive if they do not spread beyond the world of scholars. Popularizers without technical competence, unqualified textbook writers, and sometimes even charlatans control too large a part of the market for economic ideas.

Mr. Hoover is a recognized authority in this field. He began to study it by an investigation of location factors in the shoe and leather industries. For some eleven years he was professor of economics at the University of Michigan, and at about the time that this book was published became a staff member of the Council of Economic Advisors. Some planning and redevelopment officials who read his book may be rather astonished to find that he shows a keen interest and understanding of many aspects of urban growth, structure, blight, and deterioration—matters that few economists have paid much attention to. He has written with a minimum of technical language on the factors that determine existing patterns of industrial location, the forces that make for shifts and changes, the effects of various legal and institutional conditions on location, and finally on several aspects of policy, objectives, and problems.

It seems practically impossible to summarize a "distillate" of some three hundred pages on a major subject without simply paraphrasing Mr. Hoover's book. Even if an attempt of this kind should seem worth while, it clearly would run well beyond the limits of this part of URS. Perhaps, however, it may be useful to indicate the essentials of Mr. Hoover's approach and a few of his major concepts.[5] We do this only to show the relevance of his work to our interest in the subject and not to provide a substitute for reading or reference to it by redevelopers and planners.

Mr. Hoover assumes that those individuals and groups responsible for locating industries are primarily concerned in finding locations that will help to maximize the returns or earnings from the enterprises. In other words, they will try to find locations that will help to keep in-

5. Although this section of the chapter draws heavily on Mr. Hoover's book, we have not followed his explanation slavishly. Rather we have noted his basic ideas or concepts— sometimes with minor modifications of our own—and have emphasized those points of his analysis that to us seem most significant for urban planners and redevelopers.

dustrial expenses at or near a minimum and income at or near a maximum. They have to do this, of course, in a world in which the essentials of industrial production—raw and semifinished materials, power, and labor supply, as well as the markets made up of industrial and consumer purchasers—are unevenly distributed both as to quantity and quality. The crux of the problem of location is, therefore, for each plant or enterprise to find a location that represents a most favorable combination of adequate but low-cost components of production with high-return markets—both for the present and, as far as can be judged, in the future.

Admittedly, the practice of industrial location like other human efforts falls considerably short of the ideal. Admittedly, too, conditions change and many industries because of their high fixed investment cannot or do not move from locations that have become less than the best for them. Also, tradition, personal preferences, and other factors often influence initial locations and continuance in them when an analysis of expenses and income would indicate better locations elsewhere. With all these and other possible qualifications, this assumption is the foundation on which the current theory of industrial location is based.

Further this theory recognizes two broad types of costs or, more correctly, expenses. The first is *processing costs,* which are the expenses of shaping, assembling, and transforming materials into an industry's product or products. The second is *transfer costs,* which include expenses incurred both in purchasing and bringing materials and supplies to the plant and delivering and selling the products. Of course, the relative importance of these two kinds of costs varies greatly from industry to industry. For many, however, the structure of transfer costs has more influence on current decisions as to industrial location than do processing costs. Obviously this would not be true of some industries that employ a high proportion of highly skilled or other forms of specialized labor. Transfer costs, in turn, are dependent not only on distances of the plant from materials and purchasers, but also on the complex structure of rail, truck, water, and air transport charges, including handling and terminal expenses.

Although in general terms this may seem a relatively simple, common-sense type of theory, its application can become very complex, particularly when a single plant or industrial unit in one location may produce more than one product. Also it is often possible within limits to substitute certain materials for others (e.g., the proportions of ore and scrap in blast furnaces) and to vary the ratio of investment per worker in tools and machinery.

Next in this theoretical structure is the identification of four major types of industry: *material-oriented industries,* which are those in which the expenses of procuring and assembling materials and supplies are relatively large and that, therefore, tend to be located relatively close to sources of supply; *market-oriented industries; labor-oriented* and *foot-loose industries,* those in which neither material supply nor product distribution costs are predominant.[6] Incidentally, many kinds of light fabricating industries fall in the latter two classes and it would seem likely that, as a group, they would be most responsive to inducements offered by particular localities, whether in the form of good living conditions, high-quality public services, efficient local government, or more direct aid and community assistance. We shall take up some of these forms of local inducements and attractions later in this chapter.

Many of the forces that make for shifts, migration, and changes in the relative rates of industrial expansion from one locality or section to another also fit within this theoretical framework. Some of these changes are traceable to variations in the relative importance and profitableness of various markets, to the depletion of older sources of materials and to the discovery or exploitation of new ones, to shifts in consumer preferences that expand or curtail some or all markets, to modification in the structure of costs due to technical invention, new industrial processes, and the replacement of some materials by others that serve the purposes better.

Urban localities of considerable size often have certain advantages to industrial operators that sometimes induce or accelerate changes in location and, in other circumstances, may act as inhibitors or brakes on shifts that otherwise would seem indicated. For example, a large urban center may have superior facilities in the forms of a varied labor supply, producers of semifinished products that are the raw materials of fabricators, readily available subcontractors for parts of an operation, more adequate and convenient repair, servicing, warehousing, and banking, as well as substantial markets both among its other industries and among its population. These advantages of urban concentrations, within certain limits at least, may act cumulatively—i.e., they attract certain industries and the very fact of their location in the area makes it more attractive to others. Many of these advantages, it should be noted, hold quite as well for outlying parts of a large urbanized or metropolitan area as they do for near-in locations within the central city itself.

6. Mr. Hoover stresses the first two of these types; discusses the third at some length but not the term "labor-oriented" and refers only occasionally to the fourth. This four-way classification, although useful, has the dangers of oversimplification, e.g., of implying that a company in a material-oriented industry, say, is concerned only or almost entirely with material costs to it in various possible locations. Clearly this is not true. Dr. Walter Isard of Harvard suggests that a more accurate definition of material-oriented industries is that in them, by and large, savings of transport costs on materials by being located relatively close to sources of supply outweigh cost advantages of other sites.

Another part, or perhaps more accurately a corollary, of location theory in respect to changes and shifts is of particular interest to urban planners and redevelopers. Some students have suggested that the history of many manufacturing industries shows two stages. During the first an industrial enterprise is organizing and getting under way. It recruits and trains labor; selects and weeds out management personnel; develops, modifies, and perfects its processes usually in the direction of more and more simplicity, greater subdivision of labor, and consequently the use of relatively more semiskilled operatives. During this stage the advantages of location within a substantial urban area are many and obvious. In the second or more mature stage, these modifications and improvements in organization, processes, and personnel are much less significant. To be sure, they will continue in some degree, but they become relatively less important. Then, according to this corollary theory, dispersion may occur. Not always or even commonly will the original plant pick up and move to some new location, but its expansion is likely to be in other localities—often those of smaller size in other sections of the country and with more attractive living and community conditions.

In the past few paragraphs we have put down only the barest outline or skeleton of the theory of economic location that Mr. Hoover states much more thoroughly and completely. We have also tried, without distorting the basic framework, to call attention to a few points or implications of the theory that seem to us particularly pertinent to its use by persons responsible for redevelopment programs. We wish to repeat, however, that what we have written is not a summary of Hoover's summary, but only an indication of some of its major ideas and concepts. And we would emphasize that Mr. Hoover's book is valuable to urban planners and redevelopment officials not only as a competent statement of current theory on industrial location, but also for his comments and discussion on public policy and practice.

Two Other General Studies

Mr. Hoover's book shares with others of the same kind one apparently inescapable difficulty. Although he cites some illustrative material, he has set out to state certain concepts and relations rather than to substantiate or to verify them. As a matter of fact, although these concepts do seem to accord, roughly at least, with many of the known facts about industrial location and, therefore, in one sense explain them, most of the concepts are not generalizations from the facts but rather a priori deductions from the assumption of the economic man determining the location of industries. Quite probably many planners and redevelopers who will wish to study Mr. Hoover's work have a fair amount of information and acquaintance with industrial conditions and factors. For those who may feel the lack of this kind of background or who may wish to supplement what they have, two other volumes may be of interest. The first is *Industrial Location and National Resources* completed in December, 1942 by the National Resources Planning Board.[7] Although it does not cover the last decade with its many substantial and probably significant events in this field, it is still a useful and well-organized discussion of industrial location and its problems. The other is *The Structure of the American Economy* (Part I, "Basic Characteristics") put out in June, 1939 by the NRPB's predecessor, the National Resources Committee.[8] Although even further out of date, several sections of this volume, particularly chapters iii, iv, and v, still provide useful information and analysis.

Because location theory, like theories in many other social science fields, is open to the criticism that it is based too much on assumptions, deductions, and chance observations rather than flowing from carefully determined facts, we shall look briefly now at some results of a few recent studies into the factors determining decisions on industrial location as revealed by questionnaires and interviews with persons primarily responsible for these decisions. We do this in no spirit of the old, threadbare theory-versus-practice controversy. As a matter of fact, so few competent studies have been made of decisions on industrial location that by no stretch of the imagination could their results be said to controvert or verify the theoretical formulations. Rather, we wish simply to introduce our readers who do not know these studies to them and to suggest that they, too, can contribute to the knowledge and understanding of urban redevelopers and planners in this field.

INDUSTRIAL PLANT LOCATION IN THE SOUTH

Probably the best-known study of this kind was made by Mr. Glenn E. McLaughlin and Mr. Stefan Robock. Mr. McLaughlin also has a well-established reputation as a student of industrial location. Some years ago he was on the faculty of the University of Pittsburgh and a staff member of its Bureau of Business Research. Later he served as Chief of the Industrial Section of the National Resources Planning Board. During the early part of World War II he was a member of the Plant Site Board of the War Production Board. When this study was under way he was Chief of the Economics and Resources Division of the Bureau of Reclamation and later Chief Economist of the National

---

7. Washington, D.C.: Superintendent of Documents, Government Printing Office, 1943.
8. Washington, D.C.: Superintendent of Documents, Government Printing Office, 1939.

Security Resources Board. During much of the study Mr. Robock was a graduate student at Harvard University. Later he became a staff member of the Department of Justice and more recently has been with the TVA.

The study was undertaken as part of the work of the Committee of the South of the National Planning Association. It was published in June, 1949, by NPA under the title, *Why Industry Moves South.*

By interviews with responsible officers, correspondence, and some examination of company records, McLaughlin and Robock studied location decisions on eighty-eight plants that located in the South immediately after the end of hostilities in World War II—from 1945 to 1948. These plants were owned by fifty companies. All of the plants located in a thirteen-state area in the South from Texas and Oklahoma on the west to the eastern seaboard. The distribution of the plants by states was fairly wide. Thirteen of the eighty-eight went into Tennessee, twelve into Mississippi, and eleven into Georgia. South Carolina had the fewest, three, and Virginia, Oklahoma, Louisiana, Kentucky, and Alabama had four each. Eighteen major industry groups were represented. Chemicals with fifteen plants, food products with eleven, and leather goods and electrical equipment with nine each headed the list.

Most of the plants were of fairly good size. Nine-tenths of them represented investments of $100,000 or more. Those below this figure were primarily cheese, acetylene, and oxygen plants, which ordinarily are small units. Many of the plants required investments of over $10 million.

The study covered several major questions. It looked into the background of the companies to identify the facts and conditions that led to the decision to establish a new plant. (Of the eighty-eight plants, eighty-three were new branch plants of well-established and going companies.) The study also looked for the major and minor factors in the decisions on location and gave considerable attention to the governmental and community influences—taxation, housing, public services, as well as the direct inducements offered by state and local governments in the form of tax subsidies, plant sites and buildings, special financial assistance, etc.

Why branch plants?—The study arrived at a number of reasons for setting up branch plants:

1. The old plant may have reached an optimum size. Building a new plant would mean lower costs per unit than expansion of the old plant.

2. A company has decided there are substantial economies in product specialization. Some companies were convinced that production of several products under one roof was not as efficient as establishing separate plants for the different products.

3. Advances in technology cannot be utilized adequately in old plants. Perhaps the outstanding example is the switch from multi-story to single-story structures. This change has become desirable in many industries. But technical changes that utilize one-story buildings often cannot be integrated with the older multi-story operations.

4. Of major importance in the postwar period was the shortage of materials, labor, or space at the old location. Additional materials were frequently not available. In the old industrial areas the labor supply often was short in the early postwar period. Housing shortages in the big cities hindered an influx of labor. The actual space needed for expansion was not available to a number of companies. The older plants frequently were surrounded by built-up areas, residential, or otherwise.

5. Increased demand for products in the general area or section was a common consideration. It was particularly effective when the transportation rate structures favored a new location or when quicker service to customers was an important factor.

6. Materials for new processes were not available in the old region and could not be shipped in economically. An example of this is a change in nylon production that involves use of natural gas instead of coal. An old West Virginia location was supplemented by a Texas plant.

7. A deliberate decentralization policy is being followed by some companies, primarily to minimize the danger of involuntary shutdowns. Labor difficulties, shortages of materials, or hazards of weather may all cause shutdowns. Distribution of operations throughout the country make it less likely that involuntary shutdowns will occur in all of a company's operations at one time.

8. Sometimes a company did not have time to build in either a new location or at the old. Expanded production was dependent upon an available and satisfactory building.

Who does the job?—McLaughlin and Robock point out that procedures for locating new plants vary widely from company to company. The time available, the experience and ability of those making the decision, and the relative advantages to be secured from proper locations influence the methods used in arriving at the final decision.

Outside consultants were seldom used in determining locations. In the eighty-eight cases studied, outside experts were employed only six times. In three of these cases, the consultants had almost complete responsibility for recommendations on the placing of the new plant. In the fourth, the outsiders checked the location the company had picked. In the last two instances, experts were used to find a satisfactory region. The company then picked a specific location within the region. One of these companies had had unfortunate experiences in choosing locations on the basis of factory space and cheap labor.

Similarly, very few firms of those studied had full-time location experts on their own staff. The Celanese Corporation of America and E. I. du Pont de Nemours and Co. were exceptions to this generalization. These companies, with large expansion programs, do employ excellent and full-time staffs to deal with location problems. Ordinarily, however, decisions in plant location come relatively rarely and are made by special organizations set up within the companies.

McLaughlin and Robock describe briefly the make-up of some of these special committees. The personnel varied from company to company: the heads of departments concerned, one officer for each new plant, a vice-president in charge of manufacturing, or the president of the company in some of the smaller firms.

The majority of the recommendations for location decisions were made by these special *ad hoc* groups. Although some of the work done by such groups seemed to be excellent, it also seems probable that most of the poor decisions were the products of these *ad hoc* committees.

Selection of sites.—After certain preliminary analyses of markets and plant requirements had been made, the process of site location normally involved two related but separate decisions. First was a determination of the *general region* in which the new plant should be located. For the plants in the sample, this determination was made primarily in terms of one of three factors (or a combination of them); markets, materials, or labor. Which of the three was the most important was determined largely by the nature of the industry. Of the eighty-eight plants covered in the study, about 45 per cent were market-oriented, 30 per cent material-oriented, and 25 per cent labor-oriented. Once the proper region was determined, a hunt for a *specific location* was conducted in terms of the spot that best met all of the new plant's requirements.

This two-step process was not rigid or firmly formalized. As McLaughlin and Robock put it:

By selecting a satisfactory location zone on the basis of the most important location advantage, the businessman does not completely disregard all other factors. Instead, he simplifies his decision by assuming that if he selects the general area in accordance with the biggest single advantage for his type of plant, he will include specific locations which will satisfy the other essential requirements for the plant.[9]

If the company is market-oriented, the preliminary market research probably will have determined the general location of the plant. Market orientation is of two general types—orientation to consumers or to another industrial market. Plants producing for other industries usually had a relatively limited choice of location. Examples of this type were

9. *Op. cit.*, p. 25.

manufacturers of sulphuric acid, synthetic fibers, cans, glass, and paper boxes. Plants whose products go directly to consumers had more choice. In the sample studied they were represented, among others, by makers of household chemicals, farm equipment, asphalt tile, and automobile assembly plants.

McLaughlin and Robock point out that market-oriented plants generally were able to find a regional location without extensive studies. Not only were those producing for industrial markets quite restricted but those aiming at the consumer were usually quite familiar with the new territory, because they had been supplying it from another point.

Two basic patterns were common in the hunt for a location among material-oriented industries.

In the first, it was necessary to find and develop material sources that, in turn, can supply an existing market. Examples given for the postwar South are the development of meat and milk processing industries. Rising income in the South has created an expanding market for such products, but it is often necessary to persuade the local farmers to produce the necessary raw materials in quantity. In such a situation, the company tries to determine whether or not adequate material production can be realized. The specific location chosen may be in a community willing to help promote production of the material or else in a natural marketing center.

The second general pattern occurred when one or more adequate sources of supply were already in existence. Examples here were insulating board and othr paper products, phosphorous and sulphur mining plants, as well as nonferrous tubing, the manufacture of which required large amounts of electric power. Even with only one major source of supply, specific locations often were relatively numerous. With several sources, the specific location possibilities were considerably greater in number.

As a class, material-oriented industries were least influenced by locality attractiveness or inducements.

Although transportation costs are items considered in the discussion of market- and material-oriented plants, McLaughlin and Robock recognize their importance by a further analysis in a separate chapter. In general, they believe that current developments are favorable to southern locations.

Labor-oriented plants were generally those with the widest scope of location possibilities. In such industries, transfer costs are relatively small. Production can be carried out some distance from a direct line between materials and markets. Examples were makers of apparel, shoes, office and business machines.

By and large these were the industries most likely to accept a community bonus or special aid of some sort. Of course, other considerations were usually present as well. For example, a relatively small town, most of whose working population could be employed by the one company, was sometimes desired. Some companies in this group wished to avoid metropolitan centers.

The plant managers and other officials of the companies covered in this study differed considerably in their attitudes toward labor costs and allied questions. Many of them were not too impressed by low wage rates. They recognized that wage differentials between northern and southern cities, particularly those of the same size, have been narrowing and probably will continue to do so. Some of the largest companies pay the same rates in their northern and southern plants. Others pay the going rate in the locality plus a small increase to assure an adequate supply and to reduce turnover. In general, labor supply, productivity, turnover, and "attitude" were considered at least as significant as wage rates. McLaughlin and Robock also point out:

> With respect to union organization of workers at the new plant, the attitude of the industrialist varied considerably. The machinery group, made up entirely of northern companies, expected to be unionized and their expectations were confirmed. Nevertheless, every one of these companies thoroughly investigated the community history of management-labor relations before making a location decision. One company said: "It is not the unions we worry about but the type of people they sometimes have leading them." It was the opinion of another company that the unions in the South would not be so "radical" as in the North and West.
>
> The companies locating new apparel, shoe, and textile plants were interested, on the whole, in staying away from labor unions. Two of the companies had no unions in any of their plants. . . . The companies with unionized plants elsewhere placed less stress on avoiding unions than did other companies.[10]

On the whole, the labor-oriented plants required smaller investments than those primarily oriented to materials or markets. Less than a third of the labor-oriented plants cost more than $1 million and the highest estimated figure was $2.5 million. Among market and material plants, about two-thirds cost more than $1 million and many represented investments of more than $10 million.

Secondary factors.—Although the study found that the three factors —markets, materials, labor—were the prime determinants of locations, a number of secondary factors were also considered. If for a single plant location, one of the big three were the primary determinant, the other two often ranked as secondary factors with others that never were of the first order of importance. The secondary factors played their part primarily in determining locations *within* general regions, i.e., in the selection among localities rather than among regions.

10. *Op. cit.,* p. 71.

McLaughlin and Robock identify seven of these secondary factors: (1) local capital and bank credit; (2) available personnel for executive positions; (3) climate; (4) availability of buildings and sites; (5) the local industrial structure; (6) size of community; and (7) company policy in respect to centralization versus decentralization of operations. For the studies in this sample, it was clear that most of these factors were decidedly secondary. If the sample had included more new enterprises and fewer branch plants, it is conceivable that some of these factors might have been somewhat more influential.

In addition, for the plants covered top management assessed several of these factors in different ways. For example, several of the larger corporations had deliberate policies of decentralizing substantial parts of their production with a substantial degree of autonomy or discretion in the hands of plant managers. Others felt that the economies of a considerable degree of concentration of operations were significant. Different weightings of these secondary considerations were also well illustrated by the factors of local industrial structure and size of community. Some companies deliberately avoided localities in which competitors were located. They feared what seemed to them the prospect of too much competition for the available labor supply. Others favored somewhat larger communities with a fairly diversified industrial structure and prospects of substantial, if not too rapid, growth. Some of the smaller companies favored nonindustrialized communities in which they would become, at least for the time being, the main industrial employer. They feared that in larger industrial localities they might be forced into taking the least desirable and efficient members of the labor force. Although local capital and bank credit were not too important considerations for many of these branch plants whose parent companies had established sources of capital and credit, some of them, notably the food processing plants, did give considerable weight to the apparent willingness of local institutions to finance farmers in the production of livestock and dairy products that would be their primary raw materials.

On the whole it was more difficult to generalize about the operation of these secondary factors than about the primary ones.

Although discussed separately, state and local attitudes, laws, local facilities and services, and positive aids and inducements also were secondary factors of some significance for some or most of the industries. Probably the most important was the general attitude of individuals, official and nonofficial. A hospitable and friendly welcome, before and after the new plant went into production, was often mentioned in the interviews and on the questionnaires. After the three major locational factors, the almost unanimous opinion was that these favorable attitudes were important reasons for choosing southern locations. Local attitudes were effective in many ways—from such almost trivial matters as the initial response of local officials and business leaders to inquiries about their communities, to such substantial reactions as deliberate attempts of local manufacturers to discourage prospective newcomers who would draw on the same labor supply, and assurances that water, sewerage, utility or bus service would be promptly extended to a proposed site.

Activities of state planning and development agencies were of some use in gathering locational data. It was also mentioned that, for a number of reasons, state developmental agencies were not often utilized, either because of ignorance of their existence or a belief that the groups had little of value to offer. The stormy and erratic administrations of some states were an excuse for not locating in certain areas.

Some states were avoided because of high or fluctuating tax rates. The second characteristic was the more important. Some companies reported higher taxes in the South than in the North. Industries with an especial interest in taxes naturally were those with a large investment per worker.

Of significance is the relative unimportance of taxes. "It should be noted that no concern included in the survey placed its operations outside the most satisfactory zone in order to obtain a lower tax rate."[11] The tax differentials were influential only in the last stages of locational decisions. When two of several sites were found to be equally satisfactory, differing tax structures might be considered in making the final choice. But generally speaking, taxes were not of great importance in attracting companies or plants.[12]

A number of companies told McLaughlin and Robock of their concern for the general facilities of the community. What did the town have to offer workers and management personnel as a place to live? Schools, housing, churches, hospitals, municipal services, and general attractiveness were definitely taken into account. Such facilities may not be immediately translatable into dollars and cents. They probably

11. John Williams, *New Industry Comes to the South: A Summary of the Report of the NPA Committee of the South on Location of Industry*, (Washington, D.C.: National Planning Association, 1949), p. 27.

12. McLaughlin and Robock did not devote much space to discussion of tax concessions. They pointed out that an increasingly large number of companies are reluctant to accept inducements of any sort, except as a token of good faith. But tax concessions of one sort or another are fairly common in the South. Where available, companies often applied for them even if they had not considered them significant in their decisions on plant location.

Also McLaughlin and Robock have given little attention to firms that considered locating in the South and decided against it. Within this group there may have been companies kept away either by high taxes or fluctuating tax rates.

will show up in some way in the company's financial statements in the long run. Several possible sites were turned down because of inadequate general community facilities. One company has a fixed policy of rejecting any community without desirable living quarters, no matter how attractive from other points of view.

General advertising seems to have had little influence on location decisions. For all the seeming casualness of some of these decisions, it is improbable that industrialists were influenced by a half column advertisement in a weekly magazine. McLaughlin and Robock deprecate the value of shotgun attempts to secure industry. Furnishing data and making special surveys were of somewhat greater value in the cases studied.

Special inducements, bonuses and subsidies, seemed to be declining in importance. Bonuses were fairly common in the South before World War II. Companies were able to get these bonuses and were willing to accept them—notably manufacturers of shoes and textiles. These are labor-oriented enterprises with wide latitude in their choice of sites. Since they are economically able to locate at any one of numerous points and since there were more communities wanting such plants than there were plants to go into them, it is understandable that bonuses were made available and were accepted by some industries. It has been noted elsewhere that, by and large, industries or plants most susceptible to bonuses and subsidies are often of marginal desirability to most communities both because their rates of mortality are high and because their wage structures usually are low.

McLaughlin and Robock emphasize that acceptance of such inducements is increasingly less common in the South. "The great bulk of the concerns included in this survey pointed out that they received no special inducements whatsoever in selecting their plant locations. . . . Corporate executives are generally convinced that it would be poor business on their part to accept any special concession from a local community. . . ."[13] For substantial plants, such inducements are of minor significance in long-term income and outgo. Consequently, especially among the material- and market-oriented industries, subsidies of any sort were not likely to be accepted.

In summary, the industrial plants studied by Messrs. McLaughlin and Robock were largely branch plants of established companies. Most of the companies determined on a general area for a new plant from analyses of materials, markets, or labor supply. Transportation costs and facilities were usually important to material- and market-oriented plants. Within these areas specific locations were selected after weigh-

13. *Op. cit.*, p. 112.

ing a number of other or secondary factors. Here the weights assigned and the relative significance of the various factors varied greatly. On the whole it is probably fair to say that local community attitudes, the levels of public and institutional services, and general attractiveness for living were found to be rather more significant than has generally been assumed. On the other hand, within rather broad limits tax differentials were less important than many persons have supposed. Also, the industries covered in this study, with the exception of some of the textile and shoe plants, were not much influenced by state and local subsidies and special inducements.

LOCATION IN THE NEW ENGLAND STATES

Under the auspices of the Federal Reserve Bank of Boston, Mr. George H. Ellis made a somewhat similar study of industrial location practice in a sample of 106 establishments that located in New England from midyear of 1945 to mid-1948. It was summarized by Mr. Ellis in an article in the Bank's *Monthly Review*, April, 1949, under the title "Why New Manufacturing Establishments Located in New England: August 1945 to June 1948." At the time he was working on this study, Mr. Ellis was a teaching fellow in economics at Harvard University.

Of the 106 plants covered in this sample, 42 were newly organized or "new firms"; 44 were branch plants of parent firms in or outside of New England; and 20 were relocated plants—9 from within New England and 11 from other regions. All six of the New England states were represented in the sample, from Vermont with 7 plants to Connecticut with 32 and Massachusetts with 33. The total represented 15 major industry groups and one miscellaneous category. Apparel and other finished fabric products with 13 plants, textile mill products with 12, and electrical machinery with 11, headed the list. At the bottom were printing and publishing and furniture and finished lumber products with one each, and transportation equipment, lumber and basic timber products, and stone, clay, and glass products with 2 each.

As in the McLaughlin-Robock study, this New England investigation also showed that the decisions on branch plants and relocations often were reached in two steps—determination on the region and on the locality or community within the region. As Mr. Ellis puts it in his article:

. . . This distinction is fundamental for understanding the relative importance of those considerations which dominate the location decision. While a single factor frequently dominated both aspects of the decision, in most instances the region and community were selected on the basis of different considerations. This was particularly true of the decisions of branch plants and firms making relocations.[14]

New firms rarely made an explicit choice as to region. Mr. Ellis thinks that their inquiries for sites "are most aptly described as 'house hunting.'"

Mr. Ellis' summary of his findings gives relatively less attention than did that of McLaughlin and Robock to material-, market-, and labor-oriented industries. Partly this was due to the method of his study and partly to the relatively greater importance of two or three factors that do not seem to be clearly within any one of these three major influences. To be sure, materials, markets, and labor were significant considerations, but on the whole, their relative importance seems to have been somewhat less in the decisions in respect to the location of plants in New England.

Dominant factors for location in region.—In his interviews and other investigation, Mr. Ellis tried to identify for each plant the dominant or determining factor for its location in the New England region. (He did this in full recognition of the fact that "Seldom if ever is an industrial location decision based on considerations of a single factor alone.") For a few of the establishments, however, he was unable to find a single dominant factor. As a result, for the 106 plants, he classified 118 major reasons for the decision. These reasons he grouped into ten classes. With the number of firms reporting each reason or group, they were: personal reasons—37; market advantages—28; production relationships—19; material availability—11; management relationships—8; labor considerations—6; available plant—5; water supply—2; waste disposal—1; transportation facilities—1.

Even in this resumé, three of these classes of reasons—personal reasons, production relationships, and management relationships—deserve some definition. Personal reasons, which were much the most common among the new firms, included the established residence of the chief organizers and officials, their reliance on a relatively few key workers, their reputation in the area with banks, local jobbers, and wholesalers. Production relationships, as the term implies, were almost entirely limited to branch plants. The relationships usually were between the new branch plant and the parent plant of the company. Typically the branch plant assembled materials that had been fabricated in the parent plant or performed some part of the production process that began or was completed in the parent plant. Management relationships were also primarily between branch and parent plants. For several firms, top management officers have found that:

14. *Op. cit.,* p. 5.

. . . the greater the geographical distance between the parent and the branch plant the more difficulty was experienced in maintaining management supervision. It became more time-consuming for key personnel to travel from plant to plant. Orders took longer to be conveyed and executed. In those cases where a custom-built product was ordered through the parent firm, it was necessary for the sales personnel to be closely associated with the production process of the branch plant.[15]

As has just been suggested, in looking into the primary or dominant reasons for location within the region, sharp and significant differences were found among the reasons given by new firms, branch plants, relocations. Of the ten principal reasons or classes of reasons, only the branch plants were represented in each one. New firms' reasons fell into only six of the ten classes, and of these only two had more than two reasons each. Plant relocations cited a total of six classes of reasons of which only three were given more than twice.

Perhaps even more significant was the fact that of all 37 firms giving personal reasons as dominant, 29 were new firms. Similarly, of the 19 firms that assigned high importance to production relationships, 18 were branch plants. Also, of the 8 citing management relationships, 6 were branch plants. On the other hand, market advantages, material availability, and labor considerations were more evenly distributed among the three kinds of firms. Materials, however, were considerably more important to branch plants than to the new firms and relocations, and market advantages were the most important single consideration in relocations.

Selection of specific communities.—The other major question investigated was: Why did new establishments select specific communities in New England? Here as in the corresponding question on location within the region, Mr. Ellis tried to identify a principal reason or major factor for each location decision. He found this more difficult than it was in respect to regional location. As a result, he came out with a total of 198 reasons cited for the 106 plants. All of these considerations were grouped under one or another of sixteen headings. The five most common were: suitable buildings available—62; labor supply—50; personal reasons—27; suitable sites—12; transportation considerations—11. The first three of these factors together were about 70 per cent of the total number of reasons reported as dominant in locality decisions. Except for personal reasons, which again were very heavily concentrated among the new firms, the first five principal determining reasons were fairly well distributed among all three classes of plants.

Urban redevelopers undoubtedly will note that two of these principal factors, suitable buildings available and suitable sites, might be clearly related to a successful redevelopment program. Without commenting

15. *Op. cit.*, p. 6.

on this particular relationship, however, Mr. Ellis does point out that the weight given to these factors, particularly to the availability of buildings, may reflect in considerable part the time period covered by the study. Immediately after the end of hostilities in World War II, industrial space was short in many parts of the country because of the great wartime expansion. In addition, construction costs were rather high and increasing rapidly. Shortages in building materials were common and, therefore, it was difficult to get firm bids on construction projects and completion dates were often uncertain. In these circumstances, localities that had passably acceptable industrial space had a substantial advantage. This advantage might be much less significant in other times. Although the importance of labor supply, as Mr. Ellis points out, had several separable aspects, it seems likely that it, too, was more of a local advantage to some communities during this period than it might be in other times.

SOME COMMENTS ON THE TWO INVESTIGATIONS

Both the McLaughlin-Robock and Ellis studies have the earmarks of careful, competent work. We recommend them for study by urban redevelopers and planners. Here we have tried only to indicate their scope, objectives, and a few of their highlights. In concluding our brief treatment of them, a few comments on them and on their relation to the summary of location theory seem to be in order.

Both studies and particularly the one on New England indicate the considerable variety and complexity of the factors, considerations, or reasons that play important parts in decisions on industrial location. Although the factors emphasized in the theoretical formulation are clearly operative and clearly important, these investigations of location decisions by sample plants at one period of time do not give these factors quite as prominent a position as the theory does. Apparently decisions on the location of branch plants, particularly those of the larger companies, are much more likely to be based on the factors emphasized in the theory than are those of new firms or relocations of small undertakings. Not only the particular conditions of the time, but personal considerations and preferences, actions and attitudes by influential citizens and groups in the various local communities are by no means negligible forces.

Also, three factors are pointed up by these investigators, despite the fact that they do not appear as dominant factors or reasons. One of these, again, seems much more influential with the small new or relocating firms. It is the availability of funds both for venture capital and in the form of credit to operations. The second is a combination of living conditions and public services in the local community. Here it seems to be true that the larger companies are inclined to give more weight to this consideration than has been supposed. It is also probable that these conditions are more influential now than they were even a relatively few years ago. If so, we might quite reasonably expect that they will increase rather than decline in importance in the future. Finally, differentials in local tax burdens seem clearly to be less significant than has often been alleged. In the New England study this seems well established. Some state taxes, particularly the corporate income tax in some of the New England states, were looked upon as substantial disadvantages by the industries, but, with a few exceptions, this was not true of local taxes.

We also would emphasize again one limitation of studies of this kind. Useful as they are, and their usefulness will be substantially increased as more of them are undertaken over longer periods of time, they do cover only companies or plants that have decided to come into the regions and localities covered. It would seem highly desirable to supplement them with other investigations of the factors that deterred other industries from locating within the same areas. Admittedly, studies of this second kind would be rather more difficult to carry out. The task of making up the sample would be more difficult. It also might be harder to get responsible officials to talk freely about areas and localities that they did not particularly favor as locations for their enterprises. Even so, the value of this kind of investigation would seem beyond question.

Finally, it seems worth noting that local agencies directly concerned with the industrial economics of their communities can find useful allies for this kind of research. To be sure, the two studies we have cited were sponsored and largely financed by nonlocal organizations. On the other hand, many localities and certainly all regions could find other agencies directly interested in industrial location and with some resources for undertaking or at least helping to support studies of this kind.

Two other kinds of studies are worth a brief discussion in this chapter: (1) an investigation of how industrialists already established and carrying on operations within an area rate their locations in respect to various factors; and (2) a study of industrial change in an old, largely blighted industrial, and mixed area in a major metropolitan center. These may be expected to bring out facts and relationships different from those resulting from investigations of decisions on industrial location. In some circumstances these may be more or less significant than the results we have just considered. Be that as it may, all three types of investigation in competent hands may help urban planners and redevelopers in the problems that confront them.

OPINIONS FROM ESTABLISHED PLANTS

Our example of the first of these two kinds of studies was also sponsored by the Federal Reserve Bank of Boston, in collaboration with the New England Council. It was done by staff members of the Bank. Mr. Arthur A. Bright was directly in charge.[16]

Questionnaire replies were obtained from 663 manufacturers in the six New England states during the early summer of 1949. These companies had about 20 per cent of the manufacturing employment of the region. As a sample they were heavy on the larger establishments. The number per stage ranged from 35 in Maine and 38 in Vermont to 171 in Connecticut and 291 in Massachusetts.

Industrialists were asked to rate each of twenty-one industrial factors as an important advantage, of little importance, or as an important disadvantage of their existing locations. The twenty-one factors included adequacy and dependability of electric power, attitude of the community, character of the labor force (dependability, productivity, etc.), availability of labor of suitable skills, local living conditions, climate, adequacy of financing and distribution facilities, present plant site, wage rates, present plant buildings, state and local taxes, cost of electric power, availability, and cost of industrial fuel.

In tabulating the replies by state, for the region, and by industry groups, a percentage distribution among the three ratings given above was made for each of the factors, as well as for all of them combined. In addition, for each of the factors and for all of them together, an *advantage ratio* was computed. This was simply the number of firms indicating that the factor was an advantage divided by the number that indicated it was a disadvantage. For New England as a whole the advantage ratio for all twenty-one factors was 2.0, twice as many rated advantages as disadvantages. When the various items were weighted according to their relative importance as determined by other studies, the ratio was 1.4. Mr. Bright at one point makes this summary:

Of the nine major factors, the average New England producer feels that he has definite advantages in the four items relating to labor supply, labor conditions, water

16. This investigation was part of a larger study of "The Present Position and Prospects of New England Manufacturers." It was reported in three articles in the *Monthly Review* of the Federal Reserve Bank of Boston for July, August, and September, 1949. The part summarized here was in the September installment, which had the title, "New England Manufacturing . . . Its Future Prospects." In addition, six mimeographed tables were prepared. Not all of the detail in them was reported in the article in the *Monthly Review*.

supply, and living conditions. He feels that his position is essentially neutral with respect to markets and materials. He feels he is at a disadvantage with respect to tax rates, transportation costs, and power costs.[17]

The opinions of manufacturers, however, varied materially by industry groups. The best satisfied with their locations and their advantage ratios were: instruments and clocks—3.1; furniture—2.9; food—2.6; fabricated metals—2.5; chemicals—2.3; and miscellaneous products—2.3. Three of these industry groups make durable goods; three, nondurable. At the bottom of this list were makers of leather and leather products—1.5; textiles—1.3; transportation equipment—1.3; apparel—1.2; and rubber products—1.1. Four of these groups are manufacturers of nondurable goods; one makes durable goods.

It should be noted that the factors rated were reasonably specific. Thus, instead of listing simply labor, the study gave four labor factors; wage rates, relations with labor organizations, availability of labor force of suitable skills, and character of labor force (dependability, productivity, etc.). Similarly electric power was broken down into its adequacy and dependability and its cost.

Arraying in this fashion the combined opinions or judgments of responsible industrial officers certainly gives a composite picture of some significance. A breakdown by states may not be particularly helpful to local planners and redevelopers. In sizable urban areas, however, a reasonable sample might be made of local manufacturers by various major industry groups.

A study of this kind would show the relative strengths and weaknesses of a locality not as seen from outside by prospective newcomers, but as they appear to those who have had actual experience under the conditions existing at the time and place. It would indicate these relative advantages and weak spots of the locality from the point of view of industrial managements in different kinds of enterprises. Thus it could reveal sore points on some of which, perhaps, changes or improvements could be made. This is not to say, of course, that the judgment of the industrialists should dictate public policy, but simply that their estimate of existing conditions might well be considered in the shaping of that policy. It would also provide some basis for determining what types of industry might find a locality not only a likely but, in fact, a satisfactory place for a new or branch plant.

INDUSTRIAL CHANGE IN AN OLD DISTRICT

The second of these two studies and the last we shall summarize in this chapter is directly related to redevelopment in a large urban center.

17. *Op. cit.*, p. 11.

It is the work of Marcel J. De Meirleir, a graduate student in geography at the University of Chicago, and carries the formidable title, "Manufacturial Occupance in the West Central Area of Chicago."[18]

Essentially it is a descriptive study of an old and blighted near-in district of Chicago. Although many parts of the study are pertinent to urban planning and redevelopment, probably the most valuable is chapter vi, "Changes and Trends During the Last Decade." The methods used were a combination of library work on various land use studies, field inspection and mapping, a questionnaire to industrial firms in the area, and a series of interviews with industrial officers, civic leaders, and real estate men in or directly connected with the district. Staff members of both the Chicago Plan Commission and the Chicago Land Clearance Commission, the local redevelopment agency, helped at various stages of the study.

The West Central Area of Chicago lies immediately west of the central business district. It is roughly two and two-thirds miles long from east to west and slightly less than 2 miles wide. Its total area is just a little more than 5 square miles. Within this area, approximately 100,000 people are employed in industrial and commercial establishments. These included in 1944 more than 70,000 industrial employees. It is one of the major industrial districts of Chicago with 8.8 per cent of the manufacturing establishments and about 10.8 per cent of the industrial employment in the city.

Most of the industrial establishments are in the general category of light manufacturing or fabricating, storage, warehousing, and service industries. Most of the industrial buildings are the old multi-story type, which makes for a high density of manufacturing population in many parts of the area. In employment, the major manufacturers are in non-electrical machinery, electrical machinery, clothing, iron and steel products. In times past, a large proportion of the people working in the area lived in it or nearby, but with recent changes in the composition of the resident population, more and more of the employees have come from other parts of the city and metropolitan area.

Although the West Central Area is a major industrial district, it also has a substantial resident population. It was estimated in 1949 at about 172,000—up from 136,000 in 1940. This increase reversed a twenty-year decline from 194,000 in 1920. Almost 90 per cent of the residential structures were put up before 1894—41 per cent before 1885. In 1940, slightly more than 30 per cent of the structures were rated as needing major repairs or unfit for use and fully 60 per cent were in need of minor repairs.

18. Research Paper No. 11 (Department of Geography, University of Chicago, June, 1950).

In short, the district is old; its structures are largely obsolete; and the area as a whole is decidedly blighted. In general character it is industrial and mixed. Although it has some vacant land, practically all of it is in small scattered parcels. Nearly all of the area is marked by the usual characteristics of blight: obsolete and unfit buildings; poor repair and maintenance; congestion; generally poor living conditions; shifting population; and almost no opportunity for industrial expansion.

A few paragraphs from the concluding section of the chapter on trends and changes indicate their nature and complexity:

Considering the changes which took place in the West Central Area in general and in the manufacturing activities of that area, it is seen that both centrifugal and centripetal forces are active. On the one hand, under the centrifugal forces there is the tendency of emigration of the smaller establishments with local markets, mainly belonging to the subgroups I-A and I-B [e.g., printing, food processing, instruments, chemicals, primary metal products, fabricated metal products—EDITOR]. On the other hand, under the centripetal forces a relocation of manufacturing establishments takes place within the West Central Area, and others are held by the localization advantages of a central location, especially the industries of subgroups II-A and II-B which are increasing their number of employees [e.g., apparel, shoes, furniture, equipment, machinery, transportation equipment—EDITOR]. However, also a few industries of this category have moved recently, such as the A. B. Dick Company [duplicating machinery—EDITOR], and the uprooting conditions in the West Central Area are becoming worse. Thus, there is a danger that other larger establishments may follow the centrifugal trend, especially industries of subgroup II-A whose basic materials are not obtained in the metropolitan area. What is going on in the manufactural occupance of the West Central Area, especially since 1940, is not only a "decentralization," but an "emigration" from this centrally located area to the outskirts, an "immigration" into this area from other cities, and a "relocation" within the area.

The relocation of manufacturing of the West Central Area is taking the manufacturing away from the center of the city; warehousing and storage are occupying more space; smaller establishments are decreasing especially and it is feared that their position will continue to decline as the difficulties in the West Central Area increase.

Actual outward plant migrations have occurred in large numbers between the West Central Area and the districts lying immediately beyond the corporate limits, especially in the case of smaller establishments and those whose position still depends upon the Chicago Loop markets. But many establishments dependent upon the midwest have moved to less highly urbanized areas farther away, while plants dependent on basic materials are locating closer to their sources. This latter aspect is likely to increase and may swell the importance of the heavy industrial districts of the south and southeastern suburban parts of the Chicago Industrial area.

Is it to be expected that the centrifugal trend of manufacturing in the West Central Area will continue in the future? Of the 72 larger establishments asked whether their present site is still satisfactory, 49 answered in the affirmative but 7 of the 49 added that they, nevertheless, wanted to move if it was financially possible or if the "business" would not "keep them there." 23 answered negatively and expressed their intention to move "in the near future." Thus we may expect not only a continuation of the centrifugal movement but an increase in intensity.

Why do these industries want to leave their present site? They want to move for a series of reasons most of which have been mentioned in the analysis of the centrifugal forces active during the last decade. These reasons are: (1) There is a lack of space for expansion; (2) rent is too high and therefore they prefer to erect their own building but the space is not available in the West Central Area; (3) they want better, more numerous and reliable help; (4) a better building is required; (5) some are located in the path of the expressway under construction; (6) others want to get out of the slum area and congestion; (7) taxes and meddling practices are mentioned frequently; (8) there are insufficient loading facilities and space to provide for them is lacking; (9) there are nuisances and disagreements with present laws in the area.

Where do they want to move, if they leave this area? A majority prefer the northwest side of the city or the western and northwestern suburbs; only three will leave for smaller cities outside the metropolitan area, Ogbesty and Bushnell, Illinois, and Lima, Ohio.

Since World War II, the decentralization movement has accelerated, industrial expansion has reached an all-time high, and conditions in the West Central Area have become steadily less and less favorable for a manufactural occupance climate. The trends and developments have therefore reached a critical point, so that for the future there are two possibilities: (1) either the trends will continue as described, without intervention of official agencies—thus robbing the city and the West Central Area of the support of its most substantial elements, men and industry; (2) or something will be done to counteract them. "After all, the considerations which induce industries of more than merely local significance to locate in non-urban and sparsely populated areas are chiefly of a negative sort. It is not the special advantage of these areas but desire to escape from the disadvantages of congested urban living which draws industries hence."[3] ([3] *Industrial and Commercial Background for Planning Chicago*, p. 67.)

The significance of findings of this kind for the planning and execution of redevelopment programs surely requires little comment. Although the over-all picture conforms rather well to the generalizations that have been made on much less substantial evidence, this study fills in the picture for this area and adds a considerable amount of important detail. It emphasizes the often overlooked or neglected fact that industrial change in a badly blighted area often is not all in one direction. Some industries move out; others flow into the vacuum that is created; still others make minor shifts in search of better conditions within the area itself. Each of these movements and the industries that take part in them are significant as well as the net change that they produce in combination.

TWO REFERENCES

Finally, two publications of the Department of Commerce are useful reference works for urban planners and redevelopers concerned with industrial location and change. The first of these is *Basic Industrial Location Factors—Guide for Evaluating an Area's Resources for In-*

dustrial Development.[19] For a substantial number of industry groups this guide indicates the most important and the usually significant factors in their location. Much of the material is in tabular and outline form and the brief text indicates the major uses as well as the limitations of the analysis. The other is a bibliography, *Industrial Development and Plant Location (Basic Information Sources)* by Victor Roterus and Sterling R. March.[20] It covers both government and nongovernment publications, the latter subdivided into seven major categories. Although quite a few of the items listed are out of print or otherwise not available, this is nevertheless the most useful bibliography on the general subject for urban planners and redevelopers.[21]

19. Prepared by the Area Development Division, Office of Domestic Commerce (rev.; Washington, D.C.: Superintendent of Documents, Government Printing Office, June, 1947).

20. Office of Industry and Commerce, Bureau of Foreign and Domestic Commerce, December, 1950.

21. An excellent monograph, which was published after most of this section of URS had been written, is *Industrial Mobility in Michigan—A Sample Survey of Michigan Manufacturers* (Survey Research Center, University of Michigan, 1951). It is based on interviews with some 200 manufacturers in Michigan. If it had appeared earlier or this section of the study had been written later, at least a summary of the Michigan inquiry's highlights would have been included.

CHAPTER III

REGIONAL DISTRIBUTIONS AND TRENDS
IN INDUSTRIAL LOCATION

As we pointed out in chapter i, to urban planners and redevelopers the facts on broad regional distributions and trends in industrial location are useful largely as background. They indicate certain forces, but by no means the only ones, in the growth, stability, and decline of urban populations. And clearly the prospects for change in population size and composition in urban centers, as well as present conditions and those of the immediate past, often have important bearings on the character of local redevelopment programs and on the ways in which they evolve in their localities.

Most of the basic facts for our short discussion of this subject are found in Tables 1, 2, and 3. Of these, Table 1 on the distribution of production workers in manufacturing, is the most important for our purposes. Table 2, on the distribution of population, makes possible certain observations and comparisons of the relations between industrialization and population by major regions. Although these are the comparisons that are most often made, it seems to us that in many respects it is more useful to compare the distributions of industrial workers and changes in them with urban population rather than with total population for the various regions. Table 3 makes this possible.

Essential Definitions

Two of the basic terms in these tables may need definition for some readers. These are "production workers in manufacturing" and "divisions of the United States."

The Census of Manufactures for 1947 defined manufacturing establishments ". . . as those engaged in the mechanical or chemical transformation of inorganic or organic substances into new products. These activities are usually carried on in plants, factories, or mills, which characteristically use power-driven machines and materials-handling equipment."[1]

The major *industry groups* with the average numbers of their pro-

1. *Census of Manufactures: 1947*, Vol. I, "General Summary" (Washington, D.C.: Government Printing Office, 1950), p. 3.

duction workers in 1947 are: (1) food and kindred products—1,099,-478; (2) tobacco manufacturers—103,289; (3) textile mill products—1,147,194; (4) apparel and related products—972,897; (5) lumber and products, except furniture—596,118; (6) furniture and fixtures—282,780; (7) paper and allied products—388,901; (8) printing and publishing industries—438,135; (9) chemicals and allied products—466,458; (10) petroleum and coal products—169,610; (11) rubber products—214,533; (12) leather and leather products—348,529; (13) stone, clay, and glass products—405,755; (14) primary metal industries—1,010,055; (15) fabricated metal products—822,514; (16) machinery, except electrical—1,244,135; (17) electrical machinery—639,-147; (18) transportation equipment—987,142; (19) instruments and related products—181,939; (20) miscellaneous manufacturers, which includes, e.g., jewelry, musical instruments, toys, office supplies—397,-579.

As defined here, it should be noted, manufactures (or industry) does not include mining or other extractive industries, public utilities, warehousing and storage except as carried on by plants or factories as an auxiliary operation to their primary activity.

As far as possible, the Census collected information on:

. . . an establishment basis. As a rule, the term "establishment" signifies a single plant or factory and is not necessarily identical with the business unit or company which may consist of one or more establishments. A company operating establishments at more than one location is required to submit a report for each location; also, companies engaged in distinctly different lines of activity at one location are required to submit separate reports if separate payroll and inventory records are kept for each activity.[2]

Also in the 1947 Census the term *production and related workers*—usually shortened to *production workers*—designated:

". . . working foremen and all non-supervisory workers (including leadmen and trainees) engaged in fabricating, handling, packing, warehousing, shipping, maintenance, repair, janitorial and watchman services, product development, auxiliary production for plant's own use (e.g., power plant), record-keeping, and other services closely associated with the production operations."[3]

Thus it includes practically all workers and their immediate supervisors who ordinarily work in a plant, factory, or manufacturing establishment. It does not include people in top management, legal, sales, public relations, accounting, and similar positions who often are, and in large corporations with many branch plants, usually are located in offices away from the plants or factories. It is very close to the term *wage earners* used in the 1939 Census classification.

2. *Ibid.*, p. 2.
3. *Ibid.*, p. 15.

This term *production workers in manufacturing* is, therefore, very useful for our purposes both here and in the discussion in chapters v and vi. The definition accords very closely with what is usually thought of as factory or plant employment. As an index or measure of industrial location it is good in that it excludes essentially office workers of industrial companies whose place of employment and whose problems as to journey to work, etc., are much more similar to those of other office workers than to those of industrial employees. Also data for plants or manufacturing establishments are more useful for our purposes than corresponding figures for companies or corporations as units.

The term "divisions of the United States" accords less well with common usage, but is not difficult to understand. The divisions probably are more often referred to as *regions* of the United States, and we use this term for them in this chapter. The Census, however, reserves the term "regions" for four combinations of the divisions. Thus the Northeast region includes the New England and Middle Atlantic states; the North Central region includes the East North Central and West North Central divisions; the South region consists of the South Atlantic, East South Central, and West South Central divisions; and the West region is made up of the Mountain and Pacific divisions.

The make-up of the divisions, or (broad) regions, as we shall refer to them, is:[4]

New England	*West North Central*	*East South Central*	Nevada
Maine	Minnesota	Kentucky	Arizona
New Hampshire	Iowa	Tennessee	New Mexico
Vermont	Missouri	Alabama	
Massachusetts	North Dakota	Mississippi	*Pacific*
Rhode Island	South Dakota		Washington
Connecticut	Nebraska	*West South Central*	Oregon
	Kansas	Arkansas	California
Middle Atlantic		Louisiana	
New York	*South Atlantic*	Oklahoma	
Pennsylvania	Delaware	Texas	
New Jersey	Maryland		
	District of Columbia	*Mountain*	
East North Central	West Virginia	Montana	
Ohio	Virginia	Idaho	
Indiana	North Carolina	Wyoming	
Michigan	South Carolina	Colorado	
Wisconsin	Georgia	Utah	
Illinois	Florida		

The Data and Their Use

Before taking up the major facts on regional distribution and changes in industrial location that these tables indicate, we would offer a few

4. *Ibid.*, pp. x and 12.

comments on the character of the data and the measures used, particularly the percentage distribution. These are more or less warnings against misinterpretations and misunderstandings.

First, contrary to a common impression, the number of production workers in manufacturing has not increased in every decade of the approximately fifty-year period covered by Tables 1 and 2. In fact, for two of the decades, 1919 to 1929 and 1929 to 1939, the figures for the United States as a whole show decreases. For the first of these two decades the decline probably was accounted for by the disappearance of the demand created directly and indirectly by military requirements of World War I and also by the installation, during the 'twenties, of improved tools and other kinds of capital equipment that reduced the need for workers. In the second decade, the depression probably was the major factor with improved machinery and mechanical equipment also playing a part.

It is important here to realize that the number of production workers employed does not always follow closely other measures of manufacturing volume or activity. For example, in the 1919 to 1929 decade, despite the small decrease in the number of production workers, the value added by manufacture went up more than 28 per cent. Even in 1939, despite a larger drop in the number of workers, the value added figure when corrected for the change in price level was practically the same as for 1929.[5]

In short, urban planners and redevelopers for whom industrial employment figures are usually more significant than other measures of industrial activity should recognize that the number of production workers has not always increased even over fairly long periods and sometimes has moved in the opposite direction from other measures of industrial activity.

Next, in determining whether a region is faring well or poorly in industrial development, attention should be given to the numbers of production workers as well as to the percentages. The percentages alone may lead to questionable conclusions. For example, in 1929 New England had 12.4 per cent of the production workers in manufacturing of the United States (Table 1). In 1939 this proportion had fallen to 11.6 per cent; and in 1947 to 10.5 per cent. The percentages alone would seem to indicate a gradual but continuous decline. The actual numbers of production workers show a somewhat different picture. In 1929 New England had 1,098,000 workers; in 1939—969,000. Over the ten years New England lost almost 130,000 workers. Although industrial employment for the whole country also declined during this decade, New Eng-

5. For figures on value added see *ibid.*, Table 1, p. 23. Price level index from J. Frederic Dewhurst *et al.*, *America's Needs and Resources* (New York: Twentieth Century Fund, 1947), Appendix 4, Table B, p. 697.

TABLE 1

Distribution of Production Workers in Manufacturing by Divisions of the United States: 1899–1947*

Divisions	1899		1909		1919		1929		1939		1947	
	Number (thousands)	Percentage	Number (thousands)	Percentage	Number (thousands)	Percentage	Number (thousands)	Percentage	Number (thousands)	Percentage	Number (thousands)	Percentage
United States	4,713	100.0	6,615	100.0	9,096	100.0	8,828	100.0	8,340 (7,808)	100.0 (100.0)	11,916	100.0
New England	852	18.1	1,101	16.6	1,351	14.9	1,098	12.4	969 (947)	11.6 (12.1)	1,248	10.5
Middle Atlantic	1,605	34.1	2,208	33.4	2,873	31.6	2,560	29.0	2,355 (2,234)	28.3 (28.6)	3,246	27.2
East North Central	1,073	22.8	1,514	22.9	2,397	26.3	2,542	28.8	2,297 (2,181)	27.5 (27.9)	3,565	29.9
West North Central	266	5.6	374	5.7	500	5.5	474	5.4	435 (376)	5.2 (4.8)	636	5.3
South Atlantic	458	9.7	663	10.0	817	9.0	912	10.3	1,057 (978)	12.7 (12.5)	1,344	11.3
East South Central	177	3.8	262	4.0	329	3.6	378	4.3	392 (355)	4.7 (4.5)	558	4.7
West South Central	113	2.4	205	3.1	285	3.1	298	3.4	291 (259)	3.5 (3.3)	456	3.8
Mountain	44	0.9	75	1.1	109	1.2	102	1.2	86 (67)	1.0 (0.9)	116	1.0
Pacific	123	2.6	213	3.2	435	4.8	463	5.2	457 (411)	5.5 (5.3)	746	6.3

* Numbers and percentages 1899–1939 from Harold D. Kube and Ralph H. Danhof, *Changes in Distribution of Manufacturing Wage Earners, 1899–1939* (Washington, D. C.: Bureau of the Census and Bureau of Agricultural Economics, 1942), Tables 1 and 2, pp. 24 and 25. Numbers rounded. Numbers for 1939 in parentheses and for 1947 from *Census of Manufactures: 1947,* "General Summary" (Washington, D.C.: Bureau of the Census, 1950), Table 3, pp. 32–33. Numbers rounded and percentages computed. The numbers in parentheses for 1939 were recalculated from the Census of Manufactures for that year to make them more directly comparable with those of 1947.

TABLE 2

Distribution of Total Population by Divisions of the United States: 1900–1950*

Divisions	1900 Number (millions)	1900 Per-centage	1910 Number (millions)	1910 Per-centage	1920 Number (millions)	1920 Per-centage	1930 Number (millions)	1930 Per-centage	1940 Number (millions)	1940 Per-centage	1950 Number (millions)	1950 Per-centage
United States	76.0	100.0	92.0	100.0	106.0	100.0	122.8	100.0	131.7	100.0	150.6†	100.0
New England	5.6	7.4	6.6	7.1	7.4	7.0	8.2	6.7	8.4	6.4	9.3	6.2
Middle Atlantic	15.5	20.3	19.3	21.0	22.3	21.0	26.3	21.4	27.5	20.9	30.0	19.9
East North Central	16.0	21.0	18.3	19.8	21.5	20.3	25.3	20.6	26.6	20.2	30.2	20.1
West North Central	10.3	13.6	11.6	12.7	12.5	11.9	13.3	10.8	13.5	10.3	14.0	9.3
South Atlantic	10.4	13.8	12.2	13.2	14.0	13.2	15.8	12.9	17.8	13.5	21.0	13.9
East South Central	7.5	9.9	8.4	9.1	8.9	8.4	9.9	8.0	10.8	8.2	11.4	7.6
West South Central	6.5	8.6	8.8	9.6	10.2	9.7	12.2	9.9	13.1	9.9	14.5	9.6
Mountain	1.7	2.2	2.6	2.9	3.3	3.2	3.7	3.0	4.2	3.2	5.0	3.3
Pacific	2.4	3.2	4.2	4.6	5.6	5.3	8.2	6.7	9.7	7.4	14.4	9.6

* Numbers and percentages 1900–1940 from Harold D. Kube and Ralph H. Danhof, *Changes in Distribution of Manufacturing Wage Earners, 1899–1939* (Washington, D. C.: Bureau of the Census and Bureau of Agricultural Economics, 1942), Tables 3 and 4, pp. 26 and 27. Numbers for 1950 from *Population of Continental United States by Regions, Divisions and States: April 1, 1950* (1950 Census of Population—Preliminary Counts, Series PC-3, No. 1, [Washington, D.C.: Bureau of the Census]), Table 2, p. 3. Numbers rounded and percentages computed.

† Includes some 700,000 persons enumerated away from home and not allocated to their states of residence when this Preliminary Count was issued.

TABLE 3

DISTRIBUTION OF URBAN POPULATION BY DIVISIONS OF THE UNITED STATES: 1920–1950*

	1920		1930		1940		1950	
DIVISIONS	Number (mil-lions)	Per-centage	Number (mil-lions)	Per-centage	Number (mil-lions)	Per-centage	Number (mil-lions)	Per-centage
United States	54.2	100.0	69.0	100.0	74.4	100.0	95.9	100.0
New England	5.6	10.3	6.3	9.1	6.4	8.6	7.1	7.4
Middle Atlantic	16.8	31.0	20.4	29.6	21.1	28.4	24.2	25.2
East North Central	13.1	24.2	16.8	24.3	17.4	23.4	21.1	22.0
West North Central	4.7	8.7	5.6	8.1	6.0	8.1	7.3	7.6
South Atlantic	4.3	7.9	5.7	8.3	6.9	9.3	10.3	10.7
East South Central	2.0	3.7	2.8	4.1	3.2	4.3	4.5	4.7
West South Central	3.0	5.5	4.4	6.4	5.2	7.0	8.0	8.3
Mountain	1.2	2.2	1.5	2.2	1.8	2.4	2.8	2.9
Pacific	3.5	6.5	5.5	8.0	6.4	8.6	10.8	11.3

* Numbers of urban population, 1920–40, from *Statistical Abstract of the United States, 1950*, p. 41; for 1950, *Population of the United States, Urban and Rural, By States—April 1, 1950* (1950 Census of Population, Preliminary Counts, Series PC–3, No. 10, [Washington, D.C.: Bureau of the Census]), Table 1, p. 5. Numbers rounded and percentages computed.

land's decrease was somewhat greater than that for the country as a whole and its percentage of the total number of workers was less in 1939 than in 1929. During the next eight years, however, New England showed an increase of about 280,000 workers, more than twice the decline in the 1929–39 decade. Despite this fact, however, its percentage of the total in 1947 was less than in 1939. During these eight years, New England's industrial employment increased substantially, but that of the country as a whole increased even more rapidly. As a result, New England had a somewhat smaller proportion of the total at the end of the period.

Changes in the percentage figures for any region from one of the years given to another reflect changes in the *relative* industrial employment of that region to that of the country as a whole.

Third, Tables 1, 2, and 3 do not include any figures on *rates* of growth or decline from one year to another. Percentage rates, of course, could easily be computed from the numbers given for the different years. (For 1939 to 1947 they are given in Table 9.) Percentages of this kind, however, are particularly dangerous and often have been misused. This point seems significant enough to warrant an illustration.

The New England, Middle Atlantic, and East North Central regions are the most heavily industrialized parts of the country. Also, their industrial importance was established decades ago. We refer to them here as the old regions. In 1919 they had 72.8 per cent of the production workers in the United States. In the 28-year period from 1919 to 1947, two of these three regions—New England and Middle Atlantic—showed substantial declines in their percentages of total number of production workers. The proportion for all three declined from 72.8 to 67.6 per cent. This indicates that they have grown less rapidly in the number of production workers than the country as a whole. In addition, these three regions, particularly the New England and Middle Atlantic states, are the major areas that commonly are said to have suffered from various "shifts" and "migrations" of industry.

On the other hand, the South Atlantic, West South Central, and Pacific regions have grown rapidly in industry since World War I. The South Atlantic states benefited from a rapid growth, which involved some actual moves, in textile and other industries beginning in volume in the early 1920's. More recently the spotlight has been on the West South Central and Pacific areas. We call these three regions here the growth regions. In 1919 the three of them had 16.9 per cent of the production workers of the United States and in 1947 they had 21.4 per cent. Thus they had grown at a substantially higher rate than the country as a whole.

From 1919 to 1947 the old regions showed a rate of increase of 21.7 per cent in the number of production workers. Over the same period, the growth regions showed a rate of increase of 65.7 per cent. Comparisons of these rates of growth for this or shorter periods have often been interpreted to mean that the old regions are in bad shape industrially and that the growth regions may well displace them in industrial importance. Despite the percentage rates, however, from 1919 to 1947 the growth regions added approximately 1,009,000 production workers, while the old regions showed a net increase of 1,438,000—40 per cent more.

Possibly this example labors a fairly obvious point, but it seems worth some emphasis. When the base figures vary considerably in size, comparisons of rates of growth or decline have to be made with extreme caution. Also, another fact should not be overlooked. Not only major regions but other subdivisions may often show rapid rates of growth in the earlier stages of industrialization but less rapid rates as industrialization proceeds. In other words, projection of rates of growth, particularly for the less industrialized regions or divisions, may lead to questionable or even false conclusions.

Finally, although manufacturing is an important element in both the population and physical growth of most urban areas, urban planners and redevelopers should not overestimate its importance or neglect other factors. One fairly recent tabulation shows that of the total gainfully employed population, manufacturing accounted for 28.4 per cent in the New York metropolitan area, 35.0 per cent in Chicago's metropolitan area, 28.3 per cent in Boston's, 48.2 per cent in Detroit's, and 19.5 per cent in the Los Angeles area.[6] To be sure, as we have pointed

---

6. Colin Clark, "The Economic Functions of a City in Relation to Its Size," *Econometrica* (April, 1945), p. 100. For other major metropolitan areas cited the proportions were: Philadelphia, 36.6 per cent; Pittsburgh, 35.6 per cent.

out before, manufacturing employment may be basic in city growth in the sense that it brings people to cities in which they earn income that enables them to purchase the services of those who work in distribution, professional, and other nonmanufacturing activities. It is also true, however, that the existence of substantial pools of purchasing power made up in considerable part of people in nonmanufacturing activity is often a factor in the location of industries, particularly of market-oriented industries. Urban planners and redevelopers, therefore, ought to see the relative importance of these various economic factors in the life of their localities and not focus on one to the exclusion of others.

Two simple but clear examples of the operation of nonmanufacturing factors in urban growth may be noted from Tables 1 and 3. For the Pacific states the number of production workers in manufacturing increased from 435,000 in 1919 to 746,000 in 1947. This is a percentage increase of roughly 71 per cent. For the comparable period of 1920 to 1950, the urban population of the same region increased from 3,500,000 to about 10,800,000—an increase of more than 208 per cent. Also, the urban population of the United States increased by some 14,800,000 persons or about 27 per cent from 1920 to 1930 despite a slight decrease in the number of production workers in manufacturing from 1919 to 1929.

A Few Comparisons and Observations

For the periods covered by Tables 1 and 3, probably the outstanding single characteristic of the distributions of production workers and urban population by broad regions has been their relative stability. In absolute numbers, both production workers and urban population have increased substantially. When one reflects a moment on the many and diverse factors that lie behind these figures, both as to volume and distribution, he may well be astonished that the changes in their distributions are not more marked than they actually are. Certainly one general conclusion is that urban planners and redevelopers (as well as others for that matter) ought to recognize the slowness of change and not be unduly influenced by a few unusual, spectacular exceptions or by sharp differences in rates of growth for relatively short periods. It is true, of course, that the figures and proportions for large regions show greater stability than many of the corresponding figures for many smaller areas or individual cities. And it is the locality and metropolitan area figures that are usually more significant for the work of planners and redevelopers. Nevertheless, the regional figures are pertinent and their relative stability over fairly long periods of time is a fact of considerable importance.

The second over-all characteristic of these distributions is a narrowing of the differentials between the highly industrialized and the less industrialized regions. Thus, for the substantially fifty years covered by Table 1, two of the three major industrialized regions—New England, Middle Atlantic, and East North Central—have declined in the proportions of production workers and five of the six less industrialized regions have increased their proportions. In the distribution of urban population from 1920 to 1950, all three of the highly industrialized areas have shown relative declines and five of the six less industrialized regions have increased their shares.[7]

Another notable fact is the sharp increase in the total number of production workers in manufacturing from 1939 to 1947. The net change was an increase of 4,108,000 workers—52.6 per cent. Most of this, of course, was attributable to the industrial requirements and stimulus of World War II. At the height of wartime production, the number of workers was even greater than in 1947. Although the postwar boom from deferred demand, foreign aid, rearmament expenditure, and other inflationary factors has kept the level of industrial employment very high, it is still too soon to say whether or not it may fall back somewhat when, as, and if these supports are withdrawn or substantially decreased.

The last period in Table 3 is a full ten years—two years longer than the period from 1939–47 in Table 1. The ten-year increase in urban population was also substantial, 21 million or 28.9 per cent. Although considerably lower than the rate of increase for production workers, this urban population growth was largely attributable to the same forces. The difference in the percentages is accounted for in considerable part by the absorption of most of the unemployed people in the urban labor force, nonurban dwellers working in plants in urban areas, and by the war-induced employment of many women and other persons not formerly considered as industrial employees.

In some part, however, this difference may be due to war and postwar employment in industrial plants located in nonurban areas. From the information at hand it seems impossible to say whether employment of this kind has reached substantial proportions. We note the possibility here simply to suggest a question that might deserve further investigation.

Incidentally, industrial construction since World War II has been at

7. In this classification of highly and less industrialized regions the South Atlantic states are in a somewhat anomalous position. Since sometime in the 1930's they have had more production workers in manufacturing than has New England. On the other hand, the South Atlantic region has more than twice the total population so it is relatively less industrialized than New England. For our purposes here, it has not been necessary to compute indexes of industrialization.

a relatively high level. For the four years 1947 through 1950, the average dollar volume of private industrial construction work put in place, as estimated by the Department of Commerce, was $1.28 billion. In 1939 by the same estimate it was $254 million and in 1940, $442 million.[8] If these prewar figures are doubled to account roughly for the change in levels of construction cost, the postwar figures are still relatively large. Clearly they indicate that at least some industrial managers and directors anticipate a continuing high level of demand for their products.[9] They also indicate that industrial expansion of one kind or another may continue to be a major factor in urban development and redevelopment in the years immediately ahead.

A few less general observations may be made on the data in Tables 1 and 3:

1. Of the nine major regions, New England has experienced the most marked decline in proportion of production workers during the first half of this century. It is also the only region that had a smaller number of workers in 1947 than in 1919.

2. The Middle Atlantic states also showed a decline over the total period covered by Table 1. It, however, was relatively less severe than New England's.

3. With the exception of the 1929–39 decade, the East North Central region showed a slow but steady increase in the proportion of production workers. At the end of the period, 1947, it had reached first place in industrial employment among the regions.

4. The South Atlantic region also improved its relative position among the regions, but its relative increase in production workers was not great. Rather curiously, its proportion of all production workers in manufacturing increased most .rapidly in the two decades—1919 through 1929 and 1929 through 1939—in which the number of production workers for the United States as a whole declined.

5. Although the Pacific region is considerably less important industrially than is commonly supposed, during the last thirty years or so it has shown a considerable growth. Some evidence indicates that

8. *Construction and Construction Materials: Statistical Supplement*, May, 1950 (Washington, D.C.: Bureau of Foreign and Domestic Commerce, Department of Commerce, 1950), Table 7, pp. 22-27, and *ibid.*, January, 1951, Table 4, p. 8.

9. It is possible that some industrial corporations may believe that all of their present productive capacity may not be utilized for at least some period after some of the present inflationary forces decline. At that time they may be prepared to cut back production in their older plant or plants and to concentrate more of their output in the new and, therefore, presumably more efficient units. If, as some scattered evidence suggests, the newer plants are to some degree decentralized (diffused or dispersed) from major industrial centers, to the extent that this kind of cutback should occur it might produce a "delayed-action" redistribution of manufacturing employment. Unfortunately the information at hand does not enable us to do more than suggest this possibility. It is considered again in chapter v.

this region may have been growing quite rapidly industrially since the Census of Manufactures for 1947. This may account in part for the substantial increase in the proportion of its urban population in 1950 as against 1940.

Without making this discussion much longer, it seems worth-while to put down the major facts on the distribution of production workers and changes in them by major regions during the World War II and postwar period.

WAR AND POSTWAR EXPANSION

During World War II, American industrial expansion was unprecedented. Some notion of its magnitude is given by McLaughlin's estimate, quoted by Hoover,[10] that the cost of war-motivated expansion was equal to about one-third of the value of existing facilities in 1940. Of course, the somewhat higher construction costs during the war must be considered in evaluating these figures.

Table 4 gives an over-all picture of regional industrial expansion during the war period. The figures for regional shares of total value added by manufacture in 1939 are a rough index of industrial activity before World War II. For further comparison we have added the revised 1939 percentages of industrial production workers. The third column shows the regional distribution of war facilities expenditures approved from 1940 to 1944. Because not all of these facilities are transferable to peacetime industrial purposes, the column on the right shows privately financed wartime expansion, much of it, of course, with governmental aid. Presumably nearly all of this industrial capacity could be used for civilian production. It should be noted, however, that the public investment, much of which was in plant and facilities for aircraft, explosives, ammunition, and shipbuilding, was much larger in the aggregate than the private investment. According to Department of Commerce estimates for value of work put in place for the five calendar years 1940 through 1944, public investment in industrial plant totaled almost $8 billion and private investment a little less than $2 billion. For the years 1940 through 1945 the totals were for public investment $8.7 billion and for private $2.6 billion.[11]

10. Edgar M. Hoover, *The Location of Economic Activity* (New York: McGraw-Hill Book Co., 1948), p. 161.

11. *Op. cit.* in footnote 8, *Statistical Supplement,* May, 1950. These are estimates of industrial plant construction and do not include equipment. Mr. Glenn E. McLaughlin has compiled the estimated costs of wartime manufacturing facilities (plants and equipment) authorized from July, 1940 through June, 1944. His figures show almost the same proportions of public and private investment: public—$15.8 billion; private—$4.2 billion. See Table 2, p. 166, in his chap. ix, "Regional Problems of Industrialization," Seymour E. Harris (ed.), *Economic Reconstruction* (New York: McGraw-Hill Book Co., 1945).

In Table 4, the regions are arrayed in order of value added by manufacture in 1939. Ranking the regions by the order in which they received new privately financed facilities during the war and bracketing their 1939 positions in value added, yield these results: (1) East North Central [1]; (2) Middle Atlantic [2]; (3) Pacific [5]; (4) West South Central [8]; (5) South Atlantic [4]; (6) New England [3]; (7) East South Central [7]; (8) West North Central [6]; (9) Mountain [9].

No close comparisons from Table 4 would be justified because of the different units used in measuring prewar industrial activity and wartime expansion. In general, however, it seems fairly safe to say that, with

TABLE 4

REGIONAL DISTRIBUTION OF 1939 MANUFACTURING ACTIVITY AND TOTAL AND PRIVATELY FINANCED WAR FACILITIES EXPENDITURES: 1940–1944*

	PERCENTAGE OF U.S. TOTAL-VALUE ADDED BY MANUFACTURE 1939	PERCENTAGE OF U.S. TOTAL OF PRODUCTION WORKERS 1939	PERCENTAGE OF U.S. TOTAL-WAR FACILITIES EXPENDITURES APPROVED JUNE 1940–JUNE 1944	
			Total	Privately Financed
United States:	100.0	100.0	100.0	100.0
East North Central	31.5	27.9	31.1	31.3
Middle Atlantic	29.8	28.6	19.1	22.7
New England	9.8	12.1	4.9	6.5
South Atlantic	9.1	12.5	6.9	7.9
Pacific	6.5	5.3	9.2	11.0
West North Central	5.5	4.8	7.4	3.7
East South Central	3.4	4.5	6.2	5.4
West South Central	3.3	3.3	11.3	9.3
Mountain	1.1	0.9	3.9	2.2

* Edgar M. Hoover, *The Location of Economic Activity* (New York: McGraw-Hill Book Co., 1948), p. 162, from data of Glenn E. McLaughlin. Percentages of production workers in 1939 added.

the exception of the South Atlantic region (and possibly the East North Central) in respect to both total and privately financed industrial plant and the West North Central region as to private investment only, the net result of wartime expansion was to continue the process of narrowing the differentials between the heavily industrialized and the less industrialized regions of the country.

Although, as we pointed out before, the best estimates indicate that the immediate postwar years saw a quite high volume of new industrial construction, no adequate measure of its effects on the distribution of production workers by regions is available. The data of the Census of Manufactures for 1947 have two weaknesses in measuring postwar expansion. First, because no census of manufactures was taken during World War II, it is impossible to separate out with any precision the effects of wartime and postwar expansion on the changes in the number and distribution of production workers from 1939 to 1947. In general, of course, we know that the wartime influence was very great. In addition, because of construction difficulties in 1946 and 1947, it seems quite certain that a substantial proportion of the plants on which construction was started during those years was not finished and in operation by the end of 1947. These plants, therefore, were not included in the Census of that year. In chapter vi we discuss another set of data on the dollar volume of industrial construction contracts let for a four-year period beginning in July 1945. They show a surprisingly large proportion in the West South Central region and substantial amounts in the Pacific and South Atlantic states. New England's proportion is very small indeed and that of the Middle Atlantic states well below its customary proportion (Table 11). As we emphasize in chapter vi, however, we have no grounds for saying that these data are a representative sample of total industrial expansion during the immediate postwar period.

To be sure, scattered evidence in the form of reports on the expansion plans of individual companies and on some individual localities supports the belief that the Pacific and West South Central areas have made great strides in industry since World War II. These materials, too, are far from satisfactory. Even the fact that they substantiate the industrial construction contract data means very little. Quite probably these regions are growing industrially at a fairly rapid rate. Quite as surely, however, a given dollar volume of industrial expansion in a relatively less industrialized area receives much more attention than an equal or even much larger volume in a highly industrialized locality or region. Taking for granted the fact of industrial expansion in these areas, it is simply impossible to say from the facts at hand how much effect, if any, this growth has had so far upon the previously existing distribution of production workers by major regions.

In this connection the percentage rates of growth in numbers of production workers in manufacturing from 1939 through 1947 by major regions may be of interest: United States—52.6 per cent, New England —31.8 per cent, Middle Atlantic—45.3 per cent, East North Central —63.5 per cent, West North Central—69.1 per cent, South Atlantic— 37.6 per cent, East South Central—57.2 per cent, West South Central —76.2 per cent, Mountain—73.4 per cent, Pacific—81.5 per cent (Table 9). In line with our earlier warning, however, it is significant to note how relatively little difference some of these high percentage rates of growth made on the distribution of production workers in 1947. For example, the Pacific region's spectacular rate of 81.5 per cent increased its proportion of total production workers by just one percentage point over this eight-year period—5.3 per cent to 6.3 per cent.

In short, we know very little about postwar changes in the distribution of production workers in manufacturing. It seems very likely that the major trends or changes are continuing. At least some of them may be accelerating, but this is by no means certain. Until the next Census of Manufactures now scheduled for 1953, caution should be the watchword in using the results of partial surveys and opinions based on them or on more or less superficial observation.

Two Other References

Two other analyses of the subjects dealt with so far in this chapter deserve listing here. The first is the *Economic Development Atlas—Recent Changes in Regions and States* by Victor Roterus and Sterling March of the Area Development Division of the Department of Commerce. It presents in maps, tables, and short text, pertinent material not only on population and manufacturing but also on other economic characteristics by regions and states. The second is a brief article by Marion Hayes, "Regional Shifts in Industry and Population, 1899–1949," which appeared in the *Monthly Labor Review* for July, 1950.[12] Unfortunately, both of these studies use regional breakdowns that differ from the Bureau of the Census', which we have used. The *Atlas*, however, gives breakdowns by states as well so that its data could be combined into the Census' major divisions and regions.[13]

Basing-Point Pricing and Industrial Location

At least one other economic consideration should not be overlooked by those who are concerned with the probable broad patterns of industrial location in the future and their effects upon urban growth, development, and redevelopment. This is the so-called basing-point system of prices used by many major industries. More accurately, the changes that may be significant for urban planners and redevelopers seem likely to come from decisions of the United States Supreme Court holding unlawful pricing systems of this kind as they have been practiced by producers in these industries.

Unfortunately for our purpose this whole issue is complex and difficult in many of its phases. To make matters worse, the controversies that it has raised have built up a large, confusing, and often rather

12. This article was based on materials in the *Handbook of Regional Statistics*, prepared by Marion Hayes and Hyman L. Lewis of the Bureau of Labor Statistics for the Joint Committee on the Economic Report (Washington, D.C.: Government Printing Office, 1950).

13. Also useful but with rather serious weaknesses for our purposes is an article by Betty C. Churchill and Murray F. Foss, "State Estimates of the Business Population," *Survey of Current Business* (December, 1949), pp. 8–17.

murky literature that even economists not specialized in this area find hard to comprehend and deal with. Even professional students of the subject pay their compliments to the contradictions and confusions that abound in it. For example, to quote from a major recent discussion by a competent economist:

> . . . The United States Steel Corporation, for example, holds (1) that "the existence of the Pittsburgh Plus method would have a natural tendency to encourage location of mills outside of rather than at Pittsburgh"; (2) that "the location of production facilities has been due to the fundamental economic traits of the steel industry . . . rather than to any pricing system"; and (3) that without the basing-point system, "when the situation becomes highly competitive, Pittsburgh will be at a disadvantage with other areas" [citing sources of quotations from U.S. Steel representatives] I understand this to mean that the basing-point system (1) has favored locations other than Pittsburgh, (2) has favored neither other locations nor Pittsburgh, and (3) has favored Pittsburgh. . . . This, I am afraid, is somewhat confusing. . . .[14]

In fact, it is hard to escape the conclusion that some of the defenders of basing-point practices in resisting attacks on them before the Federal Trade Commission and in the courts have advanced inconsistent, if not contradictory, contentions as a kind of smoke screen to cover up some of the economic effects of the practices that are objected to.

Also it is true that much of the discussion of the evolution and abandonment of basing-point systems has given relatively little attention to their effects on industrial location. These influences are alluded to often but in much of the discussion take second place to arguments as to whether the system is discriminatory, monopolistic or in restraint of competition, conducive to unnecessarily high prices, unduly hard on small business, etc.

Offsetting to some extent these difficulties for urban planners and redevelopers who wish to understand the essentials of basing-point systems and their probable influences on industrial location are two recent books and a symposium by competent students of the subject. The first is *The Basing-Point System* by Fritz Machlup, an economist now at The Johns Hopkins University.[15] Although Mr. Machlup's book shows some indications of hurried preparation, it is on the whole well organized and well written in relatively nontechnical language. It also contains a considerable discussion of the probable effects of basing-point systems and their abandonment on industrial location both within the industries employing such methods and on other industries, largely fabricators, who purchase their products. The second work is *Monopoly and Free Enterprise* by George W. Stocking and Myron W. Watkins,

14. Fritz Machlup, *The Basing-Point System* (Philadelphia: The Blakiston Co., 1949), pp. 234–45.

15. *Op. cit.*, footnote 14.

which includes a report and recommendations by the Committee on Cartels and Monopoly of The Twentieth Century Fund.[16] Chapter vii analyzes basing-point practice and it is referred to elsewhere in the text of the work as well as in the Committee's report. Messrs. Stocking and Watkins, however, give much less attention than Mr. Machlup to effects on industrial location. The symposium is a report on a panel discussion on *Basing Point Changes and Industrial Location* arranged by the Department of Commerce.[17] Members of the panel included Mr. Glenn E. McLaughlin and Mr. Corwin D. Edwards, Director, Bureau of Industrial Economics of the Federal Trade Commission.

At the beginning of their chapter vii, Stocking and Watkins give this definition:

The basing point system is a way of quoting delivered prices. It is used mostly in sales by manufacturers to other producers or to dealers. Such prices so quoted are composed of the factory price plus a transportation charge. But the transportation charge does not always correspond to actual cost, being generally the cost from some designated production center known as a "basing point." Such a system may use one or more points in calculating delivered prices.

A good example of a simple or single basing-point system was the old form of the famous Pittsburgh plus in steel products. Under this system, steel producers in Pittsburgh and elsewhere quoted delivered prices on products that were the prices announced by a base mill in Pittsburgh plus freight charges from Pittsburgh to the point of delivery. This, of course, made for identical or nearly identical price quotations on delivered steel regardless of where it was produced or delivered.

In 1920 Chicago became a second basing point. In 1924, while the system was under inquiry by the Federal Trade Commission and attack by others, a few additional basing points were also established. Thus the earlier single basing-point system of Pittsburgh plus evolved into a multiple basing-point system.

The investigations of the Temporary National Economic Committee (TNEC), which began in 1938, listed some sixty industries that employed pricing methods that were either clearly basing-point systems or closely allied to them.[18] These included steel, pig iron, cement, corn products, industrial alcohol, asbestos roofing, cast iron pipe and many other building supplies, turbines, steel conduits, newsprint, and wood pulp.

16. New York: The Twentieth Century Fund, 1951.
17. Area Development Division, Office of Domestic Commerce, November, 1948. Mimeographed.
18. Monograph No. 21, *Competition and Monopoly in American Industry* (Washington, D.C.: Government Printing Office, 1940), and Monograph No. 42, *The Basing-Point Problem* (1941).

In 1948, after some twelve years of controversy and litigation, the United States Supreme Court ruled that the basing-point system as practiced by members of The Cement Institute was unlawful under federal statutes governing competitive practices and restraint of trade and ordered it abandoned.[19] This decision touched off a vigorous campaign by many industries to amend the basic federal statutes so as to approve basing-point practices. One such amendment was passed by the Congress but was vetoed by President Truman on June 16, 1950. As usual in such cases the decision of the Supreme Court brought new life to a controversy that had been going on more or less moderately for many years. It is replete with various interpretations of what the Court had ruled, what its *dicta* implied, and what the effects of both might be on the economy. Representatives of various basing-point industries and their supporters, of course, foresaw many dire consequences.

This is only a sketchy and, in some respects at least, an inadequate introduction to basing-point systems and the public policy controversy that they have engendered. Within the limits of this discussion it is clearly impossible for us to treat these subjects more exhaustively. The work of Messrs. Machlup, Stocking, Watkins, *et al.* seem to us, however, to deserve the attention of urban planners and redevelopers—among others. We conclude our treatment of this subject, therefore, with a brief statement of what we take to have been the most probable effects of basing-point systems on industrial location and what may be the effects of the Supreme Court decision. The latter are particularly difficult to estimate because we cannot be certain what method or methods of pricing will be substituted. Congress, of course, might amend the federal statutes so as to nullify the Supreme Court's decision. If this is not done, some students of the subject assert that the only safe course for the industries affected would be to go to a f.o.b. mill system of prices. Others deny this flatly and believe that other kinds of pricing would also meet the requirements of the Court's interpretation of the statutes.

Nevertheless, the probable effects as we see them may be summarized in a relatively few statements:

1. Basing-point systems have tended to encourage the location of plants or mills making the products covered by the systems in the localities of base-point mills. Conversely, basing-point systems discourage

19. *Federal Trade Commission* v. *The Cement Institute,* 333 U.S. 683 (1948). Anyone who wishes to sample the differences of opinion among economists on basing-point practices might refer not only to the works just mentioned but also to a series of articles in the *American Economic Review* that followed this decision: F. A. Fetter, "Exit Basing Point Pricing," and C. D. Edwards, "Basing Point Decisions and Business Practices," both in the issue of December, 1948; J. M. Clark, "Law and Economics of Basing Points," March, 1949; and G. J. Stigler, "A Theory of Delivered Price Systems," December, 1949.

the location or expansion of plants or mills in nonbasing-point localities. Machlup sums up his discussion on this point in these words: ". . . What little direct evidence is available from the historical development of the steel industry certainly reinforces our theoretical conclusion that the basing-point system in general tends to retard the decentralization of the industry in which it is employed."[20] From his earlier analysis it is clear that Machlup uses *decentralization* here in the sense of industrial location or expansion in areas other than basing-point localities.

Although this seems to have been the major result, a quite different one has been noted. Some rather small, more or less specialized producers have located near the edge of an area over which prices are determined by a basing-point. In these locations they get the benefit of the high freight costs from the distant basing point for a relatively limited market in their vicinity. Quite probably, however, this effect is limited and clearly it involves especial risks to such plants.

2. A similar influence has been at work on the location of fabricators who use materials supplied to them under basing-point systems. Largely, but not entirely, through the effects of basing-point practices on the cost of materials to such fabricators, they tend to locate and expand in or near the central or basing-point localities rather than in other parts of the country. In other words: as to the location of fabricators, basing-point systems decrease the effects of supplies of their materials outside of the basing-point localities and also lessen the influence of markets for their products in regional or nonbasing-point areas.

3. If, as a result of the Supreme Court decision, basing-point systems are abandoned, the long-term result on industrial location probably would be to encourage new plants and expansion, both of the basic producers heretofore under basing-point systems and fabricators using their products, in regions and localities whose advantages to such industries have been largely offset by the existence of basing-point practices. In more general terms, we would look for an expansion of industrial capacity in many localities and adjacent areas that have not been basing-points under previous systems.

4. These effects will not come overnight. Many of them will take years and some of them decades. Probably the influences on the location of fabricators will be seen rather more quickly than those on the location of basic industries with large fixed investments in plant and facilities.

5. It is entirely possible, but hardly predictable, that doing away with basing-point systems might result in excess capacity for some basic industrial products in erstwhile basing-point localities. If this should occur, it might lead to lower prices for these basic products in the old

20. *Op. cit.*, p. 237.

basing-point localities and thus attract to them some fabricators who might otherwise be expected to locate or expand elsewhere.

6. Although it is possible that these effects on industrial location of abandoning basing-point systems might result in lower volumes of industrial activity and manufacturing employment in some highly industrialized localities and areas (the old basing-point localities), these untoward results probably would come about so gradually that they could be largely offset by a moderate, continuing expansion of the economy as a whole. By the same token, however, a contraction of the economy in the form of a depression or a period of stable or slightly declining industrial activity might produce material hardship in some of these central or highly industrialized areas.

7. Finally, rates for trucking and water borne traffic probably will become more influential factors in the location of both primary producers, many of which have operated under basing-point systems, and their industrial customers.

One of the chief problems in trying to make out the probable effects on industrial location of basing-point systems and their passing comes from disagreements as to relative size of the savings in transportation expenses that may be made.

Thus, Corwin Edwards in the article cited in *The American Economic Review,* (p. 841) wrote:

> The (Federal Trade) Commission estimated in 1932 that unnecessary transportation in the cement industry cost slightly more than 24 cents a barrel, which was about 20 per cent of the total costs of producing and selling. I do not wish to be understood as saying that the abandonment of the basing-point system will eliminate all such transportation. . . . However, once we get rid of formulas which destroy the consumers' incentive to economize transportation, it is reasonable to suppose that the amount of cross-hauling will be substantially reduced and the cost of distribution will decline correspondingly.

On the other hand Paul Zeis, Chief of the Transportation Division, Office of Domestic Commerce, Department of Commerce, after referring in different terms to this same estimate on cement, said: "For miscellaneous products as a whole, including manufactured items, the average freight rate per ton of freight, during the year 1947, was $7.60; and . . . I think it may be said that this represents between 4 and 5 per cent of the delivered price of those same products to the consumer." He then assumes a possible 20–40 per cent saving in transportation costs and concludes: ". . . I suggest that the net saving to the consumer as a result of transportation changes may not exceed, probably won't exceed, 2 percent or 3 percent of the delivered price of those same commodities to the consumer."[21]

21. *Basing Point Changes and Industrial Location,* p. 9.

Of course, the passing of basing-point systems might result in savings to industrial purchasers from lower mill prices in addition to economies in transportation costs. This, however, is not assured.

Further speculation about savings does not seem justified here. Our purposes in this discussion of basing-point practice have been simply to open up the subject for urban planners and redevelopers who may not have had a chance to analyze it themselves and to point out that it is a changing factor in industrial location that should be watched.

Another factor of the same order is the move under way in recent years to reduce differentials in freight rates between those for the Official or Northeastern Territory (roughly east of the Mississippi and north of the Ohio and Potomac Rivers, plus some parts of Virginia) and other areas or territories. In *New York et al* v. *United States et al* (331 U.S. 284, 1946), the Supreme Court upheld an order of the Interstate Commerce Commission increasing class freight rates in the northeastern area by 10 per cent and reducing those elsewhere east of the Rocky Mountains by 10 per cent. The majority opinion (and to a lesser extent, the dissenting opinions) in this case set forth the basic structure of class freight rates and analyze many of the contentions as to its effects on industrial activity in various parts of the country.

It seems reasonable to expect that this and allied developments in freight rates may strengthen somewhat the trend we have noted toward narrowing differentials in industrialization between the heavily industrialized New England, Middle Atlantic and East North Central regions, on the one hand, and the rest of the country, on the other.

In Conclusion

In concluding this chapter, we would emphasize four conclusions or opinions that we have put forward earlier. First, an over-all view like the one we have tried to take in this chapter makes clear that, even in a dynamic economy, the distribution of industrial activity and employment changes relatively slowly. Second, facts on the broad distribution of production workers and population are useful background for urban planning and redevelopment, but after all, they are only background. Within any major region of the country, locality or subregional trends in industrial location and manufacturing employment can vary substantially from those of the region as a whole. Urban planners and developers, therefore, in their studies of economic backgrounds and bases must go beyond these regional data to the facts of their localities and of their economic hinterlands. Third, we see nothing in this industrial-economic picture that indicates that urban centers in any region of the country need not consider seriously the potentialities of redevelopment programs in their areas. Rather we suggest careful attention be given to broad regional and locality trends in industry as factors in determining the character of local redevelopment programs, including the relative emphases from locality to locality on clearance versus outlying land projects and on projects for industrial versus projects for predominantly residential reuses. Fourth, the major change in the broad distribution of industrial activity has been to narrow somewhat the differentials between the heavily industrialized and the less industrialized regions. Although this movement has been less marked than is sometimes assumed, recent economic developments, such as the apparently successful attacks on basing-point systems and on established territorial differences in some kinds of freight rates, seem likely, on balance, to make for a further narrowing of these differentials.

Finally, we would make one comment that we hope has been implicit in most of what we have put down in this chapter. It is simply that the techniques and methods of industrial and economic analysis appropriate to urban planning and redevelopment programs are still, in many respects, crude and elementary. A difficult task lies ahead in developing and refining these methods. It is a task, however, that promises worthwhile results, not only for official planning and redevelopment agencies but also for all those who are concerned with the economic and social health of urban and metropolitan areas in this country.

CHAPTER IV

SECURITY CONSIDERATIONS IN INDUSTRIAL LOCATION

IN THE checkered history of urban development and planning in this country, perhaps no chapter is on the whole more confusing and more disheartening than the record to date of the discussion and action—or more accurately, the inaction—following the advent of the atomic bomb. It would have been easy to omit any discussion of this subject here or to have dismissed it with a few generalities. How can anything really significant be said by persons whose knowledge of the basic facts about the atomic bomb, about other new military weapons—actual and prospective, and the defenses, if any, against them is limited to what has been divulged so far by military and other authorities? Even if some conclusions were arrived at from the results of the admittedly obsolete form of the bomb used against Japanese cities plus some guesses at the probable effects of later "models," the resources of URS would have been entirely inadequate for the studies that need to be undertaken on various forms of urban decentralization and industrial dispersal, on their probable costs, and on the ways and means that might be employed to bring them about.

On the other hand, the confusion of views, the inaction, the sense of futility that now exist seem to us dangerous. We have tried, therefore, in this chapter: (1) to recall for our readers in rapid summary the major happenings and ideas of this six-year period that bear upon security considerations in the development and redevelopment of cities—particularly as they are affected by industrial location; and (2) to discuss briefly six analyses and proposals that have been made on this subject. In both of these major divisions of this chapter, we have tried to set forth as objectively as possible the facts that have occurred and the ideas that have been put forward. As in other chapters, however, we have offered some comments and opinions. It is not false modesty that makes us say that whatever value this chapter may have is largely in the review of events and proposals.

TERMS AND APPROACH

Before starting on these two major parts of this chapter, one other explanation seems necessary. The major issue in nonmilitary defense measures against the destruction of urban life and property by atomic attack is commonly referred to as decentralization or dispersal of cities. *Decentralization* seems the more common term applied to cities; *dispersal* is used largely in respect to industrial plant and facilities. As used, decentralization is a loose, generic term for the spreading out of urban population and development from large concentrated centers into some other pattern or patterns. We have more to say at the beginning of chapter v about this term and its various meanings. Here we would point out that urban populations and physical development could be decentralized in a number of different ways. Not all of them would require, in theory at least, substantial changes in the industrial location pattern as it now exists. As a matter of practical fact, however, material changes in that pattern would be necessary for almost any effective decentralization of cities—certainly for any decentralization that would decrease substantially their vulnerability to atomic bombing. Here the most common term, equally general and unspecific, is *industrial dispersal*.

Both because of this fact and because we are dealing with the relations of industrial location and urban redevelopment, our analysis and comments will be centered largely on industrial location as it is related to the military vulnerability of urban centers. In a discussion of this kind no sharp line can be drawn between industrial and other forms of urban decentralization. We approach this issue, however, from the facts and possibilities of industrial location and not from a consideration of urban structure and functioning as a whole. For this reason our emphases will be somewhat different than they might otherwise have been.

ACTION ON MANY FRONTS

On August 6, 1945, President Truman, then on his way home from the Potsdam Conference, announced that an atomic bomb had been exploded over Hiroshima. His announcement indicated and later reports and investigations fully verified the horrible effectiveness of the bomb in the destruction of human life and physical property. On August 9 another bomb was dropped on Nagasaki. Although the topographic and other features of this city made the bomb's destructiveness of human life somewhat less than in Hiroshima, it was still of appalling magnitude by any comparison with other single attacks with one weapon in the history of warfare. Also, the damage to industries in Nagasaki was relatively greater in some respects than in Hiroshima.

These attacks touched off a series of governmental actions and of official, expert, and public discussion characterized by great variety and vigor. Just a few incidents of the next few months are needed to recall this period. The Japanese Empire surrendered. In September, 1945, the United States Strategic Bombing Survey established an office in Tokyo and began its study of the effects of both the conventional and atomic bombing of Japan. During 1946 its reports fully documented the terrific destructiveness of the atomic explosions. Also in the fall of 1945 came the so-called Smyth report—officially labeled *Atomic Energy for Military Purposes,* with a foreword by Major General L. R. Groves dated August, 1945.

It became known that in May, 1945, at the request of President Roosevelt, the Secretary of War had appointed a top-level committee "to consider the subject (the use of atomic energy for both war and peacetime uses) and to recommend legislation for the control and development of atomic energy."[1] Early in January, 1946, the Secretary of State appointed an official commission, headed by Dean Acheson, then Undersecretary of State, to consider the whole subject of the control of atomic energy. On January 23 this official commission appointed a board of consultants headed by David E. Lilienthal, then Chairman of the Tennessee Valley Authority. On March 28 the joint product of these two committees, the Acheson-Lilienthal report, entitled "Report on the International Control of Atomic Energy," was made public.

On June 14, 1946, Mr. Bernard Baruch as United States Representative to the United Nations Atomic Energy Commission presented this country's proposal for international control. Five days later, Mr. Andrei A. Gromyko replied for the USSR and the long and so-far fruitless tug-of-war on United Nations policy in respect to atomic power had begun.

Action on the legislative front was also under way. On October 3, 1945, President Truman sent a special message to Congress urging and making suggestions on legislation for ". . . the determination of our domestic policy for the control, use, and development of atomic energy within the United States."[2] On August 1, 1946, the Atomic Energy Act was approved. On October 28 the President named the first members of the Atomic Energy Commission. They held their first meeting on November 13, 1946.

Expert and Public Discussion

Also notable during this period was the deep concern of atomic scientists with the political and other social problems that had come from their scientific and technical achievements. Organizations of them

1. *The International Control of Atomic Energy—Growth of a Policy,* prepared by the Department of State (Washington, D.C.: Government Printing Office, no date), p. 3.
2. *Ibid.,* p. 15.

were formed. The *Bulletin of the Atomic Scientists* was founded in Chicago in 1945. On October 13, the Association of Los Alamos Scientists, with some four hundred members, put out a statement on atomic policy that emphasized, among other things, the vulnerability of our major industrial centers to atomic attack in the event of a future war.

Official action and the concern and warnings of experts were matched by a veritable gale of public discussion in newspapers, magazines, conferences, lectures, and public meetings of various kinds. This early discussion—official, expert, and public—deserves here rather more than passing notice. Although difficult to characterize briefly, it seems to have fallen into a pattern that has continued, with changes of emphasis, from then to the present day. Most of this discussion turned on one or more of three points:

1. The destructiveness of atomic bombing makes imperative an international organization to prevent wars in the future. The last possible argument for isolationism as a policy of the United States has been destroyed. We must support and strengthen the United Nations. As a part of its program and against the possibility that, despite its efforts, a war might break out in the future, the use of atomic weapons must be outlawed and some form of international control must be established to assure that atomic weapons will never again be used.

Sometimes this argument included the assertion that there was no effective defense against atomic bombing. Even if one could be devised against the kind of bombs used on Japan, it could not possibly be effective against the greater destructiveness of improved weapons of this kind. Furthermore, any future war involving the great powers would see the use of biological or bacteriological weapons that could wipe out vast segments of the population of a great country within a very short time. Although this contention in respect to biological warfare has been strongly challenged more recently, it was frequently made in these earlier days.[3]

Sometimes those who argued in this fashion went so far as to say that no other action in respect to the military use of atomic power made sense at all. If the UN failed and atomic weapons were used, even the nation that won the war, whatever that might mean, would be so horribly mangled that if civilized life were not entirely destroyed, it would not be worth living.

2. The second argument was for the United States to build up its military strength, including its atomic and other weapons, to a point where no dictator or other aggressor would dare to attack us. Although this position did not lack vociferous backers, it had a strangely familiar

---

3. *What You Should Know about Biological Warfare,* prepared by the Federal Civil Defense Administration (Washington, D.C.: Government Printing Office, 1951).

ring. Few of those who advanced it undertook to explain why the similar contention during the earlier years of the century had failed to prevent two world wars. Sometimes it was said, or at least broadly implied, that this policy had never been fully and effectively followed in the past. Aggressors could be scared out of aggression if only we made the prospects of retaliation sufficiently terrifying.

3. The third line of argument is the most germane to our concern with industrial location and its effects upon urban development and redevelopment. It suggested decentralization of our major industrial centers. It urged that this would be effective in two ways. By reducing the vulnerability of our major sources of military and industrial strength, it would deter aggression. It would reduce substantially the advantage that might come from a sneak attack with atomic or other weapons. Also, it was contended that a corollary of reduced vulnerability would be our ability to retaliate against such a sneak attack and to win any future war that such an attack would cause.

"Space is the only defense" was the slogan of those who advanced this line of argument. Although the phrase was used in other connections as well, it was applied chiefly in support of a policy of urban decentralization or industrial dispersal in the atomic age. Often it was supported further by those who believe that in addition to its defense implications, decentralization would have other results and values that, once demonstrated, would be accepted and supported by most citizens of this country.

THE SKIES DARKEN

Even while this discussion continued, relations between the United States and the USSR were deteriorating. With them, of course, went any reasonable prospect of effective international control of atomic energy. When the worsening of these relations had reached a point that might be called a break is a question of judgment that we need not go into here. However, certainly it could not possibly be dated later than the beginning of the Berlin Airlift on March 31, 1948, and probably was considerably earlier.

With these developments came a stepping up in the production of A-bombs at the centers built during World War II and an expansion by the Atomic Energy Commission of productive capacity.[4] In July, 1947, the President approved the National Security Act of 1947. Among its provisions, it established a National Security Resources Board ". . . to advise the President concerning the co-ordination of military,

4. "1951—The Payoff Year," a special report on atomic energy in *Business Week* (July 28, 1951), pp. 100 ff.

industrial and civilian mobilization, including— . . . (6) **the strategic relocation** (*sic*) of industries, services, government, and economic activities, the continuous operation of which is essential to the Nation's security."

On September 23, 1949, the President reported that our government had what was considered conclusive evidence that an atomic explosion had occurred within the territory of the USSR. On January 31, 1950, he ordered the Atomic Energy Commission to proceed with the production of the so-called H-bomb.

In August, the Department of Defense and the Atomic Energy Commission issued the long-awaited semitechnical report, "The Effects of Atomic Weapons." About the same time appeared another document prepared by these two agencies for the National Security Resources Board on "Damage from Atomic Explosion and Design of Protective Structures."

Shortly after the invasion of South Korea in late June, 1950, official and public attention turned to civilian defense measures. During the first few months particularly, some discussions of this subject bordered on near-hysteria. Magazines printed articles under such titles as "Hiroshima, U.S.A.—Can Anything Be Done about It?"[5] complete with colored drawings of fearful destruction and raging fires in various sections of major urban centers. This was no time for relatively long-range attempts to reduce vulnerability. In the spotlight were questions of public shelters, communication facilities, medical and other relief for disaster victims, and similar problems of public organization and action in the event of attack. What could be done to these ends? What organizational machinery was necessary? Who should pay the bills? *United States Civil Defense,* prepared by the National Security Resources Board and prefaced by a letter of transmittal dated September 8, 1950, deals with many of these and similar questions.

At the same time steps were taken to step up rearmament not only in this country, but in the nations of Western Europe. The Defense Production Act of 1950 passed the Congress and was approved on September 8. Later in the year the bill for what became the Federal Civil Defense Act of 1950 was introduced, was passed and approved on January 12, 1951.

In December, 1950, bills were introduced in both houses of Congress and hearings were held on proposals for several office building centers in outlying parts of the Washington metropolitan area. Similar bills were reintroduced and more hearings were held by committees of the new Congress in January and February, 1951.

Also in January, 1951, bills for a Defense Housing and Community

5. John Lear, *Collier's* (August 5, 1950).

Facilities and Services Act of 1951 were introduced in both houses. Hearings and reports followed, but up to the present time (July, 1951) final action has not been taken by the Congress. In general, these bills contemplated a defense housing program rather similiar to the one developed in the defense period before our entrance into World War II and the war housing program that followed. Although one title was based on the assumption that certain military production facilities would be in relatively isolated locations, it was clear that housing and community facilities in areas of this kind were expected to be in relatively small volume.

WHAT THIS REVIEW SHOWS

This review of ideas, proposals, and action on national security since the end of World War II is very sketchy. It would take many more pages even to catalogue all the major steps taken by the government of the United States and by various units of the United Nations. We simply have picked out a few to illustrate the scope and diversity of the problems considered, the ideas advanced, and the actions taken.

Even so, the question may well be asked: What has all this to do with industrial location or dispersal? Why do you take the time and effort to put down these events?

As we look back over the six-year record and try to make out the main lines of analysis and policy, we come back again to the three-way division of discussions and proposals that followed hard on the use of the A-bomb against Japanese cities: (1) prevent war and outlaw the use of atomic weapons by international action; (2) rearm sufficiently to deter any potential aggressor; (3) disperse industrial and military production and supporting urban populations to reduce vulnerability and to enable the economy to support quick and drastic retaliation in the event of a sneak attack with atomic weapons.

It seems clear that in general these are not mutually exclusive policy proposals. In the long run, the first and the second would be contradictory, but certainly not for the time being. Also, the proposal for dispersal would seem consistent with both of the first two.

We believe further that even our hasty resumé indicates that during the first two years or so after Japan surrendered, the first set of proposals—preventing war and outlawing atomic weapons—received the most attention, official and otherwise. Subsequently, rearmament has held the center of the stage. Throughout the whole period, to change the figure, the dispersal of industry has run a poor third.

Now we would be among the last to disparage the proposals and work toward strengthening the UN or building up military strength at home and in our allied countries, but it is fair to ask: Why has the third proposal received so little serious attention? Never in this six-year period has it been given a sizable fraction of the thought, analysis, and determined action that have gone into the other two kinds of measures. What accounts for this great disparity of interest, discussion, and preparation?

From the very beginning of this period, certainly even a casual knowledge of the history of human institutions and governmental organizations would have indicated the terrific difficulties that face the UN in grappling with the prevention of war and the outlawing of its most destructive weapons. In light of that history and the admitted difficulties of the current situation, why should any intelligent person have imagined that the chances were good for the UN to achieve these results immediately and completely without serious setbacks and resulting periods of great danger to the security of this country? Similarly, even a quick look at the record of international relations during the present century surely would raise serious questions about the efficacy of military strength as a means of maintaining peace.

We would repeat that we are not criticising adversely these policies. We believe that both were reasonable, necessary, and should continue to be pressed with vigor and persistence. Our point here is simply that in the light of the obvious difficulties that confronted these policies as means to the ultimate end, why has the dispersal proposal been so grievously neglected?

We believe we see some explanations, if not reasons, for this neglect and propose now to discuss them briefly.

Why Has Dispersal Been a Step-Child?

First, we would consider a number of possible influences that have been referred to often. It is said that after a major war effort the people of the nation naturally feel a certain degree of letdown. They are not inclined to come to grips with new and admittedly difficult proposals. They are naturally and properly concerned with the problems of postwar readjustment, inflation, the changed position of our economy in the world order (or disorder), and many personal and group problems produced or aggravated by the past war. Quite probably all these influences have been at work, but they would seem to apply quite as directly to other security measures as well. They can hardly be judged, therefore, as important factors in accounting for the differences in attention and action that we are concerned with here.

Probably more basic is the fact that in the postwar economy the more vocal and influential groups in public opinion and policy have felt no particular, direct incentive to urge industrial dispersal as a security measure. Boom conditions in construction and industrial expansion have deterred business groups from taking up seriously proposals that would add uncertainties, possibly decrease the immediate volume of some kinds of business activity, endanger certain investments in real property, and otherwise interfere with business as usual or as unusual. Similarly, ranking professional soldiers have naturally been much more interested in rearmament and the development of new military weapons, both defensive and offensive. Such matters are their profession and their life. Industrial dispersal, although approved in principle, is clearly outside their areas of special competence or interest. It has also been alleged, but by no means proved, that what might be called the leaders of thought and opinion have felt much more at home in matters of UN organization and international relations than in what may seem to many of them as a humdrum, unglamorous, semitechnical question of industrial location and real estate development. Quite possibly some of them have felt that emphasis on reducing the vulnerability of industries and urban populations generally might even tend to decrease public enthusiasm for the UN and its program. Possible influences of these kinds are, to be sure, imponderable, but it seems hard to avoid the conclusion that they account in some degree for the differential in interest and support.

Equally basic is the lack of experience with, or even understanding of, fundamental urban problems in this country. The relatively few people who know about such issues and can speak on them with some confidence and authority are not national figures. Their names are relatively unknown. Whatever they say is easily blanketed out in news reports by the pronouncements of generals, business leaders, and even by the advice of university presidents and leading intellectuals. Too many people in all walks of life seem to look upon urban centers and their physical patterns as being as relatively fixed and immutable and as far beyond the range of effective human action as the weather (before "cloud seeding"!), the tides, and the major physiographic features of the country.

Closely allied to this fact has been the nature of much of the proposals and arguments that have been made in favor of industrial dispersal. A large proportion of the arguments have been marked by what can only be called loose, overgeneralized thinking. Take, for example, the general failure to distinguish between industrial dispersal for security reasons and a wholesale scattering of urban populations and industry far and wide over the country. Nowhere have we seen any reasonable estimates of what industries and allied activities should be dispersed, of what kinds or degrees of dispersion would be necessary or optimum, of the priorities in any such program. Without these basic facts or judgments to start from, it has commonly been said, even by top federal officials, that the costs of a dispersal policy would be prohibitive. Without any question the volume of expenditure necessary to achieve a degree of dispersal that might be considered ideal as a security measure would be very great. But why in this area alone do we have to go whole-hog or none? Who can claim that the UN or the rearmament program (despite its great cost) affords perfect or nearperfect protection?

These offhand assertions of prohibitive cost have gone almost unchallenged at the very time that the nation was making new highs in both industrial and residential construction. During the decade 1940 to 1950, the urban population of the United States increased by 21.5 million persons or approximately 28.9 per cent. Despite the restrictions of a war economy for half of this period, crippling materials shortages and inflationary conditions for many years, we did provide a very substantial addition to the residential and industrial plant of the nation. A large proportion of the residential building of the decade came during the postwar years. Privately-financed industrial construction also has been much higher in dollar volume since the war than before or during it.[6] In short, the physical fabric and structure of urban centers have been changing materially at the very time that many leading citizens have been denying that it was amenable to intelligent action in behalf of national security because, by implication at least, it was too great, too fixed, too inflexible.

To be sure, this view has been challenged by some urban planners and others. Unfortunately, however, their challenges sometimes have been phrased in almost equally vulnerable terms. Some of them have actually said and others have come very close to saying that a fair degree of industrial and population dispersal could be achieved without any additional investment or expenditure. In other words, taking as given the volume of construction that is going on for housing and industrial purposes, this could be placed in a decentralized or dispersed pattern without any substantial additional expense. This is clearly a misstatement of fact as almost anyone could see who would make some

6. *Construction and Construction Materials* (Washington, D.C.: Bureau of Foreign and Domestic Commerce, Department of Commerce), *Statistical Supplement,* May, 1950, Table 7 and issue of January, 1951, Table 4. The estimated average dollar volume of private industrial construction work put in place for 1939 and 1940 was $348 million; for 1941 through 1945, $431 million; and for 1946 through 1950 was $1,335 million. Postwar building, of course, was at inflated prices. Public industrial construction for 1941 through 1945 averaged $1,714 million.

rough calculations as to the requirements for additional public facilities and services that would come from decentralizing the current volume of housing and industrial building.

It is true, however, that the differences in financial outlays between current housing and industrial construction, on the one hand, and putting much of that construction in decentralized patterns, on the other, quite surely are narrowing. In other words, the post-World War II construction boom has used up a large amount of the available unused facilities such as building sites with utility lines, schools, improved roads and streets, hospitals, retail stores, etc.

In our opinion, similarly in need of analysis is the common notion that any substantial degree of industrial dispersal could be achieved only by military direction or the advent of what is often called the garrison state. Certainly our democracy is not so helpless and sterile that we can deal effectively with industrial location and urban population patterns in the interests of national security only by military dictation. As a matter of fact, we have in operation today a number of programs for public aid that with some additions and modifications could be used as substantial inducements in behalf of less vulnerable urban centers. Mortgage insurance, financial aid to public housing, federal and state grants-in-aid for highway, airport, and other public improvements, the redevelopment title of the Housing Act of 1949, rapid amortization of expenditures for industrial plant for income tax purposes are obvious examples. These and other similar measures certainly deserve much more reasoned analysis and careful attention than anyone so far seems to have given them in this connection.

Quite probably other factors and forces have had some part in the relative neglect of industrial dispersal as a security measure. It seems to us, however, that those we have referred to briefly here are sufficient in combination to explain much of this sorry story. Although it is difficult to discuss this subject without seeming to blame, at least by implication, various agencies and individuals, this is not our intention. We do believe an opportunity has been missed. We also think that it is not too late to recover some of the lost ground and to see that we do not lose more in the future. In expressing these views, we recognize that they are simply opinions based on not much more information than the opposed notions we have been criticising. We have not had the resources nor the opportunity to analyze different kinds of industrial dispersal, their costs, their limitations, or their probable effectiveness as defense or security measures. Naturally we prefer our opinions to the opposed ones, but that is neither here nor there.

Rather we would urge that some serious attention be given to the considerable body of informed, if uninfluential, opinion among experienced urban planners and students of urban affairs that sees in industrial dispersal some promise of adding materially to the security of the nation. Why should not this opinion and the evidence for it, the contrary views and their supporting arguments, and in fact the whole issue be examined by an official commission of comparable competence and stature to, let us say, the Lilienthal committee that explored the grave potentialities and problems of international control of atomic energy. Such a commission on dispersal would have been justified, in our opinion, in late 1945 or '46. Under the conditions that exist today in our relations with Russia and in the position of the United Nations, it seems clear that the case for thorough analysis and reasoned judgment on industrial dispersal as a part of defense policy is stronger than ever before.

SOME STUDIES AND PROPOSALS

We turn now to a review of six contributions to the discussion of industrial dispersal as a security measure. We believe that this is justified not because any of these contributions or all of them together amount to a definitive analysis. Rather, some attention to these studies and proposals seems essential to a sharper definition of the points at issue and to a clearer appreciation of the level of understanding (or misunderstanding) on which the central issues have been discussed so far. In addition, we believe that both the strong and weak points of these contributions help to support our plea for further analysis without in any way prejudging the conclusions that might come from an adequate inquiry under responsible auspices.

These six contributions are: (1) the report, *The Problem of Reducing Vulnerability to Atomic Bombs,* made by Ansley J. Coale in 1947 for the Committee on Social and Economic Aspects of Atomic Energy of the Social Science Research Council;[7] (2) *National Security Factors in Industrial Location,* a pamphlet issued in September, 1948, by the National Security Resources Board; (3) the companion bills, S. 4232 and H. R. 9864, introduced in the second session of the 81st Congress and the similar bills (S. 218 and H. R. 1728) before the 82nd Congress ". . . to provide for the construction of Federal buildings outside of, but in the vicinity of, and accessible to the District of Columbia. . . ." and the hearings and Senate debate held on them; (4) the report, "The Need for Industrial Dispersal," prepared by the staff of the Joint Committee on the Economic Report and dated June 13, 1951; (5) the so-called Rains Amendment to the Defense Production Act of 1951, which was debated in the House of Representatives on July 11, 1951; and

7. Princeton: Princeton University Press, 1947.

(6) the President's "Statement of Policy on Industrial Dispersion" of August 10, 1951, and the NSRB's second pamphlet, *Is Your Plant a Target?*, which was put out at the same time and which supports the "Statement."

AN EARLY ANALYSIS

Coale's *The Problem of Reducing Vulnerability to Atomic Bombs* was one of the first major discussions of this question. Its preface by Mr. Winfield W. Riefler, Chairman of the SSRC's committee that supervised the study, was dated February 1, 1947. The work was frankly exploratory; Coale reaches no sweeping conclusions and offers relatively few specific recommendations. His work apparently was unofficial in the sense that he had few, if any, sources of technical information beyond those that were generally available to one who would look them up. Although he gave considerable attention to industrial and urban dispersal, he also took up many other aspects of vulnerability such as protection of military and civilian administrative headquarters, the location of military centers other than those for the production of war material, stock piling, transportation, and shelters for production workers and others. To be sure, many if not all of these additional subjects are related to industrial and urban patterns. They, however, do involve other questions and considerations on their own.

Mr. Coale's objective was well described by a few sentences in Mr. Riefler's preface:

> . . . It (Coale's study) is directed toward the question "Are there practicable methods by which mankind can substantially reduce its vulnerability to atomic warfare?"
>
> The study does not give a final answer to this question, nor was it the intention of the committee that it should do so. But it does analyze the problem. Only after such an analysis is it possible to form an intelligent opinion on the basic question, "Do techniques for the reduction of vulnerability from atomic weapons offer sufficient promise to merit exploration?"[8]

Despite its limitations Mr. Coale's volume probably is still the best discussion of the subject of this chapter. Its chief merit is that it is an *analysis*. It avoids sweeping, untested, or wishful generalizations about the effectiveness of dispersal, its costs, or other phases of the subject. Rather it breaks down its broad questions into a number of pertinent, more specific ones. It points out the kinds of information that should be assembled and evaluated in arriving at answers. It shows that these answers quite probably would depend on the nature of the war, when

8. *Op. cit.*, p. ix,

it might take place, and many other factors. In short, it is a competent, well reasoned introduction to a complex issue that admits of no glib answers.[9]

More specifically, the heart of Coale's work for our purpose is in chapters i and ii. The first considers reduction of vulnerability under the assumption of a generally effective agreement for international control of atomic power. If such a plan of control were put into effect but at some time were not lived up to by some nation, that nation might seize atomic energy installations and materials within its borders and conceivably might be able shortly thereafter to launch an attack against the United States—or some other nation. In these circumstances, the number of atomic bombs at its disposal would probably be limited. Coale refers to this as a limited attack. In chapter ii he makes another assumption: atomic warfare following a period in which there were no international control machinery. In this event the aggressor nation could be assumed to have a much larger number of atomic weapons at its disposal. It would be in the position to make a more or less unlimited attack—that is, it would be limited largely by the effects of retaliatory bombing and other military action against it by this and other nations.

In both of these chapters Coale examines various measures to reduce vulnerability under three headings: their possible effects in helping to prevent an attack, in contributing toward victory in the war that would follow any attack, and in minimizing casualties and aiding reconstruction of this country.

9. Another early, but brief, plea for proper analysis and study was made in Bernard Brodie (ed.), *The Absolute Weapon: Atomic Power and World Order* (New York: Harcourt, Brace and Co., 1946). In a chapter on Implications for Military Policy, Mr. Brodie has a section (pp. 99–106) on "The Dispersion of Cities as a Defense Against the Bomb." In it, he expressed serious doubt of the feasibility of wholesale rebuilding of American cities on linear or other patterns as a defense against atomic bombing. He did see promise, however, in several less sweeping measures, including relocation outside of cities of industries "especially and immediately necessary to atomic bomb warfare," accelerated suburbanization of city populations, converting cleared blighted or slum areas into "public parks or even airfields," and compartmentation of essential food, water, fuel, and medical services in large cities so that all or nearly all of them would not be paralyzed by one bomb explosion.

He concludes with this statement: "The writer is here presenting merely some general principles which might be considered in any plan for reducing our general vulnerability. Obviously, the actual content of such a plan would have to be derived from the findings of intensive study by experts in a rather large number of fields. It is imperative, however, that such a study be got under way at once. The country is about to launch into a great construction program, both for dwellings and for expanding industries. New sources of power are to be created by new dams. The opportunities thus afforded for 'vulnerability control' are tremendous, and should not be permitted to slip away—at least not without intensive study of their feasibility." (p. 106)

And this was published in 1946!

A few more sentences from Mr. Riefler's preface underline what we take to be the chief merit of Coale's study and also suggest clearly its pertinence to our discussion in this chapter:

> . . . From Mr. Coale's searching analysis, it appears that measures for the reduction of vulnerability are not limited to widespread dispersal or to "cave man" living. There are many alternatives, involving differing costs, and differing degrees of disruption. They differ also in their effectiveness, particularly by the extent to which they are integrated into a single comprehensive program. . . .
>
> Mr. Coale also shows that certain measures for the reduction of vulnerability, far from being inconsistent with the creation of an International Atomic Energy Authority, are in fact complementary to such an approach. As is indicated below, they would buttress the international approach to the control of atomic energy at its weakest point, namely, where there comes the possibility of complete breakdown of the international mechanism. . . .
>
> Mr. Coale finds that the nature and extent of measures that might be undertaken to reduce vulnerability to atomic destruction depend essentially on whether the hazard consists of atomic bombs in large numbers, such as might be produced by many countries over the course of time, or of relatively small numbers, such as might be produced in the course of a war. For the first contingency, the effort needed to minimize vulnerability approaches staggering proportions. Under such circumstances, even the most widespread decentralization loses a considerable part of its effectiveness, since if there are many bombs, there is the possibility of attacking many targets. If the atomic bomb remains a relatively scarce military weapon, however, to be conserved for use on targets of special significance, there are a variety of measures which might be employed with success for a considerable reduction of vulnerability. In either case there are considerations which our authorities should take into account, in the layout of cities, in the dispersion of plant facilities, in the location of hospitals, etc.[10]

In summary we believe that Mr. Coale's report with all of its frankly admitted limitations deserves a much wider audience and more serious consideration than apparently it has received so far. Among that audience certainly there should be many urban planners and redevelopers. If his approach of careful analysis instead of sweeping opinion were to be brought to bear on the present problem by a competent agency or group with access to the latest and best opinion on the nature and destructiveness of atomic weapons, a real foundation for an intelligent policy could be laid.

Although as we have said Mr. Coale was much more concerned with starting intelligent analysis than in drawing conclusions, his own views, as they come out rather indirectly in some sections, certainly are moderate. For example, in his last chapter on "Research and Analysis Needed," he emphasizes "the criteria of effectiveness and feasibility":

> . . . These criteria, applied on an unsubstantiated, *a priori* basis, have influenced the discussion in chapters i and ii, and the suggestions for research in this chapter. Many topics suited to the techniques of social science and apparently relevant to the

10. *Ibid.*, p. xi–xiii.

problems at hand have been consciously omitted on the grounds that they could not lead to action both effective and feasible.

An example will illustrate the type of topic which has been deliberately omitted. A primary source of vulnerability from the points of view of military strength and of civilian safety is the existence of large industrial clusters and of high population densities, both often associated with major urban areas. It might be possible to draw up a design for a new configuration of our industrial economy, a configuration capable of attaining comparable rates of industrial output, but devoid of large concentrations of plant or people. One might conceive the optimum arrangement which would minimize the danger from any particular scale of attack. The budgetary costs of the needed new construction might be computed, and the effects on industrial efficiency and national income estimated. Probably many of the less direct social consequences of abandoning metropolitan centers could be analyzed. However, the real difficulties of such a program appear when one seeks to devise methods of bringing it about, and considers whether our government has, or even should have, the needed power of enforcement; and then considers whether the public and the Congress would be likely to give support before atomic bombs had actually been used against this country. These probabilities have been deemed sufficiently small as to warrant only the mention of such a remedy in this book.

On the other hand, it would be foolhardy to state that a redistribution of industry and population cannot take place, over a long period, or to imply that the new distribution could not be one intrinsically less vulnerable than the present arrangement. This analysis has directed its attention to the problems of the next few decades—to the period during which it would probably require strong governmental intervention (or a disastrous demonstration) to reduce significantly the degree of urbanization. In the long run, developments in transportation, housing, optimum size of plant, etc., might tend to induce an industrial and demographic pattern similar to the one that consciousness of vulnerability would dictate. Such a tendency might be advanced by public persuasion and governmental inducement, and advanced more effectively if the causes of urbanization had been carefully studied.

However, it would be merely fortuitous if decisions based on individual advantage resulted eventually in a desirable dispersion of population; and, even if this dispersion occurred, the creation of more numerous, more accurate, and more powerful weapons during a long interval might well make dispersion of insignificant importance.[11]

NSRB's First Pamphlet

The first official statement on industrial dispersal as a security measure was the National Security Resources Board's pamphlet, *National Security Factors in Industrial Location.*[12] Probably it is better known than the other items we have selected for discussion in this section. If so, two brief quotations may indicate its purpose and character.

The opening section on "Purpose" reads:

This country's policies must be directed, at one and the same time, toward making every effort to build a stable peace and toward being adequately prepared in case those efforts fail. Therefore, attention must be directed to the risk of a possible

11. *Ibid.*, p. 114–15.
12. Washington, D.C.: Government Printing Office, 1948.

enemy attack against industry. The purpose of this booklet is to describe the nature of this risk and to indicate some action which industry might feasibly take. The basic concept is one of long-range planning. The immediate objective is the development of an economically practical approach to the problem of industrial security.

More specifically, the purpose of this booklet is: (*a*) to alert industrial leaders to the strategic significance of industrial plant location in the event of another war; (*b*) to suggest that industrial leaders think of strategic location or relocation of plant facilities as an added essential factor in any plans for plant expansion; (*c*) to impress upon industrial leaders the urgency for this type of thinking. Urgency, not because a national emergency is necessarily imminent, but because 12 to 14 billions of dollars are being spent annually for new plants and new equipment. A substantial portion of these plants is being located in highly concentrated industrial areas, thereby increasing vulnerability in the event of attack.

The next to the last paragraph in the pamphlet is also pertinent:

The job of dispersion is one that industry must assume, for both its own protection and that of the national security. Ours being a democratic Nation dedicated to the principles of free enterprise, the Government can neither dictate nor finance such a large-scale change in the industrial pattern. While the Government is naturally concerned with the promotion of a healthy condition in private enterprise, it also has a primary concern for the security of the Nation as a whole.

As these quotations indicate, this pamphlet is very unlike Mr. Coale's study. It makes no breakdowns of the types of danger from atomic attack, the kinds of dispersal that might be considered, other means that might be employed to reduce vulnerability. Rather, it is a brief plea directed to top officers of industrial corporations. It suggests that "It is, therefore, strategically desirable to plan industrial expansion so that further urban concentrations of more than 50,000 people may be avoided" (p. 2). This recommendation is based on the belief that urban areas less than 50,000 would be too small to justify the costs and hazards of atomic bombing. The same general opinion, with some later qualifications, is expressed also as to industrial areas of less than five square miles.

NSRB also suggested that industrialists in evaluating their present or prospective plant locations consider not only their own plants as possible targets, but also others in the immediate vicinity. Danger to Plant A is quite as great if plant B nearby becomes an atomic bomb target as if A itself would be so considered. A three-mile radius was given as a rough guide for the area of serious damage from improved A-bombs. The implication is that new plants or expansions should not be located within this distance of industrial districts that might be targets.

The pamphlet also points to some evidence that industrial dispersal already is under way for nonsecurity reasons. A further movement of this kind, therefore, might serve other ends in addition to defense and security.

We believe that the quotations and additional description of this document suggest the major criticism that has frequently been made of it. The text recalls the terrible destructiveness of atomic bombs. The frontispiece is a photograph of a great levelled section of Nagasaki. Yet the Board seemed to feel that its responsibility was limited to alerting, suggesting, and impressing. The criticism in essence is simply that the remedy bears no reasonable relation to the seriousness of the disease. We feel that this criticism is justified.

Also, although the booklet is clearly addressed to industrialists and, therefore, properly deals with facts and considerations significant to plant operation and protection, why is it practically silent on the horrible dangers to civilians who might be killed and maimed by the tens of thousands from a single atomic weapon successfully delivered against any of our large urban centers? Is this no concern of industrialists? Is the federal government's responsibility for industrial and urban dispersal as a protective measure—presumably protecting citizens as well as industrial capacity—adequately discharged by suggesting, alerting, and impressing industrialists on the dangers to their plants and facilities?

Later in this chapter we shall consider other governmental action on this front. On the whole, however, it has suffered from the same weaknesses. Is the conclusion that, in the judgment of those charged "to provide for the common defence," dispersal holds no real promise for protection. Or do they, including a majority of the Congress, believe that, even in many limited forms, it is beyond the capacities of our society? Can civilians only hope that in event of attack military defenses will stop some of the enemy's bombers and that civilian defense organizations will mitigate somewhat the horrors produced by those that would get through?

If these are the official views, why not say so and state the grounds on which they are based? If not, why has not a program commensurate with the danger been worked out, announced, and put into operation? Of course, it would encounter opposition, including charges of "crisis government" and of a "planned economy." But if the dangers and horrors of atomic attack are as they have been painted, certainly too much is at stake to allow this kind of opposition to prevail—at least without a contest.

When the NSRB's pamphlet was issued in September, 1948, it was understood that other materials on the subject would be put out later. One was to be addressed primarily to urban planners and other local officials to enable them to co-operate more effectively with industrialists who were inclined to consider seriously the decentralization or dispersal of their plants and facilities in accord with the recommendations in the first pamphlet. So far this has not been issued. The only other NSRB pamphlet on this subject to date (September, 1951) is that of August, 1951—*Is Your Plant a Target?*—which we review later in this chapter.

Officials of the Board, however, have followed up on the dispersal proposal in the first pamphlet by various addresses and in statements to the press. Some of these statements have included the opinion that a substantial degree of industrial dispersal has been taking place. Sometimes it has been admitted that apparently much of the net effect of this action has been partly hidden or partly canceled out by the continued operation of older plants in congested industrial areas and by new industrial enterprises absorbing vacant space in such areas released by dispersal of other operations. As we point out in chapters v and vi some evidence is available to support these conclusions. On the other hand, this evidence is scattered and far from conclusive. Representatives of the Board have also pointed out that from the information at hand it is very difficult, if not impossible, to say what proportion of the dispersal has been influenced primarily by strategic or security considerations and what proportion by nonmilitary factors that might have operated in any event.

A good example of an industrial policy of this kind is that of the General Electric Company. In the September, 1948 issue of the *American City,* its editors commented favorably on the arguments in the NSRB pamphlet and pointed out that in addition to their significance for national security, they conformed quite well with the magazine's long-standing argument for industrial and urban decentralization on other economic and social grounds. The following month's issue (p. 7) carried this note under the heading "General Electric's Decentralization Plan":

THE AMERICAN CITY's editorial last month, headed "Factory Dispersal for National Security and Rational Town Planning," has brought the following comment from Philip D. Reed, Chairman of the Board of the General Electric Company:

"The physical part of General Electric's decentralization program takes its pattern from economic planning rather than from any specific planning of wartime plant-dispersal. We have definitely favored building smaller plant units in our many new postwar locations for the reason that these offer better living and working conditions for our employees—easier access to schools and shopping centers, better transportation, lower taxes, more recreation facilities, and the many benefits of an economic and social character that are generally associated with life in a smaller and more cohesive community, as compared to a big city or an already overcrowded industrial area. We have no wish to be the dominant factor in the life of a community, since our experience clearly indicates that this is unhealthy both for the employee and for the company. These factors in themselves make for lower manufacturing costs.

"In addition, we know that we can produce more efficiently and in greater volume in a small, self-contained plant devoted to the making of a single product or line, than in the larger general-purpose plant which manufactures many different things. The necessity for reconversion and expansion after the last war made it possible for General Electric to develop its new plant facilities along these lines. There remain certain circumstances, of course, where large plants are still necessary, as in bringing together the skills and manpower necessary to build turbines and large rotating machinery.

"Despite the fact that our decentralization has been fundamentally economic in nature, it is nevertheless true that it automatically offers many of the security advantages which have been advocated by the National Security Resources Board, and in this respect is doubly desirable."

This statement by Mr. Reed, whose company has often been cited as one whose policies on industrial location accord with the NSRB's recommendation, suggests one distinction that may be worth noting here. As far as the physical results are concerned, it would seem to make little difference whether industrial dispersal were brought about primarily by security considerations or other factors or by some combination of the two. Questions about the influential or determining considerations or factors, however, are pertinent when one tries to form some judgment as to the effectiveness of NSRB's early policy on this front.

It is also clear that any official policy for industrial dispersal would encounter various kinds of resistances and opposition. Influential persons in the major industrial centers might object because they feared adverse effects upon their businesses, professions, or property values. Some labor unions might be sensitive to the possibility that their power at the bargaining table and in other ways might be weakened by spreading out industrial employment more and more into smaller towns— even if many of them were within the larger metropolitan areas. Many officials and citizens in the smaller localities, on the other hand, might look with considerable misgivings on the prospect of new and different kinds of economic activity within their boundaries. The first of these kinds of objection is recognized by implication in the NSRB pamphlet, and the second by a footnote at the end of the text. It would also seem beyond argument that the more vigorous the official policy for industrial dispersal the greater would be these and similar forms of opposition. Against these facts, however, should be weighed the basic considerations of military security and protection of human life that are fundamental to the entire proposal. And as we have pointed out above, any genuine attempt to strike a true balance of comparative benefits is hamstrung by the shortage of facts and the inadequate analysis of costs.

damages, and likely benefits from a well considered policy of industrial dispersal.

FEDERAL OFFICE BUILDINGS

At first glance it might seem that a proposal to decentralize a limited amount of office space for government workers to locations outside the built-up area of Washington hardly came under the heading of industrial dispersal as a security measure. The record of this attempt to date, however, deserves notice because it throws considerable light on the difficulties and misunderstandings that seem everywhere to attend the notion of dispersal.

The essential facts from this record can be briefly summarized. In the spring of 1949 the President designated the National Security Resources Board as the federal agency primarily responsible for civil defense planning. Later that year, the Atomic Energy Commission sent the Chairman of NSRB a memorandum that summarized the generally known facts on the destructiveness of atomic bombing of urban centers and stressed the vulnerability of Washington as the headquarters of vital military and other governmental services.[13] On August 30, 1950, the President sent to Congress a supplemental appropriation estimate for $139.8 million to enable the General Services Administration to construct and equip additional office building centers "within commuting distance of Washington." The accompanying explanation said that the sum requested was estimated to be required for four such centers ". . . to accommodate 35,000 to 40,000 Federal employees."[14] Congress did not make the appropriation.

At about this same time the National Capital Park and Planning Commission was preparing for publication a series of reports including *Washington Present and Future—A General Summary of the Comprehensive Plan for the National Capital and Its Environs.*[15] This plan also envisaged outlying federal office building centers and accompanying facilities. The Commission's recommendation for these developments, however, rested almost entirely upon nonsecurity or nonmilitary facts and arguments. It stressed traffic congestion. Security reasons were mentioned but not emphasized.

In December, 1950, in the closing days of the 81st Congress, identical bills were introduced in the Senate and the House of Representatives (S. 4232 and H. R. 9864). According to their titles they were "To

13. Printed in *Bulletin of the Atomic Scientists* (January, 1950), pp. 29–30.
14. Copies of the letters on this request are printed in *Dispersal of Federal Buildings— Hearings before the Subcommittee of the Committee on Public Works, United States Senate . . . on S. 4232* (Washington, D.C.: Government Printing Office, 1951), p. 3–4.
15. The Commission, Monograph No. 1, April, 1950.

authorize a program to provide for the construction of Federal buildings outside of, but in the vicinity of, and accessible to the District of Columbia. . . ." They would have authorized the Administrator of General Services to acquire sites for outlying office buildings, to see to the construction of the buildings, and ". . . all things accessory and appurtenant thereto and comprising components of respective projects, and, in addition, the provision of such utilities, roads, highways, bridges, communications, and other off-site facilities as may be necessary and appropriate: . . ." (Section 1) and also would have authorized the appropriation of $190 million for these purposes. Later in the same month, hearings on these bills were held before subcommittes of the Senate and House committees on public works. The same bills were introduced the next month in the new Congress and supplementary hearings were held.

The hearings on all four of these bills indicate clearly the difficulties this proposal has faced. The National Capital Park Planning Commission saw the need for a considerable number of these centers. Many of them would be within ten or fifteen miles of central Washington, but others "for industrial, experimental, or confidential activities" would be as far out as fifty miles or so. In testifying on the bills in December, 1950, representatives of government agencies put forward as the initial program eight centers, each of which would have office space for about 10,000 employees and would be located roughly twenty miles from the White House. Some members of the Committee seemed dubious about locations this far out.

In addition, the hearings underscored the difficulties in planning such a program that stem from the hodgepodge of local governments and planning authorities outside of the District of Columbia proper. Representatives of these outlying communities were deeply concerned over the implications of the program for their future growth and, particularly, over the burden that would be thrown on them for schools and other facilities and services. Questions from some members of the subcommittes indicated that in judging the costs of this undertaking to the federal government, they were using somewhat different standards than those that had prevailed in considering expenditures for direct military purposes.

Finally, it was clear that some of the agency representatives who testified had rather elementary notions of what such a program, if it were to be effective, would entail. For example, near the end of the testimony of Mr. Jeff Larson, Administrator of the General Services Administration, this exchange took place:

SENATOR WATKINS: Was the additional cost of educational facilities written into this estimate?

MR. LARSON: No. I did not understand your first question. I probably should have answered you initially that we assume the same type of legislation which has been referred to here would take care of the needs when the population grew around the sites. As I say, initially it is going to be a problem of transportation of the people to the sites. They are not going to live around the sites initially.

SENATOR CHAVEZ: But they will be there pretty soon. All of the surrounding country will have a regular real-estate development.

MR. LARSON: And that is desirable.

SENATOR HOLLAND: Your problem is to create new office space, and service facilities and parking facilities and transportation facilities.

MR. LARSON: That is correct.

SENATOR HOLLAND: You are not thinking in terms of housing; you are not thinking in terms of schools; you are not thinking in terms of utilities other than the kind and amount of utilities that you are going to need to service these buildings.

MR. LARSON: That is right.

SENATOR WATKINS: Have you taken into consideration the tax situation, such as you have where the Health Administration is building out there? The people going out there are taxed under the Maryland law, the nonresidents working in the area.

MR. LARSON: Well, I am not familiar with that situation. I was not aware that they were taxed, any more than anybody is taxed when they buy something.

SENATOR WATKINS: I am talking about an income tax. I understand that people living in the District and who go to Maryland to work are made to pay an extra income tax there.

MR. LARSON: I think that is a matter which the courts will eventually settle.[16]

From this view of what was needed for national security, the conclusion could well be drawn that for some indefinite period of time the security provided would be largely that of government records and equipment and of certain federal employees during working hours. If an atomic bomb were dropped on Washington during the daytime, the government files and these employees would be relatively safe, but the families of those who lived in Washington proper (rather than in its suburbs) would not. If the attack came at night, the buildings might still be standing in the morning, but some of them might have few employees left to man them.

On April 11, 1951, the Senate Committee on Public Works reported out a revised bill (S. 218, Report No. 216). It reduced the number of outlying centers to four and the authorization to appropriate to $107 million. Each center was to provide space for approximately 5,000 workers. The revised bill authorized and directed the Administrator of the General Services Administration "to demolish temporary buildings constructed by the Federal Government immediately prior to and during World War II in the District of Columbia and areas adjacent thereto at such times as space becomes available at the buildings constructed upon the sites referred to in section 1 of this Act or because of the decentralization of Government positions effectuated under sec-

16. Hearings before the Subcommittee on Public Works . . . , S. 4232, pp. 70–71.

tion 3 of this Act" (Sec. 2). Section 3 set as a goal ". . . the transfer of not less than 25,000 positions in the Federal Government from the District of Columbia and its immediate vicinity to places elsewhere in the United States. . . ." These three substantive parts of the bill were referred to in the Report and elsewhere as dispersal, demolition, and decentralization.

On April 23 the revised bill was debated by the Senate and, by a vote of 45 to 39, was sent back to the Committee on Public Works. The debate shed little or no additional light on the merits and weaknesses of the measure. Probably its more notable features were two or three. Several Senators did stress official responsibility for the protection of life as well as of official records and the continuity of the government. Also, proponents of the measure pointed out that limited dispersal (within the Washington metropolitan area—twenty miles or so from central Washington) would be almost if not quite as effective as scattering workers and functions far and wide over the country. Thus, for example, this exchange took place between Senator Watkins and Senator Holland, who was chairman of the subcommittee that considered the original bill and who was in charge of the revised measure on the floor:

MR. WATKINS: Is the Senator satisfied with the provision by which these buildings are to be placed only 20 miles from Washington?

MR. HOLLAND: I am. I heard the statements of experts, both military and civilian, both scientific and practical, who, I think, know more about the problem than anyone else in the United States, and perhaps more than anyone else in the world. They assured the committee that the distance was sufficient. To all intents and purposes, the dispersal areas would become separate targets. They would be separate targets, whether they were in Utah, Florida, California, or anywhere else, because we know that the bombers now operated by our only potential enemy can go from one end of the Nation to the other with almost equal ease.

MR. WATKINS: Will the Senator say whether or not all the experts were united on that point? Did they all agree that that was a sufficient distance?

MR. HOLLAND: They were agreed. There was not a single voice which questioned that distance, except one of the experts of the Atomic Energy Commission, who thought that a shorter distance would be sufficient. However, all agreed that the 20-mile insulating distance was completely satisfactory from the standpoint of separating the targets. A dispersal unit, involving 5,000 people, would not be a very attractive target. It would be a small area, hard to hit, and not easy to find. It would be a separate target, just as much so as though it were located in Iowa, Utah, Florida, or anywhere else in the Nation. It would not feel the impact of an attack on the District of Columbia and its immediate environs.[17]

It was also stated that the Department of Defense had endorsed the measure.[18]

17. *Congressional Record* (April 23, 1951), p. 4305.
18. *Ibid.*, p. 4321.

In addition to the admitted weaknesses of the bill, the section on "decentralization" of government employees (Sec. 3, proposing that 25,000 employees be moved out of Washington and its environs) touched off a heated debate on the size of the federal establishment, economy in government, etc. From that point on the quality of the debate was about what might have been expected.

The division on the motion of Senator Dirksen to recommit was largely on party lines with several southern Democrats joining the majority of the Republicans to send the measure back to the Committee on Public Works.

REPORT TO JOINT COMMITTEE ON THE ECONOMIC REPORT

In the summer of 1951 direct challenges were made to the view that in respect to industrial dispersal the federal government had to choose between a military dictatorship to put industrial facilities where military officers wanted them and mild suggestions to industrialists. In the first of these questionings, under the date of June 13, 1951, Senator Joseph C. O'Mahoney, Chairman of the Joint Committee on the Economic Report, had published "for the information of members of the committee and others interested . . ." a report on *The Need for Industrial Dispersal* prepared by the Joint Committee's staff.[19] In its introductory section was this statement of purpose: "This report attempts to summarize the nature and extent of the programs for directly stimulating industrial expansion and to relate them to the problems of industrial location for maximum military security and utilization of the Nation's economic resources" (p. 1).

The Committee's staff pointed out four measures for stimulating industrial expansion in the interests of the national defense program: (1) "accelerated tax amortization," provided for in Section 124A of the Internal Revenue Code and granted through certificates of necessity approved by the Defense Production Administration; (2) the Department of Defense program of military contracts for expanding privately operated and government facilities; (3) guaranteed loans; and (4) direct loans.

From the beginning of the tax amortization program in October, 1950, until late May, 1951, certificates of necessity had been granted to about $6 billion worth of industrial plant and facilities on which accelerated tax amortization of more than $4 billion had been authorized. According to the staff, the eventual size of this program had been estimated at from $10 to $12 billion. It suggested, however, that these estimates might be on the conservative side.

19. Washington, D.C.: Government Printing Office, 1951.

As to the military contracts the report said:

> . . . These contracts are financed with military funds appropriated for procurement, industrial mobilization, and for expediting production. According to an early estimate, expansion under the program is expected to reach a $5.9 billion total. Most of this money will be used for machine tools, jigs and fixtures, and other items needed to retool and reequip present plants, but a considerable proportion will be used for new structures . . . [p. 2].

The staff also reported that guaranteed loans approved to May 25, 1951, amounted to $422 million and direct loans, $563 million. Many of the facilities aided by these loans also had been allowed accelerated tax amortization. The total volume of industrial plant and facilities assisted under defense powers, therefore, is somewhat less than the total of the figures given for the four different kinds of aid. The report mentioned that a large proportion of the facilities aided up to that time had been to increase the supplies of basic materials. Because of the nature of most of these industries, the possibilities of influencing location in the interest of national security have been somewhat limited. ". . . As the industrial expansion program moves on to extend the capacity for producing finished goods, however, the way is open for using areas which are both strategically more secure and where there are reserves of manpower and other resources" (p. 4).

As the sentence just quoted indicates, the Committee's staff did not address itself here solely to defense considerations in industrial expansion. Also, much of its discussion deals with what is sometimes called *regional dispersal*—spreading out industries into broad areas not now industrialized or only slightly so. The case for this proposal rests only partly on defense considerations and, therefore, brings up some arguments both pro and con that are only indirectly if at all related to defense. Proposals of this kind are largely outside the scope of this chapter and, in any event, should be clearly distinguished from local dispersal (or industrial *diffusion* in the terminology of chapter v).

Less easily understandable is the staff's account of the criteria and procedures for handling the accelerated amortization program. The administration of the program was first in the hands of the National Security Resources Board. Later it was assigned to the Defense Production Administration. Speaking of the Executive Order of October 12, 1950, which first outlined the objectives and criteria to guide the NSRB, the report states:

> The order emphasized the need for considering, among other criteria, the necessity for and adequacy of facilities or materials or services for a particular region, the location of the facility with due regard to military security and the availability of manpower, housing, community facilities, transportation, and other elements of production. Arrangements were made under which the Department of Labor would sup-

ply NSRB or one of the delegate agencies with an analysis regarding the availability of manpower for the additional facilities for which accelerated amortization was requested. No other provision was made for reviewing the relationship of the proposed expansion to over-all economic efficiency nor was the question of military security formally evaluated. After the function of reviewing and approving certificates of necessity for accelerated tax amortization was transferred to the Defense Production Administration, the arrangement for analyzing the availability of manpower in connection with granting individual certificates was no longer observed [p. 3].

The Committee's staff points out that when the law was being considered by Congress, a memorandum was sent by Mr. Charles S. Murphy, special counsel to the President, to the House Ways and Means Committee that stated in part:

From the standpoint of the Government, this tax incentive can help get facilities built where and when they will be most useful. . . . Such special tax incentives should be of particular significance in inducing firms to select locations for new plants with primary regard for national security rather than economic considerations. It may be very desirable to ask businesses to locate new plants in places other than those they would select on the basis of cost and market considerations. Accelerated amortization may be used to compensate businesses which participate in such industrial dispersal [p. 3].

The staff also quotes from the Fifth Intermediate Report, May 28, 1951, of the House Committee on Expenditures in the Executive Departments:

One of the crucial questions which has arisen in the administration of the certificate-of-necessity program concerns the dispersal of industry. Under the present policy no effort is made by the Government to control the location of new facilities through certificates; the selection of the site is left entirely to the applicant. Quite naturally, this policy results in further concentration of industry in areas favored by economic factors wholly without regard to considerations of military security or the avoidance of knock-out blows in the event of a sudden enemy attack. Moreover, not only has the Government taken no initiative in this direction but has refused to aid, through a higher percentage certificate, an applicant who proposed to construct a facility in a location chosen primarily for reasons of military security [p. 3].

The report of the Joint Committee's staff concludes with these paragraphs:

The requirements of a defense economy operating at peak capacity and the need for strategic location against possible atomic attack make essential the increasing dispersion of industrial facilities in the United States. Present Government programs providing for accelerated tax amortization, direct guaranteed loans, (*sic*) and direct construction have tended to add to rather than relieve existing industrial concentration. There are a number of criteria which if used in guiding the direction of future expansion could do much to insure maximum military and economic security but no adequate machinery now exists for insuring that these considerations get into the procurement, amortization, or loan process.

It is recommended that the Defense Production Act be amended to the end that adequate steps be taken by all departments of Government concerned with the expansion of industrial facilities to insure a pattern of industrial development which would:

1. Consider the advantages of the present distribution of communities and production facilities and employ their present and potential productivity to a maximum.

2. In accordance with this aim, minimize the occasion for needless migration of labor, with the attendant dislocation of State, local, and family institutions.

3. Establish new or expanded facilities in areas which have greater geographic security from enemy attack.

4. Establish new or expanded plants in areas which have the potential transport, labor, and other requirements so as to economize, by avoiding undue or overconcentration in already-congested areas.

5. Develop, as natural results of plant, corporate, industrial, and geographic decentralization, the opportunities for smaller, medium-sized local businesses and industries to undertake more direct participation in the defense effort, and by opportunity for normal growth to add to the productive capacities of the economy [pp. 6 and 7].

On June 20, 1951, Representative Kersten of Wisconsin introduced a bill (H. R. 4529) to amend Section 124A of the Internal Revenue Code. In Mr. Kersten's words: "My amendment however, would permit the use of this accelerated depreciation only when the emergency facility is located in a secure area which is not likely to be subject to atomic attack."[20]

It seems to us that the staff report takes rather lightly the administrative difficulties in using the accelerated tax amortization and other aids to industries as a means of inducing industrial dispersal for security purposes. In fact, it hardly faces them at all. Certainly a flat and inflexible limitation like the one proposed by Representative Kersten would be open to serious question. If, however, a properly qualified government agency or commission had made the kind of analysis of industrial dispersal as a defense measure that we suggested earlier in this chapter, the administrative problems by no means would be insuperable. And as the Committee's staff pointed out the possibilities of using these programs as inducements to this end might be greater in the latter than in the earlier stages of industrial expansion in the current national defense job.

In a report dated July 31, 1951—*Regional Aspects of Industrial Expansion under Accelerated Tax Amortization Program*[21]—the Defense Production Administration presented an analysis with differing implications from those of the Joint Committee's staff.

DPA eliminated from its study five major industry groups on the grounds that they consisted largely of consumer goods industries not

20. *Congressional Record* (June 20, 1951), p. 7000.
21. *Defense Programs—Supplement* (Washington, D.C.: Defense Production Administration).

directly related to defense production. The five were: food and kindred products; tobacco manufacture; apparel and related products; furniture and fixtures; and printing and publishing. It then showed for each of the nine geographic regions or divisions of the country the per cent distribution of (*a*) value added by manufacture as reported by Census of Manufactures in 1947—a rough measure of industrial activity at the beginning of the post-World War II period; (*b*) capital expenditures for new plant and equipment in 1947 as reported by the Census —an indication of industrial expansion before the latest defense or rearmament period; and (*c*) dollar volume of proposed investment in plant and equipment for which certificates of necessity had been approved up to June 11, 1951—the chief program of government aid to industrial expansion in the defense period.

For three of the less industrialized regions—East South Central, West South Central, and the Mountain states—this breakdown showed a sharp rise in the proportion of aided plant and equipment investment over the proportions for value added by manufacture and for expenditures for new plant and equipment in 1947. These three regions had (*a*) 8.5 per cent of the national total of value added by manufacture in 1947; (*b*) 13.3 per cent of the total expenditures for new plant and equipment in 1947; and (*c*) 29.9 per cent of the dollar volume of proposed investment under approved certificates of necessity. Of these three regions, the West South Central had the most rapid relative shift. Its percentages were (*a*) 3.9, (*b*) 8.0, (*c*) 17.5 (p. 170).

Conversely, the three old, heavily industrialized regions had (*a*) 71.2 per cent of the 1947 total of value added by manufacture; (*b*) 62.6 per cent of the 1947 expenditures for new plant and equipment; and (*c*) 55.4 per cent of the volume under approved certificates of necessity. The percentages for the remaining three regions—West North Central, South Atlantic, and Pacific—were (*a*) 20.3, (*b*) 24.1, and (*c*) 14.7. For each of these three regions the percentages for 1947 capital expenditures for new plant and equipment was higher than that for 1947 value added, but the proportion for government aided expansion was lower than for either (*a*) or (*b*) (p. 170).

When the iron and steel industry was taken out of the dollar volume of proposed investment under approved certificates of necessity, the proportion for the first group of regions—East and West South Central and Mountain—went up from 29.9 per cent to 43.3 per cent. Iron and steel, however, accounted for about 40 per cent of the total dollar volume analyzed.

From a further breakdown of the data by industry groups, the DPA report concluded:

The Middle Atlantic States of Pennsylvania, New York, and New Jersey are receiving the lion's share of new iron and steel plants (40.3 percent). Ohio, Indiana,

Illinois, Michigan, and Wisconsin, of the East North Central Region are close behind (28.7 percent). The apportionment of 11.8 percent of proposed new iron and steel plants to the New England States is especially worth noting.

Nearly all new plants of the aluminum industry are being located in the West South Central States (67.1 percent) and in the Mountain States (27.1 percent). The bulk of new aircraft and aircraft component plants is proposed for the New England States (26.4 percent), the Middle Atlantic States (17.3 percent), and the East North Central States (34.4 percent). Half of the expansion of the chemical industry is being located in the East North Central States (23.4 percent) and the West South Central States (29.9 percent). The location of most of the new non-ferrous (other than aluminum) plants in the East North Central, West South Central, and Mountain Regions is obviously dictated by the location of raw materials, as is the concentration occurring in the expansion of the gasoline products industry, in which the West South Central States are receiving 52.3 percent of new capital proposed for the industry [pp. 179 and 181].

The DPA pamphlet concluded that its analysis shows ". . . that an appreciable degree of regional decentralization of vital manufacturing industries is taking place" (p. 169). It also warned, however, that the data on defense expansion have to be used in the light of four qualifications (p. 181): (*a*) They include both new plant and equipment. Much of the latter may be for older plants. (*b*) They do not cover expansion aided by government loans or guarantees of loans (unless, of course, accelerated tax amortization is also approved) or government-owned plants. (*c*) They are limited to manufacturing. They do not include, for example, transportation and storage facilities or power generation and distribution. (*d*) Approval of certificates of necessity does not mean that all the facilities necessarily will be built. An example of this fact may well be the proposed steel plant at New London, Connecticut, which, incidentally, probably accounts for a large proportion of the New England percentage of iron and steel expansion referred to in the quotation above.

Also, it should be clear that this analysis by DPA did not go into industrial location within the various parts of metropolitan regions or urban centers. It was limited to "regional aspects."

The Rains Amendment

On July 11, 1951, the House of Representatives (sitting as the Committee of the Whole House on the State of the Union) debated a proposed amendment by Congressman Albert Rains of Alabama to the Defense Production Act of 1950. The Rains Amendment was:

(e) Title III of the Defense Production Act of 1950 is amended by adding at the end thereof the following new section:

"SEC. 305. (a) No construction or expansion of plants, factories, or other facilities shall be (1) undertaken, or assisted by means of loans (including participation in, or guaranties, of loans), by the United States, under this act, and no equipment, facilities, or processes owned by the Government shall be installed under the authority of this act in any plant, factory, or other industrial facility which is privately owned, unless the President shall have determined that the proposed location of such construction, expansion, or installation is consistent, insofar as practicable, with a sound policy of (1) utilizing fully the human and material resources of the Nation wherever located, (2) dispersing productive capacity for purposes of national security, (3) minimizing the necessity for further concentrations of population in areas in which available housing and community facilities are presently overburdened, and (4) preventing post-emergency unemployment in localities having defense activities.

"(b) In making the determination required by subsection (a), the President shall give consideration to counties, or comparable governmental subdivisions, which—

"(1) have natural resources embracing minerals, metals, materials, and other commodities, valuable to the defense program;

"(2) are not fully utilizing their employed labor forces (as indicated by a relatively low rate of production per worker) or are not fully utilizing their natural resources;

"(3) are relatively underdeveloped industrially;

"(4) by reason of outward migration since 1930, have not retained their natural increase in population; and

"(5) are relatively less vulnerable to enemy attack by reason of geographic location, or the absence of heavy concentrations of population or vital defense industry.

"(c) The President shall make quarterly reports to the Congress on the administration of this section. Such reports shall reveal the extent to which the policy objectives of this section have been attained, the cases in which they have been found impracticable of attainment, and the criteria used in such cases. Such reports may include such recommendations as the President may deem appropriate."[22]

The background of the proposed amendment and of the debate on it is quite brief. The House Committee on Banking and Currency had been studying a number of proposed amendments to the Defense Production Act of 1950. Extensive hearings had been held. One result of the Committee's deliberations was a number of so-called committee amendments to the Act. One of these was practically identical with the Rains Amendment—except that (1) in addition to the types of industrial plants and facilities mentioned in the Rains Amendment, it referred as well to plants and facilities: ". . . certified under section 124A of the Internal Revenue Code (relating to amortization for tax purposes), . . ." and (2) it did not include subsection (a) (4) of section 305.

This committee amendment had been adopted by a vote of 17 to 5 in the Committee. Between the time that this action was taken and the debate on July 11, rather quiet, but judging from the references to it in the debate, determined and influential opposition had come from various chambers of commerce and similar organizations in the more highly industrialized states. The House debate on this matter on July 11 began on the committee amendment, but almost immediately a point of order

22. *Congressional Record* (July 11, 1951), p. 7980.

was raised against it on the grounds that it sought to amend the Internal Revenue Code under the guise of dealing with the Defense Production Act. This protest, incidentally, was supported by the Majority Leader. When the chairman sustained the point of order, Mr. Rains, a member of the Committee, introduced instead his amendment, which omitted the reference to section 124A.

Clearly the Rains Amendment dealt with other features of defense policy besides the issue of industrial dispersal. Throughout the debate, however, Mr. Rains and his chief supporters stressed dispersal as a security measure. About one-third of the way through the debate, which went on for some five hours, Congressman Multer of New York proposed an amendment to the amendment that limited it to government-owned plants and changed the references from "areas" to "localities." Mr. Rains accepted this revision. Even this watering-down was to no avail. The House rejected the Multer Amendment and then refused to approve the Rains Amendment by a vote of 79 to 134.

For our purposes here, little need be said about most of the debate. In general, it was sectionalism run wild. Nearly all of those who spoke against the amendment were Representatives from highly industrialized areas and almost the same proportion of its supporters were from the less industrialized regions. This became so obvious that many of those who spoke began by deploring sectionalism in such vital matters—and then went on with some more of it. Many of the speeches were replete with references to a planned economy, the repeal of economic laws, and similar clichés. Although it was pointed out several times that the proposed measure would apply only to new plants or expansions, the opponents constantly referred to moving industries out of their areas. The admirable qualities of the skilled workmen, the climate, and the industrial enterprisers of various regions came in for high praise.

On the other hand, very few references were made to the dangers of atomic bombing to the civilian population, including those greatly admired skilled workers. More than a few of the debaters seemed to think they had disposed of the whole issue by saying that Russian bombers by flying over the Arctic regions could reach any part of the United States. The key point of the size of industrial concentrations that would be suitable targets for atomic bombs seemed to elude not only these Congressmen, but most of those who replied to them.

Nearly all of the debate seemed to be based on the assumption that industrial dispersal was entirely a matter of locating plants in very small localities in unindustrialized regions. Only two or three times was the point clearly made that much less drastic changes in the industrial pattern of the country would add appreciably to its security. Congressman Elliott of Alabama pointed out:

Many of those who have participated in this debate have tried to make a sectional issue out of this question of the dispersal of industry. Some of our friends from New England seem to feel that the dispersal of industry would mean that industry would move from New England to the South and West. Yet, there are vast unoccupied spaces in New England where its industry could be dispersed so as to, partially at least, avoid the terrible effects of the atomic bomb.[23]

Even more pertinently, Mr. Brooks Hays of Arkansas said:

We do not say that dispersal means moving industry from one State to another or from one section of the country to another. I agree with the National Security Resources Board that only one target can be destroyed by one bomb, and that some plants 20 miles from that target might be safer than one 1,000 miles away.

And I agree with the gentleman from Alabama (Mr. Rains) that a plant change of perhaps 20 miles would meet requirements of dispersal in some instances. I would say that Mr. Wilson in locating a plant in northeast Connecticut, for example, might meet that criterion when he could not meet it by placing the plant in a congested urban area as, if the gentleman will permit me to say it, some part of the city of Hartford.[24]

In general, the Congressional Record on this debate is pertinent to our consideration here largely as evidence of the misunderstandings and loose generalizations that this issue is afflicted with in many quarters as well as an indicator of the kind of opposition that it engenders. Quite possibly the Rains Amendment attempted too much and might have been more effectively phrased. Be that as it may, in our opinion, it deserved a more thoughtful and discriminating evaluation than it received on the afternoon of July 11.

Congressmen, of course, should not be expected to be experts on all the matters that they must pass upon. Not a little of the character of this debate could be traced back to the shortcomings of those, like ourselves and some of our readers, who have failed to make clear both to the public and to their representatives the essential facts (as far as they are known) and the central issues in this whole problem. .

Neither would we have our readers believe that the debate in the House was entirely disheartening. It had its points. For example:

Mr. Gavin: Mr. Chairman, will the gentleman yield?

Mr. Hays (of Arkansas): I yield to the gentleman from Pennsylvania.

Mr. Gavin: I wish to call the attention of the gentleman to the fact that most of his forebears came from up in my district in Pennsylvania, and I am glad to see that he has developed into a real, sound, thinking statesman.

Mr. Hays (of Arkansas): Now the gentleman has embarrassed me. But I appreciate the gentleman's friendship and have always been proud of my Pennsylvania heritage.

Mr. Judd: Mr. Chairman, will the gentleman yield?

Mr. Hays (of Arkansas): I yield to the gentleman from Minnesota.

23. *Ibid.*, pp. 7996–97.
24. *Ibid.*, p. 7985.

Mr. Judd: Is that not a perfect example of the advantages of dispersal? See what happens to them when they get away.

The President's Statement of Policy

On August 10, 1951, President Truman issued a *Statement of Policy on Industrial Dispersion*. He announced that he had approved this policy on the recommendation of the Chairman of the National Security Resources Board, the Director of the Office of Defense Mobilization, and the Chairman of the Munitions Board.

The introductory paragraphs of the *Statement* mention again that a large proportion of the industrial productive capacity of the nation:

". . . lies within a relatively few densely built-up centers.

Since 1945, we have experienced a period of unprecedented industrial expansion, but, except for a few examples, there has been no pronounced trend away from these concentrations. Some eighteen billions in new plants and equipment were spent annually during the past four years, largely in areas already industrialized.

After referring to the NSRB pamphlet of September, 1948, the statement continues:

Since publication of this report, several factors have added to the urgency of the problem:

1. The evidence that Russia had a successful atomic explosion.
2. The probability that a strong enemy air attack could penetrate any defenses.
3. The outbreak of hostilities in Asia as an indication of the semi-peace conditions under which we are living.

Obviously, in the light of the above, what was, in 1948, a set of desirable objectives, is today a subject of major concern and one vital to our national security.

It is recognized that the major centers of industrial production have become highly integrated and that a part of their efficiency is due to their concentration. A dispersion policy to be effective and realistic must not be allowed to cripple the efficiency and productivity of our established industries, lest the remedy become worse than the ill. Our policy, therefore, must be directed mainly toward the dispersal of new and expanding industries.

Sites which meet dispersion security standards can be found in local marketing areas adjacent to industrial or metropolitan districts in all sections of the country.

Thus, this policy can be made to fit the economic and social pattern of any part of the country.

The fullest cooperation of industry, labor, and local and state governments, together with all of the measures which the Federal Government can take, will be needed to alleviate the present situation. With the necessary technical guidance as well as the positive inducements which we will give, much can be accomplished.

All Departments and Agencies of the Government concerned with this problem will be called upon in carrying out a coordinated policy leading to effective industrial dispersal within the concepts described above.

To this effect, the following measures will be taken:

1. To the greatest extent practicable, certificates of necessity, allocations of critical materials for construction purposes, and emergency loans growing out of

defense production will be confined to facilities which meet satisfactory standards of dispersal.

2. Primary consideration to dispersal factors will be given in locating facilities built by the Federal Government.

3. Defense contracts will be awarded, and planning under Department of Defense production allocation programs will be conducted in such a manner as to make maximum use of facilities located in dispersed sites.[25]

When the President announced this policy he also said that the Director of the Office of Defense Mobilization would be responsible for establishing "general standards with respect to dispersal. . . ."

According to newspaper stories Congressman Martin, minority leader, and some other members of the House of Representatives severely criticized this Statement of Policy. They contended that it was Executive usurpation of authority, "one-man rule" etc.[26] They maintained that the House had debated and turned down a similar policy proposal, the Rains Amendment, only a few weeks before. Possibly some of these criticisms were made to the papers before the Congressmen had seen the President's *Statement* and the NSRB pamphlet released at the same time. Be that as it may, it is clear that the emphasis in the President's policy on limited dispersal "in local marketing areas adjacent to industrial and metropolitan districts. . . ." is quite different from the conception of dispersal held by practically all who spoke against the Rains Amendment on July 11, 1951.

Also on August 10 the NSRB issued another pamphlet on this subject under the title *Is Your Plant a Target?* It was clearly implied, if not directly stated, that this pamphlet was the basis of the President's policy statement. As a matter of fact, at one or two points the language is identical.

In general, this second pamphlet seems to us a much more effective document than the one of September, 1948. Its argument is more tightly drawn and more sophisticated in the sense of recognizing more of the substantive questions and procedural difficulties that its recommendations raise. It also stated definitely that the federal government will encourage dispersal not only by means of technical information, guidance, and assistance, but also in the three direct ways mentioned in the President's Statement. In addition, the text of the pamphlet clearly referred to the dangers of atomic warfare to human life and civilian welfare as well as to industrial production.

25. Mimeographed statement, August 10, 1951 (2965), *Statement of Policy on Industrial Dispersion,* with attached letter, "To the Heads of Executive Departments and Agencies," over the name—Harry S. Truman.

26. For example, *The New York Times,* August 11, 1951, p. 1—story headed "President Orders Dispersal Policy for New Plants—Agencies Told to Give Tax and Other Aids to Plans Linked to Atomic Attack Peril—Congress Held Flouted. . . ."

The NSRB stated four basic principles of the dispersal policy:

1. It is designed to disperse new industry and expanding industry—not to move established industry.
2. No region of the country is to be built up at the expense of another.
3. Industrial dispersion can be carried out if such deployment is confined to each local marketing area.
4. State and local governments, in cooperation with private enterprise, are called upon to take the initiative in this defense objective. The Federal Government will provide encouragement and technical guidance (p. 3).

In the last few pages, the Board outlined (rather sketchily, to be sure) procedures recommended to local groups or task forces and suggested a number of pertinent considerations as to industrial deployment ". . . for security, for economical and efficient production, for sustained community benefits."

Just as we were writing this section of this chapter, the *NewsLetter* of the American Society of Planning Officials for September, 1951 came out with a leading editorial on the President's policy statement and the NSRB's booklet. The editorial comments seem to us both pertinent and well put:

The program raises a number of questions. The first one is, "Has the barn door been locked after the horse has been stolen?" Almost $9 billion dollars in certificates of necessity have been issued to date providing for five-year tax amortization programs. With increasing controls and shortage of strategic materials (for instance a recent *Wall Street Journal* advised that public utilities probably will be unable to construct much needed additions because of shortage of materials), is there any likelihood that there can be an extensive program in addition to the $9 billion dollars already authorized, a considerable part of which is already under way?

A second important question is, "How are we to get enforcement at the national level?" Responsibility is placed in the director of the Office of Defense Mobilization. Assistance at the federal level will be provided through the Area Development Division of the U.S. Department of Commerce. Who, however, at the national level will assume the responsibility of saying that a proposed new industry does not meet suitable requirements?

How will responsibility be distributed and placed at the local level? It is already obvious that many central cities, not wishing to lose potential tax base, will have no great interest in finding sites outside of their jurisdiction. This will be particularly true if the plant goes outside of a central city while most of the responsibility for housing, transportation, public health, etc., remains within the central city. Where metropolitan planning agencies exist they can, of course, provide considerable assistance in the determination of suitable locations, but candor forces the admission that there are comparatively few metropolitan planning agencies within the country. While planning agencies are quite likely to be objective about the best location for industry, there is bound to be pressure from commercial organizations and from public officials against this dispersal program which is intended—it must be repeated—not to send industries to under-developed areas, but to disperse them within metropolitan regions.

There is still another question related to this program and that is, "What will the federal government do, if anything, to assist rural areas in meeting the many problems that will be created through the establishment of industries in such areas?" There are already such areas in the United States faced with terrific problems because they do not have the knowledge or the facilities with which to provide the urban services that are required by an industry.

Already it appears that the order has been misinterpreted. We have seen one newspaper clipping from the state of Washington which estimates that the state will benefit greatly from this order. Others seem to think that the mere issuance of the order will insure a dispersal program. It isn't that simple. The problems to be faced by metropolitan areas are not lessened by this order, they are magnified. The order definitely, however, shows the need for doing planning on a metropolitan basis."

In addition, we hope it does not seem captious to say that this pamphlet deserves a better title than *Is Your Plant a Target?* Certainly a central fact in this whole issue of industrial dispersal as a defense measure is that very few individal plants would be sufficiently crucial to this country's military potential to justify making them special targets for atomic bombs. In terms of effort, materials, human life, and the prospects of retaliation, such weapons are too expensive to make and deliver to justify their use on most individual industrial establishments. Rather, it is expected that they might be used against substantial concentrations of industry and population where their terrific destructiveness would be felt in full. The gist of the argument for dispersal as a defense measure is simply that it would reduce the number of appropriate targets for atomic weapons and, therefore, would reduce also the chances of a knockout blow from a sneak attack. The title of the pamphlet certainly does not suggest this important consideration and, in fact, would even seem to deny it.

In Conclusion

As we said at the beginning of this chapter, this issue of industrial dispersal as a security and defense measure is particularly difficult to deal with in a discussion of this kind. Not only is it new and ever-changing in dimension and emphasis, but the facts available for evaluation and judgment on many crucial subpoints are entirely inadequate. Further, it has been so loosely stated, both by the proponents of dispersal and the opponents, that much time and many words have to be spent on trying to clear the ground and to define the central problems.

On the other hand, the stakes in the policy questions on this matter seem to us very great. We have tried, therefore, to bring together into a reasonably connected account several of the more important events, efforts, and suggestions on policy. We also have tried to separate out and focus attention on what we take to be the vital issues. Whether we have made any contribution to the consideration of the whole matter, we shall have to leave to the judgment of others.

Four points that have come up repeatedly in this chapter seem to us so important that they should be stated again here:

1. Large proportions of both the industry and population of this country are highly concentrated. Two sets of facts we have not cited before emphasize this. According to the Census of 1950, fourteen metropolitan areas had populations of more than 1,000,000. In these fourteen areas the aggregate population was 44,153,019 or 29.5 per cent of the total population of the United States. The fourteen metropolitan areas with the most production workers in manufacturing according to the Census of Manufacturers of 1947—the same list of cities with two exceptions—had an aggregate of 4,828,523 production workers, or 40.5 per cent of the total for the country.[27]

2. At present there is no such thing as complete or nearly complete protection against the dangers of atomic bombing. This is true not only of industrial dispersal but also of military defenses and of international control.

3. It seems likely that relatively moderate changes in the existing patterns of industrial location and urban population would reduce substantially the vulnerability of the country to atomic attack.[28] If such an attack should come, these changes might help to save lives and to reduce the extent of damage to industrial plants and equipment. If so, these changes would contribute to the ultimate end of national defense and, in some degree at least, to the ability of the nation to win the war that the attack would touch off. Besides, by reducing the possibilities of a knockout or seriously crippling blow in the first hours or days of such a war, these changes might be one deterrent to this kind of attack.

4. We still need badly the results of a thorough, competent study, under authoritative auspices, of the present-day dangers of atomic warfare to our cities and their industries, and particularly of the possibili-

27. Population figures from 1950 Census of Population, *Preliminary Counts* (Series PC-3, No. 3, Bureau of the Census, November 5, 1950), pp. 1–2. Figures on production workers in manufacturing computed from *Census of Manufactures: 1947,* Vol. I, "Summary" (Washington, D.C.: Government Printing Office, 1950), Table 3, pp. 32–33.

28. The President's *Statement of Policy* and NSRB's second pamphlet refer to dispersal "in local marketing areas adjacent to industrial or metropolitan districts." Although this clearly indicates limited dispersal, it does not make too clear the pattern or patterns that are favored by the federal authorities. Presumably their technical advisors to local officials and groups will be prepared to go further into this point. Certainly, however, some of the geographically larger metropolitan areas as defined by the Census take in very considerable territories in which industries might be dispersed. Chicago's standard metropolitan area is a good example. Quite probably, the recent Statement and pamphlet should not be taken to mean that all or nearly all dispersed industries should go outside the limits of such metropolitan areas.

ties, costs, and probable effectiveness of various patterns of industrial dispersal. Until these results are widely available, those directly responsible for action, including particularly local officials and industrialists, will be handicapped. Equally important, until the facts and the competent judgments based on them are known,[29] it will be difficult if not impossible to overcome the inertia and outright opposition that so far have prevented effective action.

29. This is not to suggest that the judgments and recommendations made to date by NSRB and other federal agencies are incompetent. Rather the point is two-fold: (1) The recommendations made so far are general in character. Local officials, industrialists and "task forces" will need much more specific advice. (2) In deciding what they can do in their localities and in seeing that it is done, these responsible local leaders will need to know not only what the federal authorities think should be done but also *why* and *how*— in terms of costs, timing, and supporting nonindustrial development. Otherwise the local officials and others will be faced with major decisions without the means to make them intelligently.

CHAPTER V

ARE INDUSTRIES DECENTRALIZING? SOME
LOCAL INQUIRIES

FOR more than half a century the concept or notion of *decentralization,* if not always the term, has been a part of the mental equipment of students of urban development and affairs. During much of this period the terms *urban decentralization, industrial decentralization,* or *decentralization* without a qualifying adjective, have been in common use. Although a critical analysis of the writing on these subjects would serve many worth-while purposes, we do not propose to undertake it here. Just a few examples will recall the variety and range of ideas and discussion that have taken place under these general headings.

In 1899 Adna F. Weber's *The Growth of Cities in the Nineteenth Century* pulled together a substantial amount of information about urban growth and structure, analyzed, and criticized much of it.[1] Although Mr. Weber's vocabulary was somewhat different from that of many later writers on this general subject, he was concerned with many of the same tendencies and problems. In 1898 Ebenezer Howard's little book, *Tomorrow: A Peaceful Path to Real Reform,* was published in Great Britain.[2] In 1902 it was reissued with minor revisions under the title *Garden Cities of Tomorrow.* Certainly throughout the Western world it has had a notable influence on a wide range of thought about urban growth and problems. The New Towns program now under way in Great Britain stems directly from Howard's proposal for a definite form and character of decentralization of major metropolitan areas or agglomerations. Again, President Franklin D. Roosevelt in his inaugural address on March 4, 1933, called attention to ". . . the overbalance of population in our industrial centers . . ." Several of the programs initiated in his first administration were directly related to the problems that he referred to in this phrase.

DIFFICULTIES IN EARLIER STUDIES

On the whole it must be admitted that much of this still growing volume of oral and written discussion on decentralization has been con-

1. New York: The Macmillan Co., 1899.
2. London: Swan Sonnenschein and Co., 1898.

fused and confusing. We say this in no spirit of captious criticism. Quite surely some of the confusion has come from loose thinking and inaccurate writing. Quite as surely much of it is traceable to complexities inherent in the subject matter and to the difficulties in finding reliable data for measuring urban growth and development. We are well aware that even today students of these phenomena, working with a full recognition of the shortcomings of many of their predecessors, find it extremely hard to avoid many of these same ambiguities and blind spots.

In general, however, it seems fair to say that much of the study and writing on this general topic has suffered from four weaknesses:

1. It has proceeded with flabby and shifting definitions and concepts.

2. The units for measuring the trends and changes under discussion have varied from study to study. As a result, very few of the findings or tentative explanations can be effectively compared. Consequently the results of analysis and speculation have not been additive.

3. When the focus has been upon industrial location and trends in it, the serious mistake has often been made of lumping together all types and kinds of industries. In fact, some of these discussions seem to proceed on the assumption that in matters of location there is some homogeneous, monolithic entity known as industry, all parts of which show substantially the same characteristics and follow the same laws. Clearly this is not a defensible assumption.

4. Much of the writing suffers from a constant admixture of analysis of facts and trends with advocacy of certain objectives and goals. Undoubtedly this is a subject on which both analyses of facts and statements of desirable objectives and goals are needed. The trouble has come from the common failure to distinguish between them, with the result that it is often hard to make out whether the discussion turns on facts or happenings, on the one hand, or on what the writer believes ought to be happening, on the other.

By no means all of the previous discussions of this subject have been marked by all of these weaknesses. They have been common enough, however, to be noted as warnings both to those responsible for further studies in this area and to those who read and evaluate their results. For these reasons and not because we believe we have avoided all of the pitfalls of logic and method in this field, we propose at the beginning of this chapter to indicate the basic concepts, definitions and units of measurement that we have used. After this we shall note briefly a few other recent investigations in this area and, after them, go on to a fuller discussion of our own study of it—including its limitations and the difficulties of interpretation that have come from it.

SOME DEFINITIONS

We take it that in common usage the noun *decentralization* means a process or procedure that results in the withdrawal or redistribution of something from a place or center in which it has previously been concentrated. *Industrial decentralization,* therefore, would be a process that has this effect upon the physical location of industrial plants and facilities. It follows that industrial decentralization may be discovered and measured, at least approximately, by changes from time to time in the percentages or other proportions of industrial personnel, investment or capacity in various areas, localities or parts of localities.

As we pointed out in the early part of our discussion on broad regional trends in industrial location (chapter iii), so-called shifts or migrations of industry are not brought about exclusively or even primarily through the picking up and moving of existing facilities, equipment and personnel. Rather the redistribution more often results from differentials in the rates of growth of industries in various areas. This holds true for nearly all the processes that properly come under the heading of industrial decentralization, whether the redistribution is between, let us say, the highly industrialized area in the northeastern part of the country and localities in some less industrialized region in the South or West, or between the central city and an outlying section of a major metropolitan area.

It is important to distinguish industrial decentralization, in this sense of a redistribution in the location of industrial plants and facilities, from decentralization as the term is widely used in discussions of industrial management and organization. In the latter usage decentralization means a devolution of some degree of management responsibility and authority from a central office or group to other units in the industrial organization. Quite often, of course, this other unit consists of officials responsible for and with headquarters in a branch plant or facility. This, however, is not always so. The unit that gains power and responsibility in decentralization of management may be, for example, a division of a corporation that makes a certain product or group of products. It may be located physically in the corporation's main plant —both before and after the change in organization. Thus industrial decentralization in the physical or location sense and in the management sense may often be related, but they are, nevertheless, clearly distinguishable.

It is also essential for our purposes to distinguish between industrial decentralization and the common notion of *urban decentralization*. We use the latter term to mean the process of withdrawal or redistribution of basic urban units, usually people, or of functions from previous centers of concentration. Although population is the usual urban element referred to in discussions of urban decentralization, it is by no means the only one. Types of land use, for example, are often used— land use for commercial purposes, retail business, industry, or residence. Sooner or later someone should devise a method for combining measures or indexes of the various phases of urban decentralization. Then we would be able to describe the phenomenon more accurately and, perhaps, might be able to discuss and evaluate it more effectively. Here, however, we simply note that industrial decentralization in our sense of the term is one phase or kind of urban decentralization.[3]

Although this is true and it is equally true that industrial decentralization in most of its conceivable forms would bring about other types of urban decentralization as well, it does seem to us necessary to distinguish between the two ideas. It would be *possible* to have certain forms and degrees of industrial decentralization within, let us say, a metropolitan area with little or no decentralization of residential or commercial land uses. Conversely, these types of land use might be partially decentralized without a corresponding change in the distribution of industrial location.

Our primary concern in this chapter is with industrial decentraliza-

3. This usage of "industrial decentralization" suggests an ambiguity with the common meaning that includes also redistribution from nonurban places of concentration, e.g., states or geographic regions, to other similar areas not so highly industrialized. We have, therefore, (1) *industrial decentralization (general)*, which includes redistribution among states, geographic regions and similar areas *as well as* changes among different kinds and sections of urban areas; and (2) *industrial decentralization (proper)*, which takes in only redistributions among cities and, within urban areas, among different parts, sections, or districts of them. This second phenomenon, industrial decentralization (proper), is one phase of *urban decentralization*. Except where otherwise indicated, this is the meaning of *industrial decentralization* in this and the following chapter.

Much of the material on urban decentralization is scattered throughout the literature of urban planning, development, and land economics. Some of the more useful, general discussions are listed in *Selected Bibliography on Urban Redevelopment* (Chicago: American Society of Planning Officials, 1951), pp. 4–7 and 29–31. *Planning*, ASPO's annual volume, also has representative discussions. See particularly, in the volume for 1948, Charles E. Merriam and Tracy B. Augur on *Decentralization—Blessing or Tragedy?* and Roger Willcox, William L. C. Wheaton, Hans Blumenfeld and Henry Cohen on *The New York Region—A Case Study of the Limits of Growth by Sprawl.*

Urban Land, the newsletter of the Urban Land Institute, has notes and brief articles from time to time. We have not referred to them often because most of them are on nonindustrial parts of the subject.

The *Journal of the American Institute of Architects*, January, 1951, consisted largely of a series of articles on "New Towns for American Defense."

Two recent British pamphlets are particularly useful: Professor W. G. Holford's *Decentralization—Great Britain*—report to the xviiith International Congress on Housing and Town Planning, [1946]; and *Dispersal—An Inquiry Made by the National Council of Social Service* (London: Oxford University Press, 1944). In addition the Barlow, Scott, and New Towns reports (cited in footnote 2, chap. ii) will repay study.

tion as we have tried to define it. From time to time we shall comment upon urban decentralization either as a general phenomenon or in its other subdivisions and aspects. We shall try to make clear when we shift from our primary subject, industrial decentralization, to its allied but broader and distinguishable phenomenon, urban decentralization.

Because industrial decentralization, even if defined and limited as we have proposed, is still a fairly inclusive concept, we have also taken over two terms used by others to indicate two of its major forms. These terms are *diffusion* and *dispersion* (or dispersal). *Diffusion* is the redistribution of industrial plant and facilities from a major area of concentration, such as a central city of a metropolitan area, to a nearby or adjacent district, such as an outlying or peripheral part of the metropolitan area. *Dispersion* means a wider redistribution, as from a major industrial concentration in a large city or metropolitan area to a number of smaller localities throughout a major economic region or even over the country as a whole.

Diffusion and dispersion in these senses have also been used, of course, to refer to the corresponding changes in the distribution of population by place of residence. Again, however, when we do not indicate this usage, we are using the terms as they apply to industrial plant and facilities.

Although this seems a useful distinction, it is not as definite and foolproof as one could wish. At what distance from a major industrial concentration does diffusion stop and dispersion begin? Fortunately our analysis of industrial location has not raised this and similar questions in very sharp form. In general, however, we have considered decentralization to be diffusion when it takes place within the limits of a definite economic area such as a standard metropolitan area. Beyond the limits of such districts (which also might include what the Bureau of the Census now terms *urbanized areas*) decentralization is dispersion. Also, in this terminology there is no clear way of labeling a redistribution from the central city of a metropolitan area to the outlying part of another or other such areas. Under this terminology, is such a move diffusion, dispersion, or something else? Again, however, our data and methods of analysis were not sufficiently refined to raise this question.[4]

4. We would also point out again that the terms we have just defined and shall use in this and the following chapter—industrial decentralization, diffusion, and dispersion— were not used in chap. iv on security considerations. There we used the common term *industrial dispersal* as roughly equivalent to industrial decentralization. This may have been a mistake and may seem rather confusing to some readers. But *dispersal* has become so common in writing on security considerations in industrial location that we decided to adopt it rather than use this other and possibly more accurate terminology. At all events, however, it should be clear that many forms of industrial decentralization—both diffusion and dispersion—would decrease the vulnerability of the industrial facilities of the country to atomic and other military attack.

In respect particularly to diffusion, two difficulties have arisen often enough to warrant notice here.

The first is more properly a matter of measurement than of definition. Most of the Census and other data on industrial location are for political or governmental units—cities, counties, etc. Clearly these vary greatly in size of area and population. These differences conceal many pertinent facts on diffusion and often make comparisons impossible or misleading. For example, the cities of Chicago and Boston are the central cities of major metropolitan areas. Chicago has a land area of more than 200 square miles; Boston—about 45 square miles. Because of this simple difference, the development of a sizable industrial area, say in Cambridge, shows up in the data as diffusion—a relative increase in industries outside of Boston proper, the central city of the metropolitan area. In the Chicago area, however, several substantial industrial districts have developed that are farther from the older industrial concentrations than the major Cambridge district is from the corresponding parts of Boston, but these Chicago districts are still within the city limits. Thus, they do not affect the proportions of industrial plant and personnel between Chicago and other governmental units within its metropolitan area and, therefore, do not show up in the usual breakdowns of data as diffusion.

This difficulty, of course, could be avoided by establishing, at least for the major metropolitan areas, a number of industrial areas or districts without reference to governmental boundary lines, and then by publishing the pertinent data by these districts. This would be no easy task but it could be done. Undoubtedly it would make possible much more precise and useful analyses of the distribution of industrial capacity and workers within metropolitan areas or regions.

The second difficulty is logical. Every once in a while someone comes out with the statement that decentralization is a nonsensical notion, a mirage. According to this view, what passes for decentralization (usually in our terms, diffusion) is simply the result of urban growth. The fallacy of this argument is clear. The existence of decentralization is a separate question from that of its causes, contributing factors, or antecedents. To be sure, it often would be significant to know or at least to be able to estimate what phases and amounts of industrial diffusion are linked primarily to urban growth and what are influenced strongly by other factors—congestion, transportation facilities, living conditions, public policies, etc. We are now very much in the dark on questions of this kind but further studies could shed considerable light on them. The point here, however, is that the fact of decentralization or diffusion, by our or almost any other definition, should not be confused with the factors that accompany and precede it or, in everyday terms, cause it.

Finally, the definition we have used for industrial decentralization takes no account of the new patterns of location that may come from the redistribution process. For example, consider two forms of redistribution of industrial plants. The first results in the building up of smaller but definitely organized or nucleated industrial districts in the outlying parts of a metropolitan area. The second might simply scatter certain small industrial plants throughout existing and developing residential districts or in predominantly commercial areas. Admittedly, this second redistribution is not very common, but it is possible and, in fact, is now proposed for certain types of industries by some urban planners and others. Our point here, however, is simply that under our terminology these two very different forms of redistribution are both industrial decentralization, diffusion. Our terminology makes no distinction between them. Although here also the data used in our study and our methods of analysis do not raise this problem, it is a weakness of the terminology and ought to be corrected. Perhaps the first form of redistribution could be called industrial diffusion with recentralization, or possibly just recentralization, and the second labeled simply diffusion. These suggestions are awkward, but here we wish only to call attention to the need for further refinement in the terminology.

Units of Measurement

Broadly speaking, in attempts to measure industrial decentralization and its opposite, concentration, four units have been used: (a) industrial plants or establishments; (b) value added by manufacture, or some other indication of industrial activity; (c) investment in plant construction; and (d) average number of production workers in manufacturing. Each of these seems to us to deserve a short comment.

Industrial plants as units of measure have been used quite frequently —particularly in locality studies. This unit has the merit of being reasonably precise. Many of the data may be taken from directories of manufactures put out by industrial associations and chambers of commerce. For not too large areas they can be checked or supplemented by field inspection. On the other hand, however, this unit has one very serious weakness. Obviously plants vary enormously in size and importance. A plant may be a small machine shop with two or three workers or a vast establishment with thousands or tens of thousands of employees. Lumping these together is the old one-horse one-rabbit error in an advanced form. In our work, therefore, we have not used this unit.

Value added by manufacture avoids most of this difficulty but it has other shortcomings for studies concerned with urban development and redevelopment. Except for the periodic censuses of manufactures, information of this kind is hard to come by. Even then it weights plants of various sizes and kinds of operation in a way that bears no direct relation to their significance in urban planning and development. Besides, over most substantial periods of time it is subject to changes in the general price level. We have not used this unit either.

Dollar volume of plant construction has much the same shortcoming as value added by manufacture for our purposes. It also has to be used carefully to make sure that the figures given include the same items. More specifically, sometimes these dollar figures include the actual or estimated cost of new plant construction with or without the cost of ancillary facilities such as parking, storage, and eating places. Sometimes they include not only construction of buildings but also outlays for machine tools and other forms of equipment. One part of our study is based on certain figures on dollar volume of industrial plant construction. They are not, however, the major reliance of our study. We used these data primarily because they were readily available to us and because we wished to have them as a rough check on the major part of our analysis. As the reader of the next chapter will see, however, they have made us much trouble.

For our and similar purposes, the average number of production workers in manufacturing is clearly the best unit for measuring industrial decentralization or concentration. Urban planners and redevelopers are concerned not only with proper locations for industrial plants in terms of their requirements for efficient operation, but also with their effects upon transit and transportation facilities, the journey to work of industrial employees, and similar matters. The production worker as a unit, therefore, is most useful because its numbers and distribution indicate more or less directly these important corollary problems and considerations. The major part of our study relies on this unit from the Census of Manufactures for 1939 and 1947.

We have mentioned before the significant differences among various kinds of industries in respect to their location requirements and the significance of various factors in determining their location and geographic distribution. The distinctions among material-, market-, and labor-oriented, as well as foot-loose industries, are in point. We would recall also, from the McLaughlin-Robock and New England studies of location practice, the differences indicated between new firms just getting started and branch plants of established and successful corporations. Facts and considerations that might be insignificant or certainly minor in the location of plants in the latter category are often determining factors in the location decisions of new firms. Unfortunately, the data for our own work measure directly only the net result of a great variety and volume of decisions on industrial location. Only by inference and interpretation is it possible to suggest certain flows and counter flows that may account for these net results. This is a weakness in the work we have done. More refined studies of individual localities and industries could avoid much of this shortcoming. However, we wish to emphasize the differences among various kinds of industries in respect to industrial location and again to warn our readers against the common error of underestimating these differences.

ANALYSES AND OBJECTIVES

The mixing together of analyses of what has been happening and preferences and objectives as to what should happen is, of course, a weakness by no means limited to industrial and urban studies. It is, however, all too common in them. Some writers on urban decentralization have started out with strong beliefs in the desirability of the garden city or other type of redistribution of industry and population. Apparently they have been unduly impressed by some facts that, in one way or another, support their views and have neglected or overlooked others that seemed to point in another direction. A similar comment could be made on other writers who apparently started out with a strong disapproval of any proposal for a new or different pattern.

Also, during the past twenty years or so changes in industrial location often have been considered in connection with depressed and poverty-stricken rural areas and, particularly during the 1930's, as a means of alleviating the distress of unemployment and underemployment of existing urban workers. These certainly are legitimate subjects for study and recommendation, but again they seem to have blinded some writers to some facts as well as to the distinction between analysis and explanation, on the one hand, and objectives and policy, on the other.

In this and the following chapter we have tried first to answer the question "Are Industries Decentralizing?" From the data we have been able to assemble and analyze that seem to us pertinent to this query, we have arrived at some tentative and admittedly inconclusive findings. We have also put forward some limited explanations or hypotheses that might account for our findings. Unless these should be borne out by further studies, they are not worth very much. We hope they may be a small contribution simply in the sense that they throw a little light on earlier studies and may suggest useful starting points for those to come. Throughout we have tried to make distinctions among findings, tentative explanations, and policy recommendations.

EARLIER STUDIES

Over the last twenty-five years or so, a number of inquiries into industrial location have been undertaken in search of facts or generalizations on what we now call industrial diffusion or dispersion. Most of them have been concerned primarily with diffusion within metropolitan areas or similar districts. Unfortunately, as we have pointed out, they have varied so in definitions, method, and scope that only their very broad conclusions are in any sense comparable and their more detailed findings are not additive. With the exception of the Goodrich-Creamer study, which we shall consider at some length in chapter vi, none of them was inclusive enough to warrant any broad generalizations—however tentative. In fact, most of them were preliminary explorations limited to one or a very few localities.

For several reasons we shall refer to them briefly here. With all their limitations and shortcomings they do make up the background of study as well as of much of the thought on this subject. Their methods, into which we shall not go in any detail, are worth looking into by those who may undertake further investigations. Their findings indicate in general some changes from time to time and certain short-term movements that may have been influenced or even determined largely by general business conditions. Also they are largely responsible for the opinion held in many planning and business circles that a phenomenon called industrial decentralization has been under way for some time in this country.

We have not tried to compile any complete list of these inquiries. We believe, however, that our sample includes most of the more significant ones and fairly illustrates the scale and scope of these undertakings.

THE REGIONAL SURVEY OF NEW YORK

Probably the most intensive analysis ever made of industrial location and movements in a metropolitan area in this country was that undertaken in the mid-1920's by the Regional Plan of New York and Its Environs. As Mr. Thomas Adams, General Director of Plans and Surveys, stated the rationale of this work: "The first thing to be done in making a study of an urban area, for the purpose of preparing a plan of physical improvement, is to ascertain the composition, volume, distribution and direction of growth of its principal economic activities. . . ."[5] A substantial proportion of the resources of the Regional Plan went into its Economic and Industrial Survey under the direction

---

5. Foreword (not paged) to *Major Economic Factors in Metropolitan Growth and Arrangement*, Vol. I, "Regional Survey of New York and Its Environs" (New York: Regional Plan of New York, 1927).

of Mr. Robert Murray Haig of Columbia University as Director and with Mr. Roswell C. McCrea also of Columbia as Consultant.

Under their direction various researchers made studies of nine of the chief industries of the New York area: chemicals, metals, food products, wood products, tobacco, printing, textiles, men's wear, and women's clothing. In addition, three nonfabricating activities were also studied: storage and marketing, finance, and retail trade. The major sources of information were the factory inspection records of the three states of New York, New Jersey, and Connecticut. The nine industries covered had almost 72 per cent of all the plants and nearly 80 per cent of all the employees on the records of the factory inspectors. For each of the industries, data were collected for the four years 1900, 1912, 1917, and 1922. The Survey set up for all these studies three zones for purposes of measuring diffusion: (1) Manhattan south of 59th Street; (2) a so-called twenty-mile zone; and (3) the outlying region. Those responsible for studying the individual industries could subdivide these zones, but their data had to be compiled for each of them.

Volume I of the Regional Survey of New York and Its Environs, *Major Economic Factors in Metropolitan Growth and Arrangement* by Messrs. Haig and McCrea, is a summary of the findings of the twelve studies plus an attempt to formulate a general or theoretical explanation of some of their major findings. The highlights of the studies may be summarized in these quotations from Volume I:

. . . These figures appear to furnish grounds for the belief that the peak of manufacturing in the center of the city was reached about ten years ago and that a process of decentralization is already under way.

When the figures are broken into the 10 industrial groups shown in the table on page 34 [the nine mentioned above and All Others—Editor], other significant facts emerge. Thus, between 1900 and 1912, the wood-products group was the only group in Zone I which actually declined in numbers. Between 1912 and 1917, metals, textiles, and tobacco also went into decline. Between 1917 and 1922, the textiles group gained slightly; but the chemical, the men's and women's clothing, and the food groups joined the ranks of those that were losing their hold in the center of the city. Printing is the only group showing a consistent record of gain in the central zone throughout the twenty-two-year period.

.   .   .   .

These general figures seem to indicate, then, that on the whole, manufacturing is certainly not more than holding its own in the center of the city and has probably already begun to be crowded out. Moreover, the figures give evidence of considerable variability in the degree of persistence with which the different industries cling to the choice central locations.

When the industries are broken still further into smaller subgroups, as is done in the table on page 35, for the years 1900 and 1922 in the center of the city, it is found that the aggregate figures conceal marked variations in the growth and decay of branches of the various industries. While the aggregate figures for the printing industry, for example, show a strong and steady growth in Zone II, amounting to about 50 per cent in the twenty-two years, the more detailed figures for the sub-groups show that photo-engraving quadrupled in this area, newspaper printing nearly trebled, book- and job-printing increased approximately the normal 50 per cent, lithography was practically static, and bookbinding declined 20 per cent. Again, while in the aggregate women's clothing about doubled in this central area, one branch, dresses and waists, trebled, and yet another branch, neckwear, lost more than half its employes. In the aggregate, the metal-products industry almost stood still in Zone I; but one branch, technical instruments, more than doubled, and another branch, heavy machinery, declined to less than half its former size. Equally striking statements can be made for practically all the other industries.

. . . .

When one begins to seek the reasons for growth and decline in the center, he is immediately impressed by the inadequacy of the terminology ordinarily used in discussing the problem. Broad terms such as "industry," "manufacture," "commerce," and "trade" are not well adapted to the task in hand. If, for example, a silk mill, formerly located on Manhattan, moves to Pennsylvania but keeps its head office and salesroom in New York, it is not accurate to say that this "industry" has left New York. What has actually happened is that there has been a territorial sub-division of functions which were formerly united in the same place, certain activities being sent to Pennsylvania and certain others kept in the metropolis. Fabrication and certain other functions have gone, but selling and many of the other functions remain. Fourth Avenue is full of establishments bearing the names of manufacturing plants, but no fabrication is in evidence. Though it is the center of the silk industry, not a loom is to be found there.

. . . .

The pressure for space in the center of New York has stimulated a great deal of relocation of functions which is difficult to catch in any statistical net. A Fifth Avenue merchant testifies that he has found it profitable in recent years to rent extensive accommodations in bonded warehouses instead of storing his imported goods in his own establishment, as was formerly his practice. Many Wall Street lawyers, finding their office space too expensive at four dollars per square foot to use for storage purposes, have sent their old files to Brooklyn, where special facilities have been established to perform this function at relatively low cost. The New York Telephone Company has tried the plan of reducing its commercial offices to mere counter-space and sending its clerical staff to low-rent quarters. A large silk manufacturer, who now uses most of his large building on Fourth Avenue as a stock-room, states that upon the completion of the new vehicular tunnel, his New York building will become strictly a sample-room and his stock-room will be in New Jersey. Even in Newark, one of New York's Jersey neighbors, the pressure for space in the shopping center has caused one large department store to establish a "service station" on cheap land, where the orders are assembled and the deliveries routed.[6]

The language of these quotations is significant because it suggests, and other parts of the volume state explicitly, a theory or conception of the nature of industrial diffusion. It is that diffusion is essentially the result of certain activities, industries in this case, being *squeezed out* of central locations by the competition for space. The assumption seems

6. *Ibid.*, pp. 33–37.

to be that, if possible, all industrial activities in a metropolitan area would prefer to be located in the central part of the central city. As the area grows, however, the competition for near-in space becomes so severe that many activities are forced out altogether and others are compelled to move out some of their subdivisions or functions.

In various rather vague and inexact forms, this notion had been current well before the Regional Survey and still is taken for granted by many people. Very often it is thought to apply to nearly all or at least a major proportion of urban residents. Thus suburbanization and other redistributions of urban population are also accounted for. It is easy to see how this idea gained currency in New York and some other congested centers with high land values in the central sections.

More recently, however, it has been called into serious question. As to urban population movement it did not seem to square too well with the facts of the 1930's when the population pressure in the central cities remained stationary or even declined, but many suburbs and other outlying areas continued to grow substantially. Also, it seems to be contradicted by many of the findings from investigations of factors determining the location of both new and branch plants.

This point is a matter of interest to more persons than students searching for a theory of industrial diffusion or urban decentralization. It has obvious implications for urban planners and redevelopers. How many of them are proceeding on the assumption, stated or implied, that nearly all kinds of industries and urban residents would actually prefer near-in locations?

REGIONAL PLAN ASSOCIATION FOLLOW-UP

In 1929 the Regional Plan Association, Inc., a voluntary, nonprofit citizens' association, was organized to further the recommendations and principles arrived at by the Regional Plan of New York and Its Environs, to keep its analytical studies up to date, and to work with local officials and others in the area who are concerned with its planning and development. The Association has done much to keep before its public the issues of over-all physical pattern and organization in this vast area. In 1944 it published a follow-up study of the economic foundation of the New York area. Based largely on preliminary work by Messrs. C. McKim Norton and Frederick P. Clark of the Association, this study was directed by Mr. Homer Hoyt and appeared under the title *The Economic Status of the New York Metropolitan Region in 1944.*[7]

In the Foreword, Mr. George McAneny, Chairman of the Board of the Association, characterized the volume in these words:

7. New York: The Regional Plan Association, Inc., 1944.

While emphasizing postwar employment, the study shows that recent trends in the economic status of the Region are slightly more favorable than that of the country as a whole, contrary to certain misconceptions derived from study of New York City alone. In other words, some of the loss or lack of gain in economic activity in New York City has been a result of shifting location of population, business and industry within the Region itself.[8]

Although this study summarized much pertinent information on the proportions of production workers in manufacturing working in the central city of the New York and other large metropolitan centers, its emphasis was on the period after 1929. For roughly the first forty years of this century, however, it showed that, contrary to a common impression, the proportionate increase in manufacturing workers outside the central city was less in the New York area than in many of the other large industrial centers of the nation.

Particularly after 1929 the New York area's industry did not grow as rapidly as some others partly because it did not include its proportionate share of such industries as automobiles, rayon, refrigerators, tires, and cigarettes—growth industries of this period. As to industrial decentralization or diffusion, the general conclusion of this study is summarized in this quotation:

This outward movement of industry is the result largely of the growth of outlying industrial areas or districts served by belt railroads and auto trucks, where one-story factories spread out over cheaper land permit all the factory processes to be conducted on one floor level without any break in the flow of manufacturing at each floor level.

The movement to the periphery has also been facilitated by the outward movement of the residential population and its greater mobility as the result of the almost universal ownership of automobiles. It is an economic movement due to shifting of industries to locations where they can operate more efficiently and while it may be regarded as detrimental to the municipal finances of the central cities, it is beneficial in promoting the development of the metropolitan regions in their entirety.[9]

CHICAGO IN THE 1920's

Although the Chicago area has never been analyzed as intensively as New York by the Regional Survey, within the past twenty years three studies of industrial location in this metropolitan area have given considerable attention to diffusion.

The first of these is *Trends in Industrial Location in the Chicago Region since 1920* by Mr. William N. Mitchell formerly of the University of Chicago.[10] It was published in 1933 and most of its data are for the decade 1920 to 1930. Mr. Mitchell made his own definition of

8. *Ibid.*, p. viii.
9. *Ibid.*, pp. 38–41.
10. Chicago: University of Chicago Press, 1933.

the Chicago region. It included eight counties, two more than the present Census definition of the metropolitan area. He added McHenry County, Illinois, at the extreme northwest corner of the area, and Porter County, Indiana, at the southeast. Admitting both the confusion of terminology and the scarcity of usable facts, Mr. Mitchell nevertheless made contributions of significance to urban planners both in helping to clarify terms and in statistical information for the period he covered. For our purposes his findings are well summarized in the following paragraphs from the concluding chapter of his monograph:

1. The Chicago region as defined for the purposes of this inquiry has become relatively more, rather than less, important industrially in this post-war period. Its share of the industry of the nation has increased more rapidly than that of either the two embracing states, Illinois and Indiana, or the east north central geographical subdivision of which it forms a part, an area which itself has registered spectacular industrial gains during the period. Apparently, the drawing power of this region's long recognized natural and acquired advantages for industry has not disappeared.

2. Intraregionally, the central nucleus, that is, corporate Chicago, has shown some tendency to decline in industrial importance in relation to the region as a whole.

3. The outlying or peripheral portions of the region have shown the same tendency relatively to decline in industrial importance. It is in this portion of the region only that important former concentrations of industry have in some instances declined actually as well as relatively.

4. Important increases in relative industrial importance have been confined to the mid-zone immediately surrounding the central nucleus.

5. Even in this mid-zone the most striking increases in relative industrial importance have occurred in suburban cities adjoining or at least in no case far removed from the corporate limits of Chicago. These developments have been chiefly to the west and south.

6. The important cities in the borderland of the region have suffered greater relative industrial decline than any other portions of the region.

7. There has been sufficient actual industrial migration to justify the conclusion that some portion at least of the intraregional industrial displacements may possibly be accounted for by plant removals from the central nucleus into surrounding less densely populated areas. Actual outward plant migrations have occurred in greatest number, by far, between corporate Chicago and that portion of the region lying immediately beyond the corporate limits.

8. Within the city proper, territorial expansion of industry reflects merely an extension of already well-defined industrial patterns into adjacent but hitherto unoccupied areas.

Two entirely different interpretations might possibly be placed upon these facts. First, it may be argued that the relatively slight evidence of outward moving industrial displacements within the region are merely the manifestation of the continuing process of growth which has given rise to large cities. Urban areas grow by accretions at the boundaries as well as by increased density at the center. It is entirely possible that the development of industrial suburbs immediately beyond the corporate limits of the city has represented nothing more than this. On the other hand, one who is impressed by the desirability of industrial decentralization might discern in the evidence some slight justification for one's hopes. If the latter interpretation is to be accepted, however, it must be with the qualification that the evidence contains no indication whatsoever that tendencies toward industrial decentralization in urban areas have as yet made their influence felt very far beyond the central zone of concentration.[11]

CHICAGO—THE LATE 1930's

In 1942 the Chicago Plan Commission published a booklet on *Industrial and Commercial Background for Planning Chicago.*[12] It is in three parts. The first is an historical review of Chicago's industrial growth; the second analyzes industrial trends in Chicago and its metropolitan area; and the third deals with commercial trends. Part II, which is of the most direct interest to us, was prepared by Mr. Albert E. Dickens of the Commission's staff, and the entire study was under the general supervision of Mr. Homer Hoyt, then Director of Research for the Commission.

Chapter iv of Part II has the title "The Decentralization of Chicago Industry." Most of the data used were for the years 1935 through 1940. Many of them were supplied by the Industrial Development Records of utility companies serving Chicago and Northern Illinois. Others came from questionnaires sent out by the Commission and the Chicago Association of Commerce.

The analysis of the figures for this five-year period were preceded by a quick review of certain facts that pointed toward industrial diffusion in the Chicago area before 1935. For example, in the eleven-year period, 1925 through 1935, 127 manufacturing establishments had moved out of Chicago to other parts of the metropolitan area. In 1929 alone, 27 plants moved out of the city. This shift was curtailed sharply during the depths of the depression but began again in 1936. In 1937, 13 plants made such moves—less than half of the 1929 number. At this point this comment is made:

> Nevertheless, despite the decreased rate of industrial migration during the post-depression recovery years, the outward movement of industry seems to be a continuous phenomenon of Chicago's industrial economy, and if past trends and responses are indexes, an acceleration in the rate of out-city industrial relocations may be anticipated if we have a marked post-war business revival.[13]

The more detailed analysis of the period 1935 through 1940 was based largely on the number of plants or *manufacturing concerns* as they are called. This weakness was partly offset, however, by two breakdowns of plants by number of wage earners and estimated annual wages. Also, some attention was given to the first of the major defense and war plants that came to this area. The analysis also has the merit

11. *Ibid.,* pp. 65–66.
12. Chicago: The Chicago Plan Commission, September, 1942.
13. *Ibid.,* p. 47.

of dealing in some detail with new plants, plants moving from Chicago proper to other parts of the metropolitan area, and plants coming into the area from outside.

During these five years, 43 plants with wage earners estimated at 6,825 moved out of Chicago to other parts of the metropolitan area. During the same period, 18 newly organized establishments located in Chicago and 24 others came in from outside of the metropolitan area. These 42 plants had an estimated 2,834 production workers. Although the balance was clearly unfavorable to the city of Chicago, it should be noted that the number of wage earners involved is relatively very small. In 1939 the Chicago area had some 480 thousand production workers and the city itself almost 345 thousand.

In addition, however, 111 plants located in the area outside of Chicago. These plus the 43 moves from Chicago proper made a total of 154. Of this total, 59 plants or 38.5 per cent moved to the area from elsewhere, and the remainder were new plants. Although no estimate is given of the aggregate employment in these 111 plants outside of Chicago proper, it was said that on the whole they were somewhat larger than the plants that located in Chicago during the same period. Of the total locations outside of Chicago (111 plus 43 from Chicago—154), 13 had from 100 to 200 employees each and 12 over 200. During this same period only two plants moved from the outlying part of the metropolitan area into Chicago itself. Thus in this five-year period Chicago had 44 additional plants (gross, not counting those that went out of business) including new ones and move-ins, and the rest of the metropolitan area had 154.

As to the over-all distribution of these additional plants:

. . . The tendency for Chicago's relocated plants to cluster on the rim of the city and in nearby suburban localities is clearly evident. In fact, three-fourths of all *relocated* industries removed to points less than 15 miles distant from the Loop. On the other hand, nearly three-fourths of the *new* industries located at points over 15 miles removed from the city's center. In general, the great majority of new industrial locations, both relocated and newly established, were made to the west and south of the city and within Cook County.

. . . .

The fact that the current trend of industrial decentralization and relocation is largely taking place on the edge of Chicago or within relatively easy commuting distance from the city tends to lessen the drain upon Chicago proper caused by the greater industrial development outside its borders. . . . (but—) The potentialities of suburban industrial development as a factor in population decentralization cannot be overlooked. In view of lower housing costs and greater living amenities in suburban regions, the tendency is inevitable for those workers whose places of employment are well outside Chicago likewise to change their residences to outlying points, thus diverting a considerable portion of their family expenditures.[14]

14. *Ibid.,* p. 49.

Those responsible for this report also hazarded ". . . what appear to be the major reasons for the one-sided industrial development of the Chicago Industrial Area. Although by no means all-inclusive, the causes set forth here represent the judgment and concensus of impartial observers, including policy-determining executives of manufacturing plants located within the city and outside its corporate limits. . . ." Four "significant reasons" were suggested:

1. Differentials in property tax burdens, both real and personal, with few exceptions favored areas outside of Chicago.

2. Building code requirements for new construction and extensions and Chicago's industrial inspection services were said by some to be onerous.

3. Land acquisition costs were lower in the suburbs and it was much easier there to accumulate sites for one-story plants.

4. The Clearing Industrial District just outside of the Chicago city limits at the southwest provided not only a location but also services that attracted many types of industry, particularly infant industries with limited capital.[15]

AND IN WORLD WAR II AND AFTER

In 1951 the Chicago Plan Commission presented a more thorough analysis in a report, *Chicago Industrial Development—Recent Trends.*[16] One section deals with "Growth of Manufacturing in Chicago and in Other Parts of the Metropolitan Area." Unlike its predecessor it does not analyze data on relocations and new plants. Instead it relies on Census of Manufactures' figures for 1939 and 1947 on the number and net change in plants or manufacturing establishments as well as on the number of production workers in manufacturing. It also makes use of data on industrial construction contracts made available to the Commission by the Territorial Information Department, a service of four utility companies in Chicago and northern Illinois. These data were compiled by TID from reports in the *Engineering News-Record.*

One of the merits of this study is that all three sets of figures are given not only for the metropolitan area, the city of Chicago, and the metropolitan area outside Chicago, but also by twenty major industry groups. Thus the changes in the relative importance of the city and the outside area can be traced back to types of industry. On the other hand, figures for the area outside of Chicago, with only one or two exceptions, are not broken down into smaller units. Thus changes in the pattern

15. *Ibid.*, p. 51. Of the 154 plants that located in the metropolitan area outside of Chicago, 28 (17 from Chicago and 11 others) went into the Clearing District—Table 17, p. 49.

16. Chicago: Chicago Plan Commission, April, 1951.

within the various parts of this large and diversified area cannot be made out in much detail from the data given.

In general, this analysis shows a continuing pattern of industrial diffusion—not a strong trend but a noticeable one. Also, it took place during a period of rapid industrial expansion in this area, as well as in the country as a whole.

Thus from 1939 to 1947 the Chicago metropolitan area showed an increase in number of plants of 3,226. Of this total, the city of Chicago gained 2,447, or 75.9 per cent. In 1939 it had had 86.0 per cent of the total number of manufacturing establishments. As a result of the war boom and the first part of the postwar period, Chicago's proportion dropped to 83 per cent. Put the other way around, in 1939 the area outside of Chicago had only 14 per cent of the total number of plants in the area and gained 24.1 per cent of the net increase from 1939 to 1947.

Five industries showed the largest proportional increases in the area outside of Chicago. They were machinery except electrical, electrical machinery, fabricated metal products, transportation equipment, leather and leather products. In all of these industry groups the percentage increase in number of plants outside of the city was one hundred or more. All of them except leather and leather products are durable or producer-goods industries. The catch-all category of miscellaneous manufactures also showed a very large percentage increase, 188.6. Within the city of Chicago, the largest percentage gains in plants were found in machinery except electrical, electrical machinery, instruments, and related products. Only the last showed more than 100 per cent increase.[17]

In the much more satisfactory unit of measurement, the number of production workers, the net changes in the basic pattern in the Chicago area were in the same directions as shown by number of plants, but also had significant differences. In rate of growth, for example, Chicago showed up rather more favorably. The 1939–47 rate of increase in production workers for the metropolitan area was 58.1 per cent, for Chicago, 54.7 per cent, and for the area outside of Chicago, 66.9 per cent. Among the major industry groups, both kinds of machinery, electrical and nonelectrical, and transportation equipment showed large increases both within Chicago and outside. In percentages, nonelectrical machinery increased more rapidly outside and electrical machinery more rapidly inside Chicago. In the area outside, the other industry groups with large percentage increases were chemicals and allied products, and lumber and products except furniture. All of these industry groups except the last are major employers in the Chicago area. Within Chicago, in addition to the two kinds of machinery and transportation equipment,

17. *Ibid.*, pp. 22 and 26. Also Table 10, p. 24.

large percentage increases were shown in instruments and related products, and petroleum and coal products. These last two groups are not major employers in the Chicago area but did have approximately 19,-000 employees each in 1947.[18]

In a rough geographic distribution of the increase in production workers during this period outside of Chicago, the remainder of Cook County showed a larger absolute increase than any of the other five counties. It gained almost 49,000 workers or 107.8 per cent. Lake County, Indiana (the county that includes Gary, Whiting, Hammond and other industrial towns at the end of Lake Michigan) gained more than 20,000 workers or 34.9 per cent. Du Page County, which is immediately to the west of Cook and partly surrounded by it, had the largest percentage increase, 109.3, but this came from an absolute gain of only 1,236 workers.[19] Although county figures are obviously very crude measures of diffusion, these figures would seem to support in general the earlier finding that industrial diffusion in this metropolitan area is taking place largely within the area immediately adjacent to the great concentration within Chicago itself. The other large concentration of industry in the area, of course, is the basic or heavy industries in the Gary region. The figures given do not show whether the substantial increase in that sector was a diffusion from existing concentrations there or whether it was a growth of them. In either event, the increase in Lake County, Indiana, does represent diffusion in respect to the Chicago metropolitan area as a whole.

This report also distributes the number and aggregate value of industrial construction contracts compiled by the Territorial Information Department from the *Engineering News-Record*. These data cover the period from January, 1946 through December, 1950—five full years. They include all contracts reported for $100,000 or more. In chapter vi we shall discuss in some detail the difficulties and limitations of these data.

For the Chicago metropolitan area, however, they totaled a very substantial number of plants and a large dollar volume during this five-year period. Within the metropolitan area the figures were for 270 plants with an aggregate value of $211,776,000. Of these totals the city of Chicago had 61 per cent of the number of plants, but only 31 per cent of the dollar volume. Conversely, the area outside of Chicago had only 39 per cent of the number of plants, but 69 per cent of the dollar volume.[20]

Finally, the writers of this report see two major factors as possible limitations on continued industrial expansion within Chicago itself—

18. *Ibid.*, Table 12, p. 29.
19. *Ibid.*, Table 13, p. 31.
20. *Ibid.*, Table 11, p. 27.

the labor supply and the supply of land available and suited to industrial use. They suggest also that to increase the supply of industrial land (a) more areas should be zoned for manufacturing and other industrial uses; and (b) a redevelopment program should be carried out to provide additional sites that would meet the requirements of present-day plants. These suggestions apparently were made without any detailed consideration of whether, in the interests of the metropolitan area as a whole, most of its future industrial expansion should take place within Chicago.

Two Detroit Studies

Within recent years the Regional Planning Commission of Detroit has put out two reports pertinent to our subject: *Movement of Manufacturing Establishments 1937–1949 and Factors Influencing Location of Plants* and *Industrial Decentralization, Detroit Region, 1940–1950 (Projection to 1970)*.[21] Both were largely the work of Mr. Paul M. Reid of the Commission's staff. The primary unit of measurement was the plant, but some use was made of the number of production workers.

The second of the two reports is the more ambitious and thorough. One useful feature of it is the division of the metropolitan area into 19 Development Areas. ". . . Within each area, townships, villages and cities that are subject to the same kind of development forces and have certain common problems have been grouped. . . ." Although this technique of analysis has certain obvious merits, particularly in a complex area such as Detroit, it makes any summary of the findings difficult without maps of these development areas and some knowledge of their makeup and characteristics.

In the earlier report, Mr. Reid estimated from local sources of data that in 1949 the Detroit area had 3,544 industrial plants—an increase of 1,654 or almost 88 per cent above the 1939 figure. For the same period, for the city of Detroit the increase was 960 plants or 57 per cent, and for the rest of the area it was 694 plants, or 344 per cent. Mr. Reid admitted that these figures of percentage increase may be too large. They are substantially greater than those from the Census of Manufactures for 1939 and 1947. The Census reported an increase of 47 per cent in the number of plants in Detroit and 222 per cent in the rest of the area for the eight years.

The significant point, however, is that both sets of data show a much larger increase of manufacturing establishments in the region outside of Detroit than in the city itself. Manufacturing employment increase in the city, according to the Census, was 61 per cent from 1939 to 1947, while the growth in the rest of the region was

21. Detroit: Detroit Metropolitan Area Regional Planning Commission, 1949 and 1951.

only 34 per cent. In Detroit, the increase was 128,016 workers and 1,052 plants. In the rest of the region, the employment growth was only 54,994 workers, but the plant increase of 1,027 was almost the same as in Detroit. Average employment per manufacturing plant in the area outside the city fell from 350 in 1939 to 146 in 1947. Within the city, this average grew from 95 in 1939 to 103 in 1947.[22]

Of the 694 additional plants in the area outside of Detroit from 1939 to 1947, 146 moved from sites within Detroit. Three major industry groups accounted for 102 of the 146 plants. These were machinery except electrical, fabricated metals, and chemicals and allied products.[23]

Officials of 63 of these 146 plants responded to a questionnaire that included a question on factors influencing the moves. Eight factors were listed and the plant representatives were asked to indicate whether each was a major factor, a minor factor, or did not apply. The eight factors in the order in which they were listed in the questionnaire were: (1) need for greater space; (2) special inducements; (3) zoning restrictions; (4) lower rental; (5) access to ground water supply; (6) labor pay rates; (7) tax rates; (8) other.

Of the seven specific factors, tax rates and need for greater space—rated as major factors by 70 per cent and 68 per cent of the plants respectively—were far and away the most significant. It should be noted, however, that the catch-all category, other reasons, was rated as a major factor in 76 per cent of the replies.[24]

The second Detroit report was based on data from both the Census of Manufactures and local sources. As its title implies, Mr. Reid not only analyzed past changes but also estimated future industrial growth in various subdivisions of the area.

In general, his statements about industrial decentralization or diffusion are more positive than those of any other study we have reviewed. For example, the Introduction includes these two paragraphs:

We all know that manufacturing in the Detroit Region has been growing by leaps and bounds. Geographical spread of plants as well as increase in industrial employment has been evident for some years. During the past decade, such developments have been phenomenal. A host of new manufacturing enterprises have been established in the municipalities and townships surrounding the city of Detroit. Many Detroit industrial firms have built branch plants or have re-established their main plants in the outlying parts of the Region. Families have moved from the city to the suburbs to be nearer their places of work and to escape crowded urban conditions. Retail business has followed this population movement; new stores, supermarkets, shops and service establishments have been built in the expanding suburban areas.

All this spells *decentralization!* The significant thing, however, is that large increases in plants and employment—both at the center and in the outlying parts—

22. 1949 Detroit report, pp. 1 and 2.
23. *Ibid.*, p. 2, Table 1, p. 11, and Table 3, p. 13.
24. *Ibid.*, pp. 3–5, and 15.

have accompanied this spread of manufacturing and population. The World War II production boom accelerated an outward trend of plant location which was already under way. Since 1945, industrial plants and employment have spread even farther into the peripheral areas.[25]

Although some of the analysis in this report was on the basis of the 19 development areas, much of it was summarized in a two-way breakdown: (1) the Central Part of the area, which is development area 11 and consists of Detroit and two cities entirely surrounded by Detroit, Highland Park and Hamtramck; and (2) Outlying Areas, the rest of the metropolitan area. According to Mr. Reid's estimates, the Central Part had 66.5 per cent of the manufacturing employment in 1940 and 65.3 per cent in 1950. Conversely, the Outlying Areas had 33.5 per cent in 1940 and 34.7 per cent in 1950. For the Central Part the rate of gain during the decade was 68.2 per cent and for the Outlying Areas was 77.8 per cent.

Although the changes in distribution between these major divisions and their rates of growth during the decade may not seem to support the strong statements on the extent and rate of decentralization, the estimates for the twenty-year period 1950 to 1970, if realized, would amount to a very substantial degree of diffusion. For these twenty years it is estimated that manufacturing employment in the metropolitan area will increase by approximately 133,000. Of this estimated total increase, less than 3,000 is estimated for the Central Part and more than 130,000 for the Outlying Areas. In other words, manufacturing employment in the Central Part is estimated to increase by 0.5 per cent and in the Outlying Areas by 57.4 per cent. If these estimates should come to pass, in 1970 the Central Part of the metropolitan area would have 54.7 per cent of the manufacturing employment of the metropolitan area and the Outlying Areas would have 45.3 per cent.[26]

This report also includes some breakdowns of numbers of plants and manufacturing employment by industries classified according to the character of their land use requirements. *Extensive* industries ". . . spread out over the land and have a low ratio of workers per acre. Steel mills and chemical plants, for example, may employ as few as 6 or 8 workers per acre." *Intensive* industries ". . . such as electrical appliances and food products—can concentrate their light production work in multi-storied buildings and thus employ from 50 to 100 workers

---

25. 1951 Detroit report, p. 1.

26. *Ibid.*, p. 28. In number of plants, the Outlying Areas gained very rapidly—see pp. 3–8 and 22. Mr. Reid also extended his analysis of both plants and employment back to 1929. Over the twenty-one-year period, 1929 to 1950, the increase in employment in the Outlying Areas was also quite impressive. The increase in these areas was over 125,000 (from 101,758 in 1929 to 227,378 in 1950) and that of the Central Part was about 138,000 (from 289,509 to 427,708). Chart B, p. 4.

per acre. . . ." Although this basic distinction is by no means new, when applied to the industries of a major region it does make possible some worth-while comparisons.

One might expect, of course, that the extensive industries, because of their land requirements, would be increasing more rapidly in the Outlying Areas than the intensive industries. During the 1940's in the Detroit area, however, Mr. Reid's figures do not show this result. For the extensive industries, the Outlying Areas in 1940 had 23 per cent of the number of plants and 42 per cent of the manufacturing employment —roughly equivalent to production workers in manufacturing. In 1940 the proportions were 34 per cent of the plants and 38 per cent of the employment. In other words, for these industries the outlying areas gained moderately in the relative number of plants but lost relatively in employment. For the intensive industries, the Outlying Areas in 1940 had 10 per cent of the plants and 7 per cent of the employment. In 1950 the proportions were 32 per cent of the plants and 23 per cent of the employment—relative gains in both.[27]

Mr. Reid attributes this unorthodox pattern of growth to two considerations. Many of the plants in the intensive industries supply parts, materials or services to some of the larger extensive industries. As units of the latter grew in the Outlying Areas their service industries clustered about or near them. Also, many of the intensive industries supplying larger plants are in sharply competitive fields. Relatively small advantages in land costs or transportation expenses may mean rather more to them than to industries operating on a wider margin between costs and prices per unit.

Two other facts might also be noted. Although many intensive industries have operated typically in multi-story buildings, some of them have been finding advantages in one-story plants with rather more space per worker than their typical ratios. Again, the years of World War II, which dominated the industrial scene for the decade of the 1940's, were unusual in many respects. Perhaps a slower industrial growth less influenced by special conditions and controls would show a different pattern in this respect.

Finally, in the analytical part of this report, five development areas were identified as the major gainers in manufacturing employment from 1940 to 1950. Their gains in employment ranged from a little less than 11,000 to 21,000. On the question of the nature or pattern of diffusion, it is significant that three of these development areas are immediately adjacent to the so-called Central Part and two of them are some little distance removed.

27. *Ibid.*, Charts C and D, pp. 6 and 7.

CINCINNATI AS AN EXAMPLE

Although not strictly speaking analyses of industrial decentralization or diffusion, a number of local planning agencies recently have made estimates of land available for industrial expansion. One example may be cited here. In the postwar *Cincinnati Metropolitan Master Plan and Official City Plan of the City of Cincinnati,* it is estimated that the metropolitan area has a "potential total" of 10,876 acres of vacant land reasonably suitable for and presumably available for future industrial use.

. . . Of this total, 6,849 acres in 100 potential sites are now physically suitable in that they are at present vacant or in open uses, are not attached to existing plant properties, and do not need major grading or filling, clearance or flood protection. The remaining 4,027 acres in 395 sites need major conditioning to make them physically suitable for industrial use. Not included in the total of 10,876 acres, there are (a) 854 acres of unused land on present sites of existing industries and (b) an undetermined quantity of acreage in sites of less than one-half acre.[28]

One significant aspect of these estimates is the distribution of this acreage in the central city and in other parts of the metropolitan area. Of the 6,849 acres now in suitable condition for industrial use in the Cincinnati area, only 755 acres are in Cincinnati; 5,292 acres are in the rest of Hamilton County; and 802 acres are in Kenton and Campbell Counties. Of the 4,027 acres requiring conditioning or preparation for industrial purposes, Cincinnati has 1,398 acres, the rest of Hamilton County—2,324, and Kenton and Campbell Counties—305.

In short, the central city, Cincinnati, has only a relatively small proportion of the land considered to be appropriate for future industrial use. Of course, some of its relatively small acreage may be more desirable for many industrial purposes than much of the larger supply outside. In broad perspective, however, it would seem that the outlying parts of the area would offer a much wider range of choice for future industrial plants. It might be reasonable to expect, therefore, that a substantial proportion of the future industrial expansion in the metropolitan area would take place outside of the central city.

Facts and prospects of this kind have been leading officials and redevelopers in central cities to urge changes in zoning as well as redevelopment projects to make available within city limits additional land for industrial purposes. As we have suggested before, however, it seems to us that proposals of this kind should be judged in terms of the desirable pattern of industrial growth for the metropolitan areas as

28. Cincinnati: City Planning Commission, 1948, p. 75.

wholes. Admittedly with existing planning machinery and the splitting up of local government in metropolitan areas, the job of making rational judgments on this question is very difficult. Nevertheless, this is a basic problem for planners and redevelopers in metropolitan areas and, unless they address themselves to it, their proposals and projects within the central city may turn out to be unfeasible or, if realized, may be regretted later.

CHAPTER VI

ARE INDUSTRIES DECENTRALIZING?
NATION-WIDE STUDIES

I N ADDITION to inquiries by local agencies into industrial diffusion in major metropolitan areas, five nation-wide studies have thrown some light on the question. Four of these we shall outline briefly here; the fifth we shall take up more thoroughly in connection with our own analysis of some more recent data. Three of the four have been published as reports by the Bureau of the Census, one in conjunction with the Bureau of Agricultural Economics. The fourth was done by the staff of the National Industrial Conference Board.

FROM 1899 TO 1929

In 1933 the Bureau of the Census issued *Location of Manufactures 1899–1929* by Mr. Tracy E. Thompson, an industrial analyst with the Bureau.[1] Rather more than half of the text of this pamphlet has to do with what was called geographic distribution, i.e., broad regional shifts and trends. One section, however, dealt with industrial and population concentration in three types of areas and another was a brief analysis of the distribution of wage jobs and population in the industrial areas, which included the ten most populous cities in the country. The first of these two parts of the study was based on a three-way breakdown of the country:

. . . (1) *Areas of primary concentration,* comprising the areas of 93 cities of 100,000 population or more; (2) *Areas of secondary concentration,* composed of the remainder of the areas of those counties within which the cities of 100,000 population are located, together with 47 other counties belonging in what the Bureau of Census defines as "industrial areas". . . and (3) *All other areas,* constituting the remainder of continental United States.[2]

This breakdown was an attempt to find out what relation, if any, existed between population and industrial density on one hand and the

1. Subtitle, "A Study of the Tendencies toward Concentration and toward Dispersion of Manufactures in the United States" (Washington, D.C.: Government Printing Office, 1933).
2. *Ibid.,* p. 29.

distribution of net additions to population and wage jobs. It should be noted, however, that in this part of the study no distinction was made between cities of 100 thousand or more that were in fact satellite centers in major metropolitan areas and other cities of substantially equal populations that were the central cities of other metropolitan or similar areas.

As in all studies of this kind that cover a substantial period of time, changes in municipal areas, unless adjusted for, are bound to influence the result in some degree. Apparently Mr. Thompson did not find it possible to make the necessary adjustments for all the areas that he covered, which admittedly would have been a difficult task, but in his opinion ". . . the modifications of corporate boundaries have not affected industrial data enough to impair seriously the value of the classification in question." Mr. Thompson also pointed out that:

> . . . Data are not available for showing in any comprehensive way the geographic redistribution of individual industries or groups of industries in the three types of areas. This is particularly unfortunate, for while the area statistics for industry as a whole indicate fairly well-defined trends, it is quite probable that data for some of the industries, if available, would show even more distinct tendencies either toward concentration or toward dispersion.[3]

For a period of thirty years the changes in the distributions of population and wage jobs that Mr. Thompson discovered do not seem very great. The areas of primary concentration in 1899 had 44.6 per cent of the total wage jobs for the country and in 1929 43.8 per cent, a decline of less than one percentage point. In population the proportions for these areas were in 1899, 22.4 per cent, and in 1929, 29.6 per cent. In other words, while the proportion of wage jobs declined very slightly during these thirty years, the proportion of population increased rather substantially.

In the areas of secondary concentration the proportion of wage jobs in 1899 was 18.4 per cent of the national total and in 1929 it was 21.1 per cent. In population the proportions were 10.7 per cent in 1899 and 14.5 per cent in 1929. In short, these areas gained moderately both in the proportions of wage jobs and population.

In the rest of the United States, the figures were: for wage jobs, 36.9 per cent in 1899, and 35.1 per cent in 1929; for population, 66.8 per cent in 1899, and 55.9 per cent in 1929. This is clearly a very slight decline in the proportion of wage jobs and a material decrease in the proportion of population.

When Mr. Thompson made this breakdown for each of the nine major divisions or regions of the country (New England, Middle Atlantic, etc.) he found a few more notable changes in the distributions

3. *Ibid.*, p. 30.

of wage jobs—but, as the national totals indicated, no clear pattern of change. Thus, in New England the proportions varied little over the thirty years. In the Middle Atlantic states the areas of primary concentration lost substantially—from 56.7 per cent in 1899 to 50.7 per cent in 1929—and the secondary areas gained from 21.7 per cent to 29.1 per cent. In the East North Central region, however, both the primary and secondary areas gained—the former from 49.7 to 52.7 per cent and the latter from 12.7 to 18.6 per cent.[4]

In this part of his analysis Mr. Thompson also traced the relocation of 287 plants (in fifty industries) that moved during 1928 and 1929. Here he found evidence of a sharp swing away from the areas of primary concentration. In their earlier locations, plants with 58.3 per cent of the wage jobs in the group of 287 manufacturing establishments were in areas of primary concentration. After relocation this proportion dropped to 27.8 per cent. The areas of secondary concentration gained noticeably from the relocation. Before the moves, plants with 33.8 per cent of the aggregate wage jobs were in these areas, and afterwards, 44.3 per cent. The rest of the country was the chief gainer in these relocations. Before these changes it had 7.9 per cent of the wage jobs, and afterwards, 27.9 per cent.

Too much significance, however, should not be attached to these figures. The 287 relocated plants had a total of 18,599 wage jobs out of a grand total of more than 8,800,000 for the country in 1929. Furthermore, practically all of the relocations took place in the four geographic divisions or regions of New England, Middle Atlantic, East North Central, and Pacific states.[5]

In Mr. Thompson's opinion, ". . . Data for the most populous ten cities of the group [that is, the group of 93 cities of 100,000 or more— EDITOR] and for their surrounding industrial areas indicate a fairly definable current of industrial dispersion." Certainly no more positive statement would have been justified by the facts. For each of these ten major areas, Mr. Thompson gave the proportions of wage jobs in the central city and in the remainder of the area. For three of the areas he also gave the proportions in cities of 100,000 population or more other than the central city. From 1899 to 1929 four of the ten central cities declined in proportion of wage jobs in their areas. These cities were New York City, Chicago, Philadelphia, and Pittsburgh. Chicago's decrease was relatively small; the others were substantial. On the other hand, six of the ten central cities actually increased their proportions of wage jobs in their areas over the thirty-year period. These cities were Detroit, Los Angeles, Cleveland, St. Louis, Baltimore, and Boston. For

4. *Ibid.*, Table 10, p. 30 and Table 13, p. 34.
5. *Ibid.*, pp. 35–39.

the aggregate wage jobs of all ten areas, the central cities' proportion in 1899 was 62.2 per cent and in 1929, 62.3 per cent. The central cities plus satellite towns of 100,000 and more in their areas had 71.4 per cent of the wage jobs in the 10 industrial areas in 1899 and 70.0 per cent in 1929.[6]

Although this hardly looks like industrial diffusion in these metropolitan areas, the breakdown of the ten central cities does suggest one possibility that might be worth further exploration. All four cities that declined in proportion of wage jobs during the first thirty years of this century were established major industrial centers at the beginning of that period. This might suggest that industrial diffusion marked by a relative decline in the number of wage jobs or of production workers in the central cities comes at a fairly mature stage in an area's industrial evolution. This possibility would be further supported by the substantial increases in the proportion of jobs in the central cities of the Detroit and Los Angeles areas during the same period. During these years these two cities certainly were in the early stages of their industrial development. On the other hand, the records of Boston and Baltimore are clearly contrary to such an explanation and those of Cleveland and St. Louis are almost as clearly contradictory. In any event, of course, ten areas are not enough to establish any generalization on the relation, if any, of industrial diffusion and industrial maturity. If some reasonably satisfactory measure of industrial maturity could be devised, the possibility of this relation between it and industrial diffusion would seem worth testing.

In his Summary, Mr. Thompson drew these very general conclusions from his entire study:

> Despite the tendency toward manufacturing decentralization, generally observable in the statistics presented in this report, industry remains quite highly concentrated in large urban centers. The dispersion which has occurred consists principally of expansion into areas adjoining the dominant population and industry centers, rather than into the thousands of smaller cities and towns throughout the country. The process also has taken the form of a relatively smaller growth of industry in the key cities of the 10 great industrial areas than in those large cities located elsewhere.[7]

FROM 1899 TO 1939

The second federal government report is *Changes in Distribution of Manufacturing Wage Earners 1899–1939* by Mr. Harold D. Kube and Mr. Ralph H. Danhof.[8] This pamphlet was the source of most of the data in Tables 1 and 2 in chapter iii. The figures for manufacturing

6. *Ibid.*, Table 17, p. 43.
7. *Ibid.*, p. 47.
8. *A Cooperative Study of the Bureau of the Census and the Bureau of Agricultural Economics* (Washington, D.C.: Government Printing Office, 1942).

wage earners were taken from various enumerations of the Census of Manufactures and adjusted for differences in definitions and coverage. From the Census of 1939 Messrs. Kube and Danhof gave figures for states and geographic divisions (regions) only, because county and city statistics were not available at the time their report was prepared. For our purposes here, therefore, the latest year covered by this study was 1937 instead of 1939.

Much of this study was concerned with broad geographic distribution by states and divisions of the country. Because we have covered some of these materials briefly in chapter iii, we shall not repeat them here. Rather we shall limit our summary to breakdowns made by Messrs. Kube and Danhof of the numbers and proportions of wage earners by three size groups of cities and the remainder of the country from 1899 to 1937, and to the same data for thirty-three major industrial areas and for the rest of the country over the same period.

The first or four-way breakdown was: (1) cities of 500,000 population or over according to the 1930 Census of Population, thirteen cities; (2) cities from 100,000 to 499,999, eighty cities; (3) cities from 25,000 to 99,999, 277 cities; and (4) the remainder of the country. Admittedly this breakdown is not too good for measuring possible diffusion of industrial workers. It is better for detecting dispersion. By and large, however, the larger cities can be taken as the areas of greatest industrial concentration and Group 4, which includes cities under 25,000 and rural parts of the country, is assumed to be the least industrialized.

From 1899 to 1937 the proportions of total manufacturing wage earners who were employed in cities in Group 1 declined slowly but quite steadily from 27.3 per cent in 1899 to 23.2 per cent in 1937. (The table that summarized these data covers the four years 1899, 1919, 1929, and 1937. For each of these years after the first the proportion of wage earners in Group 1—cities of 500,000 or over—decreased slightly.) Cities in Group 2 held about the same proportion over the period. They had 17.9 per cent of the total wage earners in 1899 and 17.8 per cent in 1937. Group 3 cities increased slightly but steadily for the four census periods from 15.3 per cent in 1899 to 18 per cent in 1937. Group 4, the remainder of the country, had 39.5 per cent in 1899, decreased to 38.1 per cent in 1919, but increased to 41.0 per cent in 1937. In general, therefore, the smaller cities and rural areas gained slightly over this period; the medium sized cities held their own, and the largest cities lost proportionately.[9]

Two interesting and possibly significant facts are brought out by

9. *Ibid.*, Table 13, p. 46. With the cities in each size group determined by the 1930 Census, the percentages were computed from the figures for the Census of Manufactures for 1899, 1919, 1929, and 1937 and the population figures for the censuses of population nearest to these dates.

comparing Messrs. Kube and Danhof's figures on rates of change in numbers of manufacturing wage earners and of population for these four groups of localities for the two periods 1919–1929 and 1929–1937. During the first of these two periods, the total population of the country increased by some 17,000,000 persons, but the number of wage earners declined by almost 270,000. In the second, the eight-year period, population increased by about 9,000,000 (actually ten years, 1930 to 1940) and the number of wage earners increased by almost the same amount as it had lost in the previous decade, about 242,000.[10]

For the 1919–1929 decade the first three groups of cities increased in population quite substantially. The rates of increase were: Group 1, 23.8 per cent; Group 2, 23.2 per cent; Group 3, 27.8 per cent. The fourth group, the rest of the country, increased in population by only 11.1 per cent. Despite these population increases, however, each of the four groups lost in number of wage earners. The rates of decrease were: Group 1, 3.8 per cent; Group 2, 6.4 per cent; Group 3, 1.5 per cent; and Group 4, 1.3 per cent. In other words, the nationwide decrease in number of wage earners was fairly evenly distributed among these four groups of localities with the medium-sized cities losing most heavily.

For the eight years 1929 to 1937, however, the picture was substantially different. Again, all four classes of localities gained in population, but much more slowly. The rates of increase ranged from 4.2 per cent for the largest cities to 8.8 per cent for Group 4—small cities and the rural parts of the country. In number of wage earners, the first two classes of cities declined—Group 1 by 4.2 per cent, and Group 2 by 3.5 per cent. On the other hand, both Groups 3 and 4 showed quite substantial rates of increase—Group 3, 6.2 per cent, and Group 4, 8.7 per cent.[11]

The rates of change shown from these figures for 1929 and 1937 certainly suggest that some kind of industrial diffusion or dispersion (or possibly both) was taking place. It must be remembered, however, that this was the period of the depression. Changes or indicated trends during such a period might or might not be continued under other conditions of general business and industrial activity.

In the two-way breakdown between the thirty-three major industrial areas and the rest of the country, the same general pattern appears from the Kube and Danhof figures. For the period 1899 to 1937 the thirty-three industrial areas increased in population by 122 per cent and in manufacturing wage earners by 88 per cent. The rest of the country, however, increased only 54.7 per cent in population, but by 98.1 per cent in number of wage earners.

10. *Ibid.*, Table 10, p. 36.
11. *Ibid.*, Table 12, p. 44.

The distribution of wage earners changed from 55.9 per cent in the industrial areas in 1899 to 58.1 per cent in 1919, and then declined to 54.6 per cent in 1937. Conversely, the rest of the country had 44.1 per cent of the total wage earners in 1899, declined to 41.9 per cent in 1919, and then increased to 45.4 per cent in 1937.[12]

In Metropolitan Districts

The third study is *The Growth of Metropolitan Districts in the United States: 1900–1940*, prepared for the Bureau of the Census by Mr. Warren S. Thompson, Director of the Scripps Foundation for Research in Population Problems at Miami University, Oxford, Ohio.[13] In our opinion Mr. Thompson's monograph deserves study by urban planners and redevelopers. He has handled skillfully the many intricate problems that arise from changing definitions of metropolitan areas in the Census of Population over these forty years.

Much of his analysis and most of his discussion were on population rather than industrial growth and change. Although this is largely outside of the scope of our analysis here, in chapter ii he established quite clearly a diffusion of population from central cities to what he called satellite areas, urban and rural, within metropolitan areas or districts. Furthermore, this movement seemed to be increasing in momentum over the period from 1920 to 1940. For the decade 1930 to 1940 Mr. Thompson also showed a diffusion of population within the boundaries of central cities from near-in districts to outlying ones in sixteen metropolitan centers. This is a type of analysis that ought to be extended not only to population but to industrial location as well within many of the larger metropolitan central cities. Mr. Thompson's method requires Census tract data grouped in concentric rings around a central point in the city. He concluded the chapter with this summary on this type of diffusion:

. . . It can be said that in general the areas near the center of the cities lost population or grew quite slowly, while the areas nearer their peripheries grew at a fairly rapid rate. In some of the smaller cities in the group of 16 for which such tabulations were made, namely. Dayton, Columbus, Nashville. and Indianapolis; in Washington, D.C.; and in Los Angeles there was no group of tracts which actually lost population but even in most of these cities the more distant tracts gained more rapidly than those near the center. In practically all the other cities the central tracts either lost population or remained about stationary while the peripheral areas gained quite rapidly. the rate of growth increasing with the increase in the length of the radius used. Thus the decentralizing trend appears to be about as great within the limits of most of these cities as it is between the central cities and their satellite areas. Only

12. *Ibid.*, Table 10. p. 36.
13. Washington, D.C.: Government Printing Office, 1948.

in Dayton is it doubtful whether there was a decentralizing trend within the city, while such a trend was clearly marked as between the city of Dayton and its satellite area.[14]

In chapter v, "Factors Affecting the Redistribution of Population Within Metropolitan Districts," Mr. Thompson specifically considered industrial location and diffusion as one of the important factors. Here his breakdown is essentially that used in the Creamer-Goodrich study that we shall discuss at some length later in this chapter. This paragraph from Mr. Thompson's text provides both a summary and a useful comment:

> But while it seems eminently reasonable to believe that this slow but steady shift of industry from central cities to satellite areas is a factor of some importance in the relatively more rapid growth of population in the satellite areas, yet we should not overlook the fact that the number of manufacturing wage earners declined in most satellite areas between 1929 and 1939 as well as in the central cities. The increase in population in most metropolitan districts and especially in their central cities during this decade must, therefore, have resulted chiefly from an expansion of non-manufacturing employment. The growth of trade and service industries, and the increasing tendency for retail stores, service establishments, etc., to be located in the periphery of large cities, are important in this connection.[15]

In chapter vii, "The Future Growth of Metropolitan Districts," Mr. Thompson distributed manufacturing wage earners for 1919, 1929, and 1939 as well as 1939 expenditures for plant and equipment by classes of counties based on the Creamer-Goodrich breakdown. These data are given for the United States and for the four major regions of the Northeastern States, North Central States, South, and West. Under the heading "Dispersion of Industry" he made this summary:

> The conclusion would appear justified that there is a slightly dispersive movement of industry away from the major industrial areas and toward those of lesser importance when the country is considered as a whole. However, when regions are considered there appear to be significant differences. . . . Thus there seems to have been at most only a mild measure of dispersion in the industry of the North.
> . . . Decentralization of industry in the South, therefore, appears to have been considerable.
> . . . Thus in the West there seems to have been a trend toward increasing centralization of industry in the major industrial areas, rather than dispersion.[16]

AN ANALYSIS FOR INDUSTRIALISTS

The last study we shall look at briefly in this section is *Decentralization in Industry* by Mr. Paul W. Dickson, a staff member of the

14. *Ibid.*, p. 9.
15. *Ibid.*, p. 17.
16. *Ibid.*, p. 25.

National Industrial Conference Board, Inc.[17] As might be expected from its authorship this study dealt with decentralization not as it affects urban structure or the broad regional distribution of manufacturing, but primarily as a problem in the management of large-scale industrial enterprises. The major emphasis, however, was on geographical location rather than on management responsibility or control. In the introductory sections this point was made clearly:

The term "decentralization" has various meanings. In industry decentralization refers to the geographic spreading out of a company's physical plant facilities. It also refers to the granting of a large degree of authority and responsibility to local plant management. Generally, the two go together, but it is possible to have physical plant decentralization without decentralization of managerial authority and responsibility. Similarly, there are many cases of managerial decentralization unaccompanied by a spreading out of physical plant. For example, many companies are organized by product divisions, with each division under a vice president or general manager charged with the over-all profit responsibility for that division. Yet, the various divisions are quite often located in the same or adjacent buildings. . . .

Decentralization is primarily a concern of those manufacturing companies with nationwide distribution that have a large degree of freedom in selecting plant locations.

.   .   .   .

. . . Major consideration is given to the geographic dispersion of plant facilities rather than to managerial decentralization, although the two often go together, as will be noted in the case studies of individual companies.[18]

This study, therefore, is germane to our purposes chiefly because it took up certain practices and considerations that influence the location of branch plants in localities of different sizes and characteristics.

Mr. Dickson surveyed 148 manufacturing companies. Although they were distributed in fourteen major industry groups and one catch-all category, he made no claim that they were a representative sample of any larger group. As has been indicated, they were large companies. Of 114 reporting on the number of plants per company, only seventeen had one each. On the other hand, thirty-six had ten or more, and seventeen had twenty-five or more plants per company. The 114 companies had a total of 1,447 plants and 1,319,941 employees—some 10 per cent of the total manufacturing employment of the country. The average number of employees per plant was 912.

Of the 148 companies covered by this study, 40 per cent were centralized, i.e., all or practically all of their facilities were in one locality. This subgroup, of course, would include the seventeen companies who reported only one plant each. As to the decentralized companies, 28 per cent of the 148 were following deliberate decentralization policies and 32 per cent were decentralized not as the result of any established

17. "Studies in Business Policy," No. 30 (New York: NICB, 1948).
18. *Ibid.*, pp. 3 and 4.

policy but through the acquisition of facilities of other companies, development of feeder plants, etc.[19]

Roughly in order of frequency, the ten chief reasons given for decentralizing plants and facilities were:

1. Proximity to important new markets.
2. Permits tapping new reservoirs of labor.
3. Small city or town location. (. . . Some of the specific advantages of the small town stressed most frequently are: more space to expand; better living conditions for employees; and less travel time between home and plant. . . .)
4. Small decentralized plant more efficient.
5. Desire to avoid dominating economic life of any one community.
6. Public relations value of being a local employer in important market areas.
7. Permits segregation of unlike operations.
8. Enables large companies to expand and yet retain features of the small company.
9. Decentralized plants serve as training centers for future top executives.
10. Human relations likely to be better in smaller decentralized plants.[20]

Among the companies not decentralizing, the chief consideration was their belief that in their industries large, highly integrated plants were most efficient. Other reasons given were the problems of top management control over a number of dispersed operations, the localization of some types of skilled labor, the unwillingness of many top executives to move away from metropolitan areas, and an existing freight-rate structure favorable to their present locations.

Mr. Dickson also separated the location of plants before 1940 and for 1940 through 1947. He had reports on 846 plants in the first class and 408 in the second. For each of these major groups he distributed the plants by major regions (Northeastern, North Central, South, and West) and by three size groups of cities; 100,000 and over; 10,000 to 99,999; and under 9,999.

The distribution of plants by geographic regions did not vary much between the two periods. As to size of city:

While only moderate shifts in the regional concentrations of manufacturing plants are noted for the period since 1940, there has been a noticeable trend away from the larger cities. The strong current preference for the more moderate-sized towns and cities reflects the trend toward decentralization. It is evidenced by the fact that 47.0 percent of the 846 plants established before 1940 were in cities of 100,000 or more, while only 34.3 percent of the 408 plants built or acquired since that date are in cities that large. Towns under 10,000 have become much more popular. For plants built or acquired since 1940, 29.4 percent are in towns in this population class, compared with 21.3 percent before 1940. The cities and towns with populations from 10,000 to 100,000 have become the most popular class, supplanting the city of 100,000 and over. Since 1940, 36.3 percent of the total plants built or purchased by

19. *Ibid.*, Tables 1, 2, and 3 and pp. 6–8.
20. *Ibid.*, p. 9.

the companies studied have been in towns or cities in this category. Before 1940 the corresponding proportion was 31.7 percent. . . .

The underlying factors in this shift include most of the reasons already given for decentralization. They comprise the economic and social advantages of the small city over the large city. Another reason not emphasized thus far is the unfavorable labor climate in some of the large cities. Many manufacturers admit frankly that they have established plants outside the highly organized urban areas in the hope of improving labor-management relations, but they report varying degrees of success. Such things as parking space for employees' cars, better living conditions for employees, space for future expansion, lower taxes, more friendly community relations, etc., are all covered under the general reasons for decentralization, but they also help to explain the increasing popularity of the smaller cities and towns.[21]

Although the findings of this study are not directly related to, or at least do not distinguish between, industrial diffusion and industrial dispersion as we are using these terms, they do indicate that probably both of these types of decentralization are a result of the policies of these larger manufacturing companies. Some evidence would point toward industrial dispersion rather than to diffusion within metropolitan areas or other relatively highly industrialized districts, but this is by no means clear.

A Partial Summary

Before going on to an examination of the Creamer-Goodrich study and our own work, which uses essentially the same breakdowns, we believe the question might well be asked at this point: What tentative conclusions, if any, can be drawn from these local and nationwide studies? This certainly is a fair question. Our answer to it is:

1. None of these studies nor all of them together amount to conclusive evidence for the existence of a marked trend toward industrial decentralization—either diffusion or dispersion. As we have noted before, they vary so much in method, units of measurement, and purpose that their results are additive only in the most general way.

2. On the whole, however, they do indicate some industrial diffusion in metropolitan areas, particularly during the period from 1920 on. Its rate has not been rapid, but possibly may have been increasing somewhat during this period. Evidence of this movement seems stronger in the very large and complex industrial centers. It may also be more noticeable in the older, more mature industrial concentrations, but this is by no means certain.

3. Some evidence also points toward industrial dispersion, particularly from the major metropolitan areas. Again, however, the picture is not clear. If such a dispersion had been under way, its rate has been quite slow.

21. *Ibid.*, pp. 12–13.

4. Quite clearly material differences as to industrial decentralization of both kinds exist among the major industry groups. Quite possibly this fact accounts for the relatively slow rates of over-all change as well as to the contradictory nature of some of the findings from these studies.

5. Plants that have left major industrial centers, whether as actual moves, expansions, or branch plants, have been both pushed or squeezed out and attracted out by positive advantages of outlying locations. Although, again, it is not possible to be definite on this point, some indications are that, in the later years of this period, the positive attractions of outlying locations have become at least as influential if not more so than the pushing or squeezing process at work in the major centers.

In saying this, we recognize that often it is difficult to distinguish sharply between these two types of forces. Those responsible for decisions on plant location naturally deal in comparisons. Factors in these comparisons may be looked at as pushing or squeezing of big city conditions or as pulling or attracting forces from outlying areas. Among the factors that push or squeeze out industrial plants, clearly one of the more important is the shortage of suitable, reasonably priced, industrial sites for the one-story plant structures that have become more and more favored by a growing number of industries. Closely allied to this factor is the preference of many industrial plants for sites that not only accommodate their present operations plus adequate parking and similar uses, but that also facilitate future extensions when and if they may be needed.

6. In metropolitan areas industrial diffusion seems to lag well behind the diffusion of population. This may be due largely to two facts. Diffusion of population, on the whole, is a less complicated matter and requires a less formidable investment per unit in building and facilities. Also, as our urban economy matures, manufacturing wage earners become a somewhat smaller proportion of the total of gainfully employed persons in most metropolitan areas. In other words, distributive trades, finance, professional, and other services are gaining in relative importance. The housing of these growing classes of urbanites can be diffused without substantial changes in the location of industrial plants.

7. Although the evidence on industrial decentralization is not conclusive one way or the other, enough is at hand indicating both diffusion and dispersion to warrant further studies, particularly of individual metropolitan areas of major industrial importance. When or if made, these studies ought to have the careful consideration of urban planners and redevelopers. If possible, they should be done by methods and with units of measurement that are sufficiently similar to make possible

comparisons and additions from locality to locality. Also, although many of the data are readily available only for major political subdivisions of metropolitan areas, at least some of these local studies ought to use other geographic breakdowns that would seem likely to bring out changes or even trends that may have been obscured by the figures on major cities and counties. Refinements of this kind, of course, will add to the costs of studies, but also to their value. They are the kind of improvement that seems possible for studies of individual localities or areas, but by their very nature as well as their cost are difficult to employ in nationwide studies.

Planning URS' Own Work

Early in the planning for the Urban Redevelopment Study the question arose of what, if anything, it should undertake on the general subject of industrialization as it relates to the possibilities and problems of urban redevelopment. For reasons we have tried to outline in chapter i, it was clear that the Study should try to come to grips with this subject. It was equally clear, however, that the subject was a large and complex one. Not only did it bristle with technical difficulties, but it was so large and had so many facets that it easily could have absorbed more than the Study's total resources. The practical question, therefore, narrowed down to: Within the limits of available time and funds, what contribution could URS make in this area, in addition, of course, to trying to define issues and summarizing and evaluating earlier studies?

Broadly speaking, two major possibilities were seriously considered. The first was to select one or possibly two industrially important metropolitan areas and in them to undertake, in collaboration with local agencies and officials, a fairly intensive investigation of industrial diffusion. If this were done, it would be with the hope, of course, that not only would the findings be of some value in themselves, but that both they and the methods used would encourage similar inquiries in other areas. The second was to make a broader but less intensive analysis, covering all or substantially all of the country, of what had been happening in recent years in industrial location whether it be decentralization, concentration, relative stability, or some combination of these. Such an undertaking would have to concentrate on a relatively few indexes of industrial location and change. At best it could only deal with major developments. It would be useful chiefly as background for the more intensive locality studies that would be essential to sound urban planning and redevelopment programs.

Choosing between these alternatives was not easy. Without going into all the pros and cons that were considered, the decision was to take the second course—the attempt to analyze what had been happening in recent years and to relate it to the best available facts and knowledge from earlier studies. One of the primary determinants of this decision was the availability of the findings and interpretations from what we have referred to earlier as the Creamer-Goodrich study.

THE CREAMER-GOODRICH STUDY

More specifically, this was one section of the Study of Population Redistribution initiated by the Social Science Research Council and organized in 1934 under the auspices of the Wharton School of Finance and Commerce of the University of Pennsylvania. It was supported by a grant from the Rockefeller Foundation.

As its title implies, this study was concerned with the distributions and movements of population within the United States, their relations to economic productivity and welfare, changes or shifts in them that might seem desirable, and the proper role, if any, of governmental policies and programs in shaping and guiding them in the future. At the time the study was initiated the country was in the midst of one of the worst depressions in its history. Unemployment was high. Terrible distress was the lot of millions of people both in cities and rural districts. The follies of the 1920's were coming home to roost and many and varied were the proposals for alleviating the suffering and dislocations that they had caused. The title of this study's final report, *Migration and Economic Opportunity,* by Carter Goodrich, its Director, and others suggests this emphasis.[22]

In addition to this report, the study put out four monographs. One of these was *Is Industry Decentralizing?* by Daniel B. Creamer.[23] Chapter vii of the final report contains the gist of Creamer's findings plus a fairly complete discussion of his methods and the meaning of his findings. Although Creamer's work was done within this broader framework, both in method and coverage it is the most useful study of this subject for urban planners and redevelopers. It seemed to us, therefore, that URS' major contribution in this area might well be made by building on Creamer's foundation. More specifically, we could extend his primary analysis of industrial diffusion and dispersion by applying his breakdowns, with one or two additions, to the figures on production workers in manufacturing from the Census of Manufactures for 1939 and 1947. Creamer had covered five Censuses from 1899 through 1933. Our extension would make available generally comparable distributions

22. The Report of the Study of Population Redistribution (Philadelphia: University of Pennsylvania Press, 1936).

23. *Study of Population Redistribution,* Bulletin 3 (Philadelphia: University of Pennsylvania Press, 1935).

of production workers for seven years over a total period of forty-eight years. In short, this addition to Creamer's work seemed to promise more useful results than anything URS could initiate and carry through on its own.

With this explanation of the part that the Creamer-Goodrich study played in the planning of URS, we turn now to a rather more detailed description of Creamer's methods and findings. His work may be outlined under three headings: (1) the breakdown of Census of Manufactures' figures on what we now call production workers in manufacturing into seven locational classes; (2) a more limited analysis of what he termed the birth, death, and morbidity rates of industries in two periods, 1928 and 1929, and 1932 and 1933; (3) an analysis of relocated plants covered by the Censuses of 1929, 1931, and 1933.

The second and third of these three parts required special tabulations and the use of unpublished Census materials. For these reasons and also because some of the data used were not collected in later Censuses, we were not able to continue these parts of Creamer's work. In this description, therefore, we propose to summarize these two sections briefly first and then turn to his major analysis, the first part mentioned above, which we did extend to the Census figures for 1939 and 1947. In order to make Parts 2 and 3 reasonably clear, however, we must first outline Creamer's basic seven-way breakdown that he used in all three parts of his work and also indicate his meanings of industrial diffusion and dispersion, which differ slightly from ours.

The Census of Manufactures for 1929 recognized thirty-three *industrial areas*. These were the major concentrations of industrial activity and employment in the country. Each industrial area had a principal city or cities—e.g., Pittsburgh, Minneapolis-St. Paul, Seattle-Tacoma, Albany-Schenectady-Troy. Each area had 40,000 or more wage earners in manufacturing in 1929. The thirty-three areas were made up of ninety-five counties and two independent cities. Creamer started with these definitions of industrial areas in 1929 and then extended his analysis based on them forward to 1931 and 1933 and backward to 1919 and 1899. In other words, he in effect marked out these areas on maps according to the Census delineation of 1929 and compiled figures for these same geographic areas for the other Census years. He then subdivided the industrial areas into three subareas, which he labeled:

A. Principal city of industrial area.
B. Large satellite cities in the industrial areas—cities of 100,000 population or more that are not principal cities. (Only five industrial areas—Boston, New York, Philadelphia, Chicago, and Los Angeles—had satellite cities in this sense.)
C. Remainder of the industrial area—sometimes referred to as the industrial periphery.

The Census also identified 103 important industrial counties outside of the industrial areas. These were sometimes referred to as areas of secondary concentration or secondary industrial counties. Of these counties, 42 had a city with 100,000 or more population in 1929. The other 61 had no city of this size, but each had 10,000 or more industrial wage earners in 1929. From these secondary areas Creamer identified three more classes of localities:

> D. A city of 100,000 or more inhabitants outside of an industrial area—referred to in tables as Other Cities of 100,000 Population.
> E. Remainder of county in which D city is located—in tables, Peripheries of (D) Cities.
> F. Important industrial county without a city as large as 100,000 inhabitants—in tables, Important Industrial Counties.

His breakdown was completed with:

> G. Remainder of the United States—in the tables, All the Rest.

As we have mentioned before, Creamer recognized two kinds of industrial decentralization, diffusion and dispersion. He defined industrial diffusion as:

> . . . the movement within an area of industrial concentration from the large, congested nuclear city to its periphery or suburbs—a reflection of metropolitan growth and increased population density. A somewhat similar type of displacement is the development of counties of only moderate industrial concentration which do not contain a large city, and are not contiguous to the metropolitan centers. Displacement in these directions will be characterized by the term "diffusion."[24]

In other words, diffusion is from a principal city to another part of an industrial area or to one of the secondary industrial counties. Dispersion, therefore, is from an industrial area or secondary industrial county to some other location in the United States.

Although these definitions of diffusion and dispersion are reasonably clear-cut, we prefer a modification of them. It seems to us that diffusion should be limited to shifts between the principal city of a major industrial area (or an industrialized metropolitan area as defined in the 1947 Census of Manufactures) to some outlying part of the same area. The studies we have reviewed earlier in this chapter indicate that this type of redistribution of industry is taking place in some volume. These major industrialized metropolitan areas have a very substantial proportion of the industrial plants and employees of the country. Also, they are in a very real sense economic units. These facts seem to support the view that redistributions of industry within them deserve a separate classification and a separate term. We propose, therefore, that

24. *Ibid.*, pp. 4–5.

industrial diffusion be limited to redistribution within these major industrial areas or districts.

This would leave three other separable kinds of industrial decentralization: (1) from an area of concentration to a secondary industrial county; (2) from an area of concentration to the remainder of the country—i.e., some part of it outside the secondary industrial counties; and (3) from a secondary county to some locality in the remainder of the United States. For most purposes these three types of redistribution might be lumped together as industrial dispersion. This is the meaning we have given the term in our own work. If it seems that the three types of redistribution should be distinguished, they might be referred to as first-, second-, and third-degree dispersion. This is a degree of refinement of definition, however, that is not needed in the work we have done.

Although the usage of these terms we prefer differs somewhat from Creamer's, the difference should make no trouble in this chapter. Any quotations, of course, will be in Creamer's usage. Other uses of the terms will be in accord with our preferred definitions unless we indicate otherwise.

CREAMER ON TYPES OF CHANGES

With this sketch of the skeleton of Mr. Creamer's work, we turn now to a summary of the second and third parts: the vital statistics of twenty-four industries in two periods of two years each, and the analysis of relocated industrial plants in three periods of two years each.

Both of these parts of Mr. Creamer's monograph have the unmistakable merit of dealing with what might be called the active margin of industrial location. In other words, the analyses in these sections of his monograph covered data only on industrial plants that in one way or another changed their status or location, i.e., they are those that started, went out of business, closed up, or moved their locations. Data on these kinds of changes are much more sensitive, of course, and show movement much more clearly than figures on the number of production workers or other unit for the country as a whole or even for major divisions or areas of it. The latter statistics at any one time or over any relatively short period of time are heavily affected by the plants that do not move or undergo any other major change in status. Thus the figures on changes might be expected to indicate beginning or incipient movements well before they have become large enough to have any substantial effect upon aggregate figures for the country, major areas, or major industry groups.

On the other hand, the figures on changes, particularly when considered by themselves, have two serious drawbacks. At least they have two characteristics that should not be overlooked in ascribing meaning to the results of any breakdowns.

The first is indicated by the question that always exists as to what degree figures on change from a small proportion of the industrial establishments in any one group or area are representative of the much larger number of industrial units in the same group or area that did not change status or location during the period under examination. At any one period of time, of course, it may well be that the industrial units that change are untypical. Some of them may be marginal industrial establishments that come and go in an unending stream. Conversely, others may be exceptionally successful units that, because of their financial strength, can make changes in location, let us say, that most other units could not consider, at least at that time. Of course, this possibility of unrepresentativeness would be less serious for analyses of these types of change made at several points over a considerable period of years. If certain kinds of shifts showed up clearly at each point, this would be some, but nevertheless not conclusive, evidence that these types of change were not surface phenomena produced by a small minority of untypical plants.

The second warning has to do with the period covered by Mr. Creamer's analyses—1928–29, 1930–31, and 1932–33. The first of these was very near the end of a substantial but spotty and uneven boom in business and industry. The other two were at the beginning and almost at the trough of the ensuing severe depression. Over-all business and industrial conditions are bound to affect the changes that Mr. Creamer dealt with. It would seem, therefore, that his findings for these periods might be of questionable validity for other points in the major business cycle.

In pointing out these limitations on these two parts of Mr. Creamer's work, we do not imply that he was blind to them. He clearly was not. Emphasizing them here, however, may be a useful warning not only in evaluating his results, but also those of some other rather similar investigations that have been undertaken by others.

In the second major part of his work, therefore, Mr. Creamer computed and compared what he called the birth rate, death rate, and morbidity rate for twenty-four industries for the years 1928–29 and 1932–33. He explained his method of arriving at birth rates in these words:

> The procedure, then, is analogous to the computation of birth rates in vital statistics. For purposes of statistical presentation, the organization of new establishments has been conceived as an organic process. For example, the number of wage jobs in new shirt factories organized in principal cities (A) in 1933 is expressed as a per

cent of the number of wage jobs in the other shirt factories located in principal cities during 1933. This is a crude birth rate which, by reducing the absolute importance of the new plants organized in well-established centers of industry and population, tends to give the proper relative weight to new plants started in each of these locational categories. For this reason it seems better calculated than a consideration of the absolute numbers to indicate a shift in locational preference over time, and is therefore the basis of the comparisons made in this section.[25]

Similarly, death rates were computed for plants that went out of business altogether, and morbidity rates for establishments that were closed up or at least not operating through an entire year. A question in the Census of Manufactures for 1929 made relatively easy the computation of birth rates for 1928–29. Although this question was not repeated in the enumeration of 1933, it was possible to compute an analogous birth rate for 1932–33 as well as the death and morbidity rates for these two years from unpublished records of the Bureau of the Census.

Because of the amount of work that would have been involved, Mr. Creamer did not cover all industries in these computations. Instead, he selected twenty-four substantial industries that in 1929 had provided 3,910,933 wage jobs, or 44 per cent of the total for that year. The list included thirteen durable goods industries with a 1929-wage-job total of more than 2.2 million and eleven semi-durable goods industries with approximately 1.7 million wage jobs.

In 1929 the durable goods industries were quite largely located in the thirty-three industrial areas, but within these areas were quite well diffused. Of their total of 2.2 million wage jobs, fully two-thirds were within the industrial areas and 40 per cent of the two-thirds were in location C—industrial peripheries. On the other hand, of the 1.7 million wage jobs in the semi-durable goods industries, only slightly more than one-half were in the industrial areas, 15.2 per cent were in location F—important industrial counties, and 29 per cent were in G—all the rest of the country.

For our purposes, Mr. Creamer's major findings on durable goods industries are summarized in this quotation:

. . . For the 1929 census the highest birth rates were in the large cities (A, B, and D) and the lowest birth rates were in the periphery areas (C and E). For the 1933 census, however, the birth rate in the "All the rest" communities was the same as in the principal cities and higher than in the other cities with 100,000 or more inhabitants. This might be interpreted as slight evidence of relative dispersion.

The survival value of the types of communities as indicated by the death rate places the principal cities and the "All the rest" localities on about the same level, both having the highest death rates. Of the important locational categories for this sample, D and C have the lowest death rates. It would seem reasonable to expect

25. *Ibid.*, p. 29.

the highest death rate in the localities with the highest birth rate, since infant mortality in the sphere of business activity as in the sphere of human activity is the most potent single determinant of the total death rate.

The measure of the importance of idle plants by types of communities is also a measure of the favorability of a given type of locality for continuous business activity. This ratio, the morbidity rate, is higher in the less densely settled localities (C, F, and G) than in the large cities (A and D). It should be noted that the morbidity rate for this sample of durable goods industries is higher than the death rate.[26]

For the semi-durable goods industries, Mr. Creamer concluded:

. . . that dispersion during the years of the deepening of the depression was restricted to the semi-durable goods industries, particularly to the clothing trades and specifically to the boots and shoes, silk and rayon, men's clothing (contract shops) and knit goods industries. At the same time for these industries and their industrial groups there was much evidence of diffusion, especially in the important industrial counties. These developments were evidenced not only by the absence of relative shrinkage in employment but also by higher birth rates and a stronger preference to locate new establishments in the smaller towns in the important industrial counties and the "All the rest" areas. It has been shown that labor costs in these four industries are a more important cost factor than in most other industries, a factor tending to impose a labor orientation in their location. This is rather clearly intimated by the data on wages per wage job.[27]

For each of the enumerations in 1929, 1931, and 1933, the Census of Manufactures had a question on changes in the name, location, ownership, or general nature of business of industrial establishments covered by it. The period covered by each question was two years, i.e., in the Census of 1929 information was requested on change of name, location, ownership, or general nature of business since January 1, 1928. Although the data from these queries were not published, the Study of Population Redistribution had access to them. From these Mr. Creamer undertook an ingenious analysis showing the moves from and to his seven location categories, A to G. For our purposes, the following paragraphs summarize his pertinent findings:

A summary classification of relocated establishments obtained from the three censuses beginning with 1929 yields several unequivocal results. The most obvious of these is the very small fraction of industry that has changed its location during this period.

Although the absolute number of wage earners involved in relocated establishments decreased in each enumeration, nevertheless, they represented about a constant percentage of wage earners in all industry ranging from 34 to $^{36}/_{100}$ths of one per cent. Thus if all changes had been in one direction, the alteration of the locational pattern would scarcely have been appreciable.[28]

26. *Ibid.*, p. 34.
27. *Ibid.*, p. 49.
28. It is interesting to note, however, that relocated plants ranged from .28 per cent to .31 per cent of the total number of plants in existence. (Table 14, p. 53.) In other words, the relocated plants averaged slightly larger in size than the average for industry as a whole. This was true for all three periods covered. Of course this may have been due to the relocation of a relatively few large plants.

Another result that seems very clear is that the bulk of the loss of wage jobs due to relocated establishments has been sustained by the principal cities of the industrial areas. . . . This loss has been shared to a lesser extent and with exception of 1930–31 by the large satellite cities (B) of the industrial areas.

The chief recipient of the gains in each case has been the industrial peripheries (C). The next largest gains were in the communities in the "All the rest" category (G) with the exception of 1928–29 when the second largest share of the gains was received by the important industrial counties (F).[29]

In short, these plant relocations, although very small in volume, showed a relatively strong tendency to diffusion within the industrial areas and a less strongly marked dispersion, particularly to location G—all the rest of the country.

CREAMER PLUS URS

As we pointed out earlier in this chapter, a large part of URS' work on industrial decentralization was undertaken as an extension of Mr. Creamer's study. We therefore shall discuss the first and major part of his work, which was presented in chapter ii of his monograph under the title "Location of the Aggregate of Wage Jobs, 1899–1933," in conjunction with our own analysis of the distribution of wage jobs or production workers in manufacturing from the Census of Manufactures for 1939 and 1947.

Although Mr. Creamer's seven location categories made possible an excellent breakdown or distribution, we felt that some minor additions might be made to it without destroying the basic framework or invalidating comparisons over the total period from 1899 to 1947. We, therefore, added four location categories: (1) the central counties of industrial areas; (2) other counties in industrial areas minus any satellite cities in them, which we have called rather awkwardly Outer Peripheries; (3) the industrial areas as a whole; and (4) areas of secondary concentration. The latter two categories, of course, are simply the totals of Creamer's locations A, B, and C, and his D, E, and F. We have computed them for the tables that draw on his work. For the Central Counties and Outer Peripheries, we computed the percentages for 1939 and 1947 but did not extend these breakdowns back to the earlier years covered by Mr. Creamer.

With these additions, therefore, we have eleven locations or location categories for industries:

> A—principal cities
> B—satellite cities
> C—industrial peripheries

29. *Op. cit.*, p. 55.

D—central counties
E—outer peripheries
F—industrial areas as a whole
G—other cities of 100,000 or more
H—peripheries of G cities
I—secondary industrial counties
J—areas of secondary concentration
K—rest of the country—all the rest

Table 5 gives the percentage distribution of wage jobs, manufacturing wage earners, or production workers in manufacturing for seven Censuses of Manufactures during the period 1899 to 1947. For the first five the results are Mr. Creamer's (with the very minor addition of the percentages for industrial areas and areas of secondary concentration as wholes) and for the last two, the work was done by URS.

Before taking up certain changes in these distributions and their possible meanings, we would point out that this forty-eight-year period might be divided into four sections:

1. Period 1 from 1899 to 1919. On the whole these were years of rapid industrial expansion. Ignoring differences in definitions and coverage of the censuses, the total number of production workers increased from roughly 4.7 million to 9.1 million—almost 94 per cent.

2. Period 2 from 1919 to 1933. Due to increased mechanization in many industries and the depression of the early 1930's, the number of production workers decreased from roughly 9.1 million to 6.0 million, or 34 per cent.

3. Period 3 from 1933 to 1939. This was the period of recovery in which the number of production workers went up from 6.0 million to 7.8 million—30 per cent.

4. Period 4 from 1939–47. This was the period of the astounding defense and war production expansion. Production workers in manufacturing increased by more than 52 per cent during these eight years—from 7.8 million to 11.9 million.

With Mr. Creamer we would also point out that in dealing with figures for cities over a substantial period of time some distortion occurs from changes in city boundaries. Like him, however, we are convinced that this distortion would be small for the percentages that we have calculated. Broadly speaking, the major annexations to important industrial cities mostly occurred before or very shortly after 1900. Of the annexations after that time, relatively few have affected substantial numbers of industries as measured by employment. Also concealed in the percentage distributions are the data for a very few cities whose totals could not be given by the Census because of the possibility of

TABLE 5

PERCENTAGE DISTRIBUTION AMONG TYPES OF LOCALITIES OF THE AGGREGATE OF PRODUCTION WORKERS IN MANUFACTURING IN THE UNITED STATES AND IN NINE REGIONS, 1899–1947*

(1929 Areas)

YEAR AND REGION	PRINCIPAL CITIES A	SATELLITE CITIES B	INDUSTRIAL PERIPHERIES C	CENTRAL COUNTIES OF INDUSTRIAL AREAS D	OUTER PERIPHERIES E	INDUSTRIAL AREAS AS A WHOLE F	OTHER CITIES OF 100,000 POP. G	PERIPHERIES OF G CITIES H	SECONDARY INDUSTRIAL COUNTIES I	AREAS OF SECONDARY CONCENTRATION (G+H+I) J	REST OF THE COUNTRY K
United States											
1947	32.2	2.4	19.8	42.2	9.9	54.4	7.1	1.9	8.7	17.7	27.9
1939	32.0	3.0	20.0	41.9	10.1	54.9	6.5	1.7	9.6	17.8	27.2
1933	33.1	2.6	18.7			54.4	6.7	1.6	10.3	18.6	27.0
1931	35.2	2.9	18.2			56.3	6.9	1.7	9.7	18.3	25.4
1929	35.1	2.9	18.2			56.2	6.9	1.6	9.3	17.8	26.0
1919	36.1	3.6	18.6			58.3	6.3	1.6	8.3	16.2	25.5
1899	39.5	3.7	14.6			57.8	5.9	1.1	8.4	15.4	26.8
New England											
1947	31.0	5.1	38.4	57.0	12.5	74.5			13.0	13.0	12.5
1939	30.0	5.1	38.2	54.8	13.3	73.2			14.1	14.1	12.7
1933	30.3	5.8	36.6			72.7			15.4	15.4	11.9
1931	31.3	6.1	36.1			73.5			14.5	14.5	12.0
1929	31.9	5.9	35.9			73.7			13.8	13.8	12.5
1919	31.5	6.4	35.4			73.3			13.8	13.8	12.9
1899	29.9	7.0	32.4			69.3			15.3	15.3	15.4
Middle Atlantic											
1947	41.6	5.7	27.4	49.7	19.3	74.8	2.7	1.8	8.2	12.7	12.5
1939	41.5	6.9	26.8	49.6	18.6	75.1	2.7	1.4	9.2	13.3	11.5
1933	43.4	6.6	24.2			74.2	2.6	1.2	10.6	14.4	11.4
1931	45.7	6.8	22.5			75.0	2.6	1.3	10.1	14.0	11.0
1929	44.2	7.2	23.9			75.3	2.9	1.4	9.2	13.5	11.2
1919	44.9	8.2	22.3			75.4	2.9	1.3	8.7	12.9	11.7
1899	52.0	7.0	16.2			75.2	2.7	.9	8.3	11.9	12.9
East No. Central											
1947	41.3	.9	19.0	51.1	9.1	61.1	6.4	1.6	8.5	16.5	22.5
1939	41.2	1.2	19.9	52.2	9.0	62.3	6.4	1.4	8.5	16.3	21.5
1933	43.2		18.0			61.2	6.7	1.4	8.3	16.4	22.4
1931	44.5		17.9			62.4	7.0	1.4	8.2	16.6	21.0
1929	45.8		16.8			62.6	6.8	1.4	8.7	16.9	20.5

TABLE 5 (*Continued*)

YEAR AND REGION	PRINCIPAL CITIES A	SATELLITE CITIES B	INDUSTRIAL PERIPHERIES C	CENTRAL COUNTIES OF INDUSTRIAL AREAS D	OUTER PERIPHERIES E	INDUSTRIAL AREAS AS A WHOLE F	OTHER CITIES OF 100,000 POP. G	PERIPHERIES OF G CITIES H	SECONDARY INDUSTRIAL COUNTIES I	AREAS OF SECONDARY CONCENTRATION (G+H+I) J	REST OF THE COUNTRY K
1919	45.9		17.4			63.3	6.2	1.2	7.4	14.8	21.9
1899	46.8		9.5			56.3	6.0	.8	7.9	14.7	29.0
West No. Central											
1947	42.9		4.6	45.6	2.0	47.6	7.3	1.5	2.3	11.1	41.4
1939	43.5		4.6	46.1	1.9	48.0	6.7	.6	2.2	9.5	42.5
1933	39.9		11.1			51.0	6.8	.5	1.0	8.3	40.7
1931	42.1		10.4			52.5	7.1	.7	1.2	9.0	38.5
1929	41.1		11.0			52.1	7.0	1.0	1.4	9.4	38.5
1919	39.7		10.1			49.8	7.8	1.5	.9	10.2	40.0
1899	43.3		6.2			49.5	5.0	2.6	.4	8.0	42.5
South Atlantic											
1947	7.3†		5.1	10.9	1.5	12.4	7.7	1.5†	15.9	25.1	62.5
1939	7.9†		5.5	11.5	1.8	13.3	7.7	1.4‡	17.7	26.8	59.9
1933	8.7		5.6			14.3	7.5	2.0	18.1	27.6	58.1
1931	10.1		5.4			15.5	8.8	2.1	16.7	27.6	56.9
1929	10.0		5.6			15.6	8.4	2.1	15.7	26.2	58.2
1919	12.8		5.8			18.6	10.2	2.9	11.5	24.6	56.8
1899	17.5		5.5			23.0	10.6	2.1	8.4	21.1	55.9
East So. Central											
1947			1.4§		1.4	1.4	27.8	7.9	2.5	38.2	60.5
1939			1.6§		1.6	1.6	27.8	8.7	2.5	39.0	59.4
1933							32.0	7.1	2.5	41.6	58.4
1931							33.0	8.6	2.2	43.8	56.2
1929							31.7	7.6	1.9	41.2	56.8
1919							28.6	8.0	1.5	38.1	61.9
1899							34.5	5.7	.8	41.0	59.0
West So. Central											
1947							30.7	6.6	8.3	45.6	54.4
1939							27.0	7.2	7.8	42.0	58.1
1933							28.0	6.6	9.5	44.1	55.9
1931							29.8	6.8	9.5	46.1	53.9
1929							27.1	5.0	9.1	41.2	58.8
1919							23.0	4.4	6.2	33.6	66.4
1899							29.4	.8	4.1	34.3	65.7

TABLE 5 (Continued)

YEAR AND REGION	PRINCIPAL CITIES A	SATELLITE CITIES B	INDUSTRIAL PERIPHERIES C	CENTRAL COUNTIES OF INDUSTRIAL AREAS D	OUTER PERIPHERIES E	INDUSTRIAL AREAS AS A WHOLE F	OTHER CITIES OF 100,000 POP. G	PERIPHERIES OF G CITIES H	SECONDARY INDUSTRIAL COUNTIES I	AREAS OF SECONDARY CONCENTRATION (G+H+I) J	REST OF THE COUNTRY K
Mountain											
1947							26.1	2.2	6.6	34.9	65.1
1939							21.9	3.2	7.4	32.5	67.5
1933							24.0	2.1	6.4	32.5	67.5
1931							24.1	2.0	6.4	32.5	67.5
1929							21.4	2.4	5.7	29.5	70.5
1919							21.1	2.5	6.0	29.6	70.4
1899							26.9	2.3	9.5	38.7	61.3
Pacific											
1947	34.5	.9	27.4	58.8	3.9	62.7‖	6.1	1.4	3.0	10.5	26.8
1939	35.7	.7	21.4	53.4	4.3	57.7‖	6.2	1.1	3.6	10.9	31.5
1933	39.8	.5	17.6			57.9	6.7	1.4	4.4	12.5	29.6
1931	39.4	1.2	16.1			56.7	6.9	1.4	3.7	12.0	31.3
1929	37.6	.5	16.2			54.3	6.5	1.3	4.6	12.4	33.3
1919	39.2	.9	13.8			53.9	8.0	1.2	4.0	13.2	32.9
1899	47.0		6.5			53.5	7.7	.7	2.3	10.7	35.8

* Figures through 1933 from Daniel B. Creamer, *Is Industry Decentralizing?* (Philadelphia: University of Pennsylvania Press, 1935), pp. 10–11.
A—Central cities of 1929 industrial areas.
B—Satellite Cities—cities with more than 100,000 population in 1929 in industrial areas.
C—Remainder of industrial areas—industrial areas as a whole, minus central and satellite cities.
D—Central counties of industrial areas—counties containing the central cities.
E—Outer peripheries—industrial areas minus the central counties and minus satellite cities outside of the central counties.
F—The industrial areas as a whole.
G—Other cities of more than 100,000 population in 1929.
H—Peripheries of G cities—the rest of their counties.
I—Secondary industrial counties—counties outside of industrial areas and without a city of 100,000 but *with* 10,000 wage earners or more in 1929.
J—Areas of secondary concentration—G + H + I.
K—All the rest.

The phrases "production workers," "wage earners in manufacturing," and "wage jobs in manufactures" have been used over the period. With some minor differences in definition they refer to the same kinds of employees. See page 145. Percentages given are based on averages for the years.

† Figures for the Central City of Wheeling, West Virginia, withheld by Census Bureau, but are included in the Central County (Ohio County) and Wheeling Industrial Area.
‡ Does not include figures for Henrico County, Virginia (Richmond's Periphery)—figures not available.
§ These figures are for Campbell and Kenton counties, Kentucky, which are parts of the Cincinnati industrial area. Cincinnati and the rest of its area are in the East North Central region. Mr. Creamer's tabulation did not show this inter-regional split. Possibly the volume of industry in these counties was so small before 1933 that he ignored it. It is possible also that the volume before 1933 was so small that Census rules against disclosure prevented the figures for these parts of the Cincinnati area from being published.
‖ This figure includes the production workers in Solano County, which is in the San Francisco standard metropolitan area, but which was not in the San Francisco industrial area. The total of production workers in Solano and Main Counties was 1,000 in 1947, and 995 in 1939. The industrial area had a total of 131,160 production workers in 1947, and 76,044 in 1939.

255

disclosing facts on individual plants. The data for these cities have been combined with their counties or peripheries. Because these cities are few and by definition relatively small, the effect of this treatment of them is quite insignificant in the percentage distributions.

The figures used for 1939 were the revised ones that were reported by the Census with the data for 1947. These revisions differed somewhat from the figures first reported for 1939. The revisions were made by the Census to make the data for 1939 more closely comparable to those for 1947.

Just one more preliminary explanation or warning before we take up Table 5: In comparing its percentage distributions for the United States as a whole and for the nine major divisions or regions, readers should not forget the fact that during the entire period covered by this table, industrial activity, however measured, was very unevenly distributed among the nine major regions. As a matter of fact, three or four of these regions had a very large proportion of the total production workers in manufacturing for the country as a whole. Thus, as Table 1 indicates, in 1899 the New England, Middle Atlantic, and East North Central states had 75.0 per cent of the production workers in manufacturing, and these three regions plus the South Atlantic states had 84.7 per cent of the national total. In 1939 the big three had 68.6 per cent of the total, and they plus the South Atlantic states had 81.1 per cent. (The proportions for 1939 are from the revised figures referred to above.)

What then are the salient facts from Table 5 for our purposes? What do these distributions show about industrial concentration and decentralization—both diffusion and dispersion—for this period of substantially half a century and for the four major subperiods mentioned above?

First, before looking at the subperiods, we suggest a look at the distributions for the United States for the years 1899 and 1947 to see if they indicate any significant changes or trends. We believe such an examination discloses five notable facts:

1. On the whole the broad pattern of industrial location has been quite stable. When one recalls that during these forty-eight years the number of production workers much more than doubled—approximately 4.7 million in 1899, and 11.9 million in 1947; that during this period new industries were born and grew to gigantic size while others were declining or disappearing altogether; that new processes, materials and sources of power have been developed; that consumers' tastes, habits, and standards of living have changed greatly: the similarity between the distributions in 1899 and 1947 is quite remarkable.

2. The three most inclusive groupings in the table are: (*a*) F—Industrial Areas as a Whole, (*b*) J—Areas of Secondary Concentration, and

(*c*) K—All the Rest of the Country. During this period the industrial areas declined relatively. They lost 3.4 percentage points. The areas of secondary concentration gained relatively. They picked up 2.3 percentage points. All the rest of the country also gained relatively, but only a very little. It increased its proportion by 1.1 percentage point.

3. The principal cities (A) of the thirty-three industrial areas—the major concentrations of industry in the country—declined relatively in production workers despite a very substantial absolute growth. In this distribution they lost 7.3 percentage points.

4. The industrial peripheries (C)—those parts of the industrial areas outside of the principal cities and the satellite cities of 100,000 or more—gained relatively both in the country as a whole and even more in their proportion of workers in the whole of the industrial areas. For the countrywide distribution they gained 5.2 percentage points. As a proportion of the workers in the industrial areas as a whole, they gained from 25.3 per cent in 1899 to 36.4 per cent in 1947. In our terms this is industrial diffusion. This redistribution was particularly strong in two major industrial regions, the Middle Atlantic and East North Central, and in one lesser one, the Pacific states.

5. The small relative increases in the areas of secondary concentration (J) and all the rest of the country (K) indicate a very slight degree of dispersion. In the South Atlantic states, the secondary industrial counties (I) and the rest of the country (K) both increased their proportions markedly. This region is the part of the country with the strongest trend toward dispersion over this period. In the West South Central Region, the areas of secondary concentration gained substantially but at the expense of all the rest. The gain was almost entirely in the peripheries of cities of 100,000 and over and in the secondary industrial counties. The larger cities themselves increased their proportion very slightly.

Period 1 (1899–1919).—Mr. Creamer made this summary:

It may be concluded from this statistical evidence that the latter phases of our expansion of industrial employment—1899 to 1919 for the nation but extending to 1929 for certain regions—resulted in both concentration and decentralization. There was greater concentration in the sense that a somewhat smaller proportion of wage jobs was located in the sparsely settled sections of the country, with the exception of the South Atlantic States. There was a degree of decentralization in the sense that a diminished share of the wage jobs was located in the principal cities of the industrial areas, with the exception of New England. The nature of the displacement, however, may be better characterized as a diffusion of wage jobs into the periphery or suburban areas and into the counties of moderate industrial concentration.[30]

30. *Ibid.*, p. 15. Four regions had their peaks of employment (before the defense and World War II years) in 1919: the New England, Middle Atlantic, West North Central, and Mountain states. The five who reached their corresponding peaks in 1929 were the East North Central, South Atlantic, East South Central, West South Central, and Pacific.

Among the regional distributions from 1899 to 1919, probably the most noticeable shifts were the substantial increases in the proportions of workers in the industrial peripheries (C) in the Middle Atlantic, East North Central, West North Central, and Pacific states. Industrial diffusion would seem to have started in the early years of this century in two heavily industrialized and two lesser industrialized regions. A lesser but still significant redistribution of the same kind occurred in another heavily industrialized region, New England.

Period 2.—During the period of contraction from 1919 to 1933, the principal cities continued to decline relatively. Their sharpest drop was in the two years from 1931 to 1933. The industrial peripheries held their own. The industrial areas as a whole, therefore, had the same pattern substantially as the principal cities. Secondary industrial counties, all areas of secondary concentration, and the rest of the country increased their proportions moderately. For the rest of the country the sharpest relative increase was in the last two years, 1931–33.

Here it should be remembered that these percentage distributions of production workers reflect not only changes in the distribution of plants, but also the proportions of their capacity that are utilized at the various periods. This is true, of course, both in periods of industrial expansion as well as those of contraction. In the latter, however, it seems possible that changes in distribution of workers may be affected more by differences in employment decreases in existing plants than by changes in the pattern of plant location.

Be that as it may, this fourteen-year period of contraction showed a continuing diffusion of industry within the major industrial areas. Although the proportion of all workers in the country in the industrial peripheries stayed about the same, the principal cities and the satellite cities declined relatively. Consequently the industrial peripheries had a larger percentage of the total employment in the industrial areas as a whole in 1933 (34.4 per cent) than they had in 1919 (31.9 per cent). Also during this period of contraction a slight dispersion in favor of the secondary industrial counties (I) and the rest of the country (K) took place. Here again the relative change was rather small and may reflect largely the possibility that industries located in these parts of the country suffered a little less from the over-all contraction of employment than those in the industrial areas and in the other cities of 100,000 and over and their peripheries.

Because Mr. Creamer's part of Table 5 ended with the figures for 1933, it seems appropriate to quote his general conclusion for the period covered by his analysis, 1899 to 1933:

To summarize for the entire period of thirty-four years. dispersion has occurred only in the South Atlantic region. where manufacturing establishments were already widely scattered. Only in the South Atlantic states was the per cent of wage jobs in the "All the rest" counties greater at the peak of regional employment than in 1899. At the same time in this region there was a diffusion into the counties of moderate industrial concentration. In the other seven regions, industrial displacement took the form of diffusion into the periphery areas and the important industrial counties. Such areas gained wage jobs chiefly at the expense of the principal and satellite cities of the industrial areas and, to a lesser extent, from the areas of dispersion, the "All the rest" category.[31]

Period 3.—During the industrial recovery from 1933 to 1939, the figures show that industrial diffusion within the industrial areas continued moderately. The proportion of workers in the principal cities declined moderately; the satellite cities and the industrial peripheries both gained relatively. As a result, the industrial areas as a whole increased very slightly. In the areas of dispersion—areas of secondary concentration (J) and all the rest (K)—no significant changes occurred. The areas of secondary concentration lost fractionally and all the rest gained an insignificant proportion. Industrial diffusion was still marked in the Middle Atlantic, East North Central, and Pacific states where it had shown up most prominently before. The South Atlantic states, in which dispersion had been most noticeable, showed little change during these six years. The proportion in the two major areas of dispersion (J and K combined) increased by only 1 percentage point.

Period 4.—For many persons, including ourselves, the distribution for 1947 has the most surprises. Although period 4, 1939 to 1947, includes substantially two years before the United States was actually at war and more than two years after the shooting war ended, industrial activity for this whole period was very heavily influenced by the war and its production program. The so-called defense period, during which this country began seriously to prepare for the possibility of war, started with the fall of France in June, 1940. Although from June 1940 to December 1941 the economy was not under the same degree of war direction and control as it was later, nevertheless, defense orders and production of war materials for other countries were important in industrial production. After the end of hostilities, many kinds of industrial production were strongly influenced by deferred needs and accumulated savings in the hands of individuals and industries from the high incomes of the war days.

Also, although private industrial construction boomed in 1946 and 1947—in estimated dollar volume of work put in place issued by the Department of Commerce, these were the two highest years on record through 1950—it is clear that a large proportion of the postwar industrial expansion is not reflected in the Census figures for production workers in 1947. Due largely to the premature lifting of controls on

31. Ibid., p. 21. Creamer here "deliberately disregarded" the Mountain region "because of its negligible industrial importance."

building, construction costs skyrocketed and shortages of materials and other difficulties increased greatly the length of time necessary to build and equip plants, and put them in operation. A plant not in operation, i.e., that did not have production workers actually employed and at work, did not enter into the 1947 Census figures on production workers. Quite probably, therefore, much of the high dollar volume of industrial construction in 1946 and practically all of the record volume in 1947 were not reflected in the Census figures for production workers in the latter year.

These facts should be kept in mind as we undertake the difficult task of trying to say what the comparable figures for 1939 and 1947 mean. Quite clearly the slow but previously rather steady movement toward industrial diffusion within the industrial areas was halted. The principal cities increased their proportion of production workers fractionally. Satellite cities and the industrial peripheries lost ground relatively and very slightly. For the industrial areas as a whole, the proportion went down by an insignificant amount. In the areas of secondary concentration, the proportion of workers was practically stabilized and all the rest of the country gained slightly. Only in the Pacific states did the trend toward industrial diffusion within industrial areas continue. In the South Atlantic region, the stronghold of dispersion, the areas of secondary concentration actually lost ground and all the rest gained moderately.

In short, during this eight-year period with its great increase in industrial employment, the distribution of production workers among the classes in Table 5 changed very little indeed. And this was the period during which, according to presumably well-informed observers, the industrial pattern of the country was being made over. Great plants in outlying parts of major industrial areas were widely commented upon. Certainly they were producing a sharp increase in industrial diffusion. Only less spectacular have been the coming of substantial industrial enterprises to small and medium-sized towns in the less industrialized regions of the country. Surely these had indicated a substantial degree of dispersion.

The figures for 1939 and 1947 contradict both of these widely held opinions. To be sure some of the more spectacular war production activities, e.g., shipyards in smaller coastal and some riverfront towns, were well deflated by 1947. Also, it is quite probable that during 1947 some of the mammoth plants in outlying parts of the major industrial areas were operating well below capacity and well below the number of workers that they had at the peak of war production. Nevertheless, it seems safe to say that very few, if any, observers of the industrial and urban scenes in this country during the war period would have

TABLE 6

PERCENTAGE DISTRIBUTION AMONG TYPES OF LOCALITIES OF PRODUCTION WORKERS IN MANUFACTURING IN 1939 AND OF THE INCREASE IN SUCH WORKERS, 1939–47*

(1929 Areas)

Year and Region	Principal Cities A	Satellite Cities B	Industrial Peripheries C	Central Counties of Industrial Areas D	Outer Peripheries E	Industrial Areas as a Whole F	Other Cities of 100,000 Pop. G	Peripheries of G Cities H	Secondary Industrial Counties I	Areas of Secondary Concentration (G + H + I) J	Rest of the Country K
United States											
1939..........	32.0	3.0	20.0	41.9	10.1	54.9	6.5	1.7	9.6	17.8	27.2
1939–47 increase.....	32.7	1.3	19.4	42.7	9.5	53.5	8.1	2.3	7.0	17.4	29.2
New England											
1939..........	30.0	5.1	38.2	54.8	13.3	73.2			14.1	14.1	12.7
1939–47 increase.....	34.3	5.1	39.3	63.8	9.8	78.8			9.5	9.5	11.7
Middle Atlantic											
1939.........	41.5	6.9	26.8	49.6	18.6	75.1	2.7	1.4	9.2	13.3	11.5
1939–47 increase......	42.1	3.0	28.8	49.9	21.0	74.0	2.8	2.5	6.1	11.4	14.7
East No. Central											
1939.........	41.2	1.2	19.9	52.2	9.0	62.3	6.4	1.4	8.5	16.3	21.5
1939–47 increase.......	41.3	.4	17.4	49.6	9.2	59.1	6.6	1.8	8.5	16.9	24.0
West No. Central											
1939..........	43.5		4.6	46.1	1.9	48.0	6.7	.6	2.2	9.5	42.5
1939–47 increase........	42.2		4.7	44.8	2.0	46.9	8.2	2.7	2.5	13.4	39.7
South Atlantic											
1939..........	7.9		5.5	11.5	1.8	13.3	7.7	1.4	17.7	26.8	59.9
1939–47 increase......	5.9		4.1	9.2	.8	10.0	7.6	1.6	11.2	20.4	69.6
East So. Central											
1939..........			1.6			1.6	27.8	8.7	2.5	39.0	59.4
1939–47			.9			.9	27.8	6.4	2.4	36.6	62.4
West So. Central											
1939							27.0	7.2	7.8	42.0	58.1
1939–47 increase......							35.6	5.8	8.9	50.3	49.6
Mountain											
1939.........							21.9	3.2	7.4	32.5	67.5
1939–47 increase......							32.0	.9	5.5	38.4	61.7
Pacific											
1939..........	35.7	.7	21.4	53.4	4.3	57.7	6.2	1.1	3.6	10.9	31.5
1939–47 increase.......	33.1	1.0	34.7	65.4	3.5	68.8	6.0	1.7	2.3	10.0	21.1

* For definitions see footnotes to Table 5, p. 255.

261

predicted the result shown by our figures for 1939 and 1947. We decided, therefore, to look rather more closely at this period.

Table 6 was one result of our further analysis. It gives for the United States and each of the nine regions the 1939 distribution that also appeared in Table 5. In addition, however, it shows the distribution of the 1939–47 *net increase* in production workers among the same classes of localities. We would emphasize that this second distribution is of the net increase only. It, therefore, is not a variant or part of the distributions existing in 1939 or of that in 1947; it is the difference between them.

In this table, clearly the most remarkable fact is the high similarity between the distribution of the wartime increase and the distribution of production workers at the beginning of this period. Of the net increase, the industrial areas received a smaller proportion than they had of the total number of production workers in 1939, but the difference was not very great. Areas of secondary concentration also received slightly less of the increase, but the difference there was insignificant. All the rest of the country (K) had 2 percentage points more of the increase than it had of the number of workers in 1939. This much more sensitive measure of what happened to industrial employment during the war years, the distribution of the net increase, simply strengthens the findings in Table 5.

URS' RECLASSIFICATION OF LOCALITIES

We next undertook another line of analysis. As we have pointed out earlier, we had taken the 1929 definitions of industrial areas, areas of secondary concentration and of their component parts in order to extend Mr. Creamer's useful analysis. Although this work seems well justified, it was possible, of course, that the 1929 areas had become rather out of date and, therefore, might be distorting or concealing certain significant changes in the distribution. Also, the 1947 Census of Manufactures had given up the old breakdowns by industrial areas and had adopted a new unit for the major areas of industrial concentration —standard metropolitan areas with 40,000 or more manufacturing employees. As far as we know this change had nothing whatever to do with the problem we had come upon, but a word of explanation on the change is necessary here.

For a few decades back, the Census of Population had presented figures for metropolitan districts. The definition of the metropolitan unit had varied considerably and this had hindered effective comparisons to measure what was actually happening to these important units of our economy and social life. Mr. Warren S. Thompson's monograph, which we have discussed briefly earlier in this chapter, deals competently and at some length with these changes in definition and the problems they have caused. Not only had the definitions of metropolitan districts changed, but they differed also from the definition of industrial areas used by the Census of Manufactures.

Late in World War II or immediately thereafter the Bureau of the Budget organized an Inter-Agency Committee on Standard Metropolitan Areas. Its purpose was to reach a generally satisfactory definition of metropolitan areas and to delineate the boundaries of these areas in accordance with the definition. Thus agencies of the federal government that collected, analyzed, and presented urban data would have a common definition of the important metropolitan unit. Clearly this would add greatly to the effectiveness of many kinds of statistical materials. The Inter-Agency Committee was successful in reaching a definition and at the time that the 1947 Census of Manufactures was being tabulated, eighty-seven standard metropolitan areas had been marked out. (Since then, the job of delineating the areas has been completed and there are 168 standard metropolitan areas in the continental United States.)

As its areas of major industrial concentration, therefore, the Census of Manufactures gave up the old industrial areas and in their place presented data on standard metropolitan areas with 40,000 or more manufacturing employees. The minimum number of employees (40,-000) was the same as for the old industrial areas. The SMA's, however, are on the whole broader districts than the old industrial areas. Except in New England, they are counties or combinations of counties. In New England townships are the component units. In 1947 there were fifty-three standard metropolitan areas with 40,000 or more manufacturing employees.

As the 1947 data for these newly defined areas became available, we distributed the production workers in manufacturing according to the new definition. The new classes A–E were the same for these SMA's as they had been for the old industrial areas except satellite cities (B) for which we used the 1940 population figures to determine localities of 100,000 population and more. Similarly the areas of secondary concentration (G, H, and I) were redefined according to 1940 population and 1947 figures for production workers.

With the 1947 figures, the Census of Manufactures also published comparable data on production workers for 1939. This enabled us to prepare Table 7, which is an eleven-class distribution of production workers for 1939 and 1947 based on the same rationale as Creamer's old breakdown as we had modified it. We already have indicated the changes from the 1929 to the 1947 areas, but to recapitulate: In Table 7 we used the standard metropolitan areas with 40,000 or more manu-

TABLE 7

PERCENTAGE DISTRIBUTION AMONG TYPES OF LOCALITIES OF PRODUCTION WORKERS IN MANUFACTURING IN THE UNITED STATES AND IN NINE REGIONS—1939 AND 1947*

(1947 Areas)

REGION	CENTRAL CITIES A	SATELLITE CITIES B	METRO-POLITAN PERIPH-ERIES C	CENTRAL COUNTIES OF SMA'S D	OUTER PERIPH-ERIES E	SMA'S AS A WHOLE F	OTHER CITIES OF 100,000 POPU-LATION G	PERIPH-ERIES OF G CITIES H	SEC-ONDARY INDUS-TRIAL COUNTIES I	AREAS OF SECONDARY CONCEN-TRATION (G+H+I) J	REST OF THE COUNTRY K
United States											
1947	36.1	2.1	20.0	46.3	9.9	58.2	3.5	.7	11.5	15.7	26.2
1939	35.7	2.6	19.3	45.4	9.6	57.6	3.2	.7	11.9	15.8	26.7
New England											
1947	32.6†	2.2	23.9	48.2	8.3	58.8	1.3	§	10.4	11.7	29.6
1939	31.4†	2.3	20.6	44.2	7.8	54.2‡	1.5	§	11.4	12.9	32.9
Middle Atlantic											
1947	44.2‖	5.7	30.7	53.7	21.3	80.6	.4	.2	9.2	9.8	9.5
1939	44.0‖	6.9	29.5	53.6	19.9	80.4	.4	.2	9.5	10.1	9.5
East No. Central											
1947	46.4	.9	19.1	57.9	7.6	66.4	.7	.2	14.4	15.3	18.4
1939	46.4	1.2	19.8	59.0	7.2	67.4	.5	.1	13.9	14.5	18.1
West No. Central											
1947	42.9		5.2	45.6	2.6	48.2	7.3	1.5	4.0	12.8	39.1
1939	43.5		5.1	46.1	2.5	48.6	6.7	.6	3.5	10.8	40.6
South Atlantic											
1947	9.5#		6.4	13.5	2.4	15.9	6.3	1.4**	23.3	31.0	53.1
1939	10.0#		6.7	14.0	2.7	16.7	6.5	1.3	24.8	32.6	50.7
East So. Central											
1947	12.1		7.0	17.8	1.4	19.2	15.7	2.2	8.0	25.9	55.0
1939	11.6		6.8	16.8	1.6	18.4	16.2	3.5	7.3	27.0	54.5
West So. Central											
1947	13.2		5.2	16.5	2.0	18.4	16.6	3.4	6.8	26.8	54.9
1939	13.5		5.1	16.3	2.3	18.6	12.7	4.0	6.0	22.7	58.7
Mountain											
1947							26.1	2.2		28.3	71.6
1939							21.9	3.2		25.1	75.0
Pacific											
1947	36.6	.9	29.6	61.0	6.0	67.1	4.6	1.5	2.1	8.2	24.7
1939	37.4	.7	23.2	54.9	6.4	61.3	5.3	1.6	2.3	9.2	29.5

264

TABLE 7 (Continued)

* The figures in Tables 7 and 8 are based on a different breakdown of localities than those in Tables 5 and 6. After World War II a number of agencies of the federal government, under the leadership of the Bureau of the Budget, defined 168 *standard metropolitan areas* for the continental U.S. These differ from the earlier *metropolitan districts*. Fifty-three of the largest standard metropolitan areas, i.e., those with 40,000 or more manufacturing employees in 1947, were used in reporting the 1947 Census of Manufactures. These large standard metropolitan areas differ considerably from the 33 *industrial areas* used in earlier Censuses of Manufactures. To quote from section 16 of the *General Explanations of the Census of Manufactures for 1947*, I, p. 13:

". . . Industrial areas, as defined in previous years, were groups of contiguous counties having large numbers of manufacturing wage earners. The standard metropolitan areas, on the other hand, are integrated economic and social entities which contain not only highly industrialized counties but also adjoining counties which, though primarily residential in character, contribute significantly to the industrial counties' labor force."

The Census' new definition of industrial areas, i.e., "standard metropolitan areas having 40,000 or more manufacturing employees" is shortened to SMA.

Except in New England all SMA's are counties or combinations of counties. In New England they are made up of towns.

Each of the three volumes of the Census of Manufactures for 1947 contains a definition and explanation of SMA's and a list of the SMA's with 40,000 or more manufacturing employees.

In Tables 7 and 8, the figures for standard metropolitan areas are compared for the years 1939 and 1947. The other types of localities are based on or derived from either the 1940 Census of Population or the 1947 Census of Manufactures.

A—Central cities of 1947 SMA's.

B—Satellite Cities—cities with more than 100,000 population in 1940 in SMA's.

C—Remainder of SMA's—SMA's as a whole minus central and satellite cities.

D—Central counties of SMA's—the counties containing the central cities. In New England, Central County = SMA, except in the Boston SMA.

E—Outer peripheries—SMA's as a whole minus the central counties and minus satellite cities that are outside of the central counties.

F—SMA's as a whole.

G—Other cities of more than 100,000 population in 1940.

H—Peripheries of G cities (the rest of their counties).

I—Secondary industrial counties—counties outside of SMA's and without a city of 100,000 (1940 census) but *with* 10,000 or more manufacturing wage earners in 1947.

J—Areas of secondary concentration—G + H + I.

K—All the rest of the country—not in classes A–J.

† Does not include figures for Bristol, Connecticut.

‡ Does not include a small number of workers, who in 1939 worked in the Springfield—Holyoke and Fall River—New Bedford SMA's and for whom figures are not available, as a consequence of SMA's overlapping state boundaries.

§ Middlesex County workers, by definition, belong in this category. However, part of Middlesex County is contained in the Boston SMA. To avoid double enumeration, those Middlesex County workers not included in the Boston SMA tabulations show up in Column K.

‖ Does not include figures for Rome, New York, nor Easton, Pennsylvania.

¶ Does not include figures for Wheeling, West Virginia, nor Steubenville, Ohio.

** Does not include Henrico County, Virginia.

facturing employees instead of the old industrial areas. We also used 1940 population figures for classes B and G as well as 1947 data on production workers for class I.

The net results of this reclassification of localities may be seen from a comparison of the distributions for 1939 and 1947 in Table 5 with Table 7, which covers the same years. On the whole, the changes were not very great. The new classification did increase somewhat the proportion of workers in the central cities of the major industrial concentrations as well as the proportion for those concentrations as a whole. Undoubtedly, however, the increases were not as great as some readers would have thought likely from the increase from thirty-three to fifty-three localities in this class. The moderate size of these changes is explained, of course, by the fact that a very substantial proportion of the industrial employment of the country is in a relatively few very large centers. The amount in some twenty localities that rank near the bottom of this class in size is not a large proportion of the national total.

This gain in the proportion of workers in the major areas of concentration due to the new definitions, results in small decreases in the proportions in the areas of secondary concentration (J) and all the rest of the country (K). Within the three component parts of the areas of secondary concentration, other cities of 100,000 and more (G) lost the most because a substantial number of the cities that had been in this class went over into the SMA classes. On the other hand, the secondary industrial counties gained noticeably by the new definition because the qualifying minimum of 10,000 industrial employees in the new definition was as of 1947 instead of 1929. These are all understandable shifts from the reclassification of localities and, as we have suggested before, they may have resulted in smaller changes in the percentage distributions than some readers would have anticipated.

Coming back now to the question of what happened to the distribution of industrial employees during the war period, the specific question is: Does the new distribution of Table 7 with the 1947 areas throw additional light on this war period? In general, the answer is *no*. To be sure, there are slight differences in the directions of movement. Thus the metropolitan peripheries in Table 7 showed a very slight gain from 1939 to 1947, while their counterparts in Table 5, the industrial peripheries, showed an even smaller relative loss. Similarly, the old industrial areas lost relatively from 1939 to 1947 and the SMA's as a whole gained slightly—but again, the differences are not great. In both breakdowns the areas of secondary concentration lost .1 percentage point from 1939 to 1947. The proportions for all the rest of the country differed between the two breakdowns. For the old areas in Table 5, the

TABLE 8

PERCENTAGE DISTRIBUTION AMONG TYPES OF LOCALITIES OF PRODUCTION WORKERS IN MANUFACTURING IN 1939 AND OF THE INCREASE IN SUCH WORKERS, 1939–47*

(1947 Areas)

YEAR AND REGION	CENTRAL CITIES A	SATELLITE CITIES B	METROPOLITAN PERIPHERIES C	CENTRAL COUNTIES OF SMA'S D	OUTER PERIPHERIES E	SMA'S AS A WHOLE F	OTHER CITIES OF 100,000 POP. G	PERIPHERIES OF G CITIES H	SECONDARY INDUSTRIAL COUNTIES I	AREAS OF SECONDARY CONCENTRATION (G+H+I) J	REST OF THE COUNTRY K
United States											
1939.................	35.7	2.6	19.3	45.4	9.6	57.6	3.2	0.7	11.9	15.8	26.7
1939–47 increase.......	36.9	1.1	21.3	47.9	10.4	59.3	4.0	0.7	10.7	15.4	25.2
New England											
1939.................	31.4	2.3	20.6	44.2	7.8	54.2	1.5		11.4	12.9	32.9
1939–47 increase.......	36.6	2.0	34.4	61.0	9.8	72.9	.8		7.3	8.1	19.0
Middle Atlantic											
1939.................	44.0	6.9	29.5	53.6	19.9	80.4	0.4	0.2	9.5	10.1	9.5
1939–47 increase.......	44.7	3.0	33.3	53.8	24.2	81.0	0.5	0.4	8.5	9.4	9.6
East No. Central											
1939.................	46.4	1.2	19.8	59.0	7.2	67.4	0.5	0.1	13.9	14.5	18.1
1939–47 increase.......	46.4	0.4	18.0	56.1	8.4	64.8	0.9	0.2	15.2	16.3	18.8
West No. Central											
1939.................	43.5		5.1	46.1	2.5	48.6	6.7	0.6	3.5	10.8	40.6
1939–47 increase.......	42.2		5.4	44.8	2.8	47.6	8.2	2.7	4.6	15.5	36.9
South Atlantic											
1939.................	10.0		6.7	14.0	2.7	16.7	6.5	1.3	24.8	32.6	50.7
1939–47 increase.......	8.3		5.5	12.1	1.8	13.9	5.9	1.5	19.2	26.6	59.6
East So. Central											
1939.................	11.6		6.8	16.8	1.6	18.4	16.2	3.5	7.3	27.0	54.5
1939–47 increase.......	13.0		7.4	19.5	0.9	20.4	14.9	(−0.1)	9.1	23.9	55.8
West So. Central											
1939.................	13.5		5.1	16.3	2.3	18.6	12.7	4.0	6.0	22.7	58.7
1939–47 increase.......	12.8		5.4	16.7	1.5	18.2	21.7	2.5	7.8	32.0	49.8
Mountain											
1939.................							21.9	3.2		25.1	75.0
1939–47 increase.......							32.0	0.9		32.9	67.1
Pacific											
1939.................	37.4	0.7	23.2	54.9	6.4	61.3	5.3	1.6	2.3	9.2	29.5
1939–47 increase.......	35.7	1.0	37.4	68.6	5.6	74.1	3.7	1.4	1.9	7.0	18.9

* For definitions see footnotes to Table 7, p. 265

267

TABLE 9

Increases in Production Workers in Manufacturing, 1939–47, as Percentages of Number of Production Workers in 1939 for the United States and Nine Regions by Types of Localities*

(1947 Areas)

Region	Central Cities	Satellite Cities	Metropolitan Peripheries	Central Counties of SMA's	Outer Peripheries	SMA's as a Whole	Other Cities of 100,000 Pop.	Peripheries of G Cities	Secondary Industrial Counties	Areas of Secondary Concentration (G+H+I)	Rest of the Country	Total
	A	B	C	D	E	F	G	H	I	J	K	L
United States....	54.5	22.3	58.2	55.6	57.1	54.3	66.0	57.1	47.4	51.6	49.8	52.6
New England.....	37.0	27.8	53.1	43.8	40.7	42.7	16.4		20.4	19.9	18.3	31.8
Middle Atlantic..	45.9	19.9	51.1	45.4	54.9	45.6	61.7	123.5	40.3	42.4	45.6	45.3
East No. Central.	63.5	21.0	57.8	60.3	74.0	61.1	115.1	104.5	69.5	71.4	65.9	63.5
West No. Central.	67.0		73.2	67.1	77.9	67.7	84.5	292.5	90.2	98.4	62.8	69.1
South Atlantic...	31.5		30.8	32.4	24.8	31.2	33.8	45.2	29.1	30.6	44.2	37.6
East So. Central..	63.8		62.5	66.2	33.1	63.3	52.5	(-1.7)	71.0	50.4	58.5	57.2
West So. Central..	72.0		81.2	77.9	49.7	74.5	130.0	47.7	98.7	107.3	64.7	76.2
Mountain.........							107.3	21.2		96.3	65.7	73.3
Pacific..........	77.7	123.9	131.2	101.8	70.3	98.5	56.9	69.1	67.8	61.7	52.2	81.5

* For definitions see footnote to Table 7.

K class gained slightly. In the new breakdown it lost slightly, but the amounts are insignificant.

To follow through on the new or 1947 areas, we prepared Table 8, which distributes production workers in 1939 and the net increase from 1939 to 1947 by the newly defined classes just as Table 6 did for the old breakdown. Here again some differences are noticeable and some of them are in the direction of the trends we had identified for the years ending in 1939. For example, metropolitan peripheries obtained a somewhat larger proportion of the net increase than they had of the total of production workers in 1939. On the whole, however, this table, like Table 7, brings out no new facts or relationships that help very much in explaining the differences between the findings for the war period in Tables 5 and 6 and the expectations and predictions of more or less well-informed observers.

Table 9, which gives the 1939–47 percentage rates of increase in production workers by locality classes for the United States and the nine major regions, simply substantiates what we have said about the facts in Table 8. Although these rates of increase are sensitive indicators of changes in distribution, they do not help us much here. In Table 9 the most useful comparisons are between rates of increase for the locality classes in each area and those for each of the areas as a whole. Thus, for the United States the number of production workers increased 52.6 per cent from 1939 to 1947. The rate for central cities, 54.5 per cent, shows that these areas of concentration gained more rapidly than the country as a whole. Note also that the outlying parts of metropolitan areas except the satellite cities gained even more rapidly than the principal cities—an indication of some slight diffusion.

The conclusion seems to us clear: The net effect of the war years on the distribution of production workers in manufacturing was very slight. It did not speed up the slow but rather continuous diffusion within major industrial areas nor strengthen the weaker and more sporadic indications of dispersion to areas outside of the major concentrations. Quite probably the explanation of the difference between the facts and the expectations lies in the difference between the spectacular, easily seen plant in a peripheral area or small town and the forms of industrial expansion that do not show up readily and, in fact, often seem to be swallowed up in the huge industrial areas of great cities.

What about the World War II Record?

Although this discussion of facts versus expectations seems to us appropriate here, this issue is not the primary one for our purposes.

From the facts as we have been able to discover and present them, what are the meanings for urban planners and redevelopers? Should they conclude that the war years stopped or reversed the tendency toward industrial diffusion and proved that the lesser evidences of dispersion were largely misleading? We think not. Neither do we suggest that the opposite of these possible conclusions is justified by the evidence. Before putting down our judgment or interpretation of these facts, it seems necessary to examine them and the period to which they apply rather more thoroughly than we have so far.

First, we would emphasize the well-known fact that during most of this period the industrial economy of the country, whatever label may now be put on it for those years, was in fact largely directed and controlled by the federal government. In the interests of military power the government had a major voice in determining what was to be produced and where. It had a variety of means and methods at its disposal —military orders and contracts, aids and inducements to private industry such as accelerated depreciation for tax purposes, loans, and guaranteed loans, as well as controls and limitations on nonessential production. The Department of Commerce's estimates of the dollar volume of construction work put in place for the years 1940 through 1945, inclusive, show that public industrial construction was about three and one-half times the amount of private industrial construction.[32] By and large, the industries that were pushed hardest in volume and activity were those that in peacetime produce capital and durable goods. Also speaking generally, those that were held back during the war were those that normally produced semidurable and nondurable consumer goods.

These are well-known facts, but in considering the distribution of production workers during the war period, they have a special pertinence. Although we ought to have more facts than we do on trends in the location of plants in these major categories of industry, we do have some evidence that probably the semidurable and nondurable goods industries were among those with the strongest tendencies toward dispersion in the years before World War II. Exceptions undoubtedly could be noted but on the whole this generalization is probably justified. To the degree that it may be, it would explain in part the practical stoppage of movements toward dispersion of industry during the war period. This possible explanation, however, probably would not apply to diffusion within major industrial areas.

32. *Op. cit.*, footnote 6, chap. iv. For the six years 1940 through 1945 the estimated volume of new private industrial construction was $2,595 million and for public industrial construction, $8,736 million.

Also, the 1939–47 increase in production workers was largely the result of five developments in industry during these years:

1. A very substantial proportion of the industrial plant of the country was being used at a much higher percentage of capacity in 1947 than in 1939. Heavy orders meant more workers, sometimes in extra shifts. For example, the steel industry was reported to be at 64.5 per cent of capacity in 1939 and at 93.0 per cent in 1947.[33]

To the degree that the increase in production workers came from a fuller use of plant capacity existing in 1939, its distribution among the classes of localities was determined by the prewar pattern of industrial location.

2. Part of the increase in workers undoubtedly came from extensions of existing plants, including absorption of space in other industrial structures and, to a limited extent, in buildings originally built for other uses. Here again the influence on the distribution of workers would be in the direction of the 1939 pattern rather than toward any substantial changes.

3. Conversely, due to wartime pressures and dislocations caused largely by the postwar inflation, some industries reduced operations or closed entirely. Quite probably most of these were smaller enterprises located in the prewar pattern. Most of the workers so thrown out of work were absorbed more or less rapidly by other industries.

4. An undetermined part of the increase was due to plants built and put into operation during the period. It should be stressed, however, that most of these plants were put up in times of tightening labor supply and their managements were under heavy pressures to get into volume production as fast as possible. In these circumstances, quite probably many of these factories were built in highly industrialized areas partly to tap their labor supplies in the form of previously unemployed men, retired workers, women, and young people in workers' families.

5. Finally, there probably were some actual moves—plants that closed down in one location and opened in another. Quite surely, however, the volume of these was relatively small and probably had a

---

33. *Survey of Current Business—1949 Statistical Supplement* (Washington, D.C.: Government Printing Office, 1949), p. 158. More precisely, the percentages given above were the monthly averages for 1939 and 1947 of estimated capacity for steel ingots and steel for castings. The average monthly production in 1939 was 4,400,000 short tons and in 1947—7,074,000 tons. Thus the estimated capacity in 1947 was about 12.6 per cent above that for 1939 but the actual production was about 60.8 per cent higher. The difference between these proportions is attributable to more intensive use. In steel, this would make some little difference in number of production workers. In some other types of industry a smaller differential in percentage of capacity utilized would provide relatively for a larger increase in production workers.

negligible effect upon the distribution of the increase during this period.

All of these factors were at work in determining the distribution of the 1939–47 increase in number of production workers in manufacturing. The significance for us of the similarity between that distribution and the distribution of production workers in 1939 depends very largely on the relative importance of these factors. To illustrate this let us take two simple hypothetical cases.

Suppose first that nearly all of the increase came from more intensive utilization of the industrial plants in existence in 1939. Clearly this would explain quite adequately most of the similarity between the distribution of the increase and that of production workers in 1939. Also it is clear that the distribution of an increase produced in this way would mean little to urban planners and redevelopers for the future unless, of course, there were still many under-utilized plants. More likely, if a more than 50 per cent increase of production workers had come almost entirely from more intensive use of existing plants, the future increase would depend largely upon new units. The main point is that under this assumption the distribution of the 1939–47 increase is of slight value in trying to estimate where any future increase would be located.

Or we could assume that all or nearly all of the 1939–47 increase came from plants built and put into operation during this period. Under this assumption the similarities between the distributions of the increase and of workers in 1939 would indicate that, unless some of the factors determining the recent location of the new plants should change substantially, we could expect about the same pattern for the next few years at least.

As a matter of fact, we have no means of knowing the relative importance of these five factors that contributed to the distribution of 1939–47 increase. It seems very likely that the two factors we selected for our hypothetical illustration—more intensive use of existing plants and new industrial construction—were more important than the other three. In our opinion, the first of these probably was the more influential of the two. Our evidence for this view is admittedly inadequate. It is, however, in two parts. The first is that in any period of a few years, even if they be years of active industrial construction, the addition to the total industrial plant of the nation will not be a large proportion of the total industrial plant in existence at the beginning of the period. Second, an unknown but probably fairly substantial part of all the new industrial plants built during the war years was operating at much less than its full capacity in 1947. It, therefore, did not affect the 1947 Census figures as much as it would have influenced figures, say, for

1944 or 1945 or even as much as it may affect the data on production workers in later censuses.[34]

Some of this analysis and discussion may seem to be rather lengthy and at some distance from the main point. From it, however, we draw two general conclusions as to the most likely meaning of the distribution of the 1939–47 increase in production workers for the pattern of industrial location in the future:

1. The increase during this period was so heavily influenced by war conditions and measures that it cannot be given much weight in estimating future tendencies or trends. The current (1951) mobilization and rearmament program is based on the principle that in another year or two we will have the industrial capacity for both guns and butter— i.e., capacity to keep our military strength at a high point and also to produce the goods needed for a civilian economy with high standards of consumption. If this be realized, it would seem wiser to take the pre-World War II facts and trends in industrial location (as modified, of course, by more recent events and developments) as rough indicators of the future pattern for civilian industry rather than the distribution so strongly influenced by the requirements and conditions of World War II.

2. If it be agreed that probably the distribution of the 1939–47 increase in workers was determined in considerable degree by more intensive utilization of prewar industrial plants, this, too, would suggest that this distribution was of little value in estimating future trends and tendencies. Again, therefore, we would conclude that the pre-War II facts and trends, including the moderate industrial diffusion and the

34. Because the argument of this and the immediately preceding paragraphs largely has determined our conclusions on the significance for urban planners and redevelopers of the 1939–47 distributions of production workers, we would refer the skeptical reader to the section on "War and Postwar Expansion" in chap. iii. True, we cited there McLaughlin's estimate that the cost of war-motivated industrial expansion was equal to about one-third of the value of the 1940 industrial plant of the country. This would seem, at first glance, to contradict part of our contention in the paragraph above. If, however, some allowance were made for the somewhat higher construction costs during the war, the size of this estimated increase would drop somewhat—to a percentage closer to one-fourth. Also, as we pointed out in this same section, about 80 per cent of the dollar volume of industrial construction for the five years 1940 through 1944 was in public construction—much of it in plant for aircraft, explosives, ammunition and shipbuilding. Certainly many of these war plants were not being used at or near full capacity in 1947 and, therefore, did not influence the 1947 Census data on production workers to a degree commensurate with their construction cost. As a matter of fact, many of them were closed down in 1947. According to Department of Labor estimates, the total of production workers in manufacturing in 1947 was down 11.5 per cent from the wartime peak. The number of production workers enumerated by the Census of Manufactures for 1947 was 17.5 per cent below the Department of Labor's estimated peak for the war years. (The Labor estimates are given in the 1949 Statistical Supplement, *Survey of Current Business*, p. 55.)

indications of dispersion in some regions, are better guides to probabilities for the future than the wartime experience.

In indicating that the pre-War II trends seem more reliable as indicators of future patterns than the wartime distribution, we hope two things are clear. The first is that the pre-War II period was one of slow and not-too-marked trends. The second is that we do not suggest any blind projection of these or other tendencies or trends into the future. Underlying conditions and factors change. For example, the prewar pattern of industrial location was almost entirely innocent of any influence from the prospects of air attack. Although no one can say with any assurance how influential this factor may be today or in the immediate future, it is entirely conceivable that it might become of considerable importance. Also, the 1950 Census of Population indicates an increase in the decentralization of urban populations. What effects, if any, will it have on the future industrial pattern? Again, traffic congestion, particularly of trucks and passenger cars, seems measurably worse in most American cities since War II than it had been for many years before. Has it or will it become so serious that it will have enough effect on industrial costs and the inconvenience of workers to become a significant factor in industrial diffusion or even dispersion? Studies to identify such forces and to measure their relative strengths, their increase or decline would be much more sensible and useful than to project prewar lines on a chart.

This analysis of the distribution of production workers in 1939 and 1947 and of the increase between these two years is the major part of our small contribution toward an answer for the question: *Are industries decentralizing?* Although this work has seemed to us worth doing, particularly because much of it ties onto Mr. Creamer's more ambitious project, as a guide to urban planners and redevelopers in the early 1950's it clearly has two major weaknesses. Although we have discussed both, we would put them down again for emphasis. Our data cover very little of the post-World War II period—a period of substantial industrial expansion of special significance for the immediate future of cities in this country. Also, as we have just pointed out, it is very difficult to say what the facts revealed for 1939 and 1947 mean to urban structure and planning. At best the findings are inconclusive and interpretations or meanings have to be hedged about with many qualifications.

THE TID-ENR DATA

At about this point in our work, we took up again another set of data that we had considered rather casually before. These were the *Engineering News-Record* reports on industrial construction contracts let.

The Territorial Information Department of the four major utility companies in Chicago and Northern Illinois, which we have referred to earlier, had taken off the data for all contracts of $100,000 and more. This dollar minimum had been used to screen out most relatively minor extensions or additions to existing plants. At the time we were completing our work on the statistics from the Census of Manufactures, the TID had the *Engineering News-Record* data for four years, from July 1, 1945, through June 30, 1949. Although the Department had used these materials for its own purposes and had run off a few totals by various breakdowns, it had not made any systematic analysis of them. It kindly offered them to URS for such study as we might wish to make of them.

At first we hesitated to undertake an analysis of these data. Their unit of measurement was different from the one that Mr. Creamer and URS had used in the work just described. For our purposes, dollar volume of industrial construction was a less satisfactory unit than production workers in manufacturing. Also, the TID-ENR data were for one relatively short period and, therefore, did not make possible any significant comparisons or measurements of changes in distributions. Further, the ENR's reports, although capably and conscientiously compiled, were known not to be a complete coverage of all industrial construction. For the four years from mid-1945 to mid-1949 the total volume of contracts reported above $100,000 was approximately $2.3 billion. For the same period the Department of Commerce estimates of the dollar volume of work put in place in private industrial construction totalled more than $5.5 billion. Although, again, dollar volumes of contracts let and work put in place are not directly comparable units, a difference of this magnitude substantiated the fact that the ENR reports are not a complete coverage. If properly distributed among industries and areas the TID-ENR data were more than large enough for a sample, but how could we know whether they were properly distributed?

Should we go ahead with an analysis of the TID-ENR data? We finally decided to do so. Our chief reasons were three: (1) Although breakdowns of these data would not be directly comparable with those for production workers, they might possibly throw some indirect light on some of the inconclusive findings from our work on the Census figures. (2) We might establish a base point for dollar volume data that would have some value for later investigators somewhat as Mr. Creamer's study had done for our work. (3) Some statistically rather crude breakdowns of these data had already found their way into print. They suggested a very substantial degree of decentralization of postwar industrial construction. Possibly our more detailed breakdown, adapted

TABLE 10

PERCENTAGE DISTRIBUTION AMONG TYPES OF LOCALITIES OF THE DOLLAR VOLUME OF INDUSTRIAL CONSTRUCTION CONTRACTS JULY 1, 1945, THROUGH JUNE 30, 1949, FOR THE UNITED STATES AND NINE REGIONS*

(1947 Areas)

REGION	CENTRAL CITIES	SATELLITE CITIES	METROPOLITAN PERIPHERIES	CENTRAL COUNTIES OF SMA's	OUTER PERIPHERIES	SMA's AS A WHOLE	OTHER CITIES OF 100,000 POP.	PERIPHERIES OF G CITIES	SECONDARY INDUSTRIAL COUNTIES	AREAS OF SECONDARY CONCENTRATION (G+H+I)	REST OF THE COUNTRY
	A	B	C	D	E	F	G	H	I	J	K
United States	24.6	2.0	20.9	35.8	10.3	47.5	8.3	1.1	7.5	16.9	35.6
New England	36.2	6.7	32.2	52.6	15.8	75.1			2.4	2.4	22.5
Middle Atlantic	29.6	6.9	52.6	41.5	40.7	89.1	1.0	.3	4.9	6.2	4.7
East No. Central	40.4	1.1	26.5	57.9	9.0	68.0	2.0		13.6	15.6	16.4
West No. Central	40.0		14.1	53.3	.8	54.1	5.4		3.9	9.3	36.6
South Atlantic	9.3		6.8	10.6		16.1	22.7	.3	5.7	28.7	55.3
East So. Central	6.3			6.3	5.5	6.3	19.5	.2	8.0	27.7	66.0
West So. Central	18.8		6.2	25.0		25.0	7.9	.7	8.2	16.8	58.1
Mountain							20.3	26.0		46.3	53.7
Pacific	19.3	5.3	32.8	44.5	13.0	57.5	8.4	1.7	3.6	13.7	28.8

* Data are the dollar volume of industrial construction contracts let (for amounts of $100,000 and more) as reported by the *Engineering News-Record* and compiled by the Territorial Information Department.
  For explanation of the locality breakdown see footnotes to Table 7.

from Mr. Creamer's, might be more useful and even might help to prevent hasty or partial interpretations that otherwise would be made.

We, therefore, prepared Table 10, which is a distribution of the aggregate dollar volume of private industrial construction contracts reported by the *Engineering News-Record* and compiled by the Territorial Information Department. The breakdown is the same as that for Table 7, i.e., by types of localities with the major areas of industrial concentration the standard metropolitan areas with 40,000 or more manufacturing employees and the city populations from the 1940 Census of Population.

A quick comparison of localities A, F, J, and K for the United States in Tables 7 and 10 shows very marked differences. The proportion of the dollar volume of industrial construction contracts in the fifty-three central cities (A) is 11.5 percentage points less than the corresponding proportion of production workers in 1947. For the industrially important standard metropolitan areas (F) the proportion of dollar volume is 10.7 percentage points lower than that for production workers. For the areas of secondary concentration (J), the proportion of dollar volume of contracts is 1.2 percentage points higher than the proportion of production workers in 1947. Finally, for all the rest of the country (K), the proportion of dollar volume is 9.4 percentage points above that for production workers.

It is interesting to note, however, that, although on the whole the dollar volume of industrial construction contracts was distributed less in the major industrial centers, slightly more heavily in the areas of secondary concentration, and much more heavily in the rest of the country, the proportion in the metropolitan peripheries was about the same as for production workers in 1947. Actually the dollar volume in the metropolitan peripheries was .9 of a percentage point above the proportion of production workers in 1947.

Although these comparisons are bound to be made and we have thought it well, therefore, to mention them here, we do wish to emphasize that no real significance can be attached to these or other differences between the two distributions. The difference in the units alone invalidates the comparisons. Besides, the difference in coverage of the two sets of data also rule out valid comparisons. In short, no one should conclude from Tables 7 and 10 that industrial decentralization has proceeded apace in the period after World War II.

At this point we clearly faced two problems: (1) to find some grounds for judging whether the TID-ENR figures were reasonably representative of total industrial construction for the period covered, and (2) to establish some base period for data on industrial building with which the distribution of the TID-ENR figures could be compared. Although we failed on both counts, a brief account of what we did and considered doing toward these ends may be useful to other researchers who later may use the same data and come up against the same problems.

On the question of the representativeness of the TID-ENR data, our first move was a fairly obvious one. The most inclusive figures available on industrial construction were those of the Construction Division, Office of Domestic Commerce of the Department of Commerce. As we pointed out earlier, these data were for estimated volume of construction work put in place. They are, nevertheless, derived data in the sense that they are based on contract figures. The Division estimates the lengths of time that construction work will go on after contracts are awarded and prorates the dollar volume over these periods of months. Also, as we have mentioned before, the Division's figures, making allowance for the difference in form of measurement, still showed a substantially larger dollar volume of industrial construction work than the TID-ENR data. Presumably, therefore, the figures used by the Division were from a more complete coverage than ours. The question then was the relatively simple one of finding ways of comparing the two sets of data that would indicate whether the less inclusive one, the TID-ENR figures, were roughly representative of the more inclusive data used by the Division.

We prepared, therefore, Table 11, Table 12, and breakdown (1) of Table 13. These are simple breakdowns of the TID-ENR data by major geographic regions, by city size groups, and by major industry groups as defined by the Census of Manufactures for 1939.[35] If these

TABLE 11

PERCENTAGE DISTRIBUTION OF DOLLAR VOLUME OF
INDUSTRIAL CONSTRUCTION CONTRACTS
JULY, 1945, THROUGH JUNE, 1949
BY REGIONS OF THE UNITED STATES*

Region	Per Cent
1. New England	2.9
2. Middle Atlantic	14.0
3. East North Central	22.9
4. West North Central	6.8
5. South Atlantic	12.6
6. East South Central	7.3
7. West South Central	20.4
8. Mountain	2.8
9. Pacific	10.4
Total	100.0

* See footnote to Table 10.

35. In addition to the primary purpose of these three tables, Table 13 deserves a further comment. Although breakdowns (1) and (2) cannot be closely compared, it may be significant that the percentages of dollar volume of construction contracts for food

TABLE 12

PERCENTAGE DISTRIBUTION OF DOLLAR VOLUME OF
INDUSTRIAL CONSTRUCTION CONTRACTS
JULY, 1945, THROUGH JUNE, 1949,
BY SIZE OF CITY IN 1940*

Size Group	Per Cent
1. Less than 2,500	17.3
2. 2,500–9,999	14.0
3. 10,000–24,999	15.8
4. 25,000–49,999	6.6
5. 50,000–99,999	11.2
6. 100,000–249,999	12.4
7. 250,000–499,999	9.9
8. 500,000–999,999	6.4
9. 1,000,000 or more	6.4
Total	100.0

* See footnote to Table 10.

percentage breakdowns corresponded roughly to the same ones for the Division's more inclusive figures, it might be concluded that the TID-ENR data, despite their less than complete coverage, were reasonably representative of the total volume of industrial building for the period or, at least, of the Department of Commerce's more inclusive series.

Although staff members of the Construction Division saw our problem and were willing to help in any ways they could, their data did not make possible the check on our figures that we had hoped for. The Division's estimates were based primarily on the F. W. Dodge Reports for the thirty-seven states east of the Rocky Mountains. The Division added an estimate for the eleven western states, which was derived by comparing building permit volume in the thirty-seven states covered by the Dodge Reports and that for the eleven states not so covered. In a letter dated November 30, 1949 Mr. Arnold E. Chase, Chief of the Economics and Statistics Section of the Construction Division concluded: ". . . Thus, we have no direct information of a comprehensive nature on the volume of industrial construction in the 11 Western States. This is a weakness in our value in place series with which we

---

products, textiles, chemicals, and products of petroleum and coal are substantially above the corresponding percentages of the increase in production workers for the same industry groups. Food products probably are a fairly well dispersed group of industries. Certainly textiles have been among the leaders in dispersion since the 1920's. If as the proportions in (1) and (2) of Table 13 suggest, the TID-ENR data are rather heavily weighted in these groups, this would account partly for the more dispersed pattern indicated by Table 10 as against Table 7. Chemicals and products of petroleum and coal are probably reasonably well dispersed and also have high capital investments per worker. Thus they, too, might contribute substantially to the dispersed pattern of Table 10.

On the other side, both kinds of machinery and transportation equipment were less heavily represented in the construction contract data than in proportions of the increase of production workers. Quite probably large proportions of these industry groups as well as of their recent growth have been in major metropolitan areas.

TABLE 13

PERCENTAGE DISTRIBUTION OF DOLLAR VOLUME OF INDUSTRIAL CONSTRUCTION CONTRACTS,
JULY, 1945, THROUGH JUNE, 1949, AND OF 1939–47 INCREASE IN PRODUCTION
WORKERS IN MANUFACTURING BY MAJOR INDUSTRY GROUPS*

Industry Groups	Construction Contracts (1)	Increase in Production Workers (2)
1. Food and kindred products	11.3	7.2
2. Tobacco manufactures	.2	.4
3. Textile-mill products and other fiber manufactures	6.2	1.6
4. Apparel and other finished products made from similar materials	.7	5.4
5. Lumber and timber basic products	.6	4.2
6. Furniture and finished lumber products	.7	2.3
7. Paper and allied products	7.3	2.9
8. Printing, publishing and allied industries	2.8	2.8
9. Chemicals and allied products	16.2	4.6
10. Products of petroleum and coal	16.8	1.5
11. Rubber products	.6	2.3
12. Leather and leather products	.1	.5
13. Stone, clay, and glass products	3.1	3.4
14. Iron and steel and their products, except machinery	12.4	} 17.3
15. Nonferrous metals and their products	4.0	
16. Electrical machinery	4.9	9.5
17. Machinery (except electrical)	3.0	17.2
18. Automobiles and automobile equipment	5.9	} 10.8
19. Transportation equipment except automobiles	.6	
20. Miscellaneous industries	2.7	6.2
Total	100.0	100.0

* For (1) see footnote to Table 10; (2), Table 2, p. 24, Vol. I, *Census of Manufactures: 1947*. Industry Groups are those defined in Census of Manufactures for 1939. The Territorial Information Department used these groups in compiling the data on industrial construction contracts. Because the 1939 and 1947 Census breakdowns by Industry Groups are not identical, percentages for the 1939–47 increase in production workers could not be given for all of the 1939 groups.

have long been seriously concerned." For this reason no useful comparisons could be made with our breakdowns in Tables 11, 12, and 13.

Besides, the Dodge Reports carry essentially the same kind of figures as the ones we were using. They are the results of an unofficial reporting system and, therefore, are subject to differences in coverage from area to area and possibly from one major industry group to another.

We next considered excluding from our data the figures on the eleven western states and comparing the TID-ENR data with those of the Dodge Reports for the thirty-seven eastern states. Although this might have produced some interesting results, we decided not to undertake it. It would have been a substantial job in proportion to our resources. We already had put into this part of URS' work as much or more time and money than we felt was justified. Also, such a comparison would not have answered conclusively the question whether the TID-ENR data were representative of the total volume of industrial construction for the period covered. It would have been simply a comparison of two somewhat similar, private reporting systems. From discussion and correspondence with persons who were acquainted with both sets of reports from their work in both private and official agencies, we concluded that such a comparison would not make possible a sufficiently firm answer to the question before us. We, therefore, had to drop at this point our quest for some adequate means of judging the representativeness of the TID-ENR data.

In light of these results we clearly were not justified in putting much more time and money into a search for a base year for data on industrial construction with which the TID-ENR figures for mid-1945 to mid-1949 could be compared. We did consider seriously breaking down the data that we had by years to see if the distribution among types of localities had changed materially over the four years. We did not do this, however, because we felt that the period was too short to produce meaningful results even if it were assumed that the coverage did not change much during this period. We also considered comparing the breakdowns of the data we had with the same breakdown for ENR data for some earlier year. Although the ENR data had been reported for some years before 1945, a comparison of the period 1945 to 1949 with some earlier year or years would have been quite inconclusive. We would not have known whether the coverages were approximately the same for the two periods and, of course, we would still have been in the dark on whether at either period it was reasonably representative of the total volume of industrial building. We concluded, therefore, that the results of such a comparison for our purposes would not be worth the additional time and expense.

Only one other attack on these baffling problems seems worth mentioning. For the first time the Census of Manufactures for 1939 collected data on "expenditures for plant and equipment." The statement on the official form read: "Report all permanent additions and major alterations made on contract or by own forces, which were *charged during the year* to fixed asset accounts and which are of the type for which depreciation accounts are ordinarily maintained. Exclude expenditures for replacement which are in the nature of maintenance." The form included a three-way breakdown for total expenditures of this kind: (1) expenditures for new construction and major alterations of buildings and other fixed plant and structures; (2) expenditures for new machinery and operating equipment; and (3) expenditures for plant and equipment acquired in a used condition from other owners and for land.

Largely because this was the first census for which information on these points had been requested, the replies indicated some confusion, particularly as to this three-way breakdown and, in the words of the

Census, ". . . left room for considerable latitude in interpretation."[36] The Census for 1947 included the same inquiry, but with a somewhat more detailed breakdown of the total figures.

At best, however, these data were not directly comparable with the TID-ENR or similar figures on industrial construction. The chief difference is that the Census asked only for expenditures made during the year of the enumeration. Thus, if a major extension or a new plant were built during a period extending over parts of two years, the report to the Census would be an estimate of the dollar amount of the construction in the one year. Also, if a plant were built by a new company or establishment almost entirely during the year that the census was taken but were not finished and in operation by the end of the year, it would not be reported at all. Perhaps these data for plant expenditures in 1939 and 1947 would justify some further analysis. We did not feel, however, that we could undertake it and, as we have just said, its results would not be comparable with the TID-ENR figures with which we had worked.

Mr. Warren S. Thompson, in his monograph to which we have referred earlier,[37] did make a rough comparison of the expenditures for plant and equipment in 1939 with the number of production workers in manufacturing for the same year. Table 14 is adapted from this item

TABLE 14

PERCENTAGE DISTRIBUTION AMONG TYPES OF LOCALITIES OF PRODUCTION WORKERS IN MANUFACTURING AND EXPENDITURES FOR PLANT AND EQUIPMENT AS REPORTED BY CENSUS OF MANUFACTURES FOR 1939*

(1929 Areas)

	INDUSTRIAL AREAS AS A WHOLE (1)	CENTRAL COUNTIES (2)	REST OF INDUSTRIAL AREAS (3)	AREAS OF SECONDARY CONCEN-TRATION (4)	REST OF THE COUNTRY (5)
Production Workers......	54.7	42.2	12.5	17.8	27.5
Expenditures for Plant and Equipment............	53.1	36.8	16.3	17.9	29.1

* Adapted from Warren S. Thompson, *The Growth of Metropolitan Districts in the United States: 1900–1940* (Washington, D.C.: Bureau of the Census, 1948), Table XVII, p. 25.
   Locality breakdown is based on that in Daniel B. Creamer's *Is Industry Decentralizing?* (Philadelphia: University of Pennsylvania Press, 1935).
   Thompson's percentage figures are based on the original reports of the Census of Manufactures for 1939. In URS tables the figures for 1939 were the revised ones published with those for the Census of Manufactures for 1947 and adjusted slightly to make them more nearly comparable with the 1947 data. This accounts for minor differences in percentages, e.g., Thompson's figures show 54.7 per cent of production workers in Industrial Areas in 1939; the URS-computed percentage, Table 5, is 54.4. See 1939 column of Table 1, which gives both the original and adjusted figures for 1939 for the United States and the nine major divisions or regions.

in Mr. Thompson's study. He used a simplified version of Mr. Creamer's breakdown on the 1929 areas.

Again with the warning that no close comparisons of the distributions

36. *Census of Manufactures: 1939*, I, ix, 363. The Census schedule is in Appendix B of this volume; the inquiry on this item is at p. 404.
37. *Op. cit.*, footnote 13, chap. vi.

of production workers and of dollar volume of industrial construction are justified, it is interesting to note that for the three major types of localities—industrial areas, areas of secondary concentration, and the rest of the country—the differences between the distributions of dollar volume of industrial construction and production workers in Table 14 are in the same direction as the differences shown in Tables 7 and 10. In other words, both in Table 14 on the one hand and in Tables 7 and 10 on the other, the proportion of dollar volume of construction is less than that of production workers in industrial areas, about the same in areas of secondary concentration, and somewhat higher in the rest of the country. In the figures for 1939 (Table 14) the differences for industrial areas and the rest of the country are much less than the differences for their 1947 and 1945–1949 counterparts in Tables 7 and 10, but they are in the same direction. This suggests, although it cannot be said to establish, the possibility that for some time past the dollar volume of industrial construction has been relatively less in the major industrial areas than their proportion of production workers would have indicated. If this could be accepted, it might mean either (*a*) that some form of industrial dispersion not clearly shown by other units of measurement was in fact under way; or (*b*) that plants with the larger ratios of workers to long-term capital investment favored the major industrial centers while those with lower ratios by and large went into dispersed locations; or (*c*) that both of these influences were at work.

At all events, it should not be overlooked that one of the breakdowns in Table 14 from Mr. Thompson's study includes expenditures for both plant and equipment. For the country as a whole the 1939 Census reported a much larger expenditure, actually more than two times as large, for equipment than for industrial buildings. This, of course, may largely invalidate the similarities we have just pointed out between Table 14 and Tables 7 and 10. In our opinion, however, it does not invalidate the suggestion that future research might look into the Census data on plant expenditures for 1939 and 1947, and perhaps might result in some useful comparisons and some tentative relations between the distributions of expenditures for industrial plants and the number of production workers.

The description and discussion of our work on the distribution of production workers and of the dollar volume of industrial construction contracts has necessarily involved considerable detail and many qualifications and warnings. We could have simplified this chapter considerably by leaving out entirely our treatment of the TID-ENR data. This would certainly have been justified by the facts that we do not know whether these latter data are representative of the total volume of industrial construction for the period covered and that, in any event, they are not directly comparable with those on production workers. To repeat, we have given this account of our attempts to use the figures on industrial construction in the hope that it might save steps for other students of this subject and might possibly have produced some elementary findings on which other students might build in their future work.

The Gist of the Creamer-URS Findings

To help our readers back to the essentials of our analysis before we offer a summary and conclusions for this chapter, we would call attention to the summary Table 15, which presents in a simplified break-

TABLE 15

Summary Table: Percentage Distribution among Six Types of Localities of Production Workers in Manufacturing, 1939 and 1947, of the 1939-47 Increase in Such Workers, and of the Dollar Volume of Industrial Construction Contracts, 1945-49, for the United States *

(1947 Areas)

Data	Central Cities (1)	Rest of Central Counties (2)	Metropolitan Areas Outside of Central Counties (3)	SMA's as a Whole (4)	Areas of Secondary Concentration (5)	All the Rest of the Country (6)
1947 production workers...	36.1	10.2	11.9	58.2	15.7	26.2
1939 production workers...	35.7	9.7	12.2	57.6	15.8	26.7
1939–47 increase in production workers..........	36.9	11.0	11.4	59.3	15.4	25.2
1945–49 dollar volume of industrial construction contracts.............	24.6	11.2	11.7	47.5	16.9	35.6

* For sources of data see footnotes to Tables 7 and 10. Percentage distributions taken or computed from Tables 7, 8, and 10. Locality breakdown is based on that of Table 7. Locality 1 = A of Table 7; 2 = D − A; 3 = F − D; 4 = F; 5 = J; 6 = K.

down the data on 1947 and 1939 production workers, the 1939–47 net increase in such workers, and the 1945–49 dollar volume of industrial construction contracts, TID-ENR. The line above the last distribution is another reminder that it is not directly comparable with the other three.

Are industries decentralizing? Mr. Creamer's study for the period 1899 to 1933 found (a) considerable evidence of a slow, but quite persistent diffusion of industry to the outlying parts of the major industrial areas; (b) less clear evidence of a more uncertain and spotty dispersion of industry to areas of secondary concentration (URS' definitions of diffusion and dispersion); and (c) the rest of the country held its own. Our work indicates that two of these probable trends or tendencies, (*a*) and (*c*), continued from 1933 to 1939. The areas of secondary concentration, however, lost ground slightly. For the period after 1939, the most significant distributions in Table 15 are those for the 1939 production workers and the 1939–47 increase.

When seen in the perspective of this table, these two distributions indicate that industrial workers for the country as a whole were not dispersed during the period 1939 to 1947. Areas of secondary concentration and the rest of the country both received slightly smaller percentages of the 1939–47 increase than they had of the number of production workers in 1939.

As to industrial diffusion within the major areas of concentration, the evidence is contradictory. The central cities obtained a slightly larger proportion of the eight-year increase than they had of the 1939 number of workers. This is the opposite of diffusion. On the other hand, the parts of the central counties outside of the central cities also improved their position and just a shade more rapidly than did the central cities. (In 1939 the number of workers in central counties outside central cities was 27.1 per cent of the number in the central cities; the counties' increase was 29.8 per cent of the central cities'; consequently in 1947 the number of workers in the outlying parts of the central counties was 28.3 per cent of the number in the central cities.) The outlying counties of the industrial metropolitan areas lost ground relatively. This relative loss, however, was due to the failure of the satellite cities (Class B of Tables 7, 8, 9) to obtain a proportion of the 1939–47 increase equal or nearly equal to their proportion of workers in 1939. All but one of these satellite cities were in outlying counties of the metropolitan areas. The figures for Class E in Tables 7, 8, and 9, which, unlike Class 3 in Table 14, do *not* include the satellite cities, show that the other parts of these outlying counties also gained more than their proportionate share of the 1939–47 increase. In fact, they grew in industry slightly more rapidly than the central counties and the central cities (Table 9).

In short, during these eight years of defense, war and immediate postwar expansion, the slow movement toward diffusion continued in the central counties of major metropolitan areas and, except for the satellite cities, in the outlying counties as well. When the satellite cities are included, diffusion during this period was limited to the parts of the central counties outside of the central cities. We have no explanation for the poor showing of the satellite cities over these years. Table 5, however, shows that of the six periods marked out between 1899 and 1947 by Mr. Creamer's and URS' breakdowns, in only one, 1933 to 1939, did the proportion of workers in these cities increase.

Summary and Conclusions

What then can we say in summary and as a set of conclusions from this and the preceding chapter? Without repeating the warnings and qualifications, we suggest the following statements as the major findings and the most likely meanings of the analyses that have been made so far to help answer the question: *Are industries decentralizing?*

1. This question is usually put in the form—is industry decentralizing? In this form it admits of no clear answer. Many parts of the evidence indicate, and other parts as well as informed observations suggest, that various groupings of industries are following different patterns of change and relative stability. Considerable differences are also apparent in different parts of the country. From the work done so far the details as well as some major parts of the picture are far from clear.

2. Industrial decentralization is too broad a term for much of the analysis that needs to be done. It is useful to distinguish between and to give reasonably precise meanings to *diffusion* and *dispersion* as the two main types of industrial decentralization.

3. From an over-all view of the patterns of industrial location over the past half century or so, their chief characteristic is their relative stability.

4. From the beginning of the present century until World War II, considerable evidence indicates a slow, but rather persistent diffusion of industry within the major areas or districts of industrial concentration. This diffusion was most marked in the Middle Atlantic, East North Central, and Pacific regions. During this same period the indications of dispersion were less strong and suggested a tendency that varied considerably with general business and industrial conditions. The South Atlantic states were the region for which the evidence of dispersion was strongest.

5. From 1939 through 1947 for the country as a whole, the tendency toward dispersion was stopped. Despite a relative gain by the central cities of the major industrial metropolitan areas, some diffusion continued except for the satellite cities. These changes were slight. During most of this period industrial location was heavily influenced by war conditions and regulations. It would seem unsafe to predict, therefore, that the post-World War II pattern of industrial location will necessarily follow that of the wartime years.

6. The few studies of postwar industrial location in major metropolitan areas indicate that diffusion is continuing in them. These studies, however, are so few and necessarily so cursory that no generalization can be based on them.

7. The old hypothesis that diffusion and dispersion result almost entirely from industries being pushed, or forced, or squeezed out of central areas of major industrial districts is open to serious question. Certainly influences of this kind are at work. Shortages of suitable land for industrial expansion and for new plants that may expand later is one condition that is helping to determine plant locations outside of the central parts of major industrial metropolitan areas. On the other hand, considerable evidence exists for believing that positive attractions and advantages of diffused and dispersed locations are major forces in the incipient trend toward industrial decentralization.

8. Many facts from the studies of industrial location as well as from observation suggest strongly that both diffusion and dispersion vary greatly among different kinds and groupings of industrial plants. We badly need more systematic and thorough studies of these tendencies by many kinds of industry groups or breakdowns. In general, it seems likely that capital and durable goods industries have diffused more rapidly than most others and that semidurable and nondurable consumer goods industries led the slight, pre-War II move toward dispersion. The evidence on these points, however, leaves much to be desired, and it is entirely possible that other types of industry breakdowns would yield more positive results. Evidence is at hand also for believing that the major industrial areas attract new establishments and that branch plants are more likely to be diffused or dispersed. Again, however, more thorough and rigorous study is needed.

9. Because of the strong probability that changes in location patterns vary substantially among various kinds and classes of industries, urban planners and redevelopers should beware of the mistake of assuming that tendencies or trends (or relative stability for that matter) for the country as a whole or for broad geographic regions are also characteristic of their particular localities. This assumption would be justifiable only if the industrial composition of a particular locality were the same as that for the nation as a whole or for the broad geographic region. Quite probably this would never be true. It follows, therefore, that urban planners and redevelopers ought to undertake or encourage other agencies to make careful studies of what is happening to the location of industries in their area and to its dominant industries, both within that area and elsewhere. As a practical matter, this conclusion probably is as significant as any other that can be drawn from study of this subject to date.

10. For readily understandable reasons, many of the locality studies that have been made so far have used the industrial plant as the unit of measurement. On the whole this is not a good unit. More usable results would come from studies based on production workers in manu-

facturing as the index of industrial location. Findings from such studies would be more significant in and of themselves and also would make possible useful comparisons from time to time with breakdowns of the comparable figures from the Census of Manufactures.

11. Finally, in these last two chapters as well as in the others we have tried primarily to describe, analyze, and, if and when possible, to explain what has been happening in industrial location. We hope that it has been clear that our attempts at analysis and explanation not only are, in many respects, elementary and inadequate but also that the findings are not, in any sense, directives to planners and redevelopers. We have been concerned here with existing patterns of location and past and present changes in them. We believe urban planners and re-developers should share this interest. Clearly, however, they have to do primarily with present and particularly with future patterns. In dealing with them, they need to build on as thorough an understanding as possible of past happenings and of the forces that account for them. But they also should work in another and, in some ways, an even more difficult and troubled area—of values, objectives, judgments, and recommendations as to those patterns of industrial location that will contribute to effective plant operation and, equally important, to efficient, pleasant, flexible and humane urban communities.

PART III

URBAN REDEVELOPMENT AND THE URBANITE

BY
WILLIAM L. SLAYTON
AND
RICHARD DEWEY

EDITOR'S FOREWORD

IN THE whole URS family of inquiries, essays, and monographs, including both those that reached maturity and those that died at an early age, the "Urbanite" has been the problem child. It was one of the first to be conceived and born, but ever since it has made trouble, aroused apprehensions, and, from time to time, occasioned anger and despair. Even now, as it is being sent forth into the world, the feelings of its parents, guardians, and nurses are very mixed.

We in URS have never doubted the underlying purpose and basic assumptions of this work. Cities have many aspects and can be looked at in many ways but one of the most fundamental sees them as aggregations of people and of groups of people. If or when the more drastic clearance and rebuilding forms of urban redevelopment reach the scale they should attain, they will do more to upset patterns of living, to unsettle established groups and their complex personal relationships, and to disturb institutions and organizations than any other single activity of local governments in collaboration with private and quasi-public agencies. It is unthinkable that this kind of program can be vigorously pushed for long without substantial and widespread understanding and support among many of the major groups that make up our cities. It is almost equally difficult to believe that such an operation can yield the optimum balance of benefits over costs and hardships unless many of these groups have some voice in determining what is to be done and when, and unless those agencies with official responsibility for local programs keep in the forefront of their individual and institutional minds three facts. Cities are people. The cities' buildings, utilities, and other facilities are for human use, satisfaction, and enjoyment. One of the most valuable parts of the intellectual equipment of urban planners and redevelopers in a democratic society is a clear and growing appreciation of the basic needs, wants, desires, aspirations, and motivations of human beings, particularly as they are affected by city life and environment.

Even as URS' work went slowly ahead, evidence accumulated to support these axioms. Redevelopment projects were defeated by the opposition of people in areas to be cleared. Technically acceptable redevelopment plans were sprung on unsuspecting communities. In some cities, the likely effects of redevelopment on racial and other occupancy patterns became the bitter and crucial issue. In important respects the kinds of housing proposed for many redevelopment areas have been almost the exact opposite to what little we know about the preferences and values of the people who are supposed to live in them.

Nevertheless, despite our strong convictions and what we took to be direct or indirect substantiation of them, the growth of the "Urbanite" was beset with troubles. Inquiries among planners and redevelopment officials showed widespread inability or unwillingness to have any part in testing sample surveys as a means of getting at some of the urban citizen's ideas, attitudes, and wants in respect to his housing, neighborhood, and ways and means of changing them. Despite considerable thought and talk about public relations and even public participation in planning and development, the experience available for analysis, except for the more common materials on reporting and other useful but superficial techniques, was very scarce. Even the promising experiments in Philadelphia, Cleveland, and elsewhere had not been going on long enough to furnish a substantial body of facts for analysis. We had difficulty in finding persons who knew something about planning and redevelopment and who also understood some of the work of social psychologists and sociologists and the experience in community organization and group work.

This sketch of our troubles with the "Urbanite" is not an excuse for its weaknesses nor a bid for sympathy. It is simply to make clear that this section of our work might well have been dropped at any one of several points. That it was not may be more effectual testimony than anything I could write to the fact that the longer we studied this subject in many of its aspects, the more convinced we became that the central themes of the "Urbanite" lie very near the heart of urban redevelopment as a public undertaking.

Two points made in the Preface to this volume are so pertinent to this section that I restate them briefly here.

First, the Study's resources and methods of operation did not allow us to keep up to date the factual and descriptive parts of those sections of the work that were undertaken first. Unless later developments were of first-rate significance, we did not add them. Although we would have liked to have had someone responsible for additions and revisions of all our reports up to the moment they went to the printer, this would have been a luxury at best. The issues we have tried to deal with are not fly-by-night matters that have to be caught in a split second or lost forever. The descriptive parts soon would be somewhat out of date no matter how often revised before publication. If the analyses and recommendations have merits, they will not wear off within a few months.

Also, the Preface mentions that neither the Administrative Committee nor the Director tried to require conformity in the opinions and recommendations of URS' contributors. For example, I find myself disagreeing with Mr. Dewey in some of the analysis and judgments in chapter ii, particularly in the paragraphs on the neighborhood unit. But he considered my criticisms, made use of parts of them, and put down what his study and experience have enabled him to see and believe. Despite differences with it, I hope planners, redevelopers, students of urban life and affairs will read and weigh what he has written.

William L. Slayton, who is chiefly responsible for chapters i, iii, and iv, was for several months the assistant director of URS. Before that he had been in the Planning Division of the Board of Public Land Commissioners and Municipal Reference Librarian in Milwaukee. He left URS in the spring of 1950 to join the field staff of the Division of Slum Clearance and Urban Redevelopment of the Housing and Home Finance Agency and is now Assistant Director of the National Association of Housing Officials, giving much of his time to redevelopment. In the Milwaukee sample survey discussed in chapter iii he had the generous and unfailing help of Carl Quast, chief planning analyst in Milwaukee and Willard E. Downing, associate professor of social work in the University of Wisconsin at Milwaukee, who made available the services of a graduate class for the interviewing.

Richard Dewey, who worked mostly on chapter ii, is associate professor of sociology at the University of Illinois. He, too, had been a staff member of the Planning Division in Milwaukee.

C. W.

CHAPTER I

INTRODUCTION—THE BASIC
APPROACH TO REDEVELOPMENT

MOST of the literature of urban redevelopment has dealt primarily with the technical problems of clearing and rebuilding slum and blighted areas, e.g., site selection, land acquisition, legislation, reuse values of land, finance, and interagency relations in local government. The emphasis has been on physical and procedural rather than social problems. To be sure, these are rough classifications, and many redevelopment issues, in fact, are difficult to pigeonhole. Nevertheless, the generalization in these terms can be defended; after all necessary qualifications are made, it is still substantially true.

Although these physical, administrative problems are by no means unimportant and a thorough understanding of each is necessary, their solution does not decide basic policy on the purpose and objectives of urban redevelopment. They are secondary to the prior and much more fundamental problem—redevelopment for what and for whom? This is the basic question to which those concerned with urban redevelopment should address themselves; otherwise the hope of a new day in city-building and urban living may well be disappointed.

In this perspective, urban redevelopment is a tool or set of tools to help provide an environment that meets the social and psychological, as well as the physical, needs of the people. Further, the way in which the physical needs are provided for often becomes important.

TYPES OF INVESTIGATION NEEDED

Unfortunately, little enough is known about the physical, let alone the psychological and social, needs of urban dwellers. The urban planner or redeveloper has scant information on which to base decisions about wants and needs. If he relies on available information, he can do little more than guess what type of arrangements should be provided to further the long-range interests and to fill the needs of those who, over the next generation or two at the least, for good or ill, are going to live and work in the neighborhoods and districts he is helping to shape. It seems reasonable to suggest, therefore, that he should initiate investigations and research toward answers to these basic questions as well as encourage professional scholars to do the same. He is charting a new field, one in which the guideposts are few and not clearly labeled. In making his decisions, he should remember that in him lies much of the present hope for the urban area, that urban redevelopment is the first opportunity to remake modern cities into really desirable places in which to live and work.

At the same time that the urban redeveloper is considering means whereby urban development can meet a wide range of the needs of city-dwellers, he must also consider other aspects of his job. One of these is that he is and will be constantly dealing with groups in proposed re-development areas. Urban redevelopment is a new and frightening term to many of them. It raises visions of forced moves and major up-heavals in family living. Its strangeness creates fear, and fear gener-ates opposition. Thus the redevelopment agency should give careful thought to ways and means of working effectively with these groups. This work must do more than "sell" the redevelopment program to residents and property owners in these areas. It must somehow reflect, in some degree, the ideas of these groups and create a measure of under-standing and interest in the undertaking. The specific ideas of such groups, their attitudes toward what should be done in the areas, and their feelings toward the proposed program may prove to be the answer to whether the city will be able to proceed with its redevelopment plans.

Another aspect of the urban redevelopment process that needs in-vestigation is that of public participation. If more than lip service is to be given the phrase "planning is for people," then redevelopment should become a process in which people can take some part: not just a few carefully selected or self-appointed persons but many, if possible, a large proportion of the ordinary people of the community. Planners should have as part of their equipment the ability to work with groups and individuals, to find out the needs and wants of the people. Overemphasis on the "planning board" technique and acceptance of a policy that in effect insists that the people for whom the plans are made must accept the decisions of the planners is contrary to basic demo-cratic principles. Redevelopment and planning for it hold the promise of becoming a focus for renewed democratic activity, and the approach of the redevelopment agency should be to encourage rather than dis-courage this movement. Redevelopment can arouse keen interest on the part of residents of a redevelopment area. A program in which the citizen can participate in the planning process and in fact influence, to a substantial extent, the way in which his area will be developed is an overwhelming need in a basically democratic society where, nevertheless, the relationship between the individual citizen and public policy so often seems quite weak and remote.

Three types of investigation, therefore, are suggested in this basic approach to redevelopment. The first is to ascertain the general and specific needs and desires of urban dwellers for housing, recreation, social relationships—all factors in the urban environment. The second concerns the attitudes to redevelopment plans and prospects on the part of residents, property owners, and interest groups in and near areas proposed for substantial action. Redevelopment agencies should have some knowledge of what these attitudes are, how they are formed, and how they may be discovered and measured. The third type of investigation concerns the participation of groups in the redevelopment process. This is closely related to the second approach and could well be considered an extension of it. Its importance and the different process required in its use, however, indicate that it deserves separate consideration. Chapters ii, iii, and iv deal, respectively, with these three subjects.

INFORMATION WANTED

Few question the need for information on family size, income levels, educational attainments, and similar facts as a basis for planning. The relation of such data to the size, number, and types of facilities that should be provided is readily apparent. If it is known that the community shows certain birth trends, no one questions the effect of such trends on future schoolroom requirements. When it is suggested, however, that information be assembled to ascertain the social needs of individuals in the community, eyebrows rise, tongues cluck, and the advocate is advised to stick to "more practical" problems. There has been little genuine acceptance of the thesis that social needs are as significant as physical needs and that just as much (or more) research is required to determine the social needs as is needed in ascertaining the physical.

SOCIAL RELATIONSHIPS

Urban redevelopment, then, is aimed in part at remedying such physical conditions as substandard houses and their surroundings, but more is required if the pattern of urban living is to include more than satisfaction of basic physical needs. The social problems of urban living are not as easily defined as are the physical, and as a result some tend to shy away from this type of investigation and analysis.

An example of a social problem which should be recognized is *anomie*.

The concept of *anomie* has been offered as a description of the lack of a sense of belonging, which is characteristic of some, if not many, urban dwellers. The size of the metropolis and its impersonal attitude dwarfs the importance of the individual and creates a feeling of insignificance and helplessness. One is unable to identify himself with a stable society; he finds few if any common values that he really believes in, and the result is frustrating to the individual's normal desire for close relationships and recognition. Perhaps some *anomie* may be caused by the urban pattern itself. The typical urban pattern may generate a superficial sociability that lacks the basic, warm relationships most individuals seem to require for a satisfying life. Since urban redevelopment is the first major opportunity for cities to take positive steps in the arrangement of large parts of the urban area, it is also an opportunity to provide an environment that will contribute to meeting these social needs of the urban dweller or, at least, to reducing the conditions that lead to *anomie*.

Urban redevelopment should produce an environment that will help or tend to provide the urban dweller with the type and degree of social relationships he finds necessary for a satisfying life. Thus information must somehow be gathered that will indicate the lacks in respect to these relationships. And at the same time studies must be undertaken to show if and how the man-made environment can help fill these gaps. Plans should be ". . . oriented primarily toward certain established social values which will make for satisfactory personal adjustment in an urban environment."[1]

PHYSICAL WANTS AND NEEDS

The social needs are but part of the picture. Because the redevelopment official is, in at least two senses, working for the people who live in his city, it is only sensible that he guide redevelopment so that it will meet the requirements of those for whom the job is done. If he but continues a pattern that has become accepted, he has no way of knowing whether he is providing the people with what they want or not. If he redevelops according to a pattern based on what he thinks they wish to have or need, he is setting himself up as arbiter of the people's wants. To repeat, it is essential that he discover by some means what seems most likely to meet the wants and needs of the people.

Of course, some information and knowledge are already at hand. The builder, contractor, mortgage lender, and others have for some time been providing houses and laying out subdivisions based on what they thought and the market indicated were the desires and needs of urban

1. See Judith Tannenbaum, "The Neighborhood—A Socio-Psychological Analysis," *Land Economics* (November, 1948), pp. 358–69.

dwellers. People who buy houses will naturally select those homes that best meet their needs; those builders who are best able to anticipate and supply these wants will be the ones who prosper and build the most houses. Those who fail to observe the demands of the market and do not meet the desires of the purchaser will not prosper and will soon drop out. At least, this is essentially the argument of how the urban land market does or should work.

There are, however, several limitations to the market functioning in quite such a neat and beneficent manner. Although the market may indicate to some degree what is wanted, it does not provide conclusive evidence or irrefutable proof of the needs and desires of the urbanite. The market works for some part of the population and for some of the problems, but it does not cover all the problems or all the population. The ideas, insight, and conclusions of the experienced builder are certainly not without value, but the limitations to such experience should be kept in mind.

In the first place, new housing being built is for only a proportion of the population. Only the top economic groups can afford new dwellings and exercise the freedom of choice taken for granted in the statement above on the working of the market. As one goes down the economic scale, the proportion who have relatively free choices in matters of housing becomes less and less and also the choices of those in the various groups become more and more limited. When the lowest economic groups are reached, freedom of choice has become almost complete absence of choice. At least, these people are those whose choices are most severely limited. Thus the new houses and the experiences of the builders do not reflect the needs and wants of a large segment of the population.

The builder is also limited in his insight into these problems because of the scale on which he customarily operates. Often, he works on too small a scale even to recognize, let alone attempt to meet, the problems of urbanites stemming from the community or neighborhood. Thus the builder may be able to reflect changes in desires in respect to size of bathrooms, but he can hardly cope with the need for a community center, a community organization, or social group relationships. These problems are not within his scope. If he is aware of them, it is not because he has had to try to solve them. Recently, however, large builders such as American Community Builders in Chicago and the Levitt Brothers in New York have begun to produce information of this nature. Operations of their scale have thrust upon them problems that were, to most builders at least, of only casual interest but few years ago.

A final limitation to the experience of the builder and his associates is the tendency of housing to slip into ruts or fads. A particular feature or arrangement gains currency, and for some reason it continues for several years as standard practice. Or a builder may have quirks or special ideas that cause him to produce certain fads or that keep him in a construction rut. These crazes, fads, and inertias limit the choice of the buyers and consequently the market does not reflect accurately their wants.

All this does not mean that the ideas and insights of the builders are without merit. They are certainly of value and should not be over-looked. But it is proposed here that a wider focus be given to the problem of meeting the needs and desires of the urbanite. It is necessary that present ideas be reviewed and criticized and that the problem be examined from a broader angle than heretofore. These physical wants and needs cover a wide range of subjects, primarily in the fields of space relationships, community facilities, and housing types.

As to space relationships, the urban redeveloper should find out such things as the distance different groups and kinds of people wish to be from playgrounds and parks; the distance considered desirable for schools, churches, transportation, shopping centers, theaters, etc.; the distance people wish to be from their places of work and from the center of the city. These are standards about which little is known. Discussions have been based primarily on what planners or technicians in the field have felt were reasonable and desirable. Very few criteria have been put forward that are based on findings of what various groups and sorts of people actually do consider desirable. In addition, where such standards have been proposed, little distinction has been made on the basis of the needs for different groups of people. Obviously, for example, most childless couples would have an entirely different attitude toward the location of playgrounds than would families with children and, quite surely, would have definite ideas on the location of recreational areas designed for the use of adults rather than children.

In the field of community facilities, the same observations apply. Few have bothered to find out even approximately which community facilities are considered important and necessary by different groups of people. Is some kind of a community hall desirable? Is it a necessary item for a community? What groups feel a need for it? Which are unconcerned? Is there evidence that many people's opinions on this point are subject to change? Of similar import is the subject of the shopping center. They have grown on a trial-and-error basis, a method that is but negative assurance that their location is a good one. Where should shopping centers be located and what shopping facilities should it provide? Other neighborhood characteristics also deserve considerations. Are a high degree of quietness and of cleanness necessary requisites for a "good" neighborhood or do they rate well down on many lists of important criteria? What types of people do various groups desire as their neighbors? Do these preferences change with experience? How rapidly? All of these items bear directly on decisions that the redeveloper must make. Without information on what the people want, he will have either to continue the existing pattern or substitute his predilections for information. Neither procedure is satisfactory.

For intelligent policy in respect to housing types, a wide range of information is needed. For example, the controversy between those who advocate tall, elevator apartments and those who insist that the two- or possibly three-story walk-up is the only or best answer to decent housing cannot be resolved until the preferences of groups are learned. Almost anyone is able to make guesses, but actual information on this subject is gravely inadequate. The redeveloper will presumably have fairly accurate factual data on the groups, the initial ones, at least, for whom he is redeveloping. He should also know what these groups want in housing.

This argument can easily be over simplified or even caricatured. Let it be emphasized, therefore, that more knowledge about peoples' wants and preferences will not lead to some simple utopia for urban planners, redevelopers, and architects. Many of the statements of needs and desires will be contradictory. Further investigation and analysis may reconcile apparent conflicts in evidence; some of them may still remain.

Also, as in other questions of this kind, the results of the early studies, though useful, may raise almost as many difficulties as they settle. Continued research, however, should resolve or at least clarify most of these problems. They should be able to show not only what items or factors of housing and city arrangement various persons like or dislike, but also what facts about or conditions of these people go with these attitudes and how rapidly and in what direction they are changing. Both the early and later studies should try to find the relative weights attached to the different items or qualities as well as preferences for *combinations* of features or characteristics—one set against others.

Again, some considerable understanding of what different kinds and groups of persons want (and understanding is much more than familiarity with figures from a survey) will not remove the fact that many felt needs and firm desires run counter to other considerations, such as, for example, cost and technical factors of unkeep and maintenance. Working out reasonable and balanced compromises among a wide range of desirable and desired attributes of housing, neighborhood layouts and city patterns will still be an important and fascinating part of planning. The difference could be that the kind of studies proposed here would make for more intelligent and satisfactory results.

ATTITUDES TOWARD REDEVELOPMENT

Knowledge of the social and physical needs of the urban dweller needs to be buttressed by still more information. Most redevelopment agencies feel the need for some type of public participation in this work, particularly when bonds are to be issued and a referendum is necessary. As a result, pamphlets are prepared, talks arranged, and the usual "public relations" machinery set in motion. Although this activity may be necessary and useful, it may also be quite wasteful. Urban redevelopment is such a new field and such a new term to most citizens, that these programs of necessity must shoot in the dark. Redevelopers do not know the level of information of the citizens they are trying to persuade. As a result, many programs may over- or undershoot the mark. In other words, the agency may have little knowledge on the attitudes of the citizens toward certain programs. It does not know whether, by and large, the citizens' opinions require only buttressing or whether basic explanations of purposes and methods are necessary. Thus the third type of information the redeveloper requires is on the level of understanding of urban redevelopment and attitudes toward it.

Of course, something is to be said for the information on attitudes in particular areas that the planning commission or redevelopment agency will acquire in the course of preparing its proposals. Planners and redevelopers may well point out that they are quite familiar with the attitudes of families and individuals in the area and are cognizant of their wants and needs. They can support their point by citing the protests (or statements of approval) from organizations and persons who attend public hearings. The planners and redevelopers will have reason to feel that on an area-wide basis they will be in a position to understand, as well as to know, the needs, desires, and attitudes of those in the area.

Basing one's proposals for redevelopment on this evidence, however, is questionable. If such evidence is not critically examined and checked, planners and redevelopers may find their conclusions erroneous.

In the first place, the order of proposal and attitude is reversed. If one waits until a program is well formulated, plans drawn, and ideas set, then the attitudes expressed by residents at public hearings often are of little importance. Certainly the agency becomes aware of them, but the "weight" of the attitudes must be strong indeed to change the program substantially. Thus knowledge of attitudes in such a case is of little value; it does not alter the course of action.

A second difficulty of assessing attitudes on the basis of what the agency "knows" or "hears" about the people in the area is that of representation. Some groups are very articulate; others, relatively mute. The articulate have been known to claim representation far in excess of their organization or following. Noise and push have a way of implying backing and influence. The actual feelings of the people in the area may be quite contrary to those expressed by some of their alleged spokesmen. With only public utterances to guide them, public bodies have no way of learning how representative such opinions are.

And finally, the strong likelihood of future relations with the redevelopment or planning agency should not be overlooked. The prospect of a buyer-seller relationship is often influential in guiding one's actions and deeds. Deep and emotional protest from one whose house is to be bought and razed may, of course, be sincere; but it may also be part of an act to create a favorable feeling toward increasing the purchase price of his property. More deep-seated attitudes in such instances would certainly not be revealed by a protest made to a redevelopment agency representative.

More, therefore, is needed in the determination of attitudes in redevelopment areas than the veneer of knowledge acquired through public hearings and casual work in the field. An effort needs be made to secure adequate and reliable information on attitudes.

Briefly, then, there are three types of information that the redeveloper needs and should take steps to get. The first of these is social—the peoples' wants for full and satisfying social living. The second is physical—the arrangements of space, buildings, and facilities that they think necessary for proper living. The third concerns citizens' attitudes toward urban redevelopment and their levels of understanding. Buttressed with information such as this, the redevelopment planner should be able to provide the urban community with projects that would amount to a major step toward making the urban area a desirable place in which to live, and further, that would have a good chance to be carried out.

It should be repeated, however, that the suggestion is not that one set up a procedure whereby the wants, needs, and attitudes are by some fascinating formula translated into a redevelopment plan. Perhaps some day the Mark III electronic calculator can perform this operation for planners; but that day is far off—fortunately!

Finally, the investigation of needs, wants, and attitudes is not to be a substitute for other redevelopment procedures and criteria. Rather it is but another tool, albeit an important and basic one, in the redevelopment process.

THE SAMPLE SURVEY

A promising method by which information may be obtained on wants and needs is the sample survey. Since the fiasco of the opinion polls in the 1948 presidential election, it hardly seems necessary to emphasize the need for competent direction and careful preparation. And conclusions from an analysis of the results must be tempered by consideration of all the variables and limitations that go with sample surveys on this kind of subject.

A major limitation of this approach, of course, is the difficulty of determining the underlying and long-range needs and desires of urban dwellers from their responses to questions when their experience has not taken in a wide range of the possibilities in housing and neighborhood design and living. Nearly everyone, it is said, wants a little more regardless of his standard or plane of living. Those who have always lived in the slums may have little or no basis for comparing various ways of living that are completely foreign to them. This difficulty is partly ameliorated by the ubiquitous movie and advertisement, which permit everyone to know to some degree the conditions of other ways of life. These mediums do present the difficulty, however, of providing an experience that is frequently removed from everyday reality.

There are other means, however, by which the urban dweller is given a wider range of experiences than one might expect at first glance. Though some of these are vicarious, nevertheless, they do extend his range and give him a greater choice in stating his preferences than one might assume. For example, nearly everyone has friends who live in a different part of town or in a different neighborhood from his own. In visiting these friends, he is bound to observe their environments and form some opinions about them. The slum dweller usually knows someone in "the project," and he must be indeed unobservant if on his visits he does not notice the difference in equipment and structure from that of his own.

Trips to and from work, Sunday outings, and the like take people to and through parts of town different from their own. Here, too, they are bound to observe variations from their own existence. Also the childhood environment of many slum dwellers and others often has been far different from their present existence; and though nostalgia (or in some cases revulsion) may distort the appraisal of their childhood environment, it too adds to their span of experience and permits a much more intelligent response to questions on wants and needs than one might suppose.

Although the obstacle of inadequate experience is a difficult one, it should not preclude the use of the sample survey. If sufficient attention is paid to the problems and the body of experience chalked up in ascertaining the attitudes of urban dwellers on other matters, a sizeable inroad toward meeting this problem may be made. Conceivably, the questions themselves may be designed so as to reduce this problem. The important point is the perception of the respondents. The interviewer must know how the people he talks with perceive the situation. He must at least approach an understanding of what they mean when they state various attitudes. In short, he should be something of a social psychologist.

In using the attitude survey, the emphasis should be on the wants of various groups rather than the individual, since the redevelopment planner presumably will be planning for groups rather than individuals. The purpose is not, of course, to attempt to use such an attitude survey as a basis for exact project specifications; variety and contradictions in wishes are bound to occur. Its value lies in informing the redevelopment planner about the type of redevelopment area or neighborhood he is expected to help provide. He may then provide a number of choices to meet the needs of various groups in the community. It is not the purpose of such a survey to determine what the majority of the people want and then provide just that, but instead to provide a variety in some proportion to the indicated preferences.

Present information on surveys for this type of work is rather sketchy. If enough attitude surveys were made and properly analyzed over a period of time, then some generalizations might be possible. Perhaps it would turn out that we are naïve in assuming that many people have a level of experience or information that makes an attitude survey meaningful and then, perhaps, we might discover the opposite. Experience may show that the expressed wants of the people are not valid. They may change suddenly and thus make obsolete earlier surveys. In general, however, it seems that surveys of this kind have wide possibilities, but much more experience with their use in this field is needed before valid conclusions can be drawn. The first few surveys will certainly not provide the last word on attitudes or methods, but they should give some indication at least of the possibilities of this device.

Another technique that needs further exploration and that can only be sketched here concerns methods for assessing the change in attitudes when groups undergo changes in environmental conditions. The question posed is: what changes occur in the attitudes of groups toward living conditions when they are moved to an environment substantially different from their previous environment? In short, what effect does a widened experience have on wants, desires, and preferences? How important is a greater experience in determining the basic wants and needs of urban dwellers?

The procedure here would be to ascertain the attitudes of various groups, some of whom one knows will move or be moved to a new environment. Such a group could well be those whom the housing authority or private developer contemplated for a new housing project. After the move, and at various intervals, this group could again be interviewed to ascertain the shift in attitudes; and at the same time, those who did not move could also be interviewed, as a control group. This type of investigation would throw some light on what the redeveloper could expect after he had met the original needs of various groups. It would also be valuable in ascertaining the effect of certain environmental patterns on the attitudes of certain groups.

This proposed procedure, however, raises another rather basic question that has been referred to earlier and that is applicable to fields other than urban redevelopment. This question essentially is: What is the relation between the people and, in this case, the planner? To what extent should facilities be limited by the expressed wishes of the people and to what extent should the ideas of the planners and technicians be given consideration, since presumably they have information unknown to the people and which, if it were known, would influence their choices? This is the fundamental problem of the relation between the people and the technician in a democracy and one for which there is no pat answer.

An approach to the problem might be that the technician should discover the peoples' wishes, broken down into their elements if possible, and from this information and his technical knowledge produce that which will best meet these wants. To use a simple and obvious example, the technician would not ask individuals whether they wished to live "close-in" or "out" but instead would try to find out the components of their "desirable environment," because, presumably, a respondent's wishes on living "close-in" or "out" would be based on his ideas of environmental conditions in each place. With this information and a knowledge of the type of facilities he could supply, the technician could then determine what groups would prefer to live close-in if certain environmental conditions were available and what groups would prefer suburban life in any event. Through urban redevelopment, the redevelopment planner quite possibly could provide housing and neighborhood conditions at a location "close-in" that would meet essentially the "desirable environment" specified by most of those who would ordinarily prefer to live "out."

Another means of attacking the problem is suggested in chapter iv, in which community and local district or neighborhood organizations are discussed. If the redevelopment planner can work closely with the groups for whom he is planning, he will be able, assuming he is an adroit and tactful person, to transmit much of his special knowledge to those with whom he works and to give them a better understanding of the span of their choices. This procedure is also a means of overcoming the problem of the limited experience of the respondent, for the technician can widen, verbally at least, the experience of those whose attitudes he seeks. The community organizations will also be a means of making clear to the planner the attitudes, needs, and desires of those in the area.

UNIVERSALITY

The usefulness of this type of information has been doubted on the basis of the questionable universality (i.e., within the urban culture of this country) of group attitudes. The question is whether one can expect groups with similar characteristics but separated geographically to have the same attitudes and express the same needs and desires. For example, can one expect a group of Milwaukee citizens with certain characteristics to express the same attitudes, needs, and desires as a group in Buffalo with similar characteristics? Insufficient information is available to answer the question, but offhand, one would expect that no categorical answer is possible.

On some subjects, one might well expect that the variable of geographic location would have no appreciable effect while in other cases it would be of considerable importance. To use another simple example, groups whose incomes are too low to provide for automobiles and who must use public transportation to and from work could be expected to have similar views on accessability of transportation facilities regardless of the city in which they live. Because of the difference in density and adequacy of transportation facilities in each city, however, one might expect that the distance from the transportation line expressed as "satisfactory" might vary.

The only real answer to this quite obviously important question will have to await the findings of many more surveys of this type than are now available. The possible limitation of universal application, however, should not deter an investigation of this fundamental problem. For a redeveloper who acquires information of this kind from his area for use in his area, the application of what he finds out may make the difference between real progress in making the city a decent place in which to live and merely removing unsightly buildings but doing little to improve the quality of the basic living pattern.

In short, urban redevelopment is the chance to do something positive and substantial toward making the city a better place in which to live. If it can be used to give the people a variety of choices to meet their needs and wants, it will have been used wisely. If the redeveloper-planner, however, does not know what the desires and preferences of urban groups are but instead must make his land reuse decisions on the basis of what he thinks the people should have, what he guesses they want, or what relatively small interest groups in the community think the people want or should have, then the real value and opportunity of urban redevelopment will be lost. The power that is his will have been wasted and in fact misused, for it will be only by chance or keen insight that he hits upon the real needs and wants of the urban dweller. Urban redevelopment is possibly the first opportunity for cities to remake themselves into desirable patterns. The opportunity should be seized—even at the cost of broadening the scope of professional practice and helping to test and improve new techniques of analysis and research.

CHAPTER II

NEEDS AND DESIRES OF THE URBANITE

URBAN REDEVELOPMENT AND CONSUMER ATTITUDES

EVERY step taken in urban redevelopment and city planning involves certain assumptions about the desires and needs of the people for whom the planning is being done. The following stenographic notes of a meeting of planners in one of America's largest cities illustrates both the importance of the subject of this chapter and the current confused thinking about the attitudes of those people whose lives are to be affected by the proposed redevelopment of many urban areas.

To illustrate the remarks of Mr. A, Mr. B was asked why he now hesitates with the specific plans he has developed. He said that he wants to know what groups are involved, i.e., whom his plans will affect and what the response will be. Mr. A asked why he needs to know this in order to plan—will the group using the playground affect either its location or plan? Mr. B insisted that knowledge of the needs and attitudes of the consumer is essential, and Mr. E added that the importance of attaining this knowledge lies with the timing of plans. . . .

Mr. C asked Mr. F if he did not feel that, in view of the impossibility of making immediate changes, it would be necessary to know something about the groups affected. Mr. B said that he had obtained a great deal of valuable information from "key people" in the area, and that the information so obtained was better than complete ignorance. A designed questionnaire, although it would yield more profitable results, would probably be prohibitively costly. Mr. D said that it was better to have complete ignorance than be misinformed. He and Mr. C argued with Mr. B that although such information may appear at the present sufficiently reliable, it is definitely not when at the crucial time action is to take place.

Mr. D then inquired what is the minimum information necessary, and how will it influence the action of the Planning Commission. What are the aims, the ultimate objectives of the planner? Until these objectives are known, it is impossible to know what prevents their attainment. What, for example, is the purpose of redevelopment, and what prevents the planner from accomplishing this purpose? Mr. B said that the objective of redevelopment is to prevent blight, and that the attitudes of the people are an important factor in preventing blight. Mr. E agreed, but said in addition that we are interested in the redevelopment of blighted areas as part of the city as a whole. Mr. C asked whether the negative objective—prevention of blight—was the only aim of redevelopment. Mr. A here disagreed with Mr. B, and described redevelopment as a means of creating a good environment, insisting that demolition not serve as the basis of redevelopment planning. Mr. C then asked by what criteria will the planner judge which is the first action, of a wide range of alternatives, to be taken. Mr. A said need and expediency. Thus, we seek an understanding of the social structure, so as to determine under what circumstances the "need" will be felt.

Mr. C recapitulated the arguments thus given, as the objective of redevelopment planning, the creation of good environments; knowledge of physical conditions and felt need on the part of the residents is indispensable to achieving this end. But Mr. D interposed a question as to the set of values by which *need* is determined. Mr. E said that we consider both the needs of the residents of the area and the needs of the city as a whole. Mr. D reiterated that a cautious decision must be made as to whose values are to be used as the basis for determining needs. He asserted that the reactions of people are of no consequence unless strong. With this opinion Mr. A took issue, stating that he renounces the authoritarian attitude. Mr. D asked whether it were not the purpose of the ———— City Planning Commission to have the authority and the conviction to effectuate plans. Mr. A insisted that the process of planning be democratic—that we must know the needs and aspirations of the people. Mr. C referred back to the problem of understanding the population of the area for which you are planning, and Mr. D asked *what* population this is: will the present population be there when the plans are fulfilled? Mr. A implied that we are planning for present residents of the area, that it makes a considerable difference what they think, that a plan cannot be imposed on an area. He described planning as a continuous process, creating an even more desirable physical and social environment; taking account of the organic nature of the society, the mutations in social relationships and institutions.

Mr. D said then that Mr. A describes an environment where people may live if they want to; and Mr. A added that such an environment must satisfactorily express the forces which develop in the community. But what is satisfaction? Is there agreement on aims? Some aims, certainly, are settled, and call for action. The planner is invertebrate if he fails under such circumstances to take action.

But Mr. A wanted to know whether we apply our own or other standards in determining a course of action. Mr. B was asked for his statement of the aims of planning and his reply was "to create an environment where people can realize their full capacity for healthy, happy living." Mr. D asked how he would know when such an aim was accomplished, to which Mr. A replied that we don't. . . .

Here is ample evidence that some planners at least are becoming acutely aware of the need for assigning more significant places in planning and redevelopment to attitudes and values of the general public.[1] Often the assumptions of what people need or want are not explicit in the minds of the planners; but if the redevelopment of urban areas is to result in the satisfaction of basic human needs and wants (and we take it for granted that this is the goal that justifies the planning effort), these assumptions of what is needed and desired must be based upon more than sheer habit of the planners' minds or upon their unconscious motivations. For example, few would seriously assert that what man does represents what man prefers to do. Were one to do so, he would

1. The term "values" or "social values" means those objects, situations, or conditions which people feel are important to their general welfare and satisfaction. Thus privacy, physical comfort, cleanliness, freedom from noise, nearness to friends or distance from them, preferences for apartments or for single family houses, homogeneity or variety of neighbors with regard to income, religion, nationality, or racial background, rural versus urban residence, all of these and many others are included under the heading of "social values" or simply "values." It is a convenient term used to indicate those things toward which persons have attitudes, whether negative or positive attitudes.

have to argue that, in the United States, very large numbers of urbanites prefer building lots so narrow that little, if any, sunlight penetrates the interior of the dwellings; that they frequently enjoy walking up three, four, or even five floors to reach their home; and that they elect to live with their families where dirt, noise, and unpleasant odors abound, but where ample play space for children is unknown.

Instead, it is surely true that millions of Americans live where they do because there is no practical alternative. A seller's market in housing has followed in the wake of this country's last two wars, nourished by newly found cash or credit and the snowballing effects of a protracted housing shortage. The builder and seller of housing needed to provide for only the lowest common denominator of man's needs: shelter from the weather, a minimum of privacy, a place to eat and sleep. Necessity, or even desperation, rather than the sober weighing of complex social needs and desires, forced people to buy or rent such minimal quarters. Nor are the two postwar periods unique in this respect; the situation in so-called "normal times" differs only in degree.

Lest all the fault be lodged with the designer, builder, and seller of America's housing, however, it is well to bear in mind that these persons are governed, at least in part, by what they believe to be the tastes of their clients. This is particularly true of those who can afford to buy or build their homes. One prominent architect believes that the unrealistic, sentimental attitudes of many purchasers of homes explains why it is true that

. . . his house is not often straightforward, logical, efficient; why it is likely to stand incongruously related to the confines of its narrow lot; why it takes no thought of its neighbors; why it is Spanish or Colonial or Tudor or what-not, according to the vague terminology of its occupants; why it so rarely has a charm arising out of a harmony of need and use with the possibilities of materials and the requirements of location. . . .[2]

The difficulty with designer, builder, real-estate dealer, and purchaser alike, it would seem, lies in a failure to understand the basic motivations of men. If either the seller or the buyer of housing had a greater awareness of the buyer's fundamental needs and wants, many of the errors so frequently built in concrete, wood, brick, and into the landscape would be avoided. It is unfortunately true, that although we all have been living for varying numbers of years in a social "laboratory," few of us have had the time or inclination to analyze the com-

2. Miles Colean, "Economic and Social Significance of Housing Design," *Annals of the American Academy of Political and Social Science*, CXC (March, 1937), 106–7. For an excellent study of the effects of the attitudes of home purchasers upon the ultimate design of the house, see Irving Rosow, "Modern Architecture and Social Change," M.A. thesis at Wayne University, Detroit, 1948.

plex motivations at work. The following analysis of these needs and wants may prove of some value to both designers and sellers on the one hand and to buyers and tenants on the other.

MAN'S NEEDS

Attitudes toward types of housing, residential location, lot sizes, size of community, rural and urban characteristics, and neighbors, as well as the action taken in response to these attitudes, are reflections of the basic requirements of man, both as a biological and social animal. Without assuming that the last word has been said concerning the nature of these basic needs, many students of human nature will agree with the particular requirements set forth here as fundamental. Satisfaction of these needs is essential to the "good life" regardless of where or when man might live.

It is the purpose of this study to bring into sharper focus these human requirements that are to serve as the starting point of all planning and redevelopment activity if such activity is to be realistic. Thus we will review the research bearing upon attitudes and social values, set these data against the broad-gauge thinking that social scientists have brought to bear upon basic human needs, and finally suggest specific avenues of research to be followed in the quest for further knowledge of these basic motivations of man as they are related to planning and redevelopment.

For purposes of this study, it seems desirable to divide these needs into two groups, namely, universal needs (needs which are shared by all of mankind because man is man) and cultural needs (needs which are peculiar to the culture of a given nation or smaller group within a nation).

I. Universal Needs
    A. Physiological ("Biogenic")
        1. Freedom from excessive noise
        2. Water
        3. Sunlight
        4. Air circulation and supply
        5. Freedom from excessive heat or lack of heat
        6. Conservation of time and energy
        7. Sex expression
        8. Pressure of habit
    B. Socially Acquired ("Sociogenic")
        1. Desire for recognition and approval
        2. Desire for affection and companionship
        3. Desire for variety of experiences
        4. Desire for security
II. Cultural Needs

The felt needs of man which are the products of his unique experiences within a given environment or environments. Involves the social values of the person as defined by his cultural group experience.

The categories of the needs of man presented here are not the only way in which these basic needs can be subdivided. The present state of the sciences of man allows no dogmatism about basic theories and, therefore, it would be suprising indeed if any classification of wants and needs were to find complete and general acceptance. On the other hand, the needs as presented and discussed here have the backing of a large portion of those whose vocation is the study of man's behavior. These concepts have proved useful in studying and understanding social behavior, and we employ them here as points of reference in our consideration of the relationship between planning and redevelopment efforts, on the one hand, and man's wants and aspirations, on the other. It is terms of satisfying these fundamental needs that planning is to be judged as successful or unsuccessful.

UNIVERSAL NEEDS

PHYSIOLOGICAL NEEDS

Physiologists and medical men have told us much about the biological needs of the human body. We know how much air, water, heat, and light are required to keep the body alive and also the additional amounts that make for good health. Man's needs at this level are of lessening concern for the planner or redeveloper because no planner of any standing in this country is apt to subscribe to standards that would jeopardize physiological health. As to the universality of these requirements, one must distinguish between the limits that permit man to exist and those that allow him to live in comfort. Thus, although man's auditory equipment can survive noises measuring up to 130 decibels, no planner would accept living conditions that necessitated the tolerance of noises even approaching this level. Similarly, although vitamin pills, artificial ventilation, and antiseptics make it possible to do without sunlight, windows will continue to be built in houses.

Planners must recognize that there are three levels of adequacy for these physiological requirements: (1) sheer existence, (2) efficiency, and (3) comfort. It should be clear that, as one attempts to know more about levels (2) and (3), it becomes increasingly difficult to separate purely physiological needs from cultural habits. That most of the levels of adequacy suggested here are strongly influenced by our cultural values is certain.

Freedom from excessive noise.—The Housing Commission of the League of Nations recommended that the noise within the dwelling unit in residential areas should not exceed 50 decibels and in study and sleeping rooms should be kept below 30 decibels.[3] Because of the open windows in warmer weather, the Committee recommends that the noise level near bedroom windows should not exceed 40 to 50 decibles, and nowhere in the immediate vicinity of any dwelling unit should a noise level of more than 50 to 60 decibels be permitted.

Water.—Although domestic consumption standards usually are estimated at from 50 to 100 gallons of water per person per day, this is not a universal need for many millions do with less in a month. This 100 per cent variation is needed to accommodate differences in types of development, effective economic demand, and other factors.[4] Frequent baths, it must be remembered, are not essential to human life.

Sunlight.—The standard of the Committee on the Hygiene of Housing is that at least half of the "habitable rooms in every dwelling unit receives direct sunlight for one hour or more during midday (between 10:00 A.M. and 2:00 P.M.) at the winter solstice. As the sun is then at its lowest height, the penetration specified will assure sunlight in all seasons."[5] To this is added the recommendation that in order to assure enough light for the performance of the usual household tasks without artificial lighting on clear days, the buildings be spaced at least as far apart as their vertical walls are high. Again, these are cultural standards and have little to do with sheer survival, though the Committee believes they are essential to full health. And health, as the Committee sees it, is not only more than keeping alive, it is more than the absence of identifiable disease.

Air circulation and supply.—Recent studies have lowered the older notions of our needs. It has been discovered that reduction of oxygen content and increase of carbon dioxide considerably beyond normal limits do not cause physical discomfort if temperature is kept low and the air is circulated. The chemical properties of air (except, of course, in the case of noxious fumes, etc.) are less important in maintaining comfort than the physical ones of temperature, moisture, and air movement. It has been demonstrated, however, that imperceptible body

3. "The decibel scale measures the loudness of sound, starting with one decibel, which is the threshold of human audibility (for normal hearing), and goes up to approximately 130 decibels,—which is the limit of the ear's endurance. A subway train approximates 100 decibels, a heavy traffic street 80 decibels, normal conversation about 50 decibels and whispering about 20. (The number of decibels is a measure, on a logarithmic scale, of the sound energy. Thus a sound at the 10-decibel level has 10 times as much energy as the just audible sound, and 60-decibel sound is 10 times as strong as 50-decibel sound.)" *Planning the Neighborhood,* APHA Committee on the Hygiene of Housing, Public Administration Service, Chicago, 1948. p. 32.

4. *Ibid.,* p. 14.

5. *Ibid.,* p. 29.

odors can and do impair appetites, a fact that has important implications for the design and location of residences.

Freedom from excessive heat or lack of heat.—Winslow and Herrington[6] state that:

. . . The physiological objective to be attained is clearly defined. It is fixed by the maintenance of a skin temperature of 33° (91°F.) with minimal negative heat exchange and minimal evaporation of sweat. With the ordinary winter clothing worn in the northern United States, this condition will be obtained, with varying degrees of metabolism at about the following temperatures in °F.:

	Operative Temperature	Air Temperature (assuming a cold wall)
Complete rest	78°	79° − 80°
Moderate activity	74°	75° − 76°
Considerable activity (rapid typewriting)	68°	69° − 70°

Conservation of time and energy.—Although all of the answers are not yet in, much knowledge has been accumulated on how to save the time and energy of the family, and of the housewife particularly, in the routine of daily living. This research, much of it done by home economists and architects, has been restricted largely to the inclosed space of the dwelling and especially to the kitchen. Comparable studies carried out in the exterior of the dwelling unit itself will bring further rewards in economy of energy and time. But by and large, it is not here that the most acute need for research and additional knowledge exists.

Sex expression.—At first it may seem that the planner is going rather far afield in considering the problems of sex as falling within his sphere of study. To the extent, however, that our dwellings and communities do not permit the expression of normal, adult sex behavior, to that extent these facilities are significantly inadequate. In our culture, as in most cultures, privacy is a *sine qua non* of successful marital sex relations, and the lack of privacy for such relations is surely one of the most unfortunate costs to be paid for overcrowding dwellings. Even the 1.5 persons per room, taken by the Bureau of Census as the criterion of overcrowding, probably is grossly out of line for such purposes. Housing inadequacy from this standpoint may be more serious for family welfare than inadequacies of light, water, or quiet.

Pressure of habit.—Often what seems a sensible evaluation of a living arrangement may, upon careful investigation, turn out to be nothing more than the work of habit's strong arm. Once one becomes accustomed to ways of doing things, to surroundings, and to associates, he tends to perpetuate them. Habits need not be "bad" in order to be dif-

6. C. E. A. Winslow and L. P. Herrington, *Temperature and Human Life* (Princeton, N.J.: Princeton University Press, 1949), p. 197.

ficult to break; good habits, of any sort, are equally resistant to change. In evaluating the attitudes and through them the fundamental requirements of the people for whom planning is being done, the planner must allow for the role of habit in the behavior of these people. This applies to the attitudes toward building types, toward locations with reference to the central city, toward racial and religious questions, as well as toward facilities that we generally assume to make for better living.

Habit is an inertia that at times militates against clear and rational thinking. If not recognized for what it is, it can thwart the redevelopers' attempts to meet the most important needs of the people. For illustrations of the work of habit, one need only walk or drive through almost any residential district in our cities. One example is the dormers that so frequently are built into houses without the redeeming justification of economic or other necessity. Somehow, the dormer, used originally to make attics livable, has become for many a symbol of something good and valuable, a symbol based upon habitual image rather than upon examination of the dormer as a means to some desired or necessary end. A similar habitual attitude toward housing design leads people to buy or build the steep-roofed, mullion-windowed houses that fit well into the landscape of the fairy tales by the Brothers Grimm but that are frustrating to their occupants in their daily tasks. Such habits of mind are costly in terms of bumped heads, inadequate closet space, poor light and ventilation, and much unusable space in peaked attics. The reader can supplement these examples with many of them from his own observations.[7]

Another form of habit that limits the horizon of tenants and owners results from restricted experiences. Habituation to apartment living and seeming satisfaction with it does not rule out the possibility of equal or greater satisfaction from other types of housing that the person has never known. Quite as surely the reverse is true. The same can be said of rural and urban preferences. This suggests a potential weakness of attitude surveys that seek evaluations by those interviewed of situations and conditions they have never experienced. The person who has always lived in a single-family house on a large lot and the one whose residence has always been in multi-storied, elevator-serviced apartments have developed habitual attitudes that hinder the task of evaluating the types of housing they have not known through living in them. Of course these people have opinions but too often they have them upon widespread but uncritical evaluations of housing types. One writer has stated the point: ". . . Thus, home to the American has been more an ideal to dream

7. That such habits of mind are not confined to the buyer is illustrated by the excellent criticism of traditionally oriented architects in the introduction to *Tomorrow's House* by Henry Wright and George Nelson (New York: Simon and Schuster, 1945).

of, to work for, and to write songs about than it has been the shelter of brick or wood in which he might be living; it has been more a sentiment than a reality."[8] As pointed out in chapter i, however, this limitation of experience does not vitiate the attitude study as a research tool.

SOCIALLY ACQUIRED UNIVERSAL NEEDS

Many of man's strongest motivations are not physiological in origin in the sense that they are innate or inborn. No matter what culture he may call his own, man *learns* certain basic needs, among them (1) the desire to be noticed and approved by his fellows; (2) the desire for affection or companionship; (3) the desire for a variety of experiences; and (4) the desire for the security of his possessions and his status in the community. It matters not whether he is a native of Brooklyn, Mozambique, Japan, Tibet, or Bali he will, in the process of interacting with other human beings, develop these needs. Not being instinctive or inborn makes them no less potent in directing man's behavior. As a matter of fact, millions of daily instances evidence the dominance of such socially acquired drives or needs over the basic physiological ones. Good health and even life itself are frequently sacrificed in trying to satisfy these "secondary" social needs.

Recognition.—Although the need for recognitions is not as important a consideration for the planner as for the designer of women's gowns, it is not to be ignored if urban redevelopment is to be realistic. As is true of all these basic, socially acquired motives, the desire for recognition can be fulfilled in many ways, depending upon the society in which one lives and the particular experiences he has had within that society. It is particularly important to keep this in mind in the complex urban cultures with which we are currently concerned. Some persons gain social approval from the positions they hold in the community, others from the things they possess, and still others from what they or their families have done in the past. The concentration and migration of the population of a community, the design of dwellings, and many other urban activities can be explained in part by the strength of this need for social recognition. Because it is one of the most fundamental forces involved in the shaping of the urban community, the redeveloper is ill-advised to ignore it.

Companionship and affection.—The need for companionship and affection has been taken into consideration in significant measure by planners. This is the need that lies behind the neighborhood principle or notion in city planning. The neighborhood, however, is not the only means of satisfying this basic human requirement, and research into other specific forms is essential.

8. Colean, *op. cit.*, p. 106.

Variety of experience.—Man's capacity for boredom is the root of much human motivation and determines the attitude one may take toward many objects and situations. However desirable an object or situation may be from other viewpoints, if it spells boredom to a given individual, it often will be abandoned in favor of what many others would consider substitutes of lesser value. As with other drives, the wish for variety or new experience can be met in an infinite number of ways; but it will manifest itself in one form or another within the redeveloper's sphere and he should take cognizance of it.

Security.—Man's need to feel secure explains many of his otherwise puzzling activities. Predictability is the foundation of much that we call security, and the desire to know that one's job, home, status, money, friends, and so forth are to persist is a strong influence upon human behavior. People remain at jobs they dislike, in houses that are neither practical nor comfortable, in neighborhoods that do not square with their attitudes because of the fear of uprooting themselves in quest of improved conditions. This is in part a reflection of the unpleasantness of changing habits. But, whatever the explanation, research indicates that the desire for security usually dominates our motives; and unless other drives are unusually strong, the need for security tends to maintain the status quo.[9]

It should be noted that most of our activities involve more than one of these fundamental motivations, and it is frequently difficult to establish the priority of one of them in a given act. Each is autonomous, however, and the satisfaction of one will seldom remove the need to satisfy another. A new home will not satisfy an affection-starved wife. It should be noted, too, that the fruits of planning and redevelopment efforts cannot hope to fulfil all these needs. One's occupation, education, travel, and many other activities are essential to this end.

CULTURAL NEEDS

The ways in which the universal needs of man can be met are without number, and the most casual reflection will reveal the grosser differences existing between the many cultural areas of the world. In pursuit of their needs and wants, some people put up stoically with a minimum of protection against excesses of heat, cold, and moisture, against the encroachments of the insect world, are apparently satisfied with a simple and often sporadic diet, and with relatively little clothing and adornment. Others, however, such as many urbanites of western European culture, tolerate but a narrow range of variations of tem-

9. Maurice H. Krout, "Wishes and Behavior," *Journal of Abnormal and Social Psychology,* XXIX (1934), 253–68.

perature or moisture, demand a complete absence of pestiferous insects, a diet that exceeds by far the minimal qualitative and quantitative requirements, and wear clothing and adornments that have little if any relationship to the need for protection from the elements.

Nor do we have to look to the different cultures in order to see marked variation in the ways of meeting the flexible innate and the acquired human needs. Particularly in the modern urban cultures do we find heterogeneity or variety of values to be a common characteristic. The many different attitudes that are so evident in the city scene demand full awareness and treatment by those who would shape the urban environment according to the basic wants of urban man. It is just the failure to realize the absence of any marked conformity of attitudes that has given a very unrealistic touch to some planning efforts. The needs, and therefore, the plans, have been oversimplified; diversity has been ignored, whereas it should be the keynote of urban redevelopment.

But, some may argue, our cities are bound to grow less mixed in values as we leave further behind in time the heavy immigration of Europeans to American cities, as the migration from rural areas tends to taper off, and as common experiences shape common attitudes. All of this is, to be sure, quite true, but many would counter with the statement that the essence of urbanism is heterogeneity of attitudes and values. In the absence of other motives, the desires for recognition and for new experiences will engender activities sufficiently diverse to make for considerable variation in attitudes. Being different just for the sake of being different may persist in the urban scene as long as urbanism itself. The degree to which the planner can create diversification in his plan is the degree to which he will contribute to the fulfilment of a fundamental requirement for satisfactory social life.

Not only does man vary from place to place his ways of responding to his universal needs but he varies his response from time to time as well. The fads and fashions of any given period are not inconsequential to the planner or redeveloper; and although he may not ignore them, neither should he fail to recognize them, if at all possible, as temporally limited wants. This caution is necessary lest one destroy lasting values in the fulfilment of temporary ones. One need not be a reactionary to suggest the importance of studying carefully every recommended radical change in urban living facilities. Caprice is not a virtue in planning.

Finally, in dealing with the basic needs of man, it should be noted that the complexity of desires, both innate and acquired, means that the pursuit of general satisfaction and the process of remaining alive involve constant compromises. Fulfilling one need to the exclusion of the others rarely, if ever, results in anything but disaster. One of the surest measures of the mature personality is the ability to forego the satisfaction of certain wants in order that others may be met. The happiest environment provides the opportunity for individuals to balance the satisfaction of physiological requirements, the universal social wants, and the demands made upon them by their society and its culture. The obligation of the planner in providing for such an environment is by no means to be taken lightly.

Summary

Although most planners have not been explicit about the matter, their plans and decisions are shaped by certain assumptions about the needs and wants of the people for whom they plan. Planning research and literature in recent years reveal a growing awareness of the importance of identifying these basic human needs as a first step in planning and redeveloping our cities. These needs are complex; and realistic planning demands that each requirement be recognized and given its due, lest in planning the fulfilment of one need, others be thwarted.

One should distinguish between the needs that all men share (universal needs) and those one develops because he has lived with a certain group of people in a given place or places (cultural needs). Among the former are the needs for bodily comfort (including the inertia of habit), based upon the physiological nature of man, and the needs for recognition or social approval, for variety of experiences, for companionship, and for security, which result from the interaction of man with man. The nature of the human being does not require that these basic needs be satisfied in any given manner, but is flexible enough to permit these wants to be met in almost numberless ways. The heterogeneity of city life finds its reason for being in these fundamental needs and thus is bound to be a continuing aspect of urbanism.

Constant awareness of the nature of these motives of man serves to lend caution to the planner lest he base his plans upon the shifting sands of fads and fashions, or else upon only one or two of the more enduring needs. Because the basic needs of mankind are mutually exclusive, the most satisfactory life always involves compromise. The city plan that attends only to the needs of man for physical comfort to the exclusion of an opportunity for companionship, freedom from boredom, and for recognition by his fellow man is a plan for a prison that men will abandon for a more precarious but more satisfying existence. The design of the well-rounded community provides for opportunities to fulfil, at least in moderation, not one, but all, of these human wants. It provides the consumer with a variety of choices, with chances to make his compromises in many different patterns.

SPECIFIC AREAS OF INVESTIGATION

Against this background of basic human needs, we may now take up two aspects of the urban community upon which the attitudes of its members have important bearings. The first is housing per se; the second deals with external space relations in terms of (1) distances to services, (2) the journey to work, (3) personal group relations, and (4) the relationship of the immediate area to the larger community. Wherever possible, a very brief account of the existing conditions in this country will be presented. This is done not in the naïve belief that what man does coincides with what he wants to do, but with the knowledge that most men have some latitude in choosing where they will live and work. Thus the picture of what is, if intelligently analyzed, may give some hints as to what is thought to be desirable.

As a possible aid to both redevelopment planners and to future researchers, the remainder of this chapter also includes five tabular summaries or digests of various studies on home ownership, size and characteristics of housing, external space relationships, neighborhood or personal face-to-face relations, and suburban living. All but a few of these studies deal with peoples' wants, opinions, and attitudes. Altogether some forty studies and investigations have been covered. Naturally they vary greatly in scope, purpose, thoroughness, nature of methods used, and competence of those who directed and did the work.

Several other facts about these studies and the tables should be emphasized. Including a study in a table does not mean that its methods, findings, or interpretations are approved or agreed to by the writers of this chapter or by others associated in URS. Neither does omitting a study mean disagreement or disapproval. Although a few studies appear in two (or more) tables, the digests are not intended as rounded or complete summaries. They only give a few highlights to indicate an investigation's nature and results. In other words, they are little more than checklists or annotated bibliographies. Both planners and researchers who may not know certain items should go to the articles and reports themselves. Also the studies were made over a period of twenty years or so—before and after the great depression of the 30's. Finally, no one claims that the list of studies covered is complete. The time and resources available for searching out and reviewing the investigations was limited. It is to be hoped, however, that the work may be the start of a more thorough and detailed compilation kept up to date at frequent intervals.[10]

10. Dr. Dewey did this work during the latter half of 1949 and the early part of 1950. With only one or two minor exceptions that were the results of later editing, his tables do not cover materials published after the first of 1950. If it had been possible for him

HOUSING

HOME OWNERSHIP VS. TENANCY

Although all the influences operating here are not known or understood, it is fairly certain that the desire to own one's own home is both widespread and deep-seated in American culture. John P. Dean, in his well-documented little book *Home Ownership: Is It Sound?*[11] has pointed to many of the influences or causes of this fact. Nevertheless, the arguments over the motivations behind home ownership still continue and will do so, at least until more definitive research is carried out.

Nor do the actual trends in home ownership in the United States help very much to end the disagreements involved in the ownership vs. tenancy duel. According to figures of the Bureau of the Census, since 1890 home ownership in the country as a whole declined slowly, with minor variations, from 48 per cent to 44 per cent in 1940 and then rose very sharply to 55 per cent in 1950. These over-all figures, however, do not tell the whole story because the differences between farm and nonfarm areas are significant. In the former, ownership percentages dropped from 66 in 1890 to 53 in 1940, and, because of the complex

---

to have revised his tables (and the accompanying text) in the following eighteen months during which other parts of URS were being prepared, the tables would have included most or all of the following reports that have come out since this chapter was written:

Robert Cooley Angell, *The Moral Integration of American Cities*, Part 2 of the *American Journal of Sociology* (July, 1951).

Theodore Caplow, "Incidence and Direction of Residential Mobility in a Minneapolis Sample," *Social Forces* (May, 1949), pp. 413–17.

Theodore Caplow and Robert Forman, "Neighborhood Interaction in a Homogeneous Community," *American Sociological Review* (June, 1950), pp. 357–66.

Chicago Housing Authority, *Home-To-Work, How Far Wage-Earners in Chicago's Low-Rent Housing Projects Travel to Their Jobs* (The Authority, 1951, mimeo).

———, *The Livability of Low-Rent Public Housing—A Pilot Survey of Five CHA Projects* (The Authority, 1950, mimeo).

P. D. Converse and Ramona J. Russell, "Why City Workers Live in Agricultural Villages," *Current Economic Comment* (College of Commerce and Business Administration, University of Illinois, August 1950), pp. 37–46.

Bleecker Marquette, "Exploring Housing Needs of the Aging," speech before Second International Gerontological Congress, St. Louis, September 13, 1951. Better Housing League of Cincinnati and Hamilton County, mimeo.

Robert K. Merton, Patricia Salter West, Marie Jahoda, and Hanan C. Selvin (eds.), "Social Policy and Social Research in Housing," *Journal of Social Issues*, Vol. VII, 1951, Nos. 1 and 2.

Helen Rankin, *New Town for Old, The Peterlee Survey* (London: Bureau of Current Affairs, 1949).

Real Estate Research Corporation, *Housing Market Analysis, Cook County, Illinois*, 1951 supplement, Housing Authority of the County of Cook, Chicago, 1952.

Svend Riemer, Marshall F. Dumeyer, and Blanche Halbert, *Livability of Housing: What Is it?* (National Association of Housing Officials, Chicago, 1951).

11. New York: Harper and Brothers, 1945.

factors surrounding the years of World War II, rose to 65 in 1950. In the nonfarm areas, the long-term trend is the reverse. Home ownership rose from 37 per cent in 1890 to 46 per cent in 1930; the economic depression of the thirties caused it to drop to 41 per cent in 1940; it was forced up to 53 per cent in 1950 by the combination of housing shortages, high rents, ready cash in the pockets of Americans, government measures in behalf of easy mortgage credit, and the postwar inflation. In urban areas alone the percentages were 43 in 1930, 37 in 1940, and 50 in 1950.

How accurately these trends reflect the true desires of Americans is not known, and the direct studies of attitudes may be more rewarding in this respect. Table 1, which presents digests of such studies, indicates two facts: (1) that whenever given the opportunity, most American families express their desire to own their homes, and (2) that the motivations behind home ownership are of many kinds.

Whether home ownership is desirable, however, is not solely a question of the attitudes of the prospective or present owners of homes. The studies by Blum and Candee, Rosow, and the 1937 *Architectural Forum* group (Table 1) show clearly that the dwelling means different things to different people, and this meaning must be known before one can judge the wisdom or folly of home ownership in any given case. In many instances a person may believe that home ownership is a reasonable way of attaining certain life goals or values, but actually he may find that ownership impedes their realization.

If, as the studies seem to indicate, a dwelling is for many persons a means of gratifying their desires for recognition, for new experiences, or for security, it behooves all potential and actual owners to find out if ownership does, in fact, serve these ends. How true is it that Americans accept the desirability of home ownership without questioning its relationship to their basic values? Do they defeat their attempts to realize a happy adjustment to life by saddling themselves with home ownership? Could not their needs be met through the proper kind of tenancy rather than through owning?

In an article describing the three housing developments of Sunnyside (Long Island), Radburn (New Jersey), and Chatham Village (Pittsburgh), Clarence S. Stein contrasts the sad experiences of ownership in the former two developments with the happy relationships in the rental units in Chatham Village.[12] Although the situations are not strictly comparable because of the ill-fated timing of Radburn (built just before

12. "Toward New Towns for America," *Town Planning Review*, XX, 187–282. This and companion articles have been reprinted in book form: Clarence S. Stein, *Toward New Towns for America* (Liverpool: University Press of Liverpool, 1951; distributed in this country by Public Administration Service, Chicago).

TABLE 1

STUDIES ON HOME OWNERSHIP

STUDY   1. "The Urge to Own," *Architectural Forum* (November 1937), p. 372
Scope: 1,003 interviews in 8 cities of various sizes and in various regions of the United States (Cherington-Roper staff) 43.4% owners, 56.6% renters
Findings: 91% of present home owners wish to keep on owning their homes, whereas 32.7% of renters want to keep on renting their homes.

Why prefer to own? (1) Like feeling of ownership (independence). (2) Like to fix up to suit self (this item first for women). (3) Good investment. (4) More economical in long run. (5) Assures a home for old age.

Why prefer not to own? (1) Dislike financial responsibility of owning. (2) Cannot afford kind wanted. (3) More economical to rent. (4) Future uncertain. (5) Dislike physical responsibility of owning.

In answer to question "Why do you not own home now?" 60% of answers concerned financial factors. Study concludes: "the urge to own is based more on emotional than on financial grounds, is more concerned with satisfaction of the ego than with considerations of economy. Which explains the widely held belief that gadgets continue to sell more houses than good construction . . ." (p. 377).

STUDY   2. Urban Redevelopment Study, study of south side of Milwaukee (chapter iii following)
Scope: Survey (interview) of 315 units in east, south-central part of Milwaukee—310 replies. 91 owners (of whom 70 had rented before buying) 219 tenants (of whom 37 had owned before renting). Median length of residence in house 5 years; in Milwaukee 20 years
Findings: 84.8% would prefer owning home. Reasons given for buying: forced to, no rental housing (21.2%); general desire to own (14.1%); greater personal freedom (10.6%); security (5.9%); family size (11.8%); convenience (7.1%); economic reasons (14%).

Reasons given for renting: economic reasons (61.9%); (includes homes lost for economic reasons) (24.2%); custom, habit (4.8%); greater freedom (4.8%).

STUDY   3. Melville C. Branch Jr., *Urban Planning and Public Opinion* (Bureau of Urban Research, Princeton University, Princeton, New Jersey, Sept. 1942)
Scope: Sample taken over entire country
Findings: 86% of home owners in American cities are glad they own, 10% are not.

Reasons why 10% are not satisfied: (1) Inconvenient or impractical location. (2) Too much responsibility or trouble. (3) Undesirable neighborhood environment. (4) Tied down, can't move readily. (5) Size of house not appropriate. (6) No longer good investment (p. 7).

In cities over 500,000, 30% own, 61% want to. In smaller cities, 44% own, and 75% want to (p. 9).

60% of present renters want to own; 35% do not. Why renters want to own? (1) security or stability (23%); (2) pride of ownership or possession (18%); (3) independence (17%); (4) desirable family environment (10%); (5) costs little if any more to own (8%).

TABLE 1 (*Continued*)

Why renters prefer renting: (1) no upkeep, no better business deal (30%); (2) not so much trouble or responsibility (18%); (3) unable to afford to buy or build (15%); (4) small family, single or too old (11%); (5) not tied down (10%); (6) liable to move or want to move (8%) (p. 8).

STUDY 4. "The Forum Study of the Housing Market," *Architectural Forum* (Sept. 1945)

Scope: Crossley's interviewers talked with 8,052 heads of families (both male and female), cross-section of United States population. Interviews December, 1944 to February, 1945.

Findings: 70% said it was better for them to own than to rent; 19% favored renting; 11% had no opinion. 34% said they were interested in buying or building in future. In past, 19% of home purchasers were over 45 years, now 34%. In past, 37% had been married ten years or more, now 54%.

STUDY 5. Theodore Caplow, "Home Ownership and Location Preference in a Minneapolis Sample," *American Sociological Review*, XIII (Dec., 1948), 725–30

Scope: 574 stable families (i.e., married prior to 1940, living together 1940–48 in Minneapolis).

Findings: 73.4% of renters and 86.7% of owners preferred home ownership to "long-term lease at reasonable rent." 91% felt most families should own their homes. Home owners more satisfied with housing than were tenants.

STUDY 6. Coleman Woodbury, *Apartment House Increases and Attitudes Toward Home Ownership* (Chicago: Institute for Economic Research, 1931)

Scope: Questionnaires and interviews with 1,882 persons in Chicago metropolitan area. Group included utility company employees, City Club members, members of a university faculty, organized and unorganized workers.

Findings: Concludes that 70.7% ". . . of the economic and social classes represented here still has as one of its aims or goals the ownership of a home. Whether this is a wise attitude for many of them is certainly open to question but these replies indicate that the increase in multi-family houses in the Chicago region is not caused by a wholesale change of attitude toward the relative advantages of home ownership and home tenancy . . ." (p. 74).

Reasons for owning: (1) welfare of children; (2) safety of investment; (3) forced saving; (4) amenities; (5) protection-security; (6) apartment districts lack play space; (7) apartment districts too noisy.

Reasons for renting: (1) cheaper; (2) financing costs of ownership too high; (3) tax burden too high; (4) investment in house too fixed; (5) increased freedom; (6) installment payments on a house are a dangerous practice.

STUDY 7. Irving Rosow, "Home Ownership Motives," *American Sociological Review*, XIII (December, 1948), 751–56

Scope: Investigation of 33 home owners in Detroit area in 1948. Interviews with owners and architects who built houses. With one exception, owners were earning $5,000 or more.

Findings: Distinguishes between motives of ownership as an end in itself

TABLE 1 (*Continued*)

(as family tradition or as passively accepted cultural goal) or as means to other ends, e.g., status-prestige, assertion of individualism or independence, financial ends, "psychic security" or ego satisfaction and creativity or self-expression. Business men more interested in status-prestige value and in psychic security, whereas the professional group more interested in living activities and self-expression potentialities of the house. Professional group had more specific complaints about previous dwelling (as domicile, location, etc.)

STUDY 8. Milton Blum and Beatrice Candee, *Family Behavior, Attitudes and Possessions* (John B. Pierce Foundation, New York, 1944)
Scope: 65 apartment families, and 66 families in private single-family homes. Four guided interviews with each family.
Findings: Home owners had more often lived in private homes before marriage, had planned more seriously about buying a house, were more realistic about planning an ideal dwelling. Note that house for some is of "focal" value, whereas for others it is of incidental value, is a means to an end rather than an end in itself. 90% apartment dwellers and 96% home dwellers prefer to own home.

STUDY 9. Betty Tableman, *Intra-community Migration in the Flint Metropolitan District* (Institute for Human Adjustment, University of Michigan, September, 1948)
Scope: Study of "spending units" in Flint, Michigan, metropolitan district.
Findings: Over half of all of the moves are toward home ownership.

STUDY 10. Washington (D.C.) Housing Association (1949)
Scope: 95 families who moved from public housing in D.C. during one year.
Findings: 41 of 95 who moved bought homes. Of total 95 (94), 56 were rated as "good" dwellings, 21 as "satisfactory," 11 as "substandard," and 6 as "slum."

STUDY 11. *President's Conference on Home Building and Home Ownership*, Vol. IV, 1942
Scope: Study in Buffalo
Findings: Of 788 cases, 12% reported home ownership had interfered with moving to another community to take another job; 7% felt 'ownership interfered with moving to larger or smaller house as family size changed; and 5% felt it had interfered with moving to another location to be nearer place of work or children's school (p. 102).

the economic crash of 1929), Mr. Stein, in his discussion of the Pittsburgh project, does paint an enticing picture of what rental housing can be like. This is a reversal of the common situation in which the prospective home buyer is forced by circumstances to contrast available rental units in blighted or congested, unimaginative parts of the city proper with the new, neat, and relatively uncongested areas of home ownership, i.e., the periphery of the city and the suburbs.

After critical analysis of the case for home ownership, taking into account jerry-building, overpriced houses, small lots, poor investment risks, curtailed mobility, and various forms of self-deception, John P. Dean has these words of caution for the American family, particularly for those whose financial resources are something less than strong:

Thus much housing progress seems to depend upon encouraging the American family to see its housing future not narrowly in a romantic vision of ownership, but broadly in terms of that which will best serve its total needs—and here is an acute area for consumer education. A central obstacle to enlightenment in this field lies in the constant comparison of ownership with renting. If a family seeking living space for itself and future children has to choose between the congestion of deep city living with its cramped quarters, lack of space, and high rentals and suburban home-owner neighborhoods, the latter naturally comes off better. But if we compare the home-owner neighborhood with the kind of housing we know how to build and have demonstrated we *can* build, it would surely run a poor second. . . . If families were shown places to rent where provisions were made for children, recreation, community life, and the aesthetic demands which only the harmony of green, open spaces and well-planned buildings can provide, they might by-pass the temptations of a second-rate home ownership. These families would be able to maintain flexibility for family growth, job mobility, or other pressing contingencies and at the same time achieve many advantages ordinarily thought to accompany only home ownership. If the needs of a family are well-supplied and the family is satisfied, it will not move,—it will be as stable as the home owner. The continuous moving of renters indicates either dissatisfaction with the quarters or a financial or occupational need to move. If the latter, home ownership would probably be unwise; if the former, adequate rental housing would hold them as long as it remained adequate. One wonders if either owners or renters should be held longer than that. . . .[13]

What Mr. Dean says is applicable to the housing problems of millions of Americans; undoubtedly countless families purchased a house only to discover that it not only fails to serve as a means of attaining their long-sought goals but is actually a hindrance.

One significant change that has come with the shift from an essentially rural-farm to an industrial-urban economy is the increase in the number of times that most families move during the period the children are growing up. Probably a majority of the urban families have moved more than once within the memory of even the younger children. Such moving is induced by changes of economic fortunes, by physical alterations in the particular area of the city in which the family lived, by changes in the social makeup of the neighborhood, or took place because the family outgrew its dwelling unit and moving was the only feasible means of securing a larger one. In days when the fortunes of a family were more apt to be grounded in the soil of a farm or in the son's following the father in his particular trade, moves were not the order of the day. In a social system where multiple moves are deemed desirable, renting acquires certain advantages over ownership. This fact has led

13. *Op. cit.*, pp. 135–56.

to a reduction of the former tendency to attach emotional values to the house itself. One writer puts it thus:

Among many individuals and in our past rather generally, there was a value merely in living in the same house throughout life, or having an ancestral abode to which one might return. Few of us today can realize *emotionally* the sentiment which inspired "The Old Oaken Bucket." Homesickness in the literal sense was probably a more frequent result of moving in the past than it is now. Value now attaches more to the standards of physical living or to a home of certain quality, rather than to a particular place. . . .[14]

Nevertheless, home ownership may fulfil other needs than that of satisfying or relieving homesickness. Moreover, irresponsible salesmanship, poor judgment on the part of the buyer, and inadequate protective provisions in the community design and plan do not add up to a wholesale condemnation of home ownership nor, it is certain, would Mr. Dean hold that they do. Among the many ways of satisfying the socially acquired needs for social approval and for self-expression, home ownership for many people must be counted as one of the most rewarding, if it is undertaken with due consideration of all its consequences. In several of the studies tabulated above, much was made of the point that the home is often more than a place for its occupants to live. It serves to secure "psychic" and "ego" satisfaction. The Blum and Candee study (Table 1) suggested that in the instances where the home was of "focal" interest, it was used to compensate for certain inadequacies in the situation or the personality. These observations may be accurate, in fact probably are, but this should not lead to the conclusion that there is something pathological about using the home for these ends. None of us is free of the need for "psychic" or "ego" satisfaction, and we will try to get it by one means or another. Some secure it through the professional or occupational status they enjoy and some through "social" activities. Where this is true, the home becomes incidental to these ends; and whether or not it is one's own is unimportant because there is little or no identification with it except as a place to eat, sleep, and plan the activities that are employed to gain social approval.

In a culture as heterogeneous as ours, it is obviously impossible to have the same degree of prestige or honor attached to all of the ways of making a living. Those occupations that are exclusive and somewhat mysterious from the layman's point of view provide a psychic return in addition to the monetary gain. For many urbanites, however, the "job" is merely tolerated because of the money income it yields. It provides the individual with little or no prestige or stature in his community. For such persons other means of securing recognition and other important

14. Joseph Folsom, "Changing Values in Sex and Family Relations," *American Sociological Review,* II (October, 1937), p. 723.

socio-psychological satisfactions are needed, and the ownership of a home may well provide them.[15]

This is particularly true of wives and single women in this country, most of whom are denied any career means of gaining the satisfaction all normal humans want. This need is reflected in the *Architectural Forum* study (Table 1), which showed that whereas men placed greatest value upon home ownership as a means of gaining independence, their wives assigned first place to the privilege of fixing it up to suit their own tastes. Involved here, of course, is the recognition anticipated from associates and friends.

Why, one may inquire, cannot these satisfactions be secured equally well from rental homes? The answer is threefold. First, the limitations placed upon alterations and remodeling of rented quarters are frequently too strict to permit much self-expression by the occupant. A second and probably more important reason is that, in our culture at least, most persons simply do not identify themselves with rented dwellings in anything like the same degree as with those to which they hold title, even if subject to a large and long mortgage debt. The owned house is much more an extension of the personality. In fact, it may be so much a part of the personality that approval or disapproval of the house is interpreted by the owner as an evaluation of himself. For the rented single-family or two-family house, a third and rather obvious reason lies in the danger that the tenant's efforts may lead to the sale of the house to someone who likes what the tenant has done to it.

In conclusion, John Dean's criticism of the motivations for owning a home seems correct. He points out that such values as safe and pleasant places for children to play, security of tenure, beautiful surroundings, good financial arrangements, and ample quarters are not the attributes of owned housing alone. He also warns against assuming the obligations of home ownership when circumstances of purse and family need do not warrant it. Over and above this, however, one must recognize that home ownership does provide for self-satisfaction in many instances and should be encouraged when the conditions are right. There is nothing pathological or abnormal about using the home as a means of securing psycho-social satisfactions any more than there is in employing a career in medicine, law, or the theater to the same end. Indeed, variety of means to such legitimate ends is essential; surely were nearly all of us to become physicians, no prestige would attend this profession and other means of satisfying basic wants would be sought.

15. Occasionally one encounters a form of intellectual snobbery that views the use of material goods to gain life satisfactions as a form of mental pathology and therefore less worthy than the use of education, musical talents, athletic prowess, or family heritage to the same end. It would be extremely difficult, if not impossible, to justify this position from any but a purely personal viewpoint of preference and self-reference.

WHAT IS DESIRED IN THE DWELLING UNIT?

As has been suggested before, any study of attitudes toward housing is fraught with two major difficulties. In the first place, those questioned often fail to distinguish between what they would actually desire and what they believe they can afford. Unhappily, these two realities coincide rarely, and then, almost without exception, in the upper income brackets. The second hurdle for such an attitude study is the inability of people to know what they want prior to the time that they have had first-hand experience with it.

Both difficulties were revealed in the Pierce Foundation study of attitudes toward dwellings. Those who rented or owned single-family houses and thus knew from their experiences what a few dollars will buy were much more realistic than were the apartment dwellers. In the description of an "ideal" house, only 8 per cent of the apartment dwellers were deemed to be realistic, whereas 44 per cent of the house occupants were so classified. Of those who were judged to be very unrealistic, the apartment dwellers outnumbered the house occupants by four to one.[16] Many thousands of persons have never considered the problems of housing as situations about which anything can be done, and therefore are not in positions to give opinions based upon careful analysis of their needs. As one writer said in reporting on an English study:

> To a great many people . . . the idea that they might either like or dislike their home is a novel one. They take their home for granted, and they just live there with little further thought. It is a closely interwoven part of their background, and they would normally as soon think of analyzing their own motives in going to a pub or clipping a troublesome child on the ear, as of sitting down and thinking whether and why they were not satisfied with their homes. . . .[17]

This is all too well illustrated by the replies to questions asked in a brief survey of attitudes toward housing and neighborhood made in a blighted area of a midwestern metropolis. In response to the interviewer's query, "What do you find undesirable about your house and neighborhood?" many answered, after some hesitation, that the sink needed painting, the roof needed patching, some windows were broken or cracked. These replies were given despite the fact that the houses were jammed on 30-foot lots, in poor repair, and in a residential area

16. Milton Blum and Beatrice Candee, *Family Behavior, Attitudes, and Possessions* (New York: John B. Pierce Foundation, 1944), p. 110. See also Elizabeth Coit, "Notes on Design and Construction of the Dwelling Unit for the Lower-Income Family," Part I and II, *The Octagon* (American Institute of Architects, October and November, 1941).

17. *An Enquiry into People's Homes*, A report prepared by *Mass-Observation* for the Advertising Service Guild (London: John Murray, 1943), p. 53.

TABLE 2

STUDIES ON THE SIZE AND CHARACTERISTICS OF HOUSING

STUDY 1. *The Livability Problems of 1000 Families* (Federal Public Housing Authority–National Housing Agency Bulletin No. 28, October 1, 1945)
Scope: Interviews with 1,062 families located in 51 public housing projects in eight regions. 61% of families were white, 28% were Negro, 10% Latin-Americans, 1% other. 75% in group-houses; 25% in 3 or more storied apartments. Low income groups. One-third of families interviewed in 1942, remainder in 1945.
Findings: 59% preferred one-story house. 32% preferred two-story house. 5% preferred first floor of two-storied house. 3% preferred second floor of two-storied house. 1% preferred apartment of three or more stories. 95% of those living in apartments wanted houses. Half of those wanting apartments were families of adults. Many expressed need for privacy. Prefer eating in kitchen to combination living-dining room. "The arrangement which would accomplish almost universal tenant satisfaction is the home with individual front and back entrances, the individual walk, entrance, and porch." Many want private back yard. Elderly couples desire first floor apartment or single-story house. Definite need for more storage space.

STUDY 2. *Present Housing of Former Project Tenants* (New York City Housing Authority, May 7, 1943)
Scope: Study of 251 former tenants of housing projects in New York City. Were persons who had lived in substandard dwellings prior to living in projects.
Findings: Standards raised by the experience in the housing project. 87% moved to apartments with heat and complete bath within apartment; more than two-thirds secured mechanical refrigeration. Those who preferred project to present quarters, reasons given as follows: (1) Playgrounds and facilities for children (43%), (2) Better ventilation, more light and air (26%), (3) Better planned, modern apartments (26%), (4) Clean, well-kept buildings, good service (19%), (5) Friendly, near friends and relatives (14%).
  Those who preferred present quarters: (1) Less congestion and noise (22%), (2) More privacy (13%), (3) Freedom from income and other rules (12%), (4) Better environment for children (9%). Concludes: "The problem of eliminating noise and congestion of city living has not been solved in public housing" (p. 4).

STUDY 3. "The Urge To Own," *Architectural Forum* (1937), p. 372
Scope: 1,003 interviews in eight cities in different regions
Findings: Chief objections to present housing: (1) needs general repairs, (2) too small, (3) needs painting, (4) needs papering, (5) poor arrangement, (6) rooms too small, (7) not modern.

STUDY. 4. *Urban Housing Survey* (Curtis Publishing Company, 1945)
Scope: 4,007 families interviewed in 35 states and 118 urban centers.
Findings: 66% prefer 5 or 6 rooms; 84.5% 2 or 3 bedrooms; 91.1% prefer single-family detached house; 6.4% two-family or duplex; 1% row house.

STUDY 5. Duane V. Ramsey, *What Some Slum Dwellers Want in Housing* (Henry Street Settlement, July, 1935)

TABLE 2 (*Continued*)

Scope: Study of groups on Henry Street and East Broadway. Questionnaires used to gather data in fall of 1934.

Findings: Reasons given for discontent: too cold, dark rooms, need repairs; no elevator; apartment too small; high rent; vermin; old building; no improvements, cold water; rooms too small; paint needed; dirty; poor landlord; roof leaks; no closets. "From this sampling of fact and opinion, it appears that wants of slum dwellers in new housing are modest and reasonable. In fact the very reasonableness of their wants suggests the great inadequacy of their present living arrangements and their consequent need for better housing" (p. 10).

STUDY 6. *Housing for the Family* (Women's City Club of New York, 1936).
Scope: Study of housing preferences of 1,395 housewives in slum areas of New York City. Questionnaires and interviews.
Findings: 47.2% preferred single-family house with yard; 81.6% preferred to serve meals in kitchen; 85% prefer tub to shower. Older persons preferred to remain in present location more than younger ones. "Such a thing as a living room in which no one sleeps is a luxury to which few of these aspire."

STUDY 7. *Better Housing for the Family* (Women's City Club of New York, 1948).
Scope: Follow-up of 1936 study by same club. Study of public housing projects at Clason Point (400 units in two-story row houses); East River (1,170 apartment units); Vladeck Houses (1,531 apartment units); and Queensbridge Houses (3,149 apartment units). Questionnaires and interviews.
Findings: Those in larger apartments better satisfied; Clason Point occupants (91%) find quarters satisfactory. (May be location in addition to housing as such.) Larger kitchen for family eating is a common request. Desire for more storage space and out-of-doors drying space. Tub-shower combination preferred to just shower or tub. Few want just shower. "But these advances (of public housing over slum and blighted areas) have in turn raised her values, have widened her horizons, and have stimulated her to look ahead to further improvements in her living conditions, whether or not they are immediately attainable."

STUDY 8. Walter A. Anicka, Ann Arbor, Michigan, 1949.
Scope: Letters from 20,000 newspaper readers in response to query of what they most wanted in homes.
Findings: "More living space in the house at the most economical cost, even if the frills must be sacrificed to get it. . . ." Most families indicated desire for breakfast alcove in kitchen. Expansibility for future needs also wanted.

STUDY 9. *Durable Goods Study Among Consumers and Dealers.* The Chicago Tribune, 1945.
Scope: Interviews with 10,850 families in five-state circulation area of the paper. Of these, 3,075 were in the Chicago metropolitan area.
Findings: Of the 24% who contemplated moving in the two postwar years, 57.3% now lived in apartments, 42.7% in houses. After the move 19.3% intended to live in apartments, 67.4% in houses, and 13.3% did not know what type of dwelling they would live in. Of those within the immediate area of Chicago, the corresponding figures were: now living in apartments, 74.5%; in houses, 25.5%. After move, 27.1% in

TABLE 2 (*Continued*)

apartments, 59.1% in houses, and 13.8% do not know. Those outside of the immediate vicinity of Chicago: at present, 29.9% and 70.1%. After move: 6.7%, 80.7%, and 12.6%.

STUDY 10. Real Estate Research Corporation, *Housing Market Analysis, Cook County, Illinois* (1949 Supplement, Housing Authority of the County of Cook, Chicago, 1950).

Scope: Building permit and other data on housing market and construction in 1949 in Cook County outside of Chicago and five of largest suburbs.

Findings: Size of 8805 single family houses put under construction in 1949:

1, 2, and 3 rooms	86
4 rooms	1,530
5 rooms	1,391
6 rooms	724
7 and over	169
No information	4,905

STUDY 11. Frederick Gutheim: *Houses for Family Living* (New York: The Woman's Foundation Inc., 1948).

Scope: Discussion and analysis of the varying housing needs in terms of family growth.

Findings: Breaks family growth into the early years (3), the crowded years (until last child enters school), the peak years (until last child leaves school), and later years. Good discussion of space requirements within the home.

STUDY 12. Svend Riemer: "Maladjustment to the Family Home," *American Sociological Review*, X (October, 1945), 642–48.

Scope: Questionnaires mailed to random sample (900) of Seattle housewives, members of the Parent Teachers Association. 300 filled out and mailed back.

Findings: Study revealed greater satisfaction with newer homes, but more complaints of crowding in homes built 1920–30 than in the more spacious homes built earlier. Crowding important with regard to child care and leisure-time activities of the family.

that was definitely on the down grade, being dirty, noisy, and cut through with heavy traffic.

The fact that many persons have relatively little choice of where they live has surely been responsible for some of these unrealistic answers to questions asked them about their housing. The strength of the influence of past experiences is shown by studies 1, 2, 5, and 6, in Table 2. The actual awareness that living conditions can be different from those in the slums and blighted areas seems to be all that is necessary to raise the housing standards of the occupants. In the 1936 New York City study of slum dwellers' attitudes toward housing accommodations (6 in Table 2), the requests for improvements were very modest and pertained especially to physical comforts. Once these needs are met, the occupants discover higher demands in the hierarchy of human needs and try to satisfy them.

Some of the wants that do appear to be supported by the studies on housing needs are those for larger quarters (in 1947 there were still 2,400,000 units with more than 1.5 persons per room), for single-family houses, for adequate eating space in the kitchen in lieu of combination living-dining rooms, and for more storage space. Except possibly for the desire expressed for a single-family house, the interviewees seemed to have had sufficient experience to state their needs correctly.

Many of the questions raised with regard to home-ownership are equally applicable to the prima facie preference for single-family houses. Of those replying that they would prefer a single-family house, many have never lived in one and, therefore, do not know of the responsibilities they impose on occupants. In 1940 about two-thirds of all housing units were single-family houses, but in large urban areas the proportion was much smaller. Perhaps it is significant that many of the apartment and duplex dwellers who said that they would like to own a single-family house are of the same income group as many who actually do own such homes (8 in Table 1). This suggests that the expression of such a desire is perhaps merely the reflection of a widely held ideal and does not represent a real driving motivation.

In any event, the consistent demand for larger quarters (for 5 and 6 rooms in contrast to the national average in 1947 of 4.8 rooms per unit), particularly by those with larger families, finds support in the conclusions of housing specialists who feel that sacrificing space for expensive gadgets is a gross error.[18] Although one would agree with the statement that "About the relationship between the ever-changing pattern of family life and its physical shelter, unfortunately, a minimum of controlled information is available,"[19] it does seem that with regard to room overcrowding we know enough to recommend that research should be focused upon ways and means of securing more space in all types of dwelling units for those of moderate and low income. Room arrangements, closet doors, kitchens visible from front doors, and so forth are matters about which we are less certain and quite willing to admit the necessity of further research as to their relationship to satisfaction in daily living.

Finally it is well to keep in mind that the physical structure of the

18. William Scheick, formerly co-ordinator of the Small Homes Council at the University of Illinois, has strongly voiced this opinion.

19. Svend Riemer, "Maladjustment to the Family Home," *American Sociological Review*, X (October, 1945), 642.

dwelling is not the only dependent or changeable factor in housing adjustment. As Riemer has said,

> The architect can do his best to improve the comfort of the family by an adequate residential construction. On the other hand, a great deal of waste and maladjustment in the housing field can be overcome by educational measures. . . . Traditions, peculiar habits and irrational family traits may completely thwart the efforts of the family to establish a comfortable home in a given physical shelter. . . .[20]

EXTERNAL SPACE RELATIONS

Housing constitutes but a part, albeit a major one, of the physical plant of the urban world. Another major feature of this physical setting is the space relationships between the dwelling units of various kinds and (1) services such as shopping, (2) places of enjoyment and recreational facilities; (3) the residences of friends and associates; (4) other residential areas, the open countryside, the other areas within the metropolitan region. A fifth factor, not strictly comparable to the four just listed but nevertheless related to these spatial considerations, is the nature and location of the prestige areas of the metropolitan region. Research has thrown some light upon the attitudes of urban dwellers toward these external space relationships, and certain tentative conclusions can be drawn from these studies.

DISTANCES TO SERVICES

The redeveloper or planner can rest assured that most persons would like to have the distances to services as short as possible without sacrificing other advantages. This is particularly true of the services that are used daily, such as those of neighborhood shopping centers (e.g., grocery stores and drugstores), grade schools, and playgrounds for very young children. Residents usually prefer these services to be within walking distance of the home, i.e., half a mile or less. High schools, churches, movie houses, and the special services not needed every day are satisfactorily spaced if they are not much more than one mile distant.

Many of these services, of course, are of special interest to the heads of families and to housewives whose job it is to keep the home stocked with the necessary provisions and to care for the children. To the single person or the married couple with no children at home, the location of grade and high schools is of little interest, and good restaurants may

20. Svend Riemer, "Sociological Theory of Home Adjustment," *American Sociological Review*, VIII (June, 1943), 277.

TABLE 3

STUDIES OF EXTERNAL SPACE RELATIONSHIPS

STUDY 1. Urban Redevelopment Study. Survey of Milwaukee area, see chapter iii following.
Scope: Study of 315 units in east south central Milwaukee. Area of relatively low income ($55 weekly), 1949. Rental median $27.33. Two-thirds of families had children living at home. White neighborhood, two-thirds Roman Catholic, largely of Polish origin, second and third generations. One-third single-family detached dwelling units; one-third two-family; 20% 3- and 4-family; approximately 10% 5-family or more.
Findings: Nearly 50% want to move from neighborhood. Main reasons were: noise, smoke, soot, dirt, 39%; don't like neighbors, 10%; dislike neighborhood, 6.8%; area not suitable for children, 8.4%. 27% preferred to move to suburbs; 18.8% to north side of Milwaukee; 17.6% to south side of Milwaukee; 10.7% to rural community in Milwaukee County. Of those who preferred to remain: like neighborhood, 23.4%; lived there for long time or used to neighborhood, 15.2%; economic stake in home or too expensive to move, 8.9%; close to services or place of employment, 15.2%; friends or relatives, 8.2%. Of total group, general dissatisfaction with lack of cleanness, 76%; noise, 44%; lack of open space, shrubs, trees, 48%; lack of place for neighborhood meetings, 43%.

STUDY 2. Betty Tableman, *Intra-community Migration in the Flint Metropolitan District* (Institute for Human Adjustment, University of Michigan, September, 1948).
Scope: Approximately 1% sample of households according to the 1940 census. Interviews of 488 households in March, 1948.
Findings: Intra-city migration—reasons: secure better quarters or location, 26.6%; build or buy house, 20.7%; more space required, 15.5%; forced to move, 12.1%; marriage, 10%; closer to work, 7.7%.
   Inter-city migration—reasons: to seek or take new job, 70%; better, cheaper accommodations, 8.6%; health, climate, 4.4%; closer to work, 1.1%.
   Why move to rural area? (migrants from Flint City) Less congested, 34.8%; cleaner, 15.9%; forced to move, 15.9%; larger lot, 13%; cheaper, 5.8%.
   Why select present location in preference to other rural site? Only place available, 20.3%; liked looks of subdivision or neighborhood, 15.9%; best buy, 13%; liked house, 7.2%; near major highway and transportation, 7.2%; nearer to work, 7.2%; close to school, shops, church, 5.8%; desirable lot size, 11.6%; near family and friends, 6.7%.

STUDY 3. J. Douglas Carroll, Jr., "Some Aspects of the Home-Work Relationships of Industrial Workers," *Land Economics* (November, 1949), pp. 414–22.
Scope: Massachusetts State Planning Board questionnaire study of industrial employees "all over the state." 72,048 questionnaires returned by employees in 233 industries.
Findings: Journey to work pattern of industrial employees unlike that of office workers in central business districts. ". . . the bulk of the factory workers live close to work and . . . beyond two or three miles the proportion of workers decreases as the distance from the factory increases" (p. 414).

TABLE 3 (*Continued*)

Median distance for all workers covered was 2.9 miles. By city size groups the median decreased with size of cities until the size group of 10,000 to 25,000. In two groups below this the median rose substantially.

". . . over time periods of stable employment, the pattern will tend to 'tighten up'—e.g., those workers living at great distances will move closer to work or find other jobs closer to home.

"We have uncovered the suspicion that there iş an optimum-sized community when measured by patterns of workers' travel distance and that by a curious coincidence the differences between different size groups in regard to commuting distance is similar to differences in per capita costs of government" (p. 422).

STUDY 4. Mary Shauffler, *The Suburban Community* (Ph.D. Thesis, University of Chicago, 1941).

Scope: 1,438 questionnaires circulated among residents of four Cleveland suburbs. Check-list answers.

Findings: Principal reasons given for moving to suburbs: to buy home, live in cleaner, healthier neighborhood, have better schools, more outside space for children, garden, to escape noise and traffic, to be among friends, relatives, people with whom one can have more friendly relations.

Showed distinction between upper-class and middle-class suburbanite values; for example, as to reason: "To live among people more socially desirable," the proportions checking it in the two upper class suburbs were 37.6% and 31.5%, whereas in the middle class towns they were 19.2% and 16.2%.

STUDY 5. Homer Hoyt, *The Structure and Growth of Residential Neighborhoods in American Cities* (Federal Housing Administration, Washington, D.C., 1939).

Scope: Analysis of real property surveys of major American cities.

Findings: Upper-class residential areas' location is determined primarily by the residents themselves; real estate dealers not able to do more than slightly influence direction of growth of such areas. Lines of rapid transportation important in influencing such directional movements. Middle-class residences tend to follow the lead of the more well-to-do members of the community.

STUDY 6. Melville C. Branch, Jr., *Urban Planning and Public Opinion* (Bureau of Urban Research, Princeton University, Princeton, N.J., September, 1942).

Scope: Nation-wide sample survey.

Findings: 15% dissatisfied with elementary school distance of more than one-half mile; 43% object to distances of over one mile. 8% object to high school being more than one-half mile distant; and 36% when it is more than one mile away (p. 15).

Reasons for intra-city movement: secure better quarters or to live in better location, 18%; to build or purchase home, 16%; more space required in house, 13%; rent or expense too high or house too large, 12%; forced to move, 10%; closer to employment, 10%; marriage, 5% (p. 21).

69% satisfied with neighborhood because:

Friends, friendly, kind, or neighborly (46%)

TABLE 3 *(Continued)*

Tend to own business (21%)
Nice, pleasant, or all right (15%)
My kind: same standards, interests, financial status (11%)
  One fourth dissatisfied with present neighborhood:
Desire better or different neighbors (25%)
Color, race, or religious reasons (11%)
Not friendly (9%) (p. 11)

STUDY 7. Richard Dewey, "Peripheral Expansion in Milwaukee County," *American Journal of Sociology,* LIV (September, 1948), pp. 118–25.
Scope: Analysis of 3,900 questionnaires circulated through schools in unincorporated areas of county.
Findings: Reasons for moving to unincorporated areas of Milwaukee County: (1) better for children, 32%; (2) less congested, 18%; (3) cleaner, 17%; (4) larger lot, 15%. Reasons for selecting particular site in the unincorporated area: (1) best buy at the time, 11%; (2) liked house, 10.9%; (3) close to school, 10.5%; (4) desirable lot size, 8.5%; (5) liked looks of subdivision, 8%; (6) only place available, 7%; (7) public transportation available, 6.9%; (8) close to city, 6.5%; (9) nearer to work, 6%; (10) restricted area, 3.8%; (11) near family and friends, 3%. Want grocery store, grade school, and drugstore within walking distance; beauty parlor, gas station, high school, church, parks, and movies within one mile. Public transportation deemed important by all.

STUDY 8. *Study of Employees* (small manufacturing plant). (Committee on Human Relations in Industry, University of Chicago, 1945).
Scope: Study to discover attitude of employees toward moving plant. 72% had lived in Chicago fifteen years or more, and 49% lived in same neighborhood seven or more years. Most have family obligations. Most live within walking distance of plant.
Findings: 21.4% said would quit if factory moved from present neighborhood (Lincoln Park district). Reasons: objections to public transportation—time, cost, inconvenience, safety. Only 8% will move if plant leaves Chicago area (does not include top executives and administrators); 5.8% willing to move to south side; 38% will go with company if it moves to western suburb (less than half would commute, rest would move); 48% would follow plant to northern suburb, such as Skokie; more than half would commute to northern suburb. 25% won't commute or move. 28% would commute up to and including 1 hour; 21% would commute 1 hour through 2 hours; 9% would commute more than 2 hours; 65% of those who would move with factory plan on moving to suburbs anyway. Conclude identification with neighborhood important factor in attitude against moving.

STUDY 9. Beatrice S. Friedman, *Better Housing for the Family* (Women's Club of New York City, 1948).
Scope: Study of families in four N.Y.C. public housing projects, Clason Point, East River, Vladeck Houses, and Queensbridge Homes.
Findings: 65% wished to have playgrounds in front of the building. 79% feel that child-care centers should be provided by project; 87% that there should be facilities for teen-agers; 74% and 72% respectively feel there should be rooms for adults and aged to meet socially. 9% of

TABLE 3 (*Continued*)

those in Clason Point, 32% of those in Vladeck, 56% in East River, and 54% in Queensbridge Homes wanted to live elsewhere. "Concern for the rearing of their children was mentioned as a prime factor in the reasons given by a majority of families in projects located in congested, long-established, and industrial neighborhoods for wanting to live elsewhere." "Preferences conditioned by the neighborhoods in which the project is located rather than by specific facilities provided by the project." "Social factors such as the desire to live near friends and relatives rates as only a minor consideration despite popular conception to the contrary" (p. 48).

STUDY 10. Theodore Caplow, "Home Ownership and Location Preferences in a Minneapolis Sample," *American Sociological Review,* XIII (December, 1948), 725–30.

Scope: 574 "stable" families in Minneapolis (i.e., married before 1940, lived together in Minneapolis, 1940–48).

Findings: 9% of the owners and 14% of the tenants wished to live closer to work.

No data on location.

STUDY 11. *Present Housing of Former Project Tenants* (New York City Housing Authority, May, 1943).

Scope: 251 former tenants of N.Y.C. public housing projects.

Findings: 43% preferred project to present quarters because of playgrounds and other facilities for children. 22% preferred present place to project because of less congestion and noise. Reasons why liked present neighborhood: previously lived there (27%); quiet, refined, uncongested (21%); near friends and relatives (16%); convenient to work (9%); to shopping (9%); to schools (6%).

STUDY 12. "Study of What Happened to Former Residents of Slums Who Were Forced to Make Way for Large Housing Project" (Lavanburg Foundation and Hamilton House, New York, 1933).

Scope: 386 families studied. Mostly long-time residents of area. Many wage earners walked to work.

Findings: Only 14% left the neighborhood, remainder to adjoining blocks. Significant number improved facilities in new dwellings.

STUDY 13. *Survey of Tenant Opinion in Charter Oak Terrace* (Hartford Housing Authority, 1942).

Scope: Survey of wartime housing project which included one-, two-, and three-bedroom row houses.

Findings: Percentages of those who desired specified services within project, i.e., within walking distance: super-market (66%); general or department store (37%); five-and-ten store (19%); barber shop (9%); shoe repair (9%); cleaners (6%); bakery (5%).

STUDY 14. *Why Do Tenants Move?* (Citizens Housing Council of New York, 1940).

Scope: Study of 1,219 families in two apartment areas in Manhattan and Brooklyn.

Findings: Main reasons roughly in order of importance: lower rent; apartment layout; better value; change in family size; near work; improved living standard; neighborhood; more light and air; near friends; near school; and near transportation. Some indication that the more money the less stability.

TABLE 3 (*Continued*)

STUDY 15. Duane V. Ramsey, *What Some Slum Dwellers Want in Housing* (Henry Street Settlement, New York, 1935).
Scope: Sample studies of two slum areas on East Side New York City.
Findings: Reasons given for not wanting to leave neighborhood: used to neighborhood, 30%; business here, 19%; employment here, 10%; children in school, 3%; old age, 3%.

STUDY 16. *Housing for the Family* (Women's City Club of New York, 1936).
Scope: Study of 1,395 housewives in slum areas of New York City.
Findings: 64.4% wishes to remain in neighborhood. Reasons: friends and social life, 240; work and business, 121; used to it, 73; schools (mostly sectarian), 69; low rent, 54; transportation and convenience, 49; contented, 47; always lived there, 22. Many foreign-born.

STUDY 17. Real Estate Research Corporation, *Housing Market Analysis, Cook County, Illinois, 1949 Supplement* (Housing Authority of the County of Cook, Chicago, 1950. Summary in the Authority's *Housing Digest,* September, 1950).
Scope: Area of Cook County outside Chicago and five of largest suburbs contiguous to it. Local market and construction data.
Findings: ". . . new house occupants in 1949 (most of whom came from Chicago or from outside of Cook County) gave the following as their principal reasons for moving to a new house . . .

'To get away from the city'	(17.4%)
'To get into better neighborhood'	(16.6%)
'To get near a better school'	(4.9%)
'To be nearer work'	(6.1%)
'New house prices are better here'	(10.4%)
'. . . more new houses in area . . . better selection'	(12.4%)
'To get more room'	(19.5%)
'Other reasons'	(12.7%)"

Housing Digest summary combines three reasons as "urban congestion" —more room, away from city, better neighborhood—total 53.5%.

STUDY 18. Donald L. Foley, "Local Facility Use in a Metropolis: I. Extent, II. Patterning," typescript. Some of the material appeared subsequently in Foley, "The Use of Local Facilities in a Metropolis," *American Journal of Sociology* (November, 1950), pp. 238–46.
Scope: Study of five-square-mile residential area in northwest St. Louis. Interviews with at least one member of 401 families selected at random from the district.
Findings: Concluded that "Our large cities, for all their urbanity, seem to contain an impressive degree of local community patterning within their metropolitan limits. . . . A greater degree of local facility use was found to be associated with these factors: automobile non-ownership, children and the aged, females, lack of formal education, and high residential density." Although ". . . relatively little coincidence of service area boundaries for different types of local facilities . . ." was revealed, seven "service neighborhoods" (i.e., where the majority of the basic local facilities services the same contiguous area) were delineated. But despite the fact that one of the major industrial areas of the city was within the boundaries of the study district, four-fifths of the reported

TABLE 3 (*Continued*)

employment was outside the district, with concentration in the central business district. Suggests the "natural" service neighborhoods as ". . . potential foundations for the possible strengthening through city planning or community organization of local functional areal units within the larger city."

replace the grocery store as a service wanted near the home. Nevertheless, for the majority of urban dwellers the distances preferred to the various services are those stated above. Thus, in this one aspect of external space relations the studies to date, although limited in number and scope, appear to vindicate the judgment of those persons who, like Clarence Perry, visualize the compact neighborhood unit as the ideal planning unit for a livable city. The preferred distances found in at least one study (6 in Table 3) coincide almost exactly with those set by Perry as most desirable for such a unit.

These distances, however, are those preferred by people who do their own shopping—the vast majority of the American urban populace. Many in the upper-middle and upper-income groups either do their routine buying by telephone and have the provisions delivered or have servants attend to the shopping chores. Distances to the grocery or drugstores are of less concern to them. As a matter of fact, one of the surest ways to lose status in one suburb of a certain midwestern city is for the housewife to do her own shopping for groceries. Reasonably convenient public transportation, however, is esteemed nearly as much by the upper-income groups as by other classes, not only by the breadwinners but also because of the greater freedom afforded parents if children and servants can ride the bus, street car, or train.

THE JOURNEY TO WORK—ITS IMPLICATIONS FOR URBAN DEVELOPMENT

Whatever preferences there are for nearness to employment seem to be colored by other considerations, because the majority of persons interviewed in most studies to date do not express any great concern about the distance to work. Yet many housers, planners, and others have deplored the amounts of time and money spent by workers on transportation from home to place of work. And certainly this feeling is not rare among professionals and white-collar workers in big cities. The following passage, not without its own kind of eloquence, illustrates the attitudes of many urbanites:

New York city and the metropolitan region constitute a maelstrom resulting from poor planning. Every morning hundreds of thousands of people stream into New York to work. standing on busses, crowded into trains and ferries, packed and choked in subways, and fretting in automobiles crawling fender to fender. They come from New Jersey, Westchester, Connecticut, Nassau and Suffolk Counties, while countless others pour out to those same places for the same purpose. Here in New York City hundreds of thousands stream from Brooklyn to Manhattan, the Bronx and Queens to work, and hundreds of thousands rush to their jobs on the reverse route. . . . This shuttling back and forth is costly, not only in the millions of hours wasted in traveling, but also in its impact on family life, in the deprivation of the companionship of the head of the household at times when he would be otherwise available, and in the effects upon the health of the traveler both through the loss of the equivalent amount of recreational time and through the vicissitudes of traveling in overcrowded, irritating and unhealthful means of transportation. . . .[21]

Whether or not this daily migration is as distasteful to the migrants themselves as it is to the writer of this piece is uncertain. An English writer tells us that—

The circumstances of the daily journey by public means of transportations need detailed examination in order to apportion the responsibility for strain amongst the various features. These are: first, the inconveniences of the various stages of the journey, walk to and from the station, waiting, queueing, changing vehicles; secondly, the condition in the conveyances, viz., standing sandwiched in overcrowded compartments and the stuffy atmosphere which tires and fosters contagion; further, superimposed on all other items, a constant hurry and nervous tension due to the fear of being late; and lastly, equally influencing each phase of the journey, bad weather. . . .[22]

Liepmann quoted the English Minister of Labour, Mr. Bevin, as saying that if a worker can reduce his journey to work from one or two hours to one-half or three-quarters of an hour, his production is increased by 9 or 10 per cent. However, no source of this information was given by the Minister.

There is little objective information with which to evaluate the costs of lengthy journeys to and from work. An interesting exception. is the study made in Germany some years ago, which indicated that the longer the ride between home and place of employment, the greater the number of days lost through illness.

Notwithstanding the comments cited above on the disadvantages of such long trips to work places, the studies on peoples' attitudes toward location of homes does not indicate that distance to work is one of the major considerations in selecting dwelling places. Generally less than 10 per cent of the reasons given for moving or complaints about loca-

21. Herman T. Stichman, "Housing Policy in the Expanded Region—A Return to Neighborhood Living," (an address before The Regional Plan Association, New York, November 16, 1948, (Division of Housing, State of New York) pp. 4–6.

22. Kate K. Liepmann, *The Journey to Work—Its Significance for Industrial and Community Life* (New York: Oxford University Press, 1944), p. 55.

tion fall in this category (see studies 6, 7, 10, 11, 14, 15, and 17 in Table 3).

In study 7, definite protests against the journey to work were voiced. Even here, however, in an instance where many of the employees do walk to work, the point of protest was not confined to the journey to work as such. Evidence of this is the fact that the *direction* of the journey made a difference. This reinforces the opinion that many urbanites are willing to commute long distances in order to preserve certain other advantages.[23] Additional support is the apparently greater willingness of the more-highly-paid employees of plants to commute greater distances. For example, a study of commuting by workers made in Milwaukee in 1936, found that 12 per cent of the persons employed in the city of Milwaukee lived in the suburbs, whereas 40 per cent of the executives (134 total) of plants in Milwaukee were suburban residents.[24] Incidentally, the study also revealed that 6,943 persons lived in the city of Milwaukee and worked in the suburbs (20 plants), while 4,371 lived in the suburbs and worked in Milwaukee (23 plants).

Two major factors in the urban-industrial world as we know it today and as it is likely to be for some time, place the longer journey to work in a different light from that in which it is usually viewed.

The first concerns the relationship between home and work for employees in the largest industrial plants. When a plant employs, say, fifteen to twenty-five thousand persons a considerable journey to work is unavoidable for many of them. Twenty-five thousand employees plus wives, parents, and children represent approximately eighty thousand people who are dependent upon the plant for a livelihood. And one writer adds:

> The community would be further increased by the auxiliary services which are necessary for such a number of inhabitants; the area covered by houses would render illusory the nearness between home and workplace. . . .[25]

Of course, plants (not companies) of this size are not common in most industries but they are found in the very large urban centers. Where they do exist, it does not make sense to talk about eliminating trips of some length to and from the place of work. They could be reduced in number; not every or even most employees would need to travel as far

23. Study 8 in Table 3 concerned many employees who lived close to work and therefore had not experienced lengthy trips back and forth, whereas most of the others involved persons whose residences were some distance from work and who had become accustomed to the long rides. Habits, and the unpleasant task of changing them, may play a large role in determining these different attitudes.

24. Compiled from the records of each firm in the spring of 1936 by the Joint Committee on Consolidation. Available from the offices of Citizens' Governmental Research Bureau of Milwaukee, 125 East Wells Street.

25. Liepmann, *op. cit.*, pp. 10–11.

or as long as many now do. Also, if the plants are obnoxious because of noise, dirt, or odor, it would be a doubtful gain to sacrifice the cleanliness and the absence of noise that most persons clearly wish to have in their residential areas.

The second factor that increases the value of the journey to work is the greater freedom in the choice of jobs it affords the individual:

> From the point of view of the worker, the principal significance of the journey to work is that it extends the market in which he is able to offer his labour and thus enlarges his economic independence. He is not obliged to accept a job from those firms which he can reach by walking from his home. Moreover, daily travelling puts at his disposal a more varied choice of employment in a broader range of occupations and industries, to suit his inclination, training and skill. He can more easily change his employer if he wants to, without having to move his home to another locality, with all the cost and inconvenience this would involve; this is especially important for those who own the houses in which they live. . . .[26]

The varying needs of the individual encompass more than sheer economic wants, and the freedom to change employers and to seek satisfactory work relationships should not be undervalued. Often a person may be perfectly satisfied with his neighborhood relationships, but will find it desirable to take another position within the metropolitan district. A longer journey to work will permit him and his family to continue their personal relationships with friends, associates, and the school, while, at the same time, he has a better job. It is particularly important to give the child and adolescent a continuity of personal contacts that repeated changes of residence destroy. The flexible journey to work also enables the family to remain together as a unit and still supplement its income through jobs held by other members than the family head.

Furthermore, it would be a mistake to assume that the journey to work is an unpleasant experience for everyone. Although it is rarely as much a part of one's recreation as it is for certain commuters from one suburb of Chicago who, each morning, enjoy a poker game of some twelve years' standing, many people like the opportunity to read papers or magazines enroute to job or home. Others find the automobile drive a pleasant experience, especially if the ride is shared by friends. To be sure, the journey to work is pleasant only if one can sit down and can avoid the trying and frustrating strap-hanging that is common in many of our overtaxed transportation systems. It is easier and more pleasant to ride thirty miles on a swift suburban commuters' train or rapid-transit line than to be jostled about on the slow, jerky, jam-packed surface or subway or elevated lines for a mere two or three miles.

For similar reasons the journey to work offers advantages to the

26. *Ibid.*, p. 11.

employer. A richer pool of variously skilled laborers is made available. New plants can be set up without waiting for housing in the vicinity. The dislike and bad publicity of the company-town employer are avoided.[27]

Thus, transporting large numbers of workers within the metropolitan region can be reduced in volume through careful planning and redevelopment but it will still remain as an essential and not altogether undesirable part of the urban scene.

DISTANCES TO FRIENDS AND ASSOCIATES

It is a commonplace that all human beings require companionship, friendship, affection, intimate response, call it what you will. Sometimes it is sought as a means to some end, and sometimes it is desired for its own sake. Without stressing the obvious, we would point out that peoples' external space relations (in other words, their nearness to or distance from others) have much to do with securing such companionship. Extremes are the crowded tenements of some cities and the isolated wheat ranches of the Great Plains. An American artist has caught the spirit of the latter kind of spatially induced loneliness in a painting of the farm wife, who, with her new baby, sits in the open field just to be within hailing distance of her husband who is working on a fenceless prairie.

Which of the many shades of personal contacts between' these two extremes approach the ideal is a judgment not easily made. The need varies from individual to individual, depending upon his or her life organization; and the optimum number of contacts for one person may well spell boredom or bedlam for others. The groups characterized by face-to-face, intimate contacts (called "primary groups" by the sociologists) often are assumed to be large and widespread in smaller communities and rural areas, whereas they are supposed to be small or lacking entirely in the urban scene. Without denying the greater possibility, and even probability, of involuntary anonymity and loneliness in the large city, the apparent difference here between rural and urban areas is, in part, an illusion.

Primary group relations—rural and urban.—There are two types of primary or face-to-face groups. One is made up of friends and associates whom we choose; the other consists of a larger number of people whose intimate knowledge of us and our behavior is usually unsolicited and often unwelcome. The latter is the group that differentiates many rural and small-town communities from the larger urban centers. In part, at least, it is just this sort of social visibility that causes many

27. *Ibid.*, p. 13.

persons to migrate to the metropolis. As one school teacher in a village said:

> Were I free to choose, I would elect to live in a large city. It would be interesting to have a date, buy a new dress, come in late at night just once without having it the subject of conversation in school the following day, or at the weekly meeting of some group or other. It is not that I wish to live a wild life, but I would like to think that my behavior is more exclusively my own business than is possible in ———. . . . .

The same viewpoint is well expressed by some planners in England:

> People who live in large towns are inclined to idealize village life, where everyone knows everyone else, joins keenly in social activities and takes part in running village affairs. In contrast to this intimate local life, large towns seem impersonal. . . . In spite of this apparently desirable social life, the inhabitants of country districts have shown a strong inclination to move away into towns. In part this [migration] has been due to lack of employment opportunities, and to bad physical conditions, but it has also been due to dissatisfaction with community life. There is a lack of privacy involved in being known by all one's neighbors. There is often a good deal of intolerance. Deviations in behavior from what is considered appropriate for the age or the social position of the particular person become a source of scandal or gossip. . . . Moreover, village life is often very dull. Rural life may seem attractive to the "week-ender" or to the business man contemplating retirement, but the native villager sighs for the city lights. . . .[28]

Viewed from this angle, village life has some of the same disadvantages of the "picture window" that is so often built into houses but a few feet from the street—the "picture" is on the wrong side of the window.

The most frequent migrants to urban areas from the farms are the hired hands, traditionally a mobile group. Next in order of migration are the young women, the young men, then the tenant operators. The last to leave are the owner operators.[29] Presumably many of them move after retirement. Although this marked shift in population cannot be interpreted as an unqualified rejection of all that is rural and an indorsement of all that the urban world has to offer, it is manifest evidence that, in the judgment of the migrants at least, the city serves the essential needs of people better than does rural or semirural America. Although there is considerable evidence that the economic factors loom large among the reasons for this movement to the cities, they are not the whole explanation. The ascendancy of urban values, which characterizes our period of history, must be counted among the effective motivating forces in the migration.

28. "Can Communities Be Planned?" *Planning* (Political and Economic Planning), London, Vol. XV (March 28, 1949).

29. Newell L. Sims, *Elements of Rural Sociology* (New York: Thomas Y. Crowell and Co., 1940), third edition, p. 233.

Not for everyone, however, is the village or small community a thing to avoid or to flee from. He who agrees with the accepted ideas and standards often finds a satisfying identification with the activity and ideals of the town. Also, the "big-frog-in-a-little-puddle" role is frequently a very gratifying one. Community leaders are rewarded not only by the knowledge that their status is esteemed in the abstract, but also by the actual respect of their townsmen.[30]

Probably, it is from the vantage point of such a social role that many planners view village life and thus esteem it highly. But just as high status is clearly visible in the small community, so is low status too. For those at the bottom of the social scale, village life may leave something to be desired. Not even identification with the community helps some of them to compensate for the lowly estimate in which they are held by their many intimates. The "West Madison Streets" and the "Boweries" of the metropolis count among their populations such persons, refugees from an obviously uncomfortable low-status role. The large urban community affords hiding-places for those who, for whatever reasons, fail to measure up to the standards of their fellowmen. There are no hiding places in the small town.

The neighborhood-unit principle.—This somewhat lengthy discourse on the nature of primary-group relations was undertaken to provide a background for a discussion of the neighborhood-unit principle of city planning. This principle has been set forth in its clearest form by the late Clarence Perry in 1929 in connection with plans for the greater New York area,[31] and later (1939) in his well-known book, *Housing for the Machine Age*.[32] For some twenty years prior to his first formal statement of the principle, Perry had been studying local community organization. The neighborhood-unit proposal is the end product of his thinking on the matter. In his own words:

> The formula for a city neighborhood, then, must be such that when embodied in an actual development all its residents will be taken care of as respects the following points: they will all be within convenient access to an elementary school, adequate common play spaces, and retail shopping districts. Furthermore, their district will enjoy a distinctive character, because of qualities pertaining viably to its terrain and structure, not the least of which will be a reduced risk from vehicular accidents. . . .[33]

30. In no way does this imply that the leaders of the smaller communities are less capable than their big-city counterparts.

31. "The Neighborhood Unit: A Scheme of Arrangement for the Family-Life Community," *The Regional Survey of New York and Its Environs*, Vol. VII, "Neighborhood and Community Planning," New York, 1929.

32. New York: Russell Sage Foundation, 1939.

33. *Ibid.*, pp. 50–51.

Perry listed six sub-principles of the neighborhood-unit plan:

1. *Size*. A residential unit development should provide housing for that population for which one elementary school is ordinarily required, its actual area depending upon its population density.

2. *Boundaries*. The unit should be bounded on all sides by arterial streets, sufficiently wide to facilitate its by-passing, instead of penetration, by through traffic.

3. *Open spaces*. A system of small parks and recreation spaces, planned to meet the needs of the particular neighborhood, should be provided.

4. *Institution sites*. Sites for the school and other institutions having service spheres coinciding with the limits of the unit should be suitably grouped about a central point, or common.

5. *Local shops*. One or more shopping districts, adequate for the population to be served, should be laid out in the circumference of the unit, preferably at traffic junctions and adjacent to similar districts of adjoining neighborhoods.

6. *Internal street system*. The unit should be provided with a special street system, each highway being proportioned to its probable traffic load, and the street net as a whole being designed to facilitate circulation within the unit and to discourage its use by through traffic.[34]

Perry believed that if these principles are properly applied to the planning of either vacant land on the periphery of the city or to central deteriorated (redevelopment) areas, ". . . there will result a neighborhood community in which the fundamental needs of family life will be met more completely . . . than they are now by the usual residential sections in cities and villages."[35] He realized that the neighborhood-unit pattern could not be applied to the whole city because of certain physical barriers. Further, certain cultural factors had to be considered, and some of them would modify the ideal or generalized neighborhood pattern. For example, he states that

Children of the higher-income groups who enjoy a home in the country and one in the city . . . do not need large recreational areas near their homes. They belong manifestly to the class for whom the downtown apartment units should be planned and constructed. . . .[36]

Perry's cautious position is emphasized lest one infer from the following paragraphs that the criticism of the uses made of the neighborhood-unit plan are laid at his door. As often happens, some of the disciples have gone off on tangents that lead them from the paths intended by the teacher.

As a principle for the development of cities, the neighborhood-unit idea has found many supporters among planners, architects, social workers, and some social scientists.[37] Some stress physical convenience

34. *Ibid.*, pp. 50–51.
35. *Ibid.*, pp. 50–51.
36. *Ibid.*, p. 61.
37. See James Dahir, *The Neighborhood Unit Plan: Its Spread and Acceptance* (New York: Russell Sage Foundation, 1947), chap. iv, "The Plan Makes Friends and Faces Obstacles." This book provides the most comprehensive treatment of the literature on the principle. It covers some 229 articles and books dealing directly or indirectly with the topic.

whereas others focus their attention upon the way in which the physical plan is related to the shaping of social relations. One of the latter has gone so far as to say that any living arrangement that places social behavior beyond the control of local gossip is unhealthy. Until very recently, a number of planners have rather uncritically accepted the principle as a guide for urban development and redevelopment.[38]

Despite the misinterpretations and misapplications of the principle, however, the very enthusiasm with which it has been accepted is itself evidence that Perry was looking in the right direction, even though he may not have provided us with the complete answer. *None of the following comments are to be interpreted as challenging the very real necessity of finding some way of providing social contacts for those urbanites who want and need them.* The principle should be carefully re-examined in terms of its value in making the urbanite's life easier and in molding desirable personal relationships. In the following paragraphs, some of the current misconceptions are analyzed.

Two factors, apparently, have accounted for the attempts by some planners to make *a* principle of city planning *the* principle.

The first of these is their admiration and even longing for the small-town way of life as they conceive it. Although most of the men in important planning offices are realistic in their attitudes toward Perry's principle, some are not.[39] Be it as it may, can the small town or village be safely taken as a prototype urban planning unit?

In light of the fictionalized notion of the small town that pervades this country, one must beware of the error of conceiving it as an un-stratified community, where one's primary group encompasses the whole population, where one's friends and close associates are selected at will, and where there is no social isolation. Such towns, if indeed they exist at all, must be exceedingly rare. Evidence of this is found in James West's study, *Plainville, U.S.A.*[40] He discovered that in this hamlet of a few hundred persons, primary groups were not constructed in a random fashion, nor were one's friends determined by one's physical location in the town. Whenever an unstratified society is approximated, it is because of a relative homogeneity of its members. Anything

38. A notable exception to this is found in two articles by Reginald Isaacs in the July and August, 1949, issues of the *Journal of Housing* in which he stresses the view that it is unrealistic to attempt the creation of neighborhood units in an urban setting because of the divergent interests of the family. He also attacks the principle as a tool of segregation.

39. A perusal of planning monographs will reveal the implied application of the principle in uncritical, unrealistic form, but the most explicit treatment of the yearning for the small town is found in *The City*, in itself an excellent job of movie-making, but hardly an unbiased presentation of the rural-urban picture. The enthusiastic reception of this picture throughout the country and its continued showing more than ten years after it was issued indicate that not only planners have this attitude toward the small-town way of life.

40. New York: Columbia University Press, 1945.

approaching this random development of primary groups is unlikely in an urban environment, which is typically heterogeneous.

Another difference between the neighborhood-unit as conceived for the city and its rural counterpart is that the former is an arrangement of housing and local service facilities only, whereas the latter is more nearly a complete community in that it provides employment for most of its inhabitants. This is important because the wage and salary earners of an urban neighborhood would of necessity spend more time away from home than would their opposite numbers in a small town. Thus, the urban workers would have substantially less time to spend cultivating friendships among the neighbors. This is one more obstacle that bars the path of those who would bring the small-town social setting to the metropolis.

Also it is unlikely that anything comparable to the pre-automobile rural neighborhood could be maintained in the face of the multiple attractions and stimuli of the city, which are certain to draw members of any geographical area in many different directions. Closely related is the fact that modern means of communication and transportation have reduced the need for physical nearness in maintaining friendships. The telephone and private automobile make possible daily contacts between persons living perhaps miles apart. It is not at all unusual to find primary groups of long standing whose members are widely separated. It is obvious, of course, that just such a change has taken place in many rural neighborhoods as well. Greater mobility and broadened horizons have destroyed their former cohesiveness. Rural sociologists tell us that ". . . the tendency for neighborhood lines and trade relations to break is strongest in those counties with the greatest amount of improved roads, the largest per capita ownerships of automobiles, and the greatest population per area. . . ."[41] Whether such alterations in the social pattern of the country are tragedy or gain is not .to be argued here. The point to be stressed is the unrealism of attempting to recreate in our present cities a situation that was the product of an age in which limitations of communication and transportation encouraged and even enforced community cohesiveness.

In short, a little reflection shows the futility of attempting the redevelopment of our cities on the pattern of the small town or village neighborhood in the absence of so many of its essential components.

What, then, are the implications of the analysis so far of the neighborhood-unit formula for the planning and redevelopment of the city? Does it mean that the present haphazard, nonintegrated, and confused distribution of peoples, buildings, and services is the inevitable pattern

---

41. J. H. Kolb and A. F. Wiledon, *Special Interest Groups in Rural Society* (Madison: University of Wisconsin, AES RB No. 84, 1927).

for the urban world? Is there nothing of value in the small-town social and physical pattern that can be profitably copied by the metropolitan communities? Surely there are some elements of this sort, but they must be woven carefully and skilfully into the urban pattern in its present and anticipated form.

It was pointed out above that two factors have led to overemphasis on the importance of the neighborhood-unit principle in planning. The first, which has just been discussed, is a desire to revive in urban centers an essentially rural or small-town way of life and a pattern of social organization pleasantly remembered from earlier days. The second is the fact that Perry's principle is not a unitary concept, but is usually viewed as such. Confusion came from the failure to distinguish between two distinctly different aspects of planning that have traditionally been included in the concept "neighborhood."

Most planners and others interested in the idea have failed to distinguish between physical planning for *services* (grocery store, drugstore, grade school, gas station, public transportation, and so forth) and physical planning that will influence *social relations* among the occupants of the area or unit. Planning for one of these components of the *neighborhood* does not mean that the other must also be included in the plan. Failure to recognize the complex nature of the neighborhood-unit often has meant that persons discussing it were not even talking about the same thing, and, therefore, no meeting of the minds was possible.

One way of reducing the confusion is to begin with the needs of man and not with a preconceived and largely untested planning principle. Earlier in this chapter, the basic needs and wants of man were detailed. Among them were the felt need to keep the expenditures of time and energy at a minimum as a person goes about his daily work and play. Attitude studies support this socio-psychological premise. Also, study 18 in Table 3 (Foley) shows that units for shopping and other services or, as the writer prefers to call them "service neighborhoods," do now exist in some form in at least one city. Here the evidence consists not in what the residents say they want but in what they actually do in choosing such facilities as local shops, schools, churches, and theaters. We need not assume an exact coincidence between the status quo and the ideal to see that these findings, as well as those of the attitude studies, strengthen the argument for carefully located and designed neighborhood shopping, school, recreational, and other facilities.

Easy accessibility of services, then, is one of the distinct advantages of the smaller community that should be incorporated into the urban pattern. It is an objective toward which the planner and redeveloper can work with assurance that their efforts will give satisfaction to those for whom the work is done. Perry would be highly pleased to see how closely his principle of service areas coincides with these expressed attitudes and also with the successful residential developments of Greenbelt, Greenhills, Greendale, Park Forest, and similar places that have followed the principles he laid down in 1929.

If the neighborhood-unit proposal meant no more than this, then planners and redevelopers could go ahead applying it in many parts of the city. Even here, however, the varying needs of mixed or heterogeneous populations call for caution. The planner must have clearly in mind the persons for whom he plans. For example, the service-units for areas populated largely by single persons or couples with no children necessarily would be different from those designed to serve the needs of the family districts. If the planner has in mind residential areas mixed as to age, marital status, family size, and other characteristics, then the service-units assume a still different character. Nevertheless, knowledge on the varying requirements of these several population groups is ascertainable, and the planner need not feel unsure of either his goal or of its desirability.

Things are different, however, when one turns his attention to the problem of consciously influencing primary-group relations by physical planning. Yet even on this less traveled ground, the planner or redeveloper is not without certain guide lines. It is to a consideration of these that we now turn.

Primary group relations and physical planning.—It is submitted that the goal for which planners and redevelopers should work is a social situation with a nice balance between the opportunities for personal contacts that characterize the smaller community and freedom from the censorship of gossip, a freedom that the larger urban community typically provides. In other words, the ideal situation gives the individual a primary, face-to-face group of his own choosing but frees him from the unsolicited and unwelcome social pressures of those about him. To be sure, one is never entirely free of the controlling attitudes of the larger community, nor should one be. There is, however, a type of meddlesome control not related to healthy community life that demands conformity to local ways of doing things. It is from this sort of coercion that the urban way of life can free one.

Stated in terms of basic human needs, it seems that the small community is better able to satisfy the need for companionship and affection and often provides security through the help of friends and neighbors in times of crisis. On the other hand, urbanism provides another aspect of security by freeing one from the over-the-shoulder censorship frequently found in the smaller community. The city, too, is better able to provide that variety of experiences that reduces, even eliminates, boredom from life. Moreover, until many Americans stop valuing things

TABLE 4

STUDIES OF NEIGHBORHOOD, OR PERSONAL, FACE-TO-FACE RELATIONS

STUDY 1. Robert K. Merton, "The Social Psychology of Housing," an essay in Wayne Dennis (ed.) *Current Trends in Social Psychology* (University of Pittsburgh Press, 1948).

Scope: Study of two 700-unit housing developments: one in New Jersey and one in Pennsylvania near Pittsburgh.

Findings: One-half of 1 per cent of the 700 families in one community were in any one building, but 19% of all friendships involved persons in same building. Likewise, although only 1% of population lived adjacent to any given informant, 22% of close personalities were with such neighbors. Comparable figures for those living across the street are 1% and 13%. "Clearly, quite apart from other factors, sheer propinquity played a major part in determining the patterns of personal association" (p. 44).

Of 82 people who had friends directly across the street, in 74% of cases front doors faced each other, in 22% one unit faced the other, and only in 4% did neither unit face directly across the street. Despite this, the informants accounted for friendships *wholly* in terms of common interests (p. 46).

In Hilltown (Pittsburgh) of those with previous experience in bi-racial neighborhoods, 9% said would get along fine, 72% said there would be no trouble, and 19% were fearful of race riots. Of those who had no such previous experience, the corresponding figures were: 5%, 39%, and 56% (p. 51). These differences nearly disappeared as the residents had opportunities to know the Negroes on a face-to-face basis as neighbors.

STUDY 2. Morton Deutsch and Mary Evans Collins, "Intergroup Relations in Interracial Housing: A Study of the Socio-Psychological Effects of Occupancy Pattern" (Research Center for Human Relations, New York University, Washington Square, New York. Mimeographed draft of report), later published as *Interracial Housing—A Psychological Evaluation of a Social Experiment* (University of Minnesota Press, 1951).

Scope: Study of four housing projects in two different cities, matched for percentage of Negro and white occupancy, and in terms of *integrated* (random distribution of races) and *segregated* (races in separate buildings or separate parts of the project) occupancy. Interviews usually took approximately 1½ hours. Research design called for one hundred interviews with white housewives in each of four interracial projects. Samples random. Actual samples ranged from 90 to 102. Some children also studied.

Findings: More frequent and intimate contacts between Negro and white in the integrated projects; attitudes of others toward interracial contacts more favorable in the integrated projects; also more internal group cohesiveness and greater awareness of and discussion of interracial factors in the integrated projects than in the segregated ones. More frequent and more extensive favorable attitude change toward the Negro people in the project among the housewives and children in the integrated projects; both types of project showed more frequent change in unprejudiced than in prejudiced direction in both projects; change of attitude in more prejudiced direction occurred more frequently in the segregated than in the integrated; also clear but less extensive favorable attitude changes toward the Negro in general and also toward Chinese. Those in the integrated projects recommended that the city adopt the integrated pattern in future

TABLE 4 *(Continued)*

plans, whereas those in the segregated projects recommended separate projects for the different races.

STUDY 3. Bemis Foundation Study, M.I.T., 1948 (Preliminary draft of Leon Festinger, Stanley Schachter and Kurt Back, *Social Pressures in Informal Groups*. Harper and Bros., N.Y., 1950).

Scope: Study of 270 student veteran families living in temporary project constructed and managed by Massachusetts Institute of Technology.

Findings: "More than 60% of all sociometric choices of friends were made inside the chooser's court. . . ." ". . . people who live in end houses which are rotated so that they face the street rather than into the court have many fewer friends in the court than do residents of the other houses." Concludes that "In a community of people who are homogeneous with respect to many of the factors which determine the development of friendships, the physical factors arising from the arrangement of houses are major determinants of what friendships will develop and what social groupings will be formed" (p. 151).

STUDY 4. Clifton R. Jones, "Invasion and Racial Attitudes," *Social Forces* Vol. 27 (March, 1949).

Scope: Study of effects of invasion of white neighborhood by Negroes in a border city.

Findings: Ninety-seven families, or 55.4%, expressed an attitude of indifference or more or less positive acceptance of Negro families in the area, though they expressed no open friendliness toward them; 21.7% expressed dislike for the presence of Negroes and intend to move; 22.8% were openly friendly toward their Negro neighbors. No ". . . significant change in attitude of this group as a result of their living in such close proximity to Negro families. About half of the group admitted friendship or more than casual acquaintance with Negroes prior to the settling of the latter in the area" (p. 290).

STUDY 5. Ruby Jo Reeves Kennedy, "Premarital Residential Propinquity and Ethnic Endogamy," *American Journal of Sociology*, XLVIII (March, 1943), pp. 580–84.

Scope: Study of marriage licenses in New Haven, 1931 and 1940.

Findings: As measured by the proportion of persons marrying those who lived within twenty blocks prior to marriage, New Haven marriages in 1940 involved persons living nearer to each other than in 1931. 64.43% lived within twenty blocks of each other in 1931, but 76.31% in 1940. Not an indication of the influence of nearness as such because most marriages were between members of the same racial, religious, or nationality groups.

STUDY 6. Ray H. Abrams, "Residential Propinquity as a Factor in Marriage Selection," *American Sociological Review*, VIII (June, 1943), pp. 288–94.

Scope: Study of residential addresses in Philadelphia given in first 5,000 consecutive marriage license applications. Years covered: 1885–86, 1905, 1915, and 1931.

Findings: Slightly greater proportion married persons whose premarital residences were within one, two, three, four, and five blocks in 1931 than in 1885–86, 1905, and 1915. Generally fewer in 1905 and 1915 than in 1885–86. Fewer (56.49%) in 1931 than in 1885–86 (70.09%), 1905 (66%), and 1915 (61.62%), married persons living within twenty blocks.

TABLE 4 (*Continued*)

Approximately the same percentage of persons married those from outside of the city in 1905 (18.20%), 1915 (18.80%), and 1931 (17.80%). In 1885–86 only 11.36% married outside of the city. No analysis was made in this study comparable to that of the New Haven study with regard to the in-group marriages.

STUDY 7. Richard Dewey, "Peripheral Expansion in Milwaukee County," *American Journal of Sociology*, LIV (September, 1948), pp. 118–25.

Scope: Analysis of nearly 4,000 questionnaires distributed in unincorporated areas of Milwaukee County, 1945.

Findings: Nearly 80% reported a more neighborly and community spirit than in the city. Some reported that primary group relations of long standing had been replaced by newly found friends among the neighbors of the subdivision. In the smaller subdivisions (less than fifty homes) a genuine neighborhood seemed to exist.

for their sheer size, larger communities will have the edge on smaller ones in satisfying the urge to feel important. Many residents of New York, Chicago, or Los Angeles feel themselves to be an integral part of these gargantuan communities, and this identification is reflected in the hauteur usually assumed by the big-city visitor to the "hick" town, regardless of what his station of life in the larger community may be.

Neither the fact that some people apparently are satisfied with the small-town way of life, nor that others are equally content with the present situation in the city can be accepted as proof that either is an ideal physical setting. Rather, it demonstrates once again the flexibility of human nature and its wide range of adaptability. If, however, the demands for security, recognition, variety of experience, and companionship are given relatively equal weights, something seems to be lacking in both small town and large city. The ideal physical and social setting meets all four of these needs and also provides for physical comfort and helps to economize expenditures of time and energy.

Until that happy situation is achieved, many urbanites will continue to yearn for certain aspects of the smaller community, and the villager will seek the lights and excitement of the city. The best contemporary combination of rural-urban attributes is, of course, the residential suburb,[42] but this nearly successful attempt to "have your cake and eat it too" is obviously a solution for but a fraction of the metropolitan population.

Although it is not the purpose of this chapter to indicate how the benefits of the small town can be brought to the city, it can point out certain research findings that are of value to those who do plan new and redevelopment areas. Studies 1, 2, 3, and 4 in Table 4 clearly indi-

42. Not considered here is the British "new town" or garden city, which, despite its influence on much planning thought and a little action in this country, has not yet struck any deep roots in American soil.

cate the influence that the physical arrangement of dwellings has upon the selection of friends and associates. It has also been reported that, in some smaller subdivisions in unincorporated suburban areas, physical proximity of homes has induced people to drop associations of long standing with friends in the central city and to substitute similar ties with their new neighbors. There can be no doubt that in these five instances the formation of social groups was shaped largely by the way in which the apartments were assigned and the houses were located. Lest one read too much into this type of influence, however, it is well to keep in mind that the people covered in these studies were quite homogeneous in their attitudes and preferences. Particularly in the M.I.T. study of student veterans housed in temporary units, the similarities of age, family status, wartime experience, intelligence, and interests set the social stage so that the physical arrangements of the dwellings would be the crucial factor in determining friendships. The suburban groups were also quite homogeneous as to income, education, and interests. In many urban areas such homogeneity is unknown, and in them friendships may be correlated relatively little with physical proximity.

Even the studies on the relationship between physical proximity of residences and marriage do not alter this observation. The New Haven study(5), although it shows a significant increase in the proportion of marriages between people who live within twenty blocks of one another, does not hold that this is the result of proximity. Rather, most of the marriages took place between members of the same religious and nationality groups and the spatial nearness of their residences was a product of ethnic segregation. The decrease in the proportion of persons marrying within the twenty-block area of the Philadelphia study (6) may well reflect the dispersion of groups in that city. Further, the fact that more Philadelphians are marrying persons who live within five blocks of their homes is not to be construed as proof that propinquity is overcoming all differences.

Neither, however, do we learn from these studies that physical proximity is never effective in removing the barriers of personality differences, for at times it certainly is. Nevertheless, such differences often defy the influences of nearness, and one should not expect the physical planning of a city to be a panacea for all social differences or antagonisms. If the problems of social segregation and group antagonisms are to be seen in proper perspective, it is imperative that one distinguish the different kinds of barriers to social relations.

As we have seen, some of these barriers are physical in nature—distance and awkward circulation systems in residential areas. Planning as traditionally conceived can do much to change these situations. Yet the job is not finished when this is done. Other barriers are the product, not of man's external, physical environment, but of his habitual attitudes toward ways of doing things and toward people who differ from himself. Here the planner must take into account not only the informally acquired attitudes that keep people apart, but also those taught by organizations whose existence depends upon perpetuating prejudicial attitudes. The tenacity of the habits of mind created by these formal and informal groups cannot be ignored if planning is to be both comprehensive and effective.

Traditionally, planners and even many redevelopers have not considered such direct study of attitudes as within their sphere, yet plans for urban redevelopment will remain incomplete unless a change is made in this respect. The planner may try to alter these attitudes by whatever means are at his disposal and thus to reconcile the differences, or he may simply accept these attitudes as relative invariables in terms of which other factors will be changed. The first is the logical step if the planner conceives his goal to be harmonious, iron-curtain-less, social relations; the second approach leads clearly to planned segregation of various sorts, possibly on a "separate but equal" basis. As a matter of fact, what the planner will often do is to compromise between the ideal he would aspire to and the coercive realism of the power-laden pressure groups, be they economic, national, religious, or racial.

Even if we do not at this juncture attempt to re-educate against the attitudes that keep men apart, there still remains the problem of the relationship between the physical arrangements of dwelling units and other units of the physical city and the social behavior of the people involved. What are the situations in which the redeveloper can plan for improved social interaction through altering the physical pattern of cities?

It was stated above that communication is essential to the removal of some types of negative attitudes. An example of attitudes that can be favorably influenced by the physical arrangement of dwellings is the attitude the majority of whites in this country have toward the Negroes. It is based upon the stereotype of the Negro as lazy, dirty, uneducated, untrustworthy, and given to excesses of emotional display. Now, if whites who do not like such traits should acquire Negro neighbors who happened to possess them, the physical proximity would *not* serve to reduce the negative feelings. The fact is that the studies directed by Merton (1), by Deutsch and Collins (2), and by Jones (4) indicate that antagonisms are reduced and friendships do develop where Negro and white families live near each other. The explanation lies in the similarity or comparability of interests and standards of behavior of the Negroes and whites involved. The whites learned that their previously held attitudes toward the Negro were based upon misconceptions.

This, and not the spatial nearness alone, made the reduction in antagonisms possible. Wherever barriers to mutual respect and other
forms of social interaction exist that are founded upon myth or error in
fact, it is important to facilitate communication between the groups
concerned.

> If group images are to be blurred and social cement applied there is no place
> in the world for iron curtains. Empathy is impossible without communication. If
> society wishes to secure this consciousness of obligation to common rules derived
> through the method of reciprocity, the social structure must be modified so that
> reciprocity is possible.[43]

At least in general terms, the role of the planner or redeveloper is
clear with regard to the group differences that will be affected by his
plans. He must know well the attitudes of the various groups, judge (or
accept the judgment of his agency as to) whether or not they are worthy
of survival, and, acting with the courage of his convictions, design the
physical structure accordingly. If he includes in his criteria of the good
city harmonious social relations, he must not rest his case upon the
physical design alone but should give attention to the organizations and
institutions that foster and strengthen these individual and group antagonisms. Even in such circumstances, free communication tends to
reduce the social isolation or immobility, but usually this alone does not
erase the dividing attitudes. Direct attack upon misconceptions of human nature must be included in any plan that aspires to be called "comprehensive."

LOCATION WITH REFERENCE TO THE LARGER COMMUNITY

External space relations include not only the location of dwelling
units with respect to services and the residences of friends, but also
with the location of housing districts in the over-all pattern of the
metropolitan community. If we think of this pattern as being made up
of certain natural areas, i.e., areas that have sufficient homogeneity of
people or buildings to identify them as distinct from their surroundings,
we can better discuss the relationships. Despite the lack of consensus
on the exact nature of the over-all pattern (illustrated, for example, by
the Burgess concentric-circle theory, Hoyt's sector theory, and the
criticisms of both of these made from the cultural viewpoint by Firey)
we can recognize that significant differences in land use do exist in all
large cities. Every scheme recognizes these districts:

I. Business districts
   1. Central

43. John W. Morgan, "Notes on Common Values and Social Control," *Social Forces,*
Vol. XXVII, No. 4 (May, 1949).

2. Secondary
3. Local shopping centers
II. Industrial districts
  1. Heavy
  2. Light
  3. Obnoxious
III. Residential districts
  1. Upper-income districts
  2. Middle-income districts
  3. Lower-income districts
  4. Single-person districts
  5. Family districts
IV. Transition or conversion districts
  1. From residential to business or industrial
  2. From agricultural to residential
  3. From agricultural to business or industry
  4. From one form of residential (usually single-family houses) to other forms (usually multi-family houses)
V. Suburban areas
  1. Residential suburbs
  2. Industrial suburbs
  3. Incorporated suburbs
  4. Unincorporated suburbs

Consciously or unconsciously, the urbanite selects his dwelling site with reference to these different land-use districts. In many instances, probably in most, the primary factor in his choice is economic. Nevertheless, within the same price range, preferences for cleaner areas, unmixed land uses, and for better public transportation manifest themselves in the movement and distribution of population within urban areas.

Near-downtown areas.—Although one might expect the majority of urban residents to prefer to live in the near-downtown areas, the growth processes of cities have resulted in the badly mixed land-use patterns of the transition or conversion zones. Here are found the slum and blighted areas of speculation, where the houses are, for the most part, overcrowded, neglected, and generally on the downgrade. Most of the residents of such districts are those who cannot afford or, for other reasons, are not able to live elsewhere. The one distinct advantage attending their location is the nearness to downtown areas where they shop and where many work.

Exceptions to this rule are found in the "Gold Coasts" of such cities as Chicago, Milwaukee, and the East River luxury apartments in Manhattan. In these instances the upper-income groups (as Hoyt points out in study 4 of Table 5) have taken advantage of near-downtown sites and because of river and lake are assured of buffer strips on at least one side. By virtue of their incomes, the occupants of these restricted

TABLE 5

STUDIES OF ATTITUDES TOWARD SUBURBAN LIVING

STUDY 1. Chauncy D. Harris, "Suburbs," *American Journal of Sociology*, XLIX (July, 1943), 1–13.

Scope: Analysis of suburbs of 140 Metropolitan districts according to census of 1940. Classified 352 suburbs of more than 10,000 population. *Findings:* Of the 352 suburbs of more than 10,000 population, 174 are residential and 148 industrial. The residential suburbs continued to grow during the 1930–40 period, but many of the industrial suburbs did not. Points to concentration of occupational groups in suburbs. Of the 19 cities in this country which reported the highest proportion of professional people, 16 were suburbs in metropolitan districts; of the 21 cities with the highest proportion of clerical workers 18 were suburbs (p. 6). Suburbs of more than 10,000 that were classed as residential averaged 11.7% increase in population, whereas the industrial suburbs averaged but 1.7% (pp. 10–11).

STUDY 2. Bernard Meltzer (Carnegie grant study of preferences of city size directed by W. F. Ogburn, University of Chicago, 1949).

Scope: Samples taken among railroad union members, high-school students in Chicago, and among residents of Peoria, LaSalle, and Bloomington, Illinois. 1,039 schedules filled out and analyzed. *Findings:* Regardless of present address, most of respondents stated preference for suburb, followed by middle-sized city (50,000) near big city. Correspondence between present city size and preferred size greatest in case of present residents of suburbs.

STUDY 3. Milwaukee County Regional Planning Dept., *Residential Development in the Unincorporated Areas of Milwaukee County*, 1945.

Scope: Analysis of approximately 4,000 questionnaires circulated through the schools in unincorporated Milwaukee County. Use of directories to trace movements of persons listed in *Social Register*. *Findings:* Indicates that people move to suburban area through series of short moves; appears to be a continuation of long-term centrifugal movement of population, and not true decentralization; no preference for given direction except in case of upper-income groups which followed restricted route in changing of address, viz., to upper east side along Lake Michigan, thence successively through the residential suburbs which line the lake shore. In general, migrants to the suburbs came from the peripheral areas of the central city.

STUDY 4. Homer Hoyt, *The Structure and Growth of Residential Neighborhoods in American Cities* (Federal Housing Administration, Washington, D.C., 1939).

Scope: Analysis of census and Real Property Survey statistics of all large cities in U.S. *Findings:* Higher-priced residential neighborhoods do not skip about at random in process of movement, but follow a definite path in one or more sectors of the city. Attracted by high ground, lake, bay, river, or ocean fronts where these are not used for industry. Tend to grow in directions not limited by geographical or artificial barriers, toward open country. Tend to grow toward homes of community leaders, and continue to grow in same direction for long time, follow along the fastest existing trans-

TABLE 5 (*Continued*)

portation lines. Deluxe high rent apartments tend to be established near the business centers in old residential areas.

STUDY 5. "The Fortune Survey," *Fortune* (December, 1948), p. 39.

Scope: Nation-wide sample of persons in the 18–25 and 40–55 age groups. Study directed by Elmo Roper.

Findings: "If you had your choice where would you like best to live?" Suburb: 22%; country: 21%; small city: 20%; small town: 19%; big city: 17%; no opinion: 1%.

STUDY 6. "The Fortune Survey," *Fortune* (April, 1946), p. 266.

Scope: Nation-wide sample. Study directed by Elmo Roper.

Findings: "If there were nothing to keep you from living wherever you wanted to, in what kind of location would you choose to live?"

WHERE THEY NOW LIVE	WHERE THEY WOULD LIKE TO LIVE				
			Small Town		
	Large City (per cent)	Small City (per cent)	Close to City (per cent)	Far from City (per cent)	Out in Country (per cent)
Over 100,000.............	36.2	10.4	36.5	2.8	11.1
25,000 to 100,000........	6.8	43.3	26.9	4.4	16.4
2,500 to 25,000..........	6.9	27.8	46.5	3.2	12.4
2,500 and rural non-farm..	6.1	16.4	49.0	6.9	20.5
Rural farm..............	0.6	6.5	18.1	1.1	71.7
National average.......	14.7	17.6	35.8	3.5	26.0

Concluded that "Except for farmers . . . the U.S. people show (however vague such terms as 'a small town' or 'close to a city' may be) a pronounced yearning for life in the suburbs."

districts have the advantages of short distances to shopping centers, places of employment, and of amusement and still have excellent living conditions in exclusive surroundings. But this is an exception to the general trend of peripheral expansion and dispersion of those in the upper-income levels.

What is to be the proper disposition of the near-downtown slum and blighted areas is one of the most debatable questions in all of present-day city planning. Were the sites not occupied by such incongruous physical structures in such varied states of disrepair and were the air relatively clean, certainly the proximity to the heart of the city would induce many of the upper-income groups to live there. Although the top-income groups are too small to fill the entire area now occupied by slums and blight in most large cities, there are easily enough in the upper-middle and middle-income groups, together with a certain amount of subsidized housing for the lowest-income groups, to fill the remainder.

We do not intend to suggest here ways of redeveloping these slum areas, but the general desire of the urbanite for accessibility to the central business district provides the planner with one criterion for their future use. It is well to keep in mind that for most urbanites there is no great merit in traveling some five or ten miles or more to and from work merely for the ride, however necessary the journey to work may be for the metropolitan districts as a whole.

Suburbs.—The distances most bread-winners in the suburban areas must travel suggest that there must be considerable advantages to living in the suburbs in order to compensate for the time, money, and energy spent in commuting. A quick glance at the suburbs, especially the residential ones, reveals these advantages. In the section above dealing with the reasons for moving it was clearly shown that the desire for clean, uncongested areas in which to raise children was high on the list of motives that induced the suburban trend, both to incorporated and unincorporated areas. There can be do doubt that many residential suburbs are the most satisfactory answer to this unending search for good living conditions in metropolitan areas—satisfactory, that is, from the viewpoint of the suburbanites and those who aspire to suburban residence. Although from the perspective of the entire metropolitan region suburbs are economic parasites and draw from the central city many potential and actual leaders who lose much of their identification with it, these facts do not affect the suburbs as desirable places to live. Such shortcomings as the suburbanites' occasional smugness and lack of imagination, and the distances to specialized services are prices many will pay in order to secure cleaner, more pleasing environment, superior schools, greater efficiency and honesty in government, and a stability of land-use pattern the central city rarely provides.

In broad terms, the better suburb is the best present-day compromise between the small town and the large city.[44] It is an error, however, to think of suburban life as strictly comparable with that of the small town. In the first place, the suburb usually is much more homogeneous with regard to income, occupational distribution, and education. Although there are significant differences and exceptions and the creation of primary groups is essentially a selective process, the suburb is a community of peers to a degree not known elsewhere. Whether or not it is a socially healthy or a democratic situation, surely parents in the higher-income residential suburbs of our large metropolitan communities worry less about their children meeting the "wrong" people than do many residents of central cities. Too, living in many suburbs enables one to insulate himself, if he wishes, from the disturbing sight of slum and blighted areas, protects his children from the conscience-probing experience of sitting in class or on public conveyances with ill-clothed children, and removes from direct focus the urgent problems of the central city. In short, life in suburbia pads one's conscience against the

44. See comment in footnote 42 of this chapter.

unpleasant probings of such experiences. This is neither to recommend that people seek the suburban life to relieve their consciences, nor is it an attack upon the escapism of the suburbanite. It is simply a statement of one reason why life in many residential suburbs is pleasant and why many city dwellers aspire to it.

Here also the relation between the community's size and the satisfaction of social needs is pertinent. At least to date, the suburb and the small town of similar size are different in the variation permitted in social behavior, particularly in personal habits and preferences for recreation and amusement, if not in attitudes toward the prevailing economic system. This reflects the fact that the suburbs are, for the most part, peopled by residents of the central city whose horizons have been broadened through wider experience with ways of thinking about and doing things. There are, of course, interesting exceptions to this willingness to live-and-let-live, but the schoolteachers, for instance, in the upper-class suburbs are not under the censuring eyes of the town's residents to the degree that they are in the independent community of the same size. Whether or not this will continue to be true in the long run is, of course, an unanswerable question. In at least one instance, a family head sold his home in a fashionable suburb and returned his family to a city apartment house because, he said, the suburban "friendliness" was just a cover-up for gossipy curiosity. This, however, does not characterize suburban attitudes generally.

The last, but highly important, motive for the movement of so many people to the more well-to-do suburbs is their high prestige. It is not at all uncommon to find persons moving to the suburbs from dwellings that are every bit as good as the new ones and from areas that are as clean and as well or better serviced. The difference between the two sites is the greater status attached to the suburb. Residents of industrial suburbs, for instance, when away from home are often willing to identify themselves as from, say, Chicago, Boston, Cleveland, or Milwaukee. Not so the residents of many residential suburbs who protest that they are *not* from Chicago, Boston, Cleveland, or Milwaukee, but from Evanston, Lincoln, Shaker Heights, or Whitefish Bay.

Much as one may disapprove of such "exclusive" attitudes and "snob appeal," a certain proportion of urbanites probably always will seek recognition in this way. Especially is it true in the larger metropolitan communities that most men must strive in order to maintain some degree of self-identity, some sort of individuality. A feeling that they are parts of a distinctive section of the sprawling metropolis aids them in this cause. Of course, only a few can distinguish themselves in this way, yet it will persist, either because of the efforts of planners or despite them. The problem really is how to provide such satisfaction without moving everyone to the suburbs. The task is something more than, and different from, the creation of face-to-face neighborhoods. Speculation may suggest a modified borough system; study and research may recommend something quite different. Whatever the means, man's felt-need to feel important and different will make for residential districts that are in some ways atypical, out of the ordinary, and set apart from the others.

SUMMARY

Until recently plans for urban regions have been based upon the planners' assumptions of what man's needs and wants are. Recent trends show that many planners are willing to re-examine these assumptions and to try to discover whether or not they coincide with the actual needs of the people.

Scientists are providing information regarding the basic needs of man, social as well as physiological. It is generally true that man's needs are very flexible in nature and can be satisfied by a wide range of experiences. Thus, we recognize the fundamental physical needs for physical comfort and for economy in the expenditure of energy, and the universal, socially acquired needs for (1) recognition by one's fellows, (2) affection and companionship, (3) a variety of experiences, and (4) a feeling of security. Just how these basic needs will be met is determined by the culture in which one lives. In the present instance, the influences of living in the American culture as well as experiences in the rural, urban, and suburban districts of the country have to be taken into account.

These culturally determined ways of meeting basic requirements become habits, and past experiences shape future preferences. This fact bulks large in evaluating attitudes expressed about living conditions, because it is frequently true that those questioned have not had experiences of sufficient breadth to permit them to answer the questions adequately. For example, the life-long apartment dweller may not be prepared to evaluate life in a single-family home, despite the fact that he may have been dissatisfied with the apartments. Also, widespread cultural values (say, the desire to own one's home, to live in a single-family house, for rural residence) often are uncritically accepted as valid whereas actual experience might have proved them to be otherwise.

Planners are urged to use these basic needs of man as their starting point. Any plan that might properly be called *comprehensive* must be geared to all of these complex needs, physiological and social.

Research on attitudes toward housing facilities reveals a widely expressed desire for (1) home ownership in preference to rental, (2) single-family houses, (3) more room than present houses provide. For some persons the dwelling unit is merely a means to some other end, whereas others value it for its own sake. For the latter, home owner- ship usually is a more satisfactory way of satisfying basic needs than renting. Some students of housing emphasize the point that home ownership is not always as desirable as the prospective owner believes it to be. In such instances it becomes an economic handicap, imposes responsibilities of maintenance that are burdensome, and limits mobil- ity. The same distinction applies to the desire for single-family houses; for some they are ideal, but multiple-dwelling units (not necessarily tall apartment buildings) best serve the needs of others. Variations in age, family size, marital and economic status, as well as the nature of past experiences must be weighed when housing needs are being ana- lyzed and estimated.

The studies of attitudes toward external space relationships show that most people wish to avoid certain rather obvious features of urban living (dirt, noise, congestion, traffic, small quarters) and to retain its advantages (variety of scene and experience, job opportunities, and accessibility of multiple services). The distances people prefer to travel for various services are much the same as those recommended by Clar- ence Perry in outlining his neighborhood-unit principle. In both in- stances, grocery store, drugstore, playground for children, and grade school were wanted within walking distance—one-half mile or less. Relatively few requested that places of employment be within short distances of the home, but this may be ascribed to the present planless patterning of cities and a desire to avoid living in or close to noisy and dirty industrial areas. The trip to and from work, although it consumes time, money, and energy, is an essential aspect of our present-day urban- industrial society and has value for both employer and employee. The former is provided with a larger labor pool and avoids the unpleasant "company-town" situation. The latter can shift from job to job without moving his home; and two or more members of a family can live at home while working in different places. Planning can reduce, but never eliminate, the need for some rather long journeys to work in large urban areas.

The general and at times uncritical acceptance of Clarence Perry's neighborhood-unit principle by planners has recently been questioned. In the discussion here it is adjudged valid as *a* principle of planning, but not as *the* principle or as a panacea for urban ills. The concept is not a unitary one, but includes both the physical layout of residential districts for safety, quiet, adequate open space, convenient access to shopping and other commercial facilities, and amenity as well as the desirability of establishing and maintaining primary group contacts or relations. Although these objectives are related in that Perry argued that proper layout would foster the social relations as well as assure safety and convenience, these two sets of objectives are distinguishable. Much confusion has come from failing to recognize this fact.

It is indeed a rare individual who would not prefer some of the residential districts planned as suggested by Perry to the monotonous, cramped, uneconomical, socially isolating blocks of dwellings that characterize most of our cities. Such places as Radburn (New Jersey), Baldwin Hills Village (Los Angeles), Greendale (Wisconsin), Chatham Village (Pittsburgh), or some unheralded suburban subdivisions illustrate the advantages that can be gained by planning physical facilities in accordance with the neighborhood-unit principle. But attempts to recreate in an urban setting the close-knit primary group neighborhood that existed in the pre-automobile, rural, or small-town community are doomed to failure because too many of the essential components of the latter are missing from the urban scene. It is likely that many of the ardent advocates of the neighborhood principle visualize the small community from the vantage point of one with high status, and overlook the unpleasantness of high visibility for those of lowly status. In the small, rural community, there is not only warm friendliness and mutual assistance, but also the unsolicited control of neighborhood gossip. It is possible, however, to have satisfactory primary group relations in the larger community and yet avoid the meddlesome interference of neighbors with one's life.

The influence of physical proximity upon social relationships must be carefully considered. On the one hand, the planner must realize that ingrained habits of prejudice toward persons of different religious persuasion, cultural, nationality, or racial background often persist, even grow in intensity in the face of spatial proximity. The Negro-white conflict is sharp in that part of the country where the two groups are in close daily contact. Our cities afford evidence that residential proximity is not sufficient to reduce or to eliminate quickly religious or cultural differences. There is sufficient evidence, however, to show the distinct advantage of physical nearness (spatial proximity) in establishing communication between many groups of persons who, prior to the neighboring, were definitely estranged and even in conflict. If the persons share many of the same or comparable beliefs, standards of cleanliness, honesty, and similar qualities, physical nearness usually induces friendly social relations. This is particularly true where the groups have been held apart by myth and misunderstanding. In such circumstances the reduction in prejudices and social isolation is accomplished despite the efforts of formal organizations whose existence demands intolerance of other ways of doing things. In essence, physical proximity is an essential, but not a sufficient condition for the reduction of group tensions.

In many respects, the suburb is the most satisfactory compromise between the large city and the small town yet tested on any scale in this country. Here are usually found the cleanliness, spaciousness, often better government, and often the neighborliness of the smaller town, combined with relatively easy access to the jobs, amusements, and special services of the larger central city. That the suburb is not the exact counterpart of the small town is clear. Suburbs, especially residential ones, are far more homogeneous with regard to age, income, education, occupation, and general attitudes than independent towns of comparable size. Furthermore there is a live-and-let-live atmosphere (with the possible exception of attitudes toward the prevailing economic system) in most suburbs not to be matched in the rural community. This is explained by the fact that most suburbanites migrated from the heterogeneous central city where divergent social behavior is common. The attitude studies reveal widespread satisfaction of suburbanites with their residential location, and a marked tendency for those in central cities and other towns to express preferences for suburban residence. The higher prestige of residential suburbs is an important item for many who prefer them. Although it is decidedly not democratic, this appeal to exclusiveness seems certain to be an enduring feature of urbanism.

The goal, which if reached or reasonably approximated, will fulfil the basic needs of the urbanite is a community that will combine some qualities of both small town and large city. Neither in its present form and at the current stage of cultural development satisfies all of the fundamental human requirements. The small town provides ample opportunity for companionship and friendship, for easy access to local services, and for certain forms of security. On the other hand, it may fall short of fulfilling man's need for recognition and variety of experience. The large city does provide insurance against boredom, affords wider opportunities for choice of occupation, freedom from unwanted interference with one's personal life, and permits one to identify himself with the city's greatness or, at least, bigness. Nevertheless, it may fail to meet other basic social needs of man. The city can be a very lonesome place. It can thwart natural human friendliness. It can breed suspicion and misunderstanding. It often has dissolved long-established values as to behavior and belief while putting nothing comparable in their place.

Careful planning for residential and service units will enable the urbanite to enjoy some of the conveniences of the smaller community, and physical planning for the reduction of dirt, noise, and congestion is in keeping with the desires of the vast majority of urbanites. Although it is desirable so to plan or redevelop the city that the residents can identify themselves not only with the city proper but also with smaller units, it is neither desirable nor possible to recreate the small-town way of life as such in the urban community.

CHAPTER III

ATTITUDES AND THE ATTITUDE SURVEY

THIS chapter discusses two related subjects: (1) the attitudes that urbanites hold toward redevelopment and their present living conditions, and (2) the sample survey technique as a means of ascertaining these attitudes.

The importance of consumers' attitudes to the redevelopment process has been discussed in chapter i and needs no reiteration here except to point out once more that urban redevelopment deals primarily with people and secondarily with things—land, buildings, investment returns.

Ascertaining attitudes, however, is not an exact science. Methods and techniques are still being proposed, tested, abandoned, and improved. This does not mean, however, that no guides are available or that each agency must strike out on its own, unaided. A few pilot sample surveys have been made on people's attitudes toward the physical development and characteristics of urban areas. The sample survey has been used much more widely to ascertain opinions and attitudes in other fields. Much of the experience gained in them is applicable to urban planning and redevelopment. This chapter is devoted to an account of some of those methods and techniques that have been tried out.

ATTITUDES TOWARD REDEVELOPMENT

At the outset, we suggest that redevelopment agencies should realize that in nearly all the areas in which they will be working there are many groups with differing and sometimes changing outlooks on their communities. An agency's purpose is not to learn the attitudes of the majority and to plan for them alone but to find out the views and preferences of many groups so that the agency's program may provide for the needs of each group as effectively as possible.

Most of these groups fall into obvious categories. One is geographic, i.e., by areas or districts—usually including or near to a site proposed for redevelopment. Another category is according to property ownership. The classifications here are three: tenant, owner occupant, and absentee owner. These groups can be expected to have different attitudes, all other factors being equal. Still another category is based on housing type. Owners and residents of single family homes may have

369

completely different ideas about what should be done in a district from those who own or occupy multi-family structures.

Again, owners and tenants of various kinds of commercial and industrial property can be expected to have attitudes related to their particular situations. Institutions such as churches, hospitals, and colleges in a proposed redevelopment area are likely to exert considerable influence on decisions about plans and proposals.

The outline below simply illustrates the diversity of difficulties and attitudes that might be expected on almost any sizeable clearance and rebuilding project. For several of the usual groups in project areas it suggests some of the questions their members *might* ask, the attitudes they *might* hold, and the way such a proposal *might* be seen by them and their associates. Although this outline is an example of one step that a redevelopment official might well take in his early planning, it is by no means enough. In fact, if it alone is done, the net result may be harmful. By trying to think through the kinds of response that his proposal might reasonably be expected to meet, he could easily fall into the error of assuming that his guesses and estimates correspond with the actual views and attitudes of people and groups in the areas—the old "every-one-knows-that . . ." assumption. But if the planner or re-developer will steer clear of that pitfall, he probably will conclude that both the content of his proposals and his methods of presenting them could be strengthened greatly if he had some real evidence on what people and organizations in these areas like and dislike about them; what they know about urban redevelopment; what hopes, doubts, suspicions, or hostilities it stirs up in them; if possible, what some of the bases of these attitudes are; and, from a thorough, realistic, and sympathetic analysis of such facts, how he might proceed with the greatest margin of benefits over hardship and inconvenience.

Also, he would be helped materially by similar information and understanding on at least some major groups not entirely or largely within specific project areas. Redevelopment, after all, is an undertaking unmistakeably "affected with a public interest." And the more vigorous, imaginative and potentially fruitful a local program may be, the wider and deeper will be its influences on people's pocketbooks, on their interest in their community, and on their standards and ways of day-to-day living.

OUTLINE OF POSSIBLE ATTITUDES TOWARD REDEVELOPMENT
PROPOSALS

A. Property owners in a project area
  1. Owner-occupants of one- and two-family houses that might be razed.
    a) Attitudes toward condition of property

    (1) Do they feel their property is adequate in spite of the classification "slum" or "substandard"? If so, why?

    (2) Is there a stigma attached to these labels that creates opposition? Could more palatable designations be devised? Cannot such a reaction be expected from a public announcement on the condition of their property?

    (3) Could they be persuaded to view their property in terms of minimum standards and to recognize the prohibitive cost of remodeling it to meet these standards?

 b) Attitudes toward moving from their homes and the community

    (1) How strong are their ties to their homes and the community?

    (2) Are they so strong that no form of persuasion will make them feel that a move is advantageous?

    (3) If housing of a better quality but at roughly comparable rentals and in a somewhat similar community were available, would this make much difference?

    (4) Might not some be willing to move if active and effective aid were offered to find them slightly better living quarters in a different community?

    (5) Might not some welcome the opportunity to be relieved of their property at a "good" price and to leave the community?

    (6) Could not at least most of these people be persuaded to move by offering them a generous price—maybe a little above the market value? If so, how much higher would such a price have to be? Should such a technique be employed?

    (7) What effect would offering these people relocation housing and priority of quarters in the redevelopment project have on their attitudes toward moving? How would the problem of rentals compared to their minimum ownership expenses be handled?

    (8) Is the only effective form of persuasion monetary?

    (9) What, if anything, do they wish to see done to the area?

2. Owners of rental units

 a) Small-income property

    (1) This is not necessarily an emotional problem though public statements of an emotional nature may be used as fronts for other basic objections.

    (2) Is not the problem here one of finding a place for investment that will yield comparable returns? May not one difficulty be the high return due to minimum capital and maintenance expenditures coupled with a high degree of overcrowding?

    (3) Is there any form of persuasion that would be effective for this group?

 b) Large-scale rental units

    (1) Their attitudes would seem to be only the desire to have comparable investment property. Is this, in fact, their view of things? To what extent, if any, are they holding for speculative purposes rather than for investment return?

    (2) Might not a great many welcome the opportunity of being bailed out?

    (3) Could there be any emotional ties to maintaining their property?

    (4) Would it be best to deal with members of this group individually or in a group?

3. Owners of commercial and industrial property
    a) Family owned and operated marginal stores
        (1) Is there liable to be much of an emotional tie to their property by this group? Is their attachment purely economic?
        (2) Would not this group fear dislocation and separation from their livelihood?
        (3) Could the problem be met by doing two things—first, aiding them in re-establishing their businesses in the same or a new community or, second, helping dispel the fear and lack of security such a change would entail?
    b) Absentee owners of commercial property
        (1) Is not the problem here basically economic, i.e., a "good" price would undoubtedly work as a good persuader?
        (2) Would not many of this group welcome disposition of their property? a good opportunity to bail out? If not, why not?
4. Owners of other types of property—institutions
    a) Churches
        (1) Here one might expect considerable opposition on emotional grounds, particularly if the church is an old one and is to be razed. Would this be offset, in part, by a recognition of the benefits of the proposed undertaking to the district as a whole?
        (2) An approach which bears some consideration is the offering of a new site in the area for a new church to serve the community. This raises the question of whether the membership or congregation in another location would bear any similarity to the present one.
        (3) Might there be opposition from a church group whose building would not be razed but whose congregation would be dispersed in the event of redevelopment? If so, what work could be done to change their attitudes? What could be offered them as a substitute? Would they have any suggestions?
        (4) If a church is to be razed, will not the price have to be sufficient to permit construction of a comparable new church? Might not such a policy eliminate a great many objections? Is it feasible?
    b) Fraternal organizations
        (1) Is not the basic problem here one of finding new and adequate quarters for the group?
        (2) Would such a group, in fact, welcome a move that would remove them from an undesirable area and permit installation in far better quarters?
    c) Cemeteries
        (1) This land use is included because of the undoubtedly very difficult problem of dealing with property owners. A cemetery because of legal restrictions and the emotional attitudes of property owners requires special consideration.
        (2) What form of persuasion could be used to change the attitude of this group toward moving the interred? Could not the opposition of this group completely stymie a project?
B. Tenants in the project area
    1. Residential tenants
        a) What might be the objections or attitudes of this group?
        b) Might any of these tenants be so attached to their quarters that moving would be strongly resisted? If so, would the offer of better quarters have any appreciable effect on their attitude?

c) Would not most tenants be more than happy to move if better accommodations could be found for them?

d) Are the prospective expenses of moving a cause of worry or concern? If so, how deep-rooted does this feeling seem to be? Is it in any sense a fundamental difficulty?

e) Are there any tenant attitudes attributable to race? Are Negroes more apt to resist moving because of the character of the neighborhood they would have to inhabit or because of the racial homogeneity of the community they would leave?

f) Is there a decided difference in attitude between "roomers" and "family units"? Do the former have but little attachment to the community? Do significant differences seem to go with differences in age?

2. Commercial and industrial tenants
   a) The marginal, family-operated store
      (1) Would not this group tend to fear moving to a new location and building up a new clientèle?
      (2) Might some of this group welcome a chance to leave their marginal occupation?
      (3) What would the possibilities be of providing store space in the project for this group? Would this prospect appeal to many of them?
   b) Tenants in larger quarters
      (1) What objections might this group have to moving? Is low rent an item that has kept them at their present location?
      (2) Might some be forced to discontinue the business because of moving costs and higher rent in other quarters?

C. Property-owners in the project area who would be required to rehabilitate their property
   1. Could there be any objections other than monetary to rehabilitation requirements? Would they fear competition with space in the new building proposed? Do they realize the probable relations of the rent levels?
   2. Would persuasion be easier if the city or authority were to provide low interest loans to finance the necessary rehabilitation?
   3. Would not the most effective persuasion be that of demonstrating how the value of the property would be maintained by adherence to the rehabilitation scheme? Would any weight be given to the possible effects of the project on neighborhood desirability and morale?

D. Property-owners in peripheral area
   1. Owners of residences
      a) The attitude of this group, it would seem, should be favorable since redevelopment would improve the environment of their property. Would they fear that "they would be next"?
      b) Owners of rental property, however, might also feel that the redevelopment project, if it contained housing, would be a severe competitor. Again, what do they know about the probable rent levels? Would they anticipate that the new development might improve the surrounding one, thus help rather than hurt their properties?
   2. Owners of commercial property
      a) Both owners and tenants alike might well welcome the project if it contained housing because of the new customers provided.
      b) On the other hand, if the project were to provide shopping facilities, this group would be apt to register strong opposition. Would this view go beyond generalities? Do they know how much business they now get from the project site?

3. Owners of industrial property

  a) The feeling of this group might well depend on the character of the new inhabitants of the project. An economic class that would constitute a potential labor supply could gain, in all probability, enthusiastic support from this group.

E. Property-owners in other parts of the urban area who might have some attitude toward a proposed project

  1. Downtown merchants and property owners

   a) The location of the project might be the dominant factor. If the project were outlying, would central area store owners dislike it or would they see an opportunity for a branch store? How much difference would it make within fairly broad limits?

   b) If it were a housing redevelopment project and it were to be located close to the central area, this group would tend to approve and push it. Would this attitude vary materially with the kind and size of store?

   c) Their support might be proportional to the economic level of the tenants and would be particularly strong if the economic level of the new inhabitants were greater than the present inhabitants. Again how significant would this be and would it vary much from one kind of establishment to another?

   d) This group might also be influenced by the proposed density, preferring a higher density than before. Does such a supposition have any basis in fact?

  2. Merchants and property owners in secondary business centers

   a) Their attitudes would probably be closely related to the location of the project and to the possible shift in population because of the project. But how closely related? Where is the geographic limit of their interest?

   b) How could such a group be persuaded to support a project if it tended to concentrate rather high economic groups in an area close to the central business district? Would not a great deal of work have to be done explaining the over-all benefit of the proposal and showing its beneficial long run effects, if any?

  3. Real estate men and subdivision developers in suburban and outlying areas

   a) Might not this group express considerable opposition if the project were to be centrally located? Might they not feel that their developments would drop in value because of the competition of the project?

   b) If a subsidy were granted by the city, might not this group feel they were contributing to a lessening of the demand for their property?

F. Civic groups

  1. Would not opposition from this group come from those either unalterably opposed to urban redevelopment or else inadequately informed on the terms of the proposal? Where and how, in fact, do members of these organizations get their information?

  2. Would not the chief problem here be one of a concerted and planned educational program to explain the project? To what extent do the members of these groups reflect information or positions taken by the group and vice versa?

  3. Might not these groups also reflect the attitudes of those members who have a personal interest rather than an over-all civic interest?

G. Racial groups

  1. When the area to be redeveloped is primarily a Negro community

   a) Organized Negro groups

      (1) Would not the main point be that of the disposition of the present inhabitants?

      (2) Might not there be considerable demand to provide subsidized, low-rent, Negro housing in the project area?

      (3) Might not such groups feel that the redevelopment project was but a subterfuge to reduce available housing for Negroes?

    b) Negro inhabitants of the area

      (1) Would not this group fear the loss of security from the disruption of their primary relationships?

      (2) To what extent should the racial character of the area be preserved?

2. When the area is predominantly white but the indications are that the occupancy will be mixed and may provide a higher percentage of Negro inhabitants

    a) Organized Negro groups

      (1) The tendency here would apparently be to give approval to the project.

      (2) Would there be a possible form of opposition? How about Negro business and professional men in districts now predominantly Negro in occupancy?

    b) White groups in the area

      (1) Would not the usual opposition be expected here?

      (2) Might not some of it be lessened by organizing "pro groups" to give local support to the project? Who in these areas could and would organize and head such a group?

H. Other groups

  1. Real estate boards

    a) Would not their reaction depend to a great extent on the nature of the project, the method of financing, and the possible effect on property values?

    b) Since much of their business is brokerage, might they object to redevelopment since it would consolidate holdings and maintain such holdings for long periods?

  2. Building and loan associations

    a) Might not they welcome the proposal because of investment opportunities?

    b) Would not their support depend to a great extent upon the character of the development?

This outline is not, of course, exhaustive. There are many questions and other groups that redevelopment and planning agencies would wish to know more about. But it is a starting point in the analysis of group attitudes. In closing this section, a few general comments may be in order.

First, it should be one of the objects of sample surveys to find what kinds of persons (and their approximate number) have attitudes that are primarily economic or selfish in nature. In the absence of more experience, it is very easy to assume that both the number and strength of such views are negligible ("everybody knows that") or that they are more widespread than they in fact may be.

Second, however useful one survey might be in substituting facts for personal hunches and rationalizations of one's own guesses about the attitudes of others, the value of a series of studies over a substantial period of time would be much greater. Changes, shifts, modifications of attitudes as a project or program went ahead and as the redevelopment agency followed certain policies would be prime material not only for the immediate job of determining agency tactics but also for a deeper understanding of personal and group behavior in local public affairs.

For example, what happens to bitterly opposed groups whose opposition does not stop or substantially modify a proposed project? Does this failure strengthen their oposition? Do some persons switch their attitudes or even their membership to other organizations or groups? And how about the normally favorable groups? Do they stay that way? If not, why not? Certainly an agency that is concerned solely with what various kinds and groups of people know and think about a project *before* it is carried through will never make much contribution to democratic practice in planning and redevelopment. In addition, such an agency may very well find out to its sorrow that the more it does the harder its problems become. Maybe not,—but it is a possibility. If each opposition group on each project stays opposed and those favorable lose interest either because the novelty wears off or because their support was limited to only one project, how many jobs can be done before the balance of support over active opposition in the community is reversed?

Finally, inquiries of the kind under discussion might well contain questions that would probe for possible differences of attitude toward wholesale clearance-and-rebuilding operations and gradualism—partly clearance, partly rehabilitation and conservation measures. Of course, physical conditions of buildings and site layout usually will play an important part in determining what the form of redevelopment in an area should be. Most large cities, however (and many smaller ones), have many, or at least several, areas that call for different kinds of treatment. Which one should be taken up first? Which one will arouse least opposition or strongest support? Which procedure or method would promise to do most to educate people on the benefits of redevelopment? Which method seems most likely to make the best use of the criticisms that residents of the area or others may have on its present development and of their suggestions on how it might be improved?

REACTIONS OF GROUPS TO REDEVELOPMENT PROPOSALS

By now many localities have had some experience with attitudes and group activities pro and con redevelopment projects. The records of two proposed projects in two cities, however, are of particular interest because the reactions were primarily negative and because in each the local project sponsors or initiators presented their proposal with substantially no prior work in explaining the redevelopment process or the redevelopment proposal to the citizenry at large or to the residents of the redevelopment area. In these respects they were following more or less accepted practice. This is not to say, however, the prior briefing would have changed these attitudes. It is only to suggest that it might have done so.

History of two redevelopment projects in Milwaukee.—Milwaukee's first proposal was advanced by a newly formed Urban Redevelopment Corporation. The officers of the Corporation proposed to build four large apartment buildings on four contiguous blocks close to the central business area. The Corporation planned to purchase the land needed for the buildings and asked the city to develop park and playground space about the buildings. They also asked for a tax-assessment freeze for thirty years. At the end of that period, the whole project, along with any surplus, would be turned over to the city. Scheduled rents were considerably below the rents for similar apartments of recent construction.

The Urban Redevelopment Corporation released its proposal without prior warning to the residents of the area. Its representatives had interviewed some of the people in the area, but this work was neither intensive nor extensive. Thus, the residents of the area had no adequate advance information about the proposal.

About three weeks after the proposal had been filed with the Board of Public Land Commissioners (Milwaukee's planning agency), seven residents of the area filed a petition with the city clerk opposing the project. The spokesman of the group said, ". . . the group resented designation as 'a blighted area' and would 'keep right on fighting to stop this thing.' "[1]

Shortly thereafter the Health Department submitted a report on housing conditions in these four blocks. Two blocks were labeled "slum," requiring demolition; one was considered possibly rehabilitable; and the fourth was labeled "markedly substandard, rehabilitation unlikely without demolition."

The resident group again protested publicly against the project. Its spokesman said, " 'Why can't the Redevelopment Corporation build on land that is legitimately [*sic*] purchased, instead of condemning the homes of men and women who have struggled to own their own property.' "[2]

By this time, the Red Arrow Project (it was so labeled because it was

1. *Milwaukee Journal* (August 26, 1947).
2. *Milwaukee Sentinel* (September 8, 1947).

adjacent to Red Arrow Park) had become a major issue in the City Council and in the press. A meeting of the Buildings and Grounds Committee of the Council brought out some sixty of the residents, who protested loudly. The alderman of the ward in which the project was located sided with the residents, objecting strenuously to the proposed project. Protest centered around the labeling of the area "slum" or "substandard" and the fear that the residents would not be provided with adequate housing. "Koerner [the local alderman] and his constituents bluntly told the committee that they believed the health department was wrong when it labeled the four block area as 'slum' and 'substandard.' . . ."[3] One comment was: "We bought a rooming house last year at a very high price. We are having trouble holding it even now. We have 17 people living in it and they are all satisfied. They say they have lived in worse places."[4]

The *Milwaukee Journal* sent a photographer and reporter into the area and found that "Resentment is seething in the lower fourth ward. It's a deep and unyielding bitterness against the Milwaukee Urban Redevelopment Corporation. . . . It was the word 'slum' that rankled in the minds of the residents. . . . People interviewed revealed a smoldering anger."[5] The story quoted several of the residents on their objection to slum designation and some insisted on showing the reporter their homes, inside as well as out.

That some of the opposition stemmed from a fear that under condemnation the owner would not receive an adequate price for his house is evident from the comment of one owner, "Sure I'd sell for a reasonable price, but I object to having my property condemned. I've spent $3,500 for repairs since 1940, including new plumbing. The house was a tumble-down wreck when I bought it in 1923."[6]

The proposal continued to be debated for many months, with residents of the area expressing greater and greater opposition. By the end of January, six months after the proposal had been submitted, the City Council turned down the project. The press reported, "At the morning committee session, more than 40 residents of the Red Arrow project site cheered the committee's action in voting down the proposal."[7]

The opposition from families that would have been displaced was so severe that the next redevelopment project proposed (in September, 1948) planned to use part of a playground for the site. The proposal was quite similar to the Red Arrow project, but the Corporation presenting the proposal hoped to be on safer ground as to its site. Unlike

3. *Milwaukee Journal* (September 9, 1947).
4. *Ibid.*
5. *Ibid.*
6. *Milwaukee Sentinel* (September 10, 1947).
7. *Ibid.* (January 30, 1948).

the Red Arrow project, this site was part of an area that had been designated as a redevelopment area in an official study.

Opposition to using a playground for the project developed swiftly. The local alderman vowed he would have no part of the project if it were to use a playground. Because of this opposition, a new site in the same area was found, a site from which the project would displace forty families. Also, this new site was selected suddenly with no prior warning, so here too the residents learned of their possible displacement through a newspaper story. Trouble began to brew immediately.

The mayor, however, took a personal interest in this project and appeared before both the Land Commissioners and the Common Council to urge its approval. The Commissioners' approval was given, but Council committee approval was by only a 3 to 2 vote. This close vote might have been affected by the fact that residents of the area, who were solid in their opposition, turned up two hundred strong at the committee hearing.

The real display of opposition came, however, when the Common Council went into a committee of the whole to hear from the residents of the area. The residents were out in force and each was anxious to state his case. The nature of the opposition is evident from the remarks of one woman who said, "Is this the land of the free, I ask you? You might as well tear the constitution up."[8] Another stated, "God is searching your conscience to see how you vote," and the *Milwaukee Journal* said, "She spread her arms to demonstrate the 'human cross' that the project would make of her. 'Slums!' she shrieked. 'Slums, they call us. Why, that's a terrible word—those are our homes, our shrines. We live there.' "[9]

This kind of opposition was too strong for the aldermen. The proposal was defeated, and redevelopment, for a while at least, was dead in Milwaukee.

San Francisco.—San Francisco also had an early experience with snowballing opposition to redevelopment. In this case, however, there was no specific redevelopment project nor a redevelopment corporation that wished to undertake a project. The city was carrying out the provisions of the redevelopment law in holding a public hearing on whether the area should be designated a redevelopment area. General plans of how the area might be redeveloped had been prepared and exhibited so those at the public hearing had some idea of what might be done.

The Western Addition was the area in question. At the hearing (held by the Board of Supervisors) the spokesman for the Board pointed out that not all of the buildings in the proposed area were blighted and that

8. *Milwaukee Journal* (November 9, 1948).
9. *Ibid.*

many of them would not be touched. The reactions of most of the groups within the area were almost uniformly against the designation of the area as a redevelopment area.

The spokesman for the Ministerial Alliance, an organization "representing more than 70 per cent of a minority group in this particular area,"[10] said, "A number of the members of the Alliance are planning churches, and many own churches during the present time, in this particular area. It is of vital interest to us as to whether or not the parishioners will be able to return to this area, and, if so, if the rental bracket will be such that they will be able to return to live in this particular area, as they are now living."[11]

This attitude is probably typical of institutions that rely upon the residents in the area for their existence. Probably they will oppose every clearance and rebuilding project unless some provision is made for their continued existence.

A fear that under eminent domain the owner would not receive a "fair" price for his property was expressed by a representative of the Business and Professional Alliance of San Francisco. He stated, "I would like to give a very simple illustration: A person bought a piece of property, and paid $12,000 for it. We know the actual value is about $6,000. He paid $3,000 down, and he signed a couple of promissory notes to pay the balance of $9,000. All right. The redevelopment began. The property is appraised at $6,000. He loses $3,000, and still is obligated to pay the balance on those promissory notes, and is still without a home."[12]

Fear of an unfair price under condemnation is a common attitude of those owning property in redevelopment areas. Other cities have found this same attitude.

A representative of the National Association for the Advancement of Colored People opposed the designation of the area as a redevelopment area because he felt the rights of the minority groups were not protected. He felt restrictive covenants should be prohibited if the area were redeveloped and that the present inhabitants should be given first priority to return. He said, "It is our belief that urban redevelopment, as envisioned in this law, is not adequate. We feel that it is undemocratic, because of the fact it places the burden upon the minority people to carry the burden, to see that their rights are protected. We are asking that certain guarantees be written into the law. . . . And I say

10. City and County of San Francisco, "Public Hearing on Redevelopment of the Western Addition," June 3, 1948, p. 21.
11. *Ibid.*, p. 22.
12. *Ibid.*, p. 24.

that we should temporize a bit; that we should wait until a law is written that guarantees to all American citizens those fundamental rights that democracy advocates. I feel that there should be written into the law, on the local level, certain guarantees that racial distinctive [*sic*] covenants, which are now known as 'Gentlemen's Agreements,' will not be placed on lands developed under eminent domain."[13]

Minority groups fear redevelopment will be used as a means of removing them from an area or even of reducing the total area of the city now open to them for housing. They will nearly always oppose redevelopment projects unless safeguards against these contingencies are included.

A representative of an association of real estate owners was opposed because of the subsidy the city would have to advance if the area were to be redeveloped. "Speaking purely from a personal taxpayer's point of view, if you are going to pay for this property at the market value, either a private sale or by condemnation, you owe these ladies and gentlemen a fair value, and you are going to sell it to somebody for 50 cents on the dollar, I suppose the good taxpayer is going to pay the other 50 cents. . . . Speaking for the long-lost animal, the taxpayer, I propose, on behalf of the taxpayers—I do not want to pay that 50 per cent difference."[14]

The CIO was in opposition because it felt the proposal was designed ". . . for the purpose of making huge profits, with the taxpayers help . . . ," and because the proposal would result ". . . in maintaining and extending the pattern of segregation."[15]

The Associated Home Builders although stating that they were ". . . in no position, at this time, to take a definite stand one way or the other . . ."[16] made statements that rather clearly indicated the kind of redevelopment in which they were interested. They feared public housing and felt it should not be used ". . . to guarantee to the tenants in that area, the redevelopment area, a suitable place to live with comparable rents during any demolition and reconstruction process."[17] They also wanted the city ". . . to enforce upon present property owners all local laws pertaining to health and safety factors and the building code before condemnation proceedings are commenced."[18] They also wanted the government to have little or nothing to do with redevelopment. They stated, "Any attempt to redevelop a

13. *Ibid.*, p. 27.
14. *Ibid.*, pp. 30–31.
15. *Ibid.*, p. 60.
16. *Ibid.*, p. 64.
17. *Ibid.*, p. 64.
18. *Ibid.*

local area under government control would be vigorously opposed as socialized housing."[19]

The attitude of the California College of Chiropody, located in the proposed redevelopment area, is probably typical of institutions in redevelopment areas that do not depend upon the residents of the area for their support. The college favored the project and stated that "The supervisors, as individuals and collectively, can serve the city as a whole in no better way than to see that redevelopment is carried through to completion."[20]

The Japanese American Citizens League opposed the proposal because they felt there were insufficient safeguards for minority groups. They asked that the redevelopment plan include the provision ". . . that the small businessmen and professional people now in the area be given first priority in establishing themselves in the commercial area of new buildings."[21] They also wanted assurances that those who lived in the area would be given an opportunity to return through priority on renting or buying, or through public housing for those of low income. Their fears are probably typical of all minority groups who see redevelopment as a means of moving their group from an area.

The city-wide civic groups, for the most part, were in favor of the proposal. Opposition came from residents and property-owners in the area, institutions that relied upon the residents of the area, minority groups that feared discrimination, and paradoxically both the liberal and conservative groups—the former fearing large profits and discrimination, the latter seeing the specters of governmental control and public housing.

Eventually the Western Addition was declared a redevelopment area in spite of this opposition, but similar difficulties can be expected when a specific redevelopment project is proposed.

These are examples of attitudes one can anticipate. They are gross in that they are but surface manifestations of perhaps more subtle attitudes. They have little shading but are posed in black and white. This is almost always true when public questions reach this kind of showdown. There seem to be but two sides, and one must align himself on one or the other.

Means for ascertaining gradations or shades of attitudes could be of assistance to redevelopment agencies in dealing with groups and in shaping redevelopment plans to take some account of their attitudes. Ascertaining attitudes from reactions to publicly announced redevelopment proposals is to acquire information after it is needed. Informa-

19. *Ibid.*
20. *Ibid.*, p. 66.
21. *Ibid.*, p. 67.

tion on attitudes is needed prior to the announcement of redevelopment proposals. Also, once attitudes have been stated publicly, they tend to become fixed; they resist change. One purpose of sample surveys of attitudes is to determine their susceptibility to change, and, if possible, to formulate a program, including the plans of a redevelopment project, that will change at least some attitudes from unfavorable to favorable. Thus, the real need is for a means or method for ascertaining these attitudes at an early stage.

THE SAMPLE SURVEY

The sample survey is one technique for ascertaining the attitudes of groups toward redevelopment and toward matters directly concerned with it. The technique consists essentially of interviewing a carefully selected sample of the people in whose views or attitudes the redevelopment agency is interested. Carefully done, this can produce information that reflects accurately the attitudes of various groups.

The technique, of course, is not peculiar to ascertaining attitudes as to redevelopment. In fact, it has been used in many other fields but only recently has it been suggested as a tool in planning and redevelopment. There are competent organizations set up to undertake these kinds of surveys, and they should be used or experts in the field consulted. In the hands of those unfamiliar with its limitations and vagaries, the technique may provide useless, and even misleading, information.

In planning and redevelopment, the sample survey has many uses other than that of ascertaining attitudes. Many purposes may be served in one survey.

For example, information about the residents of proposed redevelopment areas is always needed. Age, income, sex, family size, type of dwelling unit, occupation, etc., are factual data that the redevelopment agency must have for proper analysis of the area. These data are also necessary in analyzing attitudes of various groups. Thus, the work of an attitude survey is simplified if the questions on attitudes are added to the basic sample on factual data. The increase in cost is relatively slight, but the added information may be of great value.

Needs and wants of urban dwellers are really unknown. The information presented in chapter ii only scratches the surface in this field. The sample survey can include questions in this field as well as questions for descriptive facts. Such information cannot fail to be of value to the planner.

Other data that can be acquired in a basic sample survey are on the contacts individuals have of a social, business, or professional nature.

Delineating areas for redevelopment depends to some extent upon their cohesiveness and character, and the pattern of these contacts can aid in outlining such areas in a city.

The data are also of use in analyzing the importance of residence location to social contacts. Redevelopment may create or rebuild neighborhoods, and more knowledge of the relations of location and social activities and contacts is badly needed.

Thus a sample survey for redevelopment purposes has several valuable uses of which ascertaining attitudes of groups as to redevelopment is one of the most important. When used for this purpose, the technique has some limitations and some additional advantages.

One limitation, which has often been stressed, is that when an attitude or opinion question is asked in a sample survey, the respondent is expected to come forth with an answer even though he may have given the matter little or no thought. Except for the "don't know" or "no opinion" responses, some critics of opinion and attitude surveys say that there is no way to judge how off-hand or basic a respondent's opinion or attitude is. Many students of the subject deny this, but they do not seem to agree fully on ways and means of making reliable distinctions on this point—despite some promising work with scaling techniques and other devices.

Redevelopment, of course, is not a simple matter at best and questions as to attitudes on it can easily become rather complex. It is expecting much for the respondent to give a clear, firm opinion in a few minutes and with no real consideration of such a problem. As Lindsay Rogers says in his book, *The Pollsters,* "Men and women who answer questions put to them in polls have insufficient opportunities for appeals to authority. They have to give their instantaneous reactions to propositions that they may have considered for the first time."[22]

Although this may be a significant limitation of the survey technique at its present stage of development, it is less applicable to questions in which the respondent is directly interested. Redevelopment issues that affect him directly are likely to interest the respondent. Even Rogers recognizes the usefulness of local polls on local topics. He says, "Intelligently used, such local polls enable communities to know themselves better. . . ."[23] The importance, however, of weighing this limitation in light of the time available for interviews and the skill of the interviewers should not be minimized.

Asking questions on subjects about which the respondent has not thought extensively or intensively does have an advantage as well as a limitation. Often questions on a subject will stir up interest in the

22. New York: Alfred A. Knopf, 1949, p. 29.
23. *Ibid.,* p. 195.

matter and provoke more consideration of the problem by the respondent.

The sample survey technique is but a tool. It is no magic formula by which redevelopment can be made to proceed smoothly and efficiently. It is but a means of providing the planner and redeveloper with some information that will enable him to deal intelligently with urban groups and to provide in the redevelopment plans the kind of community setting various kinds and groups of urban dwellers really want.

The sample survey as a research tool was discussed by Rensis Likert and Angus Campbell in an interview with representatives of the magazine, *Business Week*. Both men are recognized authorites in the field. Some of the pertinent sections of the interview follow:

LIKERT: . . . In other words, you can't take people's expressed intentions and predict with confidence just from the expressed intentions what they are going to do. You have to know what people's needs and attitudes are, of course, but you also need to know what their circumstances are going to be when the time for action arrives.

LIKERT: . . . Taking an expressed intention at face value is dangerous. For one thing, expressed intentions for one reason or another may not give a true picture of a person's motivations. And, secondly, a simple statement of intentions may be only one piece of the pattern of information we need in making predictions.

LIKERT: . . . Let's make one thing very clear: We are not talking about polling as such. We are talking about a research tool. It is one of the most powerful research tools in the social sciences. It can be used to study the behavior of the community. It can be used to study political structure; it can be used to study the economy.

BW: Do you find you are discovering fresh and surprising things or just things that any sensible man would have known anyhow?

CAMPBELL: As for me, I look at it this way. Suppose you have two sensible people but they don't have the same ideas and you are able to show on the basis of objective research that A is right and B is wrong. You haven't got a new idea but you have a right one.

BW: Yes, you could arbitrate a difference of opinion.

CAMPBELL: In the same way you can find out what specific aspects of a program are the ones that bring the results. You see you may have a whole mass of stimuli hitting people, and it may be only a couple of them that are having any effect. But you think it is this big formula you have worked out. Actually six or eight parts of your formula may have no significance at all and may even be negative.

CAMPBELL: What the survey does really is substitute quantitative data for assumptions. The policy maker always makes some assumptions about how people understand his program or what they want. Now all you are doing as a social scientist is to provide him with objective data about those things.

BW: I think perhaps the uneasy feeling some people have about this is that an awful lot of policy makers tend to attach undue importance to immediate public reaction to their actions and you have a little area of safety in their sheer ignorance of what the immediate reaction is.

LIKERT: No, no. You haven't any safety there at all. What happens is they attach more emphasis to what they were told in a Pullman car or what some astrologer told them. I would much prefer facts to those sources of data.[24]

There are very few examples of the use of the sample survey to ascertain attitudes on redevelopment. These examples will be studied in some detail from two angles: (1) the effectiveness of the technique and (2) the results themselves. The answers to some of the questions may aid other redevelopers and planners in dealing with urban groups in preparing redevelopment plans.

THE MILWAUKEE SURVEY

The Milwaukee survey was undertaken by the Urban Redevelopment Study and the Planning Divsion of the Milwaukee Board of Public Land Commissioners. Its purpose was threefold: (1) to test the efficacy of this device in the urban redevelopment process, (2) to provide planners, redevelopers, and operating officials with a little more information about the wide range of attitudes, wants, and needs of various groups of urban dwellers, and (3) to provide the officials in Milwaukee with information about an area proposed for redevelopment. Some questions were added by a graduate student at the University of Wisconsin who was interested in differences in attitudes between tenants and owners. The Denver Community Survey schedule, which is discussed later on, was seen before the Milwaukee survey schedule was prepared, and some of the Denver questions were similar to some used in Milwaukee. All of these, however, had to do with items or questions long discussed among housers, planners, and redevelopers. Members of the staff of the National Opinion Research Center in Chicago were good enough to review the form of the questions and to advise on the preparation of the schedule.

The schedule was designed for some 300 interviews in a district in Milwaukee that had been considered as a possible redevelopment area. The area is slightly more than 200 acres and has a population of almost

24. *Business Week* (December 3, 1949), pp. 37–46.

13,000. Its residents are primarily in the lower-income groups. Many residents are foreign-born and of limited formal education. A large number of the dwelling units were rated "suitable for demolition" by the Milwaukee Health Department, which used the American Public Health Association's housing appraisal method in making its survey. The area is close to a large industrial district and, as a consequence, has more than its share of noise, dirt, and generally unpleasant environmental conditions.

The interviewers were members of Professor Willard E. Downing's class in social service case work at the University of Wisconsin in Milwaukee. The schedule is not as comprehensive as it should have been, but the limited number of interviewers and the amount of time available precluded expanding it.

Three hundred and thirteen usable interviews were recorded. The sample was selected to obtain response from occupants of houses in all conditions from good to slum and from all major parts of the area. The median family income of those interviewed was $55 per week. One-quarter earned over $66 per week, and one-quarter earned less than $34 per week. All but one of the respondents were white. Half of them had not attended high school but less than 10 per cent had had less than five years of grammar school. Two-thirds were Catholics. A third of them lived in single-family homes, a third in two-family (a very common type in Milwaukee) and the rest in multi-family structures. Two-thirds of the families had children living at home. Half of the houses were rated "Poor" (60 or more penalty points for facilities and maintenance) by the American Public Health Association housing appraisal technique. This does not mean that half of the houses in the area were "Poor," since the sample was designed to include a larger representation of residents in the poorer quarters. A little more than half of the respondents had lived in their present houses for over five years and about one-fourth for over ten years. Over two-thirds had lived in the county for over twenty years.

The schedule (a copy of which is in the Appendix) was focused on two kinds of attitude questions. The first dealt with opinions and attitudes toward the urban redevelopment process; the second concerned the needs and desires of these urban dwellers as to houses and neighborhood. Although these are two recognizable matters, they are certainly related. Both kinds of questions, of course, are important in planning for urban redevelopment.

Attitudes on redeveloping the neighborhood.—The first attitude question on the urban redevelopment process was 5: How do you feel about this neighborhood? Which *one* of the statements on this card best describes what should be done to this neighborhood? The three choices on the card (which was read to the respondent because it was found some could not read, or understand from reading, the statements on the card) were:

1. It needs complete rebuilding. Nearly all the stores and houses should be torn down and replaced by new ones.
2. Replacing some blocks in this neighborhood with new stores and houses is needed but complete rebuilding isn't necessary.
3. The neighborhood is pretty good the way it is. No rebuilding is needed because the people who live here and own property here take care of it.

A "don't know" (not on the card) was added for those who had no opinion. Of the 313 who replied to this question, 38 per cent felt the neighborhood needed no rebuilding, 43 per cent felt that some blocks needed redeveloping, 12 per cent felt the neighborhood needed complete rebuilding, and 7 per cent did not know what should be done. Thus about 60 per cent of the respondents who expressed opinions felt some redevelopment was necessary. Table 6 gives the percentages of respondents in the major subgroups who answered "No rebuilding is needed. . . ."[25]

In general, the results confirm what one might have suspected from an a priori analysis of the problem. The condition of housing in the block and the condition of the house in which the respondent lives seem to have some relation to the respondent's ideas on whether the neighborhood needs redevelopment, but the differences in percentages are too small to be significant in a statistical sense. Fewer of those living in better houses and in better blocks feel the neighborhood needs redeveloping. More important probably is the fact that over one-third of those living in homes that should be demolished or in blocks that should be torn down according to the Health Department survey still feel the area needs no rebuilding. It is this group that undoubtedly will give redevelopment agencies the most difficulty. They are the ones among whom special educational work should be done. This group, rather than civic organizations, usually should be the first concern in educational and publicity efforts. They are the ones who, through their local aldermen, can kill most quickly an urban redevelopment project. Their fears must be allayed and their needs must be met, at least in part, if their opposition is to be avoided.

Owners are naturally inclined to feel the neighborhood needs no rebuilding while tenants, who have no investment in the area, or at least in the house in which they are living, recognize the need for redevelop-

25. It should not be forgotten that many of the subgroups of this and later tables in this chapter are interdependent, i.e., the individuals in one subgroup may be largely the same as those in another. Some but by no means all of the more likely overlaps of this kind are mentioned in the text.

TABLE 6

PERCENTAGE IN INDICATED GROUPS SAYING, "THE NEIGHBORHOOD IS PRETTY GOOD THE WAY IT IS. NO REBUILDING IS NEEDED BECAUSE THE PEOPLE WHO LIVE HERE AND OWN PROPERTY HERE TAKE CARE OF IT"

(Milwaukee Survey Question 5)

Group	Percentage	Number of Cases§ in Each Group
Condition of housing in block		
Good*...	46	63
Fair†..	37	164
Poor‡...	36	86
Condition of respondent's house		
Good*...	41	85
Fair†..	44	78
Poor‡...	34	145
Need for redeveloping other neighborhoods		
There are other neighborhoods needing rebuilding..........	29#	122
There are not other neighborhoods needing rebuilding......	57#	37
Age		
Under 30 years old...................................	15#	75
30–39..	30	82
40 years old or more................................	54#	153
Tenure status		
Owner occupants....................................	52#	95
Tenants..	33#	218
Length of residence in house		
Less than 3 years....................................	27#	86
3–10 years...	38	146
Over 10 years.......................................	52#	81
Attitude toward house in which living		
The house is pretty good.............................	50#	175
It needs big repairs or should be torn down..............	24#	135
Desire to move		
Wants to move....:.................................	36	134
Doesn't want to move................................	44	142
Education		
Some high school or more............................	26#	154
No high school or less...............................	52#	153

# Indicates the difference is above the three sigma level of significance, i.e., that the percentage difference might occur at the most 2.7 times in every thousand due to chance alone.
* Less than 30 penalty points, facilities and maintenance, APHA survey rating.
† 30–59 penalty points, facilities and maintenance, APHA survey rating.
‡ 60 or more penalty points, facilities and maintenance, APHA survey rating.
§ Includes those who answered "Don't know" to Question 5.

ment more readily. Owner-occupants, therefore, constitute another group that needs considerable attention. Although the difference between the replies of owners and renters on this question is statistically significant, and was to be expected, how many side-line observers would have guessed that almost one-half of the owners would *not* have answered ". . . no rebuilding is needed . . ."?

The length of residence in the house is apparently another important factor influencing one's attitude toward the need for redevelopment. The differences in percentages is quite great, certainly significant. The longer one resides in the area, the more likely he is to accept the area as satisfactory or at least as not requiring redevelopment. There is, of course, the possibility that length of residence may be but another measure of ownership (or vice versa), since there may be a high correlation between the two.

The attitude toward the house in which one lives seems to extend to the neighborhood, a reasonable assumption. The variation in percentages is greater than the three sigma level of significance.[26] Here again, however, about half of those who thought their houses "pretty good" did *not* say ". . . no rebuilding needed . . ." in the neighborhood. It is important to note that it is the *attitude toward* not the *condition of* the house that is pertinent here. The two are not necessarily the same.[27]

The desire to move seems to have some relation to one's attitude on the need for redevelopment, but the difference in percentages is below the 95 per cent level of significance. Statistical significance of differences in percentages aside, why should only about one-third of those who say they want to move away feel that ". . . no rebuilding is needed . . ." in the neighborhood? Quite clearly much of the desire to move is not due to the physical condition of the buildings in the area. How much might be due to personal reasons, e.g., wish to be nearer friends or other members of the family who live elsewhere? How much might come from the belief that the things that are wrong with the neighborhood will not be changed by rebuilding it in whole or in part, e.g. dirt, noise? The answers to Question 12 are pertinent here. This is the kind of inquiry that a more thorough survey should probe further than was possible in the Milwaukee survey.

Education, however, is very clearly related to one's attitude on

26. In this section, "significant" when applied to differences in percentages means that such a difference would not occur more than five times out of 100 by chance alone. Significant to this extent is often called the 95 per cent level of significance and in the tables this level of significance has been indicated by *.

The 3 sigma level of significance means that the difference in percentages would not occur more than about 2.7 times out of a thousand by chance alone. It is obviously a much higher level of significance and in the tables has been indicated by #.

Readers not accustomed to this use of *significant* or *significance* should realize that it has to do solely with the probabilities of sampling (for this reason "reliability" might be a better word) and does *not* refer to the importance or meaningfulness of the facts in understanding urban life or in shaping redevelopment policy.

The formula used to ascertain the level of significance between two percentages is

$$\frac{p_2 - p_1}{\sqrt{\dfrac{p_1 q_1}{n_1} + \dfrac{p_2 q_2}{n_2}}}$$

where p_1 and p_2 are the two percentages expressed as decimals; q_1 and q_2 are $1 - p_1$ and $1 - p_2$ respectively; and n_1 and n_2 are the number of cases in each sample. If the quotient is greater than 1.96 but less than 3, then it is between the 95 per cent and three sigma levels of significance. If it is greater than 3, it is above the 3 sigma level of significance.

27. Only 12 per cent of those living in houses rated as unrehabilitatable by the APHA survey felt their homes should be torn down.

whether the neighborhood needs redeveloping. Fewer of those with the greater amount of formal education felt the neighborhood was all right than those with less than a high-school education. This would indicate that the most work needs be done among groups with less than a high-school education.

One finds also that the feeling that redevelopment is not necessary extends, apparently, beyond one's own neighborhood. Thus only 29 per cent of those who felt there were other neighborhoods in Milwaukee that should be torn down felt their own neighborhood was all right, but 57 per cent of those who thought there were not any other neighborhoods in Milwaukee that needed rebuilding also felt their own neighborhood was all right. Thus those opposing redevelopment locally might be expected to oppose it in other areas as well. This difference is well beyond the three sigma level of significance—it would happen by chance less than 2.7 times out of a thousand.

Age is also closely associated with the attitude one has on whether his neighborhood needs rebuilding. Of those under thirty, 15 per cent thought their neighborhood needed no rebuilding as compared to the 54 per cent of those forty years old or more. There is, of course, the possibility that this is but another measure of length of residence, but even so the difference in the percentages is much greater than under length of residence. Age (and probably long-established associations and habits) apparently leads one into accepting his neighborhood pretty much as it is; youth is more eager to change it. Thus the older age groups are most likely to oppose redevelopment plans, other factors being equal.

Family income and whether there are children living with the respondent had no apparent effect on the response to this question on attitude toward redeveloping the neighborhood and so have not been included in Table 6.

The group at the other extreme on attitudes toward redeveloping the neighborhood consists of those who answered that the neighborhood needed complete rebuilding. Some of the percentages are so striking that they are well worth noting. For instance, not one owner-occupant thought the neighborhood needed complete rebuilding as compared to 17 per cent of the renters. Only 4 per cent of those living in their homes for over ten years felt the neighborhood needed complete rebuilding as compared to 19 per cent of those living in the house less than three years. Only 5 per cent of those who thought the house in which they lived was "pretty good" said the area needed rebuilding, but 57 per cent of those who thought their residence should be torn down believed that rebuilding the area was necessary. Only 4 per cent of those fifty years old or more felt the neighborhood needed complete rebuilding compared to the 23 per cent of those under thirty who felt this way. A greater percentage of those wishing to move thought the neighborhood needed rebuilding (16 per cent) than those who did not want to move (9 per cent). Although only thirty-seven respondents favored complete neighborhood rebuilding, all these differences in percentages except the last are above the 95 per cent level of significance.

Attitudes toward redeveloping the neighborhood and satisfaction with neighborhood characteristics.—One would expect the association to be close between satisfaction with neighborhood characteristics and attitude on whether one's neighborhood needs rebuilding, and an examination of Table 7 bears this out. For every neighborhood characteristic listed, one finds a higher percentage of the satisfied group feeling that no rebuilding is necessary. What is more, the differences in percentages in every case but two are above the 95 per cent level of significance. The reverse is also true. Except for only one neighborhood charactristic—nearness to parks and playgrounds—a significantly

TABLE 7

ATTITUDES ON REBUILDING THE NEIGHBORHOOD BY SATISFACTION WITH
VARIOUS NEIGHBORHOOD CHARACTERISTICS AND FACILITIES

(Milwaukee Survey Question 5)

PERCENTAGE OF EACH INDICATED GROUP RESPONDING

CHARACTERISTICS OF THE NEIGHBORHOOD	Neighborhood Needs Complete Rebuilding	Neighborhood Needs Only Partial Rebuilding	No Rebuild-ing Needed	TOTAL NUMBER OF CASES IN EACH GROUP†
Nearness to parks and play-grounds				
Satisfied	12	43	38	268
Not satisfied	16	48	29	31
Cleanness				
Satisfied	1#	30#	60#	74
Not satisfied	15#	49#	30#	227
Quietness				
Satisfied	6#	36#	50#	174
Not satisfied	18#	54#	23#	133
Open space				
Satisfied	3#	38*	50#	160
Not satisfied	23#	50*	23#	141
Type of neighborhood stores				
Satisfied	10*	44	39*	280
Not satisfied	33*	41	22*	27
Nearness to organizations				
Satisfied	10#	43	39	198
Not satisfied	33#	33	28	46
Closeness to friends				
Satisfied	8#	43	42#	236
Not satisfied	28#	43	23#	61
Building for meetings				
Satisfied	6#	45	40*	171
Not satisfied	32#	37	27*	60

* Above the 95 per cent level of significance (difference in percentages is probable only five times out of 100 due to chance alone) but below the three sigma level of significance (difference in percentages is probable only 2.7 times out of 1,000 due to chance alone).
† Includes those who answered "Don't know" to Question 5.
# See footnote # Table 6.

greater percentage of those not satisfied feel the neighborhood needs complete rebuilding.

An analysis of those replying that the area needs partial rebuilding does not reveal this high an association. Where there is a significant difference, however, the higher percentages are in the "not satisfied" group, which would indicate that dissatisfaction with these neighborhood characteristics has a greater effect on attitudes toward redeveloping one's own neighborhood than does dissatisfaction with the other characteristics. Thus cleanness, quietness, and the amount of open space are quite important. If one is dissatisfied with these items, he is likely to feel the neighborhood needs at least some rebuilding.

Knowledge of redevelopment proposals.—Knowledge about redevelopment proposals in this area seems low in view of the wide publicity and bitter controversy aroused by the two redevelopment projects in Milwaukee described earlier in this chapter. A little less than half (42 per cent) said they had heard of plans to rebuild some neighborhoods (Question 7) but 9 of these percentage points should be deducted for those who could not name any of the neighborhoods they had heard were to be rebuilt (Question 7A). Over half (60 per cent) of the answers given to the question on how or where the respondent had heard about redevelopment proposals were "newspapers." "Radio" accounted for 10 per cent and "friends and neighbors" for 15 per cent. Ten per cent of the answers were that the respondent had seen the project under construction. They were referring to the Hillside public housing project, which was under construction at the time.

When the answers to the question on hearing about redevelopment proposals (Question 7) are analyzed, it is clear that members of certain groups are aware of such proposals more often than those in other groups. This analysis is presented in Table 8.

Age presents the interesting picture of greater awareness among those of early middle age (30–39) than among other ages. Youth and old age do not evidence the same degree of interest in these matters as do those in the thirties. Perhaps a campaign to show the young and old their stakes in redevelopment might increase their interest.[28]

The analysis by education is not at all surprising. Those with some high-school or more education have heard about redevelopment proposals to a significantly greater extent than those with less education. Here again the results indicate that particular attention need be paid the groups with little formal education.

When the question is analyzed by the opinions on the part the city

28. The difference between middle age and old age is the only one which is above the 95 per cent level of significance. The difference between "under 25" and "30–39" is significant at the 89 per cent level.

should play in redevelopment, the results are rather unusual. Of those who feel the city should take no part in the redevelopment process, a larger proportion have heard about specific redevelopment proposals than the percentage of those who think the city should limit its activity to buying the land, clearing, and then selling it to redevelopers. Peculiarly enough, those who feel the city should build housing on the

TABLE 8

Percentage in Indicated Groups Who Had Heard about Plans to
Rebuild Run-down Neighborhoods

(Milwaukee Survey Question 7)

Group	Percentage	Total Cases in Each Group†
Age		
Under 25................................	38	34
25–29....................................	48	40
30–39....................................	54*	81
40–49....................................	40	63
50–59....................................	36	47
60 and over.............................	30*	44
Education		
Some high-school or more education..........	49*	152
No high-school or less education.............	34*	154
Attitude on redevelopment methods		
City should buy the land, clear it, and sell to developers.............................	33*	42
City should buy the land, clear it, and build housing on it............................	48	149
City should do nothing....................	54*	61

* See footnote * to Table 7.
† Includes "Don't knows," i.e., those who said they had heard about redevelopment plans but could not name a neighborhood or district.

land as well as purchase it fall between the other two groups in percentage hearing about redevelopment proposals. There is a significant difference between the percentage in the first and second groups—the city do-nothings and the middle-roaders. Although conclusions cannot be drawn from this table, perhaps awareness of redevelopment proposals does not *ipso facto* persuade many people of the desirability of the rather elaborate public-private collaboration called for in the buy-clear-and-sell procedure. A more thorough study should go deeper into this matter. For example, would these relations hold also for people who not only had heard about a specific proposal or project but who gave evidence of knowing more than the name or approximate location of one?

Tenure and income were also analyzed for this question, but no pattern and no significant differences were found.

Attitudes on redevelopment methods.—If redevelopment is to go ahead vigorously, there must be a substantial degree of public acceptance of the part the municipality or its agency is to play. In this sense, therefore, Question 8 was basic in the Milwaukee survey. Perhaps it calls for more information and study of redevelopment than most of those interviewed had given it—and perhaps not. Even with this reservation, however, the results are startling; the respondents would give the city a much freer hand than one might have expected. Nearly half of those queried (48 per cent) gave the second answer to the question, i.e., the city should buy the land and clear it and then do the rebuilding, putting up low rent or veterans' housing. One-fifth felt the city should take no part in the redevelopment process, and 13 per cent felt the city should buy the land and clear it and then sell it to a private developer. Another fifth of the respondents were in the "don't know" category, a fairly high proportion.

Analysis of the characteristics of groups responding to this question reveals some interesting associations. Because of the large number of "don't knows" it seemed wise to analyze the "don't know" group as well as those giving other answers. Table 9 presents the analysis of the responses to this question.

The group that took the middle position—that the city should buy the land and then sell it to redevelopers—showed no significant associations with the characteristics for which the responses were analyzed and, therefore, are not included in this table.

Tenure showed a significant association with response to this question, with a significantly greater percentage of owner-occupants than tenants feeling the city should do nothing and a significantly greater percentage of tenants feeling the city should take over the whole job. This reaction is not unexpected. Owner-occupants seem to take a more conservative view on these matters than do tenants. It should not be overlooked, however, that a larger proportion of owners said the city should do the whole job (36 per cent) than said it should do nothing (28 per cent). A greater percentage of owner-occupants than tenants also have no opinion of this question, although the difference does not quite reach the 95 per cent level of significance. Quite probably few persons would have predicted this relationship.

There is also association apparently between the knowledge these people in Milwaukee have of redevelopment proposals and their ideas on what part the city should play in the redevelopment process. A significantly greater percentage of those who had heard of redevelopment proposals felt the city should have no hand in redevelopment, but at the same time a greater percentage (94 per cent level of significance) of those who had heard about redevelopment proposals thought the city should do the whole job. The seeming contradiction lies in the "don't knows." A quarter of those who had not heard of redevelopment proposals just did not have opinions on the subject; and of those who had heard, only a small percentage were "don't knows."

TABLE 9

ATTITUDES ON REDEVELOPMENT METHODS

(Milwaukee Survey Question 8)

PERCENTAGE OF INDICATED GROUP RESPONDING

GROUP	City Should Buy the Land, Tear Down the Buildings and Build Housing	City Should Do Nothing about Re-Building These Neighborhoods	Don't Know	TOTAL CASES IN INDICATED GROUP
Tenure				
Owner-occupants............	36#	28*	25‡	95
Tenants..................	54#	16*	16‡	218
Knowledge of redevelopment proposals				
Have heard................	54†	25*	10#	131
Have not heard............	43†	16*	26#	180
Age				
Under 30..................	65#	13*	7#	75
30–39....................	54	15	17	82
40–49....................	44	23	21	62
50–59....................	34	26	28	47
60 and over..............	30#	30*	30#	44
Income				
Under $40 per week........	42*	26	18	50
$40–49.99................	46	20	22	46
$50–59.99................	60*	15	18	73
$60–69.99................	57	17	7	46
$70 and over.............	48	24	11	46
Education				
Some high-school or more education................	59#	16†	14*	154
Less than some high-school education...............	38#	24†	23*	153

* and # see footnotes to Tables 6 and 7
† 94 per cent level of significance
‡ 92.5 per cent level of significance

The association between age and the role the city should play in urban redevelopment is rather striking. There is a measured progression from old to young in percentage of each age group who feel the city should do the whole job. The percentage of the younger age groups who feel the city should take over the whole job of redevelopment is greater than the percentage of the older age groups who feel this way; and the obverse is true when the response that the city should take no part is examined. The "don't know" analysis by age groups is also interesting, since here too there is a steady progression from young to old, i.e., the percentage of those who have no opinion increases with age. In short, the younger groups are more likely to have opinions on this subject, and their opinions are more likely to be that the city should undertake the redevelopment job even to the point of doing the rebuilding.

A breakdown by income produces no significant associations except in the response that the city should undertake the whole job of redevelopment. The lower- and higher-income groups had a lower percentage giving this answer than did the middle-income groups. The only difference at the 95 per cent significance level, however, is between the lower- and the middle-income group. Although the reverse of this pattern is found in the response that the city should do nothing, the differences are below the 95 per cent level of significance and therefore not reliable. There is no pattern among the "don't knows." Apparently, in this case, income has no connection with whether one has an opinion on the subject or not.

Analysis by education presents some extremely interesting and significant associations. One finds more of those with the greater education in favor of the city undertaking the entire redevelopment job than those with no high-school education. The difference is above the three sigma level. Because of the "don't knows," one might assume that here as before the significant difference was caused by those with the smaller amount of education having no opinion. If the "don't knows" are removed, however, and percentages computed on only those with opinions, one still finds the difference considerably above the 95 per cent level of significance.

The significant difference in percentages under the "don't know" answer indicates that those with the lesser education are less likely to have opinions on this subject. The difference in percentages under the answer that the city should take no part in redevelopment does not quite reach the 95 per cent level (94 per cent), but it seems to indicate that more of those with lesser education feel the city should steer clear of redevelopment activities than those with a greater amount of education. This appears to be contrary to the general opinion that those with the least education expect the government to undertake the greatest amount of activity.

Conclusions from an analysis of the response to this question are that half the people interviewed want the city to undertake the entire redevelopment job but one-fifth of those interviewed have no opinion. Tenants, younger age groups, middle income groups, and those with some high-school or higher education tend more toward having the city undertake the entire redevelopment job than the other segments of their groups. A greater percentage of the older age groups, those unaware of redevelopment proposals, and those who have not been to high school tend to have no opinion on this question.

Thus the redevelopment agency, if it wants to lessen opposition and indifference to its work, should concentrate a considerable volume of its activity on those groups that feel the municipality should take no part in rebuilding. The agency should pay particular attention to the older age groups and to those who have not attended high school. In Milwaukee, anyway, the indication would be that a great deal more work is needed in explaining redevelopment to the people in the area and in getting them to understand what redevelopment can do.

Attitudes on condition of residence.—Each respondent was asked to evaluate his residence, since some earlier experience had shown residents to be sensitive to any but laudatory comments about their houses. Since the APHA rating was also available, it was easy to check between an objective rating and an occupant's subjective evaluation. Table 10 gives the percentages of persons in various subgroups who responded that the house they occupied was "pretty good the way it is."

There is, as one would expect, a close association between APHA rating and the occupant's subjective evaluation of the residence in which he lives, with most respondents, however, rating their residences above the APHA score. Thus 43 per cent of those living in homes rated "poor" (unrehabilitable) by the APHA survey felt the condition of their homes was "pretty good." It is somewhat surprising, however, to find 25 per cent of those living in residences rated "good" by APHA feeling that the house "needs big repairs."

There is also a significant association between attitude toward one's residence and attitude toward the need for redeveloping the neighborhood. For the most part, those who are satisfied with the neighborhood also feel their residences are all right (87 of 120) and vice versa (87 of 175, not in Table 10). Of 312 replies, including 20 "don't knows," 56 per cent were satisfied with their houses, but only 38 per cent with the neighborhood.

Desire to move also seems to have a significant relation to attitude toward house. An analysis of those who said they did not want to move and those who said they did shows that more of the former expressed satisfaction with their residence.

Tenure is very closely associated with attitude toward the condition of one's residence. Eighty-six per cent of the owner occupants replied that their residence was "pretty good the way it is" compared to the 43 per cent of the tenants who felt this way. Some of this association might be due to a tendency for owner-occupants to have homes in better condition than tenants. An examination of tenure by APHA rating of the residence shows some association between tenure and better condition of residence but not to the same extent as between tenure and attitude toward condition of residence. Thus although only 41 per cent of the owner-occupants live in homes rated "good" by APHA and some 24 per cent in homes rated "fair" (total 65 per cent), some 86 per cent feel their homes are pretty good the way they are. It is unfortunate that the size of the sample is too small to permit a more detailed analysis.

Length of residence seems to be unrelated to attitude toward one's residence, unless one is to conclude from Table 10 that those living in

TABLE 10

ATTITUDES ON CONDITION OF RESIDENCE

(Milwaukee Survey Question 9)

Group	Percentage of Group Indicated Responding, "House is pretty good the way it is"	Total Cases in Indicated Group‖
APHA rating of house		
Good†	74#	84
Fair‡	63#	78
Poor§	43#	147
Attitude towards neighborhood		
Needs complete rebuilding	22#	37
Needs partial rebuilding	47	135
No rebuilding is needed	73#	120
Desire to move		
Wants to move	50*	133
Doesn't want to move	64*	143
Tenure		
Owner occupants	86#	95
Tenants	43#	218
Length of residence		
Less than 6 years	57	165
6–10 years	46*	68
Over 10 years	64*	80

Group by Satisfaction with Neighborhood Characteristics	Percentage of Group Indicated Responding, "House is pretty good the way it is"	Total Cases in Indicated Group‖
Quietness		
Satisfied	64*	174
Not satisfied	47*	133
Nearness to parks		
Satisfied	57	269
Not satisfied	45	31
Cleanness		
Satisfied	64	74
Not satisfied	54	227
Open space		
Satisfied	70#	160
Not satisfied	40#	141
Type of neighborhood stores		
Satisfied	59#	280
Not satisfied	26#	27
Closeness to friends		
Satisfied	61#	237
Not satisfied	40#	60
Nearness to organizations		
Satisfied	60	199
Not satisfied	48	46
Building for meetings		
Satisfied	60**	172
Not satisfied	47**	60

* and # see footnotes, Tables 6 and 7
† Less than 30 penalty points, facilities and maintenance, APHA survey
‡ 30 to 60 penalty points, facilities and maintenance, APHA survey
§ 60 or more penalty points, facilities and maintenance, APHA survey
‖ Includes "Don't knows" to Question 9
** 92.5 er cent level of significance

their homes less than six years or more than ten years have more of a tendency to approve their houses than those who have been living in them from six to ten years. There is a significant difference between the middle and the last group, but this pattern does not suggest any very clear conclusions.

Satisfaction with various neighborhood characteristics seems to be associated with one's attitude toward the condition of the house in which he is living. Thus, in respect to each of the eight characteristics listed in Table 10, a greater percentage of the "satisfied" groups than of the "not satisfied" groups felt their residence to be "pretty good the way it is." In not all cases, however, are the differences significant. It is hard to know whether this association means that feelings toward one's residence are likely to influence one's attitudes toward the neighborhood (or vice versa) or whether these people tend to be satisfied no matter what they are asked. The replies were not analyzed to see if this latter conclusion were true.

Looking at the other extreme, i.e., the replies that the residence should be torn down, one finds naturally the reverse of the patterns just discussed. One also finds a pattern to length of residence; as the length of residence increases, the percentage feeling the house should be torn down decreases. Thus, 15 per cent of those living in their homes for less than two years felt the house should be torn down compared to the 2 per cent of those who had lived in their home for more than ten years. This difference is above the three sigma level of significance.

Tenure presents a very striking contrast with not one owner-occupant feeling his house should be torn down compared to the 13 per cent of the tenants who felt that way.

Conclusions from this question are not too surprising. People tend to rate the condition of their residences much higher than an objective survey does, but there is still some association between the two.items. Attitude toward the condition of the house and the need for neighborhood redevelopment also corresponds. Those who do not wish to move and those who are satisfied with neighborhood characteristics seem to feel their houses are reasonably satisfactory. In short, satisfaction with one item seems to indicate satisfaction with others.

Attitudes toward moving from neighborhood.—Each respondent was asked whether he wished to move (Question 11), assuming he were to live in a house much the same as his present one. Some seventeen respondents missed the point and gave reasons for wanting to move that indicated it was a different house rather than a new neighborhood that was desired. If these are excluded, one finds about half did not wish to move (48 per cent), 45 per cent did, and 7 per cent did not know.

Reasons for wanting to move (excluding those who wished to move because they wanted a different house) were primarily the dislike of neighborhood characteristics. Thus, 44 per cent of the reasons given were because of smoke, noise, soot, or dirt. This is not surprising, because the area is quite close to a large industrial district. "Too many factories," "industrial area," "poor air," "factories too close," were characteristic comments to the question.

Dislike of the neighbors and a general dislike of the neighborhood constituted 19 per cent of the reasons. Typical of these comments were, "neighborhood is cheap," "people are not of a high class," "hate neighborhood," "not a nice neighborhood," "colored people, Mexicans," "tired of neighborhood," "not a good neighborhood." "Location not desirable," "area not suitable for children," and preference for a different part of town accounted for 18 per cent of the reasons. All other reasons were distributed among such classifications as "too far to work," "inadequate schools," "neighborhood too crowded," and accounted for the remaining 20 per cent. Only five of those saying they wished to move were unable to give reasons for their opinions.

Half of the reasons given for not wanting to move indicated a general satisfaction with the neighborhood. "Know neighbors here," "good friends in the neighborhood," "nice neighbors," "friends live on south side," "used to the neighborhood," "I'm used to the south side," "used to it here," "like it here," "lived here all of life," "the house is no good, but I like the location," "the neighborhood seems like home," "like neighborhood but not the house," "grown to like neighborhood," "neighborhood is all right," "stores nearby," "neighborhood is quiet, close to school," "peaceful and nice," "everything is very handy here," "schools and church convenient," and "near good transportation" were typical comments in response to request for reasons for not wanting to move. Some 16 per cent did not want to move unless they could better their living conditions, and some of their replies sounded quite despondent: "The same grief somewhere else would be no better," "wouldn't take this house anywhere," "would want to better self," "would move only to get a better house," etc.

The remaining reasons for not wanting to move were habit ("lived here so long," "been here so long is a part of me," "lived in neighborhood a long time"), economic stake stake in not moving such as owning one's home ("I own this house," "am buying house," "own own home"), closeness to work ("stay on south side near work," "job is here," "handy for work"), established business ("already settled with business here"), and such miscellaneous reasons as too old to move, too much trouble or expense.

Reasons for wanting to move or not wanting to move were, therefore, quite positive. If one had an opinion on whether one did or did not wish to move, he was able to give a reason for his opinion. The respondents knew, or seemed to know, whether they did or did not wish to move and why.

Because in urban redevelopment programs people will undoubtedly have to move in order to clear areas, an analysis of the characteristics of respondents to the question on desire to move is important. Anticipating their reactions and in fact trying to decide on the basis of consumer wants, as well as over-all planning considerations, who should live in the area once it is redeveloped becomes, therefore, a major task of the redevelopment agency. Thus cross-tabulations on one of the answers to this question (Number 11) are presented in Table 11.

Here as elsewhere, length of residence in the house apparently has no association with desire to move. Those living in the house for five years or less and those living in the house for over ten years both show a larger percentage of their group wanting to move than the middle group. It is unfortunate that more cases are not available so that a more detailed analysis could be made. One would naturally assume that length

TABLE 11

ATTITUDES ON MOVING TO NEW NEIGHBORHOOD

(Milwaukee Survey Question 11)

Group	Percentage in Indicated Group Stating They Wanted to Move	Total Number of Cases in Each Group†
Length of residence		
5 years or less	46	155
6–10 years	38	63
Over 10 years	49	79
Attitude toward neighborhood		
Needs complete rebuilding	61*	36
Needs partial rebuilding	47	122
No rebuilding is needed	41*	117
Attitude toward condition of residence		
Is pretty good the way it is	40*	169
Needs big repairs or should be torn down	52*	125
Tenure		
Owner-occupants	40	92
Tenants	47	205
Family status		
Children living with respondent	49*	198
No children living with respondent	37*	95
Age		
Under 30	51‡	67
30–39	49	78
40–49	48	60
50–59	41	46
60 and over	33‡	43
Income		
Under $40 per week	48	48
$40–49.99	43	44
$50–59.99	43	70
$60–69.99	71#	42
$70 and over	40#	40

TABLE 11 (Cont.)

Group (by Satisfaction with Neighborhood Characteristics)	Percentage in Indicated Group Stating They Wanted to Move	Total Number of Cases in Each Group†
Nearness to parks		
Satisfied	43	254
Not satisfied	55	29
Cleanness		
Satisfied	24#	72
Not satisfied	53#	213
Quietness		
Satisfied	34#	167
Not satisfied	60#	125
Open space		
Satisfied	35#	154
Not satisfied	56#	132
Type of neighborhood stores		
Satisfied	43*	265
Not satisfied	69*	26
Closeness to friends		
Satisfied	39#	225
Not satisfied	67#	58
Nearness to organizations		
Satisfied	43*	189
Not satisfied	59*	44
Building for neighborhood meetings		
Satisfied	41*	165
Not satisfied	57*	56

* and # See footnotes to Tables 6 and 7
† Includes "Don't knows" to Question 11, but not those who misunderstood the question (p. 400)
‡ 94.76 per cent level of significance

of residence would influence one's attitude toward moving. It might be, of course, that the houses fitted the needs of families in the middle stage of their cycles better than at either end. This is just a possible factor; it cannot be said to be supported by this finding.

As to the relation between one's attitude toward the need to redevelop the neighborhood and one's desire to move, the group that feels no rebuilding is necessary is the group that has the smallest percentage of those wanting to move. Thus one would expect those who oppose redevelopment to be those who do not wish to move from the area. This has become almost a truism but has been ignored quite often.

There is also an association between attitude toward condition of one's residence and desire to move. The group that feels their residences need extensive repairs or should be torn down have a larger percentage of its members wanting to move than has the group that feels their residences are pretty good the way they are. This is certainly an expected reaction from people who have misgivings about the condition of their houses.

There is, surprisingly enough, no significant difference when tenure is examined. A somewhat higher percentage of tenants want to move than do owners, but the difference is not significant. The difference in percentages between tenants and owner-occupants who do not want to move, however (not shown in Table 11), is almost at the 95 per cent level of significance (94.76 per cent), with 56 per cent of the owners and 44 per cent of the tenants not wanting to move. As these results indicate, substantially more tenants than renters said they did not know or could not express an opinion on this subject.

Family status shows a significant variation with a greater percentage of families with children living at home desiring to move than families with no children living at home. This would indicate generally that the area is considered unsuitable for the rearing of children by a great many of the families with children living at home. It is too bad the number of cases is insufficient to permit analysis by age of children living at home. This might be more revealing.

One's age also seems to be associated with the desire to move with the younger age groups seemingly much more willing to move than the oldsters. Thus 51 per cent of those under thirty want to move but only 33 per cent of those over sixty feel the same way. The percentages in between form a very decided pattern, and the difference between the extremes is just below the 95 per cent level of significance.

Income presents a pattern in relation to attitudes toward moving except for the group $60 to $69.99. The difference between this percentage (71) and the 40 per cent for those families earning $70 a week or more is significant at the three sigma level, but it is hardly information from which one can draw conclusions. An examination of percentages among the various income groups of those who do not want to move reveals no pattern whatsoever.

Satisfaction with neighborhood characteristics is quite closely, and not unexpectedly, associated with desire to move. All "not satisfied" groups contained a greater percentage of those wanting to move than did the satisfied groups; and in each case but "nearness to parks" the difference was statistically significant. Here again, the conclusion is not startling, but it is still important: of those who do not wish to move, there is a goodly percentage who are satisfied with the neighborhood as it is and who look upon redevelopment as unnecessary.

This analysis largely supports earlier conclusions. There is association among the groups who wish to remain, who are satisfied, who are not interested in redevelopment. It is unfortunate that more cases are not available in order to make more detailed analyses by several factors at the same time.

Satisfaction with neighborhood.—Each respondent was asked whether he was satisfied or dissatisfied with a whole list of items relating to the neighborhood. There were twelve of these items in Question 12, but the answer to six of them was so overwhelmingly "satisfied," that analysis of the replies by other factors would have been pointless. Thus 95 per cent were satisfied with "near to schools"; 97 per cent with "frequent public transportation"; 87 per cent with "near to parks and playgrounds"; 96 per cent with "stores close by"; 94 per cent with "church location"; and 91 per cent with "type of neighborhood stores." The overwhelming response to these six items certainly indicated that these characteristics, in the opinion of the respondents, were acceptable to those living in the area.

The replies to the six remaining items about the neighborhood were not so one-sided as to preclude cross-sorts by other factors, and these are presented in Table 12.

Over all, the degree of satisfaction with these items was fairly high except as to cleanness. Only 24 per cent of those responding were satisfied with the neighborhood in this respect. Both "nearness to organizations" and "a building or place for . . . meetings" drew the only substantial percentages of "don't knows"—26 and 24, respectively.

Analysis of the satisfaction with these characteristics by other factors bears out for the most part the conclusions one would have expected. There are occasional variations among the items, however, that are notable. Length of residence in one's house, for example, has a significant association with some items and not with others. Generally the percentage of those satisfied increases with length of residence; and in the cases of "amount of open space," "closeness to friends," "nearness to organizations," and "place for neighborhood meetings," this pattern is a significant one, i.e., the difference in the percentages of the extremes is above the 95 per cent level. This is also the pattern in "satisfaction with cleanness," but the difference in percentages is below the 95 per cent level of significance. When it comes to "quietness," however, those with the shortest and longest periods of residence have a greater percentage of those satisfied than the middle-age groups. Although this is the pattern, it is not at the 95 per cent level of significance.

In attitudes toward the need for redeveloping the neighborhood, the pattern is consistent for all six items and is at the significant level for all items but "nearness to organizations." The lack of significance here, however, is due to the large percentage of "don't knows" among the "partial rebuilding" and the "no rebuilding is needed" groups. If percentages are computed for only those with an opinion on satisfaction with "nearness to organizations," then the pattern becomes significant above the three sigma level.

The pattern by desire to move is consistent in every case and significant in four. Satisfaction is more prevalent among those who do not want to move than among those who do. The respondents were also consistent when giving reasons for wanting to move or not wanting to

TABLE 12

SATISFACTION WITH NEIGHBORHOOD CHARACTERISTICS

(Milwaukee Survey Question 12)

PERCENTAGE IN INDICATED GROUP RESPONDING
"SATISFIED WITH . . ."

GROUP	Cleanness	Quietness	Open Space	Closeness to Friends	Nearness to Organizations	Place for Neighborhood Meetings	TOTAL CASES IN GROUP†
All respondents.........	24	56	52	77	65	57	312
Length of residence in house							
Less than 3 years.......	19	61	45*	69*	51*	48*	85–86
3–5....................	22	51	46	73	69	53	78–79
6–10...................	29	54	50	81	74	63	64–67
Over 10 years..........	28	59	66*	87*	71*	66*	74–80
Attitude toward redeveloping neighborhood							
Needs complete rebuilding................	3#	31#	14#	49#	51	30#	36–37
Needs partial rebuilding..	17	46	45	77	66	59	131–135
No rebuilding needed....	38#	73#	68#	86#	68	61#	113–118
Attitude toward condition of residence							
House is pretty good the way it is............	27	63#	65#	84*	69	61	168–175
House needs big repairs..	20	44#	38	72	64	53	102–106
House should be torn down...............	18	52	25#	57*	54	50	27–28
Desire to move							
Wants to move........	13#	43#	41#	67#	62	52	129–133
Doesn't want to move...	33#	68#	62#	86#	69	61	137–141
Wants to move because of smoke, noise, dirt.....	7	x	x	x	x	x	74
Doesn't want to move because likes neighborhood...............	38	76	70	98	75	66	77–79
Tenure							
Owner occupants.......	29	60	63*	89#	75*	62	90–94
Tenants..............	22	55	47*	72#	61*	55	213–217
Age							
Under 30.............	8#	45#	35#	71	48#	42*	73–75
30–39................	21	45	46	74	73	62	79–82
40–49................	24	59	62	82	71	56	61–63
50–59................	35	65	65	80	77#	66	44–46
60 and over...........	47#	83#	65#	81	58	64*	42–43
Family status							
Children living at home..	21	52*	49	77	64	55	203–208
No children living at home...............	30	66*	59	76	67	60	96–99
Income							
Under $50 per week.....	30*	56	53*	77	67	61	92–95
$50–59................	24	53	55	75	65	46	70–73
$60–69................	13	46	33*	72	58	48	44–46
$70 and over..........	11*	56	46	81	59	65	44–48
Education							
Some high school or more	17#	50	40#	73	63	54	149–157
Completed grade school..	26	65	63	76	57	60	72–76
7 years grade school or less.................	37#	62	63#	83	75	59	77–78

* and # See footnotes to Tables 6 and 7
† Includes "Don't knows" to Question 12

move. Thus only 7 per cent who said they wanted to move because of smoke, noise, or dirt were satisfied with "cleanness" of the neighborhood. Also, satisfaction with each neighborhood characteristic was greater for the group that did not wish to move than for the sample as a whole.

Tenure presents a pattern on satisfaction with these neighborhood characteristics, but it is not always at a significant level. In every case, the percentage of owner-occupants that are satisfied is greater than the percentage of tenants, a situation one would expect. For three of the six characteristics, however, the difference is not great enough to be statistically significant.

Satisfaction with these neighborhood characteristics by age shows significant differences in percentages, but the pattern is not consistent among the characteristics. Thus for "cleanness," "quietness," and "open space," the percentage of those satisfied increases quite markedly with age. On "nearness to organizations" one finds a greater percentage of the middle groups (30–59) satisfied than the young (under 30) and old (60 and over) groups. Organizations, apparently, are of greater importance to those of middle age than they are to the young and old or what is judged to be satisfactory nearness varies considerably. "Closeness to friends" presents really no pattern at all with the differences in percentages being too small to permit the drawing of any conclusions. "Place for neighborhood meetings" is also inconclusive as far as age is concerned, although the difference between the extremes is a significant one. No pattern, however, emerges. Age, therefore, does not have the same association with satisfaction with each of the neighborhood characteristics.

Family status, although presenting something of a pattern, does not show a significant one. Fewer of those with children living at home are satisfied with the neighborhood characteristics than are those with no children living at home; but this difference is significant for only one characteristic, "quietness." Perhaps some of the respondents are merely reflecting the noise-generating ability of their children rather than the noise of the neighborhood. One would expect those respondents with children to have adjusted to noise and, therefore, not to be as demanding as those without children.

Analysis of satisfaction by income groups is not very revealing. In respect to three items (quietness, closeness to friends, place for meetings), a higher percentage of those in both the lower and the higher income groups are satisfied than those in the middle-income groups. This general pattern apparently corresponds with findings of other studies, i.e., the middle-income group tends more toward dissatisfaction than do the other income groups. The differences here, however, are not marked.

Education and satisfaction presents a weak and often not significant pattern: the less the education, the greater the satisfaction. In fact, this pattern is significant only for "cleanness" and "open space."

In general, then, those groups that show the greatest percentage of satisfaction with existing conditions are (1) those who have lived in their houses the longest, (2) those who feel no redevelopment is needed, (3) those who feel their residences are in pretty good condition, (4) those who do not wish to move, (5) owner-occupants, (6) the oldsters (in some respects only), (7) those without children living at home, (8) the lower and higher income groups, and (9) those with less than a grade-school education. These are very general conclusions from a single survey and should be treated as such.

Action re dissatisfactions with neighborhood.—Questions 13, 14, and 15 of the schedule were designed to determine the activity of the respondents on items about which they were dissatisfied. The response was quite discouraging. To Question 13, "Have you discussed these things you don't like with anyone else in the neighborhood?" 78 per cent responded "No"; to Question 14, "Have you talked about them with your alderman or any other public official?" 92 per cent "No"; and to Question 15, "Have you ever tried to get any organization you belong to to do anything about the things you don't like?" the response was overwhelmingly negative—97 per cent.

Only Question 13 on discussion with other people had enough affirmative responses to permit analysis by other factors. Length of residence in one's house and tenure were sorted according to response to this question, but the results were unrewarding. No pattern emerged from length of residence and the pattern from tenure was well below the level of significance. A greater percentage of tenants than owners had discussed their dissatisfactions, but the percentages did not vary enough to be statistically significant.

Kinds of neighbors preferred.—Question 16 was asked to see if people preferred heterogeneous or homogeneous neighborhoods. The ordinary expectation would be that most people would say they preferred living in a neighborhood in which the people are more or less alike in regard to race, income, religion, etc., and that only a few would state they preferred a neighborhood in which people were different in these respects. The results did not support this common assumption: 34 per cent preferred their neighbors alike; 21 per cent wanted them different; 42 per cent did not care; and 3 per cent gave no answer.

Too much weight cannot be attached to this breakdown even within the limits of this one study. Unsolicited comments indicated that in fifteen cases in the second and third categories the answer was really in error. For example, one person who replied he did not care added, "I can get along with anybody as long as they are white and American." Several who said they preferred neighbors who were different added, "Except for colored." On the other hand, twenty-two respondents (7 per cent) gave unsolicited comments that were vigorous affirmations of their beliefs in equality. For instance, one respondent said, "It's nice to

mix up with people just to show there are nice people in all nationali-
ties." Another said, "I don't think that makes any difference. Everyone
could get along with each other if they want to." Another stated, "Learn
different ways and different ideas. I think it is nice to mingle with different types of people."

One cannot be sure, of course, in the light of comments contradictory
to the stated reply, that the answers given are accurate reflections of the
real attitudes of the respondents. Inquiry on this point (as well as other
points) should be more thorough than was possible in this study. When
these responses had been adjusted for the contradictory comments,
however, they were analyzed by the following factors: education, religion, age, family status, income, tenure, and type of dwelling unit. In
every case but religion, no pattern was evident and no differences were
significant. Under religion, 48 per cent of the Protestants preferred
their neighbors to be alike but only some 34 per cent of the Catholics
so replied. On the other hand, 19 per cent of the Protestants and 21
per cent of the Catholics said they preferred a neighborhood which had
several different kinds of people. This whole subject needs much more
investigation and analysis before any really acceptable conclusions on
attitudes can be drawn.

Summary.—With all the limitations of the Milwaukee survey, which
have been mentioned often above, it seems fair to say that it produced
three kinds of findings. A quick look at them will serve as a summary of
this part of this chapter.

First, of course, the survey turned up many facts and connections between facts that clearly fall in the "everybody-knows-that" category.
No examples need be cited here. No attempt has been made in the foregoing pages to play down or to conceal these rather apparent or, at least
often anticipated, findings. For those who may say that this substantial
proportion of the findings is simply elaboration of the obvious, it might
be well to suggest that a little more precision in stating such facts and
some grounds for estimating their relative weights or significance in different circumstances will, to put it mildly, do no harm.

Closely related but quite distinguishable are the findings that seem
quite reasonable or to be expected on points, however, for which other
facts or relations of facts would have seemed just as plausible or understandable. For instance, the survey shows that, in this one area, family
income apparently has no bearing on the prevalence of the opinion or
attitude that the municipality should have nothing to do with redevelopment of blighted areas (Table 9). It is not difficult to rationalize that
finding—to convince one's self that, of course, anyone would know that.
But just suppose that the finding had been different, e.g., that the
higher the income the larger the proportion of families that would say

that the city should keep its hands off. Could this not have been just as easily rationalized? Could one not have said just as firmly, "Everybody knows that"? In other words, this survey, like many other modest undertakings of this kind, may have turned up findings that, although tentative and limited, can serve as a basis for accepting some things that everyone knows and rejecting others that, also, everyone knows or thinks he knows.

In the third class are the findings that very few if any persons would have anticipated or expected. It is not necessary to recapitulate such findings here but the reader may wish to check over those facts and connections between different facts that make up the foregoing pages to see how many of the results of this survey are different from his expectations and assumptions. For example, would he have guessed that in a neighborhood in which only 12 per cent of the respondents thought conditions justified complete rebuilding, nearly half of all who were asked and about 60 per cent of those who expressed an opinion on how redevelopment ought to be done, would say that the city should do the whole job? If not, the implications of this finding, even for a sample of one area in one city, deserve careful consideration.

Finally, perhaps it is worth pointing out again that the 313 cases of this survey often prevented the type of analysis most needed. Although simple cross-tabulations made possible more detailed conclusions than a subjective analysis, finer breakdowns would have provided much more information that might well have answered some of the questions raised but unanswerable with such a few cases.

DENVER COMMUNITY SURVEY

The Denver Community Survey was undertaken by the Opinion Research Center at the University of Denver primarily to check the validity of respondents' reports, interviewer bias, etc. Questions in the schedule were designed to facilitate an analysis of this type. In other words, it was designed as a testing of sample survey methods, techniques, and problems. Some questions, however, were on subjects related to redevelopment and planning. Some of the results, therefore, are usable as a pilot study on the usefulness of the survey technique in learning about a city area and its inhabitants.

No attempt will be made here to analyze the entire survey; only a few selected questions have been used. Other persons have analyzed or are in the process of studying the findings in some detail, but permission has been given to use these few results as additional examples of how the sample survey technique can be used on urban affairs.[29]

29. Walden Johnston at the University of Denver planned his Master's thesis to make use of some of the survey data. The Opinion Research Center at the University has been discontinued.

The survey covered 922 interviews with people from all parts of Denver. It was a random sample. Thus the data from these interviews are not comparable to those from the Milwaukee survey, because the latter was limited to one section slated for redevelopment. Nevertheless, some of the questions are quite similar, and the breakdown of the replies to these questions may be compared to the Milwaukee analysis.

Attitudes on moving from neighborhood.—Two attitude questions were available by other factors. These were on one's desire to move from the neighborhood and to move from the house in which he was living.

The first question read: "Which statement comes closest to the way you feel about this particular neighborhood?

"1. I wouldn't move away even if I had the chance.

"2. I might stay here from now on, but I'd rather move somewhere else if I were able.

"3. I plan to move away as soon as I can."

Some 57 per cent did not want to move; only 12 per cent definitely wanted to move; 30 per cent were in between but would "rather move somewhere else if I were able"; and only 1 per cent had no opinion on the subject. In the Milwaukee survey some 54 per cent wanted to move.[30] With allowance for the difference in phrasing of the question, this proportion could be compared roughly with the 42 per cent in Denver who would rather move or were determined to do so. The Denver survey sampled the city as a whole; the Milwaukee job, only one of the less desirable areas. In both, however, the potential for residential mobility is high. Has adequate attention been paid to this fact in planning the strategy of redevelopment programs?

Cross-tabulations of these replies are given in Table 13.

Family status seems definitely related to desire to move. As in the case of the Milwaukee survey, more of those without children want to remain in the neighborhood than those with children. Although in both cities the differences attributable to this factor are less than might have been supposed, except for one pair in Denver, they are great enough not to be due in all probability to chance.

Length of residence presents a definite pattern in the Denver survey when analyzed as a factor in desire to move. This is in contrast to the Milwaukee survey where no such pattern was found. In the Denver survey, as length of residence increased so did the percentage of those who would not move even if they had the chance. Actually different

30. The Milwaukee question, number 11, was designed to separate out those who wanted to move only to get out of their present houses. In other words, it tried to get at reasons of neighborhood conditions and location. In this it was only partly successful: more than 48 per cent said they wanted to move and gave the kind of reasons the question was aimed to bring out; 5.4 per cent were certain they wanted to move but insisted on reasons that amounted to a better building to live in.

items are being measured, since the Denver question was on length of residence in the city while the Milwaukee question was on length of residence in the house.

Tenure is quite significantly associated with desire to move: more of the owner-occupants than tenants say they wish to remain in the neighborhood. This is somewhat like the relation found in the Milwaukee survey with the important exception that the pattern there was not at a significant level.

Length of formal education (not used in analyzing desire to move in

TABLE 13

ATTITUDES TOWARD MOVING FROM NEIGHBORHOOD

(Denver Community Survey)

PERCENTAGES OF INDICATED GROUPS RESPONDING

GROUPS	I Wouldn't Move Away Even if I Had the Chance	I Might Stay Here from Now on, but I'd Rather Move Somewhere Else if I Were Able	I Plan to Move Away as Soon as I Can	TOTAL CASES IN EACH GROUP†
Family status				
Has children under 18..........	50#	34*	15	356
Has no children under 18.......	62#	27*	10	447
Length of residence in Denver				
1–9 years....................	48#	36*	15	265
10–19 years..................	54	30	15	135
20 or more years‡.............	62#	27*	10	514
Tenure				
Tenants.....................	41#	37#	21#	375
Owner-occupants.............	67#	26#	5#	512
Education				
Grade school or less...........	65#	27	6#	232
Some or completed high school..	54	30	14	412
Some college or more..........	51#	34	14#	262
Age				
21–29.......................	40#	41#	18#	168
30–39.......................	50	33	17	207
40–49.......................	57	30	12	175
50–59.......................	62	25	11	177
60 and over..................	73#	23#	2#	180
Socio-econ. status§				
Below average................	51*	35*	13	108
Average.....................	54#	31	13	586
Above average...............	66*#	24*	9	213
Condition of dwelling§				
Excellent....................	65#	26#	7*#	249
Good........................	60	29	10	378
Minor repairs................	46	33	20#	212
Major repairs................	40#	43#	17*	72
Condition of block§				
Excellent....................	68#	25*	6*#	175
Good........................	60	29	10	464
Minor repairs................	45	35	19#	238
Major repairs................	27#	50*	23*	30

* and # See footnotes to Tables 6 and 7. Only the extremes of a series are so indicated unless the character of the series requires further indication of significance.
† Includes those with "no opinion."
‡ Includes "no answer" since most of these were born in Denver. The question asked was "When did you move to Denver?" not "How long have you lived here?"
§ Based on estimate of interviewer.

the Milwaukee survey) shows a significant pattern with percentage of those saying they wish to remain decreasing as education increases. Education would seem to be associated with dissatisfaction with the neighborhood.

Age is also significantly associated with desire to remain in the neighborhood: the higher the age, the larger the proportion who wish to stay where they are. This corresponds to the findings of the Milwaukee survey, but was less marked there. The oldsters are those who have become accustomed to the neighborhood and who do not wish to upset their habits of many years. Perhaps they have less critical eyes than the younger age groups. In plans for relocation housing as parts of redevelopment programs, how clearly have these age differences been recognized?

Socio-economic status was gauged by the interviewer in the Denver survey, so it can hardly be accepted as more than an approximate measure. The percentage of those in the above-average group who wanted to remain in the neighborhood was significantly greater than the percentage of those in the below average group. Perhaps this indicates that more of those of higher economic status have been able to acquire a home in a satisfactory neighborhood than those in the lower economic groups. The Milwaukee survey showed no association between desire to move and income, but it was limited to a particular area and that might have been responsible for the difference.

The condition of the dwelling was also rated by the interviewer and, therefore, was highly subjective. A pattern is apparent, however, with percentage of those desiring to remain in the neighborhood increasing as the condition of the dwelling improves. A similar but by no means directly comparable pattern was found in the Milwaukee survey when desire to move was analyzed by the respondent's rating of the condition of the dwelling.

The same pattern in Denver is found when desire to move is analyzed by the condition of the block. Here again, the condition was rated by the interviewer and should be used with caution. No similar cross-tabulation was made for the Milwaukee sample.

The reasons given in Denver for holding these opinions on wanting or not wanting to move are not very illuminating. They are presented below in Table 14.

"Neighborhood characteristics" are a reason relatively more often given by those who want to move than by those who do not. Location is an important reason to those who do not want to move, but apparently it makes little contribution to the desire to move. "Neighbors" is a reason more often given by those favorable to the neighborhood than those unfavorable.

TABLE 14

REASONS FOR NOT WANTING TO MOVE OR WANTING TO MOVE

(Denver Community Survey)

	NUMBER	PERCENTAGE of Total	PERCENTAGE of Subtotal
Favorable (want to stay in neighborhood)	1208	70.6	100.0
Neighborhood characteristics........................	293	17.1	24.3
Location..	374	21.9	30.9
Neighbors...	375	21.9	31.0
Personal connections with neighborhood..............	118	6.9	9.8
Miscellaneous.....................................	48	2.8	4.0
Unfavorable (want to move from neighborhood)	503	29.4	100.0
Neighborhood characteristics........................	263	15.4	52.3
Location..	11	0.6	2.2
Neighbors...	83	4.9	16.5
Miscellaneous.....................................	146	8.5	29.0
Total..	1711	100.0	

Attitudes toward house in which living.—From the Denver survey, the second attitude question available for analysis by other factors had to do with the house in which the respondent lived. Each respondent was asked, "Which statement comes closest to the way you feel about *the place you are living in now?*" The respondent was then given the choice of the same three statements used in connection with the attitude towards the neighborhood:

"1. I wouldn't move away even if I had the chance.

"2. I might stay here from now on, but I'd rather move somewhere else if I were able.

"3. I plan to move away as soon as I can."

Over 46 per cent of the respondents said they would not move even if they had the chance; 35 per cent said they would rather move if they could; and 17 per cent were anxious to move. These replies were analyzed by other factors, and this analysis is presented in Table 15.

As one would expect, there is very high association between desire to move from the house and desire to move from the neighborhood. Apparently, one who wishes to move from the neighborhood often is also dissatisfied with the house he is living in (and probably vice versa). It might be questioned, however, whether many of those interviewed were able to make the necessary distinction between neighborhood and house in answering these questions. Some clearly did, but possibly not all.

Family status is also of some importance on this attitude. More of those with children under 18 want to leave their houses than those without children under 18. Those with children, however, seem more strongly attached to the neighborhood (Table 13) than to the house in which they are living. This is true, in lesser degree, of families without children.

Length of residence in Denver can also be associated with attitude toward residence. Significantly, more of the older residents would not move from their present houses even if they had the chance.

Tenancy is strongly related to desire to move from the house. Those who own their homes have less desire to move than those who rent. This may be rationalization of an existing situation, or it may be a measure of better houses, but the degree of association is high.

TABLE 15

ATTITUDES TOWARD MOVING FROM HOUSE IN WHICH LIVING

(Denver Community Survey)

| GROUP | PERCENTAGE OF INDICATED GROUPS RESPONDING | | | |
	I Wouldn't Move Away Even if I Had the Chance	I Might Stay Here from Now on, but I'd Rather Move Somewhere Else if I Were Able	I Plan to Move Away as Soon as I Can	TOTAL CASES IN EACH IN-DICATED GROUP†
Desire to move from neighborhood				
Wouldn't move if I could.......	70#	23#	6#	511
Might stay but would like to move.....................	19	60#	20	274
Plan to move away as soon as possible......................	7#	25#	66#	110
Family status				
Has children under 18 years of age	36#	40*	24#	355
Has no child under 18 years of age	55#	31*	12#	443
Length of residence in Denver				
1–9 years....................	36#	39	24#	263
10–19 years..................	38	43*	18	134
20 or more years‡.............	54#	31*	14#	510
Tenure				
Tenants.......	30#	39*	30#	373
Owner-occupants.............	59#	32*	8#	507
Education				
Grade school or less education	62#	26#	11*	231
Some or completed high school..	41	37	21	408
Some college or more education..	41#	40#	18*	260
Age				
21–29.......................	29#	39#	31#	167
30–39.......................	35	38	26	207
40–49.......................	45	41	14	174
50–59.......................	54	34	11	175
60 and over.................	69#	23#	5#	178
Socio-economic status§				
Below average................	39*	28	33#	108
Average.....................	44	36	18	579
Above average...............	56*	34	8#	213
Condition of dwelling§				
Excellent....................	54#	33	11#	246
Good........................	50	36	12	377
Minor repairs................	38	36	25	209
Major repairs................	24#	31	46#	72
Condition of block§				
Excellent....................	52#	35	12*#	173
Good........................	52	35	12	461
Minor repairs................	36	33	29#	235
Major repairs................	17#	47	37*	30

* and # See footnotes to Tables 6 and 7. Only the extremes of a series are so indicated unless the character of the series requires additional indication of significance.
† Includes "No opinion."
‡ Includes "No answers," since most of these were born in Denver and the question read, "When did you move to Denver?"
§ Rated by interviewer.

The length of formal education and age are also related to attitude toward the house, but in reverse ways. Those with fewer years in school and with more years on earth are more attached to their present houses.

Socio-economic status is apparently associated with desire to stay in the house in which one lives: the higher the status, the higher the proportion who wish to stay on in their present houses. Probably those of higher economic status have been able to select houses more suited to their needs and, therefore, have less desire to move than those lower in the income scales. It is interesting to note that satisfaction with present housing and neighborhoods is directly related to socio-economic status but inversely to length of education.

As would be expected, condition of dwelling is closely associated with one's desire to move from the house. The same relationship holds true for condition of the blocks. It is well to point out, however, that a goodly number do not want to move even though the houses in which they live need major repairs (24 per cent of those who live in such houses) or the blocks in which they live need major repairs (17 per cent).

Satisfaction with and importance of neighborhood characteristics.— One other question asked of all respondents was their satisfaction with certain neighborhood characteristics of their present housing and the importance they placed upon these characteristics when selecting a new neighborhood in which to live. The respondent was given a choice of three answers: very satisfied, partly satisfied, and not at all satisfied with the characteristics of the neighborhood in which he lived; and for the importance of these characteristics in selecting a neighborhood, very important, somewhat important, and not at all important. The results are presented in Table 16. Unfortunately, the data were not available for analysis by other factors.

On a few points the results may be compared to those from the similar question in the Milwaukee survey (Table 12 and accompanying discussion). The Milwaukee survey, however, covered only satisfaction with the characteristics in the present neighborhood and, in addition, permitted the respondent but two choices—"satisfied" and "not satisfied." Thus in comparing the two surveys, the first two choices in the Denver survey should be combined and compared to the first choice in the Milwaukee tabulations. Such items as "nearness to church," "closeness to public transportation," "nearness to stores," and "nearness to parks and playgrounds" are, in both surveys, characteristics with which a high percentage of the respondents are at least partly satisfied. Dissatisfaction runs highest for "cleanness," with the redevelopment area in Milwaukee quite understandably having a higher percentage (74 per cent) of respondents dissatisfied on this score than Denver. In Denver, in fact, satisfaction seemed quite high for every item. Without further breakdowns this, of course, does not mean much. It should, of course, be higher on most points than in the Milwaukee survey because in Denver the whole city was covered and in Milwaukee only one area, a proposed redevelopment area.

TABLE 16

SATISFACTION WITH AND IMPORTANCE OF NEIGHBORHOOD CHARACTERISTICS

(Denver Community Survey)

Neighborhood Characteristics	Satisfied with the Characteristics in Own Neighborhood (per cent)	Importance of Neighborhood Characteristics in Moving to New Location (per cent)
Nearness to stores		
Very	80	46
Somewhat or partly	15	39
Not at all	4	15
Nearness to schools		
Very	69	43
Somewhat or partly	10	12
Not at all	6	44
No opinion	15	1
Closeness to public transportation		
Very	85	68
Somewhat or partly	10	23
Not at all	4	9
Nearness to church		
Very	72	41
Somewhat or partly	18	38
Not at all	5	21
No opinion	4	—
Nearness to parks and playgrounds		
Very	64	23
Somewhat or partly	18	34
Not at all	11	42
No opinion	7	1
Cleanness of neighborhood		
Very	65	94
Somewhat or partly	25	5
Not at all	10	1
A strictly residential area		
Very	69	60
Somewhat or partly	20	25
Not at all	8	14
Kind of neighbors		
Very	77	70
Somewhat or partly	17	23
Not at all	3	7
No opinion	3	—

The Milwaukee survey did not include questions on the relative importance of factors in neighborhood selection, so the Denver findings should be of particular value on this point. Here again, one finds "cleanness" ranks well above all the other items with 94 per cent feeling it very important in neighborhood selection. "Closeness to public transportation" and "kind of neighbors" are next with about 70 per cent of the respondents feeling them very important. "A strictly residential neighborhood," "nearness to stores," "nearness to schools," and "nearness to church" are next, straddling the 50 per cent mark. Surprisingly enough, one finds 44 per cent who feel that "nearness to schools" is of no importance. It would be well if those so replying could be analyzed to determine their family status. Forty-two per cent also felt that "nearness to parks and playgrounds" was of no importance in neighborhood selection. Here again, family status is probably the reason, but it needs further analysis.

"Nearness to church" was another item that received a fairly large response in the choice "not at all important" (21 per cent) and even "nearness to stores" brought forth 15 per cent who held that it was of no importance.

These views are of particular importance in planning redevelopment projects, but in this form they are not very useful. They need analysis to ascertain the groups who expressed these ideas. Creating a neighborhood in line with these gross findings would not provide for the wants and needs of many urbanites.

Summary

This chapter has suggested the diversity of attitudes that may be expected toward redevelopment projects. It also has shown how group attitudes actually have affected the outcome of specific redevelopment projects. Any agency that ignores these attitudes is likely to run into trouble sooner or later.

Post facto discussion of these attitudes is not a very satisfactory means of understanding the people and the area. Steps need be taken early in redevelopment planning to learn more about the people, their attitudes, needs, and wants. The community organization (discussed in chapter iv) is one method. Another is the sample survey, a device that has uses beyond those of learning about the attitudes of residents. The Milwaukee survey is essentially a pilot study in the use of this technique. Its results, though not startling, indicate that it can be useful in analyzing an area physically suitable for rebuilding. The Denver Community Survey provides additional examples of the attitude survey technique applied to the physical development of a modern city. Although different in important respects and both limited in many ways, these two surveys supplement and support each other and help to open the way for more thorough and useful exploration and analysis by others.

In brief, then, the sample survey in urban development and redevelopment holds promise of becoming a useful means of ascertaining the attitudes of the urbanite toward various aspects of actual programs and projects and as a method of learning much more than we now know of his needs and wants.

APPENDIX

SURVEY OF MILWAUKEE NEIGHBORHOOD

No, 1, 2, 3–_____
Census Tract 4–_____
Block No. 5, 6–_____
APHA Rating 7, 8, 9–_____

ADDRESS_____

INTRODUCTION: I'm from the University of Wisconsin. We're making a study of this neighborhood. I'd like to speak with the lady of the house or the head of the house

1. RESPONDENT IS:	Male	10–1
	Female	2

2. How long have you lived in this house?	Less than 1 yr	11–1
	1–2 years	2
	3–5 years	3
	6–10 years	4
	11–15 years	5
	16–20 years	6
	Over 20 years	7

3. Where did you live before you moved to this house? (Record exact address if in city. If another city, just record name of city.)

_____ 12–R

4. How long have you lived in Milwaukee County? (Most recent move.)

	Less than 1 yr	13–1
	1–2 years	2
	3–5 years	3
	6–10 years	4
	11–15 years	5
	16–20 years	6
	Over 20 years	7

5. How do you feel about this neighborhood? Which *one* of the statements on this card best describes what should be done to this neighborhood?

(HAND CARD AND READ)

1. It needs complete rebuilding. Nearly all the stores and houses should be torn down and replaced by new ones.......................... 14–1

2. Replacing some blocks in this neighborhood with new stores and houses is needed but complete rebuilding isn't necessary...........   2
3. The neighborhood is pretty good the way it is. No rebuilding is needed because the people who live here and own property here take care of it..   3

    Don't know..   4

(UNSOLICITED COMMENTS)_____

_____

_____

6. Do you think there are any (other) neighborhoods in Milwaukee that should be torn down and rebuilt?

	Yes	15–1
	No.	2
	Don't know	3

(UNSOLICITED COMMENTS)_____

_____

_____

7. Have you heard anything about plans in Milwaukee to rebuild some run-down neighborhoods? That is, to tear down houses and other buildings and put up new ones?

	Yes	16–1*
	No	2

*(IF YES, ASK A AND B)

A. What neighborhoods did you hear about?
(DON'T READ CHOICES. JUST RECORD REPLY.)

Red Arrow Park Area (Michigan, 9th, Clybourn, 12th)	17–1
Lapham Park Area (Brown, 5th, 11th, Juneau)	2
Brady Humboldt Area (Kane, Cambridge, Brady, Humboldt)	3
Vieau Park Area (Lapham, Florida, 1st, 9th)	4
Juneau Park	5
City Hall Area	6
Other (SPECIFY)_____	R
Don't know	7

B. How or where did you hear about it?
(DON'T READ CHOICES. JUST RECORD REPLY.)

Newspapers	18–1
Radio	2
Friends or neighbors	3
Organization belongs to	4
Political or public meetings	5
Saw project under construction	6
Other (SPECIFY)_____	R
Don't know	7

(UNSOLICITED COMMENTS)_____

_____

_____

---

8. Here is a card on which 3 ways for rebuilding badly run-down neighborhoods are listed. Which *one* of them do you think would be the best way to rebuild a run-down neighborhood? Read them carefully; take your time.

(HAND CARD AND READ)

To rebuild run-down neighborhoods:
1. The city should buy the land, tear down the buildings, and sell the land to some large builders if they will put up new buildings........   19–1*
2. After buying the land and tearing down the buildings, the city itself should put up the new buildings, that is, low-rent or veterans' housing...   2
3. The city should do nothing about these neighborhoods, but let the real estate men and private builders do the whole job.............   3
   Don't know..   4

*A. (IF ANSWER IS 1.) Should the land be sold to private builders even if the city has to take a loss or sell it below cost?

	Yes	20–1
	No	2
	Don't know	3

(UNSOLICITED COMMENTS)_____

_____

_____

---

9. How do you feel about this house? Which *one* of the statements on this card best describes what needs to be done to this house?

(HAND CARD AND READ)

1. This house is pretty good the way it is. Only a few little repairs are necessary...   21–1
2. Basically the house is all right although it needs big repairs........   2
3. This house is so bad that it should be torn down   3
   Don't know...   4

(UNSOLICITED COMMENTS. If hesitant, ask for specific repairs which are necessary and do not circle the answer.)

_____

_____

---

10. If you *could* afford either, would you prefer to rent or to buy your home?

	Own	22–1
	Rent	2
	Don't know	3

---

11. If you were able to buy or rent a house the same as this one but in a different part of town, would you want to move?

	Yes	23–1*
	No	2#
	Don't know	3

*(IF YES, ASK A AND B)

A. Why do you want to move?
   (DON'T READ CHOICES. JUST RECORD ANSWER.)

Shopping facilities too far away	24–1
Smoke, noise, soot, dirt	2
Don't like neighbors	3
Too far from work	4
Schools inadequate	5
Schools hard to get to	6

Other (SPECIFY)_____ R

Don't know   7

B. Where would you like to move? (Exact location, if possible)

_____ 25–R

#C. (IF No) Why wouldn't you want to move?_____

_____ 26–R

12. Are you satisfied or dissatisfied with these things in your neighborhood?
    (HAND CARD AND READ)

		Satisfied	Not Satisfied	Don't Know
(1) Near to schools	27–	1	2	3
(2) Frequent public transportation	28–	1	2	3
(3) Near to parks and playgrounds	29–	1	2	3
(4) Cleanness—free of smoke, dirt, etc.	30–	1	2	3
(5) Quietness—not much noise from traffic or other causes	31–	1	2	3
(6) Stores close by	32–	1	2	3
(7) Church location	33–	1	2	3
(8) Open space—trees and shrubs	34–	1	2	3
(9) Type of neighborhood stores	35–	1	2	3
(10) Closeness to friends	36–	1	2	3
(11) Nearness to organizations you belong to	37–	1	2	3
(12) A building or place for neighborhood or group meetings	38–	1	2	3

(UNSOLICITED COMMENTS)_____

_____

_____

13. Have you discussed these things you don't like with anyone else in the neighborhood?

Yes	39–1
No	2
Don't remember	3

14. Have you talked about them with your alderman or any other public official?

Yes	40–1
No	2
Don't remember	3

15. Have you ever tried to get any organization you belong to do anything about the things you don't like?

Yes	41–1
No	2
Don't remember	3

16. If you were entirely free to choose, would you want to live in a neighborhood in which all the people are more or less alike or would you prefer to live in a neighborhood which had several different kinds of people? (Same income, race, religion, etc.)

Alike	42–1
Different	2
Don't care	3
Don't know	4

(UNSOLICITED COMMENTS)_____

_____

_____

17. Do you own or rent this house?

Own	43–1
Rent	2

18. (To OWNERS) Have you ever rented a place to live in (i.e., since you set up housekeeping)?

Yes	44–1*
No	2

*A. (IF YES) Why did you decide to buy?
(*Free response*)_____

_____ 45–R

19. (To RENTERS) Have you ever owned your own home (i.e., since you set up housekeeping)?

Yes	46–1*
No	2

*A. (IF YES) Why did you decide to rent?
(*Free response*)_____

_____ 47–R

20. (To RENTERS— What is your monthly rent?

(If weekly, record	(A)	Under $15.00	48–1
here $_____	(B)	$15.00–19.99	2
and multiply by	(C)	$20.00–24.99	3
4⅓.)	(D)	$25.00–29.99	4
	(E)	$30.00–34.99	5
	(F)	$35.00–39.99	6
	(G)	$40.00–44.99	7
	(H)	$45.00–49.99	8
	(I)	$50.00–59.99	9
	(J)	$60.00–69.99	X
	(K)	$70.00–& over	Y
		Refused	0

21. May I ask your age?

Under 20	49–1
20–24	2
25–29	3
30–39	4
40–49	5
50–59	6
60 and over	7
Refused	8

22. Do any children live here with you?

Yes	50–1*
No	2

*A. (IF YES) How many are

too young to go to school	51–
in grade school	52–
in high school	53–
in college	54–
other	55–

23. Please tell me which of these groups your weekly *family* income belongs in.

(HAND CARD)

(If monthly, record here $_____ and divide by 4⅓.)

(A) Under $15.00 a week	56–1
(B) $15.00–19.99 a week	2
(C) $20.00–24.99 a week	3
(D) $25.00–29.99 a week	4
(E) $30.00–39.99 a week	5
(F) $40.00–49.99 a week	6
(G) $50.00–59.99 a week	7
(H) $60.00–69.99 a week	8
(I) $70.00–79.99 a week	9
(J) $80.00–89.99 a week	X
(K) $90.00 and over a wk	Y
Refused	0

24. Race (DO NOT ASK—TO BE DETERMINED BY INTERVIEWER)

White	57–1
Negro	2
Other	3

25. Do you remember the last school you attended? What was the last grade you finished in school?

Completed college	58–1
Some college	2
Completed high school	3
Some high school	4
Completed grammar school	5
5–7 years grammar school	6
1–4 years grammar school	7
No formal school	8

26. What is your religious preference?

Protestant	59–1
Catholic	2
Jewish	3
Other	4
None	5
Refused	6

27. Dwelling unit type (to be determined by interviewer)

Single family detached	60–1
Single family row house	2
Two family	3
Three family	3
Four family	5
Five family or more	6

28. Interviewer's signature:_____

61, 62–

29. Date and time:_____

(General comments by interviewer or respondent. Indicate which.)

Study......................... 63–

CHAPTER IV

COMMUNITY ORGANIZATIONS AND REDEVELOPMENT

ALTHOUGH community organizations and associations of various kinds have been parts of the urban scene for some time and their import has not gone unnoticed, more recently they have become the subject of frequent monographs, books, and articles. The major theme of most of these discussions has been that the local community organization is an excellent means for bolstering and extending the "democratic process." It has been called the modern counterpart of the town meeting and upon it have been pinned hopes for arousing citizen interest in the affairs of his community and area. It has been hailed as a major weapon in the fight against political apathy. The organization and functions of these organizations are a substantial subject of study and it is not possible here to examine their nature, to outline and recommend measures for their creation, nor to advise on the methods by which they will function most effectively. Others have addressed themselves to these questions.

Quite recently, however, some organizations of this kind have focused their attention upon redevelopment as either their sole or a major function and have begun to think, talk, and act on community planning. This may be due in part to the growing realization that planning involves more than determining the location of public buildings and thoroughfares; but whatever the cause, it indicates that planning and redevelopment agencies may be able to consider these groups as increasingly important in preparing their plans and putting them into effect.

Examples of this recent emphasis on planning and redevelopment are not hard to find. Chicago has at least two community organizations whose function is planning and redevelopment—the South Side Planning Board and the Near West Side Planning Board. Each of these organizations was created for the purpose of helping to plan and redevelop an area in Chicago in which it is interested. Although not uninterested in arousing citizen interest and in dispelling political apathy, that is not their primary purpose. Another example can be found in Philadelphia where the South Philadelphia Coordinating Council, an organization of organizations working in south Philadelphia, created

the Neighborhood Planning Conference to replan an area and to encourage the citizens in the area to take part in the replanning.

One finds also that community councils, which originally were set up
to co-ordinate health and welfare agencies in various areas, have
branched out to take an interest in the planning of their areas. A good
example of this is in Cleveland where local area councils, which are
under the aegis of the Health and Welfare Federation, have become,
in effect, organizations of local citizens interested in the planning and
redevelopment of their neighborhoods or areas.

Usefulness to Redevelopment

The usefulness of community organizations in urban redevelopment
can be outlined under three headings.

The first of these concerns the actual planning of the area. It is here
that the community organization helps in eliciting information on the
attitudes and interests of those in redevelopment areas. That residents
of an area can assist in the planning of that area is a proposition not
universally accepted by planners. For a long time, some planners have
held the view that as technicians they are the only ones qualified to plan
or replan an area. Many would support this opinion by pointing out
that the planning agency is supposed to be the technical co-ordinating
agency for the municipality, and that its staff members are the only
persons who have the breadth of knowledge to take all factors into consideration.

Such an attitude, however, does not preclude recognition that residents of an area can help in its planning. In the first place, the planner
should be sure that the plan meets the needs and desires of those who
live or will live in the area. This was discussed in chapter ii at some
length, and the principle is just as applicable here though on a smaller
and more specific scale. If our cities are to be redeveloped, they ought
to provide the residents with the type of living that meets at least most
of their needs and wants. Kinds of housing, space relationships, community facilities, and other public works should be provided on the
basis of what the people need and want. Some means must be found for
ascertaining these needs and wants, and the use of a local organization
to discuss planning proposals is a promising means of doing so.

After all, planning is not an esoteric function, the procedures of
which can be understood only by those specially trained. Although the
term itself may cause confusion in the mind of some local residents,
many of their ideas on what should be done to the neighborhood are
certainly planning ideas. Because their formulation may not be in the
technical terms of the planner and because they may not be compre-

hensive in scope should not automatically preclude their consideration. On the contrary, the local resident's knowledge of his neighbors and their value systems may provide the planner with the kind of information that will permit him to create a community that will meet the needs of those for whom it is planned. Through them the professional planner will have richer materials to weave into the broad framework of the over-all plan.

A second reason community organizations are useful in the urban redevelopment process is that they provide a vehicle for discussing a proposed plan with the residents before it is announced. Examples of redevelopment projects that have been killed because of opposition within the redevelopment area are not hard to find. If residents of an area know nothing about its proposed redevelopment until they read about it in the papers, they are likely to take a dim view of its value. This is particularly true if they see their homes labeled "slum" and fear their homes may be taken from them without just compensation. Such an aroused group will have little difficulty in conveying their feelings to the local councilman, and he in turn will be hesitant to approve a redevelopment proposal in the face of such opposition. City councils generally give great consideration to the view of the councilman in whose ward a project is to be built; and if he is opposed to it, the chances for approval are rather slim.

If a community organization is in existence and the proposal is routed through it with careful explanations on the whole process, and if the organization represents the local residents and their ideas are given consideration in the planning, opposition that has resulted from fear and lack of understanding may be at least lessened. If, in addition, the plan reflects some or many of the ideas of the residents, they may not be anxious to oppose what they may look upon as their own handiwork.

Thus from a purely "practical" point of view, as a means of easing redevelopment through the perils of resident opposition, the community organization, if used properly, can become a valuable tool.

The third way in which a community organization can be a useful tool in the redevelopment process in effect includes the public relations and consultation aspects mentioned above. Essentially it is a means of making the democratic process more effective. Under our representative system of government, the influence of an individual on governmental policy through voting is slight. The chance for more active and more direct political activity is not great, and perhaps political apathy can be explained in part by this fact. If a technique were available whereby one could participate more directly in policy decisions and could observe the effect of such participation, his interest in political activity might increase. The community organization, if used as a democratic tool in the planning process, may provide one opportunity of this type. Thus the redevelopment process offers the community an excellent opportunity to encourage participation in planning. If lip service is to be translated into action, this is an opportunity to do it.

It is well to note that although the ideas of "grass roots" planning and public participation in redevelopment are most commendable and certainly seem a step in the right direction, one should avoid the pitfall of assuming that by working and consulting with local groups and organizations one has *ipso facto* reached all the people in an area and has become familiar with all their needs and wants. As is pointed out later in greater detail, public participation is quite limited regardless of the efforts made to encourage it. Only a small proportion of the people actually participate even on heated issues. The "grass roots" approach will not represent everyone; it does not automatically include all groups and ideas. It is but a means of getting to more people and understanding more of their ideas.

A major objection to this approach to redevelopment planning, however, is that often the area will be planned for people who do not now live in it. Thus, goes the argument, it is of no avail to consult the present residents and to plan the area in accord with their desires when it will not be their needs that will be met. Even so, it is the present residents who must move if a rebuilding job is to be done and their ideas on the rate and amount of dislocation may become one of the most important features of the redevelopment plan.

This argument clearly assumes that rather large areas are to be swept clear of their present structures and that all or nearly all the inhabitants will have to live elsewhere. Often this may be necessary or desirable, often it may not.

Furthermore, this argument ignores the basic premise on which this approach is based. It in fact begs the question since it assumes that the new use will be determined prior to consultation with the residents. This is not to say, of course, that the new use will be determined solely or even primarily by consulting with the residents of the area on their attitudes, wants, needs, and ideas. Relation to the master plan and considerations beyond that of local residents' ideas must play a large part in determining the new use, but these are not the only considerations. By consulting with the residents one may find that the redevelopment plan can be drawn up to meet in large part the wants and needs of those in the area who wish to remain and still be in accord with the other criteria that shape the plan.

An official planning agency, of course, must make broad recommendations on the use of land. A land use plan, however, does not have to prescribe the specific land uses for each block and part of a block in the city on the basis that the proposed, detailed land use is the only one suitable for that block. Adjustments by blocks and groups of blocks will always have to be made, and minor shifts of boundaries of a proposed housing project or an industrial site are not the kind of tampering with a city plan that violates planning principles. The planning agency should, in fact, lean over backward in planning a redevelopment area to see that it creates only those dislocations that are necessary in reaching its long-term goals. Final decisions on the exact land use pattern for a redevelopment area would best not be made until the local residents have been consulted. These consultations might look into the use of existing capital structures, i.e., rehabilitation, rather than demolition. It might also find some pattern of those who wish to leave and those who wish to stay and thus provide an outline for the redevelopment of the area which would create the smallest amount of disruption and friction without violating any planning values.

Also, community organizations generally represent quite large areas, areas considerably larger than most redevelopment sites. Thus even though redevelopment may result in replacement of some of the residents, it will not result in anything like complete replacement. In addition, a redevelopment plan for a large, redevelopment area, need not (and in most cases, will not) call for the razing of all structures in the area. If it is done at all carefully, it will be a culling process whereby the worst is removed and that which remains is improved. This type of careful surgery certainly suggests that a local community organization could aid in discussing the areas that should come under the knife. Even if much is razed, it will no doubt be done in stages thus permitting some residents to shift their location within the area or to move back into the area.

Experience with Community Organizations in Redevelopment

As mentioned earlier, there are many types of community organizations. Their effectiveness in the urban redevelopment process depends largely on their purposes and how they function. It also depends to a great extent on the way in which they are used in the redevelopment process. Cities and their organizations differ, and no one formula can be written indicating how local organizations can best be used, but the experience of cities with the longest records of such activity may be useful to others.

PHILADELPHIA

Philadelphia, perhaps, has had the most experience in using community organizations in planning and redevelopment. The Planning

Commission has been developing a policy on this question since 1945 and has now evolved what seems to be a workable system. It has had experience in dealing with three communities, and in each case, the procedure has been different. The first was one in which the people in the area did the planning; in the second the Planning Commission did the planning with essentially no prior consultation with the residents; and the third procedure was a compromise of the first two, i.e., the Planning Commission first met with the community organization, acquired information on what its members wanted done in the area, and then prepared plans that took these ideas into consideration. The first method may be analyzed in some detail since it occurred some little time ago. The second approach needs little discussion, because, in effect, it does not really involve community organizations in planning. The third method, however, is still in process so to speak and, therefore, cannot be evaluated to the same degree as the other two.

Southeast central area.—The most elaborate procedure, i.e., the one requiring the most work, began in 1947 but not at the instigation of the Planning Commission. The South Philadelphia Coordinating Council, primarily an organization of schools and welfare agencies in the area, took part in a survey of local conditions and as a result became interested in seeing what could be done to improve the area.

Conditions in the southeast central area were such that it could stand redevelopment. Although age in Philadelphia is not necessarily synonymous with obsolescence or deterioration, many of the very old as well as the not-so-old buildings in the area were beyond rehabilitation. On the basis of the 1940 Census of Housing, 63 per cent of the residential buildings were unfit for human habitation, or without private bath or plumbing facilities, or were in need of major repairs. Many dwellings, built for one-family use, had been converted to two-, three-, and even four-family use. The most common type of house in the area was the row house, and many of these were on lots less than fourteen feet wide. The area also contained a peculiar type of structure known as a "band-box house." The reason for the name is apparent when one realizes they are structures with but one room to a floor, each room stacked on top of another and occupied by an entire family.

The southeast central area also had little open space. Lot coverage was very high; over 70 per cent of the structures covered more than 80 per cent of their lots. Front, rear, and side yards were either very small or nonexistent.

Land use in the area was also undesirable. Residential and industrial use were intermixed, and switching yards of a railroad were within the area. The area also contained many nuisance industries—rubber vulcanizing, coal yards, junk yards, etc.

Racially, the area was mixed with a large part inhabited by Negroes. The area contained many families and persons of very low income, but also a great many in the middle-income groups. A block of completely deteriorated structures next to a block of old but well-maintained row houses was not at all uncommon.

The area also had some desirable characteristics that made it a promising redevelopment area. It was close to the center of the city and also to several industrial districts. Thus it was suitable for both industrial and white-collar workers. The area also contained substantial institutions and organizations, giving it stability and a core for redevelopment.

After the initial survey, members of the South Philadelphia Coordinating Council approached the Citizens Council on City Planning, an organization that had had some influence in the re-creation of the Philadelphia City Planning Commission, and asked its aid. The Citizens Council believed that democratic procedures could be effective in planning and felt that this was an opportunity to test some of them.

As a result, a special organization was created by the South Philadelphia Coordinating Council. It was called the Neighborhood Planning Conference and was as widely representative of the area as possible, differing in this respect from its parent organization whose representation was primarily of the schools and welfare agencies. Every known organization in the area was requested to elect delegates to the Conference; and the Citizens Council on City Planning, which served as secretariat for the Conference, worked assiduously to make sure that all organizations in the area were invited.

The planning of the initial meeting was under the direction of Dr. Julian L. Greifer, the director of a settlement house in the area and later director of the Conference. He held a preliminary session with all the delegates to discuss how the meeting should be run and what should be done as well as to shake out some of the time-consuming problems that invariably plague organizational meetings. This prior meeting proved effective in two ways. In the first place, the leaders of the conference gained information on the interests of the delegates. Secondly, it was important because of the effect it had on the attitudes of the delegates. They realized they were not to be pawns of others but, on the contrary, were themselves to determine policy and run the conference.

The plenary session was well run. Because of the prior meeting, the objectives and purpose of the Neighborhood Planning Conference were agreed upon. The job of the meeting was to select the name of the organization, appoint committees, and explain in general terms what the job of planning entailed. A questionnaire was distributed on which each delegate indicated the items in which he was particularly interested and specified the committees on which he would like to serve. Committees were appointed from this list.

The committees followed a procedure of breaking up into smaller groups to consider specific aspects of their problems. They spent time surveying the area in which they were interested and prepared maps, primarily of existing conditions. They held block meetings to which people in a block were invited to discuss their ideas on what should be done. A few of these meetings made it apparent that no one's home was sufficiently large to accommodate all those who came, and the need for a community center was impressed upon many.

These block meetings were perhaps one of the most effective procedures of the Neighborhood Planning Conference, for the simple reason that they brought the people of the area together to discuss common problems. In addition, the meetings themselves were tangible evidence of a concerted effort to get something done in the community. The history of the area had been one of much talk but few accomplishments. Because the past record had been so poor, the first attitude of most people toward the organization had been one of skepticism. After block meetings had shown that the Conference was interested in determining what the people in the area wanted and that their ideas were considered and discussed, many of the attitudes of skepticism changed materially toward hope and co-operation.

Most of the people in the area who attended these block meetings thought in terms of small planning problems rather than large ones. Dirty streets and playgrounds were the chief complaints and few had any conception of redevelopment. As one block leader stated later, "I never gave it a thought before." As block meetings were held and the Neighborhood Planning Conference worked more and more with them, it became apparent that an educational program was going on as well. For instance, to one group, the term "redevelopment" meant a housing project; and because of previous misinformation about eminent domain procedure and the prices that would be paid for property acquired (misinformation that some thought had been deliberately spread in order to defeat a housing project), the people were not receptive to the idea. As accurate information on condemnation was presented, however, and redevelopment explained more fully, the attitudes began to change until finally the group recommended the redevelopment of a sizable area.

Another by-product of the block meetings was the development of local leaders. In a letter to a staff member of the Planning Commission, one of the people most active in the Neighborhood Planning Conference stated: "One of the most interesting aspects of these meetings is the local leadership that is evident. I used to hear some . . . say that the able people had all moved out of this area. We are all beginning to see that there is a lot of local leadership—it just hasn't been found . . . except in a few instances."

One of these people who developed as a local leader stated that even after the Neighborhood Planning Conference had been dissolved the leadership status she had acquired in working for it had been maintained. As evidence she cited the number of people who came to her with their problems. She had become a recognized leader in the area and was continuing to exercise her leadership qualities. The Neighborhood Planning Conference had been a means in making her abilities known.

At first the committees were in the dark on how to remedy bad situations. Practically none of the members had technical training or knowledge of planning. They had to find out how things were done. They made trips to the city hall, to their councilman, and to other city officials. They soon began to learn something of the administration of the city government and to discover to whom complaints should be made when a deficiency was discovered. In addition, they asked administrative officials of the city to attend their meetings and to explain problems of street lighting, housing, and other matters of common concern. It was not long before many members of the committees were relatively well informed on municipal affairs.

Each committee had a consultant on whom it could call at will, and the Planning Commission sent a staff member to assist the committees whenever requested. A member of the Conference made the observation that the committee meetings moved along much better when a technical person was present than when not. The technical man was able to advise the committee on many problems as they arose and in that way saved the committee a great deal of waste motion.

At the beginning the Neighborhood Planning Conference consisted only of representatives of organizations and, as a result, was known to but a few of the people in the area. As it grew, however, membership on an individual basis was permitted, and more people in the community joined. The block meetings, regular meetings of the Conference, and excellent publicity soon made most of those in the area at least aware that such an organization existed. Part of this publicity was obtained through the schools. Classes in manual training prepared models of a part of the area showing existing conditions and what the area might look like after it had been redeveloped. Construction of these models created interest, and later a meeting was held at which the parents of children who had been active in the planning studies were honored.

The Conference was organized in February, 1946, and by May, 1947 the recommendations of the committees were ready. Public hearings were held on each committee's recommendations. In some respects the recommendations of the Committee on Housing and Living Conditions are perhaps the most interesting. The general recommendations are quoted below:

The committee on Housing and Living Conditions made a careful study of the substandard housing in the district with the cooperation of the real estate boards, the Police Department, social agencies, etc. The committee called eight meetings of neighbors at varying points in the district in order to get their opinions and recommendations. The various block meetings conducted by the committee revealed that the neighbors are more concerned with: (*a*) Clean streets. (*b*) Safety. (*c*) Recreation. (*d*) Enforcement of laws regarding sanitation and safety in housing. (*e*) Any change in their housing conditions would be an improvement. They were not clear as to what type of housing they would prefer, but if the area is improved they would like to continue living there; otherwise many would like to move.

The following suggested improvements have been arrived at:

1. The areas [here the area was described] are recommended to the redevelopment authority and the City Planning Commission for immediate replanning and redevelopment. [This area consisted of about 36 blocks.]

In making this recommendation the committee points out that much of the housing in this section is substandard. We need new houses and less crowding. The committee urges that in making new plans for this area, the standards for recreation adopted by the Neighborhood Planning Conference be kept in mind.

Furthermore, the committee suggests that vacant houses, of which it has a list, be used to temporarily house those whose homes will be torn down to be replaced by new ones.

2. The Neighborhood Planning Conference experimented with replanning the area bounded by Fitzwater, Fourth, Bainbridge and Sixth Streets. Recommendations for possible housing changes are demonstrated in the Bok model at the City Planning Exhibit.

3. Since our entire locality has all the indices of blight, the City Planning Commission should investigate the possibility of redeveloping the entire district in order to safeguard our historic sites as well as to make the district located closest to the center of the city inhabitable.

4. Since the district abounds with narrow alleys and little streets which are congested, these streets should be either blocked to traffic or redesigned in order to provide greater safety.

After adoption of the committee recommendations by the Neighborhood Planning Conference, they were presented with some ceremony to the City Planning Commission. As a result, some of the small items in the recommendations were achieved, and a few months later the area was certified by the City Planning Commission as a redevelopment area. The Neighborhood Planning Conference at this point had in effect achieved its first goal. The area had been certified for redevelopment and "grass roots" planning of a sort at least had taken hold. The leaders of the Conference felt, however, that to be effective the work should continue and that the interest that had been aroused should not be allowed to die. They attempted to secure enough funds to hire a professional worker and to put the Conference on a permanent basis, but were unable to raise the money.

The alternative decided upon was to transfer the duties and functions of the Conference to an existing organization, and the South Philadelphia Coordinating Council was the natural recipient. Thus it was given the job of seeing that the recommendations of the Conference were carried out. As a result of the Conference, however, the Coordinating Council became a much more representative organization.

Considerable dissatisfaction with the City Planning Commission was expressed over nonaction on the recommendations submitted. As a consequence, in June, 1949, the South Philadelphia Coordinating Council passed a resolution urging that the Planning Commission and the Redevelopment Authority "get into immediate action" and that a meeting be held shortly to determine the "possibility of housing developments in our district in the near future." The closing paragraph of the letter accompanying this resolution stated: "We are fearful of the let down and the sense of disappointment which is beginning to appear. If it is allowed to grow, it will defeat the purpose to which our organization has been dedicated and negate the work of several years in education and 'grass root' preparation for neighborhood change and improvement."

As this preliminary account by URS is being closed (early in 1950), the Planning Commission is in the process of preparing redevelopment plans, and an adequate program is expected to resume shortly.

Appraisals of the effectiveness of this particular approach to redevelopment depends, of course, on the part played in the undertaking by the appraiser. The staff of the Planning Commission looks upon the results of the Neighborhood Planning Conference with a different eye from that of one who was actually engaged in the work of the Conference. Generally, the Planning Commission staff have felt that the results of the Neighborhood Planning Conference were not too sound as planning recommendations, though they commend the interest aroused and the resulting participation. One more specific comment was that the proposals were either too large or too small.

On the one hand, Conference committees spent much too much time recommending individual lots for parking, designating street corners for traffic lights, etc., rather than working on redevelopment plans. These detailed recommendations were often unsound in that the cost involved in carrying them out would in no way have justified the small benefit received. For example, some parking lot recommendations would have permitted the parking of only a few cars, ten, and yet the cost to the city of acquiring the land and converting it into a parking lot would have been high. Staff members of the Planning Commission felt that the people who worked on reports and recommendations would have profited from the advice of technical men. They also felt that this attention to detail, though probably not a waste of time in all respects, was a waste as far as furthering redevelopment planning.

The Planning Commission staff also pointed out that the Conference had gone to the other extreme in recommending large, sweeping changes. There were two really large recommendations of the Conference; a park strip about five blocks long and one block wide, and a large area recommended for redevelopment. Within the proposed park strip were several historic structures that the Planning Commission hoped to keep. In addition, the Commission felt that the park strip was not well placed, that the area would be much better off with several small scattered park areas rather than one large park strip. The blocks recommended for this park strip contained both good and bad structures, some suitable for redevelopment, some for rehabilitation.

In short, the Planning Commission staff's opinion, with which few persons in similar positions would quarrel, was that the process itself was certainly valuable but that the people were unable to do the planning by themselves.

Those active in the Neighborhood Planning Conference, however, have held a different opinion and perhaps not really a contradictory one. Quite naturally they assess the results in a different light. Because they were responsible for the planning recommendations or at least had a part in their preparation, they are not likely to be critical of them. They accept them as valid and worth while. Their chief interest in the Conference was the extent to which it brought the people of the area into planning and how effective a means it proved to be in creating an understanding of the problems of redevelopment and planning. When looked at from this point of view, it would seem that the Neighborhood Planning Conference was an effective organization. A good many people in the area did become interested in redeveloping it, and they did learn something about planning and redevelopment. Most of these people have continued their interest in improving the area, and prompt action on some of their smaller recommendations has encouraged them to remain active.

The Neighborhood Planning Conference as a "grass roots" planning program has been described by Dr. Julian Greifer in *Survey Midmonthly* for December, 1947.[1] Since he was the leader of the Neighborhood Planning Conference, he might perhaps be a bit biased as to its effectiveness, but his comments seem modest and reasonable. It was a successful venture in "grass roots" planning. It undoubtedly could have

1. "Neighbors Meet the Experts," LXXXIII, 342.

been more effective, but it was an early experiment in this approach.

A summary evaluation of the effectiveness of this particular method would be that both the Planning Commission staff and Dr. Greifer were correct in their opinions. The actual planning left much to be desired, but the Conference proved an effective means of interesting people in their area and in encouraging them to be active in attempting to remedy bad conditions. The Conference changed an attitude of hostility to one of acceptance of redevelopment and, in fact, resulted in many of the people in the area actually asking that it be redeveloped. In light of the difficulty other cities have had in this respect, this is no mean accomplishment.

Poplar area.—Philadelphia's second experience in dealing with a redevelopment area requires little description. The Planning Commission admits that the technique used proved unsatisfactory, and this evaluation seems correct. It is included only to show the effects of the antithesis of the Neighborhood Planning Conference procedure.

The Poplar area is quite similar to the southeast area. It too contains much blighted property with 51 per cent of the residences in need of major repairs, without bath or plumbing facilities, or unfit for human habitation. Industrial uses are sprinkled throughout the area, and lot coverage is very high. Open space is provided only by lots made vacant by razed buildings, and this space is the repository of rubbish and filth. Overcrowding is evident.

The area is also mixed racially, to even a greater extent than the southeast central area. The Richard Allen Homes, a large public housing project, is in the area, and the intent is to redevelop around this core of good housing. (The Temple area in which another procedure was used and which is described in the following section is just north of the Poplar area.)

This area is also centrally located and close to industrial districts as well. Its eastern boundary is Broad Street, on which front many prosperous commercial establishments. The redevelopment plan stressed the advantage of this location.

In dealing with this area, the Planning Commission drew up a redevelopment plan based largely on observation of the characteristics and condition of housing and other land uses as well as some understanding of the place of this district in the pattern of the city. Consultation on what this plan should include was held with only a few people in the area; actually, the Planning Commission staff did all the planning.

Once the plan was prepared, the Planning Commission called in a local committee, which had been formed at the request of the Health and Welfare Council for the purpose of co-ordinating health and welfare activities in the area. The most active members of this committee were interested in redeveloping a particular block in the area.

At the meeting with this local committee, the Planning Commission explained the plan in some detail and asked the committee members for comments on it. The members had no background for criticizing or evaluating the proposal and, in fact, were able to make no comments at all. As one observer put it, "They merely gulped and accepted it." The Planning Commission, however, did try to work out some arrangement whereby the plan could be presented to the residents of the area at a large public meeting, and tentative arrangements were made for such a meeting. Unfortunately, however, these arrangements fell through, and the redevelopment plan was introduced to residents of the area by the newspapers.

The result was several phone calls from residents and businessmen who thought their homes or stores were to be demolished and they would have to move. No organized resistance has developed, but the people generally have the idea that nothing will be done anyway and, therefore, there is no need to worry. Knowledge of the proposed redevelopment plans by people in the area is very superficial.

At the time the redevelopment scheme was announced, there was no community organization behind the plans except the committee mentioned earlier, but plans are now under way to remedy this situation. In general, the Planning Commission feels that this approach was inadequate. Although the procedure was very similar to standard practice in many localities, it certainly leaves much to be desired.

Temple area.—From the Poplar area experience and that of the Neighborhood Planning Conference, the Philadelphia Planning Commission staff devised a technique that, in the opinion of many of its members, removes the unsatisfactory and includes the good qualities of the two earlier experiences. In essence it is a scheme whereby the people in the neighborhood participate in the planning process as it is carried on by the Planning Commission. Since the planners feel that this is the best procedure or method so far devised, in Philadelphia at least, it deserves a fairly detailed description.

The area in which this technique was tried is similar to the other areas in that it is close in, contains much blight, and is mixed racially. The area at one time consisted of large three- and four-story row houses that, in the course of time, were converted into multiple dwellings. In addition, the area is a conglomeration of uses, with commercial and industrial buildings sprinkled throughout the area. Many small storefront churches have been established and these too are located throughout the area. One large block is now a park and shortly is to be converted into a playground. There are two schools in the area and several large, substantial churches. Although none of the buildings is vacant, there is a fair amount of vacant land in the area. These vacant lots are those on which the buildings have been razed or destroyed but not replaced. A substantial proportion of these vacant parcels is concentrated in one section. The area is bounded by wide streets and railroad tracks. The major streets bounding the area are almost completely fronted with commercial establishments. Tap rooms are found throughout the area. About 90 per cent of the residents are nonwhite. A high percentage of the people are on relief. The area had been certified for redevelopment at the time this technique was undertaken.

To carry out the procedure it had in mind, the Planning Commission staff felt that there should be a local redevelopment committee for the area with which it could deal. It saw that a committee created by the Planning Commission would be suspect immediately as its creature or puppet. Fortunately, Philadelphia has an organization called the Conference on Area Planning, which is a "clearing-house for agencies at the city level which are concerned with the various phases of local planning."[2] Its membership includes many organizations that are directly concerned in local planning—the City Planning Commission, the Community Chest, the Board of Education, the Redevelopment Authority, the Citizens' Council on City Planning, the Philadelphia Housing Authority, the Philadelphia Housing Association, the Health and Welfare Council, and others. Its approval, therefore, carries considerable weight and prestige. The director of the Planning Commission raised the question of redevelopment activity in the Temple area at one of the meetings of the Conference. Those present agreed that the area office of the Health and Welfare Council would be a good means of bringing the local people together. After considerable discussion on just what should be done, the groups suggested that the Planning Commission request the assistance of the local area Health and Welfare Council office in calling a meeting of the people in the area who "can and will advise on the redevelopment of the area."[3]

With the approval of the Area Planning Conference, the director wrote the district office of the Health and Welfare Council that the Planning Commission was about to prepare a redevelopment plan for the area and that some of its staff members would like to meet with a small representative group of the area. He asked the local director of the area office of the Health and Welfare Council to call together a group of not more than twenty people, representing home owners, tenants, schools, neighborhood associations, retail business, church, in-

2. Conference on Area Planning, *Relationship between the Health and Welfare Council and the Citizens' Council on City Planning in Area Planning* (Philadelphia, February 26, 1948), p. 1.

3. "Minutes of Area Planning Conference," March 25, 1949 (Philadelphia), p. 3.

dustry, and real estate. He suggested that the meeting be devoted to (1) a discussion of the redevelopment plan, i.e., what it should be and (2) "the best means of maintaining continued contact with the various interests of the neighborhood." In forming the committee, the area Health and Welfare Council director found that many had the attitude that it would be of no purpose. They remembered previous redevelopment attempts that had been abortive. The response of one was, "Are we going to start that again? They call us together, get us all het up, and nothing happens."

At the first meeting of the committee, the director of the Planning Commission exhibited a map of existing land use in the area and told the committee that although the Commission had some ideas on how the area should be redeveloped, it did not wish to proceed with its plan until it learned what the people in the area thought should be done. He then explained what could be done under redevelopment and the tools available to the Redevelopment Authority in carrying out redevelopment plans.

The members of the committee then discussed some of the problems of the area, covering such fields as public housing and recreation. Several preliminary suggestions came from the meeting. The committee felt certain areas should be cleared and rebuilt and that both public and private housing should be included, that row houses rather than apartments were preferred, and that houses with gardens, even though close together, would be preferred to apartments. The meeting ended with the committee asking the Commission to prepare a redevelopment proposal for the area incorporating these ideas.

Before the next meeting, small scale maps of existing conditions in the area were prepared. These maps were distributed to committee members to aid them in discussing redevelopment recommendations at the meeting. Statistics on rents, population, dwelling units, income, etc., were distributed with these maps.

The Planning Commission absorbed as much information as possible from this meeting on what the people in the area wanted and prepared a redevelopment proposal for the area in which the ideas expressed at the meeting played an influential part. This was presented to the committee a few weeks later. In presenting it, the director of the Planning Commission made clear that the plan was only tentative and that it was subject to alteration.

This meeting was not too productive. Most of the time was spent on the question of whether a park in the area should be used for a redevelopment housing project. The question of public housing was also raised, and some members of the committee voiced objections. No clear decisions were reached, so the chairman appointed a subcommittee to study the tentative redevelopment plan and prepare recommendations on it.

This subcommittee met for four hours and hashed over the tentative plan thoroughly. Although the members of the subcommittee were generally favorably impressed with the scheme, they did not accept it completely. They went over it in great detail and drafted a series of recommendations. These recommendations were submitted to the entire committee, indorsed, and transmitted to the Planning Commission.

An analysis of the differences between the Planning Commission and the committee's recommendations on the proposed redevelopment indicates that for the most part they were quite minor. In some instances, the committee recommendations corrected omissions in the Commission's plan. The only major difference concerned a block that the Planning Commission had recommended for a park. The committee felt that it should remain as housing, and the Commission agreed to the suggestion. In commenting on the recommendations of the committee, the consultant on redevelopment for the Planning Commission stated that the recommendations of the committee were well made and that their differences with the Planning Commission were well taken. He added that their comments indicated they had gone into great detail in preparing their recommendations. It was his view that if the ideas of the committee were basically sound, they should be accepted by the Commission.

The Commission staff were quite willing to go along with the recommendations except on a few minor points. The next step, planned by the Commission but as yet not taken at the time this is written (early 1950), is to have the committee become active in explaining and "selling" the plan to the people in the area. The chairman of the committee feels that now is the time to develop community spirit. He would like to hold meetings in the area to inform the people of what has been done and what is planned. He would also like to expand the committee making each present committee member the chairman of a subcommittee on some phase of redevelopment. He feels strongly that those in the neighborhood should be influential in shaping the redevelopment plans for the locality.

The general idea behind this approach to redevelopment would seem excellent. One assumes that individually the people in the area do not have the technical training or time to do the planning of their area, but that they do have ideas and suggestions on what should be done. The Planning Commission draws out these ideas, fits them in with planning standards and existing conditions, and presents a plan to the people for their judgment. The relationship between the Planning Commission and the people in the area is that of an agency serving the people, trying to express their wishes where possible rather than telling them what is to be done. The principle seems a sound one from several points of view: (1) that the plan should reflect the ideas of the people in the area; (2) that representative people have knowledge about the ideas and characteristics of those who live in the area that the Planning Commission does not have; (3) that the people are more likely to accept the plan if it is thought of as their creation, and (4) that the people themselves are taking part in a democratic process in which they can see at least some of the effects of their activity.

Summary.—Although it is too early to assess the results of the Temple area approach, it would seem that the Planning Commission had hit upon an excellent technique based upon their experience with the Neighborhood Planning Conference and the Poplar area. Two questions that might be raised and that apply to the Neighborhood Planning Conference and the Poplar area as well as to the Temple area technique concern committee membership and timing of discussion on the redevelopment by the people in the area.

On the former, there is considerable need to determine how representative members of a committee should be. The whole question of leadership is an involved one, and this problem will be dealt with later on. Suffice to say that in the Temple area, committee members were selected by the area officeworker of the Health and Welfare Council and were primarily leaders in business and the professions. Most of them worked, but did not live, in the area.

On the second point, that of timing the discussion of redevelopment plans with the people of the area and by the committee itself, there seemed to be little time between the formation of the committee itself and the discussion of the proposed redevelopment plan. Although discussions are continuing between the Commission staff and the committee, it would seem that perhaps too little time elapsed between the formation of the committee and the discussion of what the plan should include. The members of the committee might have been given more time to analyze and compare notes on the area, its problems and needs, before going into the substance of a redevelopment program.

Whether this criticism has validity remains to be seen. The continuing discussion between the Planning Commission and the committee and the proposed program of extensive discussion of the redevelopment plan with the people in the area may accomplish the same, or perhaps, better results.

The major point of the Temple area approach, however, is that the people and the Planning Commission worked together in producing a plan rather than either working alone and then expecting the other to indorse and accept the result. This approach would seem to have promise as a means of using community organizations to bridge the gap in urban redevelopment between the planners and the people.

CHICAGO

Chicago has two types of community organizations. One consists of those established in connection with community chest and welfare services. As pointed out in the following section on Cleveland, this type offers interesting possibilities in the urban redevelopment process. The second type in Chicago is those organizations created specifically to help in redeveloping particular areas. They are discussed in this section.

The leading organizations of this kind in Chicago are the South Side Planning Board and the Near West Side Planning Board. Although they may seem somewhat similar to the Philadelphia organizations, they differ from them in several respects.

In the first place, neither was established through either the direct or indirect impetus of the City Plan Commission or the Land Clearance Commission (Chicago's redevelopment agency). Rather, they were created at the instigation of people and institutions in the local areas who were interested in preventing the continuation of blight and in redeveloping the areas.

A second difference between the Philadelphia and Chicago organizations is the type and amount of staff employed. In the Philadelphia organizations, the staff work was primarily secretarial—arranging meetings, recording minutes, and the like. The Chicago organizations, on the other hand, employ technicians to work on the planning of the areas. Men trained in planning are regular employees of the organizations, and it is their function to serve in a planning capacity. Availability of technical advice, therefore, is much greater in the Chicago than in the Philadelphia organizations.

A third major difference between the organizations in the two cities is the structure of the organization itself. The Chicago units are quite formally organized with boards of directors, dues, and so forth. Sets of by-laws govern their operations. The Philadelphia organizations, on the other hand, are rather loose associations of people in the area interested in getting something done.

The effect of the differences on the operation of the organizations will become apparent in the discussion of the Chicago efforts. The advantages and disadvantages of these differences will be analyzed in some detail when the experiences of all are summarized.

South Side Planning Board.—The South Side of Chicago had at one time been the fashionable spot to live and many large, substantial houses were built in the area, including those of such well-known family names as Armour, Swift, Pullman, and Field. These old houses, as they were vacated by the wealthier families after the onset of blighting factors—commerce, industry, traffic, noise, smoke, fumes—into the residential area, were subdivided into small, kitchenette units and rented to those of much lower income. Eventually, the area became almost completely blighted; and because of restrictive covenants elsewhere, it also became a Negro ghetto. Seventy-five per cent of those in the area are Negroes. The restrictive covenants also made the area extremely overcrowded. Many more people lived in the area than decent standards would allow.

The area is close to Chicago's "loop" (just a few minutes by public transportation) and also relatively close to the lake. Thus as to location it is a good area in which to live. It also contains some large and prosperous industrial establishments. As defined by the Board the area includes some 7 square miles and has a population of about 240,000 people.

Suggestions to do something to improve this area physically arose principally from the intentions of two large institutions in the area to modernize and expand their plant and facilities. Michael Reese Hospital had explored the possibility of moving to a completely new location. The cost of such a move was so great that the hospital board felt it would be far wiser to use funds in improving the present environment of its buildings. It created a planning staff to prepare for a private redevelopment of their campus area. The Illinois Institute of Technology, the second institution, had already embarked upon an expansion program. The two institutions, therefore, co-operated wholeheartedly in the planning of the surrounding community area. The amount of money available for reconstruction and new building activities was rather large, and it appeared that the institutions might be quite effective in achieving worth-while results.

As a result they joined forces and provided the initial leadership in bringing others into the community redevelopment program by creating the South Side Planning Board. The Board describes its beginning in this way:

The story of the origin of the Planning Board is an important factor in understanding its objectives and methods of operation. The Board was not organized by an individual or group. Its origin was in the spontaneous expression of individuals and organizations on the Central South Side. Its founders were people representing groups, businesses and labor unions, without regard to race, creed or color, who recognized the urgent need for replanning and redevelopment of an area which has great potentialities for the creation of a wholesome community life. These men from all walks of life realized that it is to the best interest of everyone to join efforts in furthering a program of redevelopment and to push that program to its fulfillment. They all realized that by working together more could be accomplished for the good of all. In the late spring of 1946 the group ended the first stage of organization by appointing an executive director and selecting a competent staff to carry out its program.[4]

This is perhaps "publicity license" since it gives the impression of a mass as well as "spontaneous" movement to create the Planning Board, and this is hardly what happened. Only community leaders and "important" people in the area were invited to the initial, exploratory meeting and had any part in the creation of the Board. In fact, community relations and participation, as will be seen, have been two of the Planning Board's most difficult problems.

The creation of the Planning Board, however, did not eliminate the planning staffs of the institutions. They continued their activity but, of course, became active members of the planning board.

Structurally, the Planning Board consists of a council of fifty members with an executive committee of sixteen selected from the Council. The members of the Council are all influential men. The institutions in the area are represented, of course, and most of the other members are heads of large firms in the area and the city at large. Part of the underlying *rationale* of this arrangement was that the problems of blight are not the sole concern of the present occupants of an area, but a community-wide responsibility. Thus the distance between the Board and the people in the area is considerably greater than was found in Philadelphia.

In 1950 the Land Clearance Commission signed contracts with the New York Life Insurance Company under which the commission will acquire, clear, and sell to the insurance company a 100-acre site in the area. The insurance company plans to erect several elevator apartment buildings and a few row houses. Although Negroes will be given priority in renting these apartments, Negroes in the area have opposed this move because they have felt that it is but a means of getting them out. The Chicago Housing Authority, however, has already built a housing project in the area, and most of its tenants will be Negroes.

Although the Planning Board has been aware of the need for community participation and the desirability of working with the people in the area, as indicated in the previous quote from the South Side Planning Board News, it has been unable thus far to get such a program under way. In a brochure published by the Board, under the heading "community planning" is this statement:

> To perform this essential research on social and industrial needs, it is important that we deal in what is known as community planning whereby the individuals and organizations in the area contribute their plans and desires to the development of a total plan. To plan a community without reference to the employment of the people is as bad a mistake as to plan industries without relation to the people to be

4. *South Side Planning Board News* (January, 1947), p. 2.

employed. For this purpose the South Side Planning Board is organized to obtain the best possible thinking from industry and the community on the needs, plans, and desires of the individuals and industries in the area.[5]

Although the Planning Board has always employed a well-qualified director of community relations, these good intentions have not been effectively put into practice. One who was active in the Board's program expressed the opinion that it should have spent its first year or two working with groups in the area in order to gain community support, but the shortage of money made this impossible. It was an initial decision to proceed with technical planning, although both phases should have gone ahead concurrently.

This failure in broadly based understanding and support was recognized in the Planning Board's minutes. They contain the following passage:

A brief review of the past two years activity in the Community Relations program indicated that desired results, primarily in terms of active citizen participation, had not materialized. A further review of specific community problems, attitudes of people in the community, political angles, and limited staff budget, indicated that the absence of desired results was not necessarily the fault of the Director of Community Relations, nor was the present situation being evaluated on any such personal basis. The matter was thus placed before the Board for a decision as to whether or not this staff function was to be continued as at present, or whether some other approach be initiated.[6]

A discussion of the problem at the same meeting brought forth the following comments:

Mr. . . . . expressed the view that the results achieved to date in terms of specific tangible accomplishments were practically non-existent and therefore a new approach must be worked out. Mr. . . . . pointed out many of the difficulties involved, including lack of political endorsement of the program, inability to express more or less long range planning in terms of "what will it do for me" interest of the average citizen. He also pointed out that a very important job had been done, however, primarily working through many of the South Side community organizations in securing a community reaction somewhat resigned to the fact that urban redevelopment did have some over-all benefits to the City as a whole, and that much of the overt opposition had dissipated. . . .

A motion was made and unanimously passed that Messrs. . . . . , . . . , and . . . submit a report with specific recommendations concerning a future program of community relations.[7]

A special report on the community relations problem was prepared in which the following analysis was offered.

5. *Your Investment in the South Side Planning Board Will Pay Dividends,* Chicago: South Side Planning Board (undated).

6. South Side Planning Board, Executive Committee, *Minutes of Meeting* (November 21, 1949), p. 2.

7. *Ibid.,* p. 3.

It was frankly admitted by all present that citizen interest and support for the program of the SSPB had not been secured as originally contemplated. The principal reasons outlined by Mr. . . . which have stymied the program to mobilize citizen interest and support were as follows:

1. That the very nature of the program of redevelopment, with initial emphasis upon large scale clearance and rebuilding, without adequate provision and safeguards being made for individual interests, has the appearance if not in fact being opposed to their personal interests.

2. That some political leaders of the local community have not yet endorsed or seen fit to support the planning objectives of the SSPB. And that while some have not spoken in direct opposition to the program, their silence has been construed to mean opposition.

3. That the immediate net effect of urban redevelopment operations in the South Side will reduce the number of total dwelling units, including privately owned homes, while there still exists an acute housing shortage. This shortage of housing operated to increase the difficulty which Negroes face in acquiring new homes, both within the predominant Negro residential areas as well as in other communities of the city where resistance has hardened against Negro families moving into predominantly white residential areas. Thus it is not likely that the SSPB will receive the credit that it will deserve for its several achievements until the community has become more and more aware of how these services actually benefit the welfare of the entire community.

4. That the limitations of budget and staff have not been sufficient to cope adequately with the tremendous problem, primarily educational, involved.[8]

From this analysis a conclusion was reached that might be, in part, a rationalization of the Planning Board's inability or failure to gain citizen participation:

The SSPB is a relatively new organization in the community. As such it is confronted with the problem of being "accepted" as part of the community "structure" in order to gain the citizen participation support ultimately required. In the first approach, the SSPB takes the "Back seat" to the extent that its role is to get the citizens to secure the projects required. In such a program the SSPB will receive little or no credit for gains made. Securing the credit is, of course, not the objective of the SSPB, but rather in getting the job done. However, without sufficient community support an initial practical approach of the SSPB requires that it be in a position to do things and gain credit to the extent that it become "accepted" as an integral part of the community.[9]

From this analysis and conclusion, several recommendations were made on changing the community relations approach:

1. That in view of present conditions and other limitations, the community relations program of the Board should be reoriented away from its present method of securing citizen interest and participation in a community wide planning program, to a program in which there shall be a series of improvement projects as a demonstration of what can be done to improve the community, and thus attract citizen interest and support.

8. South Side Planning Board, "Report to Executive Committee, Community Relations Program" (December 19, 1949), p. 2.

9. *Ibid.*, p. 3.

2. That such a program be a current planning function, in contrast to longer range planning objectives, including such activities of expediting interim playground locations, new schools, street and alley closings, better street lighting, improved safety and traffic regulations, enforcement of building code and other city ordinances, etc.

6. That as soon as successful projects have been demonstrated as a part of community planning and as the community gives growing evidence of its acceptance, the Board should take under consideration the desirability of resuming its program of securing direct community participation.[10]

The success of this new approach cannot be measured since it is just getting under way. The importance and difficulty of the problem of community relations, however, are well illustrated by the South Side Planning Board's experience. It recognized the need but because of several reasons was unable to secure the amount or kind of citizen participation it felt necessary for the success of a citizen's planning board.

Assessing the relations of the South Side Planning Board with the official city agencies—i.e., the Housing Authority, the Land Clearance Commission, and the Plan Commission—is somewhat more difficult particularly if an attempt is made to evaluate the influence of the South Side Planning Board on the policies of these agencies.

For example, when the Plan Commission staff began to analyze the South Side looking toward its redevelopment, it asked the South Side Planning Board for all the information it had acquired. It also asked the Board to review the reports of the Plan Commission on the South Side when they were issued. This exchange worked the other way as well for the Planning Board staff asked and received from the Commission all of the data it had on the area. The staffs of the two agencies know each other and at times have worked together.

This co-operation, however, has not extended to agreement on redevelopment policies for the area. In fact, the Board has objected with some heat to proposals of the Plan Commission. Some differences have become public controversies with the result that some antagonistic feelings have developed between the agencies.

These differences, however, do not mean that the opinions or plans of one agency have not had some influence on those of the other. Without trying to ascertain who influenced whom, there is evidence that the two agencies have come to agreement on certain matters. Probably a fair statement is that the resulting program for the South Side is different from a program that would have been prepared by either agency acting completely by itself. In this sense, therefore, one can say that the South Side Planning Board has had considerable influence upon the Plan Commission's redevelopment policy for the South Side.

In contrast to the relations between the Board and the Plan Commission, the relation between the Planning Board and the Land Clear-

10. *Ibid.*, p. 1.

ance Commission have been on a much friendlier basis. Personnel from each staff has assisted the other, and the two agencies seem to have fewer differences than the Board and the Plan Commission. These differences also are of much less magnitude or seriousness. Perhaps some of this is due to the fact that the first urban redevelopment project in Chicago, which is on the South Side, was fairly well fixed in location and character before the South Side Planning Board could say much about it. This project, however, was in harmony with the general community plan developed by the Board. Also, individuals responsible for the creation of the South Side Planning Board played principal roles in interesting the redevelopers in undertaking this project. One further reason, and an important one, is that during much of the period covered by this review the chairman of the South Side Planning Board was president of the Illinois Institute of Technology and also vice-chairman of the Chicago Land Clearance Commission.

In its relation with official organizations, therefore, the South Side Planning Board has not been without influence. Its influence, however, has been both in the nature of a "gadfly" as well as a "behind the scenes persuader."

In brief, the South Side Planning Board is an example of a local organization attempting to improve a badly run-down area. It is limited, however, to what one might call top-level participants and thus it does not represent, directly at least, the people in the area. It is removed from them and so does not necessarily reflect their interests and ideas. Although the plans and accomplishment of the Board may prove to be competent and valuable, criteria on which they have been based have been those of the technical planners and the Board. Whether they will be able to meet the needs and desires of the people in the area, or elsewhere for that matter, is not yet known.

Near West Side Planning Board.—The near West Side is an old area also close-in to the central business district. The Board is primarily concerned with an area of 1.7 square miles and a population of some 55,000. By elevated, it is less than ten minutes from the central part of the loop. It is similar to the South Side area in other respects as well. Industrial and commercial uses are sprinkled throughout the area and mixed with residences. Many residences are substandard and unfit for human habitation. Racially, the area contains nearly every nationality and race. Negroes, Mexicans, Greeks, and Italians predominate. Each of these and other groups has its own restaurants, customs, and small neighborhoods. It is typical of areas that sociologists have described as in transition. Waves of various groups have come to and left the area, but this constant movement slowed down about twenty years ago. Most of the people are poor, but many middle-income groups live in the area as well. One of the important agencies in the area is Hull House, the world-famous settlement house, around which attempts to better the community have centered.

The Near West Side Planning Board is a newer organization than its counterpart on the South Side. It was not created until the summer of 1949 although preparatory work preceded its creation by about a year and a half. It had its beginning as a delegation from the West Side Community Committee, a local committee of residents interested in the well being of their area. The committee went to the director of Hull House and asked what could be done about preventing the further deterioration of the near West Side. A temporary committee was formed to explore the subject.

This group consisted of Hull House board members, industry and business leaders, social agency people, and local residents. They hired a director and called themselves the Temporary Organizing Committee for Redevelopment of the Near West Side. Their aim was to create a Near West Side Planning Board to plan for and direct the redevelopment of the area, but they felt that much spade work should be done first to get the people and groups in the area interested in doing something and aware that something could be done.

The temporary organizing committee of twenty-two members was expanded gradually through subcommittees to about sixty-five as it began its work in interesting individuals and local groups in the work. By the time the organization meeting for the planning board was held, the work of the committee was well known in the area.

The objective of the organizing committee was to include as many local groups and as many individuals as possible in thinking about and contributing to the redevelopment of the area. The executive director of the Near West Side Planning Board stated this intent in his report on the activities of the committee. He said:

> The Committee, after long and careful discussion, has concluded that what it wants to sell to the people of the Near West Side is the IDEA OF PLANNING AND A PLANNING ORGANIZATION. The Committee has no plan, the Committee thinks that a plan made by the finest experts cannot be a successful one, unless based on a combination of local facts and desires, on the participation of as many as possible of those affected, and on the general plans of the city as a whole. The Committee thinks that to evolve such a plan is the work of many, many months. For these reasons the Committee is forced to its conclusion that it is the *steps toward planning* and the *organization for planning* that it wishes to establish, with the help of the community.
>
> The planning organization they propose is to be widely representative of all types of people sincerely interested in the future of the area. It seems to the Committee that anyone in the area must be free to participate and assist in the work of the

planning organization to the full extent of his interest and abilities regardless of the size of his dollar investment in the area.[11]

By "the people of the area" the committee meant not only the great body of residents but also the businessmen and larger property owners. Because of their influence, both through money and prestige, the committee worked with them closely to get them interested in the work. They are not unsuccessful in this approach, and many businessmen of the area cooperated with the committee fully during its organizational phase.

The importance of this early period of education, exploration, and discussion cannot be overstressed. The basic assumption was that redevelopment of the area is basically unsound unless it has support on a broad base. The temporary committee quite surely could have created an organization much sooner than it did by intensifying its approach to the businessmen and large firms. This organization could have made plans and perhaps could have had some of them accepted and executed, but the plans would not have reflected the ideas and needs of the people in the area. The proposals would not have had their understanding, participation, or approval.

The committee also thought the area should be redeveloped not for some group that lived outside the area but primarily for the people already living there. It wanted the area to be redeveloped for different kinds of people: not to be a "one-class" neighborhood. The report of the director of the temporary committee makes this very clear:

There is an assumption that poor people only live in this neighborhood. This assumption is false. There are, of course, many poor people, but when original applications were taken for the Jane Addams Houses in 1937, for instance, many more people were rejected because their incomes were too high than were accepted for admission. To rebuild this area with low-rent housing would be to create a one class neighborhood, which is bad, and to house only a small portion of those who already live here, which is worse. To carry out, on the other hand, proposals to rebuild the neighborhood with luxury housing at rents from a hundred monthly and up, so loop professional people can live where they can walk to work, is equally bad for the same reasons. The Committee feels a truly representative community planning effort will seek provision for some of all types of housing to meet the economic needs of the families who now live in the area and whose incomes are from low through medium and middle to high and even very high.[12]

The efforts of the temporary organizing committee paid off when it finally held its organization meeting. For weeks the meeting was advertised through posters, circulars, and other media all of which em-

11. Eri Hulbert, *Report of the Introductory Meeting of the Temporary Organizing Committee for Redevelopment of the Near West Side, January 25, 1949* (Chicago: Hull House), pp. 13–14.
12. *Ibid.*, p. 14.

phasized its importance to the people in the area. Five hundred people turned out for the meeting, and they were probably as good a cross-section of the population of the area as could be assembled. The meeting was well organized. The machinery for the creation of a Near West Side Planning Board and the election of members to its board was set up prior to the meeting. Before this election, the purpose of the organization was explained by the executive director of the temporary organizing committee. After his address, the meeting was opened to the floor for questions, and the questions asked indicated that those present had a much greater understanding of what it was all about than one might have guessed. Those asking the questions were not planted nor were they the best educated or the best off financially in the audience. The questioners were Negroes, Mexicans, Italians; they were shabbily and well dressed; some spoke fluently and some with heavy accents; they were shy and humble, militant and aggressive. They were everybody and anybody.

One question was, "It takes large amounts of money to rebuild. Who will finance?" Another, "What will happen to the people when a public housing project is built?" And another, "Does the present relocation housing program provide enough housing to meet the needs?" Another wanted to know, "Speaking of planning and following some of your previous remarks, you mean to say that in rebuilding the area the citizens that live within this area ought to take their earnings to rebuild this district?" Another was concerned about zoning: "What are you going to do about the present zoning that is established for industrial and business areas?" And a very basic question, "Can a Planning Board succeed in an occupied, established community?"[13]

These were questions asked by people who had a deep interest in their community and a desire to do something about improving it. They were acting as individuals who recognized their right to take part in the planning and development of their neighborhood. They were not likely to become fearful about their future because of seeing an item in the papers about the possibility of the redevelopment of their neighborhood. They were beginning to take advantage of the opportunity to inform themselves of what was going on and to take some part in the work to be done. The groundwork had been laid for successful redevelopment in the community.

It is yet too early to evaluate the work of the Near West Side Planning Board. It has just begun its work. The approach, however, appears to set a good example of the groundwork necessary for successful community participation in redevelopment. It is not an overnight job; it

13. All questions are quoted from Near West Side Planning Board, *Proceedings of the Public Meeting*, June 15, 1949, Riis School, 1018 S. Lytle Street, pp. 6–7.

takes time and effort. The process is not at all suitable for quick plans or rapid redevelopment. It seems promising, however, for long-term programs.

Summary.—The two local area organizations in Chicago differ radically in their approach. It is unfortunate that their recent creation precludes a thorough evaluation of their work and results. Generally, however, the consensus of those in official and nonofficial organizations interested in redevelopment in Chicago is that the Near West Side Planning Board has used the better approach. All agree that the Near West Side Planning Board is really a people's organization. It is based upon the interests of those who live and do business in the area and who look upon their Planning Board as a tool for improving it. The South Side Planning Board, on the other hand, is an organization "from the top down." It is built around prominent institutions and the larger industries. It is not an organization created by the people to make their neighborhood more livable.

The point might well be raised, however, whether the policy followed by the South Side Planning Board was not really a wise one in light of its conditions and makeup. This does not preclude the possibility that it would have been wiser and more effective if more concern had been shown for the needs and ideas of many groups that were in fact ignored and if the physical planning had waited a few months for a broader and more democratic base.

An interesting comment on the two organizations and their techniques or approaches was made by the director of one of the official agencies in the city. He pointed out that the fact that the Near West Side Planning Board was so close to the people made it vulnerable to movements by local politicians to prevent redevelopment. In at least one instance this is what happened in Chicago. Eventually, it may work out for the best, but for a short time at least the Near West Side Planning Board staggered from a body blow—the belief that it was aligned with, or was being taken over by, a political group anxious to forestall redevelopment in the near West Side area. Such attempts to prevent redevelopment are based, of course, upon the fear of such groups that the character of their constituency will be changed and that their political influence, therefore, will be diminished if not completely eliminated.

On the other hand, however, the South Side Planning Board, which is certainly an "aloof" organization from the standpoint of real contacts with the people, runs no danger of becoming so involved. It states its position emphatically and does not have to worry about it being changed. Whether this is a real or only an apparent advantage must await the verdict from further experience and results.

CLEVELAND

Cleveland's experience on this front in redevelopment differs markedly from both Chicago's and Philadelphia's. These two cities have organizations aimed at redevelopment planning and action; that is the reason for their existence. Cleveland, on the other hand, has no redevelopment organizations per se, but it does have community organizations that can serve as vehicles for redevelopment education and planning. In fact, these organizations have served as advocates and encouragers of rehabilitation, cleaning up areas, fixing up the houses, and similar steps toward physical improvement. To them this would be a far cry from redevelopment because to them as to most people the term conveys a picture of vast areas of toppling slums with shining new structures rising to take their place.

The value of the Cleveland experience is to demonstrate that some cities already have community organizations that may be used for redevelopment purposes, and that resources in these organizations should not be overlooked. Cleveland is perhaps a bit further advanced than most cities in this respect, but it is a good example of what is available, more or less, in other cities. Other cities could probably have been used as examples almost as well, and their absence from this account does not mean that their programs are not as far along or as adaptable to use in the redevelopment process as the work in Cleveland.

In Cleveland, the local community organizations are under the aegis of the Welfare Federation of Cleveland. The relationship of the Federation to these area councils, as they are called, can best be stated by the Federation itself:

> The Tremont Civic Association was one of the first officially organized Area Councils in the community and has been in existence about eleven years. Since that time, approximately twenty-five other Area Councils have been organized, sixteen of which are affiliated with the Welfare Federation's Committee on Area Councils. The purpose of this committee is to serve as a clearing-house and exchange of programs for the Area Councils.
>
> The Welfare Federation has recognized responsibility for cooperating with Area Councils. Insofar as it has been possible. field work service is provided by the Welfare Federation to the affiliated Area Councils.[14]

The operation and purpose of these area councils are well described in a study of their organization and function. This study was requested by the Welfare Federation in order to assess the role area councils should play and also to establish a more definite relationship with the Federation.

14. Cleveland Welfare Federation, *Area Councils Affiliated with the Welfare Federation Committee on Area Councils* (1949), p. 3.

In discussions with the committees, staff and representatives of Area Councils, there seemed to be agreement of the following basic principles in regard to the organization and operation of Area Councils:

1. Citizen participation is increasingly important in planning for the health, welfare, recreation, education and civic need of the community. When citizens have a democratic voice in creating, shaping and developing the programs of organizations and agencies designed to meet their needs they develop an understanding of the potentialities and limitations of these services which should lead to their better use and more adequate support.

2. Area Councils should be autonomous organizations, free to act in their own name on any community issue without control from a sponsoring body. If the action of Area Councils is subject to the approval of the board of any sponsoring organization, the Councils run the risk of being considered only a mouthpiece and thus lose their ability to serve the people as an effective voice with public officials, newspapers or other channels to the general public.

3. Area Councils should have consultant staff service by workers qualified through both professional training and experience in community organization. The role of the worker in bringing together in effective working relationship the diverse interests of organized groups within a small segment of the community requires special skills in interpersonal and intergroup relations. Through the Area Council, individual groups are helped to achieve status and prestige while working jointly with other organizations on special aspects of mutual problems. It is important also that the worker should have knowledge of community resources, the ability to conduct social studies on a scientific basis, a major interest in and ability to work with citizens and citizens' groups in such a way as to enable them to take leadership roles in determining and directing the programs of the Councils. The worker should also have a strong conviction of the importance of citizen responsibility for community planning and an ability to interpret the function of professional social work to citizen groups.

4. There should be formal channels between Area Councils and the Welfare Federation and other citywide planning bodies, to facilitate mutual exchange of information, guides on policies and joint planning on matters of mutual concern.[15]

It should be made clear that in Cleveland these community councils are not creatures of the Welfare Federation. The Federation has ties with the councils through the area workers who are employees of the Federation and thus there is some limitation to their actions. The Federation, however, in no way controls the area councils themselves; they are autonomous. The area councils, however, feel the need for attachment to some neutral, high-status, city-wide organization such as the Federation; and they have gravitated toward it. Several of the area councils have taken out membership in the Welfare Federation along with many other civic and service organizations in the community.

As a result, the community councils are by now considered a rather important part of the Federation. In fact, they have created a problem

15. Violet M. Sieder, *Study of Area Councils of the Welfare Federation of Cleveland,* Health and Welfare Planning Department, Community Chests and Councils of America, Incorporated, July 10, 1949, pp. 1–2. Although this is a confidential report, permission was given to quote these passages.

for the Federation in deciding just how much of the Federation's funds should be used for area workers.

For purposes of this inquiry, however, the details of the relationship between the Federation and the area councils are relatively unimportant. The important consideration is the way in which the councils serve their communities and how well suited they are as a vehicle in planning and carrying through an urban redevelopment program. A feature of these area councils that helps make them effective is their association with the Federation. It may be argued that, if area or community councils in any city are to be effective media for urban redevelopment, it is best that they be more than *ad hoc* organizations. They should have a status in the community and should be aware of and deal with all or, at least, many of the problems of the neighborhood, so that urban redevelopment proposals may be evaluated as contributions to the neighborhood welfare.

Another feature of the Cleveland setup that adds to its effectiveness is the Committee on Area Councils. This committee consists of representatives of the councils along with some Federation representatives and acts as a clearing house on area council matters. The association of members of various area councils to discuss their common problems and to criticize proposed programs counteracts any feeling or tendency toward isolation and encourages each council to think of its problems in terms of city-wide needs and considerations. The existence of an organization of area council representatives also gives the councils a status they might not otherwise enjoy.

The area councils themselves differ to some degree in their function and organization. This is to be expected in any city because of the personalities of the area workers and the differing character of the areas and their residents. In Cleveland, there has been some disagreement as to whether the councils should be (1) a council for all the professional workers in an area, i.e., health, welfare, etc., (2) a council of representatives of organizations in an area, or (3) an individual membership organization open to anyone in an area who is interested. As it has worked out, the councils have become, in effect, all three with different councils emphasizing different characteristics. There seems to be a trend, however, for these councils to gravitate toward the second classification—a council of representatives of organizations in the area. Membership at present consists of both organizations and individuals. Organizations include the PTA's, churches, women's clubs, local businessmen's groups, girl scouts, veterans groups, and local units such as block or street groups.

The area workers in the Cleveland area councils have functioned at times as leaders in the councils rather than as consultants. They have become identified with the areas in which they work and have come to act as spokesmen for them. They have assumed leadership because local leadership on a particular issue was not forthcoming. There is serious question, however, as to whether this should be the function of the area worker and whether it does not, in fact, lessen the effect and change the concept of the function of community councils.

In size, the areas served by area councils vary from a population of 20,000 to over 100,000. These are admittedly large areas, and some of the councils have tried to counteract the difficulties that go with size by developing street or neighborhood organizations, these units to be affiliated with the area councils. The councils, though not covering the entire city, do reach the larger part of the population.

As mentioned previously, the councils have in effect complete local autonomy. They have acted independently and have often been outspoken in their criticism of government action. Their programs cover almost every item of civic interest, ranging from housing to adequate street lighting, police protection, and state legislation. Any civic problem that affects their area is likely to be within their program, though they may not be able to take action on every one of the issues.

In order to be more effective in their work, the councils break down into committees, which deal with such subjects as recreation, health and education, home conservation, and public safety. Temporary committees are formed to cope with special problems as they arise. Generally, the area councils have maintained very good relations with city departments and call upon them for information. It has worked the other way too in that city departments make use of the area councils in discussing zoning and other matters that affect their districts.

The operation of three of these area councils was discussed at some length with their area workers in order to determine how effective they might be in an urban redevelopment program. In studying these area councils, particular attention was given to (1) the kind of an educational or information job they performed in their communities; (2) the degree to which the people in the area participated in the program; and (3) the extent or nature of their relations with the various governmental departments, particularly with the Planning Commission because in Cleveland the Planning Commission will play its full role in redevelopment.

Reaching the people.—On the first phase of the inquiry, the educational and information aspects of the council, one area council worker said that the people in the council have become familiar with the basic elements of local problems as the council developed. At first, they were concerned with very small items, but as they continued working with their problems their breadth of vision grew. As an example of this, the worker cited the action the council took after a woman in the area had been attacked. The first reaction of the group was that more street lights were needed. Then they realized that the number of degenerates on the street was part of the problem and eventually developd an interest in the state program for mental hygiene. Thus they progressed from looking at the problem as purely a local matter to recognizing its broader aspects. In fact, a council representative appeared before a committee of the state legislature in support of proposed legislation on mental hygiene.

Also at first, the local representatives on the council were quite impatient. They expected results to be forthcoming overnight. As they became more familiar with various problems and went into them more deeply, they lost a good bit of their impatience. One area worker stated, however, that it was necessary that their activity show some results before very long or the people lost interest.

In another area, the area worker discussed the council's work in explaining housing legislation. A housing committee of the area council was formed, and it organized housing mass meetings in the community. The purpose was to inform the people on housing needs and possibilities. This committee also tried to keep the people up-to-date on housing legislation. Street and neighborhood clubs, of which there are quite a few in this area, were asked to send representatives to this committee so that its work would be as widespread as possible. A major problem has been to make the people realize that housing will not be produced overnight. It has been difficult to keep the people working in, and enthusiastic over, housing when the aims of housing and urban redevelopment are so slow in being realized.

Another area council has used a different tack in reaching the people in the area. The area worker has been concentrating on the formation of street or block organizations, each organization to be affiliated with the area council. Where such organizations have been set up, they have been a stimulus to improving the looks of the yards and houses on the street. These street organizations also have proved an excellent recruiting ground for local leadership. New talent, so to speak, is uncovered. Men who took but a passing interest in such affairs have become quite interested in their community when given an opportunity to do something to improve it. When there is no channel through which local leadership can operate, there is little opportunity for it to rise and develop. Providing such channels, therefore, should be a major purpose of the community organization.

The concomitant of informing and reaching the people is the acquisition of information from the people on their attitudes and wants. In Cleveland, the area council workers who were interviewed indicated that this was one of their important functions and pointed out the usefulness of such information to them in their dealings with public agencies on community problems. The area workers were also strongly of the opinion that plans for the community would be much better if they reflected the attitudes and desires of the people and if they were partly the product of community participation. As one area worker (Donald Stier of the Glenville Area Council) put it: "Group discussion, investigation by people, will produce better plans in terms of human needs than plans of experts. If you can develop ways of finding it and getting it expressed through group discussion and so forth, there is more wisdom in a group of people than in a single individual no matter how expert his technical knowledge."

Extent of community participation.—The experience of the three area councils studied shows, as one might expect, that those citizens who are active are those who are, for the most part, better off financially or better educated than many others in their communities. The members of the board for each of the area councils are those whom one would consider leaders of the area because of their profession (ministers, lawyers, doctors), their business (owners or managers of relatively large businesses in the area), or their professional interest in the area (social workers, managers of housing projects). The small tenants, landlords, businessmen, and similar people are often represented in some way, but the former group is the influential one. This is not in any way astonishing, since every organization must have leadership and it is natural for those who have received recognition in other fields to become leaders here.

It does raise a question, however, of whether prominence in another field qualifies one as a leader in a community organization and whether the residents of the area might not look upon many of these individuals as unsuited to represent their interests. In other words are these prominent individuals leaders—do they have followers? This is a question that cannot be answered here, but it should be considered carefully when looking for leaders to head a community council. A community council bent upon securing as extensive participation as possible might often find that some persons not previously thought of as leaders have considerable qualities of leadership and, if given a chance to exert them, might well increase the amount of participation because of the regard in which they are held by people in the area. An example might be a local factory owner, a leader certainly in at least one sense, but one whom most people in the area, particularly if employed by him, might reject as unable to represent their interests. A local labor leader in the factory, however, might well be considered a far more acceptable spokesman of the people's interests, and his elevation to a position of leadership in the council could well convince many that their interests lay with it. This, however, is only one possible example. The point is simply that local leadership usually is not confined to one segment of a community nor to one set of professions or vocations. Neither is it synonymous with prominence or wealth.

In the area councils in Cleveland as in other cities, the emphasis on board membership has been to represent all professions and groups rather than using local acceptance or recognition as a criterion for leadership. Use of such men adds prestige and importance to the council in some quarters, particularly with public bodies, and it is certainly necessary that their interests in the area be represented. But most councils have relied heavily upon this type of representation and spent relatively little time seeking out those who qualify as real leaders among the people themselves.

In Cleveland, one of the most promising developments toward greater public participation in the work of area councils is the recent encouragement of local street or block organizations mentioned earlier. This small neighborhood approach brings the problems a citizen must confront down to an understandable scale. Many persons feel more competent to speak on matters concerning their block than on area-wide or city-wide problems. Also their interest in block or street matters often will exceed their interest in problems of larger areas. Interest in the immediate block, however, can serve as apprenticeship, so to speak, for the problems of the larger areas. Many block problems, after all, are but city problems on a small scale. This procedure should develop greater public participation.

Liaison with public bodies.—The extent to which the Cleveland area councils have worked with public bodies, particularly the Planning Commission, is important in this discussion. If they are to serve as vehicles for community participation in the urban redevelopment process, this should be a fair test of their suitability. The area councils were not formed for the express purpose of channeling the ideas of the community to public bodies; but as they grew and took up issues involving action by the city, they of necessity had to deal with public bodies, particularly departments of the city government. On matters of zoning, they found it necessary to appear before the zoning commission to support their positions. In this process, they had to learn something about the operation of government and much about zoning itself. This also applied to other fields in which they became interested—recreation, traffic, street lighting, schools. Thus the area councils have come to have a considerable familiarity with governmental organization, procedures, and personnel and also a considerable body of knowledge on local governmental affairs.

Official agencies have also used the area councils although not to the extent that they might. The city departments have consulted them on recreation, schools, and zoning matters; but the relationship has been periodic or even spasmodic rather than continuing.

One area worker stated that city and state officials have been very co-operative, particularly the Planning Commission, in submitting material and discussing plans with the area council. As an example, the area worker cited the experience of the area council and the Planning Commission working out a recreational program for the district. The council compiled considerable statistical information on the area's recreation needs and facilities and from this prepared detailed recreation plans. At this stage, it asked the Planning Commission to submit its recreation plans for the area to the area council, and the Commission agreed to do so. The two plans agreed fairly well, and the Planning Commission and the area council were able to agree on sites for playgrounds.

This same area worker said that the Planning Commission had used the area council to find out what the people in the area wanted and as a means of public presentation of plans concerning the area. As an example of the former, he cited the zoning ordinance. Because of Planning Commission discussion with the area councils on the new zoning ordinance, the ordinance now contains a zoning classification that reflects their ideas and suggestions.

An example of the use of area councils as a means of presenting Planning Commission proposals was cited by another worker. He said that the area council arranged a meeting at which the Planning Commission presented its general plan for the area. Unfortunately, the turnout was small, probably, according to this area worker, because the average resident finds it difficult to see the relationship between a general plan for a large area and his immediate concerns. Another area worker stated that the area council decides on what items they need information and submits a request to the Planning Commission. The information is then prepared for the council. Also, the Planning Commission has made it clear to the area councils that staff members and material are available to them whenever needed.

This is evidence, of course, that some liaison exists between the area councils and public bodies, but indications are that it could be exercised more frequently and perhaps more intensively than it has.

Summary.—The area councils in Cleveland provide an excellent vehicle for community participation in the urban redevelopment process. They have acquired a recognized status in the community and have learned the ropes of community organization and public participation. They have a history of interest in civic affairs, with much of the emphasis on planning, and have dealt with public bodies. They have established liaison with the Planning Commission and will automatically take part in any redevelopment, rehabilitation, or conservation proposal affecting their areas. Their value to the Planning Commission in ascertaining the attitudes, needs, and wants of the people in redevelopment areas is great, and the Planning Commission is in a good position for an active program of continuing and intensive use of the area councils for this purpose.

Not every city undertaking redevelopment will have such ready-made community organizations, but many will. The job of public participation can be eased considerably if these channels are available and if the redevelopment agency does not have to set up or encourage new community organizations. The latter procedure is seldom, if ever, satisfactory because such organizations are likely to be suspect, particularly in the crucial early days of a program.

Conclusions

The experience of community organizations in these three cities is insufficient, of course, to provide a set of policies and principles on public participation in the urban redevelopment process. Problems, personalities, and structure vary so much from city to city that no one program or procedure on this front could be recommended for all. In addition, the experience in these three cities is incomplete; the effects of the approach in each is only partially known; more time is needed to evaluate the effectiveness of their work.

Their experience, however, is of some use. Rather broad principles on the place of community organizations in redevelopment can be suggested and at least a few tentative conclusions on what to do and what not to do can be assembled.

By this time, the need for community organizations has been stated rather fully but can bear repeating.

First of all, they are a means of dealing with groups in redevelopment areas, assuaging their fears, explaining the program, at least lessening their resentment at being "pushed around" and inconvenienced. This may mean the difference between acceptance and nonacceptance of a project. Community opposition has killed many a project, and most of this opposition has been based on uninformed and misinformed people who feared they were to be displaced with no thought to their welfare. And all too often this opposition has been aggravated and directed by those who used local organizations and associations successfully whereas the planners and redevelopers did not.

Secondly, collaboration with a community organization will permit a planning or redevelopment agency to ascertain the ideas of the community on how the area should be redeveloped. By tapping this source, the agency may be able to produce better plans for the area and certainly plans more acceptable to the residents. And again, those who are opposed to redevelopment, whether for personal, political, or other reasons, have too often made effective use of local, uninformed opinions and appeals because they "got there first"—whether with or without "the mostest."

And the third basic reason for this approach is that if one believes in local participation in the planning process, then this is an excellent opportunity to put his beliefs into practice. Everyone, it seems, gives lip service at least to democratic participation in planning, agreeing that this is the only way we will obtain a broad base and acceptance of planning. When it comes to actual practice, however, one finds that some planners reject the idea, feeling that the process is too slow and the results unimpressive. The philosophical support for local participation in planning, however, is still impressive and difficult to refute. As one writing about area councils in Cleveland put it:

> The need for a broader base of participation in social planning has been more and more evident as study of community service problems has carried thinking back into the level of prevention of need for services. Attack on basic community problems requires broad community understanding and united community action.
>
> Furthermore, as public programs which require the vote of the people increase, broad community understanding is required. . . . It is probable that this kind of understanding will be improved as more people share in thinking out their problems and in aiding in the formulation of the plans which go before the people for support.[16]

Once the decision to work with community organizations has been reached, several problems arise, and the experience of the three cities can be called upon for partial solutions.

CREATION OF COMMUNITY ORGANIZATIONS

The first problem is obvious: How are community organizations set up for their part in the urban redevelopment process? In general, the answer is to use those organizations, if any, that are available. The degree to which such organizations have developed varies among cities, and the redevelopment agency must be the judge of whether those now in operation are suitable for redevelopment purposes. If they are similar to Cleveland's, they are usable.

If none have been established, or if they are so weak or ineffective as to be of no use, then steps must be taken to create them. This is a

16. W. T. McCullough, "Observations about the Area Council Movement" (Cleveland, September, 1947).

step that requires thought and care or else the local organization may be open to the charge of serving merely as a façade for the official agency, a rubber-stamp operation. The Area Planning Conference as the sponsoring or initiating agency in Philadelphia has much merit, because the Conference contains representatives from all of the organizations interested in neighborhood planning. In the formation of the Temple Area Redevelopment Committee, the Area Planning Conference requested the formation of the local committee.

Philadelphia was fortunate also in having a health and welfare worker in the area who could act as a secretary to such an organization and assume the responsibility of selecting members of the committee. This arrangement made full use of available personnel and other resources.

In cities that lack this kind of start, the responsible agencies must devise different means. If they search diligently, they probably will find some city-wide or local organization to undertake the task. If not, they will have to seek out local leaders and persuade them to create an area redevelopment committee—by this or some other name.

The problem of setting up a community organization presents technical and financial problems that often are too great to be overcome by the neighborhood. Mr. A. F. Metz, president of the Passaic-Bergen Community Planning Association, has pointed out this difficulty and suggested a means of solving the problem. In a letter of September 30, 1949, he said:

> It is my opinion that successful citizens' participation requires the support of volunteer organizations such as ours, which can provide professional technical assistance, including professional citizen organizers. This requires funds from those groups in the community in a position to finance the organization and aware of the importance which planning represents for the welfare of everyone. Although whatever leadership is available in blighted areas must be drawn upon, it seems to me practically impossible for citizens in blighted areas to organize by themselves without the necessary professional staff.

A city-wide organization willing to foot the bill for professional workers in neighborhood community councils is not always available. Those interested in forming neighborhood councils, therefore, must often look to other sources.

One means a neighborhood community organization may try in financing a professional worker is to share the expense with an adjacent area that is also interested in forming such a group and in employing a professional secretary or organizer. In Cleveland, the Federation has followed this policy by assigning its workers to two area councils. Thus more areas are served, and the cost remains the same.

An advantage of this arrangement, other than the obvious one of saving money, is, according to a spokesman of the Cleveland Federation, that it is a deterrent to the area worker's identifying himself too closely with the area in which he works. In Cleveland identification sometimes has become so complete that the area worker has become the spokesman for, and leader of, the local council. This, of course, is not in keeping with the functions of an area worker or organizer.

PREPARATORY WORK OF COMMUNITY ORGANIZATIONS

In the search for or the organization of a local community council for urban redevelopment, action should begin well in advance of actual redevelopment proposals. One cannot expect community organizations to become familiar with the field or to reach intelligent decisions on redevelopment plans when they have had insufficient time to study the problems of the area. A period of study of the subject and of the area, including discussions with the people on what is wanted and what is needed, is necessary. In his book, *The Small Community Looks Ahead*, Wayland J. Hayes states that, ". . . groups must study the problems they are to tackle and understand them fully before they take concrete action. The trouble with many campaigns, drives, and other rapidly organized procedures for social action is their superficial orientation and lack of comprehension by the people."[17]

The Philadelphia experience presents both good and bad examples on this point. The Neighborhood Planning Conference spent a year and a half in intensive study of the area before reaching any concrete proposals. The Temple Area redevelopment committee on the other hand was asked for redevelopment suggestions at its first meeting. The committee members had insufficient time to think about or study the problems of the area, and they did not have the chance to thrash out their problems to anyone's satisfaction. This meeting itself was one where policy and ideas were just beginning to take shape. Even the next meeting was similar. There the committee had before it a proposal from the Planning Commission, but it had a limited background to judge its merits. A subcommittee spent four hours examining it, but that was no substitute for a background of study and discussion. This, of course, is not the only time the committee will study the problem; discussion of the plan with the Commission is a continuing affair. Thus the lack of time for study and discussion in the initial period is being remedied.

The use of a study program in the initial stages of a community organization is a device useful in acquainting members of the community with the problem of the area. Hayes writes:

Inventories and rating devices can be utilized in another way. The people of a community can be stimulated to take stock of their own resources and liabilities. They themselves rate or measure their potentialities and failures with respect to

17. New York: Harcourt Brace and Company, 1947, p. 96.

economic status, political efficiency, sanitary and hygienic facilities, recreation and educational opportunities for young and old, and so on. Laymen, of course, cannot be expected to make exhaustive, accurate, and thoroughly objective investigations. Amateur studies, if carefully undertaken, can serve the purpose of starting widespread discussion and the initiation of planning. They should, of course, be as complete and accurate as circumstances will allow.[18]

One of the area councils in Cleveland has had considerable experience in the use of surveys to acquire information about the area and to create interest among its members. The Neighborhood Planning Conference in Philadelphia also used this technique with considerable success. Its chief value would seem to lie in making the people in the area aware of the problems and in acquainting the people gradually with what redevelopment and planning involve.

Another device useful in the preparatory work of a community organization is limiting purposely, in the initial period, the number of those who take part. This technique is described by Hayes:

The planning process may originate among very small groups and even be confined for quite a while to a minor segment of the community. Every local problem, whether it concerns the economic structure, form of government, improvement of health, development of recreation, or anything else, requires the assimilation of information and weighing a course of action before it can be satisfactorily solved. Unless motivation is sufficiently powerful to provoke and sustain the group and a considerable proportion of the community participates, the total planning effort is likely to fail. The creative leader will therefore frequently begin the planning process by deliberating with a small group (as in a workshop) who may become disciples. These will spread the work, as apostles always do, to an ever-widening audience.[19]

LEADERSHIP

Leadership suggests problems for which there is no simple answer. Who is and is not a leader, who are leaders in what fields, who should be selected for membership on boards of community organizations— these are questions that require more investigation before they can be answered. In the subject under discussion here, the problems add up to something of a dilemma because the community organization has three objectives as to selection of its leaders.

First of all, it wants its leaders to be truly representative of the people in the area. Leaders are needed who are looked upon as leaders by the people in the area and who can really represent their ideas and attitudes. Labor leaders, not too high up in the hierarchy in many civic undertakings, are often effective leaders of this type. The labor leader who represents a small group of employees on a grievance committee is a good example. A local political leader, also not too high in some

18. *Ibid.,* p. 99.
19. *Ibid.,* pp. 98–99.

hierarchies, is another example of a local leader trusted and respected by many in the community but often unknown by those selecting representatives for local organizations. Thus there is the danger that the board or committee will not actually reflect the ideas and attitudes of the community.

A second objective is to include those who are influential in the community because of their financial, business, managerial, or professional interest and success in the community. Managers or owners of businesses in the area often are important persons when it comes to gaining acceptance for redevelopment plans. The stake of such people in the community is a large one and is usually economic. A procedure for discussing and shaping redevelopment proposals that would by-pass this group would be totally unrealistic.

The third leadership objective is prestige in the eyes of public bodies and official agencies. Public bodies are composed of men no different, basically, from other men; and their attitude toward a community organization is apt to be favorable or derogatory depending upon the prestige of its representatives. Fortunately or unfortunately, a manager or other representative of a substantial industry or business will usually be given more weight than a relatively unknown individual, particularly if the latter is not well off financially.

About the only way to deal with this dilemma is to include representation from all substantial groups, balancing them as well as possible. There is a tendency in such an arrangement, however, for those in the second group to awe and consequently override those in the first. There is also a tendency to make up the controlling or executive committee predominantly from the second group (e.g., the South Side Planning Board in Chicago), and to have but token representation from the first group. If the committee or board is to be regarded by most people in the area as representing their interests (and this seems a very basic and important point), then every effort should be made to see that this first group is really represented. Prominent persons from the second kind of background will usually be relatively easy to find, and it is quite convenient and much simpler to select membership from them. The point, however, is that the community organization should be a vehicle whereby the redevelopment proposal can be discussed with the people. It is a real danger, if leaders from only the last two groups are selected, that the proposal will never reach the people but only this "top level."

Saul Alinsky in his book, *Reveille for Radicals,* has much to say on this point as well as on the problem of finding local leaders. He states the importance of using local leaders when he says:

The only way that people can express themselves is through their leaders. By *their* leaders we mean those persons whom the local people define and look up to as leaders. Native or indigenous leadership is of fundamental importance in the attempt to build a People's Organization, for without the support and co-operative efforts of native leaders any such venture is doomed to failure in the very beginning.[20]

Later on he states:

Most attempts at community organization have foundered on the rock of native leadership. The conventional community council of the past has evidenced little knowledge or understanding of the significance of indigenous leadership. Such organizations have largely confined themselves to co-ordinating professional, formal agencies which are first superimposed upon the community and subsequently never play more than a superficial role in the life of the community. It is rare today to discover a community organization in which the indigenous interest groups and action groups of the community not only participate but play a fundamental role.[21]

He devotes a complete chapter to the problem of leadership, and those who must deal with this problem would find it worth their while to read it with some care.

The difficulty of really reaching the people is illustrated from the experience of TVA in working with farmers in the valley, demonstrating the value of fertilizers and persuading the farmers to use them.

At the outset, few communities were sufficiently organized to assume responsibility for the selection of test-demonstrators. Consequently, county agents for the most part were forced to select them from community leaders—stalwarts and friends, who could afford the risk involved in a changed agricultural economy and, who, it was felt, would do a good job. Control of the program gravitated to the agent's office where clerical help and office space were available and technical supervision simplified. The resulting domination of leadership by the wealthier farmers and the concentrated administration in the agent's office delayed effective community organization and small-operator participation.[22]

Although test demonstrations on the use of fertilizers seem somewhat afield from redevelopment, the basic operation is the same, i.e., presenting a proposal to local residents and securing their participation through local organizations.

One worker for a community organization made several observations on those leaders who, in most cases, would be most articulate and informed about the area, its conditions, and the attitudes of the people. He felt that the local priest and minister, the newspaper editor, owners of large businesses, and ward leaders would be obvious choices for leadership. The school principal, in his opinion, generally would not be so good because usually he did not live in the area. The social worker

20. University of Chicago Press, 1946, p. 87.
21. *Ibid.*, p. 88.
22. Unpublished manuscript, 1947, pp. 8–9, "Citizen Participation in Administration of the TVA."

is an informed person and therefore very useful, but he is paralyzed on social action because he must obtain clearance from his organization. The local merchant is also an informed person, and the union leader can be expected to have some influence.

Hayes spends one whole chapter on community leadership. He distinguishes between "institutional" and "situational" leaders. The former as he describes them are, "All persons holding office in a community, whether elected, appointed or otherwise selected to carry out routine functions. . . ."[23]

Examples of such leaders are ministers, YMCA secretaries, social workers. His "situational" leader ". . . is a genuine member of the group and merely serves to focalize its desires and aspirations. To borrow a figure from chemistry, we might say that he is a catalytic agent, releasing the energy of a static, often paralyzed community. Under his wise direction, the people become aware of their common dangers or hardships and at the same time develop faith in their ability to deal with the situation."[24]

A means of discovering local leaders has been touched upon in the summary section on Cleveland. This is the technique of establishing block or street organizations affiliated with the larger local organization. This practice permits those who feel inadequate when facing larger area problems but competent to deal with localized problems, to speak up and take an active part in community affairs. Examples of this were evident in the Philadelphia Neighborhood Planning Conference where people who had never been called upon for leadership functions suddenly blossomed out as effective leaders. This technique is also of value in that it grooms these local leaders for larger roles. They become informed citizens and soon learn that they need not fear the problems of larger areas. These block organizations, in effect, become a farm system in preparing leadership for the community organization.

Clearly, it is one thing merely to set up some sort of an organization to be able to say one has used it to secure community participation and something else to make a determined effort to elicit local leadership and participation. The latter action requires time, effort, and patience, but, in the long run, it is the procedure that makes for better communities and for truly democratic participation in the planning process.

THE AREA WORKER OR ORGANIZER

Effective community organizations do not spring full grown from someone's idea or recognition that they are necessary to secure public participation in urban redevelopment. Organizing and managing a com-

23. *Op. cit.*, p. 76.
24. *Ibid.*, pp. 79–80.

munity organization successfully requires a great deal of work, more work usually than individuals in the community can provide. An effective local organization, therefore, requires a worker or organizer who can devote a good part or all of his time to the job. Just the mechanics of arranging meetings, handling memberships, keeping records, mailing notices, and following up assignments require someone whose job is primarily that. Citizens who participate cannot be expected to do this type of work unless the community can turn up a housewife or someone else who is willing to make the job her contribution to civic activity —and these persons are few and far between.

The need for a worker, executive secretary, or whatever he is called, then, is often the stumbling block in getting community organizations underway. That is another reason why the ready-made community unit with a professional secretary or worker is so desirable. Each of the organizations in the three cities studied had professionals of some sort whose job was that of serving the organization as administrator. Without this professional help, these organizations could not have functioned as they have.

Although redevelopment agencies will not themselves be selecting or paying these organizers or area workers, some attention should be paid to their role in the community organization and to the characteristics that make an area worker effective. Perhaps the public officials concerned with community organizations will be in a position to discuss with those making a selection the kind of person needed and what his functions should be.

In a recent publication the Welfare Federation of Cleveland has stated very well what the role and characteristics of the area worker should be:

The general responsibility of the area worker is to enable the area councils to perform their function effectively. The skills used by the worker in fulfilling his responsibility fall primarily in the general field of community organization. The worker blends his knowledge of local and city-wide needs, social problems and available resources of the community into the activities of the community council with which he works to facilitate its effective operation. He should see that all points of view are presented, and should regard the Welfare Federation and other city-wide planning groups as planning resources. He also needs to be skilled in the use of community action methods and in showing people how to do things for themselves.[25]

In Philadelphia, one of the workers in a community organization stated that the job of the organizer is to get the people to see that their plight is tied up with the welfare of the city as a whole. The organizer should see the people as neighbors, members of the community, rather

25. Welfare Federation of Cleveland, *Area Councils and Field Service in Greater Cleveland* (October, 1949), p. 4.

than as members of an organization. He added that the organization lasts a lot longer if more people take part in the doing.

As mentioned in the discussion of Cleveland's area councils, there is always the danger that the organizer may assume the leadership role. This is contrary to the purpose of community organizations and should be discouraged as much as possible. Real leadership should come from the community itself; no matter how capable the professional, he cannot match the local, indigenous leader in knowledge of the people and the area or in a following.

Community participation.—In any investigation of community organizations, the extent to which people actually participate is always difficult to measure and difficult to evaluate. There is apparently a feeling that unless a high percentage of the people in the area do take part, the community organization has failed in its major purpose.

This attitude is unfortunate, for it flies in the face of reality and demands far more than almost any organization can achieve. On this point one must think primarily in terms of securing the interest and activity of those who are inclined toward participation but who are dormant merely because no channels are available through which they can exercise their interests. Always a large number of citizens lack even this dormant interest in public affairs. It is asking far too much of a community organization to establish as a standard for measuring its success the drawing of this group into active participation. Only an issue that affects directly, drastically, and immediately their livelihood or well-being will bring many people from their shell of apathy. Urban redevelopment proposals that contemplate the demolition of homes and large-scale movements of residents is such an issue and often does bring this group into action, but the community organization in its usual operations cannot be expected to provide issues of this character. Parenthetically, it might be well to note that it is on just such an issue that a community organization can function effectively. With interest aroused and a strong urge on the part of the people to "do something," the community organization will provide a ready-made channel for the expression of this force. If a community organization is in existence, this energy can be channeled and co-ordinated into a coherent demand rather than dissipating itself on a wide front of hit-or-miss action and individual protest.

But such issues are not always at hand; community organizations must function as a focal point for issues that do not have a crusading character. They must do what they can to gather and channel the ideas of the residents, but they cannot be expected to produce wide interest or participation on such a bill of fare. What one may expect in community participation is well summed up in the following statement:

"So-called 'grass roots' participation in any district will be relative. It should be borne in mind that a Council with three hundred members in a population of sixty thousand amounts to one person out of every two hundred. One for every five hundred would be fairly good."[26]

Saul Alinsky also points out the small percentage who participate in organizations:

A critical study of the extent of popular participation in People's Organizations was made and the findings differed so radically from current assumptions that the original study was repeatedly checked. Each check-up corroborated the original findings. Conclusions showed that in the most powerful and deeply rooted People's Organizations known in this country the degree of popular participation reached a point varying between five and seven percent! [27]

Later in evaluating this condition he says:

When one realizes the limited extent of actual rank-and-file participation within American organizations it then becomes obvious why a People's Organization which includes from five to seven percent participation is as powerful as it is. In the present-day American scene 5 percent participation is a tremendous democratic phenomenon. This fact is also a tragic commentary on the unbelievable degree of apathy and disinterest on the part of American people. Unless the American people are aroused to a higher degree of participation, democracy will die at its roots— the withering disease of apathy in the roots of democracy will eventually cause its death.[28]

One means of securing greater participation is the use of block or street organizations, cells within the parent organization. The Neighborhood Planning Conference used this technique in Philadelphia and the result from the standpoint of participation and local leadership was very good. In Cleveland, some of the area councils have used the same technique, and one in particular is spending much of its effort in promoting these smaller organizations.

As has been emphasized before, the use of the block or street organization has the advantage of bringing the problems down to a size comprehensible by most people. The use of small-scale problems enables people to become familiar with planning and redevelopment at a level they can understand, and from there they may go on to comprehending problems on a larger scale. People are not likely to participate in that which they cannot understand.

Another facet to public participation is that discouragement increases proportionately with the time that elapses between laying of plans and achieving results. Planning and redevelopment are long-term tasks; results should not be expected overnight. But at the same time, results of some kind must be provided if interest is not to lag.

26. McCullough, *op. cit.*, footnote 16.
27. *Op. cit.*, p. 198.
28. *Ibid.*, p. 201.

The use of the block or street organization has an advantage here in that proposals emanating from such small units are usually correspondingly quite small—a street light, traffic signals, and the like—and the chances for reasonably quick results from such requests or recommendations are good. Success in these small matters will sustain interest in the organization. It is too much to expect active public interest and participation, at least at the outset, in plans that on the surface seem difficult to achieve and that also have to do with large areas and drastic changes. Interest must first be built on the smaller, more tangible items.

FUNCTIONS OF A COMMUNITY ORGANIZATION

The functions of a community organization have been indicated throughout the preceding pages, but it may be well, at the cost of some repetition, to tie up the views put forward at several points. The discussion so far has emphasized two things: (1) the general reasons and need for community organizations in the urban redevelopment process and (2) techniques in their organization and operation. But how do these organizations function as vehicles for public participation in, and understanding of, the redevelopment process?

Before going into specific functions, however, the general relationship between the local community organizations and the public bodies responsible for preparing redevelopment plans should be clear. The public body views the city as a whole and must weave the plans for a specific area into the framework of the entire city. It is also conversant with planning techniques; it possesses a body of knowledge about planning principles and experience; it has a considerable amount of statistical information about the various areas for which it must plan.

The community organization, on the other hand, lacks the planning techniques and often cannot see much beyond the borders of its own area. The people in the area have ideas on what they would like in their neighborhood or district and know something of their own needs. They also have an intimate, personal knowledge of the area, which the public body and its professional staff does not have.

The problem, then, is to bring these two groups together so that they may complement each other. Much has been said about the inadvisability of a public body announcing its redevelopment plans for an area without consulting those in the area. At the same time, one should not advocate that the community organization plan its area for redevelopment by itself, ignoring the city-wide planning problems and not using available planning techniques. The problem is to establish a meeting and exchange between these two groups that will produce the best available plans. Much has been said about the need for community organization, because, in most communities, the public body is in existence but the community organization is lacking. Also the tendency and, in fact, the usual practice, is to overlook the community in the preparation of plans. Advocacy of the need for the community organization, however, should not be interpreted to mean that this is the organization that will really do the redevelopment planning and that the public agency will merely do its bidding.

One of the most important functions of the community organization is that of serving as a source of information on the attitudes of the people in the area. It is the channeling of information to the public body on what the people in the area need and want, their feelings on remaining in or leaving the area, their acceptance of, or resistance to, various kinds of housing, their preferences or priorities among the many possible features of a redevelopment plan. Certainly no further elaboration of this point is needed to demonstrate its crucial importance for those planners and redevelopers whose end-objective is the welfare and happiness of those who live in urban communities. If the community organization is really a people's organization in that it reflects their attitudes or knows their attitudes with some accuracy, then the public body is able to learn about the people in the area and gauge their program in light of these attitudes and wants.

A second function changes the direction of flow—it is the channeling of ideas from the planning body to the community organization and, therefore assuming a truly representative organization, to the people in the area. The importance of this function cannot be overemphasized, for this is one of the major areas that many redevelopment planning bodies have in practice ignored. Although other planning bodies have been quick to see the need for this type of communication, they have somehow found it difficult to put their views into practice.

With the community organization, the official redevelopment organization has an excellent medium through which its proposals may be explained to the people—if the necessary effort, and it is a considerable effort, is made. Carefully prepared maps, film strips, movies, etc., can show the people the effect of nonplanning or why certain proposals of the locality cannot be carried out. They can also show the possibilities of well-planned neighborhoods and larger urban areas. Thus they may attack the common feeling of helplessness and fatalism in the face of urban conditions that most people dislike. Members of the staff of the planning body may work closely with the community organization, using their technical knowledge and human understanding to broaden the understanding of the people on planning problems and to keep local planning proposals in accord with city-wide plans. It is in the incipient stages that failures on this last point should be discovered and eliminated; for once a proposal is adopted, it may be considered almost sacred, and criticism of it may not be well received.

The third major function of the community organization rests with the organization itself unless the municipality were to provide an advisor for community organizations. This function is to arouse interest in the community on redevelopment planning. Techniques for securing public participation have already been sketched rather broadly so they need not be repeated. Here it is important to point out the necessity of creating widespread interest; for if that is not present, the organization is but a meeting of a few individuals who cannot speak for the community and who are unable to reflect the community's attitudes, ideas, needs, and wants. The major job of the community organization therefore is to create as great an interest as possible and secure genuine public participation.

The final function in this list, which by no means is exhaustive, is one that has been implicit in nearly all the other functions. This is the maintenance of relations with public bodies. The responsibility for maintaining relations belongs to both the community organization and to the public body. If no firm relations are maintained, if they are but sporadic and not continuing, then the place or role of community organizations in urban redevelopment loses much of its import.

Community organizations can play an effective and important part in urban redevelopment. Much remains to be learned about their methods, possibilities, and limitations in this field. This inquiry has only opened up the subject. More should be done on it as experience accumulates and differing schemes of operation are tried out. But these organizations offer an opportunity the value of which goes beyond the specific purposes of redevelopment. They have possibilities for democratic action that should not be overlooked and that could affect our whole conception of the role the citizen can play, locally at least, in a democracy.

PART IV

LOCAL GOVERNMENT ORGANIZATION IN METROPOLITAN AREAS: ITS RELATION TO URBAN REDEVELOPMENT

BY
VICTOR JONES

EDITOR'S FOREWORD

VICTOR JONES is a brave man. Why? Not primarily because he has been willing to study the relations of local government organization in metropolitan areas to their redevelopment. This, to be sure, is a formidable job but it is also a fascinating one that offers chances to help materially in an important sector of our public life. And besides, he is extraordinarily well equipped for the task.

Rather, his courage is shown by his willingness to write an account of his recent study and tentative conclusions at this time. Paradoxically enough, this takes courage because in recent months quite a few people genuinely concerned with urban redevelopment have begun to realize that it will not be well done, on any significant scale, in metropolitan areas as they are today. They are simply too closely tied together internally—their area and functional subdivisions are too interdependent —to make possible wise and far-sighted redevelopment in face of the existing Balkanization of governmental and quasi-public powers and responsibilities.

But if redevelopers and others are beginning to see this, even rather dimly, why is Mr. Jones so courageous? Why is he not a fortunate student of government riding an incoming tide of interest and concern with a subject he knows about and, therefore, well on the way to becoming an oracle?

The answer is clear: because he will be expected to come out with a short, simple proposal that will "answer" all the accumulated and aggravated problems from decades of neglect, indifference, shortsightedness, frustration, and inbred distrusts and dislikes. And of course his formula must be "practical"; it must "work." One can almost hear now one side of a short conversation:

"You've been working on metropolitan government and redevelopment? Fine! You're just the man I've been looking for. We've got one of the toughest setups in the whole country right here. . . . I'm really worried about that next project of ours. How can we know what should be done in that spot when we're in the dark about almost everything outside the city limits and don't know too much about what's going on inside them? You've got to help us out. But make it short, please. You see I've got to get back to the drafting room (or counting-house or Council chamber or what-have-you) right away. Some mighty important things coming up this afternoon. . . ."

Of course neither Victor Jones nor anyone else who has looked below the surface of this subject has any such pat answer or formula or would even suggest that there might be one. It would be just about as sensible to expect a nuclear physicist to write down on one sheet of paper instructions that would enable the handy man around the house to build an atomic power plant in his basement to run the family washing machine—at a total cost of not more than $20. It just is not that kind of a problem.

On the other hand, it can be dealt with over the years if enough men and women of intelligence, good-will, and persistence will really work at it. It seems to me that Mr. Jones's section of URS provides useful aid for those who wish to come to grips with one of the crucial and far-reaching issues in American public affairs.

Victor Jones has earned the reputation as one of the leading students of governmental organization and services in metropolitan areas. His *Metropolitan Government* is one of the standard works on the general subject. He is now professor of government at Wesleyan University and one of the leading spirits in its proposed Public Affairs Center.

C. W.

CHAPTER I

METROPOLITAN REDEVELOPMENT

U RBAN redevelopment" is a new term in the language. It has been given a technical meaning and to many people it is gobbledegook. The term is made up, however, by joining two common words. In the common sense of the term it suggests a conscious effort to remake the urban community—to arrest certain developments, to redirect others, and to initiate the development of some aspects of urban life that have heretofore been dormant.[1]

Urban redevelopment is much more than the clearance of existing slums. Urban communities cannot be developed and redeveloped into the kind of communities where people enjoy living, working, playing, and rearing children by the assembly, clearance, and improvement of one or a few blighted areas. Urban development is affected by the whole of governmental and by many private activities. And they in turn are influenced by the way in which the city developed and is developing.

City life is affected for good or ill by every action that local governments take or do not take. It is affected not only by the municipal program or lack of program but by the effectiveness of local governmental activities, by the efficiency with which the program is carried out, by the cost of local government, and by the allocation of those costs in the community. This is as true of the local judiciary, of the social welfare, educational, recreational, police, and public health authorities as it is of zoning, building inspection, subdivision control, public housing, transit, highway, or redevelopment agencies.[2]

The same observation can be made about state and national governments. Many of their programs are actually carried out within the city and its suburbs and all of them affect city life, directly or indirectly.

Although "urban redevelopment" is a new term, the process of developing and redeveloping urban areas has always been with us. This

1. Coleman Woodbury and Frederick A. Gutheim, *Rethinking Urban Redevelopment* (Urban Redevelopment Series No. 1, 1949).

2. See the community planning objectives listed by W. P. Shatts, "Planned Development of Metropolitan Regions," *Journal of the Engineers' Club of St. Louis* (March-April, 1945), pp. 3–4, and the list of city and state agencies which directly affect redevelopment projects in the 3d Public Report, Committee on Civic Design and Development, New York chapter, American Institute of Architects, *Interrelation of Agencies Affecting Development Projects in New York* (September, 1944), Tables B and C, pp. 13–15.

has resulted in facilities which from different points of view are satis-factory or unsatisfactory. Nevertheless, they have permitted a con-stantly increasing proportion of the people of the United States and in the rest of the world to live in and around cities. In 1950 almost 96 million people in the United States lived in urban areas as compared with 201,655 in 1790. During the last decade alone, the increase in the urban population was larger than the total population of New York state in 1950.

To make room for these millions of people to live and carry on their activities, the uses to which urban land and nearby rural land is put have changed time and again.[3] Factors other than population increase have brought changes in the use of land—new inventions, new de-mands, new goods brought into the market by new forms of communi-cation.[4]

We have always had urban development and redevelopment, then, but it has been largely unplanned and frequently the multitude of ac-tivities involved have been at cross-purposes. As Tugwell said in 1940: "We have not learned any better way to improve our cities than to let one set of business men ruin another set of business men."[5] Recogni-tion of such consequences is probably the reason many "businessmen" have joined in the movement for urban redevelopment as the successor, in some ways at least, to the much older slum-clearance movement. The literature is full of references to the economic as well as the social cost of the present uses of urban land.[6]

Urban redevelopment, in the technical sense of the term, is neces-sary to supplement other governmental and private activities and to focus them upon certain physical aspects of the problem. But land as-sembly, clearance and improvement, even if there be a plan for a desirable reuse of the land, are insufficient if directed only to the physi-cal aspects of particular projects.

The entire community must be considered in planning urban re-

3. See James Ford, *Slums and Housing* (Cambridge: Harvard University Press, 1936), pp. 17–252, for a fascinating history of the successive uses of land in Manhattan for hous-ing. See also the *Regional Survey of New York and Its Environs* (New York, 1929), Vol. II, *Population, Land Values and Government*.

4. The role of the steam railway, the electric street car, and the automobile in the de-velopment of metropolitan communities is well known. The story is summarized, along with speculations about the effect of passenger and cargo planes and helicopters, by W. F. Ogburn, "Inventions of Local Transportation and the Patterns of Cities," *Social Forces*, XXIV (May, 1946), 373–79. He concludes that "the natural processes of economics and of technology" will in the long-run lead to the dispersal of urban population but that "the natural process . . . could be speeded by governmental planning and direction."

5. R. G. Tugwell, "Decaying Hearts and Growing Peripheries," address before the San Francisco Down Town Association, *The Downtowner* (July 10, 1940).

6. See K. W. Kapp, *The Social Cost of Private Enterprise* (Cambridge: Harvard Uni-versity Press, 1950).

development projects. There are blighted areas in the suburbs and in the unincorporated fringe as well as in the central cities; there are areas of near blight and of probable deterioration; and in the rapid building up of these suburbs we are certainly sowing the seeds for the next generation's blight.

Furthermore, the pressures that affect the use of land in a metropolitan area cannot be excluded by the boundary lines of a municipal corporation. The wealthier suburbs of every metropolitan area are discovering that the most careful and precise zoning is not sufficient to protect them from the pressure of new population.[7] In fact, the Balkanization of local government in metropolitan areas has resulted in the unequal application of controls, unequalized services, unequalized tax burdens, and the frustration of citizens and officials in both central cities and suburbs.

Another reason why the entire community must be considered in the planning of urban redevelopment projects is that the success or failure of a redevelopment scheme depends in large part upon social and economic trends in the community. In some places, it will depend upon the willingness of outlying areas to receive the people displaced by land clearance as well as upon the willingness of the displaced persons to be relocated. This could mean a loss of population by the central city or congested suburb. Central cities everywhere are anxious to hold on to their populations and to increase them despite the fact that a metropolitan plan for relocation may be the only way that they can rebuild without maintaining or increasing congestion.

Most urban redevelopers recognize in a general way that blight and the obsolescent or undesirable use of land are metropolitan problems. The Federal Housing Act of 1949 instructs the Housing and Home Finance Agency to encourage metropolitan planning. Pressure to get projects underway, along with professional interest in physical accomplishment, has meant that most efforts have been directed at selecting particular projects for redevelopment and pushing through the preliminary and final planning of projects. Certainly little attention has been given to the metropolitan aspects of the problem and in some instances it is doubtful that the "city plan" itself is much more than an *ad hoc* plan to meet the requirements of federal statutes and regulations.

This is understandable. In the first place, the pressure to clear slums is real. Secondly, the funds available under congressional authorization are inadequate to finance more than a few projects in any one city. The need for redevelopment is so great that almost any project makes some

7. See, as examples, Churchill-Fulmer Associates, *Sewickley District Plan* (1947); Montclair Development Board, *A Program of Town Development* (1946); Scott Bagby, *A Comprehensive Plan for the Borough of Glen Ridge, N.J.* (1948); *A Comprehensive Plan for the Township of Cedar Grove, N.J.* (1949).

sense. At least, nearly all of them would seem to be improvements on existing conditions on these sites. The crucial question is whether these initial projects represent the maximum long-term improvement for these areas when they are considered as parts of a metropolitan community. Certainly, however, the effect of the program in many cities has been to encourage officials and interested groups to consider a plan for the city or to re-examine plans which have been laid upon the shelf.

Finally, the plain fact is that there are no adequate metropolitan plans. No metropolitan area is organized to prepare, adopt, and execute plans for the whole community. I do not advocate, however, that urban redevelopment under present congressional authorizations await the development of metropolitan plans.

But a start has to be made. It takes time to prepare plans and before that process can be begun the area to be planned must be organized for that and related purposes. It takes time to develop a politically acceptable and effective organization and even more time to bring it into being. The high stakes, however, are worth the effort and the creative thought required to win them.

This study of the organization of local government in metropolitan areas and its relationship to urban redevelopment is included in the Urban Redevelopment Study on the assumption that urban redevelopers should be among those who actively concern themselves with developing satisfactory local government in metropolitan areas. It must be made clear at the outset that a form of metropolitan government that is politically acceptable, adequately empowered, and democratically controlled has not yet been devised.

In the following chapters of this study, I shall describe the metropolitan community and the problems arising from the fact that nowhere is it politically organized. I shall then discuss the principal devices that have been tried or proposed for meeting these problems.

Again it should be emphasized that there is no "natural" form of metropolitan government. One must be worked out anew in each metropolis and, once organized, it will undoubtedly have to be reworked from time to time. The organization of a community for effective and popularly controlled government is, however, part of the whole problem of the democratic organization of the nation. The people in any one area can profit by the vast experience of successes and failures in hundreds of metropolitan areas in this country and abroad.

CHAPTER II

THE METROPOLITAN COMMUNITY[1]

Ｎ ONE of the one hundred and sixty-eight highly urbanized communities in the United States is politically organized as a community. The absence of a community-wide government in these communities is the problem considered in this study.

The importance of metropolitan areas is shown by the concentration of population in them and by their dominant influence on American culture. Almost 84 million people were living in these communities in 1950. This was 57 per cent of the country's population. In fact, the fourteen most populous metropolitan communities contained over 44 million people or almost three-tenths of the population of the United States (Table 1).[2]

TABLE 1

DISTRIBUTION OF POPULATION OF THE UNITED STATES, 1950

	Total Population	Percent of Total
United States......................	149,855,592	100
Rural...........................	53,964,053	36
Urban..........................	95,891,539	64
157 Urbanized Areas*................	68,787,978	45
Inside central cities...............	47,988,213	32
Outside central cities..............	20,799,765	13
168 Standard metropolitan areas*......	83,929,863	57
Inside central cities...............	49,023,935	33
Outside central cities..............	34,905,928	24

Source: U. S. Bureau of the Census, Series PC-3. Nos. 3, 9, 10.
* See pp. 489–90, note 12, and pp. 490–91, note 15 for definitions.

DOMINANT INFLUENCE OF METROPOLITAN WAYS OF LIFE

American society can be characterized as a metropolitan society, or as Lewis Mumford would say, a megalopolitan society, because of the

1. The discussion of the metropolitan community in this chapter is sketchy. I only intend to suggest to the reader the social factors that distinguish the metropolitan from other communities and that give rise to distinctive governmental problems. The discussion would be less sketchy if the full reports of the 1950 Census had been available at the time it was written.

2. The 168 metropolitan communities are the standard metropolitan areas as defined by the Bureau of the Census for the census of 1950. See pp. 489–90, note 12, and 490–91, note 15, for definitions of the "standard metropolitan area" and of the smaller but more densely populated urbanized area.

pervasive and often dominant influence of large urban communities on our values and on the selection of techniques to achieve them. As Gras put it in 1922, western civilization has developed from the economy of the village to that of the metropolis, which is "an organization of people having a large city as nucleus." If we understand *producers and consumers* and *goods and services* to include noneconomic symbols and practices as well as material goods and if we understand the large city to be the metropolitan community then the following statement characterizes the present social organization of the United States and of a large part of the world:

. . . metropolitan economy is the organization of producers and consumers mutually dependent for goods and services, wherein their wants are supplied by a system of exchange concentrated in a large city which is the focus of local trade and the center through which normal economic [and many other social] relations with the outside are established and maintained.[3]

McKenzie in 1933 was aware that the influence of the metropolis is cultural as well as economic and that the dissemination of urban cultural traits was bringing about a cultural leveling throughout the United States.[4] He was also concerned with the interrelations of metropolitan areas, the mapping of the hinterland subject to their influence, and the identification of the factors affecting the extent of their influence. This is what Benton Mackaye has called "the metropolitan invasion."

The recent study of Don J. Bogue shows that the entire land area of the United States is divided into metropolitan regions[5] in each of which population density, retail sales, receipts from services, wholesale sales, and value added by manufacture (all by per capita dollar value) decrease as distance from the central city increases. It would be extremely valuable to know, as Bogue suggests, the spatial pattern of influence of metropolitan centers with respect to "the functions of finance, government, education, religion, and innumerable other aspects of the institutional composition of the individual hinterland community."[6]

3. N. S. B. Gras, *An Introduction to Economic History* (New York: Harper & Bros., 1922), p. 186.

4. R. D. McKenzie, *The Metropolitan Community* (New York: McGraw-Hill Book Co., 1933), pp. 98–110, 116–25. See National Resources Committee, *Our Cities—Their Role in the National Economy* (Washington, D.C., 1937), pp. 1–53.

5. He uses the term "metropolitan community," whereas we reserve the term for the population of central cities and nearby areas among whom there are many kinds of regular daily contacts. For our purposes, the metropolitan community will be the equivalent of the standard metropolitan area as defined by the Bureau of Census. See Bogue, *The Structure of the Metropolitan Community: A Study of Dominance and Subdominance* (Ann Arbor: University of Michigan Press, 1949), p. 10.

6. *Ibid.*, p. 61. A careful reading of Bogue will repay the effort. The extensive discussion of his method of analysis will suggest similar studies of other phenomena. Much of his

CRITICISM OF METROPOLITANISM

There can be no doubt, however, that the metropolis functions as a clearing center, modifier, and distributor of the values of our civilization. This function has led many people to deplore what Lewis Mumford calls megalopolitan culture,[7] and to insist that a better culture would arise from the development of other forms of urban life to replace the metropolis. Warren S. Thompson believes that in the near future, a reorganization of the economic structure can be made which, if planned, will permit "a new pattern of population distribution purely as a matter of economic adjustment." These adjustments will be affected by the new technology arising from the increasing use of the electric motor, internal combustion engine, gas turbine, telephone, and airplane, the ultimate application of atomic energy to domestic uses, and the development of electronic devices for direct long-distance communication.

Atomic and biological warfare may make "man's very survival . . . depend on an intelligent distribution of population."

But, in addition to the purely economic aspects of the redistribution of population likely to arise from the use of these new techniques, many people are already questioning the desirability of living in the modern large city from other standpoints. They are asking whether the city has a harmful effect on health, citing the rapid increase of heart ailments, of cancer, and of mental ills; they are asking whether man will refuse to reproduce in crowded quarters once he has any choice in the matter, citing the fact that very few if any large cities are now maintaining their own numbers; they are wondering what will be the psychological effects on children raised in environments where they are insulated from most contacts with the phenomena of nature; they are asking whether it is possible for the masses of the workers who have relatively small incomes to live comfortably and decently in the crowded areas of modern cities. It is not in the least surprising that there is an increasing interest in the study of population and a growing feeling that we should no longer trust to chance to achieve a distribution in this new age which will assure not only an efficient economy, but also a larger measure of social and individual welfare.[8]

---

analysis seems to be obscured by the use of ecological terms and concepts, but throughout the study he is aware that "the term 'dominance' must be used as a class name for many different kinds of controls, most of which have never been subjected to rigorous study" (p. 13). For the general concepts, see A. H. Hawley, *Human Ecology* (New York: Ronald Press, 1950).

7. See his trilogy: *Technics and Civilization* (New York: Harcourt Brace & Co., 1934), *Culture of Cities* (New York: Harcourt Brace & Co., 1938), and *The Conditions of Man* (New York: Harcourt Brace & Co., 1944). See also the position of the southern agrarians in *I'll Take My Stand* (New York: Harper & Bros., 1930).

8. W. S. Thompson, Foreword to Bogue, *op. cit.*, p. 8. See also W F. Ogburn, "Inventions of Local Transportation and the Patterns of Cities," *Social Forces*, XXIV (May, 1946), 373–79, and the writings since World War II of Tracy Augur.

REDEVELOPMENT OF THE METROPOLIS A COMMUNITY-WIDE PROBLEM

I will not risk being called a "metropolitan provincialist" by denying that the future city will differ from the present as clearly as the present metropolis differs from the eighteenth-century town. On the other hand, I do not mind being called a "day-dreamer" because I insist that the development of the suburb and the redevelopment of blighted areas in suburb or central city should be planned with the whole community in mind.[9]

There are urban redevelopers and city planners as well as public officials and economic interest groups in both the central city and the suburbs who are interested in urban redevelopment as a means of increasing or maintaining the population of their particular segment of the community. For instance, the Dayton City Plan Board said in 1946:

> The decentralization process will cease only when cities stop growing, or when urban redevelopment and rehabilitation programs make the central portions of cities equal to or more attractive than "life in the suburbs." The quality and practicability of future urban redevelopment legislation will, in a large measure, determine the rate and conditions under which cities can meet the trend toward the suburbs through the process of urban redevelopment.[10]

Milwaukee, as another example, is openly talking about keeping its present population from wanting to move to the suburbs and is attempting to annex enough land to provide building space for new homes and new industries. The City Council in 1949 authorized the acquisition of a large area of vacant land outside its present limits as a site for a city-developed "self-sustaining suburb." There are sufficient reasons for bringing as much as possible of the metropolitan community under the jurisdiction of the central city (see chap. iv). But the official reasons given for the necessity of Milwaukee's "horizontal expansion" ignore the fact that a home or an industry built on either side of a municipal boundary line is still in the metropolitan community.

On the other hand, the Milwaukee plan for a "new town" to supplement the redevelopment of blighted areas is an imaginative and balanced approach to the development of the metropolitan area. No other American city has planned with so much insight and on such a scale to develop vacant land either inside or outside its borders.

9. See the editorial, "Industrial Dispersal," in the *News Letter* of the American Society of Planning Officials, September, 1951. See the bibliography, "Business Districts, Central and Decentralized" (U.S. Bureau of Public Roads, June 4, 1951), pp. 16–19.

10. Dayton City Plan Board, *Annexation* (1946), p. 6.

People identified with the central city and those identified with the suburbs are justified by their interests, *as they have defined them,* in fearing each other. What is needed is to place these interests into the larger community context so that the periphery is concerned with downtown and the city is concerned with the fringe. This can only be done by bringing the various interests—the dichotomy of suburb v. central city is too simple to describe them—into a working relationship with each other in the definition of objectives and in the development and support of means to achieve them. The formal organization of such relationships in metropolitan communities through governmental action is the problem we are concerned with in this study.

Definition of the Metropolitan Community

The metropolitan community has no political boundaries. Any boundary lines fixed by statute would be arbitrary at any given time with respect to all but perhaps one set of activities carried on in the community. Urban sociologists prefer, therefore, to use *ad hoc* boundary zones instead of fixed boundary lines to delimit the metropolitan community.

The application of indexes thus far brought into use, however, reveals that the boundaries of the modern community, instead of being precise lines, are blurred, if not indeterminate. Each index yields a different description of a community's margins. . . . In view of this peculiarity, and since each of the available indexes represent a more or less specialized relationship, nothing less than a combination of indexes is adequate for the fullest approximation to an appropriate boundary. But the use of a number of criteria produces a confusion of intertwined lines of demarcation. . . .[11]

For our purposes we shall take the standard metropolitan areas as defined by the Bureau of the Census as the equivalent of metropolitan communities.[12] Complete analysis of these areas must await the full

11. Hawley, *op. cit.,* pp. 248–49. See the maps reproduced on pp. 246–54. Other illustrative maps can be found in a number of local publications. See, for example, Philadelphia City Planning Commission, *Economic Base Study of the Philadelphia Area* (1949), pp. 40–43. It would be valuable if the Bureau of the Census could collect, and make available, maps of various service areas of business establishments and social agencies. This could be done as part of its regular Census of business.

12. A standard metropolitan area is defined by the Bureau of the Census in connection with each city of 50,000 or more in 1950. Each area therefore contains one, and may contain more than one, city of 50,000 or more. When two cities of 50,000 or more are within 20 miles of one another, they have ordinarily been included in the same standard metropolitan area. Standard metropolitan areas may lie in more than one state. The Bureau's report states further:

"Each standard metropolitan area has as a nucleus the county or counties containing the central city or cities. Contiguous counties are included in a standard metropolitan area when they qualify on two types of criteria. One type is concerned with the character of the

publication of the reports of the 1950 census. A richer body of data will be available for analysis from census reports, publications of other governmental agencies and many unofficial sources since the basic reporting unit of the standard metropolitan area is the county.[13] Few such data are available by minor civil divisions which were the reporting units for the old metropolitan districts as defined by the Bureau of the Census in 1920, 1930, and 1940.[14]

Comparisons cannot be made between the metropolitan districts of earlier censuses and the standard metropolitan areas of 1950. Nor can they be made with the urbanized areas which are also reported for the first time in this census.[15] For most communities the standard metro-

---

county as a place of work for non-agricultural workers and with the density of population. The other type is concerned with the extent to which contiguous counties are socially and economically integrated with the central city. Specifically, these criteria are:

"1. The county must have—(a) 10,000 nonagricultural workers, or (b) 10 per cent of the nonagricultural workers in the standard metropolitan area, or (c) at least half of its population residing in contiguous minor civil divisions with a population density of 150 or more per square mile.

"2. Nonagricultural workers must constitute at least two-thirds of the total employed labor force of the county.

"3. There must be evidence of social and economic integration of the county with the central city as indicated by such criteria as the following:

"a. 15 per cent or more of the workers residing in the contiguous county work in the county containing the largest city in the standard metropolitan area, or

"b. 25 per cent or more of the persons working in the contiguous county reside in the county containing the largest city in the standard metropolitan area, or

"c. An average of four or more telephone calls per subscriber per month from the contiguous county to the county containing the largest city in the standard metropolitan area."

In New England, where the city and town rather than the county were used to define standard metropolitan areas, the first and second criteria set forth above could not be applied. In their place a population density criterion of 150 or more persons per square mile, or 100 or more persons per square mile where strong integation was evident, has been used. U.S. Bureau of the Census, Series PC-3, No. 3, November 5, 1950.

13. Except in New England where the town is used in place of the county.

14. The best analysis of data on these and earlier definitions of metropolitan areas is Warren S. Thompson, *The Growth of Metropolitan Districts in the United States: 1900–1940* (Washington, D.C.: U.S. Bureau of the Census, 1948).

15. The urbanized areas represents the "nearby and closely settled" urban fringe in 1950 of all cities having a population of 50,000 or more in 1940 as mapped by geographers after field inspections of the areas. The following types of areas are included in a city's urban fringe if they are contiguous to the central city or if they are contiguous to an area already included in the urbanized area:

"1. Incorporated places with 2,500 inhabitants or more.

"2. Incorporated places with fewer than 2,500 inhabitants containing an area with a concentration of 100 dwelling units or more with a density in this concentration of 500 or more per square mile. This density represents approximately 2,000 persons per square mile and normally is the minimum found associated with a closely-spaced street pattern.

"3. Unincorporated territory with at least 500 dwelling units per square mile.

"4. Territory devoted to commercial, industrial, transportational, recreational, and other purposes functionally related to the central city.

"In addition, outlying noncontiguous areas, incorporated or unincorporated, meeting the residential density requirements are included in the urbanized area in the following cases.

politan area is larger and the urbanized area smaller than the old metropolitan district.

Although exact comparisons cannot be made, it is evident from a study of the changes of population during the last decade and of the distribution of population in 1950 that there is a continuation of the trends of previous decades.

1. Metropolitan communities are growing more rapidly than the country as a whole.
2. Within metropolitan communities the areas outside the central city are growing more rapidly than the central city or the older suburbs near the city.
3. The distribution of certain social characteristics of the population is different in the central city and in the suburbs.

POPULATION INCREASE CONCENTRATED IN METROPOLITAN AREAS

During every decade of the twentieth century these metropolitan communities taken together have grown more rapidly than the country as a whole.[16] The difference for the depression decade 1930–40 was very small, but for the last decade the population of standard metropolitan areas increased by 21.2 per cent as compared with an increase for the United States of 13.8 per cent (Table 2). Four-fifths of the entire in-

TABLE 2

POPULATION OF STANDARD METROPOLITAN AREAS, 1950*

AREA	POPULATION, 1950	POPULATION, 1940	POPULATION INCREASE 1940 to 1950	
			Number	Percentage
United States	149,855,592	131,669,275	18,186,317	13.8
Standard metropolitan areas...	83,929,863	69,263,204	14,666,659	21.2
Central cities	48,983,507	43,358,605	5,624,902	13.0
Outlying parts	34,946,356	25,904,599	9,041,757	34.9
Outside standard metropolitan areas	65,925,729	62,925,729	3,519,658	5.6

* From *The Municipal Year Book* (1951), p. 27.

All outlying areas within one and one-half miles of the central contiguous urban area, measured along the shortest connecting highway, are included. Also, any outlying area within one-half mile of another outlying area, itself within one and one-half miles of the central contiguous urban areas, is included." U.S. Bureau of the Census, Series PC-3, No. 9, February 1, 1951.

16. The Scripps Foundation for Research in Population Problems is now studying the growth patterns of metropolitan areas for the Housing and Home Finance Agency. "Census and other information is being analysed, and new facts gathered where necessary. Relationship of natural increase to migration in metropolitan growth is being studied. Changes in population composition of each metropolis are being compared with its physical expansion and economic development. Residential, industrial, and commercial development, and selected local government functions, are all being studied as interrelated factors in the evolution of these major urban areas." Housing and Home Finance Agency, Division of Housing Research, *Housing Research: Capsule Descriptions of Projects Started under Contract in 1950* (Washington, D.C., 1951), p. 3.

crease in population in the United States between 1940 and 1950 took place in the 168 standard metropolitan areas.[17] The counties in which metropolitan areas are located not only contain over half the country's population, but they are growing more rapidly than the nonmetropolitan areas. During the last decade the population of standard metropolitan areas increased by more than one-fifth as against an increase of one-twentieth for the remainder of the country. The population of the United States as a whole increased by a little less than one-seventh. This has been an enduring trend throughout the twentieth century which was only slowed down during the depression of the early 1930's. The median percentage of change in population between 1900 and 1940 for the metropolitan state economic areas[18] is 124.0 as compared with a median of 32.4 for the nonmetropolitan areas. The quartile distribution of these changes is shown in Table 3.

TABLE 3

QUARTILE DISTRIBUTION OF PERCENTAGE POPULATION CHANGES, 1900–1940, METROPOLITAN AND NONMETROPOLITAN STATE ECONOMIC AREAS*

	Metropolitan	Nonmetropolitan
Highest percentage decrease or lowest increase.........	18.1	−26.4
One-fourth lost population or increased by less than.....	70.6	8.8
Median...	124.0	32.4
One-fourth gained population by more than...........	218.7	83.6
Highest percentage increase.......................	5303.4	3224.8
Number of areas................................	174†	281

* Donald J. Bogue, *State Economic Areas* (U.S. Bureau of the Census, 1951), Appendix A.
† There are more metropolitan state economic areas than standard metropolitan areas since each part of the latter located in a different state is counted as a separate economic area.

This differential rate of growth in favor of metropolitan communities is an accentuated phase of the differential in favor of the urban population which has prevailed since the last decade of the eighteenth century except for the decade 1810–20.[19]

17. Increases cannot be computed for urbanized areas which were set up for the first time in the 1950 census.

18. State economic areas, used for the first time in the 1950 Censuses of population, housing and agriculture, "consist of single counties or group of counties which have similar economic and social characteristics." The portions of a standard metropolitan area which lie within different states are designated as separate state economic areas. There are, therefore, more metropolitan state economic areas than there are standard metropolitan areas. See U.S. Bureau of the Census, *State Economic Areas: A Description of the Procedure Used in Making a Functional Grouping of the Counties of the United States* (Washington, D.C., 1951). The report was prepared by Donald J. Bogue. Appendix A contains data on selected nonagricultural characteristics before 1950 arranged by economic areas. The preliminary report of population of state economic areas with the percentage changes for 1940–50 will be found in Series PC-3, No. 7, December 27, 1950.

19. Urban population, under the old definition included all people residing in incorporated places of 2,500 inhabitants or more. A few obviously urbanized civil divisions of counties were included by special rule. In 1950 a much more realistic definition of urban population was used by the Bureau of the Census: "For the 1950 census, urban territory

The rate of growth between 1940 and 1950 was uneven among the one hundred and sixty-eight standard metropolitan areas. One-fourth either lost population (seven areas) or increased at a rate less than that for the country as a whole. Half of the areas increased by more than 20.5 per cent and one-fourth by more than 33.7 per cent (Tables 4 and 5).

TABLE 4

QUARTILE DISTRIBUTION OF PERCENTAGE POPULATION CHANGES, 1940–50
STANDARD METROPOLITAN AREAS*

	Standard Metropolitan Areas	Central Cities†	Outside Central Cities
Highest percentage decrease..............	−14.9‡	−11.2§	−50.3‖
One-fourth lost population or increased by less than..................................	14.0	6.0	17.4
Median.....................................	20.5	11.6	32.2
One-fourth gained population by more than..	33.7	30.3	53.8
Highest percentage increase..............	110.4	257.0	167.8

* From U.S. Bureau of the Census, PC-3, No. 3 November 5, 1950.
† Multiple central cities are treated as one central city area.
§ Fifteen central cities lost population.
‡ Seven standard metropolitan areas lost population.
‖ The outlying parts of fifteen standard metropolitan areas lost population.

TABLE 5

NUMBER OF STANDARD METROPOLITAN AREAS, CENTRAL CITIES AND OUTLYING PARTS WITH RATES OF POPULATION CHANGE IN EXCESS OF, OR LESS THAN, THE UNITED STATES AND NONMETROPOLITAN AREAS, 1940–50*

	Standard Metropolitan Areas	Central Cities	Outlying Areas
Number decreasing or increasing at a rate less than that for the United States (13.8 per cent)	42	92	37
Number increasing faster than the United States....................................	126	76	131
Number decreasing or increasing at a rate less than that for nonmetropolitan United States (5.6 per cent)...........................	9	41	17
Number increasing faster than nonmetropolitan area....................................	159	127	151

* U.S. Bureau of the Census, PC-3, No. 3, November 5, 1950.

GROWTH OF SUBURBS FASTER THAN THAT OF CENTRAL CITIES

It is well known that the urban population does not reproduce itself and that the increase of urban population is due for the most part to

has been defined to comprise (a) places of 2,500 inhabitants or more incorporated as cities, boroughs, and villages; (b) the densely settled urban fringe, incorporated or unincorporated, around cities of 50,000 or more; and (c) unincorporated places of 2,500 inhabitants or more outside of any urban fringe. The urban territory also includes incorporated towns of 2,500 inhabitants or more except in New England, New York, and Wisconsin, where 'towns' are simply minor civil divisions of counties. All other territory is classified as rural." U.S. Bureau of the Census, Series PC-3, No. 10, February 16, 1951. See "The Development of the Urban-Rural Classification in the United States: 1874 to 1949," Series P-23, No. 1 (1949). The statement about the New England town is incorrect.

migration from abroad or from rural areas. Bogue has shown that the effect of the metropolis in concentrating population extends far beyond the confines of the metropolitan area.

Within 65 miles of the metropolis the land is more intensively occupied by urban than by rural populations. Within 35 miles of the metropolis the land is more intensively occupied by the rural non-farm than by the rural-farm populations. At distances greater than 115 miles the rural-farm population occupies the hinterland more intensively than does either the urban or the rural non-farm. At about the same point the rural non-farm surpasses the urban population in the rate of land occupancy. Thus, at the very periphery of the hinterlands, all populations occupy the land with a very low intensity and in a combination which is the complete reverse of the one found in the inner zones.[20]

In one hundred and forty-one standard metropolitan areas the central cities gained population between 1940 and 1950 at a lower rate than their suburban areas. In other words, only twenty-seven central cities grew more rapidly than their suburban areas. In two areas (Mobile and Topeka) the rate of increase for the central city was only slightly higher than for outside the central city. In twenty-five areas the central city grew much more rapidly than the suburban area. However, annexations to the central city, some quite extensive, are known to have been effected during the decade in eighteen of these areas. In Dallas and Fort Worth, the outlying areas increased in population more rapidly than the central cities despite the fact that the former annexed 39 square miles in 1945 and almost 12 square miles in 1949 and the latter annexed 35 square miles in 1946.

Between 1940 and 1950 no central city in the fourteen standard metropolitan areas of over a million population had a higher rate of increase than its suburban area. The increase in the city of Buffalo was only 0.3 per cent and its suburban area increased 109 times faster. The suburban rate was almost 29 times faster than that of Pittsburgh and around 13 times faster in the Cleveland and Minneapolis–St. Paul areas. It was nearly 7.5 times as rapid in St. Louis and Baltimore; from 4 to 6 times faster in Chicago, Detroit, Boston, San Francisco–Oakland, Washington, D.C., and the New York–Northeastern New Jersey areas; 3.5 times as rapid in Milwaukee and twice as fast in Los Angeles. Although comparisons of rates of increase are open to misinterpretation, it is significant here that in nearly all of these metropolitan areas the parts outside the central city had substantial populations in 1940. Their rates of increase, therefore, are not calculated on such small base numbers that their meaning is insignificant.

Among the eighteen standard metropolitan areas with populations between 500,000 and 1,000,000, only Houston increased more rapidly

20. *Op. cit.*, pp. 75, 88–95.

than the outlying area. This is accounted for by the largest annexation in the United States during the decade: almost 81 square miles and a population of 133,500. Despite this transfer of population and area to Houston, the population of the outlying area increased by 43.8 per cent.

In two of the fifty-eight standard metropolitan areas of 200,000 to 500,000 the central city grew more rapidly than the suburbs. The other twenty-four rapidly growing central cities were among the standard metropolitan areas of less than 200,000: eighteen out of sixty in the 100,000 to 200,000 group and six out of eighteen in the 50,000 to 100,000 group.

DISTRIBUTION OF POPULATION BETWEEN CENTRAL CITIES AND SUBURBS

When the outlying areas gain population more rapidly than the central city, there is an increase in the proportion of the metropolitan population residing outside the boundaries of the central city. This is a continuation of a long-run trend—known as the "suburban trend" or the trend toward decentralization or diffusion of the metropolitan population.[21]

Comparisons can be made with previous decades only if county population data are regrouped to conform to the 1950 definition of standard metropolitan areas. In 1940, however, a smaller proportion of the metropolitan district population lived in the central city than in 1930 in all but eight districts: Scranton–Wilkes Barre, Allentown–Bethlehem–Easton, Oklahoma City, Jacksonville, Savannah, Corpus Christi, Cedar Rapids and Lincoln, Nebraska. In some other areas, e.g., New York–Northeastern New Jersey, Springfield–Holyoke, and Columbia, South Carolina, the central cities about held their own.[23] Of the eight cities that gained relatively, only three—Scranton, Wilkes Barre (now central cities of separate areas with declining total populations) and Lincoln—continued this gain in the decade 1940–50.

In half the standard metropolitan areas of 1950 from one-third to

---

21. A number of local planning commissions have published analyses of the population of their respective metropolitan areas. See, for example, Cincinnati City Planning Commission, *Population* (Metropolitan Master Plan Study No. 1, December, 1945), Seattle City Planning Commission, *The Population of Metropolitan Seattle* (interim report, 1950), New Orleans City Planning and Zoning Commission, *Population* (chap. 3 of the Master Plan, preliminary report, 1949), Kansas City, Missouri, City Plan Commission, *The Kansas City Metropolitan Area* (1947), Detroit Regional Planning Commission, *Population Prospectus for the Detroit Region, 1960 and 1970* (1950), Kalamazoo City Planning Commission, *The Population of Kalamazoo, Michigan: Its Growth, Distribution and Characteristics* (City Plan Report No. 3, November, 1950). State and local traffic surveys often discuss population distribution in the metropolitan areas.

22. See *The Municipal Year Book* (1942), Table III-A, pp. 182–91.

four-fifths of the population lived outside the central city. In one-fourth of the areas less than half of the metropolitan population is in the central city but in another fourth of the areas over seven-tenths of the metropolitan population lives within the central city limits. In the much smaller and more thickly settled urbanized areas, a larger proportion of the population will, of course, be found in the central city. The median is 79.8 per cent as compared with the median of 61.7 per cent for standard metropolitan areas (Table 6).

TABLE 6

QUARTILE DISTRIBUTION
PROPORTION OF POPULATION WITHIN CENTRAL CITIES
STANDARD METROPOLITAN AND URBANIZED AREAS, 1950*

	Standard Metropolitan Areas (percentages)	Urbanized Areas (percentages)
Lowest proportion in central city	21.6	28.3
One-fourth with proportion in central city less than	50.5	68.3
Median	61.7	79.8
One-fourth with proportion in central city more than	71.2	89.0
Highest proportion in central city	93.6	97.8
Number of areas	168	153†

* From *Municipal Yearbook* (1951) Table II, pp. 28–31.
† Four less than listed by the Bureau of the Census. Where central cities of urbanized areas are co-central cities of a standard metropolitan area the urbanized areas are considered in this table as a single area.

Whereas there are only two standard metropolitan areas with more than 90 per cent of the population within the central city, there are

TABLE 7

DISTRIBUTION OF STANDARD METROPOLITAN AND URBANIZED AREAS BY SIZE OF AREA AND
BY PROPORTION OF POPULATION IN THE CENTRAL CITY OR CITIES, 1950*

AREA AND SIZE	NUMBER	PERCENTAGE OF AREA POPULATION IN CENTRAL CITY OR CITIES							
		20–30	30–40	40–50	50–60	60–70	70–80	80–90	90–100
Standard metropolitan areas:									
Over 1,000,000	14		2	1	5	4	2		
500,000 to 1,000,000	18		2	1	5	4	5	1	
200,000 to 500,000	58	6	8	8	13	12	9	2	
100,000 to 200,000	60		1	11	8	22	13	5	
50,000 to 100,000	18				5	4	3	4	2
Total	168	6	13	21	36	46	32	12	2
Urbanized areas:									
Over 1,000,000	12			1	2	1	4	3	1
500,000 to 1,000,000	12					1	3	4	4
200,000 to 500,000	37	1	1	4	6	9	13	3	
100,000 to 200,000	56			1	8	7	11	17	12
50,000 to 100,000	36				1	3	5	9	18
Total	153†	1	1	5	14	23	32	44	33

* From *Municipal Yearbook* (1951), Table II, pp. 28–31.
† Four less than listed by the Bureau of the Census. See note †, Table 6.

thirty-three urbanized areas in this category. It is significant that no standard metropolitan area of over 88,000 population (Manchester, New Hampshire) is in this group. The largest urbanized area with over 90 per cent of the population in the central city is San Antonio (447,-

365). Twelve standard metropolitan areas, nine under 200,000 population and none over a million, have central cities which contain from 80 to 90 per cent of their population. There are forty-four urbanized areas in this category (Table 7).

MIGRATION TO, FROM, AND WITHIN METROPOLITAN AREAS

Metropolitan communities have grown largely by the migration of people from abroad or from rural areas. This movement was considerably slowed down during the depression of the early 1930's but recovered with the increase in economic opportunities during World War II and the postwar period. Census data for 1940–50 have not yet been analyzed but a quick glance at the preliminary reports of standard metropolitan areas consisting of only one county shows that 3 per cent of the population in metropolitan Akron had moved into the area during the previous year; 5 per cent in the Indianapolis area; 11 per cent into metropolitan Miami; 5 per cent into the Syracuse area; and 7 per cent into the Seattle area. In the Scranton and Wilkes-Barre–Hazleton areas, immigration for the year was only 2 per cent but both these areas lost population heavily during the decade. In standard metropolitan areas containing more than one county, the reported number of people moving from another county or abroad would include those moving from county to county within the area.[23]

We have no published census data to indicate the extent of out-migration. But estimates based on local studies indicate that the increase in population of the central cities of Detroit (13.2 per cent), Seattle (25.6 per cent), and Kalamazoo (6.0 per cent) between 1940 and 1950 was due largely to an excess of births over deaths which, in the latter two, offset a net loss of migrants from the central city. The Detroit Regional Planning Commission reports that:

The Detroit Region from 1900 to 1920 depended heavily upon net migration for its population growth. Literally hundreds of thousands of people were attracted to this area in these two decades of expanding economic and social opportunities. From 1920 onward, however, the region received a decreasing share of its population growth from net migration. The proportion of growth from natural increase—excess of births over deaths—grew from 1920 onwards. This increase of births over deaths also grew numerically from 1920 onwards, as natural increase formed a larger share of the total population gain from decade to decade.

Population growth as a result of net migration dropped from 89.1% of the total gain in the 1910–1920 decade to 79.4% in the 1920–1930 decade. During the 1930–1940 period of the depression, net migration accounted for a mere 4.3% of total population gain. In the expanding decade of the 1940's, however, net migration came back somewhat to account for 39.5% of the total population gain.[24]

23. U.S. Bureau of the Census, Series PC-5, Table 5.
24. Detroit Regional Planning Commission, *Population Prospectus for the Detroit Region, 1960 and 1970* (1950), p. 14.

Again the suburbs are gaining more through net migration than are the central cities. It is estimated that only 2 per cent of the increase in population between 1940 and 1950 of Detroit is attributable to net migration. At the same time, 37.4 per cent of the increase in the remainder of the metropolitan area came from migration.[25] The New York City Planning Commission estimates that 750,000 people moved out of New York City between 1940 and 1950. This resulted in a net loss by out-migration of 135,000 which was turned into a net gain for the decade by an excess of 580,000 births over deaths.[26] In Seattle it is estimated that the central city lost 12,500 people through civilian migration between 1944 and 1950, while the rest of King County gained 38,000 migrants.[27] We do not know as yet the extent to which this migration is associated with the increase in the formation of new family units.

We have a much more reliable study of the movement of population to, from, and within the eight metropolitan areas of Ohio for the period 1935 to 1940.[28] A third of the migration was for short distances within the same area. This characteristic has also been observed in Milwaukee.[29] During this period in Ohio there was a net loss of population from the metropolitan to the nonmetropolitan areas. Three-tenths of the moves were in metropolitan communities. Five-sixths of the migration was from the central city to the environs with a net loss to the central cities of over 100,000 people.

This large number of outward migrants from the big cities not only confirms general observations regarding the decentralizing character of the movement in metropolitan areas, but emphasizes the fact that this movement continued to be a strong one at a time when the migrants to metropolitan centers were creating no additional pressure for outward expansion.[30]

The reasons people give to interviewers for moving, or wishing to move, are one factor in the explanation of how metropolitan communi-

25. *Ibid.*, pp. 15, 33.
26. *New York Times* (August 6, 1951).
27. Seattle City Planning Commission, *The Population of Metropolitan Seattle* (interim report, 1950), pp. 6, 43–45. The Kalamazoo City Planning Commission reports a net loss by migration from the city of Kalamazoo of 6,370 persons between 1940 and 1949. Kalamazoo City Planning Commission, *The Population of Kalamazoo, Michigan* (1950), p. 11.
28. Warren S. Thompson and Donald J. Bogue, "Sub-regional Migration as an Area of Research," *Social Forces*, XXVII (May, 1949), 392–400. For a more general discussion of internal migration before the war, see National Resources Committee, *The Problems of a Changing Population* (Washington, D.C., 1938), pp. 83–118.
29. Richard S. Dewey, *Residential Development in the Unincorporated Areas of Milwaukee County, Wisconsin* (Milwaukee County Regional Planning Department, 1946), p. 8; also in *American Journal of Sociology*, LIV (September, 1948), 120.
30. Thompson and Bogue, *op. cit.* For an analysis of 1940 census data see Ronald Freedman, *Recent Migration to Chicago* (Chicago: University of Chicago Press, 1950).

ties have developed into their present form. They must be taken into account by anyone who would guess the future development of the community or attempt to direct it. The needs and desires of the urbanite have been discussed by Richard Dewey in another monograph of the Urban Redevelopment Study.[31]

DAILY MOVEMENT OF POPULATION

Perhaps, the salient characteristic of a metropolitan community is the specialization of particular political, economic, and social activities in the specific areas. People are constantly moving, sometimes for long distances, from their homes to the places where they work, shop, or take their recreation. The number of people who commute to work, and this would include any person who drives to work or rides a public conveyance whether he lives in the central city or not, is not exactly known.[32]

By no means is all the movement of passengers and vehicles in the New York–Northeastern New Jersey Area into Manhattan south of 61st Street. But we do have estimates of such traffic for 1924, 1932, 1940, and 1948. On a typical business day in 1948, over 3,765,000 persons moved into lower Manhattan.[33] Over 64 per cent of them traveled by rapid transit. Nevertheless, some 382,000 busses, autos, and trucks moved into the area. This was a 9 per cent increase over 1940.

Most of these people and vehicles came into lower Manhattan from some other part of New York City. The Regional Plan Association estimates that about 350,000 commuters who lived in the suburbs worked in New York City in 1950. Many of them worked elsewhere in the city than in lower Manhattan.[34]

31. "Urban Redevelopment and the Urbanite," pp. 309–68.

32. The extent of the area of regular daily commutation would be a good equivalent of the area of a metropolitan community. For some decades, the Bureau of the Census has been urged to secure this information in the decennial census. The English census of 1921 reported place of work as well as place of residence but dropped the inquiry in 1931. Albert Lepawsky, "Redefining the Metropolitan Area," *National Municipal Review,* xxv (July, 1936), 417–22. See also Gerald Breese, "Demography and Urban Areal Studies," Scientific Monthly, LXXIII (July, 1951), 45.

33. Regional Plan Association, *Persons and Vehicles Entering Manhattan South of 61st Street, 1924–1948,* Regional Plan Bulletin No. 74, New York, October, 1949. For the extent of commuting and a discussion of the problems associated with it, see *Transit and Transportation* ("Regional Survey of New York and Its Environs," Vol. IV, 1928).

34. The Association finds "that commuting by railroad is less than it was twenty years ago, and that commuting by all means of transportation is only 19 per cent higher than in 1930 (although suburban families have increased 50 per cent)." *New York's Commuters: Trends of Commuter Transportation in the New York Metropolitan Region, 1930–1950* (Regional Plan Bulletin No. 77, New York. July, 1951); *New York Times* (July 7, 1951).

In Seattle in 1950, the daytime population of the central city was 113 per cent of its nighttime population. Most of the extra daytime population was in the central business district (472 per cent of its nighttime population) and in the industrial district known as the Duwamish basin (333 per cent). In the remainder of the central city, the daytime population was 71 per cent of the nighttime population and in the remainder of the metropolitan area, it was 77 per cent.[35]

Data on the movement of people by motor vehicles within certain metropolitan areas as well as in and out of the areas can be secured from traffic surveys. Most recent traffic surveys conducted by state highway departments are perhaps comparable since they use the same procedure developed by the U.S. Bureau of Public Roads, although the various state departments do not follow a uniform pattern in reporting data. The data collected by the state highway departments during the surveys, much of which has not been analyzed and published, probably comprise the best information available on commuting habits of the residents and workers in metropolitan areas.

One type of information that can be picked out of some of the traffic surveys is the purpose of the trip. Sometime these purposes can be broken down by cars moving wholly within the survey area and by those moving into or out of the area.[36] On the whole, however, the data available on commuting are scanty and unsatisfactory.

Fragmented Local Government

Both the big city slicker (there are none in the suburbs) and the suburbanite (there are none in the central city) have become literary and vaudeville types. Mr. New Yorker himself has recently said that

35. Seattle City Planning Commission, *op. cit.*, pp. 7, 10, 60–61. See the Study of the commuting of Connecticut "rural" residents in Walter C. McKain, Jr., and Nathan L. Whetten, *Occupational and Industrial Diversity in Rural Connecticut* (Storrs Agricultural Experiment Station, University of Connecticut, Bulletin 263, November, 1949).

36. In the Philadelphia area, for instance, it is reported that "The purpose of 43.6 per cent of the auto trips into or out of the survey area was work, 34.8 per cent social and recreational reasons, 7.3 per cent business, 6.6 per cent shopping, and the remaining 7.7 per cent of the trips were made for various other reasons.

Of the auto trips made entirely within the area, 34.8 per cent were made to the home of the driver, 35.5 per cent to work, 9.7 per cent for social and recreational purposes, 7.0 per cent to serve passengers, 5.0 per cent to shop, 4.3 per cent for business reasons, and the remaining 3.7 per cent for various other reasons." Pennsylvania Department of Highways, *Philadelphia-Camden Area Traffic Survey* (Harrisburg, 1950), I, 1. The two volumes of this survey contain excellent maps showing the origin and destination of traffic to and from the various sections of the area.

In Harrisburg "approximately one-half of all auto trips within the area and about one-third of all auto trips into or out of the area were made by people either going to or from work, while only 6 per cent of the trips into or out of the area and 12 per cent of the trips within the area were made by shoppers." Pennsylvania Department of High-

The commuter is the queerest bird of all. The suburb he inhabits has no essential vitality of its own and is a mere roost where he comes at day's end to go to sleep. Except in rare cases, the man who lives in Mamaroneck or Little Neck or Teaneck, and works in New York, discovers nothing much about the city except the time of arrival and departure of trains and busses, and the path to a quick lunch. . . . He has fished in Manhattan's wallet and dug out coins, but has never listened to Manhattan's breathing, never awakened to its morning, never dropped off to sleep in its night.

About 400,000 men and women come charging onto the Island each week-day morning, out of the mouths of tubes and tunnels. . . . The commuter dies with tremendous mileage to his credit, but he is no rover. His entrance and exits are more devious than those in a prairie-dog village; and he calmly plays bridge while buried in the mud at the bottom of the East River. The Long Island Rail Road alone carried forty million commuters last year; but many of them were the same fellows retracing their steps.[38]

The antagonism of suburbs and central city becomes very evident when it is proposed to change in any manner the political and government relationships among them.[39] Beyond recording these antagonisms, however, we have done little to understand them. Until we understand, for instance, the psychological and social factors involved in the usually quiet identification of the suburbanite with the metropolitan com-

---

ways, *Harrisburg Traffic Survey* (Harrisburg, 1948), p. 15. See Walter Isard and Vincent Whitney, "Metropolitan Site Selection," *Social Forces,* XXVII (March, 1949), 263–69, for a discussion of the spatial distribution of the sale of consumer goods. See Institute of Local and State Government, University of Pennsylvania, *Springfield Township Population* (Philadelphia, 1950) for data on commuting for work and shopping in a suburban township adjacent to Philadelphia.

38. E. B. White, *Here Is New York* (New York: Harper & Bros., 1949), pp. 18–21.

39. "Despite the long period of controversy, there is wide disagreement as to the form which integration should take and a palpable absence of pertinent facts on which to form sound conclusions. Even more important, the controversy has stirred up violent prejudices and bad feeling so that at the present time the problem is commonly looked upon as insoluble.

"Sentiment for integration comes mainly from officials and residents in the City of Boston. Opposition comes from the suburban communities. The advantages cited by proponents are enhancement of economic prestige in world markets, improvement of governmental services and economy in governmental costs. The remonstrants assert that economic prestige is not gained by annexations or federations, and is already provided for by federal recognition of metropolitan districts; that a loss of self-government would ensue and that governmental competence would be dragged down to the Boston level with a resulting overall deterioration.

"Bostonians assert that the suburban communities which they term the 'bedrooms' of Boston, skim the cream of community benefits and leave the central city with the pale residue of disadvantages. They call for annexation or some less severe form of cooperative effort in order that these outlying communities may share in the responsibilities and costs of the area. Suburban residents claim that they contribute heavily in trade to the central city and build up its values far in excess of any contribution which the central city may make to the suburbs. Between these conflicting points of view there has not yet been found a common ground of agreement" (*Proposals for Downtown Boston,* Urban Land Institute, October, 1940, p. 53). See my *Metropolitan Government* (Chicago: The University of Chicago Press, 1942) pp. 296–319.

munity and often with the central city itself and at the same time his intense identification with the suburban municipality when its corporate identity is threatened, it will do little good to make plans for any kind of metropolitan government.

I have already pointed out that the one hundred and sixty-eight metropolitan communities are not politically organized as communities. The government of these communities is divided among a multitude of municipal corporations, counties, and special districts and authorities. This fragmentation is particularly evident in the larger metropolitan districts. In 1940, the average number of incorporated suburban municipalities alone in the 11 metropolitan districts of over a million population was over 85 per district. The average for the same number of districts between 500,000 and 1,000,000 was almost 22. For the 38 districts between 200,000 and 500,000 population, the average number was 7; for 48 districts between 100,000 and 200,000, it was 4; and for 32 districts between 50,000 and 100,000, it was approximately 1.25.[37]

These suburban municipalities have been incorporated to provide urban governmental services to the suburban dweller. In 1940, there were 1,697 incorporated suburbs in the census metropolitan districts; in 1930, there were 1,562; and in 1920, there were 1,395. Between 1930 and 1940, there were 108 new municipalities incorporated as compared with 235 in the previous decade. Only 11 municipal corporations were dissolved by complete annexation to the central city or another suburb and 9 were disincorporated. Fifty-eight municipalities were completely annexed between 1920 and 1930 and none were disincorporated.

Most suburbs are very small. More than 52 per cent in 1940 were places of less than 5,000 population. More than 45 per cent of all

37. These paragraphs are taken from an article by the author, "Metropolitan Districts," *The Municipal Year Book* (1942), pp. 180–82. Table 3 shows the number of suburban municipalities in 1940, 1930, and 1920 and the number of new incorporations, annexed municipalities and disincorporation by intervening decades. Table 4 shows the number and percentage distribution of suburban municipalities by population groups and by size of metropolitan districts. A comparable analysis of units of government at the present time will have to await the complete publication of the 1950 census of population and of the 1952 census of governments. For the San Francisco–Oakland area, see John C. Bollens, *The Problem of Government in the San Francisco Bay Region* (Berkeley: Bureau of Public Administration, University of California, 1948), pp. 22–32; for Los Angeles, see Helen L. Jones and Robert F. Wilcox, *Metropolitan Los Angeles: Its Governments* (Los Angeles: Haynes Foundation, 1949), pp. 30–33; for Birmingham, see Weldon Cooper, *Metropolitan County* (University: Bureau of Public Administration, University of Alabama, 1949), pp. 1–7; and for Atlanta, see Local Government Commission of Fulton County, *Plan of Improvement for the Governments of Atlanta and Fulton County, Georgia* (Atlanta, 1950), pp. 4, 18.

For older studies, see my *Metropolitan Government;* National Municipal League, *The Government of Metropolitan Areas in the United States* (New York, 1930); Charles E. Merriam, Spencer Paratt, and Albert Lepawsky, *The Government of the Metropolitan Region of Chicago* (Chicago: University of Chicago Press, 1933); and National Resources Committee, *Our Cities: Their Role in the National Economy* (Washington, D.C., 1937).

suburbs were so small that their population was classified by the Bureau of the Census as rural!

FUNCTIONAL DIFFERENCES WITHIN METROPOLITAN COMMUNITIES

It is a matter of general knowledge that cities are not alike even though on the surface each city may look rather like any other city. The function of a city is to bring together in a small area many special activities which serve the inhabitants of the city and a large hinterland. The general configuration of a multitude of specialized activities in a culture in which common techniques are widely dispersed gives the appearance of similarity. But a breakdown of this configuration into its components will show a different combination for each metropolitan community.[40]

Various parts of the metropolitan community, however, differ from each other more markedly than metropolitan communities differ from each other. Everyone is aware of residential suburbs and industrial suburbs, of wealthy suburbs and of poor suburbs. One can easily see the difference between Brookline and Revere or Newton and Chelsea in metropolitan Boston or between Highland Park and Calumet in metropolitan Chicago. Despite the many ecological studies that have identified "natural" areas within central cities, we still are prone to compare incorporated suburbs with the entire incorporated central city.[41] In comparing a single large population aggregate with several smaller aggregates, the differences within the central city are blunted out and the suburbanite is able to base his claim for political independence on the assumption that a common government for many types of neighborhoods is unsatisfactory and undesirable.

The fact is that a metropolitan community is distinguished from other communities by the location of many types of economic, political, and social activities in close proximity to each other on a relatively small land area. The subareas may be identified by the use of one or several of many indexes. For example, one hundred and eighty-five

40. See W. F. Ogburn, *Social Characteristics of Cities* (Chicago: International City Managers Association, 1937); Chauncey Harris, "A Functional Classification of Cities in The United States," *Geographical Review*, XXIII (January, 1943), 86–99, and "Suburbs," *American Journal of Sociology*, XLIX (July, 1943), 1–13; Grace Kneedler Ohlson, "Economic Classification of Cities," *Municipal Year Book* (1946), pp. 32–40; E. L. Thorndike, *Your City* (New York: Harcourt, Brace & Co., 1939) and *144 Smaller Cities* (1940); P. B. Gillen, *The Distribution of Occupations as a City Yardstick* (New York: Columbia University Press, 1951); R. C. Angell, "The Moral Integration of American Cities," *American Journal of Sociology*, LVII (July, 1951), Part 2.

41. In thirteen metropolitan districts, there were in 1940 thirteen central cities which entirely surrounded twenty-nine incorporated municipalities. Los Angeles has thirteen incorporated enclaves and eleven unincorporated enclaves. R. C. Spencer, "29 Cities within Cities," *National Municipal Review*, XXXVII (May, 1948), 256–58.

neighborhoods have been mapped in the Los Angeles metropolitan area and grouped into nine social areas.[42]

The specialization of incorporated suburbs has been indicated by the Ohlson classification of cities of 10,000 population or over in 1940.[43]

TABLE 8

DISTRIBUTION OF SUBURBS OVER 10,000 POPULATION IN TWENTY-SEVEN METROPOLITAN DISTRICTS, 1940, BY COMMUTING TYPE AND RENT LEVEL*

| | | | | | TYPE OF SUBURB | | | | | | |
| | Dormitory† | | | | Balanced‡ RENT LEVEL | | | | Employing§ | | |
AREA	Low‖	Inter- medi- ate#	High**	Ex- clu- sive††	Low	Inter- medi- ate	High	Ex- clu- sive	Low	Inter- medi- ate	High
New York–N.E. New Jersey	3	18	10	3	7	6	1		9	1	
Chicago	3	5	5	3		2			5		
Los Angeles	6	8			1	3	1			1	
Philadelphia	1	1	1		1	1			3	1	
Boston	5	11	8	1	1	3			3	6	1
Detroit	2	2	1	1	1	2			4	1	
Pittsburgh		3	3		1	2			4	12	
St. Louis	1	1	2	2	1	2					
San Francisco–Oakland	1	5	2						1		
Cleveland		2	2	1						1	
Baltimore						1					
Providence	2	5			2				1	4	
Minneapolis–St. Paul										1	
Washington, D.C.	1										
Buffalo			1						1	2	
Milwaukee			2						2	1	
Cincinnati	2		1							1	
Kansas City		1									
New Orleans	1										
Atlanta		1									
Louisville	1				1						
Albany-Schenectady-Troy									1		
Birmingham		1				1					
Portland (Oregon)						1					
Dallas		1	1								
Youngstown		2							2	2	
San Diego	1										

* Grace Kneedler Ohlson, "Economic Classification of Cities," *The Municipal Year Book* (1946), pp. 32–40, and Table 4, pp. 50–70.
† Dormitory suburb: most of the people who reside in the suburb work elsewhere.
‡ Balanced suburb: the number of people who come to the city to work approximately balances the number who commute to other areas to work.
§ Employing suburb: more people work in the city than live there.
‖ Low rent level: $5 per month or more below the average rent for the metropolitan district.
Intermediate rent level: within a range of $5 below and $10 above the average rent.
** High rent level: more than $10 above the average rent.
†† Exclusive rent level: more than twice the average rent.

Building upon Chauncey Harris' classification scheme, cities were classified as dormitory suburbs, employing suburbs, and those in which these two functions are balanced.[44] Each of these types was further

42. Eshref Shevky and Molly Lewin, *Your Neighborhood: A Social Profile of Los Angeles* (Los Angeles: Haynes Foundation, 1949).
43. *The Municipal Year Book* (1946), pp. 32–40.
44. Planning surveys of suburban municipalities sometimes contain material that will help to place the suburb within the metropolitan community. See, for example, the Scott Bagby surveys of New Jersey suburbs and A. A. Shurcliff and S. N. Shurcliff, *Master Plan of Dedham, Massachusetts: Survey and Report* (1947).

classified on the basis of average rents in the suburb as compared with the average rent for the metropolitan district. Table 8 shows the number of such suburbs as of 1940 in certain of the larger metropolitan districts.

DIFFERENCES BETWEEN CENTRAL CITIES AND SUBURBS

Data from the 1950 Census are not yet available on the population and housing characteristics of individual suburbs. But the preliminary reports on population and housing characteristics of fifty-seven standard metropolitan areas with a population of 250,000 or more in 1940, based on a sample of the Census returns, enable us to make rough distinctions between the central cities and the outlying areas as a whole.[45]

TABLE 9

DISTRIBUTION OF FAMILIES AND UNRELATED INDIVIDUALS BY INCOME
GROUPS IN 11 STANDARD METROPOLITAN AREAS, 1949*

METROPOLITAN AREA	PERCENTAGE UNDER $2,500		PERCENTAGE $2,500 TO $5,000		PERCENTAGE OVER $5,000	
	Central City	Outlying Area	Central City	Outlying Area	Central City	Outlying Area
Boston......................	48	34	28	38	25	29
Cincinnati...................	48	30	37	45	15	22
Chicago.....................	34	27	41	44	25	29
Detroit......................	29	23	44	44	27	33
Indianapolis.................	38	29	41	34	21	37
Kansas City.................	47	38	37	47	16	15
Los Angeles.................	44	38	36	42	20	20
New Orleans.................	55	47	25	42	20	11
Pittsburgh...................	42	33	38	46	20	21
Providence..................	53	37	34	45	13	18
San Francisco–Oakland.........	40	28	39	50	21	22

* From U.S. Bureau of the Census, 1950, Series PC-5, Table 13.

Probably no one is surprised that the increase in the number of children under five years is greater in the suburbs than in the central city, that there is a larger proportion of married people, that families are larger, the number of dwelling units increased more rapidly, that a larger proportion of dwelling units are owner-occupied, and that the median value of dwelling units is higher. There are exceptions to this general statement, some of which may be explained by large annexations to some of the central cities during the decade. But the general

45. U.S. Bureau of the Census, Series PC-5 and HC-3 (1950). These data are based on a sample of census returns. Each number in the series, reporting a particular standard metropolitan area, contains a statement on the source and reliability of the data and a table showing "sampling variability of estimates of selected sizes." The reader is cautioned to interpret with particular care the smaller figures and the smaller differences between figures.

picture is one of differentiation in social characteristics between the central city and the suburbs.

Income is certainly an important factor in explaining certain other social characteristics of a population.[46] We can recognize this without accepting the large degree of equivalence between wealth and "goodness" postulated by E. L. Thorndike and P. B. Gillen.

The preliminary reports based upon a sample of the Census returns for eleven large standard metropolitan areas shows that the central cities have a larger proportion of their families and unrelated individuals with an income of less than $2,500 a year than do the suburban areas (Table 9). There are, conversely, a larger proportion of high-income families and unrelated individuals in the suburbs of all but two of the areas (Kansas City and New Orleans).[47] The difference is not appreciable in Pittsburgh and in San Francisco–Oakland. Only in Indianapolis is there a larger proportion of the middle-income group in the central city than in the suburbs. Detroit and its outlying area contain the same proportion of families and unrelated individuals making between $2,500 and $5,000 a year.

Summary

All of the American people should be concerned with the growth of metropolitan communities. About half of them live in a metropolitan community. One-fourth of them live in the twelve largest metropolitan areas. The remainder of the American people, even if they are not destined to move during this decade into a large city or its environs, are affected politically, economically, and socially by what happens in metropolitan areas. We are a metropolitanized people.

Metropolitan areas have no political boundaries despite the existence of problems arising from the constant dealings between the people who live in these heavy concentrations of people in a central city and those who live in its environs. Ever since the modern revolution in the means of transit and communication began, these metropolitan communities have been growing more rapidly than the rest of the country. Within metropolitan communities, the areas outside the older central settlements have been growing more rapidly than the central city or the older suburbs near the central city. The 1950 census shows that these trends are continuing at an accelerated rate.

46. Note that in the four cities whose "moral integration" was studied by Angell, 86.3 per cent (mean) of the leaders had incomes of over $7.500 and 71.4 per cent had incomes other than their salary (*op. cit.*, p. 40). See also Ogburn's comparison of wealthy suburbs and industrial suburbs (*Social Characteristics of Cities*, pp. 56–60).

47. The selective migration from the central city to suburbs noted by Dewey (*op. cit.*, p. 11) would in part explain this differential.

It is not surprising to find that certain social characteristics of the metropolitan population are different in the central city than in the suburbs. Closer analysis will show, however, that the central city as a whole should not be compared with the suburbs as a whole. The entire metropolitan area is a community of specialties. Various parts of the metropolitan community, or of the central city or of most suburbs, differ from each other more markedly than metropolitan communities differ from each other. Political or social conclusions based on such actual or alleged differences should be viewed suspiciously.

Local government in metropolitan areas is divided among many large and small municipalities, townships, counties, and special districts. This fragmented local government is faced with unsolved problems of urban life in the suburbs, in the central city, or certain parts thereof, and throughout the metropolitan area. These problems, particularly as they relate to housing and urban development and redevelopment will be discussed in the next chapter.

CHAPTER III

METROPOLITAN PROBLEMS

WHEN IS METROPOLITAN GOVERNMENT NEEDED?

WHAT does it matter if metropolitan communities are not governmental units? All parts of a metropolitan community are under the jurisdiction of some unit of local government and many parts are subject to the jurisdiction of several overlying local governments. Is this not enough government? Should we not direct our attention and energy to seeing that each governmental agency does its job efficiently and effectively?

A metropolitan government is desirable (1) when co-ordination of a function over the whole area is essential to effective service or control in any part of the area; (2) when it is desired to apply the ability-to-pay theory of taxation to the area as a whole, instead of allowing each part to support its own activities at whatever level its own economic base will allow; (3) when services can be supplied more efficiently through large-scale operations and when the advantages of large-scale operations are desired; and (4) when it is necessary in order to assure citizens a voice in decisions that affect them at their places of work and recreation as well as at their places of residence.

This does not mean that all existing units of local government must be abolished and all local government placed under a single unit with jurisdiction over the entire metropolitan area. One of the impediments to the reorganization of local government in metropolitan areas is our frequent approach to the problem as if we were limited in our possibilities to annexation (call it city-county consolidation, if you wish) or to the status quo.

Before considering the organization of government in metropolitan areas, it is necessary to consider what it is that we want the government to do. Otherwise we shall be advocating or opposing metropolitan government for wholly irrational reasons. Not that our objectives are completely rational, but, given our objectives, we have two questions to answer. First, are the problems of city life which we hope to solve metropolitan problems? Secondly, what form of governmental organization of the metropolitan community is most likely to be able to handle metropolitan problems with as little damage as possible to other

508

values that may be widely held in the community or in various parts of it? In this chapter, I am concerned with the first of these questions.

BLIGHT FOUND IN SUBURBS AS WELL AS IN CENTRAL CITIES

Blight is not, as commonly thought, the peculiar characteristic of central cities. It is to be found in various stages of intensity in all parts of the metropolitan community except in a very few parts which have been recently developed and well planned. Certainly the most acute stage of chronic blight is in the slum area of the central city. Coleman Woodbury has summed up the conclusions of numerous studies of slum areas:

Usually but not always these are near the central part of the central city of the region. Usually but not always they are predominately old residential areas, which in an advanced stage of obsolescence and deterioration are commonly called slums. Almost always, except in times of acute housing shortage and serious economic depression, they are areas of declining population. Over the years, many of them are lived in by successive waves of nationality and racial groups that, for one reason or another, are near the bottom of the economic ladder. Usually, but not always, they are areas of social disorganization—with high rates of crime, juvenile delinquency, communicable diseases; marked in varying degrees by squalor and ugliness, political and economic exploitation, social discrimination and the inevitable bitterness and resentment.[1]

Contrary to popular impression, however, suburbs are often less desirable than the central city as a place to live. The Cook County Housing Authority finds "that substantially *more than half of the suburban communities surrounding Chicago rated lower in desirability as a place of residence than the city itself.*"[2] Many metropolitan areas have their West Dallas suburbs which equal or exceed any area in the central city in the deterioration of property values and in the disorganization of social life.[3] The older suburbs adjacent to the central cities in the larger metropolitan areas are often indistinguishable from the central city itself. Every decade sees the land use of larger portions of the nearby suburbs change to that of the central city. People who are able to move aid the transition by fleeing from the congested suburb.

DILAPIDATED HOUSING

The preliminary reports based on a sample of the dwelling units enumerated in the 1950 census of housing indicate that a substantial

1. Coleman Woodbury, "Housing in the Redevelopment of American Cities," *Land Economics* (November, 1949), p. 398.
2. Cook County Housing Authority, *Housing Market Analysis, 1949 Supplement*, p. 3. The full quotation will be found on p. 515 of this chapter.
3. K. F. Baines, "Social Survey of West Dallas," unpublished M.A. thesis in sociology, Southern Methodist University, 1950.

number of the dwelling units outside the central city are dilapidated or lack running water.[4] The application of the census definition of dilapidation will not in itself give us the number of dwelling units in blighted areas.[5] But the preliminary census counts do show that the suburban areas of all larger metropolitan communities contain many dwelling units which "should be torn down, extensively repaired, or rebuilt."

In the metropolitan communities of Baltimore, Buffalo, Chicago, Dallas, Denver, Houston, Indianapolis, Kansas City, Louisville, Minneapolis–St. Paul, Pittsburgh, Portland (Oregon), St. Louis, San Antonio, San Francisco–Oakland, and Seattle, a larger proportion of the dwelling units outside the central city are dilapidated or lack running water than within the central city. In Buffalo, Houston, and Pittsburgh, the proportion outside is over twice as large as in the central city; in metropolitan Dallas, the proportion in the suburbs is over three-and-a-half times as large as in the central city; in Denver, it is almost four times as large; in Minneapolis–St. Paul, it is over five times as large; and in Portland (Oregon) over six times as large (Table 10).

In thirteen of the larger metropolitan areas, the total number of dwelling units dilapidated or lacking running water is higher in the suburbs than in the central city: Boston, Buffalo, Dallas, Denver, Kansas City, Minneapolis–St. Paul, Pittsburgh, Portland (Oregon), Providence, Rochester, St. Louis, San Francisco–Oakland, and Seattle. In the Pittsburgh and Portland (Oregon) areas over 80 per cent of dilapidated dwelling units are in the suburbs (Table 10).

More intensive analyses of the areal distribution of substandard dwelling units may be found in a few metropolitan housing surveys and in some general planning surveys.[6] Most surveys, however, are concerned only with the central city or with a particular suburb. Seldom is there an attempt to relate developments within the survey area to developments in the remainder of the metropolitan area.

The Cincinnati City Planning Commission has identified the resi-

4. U.S. Bureau of the Census, Series HC-3, Table 7 (1950). According to the Bureau of the Census, "A dwelling unit is dilapidated when it has serious deficiencies, is run-down or neglected, or is of inadequate original construction, so that the dwelling unit does not provide adequate shelter or protection against the elements or it endangers the safety of the occupants. Dilapidated dwelling units are so classified either because of deterioration, as evidenced by the presence of one or more critical deficiencies or a combination of minor deficiencies, or because of inadequate original construction, such that they should be torn down, extensively repaired, or rebuilt."

5. More than the condition of particular dwelling units is involved in blight. See Allan A. Twichell, "Measuring the Quality of Housing in Planning for Urban Redevelopment" (Urban Redevelopment Study) and "An Appraisal Method for Measuring the Quality of Housing," *American Sociological Review*, XIII (June, 1948), 278–87.

6. Most of these surveys use 1940 census data although some of them use more recent data gathered in the field.

TABLE 10

DISTRIBUTION OF DWELLING UNITS DILAPIDATED OR WITHOUT RUNNING WATER BY
CENTRAL CITY AND SUBURBAN AREA IN TWENTY-SIX STANDARD
METROPOLITAN AREAS, 1950*

STANDARD METROPOLITAN AREA	PERCENTAGE OF DILAPIDATED DWELLING UNITS IN			DISTRIBUTION OF DILAPIDATED DWELLING UNITS		
	Metropolitan Area	Central City	Outside Area	Metropolitan Area	Inside Central City	Outside Central City
Baltimore	8	7	11	100	66	34
Boston	6	7	4	100	47	53
Buffalo	8	5	11	100	36	64
Chicago	6	6	8	100	59	41
Cincinnati	6	7	6	100	68	32
Cleveland	5	6	2	100	86	14
Dallas	17	9	35	100	36	64
Denver	11	6	23	100	45	55
Detroit	5	5	5	100	68	32
Houston	13	10	20	100	60	40
Indianapolis	11	10	13	100	73	27
Kansas City	11	9	14	100	46	54
Los Angeles	3	4	3	100	51	49
Louisville	12	11	15	100	59	41
Milwaukee	5	6	2	100	90	10
Minneapolis–St. Paul	8	5	27	100	32	68
New York–Northeastern New Jersey	6	6	4	100	77	23
Philadelphia	5	5	5	100	55	45
Pittsburgh	10	5	12	100	17	83
Portland (Oregon)	7	2	13	100	12	88
Providence	5	7	4	100	44	56
Rochester	4	3	7	100	48	52
St. Louis	15	12	19	100	40	60
San Antonio	20	17	32	100	68	32
San Francisco–Oakland	4	3	4	100	48	52
Seattle	6	4	9	100	44	56

* U.S. Bureau of the Census, Series HC-3, 1950, Table 7.

dental neighborhoods in Cincinnati and the remainder of Hamilton
County and indicated the type of action needed to reclaim or protect
each neighborhood from blight. More neighborhoods within the city
than in the suburban area are in need of rehabilitation and the volume
of "bad order" housing is considerably larger within the city. Nevertheless, "some rehabilitation is needed in 9 [county] neighborhoods
and some conservation in 16. . . ."[7]

Apparently the well-to-do suburbs are more aware than other su-

7. Nineteen suburban neighborhoods are reported as "generally in good condition." As
of 1950, however, the Bureau of the Census reports 2,850 occupied dwelling units in Newport, Kentucky, which are substandard under the definition of the U.S Public Housing
Administration (Series HC-6, No. 147, December 29, 1950). "In the city, rehabilitation
is needed in 24 neighborhoods; conservation programs in 21; and 21 are in sufficiently
good condition as to need only further protection" (Cincinnati City Planning Commission,
Residential Areas [Metropolitan Master Plan Study No. 9, December, 1946], pp. 49–54).
Notice that residential neighborhoods in the Kentucky portion of the metropolitan area
are excluded from the Cincinnati count.

burbs of existing, impending, or threatened blight. This is particularly true of the suburbs nearest to the central city such as Evanston, Illinois,[8] and Montclair, New Jersey. The type of housing that worries civic leaders in these communities might well be envied in other parts of the metropolitan area.

Beyond the problem of immediate housing needs lies the important matter of redevelopment. There are 332 acres of land in Montclair occupied by dwelling units, the assessed valuation of which units averages less than $3,000. Ninety-six of the 332 acres are occupied by dwelling units assessed at less than $2,000 each. These latter may be considered blighted areas where redevelopment is immediately necessary; the remainder need attention in the reasonably near future to prevent further deterioration of larger areas surrounding them. To the extent that single-family units are assessed at less than $7,000, and multi-family dwelling units at less than $3,600 they fail to pay their proportionate share of government and school costs, and are thus subsidized by the taxes paid on other properties of higher valuation. It is of economic interest to all property owners and residents, therefore, that a program of redevelopment be initiated at the earliest possible date.[9]

The bias of the planners, if not of the town's leaders, and the parochial view of their community responsibilities, are shown in an earlier statement in the same report:

Although the census figures [1940] show no substantial change in the total population, [the distribution of average rentals by census enumeration districts] indicates that there has been an increase in the number of people of lower economic means. There is good reason to be concerned about this trend because it should be obvious that, given a high quality of interest in cultural values, the citizens who can back their interest up with economic means can provide a better community than the same citizens without those economic means.[10]

Selected data on substandard dwelling units as defined by the Public Housing Administration are reported by the Bureau of the Census for a few suburbs that purchased from the Bureau a special tabulation (Table 11). The housing authorities of Sacramento, Stockton, and Bakersfield, California, secured the special tabulation for their urban fringes[11] and seven others had the tabulations made for the entire urbanized area or for the central city and selected suburban areas.[12] These data show that the suburbs as well as the central cities are deteriorating in spots,

8. See Homer Hoyt Associates, *Economic Survey of the Land Uses of Evanston, Illinois* (Evanston Plan Commission, 1949).

9. Montclair, New Jersey, Development Board, *A Program of Town Development* (1946), p. 8. This argument, frequently expressed by large taxpayers, is discussed on pp. 520 ff. of this chapter.

10. *Ibid.*, p. 6; see also p. 21.

11. U.S. Bureau of the Census, Series HC-6, Nos. 154, 155, and 180.

12. Reading, Pennsylvania; Dallas, Texas; Texas City, Texas; Columbus, Ohio; Annapolis, Maryland; Racine, Wisconsin; and Newport News, Virginia. Series HC-6, Nos. 163, 165, 166, 178, 194, 211, 215.

TABLE 11

Occupied Substandard Dwelling Units, 1950
Certain Suburban Areas*

Metropolitan Area, Central City, and Suburbs	Total Number	Percentage Owner-Occupied	Percentage Dilapidated	Percentage Distribution of Units by Number of Persons per Room			
				1 or less	1.01 to 1.50	1.51 to 2.00	2.01 or more
New York–Northeastern New Jersey area							
Jersey City	14,637	10.0	28.3	75.0	16.1	6.2	2.4
Paterson, N.J.	9,397	15.8	32.4	77.3	14.0	5.9	2.4
Harrison, N.J.	808	14.4	32.3	75.0	16.5	6.5	1.7
West New York, N.J.	399	12.3	14.3	81.6	11.4	5.1	1.9
Hoboken, N.J.	4,847	5.2	16.6	74.5	18.6	5.6	1.2
Bayonne, N.J.	1,887	9.2	28.7	71.5	17.7	7.2	3.2
Woodbridge Township, N.J.	998	44.8	18.3	70.3	17.9	10.0	1.8
Yonkers, N.Y.	5,609	11.9	23.4	79.4	14.2	4.9	1.3
Philadelphia area							
Camden, N.J.	5,783	33.2	29.7	79.0	11.2	7.4	2.3
Detroit area							
Detroit, Mich.	46,655	14.9	42.5	62.8	19.8	12.1	4.4
River Rouge, Mich.	859	30.6	30.5	64.1	21.5	11.0	2.8
Providence area							
Providence, R.I.	27,687	15.0	12.5	79.2	14.3	5.3	0.9
Woonsocket, R.I.	7,876	11.8	11.0	84.9	11.5	3.2	0.4
Pawtucket, R.I.	10,047	19.2	6.0	86.8	10.1	2.1	0.7
Cincinnati area							
Newport, Ky.	2,850	28.0	20.1	53.6	19.3	14.9	12.2
St. Louis area							
East St. Louis, Ill.	11,147	37.2	36.8	58.8	18.7	13.5	8.2
Granite City, Ill.	2,773	44.7	29.2	60.4	21.8	12.2	5.5
Pittsburgh area							
Aliquippa, Pa.	1,483	31.4	47.5	60.0	24.1	10.9	5.0
McKeesport, Pa.	5,049	26.5	27.6	67.3	20.0	9.7	3.0
Phoenix area							
Phoenix, Ariz.	5,801	34.5	42.3	53.0	17.9	17.8	10.5
Vicinity	8,492	57.8	34.9	42.4	19.7	19.6	17.6
Sacramento area							
Sacramento	3,995	15.9	32.2	75.4	14.5	11.5	7.2
Urban fringe	4,620	51.3	39.2	47.1	19.8	18.0	13.2
Stockton area							
Urban fringe	3,819	48.7	44.1	47.5	21.7	17.0	13.4
Bakersfield (Calif.)							
Urban fringe	4,211	48.8	44.3	41.0	19.3	20.7	17.2

* U.S. Bureau of the Census, Special tabulations for local housing authorities, Series HC-6.

even though the number of individual substandard dwelling units cannot by itself indicate the extent or intensity of blight.[13]

BLIGHTED UNDEVELOPED LAND

Extensive blighted areas may contain no substandard housing at all
and no or few dwelling units of any kind. This is recognized in the
Housing Act of 1949 in the provision for redevelopment of open and
predominantly open land and of blighted industrial areas. In every
metropolitan area during the 1920's open land was subdivided in excess of the demand. Frequently, the site was unsatisfactory and the
physical layout of the subdivision was poorly planned and executed. In
many subdivisions a few of the more desirable lots were built upon and
the rest were left vacant.[14]

Much of this poorly planned and premature subdivision took place in
suburban areas.[15] Some occurred in central cities during the 1920's, but
they already had a legacy of "dead" land from previous real estate
booms. Despite the extension of zoning and subdivision controls during
the last two decades and the extensive building upon newly subdivided
land, some of the acreage subdivided since World War II will undoubtedly add to the "dead" land of the future.

It is relatively easy to put zoning and subdivision control ordinances
in the book. But they are often harmful if they are not based upon a
sound plan for the development of the municipality or the county that
is part of a general plan for the development of the metropolitan community. If exceptions are easily secured or if inspections are casual,
zoning and subdivision control ordinances are dangerous in that they

13. In 1942 R. C. Klove divided the northwestern Chicago suburbs of Park Ridge, Des
Plaines, Mt. Prospect, Arlington Heights, Palatine, and Barrington in ninety-three neighborhoods and found twenty-five to be "new but stunted," eight "old but stunted," fourteen
"declining," and one "blighted." "The Park Ridge–Barrington Area: A Study of Residential Land Patterns and Problems in Suburban Chicago" (photo-off-set, University of
Chicago Library, 1942), pp. 30–33.

14. Philip H. Cornick, *Premature Subdivision and Its Consequences* (New York: Institute of Public Administration, 1938); Robert E. Merriam, *The Subdivision of Land* (Chicago: Public Administration Service, 1942); Michigan Planning Commission, *A Study of
Subdivision Development in the Detroit Metropolitan Area* (1938); Klove, *op. cit.*, pp.
69–96.

15. Once poor planning has fixed the physical form of a subdivision, the selectivity of
the market may doom it as a place to live by those who can afford to go elsewhere. Note
the finding of Richard Dewey that "in the unincorporated units the subdivided areas
selected by residents are those of more recent date, with lots of relatively wide frontage,
and within a plat designed in conformity with modern standards. This coincides exceptionally well with the evidence cited in the foregoing section which pointed directly to
congestion and its attendant ills as the primary factor in residential decentralization"
(*Residential Development in the Unincorporated Areas of Milwaukee County* [1946],
p. 12).

will lead to a false sense of security on the part of land owners, sub-division developers, and the general public.

A principal finding in the Basic Market Analysis was that the greater portion of the County area suffered from out-dated and inadequately enforced building codes, ineffective zoning ordinances, lack of community planning and inefficient municipal services and government. As a matter of fact, the Scoring of Community Desirability study undertaken by the Housing Authority of the County of Cook and Real Estate Research Corporation found that substantially *more than half of the suburban communities surrounding Chicago rated lower in desirability as a place of residence than the city itself.*

A review of these same factors at the end of 1949 shows a discouraging lack of change in the situation reported previously. There have been a few isolated instances of sincere municipal effort at correcting those abuses which adversely affect real estate values and amenities though most community services and planning continue at the same level as in 1947–48. Those few communities which had a high degree of municipal integrity and citizen interest—principally the prestige suburbs—have continued to guard jealously the existing high level of administration without, however, there being a single noteworthy instance of improvement in the fields of planning, building codes, subdivision control or zoning, except that in Chicago Heights.[16]

The Cleveland metropolitan area provides a good illustration of the large number of vacant lots in the suburbs, many of which are delinquent on the tax and special assessment rolls. Sixty-three cities, villages and townships in Cuyahoga County had vacant sublots which comprised from 2 per cent to 100 per cent of all the sublots in the unit. All but seven of these units in 1947 exceeded Cleveland (13 per cent) in the percentage of vacant sublots. In three-fourths of the units the vacancy ratio exceeded 28 per cent; in one-half, the ratio was 50 per cent or more; and in one-fourth, it was over 65 per cent.[17] Lakewood with only 3 per cent of its sublots vacant had only 6.4 per cent of its land tax delinquent. The highest percentage of tax delinquency was in Brooklyn Village with 55 per cent of its land tax delinquent and 59 per cent of its sublots vacant. For the county as a whole, there were in 1946 approximately 230,000 parcels of land with buildings on them and almost 132,000 vacant parcels. Over 106,000 parcels were tax delinquent.[18]

16. Cook County Housing Authority, *Housing Market Analysis* 1949, Supplement, p. 3. The Real Estate Research Corporation, which makes these studies for the Housing Authority, says in the 1951 Supplement, p. 6, that "There is increased evidence of need for improved enforcement of building codes and modernization of zoning ordinances in almost all of the suburban communities studied."

17. Regional Association of Cleveland, *An Inventory of Vacant Residential Land* (1948, Publication No. 19), p. 24.

18. *Ibid.*, p. 23. See pp. 14–18 for a more detailed analysis of the problem in Euclid. The questions asked on pp. 19–22 will suggest some of the present and developing problems in Rocky River, Lakewood, Brooklyn Village, South Euclid, East Cleveland, Bratenahl, University Heights, Shaker Heights, and Cleveland Heights. See the various annual reports of the Cleveland Real Property Inventory by H. W. Green.

"Dead" land is a problem in other metropolitan areas but probably nowhere is it more serious than in metropolitan Chicago. In parts of southern Cook County, lots subdivided in the 1890's are still vacant and most of them are tax delinquent. More than half of all the parcels of land in this part of the area had been tax delinquent in 1946 for more than ten years. In Harvey, all the vacant lots (6,500) had been delinquent for more than ten years. Ninety per cent of these vacant lots were connected with sewer and water.[19] The problem is worse in the southern portion of the county, but municipalities and unincorporated areas throughout the county, including the city of Chicago, were affected by the problem.

Approximately 22 per cent of the total parcels of land within the city of Chicago had been delinquent in 1945 for over ten years. Almost 40 per cent of the parcels in suburban Cook County were chronically delinquent. Despite the severity of the problem within the central city, it is much worse in the suburbs. With only 45 per cent of the total number of parcels of land within the county, they had 60 per cent of the chronic delinquencies.[20]

The loss in tax revenues from idle and delinquent land is tremendous, but the principal concern over the problem is its social and economic effects on the community as a place to live, work, and play. Unused and chronically delinquent land has been called "dead" land by the Cook County Housing Authority because it is

land which is used by nobody and very often is, in effect, owned by nobody.
    . . . Because of the [tax] encumbrances, the lost ownership or the owner's indifference, the legal difficulties, and the tediousness of existing remedies, the land is virtually unavailable to those who can and would develop it.[21]

There are many other reasons for the movement of people into the outer fringes of metropolitan areas but the inability to use vacant land in the central city and its immediate environs prevents the exercise of a choice which would otherwise be available. Scattered developments, particularly when spread around the lengthy outer circumference, mean that utilities and governmental services must be developed or extended to the new areas. Facilities have already been installed in the older developed sections of the area and organized local governments are operating there.[22]

19. See the detailed analysis of the problem in Harvey and Skokie in Cook County Housing Authority, *"Dead" Land: A Study of Chronic Tax Delinquency and Abandonment* (Chicago, 1949), pp. 76–88.
    20. *Ibid.*, p. 8; for data by townships and selected municipalities see pp. 12 and 17. See Chicago Plan Commission, *Blighted Vacant Land* (1951).
    21. *Ibid.*, p. 1.
    22. Scott Bagby has emphasized this point in each of his planning survey reports on surburban communities in northeastern New Jersey.

The Cook County Housing Authority emphasizes the indirect costs of "dead" land: It increases the cost of servicing existing homes, requires expensive extensions to service new areas, depreciates property values in the neighborhood, increases the capital cost of housing, prevents an increase of tax revenues to the taxing unit in which the "dead" land lies, contributes to disorderly metropolitan expansion, and makes it difficult to plan for desirable and economic uses of all the land in the particular locality and in the metropolitan area.[23]

The recapture of "dead" land in a metropolitan area such as Chicago should be undertaken by a governmental unit with jurisdiction over the whole area. Only a relatively few metropolitan areas are contained within a single county and therefore have a unit of local government with area-wide jurisdiction. It may well be that the county should assume this[24] as well as other metropolitan functions even in multi-county metropolitan areas. (The potentialities of the county as a metropolitan government will be considered in chapter vii.) But certainly, the authority to recapture and plan the redevelopment of "dead" land should not be divided among the central city, the larger suburbs and the county with the latter acting only outside the larger municipalities.[25] The discussion of whether open land can be redeveloped under Title I, as "an adjunct to or a necessary part of an over-all slum clearance program"[26] is somewhat academic if the central city and the suburbs act without regard to each other, or in opposition to each other, or in ignorance of their common problems and destiny.

THE RELOCATION PROBLEM

The relocation of families displaced by redevelopment projects, whether they be Title I projects, extensive public works projects, or private developments, is another problem that should be planned and carried out without regard to municipal boundary lines. Programs underway or planned for the next few years in Chicago may be used to illustrate the size of the problem. By October, 1950, over 5,000 families and single persons had been relocated from the project sites being cleared for the Congress Street superhighway, the Veterans Administration Hospital, redevelopment project No. 1, public housing, the Chi-

23. Cook County Housing Authority, *op. cit.*, pp. 19–27.

24. As recommended by the Cook County Housing Authority, *ibid.*, pp. 34–45.

25. The Cook County Housing Authority study does not cover the problem in those areas outside its jurisdiction: Chicago, Evanston, Cicero, Berwyn, Oak Park, and Maywood. Its housing market analyses, likewise, refer only incidentally to these municipalities, but more frequently than most similar surveys in other metropolitan areas.

26. See *Redevelopment Information Service Newsletter* (National Association of Housing Officials), November 15, 1950, December 15, 1950, and January 15, 1951.

cago Medical Center, and the Illinois Institute of Technology. It was estimated as of that date that 18,600 families and single persons were yet to be relocated.[27]

In some metropolitan areas displaced persons may easily be relocated in other portions of the central city. The price for this show of independence, however, may be the location of these people on undesirable sites or in neighborhoods equally or more congested than the ones they left. In other metropolitan areas, such as those in New England where the area of the central city is small and is entirely surrounded by ancient and jealous towns, relocation under satisfactory living conditions will be exceedingly difficult. The problem is not solved but made only more acute by saying that Brookline doesn't want the Northenders and that the Northenders do not want to live in Brookline.[28]

FEW SUBURBS INTERESTED IN URBAN REDEVELOPMENT

Thus far suburban areas have shown little interest in urban redevelopment. Some suburbs have secured capital grant reservations under Title I and others are giving increasing attention in planning and rezoning to blighted areas. The Joint Committee on Housing of the 80th Congress held subcommittee hearings in thirty-one major cities of the country. Representatives of the central cities, in addition to representatives of the City Housing Authorities, were present at the hearings in each city except Dallas and San Antonio. In New York City, the only suburban witness was the director of the Westchester County Department of Planning. At Jersey City, the only suburban representative was the mayor of Orange. Representatives of the Dade County Planning Board testified at Miami, of the Duval County Zoning Commission at Jacksonville, of the Fulton County Planning Commission at Atlanta. Officials of county or metropolitan housing authorities testified at Seattle, Pittsburgh, Cleveland, and Chicago. The mayor of Gary in the Chicago area testified at the hearings held at Indianapolis. The city-parish master plan data on housing were introduced into the record at Baton Rouge. The city manager of Richmond, California, testified at San Diego and in his home area, San Francisco. Officials of a town school district and of the Camden City Planning Commission testified at Philadelphia. The mayors of four San Bernardino cities

27. "Recommendations on Relocation," submitted by the Chicago Housing and Redevelopment Coordinator to the Committee on Housing, City Council of Chicago, December 12, 1950, Tables I and II. From reading this report one would gather that Chicago is an isolated community.

28. See the editorial, "There Isn't Going To Be Any Urban Redevelopment—Unless," in American Society of Planning Officials, *News Letter* (January, 1950).

testified at Los Angeles and the officials of seven suburbs (including one from the Springfield-Holyoke area and another from the Providence area) testified at Boston. No one appeared to speak for the suburbs at Birmingham, Little Rock, Dallas, San Antonio, Houston, New Orleans, Memphis, Hartford, San Diego, Detroit, Indianapolis, Cincinnati, and Columbus.[29]

Suburban municipalities and counties in only twenty-two metropolitan areas, as of August, 1951, had capital grant funds reserved for them under Title I of the Housing Act of 1949. Eight of these metropolitan areas have populations of over 1,000,000; only two have populations of between 500,000 and 1,000,000; ten are in the 200,000 to 500,000 class; and one is in the 100,000 to 200,000 population group. There are sixty suburban incorporated municipalities with capital grant reservations. The number of suburbs in which redevelopment activity may take place is higher, however, since the eight counties with capital grant reservations will develop projects in additional municipalities.

OTHER METROPOLITAN PROBLEMS RELATED TO URBAN REDEVELOPMENT

Urban redevelopers are principally concerned with the physical rehabilitation of blighted areas, with the arrest of deterioration, and with the conservation of the city's physical plant from obsolescence. Many other people are interested in the accomplishment of particular purposes through the efficient and effective use of the city's facilities. Seldom do they consider the other uses to be made of the city or of the effect of their own plans upon these other uses.[30] What Walter Blucher says of the good traffic engineer—that he "is a good city planner who has specialized"—is equally descriptive of the educator, recreation specialist, urban redeveloper, and even of the professional city planner. "He has to be a *good* city planner—a man who understands relationships."[31]

The relationships that we must understand are both those of other problems, values, and activities to our own and those of the various geographical areas of the community to each other. If we leave it to the

29. *Study and Investigation of Housing,* Hearings before the Joint Committee on Housing, 80th Congress, 1st session. October and November, 1947, pp. 139–4632.

30. A very good illustration of this single-minded unawareness will be found in the discussions on urban traffic at the 1950 meeting of the Section on Municipal Law of the American Bar Association. The papers by Walter Blucher and Walter J. Mattison are exceptions. But Wilbur B. Smith says that the traffic engineer "attempts to find means of producing a satisfactory operation of vehicles, roads, and road users as a *system* of traffic." The papers are published in the *Virginia Law Review,* XXXVI (1950). 831–872, 989–1055.

31. *Ibid.,* p. 857.

professional city planner to deal with these relationships, we will fail to understand our own problems and we will make the task of the planning agency difficult if not impossible.

UNEQUAL GOVERNMENTAL SERVICES

Local governmental services and regulations are unequal in the various parts of every metropolitan area. Urban transit, highways, traffic control, the collection and disposal of sewage and garbage, stream and harbor pollution control, air pollution control, water supply and distribution, general and special public health activities, police, fire fighting, education, recreation, as well as housing and land use planning and control, are affected by the many units of local government responsible for their planning, execution and financing.[32] The unevenness of services and control can be seen by reading for a short time any metropolitan newspaper.[33] The result is, of course, an over-all inadequacy which cannot be dismissed as just an inconvenience to be suffered by this or that part of the metropolitan community.[34]

DISPARITY BETWEEN NEED AND FISCAL ABILITY

There has been much talk lately about the fact that most residential areas, even substantial middle-class areas, do not pay in direct taxes for the cost of the governmental services they receive.[35] This is the principal reason some groups are interested in slum clearance and in urban redevelopment. They hope that families and individuals with higher incomes can be induced to live in areas now occupied by low-income families. This may increase the proportion of the costs of local government borne by the inhabitants of a redeveloped area. But it will not solve the problem in the city as a whole; much less will it solve the problem for the metropolitan area.

This approach when taken by itself ignores the basic problems that lead to low incomes for a substantial portion of the inhabitants of cities. Moreover, it is based upon the assumption that each "natural" neigh-

32. See my *Metropolitan Government*, pp. 52–72.

33. Hardly a week passes without news stories in the New York papers about water and air pollution, highway congestion, and transit problems.

34. See the report of the Governor's Committee on Community Adjustment, "Collateral Problems Likely To Result from Location of a Steel Mill in Connecticut" (April 27, 1951). The inequality in the levels of governmental services in the East Bay section of the San Francisco–Oakland metropolitan area for the year 1939–40 are identified and analysed by Herbert A. Simon, *Fiscal Aspects of Metropolitan Consolidation* (Berkeley: University of California Press, 1943), pp. 25–56.

35. See, as examples, the publications of the Urban Land Institute, the economic surveys of Homer Hoyt, and the planning reports of Scott Bagby.

borhood should be self-sustaining.[36] But no one proposes that each ward, precinct, or block of the city be forced to pay in full for the fire or police protection it receives for the activities of the health department or for the schooling given its children.

But the larger urban community is divided into many fragments, each under separate local government. There is an easily observable disparity in metropolitan areas between the need for governmental services and the fiscal and administrative ability to meet the need. The more favored of the local units are able, with ample revenues derived from low tax rates levied on high-assessed valuations, to furnish all the services demanded by their citizens. Other units, contiguous to or within short distances of the wealthy units, can only manage to provide a semblance of desirable or necessary services.

In the Boston metropolitan area, the town of Hull had in 1949 almost $110 of assessed valuation per capita for each dollar of the tax rate. At the other extreme, Chelsea had less than $18 of assessed valuation per capita for each dollar of the tax rate. Boston had almost $37. The median was $43.25. Hull, Dover, Wellesley, Cohasset, Weston, Brookline, Newton, Winchester, Weymouth, Needham, and Walpole, in the upper quartile, range from $109.86 to $56.83. In the lowest quartile, Arlington, Waltham, Malden, Canton, Lynn, Medford, Somerville, Stoughton, Revere, and Chelsea range from $30.26 to $17.65.[37]

We have not yet answered the question of how large an area has a justifiable claim upon the taxable resources concentrated in the business and industrial sections of the central city, in the outlying industrial sections, and in the wealthier suburbs. Most discussions of the problem have been based upon the assumption that the general property tax not only is, but will continue to be, the principal source of local revenues. There are political and economic limits to increasing the tax burden on real property—although experience has shown that many alleged limits have been passed without the consequences predicted. Local governments are searching for and developing other sources of income and any realistic analysis of the problem of financing equalized

36. The reader will recognize the similarity of this position to the complaints that the big city pays more in state taxes than it receives back in state grants or that the wealthier states are taxed by the federal government to support governmental activities in the poor states. Federal grants-in-aid to Delaware are approximately 1 per cent of federal revenue collected in that state. At the other extreme, Mississippi received back 38 per cent. In fourteen states, the ratio is 5 per cent or less; in 8 states, it is between 6 and 10 per cent; in seventeen, between 11 and 20 per cent; in six, between 21 and 30 per cent; and in three states, the ratio is over 30 per cent. *New York Times,* February 26, 1951.

37. Harvard Graduate School of Public Administration, Bureau for Research in Municipal Government, *Status of Property Tax 1945 and 1949 in 43 Cities and Towns within the Boston Metropolitan Area* (1950), pp. 60–63.

services throughout the metropolitan area must include both property and nonproperty taxes.

Herbert A. Simon believes that revenues from nonproperty taxes should be used to equalize services in a metropolitan community and that property tax-rate differentials should be erased gradually "over a period of, say, thirty years, or an equalization at the end of such a period."[38] He concludes from his study of ten municipalities in San Francisco–Oakland Area that levels of services are noticeably uneven and that property values would be seriously diminished in some municipalities if they themselves have to finance from higher property taxes the increased level of services necessary to bring them up to "par."

It is possible, at the end of our lengthy inquiry, to draw two fairly definite conclusions about the fiscal aspects of metropolitan consolidation in the San Francisco Bay Area. First, with the present organization of governmental units in the area, a leveling of service through the area is practically impossible unless financed from some source other than the local property taxes of the individual units. Such a leveling would confiscate a large part of the property values in some communities, and would present a windfall to property owners in San Francisco.

Second, if the governmental units of the area were consolidated, it would be practicable and desirable to "level" governmental services throughout the area, but it would be undesirable to abolish existing differentials in property taxes. To abolish such differentials would create injustices of the same kind, though less severe, as those which would result from a locally-financed leveling of service. If it is politically impossible to maintain differentials indefinitely, they can gradually be extinguished over a period of years without serious injustice.

If our analysis is correct, metropolitan consolidation in the San Francisco Bay region is highly desirable from a fiscal standpoint. Its desirability does not follow, however, as is commonly asserted, from the inequalities of present tax rates in the area, but from the inequalities of present service levels. If we could imagine that through a different series of historical accidents the current pattern of government in the area were one of approximate equality of service levels, and consequent great inequality of tax rates, the fiscal argument for consolidation would be much less cogent than under the actual circumstances in the area today.

The same argument holds for other metropolitan areas. A demonstration that current tax rates vary throughout the area is no argument for consolidation. To show that consolidation is fiscally desirable it is necessary to prove inequalities in current levels of service—whatever the tax rates may be.[39]

Tax Rates Increasing More Rapidly in Many Suburbs than in Central Cities

Until lately, the pat explanation for the suburban migration was that taxes are lower outside the central city. Recent investigations have

38. "Since income at such a far distant date will be severely discounted, the amount of capitalization which will take place cannot be large, and such a measure would have the added advantage of providing for an eventual rationalization of the land-use pattern" (Simon, *op. cit.*, p. 24).

39. *Ibid.*, p. 56.

shown that this factor has been overrated in residential, commercial, and industrial location.[40]

Evidence is also accumulating to show that property tax rates and the per capita tax levy are increasing more rapidly in the less developed suburbs than in the central city and the older suburbs. People may move to the country but they want to live a city life. The demand for urban governmental services, which in most suburban areas cannot be supplied until the capital plant has been expanded, is increasing the cost of local government very rapidly.[41] The demand for more and better services is most insistent in many parts of the growing metropolitan area where the tax base is inadequate to produce the needed revenue.

Even though the assessed valuation per capita increased more rapidly from 1945 to 1949 in thirty-three towns and cities of the Boston metropolitan area than in Boston itself, the tax rate increased more rapidly in twenty-three suburban units and the property tax levy per capita increased more rapidly in twenty-nine suburbs. During the five years after the war, the tax rate increased from 44 per cent to 83 per cent in one-fourth of the towns and cities of the area and in one-half of the units, the increase was more than 36 per cent (34 per cent in Boston). The amount of revenue raised by property taxes increased during the same period from 67 per cent to 124 per cent in one-fourth of the units and by more than 52 per cent in over half the units, all suburban (45 per cent in Boston).[42]

The demand in suburban areas for urban services has also been directed at county governments in metropolitan areas. The resultant rise in the county tax levy and rates has not only increased the total cost of local government. Central cities are accusing the suburban areas, many of which are unincorporated, of using the county to provide services for which the taxpayers of the central city pay the major part of the cost. This concern of the central city indicates that sooner or later a larger share of the cost of urban county government may be shifted to the suburban taxpayer. In California, the League of California Cities unsuccessfully sought in 1951 the passage of legislation to require unincorporated areas to pay for all services received from the county above

40. See Coleman Woodbury's study of industrial location in this volume (pp. 118–143) and Richard S. Dewey, *Residential Development in the Unincorporated Areas of Milwaukee* (Milwaukee: Milwaukee County Regional Planning Department, 1946).

41. William L. C. Wheaton is studying the problem of "measuring and analyzing the costs of municipal services . . . [particularly in] fast-growing suburbs where municipal services are an acute problem . . . in order to calculate the relative advantages of residential development in different areas" Housing and Home Finance Agency, *Housing Research Capsule (Description of Projects Started under Contract in 1950* [1951], p. 4).

42. Harvard Graduate School of Public Administration, Bureau for Research in Municipal Government, *op. cit.*, pp. 20, 39–40.

the standard of those provided to rural areas. There is no reason to believe that California Cities will give up the fight.[43]

Newark has succeeded in getting twelve other municipalities in Essex County to increase property assessments by $38 million. Although the matter was settled out of court, the city had to file an "assessment equalization suit" before the suburbs agreed to raise assessments. As a result, the county tax rate within the central city will be reduced.[44]

COMPLICATED LOCAL GOVERNMENT MAKES DEMOCRATIC CONTROL DIFFICULT

The control of local government by its citizens is of prime importance. We too often overlook the fact that governmental organization, both areal and functional, is a factor that impedes or facilitates this control. Citizens cannot understand or control the formulation and administration of governmental policies in a complex urban community when responsibility is divided among many independent and overlapping units. The task imposed, for instance, upon a citizen of Chicago who is supposed to hold responsible a multitude of high and low officials in a dozen separate governments is an impossible one.[45] In the New York metropolitan area, as Hugh Pomeroy has recently pointed out,

. . . there continually arise Pharaohs who know not Joseph. With us here, sovereignty resides in fourteen million people, and Pharaoh is not one but a multitude. Taking the round number of 550 local units of government in the metropolitan area, and under-figuring at five members for each local legislative body, there appear 2750 municipal governing officials. Add members of boards of supervisors and boards of chosen freeholders to the legislative total, add members of planning boards, and of boards of appeals and boards of adjustment, add commissioners of housing authorities and of other special operating authorities, and the total approaches seven thousand—and this doesn't include the members of several hundred school boards. All these officials are occupying positions in which authority is exercised in making decisions and conducting activities that affect the form and character of the region.[46]

Many influential citizens of a metropolitan area are deprived of a vote in the elections of the central city because they live outside its

43. League of California Cities, "The Case for Assembly Bill 3217 and Senate Bill 769, To Eliminate the County Subsidy of Municipal Type Services to Urban Unincorporated Areas" (May, 1951) and Richard Graves, "Fringe Areas Should Pay Their Own Way," *Public Management,* XXXIV, (February, 1952), 30–33. See also George W. Bemis and Nancy Basche, *Los Angeles County as an Agency of Municipal Government* (Los Angeles: Haynes Foundation, 1946).

44. *New York Times,* September 16, 1951.

45. See Charles E. Merriam, Spencer D. Parratt, and Albert Lepawsky, *The Government of the Metropolitan Region of Chicago* (Chicago: University of Chicago Press, 1933).

46. "The Relationship of the Central City and the Metropolitan Region: From the Outside Looking In" (address delivered before the Fourth Regional Plan Conference, New York City, November 15, 1949), pp. 5–6.

boundaries, in the suburbs. They are not, however, deprived of a voice in its affairs. They participate, as influential members, in the work of civic groups who criticize the government of the central city for the high tax rate, for its "machine" domination, for the attitudes of its officials toward particular issues (as, for instance, in labor disputes or in franchise matters), for the poor quality of its services, or for the extravagance with which they are managed.

There is no doubt that suburbanites have a direct interest in the affairs of the central city or of other suburbs—in fact, of the entire metropolis.[47] They do not, and cannot, withdraw from the politics of the metropolitan area when they establish their residence beyond the borders of the central city. The element of responsibility is diluted, however, when they talk without suffrage.

Residents of the central city, on the other hand, if not vitally concerned, are vitally affected by the politics of the suburbs. The nature of the metropolitan area makes it difficult, and in some instances impossible, to formulate governmental policies for the central city alone. Disintegrated local government prohibits over-all planning and control of community life by setting up enclaves in the metropolitan electorate.[48]

SUMMARY

Contrary to the belief of some suburbanites and of some specialists, whose views are too narrowly focused upon the slum, blight in all stages of intensity is to be found throughout the metropolitan area. In suburb as well as in central city there are dwelling units unfit to live in; poorly located residential, commercial and industrial areas where blight is actual or incipient; overdeveloped subdivisions, tax delinquent and a drain upon local budgets, which are being by-passed by builders for undeveloped raw land. Few suburbs, however, have shown any interest in urban redevelopment.

The objectives of urban redevelopment are affected by the low level of many governmental services and controls. Frequently, but not always, low service levels are found in those parts of the metropolitan area where the need is great and fiscal ability to meet the need is low. This kind of problem cannot be solved by ignorance or by callous indifference to what is happening in the metropolitan community outside one's own municipality.

A metropolitan approach to these problems is facilitated or discour-

47. ". . . from the outside looking in, all the trees bend toward the center, as it were. There is never absent from one's consciousness the overwhelming fact of New York City" (Pomeroy, *op. cit.*, p. 2).

48. No one has studied party organization and behavior and other related aspects of the political process throughout a metropolitan community.

aged by the formal governmental organization of the community. In the remainder of this study, I shall discuss the principal proposals and attempts that have been made to reorganize local government in metropolitan areas.

CHAPTER IV

ATTEMPTS TO MEET THE PROBLEMS

I N 1949 Thomas H. Reed, veteran of many battles to integrate the governments of metropolitan areas, was dejected as he reviewed the defeats and apathy of the first half of the twentieth century. One year later, however, he was more sanguine as he recalled the many "reforms" in municipal government accomplished during his lifetime.

American politics is by no means spotless but let no one tell you that it is not incomparably cleaner, and American local government infinitely more honest and efficient than it was 50 years ago. When I was a senior at Harvard . . . the conception of the greater city of tomorrow had not even dawned on the minds of dreamers. I am confident that as we have solved so many other problems of organization and procedure in local government, in spite of the intense opposition of the politicians and the deadening pessimism of the public, we shall in good time—not too far off—conquer suburbanitis.[1]

Despite the lack of progress in integrating the local government of metropolitan communities, we are unable to despair. Old problems continue to bother us. New problems arise and old problems come again within the orbit of our concern as new techniques are developed for identifying them, and it is hoped, for solving them. Urban redevelopment and slum clearance activities, following the enactment of the Housing Act of 1949 with its declaration of national policy and its provisions for financial assistance to localities, force us again to seek a type of local government that will enable the objectives of urban development and redevelopment to be achieved throughout the metropolitan community.

BASIC POLITICAL PRINCIPLES OF LOCAL GOVERNMENTAL ORGANIZATION

Frequently groups concerned with a particular function or activity, as they become aware of the community-wide extent of its problems, propose that their special problem be handled in a special way over a

1. T. H. Reed, "Hope for 'Suburbanitis,'" *National Municipal Review*, XXXIX (December, 1950), 553; "Progress in Metropolitan Integration," *Public Administration Review*, IX (Winter, 1949), 1–10.

special area by a special organization. The ideal solution of the problem of governmental areas, from the point of view of interest groups and the professional administrators of particular functions, would be to redefine their boundaries so that they correspond to the geographical extent of the respective problems. Each special interest might then consider itself safe from "politics" and from the necessity of competing with other interests for the attention of a general local government and for a share of available revenue.

This, of course, would be a sense of security and independence having no relation to reality if each of the major and minor functions of government were organized in this manner. No function, moreover, can escape the effects of maladministration of related functions or of their under- or overdevelopment with respect to needs and fiscal resources. This is particularly true of the planning, control, development, and redevelopment of land uses in a metropolitan community.

Most of the discussion of metropolitan government is in terms of administrative utility. This objective always should be considered in the context of all the objectives of local government.[2] Areas should also be drawn to facilitate mass participation in formulating policies. They should be drawn so as not to impede but to ease the holding of officials responsible for their policy positions and accountable for their execution of accepted policies. Popular control of local government is unnecessarily difficult when the electors of metropolitan areas have to vote a long "jungle ballot," when they must watch simultaneously the activities of many units of government, and when the issues, because they have not proceeded from a consideration of the needs and re-

2. See the suggestive essay, "The Foundations of Local Government," by C. H. Wilson in *Essays on Local Government* (Oxford, England: Basil Blackwell, 1948).

"The second sufficient reason for attempting to restate the political theory of local government is that the institutions themselves are being submitted to thorough-going reorganisation. The great increases in the functions of local authorities, caused by the war and by the acceleration of social reform since the war, have affected in detail and in whole the character of English local government. The variety and kind of administrative development associated with these changes is yet only partially outlined but it is already clear that every fundamental aspect of local government is involved—the size of units themselves, the degree of responsible discretion which they may exercise, their status as agents of central authority, their financial standing, their relations to one another and to central government departments, the electorates on which they are based. The combined effect is likely to unsettle a large part of the established system, and by changing the regular channels of administrative business to impose on some considerable part of the system an increasingly futile and perfunctory role. The effect of each proposed reform, in education, in public health, in planning, in transport, and communications, could be separately estimated from this point of view. But it is the less easily estimable cumulative effects, the changes in general structure and in the general importance of local affairs which need to be brought before the attention. For however desirable the substantive reforms may be, the political life and constitution of the communities of town, village and shire are a subject of distinct and fundamental importance which ought not to be omitted from public consideration despite the complexity of the field" (p. 2).

sources of the entire metropolitan area, are often petty and unrelated to the larger needs of the community.

CLASSIFICATION OF PROPOSED AND ATTEMPTED SOLUTIONS

In the remainder of this study I shall be concerned with the various schemes which have been proposed or tried as a solution of the problem of local government in metropolitan areas. In the following chapters I shall discuss at length some of the more important devices. In this chapter I shall describe and classify the proposed and attempted solutions and discuss more cursorily the other devices which have been suggested or used with varying degrees of success in the United States, Canada, and England.[3]

These schemes are not mutually exclusive. Various combinations will be found in different areas. Undoubtedly any acceptable and workable proposal for metropolitan government in a particular area will have to be tailor made.[4] Both friends and foes of metropolitan reorganization are given to painting the alternatives in black and white. Our organizational ingenuity is not exhausted by the present dispersal of local government in a community among dozens or hundreds of municipalities, counties, and special districts or by their replacement with a single neat and tidy government.

We have, however, had enough experience to know that certain devices do not provide metropolis-wide planning, policy-making, and administration and that others actually increase the complexity of local government.[5]

The devices used or proposed in the United States and other countries may be classified in a number of ways. The most useful classification is on the basis of their effect on the structure of existing units of local government. Some of these devices involve few or no changes in the structural pattern of local government: (1) the grant of jurisdiction to, and the provision of services and the exercise of controls by,

3. I shall make extensive use of chapters iv and v of my book, *Metropolitan Government* (Chicago: University of Chicago Press, 1942).

4. See Local Government Commission of Fulton County, *Plan of Improvement for the Governments of Atlanta and Fulton County, Georgia* (1950) for a combination of various schemes which is considered to be feasible in metropolitan Atlanta. See Doris Darmstadter, "Metropolitan Atlanta," *City Growing Pains* (New York: National Municipal League, 1941), pp. 16–17, for a discussion of some of the factors peculiar to Atlanta.

5. Paul Studenski and others, *The Government of Metropolitan Areas in the United States* (New York: National Municipal League, 1930) is an indispensable source of information about these devices. See also E. A. Cottrell, "Problems of Local Governmental Reorganization," *The Western Political Quarterly* (December, 1949), pp. 599–609. See the forty-two-page bibliography on the government of metropolitan areas prepared by Los Angeles Municipal Reference Library (Special Adjustment Bibliography No. 4, December, 1947).

the central city outside its boundaries; (2) intergovernmental arrangements; (3) the establishment of special districts and other types of *ad
hoc* authorities; (4) metropolitan planning; (5) the extension of state
administration; and (6) the extension of federal administration.

Any of these devices could be carried so far as to result in the atro-
phy of existing units of local government. Such logic is unlikely to be
pursued to its conclusion in the welter of metropolitan politics. They
are, then, to be considered as stopgaps, as adjuncts, or as possible step-
pingstones to a more comprehensive local government for the entire
metropolitan area.

The devices which give greater promise of solving the problems of
local government in metropolitan areas require fundamental changes
in the structure of existing units: (1) annexation of contiguous territory or consolidation of adjacent municipalities; (2) city-county consolidation; (3) separation of the city from the county; (4) merging of
special authorities with either the central city or the county; (5) transformation of an area-wide special authority into a multifunctional unit
of government; (6) reorganization of the urban county and the transfer to it of metropolis-wide municipal functions; (7) establishment of
a "federated" or borough type of municipal government for the metropolitan area; and (8) creation of a metropolitan city-state.

DEVICES INVOLVING LIMITED STRUCTURAL CHANGES

Extraterritorial jurisdiction and services.—Many cities are authorized by statute to exercise police power beyond their borders.[6] As of September, 1944, twenty-eight states authorized all or some of their municipalities to control land subdivision outside their corporate boundaries. The area of extramural control varied from one to five miles. In
Louisiana the jurisdiction of cities with a planning commission is extended to land outside the boundaries "which, in the opinion of the
commission, bears relation to the municipality. . . ." In West Virginia
and South Dakota city jurisdiction extends over adjacent or contiguous
land. No such extraterritorial jurisdiction is granted to municipalities
in the following states with sizeable metropolitan centers: Florida,
Rhode Island, Connecticut, Delaware, Massachusetts, Michigan, Mis-

---

6. See *Corpus Juris Secundum,* "Municipal Corporations," Vol. 62, Sec. 141 and Vol. 63,
Sec. 952, for judicial construction of authority to exercise police power, to provide "proprietary" services and to acquire property outside municipal limits.

See also W. W. Crouch, "Extraterritorial Powers of Cities as Factors in California
Metropolitan Government," *American Political Science Review,* XXXI (April, 1937), 291.
William Anderson, "The Extraterritorial Powers of Cities," *Minnesota Law Review,* X
(1926), 475–97, 564–83; Albert Lepawsky, *Urban Government* (National Resources Committee, 1939), p. 34.

souri, New Jersey, New York, Pennsylvania (except third-class cities) and Washington.[7]

Facilities established primarily for the convenience of the inhabitants of the central city are regularly used by outsiders. In many metropolitan areas such facilities are directly available to all or portions of the suburban area.[8] Perhaps the best known are the transit facilities operated by the city of Detroit. Water is very frequently furnished by large cities to people living outside their boundaries. New York and Chicago are required by law to furnish water to certain suburban municipalities—New York to those in the vicinity of its aqueduct in Westchester County, and Chicago to those suburbs within the Chicago Sanitary District that build their mains to the city limits. Chicago charged the same rate to both inside and outside users, but since the outside "user" dealing with the city is a municipality the charge to the ultimate consumer, several municipalities away from the central city, was often five times Chicago's rate.[9] The trend since the war has been to increase charges for outside water, sewer, and fire services.[10]

The value of extraterritorial powers and services as an integrative device is very limited. In the first place, the exercise of extraterritorial powers by contiguous or nearby municipalities may lead to jurisdictional conflicts, bickering, and hard feelings rather than to co-operation between governments of a metropolitan area. All such conflicts make the task of effecting comprehensive reorganization more difficult. Adequate public policy is unlikely to emerge from a buyer-seller relationship among units of government. The second objection may be lessened as central cities increase their outside service charges.[11] But the suburbs

7. County control of subdivision in unincorporated areas is provided for in Delaware (New Castle County), Michigan, New Jersey, New York, Pennsylvania, and Washington. See the detailed analysis of state subdivision control statutes relating to housing and urban redevelopment in *Post-War Economic Policy and Planning: Housing and Urban Redevelopment:* Hearings before the Subcommittee on Housing and Redevelopment of the Senate Special Committee on Post-War Economic Policy and Planning, 79th Congress, 1st session, facing p. 1348.

8. See Weldon Cooper, *Metropolitan County: A Survey of Government in the Birmingham Area* (University: University of Alabama, Bureau of Public Administration, 1949), pp. 48–49, 66–69, 132–133, 137–139. Betty Tableman gives many examples of central-city services to the inhabitants of outlying areas. *Governmental Organization in Metropolitan Areas* (Ann Arbor: Institute of Public Administration, University of Michigan, 1951), pp. 33–40, 138–54, 173–74, 178–79.

9. *American Municipal News* (American Municipal Association, September, 1947).

10. *Ibid.;* see *The Municipal Year Book* (1947), pp. 295–99.

11. Long Beach, California in 1946–47 and Pueblo, Colorado in 1948 stopped outside sewerage and fire services to areas they were trying to annex, *The Municipal Year Book* (1949), p. 96; J. C. Bollens, "Annexation of Fringe Areas," *Public Management* (April, 1949), p. 99. Bollens reports that Cincinnati, Jacksonville, Louisville, and St. Paul have discontinued outside services. See also, *American Municipal News* (September, 1947). Cincinnati and Manitowoc (Wis.) require prior approval by suburban users of eventual annexation as a condition for outside services.

are glad to rely upon the central city to furnish them, at little or no cost, facilities and services beyond their own resources. There will be no comprehensive governmental organization of the metropolitan community as long as the central city eases the pressure of metropolitan problems upon the people who live outside its boundaries.

Intergovernmental arrangements.—A degree of integration is often secured through the more or less formal co-operation of two or more units of local government in a metropolitan area. The most formal of such arrangements is the creation of a special authority, an *ad hoc* union of governments rather than a superimposed unit of government, through which the local units involved jointly discharge one or more functions. Some of these joint agencies are almost autonomous and they will be discussed, along with special districts in chapter vi.

The state statute books contain many authorizations to units of local government to join with one another in the performance of a common function. The constitution of Missouri, for instance, gives wide authority to units of local government to "contract and co-operate" with other governmental units.[12] In California there is general statutory authority to enter into agreements but this is supplemented by a series of acts authorizing agreements in specific fields such as urban redevelopment,[13] roads and bridges, sewage disposal, water supply, health services, recreational facilities, libraries, fire protection, road camps for prisoners, and assessment and collection of taxes.[14]

Sometimes these arrangements take the form of a joint agency to perform a function. The increasing number of city-county health departments is an illustration of this type.[15] Other arrangements are based on a contract for one unit of government to perform a function for another unit. This device has been used most extensively in metropolitan Los Angeles. A majority of the municipalities in Los Angeles have a contract with the county for the performance of one or more personnel functions. Forty-one municipalities, including the city of Los

12. "Any municipality or political subdivision of the state may contract and cooperate with other municipalities or political subdivisions thereof, or with other states or their municipalities or political subdivisions thereof, or with the United States, for the planning, development, construction, acquisition or operation of any public improvement or facility, or for a common service, in the manner provided by law" (*Missouri Constitution* [1945], Art. VI, Sec. 16).

13. "Two or more communities may join in a redevelopment project, and one community may, by action of its legislative body, consent to the inclusion of part of its jurisdiction within the redevelopment plan of another community." Los Angeles City Planning Commission, *Blight: The Problem, the Remedy* (1948), p. 19.

14. See John C. Bollens, *The Problem of Government in the San Francisco Bay Region* (Berkeley: University of California, Bureau of Public Administration, 1948), pp. 102–4.

15. Generally in the field of public welfare, following the passage of the Social Security Act, and sporadically in other fields, there has been during the last two decades mandatory consolidation of functions in county departments.

Angeles, have a contract with the county for the assessment and collection of taxes. The county furnishes fire protection to West Covina. The county performs health services, above the minimum required by state law, under contract with thirty-eight cities. Similar contractual arrangements are found in many other fields.[16]

A less formal intergovernmental arrangement is a joint agreement to set up an extra-legal committee to integrate a function or activity of local government. For example, the Coordinated Purchasing Committee of Hamilton County, consisting of the purchasing agents of the city of Cincinnati, Hamilton County, the school board, the university and the public library, has adopted standard specifications for major commodities and established uniform contracting statements, bid forms, inquiry forms, and legal information forms.

The least formal of intergovernmental arrangement arises out of the daily contacts of officials and other individuals interested in a particular problem. These contacts are often very casual and lead to no action —unilateral, bilateral, or multilateral. It is possible, however, and often desirable to bring people interested in a common problem into a conference. Such meetings can easily become a waste of time but, they are also an effective means of communication if they are skilfully led and if the information to be used in the discussion has been assembled and organized before the meeting. The need for this type of effort "to coordinate" will probably increase rather than diminish under a metropolitan government.[17]

16. County of Los Angeles, Division of Administrative Research, "Interrelationship between the County and Various Municipalities," April 8, 1949; Helen L. Jones and Robert F. Wilcox, *Metropolitan Los Angeles: Its Governments* (Los Angeles: Haynes Foundation, 1949), pp. 72, 76, 92, 106, 160, 163, 175, 181, 184–85. See also Committee on Governmental Simplification, *Report* (Los Angeles, 1935); Frank M. Stewart, "City-County Contractual Relationships," *Public Management*, XIX (January, 1937), pp. 14–17; Ronald M. Ketcham, *Intergovernmental Cooperation in the Los Angeles Area* (Los Angeles: Bureau of Governmental Research, University of California, 1940); Betty Tableman, *op. cit.*, pp. 40–47, 138–54.

17. See Simon, Smithburg, and Thompson, *Public Administration* (New York: Alfred A. Knopf, Inc., 1950), pp. 63–64, 90, 152–54. The Milwaukee Redevelopment Coordinating Committee, established in 1946 by the Common Council, is an example of "co-ordinating" committees within a single unit of government. The following city agencies were represented on the committee: Board of Public Land Commissioners, Housing Authority, Health Department, Office of the Tax Commissioner, Building Inspector, Department of Public Works and City Attorney's Office (Board of Public Land Commissioners, *Blight Elimination*, Information Bulletin No. 1, January, 1950). The Los Angeles City Charter provides for a Coordinating Board of city officials "to advise with and assist the Director of planning in the preparation of the master plan and amendments or changes thereto." Los Angeles City Planning Commission, *Accomplishments, 1949* (annual report). The Baltimore Metropolitan Planning and Coordinating Committee, organized by agreement, is composed of the directors of the County and State Planning Commissions, the chairman of the City Planning Commission, the chief engineer of the State Roads Commission, the chief engineer of the State Department of Health, and representatives of Howard and Anne Arundel counties. See Nathalie Georgia, "Intergovernmental Relations in Metropolitan

Although nothing should be done to discourage intergovernmental arrangements of any sort that look toward functional integration, they will not serve in place of more comprehensive schemes. As Thomas H. Reed has said:

No single act of functional consolidation solves the metropolitan problem. In fact, it is inconceivable that it ever could be completely solved by that route. It does, however, provide for handling tough situations in a practical manner without, at any rate, increasing the existing complexity of local government areas as the creation of new special districts or metropolitan government on the borough plan may do. It is the road of easiest grade into the intricate and complicated field of metropolitanism. To vary the metaphor, it bears somewhat the same relation to the solution of the metropolitan problem as the patient untying of knot after knot has to untangling a skein of yarn. To the extent that a functional consolidation works, there is one less complexity to deal with.[18]

Special metropolitan authorities will be discussed in chapter vi.

Metropolitan planning.—It is impossible to confine planning within any particular form of governmental organization. Planning can, and in some fashion does, go on in special districts, counties, central cities and suburban municipalities. One may not agree with the objectives of the planning. Given its objectives, it often is inadequate, partial in its coverage, based upon incomplete and poorly analyzed data, and short-run in its outlook.[19] Certainly in no metropolitan community of the United States is there planning to meet the problems of metropolitan living which takes adequate account of the interrelation of the problems, of the formal and informal organization of the community, of its resources, and of the techniques proposed or used in their solution.

Planning, then, is discussed constantly throughout this study. It is discussed separately in this chapter as one of the devices for integrating the government of metropolitan areas because it is frequently claimed that it will serve that purpose.[20] The claims are not false but exaggerated. Local government in metropolitan areas can only be integrated by legislative and administrative action, of which planning is a part, upon metropolitan problems.[21]

Planning" (Unpublished Ph.D. thesis, Department of Political Science, University of North Carolina, 1950), pp. 116–17, and Maryland State Planning Commission, *A Functional Plan for the Baltimore Metropolitan District* (1948), pp. 81–93.

18. "The Metropolitan Problem—1941," *City Growing Pains*, p. 15.

19. See Coleman Woodbury, "Background and Prospects of Urban Redevelopment in the United States," this volume, pp. 636–49.

20. See *The Boston Contest of 1944* (Boston: Boston University Press, 1945) and American Society of Planning Officials, *Organization for Metropolitan Planning* (Chicago, 1943).

21. This is recognized in some of the proposals submitted in the Boston contest and in one sponsored by the American Society of Planning Officials. The authors give the planning agency what is in effect legislative power. The dilemma is not avoided by giving the planning agency only the power to negate proposals originating in other legislative bodies of the metropolitan area. I have discussed this feature of the proposals in "Government in the Future City," *Annals*, Vol. 242 (November, 1945), pp. 84–85.

The claims are in part correct because a well prepared and forcefully presented plan, even if dissociated from a unit of government, may influence those in authority to whom it is communicated.[22] Perhaps more important in the long run, the assemblage of data on the metropolitan community, the discussion of its social and economic unity, and the very existence of a metropolitan planning organization, official or unofficial, will increase the identification of individuals and groups with the metropolitan community.

But disembodied planning is not a substitute for government. This has been demonstrated by experience in the New York and other metropolitan communities where an effort has been made to develop it as a substitute. The most sweeping claims for the virtues of metropolitan planning without the support of a metropolitan government were made in 1929 by the Committee on Regional Plan of New York and Its Environs:

> In view of the facts as they are, it appears that unified government in the New York region as a whole is out of the question. It is because of this that regional planning is the more necessary, for in an important sense regional planning may be a substitute for centralization of government. If sufficient co-operation between the communities in a region can be obtained so that they will agree on the broad outline of a plan for all their areas together, and if they collaborate to carry out such a plan, they can go far toward attaining the ideal which would be possible under a united government. Moreover, the advantages of centralized government have to be set off against the serious disadvantages which it involves, such as the destruction of local autonomy and local neighborhood life. With regional planning most of the advantages of centralization are made possible, while local government remains intact with the very great values which it possesses.[23]

Although, as Walter Blucher said in reviewing planning developments during 1950, there is a "great variety of planning programs commonly included in the term 'regional planning,' . . . all taken together there is relatively little planning on a 'regional' basis."[24] An agency does not, however, need to have the terms "regional" or "metropolitan" in its title in order to be able to take account of the metropolis in planning for its own particular function or area. Many county planning agencies —particularly when they act jointly with the planning agencies of the central city and suburbs—are able to cover all or a large part of the metropolitan area.[25] A good example of a municipal planning agency

22. See the reports of the New York Regional Plan Association, *From Plan to Reality*.
23. Regional Survey of New York and Its Environs, Vol. II: *Population, Land Values and Government* (1929), p. 199.
24. *The Municipal Year Book* (1951), p. 261. The *Year Book* contains an annual review of developments in planning and zoning.
25. "Extensive and varied programs are being carried out by county planning commissions. Economic studies, population forecasting, land use surveys, zoning ordinances, subdivision regulations, highway plans, parking and traffic studies, recreation plans, public relations programs, technical aid to municipalities are all developing rapidly at the county level. A review of activities reported in these pages during recent years illustrates the rapid

looking beyond the city boundaries is the Metropolitan Master Plan Studies prepared and published by the Cincinnati City Planning Commission.[26]

Some of the metropolitan or, as they are frequently called, "regional" planning agencies are organized by statute. Others are unofficial citizen agencies supported by private funds. In some the membership is mixed.[27] The experience of these agencies, official, unofficial and mixed, in apportioning representation to the various parts of the metropolitan area is invaluable in tackling the most difficult aspect of establishing a metropolitan government. It will be discussed in chapter vii on "federated" forms of metropolitan government.

Extension of state administration.—Governmental functions assumed and directly administered by the state would result in limited functional integration throughout the metropolitan area. No significant simplification of local government structure, however, would be accomplished unless the state government assumed most of the functions of general local governments. In some states a large number of special districts could be abolished if reorganization follows state assumption of the primary responsibility for a particular function. In 1933, for instance, over 1,200 school districts in North Carolina and 450 school districts in West Virginia were consolidated into county school districts when the two states assumed financial responsibility for public education. It is, of course, possible to consolidate special districts or transfer their functions to general units of government without state assumption of the function. But certainly it is easier to do so when the state offers to pay for the function.

State assumption of a function may affect the complexity of overlapping local governments by making it unnecessary to organize a special district to operate over the area of several jurisdictions. In the San

growth in extent and importance of county planning. The accomplishments during 1950 are so numerous that only a few can be mentioned to typify the varied programs" (*ibid.*).

26. The following reports have been published: (1) *Population* (1945); (2) *Program and Progress;* (3) *Airports;* (4) *Industrial Areas;* (5) *Wholesale Produce Market;* (6) *Public Buildings;* (7) *Riverfront Redevelopment;* (8) *The Economy of the Area;* and (9) *Residential Areas.* Reports 2–9 were published in 1946.

27. The most comprehensive study of these agencies and their programs is Nathalie Georgia, *op. cit.* Betty Tableman, *op. cit.*, pp. 48–50, lists official and quasi-official planning agencies and citizens' associations. See also Regional Plan Association, Inc. (N.Y.), *Metropolitan Planning Organizations* (1947); American Society of Planning Officials, *Newsletter*, X (1944), 4, 23, 81, 93, 101; XII (1946), 15–16; John E. Vance, *Planning the Metropolitan District* (Providence Chamber of Commerce, no date); Citizen's Council on City Planning, Philadelphia Housing Association, *Organizations for Metropolitan Planning* (1949); Maryland State Planning Commission, *op. cit.;* Local Government Commission of Fulton County, *Plan of Improvements for the Governments of Atlanta and Fulton County, Georgia* (1950), p. 59; Weldon Cooper, *Metropolitan County: A Survey of Government in the Birmingham Area* (University: University of Alabama, Bureau of Public Administration, 1949), pp. 26–35.

Francisco Bay Area, for example, the state constructed and operates the San Francisco–Bay Bridge.[28] On the other hand, the state may create a special district controlled by the state rather than by local authorities or responsible to a local electorate. The Metropolitan District Commission in the Boston region, frequently praised in other areas, is an example of a state-controlled, locally financed, special district. The Port of New York Authority, the new Bi-State Development Authority in the St. Louis area, and the proposed Bi-State Authority in the Philadelphia area are likewise controlled, to the extent that they are controlled by state governments.

State governments are already carrying on activities directly in many urban centers. Highway construction and maintenance is an example of a direct state activity which is part of a complicated system of federal grants to states and of state grants to local units, accompanied by varying degrees of federal and state supervision. Despite the fact that some highways are directly built and maintained by the state, in no metropolitan area has the state assumed complete responsibility for the planning and construction of a metropolitan highway system. In many metropolitan areas the state highway department may be considered as one of the overlapping and competing units of government. Extensive plans for arterial highways are being made by state highway departments. The participation of local governments in many states in this planning is perfunctory.[29]

Several kinds of conflict between state and local officials are apparent in the relationships in highway planning in Los Angeles County as described by Miss Jamison:

Whereas the local planners want to use public hearing methods, the State highway officials desire to work as secretly as possible in planning highways. Although they do negotiate State highway details directly with local planners and acknowledge the high integrity of and good cooperation of the technicians in arranging for zoning and setback line regulations to protect future alignments, the State highway officials distrust the "politicians" who make capital of highway construction information and permit land speculators to dupe the public in the sale of private property facing proposed highways. Private organizations, such as the Automobile Club of Southern California, claim that full publicity should be given to highway alignments so that the property owners may protect themselves. The planners would prefer that a formal master plan be adopted on the State level because there is often confusion in the minds of local officials as to what is expected of them in cooperating with the State officials. As a result of these conferences sponsored by the State Reconstruction and Reemployment Commission, a committee of planners and local govern-

28. J. C. Bollens, *The Problem of Government in the San Francisco Bay Region*, pp. 116–18. The Golden Gate Bridge, however, was constructed and is operated by a special district (*ibid.*, pp. 100–102).

29. See Hebden and Smith, *State-City Relationship in Highway Affairs* (New Haven: Yale University Press, 1950).

mental engineers was formed to negotiate with the central offices of the State Highway Division and Department of Public Works for a specific declaration of policy
on highway alignment and construction standards which will serve in lieu of a
statutory master plan. Although the Commission is abolished, the local officials are
still tenaciously working for such a declaration.[30]

Hebden and Smith report an informal regional highway committee in
one state consisting of the planning engineer and director of public
works of the central city, the manager of one county and the county
engineer of another county in the area and the head of the traffic and
planning division of the state highway department. The committee
meets regularly twice a month

to select and agree upon a so-called "regional master plan" of highway development
within the central city and for an area extending five miles beyond [in which the
central city exercises planning controls]. . . . The meetings of the committee are
devoted to discussions of future improvements and plans for them, priorities of construction, revisions and other details of projects underway or proposed. On the basis
of these sessions this regional highway committee makes recommendations to the
state highway department and to the city. [The committee is] also working on
standards for right of way requirements and land width for various streets and highways in the regional area [and hope to make them part of the city's subdivision control regulations].[31]

Slow and tedious as it may seem to busy administrators,[32] this is the
way to secure co-ordination of the programs and activities of state and
local governments in metropolitan areas. It must be done function by
function by the officials responsible for the respective functions. But
steps must be taken at every stage to see that the planning and operations of each group of specialists are related to the planning and operations of other specialists.[33] The consultation must take place during the

30. J. N. Jamison, *Coordinated Public Planning in the Los Angeles Region* (Los Angeles:
Bureau of Government Research, University of California, 1948), p. 83.

31. Hebden and Smith, *op. cit.*, pp. 195–96.

32. "Another difficult problem confronting state highway departments is that of obtaining effective coordination of highway planning in metropolitan areas which arises because of the number of local governmental units concerned. . . . The task of coordinating
plans and reaching agreements with all the governmental units involved can be an extremely difficult and lengthy one. It necessitates innumerable dealings with many different
officials of all the governmental bodies concerned; and each body is keenly interested in
getting its needs and desires satisfied. Numerous times state highway officials asserted that
at times the task was almost impossible" (Hebden and Smith, *op. cit.*, pp. 193–94).

33. In the traffic surveys and urban highway plans published by state highway departments which I have examined, there is no evidence that related problems and plans have
been taken into account. According to Hebden and Smith ". . . in several instances it did
not seem that factual traffic data were being effectively used in selecting urban projects.
Even more limited use is made of basic city planning data—although New York State
is a notable exception in this respect. Information on population trends, motor vehicle
registration, land use and assessed valuations, for example, as well as traffic survey data
comprise the tools of the highway administrator. . . . States should make certain that
proper consideration is given [to the relation of project location to city growth and
development]" (*op. cit.*, pp. 183 ff.).

planning and policy formation. All too often interested parties are said to have been consulted when they have only been presented with a plan or a decision already wrapped up.

The initiative should be taken by the state not only to co-ordinate state and local activities but to foster the integration of local government in metropolitan areas. The Committee on State-Local Relations of the Council of State Governments, after pointing out that local officials must also assume responsibility, says

It is clear, nevertheless, that primary responsibility for a well-ordered system of state-local relations rests with the state governments. This responsibility springs principally from two facts: first, except for constitutional guarantees, the states are the legal masters of local government; second, the states are superior to localities in their ability to raise revenues. This dual dominance of states—in law and finances— is an incontrovertible fact. It places a heavy obligation upon the states to create an orderly and effective system of state-local relations.[34]

State governments have exercised their tutelage of local governments by a combination of neglect and indifference with innumerable legislative and administrative directions. Nowhere in the United States have state governments taken more than a sporadic *ad hoc* interest in developing local government that can meet the problems of the modern city. In law, and to a large extent in fact, municipalities and other local governments are "creatures" of the state. With the rapid growth of urban areas far beyond the boundaries of old municipalities and with the development of social, economic, and political relations among all parts of the country, problems of a kind and scope have arisen which the old types of local government are unable to handle. The response of state governments (and of the national government) has been an unplanned policy of unrelated measures designed to meet a particular problem or to prevent adequate local action. Examples of this policy are the restrictive annexation procedures, grant-in-aid programs which give particular activities a preferred place or frequently subsidize inefficient and ineffective units of government, debt and tax limitations, the partial transfer of local functions to a state agency which frequently plans and administers its activities without consultation with the local governments whose functions are parallel to, or are affected by, the activities of the state agency.[35]

British experience shows that the problem of how to organize the community or the nation to govern is not to be solved by the mere crea-

34. Council of State Governments, *State-Local Relations* (Chicago, 1946), p. 8. The importance attached by the Committee to the problem of local government in metropolitan areas is shown by the fact that almost a fifth of the report is given to a discussion of the problem. See pp. 183–224. See also Hebden and Smith, *op. cit.*, p. 34.

35. Albert Lepawsky, *Home-Rule for Metropolitan Chicago* (Chicago: University of Chicago Press, 1935); Council of State Governments, *op. cit.*

tion of new units of local government or of central agencies of supervision and control. But the same experience shows how useful and necessary it is for the central government to assume responsibility for studying and planning the organization, areal jurisdiction, functions, and relationships among governmental and nongovernmental agencies. There is nothing comparable in this country, except the 1937 report on Urbanism of the National Resources Committee, to the work of the Royal Commission on Municipal Corporations (1835), the Local Government Committee (1910–20), the Royal Commission on Local Government of Greater London (1923), the Royal Commission on Local Government (1923–29), the Royal Commission on Tyneside Local Government (1937), and the Local Government Boundary Commission (1945–49).

In two states, New Jersey and Pennsylvania, there are state agencies with broad power to investigate and study local government. In both states, however, these agencies are stopped short, by statute or by their own policy, of developing or taking the leadership in developing a state program for the reorganization of local government in metropolitan communities.

The New Jersey Local Government Board is part of the Division of Local Government in the State Department of Taxation and Finance.[36] The Board "is authorized to study all local governmental problems and to report to the governor and to the legislature concerning them. In practice, the board has concerned itself largely with fiscal problems, though it has also made some investigations of conservation, health and education, housing, postwar planning, and the problem of borough consolidation."[37]

Pennsylvania has two permanent agencies authorized to study local government. The Bureau of Municipal Affairs has apparently limited itself "to compiling financial statistics, supervising municipal borrowing, auditing, accounting, and reporting, and to certain aspects of municipal planning."[38] The Local Government Commission, a continuing joint legislative committee established in 1935, is authorized "to study and report on functions of local government; their allocation and elimination; the cost of local government and means of reducing it; and the consolidation of local government."[39] It differs from other legislative committees, not in terms of the scope of its investigative authority, but in its continuation as a permanent legislative committee. It might have,

36. The other part of the division is the director of Local Government who administers the state's fiscal supervision of local governments. He is also chairman of the Local Government Board. See Council of State Governments, *op. cit.*, pp. 37–38.

37. *Ibid.*, pp. 48–49.

38. *Ibid.*, p. 49.

39. Pennsylvania Public Law 244 (1935).

but it has not, developed into a source of state-wide leadership in the reorganization of local government. In its first report to the legislature, it reported a self-denying ordinance:

(1) that it would not make any recommendations destroying the existing structure of local government; nor (2) attempt any general revision of the codified local government law; nor (3) recommend any consolidation of any local government without the consent of the electors residing therein.[40]

The extension of federal activities.—The federal government, unlike the states, has no legal power to create or reorganize local governments except in the District of Columbia and in the territories and possessions. Despite this lack of authority, the federal government is deeply involved in urban affairs. Most urban problems are national problems. They become increasingly national as the proportion of the population living in metropolitan communities increases and as the economic and social life of the nation becomes more complex and interdependent.

The result is that many federal agencies are now partners, some are senior partners, with state and local governments in the provision of services for and in regulating the activities of urban residents. We are likely to see an extension of federal participation, guidance, and financial assistance. Since the war, Congress has passed the Highway Act of 1944, the Water Pollution Control Act of 1948, and the Housing Act of 1949.

The Housing and Home Finance Agency is instructed by Congress to encourage metropolitan planning. It has announced that it will give consideration, in reviewing project plans, "to the extent to which the general plan of the Municipality in which the project is located is related to *any* State, regional or metropolitan plans" (my italics). This policy is good in so far as it can be implemented. But that is not very far. Neither the Housing and Home Finance Agency nor any other single agency should be expected to bring about by itself any appreciable integration of planning and execution of its program, much less of related programs, within metropolitan areas.[41] In fact, if a federal agency succeeds in achieving its program objectives the result may be that functional disintegration of local government will replace territorial disintegration. Many New Deal federal agencies, enthusiastic,

40. Pennsylvania Local Government Commission, *Report to the General Assembly of 1937*, p. 9, as quoted in R. O. Johnston, "Selected Developments in Local Government and State-Local Relations in Pennsylvania Since 1930" (M.A. thesis, Department of Political Science, University of Chicago, 1949), p. 109.

41. See the discussion reported by Coleman Woodbury and William L. Slayton, "Administrative Problems in Federal Aid for Urban Development and Redevelopment" (Summary Report of the Second 1313 Conference on Urban Redevelopment, July 14–16, 1949).

impatient of delay, and careless of programs other than their own, encouraged or required the creation of local special districts and authorities.

The federal government can best contribute to an understanding of the problem of metropolitan government and to its solution by studying the relationship between the particular program interests of the various federal agencies and of local governments in metropolitan areas. This should be a co-operative enterprise, repeated at appropriate intervals. Over fifteen years, during which a world war was fought, have elapsed since the last and first study of this kind was made by the federal government.

As valuable as the urbanism studies of the National Resources Committee are,[42] it would be better to study the problem of metropolitan government in the context of all intergovernmental relations. The Hendrickson bill to establish a National Commission on Intergovernmental Relations would have required the Commission "to make a thorough and comprehensive study of [among other things] . . . the problem of geographical areas as related to governmental functions, field administration, and metropolitan communities."[43]

I am not suggesting that a bureau or agency of urban affairs be established in the national government. As John B. Blandford has said:

> I think that there is hazard, if not futility in attempting to organize around a generality or an abstraction. For example, a Department of Urban Affairs faithfully assembled would merge all relations between the communities and the Federal Government, including those with respect to airports, law enforcement, housing, wage-and-hour regulations and employment services, and would raise much too sharply and in an impractical fashion the issues of State and Federal relations. Similarly, any effort to combine all so-called welfare activities of the Federal Government would be like tearing a seamless web, and would raise at once the philosophic question as to whether all Government is not concerned with welfare or public interest in one way or another.[44]

For these very reasons, however, the operating agencies of the federal government should be organized to consider the impact of their activities upon the urban community. Periodically at least, representatives of state and local governments and of other interests involved should be associated with the federal government in the evaluation of

42. National Resources Committee, *Our Cities—Their Role in the National Economy* (1937); *Urban Government* (Vol. I of the supplementary report of the Urbanism Committee, 1939); *Regional Planning: Part II—St. Louis Region* (1936); and *Part IV—The Baltimore-Washington-Annapolis Area* (1937).

43. S. 810, 81st Congress, 1st session, and four similar bills introduced in the House: H. R. 2389, H. R. 3184, H. R. 3944, and H. R. 4507. See *National Commission on Intergovernmental Relations;* Joint Hearings before Subcommittees of the Committees on Expenditures in the Executive Departments, 81st Congress, 1st session, May 9–13, 1949.

44. *Housing and Urban Redevelopment—Part 6;* Hearings before Subcommittee of Senate Committee on Post-War Economic Policy and Planning, 79th Congress, 1st session, January 9, 1945, p. 1314.

their common problems, objectives, and of the means of solving or realizing them.

The least that the federal government should do is to study the problems of its own metropolitan area. Here Congress has exclusive jurisdiction over the central city. There has been piecemeal co-operation between federal agencies, the District of Columbia, and the suburban governments. But there has been no bringing of the pieces together. What is needed here as elsewhere is a governmental organization for continuous planning and replanning in which the parts will be related to each other and the whole will be related to the purposes of the metropolitan community. The need for an examination of the authority and the working relationships of the planning and operating agencies— federal, District of Columbia, state and local—in the Washington metropolitan area is evident from the hearings this year on the proposal to disperse federal agencies in the outer vicinity of the District of Columbia.[45]

The federal government has an opportunity and, I believe, a responsibility to act as a model to the rest of the country by recognizing that the national capital is a metropolitan community spilling over into several counties and independent cities of two states. It also has an opportunity to develop a model *approach* to a comprehensive and co-operative study of the problems and to the development of solutions. I emphasize the *approach* to metropolitan problems because I am not sure that there is any single solution that can be designated as a model.[46]

DEVICES REQUIRING FUNDAMENTAL STRUCTURAL CHANGES

Annexation and municipal consolidation.—These devices are discussed in chapter v.

City-county consolidation.—Until recent years a consolidated city-county was popularly considered to be the most desirable form of metropolitan government.[47] Except for annexation, city-county consolida-

---

45. *Dispersal of Federal Buildings:* Hearings before Subcommittee of the Senate Committee on Public Works, 82d Congress, 1st session, January 19 and 30, 1951. *Dispersal of Federal Agencies:* Hearings before Subcommittee of House Committee on Public Works, 82d Congress, 1st session, February 5, 6, and 8, 1951.

46. For a brief discussion of other ways in which federal activities may affect the government of metropolitan areas see pp. 110–21 of my *Metropolitan Government*.

47. "The reasons which have compelled citizens in some other cities in the rather distant past to consolidate city and county government because of duplication of functions do not exist in Oregon or in Multnomah County at the present time in any appreciable degree. It is possible within the scope of present laws for the citizens if they so desire to consolidate many of the small governmental taxing agencies now existing and still permit the citizens to preserve local control over their local affairs." Oregon Legislative Assembly, Interim Committee on City-County Consolidation in Multnomah County (Portland), *Report,* January 10, 1951, p. 12.

tion is more often proposed than any other scheme as a means of bringing the metropolitan population and area under one local government. Despite repeated failures to secure state legislative action, to secure state-wide approval of enabling amendments to the state constitution, or to secure the required majorities in local referenda, city-county consolidation has been proposed during the last decade in many metropolitan areas.[48] The only consolidation of city and county governments since Denver separated from the rural parts of Arapahoe County in 1909 was the consolidation of Baton Rouge and East Baton Rouge Parish in 1947.

City-county consolidation is often confused with city-county separation.[49] In fact, there is no difference between the two schemes except that in the latter the central city, with or without additional portions of the surrounding county, is separated from the remainder of the county and organized as a separate city-county. There are important problems associated with the separation of the central city and I shall, therefore, consider this device more fully in the next section of this chapter.

Including what is technically to be distinguished as city-county separation and two almost complete functional consolidations, there are thirty-six consolidated city-counties in the United States—namely, Baltimore, San Francisco, St. Louis, Denver, Philadelphia, New Orleans, New York City,[50] Boston, Baton Rouge, and the twenty-seven first-class cities of Virginia.

The Baton Rouge consolidation plan is significant, not only because it was approved by the electorate, but because it provides for three taxing and service areas: (1) an urban area consisting of the old city of 4.6 square miles and approximately 25 square miles of additional built-up territory; (2) two industrial areas where residences are forbidden and the industries must provide their own services;[51] and (3)

48. See the news notes in the *National Municipal Review* for movements in Houston, Fort Worth, Salt Lake City, Minneapolis, Atlanta, Macon, Cleveland, Portland (Oregon), Durham, Birmingham, Seattle, Hampton Roads area, Miami and other places. The most recently defeated plan to consolidate cities and counties was in the Hampton Roads area of Virginia. This plan, initiated by the Lower Peninsula Planning Commission, involved three cities and two counties. It received a majority vote of 56 per cent throughout the entire area, but was defeated by an adverse vote in each of the units except Hampton City (*National Municipal Review*, XXXIV [May, 1950], 251).

49. The most extensive study of this device, *The City-County Consolidated* (Los Angeles, published by the author, 1941) by J. A. Rush, is largely a plea for city-county separation.

50. For a short history of the expansion of New York City and Brooklyn by annexation and the consolidation in 1898 of these two cities, the county of Richmond, the remainder of Kings County and parts of the counties of Westchester and Queens see Regional Survey of New York and Its Environs, Vol. II: *Population, Land Values and Government* (1929), pp. 245–58.

51. Not less than the equivalent of 3 mills on the taxable valuation of the industrial

the remainder of the parish as a rural area where municipal services can be rendered only if special taxing districts are created to finance them.[52]

This way of establishing tax and service differentials should be closely observed in operation. Every metropolitan plan must take account of the differences in need for municipal services in various parts of the area as well as of the fear of the suburban taxpayer that integration will increase his tax burden. Differential tax areas once fixed in constitution, statute, or charter, may be very difficult to modify as the growth of the metropolitan area changes their character.[53] The problem of differential tax rates and municipal services is one of the factors that make some form of "federated" or borough type of metropolitan government attractive.

Under the Baton Rouge arrangement, the legal identity of the city and of the parish is maintained.[54] The governmental structure is affected by the retention of the separate legal identity of the two units as well as by the establishment of the three tax and service areas. Dr. Reed describes the resulting structure of the consolidated unit:

> In order to preserve the identity of the city and parish and not diffuse responsibility and increase cost, the city council was made to consist of seven members elected at large from the city, and the parish council of these same seven persons plus two elected from the parish outside the city. This ensures unity of policy as between the two units. Unity of administration is preserved by putting at its head a single official known as the mayor-president, elected by the people of the parish as a whole. He appoints the director of finance, the purchasing agent, the personnel administrator, the director of public works, and the chiefs of the fire and police departments. The cost of operating the department of finance is shared by the city and parish equally; the departments of fire and police are financed exclusively by the city. The public works department gets its money for highways and bridges, engineering, public building maintenance, and central garage from the parish, and for its divisions of sewers, refuse collection, and inspections (building, plumbing, electrical, etc.) from the city. The city and parish each have separate budgets but in the spending of the money there is no duplication or overlapping of administrative authority or personnel.[55]

---

areas is to be allocated to the city for urban purposes. This description of the Baton Rouge consolidated government is based on T. H. Reed's account, "Progress in Metropolitan Integration," *Public Administration Review,* IX (Winter, 1949), 7–10. See the short note by L. L. Moak in *Public Management* (October, 1947), p. 302.

52. Two small municipalities are continued in the rural area but they have no power to annex additional territory.

53. See the discussion of earlier experiences in Paul Studenski, *The Government of Metropolitan Areas in the United States* (National Municipal League, 1930), chap. ix, and T. H. Reed, "Taxation in the Proposed Metropolitan Government of Pittsburgh," *National Municipal Review,* XVIII (June, 1929), 389.

54. See my discussion of this aspect of city-county consolidation in *Metropolitan Government,* pp. 158–63, 215–35.

55. "Progress in Metropolitan Integration," *Public Administration Review,* IX (1949), 9. Schools and recreation are administered by special boards.

A proposal for the Birmingham metropolitan area, somewhat similar to the Baton-Rouge scheme, was made in 1947 by the research staff of the Legislative Advisory Commission for the Jefferson County Survey.

The area under consideration is a single-county metropolitan district. As such it enjoys certain advantages which should be retained in any proposal for consolidation. It follows, therefore, that any plan which would establish county boundary lines cutting across the Metropolitan District should be rejected. Two proposals which avoid such a division call for the creation of a city-county out of either the Metropolitan District or the county as presently defined. Of these two, the more desirable appears to be that of using the existing county as the territorial basis for any consolidated city-county. It may be, however, that the consolidation of the governments of all 16 municipalities with that of the county is not desirable at this time.

Accordingly, there is proposed the creation of a city-county combining the governments of Jefferson County and Birmingham with boundaries extended as above recommended. As has been noted, these two governments and their school systems embrace an overwhelming percentage of the resources and population of the area. If such a unit were created, there would then exist within present Jefferson County three types of governmental areas: (1) the central city governed by the combined unit with the present level of taxation and a correspondingly high level of services; (2) the non-urban area governed by the combined unit with a lower level of taxation and a more limited level of services; and (3) the remaining municipalities with (a) a basic level of taxation, and services provided heretofore by the county government and hereafter by the combined unit, and (b) additional services and taxes, at the discretion of the municipal governing body. The services heretofore performed for the different areas would remain essentially unchanged, except of course as they might be modified in the future.[56]

Except in metropolitan areas contained within a single county, such as Baton Rouge and Birmingham, city-county consolidation has disadvantages which reduce its usefulness as a device for integrating local government.[57] Once the difficult act of consolidation has been accomplished, it will be doubly difficult, without the Virginia type of annexation procedures, to expand the area of the city-county. Denver is the only city-county which has annexed land and it has not been able to bring the rapidly growing suburbs under its jurisdiction.[58]

56. Cooper, *op. cit.*, pp. 144–45; for a criticism of city-county consolidation as a form of government for the Atlanta metropolitan area, see Local Government Commission of Fulton County, *Plan of Improvement for the Governments of Atlanta and Fulton County, Georgia* (1950), pp. 31–33. The recommendations of this commission and the reorganization legislated by the Georgia Legislature during 1951 will be discussed in chapter viii. Discussion of the recommendations of the Civic Advisory Council of Toronto is also reserved for discussion in that chapter, but the second alternative proposed by the Council is quite similar to the proposal for Birmingham. See Committee on Metropolitan Problems, Civic Advisory Council of Toronto, *Final Report* (1951), pp. 45–51.

57. There are one hundred standard metropolitan areas lying wholly within one county. However, none of the fourteen areas of over a 1,000,000 inhabitants and only eight of the eighteen areas with a population of between 500,000 and 1,000,000 consist of only one county.

58. See the articles on Boston, Denver, New York City, New Orleans, Philadelphia, St. Louis and San Francisco in *City Growing Pains*.

Separation of the city from the county.—Out of anger and frustration, officials and taxpayers of large cities continue to make idle threats or proposals to separate the city from its county.[59] San Francisco, Baltimore, St. Louis, and Denver have withdrawn from the counties of which they were a part and have functioned for many years as a separate city-county. The only other large cities separated from a county are the independent cities of Virginia.[60] Apart from Virginia cities, there have been no city-county separations in the United States during the last forty-five years.

This device differs from city-county consolidation in that the merger of the two governmental units is preceded by the physical separation of the area of the central city, or of the city and some adjacent territory, from the remainder of the county. The old county is divided into two independent counties and the government of one of the new counties is consolidated with that of the central city.

Separation of the central city from the county is most frequently proposed in order to avoid paying county taxes to finance governmental services beyond the city limits. Los Angeles City has for many years complained that its residents are taxed by the county to provide municipal services to the thickly settled unincorporated areas of the county.[61] This year, the city along with the other members of the League of California Cities introduced bills in the state legislature to require any "municipal-type" service of a county to an urban unincorporated area to be paid for by the inhabitants of the area.[62] The legislation was opposed by the counties and it was defeated by a voice vote in the state senate.[63]

There are two basic issues raised by these arguments between cities and counties: (1) Shall suburban residents, industries, and business establishments be allowed to receive the benefits of urban government without paying their "equitable" share of the costs? (2) How can the

59. Or at times to separate from the state. During prohibition, several bills were introduced in the New York legislature to set up New York City as a separate state. See Stanley Walker, "New York City: the 49th State," *American Mercury,* December, 1935, pp. 476–80. For Chicago, see Lepawsky, *op. cit.,* p. 171; Merriam, Parratt, and Lepawsky, *The Government of the Metropolitan Region of Chicago* (Chicago: University of Chicago Press, 1933), pp. 180–83.

60. Most of the independent cities of Virginia are small. By law they become independent upon attaining a population of 10,000.

61. City of Los Angeles, Bureau of Budget and Efficiency, *Study of Local Government in the Metropolitan Area, within the County of Los Angeles* (1935), pp. 32–33, 245–46. See the criticism of the city's analysis and contentions in Committee on Governmental Simplification, *Report* (Los Angeles, 1935), pp. 84–85, 178–79, 186–90.

62. *National Municipal Review,* XL (March, 1951), 155–56. "'Urban unincorporated area' is defined as an unincorporated county territory of a minimum of one square mile, with a minimum population density of 300 persons per square mile, and subdivided into parcels of not more than five acres each with improvements on not less than one third of the parcels."

63. *Ibid.* (September, 1951), pp. 427–28.

metropolitan community be organized so that a minimum level of municipal services can be provided in every part of the community, irrespective of the ability of the inhabitants to pay the full cost of the services?

These two questions must be answered in evaluating the existing local government of a metropolitan area or in devising a reorganization of the local government. They will therefore be considered more extensively in chapter vii. I do not believe, however, that city-county separation will provide an acceptable answer to either question.[64]

An additional reason for avoiding city-county separation, even in desperation, is the difficulty of expanding the city's boundaries as the metropolitan community grows beyond its borders. San Francisco and St. Louis have been completely stopped in their efforts to reacquire the territory they gave up decades ago. Denver and Baltimore are better off because they either annexed extensive areas at the time of separation or have been able to secure annexations since by direct action of the state legislature. The independent cities of Virginia do not, of course, face this problem under their system of annexation by order of a court.

English experience since 1888 with independent county boroughs shows several things of interest to us.[65] In the first place, separation from the county has occurred much more frequently than in this country. There are eighty-three county boroughs in England. In the second place, it has been easier in England than in the United States to expand the boundaries of city-counties. One hundred and nine annexations of county territory to county boroughs were made between 1889 and 1925. The only state in this country where boundary changes have been as extensively made is Virginia. It is no accident that these frequent boundary changes in Virginia, as they were in England until 1926, are made by administrative action rather than by local referenda or state legislative action.[66]

In the third place, the idea of a city independent of the county has not yet been generally accepted in England. The proponents of the

64. See Los Angeles County, Bureau of Efficiency, *Problems Involved in the Proposed Separation of the City of Los Angeles from the County of Los Angeles* (1932). See also the discussion of the advantages and disadvantages of separating Birmingham from Jefferson County in W. Cooper, *op. cit.*, pp. 140–42.

65. The county boroughs are municipalities separate and independent of the county. "The main distinction between County Boroughs and Municipal Boroughs is this. The County Boroughs possess, roughly speaking, the combined powers of a County and a town, and are completely immune from the administrative activities of the County Council. On the other hand, the Municipal Borough is part of the County for Police, Elementary and Secondary Education, and Main Roads, and is subject to the authority of the County in other respects, . . ." Herman Finer, *English Local Government* (London: Methuen, 4th ed., 1950) pp. 68–69.

66. In Virginia, the administrative agency is a court and this means that there are many differences in procedure and approach from a nonjudicial administrative agency such as the British Ministry of Health. But there are also many similarities. This is further discussed in chapter v.

county, with friends in high places (this appears to be true even in the Labour Government) succeeded in stopping the creation of new county boroughs in 1926 and in practically stopping the extension of their boundaries. The fight between county and city developed during the 1920's into a slugging match lasting almost a decade before the Royal Commission on Local Government. The decision, although it was not based on a knockout, went to the counties. Any decision of public policy which prevents urban communities from effectively organizing to govern the metropolitan area is a defeat. Such a defeat was registered again when the Labour Government decided in 1949 to abolish the Local Government Boundary Commission and return to private bills as the means of adjusting the boundaries and organization of local government.[67]

No one knows whether the English metropolitan cities will be allowed to absorb their suburban territory. Experience there as in this country indicates that our attention should be directed to developing other devices than annexation. The separation of the big city from the county is likely to increase rather than diminish the difficulties of establishing a satisfactory method of governing the metropolis.

Running throughout the discussion of how to govern a metropolitan community is the question of whether there should be a single government or several governments and what their relationship shall be. Since government is not an institution with a single purpose but one with many closely interrelated purposes and problems, we should seek to organize the government of a metropolitan area so as to satisfy as many of the values of its inhabitants as is possible. This cannot be done by establishing a separate government for each interest. Nor can it be done by dividing the area of the whole community into small fragments each of which is organized as a separate, jealous, and suspicious governmental unit.

Several schemes for meeting the problems of governing a metropolitan community, none of which appears by itself to promise an adequate solution, have been discussed in this chapter. In the next two chapters, two other devices, annexation and the creation of special districts, are discussed at greater length. In chapter vii, I discuss three other devices which I believe are more likely to produce a satisfactory form of metropolitan government. We can make the county into a metropolitan municipality, we can create multi-purpose metropolitan districts, or we can devise a borough-type of local government.

---

67. See the *Minutes of Evidence* and the *First, Second and Final Reports* of the Royal Commission on Local Government (1923–29). The evidence is discussed critically by Herman Finer, *op. cit.*, and by W. A. Robson, *The Development of Local Government* (London: George Allen and Unwin, 1948), pp. 91–232. See also the three reports of the Local Government Boundary Commission (1947–49).

CHAPTER V

ANNEXATION

B<small>Y</small> 1940, it was generally agreed that it was no longer politically possible for large cities to extend their boundaries by annexing adjacent land. Municipal officials and interested citizens reluctantly arrived at this conclusion. Throughout the nineteenth century annexation had been frequently and sometimes drastically used to increase the area and population of cities.

Importance of Annexation during Nineteenth Century

If the area of the large cities of the country had not been extended by annexation during the past century, the metropolitan areas, with the exception of New York, would now contain no city large enough and important enough to give its name to the metropolitan district. These large urban aggregations would be under the jurisdiction of many times the number of local government units that exist today. If, for instance, there had been no annexations to Cleveland after 1830, the population of the city would have been less in 1930 than it was a hundred years before. The population of the area of the old city of 1830 has been decreasing since 1870. Boston, as delimited in 1840, contained only 148,040 people in 1930. This was just 12,000 more than the population of the same area in 1850. And St. Louis would be today a city of 5,000 people if there had been no annexations since 1840. As it is, the present city, with its enlarged area, increased in population from 1920 to 1930 by 6.3 per cent.[1]

Large amounts of land have been involved in some annexations. The largest single extension of city boundaries occurred in 1898, when New York City was consolidated with Brooklyn, part of Queens County, and Staten Island, adding approximately 255.5 square miles to the area of the city. The area of the city of Los Angeles is four and one-half times as large as it was in 1910. The annexation in 1915 of San Fernando alone added approximately 170 square miles to its area. Detroit increased its area between 1920 and 1930 by approximately 60 square

1. R. D. McKenzie, *The Metropolitan Community* (New York: McGraw-Hill Book Co., 1933), pp. 340–42, Table X.

miles. In the middle of the nineteenth century the area of Philadelphia was enlarged by 127.31 square miles when the city boundaries were made coterminous with the county limits. Two years later (1856) San Francisco gained 34.5 square miles of land and 84.8 square miles of water when it was separated from what is now San Mateo County. St. Louis gained approximately 43 square miles of territory at the time of a similar city-county separation in 1876.

FEW SIGNIFICANT ANNEXATIONS AFTER 1890

Annexations in the past half-century, however, have contributed little toward a solution of the problem of metropolitan government. Ten central cities in six of the seventeen most populous metropolitan areas annexed no territory between 1890 and 1940. These include Philadelphia, Providence, Fall River, New Bedford, St. Louis, San Francisco, St. Paul, Paterson, and Jersey City. Newark is the only central city in the New York area which resorted to annexation between 1898 and 1932, and the total amount of land added thereby was a little over 5 square miles. The area of Boston has been increased only a little over 7 square miles since 1880, and approximately 2 square miles are due to fillings on the harbor front and along the inland water courses.[2] And even in the two cities, Los Angeles and Detroit, which have resorted to annexations most extensively since 1910, there were almost 1,500,000 people in the former and 675,000 people in the latter who lived, in 1940, outside their corporate limits. In the 1930's census decade, the largest annexation to a central city was that of Willow Glen, with 4,167 people, to San Jose. Tujunga (population 2,311) was annexed to Los Angeles, and Miles Heights (population 2,042) to Cleveland. Small unincorporated areas were annexed to Pittsburgh, Cincinnati, Chicago, Buffalo, Milwaukee, San Jose, and Oakland. Parts of incorporated municipalities were annexed to Buffalo, Elizabeth, and Newark. Chicago ceded territory to two villages and Cincinnati to a township.

INCREASE OF ANNEXATIONS SINCE WORLD WAR II

Immediately after World War II, however, cities in many but not all parts of the country began to annex adjacent unincorporated land at a speed and with an enthusiasm reminiscent of the nineteenth century.[3]

2. F. H. Fay, "Planning of a City," *Fifty Years of Boston* (Boston: Boston Tercentenary Committee, 1934), p. 56; George H. McCaffrey, "The Political Disintegration and Reintegration of Metropolitan Boston" (Ph.D. dissertation, Harvard University, 1937), pp. 189–95.

3. John C. Bollens, "Annexation Isn't Dead," *Public Management* (June, 1951), pp. 126–130.

In 1950, land was annexed by 382 cities of over 5,000 population, including 223 cities of over 10,000 population. Table 12 shows the number of cities over 5,000 population completing annexations during 1935–39 and 1944–50.[4]

TABLE 12

NUMBER OF CITIES OVER 5,000 POPULATION ANNEXING TERRITORY, 1935–39 AND 1945–50

YEAR	ALL CITIES OVER 5,000		CITIES OF 5,000 TO 10,000		CITIES OVER 10,000	
	Total No. of Annexing Cities	No. of Cities Annexing ½ Sq. Mile or over	Total No. of Annexing Cities	No. of Cities Annexing ½ Sq. Mile or over	Total No. of Annexing Cities	No. of Cities Annexing ½ Sq. Mile or over
1950	382	60	159	12	223	48
1949	301	56	113	11	188	45
1948	288	59	95	7	193	52
1947	298	68	128	15	170	53
1946	259	43	105	13	154	30
1945	152	25	63	3	89	22
1939					76	
1938					45	
1937					52	
1936					45	
1935					25	

LIMITED UTILITY OF ANNEXATION TO PROVIDE METROPOLITAN GOVERNMENT

Annexation, however, is no more promising a device for bringing the metropolitan area under a metropolitan government than it was in 1942. An analysis of recent annexations shows that

1. Only a few central cities in the larger metropolitan areas have annexed land.

2. The amount of land annexed has, with a few exceptions, been small.

3. Except in Atlanta, only unincorporated land has been annexed.

4. *Significant* annexations have been confined to a few states. '

5. Opposition to annexation has already resulted in movements in several states to change the law to make annexation more difficult.

4. John C. Bollens, "Annexations in 1950," *The Municipal Year Book*, XVIII (1951), 95. These valuable surveys have been an annual feature of the *Year Book* since 1949. The data for the years 1935–39 are taken from *The Municipal Year Book*, XVI (1949), p. 92, footnote 1.

Other data on the number and extent of annexations during the nineteenth and early twentieth centuries may be found in U.S. Chamber of Commerce, Civic Department, *Municipal Annexation of Land* (Washington, D.C., 1926); Paul Studenski, *The Government of Metropolitan Areas in the United States* (New York: National Municipal League, 1930); R. D. McKenzie, *The Metropolitan Community;* Walter H. Blucher in *Freehold* for February 1, 1938; Victor Jones, *Metropolitan Government* (Chicago: University of Chicago Press, 1942), Table 13, pp. 124–25; and American Municipal Association, *Changes in Municipal Boundaries through Annexation, Detachment and Consolidation* (Chicago, 1939), pp. 8–10. See American Society of Planning Officials, "Annexation of Fringe Areas: A Selected Bibliography" (September, 1951).

Only seventy-six of the one hundred and ninety-seven central cities in standard metropolitan areas annexed territory during the six-year period, 1945–50.[5] Among the central cities in metropolitan areas of over 500,000 population, Detroit, New York City, Jersey City, Newark, Philadelphia, Baltimore, Minneapolis, St. Paul, Boston, Buffalo, Pittsburgh, St. Louis, San Francisco, Oakland, Washington, D.C., Albany, Troy, Columbus (Ohio), New Orleans, Providence, and Youngstown were either unsuccessful in their attempts to annex or made no effort to do so. Fourteen of the twenty central cities of metropolitan areas with a population between 500,000 and a million have completed annexations since the war and some of these cities have annexed large areas. But in metropolitan areas with populations between 200,000 and 500,000, only twenty-four out of sixty-nine central cities annexed land; in areas with populations between 100,000 and 200,000, only twenty-seven out of seventy-one central cities and among the eighteen central cities in metropolitan areas of less than 100,000 population, ten central cities annexed.

The fact that 38 per cent of central cities in the one hundred and sixty-eight standard metropolitan areas have successfully annexed adjacent territory since the war would be very encouraging if enough land had been annexed to bring an appreciable portion of the fringe area under the jurisdiction of the central city. Although twelve central cities have annexed over 10 square miles since 1945 including Atlanta (over 80 square miles) and four Texas cities (over 80, 55, 39, and 21 square miles respectively), almost half of the annexing cities have each acquired less than 1.5 square miles of additional territory.

Acreage is not, of course, the sole or the most important criterion by which annexation is to be judged. A small area may be highly developed and densely populated as, for example, the 2.33 square miles with a population of 10,000 annexed by Portland, Oregon, in 1950, the one-half square mile with a population of 5,500 annexed in the same year by Hayward (San Francisco–Oakland metropolitan area), or the three-fourths of a square mile, with a population of 10,500, annexed by Dallas in 1948. On the other hand, a large area may be scarcely populated as in the approximately 3 square miles, with a population of only ninety-six, annexed by San Diego in 1948.

Furthermore, population at the time of annexation may be less important as a reason for annexation than the impending or probable development of the area for residential or industrial use. Milwaukee has announced as the principal objective of its annexation program "the acquisition of a supply of vacant land sufficiently adequate to provide sites for urgently needed homes; to furnish locations for new industrial

5. The Atlanta annexation was made by the Georgia legislature in 1951.

plants and insure commercial development within the City borders."[6]

Even though developments on the periphery of the city are brought under the jurisdiction of the city by annexation, this action may be merely an evasion or a postponement of the political, social, and economic decisions necessary to solve the problems of the central city. None of the reasons given by the Dayton City Plan Board for the unavailability of vacant land in the city will be removed merely by an extension of the city's boundaries:

> All space in Dayton today is 85 per cent occupied. . . . Housing occupancy within the City limits is near its maximum. Dayton has reached its highest saturation in history. Unless territory is annexed there can be only limited additional development in Dayton inasmuch as *vacant lands are largely unavailable for improvement, chiefly as a result of location, ownership, type of holding, tax status, or impracticability of improvement because of physical characteristics.*[7]

Cities which have annexed large portions of their unincorporated fringe areas are able to bring many problem areas within the general city plan, if one exists.[8] They can, furthermore, forestall the creation of special districts or incorporated suburbs to meet the demand for controls and services considered by suburbanites to be necessary or desirable.[9] In most metropolitan areas where central cities have made extensive annexations, one of the purposes has been to claim the territory before the inhabitants can make annexation virtually impossible by incorporating as a municipality or before it can be annexed by a suburb.[10] In 1948, eighteen new towns were proposed within seven months following a plan to consolidate Miami and Dade County. Eleven were voted down at the polls and several others were successfully attacked in the courts.[11]

Such counteraction by the residents of an area which the city proposes to annex is an old device and accounts in part for the large num-

---

6. City of Milwaukee, Department of Annexation, "Annexation: Key to Prosperous Community" (1947?, unpaged).

7. Dayton City Plan Board, *Annexation* (1946), p. 11.

8. For a list of facilities in the annexed areas which were considered adequate at the time of annexation, see Table VI in *The Municipal Year Book* (1949–51). The table in the 1951 volume also lists the service needs which most influenced fringes to annex. In the volumes for 1949 and 1950, there is a column showing whether 50 per cent or more of the annexed area was developed.

9. In Los Angeles County, the larger cities are worried because densely populated areas will neither incorporate nor be annexed. Many of these areas are entirely surrounded by incorporated municipalities. See the map on p. 28 of G. W. Bemis and Nancy Basché, *Los Angeles County as an Agency of Municipal Government* (Los Angeles: Haynes Foundation, 1946).

10. See Lincoln Park Civic Advancement Association, Inc., "Dangers Lurking behind Incorporation Revealed" (Milwaukee, no date).

11. *American Municipal News* (September, 1948).

ber of incorporated suburbs near every large city.[12] Attempts to incorporate, however, have not always been successful. In Texas, the Supreme Court has held that an area cannot be incorporated after a home-rule city has announced that it intends to annex.[13]

INCORPORATED SUBURBS UNLIKELY TO BE ANNEXED

As useful as annexation may be in some metropolitan areas for bringing adjacent unincorporated territory into the city, it will not solve the problem of metropolitan government.[14] Incorporated suburbs, under the statutes of most states and under the politics of all, are safe from the central city. Some central cities, such as Minneapolis, are completely surrounded by incorporated suburbs.[15] All New England central cities are walled in by towns which are the regional equivalent of municipal corporations. Although the New England legislatures have constitutionally unrestricted power to alter the boundaries of towns and cities,[16] the cities can expect no assistance from legislatures where representation is based upon the towns.

In other parts of the country, incorporated municipalities cannot be annexed without a favorable vote in the municipality to be annexed. These suburban protections are found in some state constitutions and more frequently in general annexation statutes. Sometimes special annexation acts require a referendum. In the recent Birmingham annexation, for instance, the special legislative act required a separate majority in each incorporated municipality but provided that the votes

12. See J. Trenton Kostbade, *Hobart, Indiana, as a Suburban Development in the Calumet Extension of Metropolitan Chicago* (M.A. thesis, Geography, University of Chicago, 1948), pp. 81–83, for the story of Gary's efforts before World War I to expand by annexation, of the widespread incorporation of municipalities to prevent annexation, and of the race between "Greater Hobart" and "Greater Gary" for the same land. In 1916 the cities of the Calumet were attempting to annex each other.

13. *City of Houston* v. *State*, 142 Tex. 190; *State* v. *San Antonio*, 147 S.W. (2d) 551; *Fort Worth* v. *State*, 186 S.W. (2d) 323.

14. See Dayton City Plan Board, *Annexation* (1946), pp. 55–57, for a discussion of the advantages, disadvantages and difficulties of annexing Oakwood, a wealthy suburb, to Dayton.

15. See the articles by Roy Dunlap in the *St. Paul Pioneer Press* (March 4 and 11, 1951) and Charles A. Wright, "Are Suburbs Necessary?" 35 *Minnesota Law Review,* 341–55 (1951).

The Texas Supreme Court has held that a home-rule municipality cannot annex without its consent another municipality of "equal dignity" although it may by annexation encircle a municipality even though it be of "equal dignity" (*Houston* v. *Magnolia Park*, 276 S.W. 685).

16. The legislature has full power to annex in Connecticut, Massachusetts, Maine, and Vermont. In New Hampshire proposed changes must be ratified by two-thirds of the voters in each city or town involved (*Revised Laws* [1942], ch. 69, sec. 13). Since 1923, Rhode Island declared by statute that "the extent and boundaries of the several cities and towns shall remain as now established by law" (*General Laws* [1938], ch. 4, sec. 1).

cast in unincorporated areas should be counted in with the votes of the central city. Consequently, the combined vote favored annexation, and 136 square miles of unincorporated territory were annexed. No suburb was annexed, however, since all five were opposed.[17] In some states extraordinary majorities are required. The recent Atlanta annexations were made by the legislature after a referendum. In 1947, proposals to annex were decisively voted down in the suburbs.[18]

The extent of the suburban barrier is suggested by the number of incorporated municipalities other than the central city in 1940 in metropolitan areas where large annexations have taken place since the war. In Memphis, Fort Worth, and Oklahoma City areas, there were only three in each. But in the Atlanta area, there were eight suburban municipalities, ten in Birmingham, thirteen in Dallas, nine in Houston, nine in Kansas City, twelve in Louisville, and thirteen in Milwaukee.[19]

The central cities of the larger metropolitan areas are less expandable than those in the smaller areas. Almost 56 per cent of all the suburban municipalities of the one hundred and forty metropolitan districts of 1940 were in the eleven districts of 1,000,000 or more population. Furthermore, during the 1930's almost half of the new incorporations were in these eleven metropolitan areas. The concentration of suburbs in the larger areas may be indicated by the average number of suburbs in each district of certain sizes. In 1940 the rough averages were eighty-five for districts of more than 1,000,000 population; twenty for those between 500,000 and 1,000,000; seven for those between 200,000 and 500,000; four for the districts between 100,000 and 200,000; and for the districts between 50,000 and 100,000, the average was a little more than one.

TABLE 13

DISTRIBUTION OF METROPOLITAN DISTRICTS BY POPULATION SIZE AND BY PERCENTAGE OF POPULATION IN UNINCORPORATED AREAS, 1940*

	Over 1,000,000	500,000– 1,000,000	200,000– 500,000	100,000– 200,000	50,000– 100,000
1% or less	1				1
1%–5%	1	1			1
5%–10%	3	3	5	6	8
10%–15%	2	3	9	12	5
15%–20%	2	1	12	12	4
20%–25%	1		4	3	7
25%–30%			2	8	3
30%–35%				3	2
35%–40%				2	1
40%–45%				1	

* Washington, D.C., and New England districts excluded.

17. *American City* (December, 1949), p. 131.

18. M. Clyde Hughes, "Annexation and Reallocation of Functions," *Public Management,* XXXIV (February, 1952), 26.

19. Victor Jones, "Metropolitan Districts," *The Municipal Year Book,* IX (1942), 192–93, Table II-B.

Annexation proceedings have not only evoked proposals to incorporate the threatened area; they have in some metropolitan areas led to a struggle between central city and suburb to annex unincorporated areas before the other could do so. La Porte, in the Houston area, adopted a home-rule charter in 1949 and immediately put it to use in effecting three secret annexations to increase its area from 5 to 50 square miles and its population from 200 to 7,000.[20] Kansas City and North Kansas City have also been fighting for the same territory.

Most annexations since 1945 have occurred in twenty states with Texas, California, and Virginia in the lead, and only a few annexations in these states have been significant either as to area or to population.[21] Annexation is in fact unavailable in New England and to many central cities elsewhere such as Minneapolis and New York City.

One of the results of the recent annexation drive has been to heighten the opposition to the central city in many areas. This has shown itself in efforts to incorporate in order to forestall annexation, in spirited letters to editors of local newspapers, in organized campaigns to defeat proposals to annex, and in organized efforts to secure legislation making annexation more difficult. The most intense pressures have been brought to bear upon the legislatures of Texas and Virginia. In the latter state, the campaign is led by the League of Virginia Counties which hopes to substitute a referendum for the present judicial procedure. The League has succeeded in amending the statutes to prevent a city from annexing territory from a county with a land area of less than 60 square miles. Under a statute of 1950, no new annexation suits can be initiated, except by agreement, before July 1, 1952. In the same session, the General Assembly established a commission to study the conflict between counties and cities over annexation. It was ordered to report to the General Assembly by October 1, 1951, "with recommendations as to state policy to aid the orderly growth of urban areas, ease the impact of such growth on rural areas, and assist harmonious integration of contiguous rural areas with urban areas."[22]

20. Public Administration Clearing House, *News Bulletin* (April 21, 1950). Apart from the Atlanta consolidation, the only consolidations of municipalities reported in recent years are Britton and Oklahoma City (*ibid.*, May 25, 1950), Oak Knolls and Haltom City, Texas, in 1950, Salem and West Salem, Oregon, in 1947, the merger of two Texas municipalities to form Baytown in 1947, the consolidation of several municipalities with Weirton, West Virginia, in 1948 and of several others with Morgantown, West Virginia, in 1949 (*The Municipal Year Book*, XVIII [1951], 97).

21. See Robert E. Fryer, *Analysis of Annexation in Michigan* (Bureau of Government, University of Michigan, "Papers in Public Administration," No. 5, 1951), for a study of the results of annexation in Michigan between 1937 and 1947 and an analysis of successful and unsuccessful attempts to annex. Other studies refer only casually to unsuccessful annexations.

22. *National Municipal Review*, XXXIX (July, 1950), 351. County-municipal antagonism is aggravated in Virginia because land annexed to an independent city, therefore,

Whether annexation is worth the price of such antagonism cannot be decided in a general statement. Undoubtedly the bad feelings resulting from the "forcible annexation" of Allegheny City to Pittsburgh in 1910 effectively blocked all attempts to annex during the following decade. On the other hand, it was the fear of annexation that led the League of Third-Class Cities, Boroughs, and Townships of Allegheny County to seek an acceptable form of metropolitan government. If Pittsburgh had not pushed its annexation program, it is likely that the suburbs would have taken no interest in the problem.[23]

Cumbersome Annexation Procedures Required by Statutes

One of the results of the antagonism toward the central city, and perhaps the most effective in slowing down annexation, is the detailed, intricate, and often inconsistent statutory provisions for annexation. Delaware, Maine, Massachusetts, and Maryland have no annexation statutes; Rhode Island forbids by statute any territorial changes; Connecticut only requires prior public notice of petition to the legislature; and New Hampshire requires a favorable two-thirds vote of the voters of each town or city affected before the legislature can annex. The legislature in some of the other states can annex by special act, but the general annexation statutes of all states except those listed above with the addition of Virginia, Texas, and Missouri (home-rule cities) prescribe lengthy and cumbersome procedures.[24]

In Michigan, for example, there are different annexation procedures for home-rule cities of over 15,000 population, home-rule cities of less than 15,000 population, fourth-class cities, special charter cities, home-rule villages, and general-law villages. Each type of municipality is offered several different procedures from which it must select the one

is lost to the tax rolls of the county. For the complaint of Henrico County after the 1941 annexation by Richmond, see J. C. Houseman, "Model County Faces Problems," *National Municipal Review*, XXXIII (April, 1940), 179. The problem in Virginia is more comparable to the English problem of expanding the boundaries of county boroughs than it is to that of any other American state—unless, of course, some form of city-county separation is involved.

23. See my *Metropolitan Government*, pp. 308–12. The borough plan of 1929 received wide support in the suburbs. There was suburban opposition, aided and abetted by the U.S. Steel Corporation, which secured the requirement of a two-thirds majority in a majority of the cities, boroughs, and townships for adoption of the charter. The astounding fact is that it secured such an extraordinary majority in 58 such units (T. H. Reed, "Progress in Metropolitan Integration," *Public Administration Review*, IX [Winter, 1949], 3).

24. The statutory provisions of all states are conveniently reproduced in *Laws of the States Relating to Annexation of County Territory*, Vol. II, compiled by Jo Desha Lucas and Robert Desha Lucas (Charlottesville: League of Virginia Counties, 1950). Volume I consists of summaries of the statutes. The statutes as of 1939 are outlined in American Municipal Association, *Changes in Municipal Boundaries*.

to fit the particular situation. The Home Rule City Act provides six different procedures. These statutes contain detailed provisions for initiating the action, the form of the petition, action by the Board of Supervisors, submission to the electorate, etc., which vary according to the type of municipality involved. Michigan annexation laws are simpler than those of many states in that, with three exceptions, they "contain no requirements with respect to the amount, location, or condition of the lands that may be annexed; e.g., whether it must be contiguous, whether it must have a certain population density, etc."[25]

The minute classification of land to be annexed may be illustrated by those found in the Minnesota statutes (there are also seven classes of land which may be detached):

A. Villages:[26]
  1. Abutting on any village and not included in any other village or in any city or borough.
  2. Land owned by the village.
  3. Completely surrounded by land within the village limits.
  4. Plotted or if unplotted does not exceed 200 acres.
  5. Resident population of not less than 75 persons and no part of the land is less than 1½ miles from the village limits.
B. City or Village:[27]
  6. Population of not less than 75 persons, and not included in any incorporated city or village, but adjoining any city or village . . . , and no part of which territory is more than 1½ miles from the present limits of the city or village which it adjoins.
C. Villages, boroughs, and cities of the fourth class:[28]
  7. Property owned by the unit located outside of, but contiguous to or abutting on, the corporate limits.
D. Villages and cities of 10,000 or less:[29]
  8. Plotted into lots and blocks or outlots.
  9. Any abutting tract, piece or parcel of land owned by one person.
E. Cities of the fourth class:[30]
  10. Plotted or unplotted tracts, or a group of tracts or parcels of land, not used for agricultural purposes, and not within the corporate limits of any city or village and so conditioned as properly to be subjected to city or village government, and being contiguous to and surrounded on all sides by the corporate limits of a city of the fourth class or village.
F. Cities of the third class:[31]
  11. So conditioned as properly to be subjected to city government; wholly or partly plotted into lots and which has a resident population of not less than 500 to the square mile, taken as a whole, and not being within the limits of

25. Fryer, *op. cit.*, pp. 8–20.
26. *Minn. Stats. Annotated, 1947,* and 1949 Pocket Supplement, Sec. 412.041.
27. *Ibid.,* Sec. 413.12.
28. *Ibid.,* Sec. 413.13.
29. *Ibid.,* Sec. 413.14.
30. *Ibid.,* Sec. 413.143.
31. *Ibid.,* Sec. 413.18.

any city or village and lying adjacent to any city in the same county now or hereafter having a population of not more than 20,000, or less than 10,000.
    12. Plotted into lots and blocks or outlots.[32]
    13. Any abutting tract, piece, or parcel of land owned by one person.[33]
G. Cities of the second class:[34]
    14. Plotted into lots and blocks or outlots.
    15. Any abutting tract, piece, or parcel of land owned by one person.
H. Cities of the first class:
    16. Not exceeding 50 acres in area, adjoining and contiguous to any city of over 50,000 inhabitants.[35]
    17. Outside any incorporated municipality and adjoining and contiguous to any city of the first class having 350,000 inhabitants, within the same county in which the city of the first class is situated and which have been plotted into subdivisions approved by the council or chief governing body of such city and by the county board of such county, and in which the streets and alleys have been dedicated for public use.[36]
I. Villages and cities of the second, third, and fourth classes:[37]
    18. Property owned by unit which is outside of but contiguous to or adjoining corporate limits and used, operated or maintained as a municipal airport.

The initiative must be taken in some states by a specified number or portion of the inhabitants, qualified voters, or property owners. In other states, or in special types of annexation, the initiative may be taken by the council of the annexing city. The states vary in the procedure for completing annexation, once it is initiated. Most of them require approval by a majority vote in the area to be annexed, sometimes preceded by a three-fourths vote of the council. In a few states extraordinary popular majorities of three-fourths, four-fifths, two-thirds, or four-sevenths are required.

ANNEXATION BY ORDINANCE OR BY CHARTER AMENDMENT IN TEXAS AND MISSOURI HOME-RULE CITIES

Compared with such intricate statutory provisions, the Virginia system of judicial determination and the Texas and Missouri system of annexation by amendment of home-rule charters are simple. The principal advantage of both procedures, however, is that the initiative lies with the annexing city and, if necessary, the annexation can be carried through despite the objections of the people in the annexed territory.[38]

32. *Ibid.*, Sec. 413.19.
33. *Ibid.*, Sec. 413.19.
34. *Ibid.*, Sec. 413.22.
35. *Ibid.*, Sec. 413.23.
36. *Ibid.*, Sec. 413.24.
37. *Ibid.*, Sec. 413.60.
38. That this is the principal virtue of the procedure is indicated by the remarks of Thomas H. Reed, a close student of metropolitan government and a participant in efforts

These advantages have led many students and protagonists to envy the relatively easy annexation procedure in Virginia.[39]

The only thing in common between annexation procedures in Virginia and Texas (home-rule cities) is that an election is not required in either the annexing city or in the territory to be annexed. In Texas the courts have held that the plenary power of the legislature to change the boundaries of municipal corporations devolved upon cities with home-rule charters.[40] If the charter so provides, unincorporated adjacent territory can be annexed by ordinance or annexation can be by amendment to the charter.

The Missouri Supreme Court has recently held that, without specific statutory or constitutional authorization, home-rule cities may annex adjacent unincorporated land by amendment of their charters. In an opinion upholding the annexation by Kansas City of 20 square miles across the Missouri River in another county, the court said:

> The citizenship of the state plainly intended to give [home-rule] cities the right to determine for themselves the kind of charter under which they should live. But no intention appears to stifle growth and expansion. . . . The power to . . . annex and the right to grow in area by such annexation are necessarily and fairly implied in and are incident to the power of charter adoption and amendment expressly granted by the constitution. . . . Specific legislative authority to extend [Kansas City's] limits is unnecessary.[41]

---

in Virginia and elsewhere to reform it. "It would be well if the constitution and laws [of Virginia] provided for consolidation as an alternative to annexation on one condition— that the question be judicially determined. Left to popular vote there would be no better chance of consolidating than of annexing by the same means. In fact, the chances would be less, for consolidation would mean the utter elimination of one set of officials, and how they would fight to keep their jobs!" (Thomas H. Reed, "Progress in Metropolitan Integration," *Public Administration Review*, IX [Winter, 1949], 7.)

39. See, for example, Reed, *ibid.*, and "Annexation and the Urban Fringe Problem," *Virginia Municipal Review* (January, 1949), p. 5; Robert H. Armstrong and Homer Hoyt, "Decentralization in New York City" (New York: Urban Land Institute, January, 1941), p. 188; Fryer, *op. cit.*, pp. 53–54, 56; John C. Bollens, "City Annexation Programs and Policies," *Public Management*, XXXII (April, 1950), 79; Charles A. Wright, "Are Suburbs Necessary?" 35 *Minnesota Law Review,* 347–48 (1951); Elmer Krieger, executive secretary, Milwaukee Board of Public Land Commissioners, Memorandum to the Board on Coordination of plans for the city's expansion and the civil defense program, March 10, 1951, p. 8.

40. *City of Houston* v. *State,* 142 Texas 190—annexation by ordinance; *Eastham* v. *Steinhagan,* 111 Texas 597—annexation by Beaumont through charter amendment. See R. E. Rouer, "Power of Home Rule City to Annex Adjacent Territory," *Texas Municipalities* (April, 1947), p. 74; 62 *Corpus Juris Secundum* 126, ftn. 90; August O. Spain, "Recent Municipal Annexation in Texas," *Southwestern Social Science Quarterly* (March, 1949) and "Politics of Recent Municipal Annexation in Texas," *ibid.* (June, 1949), pp. 18–28.

41. *State ex inf. Taylor* ex rel. *Kansas City* v. *North Kansas City.* 228 S.W. (2nd) 762 (1950) as quoted by W. O. Winter, "Kansas City Leaps a River," 39 *National Municipal Review,* 447–48 (1950).

JUDICIAL DETERMINATION OF ANNEXATION QUESTIONS IN VIRGINIA

The only state in which significant annexations have been made throughout the last forty years is Virginia. This is correctly attributed to the judicial procedure by which annexation is determined and ordered. The question is not submitted, in any manner, to popular vote. To freedom from the chance of electoral disapproval must be added a well-established judicial tradition developed through a long series of annexation cases. This tradition is summarized in the maxim: "Urban areas should be under urban governments and rural areas should be in a county."[42] In 1941, the Supreme Court of Appeals announced the bovine theory of integration of fringe areas with the central city, in language that may or may not have convinced the rural and suburban counties:

> In considering the annexation of territory, it may be likened in rural parlance, to a well-fed milk cow whose head is feeding from the manger, which is the parent city supplying the feed, but whose body is largely in the areas proposed to be annexed, and whose milk is yielded and drawn therein. Continuing the analogy, it would seem desirable to have the whole cow under one jurisdiction that she might be properly looked after, nourished, stabled, and cared for, and if veterinary services be needed, instead of having two veterinarians, one for the head and one for the body, not always working together or in harmony, have one veterinarian whose skill and ability would best promote, not only the particular but the general welfare of the cow.[43]

This tradition is also supported by the old Virginia separation of all cities of 10,000 population or more from the county.

Annexation is secured by a suit against the county initiated by ordinance of the annexing city or by petition of a majority of qualified voters in the area which is sought to be annexed.[44] The ordinance or petition is filed in the circuit court of the county affected by the proposed annexation. The case is tried without a jury "upon the evidence introduced in the manner in which evidence is introduced in common law cases" by a special annexation court of three circuit court judges. One is the judge of the circuit court of the county from which territory is to be annexed. If the annexing city is a separate judicial circuit, its circuit judge is the second member of the court. Otherwise, the second judge is to be appointed by the Chief Justice of the Supreme Court of Appeals from an adjoining circuit. The third judge is appointed by the Chief Justice from a circuit court "remote from the territory to be annexed."

42. *County of Norfolk* v. *City of Portsmouth*, 186 Va. 1032 (1947). The case law is outlined by Reed, *op. cit.*, pp. 5–6 and by T. G. Hobbs, "Annexation of Surrounding Territory by Cities in Virginia," 28 *Virginia Law Review* 831–47.

43. *Henrico County* v. *Richmond*, 177 Va. 754, 760, 15 S.E. (2) 309 (1941).

44. *Code of Virginia*, 1950, Title 15, secs. 125–152.1, 358.

The statutory guides for the court in making its decision are best stated in the language of the statute itself:

> . . . If the majority of the court shall be satisfied of the necessity for and expediency of such annexation, considering the best interests of the county, and city and the best interests, services to be rendered and needs of the area proposed to be annexed and the best interests of the remaining portions of the county, and that such conditions are reasonable and fair, an order shall be entered providing for the annexation of such territory. But if a majority of the court shall be of the opinion that no annexation is necessary or expedient, considering the best interests of the county, the city and the best interests, services to be rendered and needs of the area proposed to be annexed, and the best interests of the remaining portion of the county, the motion to annex shall be dismissed.[45]

The court can order more or less territory annexed than requested in the petition to the court.

> The court shall so draw the lines of annexation as to have a reasonably compact body of land, and shall also see that no land shall be taken into the city which is not adapted to city improvements unless necessarily embraced in such compact body of land, or which the city shall not need in the reasonably near future for development. In making its decision as to the character and extent of annexation the court shall take into consideration as well, not only the development of the city but also the loss of revenue to the county and the effect that annexation may have upon the revenues of the city and the county.[46]

The discretion of the court is limited only by judicial interpretation of the statute and by a few explicit statutory provisions. No county can be reduced by an annexation order to a territory of less than 60 square miles. The city must assume a "just proportion" of existing county debt and reimburse the county for the value of permanent public improvements in the annexed territory.[47]

The decision of the annexation court may be appealed to the Supreme Court of Appeals which may affirm, reverse, or modify the judgment.[48]

In Virginia, therefore, cities have successfully annexed territory throughout the twentieth century because the statutes do not require the assent of either the qualified electors or of property owners in the annexed territory. The decision as to the necessity or desirability of

45. *Ibid.*, Title 15, sec. 135.
46. *Ibid.*
47. The court must "take into consideration the original cost of such public improvements less depreciation as well as the reproduction cost at the time of annexation less depreciation and the value to the city or town seeking annexation as well as the county or counties affected thereby . . ." (*ibid.*, sec. 128).
48. ". . . the appeal shall be heard and determined without reference to the principles of demurrer to evidence, the evidence being considered as on an appeal to chancery cases" (*ibid.*, sec. 137).

annexation and of the fairness and justice of the annexation proposal is vested in a court.

Judicial Determination of Annexation Questions in Other States

Virginia is not the only state which places this function in the courts.[49] In Arizona, territory with 25 or more inhabitants to a quarter section or fractional part thereof can be annexed by the superior court of the county upon petition of the city or of a majority of the legal voters or property owners of the territory proposed to be annexed. The trial may be by the court or by a jury. No member of the jury shall reside in the city or in the territory to be annexed. Annexation is to be ordered if "the court finds that such territory ought to be annexed to such city, and can be done without injustice to the inhabitants or persons interested."[50]

In Arkansas, the petition must come from a majority of real estate owners in the area to be annexed or from the annexing city, after approval by a majority of the electors. An annexation order is issued by the county judge if he is convinced that the petition is "right and proper" and that it "should be granted."[51]

In Indiana, all except first-class cities may annex by ordinance. But any person affected may appeal to the circuit or superior court. The court, after a hearing without a jury, shall affirm the annexation if it finds that less than 75 per cent of the property owners in the territory to be annexed have objected and if it is convinced "that the adding of such territory to the city will be for its interest and will cause no manifest injury to persons owning property in the territory sought to be annexed." However, if the court is satisfied that 75 per cent or more of the property owners have remonstrated, the annexation cannot take

49. In Atlanta, Georgia, "future extensions of the city limits may be requested by petition filed with the judge of the county superior court by the mayor and council in the name of Atlanta, or by 51 per cent of the qualified voters and owners of 51 per cent of the real property in the area affected. The judge, after a public hearing, has final authority to grant or refuse the petition. No legislative action or popular vote will be necessary" (Hughes, *op. cit.,* p. 27).

50. *Arizona Code Annotated, 1939* and 1949 Cumulative Pocket Supplement (Indianapolis: Bobbs-Merrill Co., 1940), Secs. 16–702 to 16–705.

51. *Arkansas Statutes Annotated, 1947* (Indianapolis: Bobbs-Merrill Co.) Title 19, ch. 3, Secs. 301–307. In Florida, an election must be held in both the city and in the territory to be annexed if more than ten registered voters live in the latter. Otherwise, it can be annexed by ordinance, but ten registered voters or two property owners in the territory to be annexed may petition the circuit court within thirty days for an order denying the annexation. After notice and hearing, the court may grant or deny the petition. Either party may demand a jury trial to determine the questions of fact. *Florida Statutes Annotated, 1943* and 1949 Cumulative Pocket Parts (Minneapolis: West Publishing Co.), Secs. 171.04.

place unless the court finds "from the evidence that the prosperity of such city and territory will be materially retarded and the safety of the inhabitants and property thereof endangered without such annexation."[52]

The Kentucky statutes provide for judicial proceedings to challenge annexations which, if unchallenged, may be made by municipal ordinance. Only in second-class cities must the ordinance be passed by a two-thirds vote. In the first-class cities, the issue, if it comes to court, is tried by a jury. In all other instances the "proceedings shall be tried according to the practice prescribed for equity cases, without the intervention of a jury." An appeal may be taken from the judgment unless the annexing city is in the third class or fifth class. If the judge or jury shall find that the prescribed proportion of freeholders in the area to be annexed (75 per cent if annexing municipality is a city of the first, third, fifth, or sixth class; 50 per cent if it is a second- or fourth-class city) have not remonstrated and that the annexation "will be for the interest of the city and will cause no manifest injury to the persons owning real estate" the annexation shall be approved. The annexation can be ordered even if more than 75 or 50 per cent, as the case may be, of the freeholders have remonstrated, provided that the judge or jury "finds from the evidence that a failure to annex . . . will materially retard the prosperity of the city, and of the owners and inhabitants of the territory sought to be annexed."[53]

Nebraska cities of the metropolitan class, i.e., with a population of 100,000 or more, may annex contiguous land, including cities of less than 10,000 population, by ordinance. Only agricultural lands "rural in character" are excluded.[54] Cities of the primary class (40,000 to 100,000 population) have the same power to annex and agricultural

---

52. *Burns Indiana Statutes Annotated* and 1950 Replacement (Indianapolis: Bobbs-Merrill Co.), Sec. 48–702. In Iowa, the city must sue in equity the owners of property to be annexed. The annexation of unplotted property must be approved by the voters before suit is filed. *Iowa Code Annotated* (Minneapolis: West Publishing Co., 1949), Sec. 326.26–326.31.

53. *Kentucky Revised Statutes,* 1946, Secs. 81.100–81.110, 81.140, 81.190, 81.210, 81.220, 81.230, 81.240. Louisiana statutes provide that any interested citizen of the municipality or of the territory proposed to be annexed may contest an annexation by suit filed in the district court. The question to be decided is the "reasonableness" of the proposed annexation. *General Statutes of the State of Louisiana* (Indianapolis: Bobbs-Merrill Co., 1939) and 1949 Cumulative Pocket Supplement, Sec. 5373.4. New Orleans is excepted from the statute, but there is reason to infer from its charter the power to annex by ordinance (*ibid.*, Sec. 6175[h]). See Lucas and Lucas, *op. cit.*, Part I, p. 23. Mississippi also provides for suits in the circuit court to determine the reasonableness of a proposed annexation. "Reasonable and unreasonable, as used in this section, must be construed as relating to the interests of the entire municipality" *Mississippi Code, 1942 Annotated, 1948 Supplement* (Atlanta: Harrison Co.), Secs. 3376–82.

54. *Revised Statutes of Nebraska State Statute Commission,* 1944, Supplement 1949, Sec. 14–117.

lands are not excepted.[55] Judicial action is necessary to annex land to other classes of cities and to villages:

> If the court finds the allegations of the petition to be true and that such territory, or any part thereof not smaller in area than as hereinbefore required, would receive material benefit by its annexation to such city, or that justice and equity require such annexation of such territory . . . a decree shall be entered accordingly.[56]

QUESTIONS OF VALUES AND INTERESTS MIXED WITH QUESTIONS OF FACT

The advantages of an agency to weigh the claims of proponents and opponents of the extension of municipal boundaries are clear. But it is doubtful that the process of weighing the evidence and making the decision is one that can best be done by courts of law or of equity. The evidence is not factual in the sense that the claims are of the kind from which "politics," that is to say questions of interests and values, can be excluded.

This is not to ask whether annexation is justiciable, whether it is the kind of controversy which the courts can constitutionally consider. It is justiciable if the courts consider it to be so, as they do in Virginia,

---

55. *Ibid.*, Sec. 15–104.

56. *Ibid.*, Secs. 16–108, 16–110, 17–409. In New Mexico, judicial proceedings are provided only when subdivided contiguous territory plotted into parcels of 10 acres or less is annexed. The owners of the property may join issue in the district court and a decree is to be entered if the court finds the allegations of the petition to be true. Similar action can be secured by means of an appeal from a councilmanic resolution annexing contiguous territory plotted into parcels of 5 acres or less and served by municipal public utilities (*New Mexico Statutes,* 1941, and 1949 Cumulative Pocket Supplement (Bobbs-Merrill), Secs. 14–602, 14–603.

North Dakota provides for an annexation review commission, consisting of the county judge, state's attorney, and chairman of the board of county commissioners to which an appeal can be taken from a city resolution (*North Dakota Revised Code of 1943* and 1949 Supplement, Sec. 40–5111).

In Ohio, any interested person may petition to enjoin further annexation proceedings—court of common pleas. (Page's *Ohio General Code Annotated,* 1938, and Cumulative Pocket Supplement for 1949, Secs. 3553–55).

Oklahoma provides for judicial proceedings only when the municipality has rejected a petition to be annexed, signed by three-fourths of the legal voters and by the owners of three-fourths of the real estate in the area. Annexation is ordered if the court finds "that the request of the petitioners ought to be granted and can be granted without injustice to the inhabitants or persons interested" (*Oklahoma Statutes,* 1941, Secs. 485–486).

In Pennsylvania, the court of quarter sessions may upon petition annex to a borough adjacent territory located in a township of the second class. The court "may make such order on the petition as to right and justice shall appertain" (Purdon's *Pennsylvania Statutes Annotated,* 1931, with 1949 Cumulative Pocket Supplement, Secs. 12411–12414).

The district court of Wyoming may order an annexation, upon petition of a city or town, if it is of the opinion, after inspection of the map and testimony heard, "that the prayer of such petition should be granted" (*Wyoming Compiled Statutes,* 1949, Sec. 29–1207).

Iowa, Nebraska, etc.[57] It is not justiciable, if the courts, as in Illinois, refuse to accept jurisdiction under their interpretation of the state constitution.[58]

Some conditions which must by statute exist before land can be annexed are as unambiguously factual as is possible. As the Iowa court said in 1876:

> Section 431 provides that the territory to be annexed must be abutting and contiguous to the city, and it must have been laid out into lots or parcels containing 2 acres or less. The petition must describe the territory and allege these facts. Certainly these are issuable facts, and the section provides that issues may be joined and the cause tried in the ordinary manner.[59]

Other conditions which some statutes require to be met before territory can be annexed are more ambiguously phrased because they involve competing interests.[60] The requirement that the proposed annexation materially benefit the municipality and cause no material injury to the territory annexed (Kentucky) is different in kind from the requirement that the territory proposed to be annexed be platted or contiguous or that a prescribed procedure be followed. The extent of judicial discretion in applying such criteria can be seen from the opinion of the Kentucky Supreme Court in refusing to annex a territory of approximately $1\frac{2}{3}$ square miles, of which almost a square mile had been subdivided in lots, although only a few streets had been built. There were from 1,500 to 2,000 people living in the territory.

> In our opinion, it would not be a benefit to the town itself to annex such a vast scope of territory, as it would impose upon the municipality the herculean task of providing streets, sidewalks, light, and other necessities of municipal existence; and there can be no doubt but that the annexation would result in very serious injury to the people owning the bulk of this territory, as it would subject them to municipal taxation without receiving any corresponding benefit or advantage therefrom, because lands situated within the corporate limits of a municipality are not exempt from municipal taxation on the ground that they are agricultural lands.[61]

57. See *Burlington* v. *Leebrick,* 43 Iowa 252 (1876); *Forsythe* v. *Hammond,* 142 Ind. 505 (1895); *Forsythe* v. *Hammond,* 166 U.S. 506, 41 L. ed. 1095 (1896); same case below, 18CCA 175, 34 U.S. App. 552, 71 Fed. 443 (1896) and 68 Fed. 774 (1895); *Wahoo* v. *Dickinson,* 23 Neb. 426 (1888); *Henrico County* v. *Richmond,* 106 Va. 282 (1906).

58. *Galesburg* v. *Hawkinson,* 75 Ill. 152 (1874); see annotation, 64 A L R 1373–1378.

59. *Burlington* v. *Leebrick,* 43 Iowa 252 (1876).

60. See C. B. Nutting, "Non-judicial Functions of Iowa District Courts," 19 *Iowa Law Review* 385, 389–390 (1934) and note "Detachment of Territory," 14 *Ibid.,* 235 (1929).

61. *Latonia* v. *Hopkins,* 104 Ky. 419 (1898). Also in Kentucky, the court may order land annexed if it is convinced that failure to annex would "retard the prosperity of the city." See *Park* v. *Covington,* 187 Ky. 311 (1920); as to extent of discretion, see *Lexington* v. *Rankin,* 278 Ky. 388.

In Virginia, "the court shall ascertain and determine the necessity for, or expediency of, annexation." In Nebraska, the court may order annexation "where justice and equity require it."[62]

ADVANTAGES OF AN ADMINISTRATIVE AGENCY TO DETERMINE ANNEXATION QUESTIONS

It is doubtful that litigation before a court is the best way to determine the issues of public policy involved in the expansion of municipal boundaries. If it is desired to vest the power to annex in an agency which is supposed to be motivated by interests larger than those which impel the participants in the usual annexation campaign, an administrative agency would have many advantages over the regular courts.[63] An administrative agency can give a hearing to interested parties and it can be required to prepare a "finding of facts" to justify its decision. But it has additional advantages: (1) The composition of the agency and the method of selecting its members can make it more susceptible than a court to the changing policies of the state government. (2) It can take the initiative in proposing boundary changes. (3) It can consider and foster alternative methods of solving metropolitan problems. (4) It can develop and facilitate the active participation of various local, regional, state, and national interests in the formulation and criticism of governmental organization, policies and procedures as they affect urban life.[64]

62. We are not concerned at this point with judicial review of annexation proceedings where the court determines the "reasonableness" of the annexation. Reasonableness is a statutory requirement in some states, but in most jurisdictions annexations can be challenged as unreasonable. See 62 *Corpus Juris Secundum.* 127–30 and Eugene McQuillin, *Municipal Corporations* (Chicago: Callaghan and Co., 3d ed., 1949), Sec. 7.18.

63. Notice the distinction made by the English Local Government Boundary Commission: "First, when a decision to review an area has been taken, the Commission are required to take the initiative in collecting all necessary information on which to base any action that they may take. In this respect their function differs fundamentally from that of a tribunal deciding an issue on facts and arguments presented to it. Hence the importance of the Investigation stage, which we describe later. Secondly, the Commission's decision, whether Provisional or final, represents the Commission's own proposals. They may or may not coincide with proposals made by one or more of the authorities concerned. Here, too, there is little or no analogy between our duties and that of a tribunal deciding a dispute between parties" (*Report,* 1946, p. 4).

"It is not possible by any process of arithmetic or logic to arrive at exact figures for an optimum size of a local government unit either in relation to local government as a whole or to any one function or group of functions. At best, one can—to use an engineering term—arrive at a reasonable tolerance, and it is fairly certain that even in regard to that there will be special cases demanding exceptional treatment. Moreover, the process is largely one of weighing conflicting aims and deciding where on balance the advantage lies. Opinions on these matters differ and will continue to differ" (*ibid.,* 1947, p. 10).

64. See chapter iv for a discussion of the responsibility of state governments, as legal creators of local governments, to consider these matters.

Although the English Local Government Boundary Commission was abolished before it could accomplish its assignment, the procedure laid down in the Act and developed by the Ministry and the Commission suggests an approach to the problem of government in metropolitan areas which should be seriously considered by the American states. In the first place, the Commission was subject to regulations of the Minister of Health. These regulations had to be submitted to Parliament. Furthermore, any order of the Commission altering the boundaries of a county or county borough were provisional until confirmed by Parliament. Each order laid before Parliament had to be accompanied by a "statement describing the proceedings leading to the making of the Notice, summarizing any representations made and setting out the considerations which led the Commission to make the order."[65]

General principles to guide the Boundary Commission were included in the regulations issued by the Minister of Health on November 15, 1945.[66]

1. The object of all alterations in status of local government authorities and of all alterations in the boundaries of local government areas is to ensure individually and collectively effective and convenient units of local government administration. This object is the governing principle by which the Commission are to be guided in exercising their functions under the Act.

2. In attaining this object all factors relevant to the areas under review shall be considered by the Commission. The following are some of the main factors placed in alphabetical order: (a) Community of interest. (b) Development, or anticipated development. (c) Economic and industrial characteristics. (d) Financial resources measured in relation to financial need, including in particular, but not exclusively, the average rateable value per head of population, rates raised per head of population and the estimated product of a given rate poundage. (e) Physical features including in particular, but not exclusively, suitable boundaries, means of communication and accessibility to administrative centres and centres of business and social life. (f) Population—size, distribution, and characteristics. (g) Record of administration by the local authorities concerned. (h) Size and shape of the areas. (i) Wishes of the inhabitants. The weight to be given to the several factors will vary from case to case, but each of them should be viewed in the light of the governing principle stated in the last preceding paragraph.

3. The interests of an urban centre and the surrounding countryside should not necessarily be regarded either as diverse or as complementary. All factors should be considered to discover whether on balance a blending of urban and rural territories is desirable.

4. The growth of publicly directed development in connection with housing, planning and similar activities makes it possible to foresee the course of development with greater accuracy than in the past. Where, under the practice which obtained in the past, alterations of boundaries have commonly followed such development, the

65. Local Government Boundary Commission, *Report,* 1946, Appendix A: "Note on Procedure."

66. These regulations were approved by resolution of the House of Commons on December 10, 1945, and by the House of Lords on December 13, 1945, in accordance with sections 1(3) and 3(10) of the Local Government Boundary Commission Act of 1945.

foregoing consideration may justify making alterations at an earlier stage than formerly, so that any change which may be found desirable in the light of the principles and factors mentioned in the preceding paragraphs of this schedule can be affected with less disturbance of local government administration and finance.

5. In considering the governing principle it is essential to take into account the effects of any alterations of status or boundaries on all local government authorities whose problems are, in the Commission's opinion, interrelated and likely to be substantially affected thereby. The Commission shall therefore, so far as is practicable, consider the circumstances of all such authorities at one and the same time.

6. Where the Commission are of opinion that more effective local government might be secured by a combination of local authorities for particular services or by establishing contractual arrangements between authorities for the use of particular facilities or accommodation than by any alteration of boundaries or status of the authorities, the Commission may bring the matter to the notice of the Minister of Health and may postpone the making of an order under the Act until after they have been informed of the outcome of the Minister's consideration of the matter.

7. It is not intended that the discretion of the Commission shall be limited by reference to population figures, but the following considerations are stated for the general guidance of the Commission: (a) an order reducing an existing county borough to the status of a non-county borough should not ordinarily be made unless the population of the county borough as estimated by the Registrar-General is less than 60,000; (b) in the absence of substantial agreement an order uniting a county with another county should not ordinarily be made unless the population of the smaller county as so estimated is less than 100,000.

8. The Commission shall take all the practicable steps to discourage local authorities and other persons from incurring unnecessary expense in connexion with local inquiries and other business transacted under the Act.[67]

Proceedings could be started by direction of the Minister, by application of a local authority, or by the Commission. Formal hearings were provided for by the Act, but the Commission did not get beyond the "Investigative Stage." The way the Commission conducted its early investigations suggests that this type of activity might over the long-run result in the most significant accomplishments of such a central agency. Certainly investigation and consultation should precede any formal hearings or action. It is the lack of adequate consultation and comprehensive investigation which in this country characterizes the state's relationship with and responsibility for local government. For this reason, and to make the document more easily accessible to American readers, I quote extensively from the Commission's description of the way it conducted its investigations.

Between May and December, 1946, members of the Commission and Assistant Commissioners have held 191 "conferences" with representatives of local authorities of all types, all of them at the authorities' own offices. None has lasted less than half a day and very many the whole day. Of these conferences 110 have been attended

67. See W. A. Robson's characterization of these regulations as "mere verbiage, little more than a substitute for thought" *The Development of Local Government* (London: George Allen and Unwin, 2d ed., 1948), p. 47.

by the Chairman or the Deputy-Chairman or by some other member of the Commission. We felt it important that we ourselves should become personally acquainted with the areas under review and with the members and officers of the authorities, and should have a first-hand impression of the problems as stated by the local authorities. We have learned much from these visits, which have stimulated a useful two-way flow of ideas. Valuable suggestions have been contributed by the smaller as well as the larger authorities. Experience of these meetings has convinced us that personal contact between members of the Commission and leading members and officers of local authorities in their own areas is, apart from the actual decision of cases, the most important part of our own work.

A tour of investigation begins with a meeting, held at some convenient centre, of representatives of all the local authorities concerned. This meeting, which is open to the Press, is confined to matters of procedure and no discussion of the merits of any proposals for the alteration of areas is permitted. The principles laid down by Parliament for our guidance are read in full, and a full explanation of the procedure is given. The opportunity is taken of emphasising three points: that the investigation is not merely into the proposals of an applicant authority; that proposals must be judged in the light of the governing principle which is "to ensure individually and collectively effective and convenient units of local government administration"; and that local authorities should not spend time and money in preparing elaborate proofs of evidence and statistics at this stage.

The Assistant Commissioner then held separate meetings with representatives of each local authority concerned, usually consisting of the Mayor or Chairman, the Chairmen of the more important Committees and the principal officers. The meetings take the form of round table discussions and, while a Chairman or the Clerk usually presents the facts and the proposals of his Council, the other representatives are encouraged to take part in the general discussion and very free expression of views by all is welcomed. During this tour, the Assistant Commissioner also takes the opportunity of viewing the locality, but detailed inspection of boundaries or proposed boundaries is not attempted at this stage. In few, if any, cases is it to be expected that the Commission will be able to complete the Investigation Stage after a single round of visits, and further conferences and inspections are arranged as necessary.

Without exception, local authorities have co-operated in this procedure and have welcomed its informality, its freedom from expense and the opportunity it affords for the frankest expression of opinion. For our part, we are glad to acknowledge, both for ourselves and on behalf of the Assistant Commissioners, the trouble taken by the authorities and their officers in the preparation of such factual information as we have asked for, including maps, and generally in the arrangements made for meetings. This investigation by "conferences and consultations" (to use the words of the Regulations) assists us to obtain "agreement, so far as possible, upon the facts" and to ascertain the "substantial issues in dispute," and gives us the basis for action.

To what extent the Investigation Stage will dispense with the need of the more formal procedure of public local inquiries remains to be seen. Any local authority likely to be affected has the right to require a public local inquiry with regard to any Order which the Commission propose to make. We propose to furnish the local authorities concerned with an explanation of the reasons for our proposals, so that they can decide whether they desire a further investigation by public inquiry. Some, no doubt, will feel justified in so doing, and in those cases, we shall ensure that the inquiry is conducted by an independent person of standing not previously concerned in the problems of the area. Nevertheless, the ascertaining at the Investigation Stage of the facts and the issues involved can hardly fail to reduce substantially the time and expense of any such inquiry.

Nor is our task confined to discussions with local authorities. The views of several Government Departments have been obtained on many facets of our problem, at Headquarters as well as at their Regional Offices where we have a conference as part of each investigation. The Departments extend beyond those more directly concerned with the day to day work of local authorities, vis., the Home Office, and the Ministries of Health, Education, Transport, and Town and Country Planning; and in every case under investigation we have also obtained advice from the Board of Trade and the Ministries of Agriculture and Fisheries and of Labour and National Service. To all of these, and to other Departments whom we have consulted from time to time, we give a grateful acknowledgement of their ready and valuable help.[68]

CONCLUSIONS

"Annexation isn't dead," but its serious limitations as a device for bringing metropolitan areas under a single government must be recognized. Failure to recognize these limitations will take our attention from the task of developing more promising means of solving the problem of local government in metropolitan areas.

The facts that annexation isn't dead, that it may be desirable for many reasons, even though some form of metropolitan government exists or is proposed, and that in some circumstances it may be the only course available make it highly desirable that local and state annexation policies and procedures be studied in the light of the objectives we desire to achieve through local government. Such a study should be undertaken in each state by state and local officials and other interested groups. The organization and investigative procedure of the English Local Government Boundary Commission suggests a way an official state commission might proceed in this country.

68. Local Government Boundary Commission, *Report*, 1946, pp. 8–9.

CHAPTER VI

SPECIAL DISTRICTS AND AUTHORITIES

IF ANNEXATION has disappointed those who have attempted to increase the area of the central city to cover all or most of the metropolitan area, others have been equally disappointed with their efforts to secure a metropolis-wide coverage of particular governmental functions through the establishment of special districts.[1] A few functions in some metropolitan areas are intrusted to special districts that cover most of the metropolitan area. Many of these special districts and authorities are well known: the Port of New York Authority, the Boston Metropolitan District in its various forms, the Sanitary District of Chicago, and the Metropolitan Water District of Southern California. Other important special metropolitan districts are the Akron Metropolitan Park District, East Bay Municipal Util'ty District, East Bay Regional Part District, Huron-Clinton Metropolitan Authority (Detroit), Passaic Valley Sewerage Commission, Cook County Forest Preserve District, Chicago Park District, Chicago Transit Authority, Cook County Superhighway Project District, Cleveland Metropolitan Park District, Hartford County Metropolitan District, Allegheny County Sanitary Authority, Milwaukee Metropolitan Sewerage Dis trict, Minneapolis–St. Paul Sanitary District, the Illinois-Missouri Development Commission and the Washington Suburban Sanitary District.

Two of these special districts, the Chicago Transit Authority and the Illinois-Missouri Development Commission, are creations of the last decade. We shall have to wait for the 1952 Census of Governments to get a full count of special districts established since 1942. It is clear, however, that significant metropolitan special districts are not being set up extensively enough to meet adequately many of the problems in metropolitan areas. And, by definition, a special district deals with only one function or some special phase of a function. Only a few special districts are concerned with more than one function. In no instance can they be considered equivalent to a metropolitan government.

1. For the structural organization and financial powers of metropolitan special districts, see Betty Tableman, *Governmental Organization in Metropolitan Areas* (Ann Arbor: Institute of Public Administration, University of Michigan, 1951), pp. 64–72, 155–67.

Nevertheless, the special district device must be seriously and carefully considered both as a promise of providing services for the whole community and as a threat of disintegration. In the first place, most special districts are single-purpose districts. Nowhere has there been established, nor is any existing district developing into, a general multipurpose metropolitan district.[2] Special districts are sired by special interests consisting of present or potential customers of the agency often allied with technicians and professional people involved in the activity. The logic of specialism leads to a special and independent agency of government for each special interest. A separate government for each function would be the ideal solution of the problem of governmental areas from the point of view of single-interest groups.

NUMBER OF SPECIAL DISTRICTS IN METROPOLITAN AREAS

Special districts (other than school districts) have increased in number in the United States during the last decade by 43.4 per cent. Most of the 11,900 special districts in 1951 were soil conservation, drainage, and fire protection districts and most of these were located in nonmetropolitan areas.[3]

Only 1,097 special districts, or 13.2 per cent, of the 8,299 special districts enumerated by the Bureau of the Census in 1942[4] were in the 140 metropolitan districts. Only 10.9 per cent of the special school districts were in metropolitan districts. Many special districts in metropolitan areas are outside the larger municipal corporations, since the 397 cities in the country with a population of over 25,000 in 1940 were overlain by only 522 special districts other than school districts. Only

2. See *ibid.*, pp. 62–63 (Table V), for a list of metropolitan special districts performing more than one function.

3. U.S. Bureau of the Census, *Governments in the United States in 1951* (State and Local Government Special Study Number 29, March 1952).

4. U.S. Bureau of the Census, *Governmental Units in the United States* (1942), Table 8. William Anderson counted 8,382 special districts in the same year—*The Units of Government in the United States* (1949 revision, Chicago: Public Administration Service), p. 17. See the comparison with the census count, pp. 47–49. He suggests a 2.3 per cent decrease in special districts between 1930 and 1940. But notice the following comment: "Hardest of all to deal with are the special districts other than school districts. This difficulty can be explained partly as follows: (1) No state agency is responsible for compiling and reporting the information concerning them, nor need they in most cases record with any state or county authority the fact of their organization. (2) As a rule they do not levy direct property taxes; in consequence, the state and county tax authorities are practically unaware of their existence. (3) New classes of such units are easily and frequently authorized by state legislation without much public notice. It would be necessary to read all the new legislation of every state each year in order to get on the trail of all these new units. (4) Under such laws local units are rather easily organized and as easily suspended or dissolved, and the facts are not noted anywhere. (5) Many such local units are distinctly borderline cases. Whether they are to be classed as separate units of government or not is often a disputable question" (*ibid.*, p. 5).

6.3 per cent, then, of the special districts (other than school districts) in the country were to be found in the larger cities.[5]

Illinois and California are the two states with the largest number of special districts. A principal reason for the multitude of special districts in California is their extensive use in unincorporated areas near large cities as a substitute for annexation or incorporation as a means of securing municipal services.

In the ten-year period from 1938 to 1948, fire protection districts have increased from 222 to 349; sanitary, 59 to 107; water 72 to 101; and public utility, 24 to 48. This is an increase of more than 60 per cent in these four types of districts, most of which supply services to unincorporated areas, in ten years.[6]

Anderson's enumeration also shows an increase for all types of special districts between 1930–33 and 1941 except rural road and bridge districts and urban improvement districts.[7]

Pennsylvania, under its Municipal Authorities Act of 1935, is another state with a large number of special districts. A total of 218 municipal authorities were incorporated between 1935 and 1950. The last four years were particularly productive of authorities: 26 in 1946; 22 in 1947; 33 in 1948; and 37 in 1949.[8] Only 103 of the 218 authorities incorporated since 1935 are active. Most of these are in townships and boroughs—only seven are organized as joint authorities:[9]

Name	County	Purpose	Date of Incorporation
1. Fox Chapel Authority	Allegheny	Construction of Waterworks	1938
2. Wilkinsburg Joint Water Authority	Allegheny	Acquisition of Water Company	1945
3. Womelsdorf-Robesonia Joint Authority	Berks		1949
4. Central Delaware County Authority.	Delaware	Construction of Sewage Disposal Facilities	1937
5. Lehigh Airport Authority	Lehigh	Acquisition of Airport	1946

5. U.S. Bureau of the Census, *Governmental Units Overlying City Areas* (Governmental Organization, No. 3, October, 1947), pp. 4–5. See Emmett Asseff, *Special Districts in Louisiana* (Baton Rouge: Bureau of Government Research, Louisiana State University, 1951). Betty Tableman lists the special districts in the various metropolitan areas (*op. cit.*, pp. 138–54).

6. John C. Bollens and John R. McKinley, *California City Government* (Berkley: Bureau of Public Administration, University of California Press, 1948), p. 55.

7. *Op. cit.*, p. 6.

8. T. V. Weintraub and J. D. Patterson, *The "Authority" in Pennsylvania: Pro and Con* (Philadelphia: Bureau of Municipal Research, 1949), pp. 17–18 and *National Municipal Review*, XXXIX (April, 1950), 195. However, the Pennsylvania Municipal Authorities Association lists only three authorities incorporated in 1949.

9. Pennsylvania Municipal Authorities Association, "Active Municipal Authorities in Pennsylvania as of January 1, 1950."

Name	County	Purpose	Date of Incorporation
6. Williamsport Municipal Airport Authority......................	Lycoming	Acquisition of Airport	1947
7. Joint Authority of the Borough of Townville and Townships of Steuben and Troy........................	Lycoming	To Acquire School Building for Improvement and Lease to School District for Operation	1949

Many special districts have done magnificent jobs in engineering, constructing, and financing certain public works and at times in managing them. But the special district is not used extensively enough, in either the large or small metropolitan areas to make an appreciable difference in the solution of problems that spread out over the areas of several units of local government. It is more frequently used within the area of a single municipality, township, or county, and its organization, legal status, and relationship with the units of general government differ only in degree from the innumerable (or uncounted) independent agencies and administrative boards and commissions exercising authority within the boundaries of municipalities.

NEED FOR LARGER AREAS OF POLICY FORMATION AND ADMINISTRATION

The only distinction that can be made between special districts with jurisdiction over an area larger than the central city and special districts coterminous with city boundaries and independent administrative boards and commissions is that the former may be the only politically acceptable way of handling a metropolitan problem. It is interesting to note from an examination of the recent literature in England and in the United States that, although the same arguments for special districts and authorities are to be found in both countries, the emphasis in England is upon attacking a metropolitan problem while almost equal emphasis is placed in this country upon "taking the function out of politics."

It is generally agreed in England that the joint-authority is "a device for rendering workable an admittedly imperfect system" of local government in metropolitan areas.[10] The political difficulties in creating

10. Elizabeth Howard, "Joint Authorities," *Essays on Local Government* (Oxford: Basil Blackwell, 1948), p. 230. The joint authority in England is comparable to those special districts in the United States which are composed of representatives of constituent units of local government, such as the joint municipal authorities in Pennsylvania, the Passaic Valley Sewerage District, the former Niagara Frontier Planning Board, the Metropolitan Water District of Southern California, and the Golden Gate Bridge and Highway District. See my *Metropolitan Government* (Chicago: University of Chicago Press, 1942), pp. 99–102.

In England, "the typical joint authority is set up, under Statute or under Order, when two or more local authorities see an advantage in combining to operate a service over their joint area or over part of it. It is, normally, as its name says, a federal body whose mema general metropolitan government have been taken both here and in England as establishing the necessity for resorting to *ad hoc* units. Luther Gulick says that

> Under American conditions we may expect the authority to be the chief vehicle of cooperative regional *planning and action* particularly with reference to transportation, power and metropolitan development. They cannot be handled by the traditional governments because of their territorial and fiscal straightjackets. Perhaps the authority will lead us into the promised land![11]

John Bauer, in urging that special districts be organized for each of the principal utility services in metropolitan areas, maintains that

> In the light of experience and probability, regional problems are likely to be worked out piecemeal as particular needs and pressures emerge. While comprehensive unification of municipal and economic territory will doubtless be the goal and trend, the apparent line of development will be through provision of individual metropolitan services as regional requirements begin to dominate and push aside municipal diversities and cross purposes. This is the type of adjustment that appears suited to the important utilities upon which the future metropolitan welfare depends.[12]

It was undoubtedly the same appraisal of "experience and probability" that led the Coalition Government in 1945 to urge the creation

---

bership is composed of representatives of the constituent authorities of the combined areas. It has two main forms, the distinction between which is of the first importance, that of joint board and joint committee. For the purposes of this essay, the term joint board is used to describe the joint authority which is a body corporate, with perpetual succession and a common seal, power to sue and be sued, and power to hold land for the purposes of its constitution without license in mortmain. A joint board has the power to raise loans, either itself, or, under recent statutes, through its constituent authorities. It can issue precepts upon its constituent authorities to meet its revenue expenditure, in so far as this is not met by the receipts of the undertaking it administers. In short, the joint board, once created, is an independent authority over which its constituent bodies have little or no control. Such a definition includes certain authorities usually described as joint committees: *e.g.* Joint Committees for River Pollution, the Mersey Tunnel Joint Committee, and, before the passage of the Public Health Act, 1936 S8 (3), Joint Committees for Tuberculosis.

"The term joint committee refers to those authorities which, whether created by statute, order or the will of the authorities concerned, have no corporate existence independent of their constituent and powers are controlled by, and in the majority of cases, their existence may be terminated by, their constituent authorities. This subordination, together with their inability to raise money by loan or to issue precepts upon their constituent authorities are the chief factors which differentiate them from the joint board" (Elizabeth Howard, *op. cit.*, pp. 204–5).

For other types of special authorities, particularly in metropolitan London, see W. A. Robson, *The Government and Misgovernment of London* (London: George Allen and Unwin, 1939). For the tendency to use *ad hoc* bodies in the nationalization program of the Labour Government and for the effect upon local government, see the prologue to the 1948 edition of Robson's *The Development of Local Government* (London: George Allen and Unwin).

11. Luther Gulick, "Authorities and How To Use Them," *Tax Review*, VIII (November, 1947), 52.

12. John Bauer, *Postwar Planning for Metropolitan Utilities* (New York: National Municipal League, 1945), p. 3. See also his article "Hartford Metropolitan Needs Served by Water and Sewer Board," *National Municipal Review*, XXXII (October, 1943), p. 477.

of more joint authorities as the principle means of solving the metropolitan problems of postwar England.[13] The same factors probably led the Labour Government in 1949 to dismiss the proposals of the Local Government Boundary Commission on the ground that they would require "comprehensive legislation" which the government could not undertake in view of the strong contradictory opinions among the local authorities. The Minister of Health, Mr. Aneurin Bevan, argued that with such disagreements "even a Royal Commission would fail to do more than reflect their divisions."[14]

If it be assumed that it is impossible to secure a general metropolitan government or that it is undesirable to so organize the government of the metropolises, many of the other arguments for special districts for special functions become unassailable. It is argued that a special district can bring all the territory in a service area, which can be delimited by "economic boundaries," under a single jurisdiction;[15] that capital investments can be made by a district that could not be borne by a single unit, even though it be the central city; that the costs of providing a metropolitan service can be spread among those who benefit from the service; and that it is easier to impose tolls or other service charges upon the immediate user of the facilities.[16]

All these arguments for special metropolitan districts are based upon the need of a particular activity for an area larger than those of existing units of government. They are valid arguments. As V. D. Lipman has said:

13. *White Paper on Local Government in England and Wales during the Period of Reconstruction* (Cmd. 6579/1945), pp. 4–6.

14. Herman Finer, *English Local Government* (London: Methuen, 4th ed., 1950), p. 86.

15. Bauer, *op. cit.*, Henry Grayson, *A Region in Upheaval* (Engineering Div., Detroit Edison Co., November, 1941), pp. 37, 76; John F. LaBoon, "Allegheny County Sanitary Authority," *County Commissioner* (December, 1946), p. 3; Pennsylvania Joint State Government Commission, Committee on Municipal Authorities, *Municipal Authorities* (April 10, 1945), pp. 11–12; *Report of the Local Government Boundary Commission, 1947* (London, 1948), p. 12; V. D. Lipman, *Local Government Areas* (London: Macmillan Co., 1949), pp. 238, 252, 332, 359.

16. Weintraub and Patterson, *op. cit.*, p. 6: "However this principle is not invariably followed by authorities. One notable exception is the Port of New York Authority, which makes up deficits on projects which are not self-supporting, by use of surplus revenues from more profitable projects. The same is true of the proposed Delaware River Port Authority program, which contemplates increasing bridge tolls to help finance general port development. As a result, motorists using the bridges would be required to help pay for other commercial port facilities. It should also be kept in mind that authorities are not the only means by which cost can be levied directly against users in proportion to use. Regular units of government can charge fees for services."

See *The Municipal Year Book* (1950), pp. 332–36; American Public Works Association, *Sewer Rentals* (1941); Pennsylvania State College, Institute of Local Government, *Sewer Rentals in Pennsylvania Municipalities* (1949); New York State Conference of Mayors, *Sewer Service to Outside Consumers* (1949); Michigan Municipal League, *Financing Sewage Disposal by Sewage Rentals in Michigan* (1948).

The different services performed by local authorities have each their special requirements which determine the suitability of the areas over which they operate. Some services require the provision of certain institutions or staff which cannot be economically provided unless they are guaranteed a minimum number of "consumers." Others are concerned with problems whose solution is dictated by the configuration of land, or similar geographical factors. Others, again, need a considerable and continuous tract of country in order to function to the best advantage. Yet others require above all a balance of different components in the area to be served. Finally, there will always be for any service certain considerations which are peculiar to it and derive from the special nature of the problem it is facing or the materials it employs. Any given service will, in the determination of the area most suitable for it, have to take into consideration the four general types of requirement, each in varying degree, as well as any special peculiarities of its own.[17]

PRESSURE FOR FUNCTIONAL AUTONOMY

There is no let-up in the pressure to shift responsibility for governmental activities from the general city or county government to special authorities and independent boards. Throughout the country parking authorities, traffic authorities, airport authorities, and redevelopment agencies are being added to the large number of existing police and fire commissions, sewerage commissions, soil conservation districts, school boards, water commissions, utility commissions, park boards, recreation boards, health boards, hospital boards, library boards, museum boards, housing agencies, public works boards, cemetery boards and other boards.[18]

It does not follow, however, that each function of government should be separately organized over a distinctive area. The logic can be carried further, of course, and appropriate areas designated for each of the activities that together are called a function and then for subactivities. The same considerations when applied to a complex of activities, more or less related to each other, make up the case for a general metropolitan government.

17. *Op. cit.,* p. 332.

18. See Victor Jones, "The Withering Away of the City," *Public Management,* XXXII (December, 1950), 270–74. The President's Water Resources Policy Commission recommends that "The States and Federal Government should encourage the formation of metropolitan water districts to develop and transmit necessary water to meet in the most economical way the requirements of a group of communities when those communities are dependent upon the same source of water supply or when existing water supplies prove inadequate" (*A Water Policy for the American People* [Washington, D.C., 1950], p. 184). This recommendation along with other excerpts from the report are reproduced and distributed by the Public Health Service.

The Governor's Committee on Community Readjustment in its *Report on Collateral Problems Likely to Result from Location of a Steel Mill in Connecticut* (Hartford, April 27, 1951) recommended special metropolitan districts for the Norwich-New London Area for water supply, for the collection and treatment of sanitary sewage, and for public health activities (pp. 6–8).

This does not mean that it is necessary or desirable to centralize all or even most of the functions of local government in a single metropolitan government. Undoubtedly any satisfactory and feasible metropolitan government which may be developed will be a variant of what is known as the borough or federated type.[19] But the distribution of authority between the central and constituent units should not be based on "guild" autonomy.[20] Persistently in this country and in England as government has undertaken new activities or as crises have arisen in the administration of established functions, the professionalism of one group of specialists after another has shown itself in the demand for a preferential position. The most powerful group fighting for the autonomy of public schools is the professional educators. They now claim that educational administration should be considered as a fourth branch of government and accorded the constitutional protection of separation from the other three powers.

Tugwell and others have talked the same way about planning; Bauer and others about municipal utilities; Wier and others about parks and recreation. Some housing and redevelopment officials are using the same argument—their function is so important to the general welfare and the methods of carrying out their function are so technical that their objectives can be accomplished only if they are protected against interference by nonprofessionals.

There is nothing sinister about this attitude of specialists. Every person who is responsible for doing something should feel that the activity is important to the community. It only becomes dangerous when this professional attitude is tied up with a special interest pressure group powerful enough to take the activity out of reach of the periodic determination by the community of how its limited resources will be allocated.

This is a political judgment, not a scientific application of a formula. It is so complex and continuous that the so-called budgetary control (authority to vote appropriations) of a city council over boards and commissions is insufficient. Unless important questions of policy come up to the chief administrator and the council, or can be brought up by interested or aggrieved citizens, the raising or lowering of appropriation requests once a year will be little more than a formal act of ratification. And there is always the motive and the rationalization, from the point of view of special interest, for the clientèle and staff of a quasi-independent administrative board to urge financial as well as administrative autonomy.

19. See Report of the California Assembly Interim Committee on State and Local Taxation (January, 1951), Part III, "The Borough System of Government for Metropolitan Areas."

20. Luther Gulick, "Politics, Administration, and the New Deal," *Annals*, Vol. 169 (September, 1933), p. 56.

All proponents of a new independent authority and defenders of existing boards and commissions claim the general city government cannot do the job. And it must be admitted that the actions, or lack of action, of many city governments give color to the charge.

CAN GOVERNMENT BE TAKEN OUT OF POLITICS?

The old battle cry, "Take our interest out of politics," either camouflages an attempt to substitute special politics for general politics or indicates a withdrawal from the everlasting struggle to change the political decisions being made in the community. Frequently both motives are involved. If "politics" refers to partisan or personal patronage and influence, the experience of special boards and commissions does not assure us that their independence of the city council or chief administrator will result in a merit system. Special boards and commissions, to paraphrase Anderson and Weidner, "have not been free from spoils politics but have developed methods of self-enrichment of their own."

Furthermore, the proliferation of autonomous agencies distracts the attention of important groups in the community from the general government. It encourages people with a strong interest in one aspect of community life and development to write off the general government and to feel that the community is sound if *only* it can have good schools, or if *only* it has adequate downtown parking facilities, or if *only* the slums are torn down. This is not only unfortunate because it diverts interest from securing or maintaining an active, effective, and efficient city government, but because it weakens the general government for its most important function of bringing the complementary and divergent interests of a locality together into a community.

If the proponents of administrative autonomy use the term "politics" to refer to the making of policies, then autonomy does not take the activity out of politics. It merely substitutes one kind of politics for another. It may be easier for a special interest group to play that kind of politics than to run the gauntlet of other interests. The observation has been frequently made that under an independent regulatory commission it is easy for the regulated to become the regulators. This happens easily enough in any government however organized, but it is much easier to bring about when the activity is given an organizational protection against "interference" by the chief administrator and council.

The political nature of the decisions of independent boards is well described by Luther Gulick:

The vital political problems which arise in government are not the questions of patronage. They are the questions of basic social and economic policy which serve to give fundamental direction to social and economic forces. For example, a port authority has the power to determine whether a community as a whole will expand as a raw material center or as a manufacturing center by the priorities which it gives to port facilities, loading and unloading equipment, wharfage rates, and rail and road connections. Toll rates on bridges will determine the rapidity of suburban development and the rise of real-estate values as well as the time of obsolescence of prior investments in ferries and commuter rail services.

The location of inland terminals, the creation of central bus facilities, the elimination of grade crossings, the arrangement of tunnel entrances and exits will determine the immediate and ultimate fate of entire neighborhoods, piling value increments here and destroying values there in spectacular fashion. Such a simple matter as the location of the express stops on the rapid transit system decides whether a street will be developed with high rental properties or with more modest shops and apartments. Similarly zone fares on city transit systems, and the system of water rates or electric power rates cannot fail to create their patterns of realty and housing developments and to influence the distribution of wealth and welfare for the people of the area.[21]

And Frederick L. Bird, who is certainly no enemy of independent authorities, says that:

When you stop to think of it, an independent agency in charge of a basic service, that can fix its own rates, determine its own policies for supplying service and making extensions, and formulate and approve its long-range plans, holds an almost dictatorial control over how, and where, and how much a community is to develop residentially, commercially, and industrially.[22]

ARE SPECIAL DISTRICTS DEVELOPING INTO GENERAL METROPOLITAN GOVERNMENTS?

It is often said that a metropolitan special district can be developed into a multipurpose metropolitan government. Nowhere has this occurred and after years of hopeful waiting, it appears to be an unlikely development. The two examples that have been frequently cited of special districts evolving into multipurpose metropolitan districts are the Port of New York Authority and the Metropolitan District Commission in the Boston area. The latter was organized in 1919 by consolidating three special metropolitan districts: sewage organized in 1889, parks in 1891, and water in 1895. In 1923, the Commission established a division of regional planning, but this function was transferred in 1941 to the State Planning Board.[23] Instead of giving the function of planning and financing rapid transit to the District Commission, another special district, the Boston Metropolitan District, was created

21. "Authorities and How To Use Them," *The Tax Review* (November, 1947), pp. 50–51.

22. Frederick L. Bird, "The Contribution of Authorities to Efficient Municipal Management," *The Authority* (December, 1949), p. 5.

23. The Metropolitan District Commission has ex-officio membership on the State Planning Board.

for this purpose in 1929. And in 1947, when the facilities of the Boston Elevated Railway Company became public property, another special district, the Metropolitan Transit Authority, was created to operate them.[24]

The Port of New York Authority, established in 1921 by compact between New York and New Jersey, failed to accomplish the immediate purpose for which it was created—to secure the adoption by the railroads of a comprehensive plan of integrated freight terminals and switching arrangements in order to reduce the cost of terminal distribution and collection of freight, and to make all parts of the area accessible to any railroad.[25]

But in thirty years of its existence, it has helped to tie together the two parts of the metropolitan area cut by the Hudson River by constructing and operating six bridges and tunnels. After decades of controversy, planning at cross-purposes and recrimination by state and local agencies, the Port Authority, as Frederick L. Bird put it, has conquered the interstate water boundary. It has, furthermore, taken over the development and operation under long-term leases of Port Newark and of the three major airports of the region, Newark, La-Guardia, and Idlewild.[26] A central bus terminal has been built in Manhattan, a motor freight terminal is operated in lower Manhattan, and another has been constructed in Newark. It operates a grain terminal in Brooklyn.

None of its operations are financed by taxes. All of its revenues come from service charges, mostly vehicular tolls, which are pledged as security for the Authority's bonds. Since 1931, all surplus revenues have been pooled in a general reserve fund.[27]

THE PORT OF NEW YORK AS A PROTOTYPE OF METROPOLITAN
GOVERNMENT

In considering whether the Port of New York Authority is the kind

24. Trustees of the Boston Metropolitan District, *Report* (June, 1950), pp. 3–4.

25. It did establish in 1932 a Union Inland Freight Terminal in Manhattan where less-than-carload freight is handled for eight railroads. See E. W. Bard, *The Port of New York Authority* (New York: Columbia University Press, 1942), pp. 3–173, 313–19. Only passing attention is given to this phase of the Authority's activities by Frederick L. Bird, *A Study of the Port of New York Authority* (New York: Dun and Bradstreet, 1949).

26. See Bird, *op. cit.*, for a description of the authority's operations, financing, and plans. The political negotiations among New York City, Robert Moses, the airlines, civic associations, and the Port Authority are discussed and analyzed in Herbert Kaufman's "Gotham in the Air Age," *Public Administration and Policy Development: A Case Book* (Harold Stein, ed., New York: Harcourt Brace and Co., 1952), pp. 143–97.

27. For the financing of the Authority's operations, see Bird, *op. cit.*, pp. 41–82, and Bard, *op. cit.*, pp. 226–66.

of governmental organization we desire to handle metropolitan problems, the following observations are relevant:

1. The Authority has been a successful means of establishing jurisdiction for certain limited but important purposes over a metropolitan area bisected by state boundary lines. It has recently been imitated in the St. Louis–East St. Louis and in the Philadelphia-Camden areas.

2. It does not follow, however, that a metropolitan authority with jurisdiction in two or more states has to be organized as an agency of the state government. It is probably legally, administratively, and politically easier to so organize it. But we have to decide whether we want the metropolitan community to be governed by agencies responsible—however tenuously—to the state government or by agencies of local government. If we desire the latter, then however difficult it may be, we must devise a system of local selection and representation that can operate in two or more states.

3. Complete reliance upon service charges as a source of revenue will make it impossible for an authority to undertake nonrevenue-producing activities. It is unlikely to undertake projects or functions which have low-income producing value. The problems of a metropolitan community cannot be solved by giving to an area-wide authority those functions that are self-supporting and leaving all other governmental functions to existing units of local government. Frederick L. Bird recognized this when he wrote that

> The Port Authority's limitations as an agency of regional government are implicit in the absence of a taxing power. This is sometimes cited as a defect in the plans of the two States for the cooperative development of the Port district, in that self-support through service charges is a too restrictive test of the public functions that should be performed on a regional basis.[28]

4. Even in the field of highway traffic, the Authority has acted apart from the other public agencies that are also responsible for moving and parking vehicles in the metropolitan area. This is in large part the result of the failure of other public agencies to work with the Authority.[29] Certainly, the success of the Port Authority and of Moses in facilitating the vehicular movement of passengers and goods into New York City has aggravated the problem of traffic congestion on the city

28. *Op. cit.*, pp. 186–87. He does not meet the argument, but makes the counter-claim that no "political agency even partially dependent on tax support" would have "been able to maintain the continuity of policy and planning and to develop the special techniques that are essential to the businesslike operation of public service enterprises."

29. See the newspaper files for the last two years for conflicts between the Port Authority and the governor of New York over the location of the Hudson River bridge unit of the proposed New York State Thruway and the conflict between the Authority on the one hand, and Robert Moses and the New York City Planning Commission on the other, over a third tube for the Lincoln Tunnel.

streets. There is no official plan for moving goods and people and for taking care of them when they reach their destination. There are many plans, but they have not been integrated.

By no means can the Port Authority alone be blamed for the failure to produce a metropolitan traffic-transit-transportation plan. But E. W. Bard believes that its organization, its structural relation to other agencies of government and its policies keep it from acting effectively even in this relatively narrow field as a metropolitan government.

The Port Authority was conceived to function as a regional planning agency, but was also clothed with power itself to make the plans effective in so far as appropriate through construction and operation. Other parts of the plans were premised upon action by the owners of private property or by the states or municipalities. Many aspects of these plans have been described in preceding chapters. In facing the problems of seeing them translated into reality the Port Authority has been structurally weak in certain respects. First, its proprietary powers were limited by ability to borrow upon the promise of charges to be collected. This weakness has been largely removed by the creation of a credit base or supplemental guarantee in the general reserve fund. Second, powers to regulate the use of private property in conformity with its plans were denied. Third, the autonomy of the Port Authority has so far removed it from the chief executive of either state, or for that matter of any city, as to deny it any real influence on executive policy.

On the other hand, this same autonomy does yield independence and continuity of which greater use might have been made. Actually the Port Authority's planning activities have followed narrowly in the wake of its first major effort, or else have been confined to the direct needs of its vehicular projects. An exception might be noted in the Port Authority's work with suburban transit. The techniques of coordinated study employed in that field might very well be applied to other fields, notably highway development. The greatest power possessed by the Port Authority, which it has not used to advantage, is the power of publicity. At no time since the campaign for the Comprehensive Plan has it done anything comparable to stir the public imagination. The Port Authority seems to have become frightened by the specter of controversy. Its policy has become totally receptive rather than aggressive.[30]

5. A corporate form of metropolitan government in which the selection of the authority or district commission members is once or more removed from the electoral controls may give us efficient and effective government but it cannot give us good government. It is not necessary, nor is it desirable, for all policy-making officials to be directly elected by popular vote. They should, however, be subject to the budgetary control of popularly elected legislators and their policies should be subject to debate and discussion.

Of course, any legislative body, whether it have jurisdiction over the matter or not, may debate anything it wishes. The object, however, is not futile and irresponsible talk. Our uneasiness should not be alloyed by saying that the ordinary municipal governments are frequently cor-

30. Bard, *op. cit.*, pp. 319–20.

rupt, irresponsible, ineffective, and inefficient. Our job is to make them responsible and efficient.[21] This cannot be done by slicing off the most important functions of local government and handing them over to one or several autonomous bodies.

31. See Coleman Woodbury, "The Background and Prospects of Urban Redevelopment in the United States," this volume, pp. 671 ff.

CHAPTER VII

FEDERATED FORMS OF METROPOLITAN GOVERNMENT

A METROPOLIS is not an assemblage of individuals so much as a collection of communities into which individuals are already assembled."[1] The one clear lesson we all should have learned by now from the many attempts in this country and abroad to establish metropolitan governments is that the units of local governments are tough organizations with many political and legal protections against annihilation or absorption by another government.

This alone would lead us to search for a form of metropolitan government that will preserve the identity of existing units of government.[2] Expediency can be rationalized by saying that the larger metropolitan communities are too extensive in area, have too large a population, and contain too many divergent interests to be governed as if they were small, compact, homogeneous cities.

It is not mere expediency nor pure rationalization, however, to recognize that the large metropolis of today is a social organization different in kind and in degree from earlier urban communities. Our task, as I said in chapter iv, is to devise forms of government that will provide effective services, guidance, and controls where desired over the whole of the metropolitan area, that will equalize the burden of

1. Thomas H. Reed, *Municipal Government in the United States* (New York: Appleton-Century Co., 1934), p. 351.
2. In 1946, T. H. Reed recommended as a first step in metropolitan Cleveland toward integration by means of functional consolidation, the concentration of all welfare activities in the county "with adequate support from the state for all those which are made mandatory on counties by state law. . . . Functional consolidation is possible because it does not wipe out any unit of government. It does not deprive any considerable number of people of their offices. It does not interfere with the operations of political parties" (*National Municipal Review* [February, 1946], p. 85). Perhaps the Local Government Commission of Fulton County, Georgia, had the same considerations in mind when it said:
"It is a mistake to believe that administrative changes, even drastic ones, must be accompanied by a reorganization at the political level. If anything, the reverse is true. A reshuffling of the structure and membership of the governing body might result in the loss of the most important single ingredient in any reorganization—the experience and know-how of the people already in office" (*op. cit.*, p. 33). Contrary to Dr. Reed's recommendations for Cleveland, the Atlanta Commission recommended that county "municipal" functions be transferred to the city of Atlanta after its boundaries were extended to include the suburban area.

supporting such functions of government, and that will facilitate effective citizen control of governmental policies which affect them at their places of work and recreation as well as at their places of residence.

Increasing attention has been given in the last thirty years to forms of metropolitan government in which an area-wide unit would have functions which are of "metropolitan" significance and smaller units within the area would retain control over "local" functions. This is commonly called a "federal" or "borough" type of metropolitan government. If the constituent units have autonomy with respect to the functions assigned to them, the characterization of the two-layer system as federal is sufficiently descriptive of its advantages and of the main problems involved in establishing and maintaining it.

The key problem is, of course, the determination of what is a "metropolitan" and what is a "local" function. How are these determinations to be made in the first place and how are adjustments to be made? How is the central metropolitan government to be constituted? What is to be the basis of representation?

These are crucial problems which must be solved in a manner satisfactory to those who must be satisfied in any particular metropolitan area.

THE BOROUGH PLAN OF METROPOLITAN GOVERNMENT

The nearest approach to a "federated" metropolitan government is to be found in London.[3] For a large part of that metropolis, the functions of local government are divided between the London County Council on the one hand and, on the other, twenty-eight metropolitan boroughs and the city of London. But a large part of metropolitan London lies beyond the jurisdiction of the London County Council and many functions are separately administered either by the national government or by special districts and authorities.[4]

The so-called borough system of government in New York City is not federally organized. To all intents and purposes, the government of

3. Greater Berlin, created in 1920, consisted of a central municipal government and of twenty administrative districts. Contrary to the general impression, Rowland Egger's unpublished study shows "that Berlin, under the Act of 1920 providing for municipal federalism in both administrative fact and political psychology, was far from having the unitary government that some writers attributed to it." Egger's study is his unpublished doctoral dissertation at the University of Michigan, entitled "The Government of Berlin: A Study in Metropolitan Federalism" (1933). The quotation is from "The Borough System of Government for Metropolitan Areas," Part III, Report of California Assembly Interim Committee on State and Local Taxation, January, 1951, p. 67.

4. See William A. Robson, *The Government and Misgovernment of London* (London: George Allen and Unwin, 2d ed., 1948).

New York City is unitary in form and in practice. Each of the five boroughs is coterminous with a county but neither the borough nor the county functions as a unit of government with even limited legislative powers. We need a thorough study of the operation of the offices of the borough presidents before we can decide whether the borough has more governmental and political significance than a ward in any other large city.[5]

Beginning in 1916 with the proposed charter for a federated city-county of Alameda in the Oakland (California) area, this type of metropolitan government has been unsuccessfully recommended by official charter commissions or by legislative action in Oakland, Pittsburgh, St. Louis, San Francisco, Boston and Cleveland.[6] In each of these metropolitan areas, the principal argument for the plan was that it met suburban objections to annexation or to other forms of metropolitan government. Despite the concessions to the existing units of local government, all the proposals have been voted down.[7]

A "federal" type of metropolitan government can be secured (1) by creating a new "federal" government to replace existing units of government, (2) by transferring certain municipal functions to the county, or (3) by establishing a multi-purpose special district or by transferring other functions to an existing special district. Whichever choice is made, the end result will be a large metropolitan municipality with

5. The statements of Mayor O'Dwyer's office "that the borough system provides a more effective means of citizen participation in city government than a more centralized system would" cannot be taken as conclusive of the way the borough system operates in New York City. California legislature, Report of Assembly Interim Committee on State and Local Taxation, Part III, "The Borough System of Government for Metropolitan Areas," January, 1951, p. 63.

6. The plan had been informally urged in many places before 1916. See *ibid.*, pp. 90–104, for developments in the Los Angeles area since 1906.

7. In at least two areas, Pittsburgh and Cleveland, the proposed charters of 1929 and 1936 respectively, received majority approval in the area as a whole but were defeated because they failed to receive majorities in the requisite number of suburbs. The Pittsburgh Charter was required to be approved by (1) a majority vote in the county as a whole and by (2) a two-thirds majority in a majority of the 122 municipalities and townships. Despite this handicap, the charter almost received the required majorities. See my *Metropolitan Government* (Chicago: University of Chicago Press, 1942), pp. 309–12, and Joseph T. Miller, "The Pittsburgh Consolidation Charter," *National Municipal Review*, XVIII (1929), 604.

In Ohio any county charter which transfers a municipal function to the county must be approved by four kinds of majority votes: (1) in the county as a whole, (2) in the central city, (3) in the county outside the central city, and (4) in each of a majority of the municipalities and townships in the county. *Metropolitan Government*, pp. 236–38.

The 1936 Charter for Cuyahoga County (Cleveland) was approved by the first three majorities but was held invalid by the state supreme court as vesting concurrently certain municipal functions in the county. *State* ex rel. *Howland* v. *Krause*, 130 Ohio State 455 (1936). See *Metropolitan Government*, pp. 237, 240–44. The proposed county charter of 1950 was defeated in the county as a whole. California Assembly Interim Committee on State and Local Taxation, *op. cit.*, p. 85.

jurisdiction over certain aspects of metropolitan life and with many functions left in the hands of smaller units of local government.

The principal advantages of creating a new metropolitan government with central and borough units are (1) the whole of a multi-county metropolis can be brought under its jurisdiction, (2) the existing units can be reorganized into more compact and homogeneous boroughs and (3) a more rational distribution of functions as between the metropolitan and borough governments can be effected. Its disadvantages are inherent in its advantages: the reorganization is so basic as to foretell the defeat of any such proposal.

The possibility, however, of securing popular approval of a bold plan for reorganizing local government should not be dismissed as easily as this. Certainly weak compromises have been defeated. There is reason to believe that plans proposing to be all things to all men will dissatisfy everyone and arouse the imagination and interest of none.

MULTI-PURPOSE DISTRICT AS A "FEDERAL" TYPE OF METROPOLITAN GOVERNMENT

If a special district covering all or a large part of the metropolitan area were given a number of metropolitan functions it would cease to be a special district and become a unit of general government. The lack of evidence that this is being done or is likely to be done was discussed in the preceding chapter. The Metropolitan District Commission in the Boston area is not a general metropolitan government nor is the Port of New York Authority. No other special district, however, has gone as far as these two in assuming other governmental functions.

If additional functions are transferred to special districts, basic questions of organization, responsibility, and citizen control will have to be answered. The Metropolitan District Commission is not a unit of local government but an agency of the Commonwealth of Massachusetts. The Port of New York Authority is an agency of the states of New York and New Jersey. It is largely autonomous in its relations to these two governments. It would be better to endure what we now have than to turn over to an agency twice or more removed from popular election the power to make some of the most basic decisions about the structure and physical development of the metropolitan community.

Only to a degree is there less objection to transforming a special district composed of representatives of other units of local government[8] into a metropolitan government. It is possible, and it may be desirable,

8. Examples of this type of special district in the United States are the Passaic Valley Sewage District, the former Niagara Frontier Planning Board, the Metropolitan Water District of Southern California and the Golden Gate Bridge and Highway District.

to associate formally the governments of the municipalities with the government of the metropolis. The legislative body of the metropolitan government, however, should be popularly elected. We are not concerned solely with getting things done or even with getting them done well. It is equally important that the voters of the metropolis have the opportunity to participate as full political members of the community.

THE COUNTY AS THE CENTRAL UNIT OF METROPOLITAN GOVERNMENT[9]

Another way to develop a federal form of metropolitan government is to transform the county into the central unit.[10] To some extent, the urban county has been developing in this direction by means of what is known as functional consolidation. Principally in public health, public welfare, and correction, but by no means confined to these activities, there has been a slow, continuing trend toward county administration or joint city-county administration.[11]

If the county alone administers a function or if a joint city-county agency exercises jurisdiction over the whole county, there is at least a limited functional division of responsibility between a central local government and units covering smaller parts of the metropolitan area. Functional consolidation, if carried far enough, can result in a "federal" metropolitan government. This development is more promising, of course, in metropolitan areas containing a single county. But even in metropolitan areas overlying several counties, it should be easier to secure the co-operation and collaboration of a few strong county governments than of the existing multitude of municipalities, townships, counties, and special districts.

The Committee on Metropolitan Problems of the Civic Advisory Council of Toronto has agreed upon two alternative organizations of local government in the Toronto metropolitan area. In each, there is a "federal" distribution of functions between the small units of local government and what the report calls a "senior" government for the

9. The development of the county into the central unit of metropolitan government would involve neither city-county consolidation nor city-county separation (see chap. iv).

10. See Local Government Commission of Fulton County, Georgia, *Plan of Improvement for the Governments of Atlanta and Fulton County* (1950), pp. 37–39, 46–59, for arguments to the contrary, with respect to the Atlanta metropolitan area.

11. See U.S. Bureau of the Census, *Governmental Units Overlying City Areas* (1947), Table 10, for a list of governments other than the city corporation responsible for selected local functions. For the assumption of urban functions by counties see Betty Tableman, *Governmental Organization in Metropolitan Areas* (Ann Arbor: Institute of Public Administration, University of Michigan, 1951), pp. 24–32, 93–105, 138–54, the annual articles by Clyde F. Snyder on county and township government in the *American Political Science Review,* and the newsnotes on county and township edited by Elwyn A. Mauck in the *National Municipal Review.*

metropolitan area. One plan provides for the amalgamation of the highly organized civic areas with Toronto and the creation of a limited regional authority with jurisdiction over planning, housing, arterial roads, public transportation, and major recreation facilities.

The other proposal is for the creation of a metropolitan county to include the city of Toronto and all other municipalities in the metropolitan areas. The present municipalities would be retained with their present areas, but the metropolitan county would be organized under an elective county council. It would have jurisdiction over assessment, arterial roads, public transportation, planning, housing, water supply, and sewage disposal, public health, public welfare, police protection, the co-ordination of municipal fire departments, parks, and recreation. The local municipal council, on the other hand, would be responsible for the distribution of water, collection of sewage and delivery to disposal plants or trunk sewers under county jurisdiction, collection of surface water subject to regulation as to disposal by the county, collection and disposal of garbage, roads and sidewalks (including arterial roads), street lighting, preparation and operation of local official plans of development, subdivision control, zoning for land use (excluding major land use regulation under county jurisdiction), local parks and recreation facilities, recreation programs, inspection to assist in the enforcement of such local by-laws as pertain to local deliveries, early closing, use of sidewalks, etc., and minor licensing.

The proposal for a metropolitan county was intended by the Committee to be

. . . a federal solution to the problems of the Toronto metropolitan community. It may be thought of as a form of borough system adapted to the Toronto situation, for it is more closely akin to the London borough system than to a number of so-called County plans. While the scheme contains many features familiar to local government in Ontario, certain special aspects, such as the suggested form of representation, are unique, and are put forward in the belief that they may provide a practical solution to the problems of the Metropolitan Area of Toronto.[12]

There are five reasons why more attention should be given to ways of developing the county into "the central agency of local government for some of the great complex urban areas":[13]

1. The urban and metropolitan county is already assuming functions that can be distinguished only by legal definition from municipal functions.

12. The Toronto Civic Advisory Council: Committee on Metropolitan Problems, *Final Report* (March, 1951), p. 36.
13. Ohio Institute, *County Organization and Government in Ohio* (Columbus, 1932), p. 8.

2. Other means of integrating local government in metropolitan areas have either been inadequate or have evoked intense opposition.[14]

3. The county has shown a persistent vitality even in urban communities, despite the often repeated assertion that it is doomed to disappear as a unit of local government. Difficult as it may be, it would be easier to reconstitute the county than to abolish it.

4. The central county, short of an area-wide unit of government, is more likely than any other jurisdiction to include all, or at least the major portion, of the metropolitan area. The solution sought is one that will bring as large a part as possible of the metropolitan population and area under an integrated government.

5. A "federal" form of metropolitan government can be built around the county and the municipalities.

Reorganization of Urban County Governments

But the county as commonly organized is poorly suited to assume municipal functions. The county as a pure agency of the state, with limited powers, many elective officials and many more autonomous boards and commissions, with an impotent governing body, can hardly be expected to bear the heavy responsibilities of metropolitan government. A "managerial" form of government must replace the traditional "magisterical" county, it must be recognized by legislatures and the judiciary as a municipal corporation, and it must be given ordinance-making power, before it can function successfully in its new role.[15]

14. The recent reorganization of local government in Fulton County, Georgia, involving extensive annexations to Atlanta and the reallocation of functions between city and county, was designed to prevent the county from developing into a municipal government. M. Clyde Hughes, "Annexation and Reallocation of Functions," *Public Management*, XXXIV (February, 1952), 26–30. This is satisfactory only because some 81 square miles of built-up portions of the county were annexed to Atlanta.

The League of California Cities is fighting the municipalization of the county. "We propose further to consider the problem in its more fundamental aspects, and in this connection we have concluded that what is urban should also be municipal. We are beginning to question whether our county governments should become also supercity governments and whether the multiplicity of overlapping special-purpose districts which this rapid urban growth would now require would be in the public interest.

"The urgent need for orderly government suggests that the role of county government is different from the function of municipal government and that the distinction should be restored. It will not be easy to unscramble this hodge-podge, but those same forces which work always for a solution of public issues and problems will be helping us work this one out. Those who know and understand government best don't really want bigger local governments, but they do want a more orderly and better integrated system of local government. We have lost it and we must get it back." Richard Graves, "Fringe Areas Should Pay Their Own Way," *Public Management*, XXXIV (February, 1952), 33.

15. See the data on the executive organization of urban counties with official and unofficial managers and elected executives in Tableman, *op. cit.*, pp. 20–22, Table II.

One of the principal impediments to the transformation of the county into a metropolitan government is the legal concept of the county as an administrative subdivision of the state "created almost exclusively with a view to the policy of the state at large." The legal distinction between a county and a municipal corporation is important beyond its application by the courts. It is part of the general attitude commonly held in most states that the county, even in urban areas, should be protected by means of constitutional provisions, statutes and at times, judicial decisions from the radical designs of city slickers. As was said of Atlanta's Fulton County:

> The county lacks full authority to act as a city government. It has no right of home rule—no right to set up a working charter under which it can operate without having to go back to the General Assembly for its authority every time it wants to act. It has no right of special assessment. It is hamstrung by all the laws, procedures and customs of a rural government.[16]

That judges themselves can still use the definitions that supposedly distinguish counties from municipal corporations[17] was shown in 1936 when the Ohio Supreme Court held that the new Cuyahoga County Charter was invalid. The Court made a sharp distinction between "municipal" and "county" functions. The Court held that the enacting of ordinances, the organization and maintenance of a county police force (to replace the sheriff's office), the creation of a civil service commission, and the exercise of the initiative and referendum by the county electorate were municipal powers.

The point at issue, according to the Court, was not whether any municipality had been deprived of a power but whether any power vested in municipalities by the constitution or statutes would, under the county charter, be either exclusively or concurrently exercised by the county.[18]

16. Local Government Commission of Fulton County, *op. cit.*, p. 11.

17. The classical statement of this distinction is in *Hamilton County* v. *Mighels*, 7 Ohio State 109, 118 (1857): "Municipal corporations proper are called into existence, either at the direct solicitation or by the free consent of the people who compose them. Counties are local subdivisions of the state, created by the sovereign power of the state, of its own sovereign will, without the particular solicitation, consent, or concurrent action of the people who inhabit them. The former organization is asked for, at least assented to by the people it embraces; the latter is superimposed by a sovereign and paramount authority. A municipal corporation proper is created mainly for the interest, advantage and convenience of the locality and its people. A county organization is created almost exclusively with a view to the policy of the state at large, for purposes of political organization and civil administration, in matters of finance, of education, of provision for the poor, of military organization, of the means of travel and transport, and especially for the general administration of justice. With scarcely an exception, all the powers and functions of the county organization have a direct and exclusive reference to the general policy of the state and are, in fact, but a branch of the general administration of that policy."

18. Thomas H. Reed, "County Government Reorganization," *Legal Notes on Local Government*, I (May, 1936), 5.

CONFUSION OF SUBSTANTIVE AND PROCEDURAL POWERS

Any power, whether it be substantive or procedural, which has been conferred upon municipalities by the constitution or by statutes, is considered by the court to be a municipal power. The Court pointed out specifically that ordinance-making power and the initiative and referendum had been conferred upon municipalities by the constitution and that the statutes had authorized municipalities to organize police departments and establish civil service commissions. The Court then denied that the statutes had conferred any such powers upon counties, and it ignored the fact that the statutes already authorized a sheriff to enforce municipal ordinances and that the Court itself had ruled that the sheriff was "the chief law enforcement officer in the county, with jurisdiction coextensive with the county, including all municipalities and townships."[19] In the very year that the county-charter case was taken to the court, the legislature passed an act authorizing the establishment by charter provision of "a county civil service commission, personnel office, or personnel department."[20] The Court said, however, that the power to establish a civil service commission "has never been conferred upon a county."

The most unfortunate result of the Court's decision is the confusion of substantive and procedural powers. None of the powers which the charter sought to vest in the county were substantive powers, but they were powers to enable the county to exercise its functions, none of which were challenged by the Court. Apparently the Court did not inquire whether the proposed charter authorized ordinances upon any subject that did not relate to a valid county function. It is absurd to call the power to manage personnel a "municipal" power when the particular method of management in question is used by all levels of government—national, state, and local. Professor Earl L. Shoup has pertinently asked:

Does the court mean . . . to imply that a charter county may not copy the methods, machinery, forms of terminology of a city government, without this amounting to the taking over of municipal functions? If so we find a devotion to ancient names, sublime in itself, but fatal to the intent and spirit of the constitutional home rule amendment.[21]

19. *In re Sulzmann,* 125 Ohio State 594, 597 (1932).
20. *Ohio General Code, 1936,* Sec. 2394–4.
21. Mimeographed address delivered at Western Reserve University, March 6, 1936; see S. Gale Lowrie, "Interpretation of the County Home Rule Amendment by the Ohio Supreme Court," 10 *Cincinnati Law Review,* 454–466 (1936); D. M. Postlewaite, "County Charter Vesting Municipal Power in the County," 2 *Ohio State Law Journal* (1936), pp. 308–13 (1936); T. H. Reed, "Constitutional Changes Necessary To Accomplish Local Government Reform," *Legal Notes on Local Government,* II (1936), 139–47.

The incapability of the county, as it is now organized, to function efficiently and effectively as a metropolitan government is indicated by the comment of two students of the Detroit metropolitan problem. After remarking that the sheriff is the logical officer to co-ordinate the separate police departments within a county, they dismiss the possibility as an "idea . . . too fantastic to elaborate."[22] The county has been correctly described by Richard Childs as "a dozen governments loosely tied together." There is no person or body of men in the county with sufficient power to control the administration of county functions. A large number of elected county officials

sit serene on their little independent islands of authority, caring nothing for the tax rate since the board of supervisors carries the brunt of that and caring nothing for the supervisors except for the need of getting the money out of them once a year. The supervisors on their part can starve these executives without being blamed for the resultant conditions in the jail or the poorhouse.[23]

In the city, on the other hand, administrative responsibility is relatively centralized, and there is agitation for further concentration of responsibility and for a simpler structure. In contrast to municipal government, there had been, until the past few years, little or no change since the end of the Colonial period in the essential features of county structure. Changes have been made in the size and composition of the county board and in the number and method of selection of other county officers. But the county is today, as it was a century and more ago, a congeries of public officials, most of whom are locally elected and all of whom are responsible for activities specifically imposed upon them by the state legislature or the state constitution. In fact, during the last two decades most states have authorized or created special county boards or commissions with varying degrees of autonomy to discharge the functions of welfare, assessment, library services, election administration, health, hospital construction and operation, schools, and planning. In over a fourth of the states, there are county highway, recreation, agriculture, personnel, penal, and finance boards.[24]

22. J. M. Leonard and Lent D. Upson, *The Government of the Detroit Metropolitan Area* (Detroit: Michigan Commission of Inquiry into County, Township and School District Government, 1934), p. 66.

23. R. S. Childs, *A Model State Constitution* (New York: National Municipal League, 1921), p. 40.

24. Edward W. Weidner, *County Boards and Commissions* (1947) reprinted from the *National Municipal Review*, XXXV (April, 1946), 166–71. The material is summarized in Paul W. Wager (ed.), *County Government across the Nation* (Chapel Hill: University of North Carolina Press, 1950), pp. 13–15. Neither Weidner nor Wager present their data separately for rural and urban counties. Wager and his collaborators describe a government of a particular county in each state, but only four of the counties selected are urban counties: Mercer County (Trenton), New Jersey; Bucks County (Philadelphia Area), Pennsylvania; Genesee County (Flint), Michigan; and Orange County (Los Angeles Area), California.

Many of these special boards have been established to administer the newer functions of county government.[25] The by-passing of the general county governing body is not the result alone of the tendency of special interests to seek autonomous administration. It clearly indicates a reluctance to place additional responsibilities upon the general county government as it is now organized.

Structural reorganization involves, besides other things, (1) the establishment of a representative and responsible legislative body, (2) the creation of a county executive, and (3) the departmentalization of county work under organization units responsible through the executive to the county legislative body. The fact that the problem of structural reorganization in urban counties is different from that of rural counties should be held constantly in mind. Failure to distinguish between urban and rural counties accounts for much of the unequivocal denunciation of the manager form of county government.

A Representative and Responsible County Legislative Body

The most immediate change to be made in county government is to divest the county board of its administrative duties and to increase its legislative powers. Nowhere, as yet, has this been completely realized. Los Angeles County is governed by a five-member commission which combines the function of administration and policy formation—and this despite the creation by ordinance in 1938 of the position of county administrator for the purpose of co-ordinating the administrative work of the commission. The boards of San Mateo County (suburb of San Francisco), Arlington County, Virginia, and Montgomery County, Maryland (suburbs of Washington, D.C.), Monroe County (Rochester), New York, and Nassau County and Westchester County (suburbs of New York City) are the closest approximations at the present time to a legislative body which has relinquished its administrative powers.

Since the population of the urban county, unlike that of the typical rural county, is not homogeneous, devices for assuring that the county board shall be representative are most important. The problem is to secure a legislative body small enough to do its work and large enough to represent the interests of the citizens of the county. Size alone is

25. "Administratively, Fulton County government is more complicated and has more problems than the city government.

"The County Commission, elected to set policy and look after the money, has no control over eight department heads who are elected by and responsible to the voters. The County Manager, appointed by the commission to be the executive head, has no authority over eight other officials who are also appointed by the Commission and report directly to it.

"There are eight separate agencies dealing with finances—three elected by the voters, three appointed by the Commission and two appointed by the manager. No one authority has the power to coordinate their work" (Local Government Commission of Fulton County, *op. cit.*, p. 11).

no guaranty that a council or board will be representative. Probably no county governing body in the country is less representative than the board of supervisors of Wayne County (Detroit), with its one hundred and forty-five members. There has been some discontent, on the other hand, with the small board of five supervisors for Los Angeles County. The county there has assumed many significant functions, and its budget is so large—exceeding the budget for the city of Los Angeles —that it is felt that a governing body of five members is too small to be "representative of all interests and sections of the area."[26] The Committee on Governmental Simplification recommends that the membership of the board be increased to fifteen.[27] The 1917 proposals for city-county consolidation recommended a council of not less than seventeen or more than twenty-one members.

The size of the county board and the method of selecting its members will depend upon whether the county is consolidated with its municipalities or maintains its usual relationship with other units of local government. The problem of giving representation to the citizens who live outside the central city, if for no other reason than that of political expediency, cannot be avoided. This is most frequently done by providing that a certain number of the members of the board be elected from outside the central city, as, for instance, in Cook County, where five of the fifteen commissioners are from outside Chicago. In other counties, such as Milwaukee, the supervisors are elected by districts. The system of election at large, with nominations by districts, used in

26. See Bemis and Basché, *From Rural to Urban, The Municipalized County of Los Angeles* (Los Angeles: Haynes Foundation, 1947), p. 27. "This step could be accomplished by increasing the membership of the Board from the present five members to approximately ten. Each member would be elected from a geographical division of the county. In setting up the election districts, an attempt should be made to eliminate, so far as possible, artificial or arbitrary boundaries. Attention should be paid to such major topographical features as hills and stream beds, to the pattern of local transportation, and to commercial, industrial, and recreational characteristics. The aim would be to obtain in each district a natural grouping of communities with common interests and problems.

"An advisory committee representing the governments of incorporated cities and urban districts should be set up in each of the major divisions of the county. The committee would meet regularly with the Supervisor representing the division to talk over problems and submit recommendations."

27. Committee on Governmental Simplification, *Report* (Los Angeles, 1935), p. 36. Four members of the committee dissented to the recommendation: "In our opinion a board of five or seven is satisfactory, but in no event should the number exceed nine." They thought the smaller board would be more expeditious and at the same time more thorough in its consideration of public business. They also feared (*ibid.*, p. 57) that the increase in membership would reduce the importance of each individual member and, consequently, attract men of "smaller calibre" as candidates. The Committee on County Government of the National Municipal League would set nine as the maximum membership on county boards. They admit, however, that the special problem of an "urban county attempting the integration of county and municipal government" may require a different provision (R. C. Atkinson, "Principles of a Model County Government," *National Municipal Review*, Supplement, XXII [September, 1933], 471).

several large cities, combines advantages of both methods of election.

The township-supervisor type of county board, found in Michigan and parts of New York, Illinois, and Wisconsin, may be particularly useful in a federated metropolitan government centering around the county. The county board under the new charter in Nassau County, New York, consists of six supervisors, elected by the three towns and two cities. Hempstead has two supervisors, as before, but their voting strength is reduced from 64 to 50 per cent of the total votes on the board. The composition of the county board, as proposed in 1936 by the Westchester County Commission on Government but not accepted by the board of supervisors, attempted to meet the problem of adequate representation of urban, suburban, and rural interests by giving Yonkers and the three other cities five members on the county board, a suburban township four members, and an upper township one member. "This plan or representation, which is not new in the county, except in so far as the cities are concerned, transforms the county into a genuine federation of self-governing local governments."[28] The county charter, as approved by the legislature and the electorate, provides for the continuance of the board of supervisors until such time as the electorate shall approve in a referendum the substitution of a county board of from ten to twelve members.

The Committee on Metropolitan Problems of the Civic Advisory Council of Toronto, however, is opposed to a scheme of representation in which members of the proposed Metropolitan County Council would "have a dual capacity as might result if he were a representative from a constituent municipality."[29] The Committee proposes that the county be divided into single-member urban electoral districts of from 60,000 to 100,000 population and rural electoral districts of 10,000 population. We are not told why such over-representation of rural population is considered to be desirable or necessary.

A SINGLE-HEADED COUNTY EXECUTIVE

To establish a county executive who would be responsible for the administration of all or most of the county functions would constitute the most radical departure from traditional county structure. It would substitute a government directed by a responsible official for the headless county government of today. A responsible county executive is not secured, however, by establishing the office of county president after

---

28. Westchester County Commission on Government, *Home Rule Plan of Government for Westchester County* (Report No. 3, White Plains, 1936), pp. 9–10.

29. Civic Advisory Council of Toronto, Committee on Metropolitan Problems, *Final Report* (1951), p. 37.

the Cook County (Chicago) model. According to the Act of 1893, which created the office, the president is a member of the county board; he possesses a limited veto power over the acts of the board; and he appoints the nonelective county officers. The Act did not reduce the number of elective and practically independent executive and administrative officers of the county. As a result, thirteen other county officers are not under the jurisdiction of the county president.

County government may be reorganized after the pattern of the council-mayor type of municipal government. Under this plan, the county executive is elected and bears the same relationship to the county board and the county administration as the mayor bears to the council and the city administration. Nassau and Westchester counties (New York area) and San Mateo County (San Francisco Bay area) are

TABLE 14

COUNTIES WITH MANAGER FORM OF GOVERNMENT*

County	Population 1950	Plan	Effective Date of Plan
Virginia			
Warwick	39,177	E	1945
Albemarle	26,550	E	1933
Arlington	134,990	E	1932
Fairfax	98,255	E	1952
Henrico	57,166	E	1934
Tennessee			
McMinn	31,954	S	1947
North Carolina			
Guilford (Greensboro)	190,152	E	1942
Durham	100,641	E	1930
New York			
Monroe	484,877	E	1936
Maryland			
Anne Arundel	111,187	S	1949
Montgomery	163,749	E	1948
Georgia			
Fulton	467,354	Sh	1947
California			
Sacramento	275,659	H	1933
San Mateo	234,080	H	1951
Santa Clara	288,938	H	1950

"E" indicates state optional enabling act adopted by vote of the people; "H" home rule charter drafted locally and adopted by the people; "S" special charter passed by the legislature without local referendum; "Sh" special charter passed by legislature and adopted by people in local referendum.
* *The Municipal Year Book* (1951), pp. 512–29, Table XIX.

the only counties in the United States which have an elective executive of this type. Efforts were successful in 1937, after failures in 1925 and 1927, to secure popular approval of a charter for Westchester County which provides for a county executive. The executives of the three counties are elected at large for four-year terms.

The Westchester and Nassau executives appoint the heads of all departments, boards, and commissions except a few specified by the charter to be filled by election. The San Mateo executive appoints only a building inspector, a board and a director of health and welfare, a purchasing agent, and a recreation commission. In Nassau the executive presides over the meetings of the board of supervisors and may vote in case of a tie. The executives of Westchester and Nassau may veto any resolution of the board except those relating to procedure.

The structural device most likely to insure the responsible and effective administration of the affairs of an urban or metropolitan county is the council-manager plan. Under this plan, the county board is restricted to the determination of broad policy and to general control of the administration of policy through a manager appointed by, and removable at, the pleasure of the council. There are fifteen counties in the United States with some form of county-manager government. Nine of these counties adopted the manager plan during the last decade. Three are small rural counties and twelve are in metropolitan areas (Table 14).

Despite the meager but increasing experience with the manager principle in county government, its success is sufficient to warrant further trial of the plan in the reorganization of urban-county government. Wylie Kilpatrick and Kirk H. Porter hold, however, that the manager plan cannot be adapted to the county, since the county is an administrative agent of the state. Here, again, the differences between urban and rural counties, which are becoming more distinct year by year, are overlooked. The rural county need not be reorganized according to the patterns used in urban and metropolitan counties. The apparent difficulties here would disappear if the proponents of state centralization of county function would distinguish between the needs of urban counties and those of rural counties. The existence of these differences makes the case for county home rule: all that is asked is that the local government of some two hundred and twenty urban counties with jurisdiction over more than half the population of the country be not confined to the patterns which may be deemed suitable to the 2,800 rural counties of the nation.

A variation of the manager plan is that of the appointive county executive under which the legislative body participates more directly in the administration. This is one of the two optional forms of county government provided by a Virginia act of 1932. It has been accepted thus far only in the rural county of Albemarle. The executive is the coordinating and supervisory agent of the county board. The department heads, of which the executive may be one, are appointed and removable by the board with the advice of the executive. This plan of organization is quite similar to that used in *ad hoc* school organizations. It was proposed by the Governor's Commission on County Government in Ohio as an alternative plan "to meet the needs of counties which may be unwilling to repose as broad authority in the chief executive" as provided in the manager or elected executive plans. None of the Ohio county charters proposed in 1936, however, provided for the limited executive, but three of the four charters proposed the adoption of the county-manager plan.

The San Francisco city-county charter of 1931 contains an interesting compromise between the elective and appointive executive plans. San Francisco, with its semi-independent county officers and a large number of administrative commissions and boards, never had anything approaching a pure mayor-council form of government. The 1931 charter established the office of chief administrator carrying an annual salary $2,000 greater than that of the mayor. The chief administrator is appointed by the mayor and may be removed (1) by a two-thirds vote of the supervisors, (2) by a three-fourths vote of the supervisors after a trial initiated by charges of the mayor, or (3) by recall. A large part of the city-county administration is outside the control of the chief administrator, but for all administration placed in his charge he is theoretically responsible to the mayor and the board of supervisors. He is responsible for the major departments of public works and public health. In addition, he has charge of the departments of supplies, real property, and electricity and the offices of sealer, public administrator, county clerk, registrar of voters, recorder, tax-collector, coroner, and horticultural commissioner. Most of these departments and offices have to do with what are traditionally considered to be county functions. The remainder of the administration is under the mayor or independent commissions and boards.

There is no correlation of functions in county government, as we have seen; and the county is consequently governed by a congeries of governments "loosely tied together." Obviously, it will be impossible to secure a responsible legislative body and a responsible executive without correlating the work of the county into departments under the jurisdiction of the executive.

SUMMARY

There are at least three forms of local governmental organization that can provide metropolitan government without destroying existing units of local government: (1) the borough plan, (2) the development of special districts into multi-purpose governments, and (3) the development of the county into the central unit of local government in metropolitan areas.

The urban county appears to be slowly developing along these lines. Probably the greatest impediment to a more rapid development of the county into a central government for metropolitan areas is its traditional organization. The structure of county government has resisted integration with municipal government. This diffuse and loose structural tradition has persisted, where city-county consolidation has been attempted, and has largely nullified the desired effects of integration. Contributing to the refractoriness of the county is the general attitude that the county is and should be a mere administrative agent of the state. No distinction is made between the needs of local metropolitan government of half the population of the country located in some 220 counties and the needs of the other half of the population scattered over some 2,800 rural counties. A fruitful course of action might be, first, to reorganize the urban county, to give it a municipal structure, and, then, to consolidate it with its municipalities or to enlarge its functions and transform it into an effective unit of metropolitan government.

Once the urban county has been reorganized, it will be easier to establish an integrated local government for the metropolitan area. The county government will then be structurally suited to assume functions of area-wide importance. It can be transformed into a pure municipal corporation with jurisdiction over extensive territory. Or it can be merged, along with other local units, into the structure of the central city without persisting as a vermiform appendix—a locus of patronage infection, a source of confusion, and an excuse for irresponsible government.

CHAPTER VIII

URBAN REDEVELOPERS AND THE GOVERNMENT
OF METROPOLITAN AREAS

A PROFESSIONAL urban redeveloper or planner, or anyone else who is primarily interested in the redevelopment of urban land for a more desirable use than is now made of it, may justifiably ask what forms of local government have to do with their particular and immediate interests. Why should they be concerned with the extent of the area over which local governments exercise jurisdiction? In any event, what can urban redevelopers do about the problem of governing metropolitan areas? Are there not enough students of local government, public administration experts, leaders of civic organizations, government officials, and legislators already engaged in the search for an acceptable solution? Why should people concerned with urban redevelopment divert their attention from the job they are competent to do? Are they not likely to find themselves a few years from now with no projects completed but with a lot of talking to their discredit?

The stakes in urban development and redevelopment are too high for any one of us, whatever his special and immediate interests may be, to leave the winning of them to others. In the first place, the objectives of urban redevelopment cannot be achieved by the physical redevelopment of any small portion of the city for the same or new uses. Unless the use of land in a particular project area is planned with as full a knowledge and understanding as possible of the changing land-use patterns of the entire metropolitan community, the probability is great that the redeveloped area is already on its way toward another round of blight and obsolescence. The difference here is between blind risk and calculated risk. Calculations can be made only if we are aware of the present and incipient social and economic need for land throughout the community and if plans for the development or redevelopment of each subarea of the community are related to these needs and to the plans being made for other subareas.

This is why the realization of the objectives of urban development and redevelopment depends upon the kind of local government we have in metropolitan areas—its quality and its competence to plan and to govern. Probably no one will object to this general statement even though he asks the questions listed at the beginning of this chapter. But we need a metropolitan government that is more than the sum of good government in each of the subareas of the community.

Only a government with community-wide jurisdiction can plan and provide the services, physical facilities, guidance, and controls necessary to relate functional plans with areal plans. None of the metropolitan areas has such a government today. Neither the federal nor state governments are providing this kind of metropolitan government. There are indeed good reasons why the governmental integration of metropolitan areas should not result from the direct activities of the federal and state governments.

If the government of metropolitan areas is to be a local government, we still have before us the job of devising acceptable and effective ways of organizing it. It is clear from experience, that each of the devices tried during the last one hundred years is either politically unacceptable to groups, in or out of the metropolis, powerful enough to block the measure, or when accepted has been inadequate to provide a metropolitan government for communities constantly growing more complicated and spreading over wider areas. This is not to say that annexation, city-county consolidation, special districts, and other devices have not temporarily eased the pains of metropolitan growth. In many instances, matters would be worse today if they had not been used.

But our metropolitan communities are growing so large that we can no longer content ourselves with attempting to bring the whole area under one all-purpose general local government organized according to a pattern suitable for the government of a nineteenth-century village.

The alternative most often proposed is to make the present dispersion of local government among the central city and its dozens or hundreds of suburbs tolerable for a time by taking the most pressing problem of the moment out from under general local governments and entrusting its solution to a special district or authority.

I do not believe that we are confined to these ways of organizing the local government of our metropolitan communities. I doubt that any proposal has much chance of success, unless it is based on the "federal principle" of allocating metropolitan functions to a metropolitan government and leaving other functions to less-than-metropolitan governments. I realize the difficulties—not the least of which will be to decide at any given time and place what activities are metropolitan and what are less-than-metropolitan. But we cannot escape the problem of planning and controlling big things and little things at the same time.

Perhaps even more important than the need to make metropolitan government acceptable is the need to make it amenable to citizen control. Irresponsible local government fragmented among a multitude of municipalities, counties, and special districts unable to meet the problems of metropolitan life, frustrates the citizen and leaves him helpless.

The other extreme of a giant all-purpose metropolitan municipality would certainly become too cumbersome for any ordinary group of citizens to influence.

Urban redevelopers can contribute positively to the reshaping of urban government. The first question to be asked and answered is: What do we want urban government to do? The next question follows from the first: Where among the existing or possible units of local government in metropolitan areas do we wish to place responsibility for doing the various things we wish local government to do?

These questions must be approached from several directions at the same time. There are general values that we expect to be realized through governmental action and these values are to be kept in mind and preserved irrespective of the special values of particular segments of the community. But, we expect government to accomplish many particular objectives, such as to provide an adequate supply of potable water and to distribute it where it is needed. Each member of the community has a vague interest in these governmental functions. This vague interest will become a very specific and urgent interest if the service is sufficiently inadequate or breaks down. Around each of these particular governmental activities, however, there has developed a small group of professional administrators and technicians and an active clientèle group, usually much smaller than the total body of "consumers." These special interest groups have made important contributions to the development of particular services and regulations and of administrative organization and techniques. But they frequently ignore or are unaware of the relationships among their special interests and other special interests and the general political and social values of the community.

Urban redevelopers can help us to find acceptable answers to both of these questions. They can identify the relationships between the reuse of land that they seek to bring about and the other activities carried on in an urban community. They can encourage and lead other specialists to undergo a similar reorientation. They can see to it that those who are concerned in a general way with reorganizing local government in metropolitan areas do not overlook urban development and redevelopment.

Participation in the task of establishing and maintaining effective, efficient, and democratic local government is not a luxury that can be enjoyed or rejected as a matter of taste or convenience. Urban redevelopers who isolate themselves from community problems that seem to have no immediate bearing upon the assembly, clearance, and reuse of land in a project run the peril of all isolation. Instead of being given adequate resources to do their job and then left alone to do it, they may find themselves project-wise and redevelopment-foolish.

PART V

THE BACKGROUND AND PROSPECTS OF URBAN REDEVELOPMENT IN THE UNITED STATES

BY
COLEMAN WOODBURY

EDITOR'S FOREWORD

THIS rather long essay is an attempt to sketch in some perspective several parts of the urban scene in this country, to indicate some objectives for cities in the future, and to suggest some of the basic issues that have to be faced by those who would redevelop them.

In it, I have taken for granted that cities are more than more or less closely spaced buildings—that they are also and in essence human beings, groups, and institutions. Although probably few persons would dispute this assumption in general terms, I admit that its corollaries for redevelopment seem to me more meaningful and significant near the end of URS than they did at the beginning. Possibly some readers may feel that some of the subsections of this discussion go rather far afield, but, if so, I ask them to hear out the argument and to weigh its contentions and conclusions with their own experience and observations in redevelopment and in other urban, public affairs. A second assumption, which may in fact be a corollary from the first, is that the physical remaking of our cities is such a drastic and far-reaching operation that it can be successful only as one part of an advance on a much broader front in urban life. My attempt to indicate that front and its major sectors will not, I am certain, be unanimously approved but again I only ask that it be considered without prejudice on the grounds that it deals primarily with people instead of with buildings, streets, utilities, and other land uses.

The relations of this section to other parts of URS's reports are twofold. At some points I have drawn on the findings and insights of other contributors. More often, however, I have stressed aspects of the urban scene that for one reason or another, primarily the nature of their assignments, my colleagues have largely passed by. The sections on local government finance and leadership in urban affairs are examples.

It is clear that I have covered a much larger area than any to which I would make any claim of serious scholarship. In the fields in which I have done little or no original study, I have quoted quite liberally from the writing of others to whom I am particularly indebted.

In most parts of the entire subject matter much more research and study need to be done. I am convinced, however, that both public policy

609

and research in urban affairs need today some more inclusive framework, perspective, philosophy—call it what you will—that will help to guide, to inform, and even to inspire both policy and research. This essay is not an "answer" to that need; it is a start in its direction. And only because I feel it is so necessary that thoughtful urban citizens approach some agreement on such a philosophy or intellectual perspective, I have been willing to deal in short compass with complex matters and to offer tentative judgments on issues and relationships that need much more thorough investigation, experiment, and discussion. Others, I hope, not only will criticize what I have written but also will try their hands at the same task.

Throughout these chapters I have used the first person active voice primarily because the editorial *we* and the third person passive seem to me usually awkward and rather labored.

Most of the economic data referred to are pre-Korea either because these sections were written in the summer of 1950 or because no more recent figures are available. After my essay was completed except for a final editing, the *American Journal of Sociology* published Professor Robert Cooley Angell's *The Moral Integration of American Cities*. Although I could not benefit from it in preparing this part of URS, I suggest that it might be read by those who are at all concerned with the matters dealt with in the latter part of my discourse.

C. W.

CHAPTER I

INTRODUCTION

SOMEONE has said that it is all but impossible to make out the size, shape, character, and location of a forest when one is in the middle of it. This aphorism applies to urban redevelopment as well as to other complex areas of public policy.

When the phrase first came into fairly common usage in the late 1930's, urban redevelopment was looked upon as a fairly narrow, real estate type operation. For what were taken to be fairly obvious reasons, sizable built-up areas of American cities were practically closed to new investment or development. Many of these areas were in the older, central parts of the larger cities. Their obsolescence and substandardness were thought to have ill effects on those who lived and worked in them. In addition, it was not hard to point out that their secondary influences on people, industry, business, and governmental affairs in other parts of their localities were only less unfortunate.

Following this kind of sketchy and preliminary analysis, various proposals were put forward to clear the way for new investment and building in these areas. Because one of the most obvious obstacles to new building was the difficulty of essembling suitable sites, it was proposed that various kinds of private corporations be given the power of eminent domain, under certain conditions, to enable them to acquire suitable building plots. At about the same time, or very shortly thereafter, it was recognized that even with this aid in site assembly land acquisition costs would be so high in most built-up blighted areas that they would discourage or actually prevent most desirable forms of new development. This fact led to proposals for various forms of public aid to offset these high costs. Most of these aids were to be in one or another form of tax freeze or reduction on the new development for a period of years.

When the argument had gone about this far, it became clear that this job of assembling and preparing land for redevelopment was the kind of operation for which properly constituted public agencies would have many advantages over private corporations. The next step called for state and federal financial assistance to enable local redevelopment agencies to cope with the write-off of land prices that would be necessary to attract the most appropriate forms of new development into these areas.

As local redevelopment agencies were established and began to put together programs that might qualify for state or federal aid, a whole series of questions and problems, most of which had been only dimly foreseen, came out in bold relief. Would the institutions, corporations, and individuals that had been rather glibly referred to as prospective investors in redevelopment actually come into the local programs on any substantial scale? How could municipalities and allied public agencies finance the new or enlarged playgrounds, schools, and other facilities and services that would be needed in these areas? Who could say what the best reuse of these blighted areas would be? Individual land owners or promotors? The planning commission or department? If so, on what grounds? Clearly new buildings in these locations would be in competition over many years with comparable facilities in other parts of the city or of the metropolitan region. Where were the analyses and planning from which a conscientious public official or prudent investor could draw the conclusion that this or that type of new development would stand a reasonable chance of being both profitable and a benefit to the community over a substantial period of time? How about the often overlooked blight in dead and arrested subdivision areas? Would it not make more sense to bring these less expensive areas into productive use now and take up the congested, blighted districts later? Perhaps some of the latter ought to be cleared and either left vacant or put into less intensive use for parking or similar purposes. Would not this reduce, at least a little, the vulnerability of cities to disaster in the event of heavy bombing or other military attack?

And how about the people now living in the built-up blighted areas? What was to become of them? Were either private or public housing programs providing effectively for their needs? Would it be possible to do more than a handful of scattered clearance and rebuilding projects without stirring up so much suspicion, distrust, and outright opposition that the program would be stopped altogether? What do we actually know about social organization in these areas and how it could help or retard a comprehensive redevelopment program? If the reuse of the cleared area should be housing, at what densities should it be provided in the interest of consumer needs and satisfaction, economy, and an efficient urban pattern? And finally, in light of all these costs, difficulties, and problems of clearance and rebuilding, what policies, if any, should local governments or other agencies undertake to slow down the blighting process in other areas and to give some assurance that the new development would not become blighted in the foreseeable future?

These questions by no means exhaust the list of issues and problems that have been stirred up by the pioneer redevelopment programs in urban centers throughout the country. They are, however, fairly typical. Not every locality, of course, has run into every one of them at the outset, nor do they appear always in the same form or with the same urgency. After all appropriate qualifications have been noted, however, these issues and obstacles will not be denied or explained away. In various combinations they stand—stern and menacing—athwart most local redevelopment programs today.

To be sure, many local officials and their collaborators have not come to grips with all of these issues. Some believe that they can work through one or two or a few clearance and rebuilding projects without meeting these problems head-on. Most of these people, however, are quite prepared to admit the existence of the problems and the need for long-range plans and policies for dealing with them. They hope that their experience with the first few undertakings, in which some of the difficulties can be dodged or avoided, will give them experience and insights that will stand them in good stead when the issues have to be faced directly. In other localities, these problems seem to have advanced in almost solid phalanx with the result that programs have gone ahead very slowly and high hopes for them are turning into discouragement, disgust, and despair.

Any rapid sketch of the evolution of a rather complex set of ideas and activities is almost bound to have certain elements of oversimplification, if not of caricature. I submit, however, that this is not an unfair outline of the concept of urban redevelopment over the past twelve or fifteen years. And as one who, in one capacity or another, has gone through most of the steps in this evolving scene, I certainly believe that nearly all who have taken part in it have learned from the process. Probably some of us have even established a few bench-marks or guide posts that make up a rough framework of a kind—within which we can see things in some perspective and judge particular questions with a little assurance. But do we yet know very much about the size and shape of the forest? Quite possibly we have been wandering most of the time in circles and have simply learned to describe in more detail the same trees as we come back to them from slightly different angles. Who can say he has defined all or even most of the fundamental problems, let alone assembled and assayed the facts, values, and policies for dealing with them?

In these circumstances, it seems wise to try to get out of and, if possible, above the forest to see if we can then make out more clearly what and where it is and how it relates to other parts of the wider scene. This essay is one attempt to do this. Because our experience with urban redevelopment so far has taken us further and further into the social-political-economic complex of urban life, I propose to try to deal even more broadly with several phases of this interrelated whole. It is a difficult and even dangerous job, but I believe it is worth trying.

Finally, in trying to see significant relationships and interconnections, I thought it advisable to back up quite a way in time. Maybe this perspective might reveal some broad trends or currents in American urban life and institutions. Because this was being done at approximately the midpoint of the twentieth century, I have taken approximately the past fifty years as the time dimension of this analysis.

CHAPTER II

ON THE NATURE OF CITIES

THREE ways of looking at cities have often been pointed out by students of urban affairs.[1] First, a city is a functional unit in the economy of its region, nation, and world. In various capacities, its citizens produce goods and services for themselves, for those who live in its hinterland, and often for others scattered throughout the world. Second, a city is a social structure or, if the term be properly qualified, a social organism with its own processes of growth, equilibrium, and decay, and whose people have certain social and psychological characteristics—in many respects similar but in some unlike those of nonurbanites. Third, a city is a physical plant or apparatus within which its citizens carry on, more or less efficiently and satisfactorily, a wide variety of activities—personal, family, civic, economic, and cultural.

For purposes of a rapid review and a broad evaluation of urban development over the past fifty years or so, this seems to me a useful breakdown. But why, it may be asked, is it so appropriate for this purpose? How about urban government in all its complexities and with all its problems? Where does it fit in? Why does it not deserve a separarate classification?

For many purposes it certainly does. The corporate-political city—the legal entity—with its limited area and often circumscribed powers confronts growing problems and changing needs. Even here, however, the three-way concept of the city is useful because it suggests that urban government influences and, in turn, is affected by the characteristics, functions, and problems of the economic, social, and physical city. The political city, therefore, although it clearly has its own identity, structure, characteristics, and problems, can properly be looked at and analyzed as a factor of first-rate importance in the economic, social, and physical urban complex. From day to day and year to year, for good or ill, it affects the production and distribution of goods and services. It also produces and distributes some of the more vital services of

1. For one example see Louis Wirth and Edward Sbils, "Urban Living Conditions," Part II of *Urban Planning and Land Policies*, p. 164 (Volume II of the Supplementary Report of the Urbanism Committee to the National Resources Committee, Washington, 1939).

modern urban life. And certainly no one will understand the political city who does not have some grasp of the economic interests and groups that bear upon urban government. Similarly, urban government is an integral part of the social-psychological city. Not only is it the chief reliance of its citizens for the basic protection of life and property, but during the last half-century particularly it has come to play a leading part in the battle against Lord Beveridge's four horsemen of modern society—want, disease, ignorance, and squalor. Also, it seems to me, our consideration of the physiology and pathology of the political city gains much when we see, at least dimly, their relation to the basic human wants and desires of the mass of urbanites—including those wants for recognition, respect, a feeling of importance, for companionship and collaborative effort toward common goals, and for security. Finally, as students of the political city, we suffer from ignorance about the city as a physical plant. We realize that, by and large, it is not one of the finest achievements of American civilization. We are beginning to see that its influences upon municipal services, their quality and costs, on economic efficiency, and the character of individual and family life are pervasive and deep. Its development cannot safely be left entirely to the operations of the individual landowner, speculative builder, mortgage lender, or even to the public utility company and the traffic engineer. Neither is the public stake in this process adequately served by the efforts of a number of municipal departments enforcing largely uncoordinated police power regulations.

So I propose, as the principal theme for this necessarily selective look at American urban communities during the past half-century, the interrelations of the city political with the city as an economic unit, as a social-psychological complex, and as a gigantic physical plant. Most of my discussion will take up six of what seem to me to be fundamental trends and persistent problems in American urban life. Before coming to grips with these, however, I propose to check over quickly some of the highlights of the urban scene at or around the turn of the century and to outline, but not to discuss, a few of the more noteworthy changes of the last fifty years.

CHAPTER III

CITIES AT THE BEGINNING OF THE CENTURY

To MOST nonhistorians with some vague impressions of their nation's past, the years immediately before and after 1900 probably are thought of primarily in rural rather than urban terms. The long simmering agricultural revolt was on. Populism and Free Silver were at flood tide. Many of the farmers of the country, particularly those of the Middle West, had heeded at least part of the advice to raise less corn and more hell. With the land frontier virtually closing in the early 1890's and with many of its last installments decidedly marginal for the uses to which they were put, the depression of the 1890's hit large sections of the rural population very hard indeed. Deeply in debt, often to institutions in, or controlled by, eastern urbanites, exploited, so they thought, by more and more menacing consolidations of industrial power, and all but destroyed by the deflationary policy of the federal government during the depression, the farmers were out to change a system that seemed to them unjust and intolerable.

In most people's recollection, the turn of the century also means the United States' first ventures in imperialism following the Spanish American War. As a new Pacific power, and with Admiral Mahan's book on the influence of sea power on history just a few years old, our taking over and completing the Panama Canal seemed to many people both logical and necessary.

This was also an era of great bitterness in industrial relations.[1] Violent strikes at Homestead and Pullman, the Haymarket riot and its repercussions colored much current discussion and writing. Charles A. Beard, looking at the American political scene in 1896, saw that ". . . Deep, underlying class feeling found its expression in the conventions of both parties, and particularly that of the Democrats. . . . The sectional or vertical cleavage in American politics was definitely cut by

---

1. An exception to this characterization was the short period just before and after 1900, which has been called "a honeymoon period of capital and labour." See Harold Underwood Faulkner, *The Quest for Social Justice—1898-1914* (Volume XI, *A History of American Life* (New York: The Macmillan Co., 1931) pp. 53 ff.—quoting on this point John R. Commons *et al.*, *History of Labour in the United States,* II, 524.

new lines running horizontally through society . . ."[2] With the decline of the Knights of Labor, the American Federation of Labor, which had been organized in 1886, slowly and painfully made its way against heavy odds and strong opposition. Although most of the labor unrest and struggle was in urban centers, apparently very few people at that time thought of them as urban problems or related them to the living conditions, social discrimination, and political exploitation under which so many working men suffered.

But even in the then more recognized areas of city affairs and government, things were by no means quiet. In 1888, Bryce's *American Commonwealth* had pointed to municipal government as the one conspicuous failure of the United States. (I sometimes wonder how much weight should be given to the adjective, "conspicuous.") Very little in the next decade, however, would have changed that verdict. Then came the muckrackers among whose products one of the most widely read was Lincoln Steffens' series on *The Shame of the Cities*. In characteristic style, Mr. Dooley commented on Mr. Steffens and his colleagues:

Put down that magazine, Hinnissy! Now d'ye feel better? I thought so. But I can sympathize with ye. I've been readin' thim meself. Time was when I seldom throubled thim. But wanst in a while some home-farin' wandhrer wud jettison wan in me place, and I'd frequently glance through it and find it in me lap when I woke up. The magazines in thim days was very ca'ming to the mind. Angabel an' Alfonso dashin' f'r a marriage license. Prom'nent lady authoresses makin' pomes at the moon. Now an' thin a scrap over whether Shakespear was enthered in his own name or was a ringer, with the longshot players always agin' Shakespear. But no wan hurt. Th' idee ye got fr'm these here publications was that life was wan glad sweet song. They were good readin'. I liked thim th' way I like a bottle iv white pop now an' thin.

But now whin I pick me fav-rite magazine off th' flure, what do I find? Ivrything has gone wrong. Th' wurruld is little better thin a convict's camp. Angabel an' Alfonso ar-re about to get married whin it is discovered that she has a husband in Ioway an' he has a wife in Wisconsin. All th' pomes be th' lady authoresses that used to begin: "Oh, moon, how fair!" now begin: "Oh, Ogden Armour, how awful!" Read th' horrible disclosures about th' way Jawn C. Higgins got th' right to build a bay-window on his barbershop at iliven forty-two Kosciusko Avnuee, South Bennington, Arkansaw. Read Wash'n'ton Bliffens's dhreadful assault on the board iv education iv Baraboo. Read Idarem on John D.; she's a lady, but she's got th' punch. Graft ivry'where. "Graft in th' Insurance Comp'nies," "Graft in Congress." "Graft be an Old Grafter," "Graft in Its Relations to th' Higher Life," be Dock Eliot; "Th' Homeeric Legend an' Graft; Its Cause an' Effect; Are They th' Same? Yes and No," be Norman Slapgood.

An' so it goes, Hinnissy, till I'm that blue, discouraged, an' broken-hearted I cud go to th' edge iv th' wurruld an' jump off. It's a wicked, wicked, horrible, place, an' this here counthry is about th' toughest spot in it. I don't thrust anny man anny more. I niver did much, but now if I hear th' stealthy step iv me dearest frind at th' dure I lock th' cash dhrawer. I used to be nervous about burglars, but now I'm

2. Quoted in Morton G. White, *Social Thought in America: The Revolt against Formalism* (New York: Viking Press, 1949), p. 40.

afraid iv a night call fr'm th' prisidint iv th' First National Bank. It's slowly killin' me, Hinnissy—or it wud if I thought about it.[3]

Quite probably it is easy to attribute to the muckrakers too much of the revolt against corruption and boodle in municipal government. At least it is difficult to judge their influence as against less advertised forces. It is a fact, however, that before, during, and after their exposures, other ferments were at work in the urban scene. Local leaders, like Golden Rule Jones in Toledo and Tom Johnson in Cleveland, led municipal reform movements. The brilliant and unusual political career of Charles E. Merriam as an alderman and mayoralty candidate in Chicago also attracted wide attention. Some of these local leaders, like Jones, Johnson, and Merriam, were considerably more than honest men trying only to turn the rascals out.

Because patronage was in many respects the lifeblood of bossism, the merit system seemed to some of the reformers to be the best, in fact probably the only necessary, weapon of attack. Because boss rule was synonymous with waste, economy and efficiency in government became the standard around which many of the reformers rallied. In 1906, the Bureau of Municipal Research was established in New York and similar organizations were not slow in appearing in other cities. Because many members of local legislative bodies as well as administrative officials had been profiting from the nefarious doings of the boodlers, more direct popular control of municipal legislation seemed to some to be a remedy. The initiative and referendum were put into the San Francisco charter in 1898; the recall in the Los Angeles basic law in 1903. Other cities took them up immediately thereafter. In 1899, the National Municipal League, which had been organized in 1894, published its first Model City Charter. It provided for a strong mayor-council plan of government.

Questions of metropolitan jurisdiction and state-local relations were also subjects of interest, agitation, and action. In 1889, the Chicago Sanitary District and the Boston Metropolitan Sewerage Commission were organized. In 1893, the Metropolitan Parks District for Boston's pioneering area-wide system began its work. In 1895, a similar metropolitan unit was given responsibility for water supply in that area. At the turn of the century, a controversy over a new charter in New York resulted in the borough or federated city government for greater New York. Following Missouri's lead in 1875, by the end of the century four states had adopted constitutional provisions for municipal home rule.

Neither were what we now call the welfare activities of local government overlooked in those days. For example, during the last quarter or

3. Quoted in Mark Sullivan, *Our Times—III: Pre-War America* (New York: Scribners, 1930), pp. 87–88.

third of the nineteenth century, public health became more and more a matter of local public concern and action. Following the work of such leaders and educators as Shattuck in Massachusetts and Chadwick in Great Britain and the scientific discoveries of Pasteur, Koch, and others, local health departments were established primarily to fight germ diseases, both by improved sanitation and protection against "the dissemination from person to person of communicable disease." About 1900, the scope of these agencies was widening to include basically educational work designed to teach people how to build up resistance against diseases that could not be fought effectively by the other two means.[4] The brutal housing conditions of the day, particularly in the immigrant-crowded seacoast cities of the east, called for action that at first took the form of police-power regulation. In 1901, following a commission inquiry and report, the so-called New Tenement House Law was passed in New York. In the same year, the City Homes Association, a civic organization, published a report on the same subject that provided ammunition for a long and rather indecisive fight for better standards and more effective enforcement of them in Chicago.[5]

The movement for public parks also picked up momentum rapidly around the turn of the century. In 1892, some one hundred cities were known to have municipal parks; ten years later, the figure was almost eight hundred. To be sure, many of these were crude and inadequate in many ways and even the best were largely devoted to "peaceful enjoyment amid beautiful surroundings." Civic attempts to provide children's playgrounds received a rather cold reception at first. Up until about 1900, many local park officials were actually opposed to them. One record of the early playground movement shows that in 1900 public playgrounds were in operation in only eleven cities. By 1910, however, the figure was 180.[6]

Public education also made long strides in those years. Public servants today may be heartened by the fact that in 1885 the United States Commissioner of Education felt he had to reply to the charge that providing free textbooks for pupils was Communism. By 1898, however, free textbooks were provided for by state legislation in ten states, and ten more authorized local school authorities to make them available if

4. C.-E. A. Winslow, "Public Health" in Volume XII of the *Encyclopaedia of the Social Sciences* (New York: The Macmillan Co., 1933), pp. 647–49.

5. *Tenement Conditions in Chicago* (Chicago: City Homes Association, 1901). See also Edith Abbott and others, *The Tenements of Chicago* (Chicago: University of Chicago Press, 1936) particularly chapter ii by Sophonisba P. Breckinridge.

6. *Park Recreation Areas in the United States* (Bulletin No. 462, Bureau of Labor Statistics, Department of Labor, May, 1928) and Jesse Frederick Steiner, *Americans at Play —Recent Trends in Recreation and Leisure Time Activities* (New York: McGraw-Hill Book Co., 1933), chap. ii.

they wished.[7] Despite the fact that in 1890 nineteen states had no compulsory school attendance law and in 1900 the number was fifteen, school population, both elementary and high school, was increasing rapidly at the turn of the century.[8] The average school year was lengthening, and curricula were being examined more carefully. Free libraries, not all of them public, were also becoming more and more common and more nearly adequate. An official estimate in 1900 was that there were then over 9,000 free libraries with three hundred or more volumes apiece.[9]

Although America's early tradition of decent town and city building had long been lost in the industrial revolution, the craze for land speculation, and the inanities of the then popular conception of laissez faire, the tide began to turn a little around 1900. Although many modern architects do not like to be reminded of the fact, the Chicago World's Fair of 1893 (the Columbian Exposition) had quite an influence on this change. For the first time, thousands of Americans saw large groups of urban buildings other than the mansions of the rich arranged for some purpose other than to get the largest immediate return, either by sale or rental, from a given investment in the land. They liked what they saw and some began to wonder why a little spaciousness, order, and even beauty might not be appropriate in the parts of the cities in which they and others lived. In 1900, a commission of four men, all of whom had worked on the Chicago Fair, was appointed to restudy the L'Enfant plan for Washington, D.C. In 1902, an official commission for the capital city was set up. In 1905, Mr. Daniel H. Burnham was employed by the Association for the Improvement and Adornment of San Francisco to prepare a report for a city plan. The poorly understood but much abused "city beautiful" phase of modern urban planning in America was on its way.

Near the turn of the century, too, humanitarianism seemed to run somewhat more strongly than it had in preceding decades. Settlement houses were established in the slums of most of the larger cities. Hull House under Jane Addams opened its doors in 1889, and many others followed in the next few years. It has been fashionable recently to be somewhat patronizing toward these good-spirited but presumably unrealistic people, but certainly it is arguable that their doctrine of neighborliness and decency toward the poverty-stricken, exploited slum

7. Arthur Meier Schlesinger, *The Rise of the City* (Volume X, *A History of American Life*, New York: Macmillan Co., 1933), p. 169.

8. Clifford L. and Elizabeth H. Lord, *Historical Atlas of the United States* (New York: Henry Holt and Co., 1944), p. 172.

9. Schlesinger, *op. cit.*, p. 177, citing Report for 1899–1900 of the U.S. Commissioner of Education.

dwellers, many of them immigrants getting their first impressions of American society, was at least as effective an approach to some of the diseases of the urban body politic as most of the other attacks on these ills that were made by others. Of course, their results were limited because their personnel and resources were pitifully small. At least, however, against the hardships and trials of a harsh urban existence they set up a competitive source of aid and assistance to the political boss and his followers. Someone who knew the ways of this society besides the minions of the local political machine tried to help out when the kids got embroiled with the law or when disease and death struck. And it should not be forgotten that settlement house leaders like Miss Addams had an effective hand in educating the general public on many fronts and were often effective in pressing for reforms in such fields as public health and housing. Also they and their associates made some of the earliest, first-hand studies of living and working conditions in urban slums—studies that others also used to good effect in later years.

On what I suppose could be called the intellectual front, the years around 1900 also saw the beginnings of change. The dry formalisms of economics and jurisprudence, reenforced by some forced interpretations of Darwinism, were definitely challenged. The popular version of laissez faire, which someone has said mistook for eternal principles of human society some of the less pleasant characteristics of the British shopkeeper, came under definite attack from a group of young men trained in the historical school of the contemporary German economists. Henry George's death in 1897 during his second campaign for the mayoralty of New York ended an extraordinary career that had produced a large, vigorous, and varied body of followers—many of them men of prominence and influence—who continued as a considerable if declining force in the body politic. Although Thorstein Veblen's later prestige was much greater than his immediate influence, *The Theory of the Leisure Class* was published in 1899 and *The Theory of Business Enterprise* in 1904. In 1902, Oliver Wendell Holmes took his seat on the Supreme Court of the United States, and not too long thereafter recorded his official doubt that the Fourteenth Amendment to the Constitution of the United States had enacted Herbert Spencer's *Social Statics*.[10] H. G. Wells's *Anticipations* saw a prospect for future urban communities that combined some of the merits of both city and country. Another Britisher, Ebenezer Howard, after several years of residence in this country, upon returning to his native land put down his specifications for garden cities. It is perhaps significant that the first edition of his little work was not called by its later title, *Garden Cities of Tomorrow*, but instead was labeled *Tomorrow—A Peaceful Path to Real*

10. *Lochner* v. *New York* 198 U.S. 45 (1905).

Reform. And in 1899, Adna Weber's book, *The Growth of Cities,* pulled together for the first time a mass of information on the growth of urbanism in many countries of the world. Although much of his work was descriptive, Weber clearly was concerned over many of the problems of urban life and looked to the suburban movement as a remedy apparently without foreseeing some of the serious difficulties that it in turn would produce.

This necessarily superficial summary of American urban life and affairs at about the beginning of this century has not been made for its own sake. It seems to me to suggest three conclusions that are pertinent for students of urban affairs today: (1) There was much more to the urban scene in 1900 than avaricious boodlers and a group of near-sighted, rather self-righteous reformers going around with clothespins on their noses and exhorting the "good people" to throw the rascals out. (2) Although the recognized problems of the day were differently defined and often appeared in somewhat different forms than they do now, most of them were essentially the same problems—the lack of rapport among the major classes and groups of the body politic; narrow, half-cynical pressure groups; bad housing; ineffective city planning and hodge-podge, shortsighted urban development; too limited and circumscribed municipal powers; value systems too much dominated by money and pecuniary success. And then, as now, decent people saw not only the symptoms but at least some of the causes of the urban diseases and, according to their lights, tried to do something about them. (3) Rather generally, those interested in specific reforms overestimated the effects of their pet measures. Civil service reform and municipal home rule, useful as they have been, have not remade our urban political life. Tenement house regulation, building and sanitary codes, necessary and desirable as they were and are, did not lead to decent housing for large sections of the urban population. Possibly the proponents of these and other measures lost perspective and sometimes mistook their means for the end. If so, possibly they were neither more nor less human than many of us today.

CHAPTER IV

THE PAST HALF-CENTURY

A s BACKGROUND for considering the persistent problems, a few high-lights of the last half-century's urban scene are worth noting.
Due largely to urban-located industries and service activities, the gross national product has substantially quadrupled over the last fifty years (in 1944 dollars). Almost half of this increase has come in the last twelve years, and, therefore, may not be too easy to maintain. The nation's total population has practically doubled; the number of so-called gainfully employed has more than doubled; the number of families is more than two and a half times the 1900 figure. The number of women in the labor force has increased by about 270 per cent. With the enormous stepping up of productivity has come greater economic instability and a more complex interdependence of the various sectors of the economy. Largely as a result of two inflationary splurges after the world wars, the wholesale price index has gone up about 180 per cent.

Our position in the international scene and its impact on domestic institutions are dramatically shown by an 8500 per cent increase in what have been called national security costs. In 1900, this meant expenditures for the Army and Navy; in 1949, outlays for Army, Navy, Air Force, and the Economic Co-operation Administration.[1]

During this half-century, the percentages of urban and rural population have substantially reversed themselves. In 1900, about 40 per cent of our people lived in cities, and 60 per cent in rural areas. At present, according to the Census of 1950 some 64 per cent of Americans are urbanites, and 36 per cent live on farms and in nonfarm rural areas. Although the 1950 percentages reflect a rather more inclusive definition of an urbanized area, the broad shift is unmistakable. Metropolitan areas have also increased enormously as measured by population. The Census of 1900 had no metropolitan classification. In 1910, however, the Bureau recognized forty-four metropolitan areas, which had about 28 per

1. For estimates on these and other phases of economic growth see *Business Week,* December 31, 1949, pp. 19, 20; J. Frederic Dewhurst and Associates, *America's Needs and Resources* (New York: The Twentieth Century Fund, 1947) and Robert W. Hartley, Eleanor Wolkind *et al., America's Capital Requirements* (New York: The Twentieth Century Fund, 1950).

cent of the total population. (More accurately, in the terminology of the 1910 Census, there were twenty-five metropolitan districts and nineteen districts with a central city of over 100,000 with adjacent territory.)[2] For the 1950 Census, there are one hundred and sixty-eight standard metropolitan areas, somewhat differently defined to be sure, and they include approximately 55 per cent of the total population.[3]

The characteristics and composition of the population also have shown significant changes. It is well known that the proportion of older people has been increasing and still continues to increase. Both this shift and decreases in the average hours per work week (in manufacturing industries from 51 to 39 hours)[4] have stepped up substantially the amount of leisure time available to large numbers of people. This latter change and others mentioned in the paragraphs on productivity and urbanization are both causes and effects of an almost 1900 per cent increase in union membership.[5] Occupational distribution has also shifted materially. For these relations, 1940 figures are the latest available. In 1900, the percentage of employed workers in agriculture and mining was 39; in 1940, 21. The percentages in manufacturing and mechanical industries held almost even at 27 to 28 per cent. Trade, transportation, and communication increased from nearly 19 per cent to about 25 per cent. Professional services went up from a little more than 4 per cent to more than 10 per cent.[6]

In short, our increasingly urban economy has made possible a notable increase in our standards of living. Most groups of the population have shared, in various degrees, in the increase. Although difficult to measure, municipal public services have contributed to the higher standards. Conversely, markedly higher economic productivity has made possible a level of public services that could scarcely have been foreseen at the beginning of the century. Finally, improved farming methods from hybrid corn to greater mechanization enable a proportionately smaller farm population to supply our national needs for foods and fibers. Urbanization, therefore, seems likely to continue and the responsibilities, possibilities, and difficulties of urban government and other institutions to grow.

Nearly every literate person, I suppose, knows that municipal functions and services have increased materially both in number and quality

2. Warren S. Thompson, *The Growth of Metropolitan Districts in the United States: 1900–1940* (Washington, D.C.: Government Printing Office, 1948), p. 1 and Table III, p. 6.

3. Press Release, October 17, 1950, Bureau of the Budget, Executive Office of the President. In addition the Bureau lists four metropolitan areas outside of the continental United States.

4. *Business Week,* December 31, 1949, pp. 19, 20.

5. *Ibid.*

6. Amos H. Hawley, *Human Ecology—A Theory of Community Structure* (New York: The Ronald Press Co., 1950) Table 41, p. 376.

during the last fifty years. I doubt, however, that many of them appreciate the range and scale of the increase. Let me give an example or two.

In 1900, Madison, Wisconsin, was a quiet, attractive state capital city with slightly less than 20,000 population. In 1948, it had grown to an estimated 90,000 with possibly another 20,000 within its immediate environs. During this span of years, I doubt that its municipal government was looked upon by many persons competent to judge as an outstanding example of excellence or progressiveness. On the other hand, it certainly was not near the rear of the procession. Probably it ranked comfortably above the average for cities of its size and type. It had the advantages of a fairly high average income per family in the city, relative economic stability, and location in a state that during most of the period had a progressive, able government. In 1948, the American Federation of State, County, and Municipal Employees, which has headquarters in Madison, put out a little pamphlet with the title *What Your Taxes Buy*.[7] It is largely a list of services taken on by the city government of Madison from 1900 to 1948 with the date of the initiation of each. These added services and functions were classified into seven groups: general government activities, protection to persons and property, conservation of health, sanitation and promotion of cleanliness, education, parks and recreation, and miscellaneous public service enterprises.

How many items would most persons guess were on this list of added municipal functions and services? Perhaps it isn't a fair question, but the answer is 239. Without listing them all, a sample will show their range and variety. Under general government activities are city purchasing agent (1929), city employee pensions (1943), and the appointment of a city manager (1947). Under protection of persons and property—regulation of public bathing (1901), firemen's pension fund (1908–9), plumbing inspector (1913), a substantial amendment to the zoning ordinance (1945). Conservation of health—keeping of vital statistics (1907), dairy and milk inspection (1912), cancer detection center (1947). Sanitation and promotion of cleanliness—new sewage disposal plant (1901), chlorination of water (1916), fluorination of water supply (1947). Education—manual training (1904), playground director (1907), an orthopedic school (1938–39), veteran training programs in the vocational school (1945–47). Parks and recreation—first playground (1903), park zoo and aquarium (1915–16), Monona golf course (1935), handicraft center (1930). Miscellaneous public service

7. *What Your Taxes Buy—A Survey of Municipal Services Added to the Government of Madison, Wisconsin from 1900–1948* (Madison: The American Federation of State, County and Municipal Employees, 1948).

enterprises—city airport constructed (1936–39), Madis
Authority established (1938), reestablished (1945), perm;
ans' housing development (1948).

I would guess that quite a few Madison residents would a;
remark attributed to Mr. Justice Holmes—"when I pay tax
civilization."

A somewhat similar study had been made earlier for Detroi.
Lent D. Upson who ran his records back to the incorporation of L
troit in 1824.[8] Then it had 24 functions or services. By 1900, the rol.
had increased to 140, and by 1941 to 396. During the last 41 years of
his record, therefore, 256 additional services or activities had been
added. The breakdown by decades may also be significant: from 1900
to 1910—39 new services or activities; from 1910 to 1920—86; from
1920 to 1930—71; from 1930 to 1940—58 (2 added in 1941). Apparently New Dealers and the welfare staters cannot be held responsible for all of this record. In fact, it seems to me at least arguable that
the welfare state is an application at the so-called federal level of many
of the decent motives and practical objectives that most progressive urban governments have taken more or less for granted. The welfare city
in America has been in the making for more than the past half-century.

These tabulations of municipal functions and activities have not been
included to threaten with apoplexy any statistician who might happen
upon this monograph. I realize that functions and activities are hard
to define specifically and that they vary enormously in size, cost, and
importance. The figures, however, are not the essence of these facts.
They simply indicate very roughly the expanding scale of municipal
government as it has responded to the ever growing complexities and
interdependencies of an urban and, increasingly, a metropolitan society. And the end is not yet.

8. Lent D. Upson, *The Growth of a City Government* (Detroit: Bureau of Governmental Research, 1942).

CHAPTER V

TRENDS AND PROBLEMS

I N THE remainder of this essay, I shall sketch in broad strokes six of
what seem to me the fundamental trends and persistent problems
in American city life. Some of these phenomena may seem to be
more in the nature of problems than trends; others—vice versa. I do
not suggest that these six take in all of the significant aspects of the
current scene in American cities. They clearly do not. It seems to me,
however, that they are among the more vital concerns of urban communities and that they illustrate the scope and complexity of both
present-day local government and the urban economy. Of course, these
phenomena may be separated only for purposes of analysis and discussion. In actual life, as I believe even my necessarily sketchy review of
them will show, they intertwine, interpenetrate, and overlap one another. In the order in which I shall take up these problems and trends,
they are: (1) Metropolitanism, (2) Political Problems of Social Heterogeneity, (3) Urban Planning, (4) Local Government Finance, (5)
Organizations for the Improvement of Local Government, (6) Representation and Leadership in Urban Public Affairs.

METROPOLITANISM

As I have indicated earlier, the first stages of metropolitanism on the
American urban scene were under way well before the beginning of the
past half century. Although Weber in his 1899 study used the word
"metropolis" and its derivatives rather sparingly, he was well aware of
the phenomenon and saw in it a remedy for many of the ills and troubles of urban life that clearly concerned him.[1] In 1901 Mr. Dooley addressed himself to suburbanism with characteristic remarks on *The
City as a Summer Resort*. Until about 1900 or a little before, however,
annexation by central cities had been able to reduce the governmental
problems of metropolitanism quite substantially. In more recent years,
it has been much less effective in this respect. From Census figures two
of the leading students of local government units have estimated that in

1. Adna Ferrin Weber, *The Growth of Cities in the Ninteenth Century* (New York: The
Macmillan Co., 1899) chap. ix, particularly pp. 458–75.

1942, one hundred and forty metropolitan districts had more than 15,-800 units of government. Of this total, 11,800 were school districts, 1,700 were municipalities and almost 1,100 were special districts of one kind or another.[2] One who reflects on these totals may well marvel that local government in metropolitan areas is not more an example of pure and applied chaos than it actually is.

By the 1920's, metropolitan trends and problems were beginning to attract major attention from various students of urban life and many of its leaders and officials. In 1922, N. S. B. Gras, in *An Introduction to Economic History,* recognized four major types of economies: the cultural nomadic economy, the settled village economy, the town economy, and the metropolitan economy.[3] He gave a little less than half of his book to two chapters on the metropolitan economy in England and in America. In his stimulating review, however, Professor Gras took "metropolis" to mean the largest urban complexes (he recognized eleven "full-grown" metropolitan areas in this country) rather than the more inclusive Census definition, which is the sense in which I use the term and its derivatives here. (Much simplified, this definition recognizes as a standard metropolitan area a central city of 50,000 or more persons, the remainder of the county in which this city is located, and all contiguous counties that are substantially urban in character and are linked economically and socially with the central county. In 1950 there were one hundred and sixty-eight standard metropolitan areas in the continental United States. Considerably more than half of this total population was in the fourteen areas with populations of a million or more.) In 1925, H. Paul Douglass' book on *The Suburban Trend* was published.[4] The next year, the National Municipal League set up a representative Committee on Metropolitan Government, and in 1930 its report appeared under the title *The Government of Metropolitan Areas in the United States.*[5] During the late 1920's, social scientists of various disciplines at the University of Chicago, the University of Michigan, and elsewhere were studying various phases of metropolitanism.

Despite this acceleration of interest and analysis, which reflected the accelerating growth of metropolitan areas and complexities, we have only scratched the surface of this major urban phenomenon. The interests of both scholars and local officials were diverted to other matters

2. William Anderson and Edward W. Weidner, *American City Government* (New York: Henry Holt and Co., New York, rev. ed., 1950), p. 171.

3. New York: Harper and Bros., 1922.

4. New York: The Century Co., 1925.

5. *The Government of Metropolitan Areas in the United States,* prepared by Paul Studenski with the assistance of the Committee on Metropolitan Government (New York: National Municipal League, 1930).

during the 1930's and the war years, but metropolitanism went ahead in its manifold, devious, and persistent ways. Today, by almost any standard of judgment, it is one of the most pressing and formidable problems of American urban life.

Elsewhere I have tried to sketch some of the more unpleasant phases of metropolitanism:

. . . As the conditions that made for blight and congestion began to do their miserable work, a very considerable proportion of the wealthy and well-to-do and a smaller proportion of the weaker economic classes began to seek quiet, green space, decent conditions in which to bring up children, and surroundings conducive to human dignity and self-respect by moving from the central cities. Contrary to a common impression, we have some evidence that this flight from the city usually is not one big leap but a series of shorter jumps—first within the central city itself, then often to one of the larger suburbs, and often again to a smaller town or, more and more, to unincorporated territory within the metropolitan region. With and as a result of these moves, the central cities have been losing continually a growing number of their economically stronger citizens—those who might be expected, by reason of their economic position, education, and cultural opportunities, to supply much of the leadership in the political, civic and cultural life of these centers.

Not only has this process of hit-or-miss decentralization deprived the central cities in metropolitan regions of needed potential leadership, it has also led to a splintering of the body urban outside the central cities. Most of our large metropolitan regions now have dozens of municipalities, usually overlaid to some extent by a number of special purpose districts for water supply, sewerage disposal, etc. Too often each of the municipalities is more or less at war with some or all of its fellows, as well as with the central city. It seeks to attract certain kinds of residents, or business, or industry. It tries just as hard to keep out others. The result is a growing Balkanization of the metropolitan economy. Very few if any of the citizens of these important regions can see the needs and welfare of the complex, interconnected whole. Many don't seem to care. Usually those who do see, at least darkly, and who do care, feel helpless to do more than talk about their fears and hopes.

This cumulative process of confusion and disintegration in metropolitan areas has led to financial difficulties for local governments, public utilities, school authorities, churches and other institutions, merchants in the older business districts and others. The central city loses taxpaying power while its obligations for public services remain unchanged or actually increase. Investment in community overhead in the forms of utility lines and facilities, streets, parks and playgrounds, schools, churches and other institutions, remains the same or declines very slightly in the older sections, while the demands for new investment for the same purposes in the newer areas of refuge from blight and decay increase from year to year. Because of the unplanned and unthought-out character of the growth, these additional investments are made often in costly form and often result in inefficient operating units with resulting high costs.

Merchants and other business men see their customers moving farther and still farther from their old shopping centers. These business men are worried. First a few, but now an increasing number, are trying to catch up with their departing customers by building branch stores in outlying cities or towns in the regions. But they, too, face the problems of additional overhead and possible under-utilization of their existing plant. . . .

Finally, all these phases of metropolitan confusion and deterioration have at least one common characteristic: they show no signs of curing themselves. . . . As a matter of fact, despite our general ignorance about many sectors of our metropolitan economies, we have some evidence for believing that many of these forces of blight and disintegration aggravate each other and that their effects over fairly long periods of time are cumulative.[6]

To this description, I would add here only a few brief comments:

1. More efficient means of transit and transportation, including motor cars and street widenings, have made possible the metropolitan sprawl.

2. In many of its manifestations, metropolitanism is a result of population growth and various kinds of decentralization of activities. The obvious breakdown of the process of decentralization is into industrial, commercial, and residential types.

3. The picture on industrial decentralization is not too clear. It seems relatively safe to say, however, that in *some* types of industry, new plants and expansion of existing facilities have gone more and more into locations in the outlying parts of metropolitan areas or outside of them altogether.

4. Commercial decentralization so far apparently has been largely a derivative of industrial and population movements. There are some indications that it may become a more active force in the complex scene.

5. In some of the larger industrial and commercial enterprises, decentralization of some departments, functions, or services has taken place.

6. Residential decentralization certainly has been going on—probably at a rapidly increasing rate. It is no longer exclusively or perhaps even primarily a flight of the rich. Many families of moderate and even lower income have joined the trek from the central city. One or two modest studies made recently indicate that even those families that flee farthest physically and socially from the central cities (that is, those who go into unincorporated areas in metropolitan districts) are not going "back to the land." Their standards of public services are essentially urban. Although they will put up for some time with a relatively low order of these services, they look forward to and expect what they would call improvement in them.

7. Finally, the reasons for residential decentralization are somewhat more complex than the quotation indicates. Quite clearly, many suburbanites in metropolitan areas have left the central cities not only in

6. Coleman Woodbury, "Housing in the Redevelopment of American Cities," *Land Economics* (November 1949), pp. 399–400. This article is a slight revision of one with the same title presented at the Centennial Celebration of the American Association for the Advancement of Science in Washington, September, 1948. See *Collected Papers Presented at the Centennial Celebration* (Washington, D.C.: AAAS, 1950), pp. 123–28.

search of space, quiet, and decent conditions in which to bring up their children, but in deliberate attempts to separate themselves from people of different backgrounds whose appearance and ways of life they do not understand and do not like. In many suburban areas, there is an ungodly amount of thanking-God-we-are-not-as-other-men-are. Also, many of the outward migrants have thought that in smaller cities of more homogeneous population they could supply for themselves higher standards of public services at lower costs than in the central cities—an expectation that has not always been realized.

8. To quote again: "By no means are all forms of urban decentralization bad or unfortunate. Through them some families have bettered their housing and other living conditions. Undoubtedly, many more families will do so in the future. The trouble is *not* that our larger urban areas are decentralizing; it is that this decentralizing and recentralizing process, because it is hit-or-miss, largely planless, and poorly understood, is producing only *some* of its potential gains, but many harmful and often unnecessary by-products."[7]

Political scientists, both professional scholars and practitioners, have considered quite a battery of possible ways and means of dealing with governmental problems in metropolitan areas. Some of them have only been talked about, others have been tried out—a few of them on a large scale. Perhaps the chief ones of both kinds could be listed as (1) enabling acts for central cities to provide certain public services outside their boundaries; (2) intergovernmental arrangements, largely contractual, among municipalities in the metropolitan area; (3) *ad hoc* authorities with an area of operation taking in all or most of the metropolitan district, e.g., water supply and sewage disposal districts; (4) easier annexation and consolidation of existing municipalities and of areas under or ripe for development; (5) city-county consolidation; (6) the reorganization and municipalization of county governments; (7) a federated or borough-type of metropolitan government; (8) the city-state.

Clearly these proposals vary greatly in scope, severity, and in degree of political practicability or impracticability for the near future. Quite as clearly, they cannot be analyzed here. Not as ideal or near-final solutions, but as partial remedies judged against the criteria of probable effectiveness in providing basic public services more effectively and of a reasonable degree of political feasibility over the next ten or fifteen years, I would suggest that particular attention be given to the municipalization of county governments and the creation of multi-purpose special authorities with metropolitan-wide jurisdiction.

7. *Ibid.*, p. 401.

POLITICAL PROBLEMS OF SOCIAL HETEROGENEITY

Urban sociologists, with that weakness for polysyllabic words for which many of them are noted, have often pointed to social heterogeneity as one of the chief characteristics of urban populations. This means, of course, that city populations, in comparison with those who live elsewhere, are made up of groups with a wide range of incomes, occupations, ethnic and national origins, standards and ways of life, value systems, and other social characteristics. Broadly speaking, this is true of urban dwellers the world over. It is a condition that is not hard to account for, at least in general terms. The economic life of cities calls for and rewards specialization. Trade contacts, usually centered in urban areas, add variety and lead to some cross-fertilization of cultures. Again, urban populations, by and large, do not reproduce themselves over long periods of time, or if they do in some areas, do not provide a sufficiently rapid increase for urban needs. Rural recruiting of urbanites, therefore, goes on. The traditions and practices of urban centers, particularly the larger ones, lessen the effectiveness of primary group controls that, in other circumstances, make for some degree of uniformity in outlook and values.

Quite probably during the last half-century, American cities have had this characteristic to a higher degree than those of any other major industrial nation. During the first quarter-century, the flood of immigrants, most of whom came from countries of southern and eastern Europe and many of whom settled in cities, were a major factor in metropolitan population increases. In 1930, after the quota system on immigration had been in force for several years, almost 44 per cent of our total urban population were foreign-born and first-generation Americans of foreign-born or mixed parentage. At about the time that immigration was sharply reduced and its distribution among countries somewhat changed by the quota system, the American Negro began to go more and more into cities, both in the North and in the South. American cities are socially heterogeneous with a vengeance.

Closely related to heterogeneity of urban dwellers is the fact that, as Louis Wirth has put it: "The contacts of the city may indeed be face to face, but they are nevertheless impersonal, superficial, transitory, and segmental." In other words, people in cities know relatively few other people as individuals, as more or less well-rounded persons with a full complement of characteristics, qualities, weaknesses, foibles, hopes, fears, ambitions, desires, wants, and needs. Rather they know them as customers, competitors, employees, bosses, politicians, business men, reformers, as whites or Negroes, Italians, Jews, Irishmen, as North

Siders or West Siders, homeowners or renters, the unemployed and so on ad infinitum. Inevitably, at best we see in two dimensions only most of those with whom we deal; at the worst, we develop stereotypes that support our group's particular prejudices.

These broad statements tell an old story. I doubt that many readers would question them, except perhaps in detail or on matters of emphasis. I doubt that they come as news to many. I put them down here simply as background for the suggestion, if I may paraphrase a well-known observation about American cities, that during the past half-century our inability to appreciate fully the significance of these facts for American cities, and our failure to deal effectively and democratically with the problems that stem from them have been the most serious weaknesses in American urban life.

In discussions of federal-state-local administrative relations, it is often said that in matters directly affecting the citizens of a locality, on the whole, wiser decisions are made by neighbors than by strangers. I would not like to have to argue against that proposition. But, in all seriousness, let me ask in what sense the family of an Italian laborer on the near West Side of Chicago, or the family of a Negro working in the stockyards or in the steel mills of South Chicago is a neighbor of an investment banker on Lake Shore Drive, a University of Chicago professor, a corporation president in Lake Forest, or a white-collar worker in Villa Park? Neighborliness, at least in the minimum sense of mutual respect and some acknowledged common characteristics and objectives, is possible among representatives of these and other socially heterogeneous groups. I have seen what I take to be examples of this relationship. I submit, however, that these examples are extremely rare and that the usual relationship has very little, if any, neighborly character. And if most group members are not neighbors of those in most other groups, how can the elected officials they vote for be neighbors or have the essential characteristics of neighbors?

It is most difficult to see this problem in the perspective of fifty years. I would guess that the group distinctions and divisions are less formidable today in some areas of city life and more numerous and finely drawn in others. In the phases of urban life and activity in which I have worked most during the last twenty years—urban planning, housing, and redevelopment—I find it hard to escape the conclusion that the trend is on the whole against or away from mutual understanding, respect, and trust across group and class lines. On the private or commercial side of city building, most real estate, mortgage lending, and building groups have made a fetish of homogeneous developments. Segregation of many kinds is the order of the day—not only by race and national origin, but more and more on the grounds of house ownership versus renting, by rental groups and sales prices of housing (which means, of course, by income status), by size of family, even more and more by age groups and veterans versus other civilians. All of this is supposed to contribute to human happiness, the stability of neighborhoods, and of property values. On the public front, zoning ordinances have had a major influence in the same direction. This influence seems to increase as the amendment and redrafting of ordinances add more and more finely drawn use districts. The common sense observation that slaughter houses and stamping mills should not be located next to dwellings or hospitals has been gradually extended to justify and support an increasing amount of segregation among various kinds of residential development. Even public housing officials, many of whose leaders are now in the forefront of local battles against racial segregation, feel compelled by the terms of their enabling acts, the sources of their financing, and the technical requirements of their developments to make their substantial contribution to segregation by income classes.

But one may well say: "Certainly this is a problem in American urban life. Without subscribing to all that you have said, we too feel concern. But is it essentially a problem in urban government? What can the city official or political scientist do about it except perhaps to urge that it be put high on the agenda of the educators, sociologists, social psychologists, and religious groups?"

As a partial answer, let me put forward a few questions: Why, in nearly every major city of the country, does the slate of a political party at a local election have to have such a neat balance of candidates from different racial, religious, and national origin groups—often at the cost of markedly weakening the slate as to experience and ability? Why does organized labor so often look askance at, or actually oppose, both the adoption and operation of city manager government? Why are the corrupt political machines (and I do not say they are all corrupt) able through their ward and precinct minions to win the more or less firm support of essentially decent folks who happen to be poor, economically insecure, and particularly vulnerable to the slings and arrows of modern industrial life? Why do members of these political machines look with apprehension at professional social workers, particularly those employed by official agencies in times of depression? Why are some leaders of organized minority groups willing to sacrifice substantial quantities of decent housing for their people rather than to approve its provision in established patterns? Why does the Chicago Housing Authority, an experienced agency in a city desperately in need of low-rent housing, have its program held up for months and months in a bitter wrangle over where it should build? Why do so many intelligent, well-educated, fine-spirited persons in the larger cities feel that the political life of their cities is practically closed to them as a career? Why is the outlook so dim for annexation or consolidation of municipal government in the senseless, inefficient hodge-podge that now exists in metropolitan areas? Why do so many of the more recently organized pressure groups operating on the local scene adopt, more or less without argument, about the same outlook as to their role and basically the same tactics as those made notorious by older groups?

Now clearly, none of these questions has a simple answer. If, however, one tried to answer them and to push his answers back as far as he could to human motives and cultural influences, I believe he would find at least one common element in all of them—too many of the socially heterogeneous groups in American cities simply do not understand, do not like, and do not trust too many of the others. Misunderstanding, distrust, and dislike feed upon one another. They also naturally and constantly divide people. They focus attention on conflicting interests (which do, of course, exist) and cover up the similarities and identities of interest (which, also, do exist). Members of the newer, less secure groups follow the precinct committeeman of the machine either because he genuinely likes and understands them or is clever enough to make them think he does. Their allegiance is kept, not only by the little services and favors that he does for them, but perhaps even more because he is about the only one they can see outside their own immediate group who shows signs of caring or trying to do anything for them. As individuals and groups rise in the economic and political power scales, their motto almost always seems to be: "Do unto others as they have been trying to do unto you."

I do not believe I am a sentimentalist about such matters. I do not subscribe to any fuzzy belief that the immediate, practical interests of all groups are the same. I do not deny that an important part of the functions of politicians and public administrators is to mediate among conflicting group claims and interests. Neither do I deny that for some people this process of mediation has an attraction so strong that it amounts almost to an addiction, and that to others it is an exciting object of observation and study. I cannot escape the conclusion, however, that in most American cities group and class lines are so tightly drawn that they are major obstacles to many of the potential values of urban living and a fruitful source of some of our toughest problems of policy and administration. My questions indicate some of them.

URBAN PLANNING

Here, indeed, is a subject, the condensing of which for the last half-century is a formidable task for anyone's powers. In tackling it, I certainly do not wish to make the job more difficult by enlarging the time period covered, but two pre-1900 facts do deserve mention.

First, as I have suggested before, in the early days of this country we had at least the start of a significant tradition of town and city building based on what can be fairly called, in light of the technological and social conditions of the time, planning. Many New England towns and small cities still show unmistakable evidences of this influence. In addition, such colonial towns as Philadelphia and Savannah during their early development were guided by clearly determined plans. Somewhat later, Detroit, Indianapolis, Salt Lake City, and other urban centers showed the same influences. When the city of Washington was decided upon, several of the nation's founding fathers, including notably Washington and Jefferson, took a very active interest in Major l'Enfant's plan for its physical pattern and development.

Of course, this planning was elementary in the light of today's needs and conditions. But if it had been allowed to evolve with the growth of our urban and metropolitan centers, it seems reasonable to believe that many of their most troublesome problems would today be much less difficult than they now are. In addition, this embryonic urban planning shared with the building practice of the day a tradition of reasonable space, dignity, and honest workmanship that, I regret to say, seems to have been more prevalent then than at any time since, including today. But these traditions were not allowed to continue. They were choked off by the onrush of the industrial revolution, the craze for land speculation that was one of the outstanding characteristics of our economy, and by the intellectual blight of laissez faire.

Almost the only exception of any consequence in this bleak picture of a century of city building was the start toward providing public parks, which may be dated from the beginning of Central Park in New York in 1853 and, somewhat later, the work of Charles Eliot and others in Boston. Here was a limited but definite example of land-use planning. Its rationale included a realistic concern over the evils of congestion and the human need for at least a modicum of space, quiet, and beauty in the physical environment. It is easy to underestimate the educational effect of this work on later phases of urban planning.

During the nineteenth century, there were, of course, other examples of government planning than these early efforts in urban land use, but to my knowledge, at least, no significant part of these others was urban in character or origin.

Coming now to the past fifty or sixty years, let me suggest for purposes of simplification and with due recognition of its dangers, six phases or periods in the evolution of urban planning: the city beautiful —from the 1890's to about the time of World War I; the city economic

—from about the end of World War I to the late 1920's; the growth of zoning—roughly from the early 1900's to about 1930; the period of debacle and disillusionment during most of the 1930's; the period of reconstruction from the late 1930's to the present; and early experiments with metropolitan regional planning. I shall mention just the highlights of these phases and at the end try to identify the major lines of evolution and growth in concepts and practice.

THE CITY BEAUTIFUL

The city beautiful era, beginning at the Chicago World's Fair of 1893, the revival of planning in Washington following the establishment of the McMillan Commission in 1900, early planning reports or reports for plans in San Francisco, St. Louis, Roanoke, Des Moines, New Haven, and Chicago, the last in 1909, perhaps can be fairly characterized in the words of Daniel H. Burnham, one if its chief prophets and evangelists. Its faith was largely in "noble, logical diagram [s]" that were not supposed to die. Its "watchword [was] order" and its "beacon, beauty."[8] Civic art was a common phrase. The emphasis was on civic centers, parks, parkways, waterfront uses and beautification, main thoroughfares and, quite often, transportation facilities.

To persons accustomed to think in terms of industrial relations and strife, the rural-urban conflict in state and national policy, or campaigns against municipal corruption and bossism—all live issues of the same day—Mr. Burnham and his colleagues must have seemed to be talking a different, strange language if not, in fact, moving in an entirely different world. But I would suggest that these early city planners, with all their limitations of philosophy and technique, were honestly trying to come to grips with other significant aspects of city life. And they were not blind to some of the interconnections between their realm and the urban body politic and social. For example, Messrs. Burnham and Bennett in their *Plan of Chicago* urged as one of the by-products of its recommendations that they would help to focus some of the interest and loyalty of citizens throughout Chicago on the city itself as a social and civic entity. They felt that one of Chicago's weaknesses at the time was that too many of its inhabitants identified

---

8. Although there seems to be no evidence on just when or where he made this statement, the well-known quotation attributed to Mr. Burnham is: "Make no little plans; they have no magic to stir men's blood and probably themselves will not be realized. Make big plans; aim high in hope and work, remembering that a noble, logical diagram once recorded will never die, but long after we are gone will be a living thing, asserting itself with ever-growing insistency. Remember that our sons and grandsons are going to do things that would stagger us. Let your watchword be order and your beacon beauty" (Charles Moore, *Daniel H. Burnham—Architect Planner of Cities*, Boston: Houghton Mifflin Co., 1921), II, 147.

themselves only with one section or neighborhood, and that these parochial interests were a divisive force in urban life and activity. Although they skirted or overlooked many of the problems of poor housing and substandard neighborhoods, they did point out that "Chicago has not yet reached the point where it will be necessary for the municipality to provide at its own expense, as does the city of London, for the housing of persons forced out of congested quarters [by the various public works and improvements recommended in the Plan]; but unless the matter shall be taken in hand at once, such a course will be required in common justice to men and women so degraded by long life in the slums that they have lost all power of caring for themselves."[9]

Despite such comments, however, the basic weaknesses of the work of Mr. Burnham and other planners of the period were well put in a statement by Richard T. Crane, a prominent industrialist and civic leader, shortly after the publication of the *Plan of Chicago:* "Do not misunderstand me, I have no quarrel with those who would make the city more beautiful than it is, but I would have all such schemes begin at the bottom. I would not put money into boulevards and statues, and fine bridges, and elaborate public buildings until the immediate surroundings of the poor are made better and decenter [*sic*]. I would start to build them from the bottom, not from the top. With a good foundation, there need be little worry as to what we rear from it."[10]

These early days also established two practices that, despite considerable criticism, have endured until the present day. After the original studies were made and the "plan" published, a city planning commission was usually set up. Typically, it consisted of citizens prominent in business, professional, and civic life—appointed by the mayor. It was a quasi-public body. Often in the early days a large part of its operating funds was contributed by business and civic groups; later, municipal appropriations took over most or all of the expenses. These commissions prided themselves on their relative separatism or independence from the hurly-burly of urban political life. They argued that in this position they were better able to consider the long-term growth and welfare of the community. Their advice and recommendations, therefore, would have more weight, so it was thought, than if they came from a municipal office or department. Also, Mr. Burnham and his associates were among the first of the professional city planning consultants— men or organizations whose primary function was to conduct surveys, to prepare maps, diagrams and sketches of municipal improvements, to

9. Daniel H. Burnham and Edward H. Bennett, *Plan of Chicago* (Chicago: The Commercial Club, 1909), p. 109.
10. Quoted in Wayne Andrews, *Battle for Chicago* (New York: Harcourt, Brace and Co., 1946), p. 162.

draft bills for recommended legislation, collect their fees,[11] and go on to the next job. This pattern of operation suffered a serious setback in the depression of the 1930's, and has never recovered its prior position. The limitations of this method of operation, however, account for many of the futilities and failures of orthodox urban planning.

During its early period, the Chicago Plan Commission gave much attention to public relations, publicity, and education. The plan had been made by Mr. Burnham and his associates. It had been approved by its business and civic sponsors and the City Council. It was now to be sold to the public at large. Under the Commission's first chairman, Charles H. Wacker, and its first secretary, Walter D. Moody, this campaign of publicity and education was carried on with resourcefulness, vigor, and persistence.[12] It included the well-known *Wacker's Manual of the Plan of Chicago,* which was used for years in Chicago schools as a civics textbook. In this respect at least, the Chicago Plan Commission was more farsighted than most of its contemporaries. Its activities of this kind paved the way and gave some background for much soul-searching and discussion in the later period of debacle and reconstruction.

THE CITY ECONOMIC OR THE CITY ON WHEELS

Broadly speaking, two factors accounted largely for the shift from the city beautiful to the city economic. The first was the fact that in too many cities, if the noble, logical diagrams did not in fact die, it began to become evident, as one sharp-tongued critic has said, that in and of themselves they had little power to stir anything besides men's blood. The second was the enormous increase during the 1920's in the production and use of the motor car.

This second phase, therefore, was the period of concern with traffic congestion, street widenings, superhighways, grade separations, and other capital public improvements designed to serve better the established business and residential districts, and to meet at least some of the needs for transit and other public services in the rapidly burgeoning new areas resulting from the building boom of the 1920's. Planning was argued for as good business. It maintained and created property values. It enlarged opportunities for private building and investment. It loosened the strangling hold of congestion on established districts. At least, so ran the argument and the creed.

11. Mr. Burnham, however, contributed his personal services in preparing the *Plan of Chicago.*

12. The most detailed account of this campaign—as well as one of its products—is a little known book—Walter D. Moody, *What of the City?* (Chicago: A. C. McClurg and Co., 1919).

ZONING

The growth, defense, and acceptance of urban zoning took place during, and in some respects was related to, the two phases of urban planning that I have just sketched. The rapid growth of cities in the early 1900's, their increasing diversity, the obvious shortcomings of the catch-as-catch-can type of development that had characterized them, all turned attention to some means of ameliorating the many weaknesses in city development. The chief way and means were found in an expansion of the concept of the police power of the state, which was granted for this purpose to municipal governments by charter provision or general enabling acts.

Most of the first zoning ordinances dealt only with the use of land. They restricted future development by districts according to various major types of use—residential uses of various kinds, commercial, industrial, with occasionally an unrestricted use area. Very shortly thereafter, zoning was applied to lot coverage and building height. This extension was due in no small part to the coming of iron and later steel frame buildings during the latter years of the nineteenth and the first few years of the twentieth century, and the concurrent development of high-speed elevators. These technical advances made possible a degree of land crowding much greater than anyone had imagined before their advent. In 1916, New York City passed the first comprehensive zoning ordinance—comprehensive in the sense that it covered all land in the five boroughs and applied to use, area, and height of buildings.

During the 1920's, zoning flourished mightily. Hundreds of cities adopted ordinances. A very substantial body of state and some federal court decisions gradually established its legal respectability. Its objective—to protect and advance the health, safety, and general welfare—was impeccable. Most of the high courts, although occasionally drawing the line on parts of regulations that seemed capricious or unreasonable, were on the whole quite ready to recognize the responsibility of municipal governments to control in this fashion private property rights in urban land.

Naturally enough, zoning ordinances and practice were uneven in quality from city to city. In general, the major weaknesses were (*a*) the overzoning of relatively high-income uses; (*b*) the failure to prohibit residential construction in commercial and industrial districts; (*c*) the fact that a large majority of the zoning ordinances were not based on any comprehensive land-use plan for the municipality; (*d*) in later years, too easy variations and exceptions by zoning boards of appeal; and (*e*) in metropolitan areas, the separatism and unrelatedness of ordinances applied to economically and socially interdependent but politically independent areas.

Of these weaknesses, perhaps the most serious was the preparation of zoning ordinances with no relation to a comprehensive land-use plan. In these circumstances, zoning became too often simply a protective device for certain types of established or prospective developments, but was not effective as a tool for the intelligent guidance of the future physical growth of the area. The seriousness of this weakness was shown by a survey of local planning and zoning activity made by the National Resources Committee in 1936. The Committee tabulated 1,322 urban zoning ordinances, but found only 933 official planning commissions and only 217 comprehensive plans as defined by the local planners. Significant also is the fact that this survey indicated that only eight cities had long-range, financial plans for carrying out the various public projects envisioned in the plan documents.[13]

It is not too much to say that in many circles and localities, popular and even official understanding of the relations of planning and zoning were confused or worse. This condition existed in the face of several excellent statements on this relationship made in the opinions of high courts. The drawing and enforcement of zoning ordinances were often looked upon as planning—if not as all of it, certainly as the most important part of it. Thus was added another concrete difficulty to seeing clearly the essential nature of urban planning. Again it was presented as primarily negative, restrictive, and prohibitory.

DEBACLE AND DISILLUSIONMENT

Not only did urban planning suffer a debacle in the early 1930's but the resulting disillusionment was also severe. As the depression reduced municipal revenues while adding to the need for urban services and activities, city planning and its agencies not only were found to be of little help but, even worse, they were quite generally looked upon as luxuries that could be sharply cut back or dispensed with altogether. Some exceptions might be noted to this generalization, but, by and large, it is a fair statement. The alleged strength of the quasi-independent citizen commission was found to be largely a myth. Clearly, city planning under part-time business and professional leaders aided by tiny staffs of engineers and concerned largely with public improvement projects and the regulation of private land use had provided, by and large, defective foresight and weak guidance for urban policy and development.

13. Robert Averill Walker, *The Planning Function in Urban Government* (Chicago: University of Chicago Press, 1941), p. 32.

Things looked no better as the depression deepened. It became apparent that urban land speculation, particularly the insane subdivision boom of the 1920's, had been a substantial factor in the economic collapse. Also it was seen that the growth of local government debt during the decade, which was about equal to the total reduction in federal government indebtedness, had left many cities with very thin margins of bonding power when they needed to borrow for public works or other forms of antidepression activity.

RECONSTRUCTION

But the validity of planning in American cities and the need for it were too great to allow the debacle to become a complete rout. By the mid-1930's, the scattered and shell-shocked forces were being reassembled for what may be fairly called a period of reform and reconstruction. As this era began, the National Resources Planning Board and its predecessors gave substantial aid and comfort through their support of state planning boards, directly through the Urbanism Committee, and in other ways. Reconstruction has been a complicated process, so let me simply list what seem to me to be the chief results in practice and ideas:

1. Many urban officials, planners, and other leaders have realized that what American cities must have is not "a plan" but planning—a continuing process of urban government in collaboration with its citizens, not the sporadic making of diagrams and maps.

2. This process calls for talents and skills of high quality and wide variety. Boosterism and the straight-line projection of curves of population increase are not substitutes for these abilities.

3. Planning implies objectives. What are they or what should they be? How can fine generalizations with which most citizens will agree be reduced to specific goals for the realization of which definite plans can be made? What part, if any, should planners play in this process of determining long-run objectives and shorter-term goals in accord with these objectives?

4. Planning in terms of ways and means and time priorities is just as much a part of the process as projecting physical improvements and the setting of interim goals. Capital improvement budgets are one device in this area.

5. Planning of decent quality cannot be done on the proverbial shoestring. Although the expenditures necessary for good planning are not large in comparison either with major municipal expenditures or with the capital value of the urban plant, their predepression range was hopelessly inadequate.

6. The place of planning in the structure of urban government is an unsolved problem of real importance. One view is that the old quasi-independent commission should be strengthened by giving it what amounts to a veto power on certain acts of the local legislative body. In other words, legislative actions in the form, say, of appropriations for specific public improvements or of amendments to the zoning ordinance would require a two-thirds or three-quarters vote if they contravene the recommendations of the planning commission. Others wish to give substantially the same powers to a full-time, paid commission. Still others argue for a planning office or department to perform a staff function for a strong municipal chief executive. Some suggest that this idea of planning as a staff function should be extended to the principal operating departments and that the heads of these departments should have some prominent position in the over-all planning unit.

7. Many observers and some officials believe that ways must be found to give the urban citizen, organized and as an individual, a more effective voice in planning. Public participation has become a catchword. To most who use it, it seems to mean that John Q. Citizen cannot be virtually ignored any longer. Usually it also means that his legitimate interests in planning are not adequately recognized by a publicity campaign to sell him specific activities or projects already decided upon by the experts. Beyond this, there are questions but very few, if any, answers. If planning is properly set up in the urban government, do the ballot box and the rest of the usual political process satisfy the right of public participation? If not, what other devices and machinery are needed? Better reporting? Formal advisory committees? Special machinery to enable neighborhoods or districts to make specific recommendations? What?

While the soul-searching and discussion go on, many cities have increased substantially their appropriations for planning, and a few are testing, in rather tentative fashion to be sure, some of the newer ideas. In this process of reconstruction, considerable impetus has come from loans and grants-in-aid by the federal government, first for PWA projects, then for public housing, airports, urban highways, and more recently for urban redevelopment. On the encouraging side also are an increasing number of state supreme court decisions on questions of public purpose raised by public housing and redevelopment programs. Some significance certainly should be given to the fact that the current postwar building boom, despite its many ominous characteristics, has not revived on any scale the kind of subdivision land speculation and land butchery that went on during the 1920's. Perhaps American urbanites are beginning to look upon their land units as a valuable resource and not as chips in a gambling game.

METROPOLITAN PLANNING

Although the evolution of city planning may seem on the whole clouded, confused, and not too encouraging, these adjectives apply with even greater force to the planning of metropolitan areas in this country. Here, however, the record is a much shorter one, and the experiments to date, although often timid and tentative, do show considerable inventiveness that seems to hold hope for the future. The early steps toward metropolitan planning may be illustrated by action in four localities during the 1920's.

Following an amendment to the Massachusetts constitution in 1918, the Metropolitan District Commission was established the following year to take over the functions of the three metropolitan-wide, *ad hoc* agencies mentioned earlier in this paper—those for sewage disposal, water supply, and parks. It is a state agency (a serious weakness) and consists of a commissioner and four associate commissioners appointed by the governor for five-year staggered terms. In 1923, the state legislature authorized it to set up a Division of Metropolitan Planning, which, among other things, was directed to confer with local planning agencies and to propose methods for financing projects to be undertaken. In 1941, however, the Division was abolished, and its responsibilities, staff, and materials were transferred to the State Planning Board.

After some months of discussion and exploration, the Committee on Regional Plan of New York and Its Environs began its monumental work in 1923. The Committee was composed of ten distinguished citizens of the area and was liberally financed by a private foundation. It produced a set of ten or twelve survey volumes and two thick volumes of plan recommendations. Many of the surveys and analyses by a staff under the direction of Thomas Adams, a distinguished British planner, set new standards for thoroughness of analysis and for comprehension of the complex forces and factors in metropolitan development. Following the end of the Committee's labors in the late 1920's, the Regional Plan Association of New York, Inc., was organized to follow up on the recommendations, to consult and advise with governmental bodies in the region, to make additional studies when necessary, to carry on an educational campaign, and in general to further the objectives and major recommendations of the Survey.

In 1923, the Chicago Regional Planning Association was organized, with the support of individuals, corporations, and governmental units, for a tri-state area outside the city of Chicago itself. Its survey work was limited and aimed at specific problems. It operated largely through a series of committees—on zoning, subdivision control, highways, recreation, etc. Most of these committees were made up largely of county and municipal officials in the area. Committee recommendation became effective only through the efforts of these official members or others in persuading their governmental bodies to take action in conformity with them. Although hard-hit by the depression, the Association has continued and is still at work.

In the Buffalo area, at the suggestion of Governor Alfred E. Smith the Niagara Frontier Planning Association was set up in 1924 and was supported by various individuals, industries, businesses and municipalities. In 1925, it succeeded in persuading the state legislature to authorize the creation of the Niagara Frontier Planning Board, composed of the mayors of six cities in Erie and Niagara Counties and six county supervisors, three from each of the counties. These twelve official members elected a private citizen as chairman. Its activities were financed by public funds supplied by the municipalities and counties. It is usually thought of as the first official metropolitan planning agency in the United States. After a promising start, however, it ran into difficulties and went out of existence in 1947.

After the dark days of the depression and particularly during and since the latter days of the war, metropolitan planning has revived somewhat. At present, some eighteen states have statutes that authorize some kind of metropolitan regional planning unit or operation. Citizen associations and quasi-public bodies have been established in several localities. In some of them, representatives of local governments play an active part, and in at least one have contributed financial support. Following in some respects the lead of Los Angeles County, which established a planning commission in 1927, county planning units have also been set up with various types of relations to municipal governments ranging from consultation to city contributions toward the expenses of the county planning operation. In 1949 a somewhat different approach was taken for the greater St. Louis metropolitan area. The Metropolitan Plan Association, Inc., of St. Louis successfully sponsored a Bi-State Development Agency for this Missouri-Illinois metropolitan area, which has been duly established in accordance with an interstate compact. The Agency has powers to construct, maintain, own, and operate bridges, tunnels, airports, and terminal facilities and to prepare for the consideration of local governments in the area plans affecting highways, streets, parkways, parking areas, terminals, water supply and sewage, recreation and conservation facilities, land use, etc.

What can we make out of this record of urban and metropolitan planning in America? Without in any way disparaging the work that has been done and the many admirable citizens who have developed the ideas, drafted and defended the laws, and manned the planning agencies as staff and board members, I find it hard to be sanguine about the results or the outlook. We have learned a lot. We have made some headway. But, in my opinion at least, we are running well behind the problems we are trying to cope with, and certainly behind the need for intelligent guidance and direction for the physical growth of our cities and for the public affairs of their citizens.

Keeping to generalities but trying to be a bit more specific, I think I see three major weaknesses in urban planning today.

1. Urban planning suffers from a general failure to realize the degree and range of government activity that is essential today for the best growth of urban areas and the welfare of all of their citizens. We easily mouth generalities about the tremendous complexity and the growing interdependencies of modern urban life. As individuals and families, we plan. Our civic and voluntary welfare associations and organizations plan. Our industries and businesses plan, both as separate operating units and through trade associations and committees of many kinds. We say we admire forsight and long-headedness. Most of us would admit the intellectual case for believing that urban government, as the most inclusive association of human beings in urban areas, must also plan—and act in accordance with the planning. Yet we have allowed a vague, traditional, largely unanalyzed distrust of government, the influence of some narrow and selfish interest groups, and the divisive forces in the urban body politic to keep urban governments not only from effective planning but even to keep them so split up that their planning could be only piecemeal and ineffective at best, even if all the other obstacles to rational performance were removed.

2. We have not yet arrived at a solid and defensible concept of planning as a function of urban government. Apparently we do not understand that planning is not fact-finding, research, consultation, map drawing, report writing, public relations, or education—or even a combination of some or all of these admirable activities. To be sure, each of them has its place in the planning process. All of them, however, should contribute to specific recommendations as to policy and procedure made directly to a governmental unit or units with powers commensurate with the planning recommendations and reasonably related to the needs of the body urban and politic. This is no one-shot operation, but a continuing process. Of course, the plans do not have to be adopted as proposed. Elected officials and those directly responsible to them in administrative positions should make the decisions. And these decisions, often rejecting or modifying the planning recommendations, will in turn call for more planning.

In this connection, it also seems to me that our concept of planning lags well behind the present-day powers of urban governments, limited and inadequate as these may be in some respects. In other words, our present battery of urban government powers could be made, individually and collectively, much more effective tools of human welfare if we would only plan their use more intelligently and vigorously. (Examples of these possibilities in urban redevelopment, a relatively new and embryonic activity, are outlined in three of the URS reports: "Eminent Domain in Acquiring Subdivision and Open Land" by Mr. Robbins and Mrs. Yankauer, "Urban Redevelopment Short of Clearance" by William L. Slayton, and "Measuring the Quality of Housing in Planning for Urban Redevelopment" by Allan A. Twichell.) During the past half-century, we have added substantially to the range and scope of local governmental powers. Undoubtedly in the future we shall add further to them, but today we are inclined to underestimate what could be done with and through them as they now stand or with only administrative or minor substantive changes.

3. Both our conception and practice of urban planning have lacked perspective and long-range objectives. Relatively we have spent too much time planning to correct evils that have overtaken us, to remove the unfortunate results of past policies, and to adjust differences and divergencies. Much of this, of course, has been necessary and useful, and I would not for a moment belittle it. But it seems to me no substitute for the formulation of long-term and interim objectives for our community life and affairs, for concern with the over-all pattern, density, and structure of our urban physical plant, for careful but realistic reshaping of our governmental institutions and machinery, and for anticipating future problems and difficulties and taking steps to cope with them before they are upon us in full force.

One common illustration of this distinction may make the point clearer. Planning staffs in many large cities in this country are now working on proposals for enlarged major highway systems. In some of these same cities the planners are readying redevelopment projects to clean out the messy, blighted development at the edges of major industrial areas so that important plants may expand economically without moving out of their present locations. These are examples of planning to correct evils, to improve conditions that have come partly from weak foresight or poor (or no) planning in times past. But in how many metropolitan areas have planners made even a good start toward planning for a really improved distribution of industrial areas that would include, among other things, (a) adequate space for one-story buildings, for future plant expansion, employee parking, and materials storage; (b) an over-all reduction in the journey-to-work with a consequent decrease in one factor in traffic loads; (c) opportunities for industries that prefer either centrally located or outlying sites to exercise a real choice; (*d*) the considerable protection that some plant dispersal could give against the terrible destructiveness of atomic bombing; and (*e*) quiet, clean, pleasant, and convenient residential areas available to and within the means of workers in both new and older industrial areas. Planning of this kind would meet at least some of the requirements that I have just suggested. It would be difficult; it would cost money; it would take time, study, and patience. Until possibilities of this kind are both seen and seized by planning agencies, the general observation at the beginning of this section seems to me entirely justified.

LOCAL GOVERNMENT FINANCE

The descriptive part of this section has to be short. For this there are two reasons. First, I shall have to spend some time on the controversial questions of debt policy and of how local governments can best strengthen the weaknesses that are becoming more and more apparent in their revenue systems. Second, the subject is so very complex that one is almost forced to content himself with what he thinks are a few major peaks in the mountain range, or to undertake the very substantial task of surveying the whole range and its environs. The latter is clearly out of the question here.

LOCAL GOVERNMENT REVENUES IN THE NATIONAL ECONOMY

Despite the substantial increase in the urban population from 1900 to the late 1940's and the notable increase in the number and variety of urban services taken on during this period, urban government revenues as a percentage of gross national product were substantially the same at the beginning and at the end of this period. I would guess that of the facts in this essay this one would be the most likely to startle many persons. Basically, of course, the trouble is that we have seen so many figures on gross government receipts or expenditures—usually set in a framework designed to alarm the taxpayer—that we simply do not realize how much of the increase over the years is due to changes in the value of the dollar, let alone being able to relate the government figures to the national totals in which, of course, they are a contributing factor and out of which, as expense items, they are paid.

It is true, of course, that the data on local government revenues leave much to be desired. Similarly, the estimates of gross national product, even for recent years, are subject to a substantial margin of error, and those for the early years of the century are very crude indeed. Even so, I put them forward not for finely drawn comparisons, but simply as very rough indications of proportion. In 1902, the total receipts of local governments other than counties was 3.4 per cent of the estimated gross national product. In 1942, the corresponding figure was 3.3 per cent; and in 1948, 3.2 per cent. Local governments other than counties include city corporations, school districts, townships, and special districts.[14]

Maybe the American urbanite has been getting a better deal from his local government in recent years than the shrill cries from taxpayers' associations and others would have led him to believe. And this suggestion certainly does not imply that local governments are as efficient agencies for public service as they should be or that specific improvements in their structure and operation are not very much in order.

SOURCES OF REVENUE

As to sources of revenue, the chief changes over our period have been a decline in the proportion from property taxes, and notable increases in financial aid received from other governments and, in recent years, in receipts from other taxes than those on property. Here I have used the usual four-way breakdown of local revenues—property taxes, other taxes, aid received from other governments, and charges and miscellaneous. According to the Bureau of the Census, in 1902 local governments other than counties received 74.2 per cent of their total revenues from property taxes. In 1942, the corresponding figure was 62.7 per cent and in 1948 it was 54.5 per cent. Other taxes—in 1902, 9.9 per cent; in 1942, 5.5 per cent; in 1948, 8.2 per cent. Aid from other governments—in 1902, 6.5 per cent; in 1942, 23.2 per cent; in 1948, 27.4 per cent. Charges and miscellaneous—in 1902, 9.4 per cent; in 1942, 8.6 per cent; in 1948, 9.9 per cent.[15] For city corporations only serving municipalities of 100,000 and over, the 1947 breakdown was: property taxes—55.7 per cent; other taxes—14.7 per cent; aid from other governments—19.9 per cent; charges and miscellaneous—9.7 per cent.

14. Gross national product in 1902 was approximately $41.2 billion in 1929 dollars— The Committee on National Debt Policy, *Our National Debt* (New York: Harcourt, Brace and Co., 1949), Table 11, p. 170, based on Simon Kuznets' *National Product Since 1869* (National Bureau of Economic Research, 1946). This was changed into 1902 dollars by applying the Snyder-Tucker general price index given in *Historical Statistics of the United States—1789-1945* (Bureau of the Census, 1949), p. 231. GNP for 1942 and 1948 in *Survey of Current Business* (July 1949), p. 11. Local government revenue figures for 1902 and 1942 in *Historical Review of State and Local Government Finances* (Washington, D.C.: Bureau of the Census, June, 1948), p. 16; for 1948 in *Governmental Revenue in 1948* (Bureau of the Census, August, 1949), p. 7. Probably figures for local government expenditures would have been better than those for revenues but aggregate expenditure figures were not available for 1902 or any other year near 1900. The difference between revenues and expenditures, however, would be proportionably small and would not alter materially the rough percentage comparison.

15. For 1902 and 1942, *Historical Review of State and Local Government Finances* (Washington, D.C.: Bureau of the Census, June, 1948) p. 16. For 1948, *Governmental Revenue in 1948* (Washington, D.C.: Bureau of the Census, August, 1949) Table 4, p. 9.

From 1940 to 1947, the percentage of revenue from other taxes went up from 10.1 to 14.7.[16]

GENERAL CHARACTER OF LOCAL TAXES

Nearly all taxes available to local governments are more or less regressive—some of them badly so. From most points of view, regressiveness is a bad quality in taxes regardless of what type of government collects them. It seems to me an especially unfortunate characteristic of local taxes. Even of those local taxes that are not technically regressive, the incidence of many bears little or no relation to ability to pay.

FISCAL WEAKNESS OF LOCAL GOVERNMENT

Of all three of the so-called levels of government, local government is in the weakest fiscal position both because federal and state governments have pre-empted several of the best revenue-producers and also because a city's limited geographical area makes escape from many taxes relatively easy. This fact is so generally accepted that I need not elaborate on it here. Just one comment may illustrate it: All taxes, with the exception of some inheritance and gift levies, should be paid out of income, and nearly all of them are. A good tax system, therefore, is one that fairly and effectively taps the flow of income to the persons of a locality or area. Since World War II, both the money and real incomes of the American people have been higher than ever before in peacetime. Despite these facts, since World War II most American cities, from the fabulous concentration of wealth and income that is New York City to small towns in the Middle West dependent largely on services and trade with now-prosperous farming communities, have had serious difficulties raising the necessary funds for established functions and activities—let alone for improving their quality or adding others. If it were not so serious, it would be ludicrous.

Of course it is true that generalizations like those I have just given on local government revenues are always oversimplifications and, therefore, are to be used only with certain cautions. The revenue positions and problems of American cities vary materially with such factors as population size and rate of growth, economic base and the distribution of wealth and income, standards of services, position in or outside of a metropolitan area, and the amount and character of state aids and controls. By no means are all cities in the same position as to inadequacy of revenues or the unsatisfactoriness of their major sources of revenue. It follows, therefore, that programs for improving the revenue position of specific cities must take into account many more detailed facts and

16. William Anderson and Edward W. Weidner, *American City Government* (New York: Henry Holt and Co., rev. ed., 1950), p. 575.

trends for the cities being considered than it is possible to give here. Nevertheless, the broad over-all picture is quite clear and the generalizations above seem to me defensible for the purposes of a rapid review.

LOCAL GOVERNMENT DEBT

In municipal indebtedness and debt management the current position is only a little less confused and unsatisfactory than that in local government revenues.

In 1902 local governments (including counties) had $1.9 billion dollars of long-term debt outstanding. Over the next three decades the dollar volume of local debts approximately doubled in each decade. The approximate amounts were: 1912—$4.1 billion; 1922—$9.1 billion; 1932—$16.7 billion. The large increase in the 1920's was due largely to public works in support of the building and subdivision booms referred to before. During the early 1930's serious difficulties in municipal finance, including numerous defaults and high interest rates, put the brakes on borrowing. Although defaults were dealt with quite successfully on the whole during the latter years of the decade, and partly as a result, interest rates went down and refunding was quite common, the aggregate volume of local indebtedness remained almost stationary—in 1942 it was $16.5 billion. During the years of the all-out war economy, local capital improvements were at a low volume, tax collections were good, interest rates continued to decline. Also, of course, a very substantial volume of deferred replacements and extensions of public facilities was built up. In 1946, gross local debts were down to $13.5 billion. During the first two postwar years, shortages of materials, rising costs of construction and uncertainties as to their future course held back public improvements. In 1948 and 1949, however, the backlog pressures, some leveling off of construction costs and the growing opinion that no substantial drop in them was likely in the near future led to record amounts of local borrowing. In 1949, outstanding indebtedness stood at $16.8 billion—just fractionally above its level in 1932.[17]

In this rapid sketch of local government indebtedness three other sets of facts are worth noting.

Local government indebtedness has declined spectacularly in relative size during the past half-century. The less than $2 billion of such debt in 1902 was approximately 57 per cent of total public debt outstanding at that time. The 1912 volume of $4 billion was almost 72 per cent of

17. *Governmental Debt in the United States: 1946* (Washington, D.C.: Bureau of the Census, June, 1947), p. 6, and *Governmental Debt in 1949* (Washington, D.C.: Bureau of the Census, 1949), p. 6.

the total. By contrast the $16.5 billion of local government debt in 1942 was about 18 per cent of the total and the substantially equal amount in 1949 was a little over 6 per cent of the total.[18]

In recent years enterprise debt (debt incurred to finance the production of services and goods normally sold to the public, e.g., water, gas, transit, housing) as distinguished from general governmental debt has become increasingly significant. In 1949, slightly more than 41 per cent of outstanding local government indebtedness as estimated by the Bureau of the Census was enterprise debt. Of aggregate enterprise debt almost one-third had been incurred by special districts of one kind or another and about two-thirds by municipalities.[19]

Over the last twenty years in particular the significance of interest rates on local debts as they affect the taxpayer and citizen-customer of public enterprises has been well illustrated. For some years before and during the 1920's prevailing interest rates on good local government bonds ranged from 4 per cent to 4.5 per cent. In 1932 they were well above 4.5 per cent and during 1933 they reached the modern high of 5.7 per cent with a year-round average of slightly more than 5.5 per cent. In 1934 they averaged less than 4 per cent and a strong downward trend for more than a decade reached an all-time low of 1.3 per cent in February, 1946. Since then a moderate adjustment upward brought the index in 1949 to a narrow range between 2.1 and 2.2 per cent.[20]

These figures, of course, are for bond yields—not coupon rates on outstanding bonds. The changes in interest paid, therefore, will be relatively less than changes in the rates of yield, themselves, and will lag somewhat behind changes in rates. Let me give only one example of the effect of lower interest rates on interest payments: the total long-term indebtedness of local governments in 1948 was only about 10 per cent less than in 1932 but the annual interest payments in 1948 were 37 per cent less than in 1932.[21]

So much for the elementary facts about local government indebtedness during the last fifty years. Perhaps the statistical picture for 1950 does not seem too dark. Local debt is substantially lower in proportion to urban population than it was in 1932 and as a percentage of esti-

18. *Ibid.* (1946), p. 6; *ibid.* (1949), p. 5.
19. *Ibid.* (1949), p. 7.
20. C. C. Ludwig, "Bond Issues Now for Post-War Projects," *Municipal Finance* (November, 1944), p. 13; Carl H. Chatters, *Municipal Finance from 1930 to 1950* (MS of statement prepared for U.S. Senate Committee on Expenditures in the Executive Departments, December 31, 1947), p. 15; Miner E. Phillipps, "Finance Administration," *The Municipal Year Book* (1950) (Chicago: International City Managers Association, 1950), p. 183. The basic data are from The Bond Buyer's index of yields on municipal bonds.
21. *Governmental Debt in 1949,* pp. 5 and 9.

mated national income it declined from 40 to 7.6 from 1932 to 1946.[22] Defaults have been cleared up quite satisfactorily. Lower interest rates have cut the aggregate of interest payments very substantially. High aggregate savings, particularly in the upper income brackets, and national fiscal and tax policies have been definitely favorable to municipal bonds. Why isn't the outlook fairly bright?

Of course it might be much worse but several large, dark clouds even now throw shadows over much of the scene. Here I can only call attention to three of them.

1. First, considerable evidence is at hand to show that the present and probable future requirements of local governments for capital funds are much greater than is generally appreciated even by many local officials. The backlog of major repairs and extensions of the existing public plant or facilities plus replacements deferred during the 1930's and 1940's plus new facilities needed to correct admittedly substandard conditions and to take care of future urban population growth together make up a formidable total. Not all of these capital outlays will require borrowing but in light of the current crisis in local revenues it is safe to say that a considerable proportion of them will.[23] The problems of carrying out these needed capital investments, however conservatively they may be estimated, are aggravated by the very high construction costs that seem likely to hold for the next few years at least, the overriding demands of rearmament and foreign aid with their enormous requirements for manpower and materials, and the continuing diffusion of population in nearly all metropolitan areas.

Can we arrive at any rough estimate of what these capital requirements might amount to? My attempt is not very satisfactory but perhaps it will give some notion of the order of their magnitude.

The most thorough and inclusive estimates of over-all capital requirements for the nation are found in *America's Capital Requirements —Estimates for 1946–1960* by Robert W. Hartley *et al.*[24] For our purposes this work is not too usable because the estimates are by major economic activities or functions and do not separate out, for most of the

22. *Historical Review of State and Local Government Finances,* p. 18. Slightly different percentages are given in *Governmental Debt in the United States: 1946,* p. 7. The differences probably are due to revision of the national income figures.

23. Preliminary figures for 1949 show that for 397 cities with populations of 25,000 and over, general borrowings were 70.0 per cent of capital outlays. For 1948 the proportion was 96.8 per cent. General borrowings exclude those for funding or refunding of existing debt but do include any net addition to short-term debt. For these years the latter item undoubtedly is small. From *Summary of City Government Finances in 1949* (Bureau of the Census, October, 1950) p. 4.

24. Robert W. Hartley, with the collaboration of Eleanor Wolkind and assisted by Maynard Hufschmidt and Sidney Jaffe, *America's Capital Requirements—Estimates for 1946–1960* (New York: The Twentieth Century Fund, 1950).

categories, public from private investment or break down public investment by local, state, and federal units. One major class used, however, is "urban development," which includes (1) nonfarm housing, (2) public water-supply systems, (3) public sewerage systems, (4) hospitals and health facilities, (5) educational facilities, (6) urban recreational facilities, and (7) public buildings. For each of these subclasses is an estimate of average annual capital requirements at 1940 prices for the period 1946–60. Land acquisition costs are not included. Neither are repairs of plant or facilities. Hartley does assume that all deferred replacements and extensions will be made up by 1960.

Nonfarm housing, of course, will be largely privately owned and financed. For Hartley's much larger total for this item I have substituted $945 million for public housing. This is based on the average annual volume of 135,000 units for which federal aid was authorized over a six-year period by the Housing Act of 1949. For public water, sewerage, and urban recreational facilities, I have used Hartley's figures without change. (For recreational facilities he does make a public-private breakdown.) His estimates for hospitals and schools unfortunately include rural needs. I have assumed that 50 per cent of these estimates would be a fair guess for urban, public investment for these purposes. Undoubtedly a large proportion—possibly 80 per cent—would be made by local governments of all kinds. For public buildings I have also made an outright guess—50 per cent of Hartley's figure for urban localities and 60 per cent for all local governments. Finally, I have assumed that construction costs in the early 1950's would average 100 per cent above 1940 levels.

With these changes the estimates for *annual* capital requirements for these seven subclasses of "urban development" are $4.4 billion for urban governments and $5.6 billion for all local governments. And these figures do not include any Hartley estimates or guesses of mine for streets and highways, waterfront development, civilian airports, transit systems or municipally owned utilities. In 1949 actual outlays for highway construction were 30.4 per cent of total capital outlays in cities of 25,000 and over; in 1948 the percentage was 32.9.[25] Allowances for these facilities and for land costs certainly would produce grand totals alarmingly high in the perspective of past capital investment by local governments and the outstanding local government debt of some $17 billion. These unspecified totals would also dwarf the approximate $2.9 billion of municipal bonds sold in 1948 and again in 1949—and these latter figures include refundings.

But even this is not all of the story. Most of the larger American cities, as indicated in the section on metropolitanism, have been suffer-

25. *Op. cit.*, footnote 23, p. 4.

ing from a chronic inability to replace their obsolete physical facilities for housing, commerce, and industry. To be sure, some replacement does take place in the normal course of events but it is so small in proportion to accumulating obsolescence that the areas of blight and deterioration continue to grow from year to year. This is a complex process clearly tied in with many of the weaknesses and problems of present-day urban life. Here the significant point is that high land prices, including prices on the "improvements," are one of the chief obstacles to redevelopment. The process of blight has now gone so far, however, and land prices are so inflexible that many cities are now making starts on the job of buying these areas of built-up blight, clearing them, if necessary laying them out anew, and selling or leasing the land for private (or public) reuse at prices sufficiently low to encourage new building of desirable character and density. Title I of the Housing Act of 1949 provides loan and grant aid for this process.

It is too soon to estimate the probable capital requirements for this activity or how rapidly it will go ahead. The federal statute simply enables a start to be made under one possible form of financing. Under it, federal loans are available for the land acquisition and the federal agency takes most of the loss from the high land prices. Much of the requirement for partial local matching of capital grants from the federal government may be met by public improvements in or near the area of redevelopment—improvements that would be included in other estimates of deferred replacements or correction of substandard conditions. Thus the additional capital needed for this program will not be quite as great as it might seem at first and the funds for acquisition, under the formula, are available from the federal government. Nevertheless, the job to be done is tremendously large and the capital obligations it will call for seem certain to be very substantial.

Perhaps some of this discussion seems to wander somewhat from the central subject of this subsection. Quite possibly some of it might better have been taken up in other contexts, e.g., under planning or in connection with municipal revenues. Quite surely the estimates and estimates from estimates are based on certain judgments as to standards for municipal facilities and services that cannot be explained here. The central point, however, is simply that the potential capital requirements of the near future for local governments, and particularly for urban governments, are on a scale quite different from that to which local officials and their agencies have been accustomed. Deferring a substantial volume of capital outlays for a decade or more—much longer, as a matter of fact, in urban redevelopment and some of the accepted local services—increases markedly the job load when the arrearages have to be caught up. When the serious problems thus created are aggravated by a more than 100 per cent increase in construction costs and by continued urbanization of the economy, the results are truly formidable.

Finally, I would point out that ignoring or belittling these capital needs will not solve the problems they present; it will simply shift them somewhat to other geographic areas. In other words, continued and aggravated inadequacies in municipal services and facilities seem certain to speed up the hit-or-miss, unplanned dispersal of urban populations, which, in turn, will create still more problems for developed areas and will produce demands for additional capital outlays in the newer areas to which urban population will flow in increasing volume.

2. Next, it seems worthwhile to note an old but often neglected issue in local financial policy: How can capital outlays of local government, particularly those that are financed by loans, be carried out so that they lessen rather than aggravate the major swings in the general business cycle? Despite the great improvements in the fiscal position of urban governments over the last ten or twelve years, the substantial increase in understanding of local fiscal policies, and improvements in fiscal management, I doubt that there is any more consensus on the answer to this question today than there was ten years ago among local finance officers, general administrative officials, or students of local finance.

Probably the question itself needs little elaboration or explanation. Both the observations and experience of practical men and the forms of analysis developed by Keynesian economists in recent years indicate that changes in the rate of capital investments or outlays have substantial effects upon the general level of business activity and employment. From this fairly well-established generalization it follows that those responsible for the volume and rate of capital investment, both private and public, can do much—no one can be sure just how much— toward stabilizing the volume of economic activity over the years. Clearly this question of fiscal and public policy is a significant one for all thoughtful and responsible citizens. For public officials who lived through the Great Depression of the 1930's or who can appreciate its heavy blows against the public welfare and the programs of their agencies, it is a particularly important matter.

No one can deny that the history of local finance and debts shows that these sectors of our economy have contributed to economic instability. The splurge of local capital improvements during the 1920's, which was mentioned in the section on urban planning, and the rapid decline in these outlays in the early stages of the depression are only a more recent and perhaps somewhat more extreme example of an unfortunate pattern that could be traced back over a considerable period of time.

But can we do better in the future? If so, what is to be this improved pattern of local capital outlays and how is it to be realized in practice? I think I see four or five types of current attitudes toward the question. Perhaps each of them deserves brief mention.

One attitude that indicates a shortsighted answer to these questions seems rather common in many circles today. Possibly it follows largely from the fact that the basic question has usually been put in the form: What can a better distribution of capital investment do to lessen the major downswings in economic activity? Naturally this was the formulation of the problem in the 1930's when it came in for major discussion. Now in an economy of full employment and high production, this older form of the issue seems to some people obsolete and irrelevant. Consequently, but not very logically, an attitude of relative indifference, or maybe apathy, has developed. Although this is understandable, it does not seem too unlike the legendary farmer's leaky roof—when it rained he couldn't fix it, and when it didn't rain—he didn't have to.

A related but different answer is that, as a result of changes in our economy during the last ten or fifteen years, capital outlays of local public agencies have decreased so much in *relative* volume that they are hardly worth bothering about in this relationship. When the total gross debt of local governments is only about 5 per cent of total public debt outstanding and, of course, a still smaller proportion of aggregate long-term debts, public and private, and when a record borrowing by local governments is less than $3 billion in a $250–$300 billion economy, the timing of capital outlays financed either by borrowing or out of current revenues cannot make too much difference in the economic health of the nation. In rejoinder two types of replies can be made. As I tried to indicate roughly in the preceding subsection, the future capital requirements of local government seem quite certain to be on an entirely different scale than in the past. As long as the levels of federal spending for military and foreign aid continue, let alone increase, local capital financing will not be a major influence in our economy, but it will be substantially larger than current statistics might indicate. Again, in our form of economy, no one class or kind of capital outlay normally amounts to very much in proportion to national totals of capital financing or national income. Certainly, however, this does not excuse those who are responsible for the unit expenditures that make up the total from doing their part as intelligently and conscientiously as possible.

Another view is that the federal government now has so much influence on the economy, through its own enormous operations and its various forms of stimulation and control of private enterprise, that it is in a position to avoid future downswings of disastrous proportions in employment and business activity. Some of its influence, of course, would be through its aid programs to state and local governments. The conclusion from this line of argument is that local governments ought to be prepared to respond as well as they may be able to federal fiscal policy, but that beyond this there is relatively little for them to do. This, however, seems to me to be a questionable conclusion from an argument based on an assumption that is very questionable. Compared with its economic powers twenty years ago, the federal government certainly is in a much stronger position. Its own peacetime operations, however, are still a minor part of the total economy, and many of its devices of control and inducement seem rather less effective to those who know the most about them than they do to the less well informed. Also, the major part of local capital financing is technically independent of federal control or else is influenced only in part by federal policy. Certainly until federal economic powers are much more thoroughly tested this line of argument would seem to be both false and dangerous.

The last general answer I shall mention has been implied in my comments on the others. It is simply that local government borrowing and capital outlays ought to be planned so that their economic effects are anticyclical. In other words, the volume of such outlays should be held back when general economic conditions are good and increased when recession sets in. Now, clearly, local debt and improvement policies cannot be determined entirely by any one rule. Other considerations, for example, at present the substantial backlog of deferred replacements and new public improvements, have to be taken into account.

Without going far into the mechanics of fiscal management, a few steps essential to the successful application of an anticyclical policy may be noted. As suggested before, the urban planning process should recognize its high responsibility for time priorities through such devices as capital budgets. More rational organization of local government units, particularly in metropolitan areas, would facilitate the job of assigning reasonable priorities to the wide range of local public improvements. As long as general governmental responsibility is split up among dozens or scores of municipalities, and special districts with limited objectives control a substantial portion of public investment, effective planning of capital improvement is all but impossible. Much more serious attention should be given to both local and state reserves for later capital outlays. Constitutional and statutory limits on local indebtedness have long needed drastic revision. State advice and control of local debt policies should recognize the objective of anti-depression influence. Finally, the local officials primarily responsible for planning and municipal finance ought to have the ability and training to weigh this objective wisely in comparison with other needs and requirements.

3. The last aspect of municipal indebtedness to be mentioned here is debt limits imposed by state law.

Every state in the union limits local debt by constitutional or statutory provision. In forty-six of the states there are general debt limitations of one kind or another; in Delaware and Maryland special local laws are relied upon for the same result. Practically all of the general debt limits are in the form of specified percentages of assessed valuation of property within the area of the local government. These percentages range from a low of one-fifth of 1 per cent to 40 per cent. In thirty of the states, however, the percentage is 10 per cent or less. Exemptions of debts incurred for specified purposes are common.[26]

Of the origin and development of these limits only a few elementary facts can be given here. Most of the limits were first imposed in a period from about 1850 to approximately 1885. They were companion controls to prohibitions against municipal guaranty of private borrowing and local government purchase of securities in private companies. The aim of all three classes of controls was to curb the reckless use of local credit in rapidly expanding and overly optimistic urban centers. Before and during the earlier part of this period, local governments not only increased their indebtedness rapidly for local public facilties and improvements, but also gave guaranties to private enterprises, notably railroads, which could thus be induced to locate in or to extend their services to the locality. When many of these private corporations got into trouble and when it became apparent that the whole operation was making for widespread waste and corruption, all three of these forms of state controls were set·up. States that were organized later generally copied these limitations in attempts to avoid the sorry results that had led to them in the older states.[27]

Although the constitutional and general statutory limits on local indebtedness soon showed serious weaknesses and inequities, a number of influences have kept them in operation with only minor modifications to the present time. One of these influences is the naïve and undiscriminating attitude that led one governor of New York to say in 1879 ". . . that debt, both public and private, are [sic] an unmitigated evil. . . ."[28] Another factor has been the inclination, now fortunately rarer than in times past, for untrained and shortsighted local officials

26. Committee on State-Local Relations, Council of State Governments, *State-Local Relations* (Chicago: The Council, 1946), pp. 116–17.

27. Horace Secrist, *An Economic Analysis of the Constitutional Restrictions upon Public Indebtedness in the United States* (Bulletin of the University of Wisconsin No. 637, Madison, 1914), Part II.

28. *Ibid.,* p. 63.

to borrow to cover up deficits in operating accounts and to provide funds for replacements and minor extensions of public facilities that under any reasonably prudent policy should be financed from current revenues. This has led to the so-called pay-as-you-go principle, which has become a fetish in some circles, and in its extreme form is quite as indefensible as indiscriminate borrowing. Undoubtedly also the maintenance of rigid debt limits in their customary forms despite clearly demonstrated weaknesses and evasions has been due in no small part to pressure from some organized business and civic groups that have had little or no sympathy with the expanding service and welfare activities of local government and to which economy seems usually to mean simply holding down public expenditures and investments. In many rather common circumstances the influence of these groups has often been salutary, but it also has helped prevent an intelligent understanding of the proper role of borrowing in the fiscal policies of expanding urban localities. It also has helped prevent both changes in the form of debt limitations and improvements in the revenue side of local finance that might otherwise have been made.

The weaknesses of debt limits as a percentage of assessed valuation are not hard to discover. With the relative decline in the general property tax as a source of local revenue the limits have come to bear less and less relation to the capacity of local governments to service and retire their debts. Variations in assessment are so common and so wide that the limits bear unevenly on local governments within many states. Ordinarily the limitations take little account of overlapping municipal corporations. This makes not only for weakness in the intended control, but also encourages the creation of special districts and *ad hoc* public bodies. This development in turn is clearly one of the major evils of our present system of local government and one of the greatest obstacles to intelligent fiscal planning, policy, and management. Percentage limits also tend to encourage public borrowing in times of economic prosperity when assessed valuations are increasing and conversely to hold it back when it is most needed in times of recession and depression. Someone has said that they make local borrowing "perversely elastic." Again, they put up no warning flags or in any way make borrowing more difficult until the limit is reached. Finally, the cumulative effect of these and secondary weaknesses has been to encourage exceptions and exemptions both in constitutional and statutory provisions that have gradually whittled away the effectiveness of the controls themselves without contributing to the formulation of a more rational and effective policy.

At least two substitute plans for debt limitation seem to deserve mention here.

One proposal would set the limit in terms of the effective market rate at which the bonds of a local government could be sold. The basic principle is clearly to shift the control from imposed percentages of valuations to the operations of the investment market. Although this suggestion would seem to deserve consideration, some questions might be raised about it. (Any plan, to be sure, will have some doubtful or weak points. The question is how serious the weaknesses are and how they compare on balance with those of other possible arrangements.) On this particular proposal one certainly could question whether the history of investment markets shows that they have been or are now sufficiently discriminating to be the main reliance for a plan of local debt limitation. Would not the market forces tend to encourage over-borrowing in times of prosperity and high savings among the economic groups that make up the chief market for municipals and, conversely, to make such borrowing very difficult under other economic conditions? In periods of economic change and uncertainty the specified market limit would have to be changed. If this were not done, the whole plan might become ineffective. If it were done too frequently, it would open the door for what would amount to more or less arbitrary control of municipal borrowing by state legislatures—many of them, as is well known, not too sympathetic to urban needs and requirements.

A more common and, in my opinion, more promising suggestion would base the limit of a local government's borrowing on the proportion that interest and other debt service bore to its revenues. This would have the obvious merit of relating debt burden to general fiscal capacity. The revenue figure should be not that of any one year, but a moving average over a period of years. This would prevent a sharp curtailment of borrowing capacity at the outset of a depression that might temporarily reduce local revenues sharply. The suggestion also usually exempts certain forms of revenue from the total against which debt service would be calculated. Nonrecurring grants from state or federal governments for particular purposes and most or all revolving fund income from public enterprises would be excluded under a reasonable interpretation of the principle of this method.

A supplementary proposal is that in addition to an upper limit on local borrowing, one or two intermediate limits might also be set. Borrowing beyond the intermediate limit would be possible only if additional steps were taken. These steps, for example, might be an extraordinary majority in the local legislative body, a referendum on the bond issues that would run debt service beyond the intermediate percentage, or the approval of a state tax body.

A plan of this kind would present a number of difficult decisions at critical points and these decisions might well have to be modified in the light of subsequent experience. On the whole, however, it would seem to be a substantial improvement over the traditional method.[29]

In short, local government borrowing and debt management are one of the crucial policy areas for the future or urban communities. Although the difficulties of the 1930's have been overcome and the technical position of most municipalities seems fairly satisfactory, the basic problems are very substantial and are beginning to make themselves felt. Most urban communities face unprecedented requirements for capital investment in the years just ahead. In meeting these requirements they will be handicapped by legal limitations and established practices that have been handed down from other days and other conditions. Unless these are re-examined and materially changed, our cities as physical plants will continue to become less and less adequate to the needs of modern urban living.

REVENUE REFORM AND AID FROM OTHER GOVERNMENTS

As we try to take a look in even broader perspective on our formidable mountain peaks of local finance, I think I see two great peaks that dominate the whole scene. They are closely related; in fact, they seem to be twin peaks.

First, the future of urban government as an effective servant of our constantly growing urban population and as a major contributor to a sound, healthful American society will depend in no small part on a thorough reform of the present system of local government finance—particularly on the revenue side. This fact, or perhaps more accurately, this opinion was suggested before but deserves emphasis. The case for it can be put in quite broad terms.

Since the war, our economy has been experiencing the greatest peacetime boom in history. Without subscribing to the view that this boom must inevitably be followed by a comparable bust or depression, I think it is justified to say that we cannot look forward safely to an uninterrupted continuance of the present level of economic activity and employment. Present conditions depend too much on a unique combination of economic stimulants—some of them outright inflationary in character. Let me just mention a few of them: the backlog demand for durable goods, which in housing, house furnishings and motor cars, at least, is still running strong; the unprecedented competitive position of many of our export industries that seems bound to be reduced somewhat as other national economies recover from the ravages and dislocations of war; federal government expenditures of some $25 billion a

29. One discussion of this kind of plan is in Alvin H. Hansen and Harvey S. Perloff, *State and Local Finance in the National Economy* (New York: W. W. Norton and Co., 1944), pp. 206–9.

year for military purposes, foreign aid, and financial assistance to war veterans—not counting post-Korea plans that have much more than doubled this amount.

If, in the midst of this thumping boom, most American cities, large and small, are hard put to it to come by sufficient funds for their present level of services, how can they be expected to strengthen, let alone to extend, the volume and quality of those services during somewhat less prosperous times without some considerable strengthening of their financial position? To that question I can see only one answer—they cannot. In saying this, I am not for a moment denying or belittling the possibilities of greater efficiency in the organization and functioning of urban governments—including their tax systems and their fiscal management. I think what I have said earlier about metropolitanism, planning, and other aspects of the urban scene are evidence on this point. Neither would I deny that some readjustment of price levels, which still seems possible sooner or later, might not ease a little the financial plight of our cities. Giving these two factors as much weight as past experience would appear to justify does not seem to me to invalidate the basic conclusion.

Second, in light of the basic trends in our economy and the highlights of the urban fiscal scene as I have tried to sketch them, it seems to me that the major part of the necessary increases in urban government revenues should come largely in the general category of financial aid from other governments—more specifically, in grants-in-aid and shared taxes from state and federal governments—and in tax supplements.

Because of the much stronger fiscal position of the federal government as compared with the states, a large proportion of the grants-in-aid at least and possibly of the shared taxes and tax supplements should come from or through the federal government itself. Whether the transmission route should be through state governments, which is now the prevailing practice, or directly, as in aid for public housing, urban redevelopment, and part of the airport program, seems to me basically a question of administration that I shall not go into here. I do not think any one pattern will be found absolutely best for all times, places, and programs. From some firsthand observation plus participation in aid programs, I think I see some of the substantial difficulties involved and I have become very skeptical of sweeping generalizations on this point.

In some respects these three classes of local revenues may be much the same. As I use the terms here, the essential differences among them are: (1) Grants-in-aid are payments made by state or federal governments either to help meet specific local expenditures for certain purposes or activities or, in the form of "block grants," as more general additions to local revenue. (2) Shared taxes are payments to local governments (in this case) from the yield of taxes collected by other governments—the shared proportion being determined by the collecting government either as a more or less arbitrary percentage of receipts or as a percentage of receipts from the jurisdictions of the local governments. (3) Tax supplements are additional taxes collected by a government of more inclusive jurisdiction from taxpayers in a less inclusive governmental area, and returned by it to a smaller unit under an agreement that allows the receiving government to determine, within limits, the amount of the supplementary tax. For example, local governments might be empowered to add a surtax to a state income tax. The resulting revenue from the taxpayers in the area of a local government that set such a surtax would be turned over to that government. The state would simply act as the collecting agency. Many variations and modifications are, of course, possible but these differences among the three kinds of revenues seem to me significant.

Much of the significance lies at the point indicated by the basic cause of the fiscal weakness of any one local government. Broadly speaking, fiscal weakness on the revenue side of local government may be due to one of two conditions—or a combination of the two. The two conditions are:

1. The citizens of a local government may have sufficient income to pay for all of its functions and services but the taxes it levies may be unable to reach that income in ways that yield the necessary revenues equitably. The revenue difficulties of many large and prosperous cities —New York is the extreme example—are basically of this kind. Here the tax supplement and the shared tax that return to the locality a part of what it contributes would seem to be called for, provided, of course, that the taxes supplemented or shared drew upon the income of the local community in a more effective and equitable way than additional local taxes.

2. A local government area may be so small or its citizens so poor that no reasonable tax system will raise sufficient revenues for public services and facilities at present-day standards. This seems to be the condition of many smaller local governments, particularly the lower-income dormitory towns in metropolitan areas, as well as of many large rural and semirural areas. To help these localities and areas to maintain a good quality of public services should be the primary purpose of grants-in-aid. They should not be looked upon as a substitute for consolidation of local units of government or other forms of reorganization. Often, however, the annexation of low-income areas is opposed by those municipalities of which they are parts both economically and socially. It makes no sense to condemn the citizens of such areas and

their children to poor quality public services simply at the whim of higher income groups or of officials in the larger municipalities.

In short, I am suggesting that the primary objective of shared taxes and tax supplements should be to remedy weaknesses in local tax systems and that the primary aim of grants-in-aid should be to see that low taxpaying ability is equalized somewhat in the interests of decent standards of public service. This is not to say that these are the exclusive roles of tax supplements, shared taxes, and grants-in-aid. Neither does it imply that shared taxes of supplements or grants-in-aid have any magical quality. Sharing by the states of the proceeds of a general sales tax does not make it a good tax no matter what the form of the sharing may be.

It does seem to me, however, that many current discussions of "centralization" and the feared domination of local government by state and federal policies and administrative agencies would be clarified a little by noting this difference between these two basic conditions that underlie much of the fiscal weakness of local governments. Certainly a local government that receives so-called aid from other governments in the form of payments of tax revenues collected from the citizens of that local government is not put, by the existence of such a tax, in a weak position vis-à-vis the government that does the collecting. To be sure, that government may try to impose unreasonable conditions on the local unit but the local government has a strong case, at least rationally and morally, for resisting such demands. And the history of state-local relations shows that unreasonable interference with local policy and administration has not waited upon fiscal collaboration.

This leads unavoidably to some comments on the view of those who see in *any* form of state or federal aid to local governments an inevitable loss of local strength, freedom, and "home rule." This is an argument with ramifications that run far and deep. A few comments, however, may be in order.[30]

First, it is a truism that all freedoms are relative. Here the question would seem to be not whether financial aids would impose, directly or indirectly, some conditions or limits on local freedom of action but whether these conditions, assuming a reasonably informed and alert urban citizenry, seem likely to be more arbitrary and crippling than those imposed by continuing fiscal weakness or by resort to a number of locally imposed levies that are either definitely regressive or at best

30. A thoughtful discussion of this problem is in Morton Grodzin's article, "State-Municipal Fiscal Relations: A Critical Commentary" in *National Tax Journal* (March 1950), pp. 1–17. He makes a strong case for looking behind the catchwords that beset most arguments on this subject. This is basically my plea also and if I had come upon his article before most of this section on "Local Government Finance" had been written, I might have been able to improve materially my necessarily cursory analysis.

bear no relation to ability to pay. I for one would fear the latter two kinds of restrictions much more in the long run. If it be objected that the assumption of "a reasonably informed and alert urban citizenry" begs the question, the reply certainly is that without such an assumption no satisfactory solution is possible for any of the many problems of local government—fiscal or other.

Next, in the fear of unwise and unreasonable conditions of aid to local governments we should not overlook the possibility, in fact the actuality in some existing programs, of conditions that are definitely helpful to and in the interests of good standards of public service and administration. Without lapsing into an argument *ad hominem,* it is well to ask ourselves just whose freedom and range of action is thought to be endangered and just what relation, if any, such limitations would have to the welfare of most urban dwellers. Although I would not place in one category all who are concerned about the likelihood of undesirable restrictions, it does seem clear that among those who voice their fears most loudly are some local legislators and officials who are not distinguished for their devotion to present-day improvements in local government as well as representatives of some business and civic groups with a consistent record of opposition to the newer service and welfare activities of local public bodies. It is proper, therefore, to ask whether the freedoms that may be infringed are those of local officials who are tender in the area of local patronage and influence or those of outside groups that feel that their heel-dragging can be more effective if it is applied to local agencies that are continually in a weak financial position.

Also, I suggest that we should not forget that all levels of government are agencies for public service and, despite their differences of outlook and the pulling and hauling that does take place among them, they do share a tradition of collaboration on many important matters that is not mean or inconsequential. In light of the almost certain increase in urbanization and the slow awakening to the fact that the continued prosperity and advance of our society depend more and more on what happens to the majority of our citizens who live in cities, it does not seem unrealistic to foresee a strengthening of this record of governmental co-operation that will work to the advantage of urban centers. Unquestionably this development will come slowly and with many lags and difficulties, but many of the underlying trends in our economy favor it. If this be admitted, is it not better to plan fiscal policy on this basis rather than to accept the conclusion that the record of urban governments in functions and services must now be stopped by the weakness of their revenue systems or, alternatively, that the best solution to the problems of fiscal weakness is the proliferation of a number of basically unsatisfactory taxes for which about the only defense is, as one leading student of public finance has described general sales taxes, that they rob nobody very much at any one time?[31]

Finally, very few persons would deny the truth of the old aphorism—eternal vigilance is the price of liberty. It seems to me to apply to this question of reasonable local freedom in the use of additions to their revenues from grants-in-aid, shared taxes and tax supplements. Important as the methods of revenue raising and distributing may be, and I would not deny their importance, no allocation of tax powers can be foolproof or harmoniously self-adjusting. In fact, any system that would seem to give grounds for this claim might, by this very fact, be most dangerous.

Quite possibly my discussion of fiscal aids and supplements may seem to some readers too much a case for these aids. If so, no one need look very long or far to find the arguments of those who feel that unless all or nearly all local revenues are raised by locally levied taxes the slide is greased for a downward trip to the destruction of responsible local government—or worse. It is clear that I do not share these fears. I hope it is equally clear that I admit the existence of dangers and difficulties in aid programs—broadly defined. My opinion simply is that these dangers can be coped with and that unless local governments, in co-operation with state and federal governments, set themselves to the job of making a system of revenue aids work fairly and effectively, they face one of two results—either of which would seem to me a tragedy. They are, to repeat, a halt (or reversal) in the decades-long advance of urban governments as agencies of public service and welfare, or the virtual abandonment of the ideal of a local system related in some degree to ability to pay. If the first of these two results should come, it probably at first would take the form of few, if any, improvements or additions to these services and possibly the abandoning of some. In the long run, however, it might well be that state and federal governments would be compelled to provide these services themselves. If so, what becomes then of strong, self-reliant local government?

Although grants-in-aid and, to a lesser degree, shared taxes were used increasingly during the 1930's and early 1940's and by no means have been entirely given up as a matter of policy or practice, in the years since World War II (particularly from 1946 through 1948) most of the changes in local revenue sources have been in the other direction. Nonproperty taxes and charges—sales taxes, business taxes, local

31. Harold M. Groves, *Trouble Spots in Taxation—Essays in the Philosophy of Taxation and Other Public Finance Problems* (Princeton: Princeton University Press, 1948), p. 77. Mr. Groves, however, believes that local income taxes are, or could be made into, fairly satisfactory sources of revenue.

earned income and payroll taxes, new forms of license fees, service charges for sewage disposal, garbage collection, parking, etc.—have been authorized increasingly by state governments and taken up with avidity, if not in desperation, by more and more cities.

It is not for anyone on the sidelines to criticize too sharply this development.[32] As I have indicated, however, this seems to me to be at best a process with very definite and foreseeable limits. Unless these are clearly recognized, it might easily become both a snare and a delusion. By at least several generally recognized standards, most of these are poor taxes. Most of them are highly regressive. Few, if any, have any close relation to ability to pay. By their nature and the fact that as presently levied only a very few of them are major revenue producers, their costs of assessment and collection are apt to run high. If they are taken up in substantial quantity their nuisance value is considerable. They also seem very likely to be poor producers in times of recession or depression—just when urban governments need sound and flexible sources of revenue to meet their responsibilities. In this last respect, of course, they might be no worse or even better than shared revenue from, or local tax supplements to, income taxes.

Anyone who addresses himself at all seriously, even if briefly, to the present near impasse in local government finance may take some comfort from de Tocqueville's comment: ". . . I have never been more struck by the good sense and the practical judgment of the Americans than in the manner in which they elude the numberless difficulties resulting from their Federal Constitution. . . ."[33] The problems I have just tried to outline and comment upon may well constitute the acid test of the next decade for this happy faculty that de Tocqueville recognized. Perhaps "elude" is not the best word. Certainly it is not for these problems if it suggests further temporizing and more makeshifts. And although the federal form of government undoubtedly aggravates these problems, it certainly does not create them. They have been produced by the trends toward centralization in economic and cultural life, urbanization, and higher standards of material well-being that have evolved in this and other countries during the last century or more. But the pace of these movements seems to increase and they now press insistently on our established forms of analysis and thought and on our traditionalism and inertia in political affairs. It is time to face the fact

32. They are sharply criticized in Louis Shere, "An Economist's Viewpoint on Tax Policy" in the *Annals of the American Academy of Political and Social Science* (November, 1949), pp. 166–73. Mr. Groves remarks (*op. cit.*, p. 77) that "Recent innovations and proposals in New York City leave one wondering when that supposedly enlightened metropolis will revive the medieval salt tax!"

33. de Tocqueville, *Democracy in America* (Reeve-Bowen-Bradley text, New York: Alfred A. Knopf, 1945) I, 167.

that the old practices and slogans do not provide an answer today—let alone for tomorrow.

TWO MORE PROBLEMS

Before closing this section, I would like to mention two problems that are not as basic as those I have just tried to deal with, but that in the long run I am sure will not be minor. Both deal with the relations of urban planning and the fiscal problems of cities.

One of the serious shortcomings of urban planning in this country has been the failure to develop even a rudimentary understanding of the relations between various sizes, densities, and patterns of physical development and the efficiency of essential municipal services provided within and through the physical urban plant. To be sure, from its earlier days it has been pointed out that proper zoning, through its control of land use and population density, would enable city governments to achieve some economies in the provision of water, sewers, streets, and pavements, playgrounds, and other open spaces. State supreme courts have accepted this argument and stated it forcefully in some of their favorable opinions. Also, city officials and others have realized for some years that municipal expenditures and activity in support of the unplanned subdivision orgy of the 1920's were very bad business for the many urban governments concerned. But beyond these obvious generalities, our information is scant and on the whole unreliable, and our understanding insufficient to support intelligent and vigorous action.

I am sure I do not underestimate the difficulties in the kind of analysis and research needed on this front. I do not suggest that ony one size or density or physical development will be found the optimum for municipal services over the whole range of types and kinds of urban localities. Neither do I urge that urban planning should be dedicated to the development of cities as efficient units for the provision of municipal services to the exclusion of such other considerations as human values and preferences or industrial and business needs. In short, planning should envisage more than making the physical city an economical unit for municipal services. Here, however, is a substantial, largely unexplored area that in the long run might yield facts and established relationships of real value in financial terms as our cities continue to develop and redevelop.

Second, as urban planning continues its evolution from the drawing of maps to a continuous process of guiding physical growth and the allied operation of the public machinery in urban communities, the relations of the planning official and department to the budget officer and his tasks will come more and more to the fore. This seems not only inevitable from the nature of the two operations, but practical evidence of it can be found in the relatively few cities in which planners are now charged with the preparation of what are usually called capital budgets.

What should be the relationship between these two important sets of staff officials? Can they continue to be, as they now are in a few municipal setups, co-ordinate staff advisors to the chief executive with that executive and the legislative body responsible for deciding upon issues on which the planners and budgeters do not see eye to eye (as well as, of course, on others)? Without questioning for a moment the responsibilities of the chief executive and the legislative body, does this relationship seem likely in the long run to produce the best results? Will it not too often force councilmen and mayors or city managers to decide questions that might better be resolved, at least in major part, earlier in the process of determining policy? Alternatively, could the budget officer be given clear responsibility for dealing with certain items, and the planner with others? Or just possibly, and I mention this with at least one eye on the exit, should the urban planning function in its full and proper scope be split in two so that the conventional operation of physical planning would be attached to a super-department or division of city development and capital investment, and the final task of co-ordinating its needs with the requirements for money and personnel for other subdivisions of municipal activity be lodged with the financial officer—under this or some other title? At least two other possibilities are worth weighing: Should the planning official be recognized as the top staff advisor on policy and programs, including the hard, stubborn facts and considerations that would continue to be the stock-in-trade of the finance officer? Or should the budget officer have the final say in recommendations to the chief executive on capital as well as operating budgets?

I mention this question not because I have a ready answer, but because I see it as an emerging problem that sooner or later will confront city officials in practical form. I see nothing to be gained by dodging or belittling it. Again, however, I do not suggest that there is any one best solution in the back of the book.

ORGANIZATIONS FOR THE IMPROVEMENT OF LOCAL GOVERNMENT

Several decades before the period under review, de Tocqueville also observed that ". . . Americans of all ages, all conditions and all dispositions constantly form associations." American officials and civic leaders and, through them, municipalities and other units of local government have showed themselves to be no exception to this generalization during the past half-century. Because I believe these organizations have contributed more than is commonly realized to the improvement of urban public life and to the role of local government in American society, I propose here to review briefly that contribution and a few of the problems these associations now face.

Organizations of cities and public officials have attracted relatively little attention, scholarly or otherwise. Compared with the analyses and discussions of the history, activities, methods, and machinations of organizations of business and professional men, of labor unions, or even of learned societies, associations of cities and urban officials have almost been ignored. It seems rather strange too that some of the earlier associations, particularly the local and statewide ones, kept such inadequate records that some of the elementary facts about their beginnings are difficult, if not impossible, to make out. How does it happen that officials, who are supposed to have as a class a well-developed sense of their own importance and of the perquisites of office, were so careless in recording their first formal attempts at mutual education and collaboration? Were they, contrary to their reputation in many quarters, more concerned with what they could learn and what they could do in concert than with the record of offices held, speeches made, and positions taken? Or perhaps they lacked the foresight to discern the long-term possibilities and implications of their pioneering organizations?

Three general kinds of organizations are worth noting: (1) civic reform groups—their members mostly nonofficials concerned with the improvement of government organization and administration; (2) associations of cities and other municipal units—represented through their chief executives or other officials; and (3) associations of public officials—professional, semiprofessional, technical, and trade union.[34] This is only a very rough grouping. In all of these classes, particularly the first and third, are many hybrids. For example, a few officials have been active in the civic reform groups. Attempts have been made by some of the leading organizations of this kind to encourage more officials to joint or to bring about formal affiliations with associations of cities or public officials. Again, many of the more prominent associations of officials have as members nonofficials who either are in private or consultant employment in the same field or who simply are interested in the program and objectives of the professional or technical activity.

34. This is essentially the classification suggested by Harold D. Smith in "Associations of Cities and Municipal Officials," Part IV of *Urban Government,* which is Vol. I of the *Supplementary Report of the Urbanism Committee to the National Resources Committee* (Washington, D.C.: Government Printing Office, 1939). As the title of his study indicates, however, Mr. Smith dealt almost entirely with classes (2) and (3) and very little with (1). For the history and activities of associations of cities and local officials I have drawn heavily on this study, which is still the most nearly thorough work of its kind.

Also, all three types of groups have been represented by local, state-wide, regional, and national organizations. In many of the organizations of officials, the membership has included state and federal as well as local public officials.

The pioneers of all three groups started before the turn of the century. Thus, citizen leagues were set up in Chicago in 1892 and in Boston in 1894. In the latter year, the National Municipal League, already referred to, was organized following a National Conference for Good City Government, which met in Philadelphia. The first league of cities was probably the Indiana Municipal League—founded in 1891. Similar organizations were established in Iowa, California, and Wisconsin in 1898 and in Michigan and Illinois in 1899. The League of American Municipalities, the first attempt at a nation-wide association of cities, began its uneven career in 1897. Among national associations of public officials, the earliest was the National Education Association, organized in 1857 under the name National Teachers' Association. By 1900, about ten such national organizations were in existence and another nine or so had a part of their membership among public officials. Most of these early organizations (thirteen out of the nineteen) were in the fields of health, education, and the protection of persons and property. Not until 1906, when the Municipal Finance Officers Association (first called the International Association of Comptrollers and Accounting Officers) and the Civil Service Assembly (National Assembly of Civil Service Commissioners) were organized, did the roll include associations of officials in what is often called general government as distinguished from such specialized functions as health, education, recreation, and public works.

Our primary interest here, however, is in the growth and evolution of these associations during the past fifty years. Although it is almost as hard to generalize on this front as it is to catalogue the variety of existing organizations, several broad developments may be noted both in the numerical growth and in the programs of all three kinds of organizations.

CIVIC REFORM GROUPS

By and large, civic reform groups have had a hard row to hoe. Wide fluctuations in interest have produced, stimulated, and killed off an unknown number of local civic leagues, associations, and committees. A relatively few have survived over substantial periods of time. In 1947 the National Municipal League, the outstanding nation-wide organization, had only some 2,200 members—according to the League "perhaps 2 per cent of a realistic potential"—and a budget of $74,000, up about $30,000 from 1946. Also active as nation-wide organizations and broadly representative of a somewhat larger number are the National Civil Service League, organized in 1881 with the word "Reform" in its name; the American Planning and Civic Association, organized in 1935 as a merger of the American Civic Association (1904) and the National Conference on City Planning (1909); the National Tax Association (1907), approximately half of whose members are state tax officials; the National Popular Government League (1913), which advocates the initiative, referendum and recall, and the public ownership of utilities; the Governmental Research Association (1914) made up largely of persons working for some two hundred privately supported organizations that inquire into government operations, programs, and finance; and the National Citizens Commission for the Public Schools, founded in 1949.

Undeniably civic reform groups on the whole have suffered from anemic finances. Some of them, particularly local committees and groups, have too often "quit at the top of the stretch"—to use a phrase attributed to one of their opponents in a major city. Others have gone out of training after early successes and have found it difficult or impossible to make an effective comeback. These characteristics are, of course, all interrelated and in many organizations, both local and nation-wide, have been offset in part by the persistent work of a small group of exceptionally able citizens devoted to the objectives of their organizations.

Another weakness of many of these organizations has been their class composition—by and large both their leaders and rank-and-file members have been from the better educated, well-to-do, business and professional classes of their communities. Leaders among other economic classes have had other things to do. Many labor unions have been influenced by a general distrust of strong government that goes back to the days of Samuel Gompers' dominance in the American Federation of Labor. Many, also, have been suspicious of the strong "economy" motif in civic reform. Others simply have felt that they were not wanted or carried over into this field their attitudes toward business leaders that had grown out of years of struggle for recognition and a larger share of the product of the economy. Whatever the causes, during the last fifteen years or so some signs point to a change both among those groups that have been the backbone of municipal reform and among the present generation of labor leaders. To be sure, these signs are not too numerous or compelling but they may indicate the possibility of a broader base for many civic groups. Other but allied local organizations—e.g., community chests and councils in many cities—now select their board members and other officers quite widely. Groups formerly overlooked or ignored are now accepted as a matter of course. In the programs of civic reform groups one or two changes over the past fifty years seem worth noting. Probably the major development has been the shift of emphasis from rather journalistic exposés of incompetence and corruption and general appeals to civic responsibility and probity to more expert, specialized advice and criticism over a wide range of municipal activities and services. Both local and national leaders have come to see that honesty, decent motives, and a reasonable degree of personal competence, necessary though they be to the conduct of local public affairs, are not enough to assure effective municipal government. This change in emphasis (and it is not more than that) not only has modified the work of many of the older organizations for general civic reform but also has led to the founding of both local and national groups primarily concerned with particular functions of local government, e.g., public utilities, recreation, city planning, and low-rent housing. Also, both the more general and the more specialized organizations probably now look with rather more favor than their predecessors did on research and study efforts as distinguished from the direct application of accepted "principles" for organizing and administering local government.

ASSOCIATIONS OF CITIES

The number of associations of cities increased substantially during the past half-century. Nearly all of this increase was among state leagues of municipalities—from six at the beginning of 1900 to forty-two today. During the early years of the century several regional associations of cities were organized, but none has survived. Their decline coincided roughly with the period of most rapid growth in the number of state leagues—from 1910 to 1915. Figures on the formation of state leagues, of course, tell little or nothing about the scope or effectiveness of their programs. As a matter of fact, most leagues of municipalities markedly strengthened both the character and competence of their work from about 1931 onward—when the American Municipal Association was reorganized and established with a full-time, professional secretariat in Chicago.

The League of American Municipalities seemed to grow rapidly at first and was a fairly effective organization in some respects until about 1910. Even during this period, however, membership and finances were weak and the decline continued until the League passed out of existence about 1915. In 1917 and 1918 attempts were made to set up a new national organization as a federation of the state leagues. War conditions and other difficulties stymied these efforts but in 1924 this objective was realized in the founding of the American Municipal Association. Although originally a federation of state organizations, its constitution now provides for direct membership of municipalities as well. This arrangement appeals primarily to the larger cities, few of which have been active in their state leagues.

In 1932 the United States Conference of Mayors was organized. Although its program has changed somewhat over the years, its original purpose was to give the larger cities, represented by their mayors, a means of agreeing on policy and urging action on relief and other depression-produced problems. Most of its early activities were naturally with the federal government. In more recent years the Conference's attention has shifted to other issues; for instance, at present (1950–51) it is much concerned with civilian defense.

The substantive programs of associations of cities have undergone at least two notable changes. In their earlier days they were much concerned with state legislation affecting municipalities. Probably this kind of legislation provided the issues around which most of the earlier leagues were formed. While these questions of local autonomy and state control are still very real, associations of cities more and more have been taking up problems in local government relations vis-à-vis the federal government. Naturally the depression drove their interest in this direction but other developments in federal aid for primarily urban activities have kept this issue in the forefront of their programs. Also, the service activities of these associations have grown in range and detail. Their evolution here is similar to the change in emphasis noted in the doings of civic reform groups.

The leagues and associations of cities from the beginning provided for some clearing-house functions on current problems and practices. These have been developed materially and have also been supplemented by various consultant services to members, co-operative activities, e.g., in centralized purchasing for smaller municipalities and training courses for municipal employees, co-operative research and publication, usually with university or college bureaus of municipal research, that cover problems of increasing range and complexity.

ASSOCIATIONS OF LOCAL PUBLIC OFFICIALS

The leading study of associations of local officials suggests two broad categories of them—". . . those engaged primarily in the exchange of experience for the improvement of standards of work, and those engaged in activity designed to protect or advance the economic welfare of the members. This difference in objectives is usually regarded as the major distinction between professional, semiprofessional, or technical associations, on the one hand, and the trade union, on the other."[35] Admittedly this is at best a rough guide but it serves well enough in describing recent trends in these organizations.

This same study, published in 1939, tabulated 813 state, regional and nation-wide organizations that included local officials as prominent elements in their membership. From this large group, the analysis centered on the 86 nation-wide associations. Sixty-seven of these had been organized since 1900.[36] After 1905 the formation of new organizations proceeded at a reasonably steady rate with the exception of a slow period from 1926 through 1930. With notable exceptions, organizations of professionals in both private and public employment came before most of the associations with largely or exclusively official membership. Organizations in functional fields preceded those in general government. Professional and semi-professional associations had earlier starts than "rank-and-file" organizations.

Seventy-eight of the 86 associations were in the first classification, i.e., professional, semi-professional, or technical in character; only 8 were "rank-and-file" organizations—essentially trade unions. Forty-five had full-time secretariats. In 51 of these organizations (out of 69 reporting on this point) public officials made up 50 per cent or more of the membership. In 43 of the 69, public officials were more than 90 per cent of total membership. Seven associations admitted to membership civic or philanthropic organizations; 9 let in commercial corporations—presumably largely to help pay the bills. Among activities listed, providing information to members was far and away the most common. Next came research (a term clearly susceptible of differing definitions) followed by information to the public and personnel training. Only 9 associations of the 86 engaged in legislative activity—still one of the major interests of the associations of cities.

Again, however, numbers and lists of activities are the bare bones of these—or any other organizations for that matter. They give no indication of the expanding influence and respect that some of these organizations have earned, particularly, again, during the past twenty years or so. Risking invidious, implied (but not intended) comparisons and from first-hand acquaintance alone, I would suggest that the contributions of such organizations as the International City Managers Association and the Municipal Finance Officers Association to local government and public affairs have been greater and may well be more lasting than those of much more widely advertised forces on the urban scene.

Although some of the earliest organizations of public officials had some of the characteristics of trade unions, unionization of public em-

35. *Ibid.*, p. 216.
36. *Ibid.*, Table VIII, p. 221. The text says 64 (p. 220).

ployees definitely started during the 1880's among teachers, policemen, and postal employees. For many years it grew rather more rapidly among federal employees. Here, of course, the obstacles and resistances made for slow progress at best, but by the early 1900's several organizations of postal employees were established, and in 1917, the National Federation of Federal Employees, now the largest union of workers in the public service, was founded. In contrast, of the active national organizations of local government employees (most of which also include state employees) the earliest, the American Federation of Teachers, was started in 1916 and was followed by the International Association of Fire Fighters in 1918. Not until the 1930's did unionism in local government begin to reach proportions that made it a major factor in local administration in a substantial number of communities. To be sure, city-wide employee organizations in New York, Chicago, Los Angeles, and a number of other larger cities and in several states had attained considerable strength before then but, by and large, they too took a new lease on life in the latter 1930's.[37] (In this résumé of unions of government workers, I am leaving out those public employees in crafts and callings most of whose members are in private employment and that are organized in unions predominantly of privately employed workers. e.g., printers, machinists, and construction workers.)

Like the facts on the early days of many associations of cities and of professional and technical officials, information on the beginnings of local government unions is very sketchy and uneven. It is clear, however, that so-called rank-and-file employees were organized, on the whole, well after most of the other kinds of associations dealt with in this section.

Partly as a result of this late start, the numerical strength of local government unions is not great. In 1948 the five national organizations of state and local employees had only about 2,400 locals and a total membership of slightly more than 280,000. These five unions are the Teachers and Fire Fighters, just mentioned, the American Federation of State, County, and Municipal Employees (AF of L), the United Public Workers of America (CIO) and the National Civil Service Association, unaffiliated. (Since 1948 the UPWA has been read out of the CIO and replaced by the Government and Civic Workers Organizing

---

37. My facts on public employee unions are largely from four sources: (*a*) William E. Mosher, J. Donald Kingsley, and O. Glenn Stahl, *Public Personnel Administration* (3d edition, New York: Harper & Bros., 1950), chap. 13; (*b*) *Employee Relations in the Public Service* (Chicago: Civil Service Assembly of the United States and Canada, 1942), chaps. i and v; (*c*) James W. Errant, "City-Wide Organizations of Municipal Employees" in *The Municipal Year Book* (1937), pp. 232–40; and (*d*) statistical summaries of public employee unions and of local government personnel in more recent issues of *The Municipal Year Book*.

Committee. The figure for total membership given above includes only state and local employees in the UPWA in 1948.) Without the teachers, the estimated totals were 2,000 locals and 230,000 members. For comparison, the estimated number of employees in agencies of state and local government in 1948 was 3,966,000 including teachers, 2,385,-000 not counting them. (Of these totals, 677,000 were state employees.) Union members in national organizations, therefore, were about 10 per cent of total employment outside of school authorities and about 7 per cent including schools. It should be emphasized that these figures on union membership are only for locals of essentially nation-wide organizations. They do not include strictly local unions or those affiliated only with city or state-wide organizations. Also, the breakdown of teachers versus other local employees may be inexact because some teachers may have been members of UPWA locals rather than of those of the American Federation of Teachers.

Another and more recent tabulation indicates that on January 1, 1950, of 1,072 cities with populations of 10,000 and more (1940 figures), 710 or about 66 per cent had employees in locals of one or more unions—local, state-wide, or national, affiliated, and unaffiliated. For 410 cities of 25,000 or more the proportion was 92 per cent.

In short, then, the proportion of local government employees in unions is small but some degree of unionization is now found quite generally among local government workers.

Unionism among public employees, naturally enough, has produced a variety of reactions among administrative officials, members of legislative bodies and the general public—as well as among the rank-and-file employees themselves. Consideration of most of these attitudes and opinions, even those on basic issues, is beyond the scope of this monograph. In the following paragraphs I shall touch very briefly on one or two of the actual and potential effects of unions on the improvement of administrative practice. On the other issues, perhaps one observation should be made. Probably many of the attitudes, ranging from mild apprehension to outright hostility, toward unions of public employees center on two apparently separate but related issues: (*a*) under what conditions, if any, do such unions have the right to strike? and (*b*) under what conditions and by what means are such unions justified in acting as "pressure groups" on legislative bodies in their quest for higher pay, more security of employment, and better working conditions?

Clearly these are not easy questions of policy but I would suggest that they should not blind us to other phases or aspects of unionism among public employees. Some of the record of unions, both among government and privately employed workers, shows that, under intelligent leadership, they have been able to perform a number of services of value both to their members and, directly or indirectly, to their employers. For example, they have sponsored and often administered economic and social activities such as credit unions, co-operative buying clubs, organizations for sickness and death benefits, as well as various recreational programs. They have been a means for exchanging between employees and their administrative superiors information, ideas, and suggestions on the objectives and functions of their operating units and on possible improvements in methods and practices. They have provided a means of airing grievances before they become too acute. Finally, they have contributed to the personal satisfaction of their members and to their morale by providing one formal means of satisfying their needs for collaborative effort, for a sense of recognition and belonging, and for the development of qualities of leadership in relatively small groups. This last service may seem rather intangible or perhaps elusive, but a growing body of studies by industrial relations specialists and social psychologists certainly indicates that these deep-seated desires and motives of nearly all workers should no longer be ignored or brushed aside by responsible administrators—private or public.

All of these products and by-products of competent unionism can contribute and, in fact, have contributed to the quality of administrative practice. They also seem, to me at least, to have substantial potentialities for further development. In addition, however, the record seems quite clear that unions of public employees have been among the most energetic advocates and friends of the merit system—partly, no doubt, because their members do not particularly enjoy being pawns in games of factional politicking.[38] On the other hand, some progress toward a merit system seems to be a precondition of unionization. I realize also that some other friends of civil service disagree sharply with the unions on the relative importance of various recognized parts of a merit system—e.g., on seniority rights and promotion from within —but these differences of emphasis would not seem to be insuperable. Be that as it may, the campaign for effective merit systems in the local public service is far from won and it may well be that unions of local government workers will be a useful force in the work that still needs to be done.

EVALUATION AND SUGGESTIONS

What can be said in summary and evaluation of these many and diverse organizations concerned in one way or another with the im-

38. See, for example, *Employee Relations in the Public Service*, pp. 18–21.

provement of local government? Although assaying their products is most difficult and is made more so by sizable holes in our basic information about them, it seems certain that each major type has contributed to the progress of local government in recent years. It is equally clear that each kind of organization has shown weaknesses and faces formidable problems in bettering its rather spotty record of achievements and shortcomings.

To list these problems and to put briefly my comments on them may make most of my present opinions concerning them seem much more firm than they actually are. I hope also it does not give an impression of glibness or smugness. The problems basically are how these organizations can fill certain needs revealed by their past and present programs.

The chief needs of civic reform associations, as a group, seem to me four:

1. They need to broaden their base in two respects—by enlisting the support of a wider representation of economic and occupational classes and by balancing their proper concern over economy with more effective support for at least some of the newer welfare activities of local government. More concretely, they need more members and officers from the other side of the tracks and more support for the work of such activities as public housing and nursery schools.

2. They need more effective tie-ups between action programs and research work—both that done by the better independent bureaus of municipal research as well as that of college and university units.

3. They need the results of more systematic analysis of their considerable body of experience with different forms of organizations and with different tactics. This analysis should always proceed in light of the somewhat different objectives and varying resources of local organizations. It should not assume that any one form of organization or any one set of tactics is best at all times and places.

4. They need to emphasize continuity of effort more than many of them have in times past.

Associations of cities face an increasingly difficult problem: how can they cover competently the administrative and policy issues of the many important functional fields of local government, e.g., protection, health, public works, utilities, recreation and housing, as well as of the various subdivisions of general government, e.g., top administrative supervision, finance, personnel, purchasing, public relations, and planning? This clearly raises a corollary question: How can associations of cities collaborate most effectively with professional and technical organizations of public officials? The American Municipal Association and the professional associations housed also at 1313 East 60th Street,

Chicago, have discussed these and related problems over the past several years. Although some advance has been made, no completely satisfactory arrangement has been developed. Also, the leagues of cities need a type or types of arrangements that will work well with specialized groups that do not have the advantage of physical proximity and easy access of staff members, which AMA and the other organizations enjoy at 1313.

Many of the more thoughtful leaders of associations of cities see the need for more education both of their members and of the urban citizenry in the newer functions and the changing local-state-federal relationships that growing urbanization and higher standards of living place on local governments. Some examples of these evolving functions and relationships have been mentioned already, particularly in the section on "Local Government Finance."

The most pervasive need of professional and semiprofessional organizations of officials is to find ways and means of building up professional competence and sense of responsibility while beating back the evils of particularism and devotion to partial, inflexible standards that are formulated and applied without enough attention to considerations at least partly outside of the professional fields themselves.

One illustration from my own experience on the staff of one of the newer associations, the National Association of Housing Officials, may be worth mentioning here just as an example. The programs of local housing authorities began to come of age in the late 1930's, following the provision of federal aid under the United States Housing Act of 1937. This statute made available rather generous federal subsidies in the interests of really low rentals but also required some subsidy contribution by local governments. Largely because of the hodgepodge of governmental units in most metropolitan and many nonmetropolitan areas, the most practicable means of giving this local subsidy was by property tax reduction—a payment by local housing authorities of amounts in lieu of taxes less than their projects would have paid under normal procedures for assessing property and levying taxes. These payments in lieu of taxes were authorized by enabling acts in some forty states and eventually were upheld in nearly all of them by supreme court decisions in test cases. Also, before housing projects were started, local legislative bodies adopted so-called co-operation agreements, which included acceptance of payments in lieu of taxes.

Nevertheless, many—by no means all—of the local tax and assessment officials as well as some general administrative officials were inhospitable not to say hostile to the entire plan. As a representative of housing officials (and at that time an active one, myself) I undertook to open up discussions on this matter with representatives of our fellow-officials in these other branches of local government. With exceptions, our reception was discouraging. Some—again, not all—of those with whom the housing officials talked simply refused, politely and sometimes indirectly to be sure, to discuss the issue in the broad framework of public policy and the welfare of the local communities that needed decent, low-rent housing. They saw very clearly the fiscal problems of the local governments that they and their associates served. They had been fighting a long, hard, uphill battle for reasonably uniform assessment and taxation. This objective was the keystone of their professional arch. They seemed interested in little else.

Later, with the help of some of the leaders and of the staffs of their professional associations, this attitude was substantially modified. Even at the beginning, as I have tried to make clear, some of their members were open to argument and persuasion. Also, I would admit that those of us who tried to open up the discussion on behalf of the housing officials might have been more skilful or more understanding of the position of the other officials. After all this is said, however, I cannot escape the conclusion that professional particularism and standards were here operating in a narrow and potentially dangerous manner.

Professional associations of local government officials also see the need for more effective training of personnel—both pre-entry and in-service. More progress has been made on this front than many persons realize but it is significant that those officials and organizations that have gone the furthest are among the firmest advocates of even more effort to this end.

Methods of measuring performance and efficiency in professional and technical administrative practice also have been commanding more consideration in recent years. This is a development that seems very likely to continue and to grow. In many realms of private employment and activity, of course, the profit motive is relied upon heavily as an incentive and the making of profits as a measure of efficiency. Detractors of public enterprise and government activity generally have been inclined to exaggerate the profit motive as an incentive for intelligent human effort. The old point of view is certainly on the defensive these days, particularly in fields of professional and technical activity. On the other hand, although profits as a gauge of efficiency clearly have their weaknesses, generally applicable substitutes are not easy to find. The search for them in public administrative practice, therefore, is a task of first-rate significance for many professional and technical organizations of local public servants.

Finally, organizations of local officials share with the other associations dealt with in this section, as well as with other groups, the need to counteract the false and often malicious caricature of public officials as stupid, incompetent bureaucrats—muddle-headed, lazy, arrogant, and unproductive. Fighting this common and often deliberately fostered misconception is a task of high priority in an urbanized democracy. And I would emphasize that it is not solely the responsibility of organizations of officials. They do, however, have their part. Increasingly able performance is, of course, an essential and important part of this campaign. More studies similar to Leonard White's work on the prestige value of public employment are also needed. The campaign, however, has many fronts and local government officials are beginning to see the importance of their public relations—both in their individual capacities as officials and as organized groups of self-respecting and respectable public servants. Among the issues at stake here is the ability of the public service to attract its fair share of those able and gifted persons, regardless of economic or social background, who have the abilities to serve capably in the ever more exacting professional and technical areas of the public service.

Probably the major need of unions of local government workers is for competent leadership—men and women able to command not only the loyalty and liking of their members but also the respect of administrative officials, local legislators and, in some degree, the citizenry at large. In meeting these requirements union leaders must overcome a formidable range of obstacles. And this must be done, in the next few years at least, with relatively little support from most of the organs of public information and opinion. An essential element in leadership of this quality would seem to be the ability to plan union activity and strategy without losing sight of the larger claims of local government as one of the chief agencies for the public welfare. Also, union leadership faces many difficulties, particularly in a period of inflation that works against the economic interests of almost all persons on wages and salaries, in minimizing an excessively belligerent, chip-on-the-shoulder attitude that may often seem a source of internal strength but in the longer run may prove to do more harm than good.

What about the financial weakness of nearly all of the organizations in all of the categories dealt with in this section? Certainly from one point of view it is the chief problem of most of them. Most of them, if they had more money, could do more and probably do it more effectively. But "wishing won't make it so," and most of the associations have access to sources of revenue that could yield rather more than they have to date. Is it unrealistic to suggest that more nearly adequate finances may come to those organizations who see most clearly the range of their potential services and who most diligently urge the need for those services not only as contributions to the advancement of the organizations themselves but also to the welfare and vigor of local government in our society?

REPRESENTATION AND LEADERSHIP IN URBAN PUBLIC AFFAIRS

In the vitally important area of citizen representation in urban government, three problems must be sketched: (1) urban representation in state legislatures; (2) the balancing of city-wide and neighborhood or district interests; and (3) nonvoting in local elections. Each of them, however, seems to me of pressing concern. If we could find and put into effect reasonably adequate solutions for all of them, the total result would be a substantial improvement in our urban democracy.

URBAN REPRESENTATION IN LEGISLATURES

First, although there are some exceptions, the cities in most states are still shamefully underrepresented in state legislatures. Although I do not have at hand any figures on representation from cities in the early years of this half-century, it seems likely that this problem is more serious now than it was then. In 1938, Albert Lepawsky, writing for the Urbanism Committee of the National Resources Committee, said, "In 21 of our States, the majority of the population is urban, but not one of the States grants to the urban communities their proportionate share of representation in the State legislative body. . . ."[39] Ten years later, the United States Conference of Mayors claimed that the estimated 59 per cent of the American people living in cities elected only 25 per cent of the state legislators.[40]

On this subject, may I offer three brief comments. As we have seen, the financial problems of most cities are acute. In remedying them, state-local relations should play a vital part. Offhand, it is hard to imagine a worse background for intelligent discussion and compromise on questions of this kind than this partial disfranchisement of urban citizens. Also, at the present time nearly all thoughtful public officials and students of public affairs see the need for increasing respect for government. Certainly one of the chief contributions to this end is to strengthen the belief in government as a form of human association in the interests of the general welfare rather than as a highly organized racket for group advantage. I believe the implications of the condition

39. Albert Lepawsky, "Development of Urban Government," Part I of Vol. I of the *Supplementary Report of the Urbanism Committee to the National Resources Committee* (Washington, D.C.: Government Printing Office, 1939), p. 24.

40. *Government of the People, by the People, for the People?* (The United States Conference of Mayors, Washington, D.C., 1948).

I am protesting against for citizen respect for government are clear. Finally, with the results of a new federal census now coming out, the immediate future would seem a most appropriate time to do away with this injustice.

CITY-WIDE AND NEIGHBORHOOD INTERESTS

The second major problem is how we can assure that members of local legislative bodies will combine an intelligent understanding and devotion to the welfare of the city as a whole with a sensitiveness to the legitimate interests and needs of neighborhoods and other relatively small subdivisions of the urban community. Obviously, this problem is more pressing in larger cities than in small and medium-sized ones. It is a problem of long standing, but it has been aggravated in recent years as urban governments have become more and more concerned in housing, urban redevelopment, and other phases of urban growth. It has an obviously important bearing on citizen indifference toward local public affairs, which I shall take up a little later. Although it is an urgent problem today in many cities, it would be much more so if we were to expand the governments of central cities to include more and more of their metropolitan areas. Conversely, some promising solution of this problem might well be a substantial contribution toward more rational organization of local government in metropolitan areas.

For the first of these twin objectives, the over-all interests of the city, it seems clear that the election-at-large of all or most of the local legislators has much to be said for it. In fact, I would think that it has a conclusive case both in logic and experience. Some of the arguments for proportional representation would seem to apply at least indirectly to the second objective, but I cannot see them as a satisfactory answer, even if one leaves out of account what many students hold are grave general weaknesses in this device.

Some thoughtful observers of urban affairs believe that these legitimate local interests, both of neighborhood and other groups, can be properly and effectively represented through civic associations and organized pressure groups of various kinds. Some of them urge that these groups are necessary and desirable adjuncts to the formal processes of urban government. Some also make quite a case for the opinion that organizations of this kind have largely untouched potentialities for the good of urban democracy that could and should be developed by proper leadership and intelligent experiment. Not all of these potentialities, of course, have to do with the relations of such groups to the urban political process, but many of them do.

Undoubtedly there is truth in all of these views. How much, is hard to say. Certainly I would not deny the educational and social values that come from participation in many voluntary associations of these kinds. Neither would I try in any way to silence them on the issues that come before city councils. Here, too, they have significant parts to play, and some of them play them well.

On the whole, however, I doubt seriously whether they are an adequate answer to the question of how we can best achieve the second objective. I say this undogmatically, but they have weaknesses that seem to me serious. They are too spotty and uneven, both in coverage and in quality. Too many of them seem to have reversed the motto of C. P. Scott, the great editor of the *Manchester Guardian*—"Opinions are free; facts are sacred." Quite often they represent only a part, sometimes a very small part, of the group or area that they claim to speak for. Too often, a majority of those who should take an active part in their counsels cannot or do not do so, and the leadership devolves on others who are not well qualified. Sometimes, in fact, their only qualifications seem to be personal ambition and a liking for the sound of their own voices. These groups are also hard to finance, even on small budgets. Too often their officers in trying to raise money resort to the scare or bugaboo technique with public officials, justly or unjustly, cast in the role of the bugaboos. Again, the dominant faction in such an organization can easily persuade itself that it has to concentrate on one or two immediate objectives. Maybe this is a wise decision, but too often after the leaders have gone on record for these objectives, they feel they have to pursue them to the bitter end—even at the expense of ignoring more important issues that have developed in the meantime.

Another possibility seems to me worth considering. The larger cities might have legislative bodies *similar* (not identical) in one respect to the British Parliament. They would have one chamber with full legislative powers and another with limited powers to consider, discuss, and to take formal action. Its actions, however, would be only advisory to the chamber with legislative powers. The legislative chamber would be elected at large, the advisory one by wards or other districts. The legislative unit would be small in number; the advisory one would be somewhat larger, but probably not more than thirty-five or forty members even in the largest cities.

Clearly not only the essential characteristics of this proposal, but many details of its organization and functioning would have to be explored most carefully. If the proposal has substantive merit, the relations between the two chambers would require most skilful shaping and probably reshaping as time went on. Even at a distance, a few questions may be raised. What seems most likely to be the caliber of the members of the advisory chamber? Would it have too much influence on the legislative chamber, or would it be ignored? Would the advisory body be given the right to consider all matters before the legislative chamber, or only specified ones? Would the advisory chamber slow up seriously the action of the legislative body? Could some provision be devised, possibly a three-quarters vote of the legislative body, to enable that body to take action on emergency questions without waiting for the advisory unit? Would it be better for the neighborhood or district representatives to be nonvoting members of a one-chamber council?

Quite possibly I give more attention to this particular proposal than is appropriate in an essay of this kind. If so, it is not because I am particularly enamored of this possible solution, but because I am convinced that the problem is a vital one and should have serious attention in the years not too far ahead.

NONVOTING

One of the most confusing and, in many respects, disturbing aspects of the urban political scene is nonvoting. Only less discouraging, to me at least, is the relative neglect of this phenomenon by most political scientists—particularly those concerned primarily with urban government. This is not to disparage the excellent research work done on political behavior by political scientists and more recently by sociologists, social psychologists, public opinion specialists, and others. A large part of this pioneering work, however, has centered on presidential campaigns and voting in presidential elections. Certainly the crude record of nonvoting in municipal elections is enough to incite curiosity if not alarm. Certainly we have techniques of social research that could be more widely and more effectively employed than they have been in trying to get at factors, causes, and meanings of both voting and nonvoting among urban citizens.

For the purposes of this review, perhaps the elementary facts on non-voting may be summarized in a few paragraphs.

1. Despite the fact that both scientific and popular interest in voting and, to a lesser extent, in nonvoting have been focused on presidential elections, it is almost certainly true that the proportions of potential voters who actually have voted in recent presidential elections have averaged almost twice the proportions that have gone to the polls in municipal elections. According to widely used figures, which admittedly are subject to a considerable margin of error because no one knows the number of eligible voters, the proportion of actual to eligible voters in presidential elections from 1928 through 1948 was around 60 per cent. On the basis of a few scattered studies, students of local government seem agreed that a fairly typical proportion in municipal elections is in

the neighborhood of 30 to 40 per cent—and it may be somewhat smaller. It also seems clear that this percentage varies widely in local elections from time to time and from locality to locality.

2. No adequate statistical evidence is available for determining whether nonvoting in municipal elections has increased or decreased over the last fifty years. For presidential elections some broad trends are apparent. In the latter part of the nineteenth century actual votes cast were at or above 80 per cent of potential votes. For 1900 one estimate is 85 per cent. From then until 1924 the proportion declined quite steadily to a low of about 50 to 55 per cent in 1924. This was followed by an upswing to a high of about 63 per cent in 1940. In 1944 and in 1948 the proportion declined again—to about 55 per cent in the latter year.[41]

3. In presidential elections do sizable urban areas turn out a proportionately larger vote than smaller cities and rural areas? Here the evidence is conflicting. One study, covering largely but not exclusively cities in California, found as the "first law of voting behavior" that the proportion of votes cast to potential voters in national and state-wide elections varied inversely with the population of the locality. Considerable doubt is thrown on this generalization, however, by comparisons of voting percentages at presidential elections in major centers such as New York City and Philadelphia with the figures for other parts of their states. Also the voting percentages by states in the last few presidential elections show at or near the top of the list such highly urbanized commonwealths as Massachusetts, Rhode Island, Connecticut, and Illinois.[42]

4. The pioneering study by Messrs. Merriam and Gosnell on the mayoralty election in Chicago in April, 1923, is still one of the few that have attempted by interviews to discover the reasons for, or factors in, municipal nonvoting. Of some twenty reasons tabulated for the sample covered, the most prevalent was—general indifference.[43] Maybe this does not tell us too much, but it was by all odds the most common factor

41. Bernard Barber, "*'Mass Apathy' and Voluntary Social Participation in the United States*" (unpublished Ph.D. dissertation, Department of Sociology, Harvard University, 1948) and *Voter Participation in New York and the Nation* (Chamber of Commerce of the State of New York, New York, October, 1950), p. 1. For one comparison of presidential voting in a small urban locality, see Ben A. Arneson and William H. Eells, "Voting Behavior in 1948 as Compared with 1924 in a Typical Ohio Community," *American Political Science Review* (June, 1950), pp. 432–34.

42. Charles Hickman Titus, *Voting Behavior in the United States—A Statistical Study* (Berkeley: University of California Press, 1935), pp. 17–41 and 69–70; Chamber of Commerce of the State of New York, *op. cit.;* H. F. Alderfer and Fonnette H. Luhrs, *Registration in Pennsylvania Elections, 1926–1946* (State College: The Pennsylvania Municipal Publications Service, 1948), pp. 28–29.

43. Charles E. Merriam and Harold F. Gosnell, *Non-Voting—Causes and Methods of Control* (Chicago: University of Chicago Press, 1924), particularly chap. i and ii.

identified. At least it might have led to further and more intensive analyses than it has so far.

5. One finding of a recent study on Detroit, although obviously not the basis for any generalization, seems to be worth recording here: ". . . in the nonpresidential election years the foreign born community had a higher participation percentage than had the native white group, whereas in the years of presidential elections the positions were reversed. In breaking the native white group down into its economic constituents it was learned that its laxness during nonpresidential years was confined entirely to the lower and middle income groups."[44]

6. The proportion of nonvoters varies substantially among major groups or subclasses of the urban population. Groupings by age, sex, race, foreign and native born, religion, economic status, education, and occupation show substantial differences in the proportions of nonvoters. Some of the studies have refined these classifications to minimize the overlapping and thus reveal the more influential factors.

Lazarsfeld's panel technique, used in studying a sample of voters in Erie County, Ohio, during the 1940 presidential campaign, opens the way for a next step in getting at the factors influencing the voter as he makes up his mind whether to vote, and, if so, how, in municipal elections. From his study Lazarsfeld emphasizes interactions among members of groups that help to crystallize the voters' decisions. His analysis of this process would take us rather afield here, but he does point out: ". . . For, whether the process of change involves the resolution of cross-pressures, the influence of opinion leaders or external events, or mutual interactions, the result of change is increased consistency, both within groups and within individuals. As these processes mold and modify opinions, the group members find themselves in closer agreement with each other; there is thus the simultaneous movement toward increased homogeneity within groups and increased polarization between groups which we described earlier. And correlatively, as the individual conforms more closely to his social environment, as he resolves his cross-pressures and finds vague feelings crystallized into definite opinions, many of the inconsistencies in his private set of attitudes will disappear."[45] Certainly it would be worth while to know whether, or to what degree, this process of mutual interaction among members of various groups affects nonvoting as well as decisions for whom and what to vote in municipal elections.

Because nearly all studies of urban voting behavior feature break-

44. Edward H. Litchfield, *Voting Behavior in a Metropolitan Area* (Ann Arbor: University of Michigan Press, 1941), p. 66.

45. Paul F. Lazarsfeld, Bernard Berelson, and Hazel Gaudet, *The People's Choice—How the Voter Makes Up His Mind in a Presidential Campaign* (New York: Columbia University Press, 2d edition, 1948), p. xxv.

downs by the various groups or subclasses of the population, a tentative warning may be in order. It is well put by Litchfield in the concluding section of his study of voting in Detroit from 1930 through 1938: "From the comparison of the movements of the political behavior curves in all of the different economic, race, and ethnic groups one very important conclusion emerged: the behavior curve movements in all groups occur in such a uniform manner that it is clear that the basic influences which cause those movements operate upon and are effective in all of the different groups. In the city as a whole, although economic groups are probably more solidified than are ethnic and race groups, none of the groups is so solidified but that the basic character of its political behavior is determined by influences that are city-wide. There is an appreciable element in each group which makes common cause with other unrelated elements in other groups."[46]

Quite possibly these more general influences were more noticeable in Detroit during the 1930's than they would be in other localities in less exciting and vigorous times. Be that as it may, Litchfield's observation may serve both as a useful warning and a suggestion that future studies might well probe for other factors and forces.

7. Perhaps a little light is thrown on nonvoting by the various get-out-the-vote campaigns and organizations. For many years past, efforts of this kind have been quite common. Their scopes, methods, and sponsorships have been various. Most of them have relied on pre-election publicity and exhortation. Although their methods and results have been on the whole untested, it seems safe to say that, in general, they have made little difference. To guess at the probable reasons, I would say that probably most of them have been too spasmodic, too patronizing and moralistic in tone, and too generalized to hit at specific influences or causes of nonvoting. Also, they have probably relied too heavily on advertising techniques against which a substantial proportion of the population has had to build up a fairly considerable immunity. From the material at hand, no one would be justified in saying that they have had no appreciable effect or that, if they had not been tried, voting percentages might not have fallen even lower. Certainly, however, they have not markedly changed the general pattern.

Probably, too, most get-out-the-vote campaigns have been ill considered in that they seem to have been based on the assumption that nonvoting is a relatively isolated phenomenon with few or at least negligible relationships with broader political attitudes and practices. To illustrate this defect, let me cite one of my pet peeves—those newspapers, business and civic groups that spend about fifty weeks a year spreading the notion that local government by its very nature is ineffi-

46. Litchfield, *op. cit.*, p. 68.

cient, unproductive, irresponsible, and more or less corrupt, and then about two weeks before an election break out in a series of printed and spoken exhortations on the high duties of voting. It is hard to imagine a more futile and, in many respects, more silly procedure. Anyone who really believed what most of these groups say during the fifty weeks would certainly conclude quite logically that local government is an institution with which any sensible person should have as little to do as possible. If so, why go to the trouble of registering and voting, let alone expending the time and effort to inform one's self sufficiently to vote intelligently?

In 1924 and 1925, as a follow-up of his study with Dr. Merriam on nonvoting in Chicago, Gosnell made a study of the effects of one partial remedy for nonvoting.[47] It was aimed primarily at those nonvoters who, in the previous study, had indicated that the chief reasons for their nonvoting were either ignorance or timidity regarding election methods or simple neglect—those who said they had intended to vote but had failed to do so. Some 15 per cent of the nonvoters gave one or the other of these reasons as the chief explanation for nonvoting. In addition, one or two minor reasons seemed somewhat related.

Although Gosnell's method required considerable care in sampling and in the use of control groups, the method he tested was quite simple. Before registration days and before the 1924 general election, he sent printed reminders of registration requirements and dates to members of the experimental groups. Before an aldermanic election in February, 1925, he again sent reminders to previous nonvoters. Most of the reminders were simply factual statements on cards, but two of them were cartoons intended to suggest the responsibility of the citizen to vote or the desirability (in his own interest) of voting. Gosnell concluded from his study that it was possible by these methods to increase the voting proportion by about 10 percentage points under conditions similar to those that existed in Chicago at that time.

Apparently no one else has undertaken to test similarly specific techniques aimed at offsetting other indicated reasons or factors in nonvoting. Why? Possibly because experiments of this kind are not showy and they do require considerable time, effort, and money. Also they may presuppose much more understanding of factors in nonvoting than does in fact exist. Finally, many of the influences in nonvoting discovered in the Merriam-Gosnell study do not seem amenable to direct remedy or experimental study of this kind.

What do these facts, near facts, and approximations mean for urban political and social life? On this question it is possible to make out two broad schools of thought, or at least, of opinion.

47. Harold F. Gosnell, *Getting Out the Vote—An Experiment in the Stimulation of Voting* (Chicago: University of Chicago Press, 1927).

Members of the first school view most aspects of nonvoting with alarm. Perhaps a better word would be anxiety or concern. Some are quite indignant. To them, most nonvoters are slackers. For quite insufficient and often trivial reasons, they shirk their primary duty and responsibility as citizens. For centuries the ballot has been the objective of long, hard struggles by a succession of groups or classes within western society. Now, in this country where a very large proportion of adult citizens have the right to vote, many of them fail to use it. Other members of this same general school hint darkly that the extent and character of nonvoting suggest strongly, if in fact they do not indicate a dangerous apathy, anomie, a psychological alienation of substantial numbers of persons from the values and standards of the society.

Whether or not one agrees or disagrees in the main with these views, he should realize that by no means are they based entirely upon the relatively slight foundation of the studies referred to above. Many of the persons who hold one or the other of these distinguishable but related estimates of the situation have arrived at them from years of observation and first-hand experience in civic and local political affairs. And sections of the Merriam-Gosnell study can be taken to support their conclusions, at least in part.

In the mayoralty election in Chicago in 1923, 51 per cent of the eligible voters did not vote. In a carefully selected sample of more than 5,300 nonvoters who were interviewed in the Merriam-Gosnell study, more than 25 per cent, as pointed out above, gave reasons for their nonvoting that could only be classified as general indifference. In addition, five other related reasons were tabulated: indifference to particular election, disgust with politics, disgust with own party, belief that ballot box is corrupted, disbelief in all political action. No one of these was a frequently given reason, but, together with general indifference, they were given as the chief reasons by over 35 per cent of those interviewed. The same combination of reasons was given by more than 42 per cent of the sample who had not even registered for the election. In addition, many of those interviewed gave combinations of reasons neither or no one of which they could distinguish as chiefly responsible for their inaction. For the sample of all nonvoters, general indifference accounted for almost 37 per cent of all reasons assigned either singly or in combinations, and the set of six allied reasons were slightly more than 50 per cent of all reasons given. Assuming the reliability of this sample study, it would seem, therefore, that at that time a proportion between one-fourth and one-sixth of the total voting population of Chicago was either indifferent to voting or even less inclined to take part in this simple, basic act of political democracy.[48]

Is this a healthy condition for a large urban community? Of course

48. Merriam and Gosnell, *op. cit.*, p. 37, and Appendix A, pp. 259–61.

no generalization can be safely based on any one study of this kind. As usual, several qualifications, refinements, and interpretations could be put on the figures that might change their implications somewhat. Furthermore, a 1934 study in Greencastle, Indiana, a city of approximately 5,000, showed that in an unusually active election in which some 85 per cent of the potential voters actually voted, general indifference, lack of interest in the particular election, disgust with politics and with the 1934 election accounted for almost 30 per cent of those who failed to go to the polls or less than 5 per cent of the total electorate.[49]

The other school, in general, is much more complacent about non-voting. In fact, the common characteristic of most of its members is that they say in effect "tut tut" to the alarmed or concerned. Some are quite top-lofty about the whole thing. Those who are deeply concerned about nonvoting are "utopians"—a label that, amusingly enough, seems to be considered particularly devastating when applied to one concerned with social studies and problems. Others point out that in our society prevailing norms or hierarchies of values put economic and family responsibilities above those of political life. This, of course, might well be admitted without being taken as an answer to the questions and fears of the alarmed. Still others assert with relatively little supporting evidence that many, perhaps most, nonvoters are reasonably satisfied with governmental conditions in their localities and, therefore, see nothing to be gained by voting.[50] At least one scholar has a variant of this to the effect that an abnormally high proportion of voting, say 90 per cent or over, would be the signal of a dangerous fever in the body politic that might lead to violence or other nonconstitutional action.[51] Maybe so, but certainly very few urban localities would seem to have to worry about this contingency, at least at present. Of course, a fever may indicate a serious pathological condition, but a continually subnormal temperature may be an equally serious symptom. Query: what is the normal temperature on this scale in the sense that 98.6 degrees Fahrenheit is usually taken to mean a healthful degree of warmth in most human bodies?

Again, members of this school also rely rather more on observation, personal experience, and common sense than they do on scientific studies. Many of them, moreover, would join with many of what I have

49. Harold Zink, *Government of Cities in the United States* (New York: The Macmillan Co., New York, rev. ed., 1948), pp. 148–50.

50. On this point the most commonly quoted study is Gordon M. Connelly in collaboration with Harry A. Field, "The Non-Voter—Who He Is, What He Thinks," *Public Opinion Quarterly* (Summer, 1944), pp. 175–88. This analysis covered voters and nonvoters in the 1940 presidential election.

51. Francis G. Wilson, "The Inactive Electorate and Social Revolution," *Southwestern Social Science Quarterly* (March, 1936), pp. 73–84. See also his article, "The Pragmatic Electorate," *American Political Science Review* (February, 1930), pp. 26–37.

called the alarmed in urging the need for further studies on a much larger scale than those of the past and making use of the most reliable techniques so far developed.

A review of the kind undertaken in this essay requires the reviewer to state his opinion on at least the major questions raised. Although most of this difficult task will be undertaken in the concluding sections, perhaps I should say here what in general I think is the most likely interpretation of what facts we have about nonvoting in urban elections. On the whole, I lean rather more to the alarmed or concerned than to the complacent view. Alarm is clearly not the best word for my attitude nor for that of many others who fall in the same general category. We do not sit up nights straining our ears for the creaking, cracking, and groaning that must come from deterioration of the urban body politic. On the other hand, it seems to me that in any society that calls itself a democracy, voting should be more than a rather crude way for a minority to make certain necessary decisions and to decide who is to make the others. High percentage voting may not be the most accurate or sensitive index of healthful, meaningful social cohesion. Casual observation indicates that it is not. But I do believe these aspects of urban life are more than casually related. I can see very little, if anything, in the imperfect information we have on urban voting that gives much assurance that the urban body politic is evolving in directions or at speeds that are in any way commensurate with the increasing complexity of the problems of urban life in America. And certainly I would join with many others in supporting the observation that ". . . about all that can be concluded about voting in state and local elections is that scholars have a wonderful opportunity to narrow our area of ignorance."[52]

Finally, looking toward this further study I would suggest that we should press our research beyond discovering and verifying certain influences or factors in nonvoting. We should try also to reach some further understanding of the belief- and value-systems of those classes or subclasses of urban populations that may make widespread nonvoting among their members a quite normal, even reasonable, occurrence.[53] So far most of us have applied to the raw facts of nonvoting our own middle-class, rather intellectualized view of things (the standards of our own subculture, perhaps) and, consequently, have achieved only limited insight and rather too much indignation, rationalization, or

52. V. O. Key, *Politics, Parties, and Pressure Groups* (New York: Thomas Y. Crowell Co., New York, 1948), p. 614.

53. What I have in mind here may be illustrated, in other areas, by Allison Davis, *Social-Class Influences upon Learning* (Cambridge: Harvard University Press, 1950) and his essay "The Motivation of the Underprivileged Worker" in William Foote Whyte, ed., *Industry and Society* (New York: McGraw-Hill Book Co., 1946), pp. 84–106.

frustration. Also, I would hope that in further studies ways and methods could be devised for testing the significance, relative to other factors, of two common features of current urban government: (*a*) the failure of local parties to present to prospective voters clear-cut issues or alternatives on major questions of policy; and (*b*) the diffused responsibility for many vital local public services.

LEADERSHIP AND MORALE

One of the latest of the major foreign commentators on American society has written:

Despite the democratic organization of American society with its emphasis upon liberty, equality of opportunity (with a strong leaning in favor of the underdog), and individualism, the idea of leadership pervades American thought and collective action. The demand for "intelligent leadership" is raised in all political camps, social and professional groups, and, indeed, in every collective activity centered around any interest or purpose—church, school, business, recreation, philanthropy, the campus life of a college, the entertaining of a group of visitors, the selling of a patent medicine, the propagation of an idea or of an interest. As a standard demand it appears with great frequency in public speeches and newspaper editorials and will seldom be absent even when the social reformer or the social scientist speaks.

If an ordinary American faces a situation which he recognizes as a "problem" without having any specific views as to how to "solve" it, he tends to resort to two general recommendations: one, traditionally, is "education," the other is "leadership." The belief in "education" is a part of, or a principal conclusion from, the American Creed. The demand for "leadership" plays on a different plane of his personality. It is a result less of a conscious ideological principle than of a pragmatic approach to those activities which require the cooperation of many individuals. For this reason it is also much less a part of Americans' self-knowledge. While the democratic Creed and the belief in education are an ever present popular theory with highest national sanctions—held conscious not only by affirmative references in practically every solemn public utterance, but also maintained by an ever growing literature—it will be found that Americans in general are quite unaware that the leadership idea is a particular characteristic of their culture. . . .[54]

Some ten years ago, an American, then a business executive who has written much on business and social questions, began one article with this paragraph:

Leadership has been the subject of an extraordinary amount of dogmatically stated nonsense. Some, it is true, has been enunciated by observers who have had no experience themselves in coordinating and directing the activities of others; but much of it has come from men of ample experience, often of established reputations as leaders. As to the latter, we may assume that they know how to do well what they do not know how to describe or explain. At any rate, I have found it difficult not to magnify superficial aspects and catch-phrases of the subject to the status of funda-

54. Gunnar Myrdal (with Richard Sterner and Arnold Rose), *An American Dilemma* (New York: Harper and Bros., 1944), p. 709.

mental propositions, generalized beyond all possibility of useful application, and fostering misunderstanding.[55]

Although these observations still have a considerable degree of validity, both may be less true today than they were when they were made a few years ago. Over the past several years, thoughtful Americans have become increasingly concerned about the place and character of leadership in many sectors of our common life. Professional students, particularly those in the social sciences, have addressed themselves more and more to various phases of leadership. On the whole, this kind of inquiry has more often been centered on industrial relations, military organization, education, the formation and functioning of small groups, than in urban government and institutions. Students of the latter subjects, however, have made some contributions to the general advance in analysis and understanding. In addition, many of them, as well as students of leadership in other fields, would agree that this whole complex subject is an excellent example of an area in which various research techniques and forms of analysis can both supplement and strengthen one another.

Approaches to an understanding of leadership.—Although I shall come back to this point a bit later, it may be useful to note here briefly the major approaches or types of investigation made in recent years. Four may be distinguished, with the usual warning that they are by no means air-tight categories but grade from one to the next:

1. Probably the first and in some ways the most simple in method is the direct study of outstanding leaders in various walks of life. From biographies, personal acquaintance, and more intensive analyses of their leadership roles, various common qualities or attributes of leaders are identified. Thus, Ordway Tead in *The Art of Leadership* notes ten such qualities:[56] physical and nervous energy, a sense of purpose and direction, enthusiasm, friendliness and affection, integrity, technical mastery, decisiveness, intelligence, teaching skill, and faith. Although others have reached conclusions somewhat differently phrased and with some differences in emphasis, by and large, one who compares their analyses finds a substantial degree of agreement among them.

Although this approach has yielded useful results and may do so again, those who followed it seemed before long to come up against a blank wall. Possibly this is stating their difficulty too strongly; at least they found it hard to press their analyses beyond these tabulations of personal qualities and attributes. Although it is quite apparent that

55. Chester I. Barnard, "The Nature of Leadership," reprinted in *Organization and Management—Selected Papers* (Cambridge: Harvard University Press, 1948), p. 80.
56. Ordway Tead, *The Art of Leadership* (New York: McGraw-Hill Book Co., 1935), chaps. vi and *passim*.

most prominent leaders have quite a full complement of these characteristics, it is also quite clear that they have no monopoly of them.
Again, among themselves they vary greatly in the degrees to which they
show many of these qualities. Where is the key to an understanding of
leadership?

2. The next line of attack was closely related both logically and in
time. It focused on the functions performed by leaders. Often, of
course, the line between the functions or roles of leadership and the
methods and personal qualities through which these functions were
performed was not a well-defined boundary. The difference lay largely
in the angle of approach and emphasis.

For example, Charles E. Merriam in his *Systematic Politics,* in addition to discussing several common characteristics of political leaders,
points out that "More modern leadership exhibits strikingly the importance of two factors: the command of symbolism and facility in organization. Neither of these is entirely new in the history of political relations, but both are highly developed in modern times. . . ."[57] Again,
two leading social psychologists, in their recent textbook, give "Fourteen different common functions of leaders . . . the leader as an executive, as planner, as policy maker, as expert, as external group representative, as controller of internal relationships, as purveyor of rewards
and punishments, as arbitrator and mediator, as exemplar, as group
symbol, as surrogate for individual responsibility, as ideologist, as father figure, and as scapegoat."[58]

Here also, the classifications from this kind of analysis have added to
our understanding and have provided a framework within which various aspects of leadership could be seen more clearly and steadily. In
general, however, this approach seems to share some of the same limitations as the first.

3. In trying to get around the barriers that were encountered in the
first two paths into this area, several investigators hit upon the probability that, as one has put it, the leader should be seen and studied in
context. Dr. Merriam in his study *Political Power* put it: "The leader
is a function of the social pattern and cannot be understood apart from
it." In other words, we might explain more satisfactorily why some
leaders are successful and why some functions of leadership are performed more effectively than others if we looked more carefully at the
groups and organizations that are being led. Quite early it was demonstrated that group size, formality of organization, age and tradition,

57. Charles E. Merriam, *Systematic Politics* (Chicago: University of Chicago Press,
1945), p. 108.
58. David Krech and Richard S. Crutchfield, *Theory and Problems of Social Psychology*
(New York: McGraw-Hill Book Co., 1948), pp. 417–39. This listing is in a summary on
p. 438.

and degree of autonomy were among the group characteristics that determined, in considerable part, the demands on their leaders.

4. The last of these four approaches is, again, a moderate extension of the rationale of the third. It seems to me well, if rather formally, stated in these words:

> . . . *leadership is a relation between leader and follower;* it is a relation that varies with (*a*) the behavior of the leader, (*b*) the predispositions or expectancies of the follower and (*c*) the supra-individual characteristics of the social situation in which leadership occurs. We need to deal with all three of these factors and their interrelation if we are to create meaningful general statements about leadership.
>
> There is some justification for regarding the follower as the most crucial factor in any leadership event and for arguing that research directed at the follower will eventually yield a handsome pay-off. Not only is it the follower who accepts or rejects leadership, but it is the follower who *perceives* both the leader and the situation and who reacts in terms of what he perceives. And what he perceives may be, to an important degree, a function of his own motivations, frames of references, and "readinesses."
>
> For the present purposes, and as an example of the sort of reasoning involved in this approach, we can think, hypothetically, in terms of followers' *needs.* We can imagine stable needs relatively common to all members of a given culture or of segments thereof. Or we can think of needs that are highly individual but still stable attributes of any given follower. And we can imagine follower needs that will vary widely as the objectively defined situation changes. In any given situation, we can conceive of determining with reasonable accuracy what are the principal needs of the followers. And once we know these needs we can predict what the leader must do to meet them, for the function of the leader, in order to win acceptance, is to *meet the needs of the followers.* If he meets these needs successfully, he is accepted. If he does not, he is merely tolerated or, if the followers are free, rejected. In the case either of rejection or mere toleration the relation between him and his followers is not of a sort that leads to adaptive group action. As the situation changes, or as membership in the group is changed, the needs of the followers will fall into a different pattern and different demands will be made on the leader. The leader may or may not be so constituted that he can meet a changed pattern of needs. The military officer who can fill his function under combat conditions and be followed unquestioningly may not often be able to establish the most effective relation with followers who are on the other side of a Navy Department desk. He often cannot meet widely differing patterns of follower needs. . . .[59]

The framework of this approach easily justifies the linking together of two social phenomena that sometimes, as a matter of common sense, are looked at together, but, on the other hand, are often considered as separate subjects—leadership and morale. The monumental study of army life during World War II, *The American Soldier,* by Stouffer and others illustrates the fruitfulness of this dual approach in the hands of

---

59. Fillmore H. Sanford, *Authoritarianism and Leadership* (Philadelphia: Institute for Research in Human Relations, 1950), pp. 3–5. In this same chapter, Dr. Sanford reviews leadership studies in more technical and precise language but in essentially the same classifications as I have used.

skilled investigators. Although the suggestion is still to be tested, I believe a similarly oriented approach to political and civic leadership in urban communities might also be enlightening.

Before going on to some of the preliminary findings from this kind of research and their possible application to public questions and programs in urban communities, two warnings seem to be in order.

None of the four paths of exploration is likely to make the others useless; none is likely to prove to be futile in the total effort to understand leadership and followership in human affairs. Although identifying and classifying the attributes and functions of established leaders seems to have reached some point of diminishing returns, it may well be that further work on the context or situations in which leaders operate and on the needs of various kinds of groups will open up new possibilities in the older lines of investigation. This likelihood is clearly recognized by many of those who are now engaged in some of the more promising explorations in the newer fields.

Again, persons interested in urban development and in public programs directly related to it ought not to sell short the work of social psychologists, sociologists, cultural anthropologists, and others in industrial relations, military organization, and group dynamics. (Incidentally, the word "dynamics" in this phrase has been defined as "Nothing more esoteric . . . than . . . adjustive changes occurring in the group structure as a whole, as produced by changes in any part of the group."[60]) Like most bodies of research and exploration in a new and complex area of study, this work is uneven. Some of it may seem to be unduly concerned with rather limited devices and techniques, possibly aimed, for example, to strengthen the hand of management in dealing with labor unions across the bargaining table or to reduce sources of friction in industrial plants. Other parts may seem unduly weighted down with cumbersome terminology that reminds one of the old remark about the systematic misuse of abstruse terms devised for that particular purpose. At all events, one unavoidably will come upon variations in basic notions or concepts, differences in vocabulary, and many more questions and suggestions for research than tested principles.

Many of the more thoughtful investigators in these other areas, however, are feeling their way toward principles or theories (in the correct sense of tested generalizations) on human behavior and its determinants that eventually may have real validity when applied to various phases of the urban scene. Considerable evidence on this point could be put down. Let me give only two quotes from one leading student of industrial relations. E. Wight Bakke of Yale University in a symposium on *Research Frontiers in Human Relations* said:

60. Krech and Crutchfield, *op. cit.*, p. 19.

. . . Although it is true that all research is in the nature of frontier activity, I should like to speak of a relatively recent emphasis and approach in industrial relations research to which that definition would seem particularly applicable. Those representing this emphasis and approach are interested primarily in the development of a fundamental theory of human behavior useful in understanding the activity and relations of people, not only in industrial life, but in whatever area of social interaction they are involved. In other words, they are as much concerned to develop a social science as to increase our knowledge of the facts of industrial relations or to suggest solutions for particular problems in the relations among workers, union leaders, and management.[61]

Later on in his statement Mr. Bakke elaborated this point:

. . . those whose purposes I have been describing are convinced that the most pressing present need is for studies not only of personnel policies but of the nature of persons; not only of incentive systems, but of human incentives; not only of collective bargaining procedures, but of the factors that mold the attitudes and actions of the bargainers; not only of bargaining issues, but of the structures of living of the parties which give them varying and conflicting 'slants' on the issues; not only of the structure of management and unions, but of the compulsions those structures impose upon the actions and thought of the men who represent them; not only of techniques for organizing enterprises or unions, but of the principles of effective association and group solidarity and teamwork.

At the risks of belaboring this point and of weighting down this part of my monograph with quotations, may I also point out that leading students of local government and public programs have recognized these substantive relations among forms of human behavio, in these various so-called fields. For example, William Anderson writing on state and local governments in a volume on *Research in Political Science* has said:

"The people, both as individuals and as groups, also call for intensive study in any well-rounded and comprehensive investigation of local government. In a sense the institutions of local government are merely formalized or crystallized aspects of the political behavior of the people. But in addition to the formalized are all the informal, the spontaneous and unregulated phases of human behavior. Non-voting and other forms of non-participation, resistance to regulations and taxes, attempts to take unfair advantage of public services and facilities,—these and other modes of unregimented behavior appear with infinite variations among the millions of citizens affected by local government. Given a uniform law to enforce or administer, even the officials themselves respond to it, interpret it, and apply it with almost endless variations. Actual uniformity is almost never, if ever attained. Human inventiveness, and intractability seem to be almost without limit, and this fact is probably nowhere better revealed than in the operation of local government. It appears, indeed, that man-made laws have relatively less, and individual human traits and behavior relatively more influence and free play in local government than at higher levels of administration. In many respects local government as a study is close to sociology,

61. "Industrial Relations Research" in *Research Frontiers in Human Relations* (Philadelphia: The American Philosophical Society, 1948), pp. 376–80.

while the attitudes and knowledge of the psychologist are also especially pertinent in this field.[62]

In a rather different connection, John Gaus in his presidential address to the American Political Science Association offered this advice:

. . . How can the knowledge of the expert be made more available to the layman? I think we shall not contribute much to an answer if we consider this a one-way process. My suggestion that, in addition to our concern for organization and process, the techniques of legislation or of adjudication, we acquaint ourselves with a substantive problem was made partly with this problem in mind. In such a study— perhaps in some civic activity in his local community, for example, the political scientist will learn as much as he teaches. He will better know how much time and energy and knowledge of what proportion of his neighbors are available for a political problem; of the distractions and apparent irrelevancies that intervene; of the special resources of knowledge and wisdom or liabilities of suspicion and hatred that must be envisaged in formulating a political problem or attempting its solution. If the political scientist has something to give, he will probably find that it wins respect. The incident may be local and petty, but the general truths it conveys may be widely applicable in his work. One does not need to sentimentalize about popular participation in affairs to recognize that the expert is more likely to be an expert if he knows better what people are concerned about, and how to explain the meaning, hitherto hidden to them, of events and institutions bound to affect them. His very research and teaching will have to become another item of weight, however tiny, against the failure of nerve and faith in human effort. . . .[63]

The last few pages have been more or less of a digression. In them, I have tried to sketch several of the ways in which leadership is now being looked at and researched into by various individuals and organizations, as well as to suggest what I take to be the probability that the results of these studies may add to our understanding of the place leaders, followers, group morale, and a feeling of social cohesion or solidarity may have in the development and redevelopment of urban communities. Now I wish to try to sharpen the focus of the argument. More specifically, what can be said in reply or at least in response to four questions:

1. Without going into too many niceties of definition, what do we mean by leadership?

2. Are American urban communities today equipped with leadership reasonably able to cope with the range and character of problems that have been dealt with earlier in this essay? In short, is urban leadership today adequate?

3. What, if anything, have recent studies of the leadership process turned up that helps us in analysis and action on these urban problems?

62. Ernest S. Griffith, ed., *Research in Political Science* (Chapel Hill: The University of North Carolina Press, 1948), p. 87.

63. John Gaus, "A Job Analysis of Political Science," *American Political Science Review* (April, 1946), p. 227.

4. How should we try to proceed from here in mobilizing understanding, action, and support in attacking these formidable problems?

What is leadership?—Its essence, at least in my view, is the ability to unite a group of persons in working together for certain purposes or ends. Often, of course, a leader may operate in a group that has been formed well before he comes on the scene; sometimes he may be a force in the formation or reorganization of the group. In either event he helps to define its purposes or ends, by one method or another mediates among or harmonizes conflicting interests or objectives, plays a major part in planning the strategy for achieving these ends, looks to the timing of various steps in the campaign strategy, fights off or in some other way counteracts divisive forces both within and outside of his group, helps to keep up its morale and cohesion, and represents it in competition, conflict, or collaboration with other groups. In all that he does, his relative success is determined not only by his own abilities and methods, but also by the characteristics, needs, and value systems of his followers.

On the urban scene, it is equally important to point out the limitations on leaders and at least some of the things that they are not. Although practically all leaders have some degree of disciplinary power in that they can measure out at least some rewards and direct or indirect punishment, their powers, particularly in the more informal groups, are primarily derived from the groups' members. A leader who alienates substantial segments of his following soon finds that he no longer is a leader. Even before his successor may appear, his powers decline and either an outright revolt or a creeping lethargy makes him ineffective. Once this process starts, it is most difficult to reverse. Although the commander, man-on-horseback type of leader, who probably has received more than his fair share of attention in recent years as compared with that given to less spectacular types, may seem an exception to some of these observations, closer analysis has shown that the exceptions are often more apparent than real. Most leaders, in short, lead rather than command or drive their followers in the kinds of groups and organizations with which we are here concerned.

At this point, it should be noted that sizable urban communities, although they may have some of the social and psychological characteristics of a group, are made up of subgroups, each of which may have leaders of some type or ability. From this it follows that the need for leadership in governmental and civic affairs in urban centers is not a matter of one or even two or three leaders, but many, each able to lead and represent one of these many and various subgroups. Probably the failure to recognize or at least to act on this fact is still one of the chief reasons for the failure of many urban communities over the years to realize objectives that are quite widely accepted. Community-wide leaders, actual and self-appointed, simply try to do too much from the top. The army has too many generals and not enough sergeants. Some of the more gifted and lucky community-wide leaders do attain a certain degree of success for a time, but it is at least arguable that the net result of their efforts may be on the debit rather than the credit side. Their limited successes may obscure the fact that longer-term results are dependent in no small measure upon continuously effective leadership in most of the subgroups. The present difficulties of some clearance and rebuilding projects in local redevelopment programs may be an illustration of this point.

Is present urban leadership adequate?—An answer may be indicated by asking another question: Does anyone think it is? Probably few persons who have had responsible parts in recent redevelopment or allied programs would answer "yes" to either of these questions.

The shortage of leaders with a substantial community- or city-wide following, either among leaders of subgroups or individual citizens, has been recognized and commented upon so often that it hardly need be demonstrated here. In this respect, some urban localities are more fortunate than others, and, in most of them, the leadership curve rises and falls over substantial periods of time. Undoubtedly, however, the average or modal level is low and, although no accurate index is available, it may be falling.

Here some possible confusion may be avoided by recalling the sense in which the words leaders and leadership are being used. A working definition of a leader and a rough description of the essentials of his relations with his followers have just been given. By such phrases as urban leaders or leaders in urban communities, I mean not only those who usually would be called political leaders, but also civic leaders— those who have a following in programs of public as distinguished from governmental undertakings. Confusion often arises from another connotation of the words "leaders" and "leadership." In this sense, a leader is simply a distinguished practitioner in some profession, calling, or craft. Thus we speak of a leading doctor or businessman. This is simply a recognition of his unusual competence or performance in his profession or vocation and does not mean necessarily that he has any followers, least of all in programs or activities in the public interest. Leaders in this sense we have in abundance, but reliance on their names and reputations in public activities and programs is no substitute for leaders with followers and the abilities to unite them effectively in behalf of definite ends.

For our purposes here, four types of subgroups of the urban community are worth noting: (*a*) what might be called functional groups, e.g., associations of businessmen and industrialists, city-wide labor federations or councils; (*b*) area groups—district or neighborhood groups of various sizes, kinds, and degrees or organization; (*c*) combinations of these two—businessmen in a certain shopping area, property owners in a neighborhood or district; and (*d*) groups whose membership ties are racial, religious beliefs, or national origins or traditions. Do these groups, by and large, turn up leaders who make them forces in programs of city-wide significance? Do they make their followers a continuing factor in the solution of public questions that bear directly upon the group or its area?

On these points, our ignorance is wide and deep. One opinion held by observers and some actual leaders is that, by and large, the answer to both of these questions is clearly "no." Most of these smaller groups have limited objectives closely related to the obvious and immediate interests of their members. When they go beyond these relatively narrow interests, it is usually to support some charitable or welfare activity, e.g., funds for private relief agencies or a boys' camp, which usually are laudable but do not bring the group into direct contact with the underlying problems of their communities.

During recent years neighborhoods in larger urban centers have been the subject of some study and much controversy not only among sociologists, but also among persons and organizations directly concerned with urban planning, housing, and redevelopment. Much of this argument would not be pertinent here. In trying to assess the effectiveness of leadership in urban communities, however, we must face the question: Do most urban neighborhoods or local districts have recognized leaders? To be sure, this is only one of a series of questions that could be put down on this general subject, but at least it would be among the first on any list of this kind.

Although not the basis for any definitive answer, the recent study that bears most directly on this question supports in general the impression that in the larger urban areas neighborhood leadership is weak and probably declining. The findings of this study deserve some comment here.

In 1948 the Institute for Research in Human Relations, which is in Philadelphia, undertook this study on *The Identification and Acceptance of Leadership in Urban Communities*.[64] Some 960 persons were interviewed in twenty-four four-block areas in the city and county of Philadelphia. The inhabitants of one of the twenty-four locality areas were predominantly in the upper economic class; six were in the upper-

64. For the part of this study drawn on here see Ira DeA. Reid and Emily L. Ehle, "Leadership Selection in Urban Locality Areas" in the *Public Opinion Quarterly*, XIV (Summer, 1950), 262–84.

middle brackets; eleven in the lower-middle; and six in the lower economic strata. As part of the seventy-two-question interviews were: "I prefer that the person I go to for advice be _____," and "In your opinion, who are the individuals in this neighborhood who have become the leaders and have been accepted as leaders by the people around here?" The most significant findings for our purposes are:

1. Of all the persons interviewed, almost three-fifths (58.8 per cent) did not nominate any local leader "around here." The percentages varied directly with economic status—from 67.5 per cent in the top economic bracket to 49.6 per cent in the lowest.

2. Among the persons most frequently mentioned as local leaders, politicians, most often the committeemen, were much more frequently mentioned than any other vocation or calling. The acceptance of the political leaders, as would be expected, was roughly inverse to economic status. Thus, in the six upper-middle areas, political leaders were most commonly nominated as first choice of persons in two of the six areas; in the six lower economic class areas, political leaders were the most common nominees for first choice in five. In general acceptance as leaders, politicians were followed by community and welfare workers, businessmen, clergymen, and lawyers, in that order.

3. ". . . In fact, in no one area can any leader claim to have the informal or unstructured support of a majority of people in that locality."[65]

4. The directors of this study ". . . believe that the data presented here lend additional support to the thesis that the intimacy of the modern urban community as indicated in the human behavior of what we have uncritically called the 'neighborhood' has been broken up by the growth of an intricate mesh of contacts wider than those of the family, play group, and small area activities."[66] Another finding, however, contradicts the common notion that neighborhood contacts and organization have been supplanted by affiliation with other groups not organized on an area or neighborhood basis: "Throughout this study, incidentally, evidence was obtained to belie the stereotyped concept of the American as a 'joiner.' Seventy-eight per cent of the sample belong to no religious organization beyond general membership in a church, 85 per cent belong to no civic or charitable organization, 74 per cent report no affiliation with occupational groups (unions, business, or professional associations). . . ."[67]

In short, this sample study in one large urban center shows that neighborhood or local district leadership is basically weak. Although the influence, if any, of other groups and their leaders on neighborhoods

65. *Ibid.*, p. 277.
66. *Ibid.*, pp. 283–84.
67. *Ibid.*, p. 265.

needs further study, these nonarea groups have rather smaller memberships than has often been supposed.

What does this all mean to our exploration of urban leadership? Although many parts of the picture are by no means clear and some have to be filled in now by outright guesswork, it does seem that at least the larger urban communities are short in effective leadership, either city-wide or in neighborhood districts. Probably the present situation in these respects represents a falling off in leadership and urban group morale over the past few decades. Probably the mobility of urban populations has some considerable relation to these declines. Quite possibly, this movement has not been a transfer of allegiance or followership from neighborhood or other area leaders to those in vocational, civic, or religious organizations. Quite possibly identification with urban groups of any kind has declined. In this connection, nonvoting and other possible evidences of political indifference may be better evaluated. Certainly what little we know about urban groups and their leaders lends some support to the argument that nonvoting may be influenced in considerable part by apathy toward local government and toward community life and affairs in general. These, to be sure, are broad conclusions and they cannot fairly be said to be demonstrated or proved by the information at hand. I submit, however, that they are not an unlikely interpretation of what we know. Certainly it would be difficult to make most of the findings from objective studies and the experience of qualified observers support an opposite set of conclusions.

What have we learned from recent studies?—All I can hope to do here is to draw off a few findings or hypotheses about human groups and their leadership that seem pertinent to urban communities and to their neighborhood or area subgroups. I propose to sketch these ideas from three areas of study and investigation: industrial relations, group morale, and racial prejudice or ethnic hostility. In none of these areas are the findings conclusive or fully established. Many are based on studies of small samples. Much more work remains to be done on the validity of these hypotheses generally in the areas from which they were drawn as well as, of course, on their reliability in other parts of our society, e.g., urban and neighborhood organizations.

Among the leaders in studying human beings in industrial relations were Elton Mayo and his former associates at Harvard. Their years of work have led to some conclusions and points of emphasis that are significant for our purpose.[68]

68. Most of these are summarized in Elton Mayo, *The Social Problems of an Industrial Civilization* (Graduate School of Business Administration, Harvard University, 1945). An appendix outlines the Harvard work in industrial relations from 1926 to 1945 and lists books, reports, and articles by staff members.

Mayo and his colleagues emphasize two requirements of human communities: (1) to supply goods and services and (2) to maintain a substantial degree of spontaneous co-operation or collaboration among their members. As they look at history they see wide variations in the degree of effective collaboration or co-operation. They stress that it is so basically important to an industrial society that it must not be left to chance. Further, they conclude that modern industrialism, particularly in this country, ". . . has been immensely successful in respect of material and technical accomplishment, an utter failure as a cooperative system . . ."[69]

This sad result is attributable largely to two facts. First, our society, or at least the industrial part of it, has been developed on the technical side to an unprecedented degree. This has called increasingly for a degree of adaptability in our human relations—a degree far exceeding that required in any other age. In times past, human collaboration or co-operation has been most evident in exactly opposite types of human societies—the established societies in which technical change is slow and relatively inconspicuous, and in which customs and folkways slowly evolve to give most groups and individuals a recognized place and to train them in a reasonably satisfactory adjustment in their relationships and responsibilities. In addition, our failure to develop an adaptive society stems not only from relative neglect of the need for collaboration, but also from outright erroneous conceptions in economics and politics.

One of the keys to our failure is the weakness, amounting often to almost total inability, in communication among most of the important groups and subgroups within our industrial society. Most members of these groups simply cannot and often do not try to understand how the members of others define common situations or arrive at their position in respect to them. This is by no means largely a matter of language or semantics. It runs much more to questions of attitude, ways of perceiving and understanding, and deep-seated differences in the objectives or things that are held to be important—the value and belief systems of various groups.

As a result of their long and intensive research the Mayo group and others in the same field have arrived at two sets of findings that seem to me of particular value for our purposes. The experiments at the Western Electric Company and elsewhere have made clear the importance of nonmonetary, nonmaterial motivation among industrial workers. Wages and working conditions are by no means the only or maybe even the chief determinants of industrial productivity or general satisfaction. Also, in industrial settings, informal, small group organization

69. *Ibid.*, p. 54.

among workers has been found to be at least as much if not more of an influence on productivity and morale than the formal structure of industrial organization. These small groups, each with its own leader, effectively establish standards of output and performance and protect them against most forms of influence or interference from outside— including the foremen when they are not recognized leaders of the group. These small groups operate effectively even under piecework systems, when presumably the economic man should look primarily to the size of his own earnings. When these groups are largely out of sympathy with management's basic policies, methods, and objectives, as they understand them, the groups usually become centers of resistance and antagonism not only to management but often among themselves.

Finally, Mayo and some of his colleagues have pointed to the decline of the neighborhood as a unit of urban group organization. On the whole, they seem to look upon this as inevitable and feel that industry can and should become the setting for another kind of meaningful social organization in the future. They do not set up an either-or choice or suggest that any one kind of group will serve all social purposes. In fact, Mayo points out in one place that ". . . those who have been intelligent and active members of many groups possess, not only superior independence of judgment, but also a greater capacity for ease of cooperation with other persons and groups."[70] This would seem to support the view that developing methods of group collaboration and understanding within industry might encourage neighborhood group organization and collaboration within the larger urban community as well, and vice versa. Quite surely, however, better group relations within industry will not assure sound neighborhoods or vice versa.

In general, many students of industrial relations, particularly the Mayo group, are very unhappy about the present position and outlook. A quotation from Mayo makes this clear:

F. J. Roethlisberger is of the opinion that our industrial civilization of the present is improvidently living on its capital, upon the store of human goodwill and self-abnegation that many centuries of established routines of living have left us. In a recent paper in the *Harvard Business Review*, he points out that in the industrial situations we have studied we have constantly found, often in the lower levels of administration, "men of extraordinary skill in the direction of securing cooperative effort." The importance of this administrative function "is too little recognized." Indeed "a greater proportion" of such men remain at the lower levels of management because technical competence wins recognition and promotion whereas skill in handling human relations does not. Yet were it not for these men, he claims, "the unleashed forces of modern technology would spin themselves out to doom and destruction." So these men go unnoticed and unrewarded; no provision is made for

70. Elton Mayo, *The Political Problem of Industrial Civilization* (Graduate School of Business Administration, Harvard University, 1947), p. 15.

their replacement when the supply shall fail. And no university calls attention to the fact that material provision is only one of the duties of civilization, the other being the maintenance of cooperative living. Of these two duties it may be said that in any society at a given time the neglected factor becomes the more important. This is our situation now; our theory of civilization acts on the assumption that if technical and material advancement is maintained, human cooperation will *somehow* be inevitable.

Morale, the maintenance of cooperative living, is commonly spoken as an imponderable, an intangible; and these epithets serve to justify the idea that the study of such matters is beneath the notice of the engineer, the economist, the university. Yet the instances I have presented do not seem to support this contemptuous dismissal. . . . The fact is that those who refer to such matters as imponderable are themselves ignorant of methods by which they can systematically set about the task of improving the cooperative morale in a working department, and are irked by any implication that this is a proper duty of the administrator. Such men therefore rely upon a confident, or even jolly, manner, upon knowing everyone's first name and using it, upon expedients such as saying "Good morning" to everyone they meet. And it is these same persons who express contempt for "sentimental" methods. This, as a substitute for intelligent inquiry and understanding, would be comic in an isolated instance; but, when twentieth-century civilization can, in general, show nothing better, the comic element recedes and tragedy takes its place. There is not much time left us; society, within the nation and without it, is breaking down into groups that show an ever increasing hostility to each other; irrational hates are taking the place of cooperation. This, historically, has been the precursor of downfall for many valiant civilizations. . . . Social life resembles biological in at least one aspect; when normal process ceases, pathological growth begins. It is a short step from friendship or tolerance to distrust and hatred when the normal social relationships disintegrate.[71]

It is a revealing commentary on Mayo's critique of our society that so much of both research and general interest in group morale can be traced more or less directly to our nation's part in the two world wars of the past generation. It is easy to see, however, why questions of morale are fundamental in a vast military organization made up largely of nonprofessional soldiers. And we certainly should be grateful both to the social scientists and to their superiors in the military services who made possible the kinds of investigation summarized in the volumes on *The American Soldier.*[72] Anyone who struggles with an essay like this one, however, may be pardoned for wishing that some of the social-psychological phases of urban life and institutions could command both the interest and resources necessary for a comparable investigation. Be that as it may, right now our task is to select from this

71. Mayo, *Social Problems,* pp. 117–18. In citing here the work of Mayo and his followers, it does not seem necessary or pertinent to comment on his alleged lack of appreciation for political processes and their relations to group interests and conflicts.

72. *The American Soldier,* four volumes prepared under the auspices of a Special Committee of the Social Science Research Council (Princeton: Princeton University Press, 1949). References here are to Vol. I, subtitled *Adjustment during Army Life,* and Vol. II, subtitled *Combat and Its Aftermath,* both by Samuel A. Stouffer *et al.*

store of information and analyses a few items that seem particularly pertinent to the urban problems we are trying to understand.

When the Research Branch was asked by the Information and Education Division of the Army to forecast problems that might arise at the end of the shooting in World War II, as the later report on this assignment pointed out the predictions were in part deductions from certain "general sociological propositions" including:

1. In general, people are able to suppress their individualistic concerns and interests which handicap them in the performance of their part in a collective enterprise under the following conditions:

a) When they are aware of a significant personal stake in the goals of the group effort and of the necessity for total group effort to achieve those goals; or

b) When they identify their own safety and welfare with that of the group and are aware of a threat to the security of the group

c) When they are aware of the nature and significance of their roles in the collective enterprise

d) When they are aware of the negative effects of failures to subordinate individualistic interests to group purposes and effort

2. Similarly people generally are able to suppress intragroup antagonisms which undermine the unity and efficiency of the group, when they are aware of the handicap these antagonisms present in the achievement of group goals or in maintaining the security of a group against external threat.

3. . . . .

4. When the conditions outlined above do not obtain, it is still possible to secure group discipline by coercive measures. But an army or any other group which has to rely on such measures to any great extent is highly vulnerable to stresses and strains.

5. When collective goals are achieved or abondoned or outer threats are removed, the hitherto suppressed individualistic concerns and interests and the latent internal antagonisms reassert themselves and cease to be subordinated to group interests. Under such conditions, the problem of group discipline and unity becomes acute.[73]

Incidentally, this quotation suggests a warning made by two other scholars about outside threats or dangers as factors in group morale. Their comment is not in opposition to the quotation, but rather to the "glib and frequently cynical belief held by many leaders that all that is necessary to heighten morale or decrease intragroup antagonism is to find a suitable and 'dangerous' out-group. . . ."[74] The limitation is that threats or fear increase morale provided the persons threatened already have some sense of solidarity. If not, the threat or fear may result in panic rather than in effective common action. Beyond question the crisis of Dunkirk united the British people in a war that none of them wanted and a considerable proportion of them thought unnecessary and avoidable. In the face of a similar military crisis, however, the French nation fell apart.

73. Stouffer, *et al.,* Vol. II, p. 550.
74. Krech and Crutchfield, *op. cit.,* p. 416.

These same two writers, drawing upon several studies that I shall not refer to, list several determinants of group morale:

Positive goals . . . In the absence of clear over-all objectives, groups cannot hope to achieve a high order of synthesis and will easily deteriorate. . . .

Satisfaction of "accessory" needs . . . Many people feel a strong wish to participate in activities with others, and such desire for participation may be related to needs for self-expression, prestige, recognition, and the like. These "accessory" functions of groups are extremely important. Better group morale can be expected, other things being equal, in groups that so function as to permit the optimal degree of feelings of participation, self-expression, and recognition on the part of its members. . . .

Sense of advance toward goal . . . It is also necessary to have some feeling of moving toward the goal. As laboratory and clinical studies have shown, very small amounts of encouragement and success and small steps toward the goal are frequently effective in sustaining and enhancing motivation. . . .

Level of aspiration and level of achievement . . . ". . . To develop and to maintain high goals, and at the same time, to keep the plan of the next action realistically within the limits of what is possible, seems to be one of the basic objectives for and a criterion of high morale.

Time perspective . . . For optimal conditions of morale, the group members should understand clearly the relevance of present activities to the main ultimate group objective. The future steps to be taken in achievement of the goal should be explicitly laid out, so that the person has a clear cognitive structure concerning the general plan of the action to be followed. . . .

Lewin . . . has pointed out that the relationship between high morale and long-range time perspective is reciprocal; i.e., not only does a long-range time perspective help maintain high morale in a group, but a group that has high morale, for whatever reason, also tends to develop a long-range time perspective. . . .

Equality of sacrifice or gain within the group. One of the deadliest weapons in the arsenal of psychological warfare is propaganda aimed at convincing some segments of the enemy group that they are suffering more hardships or are gaining fewer benefits than other segments of the group. . . . In the first stages of the bombing of London, the poorer districts in the East End were attacked almost exclusively, and the resentment of the people in this section toward the more favored in other parts of the city grew dangerously ugly. With the bombing of Buckingham Palace, however, there was a swift change in morale, the people now feeling that all were in it equally.

Feelings of solidarity, identification, and involvement . . . The sense of "togetherness," of joining with others in a common enterprise, seems by itself to make for stronger morale. . . . An individual who, alone, might easily become discouraged or intimidated can sustain his faith and keep fighting if he is with his gang. . . . The feeling of solidarity in the group seems to provide a defense against demoralization. . . . It might be safe to conclude, therefore, that a group formed on the basis of a deep emotional attachment, as in friendship among its members, will demonstrate a higher morale in all sorts of activities even though these activities have nothing to do with the basis of friendship as such . . .[75]

Looking again at *The American Soldier,* one or two excerpts from a chapter, "Attitudes toward Leadership," seem pertinent. Discussing attitudes toward officers, one of the conclusions reached is:

75. *Ibid.,* pp. 408–14.

At a given time period, the smallest proportion of favorable attitudes tended to be found in the relatively inactive overseas theaters; the highest proportion of favorable attitudes tended to be found among combat groups; the proportion favorable among troups in the United States who had not gone overseas tended to be intermediate between these two groups . . .

. . . Army life, for most civilian soldiers, was a succession of deprivations and frustrations, and it is not surprising that the blame should have been personalized and focused on those in authority. The fact that combat soldiers had more favorable attitudes than others toward their officers could be attributed in part to the opportunity to discharge their aggression directly against the enemy. But this would be much too simple a view of the matter. Among combat troops, whether air or ground, officers and enlisted men shared the common experiences of deprivation, danger, and death. Social differentiation and special privileges were at a minimum. In rear areas and inactive theaters and, to a lesser extent, in the United States, the privileges enjoyed by the officer class were so much out of line with democratic tradition and so unjustified in the eyes of the men that a smoldering resentment, which was to burst into flame with the end of the war, probably was inevitable.

Why was the criticism of officers even more acute in inactive theaters and in rear areas of active theaters than in the United States? The most plausible hypothesis seems to turn on the concept of *scarcity*. If the supply of attractive women, liquor, or entertainment is severely limited, as was the case in many overseas areas, the problem of equitable distribution is much more acute than if there is plenty to go around. The charge which enlisted men repeated in theater after theater was that the officers used their rank to monopolize these desired objects. This was not expressed merely in indictments of particular officers, although some were more conspicuous in giving offense than others. It was an indictment of a *system*—a system by which a privileged minority acquired, through their authoritarian position, a preponderant share of the scarce objects which were craved by others.[76]

Later the discussion turned to group rewards and the investigators ventured to suggest certain conditions for their success. One of these conditions is worth noting here:

Group rewards . . . would seem most likely to be effective when. . . .
The men learn to expect that everyone in the group will be benefited by the group reward, rather than a few individuals. This is primarily a function of the type of reward which is promised (e.g., everyone will be given time off versus increasing the number of men who will be given furloughs). One of the major ways in which this condition may be expected to facilitate group pressures is by eliminating the suspicion that those members of the group who are most active (the "informal organizers") are expecting to obtain the reward just for themselves.[77]

Of all the social-psychological ills of urban society, racial or ethnic prejudice, discrimination, and conflict have received by all odds the most intensive study and the most ambitious remedial programs in recent years. Much of both the study and programs includes prejudice against religious groups as well. In anti-Semitism, particularly, the ethnic and religious prejudices are tightly intertwined. This is not to imply that these social pathologies have received as much attention

76. Stouffer *et al.,* Vol. I, pp. 364–69.
77. *Ibid.,* p. 428.

by scholars, educators, officials, or others as they deserve. There is, however, a large and growing literature on these subjects. It is so large and varied that it could not be satisfactorily summarized within the limits of one section of an essay of this kind. Fortunately, thanks to the incisiveness of some of the research and the vigor of some of the educational and action programs, most reasonably informed and thoughtful persons have some knowledge of the main features of these intergroup tensions and hostilities. I will limit myself, therefore, to two or three comments on what seem to me to be fundamentals of these conditions that may well apply to other sore points in the relations among the widely varying groups in urban communities.

My first comment is a confession of doubt or perhaps of disagreement with one of the main tenets of many writers on racial and religious prejudice. They distinguish and sometimes stress the scientific and practical significance of the distinction between prejudice based on racial and religious characteristics, on the one hand, and prejudice against occupational, economic, political, or educational groups, on the other. Most of this seems to me a distinction without a difference, or, more accurately, without a significant difference.

It seems quite generally agreed that the essence of prejudice is prejudgment of individuals in a group on minor, trivial, or insignificant characteristics that are held to be closely connected with disliked action or qualities. A dark skin is enough to show that any individual with one is slovenly and irresponsible. A facial conformation or accent that is commonly thought to be characteristic of Jews is evidence of craftiness and unreliability. This attitude easily leads the prejudiced person to forms of action against Negroes, Jews, or others quite contrary to the norms, values, or ideals that the person thinks he holds and that ordinarily determine most of his behavior vis-à-vis others. Thus he believes in fair play, but will not hire a qualified Jew for his office staff, or he believes that anyone who works hard and steadily ought to earn enough to support himself and his family in decency but becomes incensed when Negroes try to get more than starvation wages. In its more virulent forms prejudice clearly amounts to looking upon and treating members of certain groups or classes as different kinds of human beings. In some vague way this is held to justify the prejudiced person in discriminatory treatment and in almost any kind of tactics when he is thrown into competition or conflict with them.

Now all this has been said many times, and I would readily admit that within the boundaries of Western civilization racial and religious prejudice have been the cause of untold human misery, particularly in recent years. It seems to me, however, that the essential characteristics of discrimination are quite as apparent and its consequences quite as demonstrable when the group discriminated against is characterized not by skin color or religious creed but, for example, by residence in a slum area, the receipt of public relief funds, holding a political job, radical or liberal opinions, low or high income, or employment in a government bureau. Not all kinds of prejudice, of course, are equally common or equally severe among all prejudiced persons, but when I try to look at the essentials of prejudice as a trait of many human beings and at its consequences in a democratic society, I can only conclude that the difference between racial and religious prejudice and many other kinds is a difference in degree only.

From this I would argue also that persons who are particularly concerned with racial and religious prejudice, whether as investigators, educators, or leaders of action, may be doing some disservice to the society that otherwise they are serving very well indeed. By insisting on the unique character of racial and religious prejudice and more or less divorcing it in the public mind from other kinds, they may encourage neglect of these other types and raise hopes for their programs that cannot be realized by them alone.

From the analysis of racial and religious tensions and hostility have come various additions to, and clarifications of, our understanding of contemporary society. We have learned again, for example, that group membership and relations with others in a group often have substantial influences on the attitudes as well as the actions of individuals. The old conceptions of mechanical causation and effect in human relations have had to give way to rather more complex but meaningful ideas. Often a social system or set of group relations seems to be in what is often called an unstable equilibrium; a minor change or influence may be enough to touch off a cumulative series of changes. On the other hand, slowness and resistance to many kinds of change, at least beyond certain limits, has been amply demonstrated but awaits further study.

Finally, some guides and suggestions for public policy are worth noting. Although qualified in their original context, several of what seem to me fairly reliable policy guides—not limited to programs against racial and religious prejudice—have been put quite succinctly: .

(*a*) The effects of isolated actions or programs are likely to be small. Frequently these effects will be attenuated, obscured, or reversed by other factors operative in the total situation.

(*b*) The effects of a given action or program are not necessarily confined to the most direct or obviously related areas. Both research and action must be sensitized to the possibility of repercussions which are indirect and far reaching.

(*c*) Other things being equal, programs of action are likely to have greatest effects when they operate simultaneously on several strategic factors, rather than upon one or a few.

(*d*) Causal inferences must be made with great care, and in the light of all the possibly relevant known factors.

(*e*) Panaceas for control of group hostility definitely will not be found.[78]

How do we proceed from here?—As suggested by this question, I shall try in this and the following section to put down some conclusions or applications of current understanding of leadership and followership to urban community problems, in the hope that these suggestions may lead others to more penetrating and useful recommendations. Again, however, I would ask the reader to look at this task in broad perspective.

My thesis is that, to have substantial validity, policies and proposals as to leadership and morale in urban communities must be based on an understanding of the nature of human nature—as it is found in present-day social organizations. Although this is no new idea, it has been so generally slighted or ignored that a little support for it here may be in order. In the introduction to his *Human Nature in Politics* (first published in 1908) Graham Wallas wrote:

> The only form of study which a political thinker of one or two hundred years ago would now note as missing is any attempt to deal with politics in its relation to the nature of man. The thinkers of the past, from Plato to Bentham and Mill, had each his own view of human nature, and they made those views the basis of their speculations on government. But no modern treatise on political science, whether dealing with institutions or finance, now begins with anything corresponding to the opening word of Bentham's "Principles of Morals and Legislation"—"Nature has placed mankind under the governance of two sovereign masters, pain and pleasure"; or to the "first general proposition" of Nassau Senior's "Political Economy," "Every man desires to obtain additional wealth with as little sacrific as possible." In most cases one cannot even discover whether the writer is conscious of possessing any conception of human nature at all."[79]

More than four decades later, Leonard D. White, speaking on *Political Science, Mid-Century,* looked at four tasks confronting those in his discipline: "A second task, now on our doorstep, is to reach a more profound understanding of political behavior, with help from the anthropologists, psychologists, sociologists, and the medical profession . . . ,"[80] Elsewhere in the same talk, he warned his colleagues who, undeterred by the fate of economists addicted to an abstraction often labeled the economic man, are trying to formulate their science around the phenomena of power:

78. Robin M. Williams, Jr., *The Reduction of Intergroup Tensions: A Survey of Research on Problems of Ethnic, Racial, and Religious Group Relations* (New York: Social Science Research Council, 1947), p. 44. In some of the preceding pages of my essay, I have drawn less directly on Mr. Williams' analysis.

79. Graham Wallas, *Human Nature in Politics* (New York: F. S. Crofts and Co., 3d ed., 1921), p. 35.

80. Leonard D. White, "Political Science, Mid-Century," *The Journal of Politics* (February, 1950), pp. 17, 18.

. . . This proposition does set the stage for the formulation of hypotheses, for observation of a framework of related propositions that tend to give form to what still remains substantially formless. But political scientists are equally interested in the phenomena of co-operation, an aspect of our public life that is of obvious importance, if often overlooked. Much hard thinking is required of us on this professional front.

And the influences of various conceptions of human nature are by no means limited to professional scholars and their work. Like the man who had been speaking prose all of his life without knowing it, all of us have some general notions about the basic nature of human beings. Sometimes we put them into words; sometimes we act on them without making the effort to state them or to criticize them. The prominent corporation executive who said that the best incentive for industrial workers is a line of men at the gate had a very definite conception of human nature. Perhaps if he had taken the trouble to examine it thoroughly, the policies of his company at a critical juncture in its history might have been considerably more fruitful than they were.

The review of urban institutions and problems in this essay has shown something of their range, complexity, and seriousness. I believe it has become apparent that the conventional machinery, ideas, and relationships for dealing with many of these problems are not fully adequate for the task. As a matter of fact, some of them are pitifully inadequate. Among those problems that might well cause more serious concern are the low morale and the scarce and ineffective leadership in most urban communities—particularly the larger ones that most need good leadership and high community morale. One of the reasons many urban centers lack both is that their leaders are trying to lead without knowing definitely who their followers are or what, by and large, determines their attitudes and behavior. Morale, both in urban communities as a whole and in many of their subgroups, is sickly not only because their leadership is poor, but because many of the institutions, customs, and folkways of some groups cut them off from communication with others. Poor morale is just another name for the resulting lack of a feeling of solidarity, of cohesion or community spirit. In this environment problems of physical development, planning, government finance, and metropolitanism continue to grow because no comprehensive, determined attack is made upon them. Further, their continuing growth makes it easier for many individuals and groups to conclude that nothing can be done about them. This conviction lowers morale still further and another vicious circle is started.

Although in many urban centers the process has not gone this far, certainly in relatively few of them has it not begun at all. Quite probably the key, or at least a key, to understanding this process and devising ways and means of stopping or reversing it lies in the broad area of human motivation[81]—the factors in, influences on, and determinants of human behavior or action, the felt needs, wants, desires, and cravings of the vast range and variety of human beings in urban communities. What makes them tick? What determines, by and large, the extent and character of their social action as members of families, lodges, neighborhood groups, unions, civic organizations, trade associations, churches, the urban community itself? Are there some common elements that at least help to explain much of this varied and often apparently contradictory activity? If so, these common factors in human behavior should help us understand many of the things that go on around us and also should help us to cope with some of the problems and trends that now seem to be going on their irresponsible way.

All well and good, one may say, but what is this nature of human nature in modern society that you refer to? How do you characterize or describe it? What light, if any, does it throw on questions of urban leadership and community morale?

As has been pointed out before in this discussion, there are no simple answers in the back of the book for such questions. We simply do not know enough about the social life of human beings to construct a true theory of social behavior—a generalization or set of generalizations that will explain all or nearly all of the many things human beings do in their life with others. In the absence of such a basic understanding, no one and no group can outline proposals or policies on these urban problems that will *fully* stand the test of applying them.

Although these are obvious remarks, it does not follow from them that we know nothing about human motives and human behavior that can guide us. On the contrary, we have learned quite a lot, particularly in recent years, from the kinds of experience and investigation that I have tried to sketch briefly in the preceding sections. Further, some students of human behavior and social problems, aided no little by the experience of so-called practical men in various urban activities, have tried to reduce their findings to relatively brief compass. From several attempts of this kind, I have chosen three that seem to be particularly meaningful for our purposes here. Most students of these matters may well feel that statements of this kind should be analyzed—broken down further and perhaps rephrased in more elementary terms of individual tensions, psychological fields, group dynamics, personality types, etc. Maybe so, but I submit that in their present form they throw light

81. To avoid becoming entangled in controversies among various schools of psychologists with their different concepts and terminology, I would point out that I use "motivation" in the broad sense of a "general name for the fact that an organism's acts are partly determined by its own nature or internal structure" (Gardner Murphy, *Personality* [New York: Harper and Bros., 1947], pp. 991–92).

on many of the problems and issues that redevelopment officials, city planners and civic leaders often find most troublesome.

One of the best-known generalizations about human motives in social life is W. I. Thomas' "four wishes": for security, response, recognition, and new experience. In seeking security, men try to assure for themselves physical and economic necessities, property, jobs, and protection against illness, accidents, and misfortunes in a changing economic and social order. The wish or need for response may account for the gregariousness or joining proclivities of most persons. It lies at the foundations of family life and group activity. To satisfy the need for recognition, people work for respect, position, prestige, and status among their fellows—particularly among those with whom they are associated in groups of different kinds. New experience implies a need for some change, adventure, and a dislike of extreme routine. Probably as a determinant of human action it usually operates within the more inclusive need for security.

Wight Bakke, whom I quoted before, has been concerned for many years with the goals or objectives that determine the behavior of both workers and managers in industrial society. One of his colleagues has quoted a summary of his conclusions from an unpublished manuscript:

> In our studies we have identified goals of two sorts. First, men want to have the experience of security, progress, and justice. Second, these goals are realized or not as experiences in attempting to reach the following six goals:
> 1. *Respect of fellows.* The desire to play a socially respected role.
> 2. *Creature sufficiency.* The desire to have that degree of creature sufficiency (food, clothes, shelter, health, etc., and the means to provide them) enjoyed by the most favored of one's customary associates.
> 3. *Increasing control over one's affairs.* The desire to have one's decisions and actions effective in shaping the course of his own life and to reduce the control exercised by others.
> 4. *Understanding.* The desire to comprehend the forces and factors that operate in one's world, to "know the score."
> 5. *Capacity performance.* The desire to utilize in living the full range of capacities possessed, both actual and potential.
> 6. *Integrity or wholeness.* The desire to experience consistency within one's self, among the parts of one's world, and a significant relationship to that world.
>
> It is recognized that the force of these objectives and their specific content may vary among individuals and among groups, and indeed within the individual and group over a period of time, but there appears to be a significant persistence of these motivations. In this study, for purposes of simplification, we have reduced these goals to a more general statement of the objectives as security, recognition, and self-expression, while preserving the content.[82]

Finally, Robert S. Lynd in his book, *Knowledge for What?*, has formulated and explained a number of "persistent cravings of human

82. Quoted from Neil W. Chamberlain, *The Union Challenge to Management Control* (New York: Harper and Bros., 1948), pp. 247–48.

personalities." His exposition of them seems to me to warrant a rather long quotation:

Since it is human beings that build culture [defined earlier by Lynd "not . . . in the refined sense of *belles lettres* and sophisticated learning," but as ". . . all the things that a group of people inhabiting a common geographical area do, the ways they do things, and the ways they think and feel about things, their material tools and their values and symbols."—EDITOR] and make it go, the social scientist's criteria of the significant cannot stop short of those human beings' criteria of the significant. The values of human beings living together in the pursuit of their deeper and more persistent purposes constitute the frame of reference that identifies significance for social science. But the situation is confused by the fact that the social scientist at work on any single culture confronts in the behavior of people two sets of emphases upon what is significant: those stereotyped emphases which human beings *enmeshed in that particular culture* exhibit as they live towards the goal sanctioned most prominently by *that culture's* traditions and the example of its conspicuous leaders; and a more general order of emphases, common to human beings everywhere as persons living with their fellows, around which the selected emphases of single cultures oscillate. These later may be characterized as the deeper and more primitive cravings of personalities.

This is not to suggest that there is a "natural man" independent of culture; but simply that human beings, structured and functioning organically alike, subjected at birth and in early infancy to many broadly common types of experience, and growing up inevitably dependent on each other, develop a set of roughly similar underlying cravings. The point here is that, in addition to their more immediately biological life-processes and in addition to their culturally conditioned ways of behaving, human beings develop needs that are less directly referable to either of the above than to certain bald and unescapable *human experiences*. . . .

What, then, are these values and cravings of the human personality? Adequate answer to this question awaits further research by a wide group of specialists, ranging all the way from biochemistry to each of the social sciences, the arts, and the humanities. But life does not wait upon the perfect formulation. One must take one's awareness at each given moment and use it. The following suggestions as to the persistent cravings of human personalities are set down not because these cravings as here stated have been finally proved by science, but because human behavior keeps continually affirming and reaffirming them. . . . The items are pitched on a level at which "cravings" and "values" are synonymous, adhering to the level of personality and avoiding, on the one hand, cravings for such things as food, shelter, and sex, in their purely biological aspects, and, on the other hand, such explicitly cultural values as a mink coat or a midwinter vacation in Florida. The point to be stressed here is not detail and nomenclature, but the fact of the generality of such desires—call them what one will—in human beings. . . .

1. The human personality craves to live not too far from its own physical and emotional tempo and rhythm. While capable of large adjustment in these respects, the personality suffers strain when the institutional demands of the culture cut too coercively across this personally natural tempo and rhythm. . . .

As a part of this craving to maintain a tempo and rhythm natural to it, the personality craves periods of latency and private recoil during which time, space, and other persons can be taken on its own terms without coercion.

2. The human personality craves a sense of growth, of realization of personal powers, and it suffers in an environment that denies growth or frustrates it erratically or for reasons other than the similar need for growth in others. . . .

3. The human personality craves to do things involving the felt sense of fairly immediate meaning. This sense of immediate meaning may derive from the interest in doing an intrinsically interesting new thing, i.e., the exhilaration of "getting the hang of it"; from the fun of doing something that *is* fun; from the sense of personal power involved in exercising one's craftsmanship; or even from doing something possessing slight intrinsic meaning but with a heavy, reasonably sure instrumental relationship to something else that has great immediate meaning. But immediate meaning tends to be dissipated when the activity in hand is too distasteful; or when the line of instrumentalism from doing something with little or no intrinsic meaning to the something else that has immediate meaning is over-prolonged or too markedly unreliable. . . .

4. The human personality craves physical and psychological security (peace of mind, ability to "count on" life's continuities, and so on) to the degree that will still leave with the individual control over the options as to when to venture (for the fun of it, for the values involved) into insecurity.

5. But the human personality is active and cherishes in varying degrees the right to exercise these optional insecurities. It craves novelty (the learning and doing of new things), provided this can be taken on the personality's own terms, i.e., "in its stride." It craves risk as exhilarating—when it *is* exhilarating. But risk is exhilarating only at the points of peak energy storage in the individual's rhythms of personal living; and when risk is continuous or forced upon one the personality is put under unwelcome strain which invites discomfort, demoralization, and regression. . . .

6. As a corollary of the preceding, the human personality craves the expression of its capacities through rivalry and competition, with resulting recognition of status— but, again, under the same circumstances as noted in 5 above: only when energy and interest are ready for it and the personality is "set to go" and to go on its own terms. . . . But the human personality does not crave competition when the latter is continuous, enforced, or too threatening. It seems safe to say that most human personalities do not crave as pervasive and continuously threatening competition as they tend to be subjected to in our culture.

7. But if rivalry and the status it yields provide some of the arpeggios of living, the more continuous melody is the craving of the personality for human mutuality, the sharing of purposes, feeling, and action with others. The personality craves to belong to others richly and confidently and to have them belong in turn to it. It craves the expression and the receipt of affection. It craves to be actively accepted and given secure status as a person, *for* the person that it is—as well as for the work it can do. Sympathy is normal to it. Conversely, it suffers when forced to live in physical or psychological isolation. . . .

8. The human personality craves coherence in the direction and meaning of the behavior to which it entrusts itself in the same or different areas of its experience. Contradictions and unresolved conflicts within the rules it learns from the culture create tensions and hinder functional satisfaction. Here is the point at which such aspects of our culture as the dual allegiance to the contradictory values of aggressive dominance and of gentleness and mutuality . . . throw us continually into tension.

9. But the human personality also craves a sense of freedom and diversity in living that gives expression to its many areas of spontaneity without sacrificing unduly its corresponding need for basic intergration of continuities. . . . And, conversely, it dislikes monotony, routine, and coercion that cramp and flatten out the rhythms of living and force a canalization of energy expenditure that deadens spontaneity.

The preceding itemization of persistent cravings of the human personality might be condensed or expanded. Some of these cravings fall into contrasting pairs—security and risk, coherence and spontaneity, novelty and latency, rivalry and mutuality. Confronted with such contrasting tendencies, there is some disposition to dismiss the whole matter and to say that they cannot ever be reconciled. The important thing for the social scientist to note, however, is that these pairs do not represent contradictions any more than sleep is a contradiction of waking. They are but different phases in the rhythm of living. Obviously, no individual craves the independent maximization of each of these values, or of all of them at the same instant. That would involve an anarchy within the personality that would be intolerable. . . . The task of the sciences of human behavior, therefore, is not to "reconcile" these different needs, but to discover the flexible cultural patterning in which their varied expressions in personality can find most adequate expression in the sequences of living.[83]

Now clearly these statements of the factors in human behavior in society vary considerably. Besides the differences in terminology and emphasis, some differences in content are quite apparent. On the other hand, among these and other formulations a substantial agreement does show through. And the general conceptions of human motivation that emerge from these kinds of analysis have a marked degree of realism. Compared with them the economic man, the power man, and what Mayo called the rabble hypothesis—"that mankind is a horde of unorganized individuals actuated by self-interest"—seem sophomoric, one-sided, and even distorted.

For our purposes I would suggest that tentative agreement might be reached on the following common determinants of much human behavior: needs or wants for (*a*) security; (*b*) respect and recognition at the hands of one's fellows; (*c*) a sense of growth and accomplishment, direct or not too indirect; (*d*) a feeling of integrity and consistency among one's actions and beliefs; (*e*) freedom and diversity, which imply real choices at least at some points in one's day-to-day life and at least occasional relief from routines and coercions; (*f*) at least a few reasonably concrete, commonly understood objectives for the various groups and subgroups with which one is associated; (*g*) communication, which implies both a chance to speak out and to understand what is being done by other groups in society that affects one's life and activities; (*h*) as well as, of course, material goods and services to meet the basic physical requirements of life.

This formulation is not original; it clearly is a rephrasing of the formulations of Lynd, Bakke, and Thomas, as well as of some others not quoted here. It also draws on the analysis of group morale, leadership, and followership discussed before. As Lynd has pointed out, however, niceties of definition and terminology are not important at this stage of our knowledge and study—at least not for those who are

83. Robert S. Lynd, *Knowledge for What?* (Princeton: Princeton University Press, 1939), pp. 189–98.

concerned primarily with public policy and programs. More knowledge and deeper understandings should be forthcoming from present and future research and experience. Meanwhile urban institutions and agencies, including local governments, can apply what we now know about human nature and behavior in these other settings as well as in their own, confident that it will take them toward more democratic and, quite probably, more widely approved results.

Quite surely, for example, leaders who thoughtfully recognize these characteristics of human beings in their social behavior would be much more effective than most of those who now act as leaders in many sectors of urban life. Similarly, if or when the patterns of the physical city and also the organization of its economic and political agencies can be shaped to help most of its citizens to satisfy these cravings or wants in their day-to-day living, the force of community morale would be multiplied many times. Few, if any, of the roadblocks to further improvement that now seem so formidable would continue long as *major* obstacles. Finally, it seems clear that the parts of our existing economic, governmental, and social institutions and activity that deny or thrwart these motivations are largely responsible for most of the mutual distrust, suspicion, cynicism, and low morale that we have already noted in several connections.

Without confusing an already complex picture at least two warnings should be given for those who are trying to move from some understanding of human behavior to questions of public and social policy in urban localities. First, these compact formulations of human needs and other determinants of behavior do not tell us in what circumstances one combination of these factors may be more influential than another. Here, for the present at least, the leader must rely largely on his own observations and more or less intuitive understanding. Second, an important intermediate step must be taken between a recognition of these basic motivations and the specific activities of persons and groups. What activities, for example, yield to the members of specific groups satisfactions in the form of recognition, security, or a sense of accomplishment? Put the other way around, how do members of specific groups look upon or, as the psychologists say, perceive particular activities or programs.

Clearly, the leader of urban groups and programs must first find out what activities are looked upon by his followers as filling some or most of these basic needs, wants, or aspirations—for respect, security, integrity, a sense of growth, etc. Their original perceptions on this score are, of course, subject to modification, but at least they are important starting points. New programs (e.g., the clearance and rebuilding type of redevelopment) must be explained so that members of many groups understand not only their immediate concrete objectives, but also the meaning of them for the lives of those directly and indirectly affected. To achieve this end we clearly must improve the communication among different groups and between their leaders and followers. This may well be a long, slow, and often discouraging process, but it would seem to be one that must be gone through if we are to develop the understanding and consensus essential for substantial achievement in programs that require the collaboration of many groups and organizations.

Once these processes of communication and the search for some degree of understanding and agreement are underway not only in respect to redevelopment, but also as to education, recreation, public health, urban planning, local government organization and finance, public and civic welfare activities, law enforcement, juvenile delinquency, and other phases of modern urban life, we may hopefully expect not utopia, not the uninhibited reign of sweetness, reason, and light, but the gradual emerging of a consensus as to certain over-all goals and values of urban living. These will be additions to, a replacement for some, and a strengthening of other values developed in generations past in an essentially nonurban America. As we all know, these values have fared badly in recent years in most American metropolitan communities. They have lost their meaning and the allegiance that they used to hold on the beliefs and ideals of large numbers of American citizens. Urban living with its diversity, complexity, money standards, and impersonal character has dissolved or seriously weakened these older systems of beliefs and values. This weakening has been both a cause and an index of the low morale, indifference, and splintering of the urban body social and politic that we have discussed before.

The development of a valid, revitalized system of commonly understood and accepted beliefs and values is the crucial task of urban communities over the next generation or so. If the job can be done even moderately well, it will open the door for the making of physical, economic, political, and social cities that realize at least some of the potentialities of our highly developed technical competence. If we fail at this task, I at least can see little long-term hope for many worthwhile programs and activities, including urban redevelopment in the usual sense of that term.

Again, two warnings: First, I hope no one understands me to mean that specific programs of city rebuilding, public education, or local finance must wait upon this regeneration of urban consensus and values. Quite the opposite: I believe we will get the new system of valid beliefs and agreed-upon values by working at these specific programs *if* we work at them in the right way—by methods devised in full recognition of the fundamental human needs in society and of the contributions these specific activities can make to the broader, less tangible objective of consensus and morale. Second, by consensus on these emerging values in urban life I do not mean that we shall ever accomplish, at least for a long time to come, anything approaching complete understanding and agreement among all groups and subgroups of urban communities. There simply are too many conflicts of interest and attitude more or less built into our economic and social order. Furthermore, *some* kinds of conflict quite surely are unavoidable and possibly desirable in a flexible, evolving society. Other conflicts, however, cannot be so characterized but as long as they exist, they will make imperfect our communication and consensus on nearly all aspects of our common urban life. Many of these obstacles are themselves being changed slowly and painfully and, although they may be annoying or even serious obstacles, they need not defeat the development of some valid objectives, values, or ideals for urban communities. As Louis Wirth in discussing consensus on an even broader plane put it:

Consensus in mass democracies, therefore, is not so much agreement on all issues, or even on the most essential substantive issues, among all the members of society, as it is the established habit of intercommunication, of discussion, debate, negotiation and compromise, and the toleration of heresies, or even of indifference, up to the point of "clear and present danger" which threatens the life of society itself. Rather than resting upon unanimity, it rests upon a sense of group identification and participation in the life of a society, upon the willingness to allow our representatives to speak for us even though they do not always faithfully represen. our views, if indeed we have any views at all on many of the issues under discussion, and upon our disposition to fit ourselves into a program that our group has adopted and to acquiesce in group decisions unless the matter is fundamentally incompatible with our interests and integrity.[84]

Although I would not commit anyone to my analysis and argument on this issue, it is a fact that leaders in various local public undertakings have seen and acted upon the necessity for wider citizen participation in their programs. Public school administrators in many localities are one example. Among local planning and redevelopment agencies, those in Philadelphia, to mention only one locality, have been working on this front and have accumulated useful experience on methods and ways and means. Probably most of these officials have been concerned more with the fairly immediate objectives of their own activities than with the social-psychological health of the urban body as a whole and with its influence on the whole range of governmental and public services. I am certain, however, that many of them do see these by-products and implications of what they have been doing.

Urban government and consensus.—The final question in this sec-

84. Louis Wirth, "Consensus and Mass Communication," *American Sociological Review* (February, 1948), pp. 9–10.

tion on leadership and urban morale is: Can urban local government, taken broadly to include not only official agencies but related civic, neighborhood, and other group organizations concerned with the same issues, become *a* major means for attaining the degree and kind of consensus just referred to? My answer is yes, *if;* or no, *if—*.

Yes, if we deliberately use the many powers and activities of these organizations to raise the level of communication among urban groups and classes. Much of what I have tried to say above might be recapitulated in explanation of this statement, but this should not be necessary. At present, however, too many group leaders are doing just the reverse —they appeal to misunderstandings and dislike among groups as their chief bid for power, which often turns out to be limited and transitory.

Those who look upon communication among urban groups and individuals as an impossible ideal, I would ask to consider one implication of such a formulation as Lynd's on the basic needs or cravings of human beings. If one admits the existence of such basic human needs (whether or not he agrees with Lynd's statements about them), it seems to me he must admit the possibility of two-way or multi-way communication. Those of one group or class who say they would like to but simply cannot talk or in other ways communicate effectively with those from some other groups are simply too diffident or too easily discouraged or prejudiced. Prejudice, as it was discussed above, is a prejudgment of individuals often justified on the grounds that they are different kinds of human beings. Once the error of this view is recognized, the possibility of some degree of communication, imperfect though it may be, is clear. And communication is not dependent entirely upon formal organization and formal means; informal contact is also an effective method.

Also I would suggest that communication among groups and classes can be furthered somewhat by the proper design and management of new or redeveloped residential areas. We are just beginning to learn a little about the effects of the physical layout of residential neighborhoods on the organization of informal groups and the formation of friendships.[85] The little we know does suggest strongly that the effects of physical design and arrangement run much deeper than has commonly been assumed. Also, we have begun to question seriously the advisability, from many points of view, of the residential district or neighborhood limited largely to one income group, to one type of tenure, to one vocational, educational, or racial group. This is not an argument for hit-and-miss admixtures of all types and kinds of families in every residential district, but it does suggest that more variety and

85. Leon Festinger *et al.*, *Social Pressures in Informal Groups* (New York: Harper and Bros., 1950).

less uniformity will make for added interest, variety, and eventually a considerable degree of mutual respect and understanding.

In short, our local public and civic agencies have at their command many effective means for facilitating communication among groups and classes. In the hands of intelligent leaders with an appreciation of what is at stake, substantial progress toward this objective is entirely possible.

Yes, if we recognize and use informal group organizations and their leaders. One of the characteristics of most human groups is that they are made up of subgroups. As pointed out before, industrial and other studies have shown the importance of the very small, informal groups in the lives of their members. Quite clearly they exist in the civic and public life of our urban centers. By and large our urban leaders, except some of the more intelligent machine politicians, have practically ignored them. It seems easier and more effective to work with more prominent and vocal organizations. Too often, however, these civic organizations of well-known business and professional people start a worth-while program and get considerable publicity and support for it. Sooner or later, however, it is stymied by what looks like indifference or stupidity but may actually be the resistence of scores of little local groups that do not understand what it is about, whose members, like most of the rest of us, fear what they do not understand, and who get satisfaction and recognition by resisting what seems to them to be pushing around by some of the high and mighty.

Yes, if our local political parties will come to stand for something on local issues and programs.

Perhaps I should have mentioned before that in the earlier years of the century some civic reformers became much concerned over the influence of national party slogans, issues, and labels in local elections. They pointed out that it made very little sense to vote for or against a candidate for councilman or mayor because he claimed to be a member of a party whose position on the tariff one agreed or disagreed with. They favored nonpartisan elections for local offices. They urged the electors to vote for good candidates regardless of party label. They asserted there was no Democratic, Republican, or Socialist way to collect the garbage.

With the irrelevance of *some* national political issues to local elections, one can only agree. From this major premise, the reformers developed an argument that is a classic example of throwing out the baby with the bath. Just because some national political issues were clearly out of place in local elections, it did not follow that all of them were or that there were not issues of local importance on which local parties ought to take stands and on which local electors ought to have a chance to vote. Further, although the plea for well-qualified or good candidates certainly was valid within limits, it surely was pressed way beyond those limits. It then became essentially meaningless. What is a good candidate? To well-to-do business and professional citizens with a highly developed sense of the business virtues and practices, a good candidate clearly was a good organizer, an economical operator, a man who got a dollar's worth of material or service for a dollar expended, even if he were rather callous to widespread human misery in many parts of the city. To the unskilled wage-earner and other citizens at or near the bottom of the economic heap, a good candidate quite as reasonably was one who knew something about their trials and troubles, who was willing to help them occasionally with a job or reference, and who talked their language, even if he associated with gamblers and other shady characters and his fingers were rather sticky when handling public money.

Today there may be no Republican, Democratic, or Socialist way of collecting the garbage, but no thoughtful person really believes that local government is limited to or properly typified by garbage collection. And certainly there are conservative and liberal views today on how local governments should raise their operating revenues, on public borrowing and other phases of fiscal policy, on public housing, on planning, on the distribution of governmental powers in metropolitan areas, on the size of school expenditures—including the level of teachers' salaries, and on many other concrete, important local questions. It seems to me entirely in keeping with democratic theory and practice for local parties to take stands on questions of this kind. If this be done with some decent respect for honest statement and a tolerance of others' opinions, it can help invigorate local government. It can also make clear the areas of agreement and the areas of conflict in the unending process of achieving some degree of consensus on ultimate values. At best, of course, this is a rough and ready process, but quite as clearly it does have educative value; it helps set immediate and medium-term objectives; it does provide another means for letting many citizens know what are the possibilities open to them from some of the newer public services and programs.

Unless local political parties, whatever their names or organization, perform this function, the legislative side of local government will continue to exemplify what a student of Congress has said about one of its functions: "In the absence of a widely recognized crisis, legislative policy-making tends to be fought out at the level of largely irresponsible personal and group strategems and compromises based upon temporary power coalitions of political, administrative, and non-

governmental interests."[86] And when legislative activity is so characterized, local administration certainly struggles in deep water with a great
millstone around its neck. About the only ones who would gain from
a continuance of this state of affairs would be the more irresponsible
political hacks and some so-called respectable citizens who support
such politicians because they, too, are all for the status quo and against
change.

A neat example of the untenableness of this garbage-collection type
of argument today is in the short history of the federal Housing Act of
1949, which provided, among other things, for federal financial aid to
local authority housing and redevelopment. Many phases of this measure, particularly the provision for public housing, had been fought
over for years in Congress. They had been bitterly and persistently opposed by the so-called real estate lobby—a group of trade associations
of real estate men, mortgage lenders, building material suppliers, and
private builders. As this fight wore on, the bill, despite effective support
by Senators Taft and Tobey and some other Republicans, became more
and more a Democratic and administration measure. Finally, in 1949,
the lobby and other opponents were beaten; the measure passed Congress on votes that more nearly approached party lines than those on
any other major housing measure considered by the Congress.

Immediately the trade associations announced that they would
transfer their opposition to local communities in which agencies would
try to get federal aid for local authority housing under this Act. This
they did with vigor and often with the crudest of measures—smears,
name calling, charges of Communism, etc. And who opposed them?
With some exceptions it was not the local parties whose federal counterpart had passed the measure and that claimed credit for it, but pick-up
teams of civic, religious, welfare, and minority groups.

This certainly is not a garbage-collection issue. Nor is it, in my
opinion at least, responsible democratic government.

In urging this view I do not say, as some others do say or imply, that
all or nearly all urban public programs should be objects of factional
or party contention. Among large sections of urban populations a substantial agreement exists on the need for and the approximate level of
many important services. And as I pointed out in the early part of this
essay, the area of this agreement seems to have been increasing—slowly
but quite steadily. It makes no sense to pick a fight on these matters
just to have a fight. Nor is public controversy the *only* means of political and civic education. It is quite as essential to civic health that

86. Stephen Kemp Bailey. *Congress Makes a Law—The Story Behind the Employment
Act of 1946* (New York: Columbia University Press, 1950), p. 236.

these agreed-upon items be recognized and the fact of agreement be respected and acted upon. None of these opinions, it seems to me, conflicts with the case for believing that local political parties should take stands on important, unsettled local issues and programs, present and proposed.

Yes, if we can devise an effective means for citizen participation in local public affairs in addition to the ballot box, occasional public hearings on specific projects or undertakings, and scattered pressure groups. Earlier in this essay I ventured one or two suggestions on this point. I do not believe they are important enough to be restated here, nor that they represent by any means the best that can be done on this score.

In some respects this objective is closely related to the one above. Certainly if local political parties were organized to present substantive issues and to help develop at least a common-sense philosophy on them, they would become a much more effective means of participation in public affairs than they now are.

Yes, if we undertake to build physical neighborhood units and social neighborhoods as one specific means of satisfying in part what Lynd has called the cravings of the human personality for physical and psychological security, for the sharing of purposes, feelings, and action with others, for ". . . periods of latency and private recoil during which time, space and other persons can be taken on its own terms. . . ." for some degree of freedom and diversity that offset the monotony, routine, and coercion of many phases of modern urban life. Even with the phrase *in part* emphasized, this may seem like a sizable claim for the planning and development of new neighborhoods. It is a considerable claim but, I think, a defensible one.

Here I part company with those who believe the neighborhood is doomed in modern cities and that its functions must be transferred to group organizations in industry or other settings. I do not see any necessary conflict between neighborhood groups and these other types of organizations. To the extent that each gives opportunities for human expression and development, so much the better. Neither am I suggesting replicas of small town neighborhoods of the past or present. Big city neighborhoods most certainly are and will be different in many respects. They can, however, show what I take to be the essential characteristics of neighborhoods: (1) a physical pattern and focus rather than a continuation of the formless sprawl of so much recent urban development; and (2) some sense of human or social solidarity or "togetherness," which naturally grows up when people have opportunities, over a period of time, for informal, uncoerced, relaxed contacts as human beings—

not as rivals, customers, competitors, or as ethnic, nationality, or class types.

The decline of the neighborhood in large cities is due to many factors. One of them deserves consideration here: the fact that many residential districts of large American cities show most of the inadequacies and few of the virtues of modern industrialism or, for that matter, of any sector of our society.

In more concrete terms an industrial worker, a clerk in a department store, or a bookkeeper in an office puts in his working hours with many of his basic human needs denied by the routines of his work and by the partial, impersonal character of most of his relations with his employers and their customers. At the end of the working day, he fights his way into a bus or streetcar or subway car where, under the conditions of mass transportation in most large urban centers today, for from fifteen or twenty minutes to an hour or more he is further regimented and, in fact, shoved around. At the end of this ordeal he finds himself in a mean, unpleasing street and later in an inconvenient, often crowded apartment or house where his contacts with persons outside his own family are apt also to be casual and impersonal—unless he gets into a row with some of them. Even his family life may be measurably circumscribed and regimented by the demands of other members of the family in too small quarters. He does not ordinarily complain too much about all this—in fact, he may look upon it as largely unavoidable. He gets a little relief from the routine by playing with his children, making a few friends at the shop or office, getting out in the country occasionally over the weekend, once in a while going to a ball game or prize fight, or taking in numberless Hollywood epics at the "neighborhood" theater where his taste for the drama, if any, is seldom served but where his taste for popcorn can be temporarily satisfied and where at least he can escape into some kind of make-believe world unlike the one he knows.

Now this is a deliberate caricature. Not every low-wage and salary worker in a large city lives like this, but I submit that most of them share many of these and other forms of inconvenience, regimentation, frustration, and boredom—at work, at home, and going back and forth. No one of them is in itself intolerable, but the combination, repeated over and over, day after day and month after month, certainly does not strengthen the human spirit or feed the human personality. In these circumstances it is only natural that urban dwellers move around from place to place when there are any vacant places to move to, and that neighborhood spirit, identification, and activities deteriorate.

Further, the evidence is against those who assert that this is all the worker and his family want or would know or learn how to use. The eagerness with which many such families rush to buy small houses in outlying sections whenever the price is at all possible for them contradicts this assertion. The wage-earner will put up with even greater inconvenience and loss of time in travel to and from work in order to get some improvement in neighborhood and housing. He and his family will take long-shot chances on the quality and purchase price of a new house as well as on their ability to meet long-term mortgage payments in order to break out of the drabness, discomfort, and monotony of living conditions in so many older urban districts.

Now suppose this urban worker could come home to a modern neighborhood setting, not too far from his place of work. It would be reasonably insulated from the noise, confusion, and danger of heavy traffic. It would have a low enough density so that open space, trees, even gardens would be possible—if he or any one of his neighbors wanted one. His living space would be reasonably adequate and convenient; school buildings, neighborhood centers, playgrounds, and other facilities would be at hand to serve the members of the family in those activities that could not be taken care of readily within the dwelling space. He would have a chance to meet some of his neighbors on some other subjects than why the radio is played so loudly or how it happened that the kids got into a fight. The layout of the neighborhood would give some sense of relaxation, variety, and beauty. Perhaps the air might be only moderately dirty so that the housewife's whole life would not need to be an unending fight against grime. The worker would have a chance to do something of an evening or weekend without drugging himself with commercial entertainment. On the other hand, TV being willing, the movie, ball game, and prize fight would be available when he wanted to see them.

Again, this is an idealized picture. It is, however, an entirely possible one. And I submit that neighborhood living of this kind offers opportunities for satisfying in part some of these basic needs and cravings that we have noted. In these circumstances, I would not despair of neighborhood values even under our present industrial order. Further, I would believe that many urban workers living under these conditions would develop again some pride in their neighborhood, some interest in its continuing welfare, and at least might become reasonably open-minded to appeals of other and somewhat more remote issues of public importance in the urban community at large.

Let me emphasize that providing pleasant, humane neighborhood settings is only one of the things that must be done if urban workers and their families are to get more satisfaction, growth, and self-respect out of life. It is no panacea for urban ills nor a snake oil to cure all the diseases of man in society. I have tried to draw these contrasting pictures, however, because in actual urban life the influences of physical environment take place in these simple, persistent, undramatic ways and too much of our talk and analysis of them covers up the homely realities with abstractions and jargon.

On the other hand, it is entirely possible that urban leadership and morale in governmental and other public affairs will continue to lose ground. It is not too difficult to point out at least a few conditions under which the answer to the question is no, if—.

No, if we fail to formulate and put before urban citizens a conception of urban government, its functions and potentialities, that shows them in their proper stature and significance. Evidence can be found on every hand of our past failure to do this. Two general notions or characterizations of urban government and affairs seem to have had the field more or less to themselves—with, of course, some notable exceptions.

One is that urban government is essentially a necessary evil. It attracts almost exclusively third-rate people and is shot through and through with graft and corruption. "Good citizens" have to clean house occasionally, but the record shows that about all that can realistically be expected is that these periodic reform movements keep things from getting measurably worse. The other is that local government, however defined, is a humdrum affair of collecting garbage, repairing streets, chasing miscreants, and putting out fires. All this is important work in the sense that keeping a house painted and the foundations repaired is important, and it ought to be faithfully and efficiently done. At best, however, it lacks intellectual content and calls for a lower order of abilities than the "large affairs" of national government, international relations, large-scale industry, or the leading professions.

Not only are these general views widespread among many groups and classes of both urban and rural Americans, but they apparently are also common in scientific and academic circles, the second even among students of political science itself. For example, a friend of mine recently became head of the political science department of an institution in a large metropolitan center. He had plans to strengthen materially the course and research work on urban problems and development. Because a very large proportion of the student body came from this great metropolitan area, he assumed that this program for his department would tap a latent pool of interest and action. Somewhat to his chagrin, he found that the student body, and to some extent his colleagues, did not share his enthusiasm. Relatively few of the students had more than a casual interest in such matters; a large proportion of them wished to specialize in international relations, international administration, or some intellectually respectable phase of national government and administration.

Or one could look at the 1948 directory of the American Political Science Association. In addition to the usual biographical data, members were asked to list their fields of special interest. In the back part of the directory, these are recapitulated under twenty-six classes of subject matter. Under the heading of international relations, for example, are almost 1050 names; under national government, some 1075; under local government, about 500.[87]

No one in his right mind, of course, could deny the high importance of international relations and effective central government in the present-day world. They deserve all the attention they are receiving in universities and colleges as well as elsewhere. I mention them here simply to cite the disparity between the popularity and prestige that attend them and the relative neglect that seems the current fate of local government in many quarters.

One of the main lines of argument in this essay could be summarized by saying that both of these common conceptions of urban government are one-sided and misleading. To be sure, corruption is often found in local public affairs. To be sure, many local officials and many local political and civic leaders are not paragons of intellectual power and social insight. To be sure, local governments perform a large number of homely housekeeping tasks. On the other hand, many local governments maintain high standards of probity and efficiency in their affairs. Probably local governments by and large compare favorably in these respects with prevailing standards in business, industry, and in many of the professions. And many local leaders, although they seldom are glamorized in the weekly magazines or elsewhere, have as many brains, as much understanding, and as high ideals as better known figures in the State Department, the Congress, or the military establishment. Finally, this entire monograph is a waste of time, money, and paper if it has not at least indicated in outline form some problems and issues of urban communities that seem likely to yield only to the best intellectual powers and social skill, including the qualities of human leadership.

No, if we continue to cling in our conceptions of social values and in planning the strategy of public programs to the old, essentially undemocratic view that those individuals and groups who can climb in the economic scale deserve particularly well of their community in other respects as well, while those who do not climb economically are,

87. *Directory of the American Political Science Association, 1948* (The Association, 1948), pp. 274–79, 281–83, 284–88.

by that very fact, relegated to a lower order of consideration in public affairs and activities. It seems to me no one can deny the prevalence and the ill effects of this attitude on urban government and local public affairs. It helps account for many of the superficial and short-sighted characteristics of other worth-while campaigns for strengthening and improving local government. The natural resentment against it by the parties of the second part certainly is a substantial factor in the tensions and mistrust that bedevil and often defeat useful public and civic undertakings.

No, if both leaders and followers in the more prominent and influential urban groups continue to excuse their inability to communicate with and understand others on the grounds of their moral substandardness or intellectual obtuseness. This is closely related to the point above, but it does, I believe, deserve a separate statement. As has often been pointed out, communication is a two-way process—it means listening and trying to understand as well as talking, writing, or in other ways trying to make oneself understood. And certainly across group and class lines it requires patience, imagination, tolerance, and an enormous amount of good will.

From a slightly different angle, Chester I. Barnard writes to the same point in the essay from which I quoted earlier:

. . . Leaders of the future, in my opinion, will generally need to be intellectually competent. However, the main point, which I wish greatly to emphasize, is that intellectual competency is *not* a substitute, at least in an important degree, for the other essential qualities of leadership.

Though it may be unpleasant to some, I have laid stress upon my opinion in this matter for two principal reasons. The first is that under present trends an excessive emphasis is placed upon intellectual (and pseudo-intellectual) qualifications by responsible "selecting" authorities, which artificially limits the supply of leaders. The same excessive emphasis upon the intellectual is made by followers who are intellectuals. Thus it is often difficult for them (experts and professionals of many kinds) who have no administrative capacity (or interest) to follow even extraordinary leaders. This is a form of conceit frequently accompanied by exhibitions of temperament and disruptiveness, and by false, ruthless, and irresponsible professions of individualism and freedom, especially professional and academic freedom. All this tends to a limitation of the supply of competent leaders, because it discourages men from undertaking the work of leadership, and it restricts their effectiveness.

My second reason is that a general condition amounting to intellectual snobbishness, it seems to me, has a great deal to do with industrial unrest. I see this in the propensity of educated people, whatever their economic status or social position, to underestimate the intelligence and other important personal qualities of workmen; in the tendency of some supervisors, quite honestly and sincerely, to blame failure to lack of brains in subordinates instead of to the stupidity of instructions; in the assumption of some men that "pure bunk" dressed up in "high brow" jargon is effective in dealing with people; in the excessive popularity of white-collar occupations; in the desire of so many intellectuals to tell others how to eat, save money, dress, marry, raise families, and take care of their own interests. These are symptoms of attitudes and it is the latter, not the symptoms, which are important. They cause division of interest artificially and lack of sympathetic understanding that are destructive of cooperation and cannot be corrected by mere "measures of good will."

I am well aware that there are differences in the intellectual capacities of men and know that such differences are important, especially as respects the ability to acquire knowledge and understanding by study in those matters which can only be learned in this way. Nevertheless, after a fairly long experience in dealing with many classes of men and women individually and collectively, the destructive attitudes I am attacking seem to me to be unwarranted by anything I know about intellect, education, or leadership. Intellectual superiority is an obtrusive thing which even intellectuals dislike in others except as they *voluntarily* give it their respect.[88]

Let me cite just one example from the program of URS that illustrates how this attitude, often quite unconsciously, influences the approach to important urban programs. Quite early in the Study, it seemed to members of URS that we might experiment a bit with the methods and techniques of public opinion and attitude research to see if they would produce results that might contribute to local redevelopment undertakings. More specifically, by a careful use of these methods of inquiry could we find out what representative residents of blighted areas knew about urban redevelopment, what they might think about a proposal to clear and rebuild their neighborhood or area, from what sources they received their information, what influenced them in making up their minds, what they liked or disliked about their present neighborhoods, what ideas, if any, they might have as to what should be done with them and by whom?

Because investigations of this kind on any substantial scale are rather expensive, we sent out a letter suggesting this type of inquiry to quite a few active redevelopment officials in cities throughout the country and offering to share the expenses of one or two test runs. With a few exceptions, the response from these leaders showed clearly that they disliked the idea or even thought it fantastic or silly. Although they were too polite to put their views bluntly, there was no mistaking them. They knew where the blighted areas in their localities were and when necessary could define them quite accurately. They knew or could find out which ones should be cleared first for rebuilding. They knew what use should be made of these areas or, if they were not too sure about this, they certainly knew more about it than anyone else, particularly the people who lived in those areas. Naturally, when certain areas were selected for clearance, "public relations" would be used to sell the idea to occupants of the areas. It would be a waste of time and money to inquire into the residents' attitudes, sources of informa-

88. Chester I. Barnard, "The Nature of Leadership" in *Organization and Management —Selected Papers* (Cambridge: Harvard University Press, 1948), pp. 98–100.

tion, acceptance or rejection of the official proposals. They just could not be expected to have any worth-while ideas on such matters. Besides, the officials would find out enough or too much about the occupants' reactions through complaints that would be made when the first steps in the local programs were announced!

I am certain that the response would have been quite the same if a similar suggestion had been made to officials concerned with almost any other local public program. It is also quite clear that other factors were at work in shaping their responses besides the one I am stressing here. Probably if a similar letter went out today rather more local redevelopers would see some merit in it. I cite this minor incident here, however, simply to illustrate how far this basic attitude of many able governmental and civic leaders influences their whole philosophy and approach to their jobs.

And finally, *no, if* informed and democratic local groups continue to hope for superbly equipped, spectacularly able leaders or even a series of them who will be able to attract and organize great sections of the urban citizenry and with this support to force through reforms and far-reaching constructive programs that will remake our urban plant, institutions and life. The corollary of this hope is that such leaders will not need to build on a prosaic groundwork laid through years of hard, patient education, communication, and organization. Here again, probably few persons would put the matter quite this bluntly, but certainly it is in the back of many minds both as a hope and a partial excuse for not getting down to the difficult, unspectacular foundation work. Occasionally in the past we have seen local leaders who for a time seemed to meet all or most of these qualifications. Some of them were mentioned earlier in this discourse. On the whole, however, their influence reached a relatively quick peak and then receded almost as rapidly. As long as this conception of leadership is common it will postpone the recognition both of the real leaders who are at hand and of how they might be expected to operate.

This section on leadership and urban morale has become long and possibly more than a little complex. In my opinion, however, it has at least the merit of trying to deal with some truly significant influences and considerations in urban life. As I have tried to survey the evolution of urban communities over the past half century, it seems to me that in this area the general scene is by all odds the darkest and the outlook most obscure and discouraging. When I tried to find out why this is so or to suggest what might be done about it, I found what seems to me a confusion of tongues and a neglect of basic reality. I have tried, therefore, to look for human and social factors sufficiently fundamental to warrant somewhat different approaches in practice for the kinds of public programs that a complex and growing urbanism requires in a democratic society.

Summary.—Essentially, then, I have been trying to state, defend, and sometimes to illustrate a few propositions about leadership and morale in urban communities. In short, they are:

1. Both the major current issues and the potentialities of the common life of urban communities require many able leaders and a fairly high morale among most of the many subgroups of these communities. In fact they require many more able leaders and a higher degree of morale than is commonly found today.

2. Without better leaders and higher morale many necessary, important programs in urban communities, including urban redevelopment, will continue to go slowly, haltingly, and imperfectly. Practical results will never achieve nor even approach their possibilities.

3. Effective leadership and good morale are not fundamentally the product of certain techniques, methods, or tricks of the trade.

4. Rather they depend primarily upon a recognition that nearly all human beings share certain basic needs, wants, and aspirations. The true leader understands this and helps his followers shape programs that appeal to these aspirations and help to satisfy these wants. At bottom morale is a by-product in a group whose members feel that they and their leaders are working, with at least some effect, on a program or programs of this kind.

5. In democratic urban communities these fundamental wants may be filled, at least in considerable part, by (*a*) the organization and normal functioning of economic, political and other social institutions, (*b*) the informal social relations encouraged by the pattern of the physical neighborhood and city and (*c*) by the very processes of shaping institutions and physical patterns to these ends.

6. When a substantial number of urban groups with this kind of leadership work together in this way for common ends, we may expect to see emerging a meaningful system of values and an urban-community-wide consensus that will give a sense of direction and significance to many activities that otherwise might seem separated, contradictory, or even futile.

7. This is no pipe dream. At various times in the history of this and other countries substantial segments of the population have attained such a consensus and have given their faith and allegiance to a widely held system of beliefs or values.

8. Urban government, taken broadly to include not only official agencies and their programs but also the related civic, neighborhood, and other groups and their activities, could play a major part in this

process of establishing two-way or multi-way communication among groups, of developing consensus and values.

9. Although all this seems basically true, it does not mean that we can look forward to the disappearance of group and class conflicts in urban life. Rather we can expect that these processes of leadership, group activity, communication, and consensus can reduce conflicts and prevent them from becoming insuperable barriers to the physical and social improvement of urban living.

10. By no means is there anything inevitable about these processes. Over the next generation at least the evolution of urban affairs could quite as readily, probably even more readily, go in the opposite direction.

CHAPTER VI

A NOTE ON PSYCHOSOMATIC URBANISM

FOR readers who may have persevered thus far and others who may have had misgivings from looking at the Contents and have started reading at this point, one criticism of the scope of this discussion will be discussed briefly. At or before this point some readers and scanners of this writing may say in effect:

"The discussion goes much too far afield. We grant that urban redevelopment is more than picking out one or two areas of centrally located blight, buying them up, clearing off the old buildings, and turning them over to private or public agencies for new construction. Sizable cities will need plans and programs for dealing with different kinds of blighted districts in different parts of their areas. We can see the crucial importance of competent, comprehensive urban planning in preparing and later in modifying redevelopment programs. We recognize the difficulties that come primarily from the diffusion and confusion of governmental powers and responsibilities in metropolitan areas. Further, urban redevelopment is an expensive process and the cities themselves must be prepared to shoulder part of the cost as well as to take most of the benefits. We see the pertinence, therefore, of an analysis and reshaping of sources of local revenue and other phases of local fiscal policy.

"But urban redevelopment has a definite, tangible objective. That objective is to remake all kinds of blighted areas into districts that will fit into an intelligent plan for the future of an urban center or metropolitan region. This is no mean goal, but after all, what have organizations of local officials, associations of municipalities, under-representation of urban areas in legislature, nonvoting, or even ineffective leadership and group antagonisms to do with either the objectives or processes of redevelopment? To be sure, in one sense nearly all phases of urban life and institutions are interrelated, but we cannot see that the connections between urban redevelopment and many of the phases of urban society that you have been writing about are close or particularly meaningful. Are you not guilty of widening the focus of your treatment until it has become blurred? To the extent that redevelopment officials, supporters and students of the redevelopment process take seriously what you put down, are you not running the danger of discouraging them or leading them to discount heavily all that you say on the subject?"

Although obviously I do not agree with this criticism, it certainly is a view that deserves attention and, if possible, an equally straightforward reply. As a matter of fact, it seems to me that two replies can be made.

The first assumes the same general objective of urban redevelopment —to remake all kinds of blighted areas so that they can perform their social and economic functions as parts of an intelligently planned urban locality or metropolitan area. It argues, however, that all of these characteristics and conditions of urban communities—e.g., group antagonisms and mutual mistrust, poor leadership and morale, professional standards among local public servants, regressive taxation, widespread citizen indifference to local public issues and problems, the general low esteem in which urban government is held, etc.—do as a matter of fact have real and continuous influence on urban communities and on local redevelopment programs as well. This influence contributes to the blighting of certain areas of cities. It has delayed a vigorous attack on blight in many localities until it has become alarmingly widespread and difficult to cope with. It has encouraged the general opinion that not very much can be done about blighted areas and, therefore, that it is the part of wisdom for all persons and families who can, to get out of them to newer areas in the suburbs or elsewhere. It breaks out in virulent and often ill-tempered opposition to specific redevelopment undertakings and projects. Residents in these areas, small business men, and even some small industrialists fight tooth and nail against well-conceived redevelopment projects. They oppose them through their aldermen; they try to discredit them through meetings and publicity campaigns; they go to court to oppose them. To the extent that their opposition is grounded in a natural disinclination to be disturbed or inconvenienced or on a sentimental attachment to things as they are, it may be largely unavoidable and certainly is understandable. But much of the opposition clearly is based on misunderstanding, on suspicion of the motives and ends of redevelopment officials and their supporters, on fear that certain economically powerful individuals and groups are imposing on weaker ones for their own narrow interest or gain.

This argument may be illustrated by an analogy to psychosomatic medicine—at least as one layman partially understands it. Over the years both researchers in medical sciences and practicing doctors have become aware of certain important interconnections between physical processes and functioning, on the one hand, and mental and emotional conditions on the other. These connections were not clearly seen as long as the prevailing view was that men had physical bodies, which worked in certain ways and were subject to certain forms of disease and breakdown, and also had mental-emotional natures, which also worked in certain ways and were subject to certain pathologies, and that the two were separate and distinct. When, however, this separation was seen to be largely a product of men's thinking and talking, some remarkable discoveries were forthcoming. It was found, for example, that deficient output of certain glands in the so-called physical body could be a chief factor in mental weakness and in emotional instability. Also, it was demonstrated that certain mental-emotional states, such as deep-seated anxieties and frustrations, could produce symptoms of physical illness without any organic base or explanation, or even might contribute importantly to physical lesions such as stomach ulcers.

As far as I know there is no neat, compact theoretical explanation of these demonstrated relations between what we ordinarily call mind, spirit, and body. But this fact is not deterring either researchers in medical sciences or many clinicians and practicing doctors. Slowly, carefully, painstakingly they are exploring and often demonstrating certain empirical relationships. They are devising and improving forms of treatment: electric and insulin shock; surgical techniques; the injection of hormones; the psychological analysis of fears and anxieties; and even the therapeutic effects of certain forms of group life and relations.

Similarly I suggest that an urban community has both a *soma* and a *psyche*. The soma is the buildings and all the other physical facilities and equipment that serve the common life of urban citizens. It functions in certain readily observable and some more obscure ways. The psyche consists of the basic needs, wants, cravings, and aspirations of human beings in urban environments—those underlying characteristics of human behavior that Lynd and others have tried to identify as they are shaped by the many forces of group-social living and the cultural heritage of urban communities in America. It also includes the resulting attitudes, beliefs, and values that both determine in part and justify in part what urban residents say and do as individuals and as members of organizations and informal groups.

It seems to me the analogy holds still further. We do not have today any neat, inclusive theoretical explanation of the structure and functioning of either the city physical and economic or of the city psychological and social—let alone of the relations between them. It seems highly unlikely that an inclusive theoretical explanation of this kind will be reached in our lifetimes. Maybe it will never be put together— we simply do not know. But it certainly does not follow from these facts that we should concern ourselves solely with one or the other of these aspects of urban communities, ignore the other, or deny the interconnections between them. Those connections do exist; they can be seen and demonstrated in urban centers throughout the land. It is eminently reasonable, therefore, to recognize them, to learn as much as we can about them, to call them to the attention of others, and to use our common store of understanding and insight both in specific programs of urban redevelopment and as a basis for further investigation of other interconnections that may lie somewhat further below the surface.

It is essentially this rationale that accounts for my attempt to treat in this monograph some aspects of urban life and institutions that ordinarily are not considered within the province of urban redevelopment. And I would point again to one further fact: As discussion of urban redevelopment and concrete local programs for accomplishing it have gone ahead in recent years, it is a common experience to discover more and more evidence of these interconnections between the physical-economic and the social-psychological cities. As far as I can see, that process of discovery is still going on. Further, it shows no signs of having reached a point of diminishing returns.

The other reply to the objection stated at the beginning of this section depends on a rather different definition of urban redevelopment. That definition, in turn, comes from a different approach to and a different evaluation of the ills of urban communities.

From this approach it appears that blighted areas are only one of the ills of urban communities, and probably not the most significant. Dislocations and malfunctioning in the social-psychological city are put at the top of the list. Weakening of group ties and value systems are probably put first. More and more urban citizens find that they have less and less to live for in the common life of their communities. Very few objectives in life seem worth the effort except the minimum requirements of physical existence. They admit they believe in relatively little. They share little or no feeling of responsibility for a group or community life, whether in informal organizations, neighborhood or functional groups, or urban government itself. They are more or less psychologically isolated from all but a few persons, and this helps to make them apathetic, cynical, and prejudiced. Often about the only way they can be roused out of their lethargy is by some crude demagogue who blames all their troubles on some likely looking scapegoat, appeals to their prejudices, and promises them the world with a fence around it. Of course, most of the observers and students of urban communities who are concerned by what they see as signs of social disorganization and deterioration would not claim that most urban citizens and their organizations would show all or nearly all of these signs of extreme decline. They would say, rather, that they see a growth and spread of these conditions both in their less virulent and more extreme forms. They are less alarmed over the existing conditions than with what seems to them to be the trend and what some of them take to be the relentless and almost unavoidable forces behind it.

Now, most of the persons who share these views in some form or other have not ordinarily used the phrase urban redevelopment in their writing and talking. To them, however, it clearly would mean a program or process of reviving and strengthening the social-psychological aspects of urban life and institutions. How this might be done would depend largely on varying estimates of the seriousness of the malady, the nature and potentialities of urban society, and the factors and forces that have contributed to the present state of affairs. Some of these forms of analysis and a few of the judgments as to influences and determining factors have been mentioned briefly in earlier sections of this essay.

Clearly persons with this orientation and estimate of urban society would not share the criticism or objection that is under examination. In fact, most of them quite probably would make the opposite criticism of this essay. To them I undoubtedly have given altogether too much attention to physical blight and deterioration as well as to the structure and mechanics of urban government, local taxation, etc.

Although I do not share the more extreme views of members of this school, no one should refuse to listen to their diagnosis and prognoses simply because he thinks they are not properly called urban redevelopment. The basic question is not to define a phrase, but to find some way of understanding urban communities both as they are and as they might become. Certainly if I had to choose between two extremists—one who refused to look beyond physically blighted areas and their immediate causes in obsolescence, land prices, overcrowding, etc., and another limited only to the psychological and social factors in the deterioration of group morale and value systems—I would take the latter simply on the grounds that in the long run what he might accomplish would help make possible what the former would like to do. But this is no either-or question; no one has to make such a choice; the basic problem is falsely stated in such terms.

Rather than arguing any point of this kind, it seems to me more worth while to suggest to sociologists, social psychologists, and others who naturally approach urban problems in this way that they do not make the mistake of underestimating the probable influence of physical conditions in urban areas, of land use patterns, of the ownership, finance, operation, and maintenance of housing and other physical facilities upon community life and behavior. Naturally many of them are apt to do this. Besides, they have some grounds for suspecting the significance of these relations as they have been set forth in some earlier studies. These studies simply show the concentration of physical, social, and psychological ills in blighted residential areas and slums. Some, but by no means all, of the persons who made these tabulations drew or implied the conclusion that blighted and slum conditions were "the cause" of these results. As a matter of fact, however, this conclusion was less often drawn than is sometimes charged. In addition, more recent and careful studies have avoided this pitfall while at the same time they have given substantial grounds for the working hypothesis that intelligent planning and physical improvement in urban centers can contribute substantially to improving other phases of community life as well.

So again I come back to the psychosomatic relationship as the most valid and useful conception today for guiding urban leaders and students of urban affairs as they try to lay out the scope and to assess the potentialities of urban redevelopment.

CHAPTER VII

IN CONCLUSION

A PRIMARY purpose of this monograph has been to provide a conspectus on the ever-growing, ever-changing, and ever-complicating urban scene in America over the last few decades. Now this attempt faces the acid test. From this review is it possible to draw off any basic trends, directions of evolution, developing relationships—call them what you will—that will give framework and meaning both to what has happened and to what urban redevelopers might help to happen in the years ahead?

First of all it can be said that over this period urban government and its allied quasi-official and voluntary associations have shared and have added to a respectable tradition of human association and human service. I say this without apology and fully recognizing the corruption, venality, and cynicism that have often been found in local public affairs. They were found at and around the beginning of the century; as this is being written they are being brought to light again in investigations of the influence of gamblers and hoodlums on some local officials in some localities throughout the country. No one can deny these facts. It is no novelty in American life to find wealthy men who think they can buy their way into positions of privilege and power. It is not news that there are people on the payroll of public and other agencies who are willing to take money and special advantages that can readily be turned into money. No one should be astonished to find that some of these more or less willing recipients are among the ill-paid, little-recognized, often-scorned employees of urban government.

Apparently, however, the sensationalism of many of our newspapers and other means of news dissemination constantly blind us to the existence of other local employees who do not take graft, who do their jobs faithfully and well, who put up with a more or less steady fire of ridicule and scorn from demagogues of the hate-government stripe.

But the record of the last fifty years in perspective is quite clear. Both the scope and the competence of local public services have grown steadily and often remarkably. Public agencies are now performing as a matter of more or less routine operation dozens of services that were unknown or even unthought of forty or fifty years ago. Although these same demagogues have tried to spread the idea that nearly all of the welfare services of government are unproductive and a drag on economic progress, the record contradicts them at every turn. Our increasingly urban society has become more and more efficient as a productive mechanism. Some considerable portion of that improvement is due in part to both the quantity and quality of urban municipal and civic services. And this record, spotted and spotty though it be, is the more notable for two facts.

During at least the first three decades of the century, this development of the welfare city went ahead despite a very unfavorable intellectual climate in many other sectors of urban life. Urban land and its physical improvements were generally treated as objects of speculation and exploitation, subject only to rather mild and not too well enforced police power regulations. Supplies of cheap labor were drawn to many urban centers, sometimes as the result of deliberate recruiting campaigns, and were herded into slum areas. While there the conditions under which they were forced to live were cited as evidence of their low standards of behavior and their lack of ability and ambition. Many of those who profited most from these and other types of speculation and exploitation were among the first to pull out of the larger cities to more pleasant surroundings in suburban areas where they resisted both attempts to make these areas parts of an inclusive urban governmental organization or to subject them to the kinds of real-estate development that were common in the central city itself. To be sure, happenings of this kind aggravated the need for educational and welfare programs, but they certainly were not congenial to humane standards and professional competence in their performance.

Again these welfare programs and activities were initiated and carried forward with relatively little ideological dispute and recrimination. To some considerable degree the need for the various activities or urban government were considered more or less on their merits. Once started, their course was again much more influenced by the results and the further appreciation of needs than by high-flown generalizations. On balance, this may be considered as a merit or a weakness, but by and large it is a fact from the record, and it contrasts sharply with the kind and level of discussion, and particularly the opposition, advanced in recent years to federal governmental aid in these same and allied fields of activity.

In short, at the beginning of the twentieth century urban government was by no means the unrelieved morass of stupidity and venality that it is sometimes painted. It held the start of many improvements in governmental organization and procedure, as well as the beginnings of many welfare activities now generally accepted as necessary and desirable. During the five decades, both the scope and the quality of urban government increased notably. Although the rate of improvement was by no means constant over the years, it has affected nearly every phase of urban public affairs—from the structure, over-all organization and control of governmental affairs through top-level administrative procedures in budgeting, personnel, and purchasing to the more specialized professional areas such as public health and relief programs. Although the problems of urban living have also grown in size and complexity—sometimes at a rate greater than the improvement in governmental administration—the record of the fifty years is on the whole one of increasing competence and growing contributions to the levels and standards of common life in urban communities. Although this is no grounds for smugness or self-satisfaction, it does give confidence for the future.

A closer view of this same scene, however, indicates that much of the improvement has taken place within the limits of various functional or professional activities in the local public service. Some exceptions, of course, should be noted—e.g., the increasing acceptance of the council-manager form of government. But by and large the generalization stands: advances in specialized and functional areas attributable largely to specialized groups or organizations of citizens and to the growing sense of professional competence and pride among various classes of the public service.

One distinguished student once pointed out that ". . . every branch of science is expert, not merely at devising methods of studying certain provinces of life, but also at creating inhibitions and defense mechanisms which bar the way to a complete and adequate knowledge of society."[1] A corresponding tendency may also be seen in urban affairs. Specialization and professionalization make for concrete advances. Unless they be supplemented by other conceptions and influences, however, they make for piecemeal progress at best and often discourage and impede other equally desirable developments. Many examples of this are at hand. A recent one, happily now largely corrected, was the indifference and often outright opposition of specialists in housing, building, and tenement house codes to the advent of local authority housing for low-income families.

The crucial tasks for the next decades would seem to be, therefore, to consolidate gains, to strengthen weak places in the common line against urban ills, and to develop a strategy or plans of urban growth and activities based on a wise appreciation not only of urban problems, but also of those longer-term goals and wants of human beings in urban

1. Karl Mannheim, *Man and Society in an Age of Reconstruction* (New York: Harcourt, Brace and Co., 1940), pp. 27–28.

groups and communities. This means much more study, attention, and understanding of the intangible but mighty forces of group morale, basic human needs and aspirations, and first-class leadership. More concretely, it means a re-evaluation and reformulation of the place and character of urban planning. It will require that we stop ducking, dodging, and improvising against the steady pressures of metropolitanism in our increasingly metropolitan urban life. Finally, it will require most urban communities to face up to the serious financial impasse that past conceptions and traditional practices have brought in their train.

These are truly formidable items on the agenda for the present and near future. No one who appreciates or understands them even casually can take them lightly or write them down as secondary problems that can be muddled through in some half-blind fashion. And I would emphasize again that their requirements for understanding, social philosophy or sense of direction, and practical approach by and large are not substitutes for but additions to the factors of group interest and professionalization that have accounted for so much of the improvement in local public affairs during the last generation or two.

And although it may seem trite, I believe it is a true observation that urban communities through their governmental and less formal institutions either make some headway during the next few years toward consolidating gains and developing some over-all conception of their future pattern and objectives, or else they begin to lose ground in many of the sectors in which they have made the most headway during the decades just past. City growth is on the whole continuing. During the decade of the 1940's the net addition to urban population amounted to some 14 million persons. Metropolitanism also continued unabated. As pointed out earlier, approximately 56 per cent of the population of the United States now lives in metropolitan areas recognized by the Bureau of the Census. About 30 per cent of the population lives in the fourteen metropolitan centers with a population of a million or more. The production side of our economy, both in agriculture and nonagricultural activity, continue to favor the urbanization of our society. With this continuing city growth goes increasing complexity—economic, governmental, and social—and this complexity, in turn, means that the interconnections and interdependence of various segments of urban life become more and more significant in the vigor and health of the whole.

Also I think our review of the past half century showed a significant break or hiatus in urban affairs at or about the onset of the great depression of the early 1930's. Many issues of metropolitan growth, local government, local finance, control of land use, relations among state, federal, and local governmental agencies, and urban planning were being sharpened during the late 1920's. The disaster of the depression temporarily shoved many of these issues into the background and sub-stituted for them another set of problems and questions. As soon as some pattern began to emerge from the rather scattered attacks on these latter problems, World War II and its aftermath, including the so-called cold war, dominated the scene. But although the earlier prob-lems of urban growth, community institutions and relationships have been kept out of the spotlight of public attention for about twenty years, they did not disappear from the scene nor did they solve them-selves in obscurity. All of them are still with us—many of them in more aggravated form than when they were last in the center of the stage. Either we tackle them now with the intellectual and practical tools that promise worth-while results or else we run the very serious danger that they will continue to grow to the point at which they produce serious deterioration in the physical, economic, and social fabric of our cities. A prime example, but by no means the only illustration of this observa-tion, is the current dilemma of local government finance. And no one should assume that these financial problems are unrelated to the ques-tions of physical growth and development, on the one hand, or to frag-mentation of the urban community into mutually antagonistic and suspicious social groups, on the other.

One response to the kind of multi-sided view of urban communities and their problems that I have attempted to take may be discourage-ment. After all, one may say, the resistance and obstacles to physical and social redevelopment—particularly in the larger metropolitan cen-ters—are simply overpowering. It is a great shame, of course. And if only a start could have been made toward redevelopment in the earlier years of this century, many mistakes could have been avoided and many of our current problems would be much less serious. But the op-portunity was missed. Now the great physical fabric of our cities, inef-ficient and unlovely as much of it may be, is simply too large and too expensive to yield to any likely combination of public and private pow-ers that in fact can be organized in the foreseeable future. With the enormous recent growth of our cities, the economic stake in this physi-cal plant, both in ownership and mortgage loans, is too heavy. In public facilities and services the arrearages of repair, maintenance, and re-placement are simply staggering. No sober person can see how they can be made up in the immediate future even without adding new services and programs. Admit that many of the group and class antagonisms and suspicion among urban populations are unfortunate and undemocratic. There they are. And there they continue to operate—in politics, in in-dustry, in education, in workaday philosophy, and in the very outlook of the urban citizens who make up these groups. Maybe some of these cleavages could have been prevented or some of the group barriers made less high and rigid when our cities were younger and their social organizations more fluid. But again, the opportunity was missed, and little or nothing can be done about that.

Many of those who hold this general view of things are not utter defeatists. They see a few steps that might be taken, but they are, by any reasonable measure, short steps. Certainly some of the worst slums ought to be torn down and replaced by decent buildings in which the plumbing works. But do not expect that this can be done on any sweeping scale or that the new development can make possible pleasant, comfortable, democratic neighborhoods or contribute to a revival of neighborhood spirit or to concern with standards of education, recreation, health, or other phases of the common life of urban dwellers.

Many changes could be rung on this theme. Fundamentally, however, the argument is that urban structure and institutions have simply become too large, too rigid, to allow any thorough-going reorganization or redevelopment. If only these objectives could have been seen earlier!

But is this brand of realism so realistic after all? In the light of the record, could the physical and social evolution of American cities have been much different than it actually was? When city populations are growing by leaps and bounds, when land values are rising spectacularly, when land and other forms of speculation are the accepted order of the day, when, democratic principles to the contrary notwithstanding, most persons in the well-to-do minority look upon large segments of the working population as a means to economic production and profit rather than as an end, when local governments lack an established body of professional competence, when the objective of many persons and groups is to fight their way out of the slums rather than to get rid of them, when making money is the most generally accepted index of competence and respectability—in all these and similar circumstances that existed in those earlier days, where was the groundwork for urban redevelopment of any kind?

Although the intellectual, emotional, and practical obstacles to redevelopment are formidable enough today, the favorable factors are also much more evident and much more strong, at least potentially, than they have been in times past. No one can demonstrate conclusively that the dissatisfactions with many of the physical and social conditions of urban life are widespread enough to provide a firm foundation for a true redevelopment program. Scattered evidence, however, can be found to support this opinion. Certainly a large proportion of urban dwellers do not realize clearly what vast improvements in the physical and social conditions of urban living are now technically possible. But again, there are signs or partial glimpses that indicate that this front also is by no means hopeless. And certainly the physical patterns of

American cities are still far from frozen. If they are not changing in the directions that some persons would like to see, at least they are changing. Without embracing any too-easy optimism and without denying the truly formidable obstacles that confront those who work for the improvement of urban communities, I do suggest that the record of the past few decades does not support the view that the real possibilities for urban redevelopment lie buried in the past.

Earlier in this monograph, I referred to some observations by Elton Mayo drawn chiefly from years of careful, thorough study by him and his associates of human relations in modern, large-scale industry. These are worth recalling again here. In Mayo's words:

> Every social group . . . must secure for its individual and group membership: (1) The satisfaction of material and economic needs. (2) The maintenance of spontaneous cooperation throughout the organization.
>
> Our administrative methods are all pointed at the materially effective; none, at the maintenance of cooperation. . . .[2]

Later he said flatly: ". . . Our civilization has been immensely successful in respect of material and technical accomplishment, an utter failure as a cooperative system. . . ." Also he observed that in respect to this second essential of human collaboration, evidence was at hand for believing that most organizations and institutions of our society are living on their capital accumulated during earlier and less complicated times. As this wasteful process continues we approach an eventual showdown—unless we change our ways. Throughout his later writing runs the theme that our highly developed and ever-changing technology throws on our weak fabric of human collaboration strains that are greater and more continuous than those in any other economic and social system that we know about. He urges again and again that human collaboration within and among the groups of modern society is so fundamental to its healthful evolution that it should not be left to chance.

These are strong words. And generalizations of this order are by their very nature subject to various exceptions and qualifications. I would suggest, however, that they hold substantially true for large segments of those institutions and programs that both make possible and help to determine the character and quality of the common life of urban communities.

In fact, the two-fold function of social organizations that Mayo emphasizes seems to me not only valid but to square well with the rough framework put forward at the beginning of this essay—the physical, economic, and social city, all closely interrelated and all directly af-

2. Mayo, *Social Problems*, pp. 9, 54.

fected by the character and activities of urban government. And borrowing from another distinguished student of contemporary society, it seems that the paramount purpose he saw for the democratic state is equally pertinent to urban government and its allied institutions: ". . . to serve the community and in that service to make it more of a community."[3]

Seen against this background, the record and present picture of urban life and institutions that this essay has tried to deal with reveal the same serious flaws that Mayo stressed from his much more thorough study of industrial organization and relations. The psychosomatic city is physically energetic and growing, but in many respects poorly coordinated and poorly disciplined. It has an abundance of crude power and despite several obvious weaknesses it has the makings of a strong, able servant of the common good. Mentally and emotionally, however, the metropolitan city is far from a healthful organism. It finds great difficulty in concentrating on any long-term objective. Its loyalties and sense of values are weak, wavering, and diffused. It suffers from vague but persistent feelings of anxiety, helplessness, and impotence. It shows symptoms of various neurotic and psychotic conditions of which the most alarming probably are attempts to escape from the realities of its existence and to blame its failures and anxieties on various convenient scapegoats—human nature, politicians, bankers, the masses, special interests, etc. Its condition is serious, but by no means hopeless. A prescription of little pink pills, a few setting-up exercises, and the daily reiteration that "every day in every way I am getting better and better" will not do it much good. Quite surely, however, it will respond to a regime of well-considered urban planning and redevelopment, a major operation on its fiscal system, and a continued application of difficult but simple democratic procedures in all phases of its common life. In time these may be expected to contribute to a substantial degree of human solidarity, widely shared loyalties and values, and a sense of well-being and meaningful existence.

Let me conclude with two quotations from men on whose ideas and analyses I have already drawn.

A. D. Lindsay in his study, *The Modern Democratic State*, which was finished during World War II, wrote:

If democracy is to survive, it will have to employ and use every bit of skill and knowledge and leadership it can get hold of. This complicated interdependent modern world in which we are living cannot be run without knowledge and skill, foresight and leadership. Any cult of incompetence can only lead to disaster. A modern democratic state is only possible if it can combine appreciation of skill, knowledge, and

3. A. D. Lindsay, *The Modern Democratic State*, London: Oxford University Press, 1943, Vol. I., p. 245.

expertness with a reverence for the common humanity of everyday people. It is that conception of equality which its institutions will have to express.[4]

And Gunnar Myrdal in the same chapter of *An American Dilemma* from which I quoted earlier put down these wise and eloquent words:

> . . . These two cultural traits of America [the faith in leadership and the relative inertia and passivity of large masses of the population in respect to social and political issues] have, in their historical development, been complementary. But individual activity and mass activity are not necessarily antagonistic principles. It is possible to envisage a future development where the masses in America participate more intensively in political activities of various sorts, but where, nevertheless, outstanding individuals are permitted to have a wide space for their initiative according to the great American tradition. Such a social system, if it ever developed, would realize in the highest degree the age-old ideal of a vitalized democracy. It would result, not only in a decrease in the immense class differences in America, but more fundamentally, it would effect a higher degree of integration in the society of the many millions of anonymous and atomized individuals: a strengthening of the ties of loyalty running through the entire social fabric; a more efficient and uncorrupted performance of all public functions; and a more intense and secure feeling on the part of the common citizen of his belongingness to, responsibility for, and participation in the commonwealth as a great cooperative human endeavor—a realization of a fuller life.[5]

I do not suggest that urban planners and redevelopers alone could or should carry the responsibility for realizing these great objectives. But they can and, I believe, should share in it as well as in the corresponding opportunities that the development of the physical, economic, social and governmental city still puts before those who are not too narrow, tired, confused, or cynical to recognize them. If they can see something of this city that could be and are prepared to combine with their vision years of hard, intelligent, and often unspectacular work on the multi-sided problems of a complex urban society, the prospects of urban redevelopment in the United States will become clearer and brighter in the years ahead.

4. *Ibid.*, p. 261.
5. Gunnar Myrdal (with Richard Sterner and Arnold Rose), *An American Dilemma* (New York: Harper & Bros., 1944), p. 716.

ACKNOWLEDGMENTS

ACKNOWLEDGMENTS

THROUGHOUT this volume footnotes and references in the text indicate how considerably most URS contributors have benefited from the writings of others. Both those responsible for the Study and its researchers and writers acknowledge gratefully permission given by publishers to quote from copyrighted works.

In addition, many persons helped materially and in many ways in the processes of investigation and presentation. They advised in defining and organizing the work; they supplied many materials and leads to others; from their experience, current operations and study they gave friendly and helpful criticism of preliminary drafts. We are grateful to them not only for their help but also for the encouragement most of them have given us. Of course, none of them is responsible for the methods, findings, or discussion in the parts of the Study on which he was good enough to help. At the risk of leaving out some whose assistance may not have been properly recorded in the Study's files, we list below those to whom we are particularly indebted.

II. "Industrial Location and Urban Redevelopment": Arthur Bright, Arnold E. Chase, Arthur C. Comey, Maxwell Conklin, Ernest M. Fisher, Milburn Forth, Walter Isard, Robert B. Mitchell, and Richard U. Ratcliff.

III. "Urban Redevelopment and the Urbanite": Edmund N. Bacon, Ernest J. Bohn, Francis Bosworth, Dan Cahalan, Jason N. Calhoun, Willard E. Downing, Dan Elliott, Molly Yard Garrett, Julian L. Greifer, William H. Harman, Clyde W. Hart, Eri Hulbert, Walden Johnston, Francis J. Lammer, James E. Lash, A. F. Metz, Hugh Mields, Jr., Hugh J. Parry, Carl Quast, Florence Schulson, Shirley A. Star, Donald Stier, Wilford G. Winholtz.

IV. "Local Government Organization in Metropolitan Areas. Its Relation to Urban Redevelopment": Walter H. Blucher, John C. Bollens, Carl H. Chatters, Carl Feiss, Bertram M. Gross, Annie Mae Jones, Lucile L. Keck, N. S. Keith, Marie di Mauro, Gertrude McKenna, Seward H. Mott, Orin F. Nolting, Roy Peel, Richard U. Ratcliff, Clarence E. Ridley, William L. Slayton, Richard L. Steiner, David M. Walker, Louis B. Wetmore.

V. "The Background and Prospects of Urban Redevelopment in the United States": William Anderson, Louis Brownlow, John M. Gaus, Victor Jones, Don K. Price.

Last but not least we offer our thanks to Marianne Yates who, despite unusually heavy duties at the Joint Reference Library of Public Administration Clearing House when the page proof was ready, prepared the Index.

INDEX

INDEX

Now, to *complete the square*, we take one-half of the coefficient of the x-term $[\frac{1}{2}(-6) = -3]$ and square it $[(-3)^2 = 9]$. We add the result to both sides of the equation. Thus the left side is the *square of a binomial*:

$$x^2 - 6x + 9 = -3 + 9$$
$$(x - 3)^2 = 6.$$

This equation has the pure form $u^2 = k$, where u is $x - 3$ and k is 6. By the square-root method, $u = \pm\sqrt{k}$, so

$$x - 3 = \pm\sqrt{6}$$
$$x = 3 \pm \sqrt{6} \qquad \text{[adding 3 to both sides].}$$

Therefore, the roots are $3 + \sqrt{6}$ and $3 - \sqrt{6}$. Although these roots can be put in decimal form (a common practice in technology), in this text a radical form is acceptable. The technique we have used to solve the quadratic equation is called **completing the square**.

Example 1

Solve $2x^2 + 3x - 4 = 0$ by completing the square.

Solution We begin by moving the constant term to the right side.

$$2x^2 + 3x - 4 = 0$$
$$2x^2 + 3x = 4.$$

To get the coefficient of the x^2-term to be 1, we divide both sides by 2.

$$x^2 + \frac{3}{2}x = 2.$$

Adding $[\frac{1}{2}(\frac{3}{2})]^2$, or $\frac{9}{16}$, to both sides gives

$$x^2 + \frac{3}{2}x + \frac{9}{16} = 2 + \frac{9}{16}$$
$$\left(x + \frac{3}{4}\right)^2 = \frac{41}{16}.$$

This equation is in pure form. Thus

$$x + \frac{3}{4} = \pm\sqrt{\frac{41}{16}} = \pm\frac{\sqrt{41}}{4}$$

$$x = -\frac{3}{4} \pm \frac{\sqrt{41}}{4}$$

The roots are $\dfrac{-3+\sqrt{41}}{4}$ and $\dfrac{-3-\sqrt{41}}{4}$.

Problem Set 12.2

Solve each equation by completing the square.

1. $x^2 + 6x - 1 = 0$.
2. $2x^2 + 4x - 8 = 0$.
3. $5x^2 - 20x + 5 = 0$.
4. $x^2 - 12x + 8 = 0$.
5. $y^2 - 3y - 1 = 0$.
6. $x^2 + 5x + 5 = 0$.
7. $x^2 + x - 4 = 0$.
8. $4w^2 - 8w - 3 = 0$.
9. $2x^2 - 14x + 1 = 0$.
10. $9x^2 + 9x - 2 = 0$.
11. $x^2 + \frac{1}{2}x - 1 = 0$.
12. $x^2 + 2x - \frac{1}{4} = 0$.
13. $7x + 3(x^2 - 5) = x - 3$.
14. $2x(4x - 1) = 4 + 2x$.

12.3 THE QUADRATIC FORMULA

Another method for solving a quadratic equation is by using a special formula known as the *quadratic formula*. To derive this formula, we apply the method of completing the square to the general quadratic equation $ax^2 + bx + c = 0$. Let

$$ax^2 + bx + c = 0, \qquad a \neq 0.$$

Then

$$ax^2 + bx = -c.$$

We can divide both sides by a because $a \neq 0$.

$$x^2 + \frac{b}{a}x = -\frac{c}{a}.$$

Because the coefficient of the x-term is b/a, we add the square of $\frac{1}{2}(b/a)$ to both sides:

$$x^2 + \frac{b}{a}x + \left(\frac{b}{2a}\right)^2 = \left(\frac{b}{2a}\right)^2 - \frac{c}{a}. \tag{1}$$

The left side is $\left(x + \dfrac{b}{2a}\right)^2$ and the right side is

$$\frac{b^2}{4a^2} - \frac{c}{a} = \frac{b^2}{4a^2} - \frac{4ac}{4a^2} = \frac{b^2 - 4ac}{4a^2}.$$

Thus Eq. 1 becomes

$$\left(x + \frac{b}{2a}\right)^2 = \frac{b^2 - 4ac}{4a^2}$$

$$x + \frac{b}{2a} = \pm\sqrt{\frac{b^2 - 4ac}{4a^2}} = \pm\frac{\sqrt{b^2 - 4ac}}{2a}.$$

Solving for x, we obtain

$$x = -\frac{b}{2a} \pm \frac{\sqrt{b^2 - 4ac}}{2a},$$

$$x = \frac{-b \pm \sqrt{b^2 - 4ac}}{2a}. \tag{2}$$

It can be shown that the two values $\dfrac{-b + \sqrt{b^2 - 4ac}}{2a}$ and $\dfrac{-b - \sqrt{b^2 - 4ac}}{2a}$ do indeed satisfy $ax^2 + bx + c = 0$. Equation 2 is called the **quadratic formula**.

QUADRATIC FORMULA

If $ax^2 + bx + c = 0$, where $a \neq 0$, then

$$x = \frac{-b \pm \sqrt{b^2 - 4ac}}{2a}.$$

These values of x are the roots of the above quadratic equation.

The quadratic formula, along with the hypothesis that precedes it, should be memorized. Be sure to write it correctly. For example, $x \neq -b \pm \dfrac{\sqrt{b^2 - 4ac}}{2a}$ because $-b$ must be divided by $2a$.

Example 1

Solve $2x^2 + 5x - 3 = 0$ by the quadratic formula.

Solution Here $a = 2$, $b = 5$, and $c = -3$, so

$$x = \frac{-b \pm \sqrt{b^2 - 4ac}}{2a} = \frac{-5 \pm \sqrt{(5)^2 - 4(2)(-3)}}{2(2)}$$

$$= \frac{-5 \pm \sqrt{25 + 24}}{4} = \frac{-5 \pm \sqrt{49}}{4} = \frac{-5 \pm 7}{4}.$$

Thus the solutions are

$$x = \frac{-5 + 7}{4} = \frac{2}{4} = \frac{1}{2} \quad \text{and} \quad x = \frac{-5 - 7}{4} = \frac{-12}{4} = -3.$$

Example 2

Solve $4t^2 + 9 = 12t$ by the quadratic formula.

Solution First we rewrite the equation so that it has the general form $at^2 + bt + c = 0$.

$$4t^2 - 12t + 9 = 0.$$

Here $a = 4$, $b = -12$, and $c = 9$, so

$$t = \frac{-b \pm \sqrt{b^2 - 4ac}}{2a} = \frac{-(-12) \pm \sqrt{(-12)^2 - 4(4)(9)}}{2(4)}$$

$$= \frac{12 \pm \sqrt{144 - 144}}{8} = \frac{12 \pm 0}{8}.$$

Notice that we get the same value whether we use the $+$ sign or the $-$ sign. Thus the only solution is

$$t = \frac{12}{8} = \frac{3}{2}.$$

We consider $\frac{3}{2}$ to be a double root.

Example 3

Solve $x^2 + x + 1 = 0$ by the quadratic formula.

Solution Here $a = 1$, $b = 1$, and $c = 1$.

$$x = \frac{-b \pm \sqrt{b^2 - 4ac}}{2a} = \frac{-1 \pm \sqrt{1^2 - 4(1)(1)}}{2(1)}$$

$$= \frac{-1 \pm \sqrt{-3}}{2}.$$

Because $\sqrt{-3}$ is not a real number, the given equation has no real solutions.

The number $b^2 - 4ac$ that appears under the radical sign in the quadratic formula is called the **discriminant** of the quadratic equation $ax^2 + bx + c = 0$. Looking back at Example 1, we see that the discriminant 49 is positive and the equation has exactly two different real solutions. In Example 2, the discriminant is zero and the equation has exactly one real solution (a double root). In Example 3 the discriminant, -3, is negative and the equation has no real solutions. Thus the discriminant tells us about the nature of the roots of a quadratic equation without the need for us to solve the equation.

DISCRIMINANT	
$b^2 - 4ac$	Nature of Solution
Positive	Two different real solutions
Zero	One real solution (double root)
Negative	No real solutions

Example 4

Use the discriminant to determine how many real solutions the given equation has.

a. $2x^2 - 4x + 5 = 0$.

Solution   Here $a = 2$, $b = -4$, and $c = 5$, so the discriminant is

$$b^2 - 4ac = (-4)^2 - 4(2)(5) = 16 - 40 = -24 < 0.$$

Because the discriminant is negative, there are no real solutions.

b. $x^2 - 6x + 6 = 0$.

Solution   The discriminant is

$$b^2 - 4ac = (-6)^2 - 4(1)(6) = 36 - 24 = 12 > 0.$$

A positive discriminant means that there are two different real solutions.

c. $x^2 - 10x + 25 = 0$.

Solution   The discriminant is

$$b^2 - 4ac = (-10)^2 - 4(1)(25) = 100 - 100 = 0.$$

Because the discriminant is zero, there is one real solution. It is a double root.

What is the best way of solving a quadratic equation $ax^2 + bx + c = 0$? The quadratic formula can be used for *any* quadratic equation. However, if there is no

x-term involved, use the square-root method. For example, to solve $5x^2 - 2 = 0$ we have

$$5x^2 - 2 = 0,$$

$$5x^2 = 2$$

$$x^2 = \frac{2}{5}$$

$$x = \pm\sqrt{\frac{2}{5}} = \pm\frac{\sqrt{10}}{5}.$$

If there are x^2- and x-terms but no constant term ($c = 0$), use factoring. For example, to solve $4x^2 + 3x = 0$ we have

$$4x^2 + 3x = 0$$

$$x(4x + 3) = 0.$$

$$x = 0. \quad \Big| \quad 4x + 3 = 0$$

$$4x = -3$$

$$x = -\frac{3}{4}.$$

For the equation $ax^2 + bx + c = 0$, where a, b, and c are all different from 0, try factoring first. If that appears to be too difficult, use the quadratic formula.

Problem Set 12.3

In Problems **1–12**, *solve each equation by using the quadratic formula.*

1. $x^2 + 3x + 1 = 0$.
2. $x^2 - 4x + 2 = 0$.
3. $x^2 - 6x + 9 = 0$.
4. $x^2 + x - 3 = 0$.
5. $2y^2 + 3y - 4 = 0$.
6. $3r^2 + 6r - 2 = 0$.
7. $4t^2 = -20t - 25$.
8. $9z(z - 1) = 3z - 4$.
9. $5x(x + 2) + 6 = 3$.
10. $(4x - 1)(2x + 3) = 18x - 4$.
11. $2 - 2x - 3x^2 = 0$.
12. $1 + 8x - 4x^2 = 0$.

In Problems **13–52**, *solve by any method.*

13. $x^2 - 36 = 0$.
14. $x^2 + 4x - 1 = 0$.
15. $x^2 + 6x - 7 = 0$.
16. $x^2 - x - 20 = 0$.
17. $z^2 = 2z$.
18. $4z^2 - 25 = 0$.
19. $x^2 + 4x + 2 = 0$.
20. $x^2 - 5x + 3 = 0$.
21. $y^2 + 16y + 64 = 0$.
22. $3y^2 - y - 4 = 0$.
23. $3x^2 - 4x - 2 = 0$.
24. $3 + x - 4x^2 = 0$.
25. $5w^2 - 21w + 4 = 0$.
26. $2x^2 - 6x + 2 = 0$.

27. $(x + 2)^2 = 5$.

28. $2m^2 - 11 = 0$.

29. $5x^2 + 4x = 0$.

30. $y(y - 5) = 0$.

31. $4 + 4y - y^2 = 0$.

32. $4y^2 + 12y + 9 = 0$.

33. $1 - 6y + 9y^2 = 0$.

34. $7 - y - y^2 = 0$.

35. $s^2 + 9 = 7s$.

36. $x^2 - 16 = 8 - 2x$.

37. $x^2 + 3x = 12 - 2x - x^2$.

38. $3x(2x - 5) = -4x - 3$.

39. $y(y + 4) = 5$.

40. $(y + 1)^2 = 2y^2$.

41. $z^2 = 2(z - 1)(z + 2)$.

42. $z^4 - 6z^2 + 7 = z^2(z^2 + 1)$.

43. $(2x + 1)^2 = 8x$.

44. $2x(x + 1) = (x - 1)(x + 1)$.

45. $\dfrac{2x^2 - 5x}{3} = x - 1$.

46. $\dfrac{x^2}{3} + 2x = x + 1$.

47. $\dfrac{x^2}{3} = \dfrac{11}{6}x + 1$.

48. $5x^2 - \dfrac{7}{2}x = \dfrac{x + 2}{2}$.

49. $0.01x^2 + 0.2x - 0.6 = 0$.

50. $6x^3 + 8x^2 - 10x = 0$.

51. $2x^2 - \sqrt{3}x - 4 = 0$.

52. $\sqrt{8}x^2 + \sqrt{5}x - \sqrt{2} = 0$.

In Problems **53–60**, *use the discriminant to determine the nature of the roots.*

53. $3x^2 - 5x - 2 = 0$.

54. $x^2 + 4x + 5 = 0$.

55. $9t^2 + 12t + 4 = 0$.

56. $4t^2 + 12t + 9 = 0$.

57. $3x^2 - 4x + 3 = 0$.

58. $4x^2 - 17x + 15 = 0$.

59. $(3x - 1)(x + 2) = 2x$.

60. $x(x - 4) - 3(2 - x) + 7 = 0$.

61. If $3x^2 - 5xy - 4y^2 = 0$, solve for x by treating y as a positive constant.

62. If $2x^2 + 6xy - 9y^2 = 0$, solve for y by treating x as a positive constant.

63. Given the equation of motion

$$s = v_0 t + \tfrac{1}{2}at^2,$$

find t (in seconds) if $s = 15$ m, $v_0 = 18$ m/s, and $a = -9.8$ m/s^2. Here s, v_0, and a are displacement, initial velocity, and acceleration, respectively.

64. When a projectile is fired so that its initial velocity in the vertical direction is 30 m/s, its height s above its starting level after t seconds is given by

$$s = 30t - 4.9t^2.$$

When will the projectile be at a height of 32 m above its starting level?

65. In a circuit carrying a current i (in amperes), the power P dissipated (in watts) is given by

$$P = i^2R + iV.$$

In one circuit, $R = 10\ \Omega$, $V = 24$ V, and $P = 30$ W. Find i (assume $i > 0$).

66. A company parking lot is 120 ft long and 80 ft wide. Because of an increase in personnel, it is decided to double the area of the lot by adding strips of equal width to one end and one side. Find the width of one such strip.

67. A chemist took some acid from a full beaker containing 81 cm^3 of pure acid and then filled up the beaker with pure water. He then took the same amount from the acid-water mixture and found that 64 cm^3 of pure acid remained in the beaker. How many cubic centimeters did he take each time?

68. An open box is to be made from a square piece of tin by cutting out a 3-cm square from each corner and folding up the sides (see Fig. 12.7). The box is to contain 75 cm³. Find the dimensions of the square piece of tin that must be used.

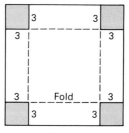

FIGURE 12.7

69. In studying the dynamic behavior of galvanometers, one encounters the equation

$$Jm^2 + Dm + S = 0,$$

where J, D, and S are physical quantities that determine the characteristics of the motion of the galvanometer coil. Solve the equation for m.

70. In Problem 69, a galvanometer is said to be *overdamped* when $\dfrac{D^2}{4J^2} > \dfrac{S}{J}$, *underdamped* when $\dfrac{D^2}{4J^2} < \dfrac{S}{J}$, and *critically damped* when $\dfrac{D^2}{4J^2} = \dfrac{S}{J}$. For each case, what is the nature of the roots of the equation in Problem 69?

71. A platinum resistance thermomometer of certain specifications operates according to the equation

$$R = 10.000 + (4.124 \times 10^{-2})T - (1.779 \times 10^{-5})T^2,$$

where R is the resistance of the thermometer at temperature T (in degrees Celsius). If $R = 13.946\ \Omega$, find the corresponding value of T. Assume that such a thermometer is useable only if $T < 600°C$.

12.4 QUADRATIC FUNCTIONS

Now that we have considered methods of solving quadratic equations, we turn our attention to properties of the graph of a *quadratic function*, which is a polynomial function of degree 2.

> A function f is a **quadratic function** if
>
> $$f(x) = ax^2 + bx + c$$
>
> where a, b, and c are real numbers and $a \neq 0$.

For example, the functions $f(x) = x^2 - 3x + 2$ and $F(t) = -3t^2$ are quadratic. However, $g(x) = \dfrac{1}{x^2}$ is *not* quadratic because it cannot be written in the form $g(x) = ax^2 + bx + c$.

The graph of the quadratic function $y = f(x) = ax^2 + bx + c$ is called a **parabola** and has a shape like the curves in Fig. 12.8. If $a > 0$, the graph extends upward indefinitely and we say that the parabola *opens upward* [Fig. 12.8(a)]. If $a < 0$, the parabola *opens downward* [Fig. 12.8(b)].

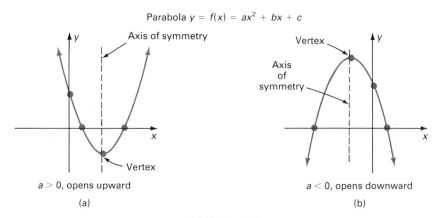

Parabola $y = f(x) = ax^2 + bx + c$

(a) $a > 0$, opens upward

(b) $a < 0$, opens downward

FIGURE 12.8

Each parabola in Fig. 12.8 is *symmetric* about a vertical line, called the **axis of symmetry** of the parabola. That is, if the page were folded on one of these lines, then the two halves of the corresponding parabola would coincide. The axis (of symmetry) is *not* part of the parabola, but it is a useful aid in sketching the parabola.

In Fig. 12.8 each parabola has a point, called the **vertex**, where the axis of symmetry cuts the parabola. If $a > 0$, the vertex is the "lowest" point on the parabola. This means that $f(x)$ has a minimum value at this point. By "completing the square" on $ax^2 + bx + c$, we can determine not only this minimum value but also where it occurs. Let

$$f(x) = ax^2 + bx + c = (ax^2 + bx) + c.$$

To complete the square we add and subtract $b^2/(4a)$:

$$f(x) = \left(ax^2 + bx + \frac{b^2}{4a}\right) + c - \frac{b^2}{4a}$$

$$= a\left(x^2 + \frac{b}{a}x + \frac{b^2}{4a^2}\right) + c - \frac{b^2}{4a}.$$

$$f(x) = a\left(x + \frac{b}{2a}\right)^2 + \frac{4ac - b^2}{4a}.$$

Because $\left(x + \dfrac{b}{2a}\right)^2 \geq 0$ and $a > 0$, it follows that $f(x)$ has a minimum value when $x + \dfrac{b}{2a} = 0$, that is, when $x = -\dfrac{b}{2a}$. The minimum value is $\dfrac{4ac - b^2}{4a}$. Thus the vertex is the point $\left(-\dfrac{b}{2a}, \dfrac{4ac - b^2}{4a}\right)$. Because the y-coordinate of this point is the same as $f\left(-\dfrac{b}{2a}\right)$, we have

$$\text{Vertex} = \left(-\dfrac{b}{2a}, f\left(-\dfrac{b}{2a}\right)\right) = \left(-\dfrac{b}{2a}, \dfrac{4ac - b^2}{4a}\right).$$

This is also the vertex of a parabola that opens downward ($a < 0$), but in this case $\dfrac{4ac - b^2}{4a}$ is the *maximum* value of $f(x)$ [see Fig. 12.8(b)].

There is exactly one point where the parabola $y = ax^2 + bx + c$ intersects the y-axis (that is, the y-intercept). It occurs when $x = 0$. The y-coordinate of this point is c, so the y-intercept is $(0, c)$ or, more simply, c. In summary, we have the following.

The graph of the quadratic function $y = f(x) = ax^2 + bx + c$ is a parabola.

1. If $a > 0$, the parabola opens upward.
   If $a < 0$, it opens downward.

2. The vertex is the point $\left(-\dfrac{b}{2a}, \dfrac{4ac - b^2}{4a}\right)$.

3. The y-intercept is c.

4. The equation of the axis of symmetry is $x = -\dfrac{b}{2a}$.

We can quickly sketch the graph of a quadratic function by first locating the vertex, the y-intercept, and a few other points, like those where the parabola intersects the x-axis. These **x-intercepts** are found by setting $y = 0$ and solving for x. Once the intercepts and vertex are found, it is then relatively easy to pass the appropriate parabola through these points. In the event that the x-intercepts are very close to the vertex, or that no x-intercepts exist, we find a point on each side of the vertex so that we can give a reasonable sketch of the parabola. Keep in mind that passing a (dashed) vertical line through the vertex gives the axis of symmetry. By plotting points to one side of this axis, we can use symmetry and obtain corresponding points on the other side.

Example 1

Sketch the graph of the quadratic function $y = f(x) = -x^2 - 4x + 12$.

Solution Here $a = -1$, $b = -4$, and $c = 12$. Since $a < 0$, the parabola opens downward. The x-coordinate of the vertex is

$$-\frac{b}{2a} = -\frac{-4}{2(-1)} = -2.$$

The y-coordinate is

$$f\left(-\frac{b}{2a}\right) = f(-2) = -(-2)^2 - 4(-2) + 12 = 16.$$

Alternatively, it is

$$\frac{4ac - b^2}{4a} = \frac{4(-1)(12) - (-4)^2}{4(-1)} = \frac{-64}{-4} = 16.$$

Thus the vertex (highest point) is $(-2, 16)$. Since $c = 12$, the y-intercept is 12. To find the x-intercepts, we let y be 0 in $y = -x^2 - 4x + 12$ and solve for x.

$$0 = -x^2 - 4x + 12$$
$$0 = -(x^2 + 4x - 12)$$
$$0 = -(x + 6)(x - 2).$$

Thus $x = -6$ or $x = 2$, so the x-intercepts are -6 and 2. Now we plot the vertex, axis of symmetry, and intercepts [see Fig. 12.9(a)]. Since $(0, 12)$ is *two* units to the *right* of the axis of symmetry, *two* units to the *left* of the axis there is a corresponding point with the same y-coordinate. Thus we get the point $(-4, 12)$. Through all points we draw a parabola opening downward [see Fig 12.9(b)].

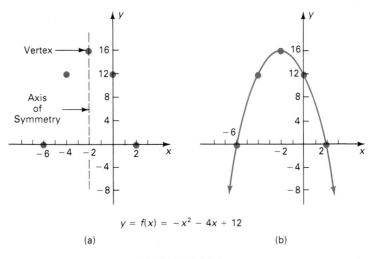

$$y = f(x) = -x^2 - 4x + 12$$

(a)　　　　　　　　　　　(b)

FIGURE 12.9

Example 2

Sketch the graph of $s = 2t^2$.

Solution   Here s is a quadratic function of t, where $a = 2$, $b = 0$, and $c = 0$. Because $a > 0$, the parabola opens upward. The t-coordinate of the vertex is

$$-\frac{b}{2a} = -\frac{0}{2(2)} = 0,$$

and the s-coordinate is $2(0)^2 = 0$. Thus the vertex is $(0, 0)$. In this case the s-axis is the axis of symmetry. A parabola opening upward with vertex at $(0, 0)$ cannot have any other intercepts. Hence to draw a reasonable graph we plot a point on each side of the vertex. If $t = 2$, then $s = 8$. This gives the point $(2, 8)$ and, by symmetry, the point $(-2, 8)$ (see Fig. 12.10).

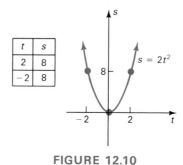

t	s
2	8
-2	8

FIGURE 12.10

Example 3

Sketch the graph of $g(x) = x^2 - 6x + 7$.

Solution   Here g is a quadratic function, where $a = 1$, $b = -6$, and $c = 7$. The parabola opens upward because $a > 0$. The x-coordinate of the vertex is

$$-\frac{b}{2a} = -\frac{-6}{2(1)} = 3,$$

and the y-coordinate is $3^2 - 6(3) + 7 = -2$. Thus the vertex (lowest point) is $(3, -2)$. Since $c = 7$, the vertical-axis intercept is 7. To find x-intercepts, we set $g(x) = 0$.

$$0 = x^2 - 6x + 7.$$

The right side does not factor easily, so we shall use the quadratic formula to solve for x.

$$x = \frac{-b \pm \sqrt{b^2 - 4ac}}{2a} = \frac{-(-6) \pm \sqrt{(-6)^2 - 4(1)(7)}}{2(1)}$$

$$= \frac{6 \pm \sqrt{8}}{2} = \frac{6 \pm \sqrt{4 \cdot 2}}{2} = \frac{6 \pm 2\sqrt{2}}{2}$$

$$= \frac{6}{2} \pm \frac{2\sqrt{2}}{2} = 3 \pm \sqrt{2}.$$

Thus the x-intercepts are $3 + \sqrt{2}$ and $3 - \sqrt{2}$, which are approximately 4.4 and 1.6, respectively. After plotting the vertex, intercepts, and (by symmetry) the point (6, 7), we draw the parabola opening upward in Fig. 12.11.

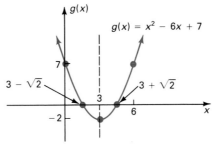

FIGURE 12.11

Example 4

Sketch the graph of $y = f(x) = 2x^2 + 2x + 3$.

Solution   This function is quadratic with $a = 2$, $b = 2$, and $c = 3$. Since $a > 0$, the graph is a parabola opening upward. The x-coordinate of the vertex is

$$-\frac{b}{2a} = -\frac{2}{2(2)} = -\frac{1}{2},$$

and the y-coordinate is $2(-\frac{1}{2})^2 + 2(-\frac{1}{2}) + 3 = \frac{5}{2}$. Thus the vertex is $(-\frac{1}{2}, \frac{5}{2})$. Since $c = 3$, the y-intercept is 3. A parabola opening upward with its vertex above the x-axis has no x-intercepts. In Fig. 12.12 we plotted the y-intercept, the vertex, and an additional point $(-2, 7)$ to the left of the vertex. By symmetry, we also get the point (1, 7). Passing a parabola through these points gives the desired graph.

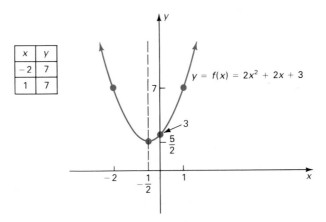

FIGURE 12.12

The following examples show some applications of quadratic functions.

Example 5

The height s of a ball thrown vertically upward from the ground is given by the equation of motion

$$s = 19.6t - 4.9t^2,$$

where s is in meters and t is elapsed time in seconds. When does the ball reach its greatest height and what is that height?

Solution   Note that s is a quadratic function of t, where $a = -4.9$, $b = 19.6$, and $c = 0$. Because $a < 0$ (the parabola opens downward), s has its maximum value at the vertex, where

$$t = -\frac{b}{2a} = -\frac{19.6}{2(-4.9)} = 2$$

and $s = 19.6(2) - 4.9(2)^2 = 19.6$. Thus the maximum height is 19.6 m, which occurs after 2 s. Figure 12.13 shows the graph of the given function. Only the part for which $t \geq 0$ and $s \geq 0$ is drawn because the elapsed time and height cannot be negative.

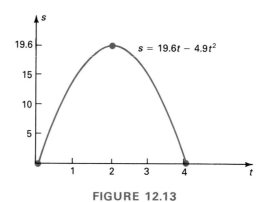

FIGURE 12.13

Example 6

A rectangle is to have a perimeter of 20 m. What should the length and width be so that the rectangle has the maximum area?

Solution   We first remark that both rectangles in Fig. 12.14 have a perimeter of 20 m, but in (a) the area is 16 m² and in (b) it is 24 m². We want to obtain the rectangle having the *largest* possible area. Let x be the length (in meters) of one side of the rectangle (see Fig. 12.15). Then the opposite side also has length x. This leaves $20 - 2x$ to be divided equally between the other

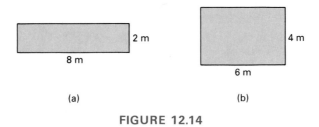

FIGURE 12.14

$$\begin{array}{c} x \\ 10 - x \boxed{} 10 - x \\ x \end{array}$$

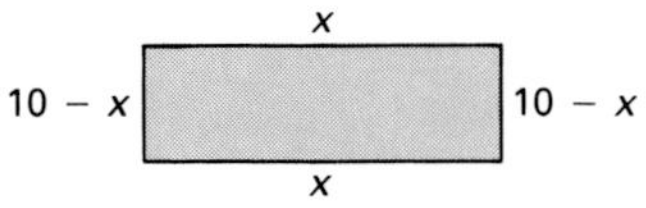

FIGURE 12.15

two sides. Thus each of these sides has length $(20 - 2x)/2$, which simplifies to $10 - x$. Let A be the area of the rectangle. Then

$$\text{Area} = (\text{length})(\text{width})$$
$$A = x(10 - x)$$
$$A = 10x - x^2.$$

Here A is a quadratic function of x, where $a = -1$ and $b = 10$. Because $a < 0$, A has a maximum value when

$$x = -\frac{b}{2a} = -\frac{10}{2(-1)} = 5.$$

Therefore, to get maximum area, the length should be 5 m and the width should be $10 - x = 10 - 5 = 5$ m. In this case the rectangle is a square whose area is 25 m².

Problem Set 12.4

*In Problems **1–8**, state whether or not the function is quadratic.*

1. $f(x) = 26 - 3x$.

2. $g(x) = (7 - x)^2$.

3. $g(x) = 4x^2$.

4. $h(s) = 6(4s + 1)$.

5. $h(q) = \dfrac{1}{2q - 4}$.

6. $f(t) = 2t(3 - t) + 4t$.

7. $f(s) = \dfrac{s^2 - 4}{2}$.

8. $g(t) = (t^2 - 1)^2$.

*In Problems **9–12**, do not include a graph.*

9. For the parabola $y = f(x) = -4x^2 + 8x + 7$, (a) find the vertex. (b) Does the vertex correspond to the highest point, or the lowest point, on the graph?
10. Repeat Problem 9 if $y = f(x) = 8x^2 + 4x - 1$.
11. For the parabola $y = f(x) = x^2 + 2x - 8$, find (a) the y-intercept, (b) the x-intercepts, and (c) the vertex.
12. Repeat Problem 11 if $y = f(x) = 3 + x - 2x^2$.

*In Problems **13–22**, graph each function. Give the vertex and intercepts.*

13. $y = f(x) = x^2 - 6x + 5$.
14. $y = f(x) = -3x^2$.
15. $y = g(x) = -2x^2 - 6x$.
16. $y = f(x) = x^2 - 1$.
17. $s = h(t) = t^2 + 2t + 1$.
18. $s = h(t) = 2t^2 + 3t - 2$.
19. $y = f(x) = -9 + 8x - 2x^2$.
20. $y = H(x) = 1 - x - x^2$.
21. $t = f(s) = s^2 - 8s + 13$.
22. $t = f(s) = s^2 + 6s + 11$.

*In Problems **23–26**, state whether $f(x)$ has a maximum value or a minimum value and find that value.*

23. $f(x) = 100x^2 - 20x + 25$.
24. $f(x) = -2x^2 - 16x + 3$.
25. $f(x) = 4x - 50 - 0.1x^2$.
26. $f(x) = x(x + 3) - 12$.

27. Express the area of the rectangle shown in Fig. 12.16 as a quadratic function of x. For what value of x will the area be a maximum?

$6 - x$

x

FIGURE 12.16

28. An object is thrown vertically upward from the ground with an initial velocity of 58.8 m/s. Its displacement s from its starting point after t seconds have elapsed is given by

$$s = -4.9t^2 + 58.8t,$$

where s is in meters. After how many seconds will the object reach its maximum height? What is the maximum height?
29. A building contractor wants to fence in a rectangular plot adjacent to a building by using the building as one side of the enclosed area. If the contractor has 200 m of fence, what should be the dimensions of the enclosed plot if the area is to be a maximum?
30. During a collision, the force F (in newtons) that acted on an object varied with time t according to the equation $F = 87t - 21t^2$, where t is in seconds.
(a) For what value of t was the force a maximum?
(b) What was the maximum value of the force?

31. The displacement s of an object from a reference point at time t is given by

$$s = 3.2t^2 - 16t + 28.7,$$

where s is in meters and t is in seconds.

(a) For what value of t does the minimum displacement occur?

(b) What is the minimum displacement of the object from the reference point?

32. An 8 μC charge is divided into two parts having charges of q and $(8 - q)$ μC, respectively. When placed 1 m apart, the Coulomb electrical force F between these charges is given by

$$F = 8kq - kq^2,$$

where k is a positive constant. For what value of q will F be a maximum?

33. When a horizontal beam of length l is uniformly loaded, the moment equation is

$$M = \frac{wlx}{2} - \frac{wx^2}{2},$$

where w is related to the load and x is measured from the left end of the beam.

(a) For what value of x is M a maximum (assume $w > 0$)?

(b) What is the maximum value of M?

(c) For what values of x does $M = 0$?

34. Find two numbers whose sum is 40 and whose product is a maximum.

35. A company has set aside \$3000 to fence a rectangular portion of land adjacent to a stream by using the stream for one side of the enclosed area. The cost of the fencing parallel to the stream is \$5 per foot installed, and the fencing for the remaining two sides is \$3 per foot installed. Find the dimensions of the maximum enclosed area. *Hint*: If the side opposite the stream has length x, first show that each of the other two sides has length $(3000 - 5x)/6$.

12.5 EQUATIONS LEADING TO QUADRATIC EQUATIONS

Some equations that are not quadratic can lead to quadratic equations by algebraic operations. We shall consider three such types: fractional equations, radical equations, and equations in *quadratic form*.

Fractional Equations

Recall that to solve a fractional equation, we first clear fractions by multiplying both sides by the L.C.D. of the fractions involved. This operation does not guarantee that the resulting equation is equivalent to the original equation, so it is important that any roots of the resulting equation be checked by substituting them into the *original* equation.

Example 1

Solve $\dfrac{x}{x+4} = \dfrac{2}{x}$.

Solution Multiplying both sides by the L.C.D., $x(x+4)$, and simplifying, we get

$$x(x+4)\cdot\frac{x}{x+4} = x(x+4)\cdot\frac{2}{x}$$

$$x^2 = 2(x+4)$$

$$x^2 = 2x + 8$$

$$x^2 - 2x - 8 = 0 \qquad \text{[quadratic equation]}$$

$$(x+2)(x-4) = 0 \qquad \text{[factoring]}.$$

$x + 2 = 0$	$x - 4 = 0$
$x = -2.$	$x = 4.$

The values $x = -2$ and $x = 4$ satisfy the original equation (verify this), so they are the solutions.

Example 2

Solve

$$\frac{y+1}{y+3} + \frac{y+5}{y-2} = \frac{7(2y+1)}{y^2+y-6}. \tag{1}$$

Solution Noting that $y^2 + y - 6 = (y+3)(y-2)$, we conclude that the L.C.D. is $(y+3)(y-2)$. Multiplying both sides by the L.C.D., we have

$$(y+3)(y-2)\left(\frac{y+1}{y+3} + \frac{y+5}{y-2}\right) = (y+3)(y-2)\cdot\frac{7(2y+1)}{(y+3)(y-2)}$$

$$\frac{\cancel{(y+3)}(y-2)(y+1)}{\cancel{y+3}} + \frac{(y+3)\cancel{(y-2)}(y+5)}{\cancel{y-2}} = \frac{\cancel{(y+3)}\cancel{(y-2)}\cdot7(2y+1)}{\cancel{(y+3)}\cancel{(y-2)}}$$

$$(y-2)(y+1) + (y+3)(y+5) = 7(2y+1)$$

$$y^2 - y - 2 + y^2 + 8y + 15 = 14y + 7$$

$$2y^2 + 7y + 13 = 14y + 7$$

$$2y^2 - 7y + 6 = 0 \qquad \text{[quadratic equation]}.$$

$$(2y-3)(y-2) = 0 \qquad \text{[factoring]}.$$

$2y - 3 = 0$	$y - 2 = 0$
$2y = 3$	$y = 2.$
$y = \dfrac{3}{2}.$	

Thus $\frac{3}{2}$ and 2 are *possible* solutions of the given equation. We find that 2 is *not* a solution of Eq. 1 because substitution leads to a denominator of zero. However, you should check that $\frac{3}{2}$ does indeed satisfy Eq. 1. Thus the only solution is $\frac{3}{2}$.

Example 3

The rate of the current in a stream is 3 km/h. A person rowed upstream for 3 km and then returned to the starting point. The round trip took a total of 1 h 20 min. At what rate could the person row in still water?

Solution Let r be the rate (in kilometers per hour) at which the person can row in still water. Because the rate of the current is 3 km/h, the person's rate upstream was $r - 3$, and downstream it was $r + 3$. Since time = distance/rate and distance = 3 for each rate, we have

$$\left(\begin{array}{c} \text{time} \\ \text{upstream} \end{array}\right) + \left(\begin{array}{c} \text{time} \\ \text{downstream} \end{array}\right) = \text{total time}$$

$$\frac{3}{r - 3} + \frac{3}{r + 3} = \frac{4}{3}. \qquad \left[1 \text{ h } 20 \text{ min} = \frac{4}{3} \text{h} \right]$$

Multiplying both sides by $3(r - 3)(r + 3)$ and simplifying, we obtain

$$3(3)(r + 3) + 3(3)(r - 3) = 4(r - 3)(r + 3)$$
$$9r + 27 + 9r - 27 = 4[r^2 - 9]$$
$$18r = 4r^2 - 36$$
$$0 = 4r^2 - 18r - 36$$
$$0 = 2r^2 - 9r - 18 \qquad \text{[dividing both sides by 2]}$$
$$0 = (2r + 3)(r - 6).$$

$$2r + 3 = 0 \qquad \bigg| \qquad r - 6 = 0$$
$$r = -\tfrac{3}{2}. \qquad \bigg| \qquad r = 6.$$

The values $-\frac{3}{2}$ and 6 satisfy the original equation. But r is a rate, a positive number, so the only acceptable answer is 6 km/h.

Radical Equations

Recall that when solving a radical equation, we raise both sides to the same power to eliminate the radical. Again, you must check that any solutions obtained satisfy the *original* equation.

Example 4

Solve $\sqrt{x + 2} - x + 4 = 0$.

Solution It is best to rewrite the equation so that the radical is by itself on one side.

$$\sqrt{x + 2} = x - 4$$
$$x + 2 = (x - 4)^2 \qquad \text{[squaring both sides]}$$
$$x + 2 = x^2 - 8x + 16$$
$$0 = x^2 - 9x + 14$$
$$0 = (x - 7)(x - 2) \qquad \text{[factoring]}$$
$$x = 7 \quad \text{or} \quad x = 2.$$

Now we check these values in the *original* equation.

Replacing x by 7 gives $\sqrt{7 + 2} - 7 + 4 = 0$, or $3 - 7 + 4 = 0$, which is *true*.

Replacing x by 2 gives $\sqrt{2 + 2} - 2 + 4 = 0$, or $2 - 2 + 4 = 0$, which is *false*.

Thus the only solution is 7.

Example 5

Solve $\sqrt{x + 6} - \sqrt{2x + 5} = -1$.

Solution It is best to rewrite the equation so that only one radical expression appears in the left side:

$$\sqrt{x + 6} = \sqrt{2x + 5} - 1.$$

Squaring both sides and simplifying, we have

$$x + 6 = 2x + 5 - 2\sqrt{2x + 5} + 1$$
$$2\sqrt{2x + 5} = x.$$

Squaring both sides again gives

$$4(2x + 5) = x^2$$
$$8x + 20 = x^2$$
$$x^2 - 8x - 20 = 0$$
$$(x - 10)(x + 2) = 0$$
$$x = 10 \quad \text{or} \quad x = -2.$$

Substitution shows that the original equation is satisfied only for $x = 10$. Thus the solution is 10.

Equations in Quadratic Form

Sometimes an equation that is not quadratic can be transformed into a quadratic equation by an appropriate substitution and then solved by the methods we have discussed. Such equations are said to be **quadratic in form** because they can be written as

$$a(\ )^2 + b(\ ) + c = 0,$$

where the missing expressions inside the parentheses are identical. For example, the equation

$$x^4 - x^2 - 6 = 0 \tag{1}$$

is quadratic in form because it can be written

$$(x^2)^2 - (x^2) - 6 = 0. \tag{2}$$

Equation 1 is of the fourth degree, whereas Eq. 2 is considered quadratic in the variable x^2. The following examples show how to solve these kinds of equations.

Example 6

Find all real solutions of $x^4 - x^2 - 6 = 0$.

Solution   From the preceding discussion, the equation may be rewritten as

$$(x^2)^2 - (x^2) - 6 = 0.$$

Now we make a substitution. If we replace x^2 by w, the resulting equation is quadratic in the variable w.

$$w^2 - w - 6 = 0$$
$$(w - 3)(w + 2) = 0.$$

$w - 3 = 0$	$w + 2 = 0$
$w = 3.$	$w = -2.$

Finally, we replace w by x^2 and solve for x.

$x^2 = 3$	$x^2 = -2$
$x = \pm\sqrt{3}.$	No real solution.

Thus the real solutions are

$$x = \pm\sqrt{3}.$$

An alternative method of solving the given equation is by factoring.

$$x^4 - x^2 - 6 = 0$$

$$(x^2 - 3)(x^2 + 2) = 0.$$

$x^2 - 3 = 0$	$x^2 + 2 = 0$
$x^2 = 3$	$x^2 = -2.$
$x = \pm\sqrt{3}.$	No real solution.

Example 7

Find all real solutions of $\dfrac{1}{x^6} + \dfrac{9}{x^3} + 8 = 0$.

Solution   The equation is quadratic in form because it can be written as

$$\left(\frac{1}{x^3}\right)^2 + 9\left(\frac{1}{x^3}\right) + 8 = 0.$$

By substituting the variable w for $1/x^3$, we obtain a quadratic equation in w.

$$w^2 + 9w + 8 = 0$$

$$(w + 8)(w + 1) = 0$$

$$w = -8 \quad \text{or} \quad w = -1.$$

Returning to the variable x, we have

$$\frac{1}{x^3} = -8 \quad \text{or} \quad \frac{1}{x^3} = -1.$$

Equivalently,

$$x^3 = -\tfrac{1}{8} \quad \text{or} \quad x^3 = -1,$$

from which

$$x = -\tfrac{1}{2}, -1.$$

Checking, we find that both values of x satisfy the original equation.

Problem Set 12.5

*In Problems **1–16**, solve the given fractional equation.*

1. $\dfrac{x}{3} = \dfrac{6}{x} - 1.$

2. $\dfrac{1}{2x} - \dfrac{2x - 3}{4x} = \dfrac{3x}{4}.$

3. $\dfrac{1}{x^2} + \dfrac{6}{x} + 8 = 0.$

4. $\dfrac{1}{x} - \dfrac{2}{3x} = 3x.$

5. $\dfrac{3}{x-4} + \dfrac{x-3}{x} = 2.$

6. $\dfrac{1}{x^2} + \dfrac{1}{x} - 12 = 0.$

7. $\dfrac{2}{x-2} = \dfrac{x+1}{x+4}.$

8. $\dfrac{x}{x-1} = \dfrac{4}{x}.$

9. $\dfrac{x^2}{x-1} + 1 = \dfrac{1}{x-1}.$

10. $\dfrac{4-x}{x} + \dfrac{8}{4+x} = 1.$

11. $\dfrac{2}{x-1} - \dfrac{6}{2x+1} = 5.$

12. $\dfrac{x+1}{x} - \dfrac{6}{x+5} = \dfrac{3}{x}.$

13. $\dfrac{3}{x} - \dfrac{4}{x+2} = \dfrac{5}{3}.$

14. $x + \dfrac{2x}{x-2} = \dfrac{4}{x-2}.$

15. $\dfrac{3}{x+1} + \dfrac{4}{x} = \dfrac{12}{x+2}.$

16. $\dfrac{2}{x^2-1} - \dfrac{1}{x(x-1)} = \dfrac{2}{x^2}.$

In Problems 17–28, solve the given radical equation.

17. $\sqrt{x+2} = x - 4.$

18. $3\sqrt{x+4} = x - 6.$

19. $z + 2 = 2\sqrt{4z-7}.$

20. $x + \sqrt{x-2} = 0.$

21. $\sqrt{x+7} - \sqrt{2x} = 1.$

22. $\sqrt{3x} - \sqrt{5x+1} = -1.$

23. $\sqrt[3]{x^2+2} = 3.$

24. $\sqrt{x} + \sqrt{2x+7} - 8 = 0.$

25. $\sqrt{x} - \sqrt{2x+1} + 1 = 0.$

26. $\sqrt{x-2} + 2 = \sqrt{2x+3}.$

27. $\sqrt{x+5} + 1 = 2\sqrt{x}.$

28. $\sqrt{\sqrt{x}+2} = \sqrt{2x-4}.$

In Problems 29–44, find all real solutions of the given quadratic-form equation.

29. $x^4 - 5x^2 + 6 = 0.$

30. $x^4 - 3x^2 - 10 = 0.$

31. $\dfrac{2}{x^2} + \dfrac{3}{x} - 2 = 0.$

32. $x^{-2} + x^{-1} - 12 = 0.$

33. $x^{-4} - 9x^{-2} + 14 = 0.$

34. $\dfrac{1}{x^4} - \dfrac{9}{x^2} + 8 = 0.$

35. $x - 2\sqrt{x} - 3 = 0.$

36. $6x - 5\sqrt{x} + 1 = 0.$

37. $(x-3)^2 + 9(x-3) + 14 = 0.$

38. $(x+5)^2 - 8(x+5) = 0.$

39. $\dfrac{1}{(x-2)^2} - \dfrac{12}{x-2} + 35 = 0.$

40. $\dfrac{2}{(x+4)^2} + \dfrac{7}{x+4} + 3 = 0.$

41. $(x^2+2)^2 - 12(x^2+2) + 11 = 0.$

42. $(x^2-5)^2 - 9(x^2-5) - 36 = 0.$

43. $y^{2/3} + y^{1/3} - 2 = 0.$

44. $2y^{-2/3} - 5y^{-1/3} - 3 = 0.$

45. In the ac circuit shown in Fig. 12.17, the impedance Z (in ohms) is given by

$$Z = \sqrt{R^2 + X^2},$$

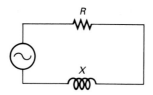

FIGURE 12.17

where R is the resistance (in ohms) and X is the reactance (in ohms). If $Z = 10$ and $R = 8$, find X if $X > 0$.

46. In a series ac circuit, resonance occurs when

$$2\pi f_r L = \frac{1}{2\pi f_r C},$$

where f_r is a resonant frequency, L is inductance, and C is capacitance. Solve for f_r if $f_r > 0$.

47. An object is 120 cm from a wall. In order to focus the image of the object on the wall, a converging lens with a focal length of 24 cm is used. The lens is placed between the object and the wall at a distance of p centimeters from the object, where

$$\frac{1}{p} + \frac{1}{120 - p} = \frac{1}{24}.$$

Find p to one decimal place.

48. If $\omega L = \dfrac{1}{\omega C}$ and $2\pi f_r = \omega$, show that

$$f_r = \frac{1}{2\pi\sqrt{LC}}.$$

Assume that all quantities are positive.

49. A boat traveled 36 km upstream on a river where the rate of the current was 3 km/h. It then returned. The round trip took 5 h. Find the speed of the boat in still water.

50. A land investment company purchased a parcel of land for $7200. After having sold all but 20 acres at a profit of $30 per acre, the entire cost of the parcel had been regained. How many acres were sold?

51. A small boat moving easterly out to sea with a speed of 10 m/s is 100 m from the nearest point A of a straight shoreline. A faster boat with a speed of 15 m/s starts from point B, which is 100 m south of A, to meet it. After how many seconds will the boats meet?

52. If a resistance R and reactance X are connected in parallel, the impedance Z of the circuit is given by

$$Z = \frac{RX}{\sqrt{R^2 + X^2}}.$$

Solve this equation for X.

53. The frequency of a damped vibration, ω_d (in radians per second), is given by

$$\omega_d = \sqrt{1 - d^2}\,\omega_n,$$

where ω_n is the natural frequency of the undamped vibration and d, a unitless constant, is called the *damping factor*. If $\omega_n = 25.4$ rad/s and $\omega_d = 24.1$ rad/s, find the damping factor, which is positive.

54. The mass m of an object moving with speed v (in meters per second) is given by

$$m = \frac{m_0}{\sqrt{1 - \dfrac{v^2}{c^2}}},$$

where m_0 is the rest mass of the object and $c = 3 \times 10^8$ m/s is the speed of light in vacuum. If $m = 1.5m_0$, find v. (Assume $v > 0$.)

55. There are several rules for determining doses of medicine for children when the adult dose has been specified. Such rules may be based on weight, height, and so on. If A = age of child, d = adult dose, and c = child's dose, here are two rules.

$$\text{Young's rule:} \quad c = \frac{A}{A + 12}\,d.$$

$$\text{Cowling's rule:} \quad c = \frac{A + 1}{24}\,d.$$

At what age are the children's doses the same under both rules? Round your answer to the nearest year.

12.6 NONLINEAR SYSTEMS

A system of equations in which at least one of the equations is not linear is called a **nonlinear system**. A nonlinear system may often be solved by substitution. Of course, the system might be solved graphically, but we can only approximate the solutions in that case.

In our first example, we handle a system in which one equation is linear and the other is quadratic.

Example 1

Solve the nonlinear system

$$\begin{cases} x^2 - 2x + y - 7 = 0 & (1) \\ 3x - y + 1 = 0. & (2) \end{cases}$$

Solution   We shall solve Eq. 2 for y and substitute into Eq. 1. From Eq. 2 we have

$$y = 3x + 1. \tag{3}$$

Substituting $3x + 1$ for y in Eq. 1 gives an equation in one unknown.

$$x^2 - 2x + (3x + 1) - 7 = 0$$
$$x^2 + x - 6 = 0$$
$$(x + 3)(x - 2) = 0$$
$$x = -3 \quad \text{or} \quad x = 2.$$

Setting $x = -3$ in Eq. 3 gives $y = -8$; if $x = 2$, then $y = 7$. You should check that each pair of values satisfies the given system. The solutions are

$$x = -3, \quad y = -8 \quad \text{and} \quad x = 2, \quad y = 7.$$

We can see these solutions geometrically in the graph of the system in Fig. 12.18. Notice that the graph of Eq. 1 is a parabola and the graph of Eq. 2 is a line. The solutions correspond to the intersection points $(-3, -8)$ and $(2, 7)$.

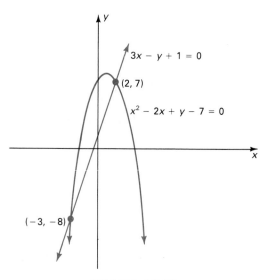

FIGURE 12.18

Example 2

Solve the nonlinear system

$$\begin{cases} x^2 + y^2 = 4 & (4) \\ 9x^2 + y^2 = 9. & (5) \end{cases}$$

Solution   Solving Eq. 4 for y^2 gives

$$y^2 = 4 - x^2. \tag{6}$$

Substituting for y^2 in Eq. 5, we have

$$9x^2 + 4 - x^2 = 9$$

$$8x^2 = 5$$

$$x^2 = \frac{5}{8}$$

$$x = \pm\sqrt{\frac{5}{8}} = \pm\frac{\sqrt{10}}{4}.$$

Substituting $x = \sqrt{10}/4$ in Eq. 6 gives $y = \pm\frac{3}{4}\sqrt{6}$. Substituting $x = -\sqrt{10}/4$ in Eq. 6 gives $y = \pm\frac{3}{4}\sqrt{6}$. The four solutions are

$$x = \frac{\sqrt{10}}{4}, \quad y = \frac{3\sqrt{6}}{4}, \qquad x = \frac{\sqrt{10}}{4}, \quad y = -\frac{3\sqrt{6}}{4},$$

$$x = -\frac{\sqrt{10}}{4}, \quad y = \frac{3\sqrt{6}}{4}, \qquad x = -\frac{\sqrt{10}}{4}, \quad y = -\frac{3\sqrt{6}}{4}.$$

The graph of the given system is shown in Fig. 12.19. The four points of intersection correspond to the four solutions.

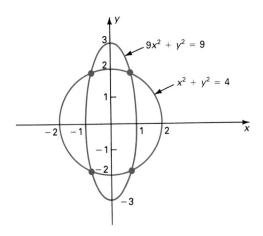

FIGURE 12.19

Example 3

Solve the system

$$\begin{cases} y = \sqrt{x + 2} \\ x + y = 4. \end{cases}$$

Solution Solving the second equation for y gives

$$y = 4 - x. \tag{7}$$

Substituting into the first equation gives

$$4 - x = \sqrt{x + 2}$$
$$16 - 8x + x^2 = x + 2 \quad \text{[squaring both sides]}$$
$$x^2 - 9x + 14 = 0$$
$$(x - 2)(x - 7) = 0$$
$$x = 2 \quad \text{or} \quad x = 7.$$

Thus $x = 2$ or $x = 7$. From Eq. 7, if $x = 2$, then $y = 2$; if $x = 7$, then $y = -3$. Although the pair $x = 2$ and $y = 2$ satisfies the given system, the pair $x = 7$ and $y = -3$ does not. Thus the solution is $x = 2$, $y = 2$.

Example 4

Find all real solutions of

$$\begin{cases} 2x^2 + xy - y^2 = 20 & \tag{8} \\ xy = 6. & \tag{9} \end{cases}$$

Solution From Eq. 9, if $x \neq 0$, then $y = 6/x$. Substituting in Eq. 8, we have

$$2x^2 + x\left(\frac{6}{x}\right) - \left(\frac{6}{x}\right)^2 = 20$$
$$2x^2 + 6 - \frac{36}{x^2} = 20$$
$$2x^4 + 6x^2 - 36 = 20x^2 \quad \text{[multiplying both sides by } x^2\text{]}$$
$$2x^4 - 14x^2 - 36 = 0$$
$$x^4 - 7x^2 - 18 = 0 \quad \text{[dividing both sides by 2]}$$
$$(x^2 - 9)(x^2 + 2) = 0$$
$$(x + 3)(x - 3)(x^2 + 2) = 0.$$

Setting the first two factors equal to zero gives $x = \pm 3$. Substituting these values of x into the equation $y = 6/x$ gives the solutions $x = 3$, $y = 2$ and $x = -3$, $y = -2$, which check in the given system. The factor $x^2 + 2$ does not give rise to real solutions.

Problem Set 12.6

In Problems **1–20**, *solve the nonlinear systems.*

1. $\begin{cases} y = x + 1 \\ x^2 + y^2 = 1. \end{cases}$

2. $\begin{cases} y = 4 - x^2 \\ 3x + y = 0. \end{cases}$

3. $\begin{cases} p^2 = 4 - q \\ p = q + 2. \end{cases}$

4. $\begin{cases} y = x^2 \\ x + y - 6 = 0. \end{cases}$

5. $\begin{cases} y^2 - x^2 = 28 \\ x - y = 14. \end{cases}$

6. $\begin{cases} y^2 - x = 0 \\ 3x - 2y - 1 = 0. \end{cases}$

7. $\begin{cases} y = 4x - x^2 + 8 \\ y = x^2 - 2x. \end{cases}$

8. $\begin{cases} q^2 + p^2 - 2pq = 1 \\ 3q - p = 5. \end{cases}$

9. $\begin{cases} x^2 - y = 8 \\ y - x^2 = 0. \end{cases}$

10. $\begin{cases} y = x^3 \\ x - y = 0. \end{cases}$

11. $\begin{cases} 2x^2 - 3y^2 = 6 \\ 3x^2 - 2y^2 = 19. \end{cases}$

12. $\begin{cases} 2x^2 - 5y^2 = 10 \\ 3x^2 + 15y^2 = 195. \end{cases}$

13. $\begin{cases} y = \sqrt{x + 14} \\ x - y = -2. \end{cases}$

14. $\begin{cases} y^4 - x^2 = 2x + 4 \\ y = \sqrt{x + 1}. \end{cases}$

15. $\begin{cases} p = \sqrt{q} \\ p = q^2. \end{cases}$

16. $\begin{cases} x = y^2 \\ y = x^2. \end{cases}$

17. $\begin{cases} w^2 = z^2 + 14 \\ z = w^2 - 16. \end{cases}$

18. $\begin{cases} z = w + 6 \\ w = 3\sqrt{z + 4}. \end{cases}$

19. $\begin{cases} y = \dfrac{x^2}{x - 1} + 1 \\ y = \dfrac{1}{x - 1}. \end{cases}$

20. $\begin{cases} y = \dfrac{4}{x} \\ 3y = 2x + 2. \end{cases}$

21. In making stress tests, a technician uses four square sheets of glass. Exactly three of the sheets are identical in size. The sum of the areas of the four sheets is 156 m², and the sum of their perimeters is 96 m. Find the possible sizes of the sheets.

22. When wet, a rectangular cloth shrank one-eighth in length and one-sixteenth in width. The original area of the cloth was reduced by 5.75 m², and the total length of the four sides was reduced by 4.25 m. Find the original length and width of the cloth.

23. A body A of mass 5 kg moving with a speed of 3 m/s underwent a completely elastic collision with a body B of mass 2 kg initially at rest. The principles of conservation of linear momentum and kinetic energy yield the system of equations

$$\begin{cases} 5(3) = 5V_A + 2V_B \\ \tfrac{1}{2}(5)(3^2) = \tfrac{1}{2}(5)V_A^2 + \tfrac{1}{2}(2)(V_B^2), \end{cases}$$

where V_A and V_B are the speeds of bodies A and B after the collision. Find V_A and V_B.

24. Two bodies A and B are moving at constant rates and in the same direction around a circle 36 m in circumference. A makes one revolution in 3 s less time than it takes B, and A and B meet every 18 s. What are their rates?

25. The equivalent capacitance C of two capacitors C_1 and C_2 connected in parallel is given by

$$C = C_1 + C_2.$$

If the capacitors are connected in series, the equivalent capacitance is given by

$$C = \frac{C_1 C_2}{C_1 + C_2}.$$

When two capacitors are connected in parallel, the equivalent capacitance is 9 μF; when connected in series the equivalent capacitance is 2 μF. Find the values of C_1 and C_2.

26. When two capacitors C_1 and C_2 are connected in parallel, the equivalent capacitance is 3.90 μF. When the same capacitors are connected in series, the equivalent capacitance is 0.867 μF. Find C_1 and C_2. (See Problem 25.)

27. A uniform beam is L meters long and weighs W newtons. When a pivot is placed 2.5 m from the left end, the beam can be balanced by a 30-N force applied at its left end [see Fig. 12.20(a)]. When the 30-N force is applied to the right end of the beam, the beam can again be balanced at the same pivot when a force of 96 N is applied to the left end [see Fig. 12.20(b)]. Find L and W. *Hint*: It may help to review Example 7 in Sec. 4.5.

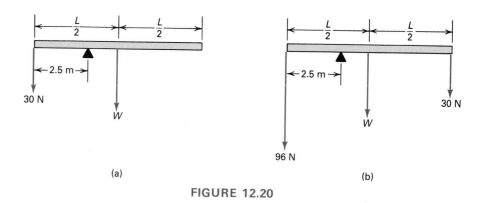

(a)   (b)

FIGURE 12.20

12.7 REVIEW

Important Terms

Section 12.1   Second-degree equation, quadratic equation, repeated root, double root, square-root method.

Section 12.2   Pure quadratic equation, completing the square.

Section 12.3   Quadratic formula, discriminant.

Section 12.4 Quadratic function, parabola, axis of symmetry, vertex, x-intercepts.

Section 12.5 Quadratic in form.

Section 12.6 Nonlinear system.

Formula Summary

QUADRATIC EQUATIONS

Quadratic equation: $ax^2 + bx + c = 0$
$(a \neq 0)$.

Square-root method: If $u^2 = k$, then $u = \pm\sqrt{k}$.

Quadratic formula: $x = \dfrac{-b \pm \sqrt{b^2 - 4ac}}{2a}$.

Discriminant: $b^2 - 4ac$.

PARABOLAS

Quadratic function: $y = f(x) = ax^2 + bx + c$.
$a > 0$, opens upward.
$a < 0$, opens downward.

Vertex $\left(-\dfrac{b}{2a}, \dfrac{4ac - b^2}{4a}\right)$.

y-intercept c.

Axis of symmetry $x = -\dfrac{b}{2a}$.

Review Questions

1. A quadratic equation is of the __(a)__ degree and can be written in the form __(b)__.

2. True or false: Every quadratic equation has two different roots. _____

3. The discriminant of $ax^2 + bx + c = 0$ is $(b^2 - 4ac)(\sqrt{b^2 - 4ac})$.

4. If the discriminant of a quadratic equation is __(positive)(negative)(zero)__, then there are no real solutions.

5. If the discriminant of $ax^2 + bx + c = 0$ is __(positive)(zero)__, then the equation has only one real solution.

6. The roots of $x^2(x - 2)(2x + 1)$ are equal to _____.

7. The roots of $x^2 - 4 = 0$ are equal to _____.

8. In the equation $(x - 5)(x - 5) = 0$, the root 5 is called a _____ root.

9. If the graph of $f(x) = ax^2 + bx + c = 0$ intersects the x-axis at exactly one point, then the equation $f(x) = 0$ has a _____ root.

10. The roots of $x^2 + 100x = 0$ are equal to _____.

11. The equation $x^{2/3} + 3x^{1/3} - 6 = 0$ is quadratic in form. We can transform the equation into a quadratic equation in w if we substitute w for _____.

12. To complete the square in the equation $x^2 - 7x = 0$, you would add the number _____ to both sides.

13. The discriminant of $2x^2 - 4x + 3 = 0$ is equal to _____.

14. The nonlinear system

$$\begin{cases} x^2 - 2xy - y^2 = 6 \\ 2x - y = 3 \end{cases}$$

can be solved easily for x by solving the $\dfrac{\text{(first)(second)}}{\text{(a)}}$ equation for y and substituting this value in the $\dfrac{\text{(first)(second)}}{\text{(b)}}$ equation.

15. The graph of $f(x) = 7x^2 + 3x - 5$ is called a _____.

16. The parabola $g(x) = x^2 - 1$ opens $\underline{\text{(upward)(downward)}}$.

17. The vertex of the parabola $f(x) = x^2 - 6x + 1$ occurs when $x = $ _____.

18. The graph of $y = -2x^2 + 4x - 3$ has a $\dfrac{\text{(high)(low)}}{\text{(a)}}$ point when $x = $ __(b)__.

Answers to Review Questions

1. (a) Second, (b) $ax^2 + bx + c = 0$, $a \neq 0$.   2. False.   3. $b^2 - 4ac$.   4. Negative.
5. Zero.   6. $0, 2, -\frac{1}{2}$.   7. ± 2.   8. Double, or repeated.   9. Double.
10. $0, -100$.   11. $x^{1/3}$.   12. $\frac{49}{4}$.   13. -8.   14. (a) Second, (b) First.
15. Parabola.   16. Upward.   17. 3.   18. (a) High, (b) 1.

Review Problems

In Problems 1-10, solve by factoring.

1. $x^2 - 10x + 25 = 0$.   2. $x^2 - 2x - 8 = 0$.   3. $x^2 - 2x - 24 = 0$.

4. $x^2 + 6x + 9 = 0$.   5. $12x^2 - 20x + 3 = 0$.   6. $4x^2 - 5x - 6 = 0$.

7. $x^2 - 12 = 0$.   8. $x^2 - 28 = 0$.   9. $2x^3 - x^2 = 0$.

10. $x^4 - 9x^2 = 0$.

In Problems 11-14, solve by completing the square.

11. $x^2 - 10x + 1 = 0$.   12. $x^2 + 8x - 5 = 0$.

13. $4x^2 + 12x - 2 = 0$.   14. $2x^2 - 2x - 3 = 0$.

In Problems **15–20**, *solve by the quadratic formula.*

15. $x^2 - 6x + 7 = 0.$

16. $x^2 + 3x - 5 = 0.$

17. $4x^2 + 4x + 1 = 0.$

18. $3x^2 - 2x - 6 = 0.$

19. $2x + 5 - 2x^2 = 0.$

20. $25 - 20x + 4x^2 = 0.$

In Problems **21–44**, *solve.*

21. $16x^2 - 9 = 0.$

22. $25x^2 - 3 = 1.$

23. $y^2 + 2y - 24 = 0.$

24. $y^2 + 4y - 21 = 0.$

25. $(z + 4)^2 = 36.$

26. $4z(z + 2) = -8 - 4z.$

27. $3(t + 1) = 2t^2.$

28. $100t^2 = 100t.$

29. $(x + 1)(x + 2) = 4.$

30. $x^2 + 5 = 8 - x.$

31. $4x^2 + 10x = -\dfrac{25}{4}.$

32. $\dfrac{3}{4}(x^2 - 2) = x.$

33. $\dfrac{x}{x - 1} - \dfrac{9}{x + 3} = 0.$

34. $\dfrac{1}{x^2} - \dfrac{9}{x} + 8 = 0.$

35. $\dfrac{x + 1}{x} + \dfrac{2x}{x - 2} = \dfrac{5x + 1}{x}.$

36. $\dfrac{6x + 7}{2x + 1} - \dfrac{6x + 1}{2x} = 1.$

37. $\dfrac{x}{x - 1} - \dfrac{2}{x} + \dfrac{x - 2}{x^2 - x} = 0.$

38. $\sqrt{z^2 + 9} = 5.$

39. $\sqrt{2x + 1} = x - 7.$

40. $\sqrt{x} - \sqrt{x + 1} = 6.$

41. $x^{2/3} - x^{1/3} - 12 = 0.$

42. $2x^4 - 11x^2 + 12 = 0.$

43. $x^{-2} + 10x^{-1} + 25 = 0.$

44. $x + 1 + 2\sqrt{x} = 0.$

In Problems **45–48**, *solve each nonlinear system.*

45. $\begin{cases} x^2 - y + 2x = 7 \\ x^2 + y = 5. \end{cases}$

46. $\begin{cases} x^2 + y^2 = 5 \\ x + y - 3 = 0. \end{cases}$

47. $\begin{cases} y - 3 = \sqrt{x + 2} \\ x + y = 3. \end{cases}$

48. $\begin{cases} y = \dfrac{18}{x + 4} \\ x - y + 7 = 0. \end{cases}$

In Problems **49–52**, *graph each quadratic function. Give all intercepts and the vertex.*

49. $y = f(x) = 9 - x^2.$

50. $s = g(t) = 8 - 2t - t^2.$

51. $y = h(t) = t^2 - 4t - 5.$

52. $y = (2x - 1)^2.$

53. Find the maximum value of y if $y = -3x^2 + 6x - 4.$

54. Find the minimum value of y if $y = 4x^2 + 16x - 6.$

55. In studies of electrical networks, the following equation occurs:

$$S^2 + \frac{R}{L}S + \frac{1}{LC} = 0.$$

Show that

$$S = -\frac{R}{2L} \pm \sqrt{\left(\frac{R}{2L}\right)^2 - \frac{1}{LC}}.$$

56. The kinetic energy K of a particle is given by $K = \frac{1}{2}mv^2$, where m is the mass and v $(v > 0)$ is the speed of the particle. The momentum p of the same particle is given by $p = mv$. Show that $p = \sqrt{2mK}$.

57. Suppose the height h of an object thrown straight upward from the ground is given by

$$h = 44.1t - 4.9t^2,$$

where h is in meters and t is elapsed time in seconds.
(a) After how many seconds does the object strike the ground?
(b) When is the object at a height of 88.2 m?
(c) After how many seconds is the object at its maximum height?
(d) What is the maximum height of the object?

58. In the kinetic theory of gases, it is shown that at a given temperature the kinetic energy of different gas molecules is the same. (See Problem 56.) Given that

$$\tfrac{1}{2}m_1v_1^2 = \tfrac{1}{2}m_2v_2^2,$$

show that if $v_2/v_1 > 0$, then

$$\frac{v_2}{v_1} = \sqrt{\frac{m_1}{m_2}}.$$

59. An open box is to be made from a square piece of tin by cutting out a 6-cm square from each corner and turning up the sides. The box will contain $150\,\text{cm}^3$. Find the *area* of the original square.

60. A square plot, 12 m by 12 m, is to be used for a garden. It is decided to put a pavement of uniform width inside the plot bordering three of the sides so that $80\,\text{m}^2$ of the plot is left for flowers. How wide should the pavement be?

13

Complex Numbers

Every applied problem encountered thus far in our study of technical mathematics has had a solution in the real number system. There are, however, many problems in applied mathematics that have *no* solutions in that system. To solve such problems, we shall expand our number system and create a new one. Our new system, called the *system of complex numbers*, includes the real numbers and provides solutions to previously unsolvable problems.

Moreover, with some problems in science and engineering, a solution in the real number system exists, but the characteristics of that system make it tedious to obtain the solution. In such problems—for example, the analysis of ac circuits in electrical engineering—the complex number system allows a much simpler and compact solution. In the following section you will see that the need for complex numbers arises quite naturally from consideration of solving certain equations.

13.1 THE *j*-OPERATOR AND COMPLEX NUMBERS

In the previous chapter we saw that a quadratic equation may have no solution in the real number system. For example, consider the equation $x^2 = -1$. Since the square of any real number is nonnegative, there is no real number x whose square is -1. That is, the symbol $\sqrt{-1}$ does not make sense in the real number system. Thus $x^2 = -1$ has no real solution. Similarly, there are no real solutions of the equations $x^2 = -2$ and, more generally, $x^2 = -a$, where $-a$ is negative (note that if $-a$ is negative, then a is positive). To overcome this situation, we shall extend the real number system so that the new system will indeed provide solutions to equations like $x^2 = -1$. In fact, by considering only $\sqrt{-1}$, we shall be able to handle a square root of *any* negative number.

To begin, we introduce (or invent, so to speak) a new type of number that, by its definition, is a solution of the equation $x^2 = -1$.

The *j*-**operator**, denoted by j, is that number which when squared is equal to -1; that is,

$$j^2 = -1.$$

From this definition, j is a square root of -1, so we write

$$j = \sqrt{-1}.$$

Since j is not a real number, we call it (according to custom) the **imaginary unit**. Do not let the term *imaginary* fool you. It does not mean that j is "impossible" or "does not exist" but means only that j does not belong to the set of real numbers. Indeed, the practical applications of j to topics such as electrical theory are extensive.*

By taking the product of j and a real number, for instance, $2j$, $-5j$, and $6.4j$, we obtain what is referred to as a *pure imaginary number*.

A **pure imaginary number** is a number that can be expressed in the form bj, where b is a real number.†

In performing operations with j, we follow the usual algebraic rules for real numbers. To illustrate, we consider powers of j:

$$j^1 = j,$$
$$j^2 = -1 \qquad \text{by definition,}$$
$$j^3 = j^2 \cdot j = (-1) \cdot j = -j,$$
$$j^4 = j^2 \cdot j^2 = (-1)(-1) = 1,$$
$$j^5 = j^4 \cdot j = 1 \cdot j = j,$$
$$j^6 = j^4 \cdot j^2 = 1 \cdot (-1) = -1, \qquad \text{and so on.}$$

The preceding cyclic pattern continues, so any positive integral power of j must be one of four possible numbers: j, -1, $-j$, or 1. The pattern also suggests an easy way to simplify j^n, where n is a positive integer. First, we divide n by 4 and find the remainder r, which is either 1, 2, 3, or 0. Then we raise j to the rth power; that is, $j^n = j^r$.

---

* In mathematics, the symbol i is preferred instead of j. However, in electrical theory the use of j avoids confusion with the use of i for electrical current. We adopt that symbol here.

† In electrical theory, bj is usually written jb. For example, $2j$ is written $j2$, which should not be confused with j^2.

Example 1

Simplify the following powers of j.

a. j^{35}.

Solution Since $35 \div 4$ is 8 with a remainder of 3,

$$j^{35} = j^3 = -j.$$

In other words,

$$j^{35} = (j^4)^8 \cdot j^3 = (1)^8 \cdot j^3 = j^3 = -j.$$

b. j^{26}.

Solution Since $26 \div 4$ is 6 with a remainder of 2,

$$j^{26} = j^2 = -1.$$

c. j^{40}.

Solution Since 40 is a multiple of 4, dividing 40 by 4 results in a remainder of 0. Thus

$$j^{40} = j^0 = 1.$$

Our claim that $j^0 = 1$ is reasonable because

$$j^{40} = (j^4)^{10} = (1)^{10} = 1.$$

To generalize the notion of $\sqrt{-1}$, we express a square root of *any* negative number as the product of a real number and j in the following manner:

> If a is a positive number, then
>
> $$\sqrt{-a} = j\sqrt{a}.$$

Thus

$$\sqrt{-4} = j\sqrt{4} = j(2) = 2j.$$

Example 2

Write the following numbers in terms of j.

a. $\sqrt{-2} = j\sqrt{2}.$

b. $-\sqrt{-9} = -(j\sqrt{9}) = -[j(3)] = -3j.$

c. $\sqrt{-32} = j\sqrt{32} = j(4\sqrt{2}) = 4j\sqrt{2}.$

d. $\sqrt{-\dfrac{1}{16}} = j\sqrt{\dfrac{1}{16}} = \dfrac{1}{4}j = \dfrac{j}{4}.$

By combining the real number system with the concept of a pure imaginary number, we are led to the notion of a *complex number*, which is the sum of a real number and a pure imaginary number.

A **complex number** is one of the form $a + bj$, where a and b are real numbers. The number a is called the **real part** of $a + bj$, and b is called the **imaginary part**.

Some examples of complex numbers are $2 + 3j$, $-4 + j$, and $-3 - 5j$, which is $-3 + (-5)j$. The real part of $-3 - 5j$ is -3 and the imaginary part is -5. If $a = 0$, then $a + bj$ is bj, a *pure imaginary number*. If $b = 0$, then $a + bj$ is a, a *real number*. Thus *every real number is also a complex number with imaginary part zero*. For example, the real number 3 is the complex number $3 + 0j$. Complex numbers that are not real are called **imaginary numbers**. Thus the complex number 7 is real, but the complex number $7 + 2j$ is imaginary.

The complex number $a - bj$ is called the **complex conjugate** (or simply the **conjugate**) of the complex number $a + bj$, and vice versa. For example, the conjugate of $2 + 3j$ is $2 - 3j$, the conjugate of $-3 - 4j$ is $-3 + 4j$, and the conjugate of 6 is 6 because the conjugate of $6 + 0j$ is $6 - 0j$, or 6.

Example 3

	Complex Number	Real Part	Imaginary Part	Conjugate
a.	$3 + 4j$	3	4	$3 - 4j$
b.	$-3 - j$	-3	-1	$-3 + j$
c.	-7	-7	0	-7
d.	$-j$	0	-1	j
e.	$\sqrt{-4}$	0	2	$-2j$
f.	$\sqrt[3]{-1}$	-1	0	-1
g.	0	0	0	0

Observe in Part f that $\sqrt[3]{-1}$ is a real number; $(-1)^3 = -1$, so $\sqrt[3]{-1} = -1$. Note in Parts c, f, and g that a real number is equal to its conjugate. Finally, in Part g we note that *zero is the only complex number that is both real and pure imaginary.*

Now that we have defined a complex number, we must be precise regarding when two complex numbers are equal.

EQUALITY OF COMPLEX NUMBERS

$a + bj = c + dj$ if and only if $a = c$ and $b = d$.

This means that **two complex numbers are equal if and only if they have the same real parts and the same imaginary parts.** Thus $2 - 3j = -3j + 2$ and $0.2 + j = j + \frac{1}{5}$, but $4 + 2j \neq 2 + 4j$ and $3 - j \neq j - 3$.

Example 4

Solve each of the following equations if x and y are real numbers.

a. $2 - 5j = x + yj$.

    Solution   By the definition of equality of complex numbers, we can equate the real parts of both sides of the equation:

$$2 = x.$$

    Equating imaginary parts gives

$$-5 = y.$$

    The solution is $x = 2$ and $y = -5$.

b. $x - y + xj = 3 + 2j$.

    Solution   Equating real parts of both sides of the equation gives

$$x - y = 3. \tag{1}$$

    Equating imaginary parts gives

$$x = 2.$$

    Substituting this value of x in Eq. 1 gives $2 - y = 3$, from which $y = -1$. The solution is $x = 2$ and $y = -1$.

Example 5

Solve $x^2 + x + 1 = 0$ by the quadratic formula.

Solution   Here $a = 1$, $b = 1$, and $c = 1$.

$$x = \frac{-1 \pm \sqrt{1^2 - 4(1)(1)}}{2(1)} = \frac{-1 \pm \sqrt{1-4}}{2}$$

$$= \frac{-1 \pm \sqrt{-3}}{2} = \frac{-1 \pm j\sqrt{3}}{2}.$$

Thus

$$x = -\frac{1}{2} + \frac{\sqrt{3}}{2}j, \quad -\frac{1}{2} - \frac{\sqrt{3}}{2}j.$$

Note that the solutions are a pair of conjugates. Whenever the discriminant of a quadratic equation is negative (here it is -3), there are two different imaginary solutions (conjugates).

We conclude this section by again remarking that complex numbers have wide applications in electrical theory. For example, the impedance of an ac circuit can be expressed in the form $a + bj$, where the real part represents the resistance of the circuit and the imaginary part represents the reactance of the circuit. Later in this chapter you will see how complex numbers are used in situations of this type.

Problem Set 13.1

In Problems 1–8, simplify the expressions.

1. j^9.

2. j^{14}.

3. j^{15}.

4. j^{488}.

5. $-j^{66}$.

6. j^{243}.

7. j^{324}.

8. $j^2 \cdot j^3 \cdot j^4$.

In Problems 9–20, write each number in terms of j.

9. $\sqrt{-81}$.

10. $\sqrt{-36}$.

11. $-\sqrt{-25}$.

12. $\sqrt{-27}$.

13. $\sqrt{-32}$.

14. $\sqrt{-144}$.

15. $\sqrt{-\frac{1}{4}}$.

16. $-\sqrt{-\frac{1}{100}}$.

17. $\sqrt{-0.09}$.

18. $\sqrt{-0.04}$.

19. $\sqrt{-\pi^6}$.

20. $\sqrt{-4^{10}}$.

In Problems 21–36, for each complex number state (a) the real part, (b) the imaginary part, and (c) the conjugate. Simplify first, if necessary.

21. $-6 + 5j$.

22. -2.

23. $-31j - 2$.

24. $-3 + 5j$.

25. $-3j$.

26. $2 - \sqrt{-9}$.

27. $7 + \frac{3}{5}j$.

28. πj.

29. j^{17}.

30. j^2.

31. 7.

32. $-\sqrt[3]{-64}$.

33. $\sqrt[3]{-8}$.   34. $6 + \sqrt{-3}$.   35. $-\sqrt{-49}$.

36. 0.

In Problems **37–40**, *solve the equations if x and y are real numbers.*

37. $2x + yj = 4 - 6j$.   38. $x - 2j = 17 + yj$.

39. $(x + y) + (x - y)j = 18 - 14j$.   40. $x + (x - y)j = 4j$.

41. Two ac voltages are given by the expressions $\frac{3}{2} + (y + 1)j$ and $(7 + x) - 3j$, respectively. If the voltages are equal, what are the values of x and y? (Assume that x and y are real numbers.)

42. What can be said about a complex number that is equal to its conjugate?

43. Determine whether the following statements are true or false.

    (a) $\frac{1}{2} + 2j = 2j + 0.5$.

    (b) $3 - \sqrt{-5} = 3 - j\sqrt{5}$.

    (c) $\sqrt[3]{-27} = 3j$.

    (d) $5 - 6j = (7 - 2) + (4 - 10)j$.

44. Suppose $a + bj = 0$. To what must $a^2 + b^2$ be equal?

In Problems **45–60**, *solve the equation.*

45. $x^2 - 4x + 5 = 0$.   46. $x^2 - 2x + 2 = 0$.   47. $x^2 + 2x + 3 = 0$.

48. $2x^2 - 4x + 5 = 0$.   49. $x^2 - 2x + 4 = 0$.   50. $3t^2 - 3t + 1 = 0$.

51. $x^2 + 4 = 0$.   52. $x^2 + 8 = 0$.   53. $6r^2 + 8r + 3 = 0$.

54. $x^2 = x - 1$.   55. $-3r^2 + 5r = 4$.   56. $x(x + 5) = 5(x - 5)$.

57. $1 + x^2 = 0$.   58. $(x + 1)^2 = -4$.   59. $x(4x - 3) = x^2 - 2$.

60. $\dfrac{x^2}{5} + 2 = x$.

61. A Maxwell bridge is an ac bridge circuit that permits the inductance L_x and resistance R_x of a coil to be measured. A theoretical analysis of the circuit yields the equation

$$R_x + j\omega L_x = R_2 R_3 \left(\frac{1}{R_1} + j\omega C_1 \right).$$

Determine the resistance and inductance of a coil in terms of the circuit constants R_1, R_2, R_3, C_1, and ω.

13.2 OPERATIONS WITH COMPLEX NUMBERS

Algebraic operations with complex numbers are defined in such a way that the usual rules for real numbers apply, such as the commutative, associative, and distributive laws. We begin with addition and subtraction.

ADDITION AND SUBTRACTION OF COMPLEX NUMBERS

$$(a + bj) + (c + dj) = (a + c) + (b + d)j.$$

$$(a + bj) - (c + dj) = (a - c) + (b - d)j.$$

That is, the sum (or difference) of two complex numbers is a complex number whose real part is the sum (or difference) of the real parts of the given numbers and whose imaginary part is the sum (or difference) of their imaginary parts.

Example 1

a. $(2 + 3j) + (4 + j) = (2 + 4) + (3 + 1)j = 6 + 4j.$

b. $(5 + 2j) - (3 + 6j) = (5 - 3) + (2 - 6)j = 2 - 4j.$

Rather than memorize the preceding definitions, you can add or subtract complex numbers in a more direct and efficient way. Simply apply the usual rules for removing parentheses and combining like terms. Consider j as you would any other literal number.

> **Add or subtract complex numbers as you would ordinary algebraic expressions. Treat j like any other literal number.**

Example 2

Perform the indicated operations.

a. $(-1 - 2j) + (1 - 6j) = -1 - 2j + 1 - 6j = -8j.$

b. $(3 - 4j) - (-4j) = 3 - 4j + 4j = 3.$

c. $2 + (8 - 3j) = 2 + 8 - 3j = 10 - 3j.$

d. $5 - 2j - (-6 + j) = 5 - 2j + 6 - j = 11 - 3j.$

e. $\sqrt{8} + \sqrt{-\frac{3}{2}} - \sqrt{-24} = \sqrt{8} + j\sqrt{\frac{3}{2}} - j\sqrt{24}$

$$= 2\sqrt{2} + \frac{1}{2}j\sqrt{6} - 2j\sqrt{6}$$

$$= 2\sqrt{2} - \frac{3}{2}j\sqrt{6}.$$

Note that the complex numbers $\sqrt{-\frac{3}{2}}$ and $\sqrt{-24}$ were *first* placed in $a + bj$ form before we proceeded to other operations.

Before discussing multiplication, we give you a **note of caution!** Recall that when radicals were studied, we used the rule $\sqrt{a}\sqrt{b} = \sqrt{ab}$. However, this rule is true provided a and b are nonnegative *real* numbers. The rule does *not* apply when both a and b are negative. Using this rule in the latter case leads to incorrect results. For example, applying it to $\sqrt{-1}\sqrt{-1}$ gives

$$\sqrt{-1}\sqrt{-1} = \sqrt{(-1)(-1)} = \sqrt{1} = 1,$$

which is false because

$$\sqrt{-1}\sqrt{-1} = j \cdot j = j^2 = -1.$$

Thus, to help avoid errors in computations, *always express square roots of negative numbers in the bj form **before** performing any algebraic operations with them.*

The complex numbers $a + bj$ and $c + dj$ are multiplied the same way binomials are. We make use of the distributive law and the fact that $j^2 = -1$.

$$(a + bj)(c + dj) = a(c + dj) + bj(c + dj)$$

$$= ac + adj + bcj + bdj^2$$

$$= ac + (ad + bc)j + bd(-1),$$

$$(a + bj)(c + dj) = (ac - bd) + (ad + bc)j.$$

MULTIPLICATION OF COMPLEX NUMBERS

$$(a + bj)(c + dj) = (ac - bd) + (ad + bc)j.$$

More simply:

Multiply complex numbers as you would algebraic expressions. However, all complex numbers should be expressed in the form $a + bj$ before multiplying them, and whenever j^2 occurs, it should be replaced by -1.

Example 3

Perform the indicated operations.

a. $(3 + 2j)(2 - 5j) = 3(2 - 5j) + 2j(2 - 5j)$

$$= 6 - 15j + 4j - 10j^2$$

$$= 6 - 11j - 10(-1)$$

$$= 16 - 11j.$$

b. $j(-2 + 3j) = -2j + 3j^2 = -2j + 3(-1) = -3 - 2j.$

c. $(8j)(4j) = 32j^2 = 32(-1) = -32.$

d. $(-3 - 4j)(2 - j) = -3(2 - j) - 4j(2 - j)$

$$= -6 + 3j - 8j + 4j^2$$
$$= -6 - 5j + 4(-1)$$
$$= -10 - 5j.$$

e. $(4 + 5j)^2$.

   Solution   We treat this as a square of a binomial:

$$(4 + 5j)^2 = (4)^2 + 2(4)(5j) + (5j)^2$$
$$= 16 + 40j + 25j^2$$
$$= 16 + 40j + 25(-1)$$
$$= -9 + 40j.$$

f. $2\sqrt{-4}(3 - 2\sqrt{-3}) + j = 2(2j)(3 - 2j\sqrt{3}) + j$

$$= (4j)(3 - 2j\sqrt{3}) + j$$
$$= 12j - 8j^2\sqrt{3} + j$$
$$= 13j - 8(-1)\sqrt{3}$$
$$= 8\sqrt{3} + 13j.$$

g. $(2 + 3j)(2 - 3j) = (2)^2 - (3j)^2 = 4 - 9j^2 = 4 - 9(-1) = 13$. Here we used the special product $(a + b)(a - b) = a^2 - b^2$.

In Part g of Example 3, the product of a complex number and its conjugate was a real number. This is true in general because

$$(a + bj)(a - bj) = a^2 - (bj)^2 = a^2 - b^2j^2 = a^2 - b^2(-1) = a^2 + b^2,$$

which is *always* a real number.

> **PRODUCT OF CONJUGATES**
>
> $(a + bj)(a - bj) = a^2 + b^2,$ a real number.

We emphasize that *the product of conjugates is a **sum** of squares of real numbers*:

$$(5 + 2j)(5 - 2j) = 5^2 + 2^2 = 29.$$

Do *not* write the product as a difference:

$$(5 + 2j)(5 - 2j) \neq 5^2 - 2^2 = 21.$$

(Students commonly make this error.)

Since the product of a complex number and its conjugate is a real number, to perform the division $(a + bj)/(c + dj)$ we are motivated to multiply *both* the numerator and denominator by the conjugate of the *denominator*. The resulting denominator is a real number, so the quotient can easily be put in the form $a + bj$. The procedure resembles that of rationalizing the denominator of an algebraic expression.

$$\frac{a + bj}{c + dj} = \frac{a + bj}{c + dj} \cdot \frac{c - dj}{c - dj}, \qquad c + dj \neq 0$$

$$= \frac{ac - adj + bcj - bdj^2}{c^2 + d^2}$$

$$= \frac{(ac + bd) + (bc - ad)j}{c^2 + d^2}$$

$$= \frac{ac + bd}{c^2 + d^2} + \frac{bc - ad}{c^2 + d^2}j.$$

DIVISION OF COMPLEX NUMBERS

$$\frac{a + bj}{c + dj} = \frac{ac + bd}{c^2 + d^2} + \frac{bc - ad}{c^2 + d^2}j.$$

More simply:

To find the quotient of two complex numbers, multiply both the numerator and denominator by the conjugate of the denominator and simplify.

Example 4

Find $\dfrac{2 - j}{3 + 2j}$.

Solution We multiply both the numerator and denominator by the conjugate of the denominator, $3 - 2j$:

$$\frac{2 - j}{3 + 2j} = \frac{(2 - j)(3 - 2j)}{(3 + 2j)(3 - 2j)}$$

$$= \frac{6 - 4j - 3j + 2j^2}{3^2 + 2^2}$$

$$= \frac{6 - 7j + 2(-1)}{9 + 4}$$

$$= \frac{4 - 7j}{13} = \frac{4}{13} - \frac{7}{13}j.$$

Example 5

a. $\dfrac{-3 + 4j}{4 - 3j} = \dfrac{(-3 + 4j)(4 + 3j)}{(4 - 3j)(4 + 3j)}$

$$= \dfrac{-12 - 9j + 16j + 12j^2}{4^2 + 3^2} = \dfrac{-12 + 7j + 12(-1)}{16 + 9}$$

$$= \dfrac{-24 + 7j}{25} = -\dfrac{24}{25} + \dfrac{7}{25}j.$$

b. $\dfrac{2}{1 - j} = \dfrac{2(1 + j)}{(1 - j)(1 + j)} = \dfrac{2 + 2j}{1^2 + 1^2}$

$$= \dfrac{2 + 2j}{2} = \dfrac{2}{2} + \dfrac{2}{2}j = 1 + j.$$

c. $\dfrac{6}{5j} = \dfrac{6(-5j)}{5j(-5j)} = \dfrac{-30j}{5^2} = \dfrac{-30j}{25} = -\dfrac{6}{5}j.$

Alternatively, if the denominator of a fraction is a pure imaginary number, as it is in $\dfrac{6}{5j}$, we can simply multiply the numerator and denominator of the fraction by j. Thus

$$\dfrac{6}{5j} = \dfrac{6(j)}{5j(j)} = \dfrac{6j}{5j^2} = \dfrac{6j}{-5} = -\dfrac{6}{5}j.$$

d. $j^{-7} = \dfrac{1}{j^7} = \dfrac{1}{j^3} = \dfrac{1}{-j} = \dfrac{1(j)}{(-j)j} = \dfrac{j}{-j^2} = \dfrac{j}{1} = j.$

Example 6

If $f(z) = z^2 + 6z + \dfrac{1}{z}$, find $f(3j)$.

Solution

$$f(3j) = (3j)^2 + 6(3j) + \dfrac{1}{3j}$$

$$= 9j^2 + 18j + \dfrac{1(j)}{(3j)j} = -9 + 18j + \dfrac{j}{3j^2}$$

$$= -9 + 18j - \dfrac{1}{3}j = -9 + \dfrac{53}{3}j.$$

Example 7

When elements of a circuit are connected in *series*, the total impedance Z of the circuit is the *sum* of the individual impedances. Suppose that a resistor, a capacitor, and an inductor are connected in series. If their impedances, in ohms, are 180, $10 + 60j$, and $22 - 110j$, respectively, find the circuit impedance.

Solution   Letting $180 = Z_1$, $10 + 60j = Z_2$, and $22 - 110j = Z_3$, we have

$$Z = Z_1 + Z_2 + Z_3$$
$$= (180) + (10 + 60j) + (22 - 110j)$$
$$= 212 - 50j \; \Omega.$$

Example 8

When two elements of an electrical circuit are connected in *parallel*, the total impedance Z of the circuit is given by

$$Z = \frac{Z_1 Z_2}{Z_1 + Z_2},$$

where Z_1 and Z_2 are the impedances of the two elements. Suppose capacitive and inductive elements are connected in parallel. If their impedances (in ohms) are $7 - 12j$ and $3 + 26j$, find the circuit impedance (in ohms).

Solution   Letting $7 - 12j = Z_1$ and $3 + 26j = Z_2$, we have

$$Z = \frac{(7 - 12j)(3 + 26j)}{(7 - 12j) + (3 + 26j)} = \frac{21 + 182j - 36j + 312}{10 + 14j} = \frac{333 + 146j}{10 + 14j}$$

$$= \frac{333 + 146j}{10 + 14j} \cdot \frac{10 - 14j}{10 - 14j} = \frac{3330 - 4662j + 1460j - 2044j^2}{100 + 196}$$

$$= \frac{5374 - 3202j}{296} = \frac{5374}{296} - \frac{3202}{296}j = 18.16 - 10.82j.$$

Problem Set 13.2

In Problems **1–54**, *perform the indicated operations.*

1. $(3 - 5j) + (-6 + 4j)$.
2. $(-2 + 6j) + (7 + 4j)$.
3. $(7 - 3j) - (9 - 6j)$.
4. $(4 + 3j) - (5j - 6)$.
5. $2j + 3j - 3$.
6. $2j - 6j + 4j$.
7. $(2 - j) + (3 + j) - (4 - j)$.
8. $4(2 + j) - 3(6 + 2j) + 7j$.
9. $(2 + j)(3 + j)$.
10. $(1 + j)(6 - 2j)$.
11. $(4 + 3j)(5 - 2j)$.
12. $(-2 - j)(-3 + j)$.
13. $2(2 - j)(3 + 2j)$.
14. $2(-5 + j)(-5 - j)$.
15. $(2j^2)(3j)^2$.
16. $j(2j)(3j)(4j)$.
17. $3j(2 - 5j)$.
18. $(8j)(2j)^2(1 + j)$.

19. $(3 + 2j)^2$.

20. $(8 - 4j)^2$.

21. $(5 + 2j)(5 - 2j)$.

22. $(-4 - 2j)(-4 + 2j)$.

23. $\dfrac{3 + 4j}{2}$.

24. $\dfrac{10 - 8j}{5}$.

25. $\dfrac{3 - j}{4 + j}$.

26. $\dfrac{1 - j}{1 + j}$.

27. $\dfrac{2 - j}{3 - j}$.

28. $\dfrac{2 - j}{2 + j}$.

29. $\dfrac{2}{1 - 4j}$.

30. j^{-5}.

31. $\dfrac{3}{2j}$.

32. $\dfrac{3}{2(1 - j)}$.

33. $\dfrac{4 - 2j}{-j}$.

34. $\dfrac{1}{j} + \dfrac{2}{j}$.

35. $\dfrac{5 + 3j}{5 - 6j}$.

36. $\dfrac{2 + 3j}{4 - 2j}$.

37. $\sqrt{-4} + 2\sqrt{-8} + 3\sqrt{12}$.

38. $5 - 2\sqrt{-16} + (3 - \sqrt{-2})$.

39. $\sqrt{-2}\sqrt{-20}$.

40. $(-\sqrt{-4})(-\sqrt{-5})(-\sqrt{-20})$.

41. $(6 + 2j)(-7 - \sqrt{-4})$.

42. $(2 - \sqrt{-3})(3 + \sqrt{-12})$.

43. $(3 - \sqrt{-25})^2$.

44. $(2j - \sqrt{-64})^2$.

45. $\left(\dfrac{1}{3} - \dfrac{4}{5}j\right)\left(\dfrac{3}{8} + \dfrac{2}{7}j\right)$.

46. $\dfrac{\sqrt{-12}}{\sqrt{-9}}$.

47. $\dfrac{1}{(-4 + 3j)(2 + 4j)}$.

48. $\dfrac{5}{(2 + j)(2 - j)}$.

49. $(2 - j)(3 + j)(1 + j)$.

50. $(1 + j)^2(1 - j)$.

51. $\dfrac{\dfrac{2}{3} - \dfrac{j}{2}}{\dfrac{1}{3} + \dfrac{j}{4}}$.

52. $\dfrac{\dfrac{1}{3} + \dfrac{j}{4}}{\dfrac{2}{3} + \dfrac{j}{2}}$.

53. $\dfrac{(6 + 2j)(4 - 3j)}{(1 + j)^2}$.

54. $5 + 2j + (1 + j)^{-2}$.

55. If $f(z) = z^2 - 2z + 1$, find $f(1 + j)$.

56. If $f(z) = 2z^2 - z + 1$, find $f(2 - j)$.

57. In electrical theory, impedance Z (in ohms) is given by

$$Z = \frac{V}{I},$$

where V is voltage (in volts) and I is current (in amperes).

(a) Find Z if $V = 5 + 5j$ and $I = 3 + 4j$.

(b) Find V if $Z = 1 + j$ and $I = 1 - j$.

58. The voltage V across a circuit element is given by $V = IZ$, where V is in volts, I is in amperes, and Z is in ohms. Find the voltage across an element if $I = 4 - 3j$ and $Z = 8 - 15j$.

59. Figure 13.1 shows part of an electrical circuit. Kirchhoff's laws imply that $I_1 + I_2 = I_3$. Find I_2 if $I_1 = 7 + 2j$ and $I_3 = 9 - 5j$.

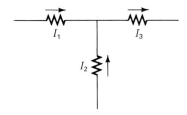

FIGURE 13.1

60. A student said that $-1/j = j^2/j = j$. Is this correct?

61. A resistor, a capacitor, and an inductor are connected in *series*. Their impedances (in ohms) are 8, $3 - 7j$, and $2 + 15j$, respectively. Find the circuit impedance (see Example 7).

62. If the resistor and capacitor in Problem 61 were connected in *parallel*, find the impedance of the combination (see Example 8).

63. If the capacitor and inductor in Problem 61 were connected in *parallel*, find the circuit impedance (see Example 8).

64. The impedance Z of a combination series-parallel circuit is given by

$$Z = Z_1 + \frac{Z_2 Z_3}{Z_2 + Z_3},$$

where $Z_1 = 1 + 3j$, $Z_2 = 1 + j$, and $Z_3 = 1 + 2j$. Find Z (in ohms).

65. In finding the Thévenin equivalent for a complex circuit, the open-circuit voltage V_0 must be found, where

$$V_0 = V_2 + \frac{Z_2}{Z_1 + Z_2}(V_1 - V_2).$$

Given that $V_1 = 2 + 0j$, $V_2 = 0.707 + 0.707j$, $Z_1 = 1 + 2j$, and $Z_2 = 2 + 3j$, find V_0.

66. The Hay bridge is an ac circuit used in electrical measurements. It is governed by the equation

$$\left(R_1 - j\frac{1}{\omega C_1}\right)(R_x + j\omega L_x) = R_2 R_3.$$

Express R_x and L_x in terms of the other circuit constants.

13.3 POLAR FORM OF A COMPLEX NUMBER

Real numbers can be geometrically represented by points on a *line*, whereas complex numbers are represented by points in a rectangular coordinate *plane*. By one method the complex number $a + bj$ is represented by the point (a, b). The abscissa a corresponds to the real part of $a + bj$, and the ordinate b corresponds to the imaginary part of $a + bj$ [see Fig. 13.2(a)]. For example, in Fig. 13.2(b) the number $2 + 3j$ is represented by the point $(2, 3)$ in the first quadrant; the number $-3 - j$ is

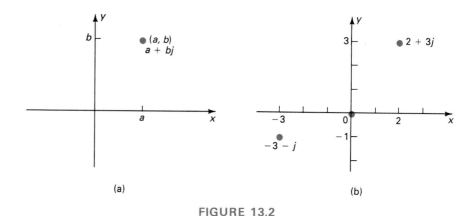

(a)

(b)

FIGURE 13.2

represented by the point $(-3, -1)$ in the third quadrant. The origin $(0, 0)$ corresponds to 0 or $0 + 0j$. Since the points in the plane are considered here to represent complex numbers, we refer to the plane as the **complex plane** (also called the *Argand plane*).

Observe in Fig. 13.3 that the point $(a, 0)$ on the x-axis corresponds to the real number $a = a + 0j$, whereas the point $(0, b)$ on the y-axis corresponds to the pure imaginary number $bj = 0 + bj$. For these reasons the x-axis is called the **real axis** and the y-axis is called the (pure) **imaginary axis**. The fact that $(0, 0)$ lies both on the real axis *and* the imaginary axis gives a geometric picture of the previous statement in Example 3 of Sec. 13.1 that zero is both a real and a pure imaginary number.

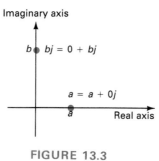

FIGURE 13.3

Since the complex number $a + bj$ can be represented by the point (a, b), we can speak of the *point* $a + bj$ and no confusion should arise. Also, $a + bj$ is called the **rectangular form** of a complex number.

Example 1

Locate the points in the complex plane that correspond to the complex numbers $2 + j$, $3 - 2j$, $-1 - 2j$, $-1 + 3j$, -3, 2, j, and $-3j$.

Solution See Fig. 13.4.

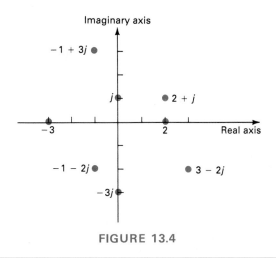

FIGURE 13.4

The complex number $a + bj$ can also be represented in the plane by the vector **OP** from the origin to the point $P(a, b)$, as indicated in Fig. 13.5. Hence we can speak interchangeably of the *complex number* $a + bj$, the *point* $a + bj$, and the *vector* $a + bj$.

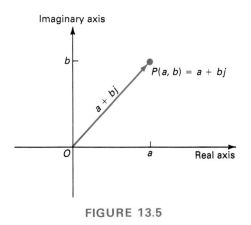

FIGURE 13.5

Addition and subtraction of complex numbers can be interpreted geometrically as addition and subtraction of vectors in standard position. In Fig. 13.6, the vector

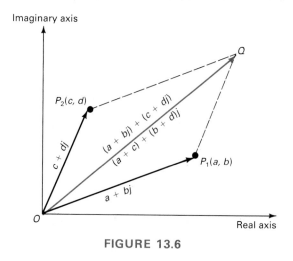

FIGURE 13.6

representing $a + bj$ has terminal point $P_1(a, b)$, and the vector for $c + dj$ has terminal point $P_2(c, d)$. Vector **OQ** is the diagonal of the parallelogram having these vectors for adjacent sides, and **OQ** is the vector representing the sum

$$(a + bj) + (c + dj) = (a + c) + (b + d)j.$$

Example 2

Geometrically find the sum $(2 + 3j) + (3 + j)$.

Solution   The sum of $2 + 3j$ and $3 + j$ is represented geometrically by the diagonal vector $5 + 4j$ of the parallelogram with the given vectors for adjacent sides (see Fig. 13.7).

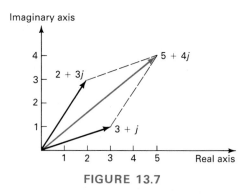

FIGURE 13.7

The subtraction $(a + bj) - (c + dj)$ can be expressed geometrically as the vector sum $(a + bj) + (-c - dj)$, where the vector representing $-c - dj$ is a vector equal in magnitude but opposite in direction to the vector $c + dj$.

Example 3

Geometrically determine the difference $(2 + j) - (3 - 2j)$.

Solution   In Fig. 13.8, the difference $(2 + j) - (3 - 2j)$ is represented by the diagonal vector $-1 + 3j$ of the parallelogram which has as adjacent sides the vector for $2 + j$ and the vector which is equal in magnitude but opposite in direction to $3 - 2j$ (that is, $-3 + 2j$).

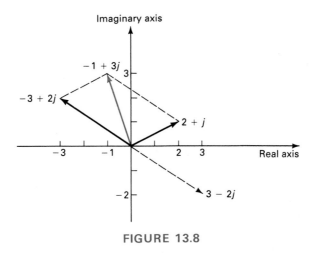

FIGURE 13.8

Figure 13.9 shows a vector **OP** representing the complex number $a + bj$. The angle θ that **OP** makes with the positive real axis is called an **amplitude**, or **argument**,

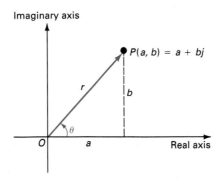

FIGURE 13.9

of $a + bj$. The length r of **OP** is called the **absolute value**, or **modulus**, of $a + bj$ and is always positive or zero. It is also called the **magnitude** of $a + bj$ and may be denoted by $|a + bj|$. From Fig. 13.9 we conclude that $\cos \theta = a/r$, so

$$a = r \cos \theta. \tag{1}$$

Similarly, $\sin \theta = b/r$, or

$$b = r \sin \theta. \tag{2}$$

Moreover,

$$\tan \theta = \frac{b}{a}, \tag{3}$$

$$r = |a + bj| = \sqrt{a^2 + b^2}. \tag{4}$$

By using Eqs. 1 and 2, we can express $a + bj$ in terms of r and θ:

$$a + bj = r \cos \theta + (r \sin \theta)j = r(\cos \theta + j \sin \theta).$$

We speak of $r(\cos \theta + j \sin \theta)$ as being a **trigonometric form**, or **polar form**, of $a + bj$. Polar form is often denoted by the symbol $r\underline{/\theta}$, which is read r *at angle* θ. Another abbreviation is r cis θ.

> **POLAR FORM**
>
> $$a + bj = r(\cos \theta + j \sin \theta) = r\underline{/\theta}.$$

We remark that a complex number does not have a unique polar form. That is, in Fig. 13.9 there is only one choice for r, whereas the argument of $a + bj$ could be any one of infinitely many angles that are coterminal with the indicated argument θ, such as $\theta + 360°$ and $\theta - 360°$. However, when we choose θ such that $0° \leq \theta < 360°$, we may call θ the **principal argument**.

Example 4

Locate the number $2(\cos 300° + j \sin 300°)$ in the complex plane and express the number in rectangular form.

Solution The absolute value r is 2 and the amplitude θ is $300°$, so the number is represented by the vector of length 2 (units) that makes an angle of $300°$ with the positive real axis (see Fig. 13.10). The number can also be written as $2\underline{/300°}$.

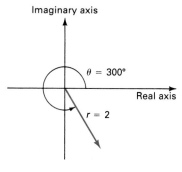

Imaginary axis

$\theta = 300°$

Real axis

$r = 2$

FIGURE 13.10

To convert from polar form to rectangular form, we can use Eqs. 1 and 2.

$$a = r \cos \theta = 2 \cos 300° = 2\left(\frac{1}{2}\right) = 1.$$

$$b = r \sin \theta = 2 \sin 300° = 2\left(-\frac{\sqrt{3}}{2}\right) = -\sqrt{3}.$$

Thus

$$2(\cos 300° + j \sin 300°) = a + bj = 1 - j\sqrt{3}.$$

More directly, we can simply substitute for the trigonometric values:

$$2(\cos 300° + j \sin 300°) = 2\left[\frac{1}{2} + j\left(-\frac{\sqrt{3}}{2}\right)\right] = 1 - j\sqrt{3}.$$

Example 5

Express each of the following complex numbers in rectangular form.

a. $4(\cos 45° + j \sin 45°)$.

Solution By substitution we have

$$4(\cos 45° + j \sin 45°) = 4\left(\frac{\sqrt{2}}{2} + j \cdot \frac{\sqrt{2}}{2}\right) = 2\sqrt{2} + 2j\sqrt{2}.$$

b. $8(\cos 90° + j \sin 90°)$.

Solution

$$8(\cos 90° + j \sin 90°) = 8(0 + j \cdot 1) = 8j.$$

c. $3\underline{/150°}$.

Solution

$$3\underline{/150°} = 3(\cos 150° + j \sin 150°)$$

$$= 3\left(-\frac{\sqrt{3}}{2} + j \cdot \frac{1}{2}\right) = -\frac{3\sqrt{3}}{2} + \frac{3}{2}j.$$

d. $24.3\underline{/27.4°}$.

Solution

$$24.3\underline{/27.4°} = 24.3(\cos 27.4° + j \sin 27.4°)$$

$$= 24.3(0.8878 + 0.4602j)$$

$$= 21.6 + 11.2j.$$

Some calculators have the capability to perform conversions from polar form to rectangular form. It involves keying in the values of θ and r (in a particular order). Then the values of a and b in $a + bj$ are displayed sequentially. A reverse procedure is used for conversion from rectangular form to polar form. You should check the manual that came with your calculator to see if your calculator has this capability.

To convert a complex number from rectangular form to polar form, we make use of Eqs. 3 and 4:

$$\tan \theta = \frac{b}{a}, \qquad r = \sqrt{a^2 + b^2}.$$

The next example shows the procedure.

Example 6

The impedance Z of an inductor is given by $Z = R + X_L j$, where the real part R represents the resistance of the inductor and the imaginary part X_L represents the inductive reactance (see Fig. 13.11). (Assume that Z, R, and X_L are measured in ohms.) If $Z = 2 + 2j$, express Z in polar form.

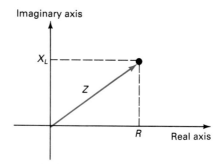

FIGURE 13.11

Solution   First, we note that $2 + 2j$ lies in the first quadrant. In Fig. 13.12, $2 + 2j$ is geometrically represented by both the point $(2, 2)$ and the vector from the origin to $(2, 2)$.

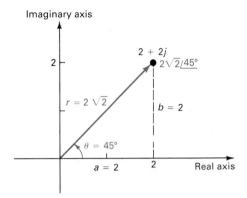

FIGURE 13.12

Second, for the absolute value r, we have $a = 2$ and $b = 2$, so

$$r = \sqrt{a^2 + b^2} = \sqrt{2^2 + 2^2} = \sqrt{8} = 2\sqrt{2}\ \Omega$$

Now, to find the amplitude θ we have

$$\tan \theta = \frac{b}{a} = \frac{2}{2} = 1.$$

Thus θ is a first-quadrant angle with a tangent of 1. Using our knowledge of special angles, we conclude that θ could be $45°$, $45° + 360°$, $45° - 360°$, and so on for other coterminal angles. However, in general *we usually choose θ such that* $0° \leq \theta < 360°$. Thus we choose $\theta = 45°$. (That is, $45°$ is the principal argument.) We can now write

$$2 + 2j = r(\cos \theta + j \sin \theta)$$

$$= 2\sqrt{2}(\cos 45° + j \sin 45°) \quad \text{or} \quad 2\sqrt{2}\underline{/45°}\ \Omega.$$

Because, in general, there are two choices for θ such that both $\tan \theta = b/a$ and $0° \leq \theta < 360°$, the correct choice will be evident by first determining the quadrant in which the point $a + bj$ lies. For our situation above, $\tan 45° = 1$ and $\tan 225° = 1$, but we must choose $\theta = 45°$ because $2 + 2j$ lies in the first quadrant.

Example 7

Express $-3 + 3j\sqrt{3}$ in polar form.

Solution   The point $-3 + 3j\sqrt{3}$ lies in the second quadrant (see Fig. 13.13).

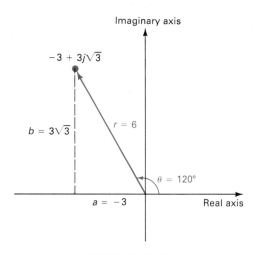

FIGURE 13.13

Since $a = -3$ and $b = 3\sqrt{3}$, we have

$$r = \sqrt{a^2 + b^2} = \sqrt{(-3)^2 + (3\sqrt{3})^2} = \sqrt{9 + 27} = 6$$

and

$$\tan \theta = \frac{b}{a} = \frac{3\sqrt{3}}{-3} = -\sqrt{3}.$$

For $\tan \theta = -\sqrt{3}$, θ may be either $120°$ or $300°$ (from our knowledge of special angles). But $-3 + 3j\sqrt{3}$ is in the second quadrant, so the correct choice is $120°$. Therefore,

$$-3 + 3j\sqrt{3} = 6(\cos 120° + j \sin 120°).$$

In Example 7, a typical direct calculator result for an angle with a tangent of $-\sqrt{3}$ (or -1.732) is $-60°$. That result is *unacceptable* because the problem requires the amplitude to be a second-quadrant angle. As discussed in Sec. 7.1, we should first find the acute reference angle whose tangent is $\sqrt{3}$ (we omit the negative sign). A calculator result is $60°$. Thus $\theta = 180° - 60° = 120°$. We emphasize that due to our preference for θ to lie between $0°$ and $360°$, we choose $6\underline{/120°}$ as our answer. You should realize, however, that $6\underline{/-240°}$ could be used as a polar form for the given number. Similarly, in Example 6 another polar form for $2 + 2j$ is given by $2\sqrt{2}[\cos(-315°) + j \sin(-315°)]$. The amplitude for the complex number zero can be any angle.

Example 8

The voltage across an inductor in an ac circuit is $3 - 4j$ volts. Express that voltage in polar form.

Solution   The vector $3 - 4j$ lies in the fourth quadrant. We have

$$r = \sqrt{(3)^2 + (-4)^2} = \sqrt{25} = 5 \text{ V}$$

and

$$\tan \theta = \frac{b}{a} = \frac{-4}{3} = -\frac{4}{3} = -1.3333.$$

The reference angle with a tangent of 1.3333 is 53.1°. Because θ is a fourth-quadrant angle, we choose θ to be $360° - 53.1° = 306.9°$. We then have

$$3 - 4j = 5\underline{/306.9°} \text{ V.}$$

The polar form of a real number or a pure imaginary number is easy to find, as the following example shows.

Example 9

Express each of the following complex numbers in polar form.

a. 2.

Solution   The point 2, or $2 + 0j$, lies on the positive real axis and is two units from the origin [see Fig. 13.14(a)]. Therefore, $\theta = 0°$, $r = 2$, and we have $2 = 2(\cos 0° + j \sin 0°)$.

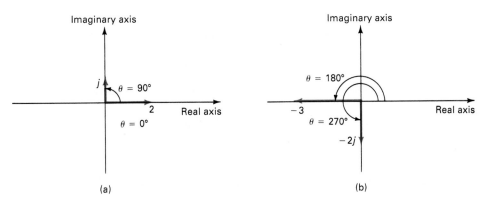

FIGURE 13.14

b. j.

Solution　The point j, or $0 + 1j$, lies on the positive imaginary axis and is one unit from the origin [see Fig. 13.14(a)]. Thus $\theta = 90°$ and $r = 1$. Therefore, $j = 1(\cos 90° + j \sin 90°)$.

c. -3.

Solution　By inspection of Fig. 13.14(b), clearly $r = 3$ and $\theta = 180°$, so $-3 = 3\underline{/180°}$.

d. $-2j$.

Solution　From Fig. 13.14(b) we have $r = 2$ and $\theta = 270°$. Hence $-2j = 2\underline{/270°}$.

Example 10

The total impedance Z (in ohms) of a circuit is given by

$$Z = Z_1 + Z_2,$$

where $Z_1 = 4\underline{/0°}$ and $Z_2 = 8\underline{/90°}$. Find the magnitude (in ohms) and amplitude of the circuit impedance and express the circuit impedance in polar form.

Solution

$$Z = Z_1 + Z_2 = 4\underline{/0°} + 8\underline{/90°}$$
$$= 4(\cos 0° + j \sin 0°) + 8(\cos 90° + j \sin 90°)$$
$$= 4[1 + j(0)] + 8[0 + j(1)] = 4(1) + 8(j),$$
$$Z = 4 + 8j.$$

The magnitude (r) of Z is given by

$$|4 + 8j| = \sqrt{4^2 + 8^2} = 8.94.$$

To find the amplitude θ, we have

$$\tan \theta = \frac{8}{4} = 2.$$

Since $4 + 8j$ lies in the first quadrant, we choose

$$\theta = 63.43°.$$

Thus the magnitude of the circuit impedance is $8.94\,\Omega$, the amplitude is $63.43°$, and in polar form we have

$$Z = 8.94\underline{/63.43°}\ \Omega.$$

Example 11

In Example 7 of Sec. 13.2, the circuit impedance Z (in ohms) is given by

$$Z = 212 - 50j.$$

Find the magnitude (in ohms) of the circuit impedance and express the circuit impedance in polar form.

Solution The magnitude of Z is

$$\sqrt{(212)^2 + (-50)^2} = 217.8.$$

Also,

$$\tan \theta = \frac{-50}{212},$$

from which we find that $\theta = 346.7°$, because Z is in the fourth quadrant. Thus in polar form we have $Z = 217.8\underline{/346.7°}$.

Example 12

In Example 8 of Sec. 13.2, the circuit impedance Z (in ohms) is given by

$$Z = 18.16 - 10.82j.$$

Find the magnitude (in ohms) of the circuit impedance and the *phase angle* θ, which is the amplitude of Z.

Solution The magnitude of the circuit impedance is

$$\sqrt{(18.16)^2 + (-10.82)^2} = 21.1.$$

The phase angle θ is given by

$$\tan \theta = \frac{-10.82}{18.16},$$

from which $\theta = 329.2°$, because Z lies in the fourth quadrant.

Just as complex numbers can be represented by vectors, liberal adaptation permits vector quantities such as force and velocity to be represented by complex numbers. As a result, problems which involve finding the resultant of a number of vector quantities may be solved by means of algebra of complex numbers. That is, the resultant of two or more vectors can be obtained by first expressing each vector as a complex number and then adding these numbers in the usual manner. In the following example, we shall find the resultant of three forces acting at the same point (that is, *concurrent forces*).

Example 13

Use complex algebra to find the resultant of the following system of forces that act at the origin:

$$A = 30 \text{ N}, \qquad \theta_A = 44°,$$
$$B = 40 \text{ N}, \qquad \theta_B = 121°,$$
$$C = 20 \text{ N}, \qquad \theta_C = 209°,$$

where θ is the angle that the given force makes with the positive x-axis. The system is shown in Fig. 13.15.

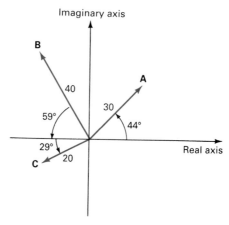

FIGURE 13.15

Solution   After first writing each force in polar form, we express them in rectangular form:

$$\mathbf{A} = 30(\cos 44° + j \sin 44°) = 21.58 + 20.84j,$$
$$\mathbf{B} = 40(\cos 121° + j \sin 121°) = -20.60 + 34.29j,$$
$$\mathbf{C} = 20(\cos 209° + j \sin 209°) = -17.49 - 9.70j.$$

We now add the real parts and add the imaginary parts to obtain the resultant.

$$\mathbf{A} + \mathbf{B} + \mathbf{C} = -16.51 + 45.43j = 48.3 \underline{/110.0°}.$$

Thus the magnitude of the resultant is 48.3 N and its direction is $\theta = 110.0°$.

Problem Set 13.3

In Problems 1–18, express the given complex number in polar form. Do not use a calculator in Problems 1–16.

1. $4 + 4j$.

2. $-\sqrt{3} + j$.

3. $2 - 2j\sqrt{3}$.

4. -4.

5. $5j$.

6. $1 + j\sqrt{3}$.

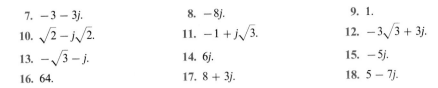

7. $-3 - 3j$.

8. $-8j$.

9. 1.

10. $\sqrt{2} - j\sqrt{2}$.

11. $-1 + j\sqrt{3}$.

12. $-3\sqrt{3} + 3j$.

13. $-\sqrt{3} - j$.

14. $6j$.

15. $-5j$.

16. 64.

17. $8 + 3j$.

18. $5 - 7j$.

In Problems **19–34,** *locate the given number in the complex plane and express it in rectangular form. Do not use a calculator in Problems* **19–30.**

19. $2(\cos 30° + j \sin 30°)$.

20. $3(\cos 240° + j \sin 240°)$.

21. $6(\cos 120° + j \sin 120°)$.

22. $4(\cos 210° + j \sin 210°)$.

23. $2(\cos 315° + j \sin 315°)$.

24. $3(\cos 150° + j \sin 150°)$.

25. $3(\cos 270° + j \sin 270°)$.

26. $2(\cos 180° + j \sin 180°)$.

27. $4/0°$.

28. $4/240°$.

29. $3/330°$.

30. $\frac{1}{2}/90°$.

31. $2/15°$.

32. $3/40°$.

33. $2/245°$.

34. $4/340°$.

35. If all complex numbers with an absolute value of 1 were plotted in the complex plane, what geometric figure would they form?

36. If $3(\cos 220° + j \sin 220°) = a + bj$, find a and b.

37. If $4(\cos 500° + j \sin 500°) = a + bj$, find a and b.

38. If $2(\cos 0° + j \sin 0°) = a + \left(\dfrac{b}{c}\right)j$, find a.

In Problems **39–42,** *express the given number in rectangular form.*

39. $3[\cos(-205°) + j \sin(-205°)]$.

40. $7\left(\cos \dfrac{\pi}{5} + j \sin \dfrac{\pi}{5}\right)$.

41. $0.75/-42°$.

42. $1/-100.3°$.

43. The impedance of an inductor is $6.2 + 0.8j\,\Omega$. (a) Express the impedance in polar form. Find the (b) resistance and (c) inductive reactance of the inductor (see Example 6).

44. The impedance of a branch of a circuit is $1.5 - 2.3j$ ohms. Express that impedance in polar form.

45. Express a voltage of $23 - 46j$ volts in polar form.

46. Find a polar form of the conjugate of the voltage in Problem 45.

47. The voltage across an inductor in an ac circuit is $11.2/72°$ V. Express the voltage in rectangular form.

48. The electric current in a circuit is $0.026/26°$ A. Express that current in rectangular form.

49. Find the acute angle between the vectors $\mathbf{V} = 2 + 3j$ and $\mathbf{I} = 4 + j$.

50. Arrange the following numbers in order of decreasing absolute value: $4 + 3j$, $-6j$, and $5 - 5j$.

In Problems **51–54,** *geometrically construct the sums and differences.*

51. $(2 - 3j) + (-4 + 3j)$.

52. $(8 - 4j) + (-6 - 2j)$.

53. $(3 + 2j) - (2 + 4j)$.

54. $(3 + 5j) - (5 + 2j)$.

SEC. 13.3 Polar Form of a Complex Number **503**

55. Find the value of $20\underline{/46°} + 34\underline{/62°}$ and express your answer in polar form.

56. If $Z_1 = 30 + 10j$ and $Z_2 = 20 - 46j$, find the polar form for Z_T if $Z_T = Z_1 + Z_2$.

57. When two elements of an electrical circuit are connected in parallel, the total impedance Z of the circuit is given by

$$Z = \frac{Z_1 Z_2}{Z_1 + Z_2},$$

where Z_1 and Z_2 are the impedances of the two elements. If $Z_1 = 2 - 3j$ and $Z_2 = 3 + 4j$, find the (a) magnitude, (b) amplitude, and (c) polar form of the circuit impedance. (Assume that Z, Z_1, and Z_2 are in ohms.)

In Problems 58–61, find the resultant of the given vectors in the manner of Example 13. Give your answer in polar form.

58. $A = 20, \theta_A = 125°,$
$ B = 30, \theta_B = 315°,$
$ C = 10, \theta_C = 70°.$

59. $A = 100, \theta_A = 310°,$
$ B = 120, \theta_B = 35°,$
$ C = 50, \quad \theta_C = 40°.$

60. $A = 200, \theta_A = 42°,$
$ B = 100, \theta_B = 85°,$
$ C = 50, \quad \theta_C = 155°.$

61. $A = 120, \theta_A = 80°,$
$ B = 49, \quad \theta_B = 125°,$
$ C = 85, \quad \theta_C = 215°.$

13.4 EXPONENTIAL FORM OF A COMPLEX NUMBER

It is not uncommon for an engineer to encounter, and indeed perform, computations involving the *exponential form* of a complex number. This form makes use of a special irrational number that is symbolized by the letter e and is approximated by

$$e \approx 2.71828.$$

The number e plays an important role in mathematics; you will encounter it again in Chapter 15.

A complex number $z = a + bj$ having polar form $r(\cos\theta + j\sin\theta)$ can also be expressed in the **exponential form** defined by

$$\boxed{z = re^{j\theta},}$$

where

$$\boxed{e^{j\theta} = \cos\theta + j\sin\theta.}$$

The last equation is called **Euler's formula** and requires that θ be in radians. Our definition of the exponential form $re^{j\theta}$ allows the usual rules for exponents to hold, as will be illustrated in the next section.

Example 1

Express $4 - 4j$ in exponential form.

Solution In polar form we have $4 - 4j = 4\sqrt{2}(\cos 315° + j \sin 315°)$, which in terms of radians is $4\sqrt{2}\left(\cos \dfrac{7\pi}{4} + j \sin \dfrac{7\pi}{4}\right)$. Thus $r = 4\sqrt{2}$ and $\theta = \dfrac{7\pi}{4}$, so

$$4 - 4j = re^{j\theta} = 4\sqrt{2}e^{7\pi j/4}.$$

Example 2

Express $3.2(\cos 23.6° + j \sin 23.6°)$ in exponential form.

Solution Here $r = 3.2$ and in terms of radians we have $\theta = 23.6° = 0.412$. Thus

$$3.2(\cos 23.6° + j \sin 23.6°) = 3.2e^{0.412j}.$$

Example 3

Express $3.5e^{1.65j}$ in polar and rectangular forms.

Solution We can immediately write a polar form, which is then used to obtain the rectangular form.

$$
\begin{aligned}
3.5e^{1.65j} &= 3.5(\cos 1.65 + j \sin 1.65) \qquad \text{[polar form]} \\
&= 3.5(-0.0791 + 0.9969j) \\
&= -0.28 + 3.49j \qquad\qquad\quad \text{[rectangular form]}.
\end{aligned}
$$

Problem Set 13.4

In Problems 1–12, express the given complex number in exponential form. If possible, do not use a calculator.

1. $1 + j$.

2. -6.

3. $-2\sqrt{3} + 2j$.

4. $-3 - 3j$.

5. $-7j$.

6. $1 - j\sqrt{3}$.

7. $-4.6 - 7.8j$.

8. $-0.46 + 1.53j$.

9. $2.8(\cos 14.6° + j \sin 14.6°)$.

10. $7.3(\cos 123.6° + j \sin 123.6°)$.

11. $3.7(\cos 2.46 + j \sin 2.46)$.

12. $3\left(\cos \dfrac{\pi}{5} + j \sin \dfrac{\pi}{5}\right)$.

In Problems 13–20, *express the given complex number in polar and rectangular forms. If possible, do not use a calculator.*

13. $e^{\pi j/2}$.

14. $2e^{(4/3)\pi j}$.

15. $3e^{3\pi j/4}$.

16. $4e^{\pi j}$.

17. $2e^{(5\pi/6)j}$.

18. $e^{(3\pi/2)j}$.

19. $4e^{2.35j}$.

20. $1.6e^{3.01j}$.

21. Express $e^{j\omega t}$ in polar form.

13.5 OPERATIONS IN POLAR FORM

Multiplication or division of complex numbers is easily performed when the numbers are in polar form. We can determine a formula for the product of two complex numbers by considering the product of the exponential forms $r_1 e^{j\theta_1}$ and $r_2 e^{j\theta_2}$. From rules of exponents, we have

$$(r_1 e^{j\theta_1})(r_2 e^{j\theta_2}) = r_1 r_2 e^{j\theta_1 + j\theta_2} = r_1 r_2 e^{j(\theta_1 + \theta_2)}.$$

In polar form this gives the following rule:

MULTIPLICATION IN POLAR FORM

$$r_1(\cos \theta_1 + j \sin \theta_1) \cdot r_2(\cos \theta_2 + j \sin \theta_2) = r_1 r_2 [\cos(\theta_1 + \theta_2) + j \sin(\theta_1 + \theta_2)].$$

Therefore, *the product of two complex numbers in polar form is a complex number in which the absolute value is the product of the absolute values of the given numbers and the amplitude is the sum of the amplitudes of the given numbers.* More compactly we have

$$(r_1 \underline{/\theta_1})(r_2 \underline{/\theta_2}) = r_1 r_2 \underline{/\theta_1 + \theta_2}.$$

Example 1

Find each of the following products and express the answer in rectangular form.

a. $2(\cos 10° + j \sin 10°) \cdot 4(\cos 20° + j \sin 20°)$.

Solution The product of the absolute values is $2 \cdot 4 = 8$ and the sum of the amplitudes is $10° + 20° = 30°$. Thus

$$2(\cos 10° + j \sin 10°) \cdot 4(\cos 20° + j \sin 20°) = 8(\cos 30° + j \sin 30°)$$

$$= 8\left(\frac{\sqrt{3}}{2} + \frac{1}{2}j\right)$$

$$= 4\sqrt{3} + 4j.$$

b. $(8/-35°)(5/160°) = (8 \cdot 5)/-35° + 160° = 40/125°$

$$= 40(\cos 125° + j \sin 125°)$$

$$= -22.9 + 32.8j.$$

c. $(3/9°)(4/30°)(2/-6°).$

Solution   The preceding rule can be extended so that it applies to a product of any number of complex numbers. Thus

$$(3/9°)(4/30°)(2/-6°) = (3 \cdot 4 \cdot 2)/9° + 30° - 6° = 24/33°$$

$$= 24(\cos 33° + j \sin 33°)$$

$$= 20.1 + 13.1j.$$

Multiplication of the complex number $a + bj$ by j has special geometrical significance. If $a + bj = r(\cos \theta + j \sin \theta)$ and $j = 1(\cos 90° + j \sin 90°)$, then by the preceding rule we have

$$(a + bj)j = r[\cos (\theta + 90°) + j \sin (\theta + 90°)],$$

which is the vector obtained by rotating $a + bj$ counterclockwise through an angle of 90°. Thus *the effect of multiplying a vector by j is to rotate the vector counterclockwise by 90°.* It is based on this rotational effect that we speak of j as an *operator.*

We now turn our attention to the quotient of two complex numbers. Using laws of exponents gives

$$\frac{r_1 e^{j\theta_1}}{r_2 e^{j\theta_2}} = \frac{r_1}{r_2} e^{j\theta_1 - j\theta_2} = \frac{r_1}{r_2} e^{j(\theta_1 - \theta_2)}.$$

In polar form this means:

DIVISION IN POLAR FORM

$$\frac{r_1(\cos \theta_1 + j \sin \theta_1)}{r_2(\cos \theta_2 + j \sin \theta_2)} = \frac{r_1}{r_2} [(\cos (\theta_1 - \theta_2) + j \sin (\theta_1 - \theta_2)].$$

Therefore, *the quotient of two complex numbers in polar form is a complex number in which the absolute value is the absolute value of the numerator divided by the absolute value of the denominator and the amplitude is the result of subtracting the amplitude of the denominator from that of the numerator.* More compactly we have

$$\frac{r_1/\theta_1}{r_2/\theta_2} = \frac{r_1}{r_2} /\theta_1 - \theta_2.$$

Example 2

Perform the indicated operations and express the answer in polar form and rectangular form.

a. $\dfrac{3(\cos 75° + j \sin 75°)}{6(\cos 15° + j \sin 15°)} = \dfrac{3}{6}[\cos (75° - 15°) + j \sin (75° - 15°)]$

$$= \frac{1}{2}(\cos 60° + j \sin 60°) \qquad \text{[polar form]}$$

$$= \frac{1}{2}\left(\frac{1}{2} + j\frac{\sqrt{3}}{2}\right)$$

$$= \frac{1}{4} + j\frac{\sqrt{3}}{4} \qquad\qquad \text{[rectangular form]}.$$

b. $\dfrac{8\underline{/10°}}{3\underline{/-20°}} = \dfrac{8}{3}\underline{/10° - (-20°)} = \dfrac{8}{3}\underline{/30°} \qquad \text{[polar form]}$

$$= \frac{8}{3}(\cos 30° + j \sin 30°)$$

$$= \frac{8}{3}\left(\frac{\sqrt{3}}{2} + \frac{1}{2}j\right) = \frac{4\sqrt{3}}{3} + \frac{4}{3}j \qquad \text{[rectangular form]}.$$

c. $\dfrac{(3\underline{/10°})(5\underline{/140°})}{7\underline{/230°}} = \dfrac{15\underline{/150°}}{7\underline{/230°}} = \dfrac{15}{7}\underline{/150° - 230°}$

$$= \frac{15}{7}\underline{/-80°} \qquad \text{[polar form]}$$

$$= \frac{15}{7}[\cos (-80°) + j \sin (-80°)]$$

$$= 0.37 - 2.11j \qquad \text{[rectangular form]}.$$

In general, addition (or subtraction) cannot be performed in polar coordinates. For example

$$2\underline{/35°} + 5\underline{/10°} \ne 7\underline{/45°}.$$

However, in the sense of adding like terms, it can be performed when the **amplitudes** are the same. Thus

$$3\underline{/10°} + 6\underline{/10°} = 9\underline{/10°}.$$

When adding complex numbers in polar form, we convert to rectangular **form** to perform the addition. Example 3a shows the procedure.

Example 3

Perform the indicated operations and express the answer in polar form.

a. $\dfrac{24/10°}{4/100°} + \dfrac{25/0°}{2.5/-123°} = 6/-90° + 10/123°$

$$= (0 - 6j) + (-5.45 + 8.39j)$$

$$= -5.45 + 2.39j = 5.95/156.3°.$$

b. $\dfrac{1}{(2.3/15.4°)(1.8/13.8°)} = \dfrac{1/0°}{4.14/29.2°} = 0.24/-29.2° = 0.24/330.8°.$

Example 4

A capacitive element with impedance $Z_1 = 13.9/-59.7°\ \Omega$ and an inductor with impedance $Z_2 = 26.2/83.4°\ \Omega$ are connected in parallel. Find the circuit impedance Z (in ohms).

Solution Using the formula from Example 8 of Sec. 13.2, we have

$$Z = \dfrac{Z_1 Z_2}{Z_1 + Z_2} = \dfrac{(13.9/-59.7°)(26.2/83.4°)}{13.9/-59.7° + 26.2/83.4°}$$

$$= \dfrac{364.2/23.7°}{(7.01 - 12.0j) + (3.01 + 26.0j)}$$

$$= \dfrac{364.2/23.7°}{10.02 + 14.0j} = \dfrac{364.2/23.7°}{17.2/54.4°}$$

$$= 21.2/-30.7° = 21.2/329.3°.$$

Problem Set 13.5

In Problems **1–14**, *perform the indicated operations and give the answers in polar form.*

1. $2(\cos 17° + j \sin 17°) \cdot 4(\cos 43° + j \sin 43°).$
2. $4(\cos 125° + j \sin 125°) \cdot 5(\cos 85° + j \sin 85°).$
3. $3 \cos 105° + j \sin 105°) \cdot 2(\cos 105° + j \sin 105°).$
4. $5(\cos 324° + j \sin 324°) \cdot 3(\cos 126° + j \sin 126°).$
5. $\dfrac{30(\cos 145° + j \sin 145°)}{3(\cos 100° + j \sin 100°)}.$
6. $\dfrac{25(\cos 384° + j \sin 384°)}{5(\cos 174° + j \sin 174°)}.$
7. $\dfrac{18(\cos 284° + j \sin 284°)}{3(\cos 59° + j \sin 59°)}.$
8. $\dfrac{32(\cos 125° + j \sin 125°)}{16(\cos 170° + j \sin 170°)}.$
9. $2/44° \cdot 2/11°$
10. $9/39° \cdot 8/28°.$
11. $1/46° \cdot 3/-12° \cdot 7/37°.$
12. $3/-45° \cdot 4/-87° \cdot 0.5/64°.$
13. $\dfrac{2/134°}{4/-250°}.$
14. $\dfrac{4/251°}{5/264°}.$

In Problems **15–22**, *perform the indicated operations and give the answers in rectangular form.*

15. $\dfrac{(3/325°)(12/254°)}{18/9°}$.

16. $\dfrac{4/275°}{(2/44°)(50/19°)}$.

17. $\dfrac{(4/77°)(4/157°)}{(3/200°)(2/50°)}$.

18. $\dfrac{(3/46°)(5/295°)}{(4/200°)(3/23°)}$.

19. $\dfrac{(7/-10°)(4/15°)}{(3/41°)(2/-63°)}$.

20. $8/-10° + 4/15°$.

21. $\dfrac{10/10°}{4/60°} + \dfrac{15/5°}{3/0°}$.

22. $\dfrac{5/-4° + 6/5.6°}{(5/-4°)(6/5.6°)}$.

23. If a capacitor of impedance $6/275°$ (Ω) and an inductor of impedance $8/40°$ (Ω) are connected in parallel, find the circuit impedance and express the answer in rectangular form. (See Example 4.)

24. The voltage V (in volts) across a circuit with an impedance Z (in ohms) and carrying a current I (in amperes) is given by $V = IZ$. Find V if $I = 1.5/38°$ and $Z = 6/48°$. Express the answer in both polar and rectangular forms.

25. In Problem 24, if the current in the circuit is $4/50°$ and the voltage is $20/30°$, find the impedance of the circuit and express the answer in polar form.

26. Given that the impedance Z of a circuit element is the reciprocal of its admittance Y, find the impedance if $Y = 0.5/30°$. Give your answer in polar form.

27. In the analysis of a mechanical network, the following determinant was encountered:

$$\Delta = \begin{vmatrix} 10 & -0.5 & 0.25/90° \\ 0 & 1.3/20.1° & -0.8/71.2° \\ 0 & -0.8/72.3° & 0.6/62.6° \end{vmatrix}.$$

Find Δ in rectangular form. *Hint:* Expand along the first column.

28. Show that the effect of dividing a complex number $a + bj$ by j is to rotate the vector for $a + bj$ clockwise by $90°$.

29. Show that $\dfrac{1}{r/\theta} = \dfrac{1}{r}/-\theta$.

13.6 DE MOIVRE'S THEOREM

To evaluate an expression such as $(\sqrt{3} + j)^5$, it is obvious that using repeated multiplication would be rather laborious. Fortunately, using polar form reduces the work considerably. To see why, observe that the nth power of $r(\cos\theta + j\sin\theta)$ is given by

$$[r(\cos\theta + j\sin\theta)]^n = (re^{j\theta})^n = r^n e^{n\theta j}$$

$$= r^n(\cos n\theta + j\sin n\theta).$$

That is, **to raise a complex number to a power n, we raise its absolute value to the nth power and multiply its amplitude by n.** This important result, which is true for any integer n, is known as *De Moivre's theorem.*

DE MOIVRE'S THEOREM

$$[r(\cos\theta + j\sin\theta)]^n = r^n(\cos n\theta + j\sin n\theta).$$

For example, to find $(\sqrt{3} + j)^5$, we first write $\sqrt{3} + j$ in polar form.

$$\sqrt{3} + j = 2(\cos 30° + j\sin 30°).$$

Thus

$$
\begin{aligned}
(\sqrt{3} + j)^5 &= [2(\cos 30° + j\sin 30°)]^5 \\
&= 2^5[\cos(5\cdot 30°) + j\sin(5\cdot 30°)] \qquad \text{[De Moivre's theorem]} \\
&= 32(\cos 150° + j\sin 150°) \\
&= 32\left(-\frac{\sqrt{3}}{2} + \frac{1}{2}j\right) \\
&= -16\sqrt{3} + 16j.
\end{aligned}
$$

Example 1

Evaluate by using De Moivre's theorem and give the answer in rectangular form.

a. $\quad [2(\cos 10° + j\sin 10°)]^6 = 2^6[\cos(6\cdot 10°) + j\sin(6\cdot 10°)]$

$$= 64(\cos 60° + j\sin 60°)$$

$$= 64\left(\frac{1}{2} + j\frac{\sqrt{3}}{2}\right) = 32 + 32j\sqrt{3}.$$

b. $\quad (3\underline{/30°})^{-3} = 3^{-3}\underline{/-3\cdot 30°} = \dfrac{1}{27}\underline{/-90°} = \dfrac{1}{27}[0 + j(-1)] = -\dfrac{1}{27}j.$

Example 2

Evaluate $(1 + j)^{12}$ by using De Moivre's theorem and give the answer in rectangular form.

Solution First we write $1 + j$ in polar form.

$$1 + j = \sqrt{2}(\cos 45° + j\sin 45°).$$

Applying De Moivre's theorem gives

$$
\begin{aligned}
[\sqrt{2}(\cos 45° + j\sin 45°)]^{12} &= (\sqrt{2})^{12}[\cos(12\cdot 45°) + j\sin(12\cdot 45°)] \\
&= (2^{1/2})^{12}(\cos 540° + j\sin 540°) \\
&= 2^6[-1 + j(0)] \\
&= -64.
\end{aligned}
$$

Example 3

Evaluate by using De Moivre's theorem and give the answer in rectangular form.

a. $(3 + 2j)^4$.

Solution   In polar form we have

$$3 + 2j = \sqrt{13}\underline{/33.69°}.$$

Applying De Moivre's theorem gives

$$(3 + 2j)^4 = (\sqrt{13}\underline{/33.69°})^4 = (13^{1/2})^4\underline{/4 \cdot 33.69°}$$

$$= 13^2\underline{/134.76°} = -119.0 + 120.0j.$$

b. $\dfrac{(2 + 2j)^{15}}{(\sqrt{3} + j)^{21}} = \dfrac{(\sqrt{8}\underline{/45°})^{15}}{(2\underline{/30°})^{21}} = \dfrac{(2^{3/2})^{15}\underline{/15 \cdot 45°}}{2^{21}\underline{/21 \cdot 30°}}$ [since $\sqrt{8} = (2^3)^{1/2} = 2^{3/2}$]

$$= \dfrac{2^{45/2}\underline{/675°}}{2^{21}\underline{/630°}} = 2^{3/2}\underline{/45°}$$

$$= 2\sqrt{2}\left(\dfrac{\sqrt{2}}{2} + j\dfrac{\sqrt{2}}{2}\right)$$

$$= 2 + 2j.$$

We conclude this section by using De Moivre's theorem to solve the equation $w^n = z$ for w, where w and z are complex numbers and n is a positive integer. That is, we want to find an nth root of a complex number z. Suppose $z = r(\cos \theta + j \sin \theta)$ and $w = \rho(\cos \varphi + j \sin \varphi)$, where ρ and φ are the Greek letters rho and phi, respectively. Then substituting into $w^n = z$ gives

$$[\rho(\cos \varphi + j \sin \varphi)]^n = r(\cos \theta + j \sin \theta),$$

or, by De Moivre's theorem,

$$\rho^n(\cos n\varphi + j \sin n\varphi) = r(\cos \theta + j \sin \theta).$$

Both sides of this equation represent the same number. But two numbers in polar form represent the same number if, in addition to having the same absolute value, their amplitudes are coterminal angles. In other words, $n\varphi$ can differ from θ by any integral multiple of $360°$ (or 2π if θ is in radians). Symbolically, this means that

$$n\varphi = \theta + k \cdot 360°$$

$$\varphi = \frac{\theta}{n} + \frac{k \cdot 360°}{n}, \qquad \text{where } k \text{ is an integer.}$$

Also, $\rho^n = r$ is true if $\rho = \sqrt[n]{r}$, the positive nth root of r. Thus the nth roots of z are given by the following formula:

---

nTH ROOTS OF A COMPLEX NUMBER

The nth roots of $r(\cos \theta + j \sin \theta)$ are denoted by w_k and are given by

$$w_k = \sqrt[n]{r}\left[\cos\left(\frac{\theta}{n} + \frac{k \cdot 360°}{n}\right) + j \sin\left(\frac{\theta}{n} + \frac{k \cdot 360°}{n}\right)\right],$$

where $k = 0, 1, 2, \ldots, n - 1$.

Each of the n values of k from zero to $n - 1$ gives a different root. For $k > n - 1$, repetition of a previous root occurs. In summary, there are exactly n different complex nth roots of a nonzero complex number. These roots have the same absolute value.

Example 4

Find the six sixth roots of -64. That is, find the six solutions of the equation $x^6 = -64$.

Solution We first express -64 in polar form:

$$-64 = 64(\cos 180° + j \sin 180°).$$

Thus $r = 64$, $\theta = 180°$, and $n = 6$. Denoting the sixth roots by w_k and substituting in the preceding formula, we get

$$w_k = \sqrt[6]{64}\left[\cos\left(\frac{180°}{6} + \frac{k \cdot 360°}{6}\right) + j \sin\left(\frac{180°}{6} + \frac{k \cdot 360°}{6}\right)\right]$$

$$= 2[\cos(30° + k \cdot 60°) + j \sin(30° + k \cdot 60°)], \qquad k = 0, 1, \ldots, 5.$$

Next we successively replace k by $0, 1, \ldots, 5$. This gives the roots $w_0, w_1, \ldots, w_5$.

If $k = 0$,

$$w_0 = 2(\cos 30° + j \sin 30°) = 2\left(\frac{\sqrt{3}}{2} + \frac{1}{2}j\right) = \sqrt{3} + j.$$

If $k = 1$,

$$w_1 = 2(\cos 90° + j \sin 90°) = 2(0 + j) = 2j.$$

If $k = 2$,

$$w_2 = 2(\cos 150° + j \sin 150°) = 2\left(-\frac{\sqrt{3}}{2} + \frac{1}{2}j\right) = -\sqrt{3} + j.$$

If $k = 3$,

$$w_3 = 2(\cos 210° + j \sin 210°) = 2\left(-\frac{\sqrt{3}}{2} - \frac{1}{2}j\right) = -\sqrt{3} - j.$$

If $k = 4$,

$$w_4 = 2(\cos 270° + j \sin 270°) = 2(0 - j) = -2j.$$

If $k = 5$,

$$w_5 = 2(\cos 330° + j \sin 330°) = 2\left(\frac{\sqrt{3}}{2} - \frac{1}{2}j\right) = \sqrt{3} - j.$$

You may verify that for $k > 5$, no new roots are obtained. As geometrically shown in Fig. 13.16, the roots correspond to equally spaced points on a circle with center at the origin and radius 2. They appear as vertices of a regular six-sided polygon in the complex plane.

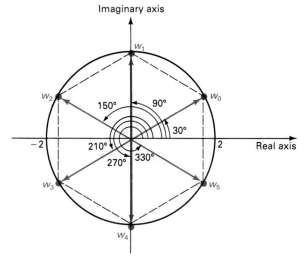

FIGURE 13.16

Example 5

Find the three cube roots of $-1 + j\sqrt{3}$.

Solution   We have

$$-1 + j\sqrt{3} = 2(\cos 120° + j \sin 120°).$$

Thus $r = 2$, $\theta = 120°$, and $n = 3$, so

$$w_k = \sqrt[3]{2}\left[\cos\left(\frac{120°}{3} + \frac{k \cdot 360°}{3}\right) + j \sin\left(\frac{120°}{3} + \frac{k \cdot 360°}{3}\right)\right]$$

$$= \sqrt[3]{2}[\cos(40° + k \cdot 120°) + j \sin(40° + k \cdot 120°), \qquad k = 0, 1, 2.$$

Thus

$$\text{If } k = 0, \qquad w_0 = \sqrt[3]{2}(\cos 40° + j \sin 40°),$$

$$\text{If } k = 1, \qquad w_1 = \sqrt[3]{2}(\cos 160° + j \sin 160°),$$

$$\text{If } k = 2, \qquad w_2 = \sqrt[3]{2}(\cos 280° + j \sin 280°).$$

See Fig. 13.17. Note that this problem could have been posed by saying, "Solve the equation $x^3 = -1 + j\sqrt{3}$."

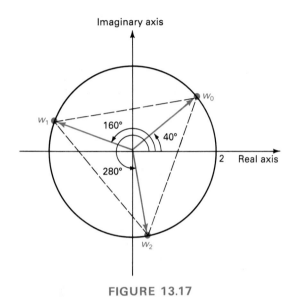

FIGURE 13.17

Problem Set 13.6

In Problems 1–20, use De Moivre's theorem to evaluate the expression. Give your answer in both polar and rectangular forms. Do not use a calculator.

1. $[2(\cos 10° + j \sin 10°)]^3$.

2. $[3(\cos 25° + j \sin 25°)]^6$.

3. $[\sqrt{2}(\cos 15° + j \sin 15°)]^8$.

4. $[2(\cos 150° + j \sin 150°)]^4$.

5. $(\cos 40° + j \sin 40°)^{-6}$.

6. $[2(\cos 45° + j \sin 45°)]^{-3}$.

7. $(\sqrt{2} + j\sqrt{2})^5$.

8. $(-\sqrt{2} - j\sqrt{2})^4$.

9. $(-\sqrt{3} + j)^4$.

10. $\left(-\dfrac{\sqrt{3}}{2} - \dfrac{1}{2}j\right)^5$.

11. $(\sqrt{3} + j)^4$.

12. $\left(-\dfrac{1}{2} - j\dfrac{\sqrt{3}}{2}\right)^4$.

13. $(-\sqrt{2} + j\sqrt{2})^6$.

14. $(1 + j)^7$.

15. $(1 - j)^{10}$.

16. $(-\sqrt{2} + j\sqrt{2})^4$.

17. $\dfrac{(\sqrt{2} + j\sqrt{2})^{10}}{(\sqrt{3} + j)^{10}}$.

18. $\dfrac{(1 - j)^{15}}{(1 + j)^{12}}$.

19. $(-2 + 2j)^{-8}$.

20. $(1 - j\sqrt{3})^{-4}$.

In Problems **21–30**, *find the indicated roots. Give the answer in rectangular form if you can do so without using a calculator.*

21. Cube roots of 1.

22. Fourth roots of 16.

23. Square roots of $-8j$.

24. Cube roots of -4.

25. Square roots of j.

26. Fourth roots of $\frac{1}{2}(1 - j\sqrt{3})$.

27. Fourth roots of $2(-1 + j\sqrt{3})$.

28. Fifth roots of $1 + j$.

29. Sixth roots of $2 - 2j\sqrt{3}$.

30. Sixth roots of $-1 - j$.

In Problems **31–36**, *solve the given equation. Express your answer in rectangular form if you can do so without a calculator.*

31. $x^3 = 1$.

32. $x^4 = 1$.

33. $x^5 - 1 = 0$.

34. $x^6 - 1 = 0$.

35. $x^3 = 1 + j$.

36. $x^3 = -\sqrt{2} - j\sqrt{2}$.

13.7 REVIEW

Important Terms and Symbols

Section 13.1 j-operator, j, imaginary unit, pure imaginary number, complex number, $a + bj$, real part, imaginary part, imaginary number, (complex) conjugate, equality of complex numbers.

Section 13.3   Complex plane, real axis, imaginary axis, rectangular form, amplitude, argument, absolute value, magnitude, modulus, $|a + bj|$, polar form, $r(\cos\theta + j\sin\theta)$, $r\underline{/\theta}$, principal argument.

Section 13.4   Exponential form, Euler's formula.

Section 13.6   De Moivre's theorem, nth roots of a complex number.

Formula Summary

j-OPERATOR
$j^2 = -1, \qquad j = \sqrt{-1}$

POLAR FORM OF COMPLEX NUMBER

$$a + bj = r(\cos \theta + j \sin \theta) = r\underline{/\theta},$$

where $r = \sqrt{a^2 + b^2}$ and $\tan \theta = \dfrac{b}{a}$.

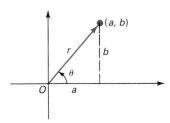

OPERATIONS IN POLAR FORM

$$(r_1\underline{/\theta_1})(r_2\underline{/\theta_2}) = r_1 r_2\underline{/\theta_1 + \theta_2}. \qquad \frac{r_1\underline{/\theta_1}}{r_2\underline{/\theta_2}} = \frac{r_1}{r_2}\underline{/\theta_1 - \theta_2}.$$

DE MOIVRE'S THEOREM

$$[r(\cos \theta + j \sin \theta)]^n = r^n(\cos n\theta + j \sin n\theta)$$

EXPONENTIAL FORM

$$z = re^{j\theta},$$

where $e^{j\theta}$ is given by Euler's formula

$$e^{j\theta} = \cos \theta + j \sin \theta.$$

Review Questions

1. The powers j^2, j^3, j^4, j^5, and j^{-2} are equal, respectively, to _____.

2. The real part of $3 - 4j$ is ___(a)___ and the imaginary part is ___(b)___.

3. Among the numbers $\sqrt[3]{-8}$, $\sqrt{-2}$, and $\sqrt{(-2)(-2)}$, which are pure imaginary? _____

4. The number $a + bj$ is the conjugate of what number? _____

5. The product of a complex number and its conjugate is $\underset{\text{(always)(sometimes)}}{}$ a real number.

6. In the representation of a complex number $a + bj$ in the complex plane, the absolute value of $a + bj$ is the distance from $(0, 0)$ to the point ___(a)___. This distance is given by the expression ___(b)___.

7. Representation of a complex number in polar form $\underset{\text{(is)(is not)}}{}$ unique.

8. A polar form for 8 is _____.

9. In rectangular form, $3(\cos 270° + j \sin 270°)$ is equal to _____.

10. The division $\dfrac{1}{1 - j}$ is performed by multiplying the numerator and denominator by

_____.

11. $\sqrt{(-2)(-2)}$ equals ___(a)___ but $\sqrt{-2}\sqrt{-2}$ equals ___(b)___.

12. The nth roots of 1 lie on a circle of radius ___(a)___ and determine the vertices of a regular polygon of ___(b)___ sides.

13. The imaginary part of a complex number $\underset{\text{(is)(is not)}}{}$ a real number.

14. If $1 + zj = 0$, then z equals _____.

15. The square of a pure imaginary number $\underset{\text{(is)(is not)}}{}$ a real number.

16. In the complex plane, the vector representing the number $-2 + j\sqrt{3}$ has its initial point at ___(a)___ and terminates at the point ___(b)___.

17. If z is a sixth root of $-2 + j\sqrt{3}$, then z^6 equals _____.

18. In the complex plane, $e^{j\theta}$ is a point on a circle with radius _____.

Answers to Review Questions

1. $-1, -j, 1, j, -1$.   2. (a) 3,   (b) -4.   3. $\sqrt{-2}$.   4. $a - bj$.   5. Always.
6. (a) (a, b),   (b) $\sqrt{a^2 + b^2}$.   7. Is not.   8. $8(\cos 0° + j \sin 0°)$.   9. $-3j$.   10. $1 + j$.
11. (a) 2,   (b) -2.   12. (a) 1,   (b) n.   13. Is.   14. j.   15. Is.
16. (a) $(0, 0)$,   (b) $(-2, \sqrt{3})$.   17. $-2 + j\sqrt{3}$.   18. 1.

Review Problems

In Problems 1–20, perform the operations and simplify.

1. $(8 - 3j) + 2(6 + 4j)$.
2. $9j^2 - 3j + 2j^3$.
3. $(4 + 3j) - (6 + j) + 10j$.
4. $3j(1 + 2j)$.
5. $(1 + 2j)(3 + 4j)$.
6. $(1 - j)^2$.
7. $(2 + j)(2 - j)$.
8. $(2 - 5j) + j(6j)$.
9. $\dfrac{4 + 2j}{3 + j}$.
10. $\dfrac{3j}{6 - 2j}$.
11. $-\sqrt{-3} + \sqrt{-12} + 2$.
12. $\sqrt{-8}(1 - \sqrt{-2})$.
13. $(1 + \sqrt{-4})(1 + \sqrt{-9})$.
14. $\dfrac{2}{2 + \sqrt{-25}}$.

15. $8 + 2j - j(2 + j) + 5j^3 - \sqrt{-4}$.

16. $(2 + j)(3 - 3j) - 6j(j + 7)$.

17. $\dfrac{7}{j + 2}$.

18. $\dfrac{j - 6}{5 + 2j}$.

19. $\dfrac{2 + j}{(1 + j)(2 - j)}$.

20. $(3 + 2j)(3 - 2j) - (1 + 3j)^2$.

In Problems 21-24, solve the equations.

21. $2x - 5 - 2x^2 = 0$.

22. $3x^2 - 2x + 6 = 0$.

23. $3(t - 1) = 2t^2$.

24. $x^2 + 5 = -1(1 - x)$.

In Problems 25-32, express in polar form.

25. $4\sqrt{2} + 4j\sqrt{2}$.

26. $\dfrac{3}{5} - \dfrac{3\sqrt{3}}{5}j$.

27. $-\dfrac{\sqrt{3}}{2} + \dfrac{j}{2}$.

28. $-27j$.

29. $7 - 8j$.

30. $-0.3 - 0.2j$.

31. $3e^{\pi j/4}$.

32. $2e^{1.5j}$.

In Problems 33-38, express in rectangular form.

33. $\sqrt{3}(\cos 315° + j \sin 315°)$.

34. $\frac{1}{2}(\cos 210° + j \sin 210°)$.

35. $\sqrt{2}(\cos 135° + j \sin 135°)$.

36. $\frac{2}{3}(\cos 60° + j \sin 60°)$.

37. $3(\cos 22.1° + j \sin 22.1°)$.

38. $2.4\underline{/320.7°}$.

In Problems 39-45, perform the indicated operations and give each answer in polar and rectangular forms.

39. $2(\cos 341° + j \sin 341°) \cdot 3(\cos 109° + j \sin 109°)$.

40. $(1.4\underline{/40°})(7.5\underline{/75.2°})$.

41. $\dfrac{\sqrt{8}(\cos 284° + j \sin 284°)}{\sqrt{2}(\cos 59° + j \sin 59°)}$.

42. $\dfrac{0.780\underline{/42°}}{0.156\underline{/73°}}$.

43. $[2.4(\cos 10° + j \sin 10°)]^5$.

44. $\dfrac{(3\underline{/23°})^4}{(2\underline{/17°})^5}$.

45. $\dfrac{[2(\cos 22° + j \sin 22°)]^8 \cdot [3(\cos 125° + j \sin 125°)]^5}{[3(\cos 78° + j \sin 78°)]^4 \cdot [2(\cos 139° + j \sin 139°)]^2}$.

In Problems 46-48, give all answers in polar form.

46. Find all square roots of $-1 + j\sqrt{3}$.

47. Find all fifth roots of $-\sqrt{2} - j\sqrt{2}$.

48. Find all eighth roots of 1.

In Problems 49-52, express in exponential form.

49. $5j$.

50. $-1 + j\sqrt{3}$.

51. $-1 + j$.

52. 9.

SEC. 13.7 Review **519**

53. In the analysis of a circuit, the current was found to be $100/(4 + 6j)$ amperes. What is the absolute value of the current?

54. In an alternating current series circuit, the admittance Y is expressed as the reciprocal of the impedance Z. If $Z = 16.8 - 22.1j$, find Y.

55. The current I through a particular circuit is given by $I = V/Z$, where I is in amperes, voltage V is in volts, and impedance Z is in ohms.
    (a) Find I if $V = 8.1 - 2.0j$ and $Z = 5.6 - 0.3j$.
    (b) Find Z if $I = 1 + j$ and $V = 1 - j$.

56. Suppose $R + \left(\omega L - \dfrac{1}{\omega C} \right) j = re^{j\theta}$. Find r and $\tan \theta$.

14

Variation

14.1 DIRECT VARIATION

In both science and engineering, the concept of *variation* is used to describe special types of functional relationships between variable quantities. In this chapter we shall discuss the three types of variation that occur, namely, *direct variation, joint variation,* and *inverse variation.*

If x and y are variables and the ratio of y to x is constant, we refer to the relationship between x and y as **direct variation**. For instance, the equation

$$\frac{y}{x} = 4 \tag{1}$$

defines a direct variation relationship between x and y. Table 14.1 shows some typical values for x and y as well as the constant quotient y/x. To describe the way in which x

TABLE 14.1

x	y	$\dfrac{y}{x}$
1	4	$\frac{4}{1} = 4$
3	12	$\frac{12}{3} = 4$
5	20	$\frac{20}{5} = 4$

521

and y are related, we say that y *varies directly as* x, or y *is directly proportional to* x. The constant 4 is called the *constant of variation*, or the *constant of proportionality*.

We can view direct variation another way. By writing Eq. 1 as

$$y = 4x, \tag{2}$$

we conclude that saying "y is directly proportional to x" means that y is a constant multiple of x. That is, Eq. 2 has the form

$$y = kx, \tag{3}$$

where k is a constant. It is worth noting that Eq. 3 defines a linear function, so the relationship "y is directly proportional to x" gives rise to a straight-line graph.

As another example of the constant-multiple approach to direct variation, consider the formula for the circumference of a circle:

$$C = 2\pi r.$$

This states that the circumference C varies directly as the radius r. Here the constant of variation is 2π because $C = (2\pi)r = kr$.

We shall now give a more general definition of direct variation so that it applies when y is a constant multiple of a *power* of x, such as x^2 or x^3.

The statement **y varies directly as the nth power of x** (for $n > 0$), or **y is directly proportional to the nth power of x**, means that

$$y = kx^n,$$

where k is a nonzero constant called the **constant of variation**, or the **constant of proportionality**.

Example 1

The formula

$$A = \pi r^2 \qquad (r > 0)$$

expresses the area A of a circle as a function of the radius r (in centimeters). It states that the area is directly proportional to the *square* of the radius. Here the constant of proportionality is π. The graph of $A = \pi r^2$ (see Fig. 14.1) shows that the greater the radius, the greater is the area. It is typical for direct variation (with $k > 0$) that the value of the dependent variable increases as the value of the independent variable increases.

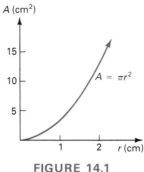

FIGURE 14.1

If we have a direct variation relationship and are given a pair of corresponding values for the variables involved, we can determine the constant of variation k. As a result, we can then obtain the specific formula that expresses the relationship. The next two examples illustrate the steps to follow.

Example 2

Suppose y varies directly as x^3, and $y = 4$ when $x = 2$. (a) Find the function that relates x and y. (b) Find y when $x = 10$.

Solution

a. Because y varies directly as x^3, by definition we have

$$y = kx^3. \tag{4}$$

We are given that $y = 4$ when $x = 2$. Substituting these values into Eq. 4 and solving for k give

$$4 = k(2)^3$$
$$4 = 8k$$
$$k = \tfrac{4}{8} = \tfrac{1}{2}.$$

Replacing k in Eq. 4 by $\tfrac{1}{2}$ gives the function that relates y and x.

$$y = \frac{1}{2}x^3. \tag{5}$$

(You should realize that k can be determined if *any* pair of corresponding values of y and x are known, except $y = 0$ when $x = 0$.)

b. Setting $x = 10$ in Eq. 5, we obtain the corresponding value of y.

$$y = \frac{1}{2}(10)^3 = \frac{1}{2}(1000) = 500.$$

Example 3

Hooke's law states that if the elastic limit is not exceeded, the force F exerted by a spring on an attached body is directly proportional to the displacement x of the end of the spring from its unstretched position. If a 40-N force results from a displacement of 5 cm, what displacement corresponds to a 10-N force?

Solution Because F is directly proportional to x, we have $F = kx$. From the given data, $F = 40$ N when $x = 5$ cm. We proceed to find k.

$$F = kx \qquad (6)$$

$$40 \text{ N} = k(5 \text{ cm})$$

$$k = \frac{40 \text{ N}}{5 \text{ cm}} = 8 \frac{\text{N}}{\text{cm}}.$$

Therefore, from Eq. 6, the equation that relates F and x is

$$F = \left(8 \frac{\text{N}}{\text{cm}}\right)x. \qquad (7)$$

To find x when $F = 10$ N, we substitute into Eq. 7:

$$10 \text{ N} = \left(8 \frac{\text{N}}{\text{cm}}\right)x$$

$$x = \frac{10 \text{ N}}{8 \text{ N/cm}} = \frac{5}{4} \text{ cm}.$$

In the last step, observe the algebraic treatment of the units involved.

The definition of direct variation can be extended to the case where one variable varies directly as the *product* of powers of other variables. We call this **joint variation**.

> The statement y **varies jointly as** x^m **and** z^n, or y **is directly proportional to the product of** x^m **and** z^n, means that
>
> $$y = kx^m z^n$$
>
> for some nonzero constant k (where $m, n > 0$).

Example 4

Suppose y varies jointly as the square of x and the cube root of z. If $y = 1$ when $x = 1$ and $z = 2$, find y when $x = 2$ and $z = 16$.

Solution Because y varies jointly as the square of x and the cube root of z,

$$y = kx^2 \sqrt[3]{z}. \qquad (8)$$

Substituting the given values ($y = 1$, $x = 1$, $z = 2$) and solving for k, we have

$$1 = k(1)^2 \sqrt[3]{2}$$

$$k = \frac{1}{\sqrt[3]{2}}.$$

Thus from Eq. 8,

$$y = \frac{1}{\sqrt[3]{2}} x^2 \sqrt[3]{z}.$$

When $x = 2$ and $z = 16$,

$$y = \frac{1}{\sqrt[3]{2}} (2)^2 \sqrt[3]{16} = 4 \sqrt[3]{\frac{16}{2}} = 4\sqrt[3]{8} = 8.$$

Example 5

The kinetic energy K of a particle is directly proportional to the product of the mass m of the particle and the square of the particle's speed v. When a particle of mass 0.1 kg has a speed of 20 m/s, its kinetic energy is 20 kg m^2/s^2. What is the kinetic energy of the same particle when its speed is 10 m/s?

Solution From the statement of the problem,

$$K = kmv^2.$$

Substituting the data and solving for k,

$$20 \frac{\text{kg m}^2}{\text{s}^2} = k(0.1 \text{ kg})\left(20 \frac{\text{m}}{\text{s}}\right)^2$$

$$20 \frac{\text{kg m}^2}{\text{s}^2} = 40k \frac{\text{kg m}^2}{s^2}$$

$$k = \frac{1}{2}.$$

Thus

$$K = \frac{1}{2} mv^2.$$

Note that here the constant of proportionality has no units associated with it. Now, when $m = 0.1$ kg and $v = 10$ m/s,

$$K = \frac{1}{2} (0.1 \text{ kg})\left(10 \frac{\text{m}}{\text{s}}\right)^2$$

$$= 5 \frac{\text{kg} \cdot \text{m}^2}{\text{s}^2}.$$

You may recall from Sec. 3.5 that this basic SI unit of energy, kg·m^2/s^2, is called a joule (J). Thus $K = 5$ J.

Example 6

The volume V of a cylinder varies jointly as the height h and the square of the radius r.

a. Suppose that two cylinders have heights h_1 and h_2, radii r_1 and r_2, and volumes V_1 and V_2, respectively. Find a general formula, in the form of a proportion, that relates these values but does not involve the constant of variation.

Solution   We have

$$V = kr^2h.$$

For the first set of values, V_1, r_1, and h_1,

$$V_1 = kr_1^2h_1.$$

Thus

$$\frac{V_1}{r_1^2 h_1} = k. \qquad (9)$$

Similarly, for the second set of values, V_2, r_2, and h_2,

$$\frac{V_2}{r_2^2 h_2} = k. \qquad (10)$$

From Eqs. 9 and 10 and substitution we get the proportion

$$\frac{V_1}{r_1^2 h_1} = \frac{V_2}{r_2^2 h_2}. \qquad (11)$$

b. How is the volume affected if h is increased by 20% and r is decreased by 10%?

Solution   Let the initial set of values of V, r, and h be V_1, r_1, and h_1. Because h is increased by 20%, its new value is $h_1 + 0.2h_1$, or $1.2h_1$. The new value of r is $r_1 - 0.1r_1$, or $0.9r_1$. We denote the new value of V by V_2. Substituting these values into Eq. 11 gives

$$\frac{V_1}{r_1^2 h_1} = \frac{V_2}{(0.9r_1)^2(1.2h_1)}.$$

Solving for V_2 and simplifying,

$$V_2 = \frac{(0.9r_1)^2(1.2h_1)V_1}{r_1^2 h_1}$$

$$= \frac{(0.81r_1^2)(1.2h_1)V_1}{r_1^2 h_1}$$

$$= (0.81)(1.2)V_1,$$

$$V_2 = 0.972V_1.$$

Thus the volume is 97.2% of its initial value. Equivalently, the volume is decreased by 2.8%.

Problem Set 14.1

In Problems 1–6, express the given statement as an equation.

1. s varies directly as t.
2. z varies directly as $\sqrt{w}$.
3. y is directly proportional to the fourth power of x.
4. V is directly proportional to the cube of r.
5. w varies jointly as x^2 and $\sqrt{z}$.
6. s is directly proportional to the product of x, the square of y, and the cube root of z.

In Problems 7–10, find the constant of variation.

7. y is directly proportional to x^2, and $y = 18$ when $x = 3$.
8. s is directly proportional to t^3, and $s = 10$ when $t = 2$.
9. w is directly proportional to the product of s^3 and z^2, and $w = 1$ when $s = 8$ and $z = \frac{1}{2}$.
10. F varies jointly as the product of q_1 and q_2, and $F = 40$ when $q_1 = 2$ and $q_2 = 6$.

11. Suppose y varies directly as x, and $y = 8$ when $x = 2$.
    (a) Find the function that relates y and x.
    (b) Find y when $x = 6$.
12. Suppose y is directly proportional to x^3, and $y = 16$ when $x = 2$.
    (a) Find the function that relates y and x.
    (b) Find y when $x = 3$.
13. Suppose y is directly proportional to x^2, and $y = 2$ when $x = 4$. Find y when $x = 6$.
14. Suppose y is directly proportional to $\sqrt{x}$, and $y = 4$ when $x = 25$. Find y when $x = 16$.
15. Suppose y varies jointly as x and z^2, and $y = 6$ when $x = 2$ and $z = \frac{1}{2}$. Find y when $x = 4$ and $z = \sqrt{2}$.
16. Suppose y varies jointly as $\sqrt{x}$ and $\sqrt{z}$. Find y when $x = 4$ and $z = 8$, if $y = 11$ when $x = 2$ and $z = 1$.
17. The elongation of a supporting cable varies directly as the load if the elastic limit is not exceeded. Find the elongation (in centimeters) when the load is 1000 N, if a load of 300 N causes an elongation of 0.6 cm.
18. The volume V of a sphere is directly proportional to the cube of the radius r. If a sphere has a volume of 36π cm^3 when the radius is 3 cm, find the volume when the radius is 5 cm.
19. If a body is dropped from rest and falls freely, the distance d that it falls below its starting point is directly proportional to the square of the elapsed time t. If a body falls 144 ft in 3 s, how far does it fall in 4 s?
20. In the equation $f = \dfrac{1}{2L}\sqrt{\dfrac{T}{m}}$, where m is a constant, the frequency f of a vibrating string of fixed length L is directly proportional to the square root of the tension T in the string, because

$$f = \frac{1}{2L\sqrt{m}}\sqrt{T} = k\sqrt{T}.$$

Show that T is directly proportional to the square of the frequency.

21. The weight W of an object is directly proportional to the product of the mass m of the object and the acceleration g due to gravity. Suppose a mass of 2 kg weighs 19.6 N on the earth's surface, where $g = 9.80$ m/s^2.
    (a) Find a formula for W and simplify by using the fact that 1 N $= 1$ kg·m/s^2.
    (b) Find what the same mass would weigh on the moon where $g = 1.67$ m/s^2.

22. Experiments indicate that thin rods, when heated, expand principally in one dimension along their lengths. The change in length of a rod, ΔL, varies jointly as the original length of the rod, L_0, and the change in temperature, Δt. Suppose a rod is initially 20 cm long at 50°C and then 20.0072 cm long at 80°C. Find its length at 110°C.

23. When a substance is heated without changing its state, the amount Q of heat added to the substance is directly proportional to the product of the mass m of the substance and the change in temperature, Δt. Suppose it requires 60 calories of heat to raise the temperature of 100 g of lead from 50° to 70°C. How many more calories are necessary to raise the temperature of the same mass an additional 10 Celsius degrees?

24. Total internal reflection of a light ray takes place at the boundary of two surfaces if the angle of incidence is greater than the critical angle for those surfaces. The sine of the critical angle θ_c varies directly as the ratio n_2/n_1 of the indices of refraction of the two surfaces. If the index of refraction of air is $n_2 = 1.00$ and that of glass is $n_1 = 1.50$ and the critical angle for an air-glass boundary is 42°, find the critical angle for an air-water boundary if the index of refraction of water is $n_1 = 1.33$. Give your answer to the nearest degree.

25. Experiments indicate that the potential difference V across an ohmic conductor varies jointly as the current i and the resistance R. This is known as Ohm's law. Suppose a conductor having a fixed resistance of x ohms has a potential difference of 30 V across it when it carries a current of 2 A. What is the potential difference across the same conductor when $i = 6$ A?

26. The angular deflection θ of a galvanometer is directly proportional to the product of the current i through the coil and the number n of turns in the coil. If a galvanometer deflects 60° for a current of 6 A, what would be the deflection, in radians, if the current is reduced to two-thirds of its original value?

27. When a space capsule is launched from a planet (or satellite), it can be shown, under simplifying assumptions, that the capsule must be given an initial speed (or escape velocity) v if it is to escape the planet's gravitational field and that v varies jointly as the square root of the radius r of the planet and the square root of the acceleration g due to gravity. The escape velocity on the earth is about 11.2 km/s. The radius of the earth is (approximately) four times that of the moon and the acceleration due to gravity on the earth is six times that of the moon. Find the escape velocity on the moon.

28. The potential V at a given point due to a number of distinct point charges varies directly as the algebraic sum of the ratios of the charges to the distances of the charges from the given point. Consider three point charges, two positive and one negative, all having magnitude q and equidistant from a given point. How is the potential at the given point affected if the negative charge is doubled in magnitude and one of the positive charges is moved three times as far away from the given point?

29. The volume V of a sphere is directly proportional to the cube of its radius r. If two spheres have volumes V_1 and V_2, and radii r_1 and r_2, show that the ratio of the volumes of the spheres is equal to the ratio of the cubes of their corresponding radii; that is,

$$\frac{V_1}{V_2} = \frac{r_1^3}{r_2^3}.$$

14.2 INVERSE VARIATION

Another type of functional relationship is known as *inverse variation*. This describes the situation when the *product* of two quantities is constant. For example, if

$$xy = 4$$

or, equivalently,

$$y = \frac{4}{x},$$

we say that y is **inversely proportional** to x. Here is a more general definition.

The statement y **varies inversely as the nth power of x** (for $n > 0$), or y **is inversely proportional to the nth power of x**, means that

$$y = \frac{k}{x^n},$$

where k is a nonzero constant called the **constant of variation** or the **constant of proportionality**.

For example, if y is inversely proportional to the square of x, then

$$y = \frac{k}{x^2}.$$

Figure 14.2 shows the graph of this function for $x, k > 0$. Observe that the values of y *decrease* as the values of x increase. As the values of x get smaller, the values of y get larger. *This is characteristic of inverse variation.* (Recall that with *direct* variation, the values of x and y get larger *together* or they get smaller *together*.)

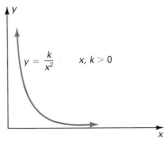

$$y = \frac{k}{x^2} \qquad x, k > 0$$

FIGURE 14.2

Example 1

If y varies inversely as the cube root of z, and $y = 2$ when $z = 2$, find y when $z = 8$.

Solution   Because y varies inversely as $\sqrt[3]{z}$,

$$y = \frac{k}{\sqrt[3]{z}}.$$

When $z = 2$, then $y = 2$:

$$2 = \frac{k}{\sqrt[3]{2}}$$

$$k = 2\sqrt[3]{2}.$$

Thus the function that relates y and z is

$$y = \frac{2\sqrt[3]{2}}{\sqrt[3]{z}}.$$

When $z = 8$,

$$y = \frac{2\sqrt[3]{2}}{\sqrt[3]{8}} = \frac{2\sqrt[3]{2}}{2} = \sqrt[3]{2}.$$

Example 2

The weight W of an object on or above the earth's surface is inversely proportional to the square of the distance r of the object from the center of the earth. Take the radius of the earth to be 6.37×10^6 m. If an astronaut weighs 800 N on the earth, what is the corresponding weight at an altitude of 5.63×10^6 m above the earth's surface?

Solution   Because W is inversely proportional to r^2,

$$W = \frac{k}{r^2}.$$

On the earth's surface, we have $W = 800$ N and $r = 6.37 \times 10^6$ m. Thus

$$800 \text{ N} = \frac{k}{(6.37 \times 10^6 \text{ m})^2}$$

$$k = 3.25 \times 10^{16} \text{ N} \cdot \text{m}^2.$$

At an altitude of 5.63×10^6 m, we have

$$r = (6.37 \times 10^6) + (5.63 \times 10^6)$$

$$= 1.20 \times 10^7 \text{ m}$$

and

$$W = \frac{k}{r^2} = \frac{3.25 \times 10^{16} \text{ N} \cdot \text{m}^2}{(1.20 \times 10^7 \text{ m})^2} = 226 \text{ N}.$$

Example 3

The resonant frequency f_r of a series ac circuit containing an inductance L and a capacitance C varies inversely as the square root of the product of L and C. If $f_r = 10{,}000/\pi$ hertz (Hz) when $L = 5 \times 10^{-3}$ henries (H) and $C = 5 \times 10^{-7}$ farads (F), find f_r in terms of π when $L = 4 \times 10^{-3}$ H and $C = 9 \times 10^{-7}$ F.

Solution   Because f_r varies inversely as $\sqrt{LC}$,

$$f_r = \frac{k}{\sqrt{LC}}$$

Substituting the given data,

$$\frac{10{,}000}{\pi} = \frac{k}{\sqrt{(5 \times 10^{-3})(5 \times 10^{-7})}}$$

$$k = \frac{10{,}000}{\pi} \sqrt{(5 \times 10^{-3})(5 \times 10^{-7})}$$

$$= \frac{10{,}000}{\pi} \sqrt{25 \times 10^{-10}}$$

$$= \frac{10{,}000}{\pi} (5)(10^{-5}) = \frac{0.5}{\pi} = \frac{1}{2\pi}.$$

Thus

$$f_r = \frac{1}{2\pi\sqrt{LC}}.$$

If $L = 4 \times 10^{-3}$ and $C = 9 \times 10^{-7}$,

$$f_r = \frac{1}{2\pi\sqrt{(4 \times 10^{-3})(9 \times 10^{-7})}} = \frac{1}{2\pi(6 \times 10^{-5})}$$

$$= \frac{10^5}{12\pi} \text{ Hz}.$$

Sometimes a variable simultaneously varies directly as one quantity and inversely as another quantity. We speak of this situation as **combined variation**, which Example 4 illustrates.

Example 4

If y varies directly as x and inversely as z, find y when $x = 6$ and $z = 2$, if $y = 4$ when $x = 5$ and $z = 4$.

Solution   We express the fact that y varies directly as x and inversely as z by writing

$$y = \frac{kx}{z}.$$

Now, $y = 4$ when $x = 5$ and $z = 4$; therefore

$$4 = \frac{k \cdot 5}{4}$$

$$k = \frac{16}{5}.$$

Thus

$$y = \frac{\frac{16}{5}x}{z} = \frac{16x}{5z}.$$

When $x = 6$ and $z = 2$, we have

$$y = \frac{16(6)}{5(2)} = \frac{48}{5}.$$

Problem Set 14.2

*In Problems **1–8**, express the given statement as an equation.*

1. y is inversely proportional to the cube of x.
2. s varies inversely as $\sqrt{t}$.
3. w varies inversely as the product of m_1 and m_2.
4. R is directly proportional to l and inversely proportional to the square of d.
5. w varies directly as the square of x and inversely as z.
6. y varies jointly as x and z^2 and inversely as the cube of w.
7. w varies jointly as a and b and inversely as c and d.
8. y varies directly as x^2 and inversely as s and t.

*In Problems **9–12**, find the constant of variation.*

9. y varies inversely as $\sqrt{x}$, and $y = 2$ when $x = 4$.
10. s is inversely proportional to t^2, and $s = 9$ when $t = 2$.
11. p is directly proportional to w and inversely proportional to d^2; $p = 4$ when $w = 2$ and $d = \sqrt{2}$.

12. z varies inversely as x and y^2; $z = 4$ when $x = 2$ and $y = 2$.

13. Suppose y is inversely proportional to x, and $y = 12$ when $x = 3$.
    (a) Find the function that relates y and x.
    (b) Find y when $x = 4$.

14. Suppose p is inversely proportional to t^3, and $p = \frac{1}{36}$ when $t = 3$.
    (a) Find the function that relates p and t.
    (b) Find p when $t = 2$.

15. Suppose r varies directly as s and inversely as t^2, and $r = 10$ when $s = 1$ and $t = 2$.
    (a) Find the function that relates r to s and t.
    (b) Find r when $s = 4$ and $t = 9$.

16. Suppose Q varies directly as $\sqrt{u}$ and inversely as v, and $Q = 1$ when $u = 4$ and $v = 4$. Find Q when $u = 9$ and $v = 2$.

17. Suppose y varies directly as x^2 and inversely as z, and $y = 8$ when $x = 2$ and $z = 2$. Find y when $x = 3$ and $z = 4$.

18. Suppose y varies jointly as x^2 and z and inversely as $\sqrt{w}$, and $y = 12$ when $x = 1$, $z = 3$, and $w = 4$. Find y when $x = 4$, $z = 2$, and $w = \pi^2$. Give your answer in terms of π.

19. Suppose a varies jointly as b^2 and c^3 and inversely as d^2, and $a = 25$ when $b = 2$, $c = 2$, and $d = 2$. Find a when $b = 3$, $c = 2$ and $d = 1$.

20. Suppose y varies directly as x and inversely as $\sin z$, and $y = 7$ when $x = 4$ and $z = \pi/2$. Find y when $x = \sqrt{2}$ and $z = \pi/4$.

21. Newton's second law of motion states that when a mass m is acted upon by a force F, the acceleration a of the mass is directly proportional to F and inversely proportional to m. If a mass of 50 kg initially at rest on a horizontal surface is acted upon by a force of 500 N, the acceleration is 10 m/s^2. What force would give a mass of 30 kg an acceleration of 75 m/s^2?

22. The resistance of a copper wire varies directly as its length and inversely as its cross-sectional area. A copper wire of length 500 cm and radius 0.2 cm has a resistance of 0.025 Ω. What will the resistance be for the same copper wire of length 1000 cm and radius 0.1 cm?

23. Under certain conditions, the illumination E of a surface varies directly as the intensity I of the light source and inversely as the square of the distance r of the surface from the source. What is the effect on the illumination if the intensity and distance are both doubled?

24. Coulomb's law states that the force F of attraction or repulsion between two electrostatic point charges of magnitudes q_1 and q_2 is directly proportional to the product of the magnitudes of the charges and inversely proportional to the square of the distance r between them. If the magnitude of one charge is doubled and the distance between charges is reduced by a factor of one-half, how is the force affected?

25. In Example 2, at what altitude above the earth's surface must the astronaut be if his weight is to be 1% of his weight on the earth's surface?

26. The capacitance of a parallel-plate capacitor varies directly as the area of either of its plates and inversely as the separation of its plates. If the plates are 5 mm apart and 2 m^2 in area, the capacitance is 3.54×10^{-9} F. For square plates separated by 1 mm, what must be the length of a side for the capacitance to be 1 F? Based on your answer, would you expect to find a 1-F parallel-plate capacitor in practice?

27. Newton's law of gravitation states that the attractive force F between masses m_1 and m_2 varies directly as the product of the masses and inversely as the square of the distance r

between their centers. If the centers of two 10-kg masses are 1 m apart, then $F = 6.67 \times 10^{-9}$ N. Find F when two 100-kg masses are 1 m apart.

28. Given a volume V containing n moles of gas at temperature T, the ideal gas law states that the pressure P of the gas is directly proportional to the product of n and T and inversely proportional to V. If the volume of a particular sample of an ideal gas is reduced to one-third its original value during an isothermal process, one that takes place at constant temperature, what happens to the pressure of the gas?

29. Suppose that in a laboratory experiment you took measurements of two related quantities, x and y, and obtained the following pairs of values:

x	3	6	12
y	240	60	15

Based on these data, would you conjecture that x varies inversely as y, or inversely as $\sqrt{y}$? To support your conclusion, find an equation that relates x and y.

30. In studies of electric fields, it is shown that the electric field intensity E at a distance r from an isolated point charge varies directly as the charge q and inversely as the square of the distance r. If a point charge of 2×10^{-9} C sets up an electric field intensity of 2 N/C at a distance of 3 m from the charge, what is the electric field intensity for the same charge at a distance of 6 m from the charge?

31. The volume V of a gas varies directly as its absolute temperature T and inversely as its pressure P. If two different sets of conditions are V_1, T_1, P_1 and V_2, T_2, P_2, show that

$$\frac{V_1 P_1}{T_1} = \frac{V_2 P_2}{T_2}.$$

14.3 REVIEW

Important Terms and Symbols

Section 14.1   Direct variation, y varies directly as x^n, y is directly proportional to x^n, constant of variation (k), constant of proportionality, joint variation.

Section 14.2   Inverse variation, y varies inversely as x^n, y is inversely proportional to x^n, combined variation.

Formula Summary

Direct variation	$y = kx^n$.
Joint variation	$y = kx^m z^n$.
Inverse variation	$y = \dfrac{k}{x^n}.$

Review Questions

1. The statement that y varies directly as x means that the ratio of y to x is a _____.
2. If y is directly proportional to the product of x and w, then $y = kxw$. For this statement we can also say that y varies _____ as x and w.
3. If $y = kL^2/\sqrt{w}$, then y varies ___(a)___ as L^2 and ___(b)___ as $\sqrt{w}$.
4. If y varies inversely as x^2, then the _____ of y and x^2 is a constant.

Answers to Review Questions

1. Constant.   2. Jointly.   3. (a) Directly, (b) Inversely.   4. Product.

Review Problems

1. Suppose y varies directly as x and inversely as w, and $y = 7$ when $x = 2$ and $w = 3$. Find y when $x = 1$ and $w = 4$.
2. Suppose y varies directly as x^2 and inversely as $\sqrt{w}$. If $y = 2$ when $x = 3$ and $w = 4$, find y when $x = \frac{1}{3}$ and $w = 9$.
3. Suppose y varies jointly as x^2 and w and inversely as z. If $y = 1$ when $x = 1$, $w = 2$, and $z = 3$, find y when $x = 3$, $w = 2$, and $z = 1$.
4. Suppose y varies directly as $x^{3/2}$ and inversely as $\sqrt{z}$, and $y = 8$ when $x = 4$ and $z = 3$. Find y when $x = 2$ and $z = 12$.
5. When a rod or cable is subjected to a stretching force, the stress is directly proportional to the strain produced. If, for a particular steel wire, the stress is $6.9 \times 10^7 \, \text{N/m}^2$ when the strain is $1/3000$, what is the stress when the strain is $1/2000$?
6. When an object is released from rest and falls freely, its speed varies directly as the square root of the product of the acceleration due to gravity and the distance fallen. Take the acceleration due to gravity to be $9.8 \, \text{m/s}^2$. If a body acquires a speed of $9.9 \, \text{m/s}$ after falling a distance of 5 m, what is its speed after falling 8 m?
7. Determine whether the given statement is true or false.
   (a) If y varies directly as x, then x varies directly as y.
   (b) If y varies inversely as x, then x varies inversely as y.
   (c) If y is inversely proportional to x, it is typical that y increases as x increases.
8. If I varies inversely as the square of d, what is the effect on I if d is tripled?
9. When a body travels in a circle at a constant speed, it is acted upon by a centripetal force, which varies jointly as the mass of the body and the square of its speed and inversely as the radius of the circle. If a 2-kg mass traveling in a circle of radius 5 m with a speed of 10 m/s is acted upon by a centripetal force of 40 N, what force acts upon a 3-kg mass traveling in a circle of radius 6 m at a speed of 8 m/s?
10. In some spectographic instruments, a charged particle is projected perpendicularly in a field of magnetic induction B. Under this condition the particle travels in a circle of radius R. The radius is directly proportional to the product of the mass m and speed v of the particle and inversely proportional to the product of the charge q on the particle and the magnetic induction B. If a charge of mass m_0 travels in a circle of radius 2 m in a magnetic field, what must be the mass of a charged particle with three times the charge if it is to travel in the same circle in the same field with the same speed?

11. The rate at which heat is transferred through a metal rod varies jointly as the cross-sectional area of the rod and the difference in temperature between its ends and inversely as the length of the rod. If 12,500 cal/s (calories per second) is transmitted through an aluminum rod 0.5 cm long of cross-sectional area 500 cm² when the temperature difference between its ends is 25 C°, at what rate is heat transferred through a rod of the same material and length if its cross-sectional area is 600 cm² and the temperature difference is 80 C°?

12. Under certain conditions, the velocity of an object varies jointly as its acceleration, which is constant, and the time it has been in motion.
    (a) If the velocity is 29.4 m/s after 3 s, what is the velocity after $\frac{1}{2}$ s?
    (b) If the acceleration is 9.8 m/s², what is the constant of variation?

15

Exponential and Logarithmic Functions

15.1 EXPONENTIAL FUNCTIONS

It is not unusual for a physical quantity, such as the charge on a discharging capacitor, the temperature of a cooling body, and the amount of a radioactive substance, to be described mathematically by a function involving a constant raised to a variable power, like $f(x) = 2^x$. Such functions are called *exponential functions*. Do not confuse the exponential function $f(x) = 2^x$ with the *power function* $g(x) = x^2$, which has a variable base and a constant exponent.

The **exponential function** with base b is defined by

$$f(x) = b^x,$$

where $b > 0$, $b \neq 1$, and the exponent x is any real number.

The reason we excluded $b = 1$ is because $1^x = 1$ for all x.

Since the exponent in b^x can be any real number, you may wonder how we assign a value to an irrational power, like $6^{\sqrt{2}}$. Stated simply, we use approximations. First, $6^{\sqrt{2}}$ is approximately $6^{1.4} = 6^{7/5} = \sqrt[5]{6^7}$, which *is* defined. Better approximations are $6^{1.41} = 6^{141/100} = \sqrt[100]{6^{141}}$, and so on. In this way the meaning of $6^{\sqrt{2}}$ becomes clear.

537

Some functions that do not appear to have the exponential form b^x can be put in that form by applying rules for exponents. For example, $2^{-x} = 1/(2^x) = (\frac{1}{2})^x$ and $3^{2x} = (3^2)^x = 9^x$.

Figure 15.1 shows the graphs of the exponential functions $y = 2^x$, $y = 3^x$, and $y = (\frac{1}{2})^x$. Notice the following:

1. The domain of an exponential function is all real numbers.
2. The range is all positive real numbers. Thus b^x is positive for all x.
3. Since $b^0 = 1$ for every base b, each graph has y-intercept $(0, 1)$. There is no x-intercept. Each graph always lies above the x-axis.

x	2^x	3^x	$\left(\dfrac{1}{2}\right)^x$
-2	$\dfrac{1}{4}$	$\dfrac{1}{9}$	4
-1	$\dfrac{1}{2}$	$\dfrac{1}{3}$	2
0	1	1	1
1	2	3	$\dfrac{1}{2}$
2	4	9	$\dfrac{1}{4}$
3	8	27	$\dfrac{1}{8}$

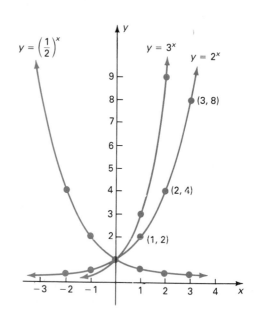

FIGURE 15.1

We also see in Fig. 15.1 that the graph of $y = b^x$ has one of two basic shapes, depending on whether $b > 1$ or $0 < b < 1$:

4. If $b > 1$, as in $y = 2^x$ and $y = 3^x$, then the graph of $y = b^x$ *rises* from left to right. That is, as x increases, y also increases. But y can also take on values very close to zero. (In quadrant II observe how the graph of $y = 3^x$ gets close to the x-axis. For example, if $x = -100$, then $3^x = 3^{-100} = 1/3^{100}$ is a number close to zero.) Notice also that in quadrant I, the greater the value of b, the more quickly the graph rises. (Compare the graphs of $y = 2^x$ and $y = 3^x$.)
5. If $0 < b < 1$, as in $y = (\frac{1}{2})^x$, then the graph of $y = b^x$ falls from left to right. As x increases, then y *decreases* and gets closer to 0.

One of the numbers most useful for a base in an exponential function is a certain irrational number denoted by the letter e, in honor of the Swiss mathematician and physicist Leonhard Euler (1707–1783):

$$e \text{ is approximately } 2.71828$$

Although e may seem to be a strange number to use as a base for an exponential function, it arises quite naturally in applied mathematics, science, and engineering technology. It occurs in many problems involving natural growth or decay.

Values of e^x can be obtained conveniently by using the $\boxed{e^x}$ key on a calculator (or $\boxed{\text{INV}}$ $\boxed{\text{LN}}$ on some calculators). For example, to find $e^{2.45}$, we key in 2.45 and press the $\boxed{e^x}$ key. You should verify that the (rounded) display is 11.588. The $\boxed{y^x}$ key can also be used to find values for an exponential function. (See Sec. A.5 in Appendix A for a further discussion.) The graph of $y = e^x$ is shown in Fig. 15.2.

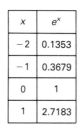

x	e^x
-2	0.1353
-1	0.3679
0	1
1	2.7183

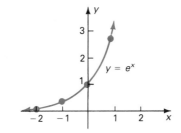

FIGURE 15.2

There are many physical quantities for which the rate of growth or decay at any time is proportional to the amount of the quantity present at that time. Examples are bacteria growth, decay of a radioactive element, and the decay of a current in some electrical circuits. Such growth or decay can be described in terms of a function of the form

$$Q = Q(t) = Q_0 e^{kt}, \tag{1}$$

where Q is the amount of the quantity at time t, and Q_0 and k are constants. Due to the form of Eq. 1, we say that the quantity has **exponential growth** if $k > 0$ and **exponential decay** if $k < 0.$* *If* $t = 0$ in Eq. 1, then

$$Q = Q_0 e^0 = Q_0(1) = Q_0.$$

Thus Q_0 represents the amount of the quantity present when $t = 0$; that is, Q_0 is the initial amount.

---

* Note that $e^{kt} = (e^k)^t = b^t$, where $b = e^k$. If $k > 0$, then $b > 1$ and so e^{kt} increases as t increases. If $k < 0$, then $0 < b < 1$ and e^{kt} decreases as t increases.

With exponential decay, to stress that k is negative it is customary to replace k by $-\lambda$, where λ (lambda) is a positive constant called the **decay constant**. Thus Eq. 1 becomes

$$Q = Q(t) = Q_0 e^{-\lambda t}. \tag{2}$$

Example 1

Suppose that the number Q of milligrams of a radioactive substance present after t years is given by the exponential decay function

$$Q = Q(t) = 100e^{-0.035t}.$$

How much of the substance is present initially? How many milligrams are present after 20 years?

Solution Comparing the given equation to Eq. 2 gives $Q_0 = 100$. Thus there are 100 mg present initially. That is, the value of $Q(t)$ is 100 when $t = 0$. After 20 years the amount present is $Q(20)$:

$$Q(20) = 100e^{-0.035(20)} = 49.66 \text{ mg}.$$

The time required for one-half of a radioactive substance to decay is called the **half-life** of the substance. It is the value of t for which $Q = Q_0/2$ in Eq. 2. For example, the half-life of radioactive carbon 14 (^{14}C) is approximately 5600 years. Figure 15.3 shows the graph of radioactive decay.

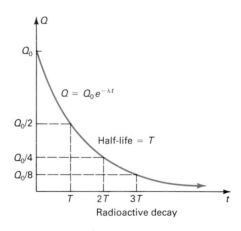

Radioactive decay

FIGURE 15.3

Problem Set 15.1

*In Problems **1–4**, graph the function.*

1. $y = 4^x$.   **2.** $y = (\frac{1}{3})^x$.   **3.** $f(t) = (\frac{1}{4})^t$.   **4.** $f(t) = 3^{t/2}$.

*In Problems **5–8**, use a calculator to find the value of the given number to four decimal places.*

5. $e^{2.4}$.   **6.** $e^{0.06}$.   **7.** $e^{-4.2}$.   **8.** $e^{-3.67}e^{2.87}$.

*In Problems **9–14**, find the function values. A calculator is not needed except for the last part of each problem, for which you should give your answer to four decimal places.*

9. $f(x) = 9^x$; $f(2)$, $f(-2)$, $f(\frac{1}{2})$, $f(2.8)$.

10. $g(x) = 4(3)^x$; $g(0)$, $g(2)$, $g(-1)$, $g(e)$.

11. $h(t) = 3(16)^{t/2}$; $h(1)$, $h(\frac{1}{2})$, $h(-\frac{1}{2})$, $h(-3.2)$.

12. $f(t) = 5 - (\frac{1}{2})^t$; $f(2)$, $f(3)$, $f(-3)$, $f(-4.3)$.

13. $g(x) = 1 + 2(\frac{1}{8})^{1-x}$; $g(1)$, $g(-1)$, $g(\frac{1}{3})$, $g(-e)$.

14. $h(x) = \dfrac{6(0.25)^{(4-x)/2}}{5}$; $h(0)$, $h(2)$, $h(3)$, $h(-0.4)$.

15. The number Q of milligrams of a radioactive substance present after t years is given by $Q = 75e^{-0.0244t}$.
   (a) How much of the substance is present initially?
   (b) How many milligrams are present after 14 years?

16. Show that the exponential decay function in Problem 15 can be expressed as $Q = 75(0.976)^t$.

17. The decaying current i, in amperes, in an ac circuit is given by $i = 10e^{-2t} \sin(100t)$, where time t is in seconds and the angle $100t$ is in radians. Find the current when $t = 1.2$ s.

18. The charge q on a discharging capacitor is given by $q = 8e^{-2.8t}$, where t is time in seconds and q is in microcoulombs. Find q when $t = 0.3$ s.

19. A function used in statistics is

$$f(x) = \frac{1}{\sqrt{2\pi}} e^{-x^2/2}.$$

Find $f(0)$, $f(-1)$, and $f(1)$. Give your answers to three decimal places.

15.2 LOGARITHMIC FUNCTIONS

The next functions of interest to us in this chapter are *logarithmic functions*, which are related to exponential functions. Figure 15.4 shows the graph of the exponential function $s = f(t) = 2^t$. Here f sends an input number t into a *positive* output number s. For example, f sends 2 into 4: $f(2) = 4$.

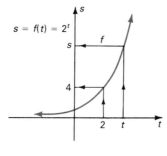

FIGURE 15.4

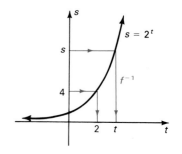

FIGURE 15.5

Now look at the same curve in Fig. 15.5. The direction of the small arrows conveys a different functional relationship. With each positive number s on the vertical axis, we can associate exactly one value of t. For example, with $s = 4$ we associate $t = 2$. By thinking of s as an input and t as an output, we have a function that sends values of s into values of t. We shall denote this function by f^{-1} (read f inverse). Thus

$$f^{-1}(4) = 2.$$

We caution you that the -1 in f^{-1} is not treated as an exponent, so f^{-1} does not mean $1/f$.

The functions f and f^{-1} are related. Figure 15.6 shows that f^{-1} *reverses* the

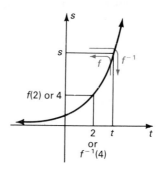

FIGURE 15.6

action of f, and vice versa. For example,

f sends 2 into 4   and f^{-1} sends 4 into 2.

More generally, for all possible values of s and t, we have $f(t) = s$ and $f^{-1}(s) = t$. The domain of f^{-1} is the range of f (all positive real numbers), and the range of f^{-1} is the domain of f (all real numbers).

We give a special name to f^{-1}. It is called the **logarithmic function with base 2** and is written as $\log_2$ [read *logarithm* (or log) *base* 2]. Thus $f^{-1}(4) = \log_2 4 = 2$, and we say that the *logarithm* base 2 of 4 is 2.

In summary,

$$\text{If } s = 2^t, \quad \text{then} \quad t = \log_2 s. \tag{1}$$

We now generalize our discussion to other bases. In Eq. 1, replacing 2 by b, s by x, and t by y gives the following definition.

The **logarithmic function** with base b, where $b > 0$ and $b \neq 1$, is denoted by $\log_b$ and is defined by

$$y = \log_b x \quad \text{if and only if} \quad b^y = x.$$

The domain of $\log_b$ is all positive numbers, and the range is all real numbers.

A logarithmic function reverses the action of the corresponding exponential function, and vice versa. Because of this, each logarithmic function is called the *inverse* of its corresponding exponential function, and that exponential function is the inverse of its corresponding logarithmic function.

Always remember: When we say that the log base b of x is y, we mean that b raised to the y power is x.

$$\log_b x = y \quad \text{means} \quad b^y = x.$$

In this sense, *a logarithm of a number is an exponent.* It is the power to which we must raise the base to get the number. For example,

$$\log_2 8 = 3 \quad \text{because} \quad 2^3 = 8.$$

We say that $\log_2 8 = 3$ is the **logarithmic form** of the **exponential form** $2^3 = 8$.

Example 1

	Exponential form		Logarithmic form
a. Since	$5^2 = 25,$	then	$\log_5 25 = 2.$
b. Since	$3^4 = 81,$	then	$\log_3 81 = 4.$
c. Since	$10^0 = 1,$	then	$\log_{10} 1 = 0.$

Example 2

	Logarithmic form		Exponential form
a.	$\log_{10} 1000 = 3$	means	$10^3 = 1000.$
b.	$\log_{64} 8 = \frac{1}{2}$	means	$64^{1/2} = 8.$
c.	$\log_2 \frac{1}{16} = -4$	means	$2^{-4} = \frac{1}{16}.$

Example 3

Graph the function $y = \log_2 x$.

Solution   It can be awkward to substitute values of x and then find corresponding values of y. For example, if $x = 3$, then $y = \log_2 3$, which is not easily determined. An easier way to plot points is to use the equivalent exponential form $x = 2^y$. We choose values of y and find the corresponding values of x. For example, if $y = 0$, then $x = 1$. This gives the point $(1, 0)$. When $y = 2$, then $x = 2^2 = 4$, and when $y = -1$, we have $x = 2^{-1} = \frac{1}{2}$. This gives the points $(4, 2)$ and $(\frac{1}{2}, -1)$. Other points are shown in Fig. 15.7. From the graph you can see that the domain is all positive real numbers. Thus *negative numbers and 0 do not have logarithms*. The range is all real numbers. Observe that as x increases, y increases. Numbers between 0 and 1 have negative logarithms, and the closer such a number is to 0, the more negative is its logarithm. The log of 1 is 0, which corresponds to the intercept $(1, 0)$. There is no y-intercept. This graph is typical for a logarithmic function with $b > 1$.

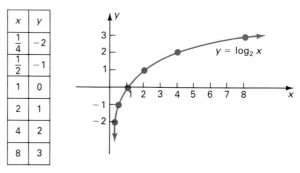

x	y
$\frac{1}{4}$	-2
$\frac{1}{2}$	-1
1	0
2	1
4	2
8	3

FIGURE 15.7

For many functions f, if $f(m) = f(n)$, this does not imply that $m = n$. For example, if $f(x) = x^2$ and $m = 2$ and $n = -2$, then $f(m) = f(n)$, but $m \neq n$. This is not the case for a logarithmic function. Because the graph in Fig. 15.7 is always rising, it is obvious that if two numbers are different, then their logarithms (y-values) are different. This means that if $\log_2 m = \log_2 n$, then $m = n$. Generalizing to base b, we have the following property:

$$\boxed{\text{If } \log_b m = \log_b n, \quad \text{then} \quad m = n.}$$ (1)

There is a similar property for the exponential function:

$$\boxed{\text{If } b^m = b^n, \quad \text{then} \quad m = n.}$$ (2)

Logarithms with base 10 are called **common logarithms**. The subscript 10 is usually omitted from the notation:

$$\log x \quad \text{means} \quad \log_{10} x.$$

Logarithms with base e are called **natural logarithms**. We use the notation ln for such logarithms:

$$\ln x \quad \text{means} \quad \log_e x.$$

Common and natural logarithms of numbers can be found with a calculator by using the log and ln keys, respectively. For example, you should verify that $\ln 2 \approx 0.69315$. This means that $e^{0.69315} \approx 2$. A discussion of these keys is found in Sec. A.7.

Figure 15.8 shows the graphs of $y = e^x$ and $y = \ln x$ on the same set of axes. If a mirror were placed along the line $y = x$, then each graph would be the mirror image of the other graph. The reason for this is that $y = e^x$ and $y = \ln x$ are inverses of each other, so the corresponding values for x and y are reversed. For example, $y = e^x$ crosses the y-axis at $(0, 1)$, so $y = \ln x$ crosses the x-axis at $(1, 0)$.

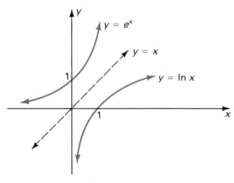

FIGURE 15.8

Example 4

Find each of the following without the aid of a calculator.

a. $\log 100$.

   Solution   Here the base is 10. Thus $\log 100$ is the power to which we must raise 10 to get 100. Since $10^2 = 100$, $\log 100 = 2$.

b. $\ln 1$.

   Solution   Here the base is e. Because $e^0 = 1$, $\ln 1 = 0$.

c. log 0.1.

Solution Since $0.1 = \frac{1}{10} = 10^{-1}$, log $0.1 = -1$.

d. ln e^{-1}.

Solution Since ln e^{-1} is the power to which e must be raised to get e^{-1}, clearly we have ln $e^{-1} = -1$.

e. $\log_{36} 6$.

Solution Because $36^{1/2}$ (or $\sqrt{36}$) is 6, $\log_{36} 6 = \frac{1}{2}$.

Example 5

Solve each equation for x.

a. $\log_3 x = 4$.

Solution In exponential form, $3^4 = x$. Thus $x = 81$.

b. ln $(x + 1) = 7$.

Solution The exponential form gives $e^7 = x + 1$. Thus $x = e^7 - 1$.

c. $\log_x 49 = 2$.

Solution In exponential form we have

$$\log_x 49 = 2$$
$$x^2 = 49$$
$$x = \pm 7.$$

A negative number cannot be a base for a logarithm, so we disregard $x = -7$ and choose $x = 7$.

d. $e^{0.2x} = 6$.

Solution In logarithmic form,

$$0.2x = \ln 6$$

$$x = \frac{\ln 6}{0.2} = 8.959.$$

e. $x + 1 = \log_4 16$.

Solution   Because $\log_4 16$ is 2, we have $x + 1 = 2$, from which $x = 1$. If you did not recognize that $\log_4 16 = 2$, then you could solve the equation in the following way.

$$x + 1 = \log_4 16$$

$$4^{x+1} = 16 \qquad \text{[converting to exponential form]}$$

$$4^{x+1} = 4^2.$$

From Property (2), $x + 1 = 2$, so $x = 1$.

When the logarithm of a number N is known, the process of finding N is referred to as finding the **antilogarithm**. Because this involves reversing the action of the logarithmic function, we can make use of the 10^x, e^x, or y^x exponential keys on a calculator, as Example 6 shows.

Example 6

a. If $\log N = 4.86052$, find N. That is, find antilog 4.86052.

Solution   Because $\log N = 4.86052$, in exponential form we have

$$N = 10^{4.86052} = 72{,}530.$$

That is, antilog $4.86052 = 72{,}530$.

b. If $\ln N = -5.37737$, find N. That is, find $\text{antilog}_e (-5.37737)$.

Solution

$$\text{antilog}_e (-5.37737) = e^{-5.37737} = 4.620 \times 10^{-3}.$$

Thus $N = 4.620 \times 10^{-3}$.

In the previous section the exponential decay function $Q = Q_0 e^{-\lambda t}$ was discussed. Recall that the value of t when $Q = Q_0/2$ is the half-life of a radioactive substance. We wish to find a formula for this value of t.

$$\frac{Q_0}{2} = Q_0 e^{-\lambda t}$$

$$\frac{1}{2} = e^{-\lambda t} \qquad \text{[dividing both sides by } Q_0 \text{]}.$$

In logarithmic form we have

$$-\lambda t = \ln \frac{1}{2} = -0.69315,$$

which means

$$t = \frac{0.69315}{\lambda}.$$

(3)

Note that the half-life depends on λ. That is, it depends on the substance and not on the amount of the substance.

Example 7

If 60% of a radioactive element remains after 50 d, find the decay constant and the half-life of the element.

Solution   We use the function $Q = Q_0 e^{-\lambda t}$, where Q_0 is the amount of the element present at $t = 0$ and λ is the decay constant. Because $Q = 0.6Q_0$ when $t = 50$, we have

$$0.6Q_0 = Q_0 e^{-50\lambda}$$

$$0.6 = e^{-50\lambda}$$

$$-50\lambda = \ln 0.6 \qquad \text{[logarithmic form]}$$

$$\lambda = -\frac{1}{50}\ln 0.6 = -\frac{1}{50}(-0.51083)$$

$$= 0.01022.$$

Thus the decay constant is 0.01022. The half-life, from Eq. 3, is

$$\frac{0.69315}{\lambda} = \frac{0.69315}{0.01022} = 67.82 \text{ d}.$$

Note that the unit of λ is the unit of 1/time. Here the unit is $1/\text{day} = (\text{day})^{-1}$.

Problem Set 15.2

In Problems 1–16, write each exponential form logarithmically and each logarithmic form exponentially.

1. $4^3 = 64$.

2. $2 = \log_{12} 144$.

3. $10^5 = 100{,}000$.

4. $\log_9 3 = \frac{1}{2}$.

5. $\log_2 64 = 6$.

6. $4^4 = 256$.

7. $\log_8 2 = \frac{1}{3}$.

8. $8^{2/3} = 4$.

9. $6^0 = 1$.

10. $\log_{1/2} 4 = -2$.

11. $\log_2 x = 14$.

12. $10^{0.48302} = 3.041$.

13. $e^2 = 7.3891$.

14. $e^{0.33647} = 1.4$.

15. $\ln 3 = 1.0986$.

16. $\log 5 = 0.6990$.

In Problems **17** *and* **18**, *graph the function.*

17. $y = f(x) = \log_3 x$.   18. $y = f(x) = \log_{1/2} x$.

In Problems **19–22**, *use a calculator to find the value of the given number to four decimal places.*

19. $\ln 7.34$.   20. $\ln 3.1$.   21. $\log 0.2538$.   22. $\log 5988$.

In Problems **23–36**, *find the value of each number without the aid of a calculator.*

23. $\log_6 36$.   24. $\log_2 32$.   25. $\log_3 27$.
26. $\log_{27} 3$.   27. $\log_{16} 4$.   28. $\log_7 7$.
29. $\log 10$.   30. $\log 10,000$.   31. $\log 0.01$.
32. $\ln e^4$.   33. $\log_5 1$.   34. $\log_2 \sqrt{2}$.
35. $\log_2 \frac{1}{8}$.   36. $\log_5 \frac{1}{25}$.

In Problems **37–60**, *find x without the aid of a calculator.*

37. $\log_3 x = 2$.   38. $\log_2 x = 4$.   39. $\log_5 x = 3$.
40. $\log_4 x = 0$.   41. $\log x = -1$.   42. $\ln x = 1$.
43. $\ln x = 2$.   44. $\log_x 100 = 2$.   45. $\log_x 8 = 3$.
46. $\log_x 3 = \frac{1}{2}$.   47. $\log_x \frac{1}{6} = -1$.   48. $\log_x y = 1$.
49. $\log_4 16 = x$.   50. $\log_3 1 = x$.   51. $\log 10^{-7} = x$.
52. $\log_2 \frac{1}{16} = x$.   53. $\log_{25} 5 = x$.   54. $\log_9 9 = x$.
55. $\log_3 x = -4$.   56. $\log_x (2x - 3) = 1$.   57. $\log_x (6 - x) = 2$.
58. $\log_8 64 = x - 1$.   59. $2 + \log_2 4 = 3x - 1$.   60. $\log_3 (x + 2) = -2$.

In Problems **61–68**, *find x to three decimal places.*

61. $e^{3x} = 2$.   62. $e^{2x-5} + 1 = 4$.   63. $0.1e^{0.1x} = 0.5$.
64. $3e^{2x} - 1 = \frac{1}{2}$.   65. $\log x = 2.35$.   66. $\log x = -0.78$.
67. $\ln x = -0.03$.   68. $\ln x = 4.295$.

69. Evaluate $\ln 54 - (\ln 17.2)^2$. Give your answer to four decimal places.
70. Evaluate $\log 87 + 3 \log 0.834$. Give your answer to four decimal places.
71. In chemistry, the acidity or basicity of an aqueous solution at room temperature is determined by finding the pH of the solution. If the hydrogen-ion concentration (in moles per liter) is denoted by $[H^+]$, then the pH is given by

$$pH = -\log [H^+].$$

If pH < 7, the solution is acidic. If pH > 7, it is basic. If pH $= 7$, the solution is said to be neutral.
(a) What is the pH of vinegar with $[H^+]$ equal to 3×10^{-4}?
(b) An ammonia cleaning solution has a pH of 7.85. What is the $[H^+]$ of this solution?

72. If $\ln \dfrac{V}{V_0} = -\dfrac{t}{RC}$, solve for V.

73. The intensity level β of a sound wave of intensity I is defined by

$$\beta = 10 \log \frac{I}{I_0},$$

where I_0 is a standard reference intensity taken to be 10^{-12} W/m², which approximately corresponds to the faintest audible sound. The intensity level is measured in decibels (db). If a second source has an intensity of 3×10^{-10} W/m², what is its intensity level to the nearest tenth of a decibel?

74. The work, in joules, done by a 1-kg sample of nitrogen gas as its volume changes from an initial value V_i to a final value V_f during an isothermal (constant-temperature) process is given by

$$W = 8.1 \times 10^4 \ln \frac{V_f}{V_i}.$$

If such a sample expands isothermally from a volume of 3 L to a volume of 7 L, determine the work done by the gas to the nearest hundred joules.

75. Atmospheric pressure p varies with the altitude h above the earth's surface. For altitudes up to about 10 km, the pressure p (in millimeters of mercury) is given approximately by

$$p = 760e^{-0.125h},$$

where h is in kilometers.
(a) Find p at an altitude of 7.3 km.
(b) At what altitude will the pressure be 400 mm of mercury?

76. In studies of electric fields, one may encounter a device called a cylindrical capacitor, two concentric cylindrical conductors. The capacitance per unit length of such a device, in microfarads per meter, can be shown to be *inversely* proportional to

$$\ln \frac{r_0}{r_i},$$

where r_0 and r_i are the radii of the outer and inner cylinders, respectively. If the capacitance per unit length of a particular cylindrical capacitor is 10 μF/m when the outer radius is twice the inner radius, find the capacitance per unit length when it is three times the inner radius.

77. If 30% of the initial amount of a radioactive sample *remains* after 100 s, find the decay constant and the half-life of the element. (Refer to Example 7.)

78. If 30% of the initial amount of a radioactive sample *has decayed* after 100 s, find the decay constant and the half-life of the element. (Refer to Example 7.)

79. Radon has a half-life of 3.82 d.
(a) Find the decay constant.
(b) What fraction of the original amount of it remains after 7.64 d? *Hint:* The fraction of the original amount at any time is given by Q/Q_0.

15.3 PROPERTIES OF LOGARITHMS

Because logarithms are exponents, their properties can be obtained by using properties of exponents. For example, we shall consider the logarithm of a product, such as $\log_b (mn)$. If we let $x = \log_b m$ and $y = \log_b n$, then $b^x = m$ and $b^y = n$. Therefore,

$$mn = b^x b^y = b^{x+y}.$$

Thus $mn = b^{x+y}$. Converting this to logarithmic form gives $\log_b (mn) = x + y$. But, from above, x is $\log_b m$ and y is $\log_b n$. Thus we have our first property.

PROPERTY 1

$$\log_b (mn) = \log_b m + \log_b n.$$

That is, *the logarithm of the product of two numbers is the **sum** of the logarithms of the numbers.* For example, $\log (3 \cdot 5) = \log 3 + \log 5$.

In some of the examples and exercises that follow, we shall use Table 15.1, which gives the values of a few common logarithms to four decimal places. This table, which you should verify with a calculator, is useful in illustrating the many properties of logarithms.

TABLE 15.1 Common Logarithms

x	log x	x	log x
2	0.3010	7	0.8451
3	0.4771	8	0.9031
4	0.6021	9	0.9542
5	0.6990	10	1.0000
6	0.7782	e	0.4343

Example 1

Use Table 15.1 to find each of the following. Check the answers with a calculator.

a. log 15.

> **Solution**   Log 15 is not in Table 15.1. But we can write 15 as the product $3 \cdot 5$. Thus

$$\log 15 = \log (3 \cdot 5)$$
$$= \log 3 + \log 5 \qquad \text{[Property 1]}$$
$$= 0.4771 + 0.6990 \qquad \text{[Table 15.1]},$$
$$\log 15 = 1.1761.$$

A calculator value for log 15 is the same.

b. log 56.

Solution

$$\log 56 = \log (8 \cdot 7) = \log 8 + \log 7 = 0.9031 + 0.8451 = 1.7482,$$

which agrees with a calculator value for log 56.

The next two properties can be proved in the same way as Property 1.

PROPERTY 2

$$\log_b \frac{m}{n} = \log_b m - \log_b n.$$

That is, *the logarithm of a quotient is equal to the logarithm of the numerator minus the logarithm of the denominator.* For example, $\log \frac{2}{3} = \log 2 - \log 3$.

PROPERTY 3

$$\log_b m^n = n \log_b m.$$

That is, *the logarithm of the nth power of a number is equal to n times the logarithm of the number.* For example, $\log 2^8 = 8 \log 2$. Note that $\log 2^8 \neq (\log 2)^8$.

Make sure that you clearly understand Properties 1–3. They do *not* apply to the log of a sum $[\log_b (m + n)]$, log of a difference $[\log_b (m - n)]$, or quotient of logs $[\log_b m/\log_b n]$. For example, the logarithm of a sum is *not* the sum of logarithms. In general,

$$\log_b (m + n) \neq \log_b m + \log_b n,$$

$$\log_b (m - n) \neq \log_b m - \log_b n,$$

$$\frac{\log_b m}{\log_b n} \neq \log_b (m - n),$$

and

$$\frac{\log_b m}{\log_b n} \neq \log_b \left(\frac{m}{n}\right).$$

Example 2

Use Table 15.1 to find each of the following. Check the answers with a calculator.

a. $\log \dfrac{9}{2}$.

Solution

$$\log \frac{9}{2} = \log 9 - \log 2 \qquad \text{[Property 2]}$$

$$= 0.9542 - 0.3010 \qquad \text{[Table 15.1]},$$

$$\log \frac{9}{2} = 0.6532.$$

b. log 64.

Solution

$$\log 64 = \log (8^2)$$

$$= 2 \log 8 \qquad \text{[Property 3]}$$

$$= 2(0.9031) \qquad \text{[Table 15.1]},$$

$$\log 64 = 1.8062.$$

c. $\log \sqrt{5}$.

Solution

$$\log \sqrt{5} = \log (5^{1/2}) = \frac{1}{2} \log 5 = \frac{1}{2} (0.6990) = 0.3495.$$

d. $\log \frac{16}{21}$.

Solution

$$\log \frac{16}{21} = \log 16 - \log 21$$

$$= \log (4^2) - \log (3 \cdot 7)$$

$$= 2 \log 4 - [\log 3 + \log 7]$$

$$= 2(0.6021) - [0.4771 + 0.8451] = -0.1180.$$

Note the use of brackets in the third line. It is wrong to write $2 \log 4 - \log 3 + \log 7$. A calculator value for $\log \frac{16}{21}$ is -0.1181. The difference in the results is due to rounding in Table 15.1.

Example 3

a. $\log[(a)(b)(c)] = \log[(ab)(c)]$

$$= \log (ab) + \log c$$

$$= \log a + \log b + \log c.$$

This technique can, of course, be extended to the logarithm of any number of factors.

Do not confuse $\ln x^2$ with $(\ln x)^2$. We have

$$\ln x^2 = \ln (x \cdot x),$$

$$\text{but} \quad (\ln x)^2 = (\ln x)(\ln x),$$

which can be written as $\ln^2 x$. Thus in $\ln x^2$ we square x; in $(\ln x)^2$, or $\ln^2 x$, we square $\ln x$.

c. $\log [a(b + c)] = \log a + \log (b + c)$. Note that $\log (b + c)$ cannot be simplified.

Example 4

a. Write $\log \dfrac{1}{x^2}$ in terms of $\log x$.

Solution

$$\log \frac{1}{x^2} = \log x^{-2} = -2 \log x \qquad \text{[Property 3]}.$$

b. Write $\log x - \log (x + 3)$ as a single logarithm.

Solution

$$\log x - \log (x + 3) = \log \frac{x}{x + 3} \qquad \text{[Property 2]}.$$

c. Write $3 \log_2 10 + \log_2 15$ as a single logarithm.

Solution

$$3 \log_2 10 + \log_2 15 = \log_2 (10^3) + \log_2 15 \qquad \text{[Property 3]}$$
$$= \log_2 [(10^3)15] \qquad \text{[Property 1]}$$
$$= \log_2 15{,}000.$$

d. Write $\ln 3 + \ln 7 - \ln 2 - 2 \ln 4$ as a single logarithm.

Solution

$$\ln 3 + \ln 7 - \ln 2 - 2 \ln 4$$
$$= \ln 3 + \ln 7 - \ln 2 - \ln (4^2)$$
$$= \ln 3 + \ln 7 - [\ln 2 + \ln (4^2)]$$
$$= \ln (3 \cdot 7) - \ln (2 \cdot 4^2)$$
$$= \ln 21 - \ln 32$$
$$= \ln \frac{21}{32}.$$

e. Write $-\log \dfrac{x}{2}$ without using a minus sign.

Solution

$$-\log \frac{x}{2} = (-1) \log \frac{x}{2}$$

$$= \log \left(\frac{x}{2}\right)^{-1} \qquad \text{[Property 3]}$$

$$= \log \frac{2}{x}.$$

Example 5

a. Write $\ln \dfrac{x^5 y}{zw}$ in terms of $\ln x$, $\ln y$, $\ln z$, and $\ln w$.

Solution

$$\ln \frac{x^5 y}{zw} = \ln (x^5 y) - \ln (zw)$$

$$= \ln (x^5) + \ln y - (\ln z + \ln w)$$

$$= 5 \ln x + \ln y - \ln z - \ln w.$$

b. Write $\log \sqrt[3]{\dfrac{x^2}{x-4}}$ in terms of $\log x$ and $\log (x-4)$.

Solution

$$\log \sqrt[3]{\frac{x^2}{x-4}} = \log \left(\frac{x^2}{x-4}\right)^{1/3} = \frac{1}{3} \log \frac{x^2}{x-4}$$

$$= \frac{1}{3} [\log (x^2) - \log (x-4)]$$

$$= \frac{1}{3} [2 \log x - \log (x-4)].$$

Because $b^0 = 1$ and $b^1 = b$, by converting to logarithmic forms we have two more properties of logarithms:

> **PROPERTY 4**
> $\log_b 1 = 0.$
>
> **PROPERTY 5**
> $\log_b b = 1.$

Example 6

Find each of the following.

a. log 1.

Solution

$$\log 1 = \log_{10} 1 = 0 \qquad \text{[Property 4]}.$$

b. ln e.

Solution

$$\ln e = \log_e e = 1 \qquad \text{[Property 5]}.$$

c. log 1000.

Solution

$$\log 1000 = \log_{10} 10^3 = 3 \log_{10} 10$$
$$= 3 \cdot 1 \qquad \text{[Property 5]}$$
$$= 3.$$

d. log (10^n).

Solution

$$\log (10^n) = n \log_{10} 10 = n \cdot 1 = n.$$

We can generalize the result of Example 6(d):

> **PROPERTY 6**
>
> $\log_b b^n = n.$

For example, log $10^9 = 9$ and ln $e^8 = 8$.

Example 7

a. Find $\log_7 \sqrt[9]{7^8}$.

Solution

$$\log_7 \sqrt[9]{7^8} = \log_7 (7^{8/9}) = \frac{8}{9} \qquad \text{[Property 6]}.$$

b. Find $\log_3 \frac{27}{81}$.

Solution

$$\log_3 \frac{27}{81} = \log_3 \frac{3^3}{3^4} = \log_3 (3^{-1}) = -1 \qquad \text{[Property 6]}.$$

c. Find $\ln (e^2) + \log \frac{1}{10}$.

Solution

$$\ln (e^2) + \log \frac{1}{10} = 2 + \log 10^{-1} = 2 + (-1) = 1.$$

d. Find $\log \frac{200}{21}$ by using Table 15.1.

Solution

$$\log \frac{200}{21} = \log 200 - \log 21 = \log (2 \cdot 10^2) - \log (3 \cdot 7)$$

$$= \log 2 + \log (10^2) - (\log 3 + \log 7)$$

$$= \log 2 + 2 - \log 3 - \log 7$$

$$= 0.3010 + 2 - 0.4771 - 0.8451$$

$$= 0.9788.$$

Our last property is:

PROPERTY 7

$b^{\log_b n} = n$ and, in particular, $10^{\log x} = x$ and $e^{\ln x} = x$.

Property 7 is true because it states, in logarithmic form, that $\log_b n = \log_b n$.

Example 8

a. $e^{\ln 2x} = 2x$, by Property 7.

b. $10^{\log x^2} = x^2$, by Property 7.

Problem Set 15.3

*In Problems **1–48**, use Table 15.1 and properties of logarithms to find each value.*

1. $\log 5$.
2. $\log 3$.
3. $\log 21$.
4. $\log 14$.
5. $\log 35$.
6. $\log 12$.
7. $\log 25$.
8. $\log 49$.
9. $\log \frac{9}{4}$.
10. $\log \frac{7}{3}$.
11. $\log \frac{1}{2}$.
12. $\log \frac{7}{9}$.
13. $\log (8^5)$.
14. $\log (4^{-3})$.
15. $\log \dfrac{1}{5^4}$.
16. $\log 2^{0.01}$.
17. $\log \sqrt{2}$.
18. $\log \sqrt[3]{4}$.
19. $\log \sqrt[3]{6^2}$.
20. $\log \dfrac{1}{\sqrt[3]{5}}$.
21. $\log \frac{14}{5}$.
22. $\log \frac{3}{35}$.
23. $\log \frac{15}{28}$.
24. $\log \frac{81}{25}$.
25. $\log 10{,}000$.
26. $\log 10^{10}$.
27. $\log 0.01$.
28. $\log (0.1)^3$.
29. $\log 300$.
30. $\log \sqrt[3]{400}$.
31. $\log \frac{100}{9}$.
32. $\log \frac{1}{600}$.
33. $\log \frac{27}{5000}$.
34. $\log \sqrt{\frac{8}{3}}$.
35. $\log_7 7^{48}$.
36. $\log_4 \sqrt[5]{4}$.
37. $\log_5 \sqrt[4]{5^3}$.
38. $\log_2 \dfrac{1}{\sqrt{2}}$.
39. $\ln e^4$.
40. $\ln \dfrac{1}{e}$.
41. $\log_2 \dfrac{2^6}{2^{10}}$.
42. $\log_3 (3^5 \cdot 3^4)^6$.
43. $\log [(10\sqrt{10})^3]$.
44. $\log_5 \dfrac{25}{\sqrt{5}}$.
45. $\log_7 \dfrac{\sqrt[3]{49}}{7}$.
46. $\log_8 (64\sqrt[4]{8})$.
47. $\log 10 + \ln (e^2)$.
48. $(\log 100)(\ln \sqrt{e})$.

*In Problems **49–62**, write each expression as a single logarithm.*

49. $\log 7 + \log 4$.
50. $\log_3 10 - \log_3 5$.
51. $\log_2 (x + 2) - \log_2 (x + 1)$.
52. $\log (x^2) + \log x$.
53. $2 \ln 5 - 3 \ln 4$.
54. $3 \log_7 2 + 2 \log_7 3$.
55. $\frac{1}{2} \log_4 2 + 3 \log_4 3$.
56. $\frac{1}{3} \ln x - 5 \ln (x - 2)$.
57. $\log_3 x + \log_3 y - \log_3 z$.
58. $\ln x + \ln (x - 1) - 2 \ln y$.
59. $\log_2 5 + 2 \log_2 3 - \log_2 7$.
60. $\frac{1}{2}(\log_3 x + \log_3 y)$.
61. $2 \ln x + 3 \ln y - 4 \ln z - 2 \ln w$.
62. $\log_6 5 - 2 \log_6 \frac{1}{5} - 2 \log_6 4$.

*In Problems **63–72**, write the given expression in terms of $\log x$, $\log y$, and $\log z$.*

63. $\log (xy)$.
64. $\log (x^2 yz)$.
65. $\log \dfrac{x}{z^2}$.
66. $\log x^6$.
67. $\log \sqrt{x}$.
68. $\log \dfrac{xy^2}{z^3}$.

69. $\log (xy^2)^6$.

70. $\log \dfrac{y\sqrt[3]{x}}{z^2}$.

71. $\log \sqrt[6]{\dfrac{x^2y^3}{z^5}}$.

72. $\log \dfrac{1}{y\sqrt{z}}$.

In Problems 73–78, write each expression in terms of log x, log (x + 2), and log (x − 3).

73. $\log [x(x + 2)(x − 3)]$.

74. $\log \dfrac{x^2(x + 2)}{x − 3}$.

75. $\log \dfrac{\sqrt{x}}{(x + 2)(x − 3)^2}$.

76. $\log [(x − 3)\sqrt{x(x + 2)}]$.

77. $\log \sqrt{\dfrac{x^2(x − 3)^3}{x + 2}}$.

78. $\log \dfrac{1}{x(x − 3)^2(x + 2)^3}$.

For an aqueous solution at room temperature, the product of the hydrogen-ion concentration, $[H^+]$, and the hydroxide-ion concentration, $[OH^-]$, is 10^{-14} (where the concentrations are in moles per liter):

$$[H^+][OH^-] = 10^{-14}.$$

In Problems 79 and 80, find the pH of a solution (see explanation in Problem 71 of Problem Set 15.2) with the given $[OH^-]$ if $pH = -\log [H^+]$.

79. $[OH^-] = 10^{-4}$.

80. $[OH^-] = 3 \times 10^{-2}$.

81. The intensity level β (beta) of a sound wave of intensity I is given by

$$\beta = 10 \log \frac{I}{I_0},$$

where I_0 is a standard reference intensity taken to be 10^{-12} W/m², which approximately corresponds to the faintest sound that you can hear. The intensity level is measured in decibels (db). For example, the intensity level of an ordinary conversation is 40 db, and that for a subway train is 100 db. Find the intensity level of the sound of rustling leaves, which has an intensity of 10^{-11}.

82. In Problem 81, suppose that two sound sources have intensities I_1 and I_2. Show that the *difference* in the intensity levels of the sounds is given by

$$\beta_2 - \beta_1 = 10 \log \frac{I_2}{I_1}.$$

83. According to Richter,* the magnitude M of an earthquake occurring 100 km from a certain type of seismometer is given by $M = 3 + \log A$, where A is the recorded trace amplitude (in millimeters) of the quake.

(a) Find the magnitude of an earthquake that records a trace amplitude of 1 mm.

(b) If a particular earthquake has amplitude A_1 and magnitude M_1, determine the magnitude of a quake with amplitude $100A_1$. Express your answer in terms of M_1.

* C. F. Richter, *Elementary Seismology* (San Francisco: W. H. Freeman, 1958).

15.4 CHANGE OF BASE

Our next property of logarithms allows us to convert logarithms from one base to another. Let

$$x = \log_b N.$$

Then, in exponential form,

$$b^x = N.$$

Taking the logarithm (base a) of both sides, we have

$$\log_a (b^x) = \log_a N$$
$$x \log_a b = \log_a N$$
$$x = \frac{\log_a N}{\log_a b}.$$

However, from before, $x = \log_b N$. Thus we have the *change of base formula*:

> **CHANGE OF BASE FORMULA**
> $$\log_b N = \frac{\log_a N}{\log_a b}.$$

This formula allows us to find a logarithm with base b in terms of logarithms with base a. In particular, from the change of base formula with $a = e$, we have

$$\log_b N = \frac{\ln N}{\ln b} \tag{1}$$

With this formula we can find logarithms with base b by using natural logarithms. Letting $b = 10$ in Eq. 1 gives

$$\log N = \frac{\ln N}{\ln 10}.$$

Thus

$$\ln N = (\ln 10)(\log N),$$

or

$$\textbf{ln } N = \textbf{2.30259 log } N. \tag{2}$$

It also follows that

$$\log N = 0.43429 \ln N. \tag{3}$$

Example 1

Find $\log_5 8$ by using common logarithms.

Solution Using the change of base formula with $b = 5$, $N = 8$, and $a = 10$ gives

$$\log_5 8 = \frac{\log 8}{\log 5} = 1.2920.$$

We remind you that $\dfrac{\log 8}{\log 5} \neq \log (8 - 5)$ and $\dfrac{\log 8}{\log 5} \neq \log \dfrac{8}{5}.$

Example 2

Find $\log_4 20$ by using natural logarithms.

Solution Using Eq. 1 with $b = 4$ and $N = 20$, we have

$$\log_4 20 = \frac{\ln 20}{\ln 4} = 2.1610.$$

Problem Set 15.4

In Problems **1–6**, *find the values of the logarithms.*

1. $\log_5 27$.
2. $\log_2 15$.
3. $\log_7 0.67$.
4. $\log_{100} 25$.
5. $\log_6 0.00032$.
6. $\log_5 0.5$.

15.5 EXPONENTIAL AND LOGARITHMIC EQUATIONS

An equation in which the unknown appears in an exponent is called an **exponential equation**. An exponential equation can generally be solved by first taking logarithms of both sides and using properties of logarithms. Although we may use logarithms to any base, we usually use either common or natural logarithms because these can be obtained with a calculator.

Example 1

Solve $6^x = 8.2$.

Solution Taking natural logarithms of both sides, we have

$$\ln 6^x = \ln 8.2.$$

Using Property 3,

$$x \ln 6 = \ln 8.2$$

$$x = \frac{\ln 8.2}{\ln 6} = 1.1743.$$

Example 2

Solve $5^{2x+1} = 36$.

Solution Taking common logarithms of both sides, we have

$$\log 5^{2x+1} = \log 36$$

$$(2x + 1)(\log 5) = \log 36$$

$$2x + 1 = \frac{\log 36}{\log 5}$$

$$2x = \frac{\log 36}{\log 5} - 1$$

$$x = \frac{\log 36}{2 \log 5} - \frac{1}{2}$$

$$x = 0.61328.$$

Example 3

A 6-μF capacitor is charged by connecting it in series with a 2-MΩ resistor and a 100-V battery. In the charging circuit the current i (in amperes) follows an exponential decay given by

$$i = \frac{\mathcal{E}}{R} e^{-t/(RC)}, \tag{1}$$

where C is the capacitance (in farads), R is the resistance (in ohms), and $\mathcal{E}$ is the emf (in volts). In how many seconds after the connection is made will the current in the circuit be 20 μA?

Solution Substituting the given values into Eq. 1 gives

$$20 \times 10^{-6} = \frac{100}{2 \times 10^6} e^{-t/[(2 \times 10^6)(6 \times 10^{-6})]}$$

$$0.4 = e^{-t/12}. \tag{2}$$

Now we solve $e^{-t/12} = 0.4$. Taking natural logarithms of both sides, we have

$$\ln e^{-t/12} = \ln 0.4$$

$$-\frac{t}{12} = \ln 0.4 \qquad \text{[Property 6]}$$

$$t = -12 \ln 0.4$$

$$t = 11.0 \text{ s.}$$

Equation 2 can also be solved by first expressing it in an equivalent logarithmic form:

$$-\frac{t}{12} = \ln 0.4$$

$$t = -12 \ln 0.4 = 11.0 \text{ s.}$$

An equation involving a logarithm of an expression containing the unknown is called a **logarithmic equation**. A logarithmic equation can generally be solved by rewriting it in exponential form, as the following examples show.

Example 4

Solve $\log_2 x + \log_2 (x + 4) = 5$.

Solution We first write the left side as a single logarithm by using Property 1:

$$\log_2 [x(x + 4)] = 5.$$

In exponential form we have

$$x(x + 4) = 2^5$$

$$x^2 + 4x = 32$$

$$x^2 + 4x - 32 = 0 \qquad \text{[quadratic equation]}$$

$$(x - 4)(x + 8) = 0$$

$$x = 4 \quad \text{or} \quad x = -8.$$

We must reject $x = -8$ because the given equation is not defined for negative x (the logarithm of a negative number is not defined). Thus only 4 is a solution.

Example 5

Solve $\log (x + 1) - \log (x - 1) = \log x$.

Solution   Simplifying the left side gives

$$\log \frac{x + 1}{x - 1} = \log x.$$

Recall that if the logarithms of two numbers are equal, then the numbers are equal. Thus

$$\frac{x + 1}{x - 1} = x$$

$$x + 1 = x(x - 1)$$

$$x + 1 = x^2 - x$$

$$0 = x^2 - 2x - 1.$$

Using the quadratic formula gives $x = 1 \pm \sqrt{2}$. However, the given equation is not defined for $x = 1 - \sqrt{2}$. The solution is $1 + \sqrt{2}$.

Problem Set 15.5

In Problems 1–18, solve the equation.

1. $12^x = 17$.
2. $2^{8x} = 9$.
3. $3^{x-2} = 14$.
4. $5^{2x-4} = 96$.
5. $2^{-t} = 9$.
6. $3^{t/2} = 0.056$.
7. $e^{3t+1} = 35$.
8. $e^{1-t} = 354$.
9. $x^{2.56} = 26$.
10. $t^{2.5} = 24.71$.
11. $\log (x - 3) = 3$.
12. $\log_2 (x + 1) = 4$.
13. $\log (2x + 1) = \log (x + 6)$.
14. $\log x + \log 3 = \log 5$.
15. $\log x - \log (x - 1) = \log 4$.
16. $\log_2 x + 3 \log_2 2 = \log_2 \left(\dfrac{2}{x}\right)$.
17. $\log (3x - 1) - \log (x - 3) = 2$.
18. $\log_3 (2x + 3) = 4 - \log_3 (x + 6)$.

19. The magnitude of the force F (in newtons) driving a piston varies with the distance x (in meters) of the piston from its central position according to the equation

$$F = 135x^{-7/5}.$$

  (a) Find the force acting when the piston is 8.0 cm from its central position.
  (b) How far is the piston from its central position when $F = 1000$ N?

20. A sound source has an intensity level of 100 db. Find its intensity in watts per square meter. Refer to the formula in Problem 73 in Problem Set 15.2.

21. A 2-μF capacitor is charged by connecting it in series with a 4-MΩ resistor and a 200-V source.
    (a) Find the current in the circuit at $t = 0$, which is the instant the connections are made. (Refer to Example 3.)
    (b) For what value of t will the current in the circuit be 10 μA?

22. Suppose the number Q of milligrams of a radioactive substance present after t years is given by

$$Q = 100e^{-0.035t}.$$

    (a) How many milligrams are present after 0 years?
    (b) After how many years will there be 50 mg present?

23. In one city the population P grows at the rate of 2% per year. The equation $P = 1,000,000(1.02)^t$ gives the population t years after 1983. Find the value of t for which the population is 1,500,000.

24. A capacitance C is charged by connecting it in series with a resistance R and an emf $\mathcal{E}$.
    (a) Show that the initial current in the circuit (at $t = 0$) is $\mathcal{E}/R$. (See Example 3.)
    (b) The *capacitive time constant* τ_C is given by $\tau_C = RC$. Show that when $t = \tau_C$, the current has decayed to $1/e$ of its initial value.
    (c) In Part (b), approximately what percentage of the initial current does that represent?

25. The water in a midwestern lake contains sediment, and the presence of the sediment reduces the transmission of light through the water. Experiments indicate that the intensity of light is reduced by 10% by passage through 20 cm of water. Suppose that the lake is uniform with respect to the amount of sediment contained by the water. A measuring instrument can detect light at the intensity of 0.17% of full sunlight. This measuring instrument is lowered into the lake. At what depth will it first cease to record the presence of light?

26. A translucent material has the property that although light passes through the material, its intensity is reduced. A particular translucent plastic has the property that a sheet 1 mm thick reduces the intensity of light by 10%. How many such sheets are necessary to reduce the intensity of a beam of light to about 50% of its original value?

15.6 LOGARITHMIC AND SEMILOGARITHMIC GRAPH PAPER

In technical work there is sometimes a need to conveniently graph a function $y = f(x)$ when both x and y range over wide intervals of values. In such cases it may be best to show not how y varies with x, but how log y varies with log x. For example, if $10 \le x \le 1000$, then $1 \le \log x \le 3$. Clearly, the latter interval is easier to work with on an axis.

If such a graph is desired, we can sketch it without having to determine the logarithms of any numbers. We use a special **logarithmic graph paper** (or **log paper**) on which both axes are ruled with logarithmic scales in base 10 (see Fig. 15.9). Plotting a point (x, y) on log paper is equivalent to plotting the point $(\log x, \log y)$ on ordinary graph paper. The 1 that is preprinted on log paper can represent only an integral power of 10, such as 1, 10, 100, 0.1, 0.01, and so on. If the 1 represents 10, then the 2 represents 20. A **cycle** is the distance between two numbers having logarithms that are consecutive integers. For example, from 1 to 10 is one cycle; from 10 to 100 is one cycle. Log paper is described by the number of cycles on each axis. For example, Fig. 15.9 has two cycles on the vertical axis.

A similar type of graph paper, called **semilogarithmic graph paper**, is shown in Fig. 15.10. One axis is ruled logarithmically (base 10) and the other axis is ruled linearly, like ordinary graph paper. This paper is used when only *one* variable has a wide range of values.

A significant advantage of log paper is that the graph of the **power function** $y = ax^m$, where a and x are positive, appears as a straight line on log paper. To show why, we take the common logarithm of both sides and simplify:

$$\log y = \log ax^m$$

$$\log y = \log a + \log x^m$$

$$\log y = \log a + m \log x. \tag{1}$$

If we substitute y_L for $\log y$, x_L for $\log x$, and b for the constant $\log a$, then Eq. 1 becomes

$$y_L = mx_L + b,$$

which is an equation of a straight line with slope m and y-intercept $\log a$. Thus an equation of the form $y = ax^m$ appears as a straight line on log paper. The exponent m of $y = ax^m$ is the slope of the line. Moreover,

> If the graph of data is a straight line on log paper, then the data are related by a function of the form $y = ax^m$.

Similarly, we shall show that the graph of the exponential function $y = ab^x$, where a and b are positive, is a straight line on semilog paper if y is on the logarithmic scale. Taking logarithms of both sides gives

$$\log y = \log a + x \log b.$$

Substituting y_L for $\log y$, k for the constant $\log a$, and m for the constant $\log b$ gives

$$y_L = mx + k,$$

whose graph is a straight line. Moreover,

> If the graph of data is a straight line on semilog paper, then the data are related by a function of the form $y = ab^x$.

Example 1

Sketch the graph of the power function $y = 3x^2$, for $1 \leq x \leq 5$, on log paper.

Solution Using Table 15.2, we note that two logarithmic cycles will be needed for y: one cycle for 3 and one cycle for 12, 27, 48, and 75. The graph, shown in Fig. 15.9, is a straight line,

TABLE 15.2

x	1	2	3	4	5
y	3	12	27	48	75

as expected. Using a *ruler* to measure Δx and Δy, you should verify that $\Delta y / \Delta x = 2$. The slope may also be found analytically. Choosing the points $(1, 3)$ and $(5, 75)$, we have

$$\frac{\Delta y}{\Delta x} = \frac{\log y_2 - \log y_1}{\log x_2 - \log x_1} = \frac{\log 75 - \log 3}{\log 5 - \log 1} = 2.$$

In particular, note that using the same points you must *not* write

$$\frac{\Delta y}{\Delta x} = \frac{75 - 3}{5 - 1} = 18,$$

for the data do not give a straight line on ordinary graph paper.

Example 2

Suppose that the data in Table 15.3 are plotted on log paper and the resulting points lie on a straight line. Determine an equation that relates y as a function of x.

TABLE 15.3

x	1.4	2.5	6.1	11.4	17.5
y	24.5	7.68	1.29	0.369	0.157

Solution Because the data determine a straight line on log paper, the equation is a power function of the form $y = ax^m$. To find the slope m of the line, we may use the slope formula

$$m = \frac{\log y_2 - \log y_1}{\log x_2 - \log x_1}$$

and two of the data points, such as $(17.5, 0.157)$ and $(1.4, 24.5)$. This gives

$$m = \frac{\log 24.5 - \log 0.157}{\log 1.4 - \log 17.5} = -2.0.$$

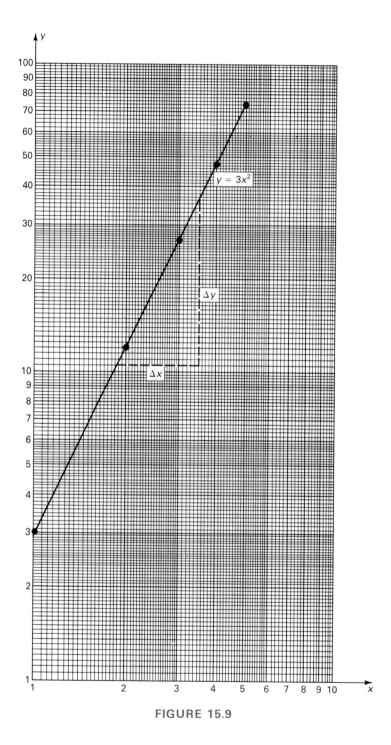

FIGURE 15.9

Thus $y = ax^{-2} = a/x^2$. To find a, we substitute a data point, such as $(1.4, 24.5)$, into the equation and solve for a.

$$24.5 = \frac{a}{(1.4)^2}$$
$$a = 24.5(1.4)^2 = 48.0.$$

Thus $y = \dfrac{48}{x^2}$.

Example 3

Sketch the graph of the exponential function $y = e^x$, for $-1 \leq x \leq 4$, on semilog paper.

Solution From Table 15.4 we conclude that three cycles will be needed for y. The graph, shown in Fig. 15.10, is a straight line, as expected.

TABLE 15.4

x	-1	0	1	2	3	4
y	0.37	1	2.72	7.39	20.1	54.6

Example 4

A student found that plotting data from an experiment resulted in a straight-line graph on semilog paper. If two of the data points are $x = 1$, $y = 2.81$, and $x = 4$, $y = 5.12$, find an equation that approximates the data.

Solution We assume that the equation has the form $y = ab^x$. Substituting the given values gives the system

$$\begin{cases} 2.81 = ab & (1) \\ 5.12 = ab^4. & (2) \end{cases}$$

From Eq. 1, $a = 2.81/b$. Substituting into Eq. 2 gives

$$5.12 = 2.81b^3$$
$$b^3 = \frac{5.12}{2.81}$$
$$b = 1.22.$$

Thus $y = a(1.22)^x$. At the data point $(1, 2.81)$ we have

$$2.81 = a(1.22)$$
$$a = 2.30.$$

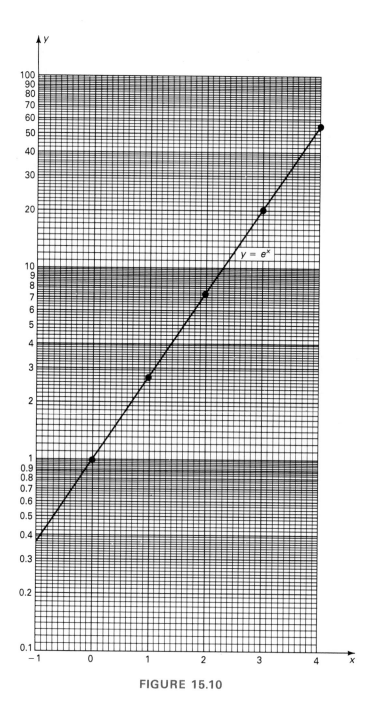

FIGURE 15.10

Therefore, the data are approximated by the equation

$$y = 2.3(1.22)^x.$$

We remark that because $\ln 1.22 = 0.199$, then $1.22 = e^{0.199}$, so the answer can be expressed as $y = 2.3e^{0.199x}$.

Problem Set 15.6

1. Consider the function $y = e^{-x}$ for $1 \le x \le 6$.
   (a) Will the graph be a straight line on semilog paper or on log paper?
   (b) On the appropriate paper, use the points corresponding to $x = 1$ and $x = 6$ to sketch the straight-line graph.
   (c) From your graph, estimate e^{-x} for various values of x between 1 and 6 and compare your results to values found with a calculator.

2. Consider the function $y = \sqrt{x}$.
   (a) Will the graph be a straight line on semilog paper or on log paper?
   (b) On the appropriate paper, use the points corresponding to $x = 1$ and $x = 100$ to sketch the straight-line graph.
   (c) From your graph, estimate the square roots of various numbers between 1 and 100 and compare your results to values found with a calculator.

3. During an experiment, the data shown in Table 15.5 were recorded. Plot the data on log paper and semilog paper.
   (a) On which paper do the points lie on a straight line?
   (b) Find an equation that approximates the data.

TABLE 15.5

x	1	4	8	12	16	20	24
y	600	150	75	50	37.5	30	25

4. Table 15.6 gives the barometric pressure p, in millimeters of mercury, at various altitudes h, in meters.
   (a) Plot the data on semilog paper.
   (b) Determine an equation for p as a function of h. Give your answer in two forms, like in Example 4.

TABLE 15.6

h (m)	0	500	1000	1500	2000	2500
p (mm)	760	716	674	635	598	563

5. Data from an experiment produced a straight line on semilog paper. If two of the data points are $x = 2$, $y = 3.61$ and $x = 4$, $y = 32.6$, find an equation that approximates the data.

6. Data from an experiment produced a straight line on log paper. If two of the data points are $x = 3$, $y = 3.46$ and $x = 8$, $y = 4.80$, find an equation that approximates the data.

7. The period T of a simple pendulum was measured for various lengths L. The results are given in Table 15.7. Plot the data on log paper and semilog paper.
   (a) On which paper do the points lie on a straight line?
   (b) Find an equation for T as a function of L.

TABLE 15.7

L (m)	0.2	0.4	0.6	0.8	1.0	1.2
T (s)	0.89	1.26	1.55	1.79	2.00	2.20

15.7 REVIEW

Important Terms and Symbols

Section 15.1   Exponential function, $f(x) = b^x$, e.

Section 15.2   Logarithmic function, $y = \log_b x$, logarithmic form, exponential form, antilogarithm, common logarithm, $\log x$, natural logarithm, $\ln x$.

Section 15.4   Change of base formula.

Section 15.5   Exponential equation, logarithmic equation.

Section 15.6   Logarithmic graph paper, semilogarithmic graph paper.

Formula Summary

> *Exponential function* $f(x) = b^x$
> *Logarithmic function* $y = \log_b x$ means $b^y = x$

$$e \approx 2.71828$$

PROPERTIES OF LOGARITHMS

$$\log_b (mn) = \log_b m + \log_b n \qquad \log_b \frac{m}{n} = \log_b m - \log_b n$$

$$\log_b m^n = n \log_b m \qquad\qquad \log_b 1 = 0$$

$$\log_b b = 1 \qquad\qquad\qquad \log_b b^n = n$$

$$b^{\log_b n} = n$$

Review Questions

1. A function of the form $f(x) = b^x$ is called an _____ function.
2. Is the value of e closer to 2 or to 3? _____
3. If $\log_b x = y$, then $b^y = $ _____.
4. The base in $\log x$ is _____.
5. The base in $\ln x$ is _____.
6. The domain of the exponential function $f(x) = b^x$ is __(a)__ and its range is __(b)__.
7. The domain of the logarithmic function $g(x) = \log_b x$ is __(a)__ and its range is __(b)__.
8. The graph in Fig. 15.11 is typical of a(n) __(exponential)(logarithmic)__ function.

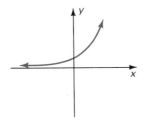

FIGURE 15.11

9. If $\log_2 (x + 1) = \log_2 4$, then $x = $ _____.
10. If $\log x = 1.2222$, then $\log\sqrt{x} = $ _____.
11. $\log 10^{5x} = $ _____.
12. $\ln \dfrac{x^2 y^3}{z^4} = $ __(a)__ $\ln x + $ __(b)__ $\ln y - $ __(c)__ $\ln z$.
13. The graphs of $y = e^{x+2}$ and $y = e^2 e^x$ __(are)(are not)__ identical.
14. $\log_5 5 = $ _____.
15. $\log_3 1 = $ _____.
16. If $\log x = 0.62148$, then $10^{0.62148} = $ _____.

Answers to Review Questions

1. Exponential.   2. 3.   3. x.   4. 10.   5. e.
6. (a) All real numbers,   (b) All positive numbers.
7. (a) All positive numbers,   (b) All real numbers.   8. Exponential.   9. 3.
10. 0.6111.   11. $5x$.   12. (a) 2, (b) 3, (c) 4.   13. Are.   14. 1.   15. 0.   16. x.

Review Problems

In Problems **1–4**, *find the given function values.*

1. $f(x) = 4 + 3^{2x}$; $f(0)$, $f(1)$, $f(-\frac{1}{2})$.
2. $g(t) = 4(9)^{t/2}$; $g(1)$, $g(-1)$, $g(3)$.
3. $h(s) = 100e^{(s+3)/2}$; $h(-3)$, $h(5)$, $h(-6)$.
4. $F(x) = 6 - 3(\frac{1}{2})^{x+4}$; $F(-3)$, $F(-1)$, $F(-6)$.

In Problems **5** *and* **6**, *graph the given function.*

5. $y = \log_5 x$.

6. $y = 5^x$.

In Problems **7–12**, *write each exponential form logarithmically and each logarithmic form exponentially.*

7. $3^5 = 243$.

8. $\log_7 343 = 3$.

9. $\log_{16} 2 = \frac{1}{4}$.

10. $10^5 = 100,000$.

11. $e^4 = 54.598$.

12. $\log_9 9 = 1$.

In Problems **13–18**, *find the values.*

13. $\log_5 125$.

14. $\log_4 16$.

15. $\log_2 \dfrac{1}{16}$.

16. $\log_{1/3} \dfrac{1}{9}$.

17. $\log_{1/3} 9$.

18. $\log_4 2$.

In Problems **19–24**, *determine the common logarithm of the given number to five decimal places.*

19. 634.82.

20. 0.00064321.

21. 8.62×10^{16}.

22. 0.084138.

23. 6047.1.

24. 9.72×10^{-3}.

In Problems **25–28**, *determine the natural logarithm of the given number to five decimal places.*

25. 0.632.

26. 468.

27. 4.72.

28. 0.000014.

In Problems **29–32**, *determine the value of N to four decimal places.*

29. $\ln N = 1.13465$.

30. $\log N = 8.19893$.

31. $\log N = -0.68078$.

32. $\log N = 3.69037$.

In Problems **33–50**, *find x.*

33. $\log_5 \dfrac{1}{25} = x$.

34. $\log_x 1000 = 3$.

35. $\log x = -2$.

36. $\log_8 64 = x$.

37. $\log_x 81 = 2$.

38. $\log_3 x = \dfrac{1}{2}$.

39. $\log_x (4x - 9) = 1$.

40. $\log_4 (x - 6) = 2$.

41. $\log_6 x = 3.265$.

42. $e^{0.3x+1} = 6$.

43. $7^{1.6x} = 3.429$.

44. $\log_e \pi = x$.

45. $\log x = 0.$

46. $\ln \dfrac{1}{e} = x.$

47. $\log_x (2x + 3) = 2.$

48. $\log (4x + 1) = \log (x + 2).$

49. $e^{\ln(x + 4)} = 7.$

50. $\log x + \log 2 = 1.$

In Problems **51–56**, write each expression as a single logarithm.

51. $2 \log 5 - 3 \log 3.$

52. $6 \ln x + 4 \ln y.$

53. $2 \ln x + \ln y - 3 \ln z.$

54. $\log_6 2 - \log_6 4 - 2 \log_6 3.$

55. $\dfrac{1}{2} \log_2 x + 2 \log_2 (x^2) - 3 \log_2 (x + 1) - 4 \log_2 (x + 2).$

56. $3 \log x + \log y - 2 (\log z + \log w).$

In Problems **57–62**, write each expression in terms of $\ln x$, $\ln y$, and $\ln z$.

57. $\ln \dfrac{x^2 y}{z^3}.$

58. $\ln \dfrac{\sqrt{x}}{(yz)^2}.$

59. $\ln \sqrt[3]{xyz}.$

60. $\ln \left[\dfrac{xy^3}{z^2} \right]^4.$

61. $\ln \left[\dfrac{1}{x} \sqrt{\dfrac{y}{z}} \right].$

62. $\ln \left[\left(\dfrac{x}{y} \right)^2 \left(\dfrac{x}{z} \right)^3 \right].$

63. If $\log 3 = x$ and $\log 4 = y$, express $\log (16 \sqrt{3})$ in terms of x and y.

64. Express

$$\log \frac{x^2 \sqrt{x + 1}}{\sqrt[3]{x^2 + 2}}$$

in terms of $\log x$, $\log (x + 1)$, and $\log (x^2 + 2)$.

65. Find $\log_3 4$.

66. Data from an experiment produced a straight line on log paper. If two of the data points are $x = 2$, $y = 26.4$ and $x = 4$, $y = 278.6$, find an equation that approximates the data.

67. Data from an experiment produced a straight line on semilog paper. If two of the data points are $x = 2$, $y = 49$ and $x = 3$, $y = 171.5$, find an equation that approximates the data.

68. If 95% of a radioactive substance remains after 100 years. find the decay constant and, to the nearest percent, give the percentage of the original amount present after 200 years.

69. The following equation was encountered in statistical biology:

$$R = 2\sigma \sqrt{2 \log \left(\frac{n}{\sigma \sqrt{2\pi}} \right)}.$$

Find R if $\sigma = 2.378$ and $n = 1000$.

70. When a solenoid of inductance L (in henries) and resistance R (in ohms) is connected to a battery of emf $\mathcal{E}$ (in volts), the current i (in amperes) in the circuit is given by

$$i = \frac{\mathcal{E}}{R} (1 - e^{-Rt/L}).$$

A solenoid with an inductance of 60 H and a resistance of 20 Ω is connected to a 100-V battery. For what value of t will the current be 2.5 A?

16

Graphs of the Trigonometric Functions

When we studied the trigonometric functions in Chapters 6 and 7, no consideration was given to their graphical characteristics. To properly understand the behavior of the trigonometric functions, an analysis of their graphs is essential. These graphs have wide application in mathematically describing several occurrences in nature, such as wave motion, vibrations and simple harmonic motion, and certain electrical phenomena. In this chapter we shall consider the graphs of the six trigonometric functions and some of their variations. You will see that, in comparison to the graphs of algebraic functions, these graphs have strikingly unique features.

16.1 THE GRAPH OF THE SINE FUNCTION

We begin with the graph of the basic sine function,

$$y = f(x) = \sin x,$$

where x is in radians. Table 16.1 lists some values of x between 0 and 2π along with the corresponding y-values. The points (x, y) are plotted in Fig. 16.1 and connected by a smooth curve.

Because the angles x and $x + 2\pi$ are coterminal angles, we have $\sin (x + 2\pi) = \sin x$. For example, $\sin (\pi + 2\pi) = \sin \pi$. This means that the graph of $y = \sin x$ repeats itself every 2π radians. In other words, as x increases from 2π to 4π, from 4π to 6π, and so on, $\sin x$ behaves exactly as it does as x increases from 0 to 2π. This is

TABLE 16.1

x (rad)	y = sin x	x (rad)	y = sin x
0	0	$\dfrac{7\pi}{6}$	$-\dfrac{1}{2} = -0.5$
$\dfrac{\pi}{6}$	$\dfrac{1}{2} = 0.5$	$\dfrac{4\pi}{3}$	$-\dfrac{\sqrt{3}}{2} \approx -0.87$
$\dfrac{\pi}{3}$	$\dfrac{\sqrt{3}}{2} \approx 0.87$	$\dfrac{3\pi}{2}$	-1
$\dfrac{\pi}{2}$	1	$\dfrac{5\pi}{3}$	$-\dfrac{\sqrt{3}}{2} \approx -0.87$
$\dfrac{2\pi}{3}$	$\dfrac{\sqrt{3}}{2} \approx 0.87$	$\dfrac{11\pi}{6}$	$-\dfrac{1}{2} = -0.5$
$\dfrac{5\pi}{6}$	$\dfrac{1}{2} = 0.5$	2π	0
π	0		

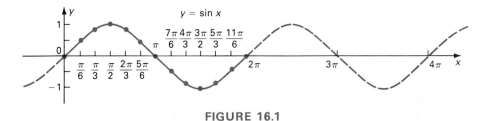

FIGURE 16.1

indicated by the dashed curve in Fig. 16.1 and gives the graph a characteristic wavelike appearance. To describe the repetition, or *periodicity*, we say that the sine function is *periodic*. In general:

PERIODIC FUNCTION

A (nonconstant) function f is called a **periodic function** if there is a positive number p such that $f(x + p) = f(x)$ for all x in the domain of f. The least such value of p is called the **period*** of f.

Thus the sine function has period 2π.

* More precisely, p is called the *fundamental* period. Actually, since $\sin(x + 4\pi) = \sin x$, the number 4π is a period of $y = \sin x$. However, because 2π is the *smallest* positive number p such that $\sin(x + p) = \sin x$, we call 2π *the* (fundamental) period.

We emphasize that Fig. 16.1 shows merely a portion of the basic sine curve, for $y = \sin x$ is defined for all values of x and its graph extends indefinitely to the right and to the left.

The graph of $y = \sin x$ over an interval of length one period (2π) is called a **cycle** of the sine curve. Notice in Fig. 16.1 that the cycle from $x = 0$ to $x = 2\pi$ has four basic parts in its pattern:

1. From $x = 0$ to $x = \pi/2$, the curve *rises* from $y = 0$ to $y = 1$.
2. From $x = \pi/2$ to $x = \pi$, the curve *falls* from $y = 1$ to $y = 0$.
3. From $x = \pi$ to $x = 3\pi/2$, the curve continues to *fall* from $y = 0$ to $y = -1$.
4. From $x = 3\pi/2$ to $x = 2\pi$, the curve *rises* from $y = -1$ to $y = 0$.

Thus the zeros of the sine function are 0, π, 2π, and so on.

For any periodic function, one-half of the difference of the maximum and minimum values is called the **amplitude** of the function. You can see that the maximum value of $\sin x$ is 1 and the minimum value is -1. Thus the amplitude of $y = \sin x$ is 1 because

$$\frac{1}{2}[1 - (-1)] = \frac{1}{2}(2) = 1.$$

In summary we have:

> The sine function $y = \sin x$ has period 2π and amplitude 1.

One simple variation of the sine function is a function of the form

$$y = a \sin x, \qquad \text{where } a \text{ is a constant.}$$

As $\sin x$ varies between 1 and -1, the values of $a \sin x$ vary between a and $-a$. In fact, the y-value of each point on the curve $y = a \sin x$ is just a times the corresponding y-value on the curve $y = \sin x$. Thus the graphs of $y = a \sin x$ and $y = \sin x$ may differ in a vertical sense. The period is 2π in both cases. If a is positive, the graph of $y = a \sin x$ resembles the basic sine curve. If a is negative, then when $\sin x$ is positive, $a \sin x$ is negative; when $\sin x$ is negative, $a \sin x$ is positive. As a result, the graph of $y = a \sin x$ appears like an *inverted* sine curve. However, regardless of a, the amplitude of $y = a \sin x$ is $|a|$.

> The amplitude of $y = a \sin x$ is $|a|$, and the period is 2π. If $a > 0$, the shape is that of a basic sine curve; if $a < 0$, the shape is that of an inverted sine curve.

Example 1

Sketch the graph of $y = 2 \sin x$ over one period.

Solution Here $a = 2 > 0$. Thus the graph is a sine curve with amplitude 2 and period 2π. To draw the graph, we sketch a basic sine curve and label the axes to indicate the amplitude and period. See Fig. 16.2.

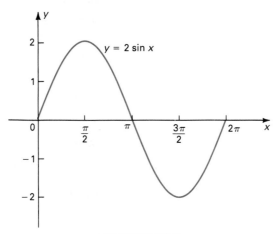

FIGURE 16.2

Example 2

Sketch the graph of $y = -2 \sin x$ over one period.

Solution The amplitude is $|a| = |-2| = 2$ and the period is 2π. Since $a < 0$, the basic shape is an *inverted* sine curve. See Fig. 16.3.

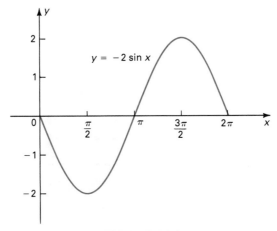

FIGURE 16.3

A more general variation of the sine function is

$$y = a \sin (bx + c) \qquad a, b, c \text{ constants, } b > 0.$$

(The equation $y = a \sin x$ is a special case where $b = 1$ and $c = 0$.) The quantity $bx + c$, which represents an angle, is called the **argument** of the sine function. As before, the amplitude is $|a|$. The shape is still that of a sine curve if $a > 0$ or an inverted sine curve if $a < 0$. However, the graph may be affected in a *horizontal* way, depending on b and c.

To show why, we consider the graph of

$$y = 3 \sin \left(2x + \frac{\pi}{2} \right).$$

Here $a = 3$, $b = 2$, and $c = \pi/2$. The amplitude is 3, and the shape is that of a sine curve because $a > 0$. Recall that we obtain one cycle of the curve $y = \sin \theta$ whenever θ ranges over an interval of length 2π. Similarly, we obtain one cycle of

$$y = 3 \sin \left(2x + \frac{\pi}{2} \right)$$

as the argument, $2x + \dfrac{\pi}{2}$, ranges over an interval of length 2π, such as from zero to 2π. Thus a cycle *begins* when

$$2x + \frac{\pi}{2} = 0$$

$$2x = -\frac{\pi}{2}$$

$$x = -\frac{\pi}{4}.$$

The previous cycle *ends* when

$$2x + \frac{\pi}{2} = 2\pi$$

$$2x = \frac{3\pi}{2}$$

$$x = \frac{3\pi}{4}.$$

The period is the length of the interval from $-\pi/4$ to $3\pi/4$, which is

$$\frac{3\pi}{4} - \left(-\frac{\pi}{4} \right) = \pi.$$

Thus the curve completes one cycle as x varies over an interval of length π, for over that interval the argument $2x + \dfrac{\pi}{2}$ varies over an interval of length 2π.

When we draw the cycle of $y = 3 \sin\left(2x + \dfrac{\pi}{2}\right)$ that begins at $x = -\pi/4$ and ends at $x = 3\pi/4$, we must keep in mind that a cycle of a sine curve has four basic parts. To aid us, therefore, on the x-axis we shall label the values of x where y has a maximum value (3) or minimum value (-3) or is 0. These values of x are equally spaced and are found by dividing the period by 4 (this gives $\pi/4$) and successively adding the result to the beginning x-value, $-\pi/4$:

$$-\frac{\pi}{4} + \frac{\pi}{4} = 0; \qquad 0 + \frac{\pi}{4} = \frac{\pi}{4}; \qquad \frac{\pi}{4} + \frac{\pi}{4} = \frac{2\pi}{4} = \frac{\pi}{2}; \qquad \frac{\pi}{2} + \frac{\pi}{4} = \frac{3\pi}{4}.$$

Thus the important values of x are:

$$-\frac{\pi}{4}, \quad 0, \quad \frac{\pi}{4}, \quad \frac{\pi}{2}, \quad \text{and} \quad \frac{3\pi}{4}.$$

Finally, we draw a sine curve such that y has a value of 0 at $x = -\pi/4$, then rises to a maximum value of 3 at $x = 0$, decreases to 0 at $x = \pi/4$, then continues to decrease to the minimum value of -3 at $\pi/2$, and then rises to the value of 0 at $x = 3\pi/2$. See Fig. 16.4.

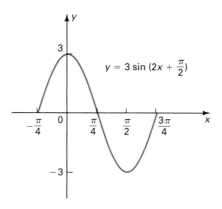

FIGURE 16.4

More generally, we obtain a cycle of $y = a \sin(bx + c)$ when the value of the argument ranges from 0 to 2π. The cycle begins when

$$bx + c = 0, \quad \text{or} \quad x = -\frac{c}{b},$$

and it ends when

$$bx + c = 2\pi, \quad \text{or} \quad x = -\frac{c}{b} + \frac{2\pi}{b}.$$

Thus the period p is given by

$$p = \left(-\frac{c}{b} + \frac{2\pi}{b}\right) - \left(-\frac{c}{b}\right) = \frac{2\pi}{b}.$$

Because the period is $2\pi/b$, we conclude that b gives the number of cycles in the interval from zero to 2π.

Furthermore, depending on the values of b and c, the graph of $y = a \sin (bx + c)$ may be shifted horizontally to the right or left with respect to the graph of the basic sine function. The quantity $-c/b$ is called the **displacement** (or **phase shift**) and represents the amount by which the graph of $y = a \sin (bx + c)$ is shifted in comparison to the basic sine curve. That is, a cycle of $y = \sin x$ begins when $x = 0$, but a cycle of $y = a \sin (bx + c)$ begins when $x = -c/b$. If the displacement is positive, the shift is to the right; if the displacement is negative, the shift is to the left. For example, given the function

$$y = 3 \sin \left(2x + \frac{\pi}{2}\right),$$

the displacement d is given by

$$d = -\frac{c}{b} = -\frac{\pi/2}{2} = -\frac{\pi}{4} < 0,$$

which agrees with the fact that the cycle shown in Fig. 16.4 begins to the *left* of the origin at $x = -\pi/4$.

The preceding discussion leads to a procedure for sketching the graph of $y = a \sin (bx + c)$, where $b > 0$.

1. *Find the amplitude. It is $|a|$.*
2. *Find the shape of the curve, that is, regular sine curve pattern ($a > 0$) or inverted sine curve pattern ($a < 0$).*
3. *Solve $bx + c = 0$ to find a value of x when a cycle begins. Call this value x_b.*
4. *Solve $bx + c = 2\pi$ to find the value of x when the cycle in Step 3 ends. Call this x_e.*
5. *Find the period p:*

$$p = \frac{2\pi}{b}.$$

6. *Find the x-values of "important" points. By important, we mean those points where the function has a maximum, minimum, or zero value. One of these is x_b. To find the others, divide p by 4 and successively add this result to x_b. Also label the y-axis to show the maximum and minimum values.*

A general sketch of $y = a \sin (bx + c)$ appears in Fig. 16.5. The following should be noted.

1. a affects amplitude and shape (that is, regular or inverted pattern).
2. b affects the period.
3. b and c affect displacement.

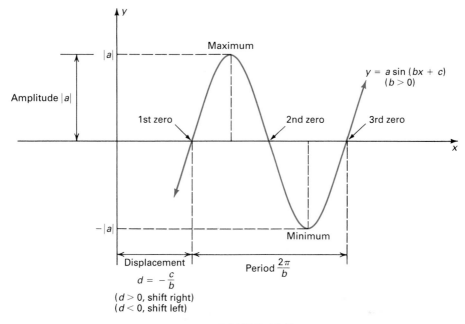

FIGURE 16.5

Example 3

Sketch the graph of $y = -2 \sin (\frac{1}{2}x)$.

Solution

1. The amplitude is $|a| = |-2| = 2$.
2. Since $a < 0$, the shape is that of an *inverted* sine curve pattern.
3. If $\frac{1}{2}x = 0$, then $x = 0$. A cycle begins when $x_b = 0$.
4. If $\frac{1}{2}x = 2\pi$, then $x = 4\pi$. The above cycle ends when $x_e = 4\pi$.
5. The period p is:

$$p = \frac{2\pi}{b} = \frac{2\pi}{\frac{1}{2}} = 4\pi.$$

SEC. 16.1 The Graph of the Sine Function **583**

6. Since $p/4$ is π, the x-values of important points are:

$$0, \qquad 0 + \pi = \pi, \qquad \pi + \pi = 2\pi, \qquad 2\pi + \pi = 3\pi, \quad \text{and} \quad 3\pi + \pi = 4\pi.$$

Important points: when $x = 0$, π, 2π, 3π, and 4π.

One cycle of the graph is drawn in Fig. 16.6. Note that in the interval from zero to 2π, there is one-half ($b = \frac{1}{2}$) cycle of $y = -2\sin\left(\frac{1}{2}x\right)$.

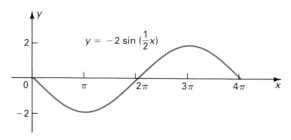

FIGURE 16.6

Example 4

Sketch the graph of $y = \sin\left(\pi x - \dfrac{\pi}{4}\right)$.

Solution

1. The amplitude is $|a| = |1| = 1$.
2. Because $a > 0$, the shape is that of a regular sine curve pattern.
3. If $\pi x - \pi/4 = 0$, then $\pi x = \pi/4$, so $x = \frac{1}{4}$. Thus a cycle begins when $x = \frac{1}{4}$, so $x_b = \frac{1}{4}$.
4. If $\pi x - \pi/4 = 2\pi$, then $\pi x = 9\pi/4$, so $x = \frac{9}{4}$. The previous cycle ends when $x = \frac{9}{4}$, so $x_e = \frac{9}{4}$.
5. The period p is given by

$$p = \frac{2\pi}{b} = \frac{2\pi}{\pi} = 2.$$

6. Since $p/4$ is $\frac{2}{4}$, the x-values of important points are: $\frac{1}{4}$, $\frac{1}{4} + \frac{2}{4} = \frac{3}{4}$, $\frac{3}{4} + \frac{2}{4} = \frac{5}{4}$, and so on.

Important points: when $x = \dfrac{1}{4}, \dfrac{3}{4}, \dfrac{5}{4}, \dfrac{7}{4}$, and $\dfrac{9}{4}$.

One cycle of the graph is shown in Fig. 16.7.

584 CHAP. 16 Graphs of the Trigonometric Functions

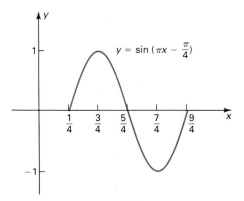

$$y = \sin\left(\pi x - \frac{\pi}{4}\right)$$

FIGURE 16.7

Example 5

Sketch the graphs of $y = \sin x$ and $y = \sin 3x$ on the same coordinate plane.

Solution   The graphs appear in Fig. 16.8. The period of $y = \sin 3x$ is $2\pi/b = 2\pi/3$. Note that in the interval from zero to 2π, there are three ($b = 3$) cycles of $y = \sin 3x$.

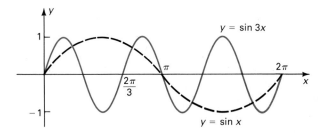

FIGURE 16.8

Example 6

When an object vibrates in simple harmonic motion, its displacement y from its equilibrium position as a function of time t can written in the general form

$$y = A \sin\left(2\pi ft + \varphi\right),$$

where $|A|$ is the *amplitude* of the motion, f is the *frequency* in cycles per second (or hertz), and φ is the *phase constant*. Suppose a mass attached to a spring undergoes simple harmonic motion according to the equation

$$y = 0.60 \sin\left(\frac{\pi}{2}t - \frac{\pi}{4}\right),$$

where y is in meters and t is in seconds. Find the amplitude, frequency, and period of the motion.

Solution   Comparing the given equation to the general form, we have an amplitude of $A = 0.60$ m. Because the coefficient of t must correspond to $2\pi f$, we have

$$2\pi f = \frac{\pi}{2}, \qquad f = \frac{1}{4}.$$

Thus the frequency of the motion is $f = \frac{1}{4}$ cycle per second, or $\frac{1}{4}$ Hz. The period p is given by

$$p = \frac{2\pi}{b} = \frac{2\pi}{\pi/2} = 4 \text{ s}.$$

Note that the period and frequency of a simple harmonic motion are reciprocals of one another.

Problem Set 16.1

In Problems 1–18, draw one cycle of each curve. Give the amplitude A and period p.

1. $y = 3 \sin x$.

2. $y = \dfrac{1}{2} \sin x$.

3. $y = -4 \sin x$.

4. $y = -1.2 \sin t$.

5. $y = \sin 2x$.

6. $y = \sin \dfrac{x}{2}$.

7. $y = 2 \sin \dfrac{1}{3} t$.

8. $y = 3 \sin 6x$.

9. $y = -4 \sin 3x$.

10. $y = 1.2 \sin \dfrac{3\pi x}{2}$.

11. $y = \sin \left(x + \dfrac{\pi}{4} \right)$.

12. $y = -3 \sin \left(x - \dfrac{\pi}{6} \right)$.

13. $y = 4 \sin \left(2t - \dfrac{\pi}{2} \right)$.

14. $y = -\dfrac{1}{4} \sin \left(t + \dfrac{\pi}{2} \right)$.

15. $y = -2 \sin \left(\dfrac{x}{2} - \dfrac{2\pi}{3} \right)$.

16. $y = 2 \sin \left(2x - \dfrac{2\pi}{3} \right)$.

17. $y = \sin \left(\pi x - \dfrac{\pi}{2} \right)$.

18. $y = 3 \sin \left(\dfrac{2}{3}\pi x - \dfrac{3\pi}{2} \right)$.

19. Draw the graphs of $y = \sin x$ and $y = \sin 2x$ on the same coordinate plane. How many cycles of $y = \sin 2x$ are there for each cycle of $y = \sin x$?

20. Draw the graph of $y = 2 \sin \dfrac{x}{4}$ from $x = -2\pi$ to $x = 4\pi$.

21. If the equation $y = 2.3 \sin (8.7t - 1.2)$ describes the harmonic motion of a particle, where t is in seconds and y is in meters, find (a) the period and (b) the frequency. (See Example 6.)

22. Repeat Problem 21 if $y = 4 \sin \omega t$, where ω is a constant.

23. The transverse wave traveling on a stretched string is of the form $y = 2 \sin [\pi(2x - 20t)]$, where t is time in seconds. Sketch one cycle of this wave when $t = 2$ s.

24. The velocity v of a particle undergoing simple harmonic motion is given by the relation $v = -2\pi fA \sin(2\pi ft)$, where f is the frequency in hertz, A is the maximum displacement from the equilibrium point, and t is time in seconds. Sketch the graph of this equation for a frequency of 50 Hz and $A = 10$ m.

25. The horizontal range R of a projectile having an initial speed v_0 and projected at an angle θ above the horizontal is given by

$$R = \frac{v_0^2}{g} \sin 2\theta.$$

(a) Draw one cycle of the graph of this equation.
(b) At what angle of projection, θ, does your graph indicate the horizontal range is maximum? We point out that the graph has physical significance for the first half-cycle only, for an object must be projected *above* the horizontal.

26. When the coil of a generator rotates in a magnetic field, the induced voltage $\mathcal{E}$ in the coil as a function of time is given by the expression

$$\mathcal{E} = \mathcal{E}_m \sin(\omega t - \varphi),$$

where $\mathcal{E}_m$ is the maximum induced voltage, ω is the angular speed of the coil in radians per second, t is the time in seconds, and φ is the phase angle in radians. Let $\mathcal{E}_m = 20$ V, $\omega = \dfrac{\pi}{4}$ rad/s, and $\varphi = \dfrac{\pi}{2}$ rad. Sketch one cycle of the curve and determine, from your graph, the induced voltage when $t = 6$ s.

16.2 THE GRAPH OF THE COSINE FUNCTION

Using the data in Table 16.2, we have sketched the graph of the basic cosine function $y = \cos x$ in Fig. 16.9. Like the sine function, the period of $y = \cos x$ is 2π and the amplitude is 1. For the cycle from $x = 0$ to $x = 2\pi$, there are four basic parts.

TABLE 16.2

x	0	$\dfrac{\pi}{6}$	$\dfrac{\pi}{3}$	$\dfrac{\pi}{2}$	$\dfrac{2\pi}{3}$	$\dfrac{5\pi}{6}$	π	$\dfrac{7\pi}{6}$	$\dfrac{4\pi}{3}$	$\dfrac{3\pi}{2}$	$\dfrac{5\pi}{3}$	$\dfrac{11\pi}{6}$	2π
$y = \cos x$	1	0.87	0.5	0	−0.5	−0.87	−1	−0.87	−0.5	0	0.5	0.87	1

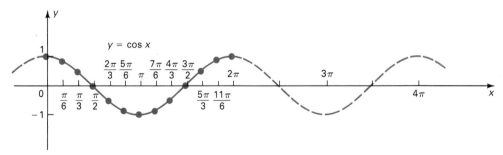

FIGURE 16.9

1. From $x = 0$ to $x = \pi/2$, the curve *falls* from $y = 1$ to $y = 0$.
2. From $x = \pi/2$ to $x = \pi$, the curve continues to *fall* from $y = 0$ to $y = -1$.
3. From $x = \pi$ to $x = 3\pi/2$, the curve *rises* from $y = -1$ to $y = 0$.
4. From $x = 3\pi/2$ to $x = 2\pi$, the curve continues to *rise* from $y = 0$ to $y = 1$.

Comparing the cosine curve in Fig. 16.9 to the sine curve in Fig. 16.1, you can see that the cosine curve is simply the sine curve shifted $\pi/2$ to the left. This means that

$$\sin\left(x + \frac{\pi}{2}\right) = \cos x.$$

In fact, the complete discussion in Sec. 16.1 of amplitude, inversion, period, and displacement also applies to variations of the cosine function, that is, to functions having the form $y = a\cos(bx + c)$ where $b > 0$. The following examples will illustrate this.

Example 1

Sketch the graph of $y = 3\cos 6x$.

Solution

1. The amplitude is $|a| = |3| = 3$.
2. Because $a > 0$, the shape is that of a regular cosine curve.
3. If $6x = 0$, then $x = 0$. A cycle begins when $x_b = 0$.
4. If $6x = 2\pi$, then $x = \pi/3$. The above cycle ends when $x_e = \pi/3$.
5. The period p is:

$$p = \frac{2\pi}{b} = \frac{2\pi}{6} = \frac{\pi}{3}.$$

6. Important points: when $x = 0, \dfrac{\pi}{12}, \dfrac{\pi}{6}, \dfrac{\pi}{4}$, and $\dfrac{\pi}{3}$.

One cycle of the graph is drawn in Fig. 16.10.

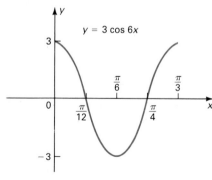

FIGURE 16.10

Example 2

Sketch the graph of $y = -2 \cos{(7x - \pi)}$.

Solution

1. The amplitude is $|a| = |-2| = 2$.
2. Because $a < 0$, the curve has an *inverted* cosine curve pattern.
3. If $7x - \pi = 0$, then $x = \pi/7$. A cycle begins when $x_b = \pi/7$.
4. If $7x - \pi = 2\pi$, then $x = 3\pi/7$. The above cycle ends when $x_e = 3\pi/7$.
5. The period p is:

$$p = \frac{2\pi}{b} = \frac{2\pi}{7}.$$

6. Important points: when $x = \dfrac{\pi}{7}, \dfrac{3\pi}{14}, \dfrac{2\pi}{7}, \dfrac{5\pi}{14}$, and $\dfrac{3\pi}{7}$.

One cycle of the graph is drawn in Fig. 16.11.

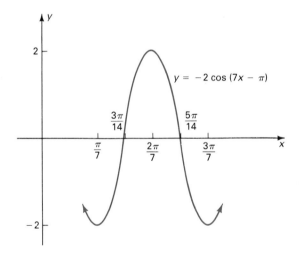

FIGURE 16.11

In the study of electrical circuits, we often find it necessary to deal with the *phase relationship* between trigonometric functions having the same period. For example, in ac circuits the voltage and current are both expressible as cosine or sine functions. The graphs of these functions do not necessarily pass through their zero (or maximum) values at the same instant of time. If they do not rise and fall together, a *phase difference* is said to exist between them.

In Fig. 16.12 we have indicated three different phase relationships that exist between a voltage V and a current I in an ac circuit. Figures 16.12 (a), (b), and (c),

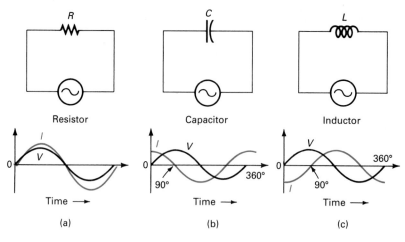

FIGURE 16.12

respectively, represent an ac generator connected in series to a pure resistor R, a pure capacitor C, and a pure inductor L. In (a), the current and voltage are said to be *in phase* because they pass through their zero values and maximum values at the same instant of time. This relationship is characteristic of a purely resistive ac circuit. In (b), the current and voltage are said to be 90° *out of phase* because their corresponding maximum values and zero values occur $\frac{1}{4}$ cycle apart. Note that in discussing phase relationships the engineer speaks in terms of *electrical degrees*, where 1 cycle represents 360 electrical degrees. More specifically we say that in (b) the current *leads* the voltage by 90° because it reaches its maximum (or zero) value $\frac{1}{4}$ cycle, or 90 electrical degrees, earlier than the voltage does as we view the curves from left to right. Equivalently, we can say that the voltage *lags* the current by 90°. This is characteristic of a purely capacitive ac circuit. Finally, in (c) the voltage *leads* the current by 90°—characteristic of a purely inductive ac circuit.

Problem Set 16.2

In Problems 1–12, draw one cycle of each curve. Give the amplitude A and the period p.

1. $y = \frac{1}{2} \cos x.$

2. $y = -3 \cos x.$

3. $y = 4 \cos 4t.$

4. $y = \frac{1}{2} \cos 5x.$

5. $y = -4 \cos 3x.$

6. $y = \cos\left(4x - \dfrac{\pi}{2}\right).$

7. $y = 2 \cos\left(x + \dfrac{\pi}{3}\right).$

8. $y = \cos\left(\dfrac{1}{4}x\right).$

9. $y = -2 \cos\left(\dfrac{x}{2} - \dfrac{2\pi}{3}\right).$

10. $y = 3 \cos\left(x - \dfrac{\pi}{6}\right).$

11. $y = \cos\left(\pi x - \dfrac{\pi}{2}\right).$

12. $y = 2 \cos(3x + 1).$

13. The voltage across an inductor in an ac circuit can be described mathematically by the equation $y_1 = 2 \cos 3x$. The voltage across another component in the same circuit is given by $y_2 = \cos\left(3x - \dfrac{\pi}{2}\right)$. What is the phase relationship between these two voltage signals— that is, which of the curves leads the other and by how many electrical degrees?

14. If a uniform metal disk with its plane horizontal is suspended by a wire attached to its center, the device is called a torsional pendulum. If the disk is now rotated through an angle in the horizontal plane and released, it will execute simple angular harmonic motion. For such motion the angular displacement θ from the equilibrium position is given by the equation

$$\theta = \theta_m \cos(\omega t + \alpha),$$

where θ_m is the maximum displacement in radians, ω is the angular frequency in radians per second, t is time in seconds, and α is the phase angle in radians. Draw one cycle of the graph of this equation if $\omega = \pi$ and $\alpha = \pi/2$.

15. In a series ac circuit having a current $I = 2 \sin(120\,\pi t)$, the voltage across a pure capacitor as a function of time is given by $V = -3\cos(120\,\pi t)$. Sketch the graph of both of these equations on the same coordinate plane and determine the phase difference between I and V.

16.3 THE SINE CURVE AND HARMONIC MOTION

When a particle moves around a circle at a constant speed, the projection of the particle on a diameter of the circle, which we shall describe, is said to be in *simple harmonic motion*. In physics, a discussion of simple harmonic motion (SHM) is often presented with a geometric approach. Because that technique illustrates the natural occurrence of sine and cosine curves in a technical context, it is worthy of our brief consideration.

Figure 16.13 shows a particle P on a circle with radius A and center at the origin. We shall assume that the particle is moving counterclockwise around the circle at a constant angular speed ω, which is measured in radians per second. The radius vector from O to P represents the position of P with respect to O.

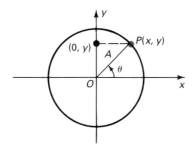

FIGURE 16.13

As the radius vector rotates counterclockwise from an initial position along the positive x-axis, it generates a positive angle θ. If $\theta = 0$ when time $t = 0$, then t seconds later we have

$$\theta = \omega t. \tag{1}$$

Because there are 2π rad in one revolution, the angular speed ω is related to the frequency f (the number of revolutions completed by P in a second) by the equation

$$\omega = 2\pi f. \tag{2}$$

From Eqs. 1 and 2 we can write

$$\theta = 2\pi ft. \tag{3}$$

When the particle, and therefore the endpoint of the radius vector, is at (x_1, y_1), then $\sin \theta_1 = y_1/A$ (Fig. 16.14). When the particle is at (x_2, y_2), then $\sin \theta_2 = y_2/A$. In

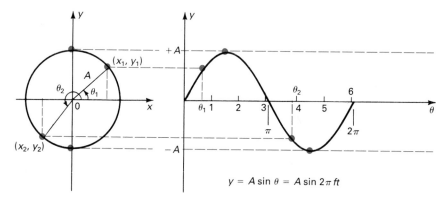

$$y = A \sin \theta = A \sin 2\pi ft$$

FIGURE 16.14

fact, regardless of the position (x, y) of particle P we have

$$\sin \theta = \frac{y}{A} \quad \text{or} \quad y = A \sin \theta. \tag{4}$$

Thus we conclude that for any position (x, y) of particle P, the value of the ordinate y is expressible in terms of the sine of the generated angle. Moreover, from (4) and (3), we have

$$y = A \sin \theta = A \sin 2\pi ft. \tag{5}$$

The resulting graph of $y = A \sin \theta$ for one counterclockwise revolution of the radius vector is also shown in Fig. 16.14. This sine curve was obtained as follows: For a given value of θ, the ordinate of a point on the curve $y = A \sin \theta$ is the same as the ordinate of the position of the particle for the same value of θ. This is indicated by the dashed lines. The values of θ along the horizontal axis are in radians. Observe, for example, that when the particle moves in the third or fourth quadrants, its ordinate is negative. Therefore, the graph of $y = A \sin \theta$ falls below the θ-axis for θ between π and 2π. Although only a portion of the curve is shown, it should be realized that the curve continues in this manner indefinitely. Similarly, you should realize that values of $A \sin \theta$ for negative angles could be found by considering *clockwise* rotation of the radius vector.

When the particle P is at point (x, y) the point $(0, y)$ is called the **projection** of P on the y-axis (refer back to Fig. 16.13). If P begins at $(A, 0)$ and travels once around the circle, then its projection travels on the y-axis from $(0, 0)$ to $(0, A)$, then to $(0, -A)$, and back to $(0, 0)$. Thus the projection will move up and down on the diameter of the circle joining $(0, A)$ and $(0, -A)$. The motion of the projection on the y-axis is an example of SHM. The period of the SHM is the same as the time of one revolution of P around the circle. The frequency of the SHM is the same as the number of revolutions per second that P makes around the circle.

Equation 5, which gives the y-axis position of the projection executing SHM along the y-axis, is restricted in the sense that if $t = 0$, then $y = 0$. For a real motion we might expect that if $t = 0$, then y could have some other value between $-A$ and A. That is taken care of in the following more general form of the equation for SHM.

$$y = A \sin (2\pi ft + \varphi), \tag{6}$$

where φ is called the phase constant. In particular we note that if $\varphi = \pi/2$, then the curve generated in the manner of Fig. 16.14 is

$$y = A \sin \left(2\pi ft + \frac{\pi}{2} \right) = A \cos 2\pi ft,$$

a cosine curve [this follows from the fact that $\sin \left(x + \dfrac{\pi}{2} \right) = \cos x$, which was stated in Sec. 16.2]. Simple harmonic motions are described in terms of both sine and cosine functions.

16.4 GRAPHS OF TANGENT, COTANGENT, SECANT, AND COSECANT

Whereas the graphs of the sine and cosine functions are both smooth curves exhibiting wavelike appearances, the graphs of the remaining trigonometric functions are strikingly different. Consider the function

$$y = \tan x.$$

In Table 16.3 are x- and y-values for $y = \tan x$ (some y-values are approximate). The dashes when $x = \pm \pi/2$ and $x = \pm 3\pi/2$ mean that $\tan x$ is not defined there. Figure 16.15 shows the graph of $y = \tan x$. As expected, there are no points on the graph when $x = \pm \pi/2, \pm 3\pi/2$. But for x near these values, $\tan x$ increases or decreases without bound. The graph gets very close to the vertical lines $x = \pm \pi/2, \pm 3\pi/2$, but

TABLE 16.3

x	0	$\dfrac{\pi}{6}$	$\dfrac{\pi}{3}$	$\dfrac{\pi}{2}$	$\dfrac{2\pi}{3}$	$\dfrac{5\pi}{6}$	π	$\dfrac{7\pi}{6}$	$\dfrac{4\pi}{3}$	$\dfrac{3\pi}{2}$
$y = \tan x$	0	0.6	1.7	$—$	-1.7	-0.6	0	0.6	1.7	$—$

x	$-\dfrac{\pi}{6}$	$-\dfrac{\pi}{3}$	$-\dfrac{\pi}{2}$	$-\dfrac{2\pi}{3}$	$-\dfrac{5\pi}{6}$	$-\pi$	$-\dfrac{7\pi}{6}$	$-\dfrac{4\pi}{3}$	$-\dfrac{3\pi}{2}$
$y = \tan x$	-0.6	-1.7	$—$	1.7	0.6	0	-0.6	-1.7	$—$

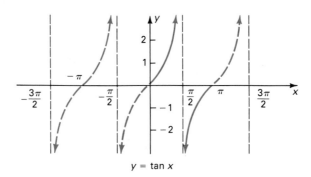

$y = \tan x$

FIGURE 16.15

does not touch them. These lines are called **vertical asymptotes** for the curve; they are lines near which the function "blows up." However, they are *not* part of the graph. We also see that the portion of the graph between $x = 0$ and $x = \pi$ repeats itself. Thus

$$y = \tan x \text{ has period } \pi.$$

That is, $\tan (x + \pi) = \tan x$. Only three cycles of $y = \tan x$ are shown in Fig. 16.15, but it should be clear that the graph continues both to the left and right. Because $\tan x$ has no maximum or minimum values, no amplitude is assigned to it.

The graph of $y = \csc x$ can be conveniently sketched if we use the reciprocal relationship

$$\csc x = \frac{1}{\sin x}.$$

We first sketch the sine function (see the dashed curve in Fig. 16.16). For a point (x, y) on the graph of $y = \sin x$, we estimate the value of y. The reciprocal of this value is then the ordinate of the corresponding point on $y = \csc x$ with the same abscissa. For example, when $\sin x = \frac{1}{2}$, then $\csc x = 2$; when $\sin x = 1$, then $\csc x = 1$; and so on. In

594 CHAP. 16 Graphs of the Trigonometric Functions

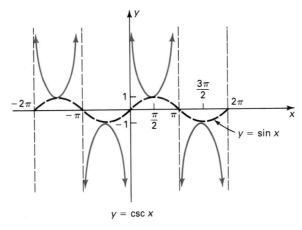

$$y = \csc x$$

FIGURE 16.16

this way we can get the entire graph of $y = \csc x$. The solid curve in Fig. 16.16 shows two cycles. Just as $\sin x$ has period 2π,

$$y = \csc x \text{ has period } 2\pi.$$

For $x = 0, \pi, 2\pi$, and so on, $\sin x = 0$. Thus $\csc x$ is not defined for these values. The lines $x = 0, \pi, 2\pi$, and so forth are vertical asymptotes. No amplitude is assigned to $y = \csc x$.

By similar reasoning we can also sketch the graphs of

$$y = \cot x = \frac{1}{\tan x} \quad \text{and} \quad y = \sec x = \frac{1}{\cos x}.$$

These graphs, with the graphs of the corresponding reciprocal functions shown by dashed curves, are indicated in Figs. 16.17 and 16.18. Note that when $\tan x = 0$, $\cot x$

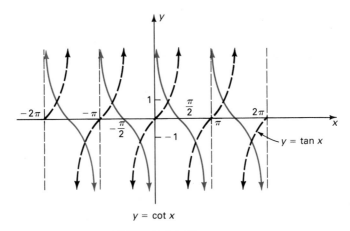

$$y = \cot x$$

FIGURE 16.17

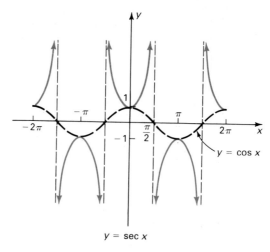

FIGURE 16.18

is undefined; when $\tan x$ is undefined, $\cot x = 0$. It should be clear that $\cot (x + \pi) = \cot x$ and $\sec (x + 2\pi) = \sec x$. That is,

> $y = \cot x$ has period π.
>
> $y = \sec x$ has period 2π.

No amplitudes are assigned to these functions.

Problem Set 16.4

1. Draw the graph of $y = \csc x$. Use this graph to find all angles x between zero and 4π for which $\csc x = -1$.

2. Draw the graph of $y = \cot x$. Use this graph to find all angles x between zero and 2π for which $\cot x = 0$.

3. Draw the graph of $y = \tan x$. Use this graph to find all angles x between $-\pi/2$ and $5\pi/2$ for which $\tan x = 0$.

4. Draw the graph of $y = \sec x$. Use this graph to find all angles x between $-5\pi/2$ and $5\pi/2$ for which $\sec x = 1$.

16.5 ADDITION OF ORDINATES

In certain applications, physical phenomena are representable mathematically as sums or differences of trigonometric functions. The graphs of such combinations of trigonometric functions may be sketched by a technique known as **addition of**

ordinates. We shall illustrate this method by sketching the curve $y = \sin x + \cos x$. This equation can be thought of as representing the sum of two functions:

$$y = y_1 + y_2, \qquad \text{where } y_1 = \sin x \quad \text{and} \quad y_2 = \cos x.$$

We first sketch the graphs of $y_1 = \sin x$ and $y_2 = \cos x$ on the same coordinate plane, as shown in Fig. 16.19. These graphs are then combined by adding the ordinates

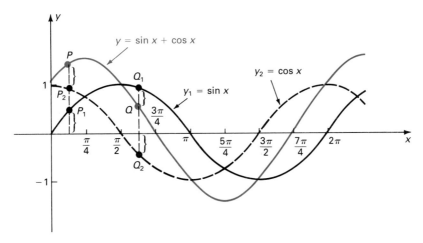

FIGURE 16.19

(y-values) corresponding to the same abscissa (x-value). For example, point P is obtained by measuring the ordinate of P_1 (see the lower brace) and adding it algebraically to the ordinate of P_2 (see the upper brace). To obtain point Q, we add the negative ordinate of point Q_2 to the ordinate of Q_1. After a suitable number of points are obtained in this manner, they are connected by a smooth curve. Thus we obtain the graph of $y = \sin x + \cos x$. Engineers often speak of this addition of ordinates as the *principle of superposition*.

Example 1

Sketch the graph of $y = \sin x + \frac{1}{3}\sin 3x$.

Solution   We first sketch the graphs of $y_1 = \sin x$ and $y_2 = \frac{1}{3}\sin 3x$ on the same coordinate plane (see Fig. 16.20). Note that $\sin x$ has amplitude 1 and period 2π, but $\frac{1}{3}\sin 3x$ has amplitude $\frac{1}{3}$ and period $2\pi/3$. Next, at various values of x we add the y-values of the two graphs. We then connect the points by a smooth curve.

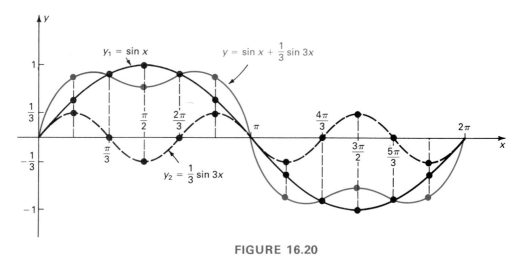

FIGURE 16.20

The French mathematician J. Fourier (1768–1830) showed that we can analyze extremely complicated periodic waves as a combination of relatively simple waves. By his technique, well known in engineering as Fourier analysis, a periodic function may be represented as an infinite series—that is, an unending sum of terms—each term of which is a sine or cosine function. Example 2 gives an illustration.

Example 2

The dashed curve of Fig. 16.21(a) is a sawtooth waveform, a periodic curve commonly associated with the oscilloscope. Figure 16.21(b) shows the graphs of the first six terms of the

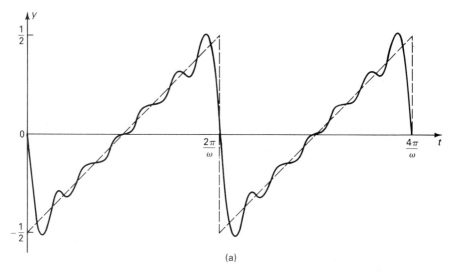

(a)

FIGURE 16.21

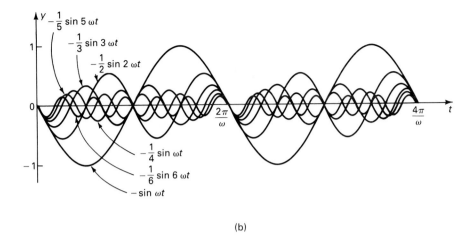

$-\frac{1}{5}\sin 5\,\omega t$

$-\frac{1}{3}\sin 3\,\omega t$

$-\frac{1}{2}\sin 2\,\omega t$

$-\frac{1}{4}\sin \omega t$

$-\frac{1}{6}\sin 6\,\omega t$

$-\sin \omega t$

(b)

FIGURE 16.21 (Reprinted from R. Resnick and D. Halliday, *Physics*, 1st ed., by permission of John Wiley & Sons, Inc.)

Fourier series for that periodic wave. The solid curve in Fig. 16.21(a) is the sum of the first six terms of the Fourier series found from the graphs in (b) by the technique of addition of ordinates. The solid curve can be seen to be a fairly close approximation of the sawtooth waveform. As additional terms of the Fourier series are included, the approximation continually improves. Hence, the sawtooth waveform has been expressed as a sum of relatively simple sine curves.

Problem Set 16.5

In Problems 1–8, sketch the graph of the given equation over the given interval by means of addition of ordinates.

1. $y = 2 + \sin x$; 0 to 2π.
2. $y = 1 + \cos x$; 0 to 2π.
3. $y = \sin x + \sin 2x$; 0 to 2π.
4. $y = \sin 2x + 2 \sin x$; 0 to 2π.
5. $y = \sin 2x + \cos 3x$; 0 to π.
6. $y = 4 \sin x - 3 \cos x$; 0 to 2π.
7. $y = x + \sin x$; 0 to 3π.
8. $y = \cos 3x - \sin 2x$; 0 to π.

9. Consider a string fixed at both ends in which a wavetrain is initiated by plucking the string. Waves will be reflected from both ends of the string with the resulting shape of the string determined by the sum of the two waves, one traveling to the right and the other traveling to the left. Suppose the wave traveling to the right is given by $y_1 = 2 \sin \pi(x - t)$ and the one to the left is given by $y_2 = 2 \sin \pi(x + t)$. Find the shape of the string as a function of position at $t = 3$ s.

16.6 INVERSE TRIGONOMETRIC FUNCTIONS

The equation $w = \sin t$ defines w as a function of t. However, it does not define t as a function of w. To see why, let the input w be $\frac{1}{2}$. Then the output is a value of t such that

$$\frac{1}{2} = \sin t.$$

Because the sine function is periodic, this equation has many solutions. Some are $\pi/6$, $5\pi/6$, $13\pi/6$, and $-7\pi/6$, as shown in Fig. 16.22.

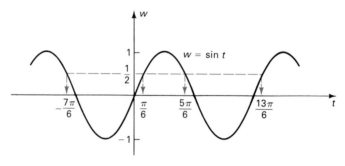

FIGURE 16.22

Because there is more than one output for a single input, the equation $w = \sin t$ does *not* define t as a function of w. However, if we restrict the domain of $\sin t$ so that

$$-\frac{\pi}{2} \le t \le \frac{\pi}{2},$$

then to each input w (where $-1 \le w \le 1$) there corresponds exactly one output t (see Fig. 16.23) and we *do* have a function of w.

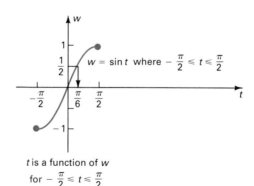

t is a function of w

for $-\dfrac{\pi}{2} \le t \le \dfrac{\pi}{2}$

FIGURE 16.23

For example, if the input is $w = \frac{1}{2}$, then the output t must be $\pi/6$ because

$$\sin \frac{\pi}{6} = \frac{1}{2} \quad \text{and} \quad -\frac{\pi}{2} \le \frac{\pi}{6} \le \frac{\pi}{2}.$$

Similarly, if $w = -1$, then $t = -\pi/2$ because

$$\sin\left(-\frac{\pi}{2}\right) = -1 \quad \text{and} \quad -\frac{\pi}{2} \le -\frac{\pi}{2} \le \frac{\pi}{2}.$$

This function of w that reverses the action of the restricted sine function is called the **inverse sine function** (or the **arcsine function**) and is denoted by $\sin^{-1}$ (or arcsin), where the -1 is not an exponent but is simply part of this new symbol. (This function is also written with a capital first letter as Sin^{-1} or Arcsin.) Thus

$$t = \sin^{-1} w.$$

For example, we have just shown that $\sin^{-1}\left(\frac{1}{2}\right) = \pi/6$ and $\sin^{-1}(-1) = -\pi/2$.

In the equation $t = \sin^{-1} w$, let us replace the input w by x and the output t by y. Then to say that y is the inverse sine of x, that is,

$$y = \sin^{-1} x,$$

means that $\sin y = x$, where $-\pi/2 \le y \le \pi/2$. Note that the domain of $y = \sin^{-1} x$ consists of all x such that $-1 \le x \le 1$. In summary we have:

$$y = \sin^{-1} x \text{ means } \sin y = x,$$

$$\text{where } -1 \le x \le 1 \text{ and } -\frac{\pi}{2} \le y \le \frac{\pi}{2}.$$

Restricting the domains of the cosine and tangent functions allows us to define inverse functions for them as follows:

$$y = \cos^{-1} x \text{ means } \cos y = x,$$

$$\text{where } -1 \le x \le 1 \text{ and } 0 \le y \le \pi.$$

$$y = \tan^{-1} x \text{ means } \tan y = x,$$

$$\text{where } x \text{ is any real number and } -\frac{\pi}{2} < y < \frac{\pi}{2}.$$

Example 1

Find each of the following.

a. $\sin^{-1} \dfrac{\sqrt{2}}{2}$.

Solution $\sin^{-1}(\sqrt{2}/2)$ is the angle y between $-\pi/2$ and $\pi/2$ such that $\sin y = \sqrt{2}/2$. Clearly $y = \pi/4$, so $\sin^{-1}(\sqrt{2}/2) = \pi/4$.

b. $\cos^{-1}\frac{1}{2}$.

Solution $\cos^{-1}\frac{1}{2}$ is the angle y between 0 and π such that $\cos y = \frac{1}{2}$. Thus $y = \pi/3$, so $\cos^{-1}\frac{1}{2} = \pi/3$.

Example 2

Find each of the following.

a. $\cos^{-1}\left(-\dfrac{\sqrt{3}}{2}\right)$.

Solution $\cos^{-1}(-\sqrt{3}/2)$ is the angle y between 0 and π such that $\cos y = -\sqrt{3}/2$. Since $\cos y$ is negative, y must lie between $\pi/2$ and π. If the reference angle is y_R, then $\cos y_R = \sqrt{3}/2$, so $y_R = \pi/6$. Thus $y = \pi - \pi/6 = 5\pi/6$. Hence $\cos^{-1}(-\sqrt{3}/2) = 5\pi/6$.

b. $\tan^{-1}(-1)$.

Solution $\tan^{-1}(-1)$ is the angle y between $-\pi/2$ and $\pi/2$ such that $\tan y = -1$. Since $\tan y$ is negative, y must lie between $-\pi/2$ and 0. If its reference angle is y_R, then $\tan y_R = 1$, so $y_R = \pi/4$. Thus $y = \tan^{-1}(-1) = -\pi/4$.

Example 3

Find each of the following.

a. $\sin\left(\sin^{-1}\dfrac{1}{4}\right)$.

Solution $\sin^{-1}\frac{1}{4}$ is an angle y such that $\sin y = \frac{1}{4}$. Thus

$$\sin\left(\sin^{-1}\frac{1}{4}\right) = \sin(y) = \frac{1}{4}.$$

As a general rule,

$$\boxed{\sin(\sin^{-1} x) = x.}$$

b. $\cos (\sin^{-1} 0)$.

   Solution   Since $\sin^{-1} 0 = 0$, then

$$\cos (\sin^{-1} 0) = \cos (0) = 1.$$

c. $\sin^{-1} \left(\sin \dfrac{5\pi}{6} \right)$.

   Solution

$$\sin^{-1} \left(\sin \frac{5\pi}{6} \right) = \sin^{-1} \left(\frac{1}{2} \right) = \frac{\pi}{6}.$$

   Note that $\sin^{-1} [\sin (5\pi/6)] \neq 5\pi/6$. Compare this with the rule in Part a.

The remaining inverse trigonometric functions, which are not frequently used, are as follows:

> $y = \cot^{-1} x$ means $\cot y = x$, where
> x is any real number and $0 < y < \pi$.
>
> $y = \sec^{-1} x$ means $\sec y = x$, where
> $x \leq -1$ or $x \geq 1$ and $-\pi \leq y < -\dfrac{\pi}{2}$ or $0 \leq y < \dfrac{\pi}{2}$.
>
> $y = \csc^{-1} x$ means $\csc y = x$, where
> $x \leq -1$ or $x \geq 1$ and $-\pi < y \leq -\dfrac{\pi}{2}$ or $0 < y \leq \dfrac{\pi}{2}$.

The graphs of some inverse trigonometric functions are shown in Fig. 16.24.

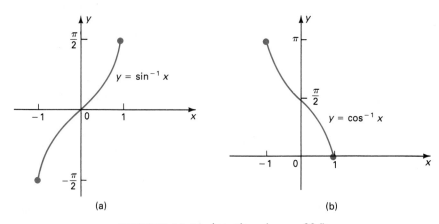

(a)   (b)

FIGURE 16.24 (*continued on p. 604*)

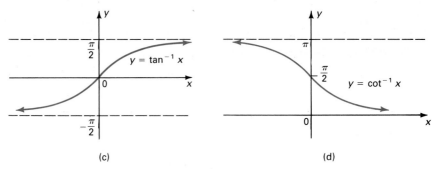

(c)   (d)

FIGURE 16.24 (*cont.*)

Problem Set 16.6

In Problems 1–22, find the value.

1. $\sin^{-1} 1$.

2. $\sin^{-1} \dfrac{\sqrt{3}}{2}$.

3. $\cos^{-1} \dfrac{\sqrt{3}}{2}$.

4. $\arccos(-1)$.

5. $\tan^{-1} 0$.

6. $\sin^{-1}\left(-\dfrac{\sqrt{2}}{2}\right)$.

7. $\sin^{-1}\left(-\dfrac{1}{2}\right)$.

8. $\cos^{-1} 0$.

9. $\arctan 1$.

10. $\tan^{-1}(-\sqrt{3})$.

11. $\cos^{-1}\left(-\dfrac{\sqrt{2}}{2}\right)$.

12. $\cos^{-1}\left(-\dfrac{1}{2}\right)$.

13. $\sin\left(\sin^{-1}\dfrac{1}{3}\right)$.

14. $\cos\left[\cos^{-1}\left(-\dfrac{1}{5}\right)\right]$.

15. $\cos\left(\sin^{-1}\dfrac{1}{2}\right)$.

16. $\sin[\cos^{-1}(-1)]$.

17. $\cot(\cos^{-1} 0)$.

18. $\tan(\cos^{-1} 1)$.

19. $\cos[\tan^{-1}(-1)]$.

20. $\sin\left(\tan^{-1}\dfrac{\sqrt{3}}{3}\right)$.

21. $\sin^{-1}\left(\sin\dfrac{2\pi}{3}\right)$.

22. $\sin^{-1}\left(\sin\dfrac{\pi}{3}\right)$.

16.7 THE OSCILLOSCOPE AND LISSAJOUS FIGURES

We now consider the generation of *Lissajous figures* on the screen of a cathode-ray oscilloscope. The oscilloscope is one of the most useful and versatile instruments available to the engineer.

The heart of an oscilloscope is the cathode-ray tube in which a narrow beam of high-speed electrons strikes a special screen which fluoresces; that is, it gives off visible light at the point where the beam strikes the screen. The position at which the beam strikes the screen can be controlled by two pairs of *deflection plates*. Depending on its polarity, a voltage signal applied to the horizontal deflection plates will cause the beam to move to the right or to the left; a signal applied to the vertical deflection plates will cause the beam to move up or down.

When sinusoidal signals (that is, signals represented by sine or cosine curves) are applied to the two pairs of deflecting plates, the path traced out by the fluorescent dot formed by the impinging electron beam forms a pattern on the screen of the oscilloscope. Furthermore, the pattern will remain stationary as long as the amplitudes and phase relationships of the signals applied to the deflection plates do not change.

Let us consider a simple situation. Suppose a voltage signal in the shape of a sine curve is applied to the vertical deflection plates with *no signal* applied to the horizontal deflection plates. This situation is illustrated in Fig. 16.25 where, for

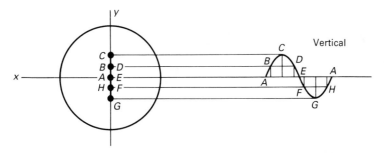

FIGURE 16.25

convenience, we show rectangular coordinate axes on the screen of the oscilloscope. With no signal applied to the horizontal deflection plates, the dot will not move to the left or right and, hence, it will remain on the y-axis. Its motion on the y-axis is controlled by the signal applied to the vertical deflection plates as shown in Fig. 16.25. The dot is at the center of the screen when the voltage applied to the vertical deflection plates is at point A on the voltage signal. The dot moves upward along the y-axis and reaches a maximum height at point C as the voltage applied to the deflection plates reaches its maximum value at point C.* Then, corresponding to a decreasing voltage signal between points C and G, the dot moves downward along the y-axis, reaching its lowest position at point G. Since the voltage signal increases to its original value in the last quarter of the cycle between points G and A, the dot will rise along the y-axis and return to its initial position. If the frequency of the signal to the vertical deflection plates were, for example, 60 cycles per second, the travels of the dot outlined above would be repeated 60 times each second. It is not surprising then that we should "see" a *stationary* vertical line on the oscilloscope screen.

It should be clear that if the sinusoidal voltage shown in Fig. 16.25 were applied to the horizontal deflection plates with no signal applied to the vertical deflection

---

* Because of a scaling factor, these heights may not necessarily be the same.

plates, the dot would trace a path back and forth along the x-axis and we should "see" a horizontal line on the oscilloscope screen.

When sinusoidal signals are simultaneously applied to both sets of deflection plates, the pattern which results depends on the amplitudes, frequencies, and phase relationships of the two signals. The pattern observed on the screen when the ratio of the frequencies of the two signals can be expressed as a ratio of integers is called a **Lissajous figure**.

As an example let us consider voltage signals that have the *same* frequency f, *different* amplitudes, and are 90° out of phase with one another. The mathematical forms of such voltage signals applied to the horizontal and vertical deflection plates are given by Eqs. 1 and 2:

$$V_x = 4 \sin (\omega t), \tag{1}$$

$$V_y = 2 \cos (\omega t). \tag{2}$$

In each case we assume the value of ω is the same; it represents the constant quantity $2\pi f$, called the *angular frequency*. The physical situation is illustrated in Fig. 16.26. By

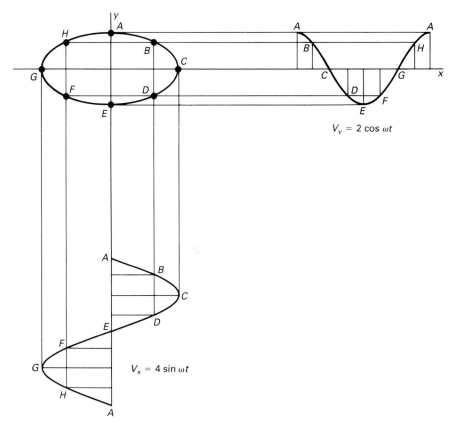

FIGURE 16.26

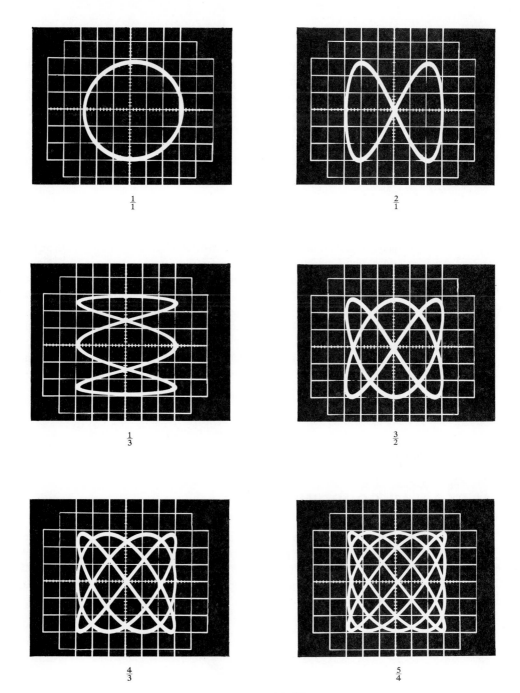

$\frac{1}{1}$

$\frac{2}{1}$

$\frac{1}{3}$

$\frac{3}{2}$

$\frac{4}{3}$

$\frac{5}{4}$

FIGURE 16.27

considering the horizontal and vertical deflections simultaneously, it should be clear that these voltage signals will result in the generation of the Lissajous figure shown, which is called an *ellipse*. Moreover, it should be apparent that if the amplitudes of the two signals were the same, the Lissajous figure would be a circle.

An important application of Lissajous figures is in the calibration of signal generators or, indeed, in any instance where a frequency comparison is desired. Photographs of actual Lissajous patterns for various values of the ratio f_y/f_x, where f_y and f_x are the frequencies of the vertical and horizontal signals, respectively, are shown in Fig. 16.27. Each of these patterns was generated by using signals of equal amplitudes to the vertical and horizontal deflection plates.

Problem Set 16.7

1. Construct a diagram similar to Fig. 16.26 and determine the resulting pattern on the screen if $V_x = 2 \sin \omega t$ and $V_y = 2 \sin \omega t$.

2. In Problem 1, if the amplitude of the vertical deflection signal were increased while that of the horizontal deflection signal remained the same, how would the pattern on the screen change?

3. How would the pattern of Fig. 16.26 appear if the deflection voltages were switched, that is, if the vertical signal were applied to the horizontal deflection plates and the horizontal signal were applied to the vertical deflection plates?

4. As an example of the Lissajous patterns generated for ratios of vertical to horizontal frequencies which are expressible by integers, construct a diagram for

$$V_x = \sin 2\pi t$$

and

$$V_y = \sin 4\pi t,$$

which illustrates the ratio $f_y/f_x = 2/1$.

16.8 POLAR COORDINATES

Besides representing a point in a plane by its rectangular coordinates (x, y), we can use another system called the **polar coordinate system** to represent points. We shall impose such a system on a rectangular coordinate plane. Here the origin O is called the **pole**, and the positive x-axis is called the **polar axis** (see Fig. 16.28). For any point

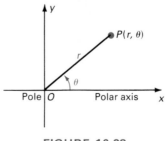

FIGURE 16.28

P (except the pole), let r be the distance from the pole to P, and let θ be the angle (in radians or degrees) from the polar axis to the line segment OP. We consider θ to be positive if measured counterclockwise from the polar axis, and negative if measured clockwise. The pair of numbers r and θ locate P, and we refer to the ordered pair (r, θ) as **polar coordinates** for P. For example, Fig. 16.29 gives some points and a polar-coordinate representation of each point. The pole has polar coordinates $(0, \theta)$, where θ is any angle.

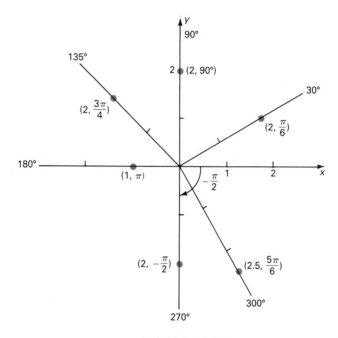

FIGURE 16.29

With rectangular coordinates each point has exactly one representation, whereas with polar coordinates there are infinitely many ways to represent a given point. For example, the point $(3, \pi/6)$ in Fig. 16.30(a) can also be represented by $\left(3, \dfrac{\pi}{6} + 2\pi\right)$. Similarly, $(2, 90°)$ and $(2, -270°)$ are polar coordinates for the same point [see Fig. 16.30(b)].

For positive values of the r-coordinate, the point located by (r, θ) is on the terminal side of θ. Actually, we can also permit negative values of the r-coordinate. We consider the polar coordinates $(-r, \theta)$, where $r > 0$, to locate the point that is a distance of r from the pole but that is on the backward extension of the terminal side of θ drawn through the pole. This means that if θ is in degrees, then $(-r, \theta)$ and $(r, \theta + 180°)$ represent the same point, as shown in Fig. 16.31(a). Another example is given in Fig. 16.31(b).

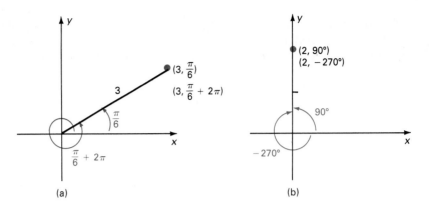

FIGURE 16.30

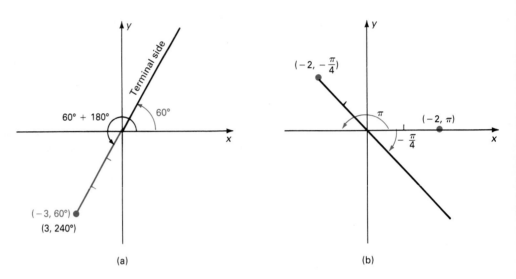

FIGURE 16.31

From Fig. 16.32 and our knowledge of trigonometry, it follows that if P has rectangular coordinates (x, y) and polar coordinates (r, θ), then we have the following:

$$x = r \cos \theta, \qquad y = r \sin \theta,$$

$$r^2 = x^2 + y^2,$$

$$\tan \theta = \frac{y}{x}, \qquad \text{for } x \neq 0.$$

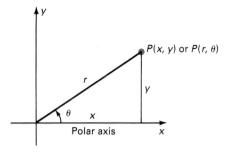

FIGURE 16.32

These relationships* are used to convert from polar coordinates to rectangular coordinates, and vice versa, as Example 1 shows.

Example 1

Find the rectangular coordinates of the point with polar coordinates $(4, 3\pi/4)$.

Solution   We use the relationships $x = r \cos \theta$ and $y = r \sin \theta$.

$$x = r \cos \theta = 4 \cos \frac{3\pi}{4} = 4\left(-\frac{\sqrt{2}}{2}\right) = -2\sqrt{2}.$$

$$y = r \sin \theta = 4 \sin \frac{3\pi}{4} = 4\left(\frac{\sqrt{2}}{2}\right) = 2\sqrt{2}.$$

The rectangular coordinates of the point are $(-2\sqrt{2}, 2\sqrt{2})$.

Example 2

Find polar coordinates of the point with rectangular coordinates $(3, -5)$.

Solution   Figure 16.33 shows the given point and indicates that we shall choose $r > 0$ and $0 \le \theta < 2\pi$ for convenience. We have

$$r^2 = x^2 + y^2 = 3^2 + (-5)^2 = 34,$$

so

$$r = \sqrt{34} = 5.83.$$

* Although Fig. 16.32 assumes P is in Quadrant I and $r > 0$, the boxed rules also apply to all other situations.

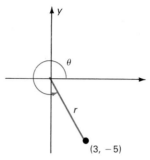

FIGURE 16.33

Also,

$$\tan \theta = \frac{y}{x} = \frac{-5}{3}.$$

Since $\tan \theta$ is negative and $(3, -5)$ lies in the fourth quadrant, we choose $\theta = 300.96°$. Thus the point has polar coordinates $(5.83, 300.96°)$. Choosing $r = -\sqrt{34}$ and $\theta = 300.96° - 180° = 120.96°$ also gives a polar representation of the point.

The **graph of a polar equation** in the variables r and θ consists of all points (r, θ) that satisfy the equation. The remaining examples illustrate the sketching of polar equations.

Example 3

Sketch the graph of the polar equation $r = 2$.

Solution The equation can be thought of as $r = 2 + 0\theta$. Thus for *any* value of θ we have $r = 2$. Therefore the graph is a circle of radius 2 (see Fig. 16.34).

θ	r
0°	2
30°	2
60°	2
90°	2
120°	2

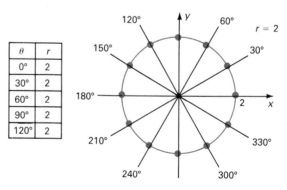

FIGURE 16.34

Example 4

Sketch the polar graph of $r = 2 \sin \theta$.

Solution   Choosing typical values of θ between $0°$ and $360°$ and finding the corresponding values of r, we obtain Table 16.4.

TABLE 16.4

θ	$0°$	$30°$	$45°$	$60°$	$90°$	$120°$	$135°$	$150°$	$180°$
r	0	1	$\sqrt{2}$	$\sqrt{3}$	2	$\sqrt{3}$	$\sqrt{2}$	1	0

θ	$210°$	$225°$	$240°$	$270°$	$300°$	$315°$	$330°$	$360°$
r	-1	$-\sqrt{2}$	$-\sqrt{3}$	-2	$-\sqrt{3}$	$-\sqrt{2}$	-1	0

Connecting the points by a smooth curve gives Fig. 16.35. Because the sine function has period $360°$, we shall not obtain any new points for $\theta > 360°$ or $\theta < 0°$. In fact, for θ between $180°$ and $360°$, note that $r < 0$ and the corresponding points are the same as those for θ between $0°$ and $180°$. It can be shown that the graph is a circle.

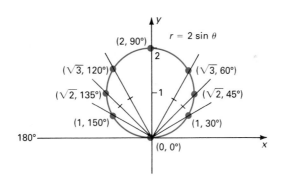

FIGURE 16.35

Example 5

Sketch the graph of the polar equation $r = \theta$, where $\theta \geq 0$.

Solution   See Fig. 16.36. The graph, which is an unending spiral, is called the *spiral of Archimedes.* Here, θ must be in radians. Observe that as θ increases, r increases.

θ	r
0	0
$\dfrac{\pi}{4}$	0.8
$\dfrac{\pi}{2}$	1.6
π	3.1
$\dfrac{3\pi}{2}$	4.7
2π	6.3
$\dfrac{5\pi}{2}$	7.9

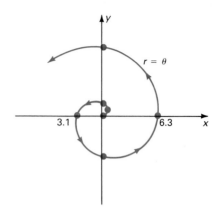

FIGURE 16.36

Sketching polar graphs can be made less time consuming if *polar coordinate graph paper* is used. This paper consists of concentric circles and rays (like spokes on a wheel) and is shown in Fig. 16.37.

Example 6

Sketch the graph of $r = 2(1 + \cos \theta)$ on polar coordinate graph paper.

Solution   Figure 16.37 shows the graph, which is called a *cardioid*.

$r = 2(1 + \cos \theta)$

θ	r	θ	r
0°	4	210°	0.3
30°	3.7	240°	1
60°	3	270°	2
90°	2	300°	3
120°	1	330°	3.7
150°	0.3	360°	4
180°	0		

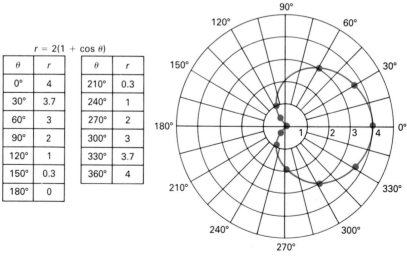

FIGURE 16.37

Problem Set 16.8

In Problems 1–12, plot the points that have the given polar coordinates.

1. $(1, 30°)$.

2. $\left(2, \dfrac{\pi}{2}\right)$.

3. $(2, -60°)$.

4. $(3, 45°)$.

5. $(1.5, 180°)$.

6. $\left(3, \dfrac{3\pi}{4}\right)$.

7. $\left(-3, \dfrac{5\pi}{6}\right)$.

8. $\left(2, \dfrac{5\pi}{4}\right)$.

9. $(-2, -60°)$.

10. $(-3, 0)$.

11. $(2.5, 195°)$.

12. $\left(-4, -\dfrac{\pi}{2}\right)$.

In Problems 13–22, find rectangular coordinates for each point that has the given polar coordinates.

13. $(3, 60°)$.

14. $(0, -\pi)$.

15. $\left(2, \dfrac{3\pi}{4}\right)$.

16. $(4, 0)$.

17. $(5, -150°)$.

18. $\left(\dfrac{3}{5}, -\dfrac{5\pi}{3}\right)$.

19. $\left(-2, \dfrac{7\pi}{4}\right)$.

20. $(3, 270°)$.

21. $(-5, -20.6°)$.

22. $(0, 0)$.

In Problems 23–34, find polar coordinates (with $r > 0$) for each point that has the given rectangular coordinates.

23. $(0, 2)$.
24. $(2, 2)$.
25. $(1, -\sqrt{3})$.
26. $(3, -3)$.

27. $(-4, 0)$.
28. $(-4, -4)$.
29. $(-2, 2\sqrt{3})$.
30. $(0, -8)$.

31. $(2.41, 5.64)$.
32. $(-2.1, 5.3)$.
33. $(-4, -6)$.
34. $(5, -6)$.

In Problems 35–46, sketch the graph of the given polar equation.

35. $r = 1$.

36. $\theta = \pi/3$.

37. $r = 2\cos\theta$.

38. $r = \sin\theta$.

39. $r = 2\theta$, where $\theta \geq 0$.

40. $r = 1 + \cos\theta$.

41. $r = 2(1 - \cos\theta)$.

42. $r = 1 + 2\cos\theta$.

43. $r = \sin 3\theta$.

44. $r = \cos 2\theta$.

45. $r^2 = \cos 2\theta$.

46. $r = 1 + 2\sin\theta$.

16.9 REVIEW

Important Terms and Symbols

Section 16.1   Periodic function, period, cycle, amplitude, displacement (phase shift).

Section 16.4   Vertical asymptotes.

Section 16.5   Addition of ordinates, principle of superposition.

Section 16.6   Inverse trigonometric function, $\sin^{-1}$, arcsin, $\cos^{-1}$, arccos, $\tan^{-1}$, arctan, $\cot^{-1}$, $\sec^{-1}$, $\csc^{-1}$.

Formula Summary

Graph of $y = a \sin (bx + c)$, $(b > 0)$

Amplitude: $|a|$

Shape: regular for $a > 0$;

inverted for $a < 0$.

Period: $\dfrac{2\pi}{b}$.

Displacement: $-\dfrac{c}{b}$.

The same is true for $y = a \cos (bx + c)$.

INVERSE TRIGONOMETRIC FUNCTIONS

$y = \sin^{-1} x$ means $\sin y = x$ where $-\dfrac{\pi}{2} \leq y \leq \dfrac{\pi}{2}$.

$y = \cos^{-1} x$ means $\cos y = x$ where $0 \leq y \leq \pi$.

$y = \tan^{-1} x$ means $\tan y = x$ where $-\dfrac{\pi}{2} < y < \dfrac{\pi}{2}$.

CONVERSION BETWEEN POLAR AND RECTANGULAR COORDINATES

$$x = r \cos \theta, \qquad y = r \sin \theta,$$

$$r^2 = x^2 + y^2,$$

$$\tan \theta = \frac{y}{x}, \qquad \text{for } x \neq 0.$$

Review Questions

1. The period of $y = 4 \sin 18x$ is equal to ___(a)___. The amplitude is ___(b)___.

2. The values of $y = 3 \sin\left(\dfrac{6}{97}x - \dfrac{2\pi}{63}\right)$ range from a minimum of ___(a)___ to a maximum of ___(b)___.

3. In comparison to the graph of $y = \sin x$, the graph of $y = \sin\left(x + \dfrac{\pi}{2}\right)$ ___(leads)(lags)___ by $\pi/2$.

4. The periods of $y = \sin x$ and $y = \cos x$ are both equal to ___(a)___, but the periods of $y = \tan x$ and $y = \cot x$ are both equal to ___(b)___.

5. The graph of $y = \sin x$ is the same as the graph of $y = -\cos x$ displaced $\pi/2$ radians to the ___(left)(right)___.

6. $\text{Sin}^{-1} x$ is the angle in the interval from $-\dfrac{\pi}{2}$ to $\dfrac{\pi}{2}$ with sine of _____.

7. $\text{Cos}^{-1} x$ is the angle in the interval from ___(a)___ to ___(b)___ with cosine of ___(c)___.

8. $\text{Tan}^{-1} x$ is the angle in the interval from ___(a)___ to ___(b)___ with tangent of ___(c)___.

9. The angles 0, $\pm 2\pi$, $\pm 4\pi$, and so on, all have a cosine of 1. But $\cos^{-1} 1 = $ _____.

10. True or False: Every point in the plane has one and only one representation in polar coordinates. _____.

Answers to Review Questions

1. (a) $\pi/9$, (b) 4.   2. (a) -3, (b) 3.   3. Leads.   4. (a) 2π, (b) π.   5. Left.   6. x.
7. (a) 0, (b) π, (c) x.   8. (a) $-\pi/2$, (b) $\pi/2$, (c) x.   9. 0.   10. False.

Review Problems

In Problems 1–10, sketch one cycle of each curve. In 1–8, give the amplitude A and period p.

1. $y = -\sin 3x$.

2. $y = 3 \cos 6x$.

3. $y = 4 \cos\left(x - \dfrac{\pi}{2}\right)$.

4. $y = 2 \sin\left(3x + \dfrac{\pi}{2}\right)$.

5. $y = 3 \cos\left(2x + \dfrac{\pi}{6}\right)$.

6. $y = -\cos\left(\dfrac{x}{2} - \dfrac{\pi}{3}\right)$.

7. $y = \tan x$.

8. $y = \sec x$.

9. $y = \sin 2x + 2 \cos x$.

10. $y = 2 \sin x - \cos x$.

In Problems 11–24, find the value of the given expression.

11. $\arcsin(-1)$.

12. $\arccos \dfrac{1}{2}$.

13. $\arctan \dfrac{\sqrt{3}}{3}$.

14. $\sin^{-1}\left(-\dfrac{\sqrt{3}}{2}\right)$.

15. $\cos^{-1}\left(-\dfrac{\sqrt{3}}{2}\right)$.

16. $\tan^{-1}(-1)$.

17. $\tan (\cos^{-1} 1)$.

18. $\cos \left(\sin^{-1} \dfrac{\sqrt{2}}{2} \right)$.

19. $\sin [\tan^{-1} (-\sqrt{3})]$.

20. $\csc (\cos^{-1} 0)$.

21. $\sin (\sin^{-1} 0.8)$.

22. $\tan^{-1} (\tan 2\pi)$.

23. $\cos^{-1} (\cos 3\pi)$.

24. $\cos \left[\cos^{-1} \left(-\dfrac{1}{10} \right) \right]$.

In Problems 25–28, find rectangular coordinates for the point with the given polar coordinates.

25. $(1, 315°)$.

26. $(-3, 50°)$.

27. $(5, -210°)$.

28. $(2, \pi)$.

In Problems 29–32, find polar coordinates for the point with the given rectangular coordinates.

29. $(1, -1)$.

30. $(-7, 8)$.

31. $(-4, 0)$.

32. $(1, \sqrt{3})$.

In Problems 33–36, sketch the given curve in polar coordinates.

33. $r = 2(1 - \sin \theta)$.

34. $r = 1 - 2 \sin \theta$.

35. $r = 2 - \sin \theta$.

36. $r = e^{\theta/6}$, for $\theta \geq 0$.

17

Trigonometric Formulas and Equations

17.1 BASIC IDENTITIES

In Chapter 6 the following basic trigonometric relations were given:

$$1. \quad \csc \theta = \frac{1}{\sin \theta}, \qquad \sin \theta = \frac{1}{\csc \theta}.$$

$$2. \quad \sec \theta = \frac{1}{\cos \theta}, \qquad \cos \theta = \frac{1}{\sec \theta}.$$

$$3. \quad \cot \theta = \frac{1}{\tan \theta}, \qquad \tan \theta = \frac{1}{\cot \theta}.$$

$$4. \quad \frac{\sin \theta}{\cos \theta} = \tan \theta.$$

$$5. \quad \frac{\cos \theta}{\sin \theta} = \cot \theta.$$

Each of the preceding equations is called a **trigonometric identity** because it is true for *all* values of θ for which both sides are defined.

There are three more basic identities: Each involves a *power* of a trigonometric function. In stating them we shall abbreviate $(\sin \theta)^2$ by writing $\sin^2 \theta$ (read *sine squared theta*), and we shall use similar abbreviations for the squares of the other

619

trigonometric functions. Do not confuse $\sin^2 \theta$ with $\sin \theta^2$, which means $\sin (\theta^2)$. The three identities in various forms are:

6.	$\sin^2 \theta + \cos^2 \theta = 1$ or	$\begin{cases} \sin^2 \theta = 1 - \cos^2 \theta, \\ \cos^2 \theta = 1 - \sin^2 \theta. \end{cases}$
7.	$1 + \tan^2 \theta = \sec^2 \theta$ or	$\begin{cases} \tan^2 \theta = \sec^2 \theta - 1, \\ \sec^2 \theta - \tan^2 \theta = 1. \end{cases}$
8.	$1 + \cot^2 \theta = \csc^2 \theta$ or	$\begin{cases} \cot^2 \theta = \csc^2 \theta - 1, \\ \csc^2 \theta - \cot^2 \theta = 1. \end{cases}$

To prove these identities, let θ be any angle in standard position and (x, y) be a point on its terminal side (see Fig. 17.1). Then recall that

$$x^2 + y^2 = r^2.$$

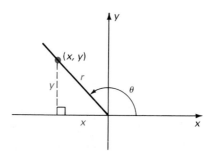

FIGURE 17.1

Successively dividing both sides of this equation by r^2, x^2, and y^2, respectively, we obtain three equations.

$$\frac{x^2}{r^2} + \frac{y^2}{r^2} = 1, \qquad 1 + \frac{y^2}{x^2} = \frac{r^2}{x^2}, \qquad \frac{x^2}{y^2} + 1 = \frac{r^2}{y^2}$$

or, equivalently,

$$\left(\frac{x}{r}\right)^2 + \left(\frac{y}{r}\right)^2 = 1, \qquad 1 + \left(\frac{y}{x}\right)^2 = \left(\frac{r}{x}\right)^2, \qquad \left(\frac{x}{y}\right)^2 + 1 = \left(\frac{r}{y}\right)^2.$$

Using the definitions of the trigonometric functions, we see that these three equations are equivalent, respectively, to the following identities:

$$\cos^2 \theta + \sin^2 \theta = 1, \qquad 1 + \tan^2 \theta = \sec^2 \theta, \qquad \cot^2 \theta + 1 = \csc^2 \theta.$$

These three identities are called the **Pythagorean identities**.

Example 1

a. $\sin^2 20° + \cos^2 20° = 1$, by Identity 6.

b. $1 + \tan^2 \dfrac{\pi}{3} = \sec^2 \dfrac{\pi}{3}$, by Identity 7.

c. $1 + \cot^2 4x = \csc^2 4x$, by Identity 8.

When using Identities 6–8 to express one trigonometric function in terms of the other function, you must consider signs. Identity 6, for example, implies that $\sin \theta = \pm\sqrt{1 - \cos^2 \theta}$. The choice of whether to use the plus sign or minus sign depends on the sign of $\sin \theta$. If θ is a first- or second-quadrant angle, use the plus sign because $\sin \theta$ must be positive there. For a third- or fourth-quadrant angle, use the minus sign.

Identities 1–8 are considered the basic trigonometric identities, and you should become totally familiar with them. They are used to simplify expressions involving trigonometric functions and to prove (or verify) other identities. In physical situations, this can mean dealing with a simpler or more suitable form of a trigonometric expression.

For example, we shall prove the identity

$$\cot x \sin x = \cos x.$$

To do this, we choose one side and make substitutions until it is the same as the other side. Usually it is best to choose the more complicated side, which in our case is $\cot x \sin x$. We must express it in terms of $\cos x$ only. Using Identity 5, we can replace $\cot x$ by $\dfrac{\cos x}{\sin x}$. Thus

$$\cot x \sin x \quad \text{becomes} \quad \frac{\cos x}{\sin x} \cdot \sin x.$$

This reduces to

$$\cos x,$$

which is the same as the right side of the given identity. Thus the identity is proved. We usually write our work in a vertical arrangement as follows:

Left side	*Right side*
$\cot x \sin x$	$\cos x.$
$= \dfrac{\cos x}{\sin x} \sin x$	
$= \cos x.$	

Example 2

Prove the identity $\sec \theta - \tan \theta \sin \theta = \cos \theta$.

Solution   Because the left side is the more complicated side, we shall try to transform it so that it is the same as the right side. In each step of the proof we will indicate the basic identity being used. We begin by expressing the left side in terms of $\sin x$ and $\cos x$ only.

$$\sec \theta - \tan \theta \sin \theta \qquad\qquad \cos \theta.$$

$$= \frac{1}{\cos \theta} - \frac{\sin \theta}{\cos \theta} \sin \theta \qquad [2, 4]$$

$$= \frac{1}{\cos \theta} - \frac{\sin^2 \theta}{\cos \theta}$$

$$= \frac{1 - \sin^2 \theta}{\cos \theta} \qquad [\text{combining}]$$

$$= \frac{\cos^2 \theta}{\cos \theta} \qquad [6]$$

$$= \cos \theta.$$

Example 3

Prove the identity $\dfrac{\tan^2 x}{1 + \sec x} = \sec x - 1$.

Solution   We shall express the left side in terms of $\sec x$ only.

$$\frac{\tan^2 x}{1 + \sec x} \qquad\qquad \sec x - 1.$$

$$= \frac{\sec^2 x - 1}{1 + \sec x} \qquad [7]$$

$$= \frac{(\sec x + 1)(\sec x - 1)}{1 + \sec x} \qquad [\text{factoring}]$$

$$= \sec x - 1.$$

Example 4

Prove the identity $\csc^2 x - \dfrac{\cos^2 x}{\sin^2 x} = 1$.

Solution   Here we can write $\dfrac{\cos^2 x}{\sin^2 x}$ as $\left(\dfrac{\cos x}{\sin x}\right)^2$ or $\cot^2 x$ (by Identity 5). Thus

$$\csc^2 x - \frac{\cos^2 x}{\sin^2 x} \qquad\qquad 1.$$

$$= \csc^2 x - \cot^2 x \qquad [5]$$

$$= 1. \qquad [8]$$

Example 5

Prove the identity $1 - \cot^4 x = 2 \csc^2 x - \csc^4 x$.

Solution

$$1 - \cot^4 x \qquad 2 \csc^2 x - \csc^4 x$$

$$= (\csc^2 x)(2 - \csc^2 x) \qquad\qquad [\text{factoring}]$$

$$= (1 + \cot^2 x)[2 - (1 + \cot^2 x)] \qquad [8]$$

$$= (1 + \cot^2 x)[1 - \cot^2 x]$$

$$= 1 - \cot^4 x \qquad\qquad [\text{multiplying}].$$

We may also prove an identity by *separately* manipulating *both* sides until they are the same. Usually we express both sides in terms of sines and cosines when no other approach to the problem is obvious. Example 6 shows this method.

Example 6

Prove the identity $\tan x + \cot x = \csc x \sec x$.

Solution

$$\tan x + \cot x \qquad\qquad\qquad \csc x \sec x$$

$$= \frac{\sin x}{\cos x} + \frac{\cos x}{\sin x} \quad [4, 5] \qquad\qquad = \frac{1}{\sin x} \cdot \frac{1}{\cos x} \quad [1, 2]$$

$$= \frac{\sin^2 x + \cos^2 x}{\cos x \sin x} \quad [\text{combining}] \qquad = \frac{1}{\sin x \cos x}.$$

$$= \frac{1}{\cos x \sin x}. \quad [6]$$

In Example 6 there was really no need to manipulate the right side, because we can take the last form of the left side and write

$$\frac{1}{\cos x \sin x} = \frac{1}{\cos x} \cdot \frac{1}{\sin x} = \sec x \csc x,$$

which agrees with the right side of the identity.

Example 7

When a ball of mass m is suspended from a string and pulled aside by a horizontal force F until the string makes an angle θ with the vertical, three forces are acting on the ball, as shown in Fig. 17.2. The downward gravitational force is mg, the tension in the string is T, and F is the supporting force. The system, being stationary, is said to be in equilibrium, and the relationships between the forces are determined by applying Newton's second law. By summing vertical and horizontal components, it can be shown that

$$T \cos \theta - mg = 0 \quad \text{and} \quad F - T \sin \theta = 0.$$

Show that $F = mg \tan \theta$.

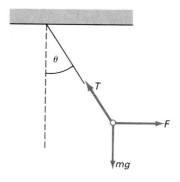

FIGURE 17.2

Solution   Solving the first equation for T, we obtain $T = mg/(\cos \theta)$. Substituting this value into the second equation gives

$$F - \left(\frac{mg}{\cos \theta}\right) \sin \theta = 0$$

$$F = mg\left(\frac{\sin \theta}{\cos \theta}\right).$$

Finally, by Identity 4, we have

$$F = mg \tan \theta.$$

Problem Set 17.1

In Problems **1–40**, *prove the identities.*

1. $\tan x \cos x = \sin x.$

2. $\cot x \tan x = 1.$

3. $\dfrac{\sin x}{\tan x} = \cos x.$

4. $\csc x \cos x = \cot x.$

5. $\dfrac{1 - \sin^2 x}{\cos x} = \cos x.$

6. $\dfrac{\cos x \tan x}{\sin x} = 1.$

7. $(1 + \cos x)(1 - \cos x) = \sin^2 x.$

8. $(\tan x)(1 - \sin^2 x) = \sin x \cos x.$

9. $\dfrac{\csc x}{\sec x} = \cot x.$

10. $\dfrac{\sin^2 x}{1 - \sin^2 x} = \tan^2 x.$

11. $\dfrac{\cos^2 \theta}{1 - \sin \theta} = 1 + \sin \theta.$

12. $\sec^2 \theta - \dfrac{\sin^2 \theta}{\cos^2 \theta} = 1.$

13. $\dfrac{1}{1 - \cos^2 \theta} = \csc^2 \theta.$

14. $\dfrac{1}{1 + \tan^2 \theta} = \cos^2 \theta.$

15. $\dfrac{1 - \cos^2 x}{1 - \sin^2 x} = \tan^2 x.$

16. $\dfrac{1}{\csc^2 x - 1} = \tan^2 x.$

17. $\dfrac{1 - \sin x}{\cos x} = \sec x - \tan x.$

18. $\dfrac{\cos^2 x}{1 - \sin^2 x} = 1.$

19. $\dfrac{1 + \tan^2 x}{\csc x} = \tan x \sec x.$

20. $\dfrac{1 + \cot^2 x}{\sec x} = \cot x \csc x.$

21. $(\sin x)(1 + \cot^2 x) = \csc x.$

22. $(1 + \tan^2 x) \cos x = \sec x.$

23. $\csc^4 \theta - \cot^4 \theta = \csc^2 \theta + \cot^2 \theta.$

24. $\dfrac{\csc^4 \theta - 1}{\cot^2 \theta} = \csc^2 \theta + 1.$

25. $\dfrac{2}{1 - \cos x} = \dfrac{2 \sec x}{\sec x - 1}.$

26. $\dfrac{\sin^2 x + \cos^2 x}{\cos^2 x} = \sec^2 x.$

27. $\dfrac{\sin x \cos y}{\sin y \cos x} = \tan x \cot y.$

28. $\dfrac{\cot x}{1 + \cot^2 x} = \sin x \cos x.$

29. $\dfrac{1}{\tan x + \cot x} = \cos x \sin x.$

30. $\dfrac{1 + \cot^2 x}{\cos^2 x \csc^2 x + 1} = 1.$

31. $\dfrac{1 + \tan x}{\sec x + \csc x} = \sin x.$

32. $\dfrac{\sin^2 x}{\cos^4 x + \cos^2 x \sin^2 x} = \tan^2 x.$

33. $\dfrac{1}{\sec x - \tan x} - \dfrac{1}{\sec x + \tan x} = 2 \tan x.$

34. $\dfrac{\cos x}{\tan x + \sec x} - \dfrac{\cos x}{\tan x - \sec x} = 2.$

35. $\dfrac{\cos^2 x - \cos^2 x \sin^2 x}{\sin^2 x - \cos^2 x \sin^2 x} = \cot^4 x.$

36. $\sin^2 x + 1 - \cos^2 x - 2 \sin^2 x \cos^2 x = 2 \sin^4 x.$

37. $\dfrac{\sin^2 x}{\cos x}\,(\tan x - \cos x \cot x) = (\sin x)(\tan^2 x - \cos x)$.

38. $\dfrac{\sin x + \tan x}{1 + \cos x} = \tan x$.

39. $\cos^4 x - \sin^4 x + 1 = 2 \cos^2 x$.

40. $(1 + \cos x)\csc x + \dfrac{1}{\csc x(1 + \cos x)} = 2 \csc x$.

41. Suppose a weight W slides down a plane, inclined at an angle θ, at constant speed. Such a situation leads to the system of equations

$$\begin{cases} W \sin \theta - \mu N = 0 \\ N - W \cos \theta = 0, \end{cases}$$

where N is a force that the plane exerts on the block and μ is a constant involved with friction. Solve this system for μ and show that $\mu = \tan \theta$.

42. When a beam of circularly polarized light falls on a polarizing sheet, the resulting amplitude E of the electric field component is given by

$$E = \sqrt{E_x^2 + E_y^2},$$

where $E_x = E_m \sin(\omega t)$ and $E_y = E_m \cos(\omega t)$. Prove that $E = E_m$. You may assume that $E_m > 0$.

17.2 ADDITION AND SUBTRACTION FORMULAS

In the theory of the interference and diffraction of electromagnetic waves, it is usual to assume that the electric field component of such a wave has the form $E_0 \sin(\omega t + \varphi)$. In this and many other situations, it is useful to express a trigonometric function of the *sum* of two angles in terms of functions of the individual angles. We can do this by using the following identities, which are called the **addition formulas**.

---

9. $\sin(x + y) = \sin x \cos y + \cos x \sin y$.

10. $\cos(x + y) = \cos x \cos y - \sin x \sin y$.

11. $\tan(x + y) = \dfrac{\tan x + \tan y}{1 - \tan x \tan y}$.

Identity 9 states that *the sine of the sum of two angles is the sine of the first angle times the cosine of the second angle, plus the cosine of the first angle times the sine of the second angle.*

In general, $\sin(x + y) \neq \sin x + \sin y$, and similarly for $\cos(x + y)$ and for $\tan(x + y)$. For example,

$$\sin(30° + 60°) = \sin 90° = 1,$$

but

$$\sin 30° + \sin 60° = \frac{1}{2} + \frac{\sqrt{3}}{2} = \frac{1 + \sqrt{3}}{2}.$$

The proofs of Identities 9–11 are given at the end of this section.

Example 1

Find $\sin 75°$ by using the trigonometric values of $45°$ and $30°$.

Solution Since $75° = 45° + 30°$, we may use Identity 9 with $x = 45°$ and $y = 30°$.

$$\sin 75° = \sin (45° + 30°)$$
$$= \sin 45° \cos 30° + \cos 45° \sin 30°$$
$$= \frac{\sqrt{2}}{2} \cdot \frac{\sqrt{3}}{2} + \frac{\sqrt{2}}{2} \cdot \frac{1}{2}$$
$$= \frac{\sqrt{6}}{4} + \frac{\sqrt{2}}{4} = \frac{\sqrt{6} + \sqrt{2}}{4}.$$

Example 2

Simplify the equation $y = \cos \left(x + \frac{\pi}{2} \right)$.

Solution We expand $\cos \left(x + \frac{\pi}{2} \right)$ by using Identity 10.

$$y = \cos \left(x + \frac{\pi}{2} \right) = \cos x \cos \frac{\pi}{2} - \sin x \sin \frac{\pi}{2}$$
$$= (\cos x)(0) - (\sin x)(1),$$
$$y = -\sin x.$$

The formulas for the functions of the *difference* of two angles will be obtained after we consider some identities that express a trigonometric function of $-\theta$ in terms of a trigonometric function of θ. We shall derive them for the case where θ is a second-quadrant angle, but the results are true for any angle θ.

Figure 17.3 shows the angles θ and $-\theta$, both in standard position, along with points on their terminal sides. These points are chosen so that they give the same

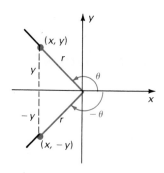

FIGURE 17.3

distance r. Notice that their first coordinates are equal, but their second coordinates differ in sign. We have

$$\sin(-\theta) = \frac{-y}{r} = -\frac{y}{r} = -\sin\theta,$$

$$\cos(-\theta) = \frac{x}{r} = \cos\theta,$$

$$\tan(-\theta) = \frac{-y}{x} = -\frac{y}{x} = -\tan\theta.$$

Since cosecant and sine are reciprocal functions, we have

$$\csc(-\theta) = \frac{1}{\sin(-\theta)} = \frac{1}{-\sin\theta} = -\csc\theta.$$

We can do the same for secant and cotangent. In summary, we have the following identities:

12. $\begin{cases} \sin(-\theta) = -\sin\theta, & \csc(-\theta) = -\csc\theta. \\ \cos(-\theta) = \cos\theta, & \sec(-\theta) = \sec\theta, \\ \tan(-\theta) = -\tan\theta, & \cot(-\theta) = -\cot\theta. \end{cases}$

For example, $\sin(-30°) = -\sin 30° = -(\frac{1}{2}) = -\frac{1}{2}$, and $\cos(-\pi/4) = \cos(\pi/4) = \sqrt{2}/2$.

Any function f such that $f(-x) = -f(x)$ for all x in the domain of f is called an **odd function**. By Identities 12, the sine, tangent, cotangent, and cosecant functions are *odd functions*. Any function f such that $f(-x) = f(x)$ for all x in the domain of f is called an **even function**. The cosine and secant functions are *even* functions.

With the previous identities, we can find formulas for the trigonometric functions of the *difference* of two angles. For example, to find $\sin (x - y)$ we have

$$\sin (x - y) = \sin [x + (-y)]$$
$$= \sin x \cos (-y) + \cos x \sin (-y) \qquad \text{[Identity 9]}$$
$$= \sin x \cos y + (\cos x)(-\sin y) \qquad \text{[Identity 12]}$$
$$= \sin x \cos y - \cos x \sin y.$$

We can do the same kind of thing with Identities 10 and 11. Thus we have the **subtraction formulas**.

---

13. $\sin (x - y) = \sin x \cos y - \cos x \sin y.$

14. $\cos (x - y) = \cos x \cos y + \sin x \sin y.$

15. $\tan (x - y) = \dfrac{\tan x - \tan y}{1 + \tan x \tan y}.$

It is worth pointing out that mathematical reference handbooks often combine identities of similar form. For example, in a typical reference source, Identities 9 and 13 might appear as follows:

$$\sin (x \pm y) = \sin x \cos y \pm \cos x \sin y.$$

Here, *either* the upper signs ($+$ and $+$) in both sides *or* the lower signs ($-$ and $-$) in both sides are chosen. Similarly, Identities 10 and 14 can be given as

$$\cos(x \pm y) = \cos x \cos y \mp \sin x \sin y.$$

Here, if the plus sign is chosen in the left side, then the minus sign is chosen in the right side, and so on.

Example 3

Find $\cos 15°$ by using a subtraction formula.

Solution Because $15° = 45° - 30°$, using Identity 14 we have

$$\cos 15° = \cos (45° - 30°)$$
$$= \cos 45° \cos 30° + \sin 45° \sin 30°$$
$$= \frac{\sqrt{2}}{2} \cdot \frac{\sqrt{3}}{2} + \frac{\sqrt{2}}{2} \cdot \frac{1}{2}$$
$$= \frac{\sqrt{6}}{4} + \frac{\sqrt{2}}{4} = \frac{\sqrt{6} + \sqrt{2}}{4}.$$

Example 4

Show that $\tan(\pi - x) = -\tan x$.

Solution From Identity 15 we have

$$\tan(\pi - x) = \frac{\tan \pi - \tan x}{1 + \tan \pi \tan x}$$

$$= \frac{0 - \tan x}{1 + (0)\tan x} = \frac{-\tan x}{1} = -\tan x.$$

Example 5

Prove the identity $\dfrac{\cos(A + B)}{\sin A \cos B} = \cot A - \tan B$.

Solution Using Identity 10 we have

$$\frac{\cos(A + B)}{\sin A \cos B} \qquad\qquad \cot A - \tan B.$$

$$= \frac{\cos A \cos B - \sin A \sin B}{\sin A \cos B}$$

$$= \frac{\cos A \cos B}{\sin A \cos B} - \frac{\sin A \sin B}{\sin A \cos B}$$

$$= \frac{\cos A}{\sin A} - \frac{\sin B}{\cos B}$$

$$= \cot A - \tan B.$$

Example 6

If $\sin \alpha = \frac{1}{3}$, $\cos \beta = \frac{3}{4}$, α is a first-quadrant angle, and β is a fourth-quadrant angle, find $\cos(\alpha - \beta)$.

Solution Angles α and β are sketched in Fig. 17.4. We shall first get values of x, y, and r for each angle. Since $\sin \alpha = \dfrac{y}{r} = \dfrac{1}{3}$, we can choose a point (x, y) on the terminal side of α so that $y = 1$ and $r = 3$. See Fig. 17-4(a). By the Pythagorean theorem, $x^2 + 1^2 = 3^2$. Thus $x^2 = 3^2 - 1^2 = 8$, so $x = 2\sqrt{2}$ because x is positive in Quadrant I. Similarly, we can get values for x, y, and r for β. See Fig. 17.4(b). By Identity 14 we have

$$\cos(\alpha - \beta) = \cos \alpha \cos \beta + \sin \alpha \sin \beta$$

$$= \left(\frac{2\sqrt{2}}{3}\right)\left(\frac{3}{4}\right) + \left(\frac{1}{3}\right)\left(-\frac{\sqrt{7}}{4}\right)$$

$$= \frac{6\sqrt{2}}{12} - \frac{\sqrt{7}}{12} = \frac{6\sqrt{2} - \sqrt{7}}{12}.$$

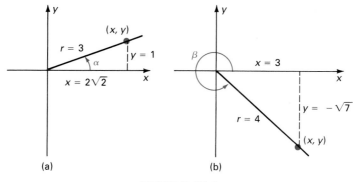

(a)   (b)

FIGURE 17.4

Example 7

Parallel and perpendicular lines: Section 8.3 made use of the facts that if two nonvertical lines L_1 and L_2 are parallel, then their slopes m_1 and m_2 are equal, and if the two lines are perpendicular, the slope of one line is the negative reciprocal of the slope of the other line—that is, $m_2 = -1/m_1$. We now prove both statements.

Figure 17.5(a) shows two parallel lines, L_1 and L_2, which are not vertical. For each line we can determine the slope by selecting two arbitrary points on the line. We choose for these points the intersections of the line with the x- and y-axes, and we define the angle α formed from the x-axis in a positive direction to the line as the **angle of inclination** of the line. Clearly, if the two lines are parallel, they must have the same angle of inclination. Furthermore,

$$m_2 = \frac{y_4 - y_3}{x_4 - x_3} = \tan \alpha$$

and

$$m_1 = \frac{y_2 - y_1}{x_2 - x_1} = \tan \alpha.$$

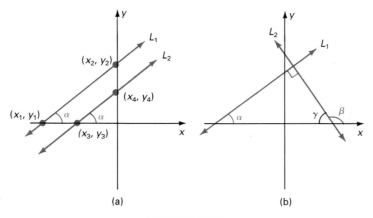

(a)   (b)

FIGURE 17.5

Hence, for parallel lines, $m_1 = m_2$. If L_1 and L_2 are horizontal lines, they both have slopes of zero.

Figure 17.5(b) shows two perpendicular lines with angles of inclination α and β. Now,

$$\alpha + \gamma + 90° = 180°,$$

and

$$\gamma + \beta = 180°.$$

Therefore,

$$\alpha + \gamma + 90° = \gamma + \beta,$$

so

$$\alpha + 90° = \beta.$$

Thus

$$\tan (\alpha + 90°) = \tan \beta.$$

Using Identities 4, 9, and 10 gives

$$\tan (\alpha + 90°) = \frac{\sin (\alpha + 90°)}{\cos (\alpha + 90°)} = \frac{\sin \alpha \cos 90° + \cos \alpha \sin 90°}{\cos \alpha \cos 90° - \sin \alpha \sin 90°}$$

$$= \frac{0 + \cos \alpha}{0 - \sin \alpha} = -\cot \alpha.$$

Thus

$$-\cot \alpha = \tan \beta \quad \text{or} \quad -\frac{1}{\tan \alpha} = \tan \beta.$$

Because $m_1 = \tan \alpha$ and $m_2 = \tan \beta$,

$$m_2 = -\frac{1}{m_1}.$$

We now consider the proofs of Identities 9–11. Assume that α and β are positive acute angles and that their sum $\alpha + \beta$ is a first-quadrant angle. (It can be shown that our results are true for any angles α and β.) Refer to Fig. 17.6 as you follow our discussion.

From any point P on the terminal side of $\alpha + \beta$, perpendiculars are constructed to the x-axis at A and to the terminal side of α at B. From B, perpendiculars are constructed to the x-axis at C and to segment AP at D. Using the angle symbol $\angle$, we have

$$\angle BPD + \angle PBD = 90°$$

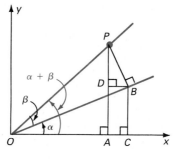

FIGURE 17.6

and

$$\angle DBO + \angle PBD = 90°.$$

It follows by substitution that

$$\angle BPD = \angle DBO.$$

But angle DBO equals angle α because they are alternate interior angles formed by parallel lines cut by a transversal. Thus $\angle BPD = \alpha$.

Now, from right triangle OCB, $\sin \alpha = \overline{CB}/\overline{OB}$, or $\overline{CB} = \overline{OB} \sin \alpha$. From triangle PDB, $\cos \alpha = \overline{DP}/\overline{PB}$, so $\overline{DP} = \overline{PB} \cos \alpha$. Therefore, from right triangle OAP, we have

$$\sin (\alpha + \beta) = \frac{\overline{AP}}{\overline{OP}} = \frac{\overline{AD} + \overline{DP}}{\overline{OP}} = \frac{\overline{CB} + \overline{DP}}{\overline{OP}}$$

$$= \frac{\overline{OB} \sin \alpha + \overline{PB} \cos \alpha}{\overline{OP}}$$

$$= \frac{\overline{OB}}{\overline{OP}} \sin \alpha + \frac{\overline{PB}}{\overline{OP}} \cos \alpha,$$

$$\mathbf{\sin (\alpha + \beta) = \sin \alpha \cos \beta + \cos \alpha \sin \beta.}$$

Similarly,

$$\cos (\alpha + \beta) = \frac{\overline{OA}}{\overline{OP}} = \frac{\overline{OC} - \overline{DB}}{\overline{OP}}.$$

From right triangle OCB, $\cos \alpha = \overline{OC}/\overline{OB}$; so $\overline{OC} = \overline{OB} \cos \alpha$. From right triangle BPD, $\sin \alpha = \overline{DB}/\overline{BP}$, or $\overline{DB} = \overline{BP} \sin \alpha$. Thus

$$\cos (\alpha + \beta) = \frac{\overline{OC} - \overline{DB}}{\overline{OP}} = \frac{\overline{OB} \cos \alpha - \overline{BP} \sin \alpha}{\overline{OP}}$$

$$= \frac{\overline{OB}}{\overline{OP}} \cos \alpha - \frac{\overline{BP}}{\overline{OP}} \sin \alpha$$

$$= \cos \beta \cos \alpha - \sin \beta \sin \alpha,$$

$$\mathbf{\cos (\alpha + \beta) = \cos \alpha \cos \beta - \sin \alpha \sin \beta.}$$

Finally,

$$\tan(\alpha + \beta) = \frac{\sin(\alpha + \beta)}{\cos(\alpha + \beta)}$$

$$= \frac{\sin \alpha \cos \beta + \cos \alpha \sin \beta}{\cos \alpha \cos \beta - \sin \alpha \sin \beta}.$$

Dividing each term of the numerator and denominator by $\cos \alpha \cos \beta$ gives

$$\tan(\alpha + \beta) = \frac{\dfrac{\sin \alpha \cos \beta}{\cos \alpha \cos \beta} + \dfrac{\cos \alpha \sin \beta}{\cos \alpha \cos \beta}}{1 - \dfrac{\sin \alpha \sin \beta}{\cos \alpha \cos \beta}},$$

$$\tan(\alpha + \beta) = \frac{\tan \alpha + \tan \beta}{1 - \tan \alpha \tan \beta}.$$

Although we could derive formulas for $\cot(\alpha + \beta)$, $\sec(\alpha + \beta)$, and $\csc(\alpha + \beta)$, they are rarely used.

Problem Set 17.2

1. Find $\cos 75°$ by using functions of $30°$ and $45°$.
2. Find $\sin 15°$ by using functions of $30°$ and $45°$.
3. Find $\sin 195°$ by using functions of $225°$ and $30°$.
4. Find $\cos 165°$ by using functions of $120°$ and $45°$.

*In Problems **5–12**, use the formulas of this section to find the given values. Rationalize your answers.*

5. $\tan 15°$.
6. $\tan 75°$.
7. $\cos 105°$.
8. $\sin 105°$.
9. $\sin 255°$.
10. $\cos 255°$.
11. $\tan 255°$.
12. $\tan 345°$.

13. If α and β are second-quadrant angles and $\tan \alpha = -\frac{1}{2}$ and $\tan \beta = -\frac{2}{3}$, find (a) $\sin(\alpha + \beta)$, (b) $\cos(\alpha + \beta)$, (c) $\tan(\alpha + \beta)$, and (d) the quadrant in which $\alpha + \beta$ lies.
14. If α is a first-quadrant angle and $\sin \alpha = \frac{3}{5}$, and β is a second-quadrant angle and $\cos \beta = -\frac{3}{4}$, find (a) $\sin(\alpha - \beta)$, (b) $\cos(\alpha - \beta)$, and (c) $\tan(\alpha - \beta)$.

*In Problems **15–20**, write each expression in terms of $\sin x$, $\cos x$, or $\tan x$, as in Example 4.*

15. $\sin(x + \pi)$.
16. $\cos(x + \pi)$.
17. $\cos\left(\dfrac{\pi}{2} - x\right)$.
18. $\sin\left(\dfrac{\pi}{2} - x\right)$.
19. $\tan\left(x + \dfrac{\pi}{4}\right)$.
20. $3 \sin\left(x + \dfrac{\pi}{2}\right)$.

21. Express $\cos 23° \cos 47° - \sin 23° \sin 47°$ as a trigonometric function value of one angle only.

22. Express $\sin 18° \cos 10° - \cos 18° \sin 10°$ as a trigonometric function value of one angle only.

In Problems 23–28, prove the given identities.

23. $\dfrac{\sin (\alpha + \beta)}{\cos \alpha \cos \beta} = \tan \alpha + \tan \beta.$

24. $\cos (\alpha + \beta) - \cos (\alpha - \beta) = -2 \sin \alpha \sin \beta.$

25. $\sin (x + y) + \sin (x - y) = 2 \sin x \cos y.$

26. $\sin (A + B) \sin (A - B) = \sin^2 A - \sin^2 B.$

27. $\dfrac{\sin (x + y)}{\sin (x - y)} = \dfrac{\tan x + \tan y}{\tan x - \tan y}$

28. $\dfrac{\sin (x + y)}{\cos (x - y)} = \dfrac{\tan x + \tan y}{1 + \tan x \tan y}.$

29. Derive Identity 14.

30. Derive Identity 15.

In Problems 31–36, without performing any calculations, determine whether the given statement is true or false.

31. $\sin (-85°) = -\sin 85°.$

32. $\sin (-225°) = -\sin 225°.$

33. $\cos (-225°) = \cos 225°.$

34. $\cos (-225°) = -\cos 45°.$

35. In a certain three-phase ac generator, the phases are expressed as $I \cos \theta$, $I \cos (\theta + 120°)$, and $I \cos (\theta + 240°)$. It is to be shown that each phase is numerically equal to the sum of the other phases but opposite in sign. To do this it suffices to show that

$$I \cos \theta + I \cos (\theta + 120°) + I \cos (\theta + 240°) = 0.$$

Show that this is indeed the case.

36. The displacement x of a certain object, undergoing harmonic motion, as a function of time t is given by

$$x = 2\sqrt{2} \cos \left(2t - \frac{\pi}{4} \right).$$

(a) By expanding the right side, show that the displacement is the sum of two different motions: a sine function and a cosine function.

(b) For the two different motions in Part a, find the contribution of each to the displacement when $t = \pi/4$.

37. For light passing symmetrically through a prism, the index of refraction, n, of glass with respect to air is given by

$$n = \frac{\sin \left[\frac{1}{2}(\alpha + \beta) \right]}{\sin (\beta/2)},$$

where α is the deviation angle and β is the angle of the apex of the prism. If $\beta = 60°$, show that $n = \sqrt{3} \sin (\alpha/2) + \cos (\alpha/2).$

38. The electric field components of two light waves vary with time at a given point as given by

$$E_1 = E_0 \sin (\omega t),$$

$$E_2 = E_0 \sin (\omega t + \varphi).$$

The electric field component is associated with the disturbance caused by the waves. **Show** that $E_1 + E_2 = E_0 (\sin \omega t)(1 + \cos \varphi) + E_0(\cos \omega t) \sin \varphi$.

39. The equation of a standing wave can be obtained by adding the displacements y_1 and y_2 associated with two waves traveling in opposite directions. Given

$$y_1 = A \sin (\omega t - kx),$$

$$y_2 = -A \sin (\omega t + kx),$$

show that the equation of the standing wave is

$$y = y_1 + y_2 = -2A \cos (\omega t) \sin (kx).$$

17.3 DOUBLE- AND HALF-ANGLE FORMULAS

Using the addition formulas, we can derive formulas that express the trigonometric functions of twice an angle in terms of functions of the angle itself. By letting $y = x$ in Identity 9, we obtain

$$\sin 2x = \sin (x + x) = \sin x \cos x + \cos x \sin x$$

$$= 2 \sin x \cos x.$$

Thus we have the following identity.

$$\boxed{\textbf{16.} \ \ \textbf{sin } 2x = \textbf{2 sin } x \textbf{ cos } x \ .}$$

Letting $y = x$ in Identity 10, we have

$$\cos 2x = \cos (x + x) = \cos x \cos x - \sin x \sin x$$

$$= \cos^2 x - \sin^2 x.$$

But since $\sin^2 x + \cos^2 x = 1$, the preceding expression can be written either as

$$\cos^2 x - \sin^2 x = \cos^2 x - (1 - \cos^2 x) = 2 \cos^2 x - 1$$

or as

$$\cos^2 x - \sin^2 x = (1 - \sin^2 x) - \sin^2 x = 1 - 2 \sin^2 x.$$

Thus we have three ways to express $\cos 2x$:

$$\boxed{\textbf{17.} \ \ \begin{cases} \cos 2x = \cos^2 x - \sin^2 x \\ \qquad \quad = 2 \cos^2 x - 1 \\ \qquad \quad = 1 - 2 \sin^2 x. \end{cases}}$$

Similarly, letting $y = x$ in Identity 11 gives Identity 18:

$$18. \ \ \mathbf{tan} \ 2x = \frac{2 \tan x}{1 - \tan^2 x}.$$

Identities 16–18 are called **double-angle formulas.**

Do not confuse $\sin 2\theta$ with $2 \sin \theta$; they are *not* the same for all values of θ. For example, if $\theta = 30°$, then $\sin 2\theta = \sin 60° = \sqrt{3}/2$, but $2 \sin \theta = 2 \sin 30° = 2(\frac{1}{2}) = 1$.

Example 1

Use a double-angle formula to evaluate $\sin 60°$.

Solution Since we want $\sin 2x = \sin 60°$, we let $x = 30°$. From Identity 16 we have

$$\sin 2x = 2 \sin x \cos x,$$
$$\sin 60° = \sin (2 \cdot 30°) = 2 \sin 30° \cos 30°$$
$$= 2 \left(\frac{1}{2} \right) \left(\frac{\sqrt{3}}{2} \right) = \frac{\sqrt{3}}{2}.$$

Example 2

If θ is a second-quadrant angle and $\sin \theta = \frac{3}{5}$, find $\tan 2\theta$.

Solution In Fig. 17.7 we drew a second-quadrant angle θ such that $\sin \theta = \frac{3}{5}$. To find x we solve $x^2 + 3^2 = 5^2$, which gives $x = -4$ (negative, because x is negative in the second quadrant). Using Identity 18 with $\tan \theta = 3/x = 3/(-4) = -\frac{3}{4}$, we have

$$\tan 2\theta = \frac{2 \tan \theta}{1 - \tan^2 \theta} = \frac{2(-\frac{3}{4})}{1 - (-\frac{3}{4})^2}$$
$$= \frac{-\frac{3}{2}}{1 - \frac{9}{16}} = \frac{-\frac{3}{2}}{\frac{7}{16}} = -\frac{24}{7}.$$

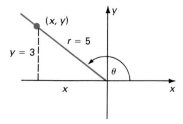

FIGURE 17.7

There are formulas, called **half-angle formulas**, that express a trigonometric function of half an angle, $\theta/2$, in terms of the angle θ itself. To derive one of these, we use the double-angle formula

$$\cos 2x = 1 - 2 \sin^2 x.$$

Letting $x = \theta/2$ gives

$$\cos\left[2\left(\frac{\theta}{2}\right)\right] = 1 - 2 \sin^2 \frac{\theta}{2}$$

$$\cos \theta = 1 - 2 \sin^2 \frac{\theta}{2},$$

which can be written

$$2 \sin^2 \frac{\theta}{2} = 1 - \cos \theta$$

$$\sin^2 \frac{\theta}{2} = \frac{1 - \cos \theta}{2}. \tag{1}$$

Solving for $\sin \theta/2$ gives the following identity, called a *half-angle formula*:

$$\boxed{\ \ \textbf{19.} \quad \sin \frac{\theta}{2} = \pm \sqrt{\frac{1 - \cos \theta}{2}}.\ \ }$$

In this formula, we use either the plus sign or the minus sign (not both). The proper choice depends on the sign of $\sin (\theta/2)$. If $\theta/2$ (*not* θ) is a first- or second-quadrant angle, use the plus sign because $\sin (\theta/2)$ is positive there. For a third- or fourth-quadrant angle, use the minus sign.

We can derive more half-angle formulas. Using the double-angle formula

$$\cos 2x = 2 \cos^2 x - 1$$

and again letting $x = \theta/2$ yields

$$\cos\left[2\left(\frac{\theta}{2}\right)\right] = 2 \cos^2 \frac{\theta}{2} - 1.$$

Rearranging terms and dividing by 2, we have

$$2 \cos^2 \frac{\theta}{2} = 1 + \cos \theta$$

$$\cos^2 \frac{\theta}{2} = \frac{1 + \cos \theta}{2}. \tag{2}$$

Thus we have another half-angle formula:

$$\cos \frac{\theta}{2} = \pm \sqrt{\frac{1 + \cos \theta}{2}}.$$

To derive a formula for $\tan(\theta/2)$, we write

$$\tan\frac{\theta}{2} = \frac{\sin\dfrac{\theta}{2}}{\cos\dfrac{\theta}{2}}.$$

Multiplying the numerator and denominator by $2\cos(\theta/2)$ gives

$$\tan\frac{\theta}{2} = \frac{\sin\dfrac{\theta}{2}}{\cos\dfrac{\theta}{2}} \cdot \frac{2\cos\dfrac{\theta}{2}}{2\cos\dfrac{\theta}{2}}$$

$$= \frac{2\sin\dfrac{\theta}{2}\cos\dfrac{\theta}{2}}{2\cos^2\dfrac{\theta}{2}}.$$

Using Identity 16 and Eq. 2, we get the identity

$$\tan\frac{\theta}{2} = \frac{\sin\theta}{1 + \cos\theta}.$$

To get another form for $\tan(\theta/2)$ we proceed as follows:

$$\tan\frac{\theta}{2} = \frac{\sin\theta}{1 + \cos\theta} \cdot \frac{1 - \cos\theta}{1 - \cos\theta} = \frac{(\sin\theta)(1 - \cos\theta)}{1 - \cos^2\theta}$$

$$= \frac{(\sin\theta)(1 - \cos\theta)}{\sin^2\theta},$$

$$\tan\frac{\theta}{2} = \frac{1 - \cos\theta}{\sin\theta}.$$

Thus we have the following half-angle formulas:

---

20. $\quad \cos\dfrac{\theta}{2} = \pm\sqrt{\dfrac{1 + \cos\theta}{2}}.$

21. $\quad \tan\dfrac{\theta}{2} = \dfrac{\sin\theta}{1 + \cos\theta}$

$\qquad\qquad = \dfrac{1 - \cos\theta}{\sin\theta}.$

In Identity 20, use the plus sign if $\theta/2$ is a first- or fourth-quadrant angle because for these quadrants the cosine function is positive. Use the minus sign for the other quadrants. Again, the proper sign depends on $\theta/2$, not θ. Note in Identity 21 that $\tan(\theta/2)$ is expressed without radicals.

If we replace $\theta/2$ by θ in Eqs. 1 and 2, we get the following identities, which are also called half-angle formulas.

$$\sin^2 \theta = \frac{1 - \cos 2\theta}{2}. \tag{3}$$

$$\cos^2 \theta = \frac{1 + \cos 2\theta}{2}. \tag{4}$$

Example 3

Use a half-angle formula to determine $\sin 75°$.

Solution   We want $\theta/2 = 75°$, so $\theta = 150°$. Since $\sin 75°$ is positive, we use the plus sign with Identity 19.

$$\sin 75° = \sin \frac{150°}{2} = \sqrt{\frac{1 - \cos 150°}{2}}$$

$$= \sqrt{\frac{1 - \left(-\frac{\sqrt{3}}{2}\right)}{2}} = \sqrt{\frac{2 + \sqrt{3}}{4}}$$

$$= \frac{\sqrt{2 + \sqrt{3}}}{2}.$$

Example 4

Find $\tan 105°$ from the trigonometric functions of $210°$.

Solution   We use Identity 21 with $\theta = 210°$.

$$\tan 105° = \tan \frac{210°}{2} = \frac{\sin 210°}{1 + \cos 210°}$$

$$= \frac{-\frac{1}{2}}{1 + \left(-\frac{\sqrt{3}}{2}\right)} = -\frac{\frac{1}{2}}{\frac{2 - \sqrt{3}}{2}}$$

$$= -\frac{1}{2 - \sqrt{3}} = -\frac{1}{2 - \sqrt{3}} \cdot \frac{2 + \sqrt{3}}{2 + \sqrt{3}}$$

$$= -\frac{2 + \sqrt{3}}{4 - 3} = -(2 + \sqrt{3}).$$

As an aid to you, Sec. 17.5 contains a summary of the identities of this chapter, along with some other identities for future reference.

Problem Set 17.3

In Problems **1–6**, *use a double-angle formula to evaluate the given trigonometric value. A calculator should not be needed.*

1. $\sin 60°$.
2. $\cos 60°$.
3. $\cos 240°$.
4. $\sin 240°$.
5. $\tan 120°$.
6. $\tan 240°$.

In Problems **7–12**, *use a half-angle formula to evaluate the given trigonometric value. A calculator should not be needed.*

7. $\sin 15°$.
8. $\cos 75°$.
9. $\cos 22.5°$.
10. $\sin 157.5°$.
11. $\tan 112.5°$.
12. $\sin 67.5°$.

In Problems **13–16**, *find* $\sin x$, $\cos x$, $\tan x$, $\sin 2x$, $\cos 2x$, *and* $\tan 2x$ *from the given information.*

13. $\cos x = \frac{3}{5}$, $\sin x$ is positive.
14. $\sec x = 5$, $\sin x$ is negative.
15. $\sin x = -\frac{1}{3}$, $\cot x$ is positive.
16. $\cos x = -\frac{1}{4}$, $\tan x$ is negative.

In Problems **17–20**, *find* $\sin x$, $\cos x$, $\tan x$, $\sin (x/2)$, $\cos (x/2)$, *and* $\tan (x/2)$ *from the given information. Assume* $0° < x < 360°$ *and use the facts that if* $0° < x < 180°$, *then* $0° < \dfrac{x}{2} < 90°$, *and if* $180° < x < 360°$, *then* $90° < \dfrac{x}{2} < 180°$.

17. $\cos x = \frac{12}{13}$, $\sin x$ is positive.
18. $\cot x = -\frac{8}{15}$, $\sin x$ is positive.
19. $\sin x = -\frac{3}{5}$, $\tan x$ is positive.
20. $\cos x = \frac{5}{13}$, $\sin x$ is negative.

In Problems **21–26**, *prove the identities.*

21. $\cos^4 x - \sin^4 x = \cos 2x$.
22. $1 + \sin 2x = (\sin x + \cos x)^2$.
23. $\sin 2x \cot x = \cos 2x + 1$.
24. $\tan \dfrac{x}{2} = \csc x - \cot x$.
25. $2 \sin \dfrac{\theta}{2} \cos \dfrac{\theta}{2} = \sin \theta$.
26. $\tan x + \cot x = 2 \csc 2x$.

27. Show that $\sin 3x = 3 \sin x - 4 \sin^3 x$. *Hint*: $\sin 3x = \sin (2x + x)$.
28. Show that

$$\sin^2 2x = \frac{1 - \cos 4x}{2}.$$

29. The index of refraction, n, of a prism whose apex angle is α and whose angle of minimum deviation is φ is given by

$$n = \frac{\sin [(\alpha + \varphi)/2]}{\sin (\alpha/2)} \qquad (n > 0).$$

Show that

$$n = \sqrt{\frac{1 - \cos \alpha \cos \varphi + \sin \alpha \sin \varphi}{1 - \cos \alpha}}.$$

30. If a projectile is fired from the ground at an angle θ with the horizontal with an initial speed v_0, the horizontal range of the projectile is given by

$$R = \frac{v_0^2 \sin 2\theta}{g}.$$

Determine another expression for R in terms of trigonometric functions of θ.

31. Suppose that the power P delivered by an ac supply at time t is given by

$$P = I^2 R \sin^2 \omega t,$$

where R is resistance and I is current. Show that

$$P = \frac{I^2 R}{2} - \frac{I^2 R}{2} \cos 2\omega t.$$

32. Use Identity 25 in Table 17.1 (see Sec. 17.5) to show that

$$\sin (\omega t + \beta) \sin (\omega t + \psi) = \frac{\cos (\beta - \psi) - \cos (2\omega t + \beta + \psi)}{2}.$$

33. Two tuning forks of nearly equal frequencies f_1 and f_2 are heard by a listener. The air-pressure variations p_1 and p_2 on the listener's eardrum are given by

$$p_1 = p_0 \cos 2\pi f_1 t$$

and

$$p_2 = p_0 \cos 2\pi f_2 t,$$

where p_0, f_1, and f_2 are constants. Use Identity 27 in Table 17.1 (see Sec. 17.5) to show that the total pressure $p = p_1 + p_2$ can be expressed as

$$p = 2p_0 \cos \left[2\pi \left(\frac{f_1 + f_2}{2} \right) t \right] \cos \left[2\pi \left(\frac{f_1 - f_2}{2} \right) t \right].$$

17.4 TRIGONOMETRIC EQUATIONS

A **trigonometric equation** is an equation involving trigonometric functions of un-known angles. An example is $2 \sin x = 1$. Solving this equation means to find all *angles* x for which the equation is true. However, we shall confine ourselves only to those solutions for which $0° \le x < 360°$. To solve a trigonometric equation we use algebra (as we would with any equation) and also trigonometric identities when they seem useful.

Example 1

Solve $2 \sin x = 1$.

Solution

$$2 \sin x = 1$$

$$\sin x = \frac{1}{2}.$$

From our knowledge of special angles, clearly $30°$ is a solution. But $\sin x$ is also positive if x is a second-quadrant angle. Thus a second-quadrant angle with $30°$ as its reference angle is a solution. It must be $180° - 30° = 150°$. The solutions are $30°$ and $150°$.

Some trigonometric equations can be solved by factoring, as Example 2 shows.

Example 2

Solve $2 \sin^2 x - \sin x - 1 = 0$.

Solution

$$2 \sin^2 x - \sin x - 1 = 0$$

$$(2 \sin x + 1)(\sin x - 1) = 0 \qquad \text{[factoring]}.$$

$$2 \sin x + 1 = 0 \qquad \qquad \sin x - 1 = 0$$

$$2 \sin x = -1 \qquad \qquad \sin x = 1.$$

$$\sin x = -\frac{1}{2}.$$

Thus either $\sin x = -\frac{1}{2}$ or $\sin x = 1$. If $\sin x = -\frac{1}{2}$, then x is a third- or fourth-quadrant angle with $30°$ as its reference angle, so $x = 210°$ or $x = 330°$. If $\sin x = 1$, then $x = 90°$. The solutions are $90°$, $210°$, and $330°$.

Example 3

Solve $\sin^2 x - \sin x - 2 = 0$.

Solution

$$\sin^2 x - \sin x - 2 = 0$$

$$(\sin x - 2)(\sin x + 1) = 0 \qquad \text{[factoring]}.$$

$$\sin x - 2 = 0 \qquad \qquad \sin x + 1 = 0$$

$$\sin x = 2. \qquad \qquad \sin x = -1.$$

Thus either $\sin x = 2$ or $\sin x = -1$. Because $|\sin x| \le 1$ for all x, the equation $\sin x = 2$ has no solution. However, $\sin x = -1$ has solution $x = 270°$. Thus the only solution of the given equation is $270°$.

Some trigonometric equations can be solved by writing the equation in terms of one trigonometric function only, as Example 4 shows.

Example 4

Solve $2 \cos x - \sec x = 1$.

Solution   We can write this equation in terms of $\cos x$ only.

$$2 \cos x - \sec x = 1$$

$$2 \cos x - \frac{1}{\cos x} = 1 \qquad \text{[Identity 2]}.$$

To clear fractions, we multiply both sides by $\cos x$.

$$2 \cos^2 x - 1 = \cos x$$

$$2 \cos^2 x - \cos x - 1 = 0$$

$$(2 \cos x + 1)(\cos x - 1) = 0 \qquad \text{[factoring]}.$$

$2 \cos x + 1 = 0$	$\cos x - 1 = 0$
$2 \cos x = -1$	$\cos x = 1.$
$\cos x = -\dfrac{1}{2}.$	

If $\cos x = -\frac{1}{2}$, then $x = 120°$ or $240°$. If $\cos x = 1$, then $x = 0°$. *We are not done yet!* Because we multiplied both sides by $\cos x$—which involves a variable—we must check each value of x in the original equation.

If $x = 0°$, then $2 \cos 0° - \sec 0° = 2(1) - 1 = 1 = \text{right side}$.

If $x = 120°$, then $2 \cos 120° - \sec 120° = 2(-\frac{1}{2}) - (-2) = 1 = \text{right side}$.

If $x = 240°$, then $2 \cos 240° - \sec 240° = 2(-\frac{1}{2}) - (-2) = 1 = \text{right side}$.

Thus the solutions are $0°$, $120°$, and $240°$.

Another method of solving some trigonometric equations involves squaring both sides, as Example 5 shows.

Example 5

Solve $\sin x + \cos x = 1$.

Solution In this equation no worthwhile substitution is obvious. One way out of this situation is to square both sides. Before squaring, a common practice is to rewrite the equation so that there is a trigonometric function on each side.

$$\sin x + \cos x = 1$$
$$\sin x = 1 - \cos x$$
$$(\sin x)^2 = (1 - \cos x)^2$$
$$\sin^2 x = 1 - 2 \cos x + \cos^2 x$$
$$1 - \cos^2 x = 1 - 2 \cos x + \cos^2 x \qquad \text{[Identity 6].}$$

Now we combine terms.

$$0 = 2 \cos^2 x - 2 \cos x$$
$$0 = \cos^2 x - \cos x \qquad \text{[dividing both sides by 2]}$$
$$0 = (\cos x)(\cos x - 1) \qquad \text{[factoring].}$$

$$
\begin{array}{c|c}
\cos x = 0 & \cos x - 1 = 0 \\
x = 90°, 270°. & \cos x = 1 \\
& x = 0°.
\end{array}
$$

Because we squared both sides, we must check all values of x in the given equation.

If $x = 0°$, then $\sin 0° + \cos 0° = 0 + 1 = 1 = $ right side.

If $x = 90°$, then $\sin 90° + \cos 90° = 1 + 0 = 1 = $ right side.

If $x = 270°$, then $\sin 270° + \cos 270° = -1 + 0 = -1 \neq $ right side.

Thus the solutions are $0°$ and $90°$.

In Example 5 we solved $0 = (\cos x)(\cos x - 1)$ by setting each factor equal to 0. You may be tempted to first divide both sides by $\cos x$. Doing this division gives $0 = \cos x - 1$, which has $0°$ as its only solution. However, from Example 5 we know that the original equation is true not only for $0°$, but for $90°$ as well. Thus by dividing by $\cos x$ we lose a solution. As we have mentioned before, it is best not to divide both sides of an equation by an expression involving a variable.

Example 6

Solve $2 \sin x \cos x = 1$.

Solution

$$2 \sin x \cos x = 1$$
$$\sin 2x = 1 \qquad \text{[Identity 16].}$$

Since 90° has a sine of 1, we set $2x = 90°$, so $x = 45°$. Also, $\sin 450° = 1$. Setting $2x = 450°$ gives $x = 225°$. Thus the solutions are 45° and 225°. Note that although 450° is beyond our usual considerations, after dividing by 2 we obtain a solution between 0° and 360°. More generally, to solve $\sin nx = k$, we consider all angles nx between 0° and $(360n)°$ with a sine of k so that we find all solutions x between 0° and 360°.

Problem Set 17.4

In Problems **1–32**, *solve for* x, *where* $0° \leq x < 360°$.

1. $\sin x = \dfrac{\sqrt{2}}{2}$.

2. $\cos x = -\dfrac{\sqrt{3}}{2}$.

3. $\tan x = -1$.

4. $\sin x = 0$.

5. $2 \cos x = 1$.

6. $\sin (x + 10°) = -\dfrac{1}{2}$.

7. $2 \cos^2 x - \cos x - 1 = 0$.

8. $\sin^2 x - 2 \sin x + 1 = 0$.

9. $\sin x + \sin x \cos x = 0$.

10. $\sin^2 x - 1 = 0$.

11. $\sin x = 2 \cos x$.

12. $2 \tan^2 x = 5$.

13. $\sin^2 x + \sin x - 1 = 0$.

14. $(\sin x)(3 \cos x - 2) = 0$.

15. $2 \sin x - \csc x = 1$.

16. $\tan x \cos x = \dfrac{1}{2}$.

17. $\sin 2x = \dfrac{\sqrt{3}}{2}$.

18. $\cos 3x = 1$.

19. $\cos x - 1 - \sqrt{3} \sin x = 0$.

20. $\cos x - \sin x - 1 = 0$.

21. $2 \sin x \cos x = -\dfrac{\sqrt{2}}{2}$.

22. $\sin 2x = \sin x$.

23. $\cos x - \cos 2x = 1$.

24. $\sin 2x \cos x = 0$.

25. $2 \sin x - \tan x = 0$.

26. $\sin x + \cos 2x = 4 \sin^2 x$.

27. $2 \tan^2 x + \sec^2 x = 2$.

28. $\sqrt{2 - \csc^2 x} = \csc x$.

29. $\sin 2x + \cos x = 0$.

30. $\tan 2x + \sec 2x = 1$.

31. $\sec^2 x + \tan x = 1$.

32. $\cot x - \csc^2 x = -1$.

17.5 REVIEW

Important Terms

Section 17.1   Trigonometric identity.
Section 17.2   Addition formulas, subtraction formulas.
Section 17.3   Half-angle formulas.
Section 17.4   Trigonometric equation.

Formula Summary

TABLE 17.1   Trigonometric Identities

1. $\csc \theta = \dfrac{1}{\sin \theta}$.

2. $\sec \theta = \dfrac{1}{\cos \theta}$.

3. $\cot \theta = \dfrac{1}{\tan \theta}$.

4. $\tan \theta = \dfrac{\sin \theta}{\cos \theta}$.

5. $\cot \theta = \dfrac{\cos \theta}{\sin \theta}$.

6. $\sin^2 \theta + \cos^2 \theta = 1$.

7. $1 + \tan^2 \theta = \sec^2 \theta$.

8. $1 + \cot^2 \theta = \csc^2 \theta$.

9. $\sin (x + y) = \sin x \cos y + \cos x \sin y$.

10. $\cos (x + y) = \cos x \cos y - \sin x \sin y$.

11. $\tan (x + y) = \dfrac{\tan x + \tan y}{1 - \tan x \tan y}$.

12. $\sin (-\theta) = -\sin \theta$. $\qquad \csc (-\theta) = -\csc \theta$.

   $\cos (-\theta) = \cos \theta$. $\qquad \sec (-\theta) = \sec \theta$.

   $\tan (-\theta) = -\tan \theta$. $\qquad \cot (-\theta) = -\cot \theta$.

13. $\sin (x - y) = \sin x \cos y - \cos x \sin y$.

14. $\cos (x - y) = \cos x \cos y + \sin x \sin y$.

15. $\tan (x - y) = \dfrac{\tan x - \tan y}{1 + \tan x \tan y}$.

16. $\sin 2x = 2 \sin x \cos x$.

17. $\cos 2x = \cos^2 x - \sin^2 x$

$$= 2 \cos^2 x - 1$$

$$= 1 - 2 \sin^2 x.$$

18. $\tan 2x = \dfrac{2 \tan x}{1 - \tan^2 x}$.

19. $\sin \dfrac{\theta}{2} = \pm \sqrt{\dfrac{1 - \cos \theta}{2}}$.

20. $\cos \dfrac{\theta}{2} = \pm \sqrt{\dfrac{1 + \cos \theta}{2}}$.

21. $\tan \dfrac{\theta}{2} = \dfrac{\sin \theta}{1 + \cos \theta} = \dfrac{1 - \cos \theta}{\sin \theta}$.

TABLE 17.1 Trigonometric Identities (*cont.*)

22. $\sin (x + y) + \sin (x - y) = 2 \sin x \cos y.$

23. $\cos (x + y) + \cos (x - y) = 2 \cos x \cos y.$

24. $\sin (x + y) - \sin (x - y) = 2 \cos x \sin y.$

25. $\cos (x + y) - \cos (x - y) = -2 \sin x \sin y.$

26. $\sin x + \sin y = 2 \sin \dfrac{x + y}{2} \cos \dfrac{x - y}{2}.$

27. $\cos x + \cos y = 2 \cos \dfrac{x + y}{2} \cos \dfrac{x - y}{2}.$

28. $\sin x - \sin y = 2 \cos \dfrac{x + y}{2} \sin \dfrac{x - y}{2}.$

29. $\cos x - \cos y = -2 \sin \dfrac{x + y}{2} \sin \dfrac{x - y}{2}.$

Review Questions

1. How many of the following expressions always have a value of 1? _____

$$\sin^2 \theta + \cos^2 \theta, \qquad \csc^2 3° - \cot^2 3°, \qquad \sec^2 \theta + \tan^2 \theta.$$

2. Which of the following statements are identities? _____

   (a) $\sin^2 \theta = 1 + \cos^2 \theta.$ (b) $\dfrac{1}{\sec \theta} = \cos \theta.$

   (c) $\sin \theta \csc \theta = 1.$ (d) $1 + \sec^2 \theta = \tan \theta.$

3. True or false: $\sin (-15°) = -\sin 15°.$ _____

4. True or false: $\cos (A + B) = \cos A \cos B + \sin A \sin B$ for all values of A and B. _____

5. If $A = 130°$, then $\cos (A/2)$ is $\underline{\text{(positive)(negative)}}$.

6. $\dfrac{2 \tan 40°}{1 - \tan^2 40°} = \tan \underline{\hspace{1cm}}°.$

Answers to Review Questions

1. Two.   2. *b, c.*   3. True.   4. False.   5. Positive.   6. 80.

Review Problems

In Problems **1–10**, *prove the given identities.*

1. $\tan x + \cot x = \sec x \csc x.$

2. $\cot^2 x \sin^2 x + \tan^2 x \cos^2 x = 1.$

3. $\csc^2 \theta \tan^2 \theta - \sec \theta \cos \theta = \tan^2 \theta.$

4. $\dfrac{\sec^2 \theta}{\cot \theta} - \tan^3 \theta = \tan \theta.$

5. $\dfrac{\sin^2 x}{1 - \cos x} = 1 + \cos x.$

6. $\sec^2 x + \csc^2 x = \sec^2 x \csc^2 x.$

7. $\cos x + \sin x \tan x = \sec x$.

8. $\sin 2x \tan x = 2 \sin^2 x$.

9. $\dfrac{1 + \cos 2x}{\sin 2x} = \cot x$.

10. $\sin^2 \dfrac{x}{2} = \dfrac{\tan x - \sin x}{2 \tan x}$.

In Problems 11–18, evaluate the given expressions if α and β are first-quadrant angles and $\sin \alpha = \frac{1}{2}$ and $\sin \beta = \frac{4}{5}$.

11. $\sin (\alpha + \beta)$.

12. $\cos (\alpha - \beta)$.

13. $\tan \dfrac{\beta}{2}$.

14. $\cos (\alpha + \beta)$.

15. $\cos 2\alpha$.

16. $\sin 2\alpha$.

17. $\tan (\beta - 45°)$.

18. $\cos \dfrac{\beta}{2}$.

19. If x is an acute angle and $\tan x = \frac{15}{8}$, find $\sin x$, $\cos x$, $\tan x$, $\sin (-x)$, $\cos (-x)$, $\sin 2x$, $\cos 2x$, $\tan 2x$, $\sin \dfrac{x}{2}$, $\cos \dfrac{x}{2}$, and $\tan \dfrac{x}{2}$.

20. If $\sin x = \frac{3}{5}$, find the trigonometric values asked for in Problem 19. Assume x is acute.

In Problems 21–24, solve the equation for x, where $0° \leq x < 360°$.

21. $\sin x \cos x - \cot x = 0$.

22. $\sin 2x - \sqrt{2} \sin x = 0$.

23. $\dfrac{\sqrt{3}}{2} + \tan^2 x + \sin x - \sec^2 x = -1$.

24. $1 + \sin 2x = 0$.

25. (a) Prove that $\sin x = \cos \left(x - \dfrac{\pi}{2} \right)$.

(b) Use your result in Part a to show that

$$\sin \left(\omega t + \dfrac{\pi}{5} \right) = \cos \left(\omega t - \dfrac{3\pi}{10} \right).$$

18

Oblique Triangles, Area, and Angular Speed

18.1 THE LAW OF SINES

In Sec. 6.4 we solved right triangles by applying the trigonometric ratios. There are two special formulas that allow us to solve a triangle that does not contain a right angle. Such triangles, which are called **oblique triangles**, are of two types, depending on the angles they contain. An **acute triangle** has three acute angles [see Fig. 18.1(a)]. An **obtuse triangle** has one obtuse angle, and this angle must be opposite the longest side [see Fig. 18.1(b)].

The first formula we look at involves the sine function and is called the **law of sines**, or the **sine law**. In stating it, we assume that a triangle has angles A, B, and C and the sides opposite these angles are a, b, and c, respectively.

> **LAW OF SINES**
> $$\frac{a}{\sin A} = \frac{b}{\sin B} = \frac{c}{\sin C}.$$

The statement in the preceding box is a shorthand way of writing three equations:

$$\frac{a}{\sin A} = \frac{b}{\sin b}, \qquad \frac{a}{\sin A} = \frac{c}{\sin C}, \qquad \frac{b}{\sin B} = \frac{c}{\sin C}.$$

650

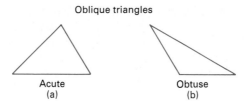

Oblique triangles

Acute
(a)

Obtuse
(b)

FIGURE 18.1

An equivalent form of the sine law is

$$\frac{\sin A}{a} = \frac{\sin B}{b} = \frac{\sin C}{c}.$$

To derive the law of sines, we have indicated both types of oblique triangles in Fig. 18.2. In each case an altitude CD has been constructed, with its length denoted by h. In Fig. 18.2(b) we have

$$\sin A = \sin (180° - A) = \sin \angle CAD.$$

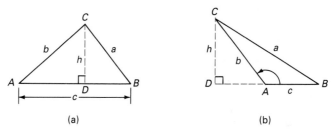

(a)   (b)

FIGURE 18.2

Therefore, for both triangles we have

$$\sin A = \frac{h}{b} \quad \text{or} \quad h = b \sin A,$$

and

$$\sin B = \frac{h}{a} \quad \text{or} \quad h = a \sin B.$$

Hence, setting the two expressions for h equal to each other, we get

$$a \sin B = b \sin A.$$

Dividing both sides by $\sin A \sin B$ gives

$$\frac{a}{\sin A} = \frac{b}{\sin B}. \tag{1}$$

In a similar way it can be shown that

$$\frac{b}{\sin B} = \frac{c}{\sin C}.$$

(2)

Combining Eqs. 1 and 2 gives the law of sines.

The sine law is used to solve a triangle when you know *either* of the following:

1. Two angles and any side.
2. Two sides and the angle opposite one of them.

Note that three specific parts must be known in order to use the sine law.

Example 1

Given two angles and any side.

Solve triangle ABC if $A = 30°$, $B = 70°$, and $a = 4$.

Solution   A sketch of the triangle is in Fig. 18.3. Angle C is easily found because we know angles A and B and also that the sum of the angles in any triangle is $180°$.

$$C = 180° - A - B = 180° - 30° - 70° = 80°.$$

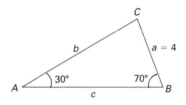

FIGURE 18.3

To find b, we pair the first and second expressions in the sine law and substitute our data. This leads to an equation with one unknown.

$$\frac{b}{\sin B} = \frac{a}{\sin A}$$

$$\frac{b}{\sin 70°} = \frac{4}{\sin 30°}.$$

Solving for b and using a calculator, we get

$$b = \frac{4 \sin 70°}{\sin 30°} = 7.518.$$

A keystroke sequence is

| 4 | × | 70 | SIN | ÷ | 30 | SIN | = | Display: 7.51754

To find c we use the sine law again.

$$\frac{c}{\sin C} = \frac{a}{\sin A}$$

$$\frac{c}{\sin 80°} = \frac{4}{\sin 30°}$$

$$c = \frac{4 \sin 80°}{\sin 30°} = 7.878.$$

Therefore, $C = 80°$, $b = 7.518$, and $c = 7.878$.

If you are given two sides and the angle opposite one of them, there may be two, one, or no triangles fitting the data. Because of these possibilities, we say that this kind of problem falls in the **ambiguous case**. To see why these situations may occur, let us assume that the given parts are a, b, and A. We shall consider the situations when $A < 90°$ or when $A \geq 90°$.

Angle $A < 90°$: If A is an acute angle, there are five possible situations:

1. If $a < b \sin A$, then the length of side a is less than the length h of the altitude (which is $b \sin a$), so side a will not meet the lower side of angle A (see Fig. 18.4).* Thus there is no triangle and, hence, *no solution*.

2. If $a = b \sin A$, then side a corresponds to the altitude and there is only *one triangle*, which is the right triangle ABC (see Fig. 18.5).

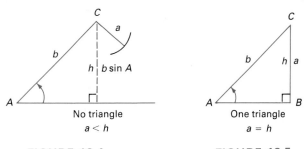

FIGURE 18.4   FIGURE 18.5

3. If $a > b$, then as a consequence $a > b \sin A$ and side a meets the lower side of angle A at exactly one point (see Fig. 18.6). In this case only *one triangle* is determined.

* Note that $\sin A = h/b$, so $h = b \sin A$.

4. If $a > b \sin A$ and $a < b$, then side a meets the lower side of angle A in two places (see Fig. 18.7). Thus *two triangles* are determined, ABC and $AB'C$, so there are two solutions. Angles B and $AB'C$ are supplementary, but B is acute and $AB'C$ is obtuse.

5. If $a = b$, there is *one triangle*, which is isosceles (see Fig. 18.8).

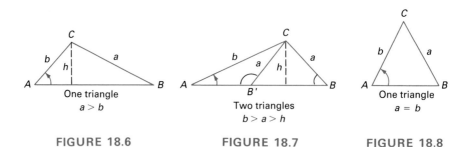

FIGURE 18.6   FIGURE 18.7   FIGURE 18.8

Angle $A \geq 90°$: If A is either a right angle or an obtuse angle, there are two possible situations:

1. If $a \leq b$, there is *no triangle* (see Fig. 18.9).
2. If $a > b$, there is *one triangle* (see Fig. 18.10).

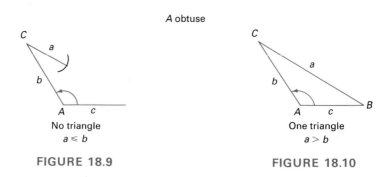

FIGURE 18.9   FIGURE 18.10

When you have a problem involving the ambiguous case, a fairly accurate sketch based on the given data will often make the number of solutions obvious. Moreover, the particular situation occurring should become clear to you after applying the sine law. For example, obtaining the result that $\sin B = 1.3$ indicates that no triangle exists, because the sine of any angle cannot be greater than 1.

Example 2

Given two sides and the angle opposite one of them.

Solve triangle ABC if $a = 6$, $b = 10$, and $A = 30°$.

Solution   We first find *B*. By the sine law,

$$\frac{\sin B}{b} = \frac{\sin A}{a}$$

$$\frac{\sin B}{10} = \frac{\sin 30°}{6}$$

$$\sin B = \frac{10 \sin 30°}{6}.$$

Using a calculator we find that

$$\sin^{-1}\left[\frac{10 \sin 30°}{6}\right] = 56.44°.$$

The keystroke sequence is

| 10 | × | 30 | SIN | ÷ | 6 | = | SIN⁻¹ | Display: 56.44269

Thus we can choose *B* = 56.44° or *B* = 180° − 56.44° = 123.56°. Therefore, two triangles are determined (see Fig. 18.11).

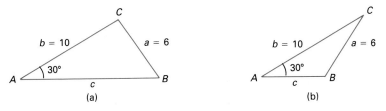

FIGURE 18.11

Case 1. If *B* = 56.44° [Fig. 18.11(a)], then

$$C = 180° - A - B = 180° - 30° - 56.44° = 93.56°.$$

Thus

$$\frac{c}{\sin C} = \frac{a}{\sin A}$$

$$c = \frac{a \sin C}{\sin A} = \frac{6 \sin 93.56°}{\sin 30°} = 11.98.$$

The keystroke sequence is

| 6 | × | 93.56 | SIN | ÷ | 30 | SIN | = | Display: 11.97684

The solution for Fig. 18.11(a) is *c* = 11.98, *B* = 56.44°, and *C* = 93.56°.

Case 2. If $B = 123.56°$ [Fig. 18.11(b)], then

$$C = 180° - A - B = 180° - 30° - 123.56° = 26.44°.$$

Thus

$$\frac{c}{\sin C} = \frac{a}{\sin A}$$

$$c = \frac{a \sin C}{\sin A} = \frac{6(\sin 26.44°)}{\sin 30°} = 5.34.$$

Thus the solution for Fig. 18.11(b) is $c = 5.34$, $B = 123.56°$, and $C = 26.44°$.

Example 3

Given two sides and the angle opposite one of them.

Solve triangle *ABC* if $b = 10$, $c = 5$, and $B = 60°$.

Solution By the sine law,

$$\frac{\sin C}{c} = \frac{\sin B}{b}$$

$$\frac{\sin C}{5} = \frac{\sin 60°}{10}$$

$$\sin C = \frac{5 \sin 60°}{10}.$$

At this point you might be tempted to think that there are two choices for *C*, as in Example 2. This is *not* the case here. Because *C* is opposite side *c*, and *c* is *not* the longest side (10 > 5), then *C cannot* be obtuse. *C* must be acute. Thus we find that

$$C = 25.66°.$$

A sketch of the triangle is in Fig. 18.12.

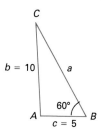

FIGURE 18.12

Now,

$$A = 180° - 60° - 25.66° = 94.34°.$$

Thus

$$\frac{a}{\sin A} = \frac{b}{\sin B}$$

$$a = \frac{b \sin A}{\sin B} = \frac{10(\sin 94.34°)}{\sin 60°} = 11.51.$$

Therefore, $A = 94.34°$, $C = 25.66°$, and $a = 11.51$. We remark that if C were chosen to be obtuse, then $C = 180° - 25.66° = 154.34°$. As a result, $B + C > 180°$, which is impossible.

Example 4

Given two sides and the angle opposite one of them.

Solve triangle ABC if $a = 2$, $b = 6$, and $A = 20°$.

Solution   By the sine law,

$$\frac{\sin B}{b} = \frac{\sin A}{a}$$

$$\frac{\sin B}{6} = \frac{\sin 20°}{2}$$

$$\sin B = \frac{6(\sin 20°)}{2} = 1.02606.$$

But the sine of an angle cannot be greater than 1, because for any angle B we must have $-1 \leq \sin B \leq 1$. Thus there is no triangle and therefore **no solution**. (A calculator gives an error message when we try to solve for B.)

Problem Set 18.1

In Problems **1–16**, *solve triangle ABC from the given information.*

1. $A = 50.1°$, $B = 98.4°$, $a = 20.31$.
2. $A = 78.3°$, $C = 41.3°$, $c = 101.12$.
3. $a = 9.23$, $b = 7.22$, $A = 80.42°$.
4. $a = 20.41$, $b = 10.72$, $A = 55.68°$.
5. $a = 7.46$, $b = 9.62$, $A = 20.46°$.
6. $a = 67.01$, $b = 95.62$, $A = 24.63°$.
7. $a = 50.41$, $b = 97.42$, $A = 58.82°$.
8. $b = 30.7$, $c = 70.5$, $B = 28.97°$.
9. $a = 7.12$, $c = 20.19$, $C = 138.82°$.
10. $b = 109$, $c = 90.5$, $B = 110.53°$.
11. $B = 60.3°$, $C = 72.1°$, $a = 80.3$.
12. $C = 20.4°$, $A = 40.4°$, $b = 50.4$.

13. $c = 5.00$, $b = 10.00$, $C = 30°$.

14. $b = 70.3$, $c = 70.3$, $C = 68.18°$.

15. $a = 6.04$, $b = 7.05$, $A = 104.24°$.

16. $a = 60.6$, $b = 60.6$, $A = 99.66°$.

17. A boat at point B can be seen from points A and C on the shore. A and C are 1650 m apart. Angles BAC and BCA are found to be 65° and 75°, respectively. How far is the boat from A?

18. In order to find the distance between points A and B, another point C is marked off. The distance from B to C is known to be 65 m. Angle ABC is measured to be 120°, and angle BCA is found to be 35°. Find the distance between A and B.

19. Two students send up a balloon with a remote-controlled camera to take a picture of the countryside. They position themselves 1.6 km apart. When the picture is taken, the balloon is between the students and the angles of elevation from the students are 46° and 70°. Find the height of the balloon.

20. From a point on the ground, the angle of elevation of the top of a building is 60°. From another point 33 m *farther* away from the building, the angle of elevation is 40°. Find the height of the building.

21. Suppose forces $F_1 = 500$ N and $F_2 = 700$ N act on a body such that the resultant force **F** forms an angle of 42° with **F**$_1$. Find F and the angle θ that **F**$_2$ makes with **F**$_1$.

22. In one of the locks of the St. Lawrence Seaway, the angle of elevation α of the top C of a Canadian landmark from a ship at point A is 55° (see Fig. 18.13). As the lock fills, the ship rises from A to B and the angle of elevation decreases to $\beta = 50°$. If the distance from B to the base of the landmark is 135 m, through what distance did the ship rise?

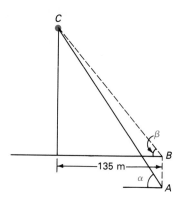

FIGURE 18.13

23. A tree grows vertically on a mountainside. Farther up the mountain, from a point 80 ft from the base of the tree, the angle of elevation of the tree top is 30° and the angle of depression of the base is 20°. Find the height of the tree.

24. A pole on level ground leans at a 10° angle from the vertical and toward the sun. The tip of the shadow cast by the pole is 35 ft from the base of the pole. The angle of elevation from the tip of the shadow to the top of the pole is 35°. Find the length of the pole.

25. Two boats simultaneously leave a harbor and sail at different constant rates and on straight-line courses that diverge by 25°. The slower boat sails at the rate of 20 mi/h. After 2 h the boats are 23 mi apart. Find the rate of the faster boat.

18.2 THE LAW OF COSINES

In addition to the sine law, the *law of cosines* is another formula that is important in solving oblique triangles. It gives a relationship between an angle of a triangle and the three sides of the triangle. To derive the law of cosines, we consider the oblique triangle ABC in Fig. 18.14, where altitude CD with length h has been constructed.

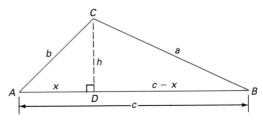

FIGURE 18.14

(Although angle A is acute, our results are also true when A is obtuse.) If we let the length of the line segment AD be x, then the length of segment DB must be $c - x$. Note that CD divides the oblique triangle into two right triangles. Applying the Pythagorean theorem to right triangle BCD, we have

$$a^2 = h^2 + (c - x)^2, \tag{1}$$

and applying it to right triangle ACD gives

$$b^2 = h^2 + x^2. \tag{2}$$

Subtracting Eq. 2 from Eq. 1 yields

$$a^2 - b^2 = h^2 + (c - x)^2 - (h^2 + x^2)$$
$$= h^2 + c^2 - 2cx + x^2 - h^2 - x^2,$$
$$a^2 - b^2 = c^2 - 2cx. \tag{3}$$

From Fig. 18.14 we have $\cos A = x/b$, so $x = b \cos A$. Substituting this value for x in Eq. 3 and rearranging terms yields the formula

$$a^2 = b^2 + c^2 - 2bc \cos A. \tag{4}$$

In a similar manner it can be shown that

$$b^2 = a^2 + c^2 - 2ac \cos B \tag{5}$$

and

$$c^2 = a^2 + b^2 - 2ab \cos C. \tag{6}$$

Equations 4–6 are known collectively as the **law of cosines**, or **cosine law**.

$$\boxed{\begin{array}{c} \textbf{LAW OF COSINES} \\ a^2 = b^2 + c^2 - 2bc \cos A. \\ b^2 = a^2 + c^2 - 2ac \cos B. \\ c^2 = a^2 + b^2 - 2ab \cos C. \end{array}}$$

The cosine law states that *the square of the length of any side of a triangle is equal to the sum of the squares of the lengths of the other two sides minus twice the product of the lengths of these sides times the cosine of their included angle.* The cosine law is used in solving an oblique triangle when you know *either* of the following.

1. Two sides and their included angle.
2. Three sides.

Note that three specific parts must be known in order to use the cosine law.

Example 1

Given two sides and their included angle.

Solve triangle *ABC* if $a = 10$, $b = 40$, and $C = 120°$ (see Fig. 18.15).

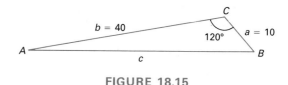

FIGURE 18.15

Solution We first use the cosine law to find side *c*.

$$c^2 = a^2 + b^2 - 2ab \cos C$$
$$= 10^2 + 40^2 - 2(10)(40) \cos 120°.$$

Using a calculator to find the square root of the right side gives

$$c = 45.8258.$$

A keystroke sequence is

Display: 45.8258

Angles A and B can now be found with the cosine law. However, we shall use the sine law to simplify our work. To find A we have

$$\frac{\sin A}{a} = \frac{\sin C}{c}$$

$$\sin A = \frac{a \sin C}{c} = \frac{10 \sin 120°}{45.8258}$$

$$A = \sin^{-1}\left(\frac{10 \sin 120°}{45.8258}\right) = 10.89°.$$

Note that A must be acute, since C is obtuse. Even if C were not obtuse, A must be acute here because a is the smallest side. Only the angle opposite the longest side has any chance of being obtuse. Finally,

$$B = 180° - A - C = 180° - 10.89° - 120° = 49.11°.$$

Thus $c = 45.83$, $A = 10.89°$, and $B = 49.11°$. Although the value of c to four decimal places was used to find A, it has been rounded to two decimal places in our final answer.

Example 2

Given three sides.

Solve triangle ABC if $a = 7$, $b = 6$, and $c = 8$ (see Fig. 18.16).

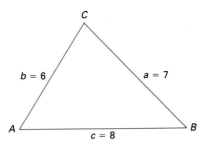

FIGURE 18.16

Solution   We first find the largest angle. Then we will know whether or not the triangle contains an obtuse angle. Because the largest angle must be opposite the longest side, it is C in this case. By the cosine law,

$$c^2 = a^2 + b^2 - 2ab \cos C$$

$$8^2 = 7^2 + 6^2 - 2(7)(6) \cos C$$

$$64 = 85 - 84 \cos C$$

$$84 \cos C = 21$$

$$\cos C = \frac{21}{84}.$$

Since cos C is positive, C is acute:

$$C = 75.52°.$$

To solve for A and B, we can use the cosine law again, but the work is easier if we use the sine law.

$$\frac{\sin B}{b} = \frac{\sin C}{c}$$

$$\sin B = \frac{b \sin C}{c} = \frac{6 \sin 75.52°}{8}$$

$$B = 46.57° \qquad (B \text{ must be acute}).$$

Finally,

$$A = 180° - B - C = 180° - 46.57° - 75.52° = 57.91°.$$

Therefore, $A = 57.91°$, $B = 46.57°$, and $C = 75.52°$.

In Example 2, with efficient use of a calculator we can find C without performing intermediate steps. The following alternative forms of the cosine law are used for such purposes:

$$\cos A = \frac{b^2 + c^2 - a^2}{2bc},$$

$$\cos B = \frac{a^2 + c^2 - b^2}{2ac},$$

$$\cos C = \frac{a^2 + b^2 - c^2}{2ab}.$$

The $\cos^{-1}$ key will give the proper angle even if it is obtuse, that is, a second-quadrant angle. In Example 2 we have

$$\cos C = \frac{7^2 + 6^2 - 8^2}{2(7)(6)}$$

$$C = \cos^{-1}\left[\frac{7^2 + 6^2 - 8^2}{2(7)(6)}\right] = 75.52°.$$

Example 3

Given triangle ABC such that $a = 9$, $b = 8$, and $c = 2$, find A.

Solution By the cosine law,

$$a^2 = b^2 + c^2 - 2bc \cos A$$

$$9^2 = 8^2 + 2^2 - 2(8)(2) \cos A$$

$$81 = 68 - 32 \cos A$$

$$32 \cos A = -13$$

$$\cos A = -\frac{13}{32} = -0.40625.$$

Because $\cos A$ is negative, angle A is obtuse. The reference angle for A is $66.03°$, so

$$A = 113.97°.$$

Alternatively, with efficient use of a calculator we have

$$\cos A = \frac{8^2 + 2^2 - 9^2}{2(8)(2)}$$

$$A = \cos^{-1}\left[\frac{8^2 + 2^2 - 9^2}{2(8)(2)}\right] = 113.97°.$$

Problem Set 18.2

In Problems **1–10**, *solve triangle ABC from the given data.*

1. $a = 20$, $b = 40$, $C = 28°$.
2. $b = 7$, $c = 13$, $A = 135°$.
3. $a = 16.1$, $b = 17.2$, $c = 18.3$.
4. $a = 7$, $b = 4$, $c = 1$.
5. $a = 14.86$, $c = 12.24$, $B = 115.23°$.
6. $a = 18.10$, $b = 24.53$, $c = 26.41$.
7. $a = 110$, $b = 85$, $c = 90$.
8. $a = 10.45$, $c = 9.83$, $B = 62.45°$.
9. $a = 116.32$, $b = 82.64$, $c = 95.24$.
10. $b = 145.87$, $c = 231.56$, $A = 29.44°$.

11. Figure 18.17 shows two forces represented by the vectors **OA** and **AB**. Find the length r of the resultant **OB** and find θ.

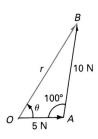

FIGURE 18.17

12. Repeat Problem 11 for the data in Fig. 18.18.

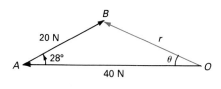

FIGURE 18.18

13. Two boats leave a dock at the same time. One travels north at 10 km/h. The other travels northeast at 20 km/h. After 3 h, how far apart are the boats?

14. Points A and B are on opposite sides of a lake. To find the distance $\overline{AB}$, another point C on the same side of the lake as A is used. It is known that $\overline{BC} = 200$ m and $\overline{AC} = 500$ m. Angle BCA is measured to be 35°. Find $\overline{AB}$.

15. Two forces act simultaneously on an object: $F_1 = 40$ N and acts due west; $F_2 = 20$ N and acts 62° east of north. Find the magnitude and direction of the resultant force acting on the object.

16. Forces acting on an object tend to give it simultaneous velocities in two directions. If $v_1 = 12$ cm/s directed due east, and $v_2 = 12$ cm/s directed 25° east of north, what is the magnitude and direction of the resultant velocity?

17. A student claims that he underwent two separate displacements of 5 m and 8 m respectively, and ended up exactly 10 m from his starting point. Find the angle between the 5-m displacement and the resultant displacement of 10 m. What is the angle between the original two displacements?

18. Two engines and separate steering mechanisms of a speedboat effectively create two velocities: one, 22 km/h, 65° east of north, and a second, 50 km/h, 52° east of north. Determine the magnitude and direction of the resultant velocity.

19. An antenna is to be erected on top of a mountain. The mountainside makes a 30° angle with the horizontal. One end of a supporting wire is to be attached to the antenna at a point 100 ft above its base. The other end is to be anchored down the mountainside at a point 50 ft from the antenna's base. What length is required for the supporting wire?

20. A plane is flying eastward at 300 mi/h and at a certain time it passes over Pittsburgh. Twenty minutes later the plane changes course and flies southeast at the same rate. One hour after passing over Pittsburgh, how far is the plane from that city?

21. A plane is flying at the rate of 400 mi/h from city A to city B on a straight-line path, which has a distance of 1500 mi. After $1\frac{1}{2}$ h, the plane changes course by 30° to avoid a storm and continues on that course for 30 min (see Fig. 18.19). Through what angle θ must the plane then turn in order to fly directly to city B?

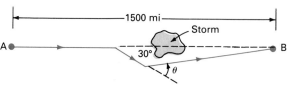

FIGURE 18.19

22. Figure 18.20 shows a cross-sectional view of a roadside sign. The sign is 7 m tall and three sections of supporting beams have lengths 2.5, 3.5, and 4.5 m, respectively. Find the distance x from the base of the sign to the bottom of the back leg.

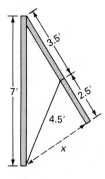

FIGURE 18.20

18.3 AREAS AND ANGULAR SPEED

Area of a Triangle

You may recall from geometry that the area of any triangle is equal to one-half the product of the lengths of its base and altitude. For each triangle ABC in Fig. 18.21, c

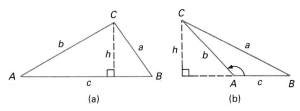

FIGURE 18.21

is the base, h is the altitude, and

$$\sin A = \frac{h}{b},$$

or

$$h = b \sin A.$$

Thus

$$\text{Area} = \tfrac{1}{2}(\text{base})(\text{altitude})$$
$$= \tfrac{1}{2}c(b \sin A).$$

$$\boxed{\textbf{Area} = \tfrac{1}{2}\boldsymbol{bc} \, \textbf{sin} \, \boldsymbol{A}.}$$

By appropriate labeling we can also show that area $= \tfrac{1}{2}ac \sin B = \tfrac{1}{2}ab \sin C$. That is, **the area of a triangle is equal to one-half the product of the lengths of any two sides and the sine of their included angle.**

Example 1

Find the area of triangle ABC if $b = 10$, $c = 15$, and $A = 35°$.

Solution   We have

$$\text{Area} = \tfrac{1}{2}bc \sin A$$
$$= \tfrac{1}{2}(10)(15) \sin 35°$$
$$= 43.02 \quad \text{square units.}$$

Example 2

Find the area of the triangle in Fig. 18.22 given that C is obtuse.

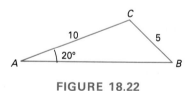

FIGURE 18.22

Solution   The area is given by $\tfrac{1}{2}ab \sin C$. To find C, we first find B by using the sine law.

$$\sin B = \frac{b \sin A}{a} = \frac{10 \sin 20°}{5}$$

$$B = 43.16° \qquad [B \text{ must be acute}].$$

Thus $C = 180° - 20° - 43.16° = 116.84°$. Therefore,

$$\text{Area} = \tfrac{1}{2}(5)(10) \sin 116.84°$$
$$= 22.31 \quad \text{square units.}$$

Area of a Sector of a Circle

Radian measure is useful when we want to find the area of a *sector* of a circle. Figure 18.23 shows a circle of radius r. The shaded region cut by the central angle θ (in

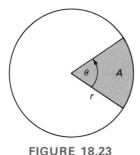

FIGURE 18.23

radians) is called a **sector** of the circle. From geometry, the area A of a sector of a circle determined by a central angle θ is directly proportional to θ. Symbolically,

$$A = k\theta.$$

But when $\theta = 2\pi$, we get the area of the entire circle, which is πr^2. Therefore, with this data we can find k:

$$\pi r^2 = k(2\pi)$$

$$k = \tfrac{1}{2}r^2.$$

Thus we get the following formula:

> For a circle of radius r, the area A of a sector with central angle θ is given by
>
> $$A = \tfrac{1}{2}r^2\theta, \qquad \theta \text{ in radians.}$$

Example 3

For a circle of radius 2 m, find the area of a sector determined by a central angle of 30°.

Solution   We first convert 30° to radians.

$$30° = 30°\left(\frac{\pi}{180°}\right) = \frac{\pi}{6}\text{ rad.}$$

By the formula for the area of a sector,

$$A = \frac{1}{2}r^2\theta = \frac{1}{2}(2^2)\left(\frac{\pi}{6}\right) = \frac{\pi}{3}\text{ m}^2.$$

Angular Speed

The **average linear speed** $\bar{v}$ of an object is the average rate of change of distance with respect to time—that is, the average speed is the ratio of distance s to time t:

$$\bar{v} = \frac{s}{t}. \tag{1}$$

In Fig. 18.24, suppose the disk of radius r is rotating counterclockwise. The segment OP serves as a reference. The **angular displacement** is the angle θ, in radians,

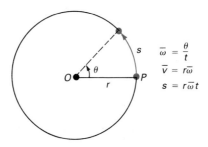

$$\bar{\omega} = \frac{\theta}{t}$$
$$\bar{v} = r\bar{\omega}$$
$$s = r\bar{\omega}t$$

FIGURE 18.24

through which the disk rotates, and the **average angular speed** $\bar{\omega}$ is the ratio of the angular displacement to time—that is,

$$\bar{\omega} = \frac{\theta}{t},$$

or

$$\theta = \bar{\omega}t. \tag{2}$$

If we assume that time is measured in seconds, the unit of $\bar{\omega}$ is radians per second. While the disk rotates through an angle θ, in radians, the point P on the rim moves a distance s given by (here we use the formula for arc length)

$$s = r\theta.$$

Thus, using Eq. 2 to substitute for θ, we have

$$s = r(\bar{\omega}t).$$

$$s = r\bar{\omega}t \qquad (\bar{\omega} \text{ in radians per second}). \tag{3}$$

To relate angular speed $\bar{\omega}$ to linear speed $\bar{v}$, we need only take the value of s from Eq. 1 and substitute it into Eq. 3:

$$\bar{v}t = r\bar{\omega}t$$

$$\boxed{\bar{v} = r\bar{\omega},}$$ (4)

where $\bar{\omega}$ is in radians per second. (More generally, in Eqs. 3 and 4, $\bar{\omega}$ is in radians per unit of time.)

Example 4

A rotating circular disk of radius 2 m makes 10 rev/s. Find (a) the angular speed of the disk, (b) the linear speed of a point on the rim, and (c) the distance moved by that point in 10 s.

Solution

a. $\bar{\omega} = \dfrac{10 \text{ rev}}{\text{s}} = 10\dfrac{\text{rev}}{\text{s}}\left(2\pi\,\dfrac{\text{rad}}{\text{rev}}\right) = 20\pi$ rad/s.

b. $\bar{v} = r\bar{\omega} = (2)(20\pi) = 40\pi$ m/s.

c. $s = r\bar{\omega}t = (2)(20\pi)(10) = 400\pi$ m.

Problem Set 18.3

*In Problems **1-6**, find the area of the triangle ABC having the given parts.*

1. $b = 6,\ c = 8,\ A = 20°$.
2. $a = 10,\ b = 5,\ C = 14°$.
3. $a = 7,\ c = 12,\ B = 130°$.
4. $a = 20,\ b = 13,\ A = 55°$.
5. $a = 40,\ A = 70°,\ b = 40$.
6. $A = 100°,\ a = 100,\ b = 80$.

*In Problems **7-10**, the radius r (in centimeters) and central angle θ of a circle are given. Find the area of the sector determined by θ. You may express your answer in terms of π.*

7. $r = 12,\ \theta = \pi/6$.
8. $r = 25,\ \theta = \pi/3$.
9. $r = 18,\ \theta = 40°$.
10. $r = 20,\ \theta = 171°$.

11. What is the angular speed, in radians per second, of a wheel that makes 900 rev/min?

12. Three concentric circles have radii of 1, 1.5, and 3 m. What is the area of the segment between the inner and middle circles bounded by radii forming a central angle of 87°?

13. A semicircular traffic rotary is to be built so that an automobile traveling at a constant speed of 30 km/h can traverse the semicircle in 12 s. What is the required radius, in meters?

14. In the traffic rotary of Problem 13, what is the average angular speed of the automobile?

15. A wheel of an automobile has a radius of 43 cm. If the automobile is traveling at a constant speed of 30 km/h, what is the angular speed of the wheel, in radians per second?

16. A drive belt runs around two pulleys, which have diameters of 20 cm and 80 cm. If the larger pulley makes 3 revolutions every second, determine each of the following.
    (a) The angular speed of the small pulley, in radians per second.
    (b) The linear speed of a point on the rim of each pulley, in centimeters per second.
    (c) The area, in square centimeters, of a sector swept out by a radius line on each pulley in 2 s.

17. The propeller of a fan rotates at a constant angular speed of 1200 rev/min. The radius of the propeller is 10 cm. Determine
    (a) the angular speed, in radians per second,
    (b) the angular displacement after 28 s,
    (c) the angular and linear speeds of a point on the propeller 2 cm from the center, and
    (d) the angular and linear speeds of a point on the rim of the propeller.

18. A circular road surrounds a lake. The road can be considered as the region between two concentric circles (they have the same center) having radii of 60 m and 67 m. Reflective material is to be applied to a portion of the road that is used as a pedestrian crossway. This portion can be considered as the region between the circles and bounded by a central angle of 5°. How many square meters of reflective material are required?

18.4   REVIEW

Important Terms and Symbols

Section 18.1   Oblique triangle, acute triangle, obtuse triangle, law of sines (sine law), ambiguous case.

Section 18.2   Law of cosines (cosine law).

Section 18.3   Sector of circle, average linear speed ($\bar{v}$), angular displacement, average angular speed ($\bar{\omega}$).

Formula Summary

SOLUTION OF OBLIQUE TRIANGLES

Law of sines: $\dfrac{a}{\sin A} = \dfrac{b}{\sin B} = \dfrac{c}{\sin C}$.

Law of cosines $a^2 = b^2 + c^2 - 2bc \cos A$.

Area of a triangle: $\text{area} = \dfrac{1}{2} bc \sin A$.

Area of a sector of circle: $A = \dfrac{1}{2} r^2 \theta$,   ($\theta$ in radians)

Linear speed: $\bar{v} = \dfrac{s}{t}$.   Angular speed: $\bar{\omega} = \dfrac{\theta}{t}$.

$s = r\bar{\omega}t$, $\bar{v} = r\bar{\omega}$ ($\bar{\omega}$ in radians per unit of time)

Review Questions

1. True or false: Given two sides and the included angle of an oblique triangle, two solutions may occur. _____.
2. The law of _____ is the first relation that is used to solve an oblique triangle when three sides are given.
3. When solving an oblique triangle where the lengths of three sides are given, you should solve first for the __(largest)(smallest)__ angle.
4. The largest angle of a triangle is found opposite the side of __(greatest)(least)__ length.
5. State in the order given, that is, a, b, and c, how many triangles are possible in each case.
   (a) $a = 30$, $b = 25$, $A = 45°$.
   (b) $a = 20$, $b = 30$, $A = 45°$.
   (c) $a = 2\sqrt{3}$, $b = 4$, $A = 60°$. _____

Answers to Review Questions

1. False.   2. Cosines.   3. Largest.   4. Greatest.   5. 1, 0, 1.

Review Problems

In Problems 1–10, solve the triangle ABC from the given data.

1. $a = 5$, $b = 4$, $C = 30°$.
2. $a = 2$, $c = 3$, $B = 60°$.
3. $B = 30°$, $C = 70°$, $b = 3$.
4. $A = 110°$, $B = 40°$, $a = 9$.
5. $a = 8$, $b = 6$, $c = 3$.
6. $a = 5$, $b = 7$, $c = 9$.
7. $A = 60°$, $a = 20$, $b = 10$.
8. $b = 5$, $c = 8$, $C = 40°$.
9. $a = 6$, $b = 8$, $A = 10°$.
10. $A = 130°$, $b = 20$, $a = 10$.

In Problems 11–14, for a circle with the given radius r, find the area of the sector with the given central angle θ. Assume answers are in square units.

11. $\theta = \dfrac{\pi}{3}$, $r = 3$.
12. $\theta = \dfrac{5\pi}{6}$, $r = 2$.
13. $\theta = 45°$, $r = 10$.
14. $\theta = 225°$, $r = 5$.

15. It is required that a circular track in the shape of a washer have an area of 2500 m². Determine the inside and outside radii of the track if the circumference of the inner edge is 91 m. If a woman runs along the very center of the track, how many revolutions must she make to run 3.2 km?

16. A phonograph turntable rotates at $33\frac{1}{3}$ rev/min. What is the linear speed of a point 2 cm from the center of the turntable?

17. Find the area of triangle ABC if $a = 25$, $b = 12$, and $C = 120°$.

18. In Fig. 18.25 are forces **AB** and **BC** represented by vectors. Find the length r of the resultant **AC**.

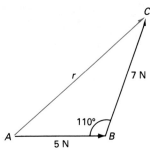

FIGURE 18.25

19. From points *A* and *B*, which are 1000 ft apart along a straight shoreline, a boat is sighted offshore at point *C*. If angle *CAB* is 80° and angle *CBA* is 85°, how far is the boat from the shoreline? Give your answer to the nearest foot.

Inequalities

19.1 LINEAR INEQUALITIES IN ONE VARIABLE

In Sec. 1.2 the inequality symbols $<$, $>$, $\leq$, and $\geq$ were introduced. In this section we shall deal with inequalities involving variables.

We begin with the notion of **intervals**, which are types of sets of real numbers that are defined in terms of inequality symbols. For example, the set of all real numbers x such that $3 \leq x \leq 5$ is called a **closed interval**. The term *closed* is used because the interval *includes* the numbers 3 and 5, which are called **endpoints** of the interval. We can denote this interval by writing $[3, 5]$, which is called **interval notation**. A bracket indicates that the endpoint *is included*. The set of all numbers x such that $a < x < b$ is called an **open interval** because the endpoints a and b are *not included*. In interval notation this set is written (a, b), where a parenthesis indicates that the endpoint is not included. Similarly, the interval $(1, 4]$, called a **half-open interval**, consists of all x such that $1 < x \leq 4$.

An interval is represented geometrically by darkening the portion of the number line that corresponds to the numbers (or points) in the interval (and by using parentheses and brackets as needed). In Fig. 19.1 the various types of intervals are shown. The infinity symbols ∞ and $-\infty$ that appear are not numbers but are merely convenient symbols for indicating that an interval extends indefinitely in some direction.

Inequalities that have their inequality symbols pointing in the same direction are said to have the *same sense*. If the symbols point in opposite directions, the

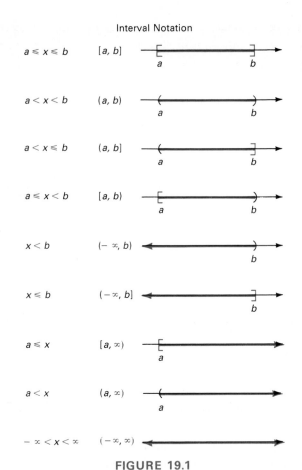

FIGURE 19.1

inequalities are said to be *opposite in sense*, or one is said to have the *reverse sense* of the other. Thus the inequalities $a < b$ and $c < d$ have the same sense, but $a < b$ and $c > d$ are opposite in sense.

As with equations, there are various types of inequalities. An **absolute inequality** is one that is true for *all* allowable values of the variables involved. A **conditional inequality** is one that is true for *some*, but not all, of the allowable values.

Example 1

a. $x^2 \geq 0$ is an absolute inequality because the square of *any* real number x is positive or zero.

b. $x^2 > 0$ is a conditional inequality because it is true if and only if x is not zero.

Solving an inequality, such as $2(x - 3) < 4$, means to find all values of the variable for which the inequality is true. This involves the application of certain rules which we now state.

1. **If the same number is added to or subtracted from both sides of an inequality, then the resulting inequality has the same sense as the original inequality.** Symbolically, [for the less than ($<$) relation],

$$\text{If } a < b, \text{ then } a + c < b + c \text{ and } a - c < b - c.$$

For example, since $7 < 10$, then $7 + 3 < 10 + 3$ or, simply, $10 < 13$.

2. **If both sides of an inequality are multiplied or divided by the same *positive* number, then the resulting inequality has the same sense as the original inequality.** Symbolically,

$$\text{If } a < b \text{ and } c > 0, \text{ then } ac < bc \text{ and } \frac{a}{c} < \frac{b}{c}.$$

For example, since $3 < 7$ and $2 > 0$, then $3(2) < 7(2)$ and $\frac{3}{2} < \frac{7}{2}$.

3. **If both sides of an inequality are multiplied or divided by the same *negative* number, then the resulting inequality has the *reverse* sense of the original inequality.** Symbolically,

$$\text{If } a < b \text{ and } c > 0, \text{ then } a(-c) > b(-c) \text{ and } \frac{a}{-c} > \frac{b}{-c}.$$

For example, $4 < 7$ but $4(-2) > 7(-2)$ or, more simply, $-8 > -14$. Also, $\dfrac{4}{-2} > \dfrac{7}{-2}$.

4. **If the sides of an inequality are either both positive or both negative, then their respective reciprocals are unequal in the *reverse* sense.** For example,

$$2 < 4 \quad \text{but} \quad \tfrac{1}{2} > \tfrac{1}{4}.$$

5. **If both sides of an inequality are positive and we raise each side to the same positive power, then the resulting inequality has the same sense as the original inequality.** Symbolically,

$$\text{If } a > b > 0 \text{ and } n > 0, \text{ then } a^n > b^n \text{ and } \sqrt[n]{a} > \sqrt[n]{b}.$$

For example, $9 > 4$, so $9^2 > 4^2$ and $\sqrt{9} > \sqrt{4}$.

Whenever one of Rules 1–3 is applied to an inequality, the resulting inequality is equivalent to the given one. (**Equivalent inequalities**, like equivalent equations, have the same solutions.) Thus to solve an inequality, we apply Rules 1–3 until the values of the variable are obvious. We shall apply these rules to solve a *linear inequality*.

> A **linear inequality** in the variable x is an inequality that can be written in the form
>
> $$ax + b < 0 \qquad (\text{or} >, \leq, \geq),$$
>
> where a and b are constants and $a \neq 0$.

In the following examples of solving linear inequalities, the given inequality will be replaced by equivalent inequalities until we isolate the variable on one side of the inequality. Whereas a linear *equation* has exactly one solution, you will see that a linear inequality has infinitely many solutions.

Example 2

Solve $2(x - 3) < 4$.

Solution

$$
\begin{aligned}
2(x - 3) &< 4 \\
2x - 6 &< 4 && \text{[distributive law]} \\
2x - 6 + 6 &< 4 + 6 && \text{[adding 6 to both sides (Rule 1)]} \\
2x &< 10 && \text{[simplifying]} \\
\frac{2x}{2} &< \frac{10}{2} && \text{[dividing both sides by 2 (Rule 2)]} \\
x &< 5 && \text{[simplifying].}
\end{aligned}
$$

Thus all real numbers less than 5 are solutions. We shall write our solution as $x < 5$ [in interval notation the solution is $(-\infty, 5)$]. For example, 1 is less than 5, so 1 is a solution. To check this we have

$$
\begin{aligned}
2(1 - 3) &< 4 \\
2(-2) &< 4 \\
-4 &< 4.
\end{aligned}
$$

Figure 19.2 shows the solution.

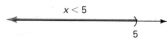

$$x < 5$$

5

FIGURE 19.2

Example 3

Solve $3 - 2x \le 6$.

Solution

$$3 - 2x \le 6$$

$$-2x \le 3 \qquad \text{[subtracting 3 from both sides (Rule 1)]}$$

$$x \ge -\frac{3}{2} \qquad \text{[dividing both sides by } -2 \text{ and changing direction of inequality (Rule 3)].}$$

The solution is $x \ge -\frac{3}{2}$. See Fig. 19.3.

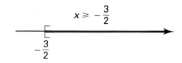

FIGURE 19.3

Example 4

Solve $\frac{3}{2}(s - 2) + 1 > -2(s - 4)$.

Solution   To clear fractions, we multiply both sides by 2.

$$2[\tfrac{3}{2}(s - 2) + 1] > 2[-2(s - 4)] \qquad \text{[Rule 2]}$$

$$3(s - 2) + 2 > -4(s - 4)$$

$$3s - 4 > -4s + 16$$

$$7s - 4 > 16 \qquad \text{[adding } 4s \text{ to both sides (Rule 1)]}$$

$$7s > 20 \qquad \text{[adding 4 to both sides (Rule 1)]}$$

$$s > \frac{20}{7} \qquad \text{[dividing both sides by 7 (Rule 2)].}$$

See Fig. 19.4

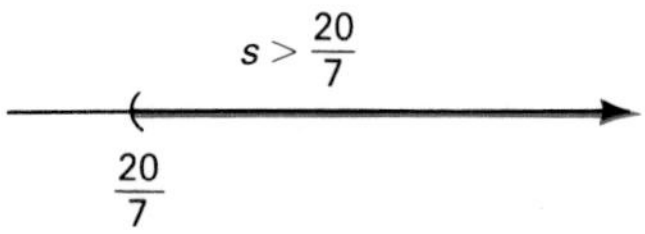

$$s > \frac{20}{7}$$

$$\frac{20}{7}$$

FIGURE 19.4

Example 5

Solve $2(x - 4) - 3 > 2x + 1$.

Solution

$$2(x - 4) - 3 > 2x + 1$$
$$2x - 8 - 3 > 2x + 1$$
$$-11 > 1 \qquad \text{[subtracting } 2x \text{ from both sides].}$$

The inequality $-11 > 1$ is never true, so there is *no solution*.

Example 6

Solve $3z + 7 > 8z - (5z - 2)$.

Solution

$$3z + 7 > 8z - (5z - 2)$$
$$3z + 7 > 3z + 2$$
$$7 > 2 \qquad \text{[subtracting } 3z \text{ from both sides].}$$

Since the inequality $7 > 2$ is always true (true for any value of z), the solution consists of *all real numbers*. We write this solution as $-\infty < z < \infty$. See Fig. 19.5.

FIGURE 19.5

Problem Set 19.1

In Problems **1–34**, *solve the inequalities and indicate your answers geometrically on the real number line.*

1. $3x > 12$.
2. $4x < -2$.
3. $4x - 13 \le 7$.
4. $3x \ge 0$.
5. $-4x \ge 2$.
6. $2y + 1 > 0$.
7. $3 - 5s > 5$.
8. $4s - 1 < -5$.
9. $3 < 2y + 3$.
10. $6 \le 5 - 3y$.
11. $2x - 3 \le 4 + 7x$.
12. $-3 \ge 8(2 - x)$.
13. $3(2 - 3x) > 4(1 - 4x)$.
14. $8(x + 1) + 1 < 3(2x) + 1$.
15. $2(3x - 2) > 3(2x - 1)$.
16. $3 - 2(x - 1) \le 2(4 + x)$.
17. $x + 2 < \sqrt{3} - x$.
18. $\sqrt{2}(x + 2) > \sqrt{8}(3 - x)$.

19. $\dfrac{5}{3}x < 10.$

20. $-\dfrac{1}{2}x > 6.$

21. $\dfrac{9y + 1}{4} \le 2y - 1.$

22. $\dfrac{4y - 3}{2} \ge \dfrac{1}{3}.$

23. $4x - 1 \ge 4(x - 2) + 7.$

24. $0x \le 0.$

25. $\dfrac{1 - t}{2} < \dfrac{3t - 7}{3}.$

26. $\dfrac{3(2t - 2)}{2} > \dfrac{6t - 3}{5} + \dfrac{t}{10}.$

27. $2x + 3 \ge \dfrac{1}{2}x - 4.$

28. $4x - \dfrac{1}{2} \le \dfrac{3}{2}x.$

29. $\dfrac{2}{3}r < \dfrac{5}{6}r.$

30. $\dfrac{7}{4}t > -\dfrac{2}{3}t.$

31. $\dfrac{y}{2} + \dfrac{y}{3} > y + \dfrac{y}{5}.$

32. $9 - 0.1x \le \dfrac{2 - 0.01x}{0.2}.$

33. $0.1(0.03x + 4) \ge 0.02x + 0.434.$

34. $\dfrac{5y - 1}{-3} < \dfrac{7(y + 1)}{-2}.$

35. The amount of current needed for a certain electrical appliance is more than 7 A but less than 9.5 A. If 12 such appliances are to be used and I represents the total number of amperes needed, describe I by using inequalities.

36. Using inequalities, symbolize the following statement: The number of working hours x to produce a blueprint is at least 15 but not more than 18.

37. If a block slides down a rough inclined plane, it can be deduced from the principle of conservation of energy that the gravitational potential energy P of the block at the top of the inclined plane is greater than the kinetic energy K of the block at the bottom of the plane. If $K = 36$ J, geometrically indicate the possible values of P on the real number line.

19.2 NONLINEAR INEQUALITIES

Let us consider how we would go about solving a nonlinear inequality such as

$$x^2 - x - 2 > 0.$$

One method is to graph the equation $y = f(x) = x^2 - x - 2$ and observe when y is greater than 0. In Fig. 19.6 we see that $y > 0$ if $x < -1$ or $x > 2$. That is, the

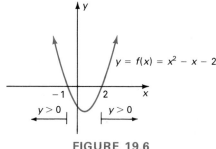

FIGURE 19.6

solution of $x^2 - x - 2 > 0$ is $x < -1$ or $x > 2$. Although this approach is easy to understand, the accuracy of the graphical technique is too limited. A more accurate method is needed.

Consider again the inequality $x^2 - x - 2 > 0$. To solve it another way, we first find the roots of the corresponding *equation* $x^2 - x - 2 = 0$. Factoring gives

$$(x + 1)(x - 2) = 0,$$

so the roots are -1 and 2, which are marked on a number line in Fig. 19.7.

FIGURE 19.7

These two roots determine three open intervals (also shown in Fig. 19.7):

$$(-\infty, -1), \quad (-1, 2), \quad \text{and} \quad (2, \infty).$$

Referring back to Fig. 19.6, we see that if x is *any* number in the interval $(-\infty, -1)$, then $f(x) > 0$. If x is *any* number in the interval $(-1, 2)$, then $f(x) < 0$, and so on. That is, given any of these three intervals, $f(x)$ does not change sign *throughout* that interval. This means that to determine the sign of $f(x)$ on one of these intervals, it is sufficient to determine its sign at *any* point in that interval. For instance, -2 is in $(-\infty, -1)$ and $f(-2) = 4 > 0$. Thus $f(x) > 0$ on the *entire* interval $(-\infty, -1)$. Because zero is in $(-1, 2)$ and $f(0) = -2 < 0$, then $f(x) < 0$ on the *entire* interval $(-1, 2)$. Similarly, 3 is in $(2, \infty)$ and $f(3) = 4 > 0$, so $f(x) > 0$ on the *entire* interval $(2, \infty)$. A summary of our results is shown in Fig. 19.8. Therefore, from these results we conclude that $x^2 - x - 2 > 0$ for $x < -1$ or for $x > 2$, so we have solved the inequality. [In interval notation we can express the solution as $(-\infty, -1)$ and $(2, \infty)$].

FIGURE 19.8

In general, for any polynomial function $P = P(x)$, the (real) zeros of P give rise to certain open intervals. On each of these intervals, $P(x)$ is always positive or always negative. Thus if $P(x)$ is positive (or negative) at a single point in one such interval, then $P(x)$ must be positive (or negative) on that *entire* interval. This fact allows us to solve inequalities without the need for graphing.

Example 1

Solve $x^2 - 4x - 12 < 0$.

Solution Let $f(x) = x^2 - 4x - 12$. First we factor $f(x)$.

$$f(x) = (x + 2)(x - 6).$$

Next we find the roots of the equation $f(x) = 0$.

Roots of $(x + 2)(x - 6) = 0$ are -2 and 6.

The roots are marked in Fig. 19.9.

FIGURE 19.9

These two roots determine three open intervals:

$$(-\infty, -2), \quad (-2, 6) \quad \text{and} \quad (6, \infty).$$

On each interval, $f(x)$ [which is the product $(x + 2)(x - 6)$] must be always positive or always negative. We test a value of x in each of them. For $-\infty < x < -2$, let us choose $x = -8$. Then the sign of $f(x)$ on $(-\infty, -2)$ is the same as the sign of $f(-8)$.

$$f(x) = (x + 2)(x - 6)$$
$$f(-8) = (-8 + 2)(-8 - 6)$$
$$= (-)(-) = +.$$

Note that it is not necessary actually to evaluate $f(-8)$ to find its sign. Knowing the signs of the factors allows us to find the sign of the product. Here $f(-8)$ is positive because there is an even number of negative factors. Thus $f(x) > 0$ for $x < -2$. For the other intervals we find that

$$f(0) = (+)(-) = -, \quad \text{so } f(x) < 0 \quad \text{for } -2 < x < 6,$$
$$f(10) = (+)(+) = +, \quad \text{so } f(x) > 0 \quad \text{for } x > 6.$$

A summary of our results is given by the *sign chart* in Fig. 19.10. Thus the solution of $x^2 - 4x - 12 < 0$ is $-2 < x < 6$ [or $(-2, 6)$] because that is the only one of the three intervals on which $f(x) < 0$.

Signs of $(x + 2)(x - 6)$

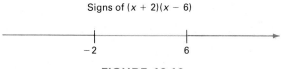

FIGURE 19.10

Example 2

Solve $x(x - 1)(x + 4) \leq 0$.

Solution   If $f(x) = x(x - 1)(x + 4)$, then the roots of the equation $f(x) = 0$ are 0, 1, and -4, which are shown in Fig. 19.11.

FIGURE 19.11

These three roots determine four intervals:

$$(-\infty, -4), \quad (-4, 0), \quad (0, 1) \quad \text{and} \quad (1, \infty).$$

Because -5 is in $(-\infty, -4)$, the sign of $f(x)$ on $(-\infty, -4)$ is the same as that of $f(-5)$. Given

$$f(x) = x(x - 1)(x + 4),$$

then

$$f(-5) = -5(-5 - 1)(-5 + 4) = (-)(-)(-) = -,$$

so $f(x) < 0$ for $x < -4$. For the other intervals we find that

$$f(-2) = (-)(-)(+) = +, \quad \text{so } f(x) > 0 \quad \text{for } -4 < x < 0,$$
$$f(\tfrac{1}{2}) = (+)(-)(+) = -, \quad \text{so } f(x) < 0 \quad \text{for } 0 < x < 1,$$
$$f(2) = (+)(+)(+) = +, \quad \text{so } f(x) > 0 \quad \text{for } x > 1.$$

Our results are summarized by the sign chart in Fig. 19.12. Thus $x(x - 1)(x + 4) < 0$ for

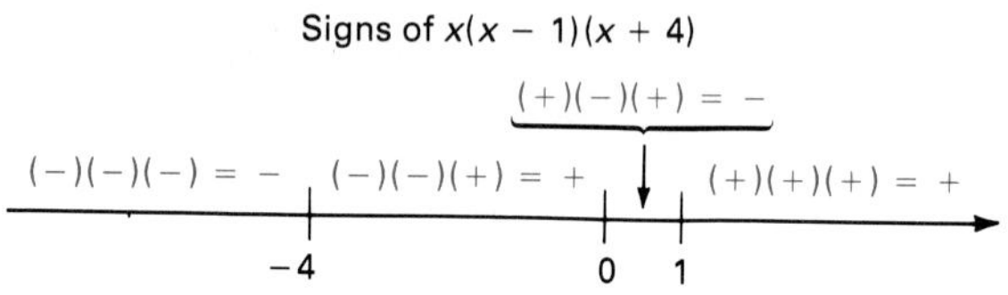

Signs of $x(x - 1)(x + 4)$

$$\underbrace{(+)(-)(+)} = -$$

$(-)(-)(-) = -$ $(-)(-)(+) = +$ $\quad\downarrow\quad$ $(+)(+)(+) = +$

$-4 \qquad 0 \quad 1$

FIGURE 19.12

$x < -4$ or for $0 < x < 1$. To take care of the equality $(=)$ part of the inequality $(\leq)$, we solve the equation

$$x(x - 1)(x + 4) = 0.$$

Since the roots are 0, 1, and -4, our solution to the inequality must include these numbers. Thus the solution consists of the intervals $(-\infty, -4]$ and $[0, 1]$; that is,

$$x \leq -4 \quad \text{or} \quad 0 \leq x \leq 1.$$

Example 3

===

Solve $\dfrac{x^2 - 6x + 5}{x} \ge 0$.

Solution   Let

$$f(x) = \frac{x^2 - 6x + 5}{x} = \frac{(x-1)(x-5)}{x}.$$

For a quotient we solve the inequality by considering the intervals determined by the roots of $f(x) = 0$, namely, 1 and 5, and those values of x for which f is undefined. Here f is undefined when $x = 0$. In Fig. 19.13 we have marked the points 0, 1, and 5. We thus consider the intervals

$$(-\infty, 0), \qquad (0, 1), \qquad (1, 5), \quad \text{and} \quad (5, \infty).$$

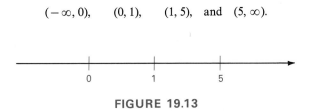

FIGURE 19.13

Determining the sign of $f(x)$ at a point in each interval, we find that

$$f(-1) = \frac{(-)(-)}{(-)} = -, \quad \text{so } f(x) < 0 \quad \text{for } x < 0,$$

$$f\left(\tfrac{1}{2}\right) = \frac{(-)(-)}{(+)} = +, \quad \text{so } f(x) > 0 \quad \text{for } 0 < x < 1,$$

$$f(2) = \frac{(+)(-)}{(+)} = -, \quad \text{so } f(x) < 0 \quad \text{for } 1 < x < 5,$$

$$f(6) = \frac{(+)(+)}{(+)} = + \quad \text{so } f(x) > 0 \quad \text{for } x > 5.$$

The sign chart is given in Fig. 19.14. Therefore, $f(x) \ge 0$ for $0 < x \le 1$ or $x \ge 5$ (see Fig. 19.15). Why are 1 and 5 included, but zero excluded?

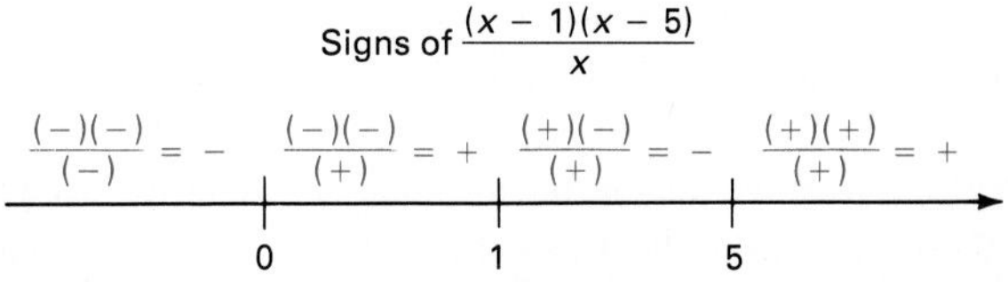

Signs of $\dfrac{(x-1)(x-5)}{x}$

$$\frac{(-)(-)}{(-)} = - \qquad \frac{(-)(-)}{(+)} = + \qquad \frac{(+)(-)}{(+)} = - \qquad \frac{(+)(+)}{(+)} = +$$

| 0 | 1 | 5 |

FIGURE 19.14

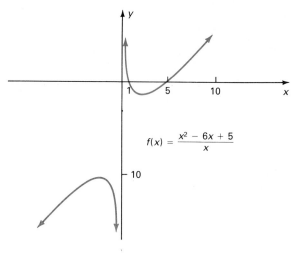

$$f(x) = \frac{x^2 - 6x + 5}{x}$$

FIGURE 19.15

Example 4

Solve $t^3 + 16t > 8t^2$.

Solution   We first rewrite the inequality so that one side is zero and then we factor.

$$t^3 - 8t^2 + 16t > 0,$$

$$t(t^2 - 8t + 16) > 0,$$

$$t(t - 4)^2 > 0.$$

The roots of $t(t - 4)^2 = 0$ are 0 and 4. From the sign chart in Fig. 19.16, we conclude that the solution is $0 < t < 4$ or $t > 4$.

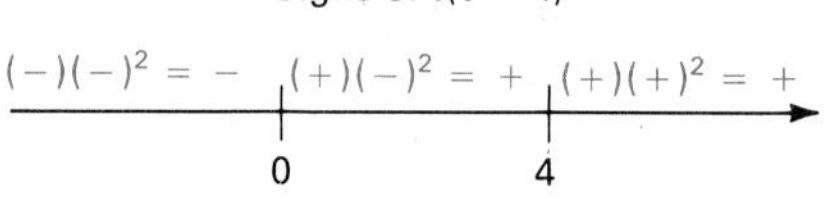

Signs of $t(t - 4)^2$

$$(-)(-)^2 = - \qquad (+)(-)^2 = + \qquad (+)(+)^2 = +$$

$$0 \qquad\qquad 4$$

FIGURE 19.16

Example 5

a. Solve the inequality $x^2 + x + 1 > 0$.

Solution   Using the quadratic formula, we find the roots of $x^2 + x + 1 = 0$ to be imaginary. We therefore turn to the graph of $y = x^2 + x + 1$ for any information it may yield (Fig. 19.17). Because for all x we have $y > 0$, the solution of $x^2 + x + 1 > 0$ is $-\infty < x < \infty$.

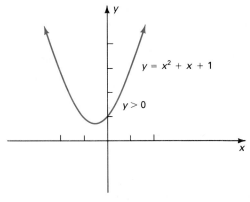

FIGURE 19.17

b. Solve $x^2 + x + 1 < 0$.

Solution From Part a, the expression $x^2 + x + 1$ is always positive. Thus the inequality $x^2 + x + 1 < 0$ has no solution.

Problem Set 19.2

In Problems **1–38**, *solve the inequalities.*

1. $(x - 1)(x - 5) < 0$.
2. $(x + 3)(x - 8) > 0$.
3. $(x + 1)(x - 3) > 0$.
4. $(x + 4)(x + 5) < 0$.
5. $x^2 - 1 < 0$.
6. $x^2 > 9$.
7. $x^2 - x - 6 > 0$.
8. $x^2 - 2x - 3 \le 0$.
9. $5s - s^2 \le 0$.
10. $t^2 + 9t + 18 \ge 0$.
11. $x^2 + 5x < -6$.
12. $x^2 - 12 > x$.
13. $x^2 + 4x - 5 \ge 3x + 15$.
14. $x^2 + 9x + 9 \le 2 - x^2$.
15. $2z^2 - 5z - 12 < 0$.
16. $5t^2 - 1 > 4t$.
17. $x^2 + 2x + 1 > 0$.
18. $x^2 + 9 \le 6x$.
19. $4(t^2 + t) - 1 \ge 2$.
20. $3s^2 \le 11s - 10$.
21. $(x + 2)(x - 1)(x - 4) > 0$.
22. $x(x + 3)(5 - x) < 0$.
23. $(x + 5)(x - 3)^2 < 0$.
24. $(x + 1)^2(x - 4)^2 > 0$.
25. $y^3 - y \le 0$.
26. $x^3 + 8x^2 + 15x \ge 0$.

27. $x^3 - 2x^2 \ge 0$.
28. $p^4 - 2p^3 - 3p^2 \le 0$.
29. $\dfrac{x - 4}{x + 8} > 0$.

30. $\dfrac{x + 3}{x + 5} < 0$.
31. $\dfrac{t}{3 - t} \le 0$.
32. $\dfrac{s - 1}{2s - 1} > 0$.

33. $\dfrac{5}{x + 2} > 0$.
34. $\dfrac{3}{9(x - 8)} < 0$.
35. $\dfrac{x + 3}{x^2 - 1} < 0$.

36. $\dfrac{x^2 - x - 6}{x + 4} > 0$.
37. $\dfrac{x^2 - 5x + 4}{x^2 + 5x + 4} \ge 0$.
38. $\dfrac{x^2 - 4}{x^2 + 2x + 1} \le 0$.

39. A company owns a 1 km by 2 km rectangular lot and needs to cut a uniform strip of trees along the outer edges of the lot. At most, how wide can the strip be if at least $\frac{3}{4}$ km^2 of the lot must remain?

40. A container manufacturer wishes to make an open box by cutting a 4-cm square from each corner of a square sheet of aluminum and then turning up the sides. The box is to contain at least 324 cm^2. Find the dimensions of the smallest sheet of aluminum that can be used.

19.3 EQUATIONS AND INEQUALITIES INVOLVING ABSOLUTE VALUE

Recall from Sec. 1.2 that the absolute value of a real number is its distance from zero on the real number line. We also gave an algebraic definition in Sec. 1.4:

$$|x| = \begin{cases} x, & \text{if } x \geq 0, \\ -x, & \text{if } x < 0. \end{cases}$$

In this definition, note that $-x$ is a positive number when x is negative. The next example shows how to solve some equations involving absolute value. In general, $|x| = d$ means $x = \pm d$, where $d > 0$.

Example 1

a. Solve $|x - 4| = 3$.

Solution   This equation states that $x - 4$ is a number three units from zero. Thus either

$$x - 4 = 3 \quad \text{or} \quad x - 4 = -3.$$

If $x - 4 = 3$, then $x = 7$; if $x - 4 = -3$, then $x = 1$. Thus $x = 1, 7$.

b. Solve $|8 - 5x| = 6$.

Solution   The equation is true if $8 - 5x = 6$ or if $8 - 5x = -6$. Solving these gives $x = \frac{2}{5}$ and $x = \frac{14}{5}$.

c. Solve $|x - 5| = -2$.

Solution   Because the absolute value of a number is never negative, there is no solution.

The numbers 5 and 9 are 4 units apart. Also,

$$|9 - 5| = |4| = 4,$$
$$|5 - 9| = |-4| = 4.$$

In general, we may intepret $|a - b|$ or $|b - a|$ as the *distance* between a and b. For example, to solve the equation $|x - 4| = 3$ in Part a of Example 1 means to find all numbers x that are exactly 3 units from 4. Thus x can be 1 or 7. We also remark that $|a - b| = |b - a|$.

Let us turn now to inequalities. For example, if $|x| < 3$, then x is less than 3 units from 0. Thus x must lie between -3 and 3. That is, $-3 < x < 3$ [Fig. 19.18(a)]. However, if $|x| > 3$, then x must be more than 3 units from 0. Thus, one of two things must be true: Either $x > 3$ *or* $x < -3$ [Fig. 19.18(b)]. We can extend these ideas. If $|x| \le 3$, then $-3 \le x \le 3$. If $|x| \ge 3$, then $x \ge 3$ or $x \le -3$.

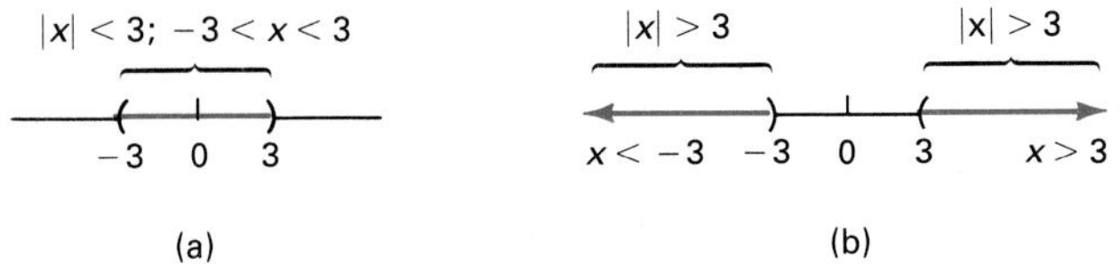

(a)   (b)

FIGURE 19.18

In general, the solutions of $|x| < d$ or $|x| \le d$, where d is a positive number, consist of one interval. However, when $|x| > d$ or $|x| \ge d$, there are two intervals in the solution. More precisely we have the following rules.

ABSOLUTE-VALUE INEQUALITIES

If $d > 0$, then

1. $\quad |x| < d \quad$ means $\quad -d < x < d;$
   $\quad |x| \le d \quad$ means $\quad -d \le x \le d.$

2. $\quad |x| > d \quad$ means $\quad x < -d$ or $x > d;$
   $\quad |x| \ge d \quad$ means $\quad x \le -d$ or $x \ge d.$

Example 2

Solve the following absolute value inequalities.

a. $|x - 2| < 4$.

Solution The number $x - 2$ must be less than 4 units from 0. By Rule 1, this means that $x - 2$ lies between -4 and 4. Thus $-4 < x - 2 < 4$. We may set up the procedure for solving this inequality as follows:

$$-4 < x - 2 < 4$$

$$-4 + 2 < x < 4 + 2 \qquad \text{[adding 2 to each member]}$$

$$-2 < x < 6.$$

b. $|3 - 2x| \le 5.$

Solution

$$-5 \le 3 - 2x \le 5 \qquad \text{[Rule 1]}$$

$$-5 - 3 \le -2x \le 5 - 3 \qquad \text{[subtracting 3 from each member]}$$

$$-8 \le -2x \le 2,$$

$$4 \ge x \ge -1 \qquad \text{[dividing each member by } -2 \text{ and changing the direction of inequalities]}$$

$$-1 \le x \le 4 \qquad \text{[rewriting].}$$

Example 3

Solve the following inequalities.

a. $|x + 5| \ge 7.$

Solution   The number $x + 5$ must be *at least* 7 units from 0. By Rule 2, either $x + 5 \ge 7$ or $x + 5 \le -7$. Solving these inequalities, we have

$$x \ge 2 \quad \text{or} \quad x \le -12.$$

b. $|3x - 4| > 1.$

Solution   By Rule 2, either $3x - 4 > 1$ or $3x - 4 < -1$. Thus either $3x > 5$ or $3x < 3$. The solution is

$$x > \frac{5}{3} \quad \text{or} \quad x < 1.$$

Example 4

Use absolute value notation to express each statement.

a. x is less than four units from 7.

Solution   Since the distance between x and 7 is less than 4, we must have

$$|x - 7| < 4.$$

b. x differs from 2 by at least 3.

Solution

$$|x - 2| \ge 3.$$

c. $x < 9$ and $x > -9$ simultaneously.

Solution

$$|x| < 9.$$

d. x is more than two units from -3.

Solution

$$|x - (-3)| > 2,$$
$$|x + 3| > 2.$$

e. x is less than σ (sigma) units from μ (mu).

Solution

$$|x - \mu| < \sigma.$$

The following are four basic properties of absolute value:

BASIC PROPERTIES OF ABSOLUTE VALUE

1. $|ab| = |a| \cdot |b|$.

2. $\left|\dfrac{a}{b}\right| = \dfrac{|a|}{|b|}$.

3. $|a - b| = |b - a|$.

4. $|a + b| \leq |a| + |b|$.

Example 5

a. $|(-7) \cdot 3| = |-7| \cdot |3| = 21$; $|(-7)(-3)| = |-7| \cdot |-3| = 21$.

b. $|4 - 2| = |2 - 4| = 2$.

c. $|7 - x| = |x - 7|$.

d. $\left|\dfrac{-7}{3}\right| = \dfrac{|-7|}{|3|} = \dfrac{7}{3}$; $\left|\dfrac{-7}{-3}\right| = \dfrac{|-7|}{|-3|} = \dfrac{7}{3}$.

e. $\left|\dfrac{x-3}{-5}\right| = \dfrac{|x-3|}{|-5|} = \dfrac{|x-3|}{5}$.

f. $|2 + 3| = 5 = |2| + |3|$, and $|2 + (-3)| = 1 < |2| + |-3|$.

Problem Set 19.3

*In Problems **1–30**, solve the given equation or inequality.*

1. $|x| = 6$.

2. $|-x| = 3$.

3. $\left|\dfrac{x}{3}\right| = 2$.

4. $\left|\dfrac{4}{x}\right| = 8$.

5. $|x - 5| = 8$.

6. $|4 + 3x| = 2$.

7. $|5x - 2| = 0$.

8. $|7x + 3| = x$.

9. $|7 - 4x| = 5$.

10. $|1 - 2x| = 1$.

11. $|x| < 3$.

12. $|x| < 10$.

13. $|x| > 6$.

14. $|x| > 3$.

15. $|2x| \leq 2$.

16. $|4x| \leq 3$.

17. $|3x| \geq 9$.

18. $\left|\dfrac{x}{2}\right| \geq 3$.

19. $|x - 4| < 16$.

20. $|y + 5| \leq 6$.

21. $|y + 1| \geq 6$.

22. $|x - 2| \geq 4$.

23. $|3x - 5| \leq 1$.

24. $\left|\dfrac{x}{3} - 5\right| < 4$.

25. $|1 - 3x| < 2$.

26. $|4x - 1| > 7$.

27. $|\tfrac{1}{2} - t| > \tfrac{1}{2}$.

28. $|5 - 2x| > 1$.

29. $\left|\dfrac{3x - 8}{2}\right| \geq 4$.

30. $\left|\dfrac{x - 8}{4}\right| \leq 2$.

31. Why does $|x - 5| < -12$ have no solution?

32. Why does every value of x satisfy $|2x + 1| > -1$?

33. Using the absolute value symbol, express each fact.
    (a) x is less than three units from 7.
    (b) x differs from 2 by less than 3.
    (c) x is no more than five units from 7.
    (d) The distance between 7 and x is 4.
    (e) $x + 4$ is less than two units from the origin.
    (f) x is between -3 and 3 but is not equal to 3 or -3.
    (g) $x < -6$ or $x > 6$.
    (h) $x - 6 > 4$ or $x - 6 < -4$.
    (i) The number of hours, x, that a machine will operate efficiently differs from 105 by less than 3.

34. Show that if $|x - \mu| \leq 2\sigma$, then $-2\sigma + \mu \leq x \leq 2\sigma + \mu$.

35. In the manufacture of a certain machine, the average dimension of a part is 0.01 cm. Using the absolute value symbol, express the fact that an individual measurement x of a part does not differ from the average by more than 0.005 cm.

19.4 LINEAR INEQUALITIES IN TWO VARIABLES

Suppose that a chemical manufacturer has 60 kg of a certain chemical element and uses it all to manufacture x units of compound A and y units of compound B. If each unit of A requires 2 kg of the element and each unit of B requires 3 kg, then the possible combinations of A and B that can be produced must satisfy the equation

$$2x + 3y = 60, \qquad \text{where } x, y \geq 0.$$

The solution is represented by the line segment in Fig. 19.19. For example, if 15 units of A are made, these require 30 kg of the element. Since 60 kg of the element must be used, 10 kg of B must be made (these require 30 kg of the element). Thus the point (15, 10) is on the line.

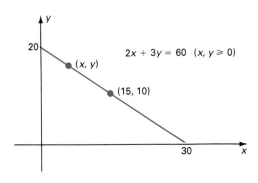

FIGURE 19.19

On the other hand, suppose the manufacturer does not necessarily wish to use the *total* supply of the element. In this case, the possible combinations are described by the inequality

$$2x + 3y \le 60, \qquad \text{where } x, y \ge 0. \tag{1}$$

When linear inequalities in *one* variable were discussed in Sec. 19.1, their solutions were represented geometrically by *intervals* on the real number line. However, for an inequality in *two* variables, as in Inequality 1, the solution is usually represented by a *region* in the coordinate plane. We shall find the region corresponding to (1) after considering such inequalities in general.

A **linear inequality** in the variables x and y is an inequality that can be written in the form

$$ax + by + c < 0 \qquad (\text{or } \le 0, \ge 0, > 0),$$

where a, b, and c are constants and a and b are not both zero.

Geometrically, the solution of a linear inequality in x and y consists of all points in the plane whose coordinates satisfy the inequality. In particular, the graph of a nonvertical line $y = mx + b$ separates the plane into three distinct parts (see Fig. 19.20).

1. The line itself, consisting of all points (x, y) with coordinates that satisfy $y = mx + b$.

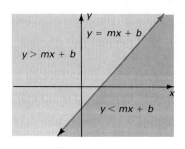

FIGURE 19.20

2. The region lying above the line, consisting of all points (x, y) that satisfy $y > mx + b$.

3. The region below the line, consisting of all points (x, y) satisfying $y < mx + b$.

For a vertical line $x = a$, we speak of regions to the right $(x > a)$ or the left $(x < a)$ of the line (see Fig. 19.21).

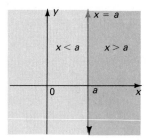

FIGURE 19.21

To apply these facts, we shall solve $x + y < 4$. We first sketch the corresponding *line* $x + y = 4$ by choosing two points on it, for instance the intercepts $(4, 0)$ and $(0, 4)$ (see Fig. 19.22). By writing the inequality in the equivalent form $y < -x + 4$,

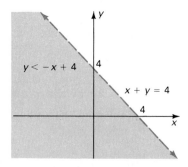

FIGURE 19.22

we conclude from number 3 in the previous list that the solution consists of all points below the line. Part of this region is shaded in Fig. 19.22. Thus if (x, y) is *any* point in this region, then y is less than the number $-x + 4$. For example, the point $(-2, 1)$ is in the region and $1 < -(-2) + 4$. You must realize that this check with a single point does *not* guarantee that our solution is correct. However, if the given inequality is *not* satisfied by the chosen point, then our solution is not correct. Moreover, if we had required that $y \leq -x + 4$ instead of $y < -x + 4$, then the line $y = -x + 4$ would also have been included in the solution as indicated by the solid line in Fig. 19.23. We shall adopt the conventions that **a solid line *is included*** and that **a broken line *is not* included in the solution**.

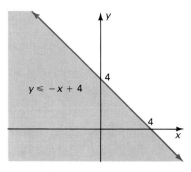

FIGURE 19.23

Example 1

Find the region described by $y \leq 3$.

Solution   Since x does not appear, the inequality is assumed to be true for all values of x. The solution consists of the line $y = 3$ *and* the region below it (see Fig. 19.24), because the y-coordinate of each point in that region is less than 3.

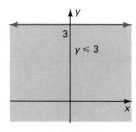

FIGURE 19.24

Example 2

Find the region described by $x \leq 4$.

Solution   Because y does not appear, the inequality is assumed to be true for all values of y. The solution consists of the line $x = 4$ and the region to the left of the line (see Fig. 19.25).

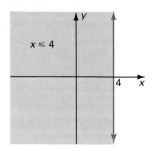

x ≤ 4

FIGURE 19.25

Example 3

Solve $2(2x - y) < 2(x + y) + 4$.

Solution We first rewrite the inequality in an equivalent form so that y alone appears to the left of the inequality symbol:

$$2(2x - y) < 2(x + y) + 4$$

$$4x - 2y < 2x + 2y + 4$$

$$-4y < -2x + 4$$

$$-y < -\frac{x}{2} + 1$$

$$y > \frac{x}{2} - 1.$$

In the last step, the sense of the original inequality was changed because we multiplied both sides by -1, a negative number. We now sketch the line $y = (x/2) - 1$ by using the points $(2, 0)$ and $(0, -1)$. Then we shade the region above the line (see Fig. 19.26). Every point in this region is a solution.

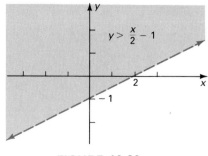

$y > \frac{x}{2} - 1$

FIGURE 19.26

The solution of a *system* of inequalities consists of all points whose coordinates simultaneously satisfy all the given inequalities. Geometrically, it is the region that is common to all the regions determined by the given inequalities. For example, let us solve the system

$$\begin{cases} y - 3x < 6 \\ x - y \le -3. \end{cases}$$

This system is equivalent to

$$\begin{cases} y < 3x + 6 \\ y \ge x + 3. \end{cases}$$

Note that each inequality has been written so that y is isolated on one side. Thus the appropriate regions with respect to the corresponding lines will be apparent. We first sketch the lines $y = 3x + 6$ and $y = x + 3$ and then shade the region that is simultaneously *below* the first line and *on or above* the second line (see Fig. 19.27). This region is the solution. When sketching the lines, **you should draw dashed lines everywhere until it is clear which portions of the lines are to be included in the solution**.

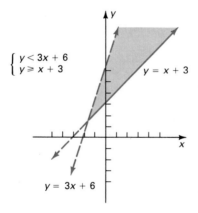

FIGURE 19.27

Example 4

Find the region described by

$$\begin{cases} 2x + 3y \le 60 \\ x \ge 0 \\ y \ge 0. \end{cases}$$

Solution This system relates to Inequality 1 in the discussion at the beginning of this section. The inequalities $x \geq 0$ and $y \geq 0$ restrict the solution to points that are both on or to the right of the y-axis *and* also on or above the x-axis. The desired region is indicated in Fig. 19.28.

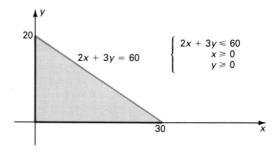

FIGURE 19.28

Example 5

Solve the system

$$\begin{cases} 2x + y > 3 \\ x \geq y \\ 2y - 1 > 0. \end{cases}$$

Solution The system is equivalent to

$$\begin{cases} y > -2x + 3 \\ y \leq x \\ y > \tfrac{1}{2}. \end{cases}$$

We sketch the lines $y = -2x + 3$, $y = x$, and $y = \tfrac{1}{2}$ and then shade the region that is simultaneously *above* the first line, *on or below* the second line, and *above* the third line (see Fig. 19.29). This region is the solution.

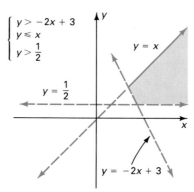

FIGURE 19.29

Problem Set 19.4

Sketch the region described by the following inequalities.

1. $y > 2x$.
2. $y < 3x - 4$.
3. $2x + 3y \le 6$.
4. $x + 3y > 12$.
5. $x + 5y < -5$.
6. $3x + y \le 0$.
7. $-x \ge 2y - 4$.
8. $2x + y \ge 10$.
9. $2(x + y) > 2(2x - y)$.
10. $-x < 2$.
11. $\frac{3}{2}x + \frac{4}{3}y > \frac{3}{2}(x - y)$.
12. $2(x^2 + 4x + y) > 4(x^2 - y + 1) - 2x^2$.
13. $\begin{cases} y \le 2x \\ x > 2y. \end{cases}$
14. $\begin{cases} x - y < 1 \\ y - x \le 1. \end{cases}$
15. $\begin{cases} 3x - 2y < 6 \\ x - 3y > 9. \end{cases}$
16. $\begin{cases} 2x + 3y > -6 \\ 3x - y < 6. \end{cases}$
17. $\begin{cases} 2x + 3y \le 6 \\ x \ge 0. \end{cases}$
18. $\begin{cases} 2y - 3x < 6 \\ x < 0. \end{cases}$
19. $\begin{cases} 2x - 2 \ge y \\ 2x \le 3 - 2y. \end{cases}$
20. $\begin{cases} \frac{3}{2}x - \frac{3}{4}y \ge 1 \\ x(x + 1) - 5 \le xy - x(y - x). \end{cases}$
21. $\begin{cases} x - y > 4. \\ x < 2 \\ v > 1. \end{cases}$
22. $\begin{cases} 2x + y < -1 \\ y > -x \\ 2x + 4 < 0. \end{cases}$
23. $\begin{cases} y < 2x + 1 \\ y > 1 \\ x > \frac{1}{2}. \end{cases}$
24. $\begin{cases} 4x + 3y \ge 12 \\ y \ge x \\ 2y \le 3x + 6. \end{cases}$
25. $\begin{cases} 5y - 2x \le 10 \\ 4x - 6y \le 12 \\ y \ge 2. \end{cases}$
26. $\begin{cases} 3x + y > -6 \\ x - y > -5 \\ x \ge 0. \end{cases}$

19.5 REVIEW

Important Terms and Symbols

Section 19.1 Interval, closed interval, endpoint, interval notation, open interval, half-open interval, $[a, b]$, (a, b), $(a, b]$, $[a, b)$, $(-\infty, b)$, $(-\infty, b]$, $[a, \infty)$, (a, ∞), $(-\infty, \infty)$, sense of inequality, absolute inequality, conditional inequality, equivalent inequalities, linear inequality in x.

Section 19.4 Linear inequality in x and y, system of inequalities.

Formula Summary

LINEAR INEQUALITIES

1. If $a < b$, then $a + c < b + c$.

2. If $a < b$ and $c > 0$, then $ac < bc$ and $\dfrac{a}{c} < \dfrac{b}{c}$.

3. If $a < b$ and $c < 0$, then $ac > bc$ and $\dfrac{a}{c} > \dfrac{b}{c}$.

Multiplication or division by a negative number reverses the sense of the inequality.

ABSOLUTE-VALUE EQUATIONS AND INEQUALITIES

If $d > 0$, then

1. $|x| = d$ means $x = \pm d$.

2. $|x| < d$ means $-d < x < d$.

3. $|x| > d$ means $x < -d$ or $x > d$.

PROPERTIES OF INEQUALITIES

1. $|ab| = |a||b|$.

2. $\left|\dfrac{a}{b}\right| = \dfrac{|a|}{|b|}$.

3. $|a - b| = |b - a|$.

4. $|a + b| \le |a| + |b|$.

Review Questions

1. True or false: If $x > -3$, then $-x > 3$. ___(a)___

   If $x > 4$, then $2x > 8$. ___(b)___

   If $2 < x < 3$, then both $x > 2$ and $x < 3$. ___(c)___

2. The solution of $4x \le 12$ is _____.

3. The solution of $x + 1 < x + 2$ is _____.

4. The solution of $x - 2 \ge x + 1$ is _____.

5. The solution of $|x - 5| = 0$ is _____.

6. The solution of $-3 \le x - 4 \le 3$ is _____.

7. If $-x > 0$, then $|x| = $ _____.

8. In absolute value notation, the fact that $2x$ is less than seven units of 4 would be written _____.

9. True or false: The inequality $x > 2$ is equivalent to $x^2 > 4$. _____

10. The inequality $x \geq 4$ is satisfied by all points to the _____ (right)(left) _____ of the line $x = 4$ and
    _____ (a)

    _____ (includes)(excludes) _____ the line itself.
    _____ (b)

11. If $y_1 \geq m_1 x + b_1$ and $y_2 \leq m_2 x + b_2$ is a system of inequalities, which of the regions 1, 2, 3, or 4 in Fig. 19.30 would correspond to the solution? _____

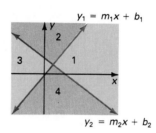

FIGURE 19.30

Answers to Review Questions

1. (a) False, (b) True, (c) True.   2. $x \leq 3$.   3. $-\infty < x < \infty$.   4. $\emptyset$.   5. 5.
6. $1 \leq x \leq 7$.   7. $-x$ 8. $|2x - 4| < 7$.   9. False.   10. (a) Right, (b) Includes.
11. 3.   ·

Review Problems

In Problems 1–34, solve the inequalities and equations.

1. $3x + 5 < 6$.

2. $3(x + 1) > 9$.

3. $4 - 2x \geq 8$.

4. $-2(x + 6) \leq x + 4$.

5. $3(t + 4) < 9 + 6t$.

6. $5(s + 3) > 2(s - 1)$.

7. $\frac{1}{3}(x + 2) \geq \frac{1}{4}x + 4$.

8. $\frac{x + 1}{5} \leq \frac{x}{10} + 2$.

9. $x^2 + 4x - 12 < 0$.

10. $x^2 + 11x + 28 > 0$.

11. $y^2 > 6y$.

12. $z^2 + 6z < -5$.

13. $2x^2 + 5x \geq x^2 - 4x - 20$.

14. $3x(x - 4) \leq 2x^2 - 27$.

15. $x(3x + 2) < 1$.

16. $6x(x - 1) > 1 - 5x$.

17. $(x + 4)(x - 5)(x - 9) > 0$.

18. $(x + 2)(x + 4)^2 < 0$.

19. $p^3 - 8p^2 \leq 0$.

20. $r^3 - 9r \geq 0$.

21. $\frac{x + 9}{x + 2} \geq 0$.

22. $\frac{x + 3}{x^2 - 3x + 2} \leq 0$.

23. $\frac{x^2 - 6x + 9}{x^2 + 7x + 10} > 0$.

24. $\dfrac{x^2 + 2x - 8}{x^2 - 25} < 0.$

25. $|3 - 2x| = 7.$

26. $\left|\dfrac{5x - 8}{13}\right| = 0.$

27. $|3x| > 6.$

28. $|x + 4| \le 6.$

29. $|4x - 1| < 1.$

30. $\left|\dfrac{5x - 8}{12}\right| \ge 1.$

31. $|4 - 2x| \ge 4.$

32. $|-1 - x| < 1.$

33. $|x + \frac{1}{2}| \le \frac{3}{2}.$

34. $|\frac{2}{3}x - 5| > 4.$

*In Problems **35–38**, sketch the region described by the given system.*

35. $\begin{cases} 2x + y < 4 \\ -y + 2x > 5. \end{cases}$

36. $\begin{cases} 3x + 2y > 5 \\ -3y + 5x < 7. \end{cases}$

37. $\begin{cases} x - y < 4 \\ y - x < 4. \end{cases}$

38. $\begin{cases} y \ge 5 \\ 2x - y < -2. \end{cases}$

39. $\begin{cases} x + y > 1 \\ 3x - 5 \ge y \\ y > 2x. \end{cases}$

40. $\begin{cases} 3x + y > -4 \\ x - y < -5 \\ x > 0. \end{cases}$

41. Show that if $|y - L| < \epsilon$, then $L - \epsilon < y < L + \epsilon.$

Sequences and Series

20.1 SEQUENCES AND SERIES

Suppose an object starts from rest and travels in a straight-line path with a constant acceleration of $4 \, \text{m/s}^2$. It is shown in physics that the distance s (in meters) of the object from its starting point at time t (in seconds) is given by the function $s = f(t) = 2t^2$. Let us restrict t to positive integral values; that is, we take the domain of f to be the positive integers. We find that if $t = 1$, then $s = 2$; if $t = 2$, then $s = 8$; and so on. Thus we have the following correspondence:

$$\begin{array}{ccccccc}
\text{Domain} & 1 & 2 & 3 & 4 & \cdots & n & \cdots \\
& \downarrow & \downarrow & \downarrow & \downarrow & & \downarrow & \\
\text{Range} & 2 & 8 & 18 & 32 & \cdots & 2n^2 & \cdots.
\end{array}$$

In mathematics we use the term **sequence** to describe a function, such as the preceding one, whose domain consists of the positive integers. Thus the function

$$f(n) = 2n^2,$$

where n is any positive integer, is a sequence. With sequences, instead of using the function-value notation $f(n)$, we commonly use the letter a along with subscript notation, so we write $f(n)$ as a_n. That is, when the input is n, the output is a_n. For

701

example, $f(1)$ becomes a_1 and $f(2)$ becomes a_2. If $a_n = 2n^2$, we have $a_1 = 2(1)^2 = 2$, $a_2 = 2(2)^2 = 8$, $a_3 = 2(3)^2 = 18$, and so on.

When we list the function values of a sequence in the order

$$a_1, a_2, a_3, \ldots, a_n, \ldots,$$

this arrangement also defines the sequence, and the values are called **terms** of the sequence. The *first term* is a_1, the *second term* is a_2, and so on. The **nth term**, or **general term**, is a_n. When specific values for $a_1, a_2, \ldots$ are listed, a_n is usually indicated by a rule for the sequence. For example, if the general term is $a_n = 2n^2$, then the sequence is

$$2, 8, 18, 32, \ldots, 2n^2, \ldots. \tag{1}$$

A sequence with general term a_n is often denoted by the symbol $\{a_n\}$. For example, the sequence in (1) can be denoted $\{2n^2\}$.

We also use the term *sequence* when the domain is a *finite* set of consecutive positive integers. For example, if $a_n = n^2$ and $n = 3, 4, 5$, and 6, then the sequence is

$$9, 16, 25, 36. \tag{2}$$

The sequence in (1) is called an **infinite sequence**, and the sequence in (2) is called a **finite sequence** because it has a first term *and* a last term. Unless otherwise specified, we shall assume that the sequences we deal with have domains consisting of the positive integers.

Example 1

Find the first four terms of the sequence with the given general term.

a. $a_n = \dfrac{2n}{3n + 1}$.

Solution In the expression $\dfrac{2n}{3n + 1}$, we successively replace n by the integers 1, 2 3, and 4.

$$n = 1, \quad a_1 = \frac{2(1)}{3(1) + 1} = \frac{2}{4} = \frac{1}{2}.$$

$$n = 2, \quad a_2 = \frac{2(2)}{3(2) + 1} = \frac{4}{7}.$$

$$n = 3, \quad a_3 = \frac{2(3)}{3(3) + 1} = \frac{6}{10} = \frac{3}{5}.$$

$$n = 4, \quad a_4 = \frac{2(4)}{3(4) + 1} = \frac{8}{13}.$$

Thus the first four terms are $\frac{1}{2}, \frac{4}{7}, \frac{3}{5}$, and $\frac{8}{13}$.

b. $a_n = (-1)^{n+1} 2^n$.

Solution

$$n = 1, \quad a_1 = (-1)^{1+1} 2^1 = (1)(2) = 2.$$

$$n = 2, \quad a_2 = (-1)^{2+1} 2^2 = (-1)(4) = -4.$$

$$n = 3, \quad a_3 = (-1)^{3+1} 2^3 = (1)(8) = 8.$$

$$n = 4, \quad a_4 = (-1)^{4+1} 2^4 = (-1)(16) = -16.$$

The first four terms are $2, -4, 8$, and -16. Note that these terms alternate in sign because of the factor $(-1)^{n+1}$.

Example 2

Find a general term for the given sequence.

a. 2, 4, 6, 8, ...

Solution Here $a_1 = 2, a_2 = 4, a_3 = 6$, and $a_4 = 8$. Looking for a pattern, we observe that $a_1 = 2(1), a_2 = 2(2), a_3 = 2(3)$, and $a_4 = 2(4)$. That is, the value of each term is twice the number of that term. Thus a general term is given by $a_n = 2n$.

b. $x, x^2, x^3, x^4, \ldots$.

Solution By inspecting the terms, we see that a general term is $a_n = x^n$.

If we have a sequence, then an indicated sum of its terms is called a **series**. For example, given the (finite) sequence

$$2, 3, 4,$$

the corresponding series is

$$2 + 3 + 4.$$

Similarly, the series that corresponds to

$$x, x^2, x^3, \ldots, x^n$$

is

$$x + x^2 + x^3 + \cdots + x^n.$$

To represent such sums we can use **sigma** (or **summation**) **notation**, so named because the Greek letter Σ (sigma) is used. For example, the symbol

$$\sum_{k=1}^{3} (2k + 5)$$

denotes the sum of those numbers obtained from the expression $2k + 5$ by first replacing k by 1, then by 2, and finally by 3. That is, k takes on consecutive integer values from 1 to 3. Thus

$$\sum_{k=1}^{3} (2k + 5) = [2(1) + 5] + [2(2) + 5] + [2(3) + 5]$$

$$= 7 + 9 + 11 = 27.$$

The expression $\sum_{k=1}^{3} (2k + 5)$ may be read *the sum of $2k + 5$ from $k = 1$ to $k = 3$*. The letter k is called the **index of summation**; the numbers 1 and 3 are called the **limits of summation** (1 is the *lower limit* and 3 is the *upper limit*). The letter used for the index is a "dummy" symbol in the sense that it does not affect the sum of the terms. Any other letter may be used. For example,

$$\sum_{j=1}^{3} (2j + 5) = 7 + 9 + 11 = \sum_{k=1}^{3} (2k + 5).$$

With sigma notation, the series $2 + 3 + 4$ may be written

$$\sum_{n=2}^{4} n.$$

We say that the **expanded form** of $\sum_{n=2}^{4} n$ is $2 + 3 + 4$. The series $x + x^2 + \cdots + x^n$ may be written

$$\sum_{k=1}^{n} x^k.$$

Example 3

Evaluate each of the following.

a. $\sum_{k=4}^{7} \dfrac{k^2 + 3}{2}$.

   Solution   Here the sum begins with $k = 4$.

$$\sum_{k=4}^{7} \frac{k^2 + 3}{2} = \frac{4^2 + 3}{2} + \frac{5^2 + 3}{2} + \frac{6^2 + 3}{2} + \frac{7^2 + 3}{2}$$

$$= \frac{19}{2} + \frac{28}{2} + \frac{39}{2} + \frac{52}{2} = \frac{138}{2} = 69.$$

b. $\displaystyle\sum_{n=0}^{2} (-1)^n(2^n - 1)$.

Solution Here the sum begins with $n = 0$.

$$\sum_{n=0}^{2} (-1)^n(2^n - 1) = (-1)^0(2^0 - 1) + (-1)^1(2^1 - 1) + (-1)^2(2^2 - 1)$$

$$= (1)(0) + (-1)(1) + (1)(3)$$

$$= 0 - 1 + 3 = 2.$$

c. $\displaystyle\sum_{n=1}^{4} 2$.

Solution The 2 can be thought of as $2 + 0n$. Thus

$$\sum_{n=1}^{4} 2 = 2 + 2 + 2 + 2 = 8.$$

Problem Set 20.1

In Problems 1–14, find the first four terms of the sequence that has the given general term.

1. $a_n = 3n$.

2. $a_n = \frac{1}{2}n$.

3. $a_n = n^2 + n$.

4. $a_n = 2n^2 + 4$.

5. $a_n = \dfrac{n^2 - 1}{n^2 + 2}$.

6. $a_n = \dfrac{n}{2^n}$.

7. $a_n = x^{2n}$.

8. $a_n = (2n)^2$.

9. $a_n = (-1)^{n+1}n^2$.

10. $a_n = (-1)^n(2n)^2$.

11. $a_n = \sin\dfrac{n\pi}{2}$.

12. $a_n = \cos\left(\dfrac{n\pi}{2}\right)$.

13. $a_n = \dfrac{e^n}{2}$.

14. $a_n = \dfrac{\sin nx}{n^2}$.

In Problems 15–22, find a general term for the given sequence.

15. $1, 2, 3, 4, \dots$.

16. $0, -1, -2, -3, \dots$

17. $3, 6, 9, 12, \dots$.

18. $1, \frac{3}{2}, 2, \frac{5}{2}, \dots$.

19. $1, 3, 9, 27, \dots$.

20. $x^2, x^4, x^6, x^8, \dots$.

21. $\frac{1}{2}, -\frac{1}{3}, \frac{1}{4}, -\frac{1}{5}, \dots$.

22. $-\frac{1}{2}, \frac{1}{3}, -\frac{1}{4}, \frac{1}{5}, \dots$.

In Problems 23–32, evaluate the given sum.

23. $\displaystyle\sum_{k=1}^{5} (k + 4)$.

24. $\displaystyle\sum_{k=4}^{7} (5 - 2k)$.

25. $\displaystyle\sum_{n=0}^{3}(3n^2 - 7)$.

26. $\displaystyle\sum_{n=2}^{4}\frac{n+1}{n-1}$.

27. $\displaystyle\sum_{n=1}^{3}3$.

28. $\displaystyle\sum_{n=1}^{5}1$.

29. $\displaystyle\sum_{k=3}^{4}\frac{(-1)^k(k+1)}{2^k}$.

30. $\displaystyle\sum_{n=1}^{4}(n^2+n)$.

31. $\displaystyle\sum_{n=1}^{3}2\left(\frac{1}{2}\right)^n$.

32. $\displaystyle\sum_{n=0}^{3}(-1)^n\frac{1}{n+1}$.

In Problems **33** *and* **34**, *write the series in expanded form.*

33. $\displaystyle\sum_{k=1}^{4}\sin kx$.

34. $\displaystyle\sum_{k=1}^{4}\frac{\cos kx}{k}$.

20.2 ARITHMETIC PROGRESSIONS

If you look for the pattern of the terms in the sequence

$$1, 3, 5, 7,$$

you may notice that by adding 2 to any term, you get the next term. This means that the difference between any term and the term preceding it is 2:

$$3 - 1 = 2, \qquad 5 - 3 = 2, \qquad 7 - 5 = 2.$$

We call the sequence 1, 3, 5, 7 an *arithmetic progression* (or *arithmetic sequence*) with *common difference* 2. Here is a more general definition.

> A sequence in which each term after the first can be obtained by adding the constant d to the preceding term is called an **arithmetic progression** with **common difference** d.

Example 1

Suppose the first term of an arithmetic progression is 6 and the common difference d is 5. Then

$$a_1 = 6,$$
$$a_2 = 6 + 5 = 11,$$
$$a_3 = 11 + 5 = 16,$$
$$a_4 = 16 + 5 = 21, \qquad \text{and so on.}$$

Thus the arithmetic progression is

$$6, 11, 16, 21, \ldots.$$

Example 2

a. In the arithmetic progression

$$\frac{1}{3}, \frac{2}{3}, 1, \frac{4}{3}, \ldots$$

we can find d by choosing *any* two consecutive terms and subtracting the first one from the second one. For example, subtracting the first term from the second term gives

$$d = \frac{2}{3} - \frac{1}{3} = \frac{1}{3}.$$

b. The sequence

$$2, -1, -4, -7, \ldots$$

is an arithmetic progression, because if we add -3 to *any* term, we get the next term:

$$2 + (-3) = -1, \qquad -1 + (-3) = -4, \qquad \text{and so on.}$$

We can find a formula for the nth term of an arithmetic progression with first term a_1 and common difference d. In this progression we have

$$a_2 = a_1 + d$$
$$a_3 = a_2 + d = (a_1 + d) + d = a_1 + 2d$$
$$a_4 = a_3 + d = (a_1 + 2d) + d = a_1 + 3d.$$

Remaining terms can be obtained in a similar manner. Thus the arithmetic progression is

$$a_1, \quad a_1 + d, \quad a_1 + 2d, \quad a_1 + 3d, \ldots.$$

Each term is the sum of a_1 and a number that is a multiple of d. That number is d times one *less* than the number of the term. For example, the tenth term is

$$a_{10} = a_1 + (10 - 1)d = a_1 + 9d.$$

More generally, we have the following formula for the nth term of an arithmetic progression.

> The nth term, a_n, of an arithmetic progression with first term a_1 and common difference d is given by
>
> $$a_n = a_1 + (n - 1)d. \tag{1}$$

In Example 2, the nth term of the arithmetic progression in Part a is $a_n = \frac{1}{3} + (n - 1)\frac{1}{3} = \frac{1}{3} + \frac{1}{3}(n - 1)$; in Part b it is $a_n = 2 + (n - 1)(-3) = 2 - 3(n - 1)$.

Example 3

Find the eighteenth term of the sequence

$$7, 13, 19, \ldots.$$

Solution This sequence is an arithmetic progression with $a_1 = 7$ and $d = 6$. To find a_{18}, we use Eq. 1 with $n = 18$.

$$a_n = a_1 + (n - 1)d$$
$$a_{18} = 7 + (18 - 1)6 = 7 + (17)6 = 109.$$

Example 4

The third term of an arithmetic progression is 2 and the tenth term is -26. Find a_1 and d.

Solution We have $a_3 = 2$ and $a_{10} = -26$. Using Eq. 1 with $n = 3$ and $a_3 = 2$ gives

$$2 = a_1 + (3 - 1)d$$
$$2 = a_1 + 2d. \tag{2}$$

Using Eq. 1 with $n = 10$ and $a_{10} = -26$ gives

$$-26 = a_1 + (10 - 1)d$$
$$-26 = a_1 + 9d. \tag{3}$$

Equations 2 and 3 form a system of equations.

$$\begin{cases} 2 = a_1 + 2d & (4) \\ -26 = a_1 + 9d. & (5) \end{cases}$$

Multiplying Eq. 4 by -1 and adding it to Eq. 5, we have

$$-28 = 7d$$
$$-4 = d.$$

Substituting -4 for d in Eq. 4 gives

$$2 = a_1 + 2(-4)$$
$$2 = a_1 - 8$$
$$10 = a_1.$$

Thus $a_1 = 10$ and $d = -4$.

Example 5

A particle has an initial speed of 5 m/s and travels in a straight line with an acceleration of 2 m/s². The values of the speed of the particle, in meters per second, at positive integral values of time t (in seconds) form the arithmetic progression

$$7, 9, 11, 13, \ldots, 5 + 2t, \ldots.$$

Find the speed of the particle when $t = 100$ s.

Solution   Here the first term $a_1 = 7$ corresponds to the time $t = 1$, the second term $a_2 = 9$ corresponds to $t = 2$, and so on, and $d = 2$. We need to find a_{100}, which corresponds to $t = 100$. In Eq. 1 we set $a_1 = 7$, $d = 2$, and $n = 100$.

$$a_n = a_1 + (n - 1)d$$
$$a_{100} = 7 + (100 - 1)(2) = 205.$$

Thus the speed is 205 m/s.

We can find a formula for the sum S_n of the first n terms of an arithmetic progression. Suppose that $a_1, a_2, \ldots$ is an arithmetic progression. Then $a_2 = a_1 + d$, $a_3 = a_1 + 2d$, and so on. Thus

$$S_n = a_1 + a_2 + a_3 + \cdots + a_n$$

or $\qquad S_n = a_1 + (a_1 + d) + (a_1 + 2d) + \cdots + [a_1 + (n - 1)d].$ $\qquad$ (6)

In an arithmetic progression, we can find a term by subtracting d from the term that follows it. Thus the terms in the sum S_n can be written in reverse order to give

$$S_n = a_n + (a_n - d) + (a_n - 2d) + \cdots + [a_n - (n - 1)d]. \qquad (7)$$

Adding corresponding sides of Eq. 6 and Eq. 7 gives

$$
\begin{aligned}
S_n &= a_1 &&+ (a_1 + d) + \cdots + [a_1 + (n - 1)d] \\
S_n &= a_n &&+ (a_n - d) + \cdots + [a_n - (n - 1)d] \\
\hline
2S_n &= (a_1 + a_n) + (a_1 + a_n) + \cdots + (a_1 + a_n).
\end{aligned}
$$

On the right side of the last equation, the number $a_1 + a_n$ occurs n times. Thus

$$2S_n = n(a_1 + a_n).$$

By dividing both sides by 2, we have the following result.

> The sum S_n of the first n terms of an arithmetic progression is given by
>
> $$S_n = \frac{n}{2}(a_1 + a_n), \qquad (8)$$
>
> where a_1 is the first term and a_n is the nth term.

Example 6

Find the sum of the first eight terms of the series

$$1 + 4 + 7 + \cdots.$$

Solution   The terms form an arithmetic progression with $a_1 = 1$ and $d = 3$. The eighth term is given by

$$a_n = a_1 + (n - 1)d$$
$$a_8 = 1 + (8 - 1)3 = 22.$$

We can now find the sum by using Eq. 8.

$$S_8 = \frac{8}{2}(a_1 + a_8) = 4(1 + 22) = 92.$$

Example 7

Find the sum of the odd integers between 20 and 60.

Solution   The odd integers between 20 and 60 form an arithmetic progression with $d = 2$. Here $a_1 = 21$ and $a_n = 59$. To find n, we have

$$a_n = a_1 + (n - 1)d$$
$$59 = 21 + (n - 1)2$$
$$38 = 2n - 2$$
$$40 = 2n$$
$$20 = n.$$

That is, 59 is the twentieth term of the arithmetic progression. Using Eq. 8 gives

$$S_{20} = \frac{20}{2}(21 + 59) = 800.$$

We can find another formula for S_n besides Eq. 8. Replacing a_n in that equation by $a_1 + (n + 1)d$, we have

$$S_n = \frac{n}{2}(a_1 + a_n)$$

$$= \frac{n}{2}[a_1 + a_1 + (n - 1)d].$$

Thus

$$S_n = \frac{n}{2}[2a_1 + (n-1)d].$$

To redo Example 6 by using this formula, we have

$$S_8 = \frac{8}{2}[2(1) + (8-1)3] = 4[2 + 21] = 92.$$

Example 8

Derive a formula for the sum of the first k positive integers.

Solution   The terms of the series

$$\sum_{n=1}^{k} n = 1 + 2 + 3 + \cdots + k$$

form an arithmetic progression with $a_1 = 1$, $d = 1$, and k terms. Thus, by Eq. 8, we have

$$\sum_{n=1}^{k} n = \frac{k(k+1)}{2}. \tag{9}$$

For example, to find the sum of the first 25 positive integers we set $k = 25$:

$$\sum_{n=1}^{25} n = \frac{25(25+1)}{2} = 325.$$

Problem Set 20.2

In Problems 1–10, for those sequences that are arithmetic progressions, find the indicated term.

1. 2, 6, 10, ...; a_6.
2. 4, 9, 14, ...; a_5.
3. 13, 1, -11, ...; a_8.
4. 13, 0, -13, ...; a_7.
5. 4, 1, -1, ...; a_5.
6. 4, 1, $\frac{1}{4}$, ...; a_7.
7. $\frac{1}{3}$, $\frac{2}{3}$, 1, ...; a_{11}.
8. a, $-a$, $-3a$, ...; a_9.
9. 0.4, 0.8, 1.2, ...; a_{10}.
10. -3, -1, 1, ...; a_6.

In Problems **11–20**, *find the indicated sum.*

11. $2 + 4 + 6 + \cdots$; S_{10}.

12. $1 + 5 + 9 + \cdots$; S_9.

13. $15 + 10 + 5 + \cdots$; S_{16}.

14. $-\frac{1}{3} + \frac{1}{3} + 1 + \cdots$; S_{12}.

15. $2 + 0 - 2 - 4 - \cdots$; S_{12}.

16. $14 + 7 + 0 + \cdots$; S_9.

17. $-10 + 6 + 22 + \cdots$; S_{10}.

18. $\frac{3}{6} + \frac{2}{6} + \frac{1}{6} + \cdots$; S_9.

19. $3 + 6 + 9 + \cdots + 27$.

20. $7 + 9 + 11 + \cdots + 33$.

21. The fourth term of an arithmetic progression with $d = 14$ is 86. Find (a) the first term and (b) the eighth term.

22. The first term of an arithmetic progression is 16. The tenth term is 10. Find d.

23. The sixteenth term of an arithmetic progression is 28. The first term is -4. Find d.

24. In an arithmetic progression, $a_1 = 6$, $a_n = 26$, and $d = 4$. Find n.

25. The fourth term of an arithmetic progression is 11 and the eleventh term is 32. Find a_1 and d.

26. The third term of an arithmetic progression is -2 and the tenth term is 12. Find the first term.

27. Find the sum of the first 100 positive integers.

28. Find the sum of the odd integers between 30 and 80.

In Problems **29–32**, *find the values of the indicated quantities for the arithmetic progression that has the given properties.*

29. $a_{13} = 42$, $d = 2$; a_{16}, S_{16}.

30. $a_9 = 20$, $d = 1$; a_{16}, S_{16}.

31. $a_1 = -30$, $d = 3$, $S_n = 69$; n, a_n.

32. $a_1 = 12$, $a_n = 42$, $d = 2$; n, S_n.

33. The length of the first swing of a pendulum is 10 cm, and because of resistance, each succeeding swing is $\frac{1}{4}$ cm less. What is the length of the thirteenth pendulum swing?

34. How many swings of the pendulum in Problem 33 are completed before the pendulum comes to rest?

35. If a person saves 1¢ the first day, 2¢ the next day, 3¢ the next day, and so on, how much money will the person have at the end of 30 days?

36. In a vacuum, an object falls approximately 4.9 m the first second, 14.7 m the next, 24.5 m the next, and so on. How far does it fall in 10 s?

37. A display in a supermarket consists of boxes piled up in the form of a pyramid. There are 20 boxes on the bottom layer and each successive layer has two fewer boxes. How many boxes are in the display?

38. It can be shown that the sum of the squares of the first k positive integers is given by

$$\sum_{n=1}^{k} n^2 = \frac{k(k+1)(2k+1)}{6}.$$

Find the sum of the squares of the first ten positive integers.

39. It can be shown that the sum of the cubes of the first k positive integers is given by

$$\sum_{n=1}^{k} n^3 = \frac{k^2(k+1)^2}{4}.$$

Find the sum of the cubes of the first ten positive integers.

20.3 GEOMETRIC PROGRESSIONS

In the sequence

$$3, 6, 12, 24, 48,$$

each term, after the first, can be obtained by multiplying the preceding term by 2. This means that the ratio (or quotient) of every two consecutive terms is 2:

$$\frac{6}{3} = 2, \qquad \frac{12}{6} = 2, \qquad \text{and so on.}$$

We call the sequence 3, 6, 12, 24, 48 a *geometric progression* (or *geometric sequence*) with *common ratio* 2. Here is a more general definition.

> A sequence in which each term, after the first, can be obtained by multiplying the preceding term by the constant r is called a **geometric progression** with **common ratio** r.

Example 1

Suppose the first term of a geometric progression is 3 and the common ratio r is $-\frac{1}{2}$. Then

$$a_1 = 3$$

$$a_2 = 3\left(-\frac{1}{2}\right) = -\frac{3}{2}$$

$$a_3 = \left(-\frac{3}{2}\right)\left(-\frac{1}{2}\right) = \frac{3}{4}$$

$$a_4 = \frac{3}{4}\left(-\frac{1}{2}\right) = -\frac{3}{8}, \qquad \text{and so on.}$$

Thus the geometric progression is

$$3, -\frac{3}{2}, \frac{3}{4}, -\frac{3}{8}, \ldots$$

Example 2

a. The sequence

$$4, 0.4, 0.04, 0.004$$

is a geometric progression with $r = 0.1$. For example, the ratio of the second term to the first term is $0.4/4 = 0.1$.

b. The sequence

$$\frac{1}{2}, 1, 2, 4, \ldots$$

is a geometric progression with $r = 2$. Verify this.

We can find a formula for the nth term of a geometric progression. Suppose a geometric progression has first term a_1 and common ratio r. Then

$$a_2 = a_1 r$$
$$a_3 = a_2 r = (a_1 r)r = a_1 r^2$$
$$a_4 = a_3 r = (a_1 r^2)r = a_1 r^3, \quad \text{and so on.}$$

Thus the geometric progression is

$$a_1, a_1 r, a_1 r^2, a_1 r^3, \ldots.$$

In each term the exponent for r is one less than the number of the term. For example, the tenth term is $a_{10} = a_1 r^{10-1} = a_1 r^9$. More generally, we have the following formula.

> The nth term, a_n, of a geometric progression with first term a_1 and common ratio r is given by
> $$a_n = a_1 r^{n-1}. \tag{1}$$

Example 3

Find the fifth term of the geometric progression

$$2, -\frac{1}{2}, \frac{1}{8}, \ldots.$$

Solution Here $a_1 = 2$ and $r = (-\frac{1}{2})/2 = -\frac{1}{4}$. Using Eq. 1 with $n = 5$ gives

$$a_n = a_1 r^{n-1}$$
$$a_5 = 2\left(-\frac{1}{4}\right)^{5-1} = 2\left(-\frac{1}{4}\right)^4 = \frac{1}{128}.$$

Example 4

The first term of a geometric progression is 3 and the sixth term is $\frac{3}{32}$. Find the common ratio r.

Solution Here $a_1 = 3$ and $a_6 = \frac{3}{32}$. Using Eq. 1 with $n = 6$, we have

$$a_1 r^{n-1} = a_n$$

$$3r^5 = \frac{3}{32}$$

$$r^5 = \frac{1}{32}$$

$$r = \frac{1}{2} \quad \text{[taking the fifth root of both sides].}$$

Example 5

A person invests a principal of $100 and earns interest of 6% at the end of each year. If none of the interest is withdrawn, how much is the investment worth at the end of 5 years?

Solution At the end of the first year, the value of the investment is the sum of the original investment and the interest:

$$100 + 100(0.06) = 100(1 + 0.06) \quad \text{[factoring]}$$

$$= 100(1.06).$$

This amount is the principal on which interest is earned for the second year. At the end of that year, the value of the investment is the sum of principal and interest, or

$$100(1.06) + [100(1.06)]0.06 = 100(1.06)[1 + 0.06] \quad \text{[factoring]}$$

$$= 100(1.06)^2.$$

Similarly, the value of the investment at the end of the third year is $100(1.06)^3$, and so on. These values,

$$100(1.06), \ 100(1.06)^2, \ 100(1.06)^3, \ \ldots,$$

form a geometric progression with common ratio 1.06. In general, the value of the investment at the end of n years is

$$100(1.06)^n.$$

Thus, at the end of 5 years, the value is $100(1.06)^5$ dollars. (A calculator value is $133.82.) Because the interest is reinvested, the person is earning "interest on interest," called *compound interest*.

We can find a formula for the sum S_n of the first n terms of a geometric progression. Since

$$S_n = a_1 + a_1 r + a_1 r^2 + \cdots + a_1 r^{n-1}, \tag{2}$$

multiplying both sides by r gives

$$rS_n = a_1r + a_1r^2 + a_1r^3 + \cdots + a_1r^n. \tag{3}$$

Subtracting Eq. 3 from Eq. 2 and factoring, we have

$$S_n - rS_n = a_1 - a_1r^n$$
$$S_n(1 - r) = a_1(1 - r^n).$$

If $r \neq 1$, then dividing both sides by $1 - r$ gives the following result.

The formula

$$S_n = \frac{a_1(1 - r^n)}{1 - r} \tag{4}$$

gives the sum S_n of the first n terms of a geometric progression with first term a_1 and common ratio r.

From Eq. 4 we can get another formula for S_n that involves a_n. We have

$$S_n = \frac{a_1(1 - r^n)}{1 - r} = \frac{a_1 - a_1r^n}{1 - r}$$
$$= \frac{a_1 - (a_1r^{n-1})r}{1 - r}.$$

From Eq. 1, $a_1r^{n-1} = a_n$, so we have

$$S_n = \frac{a_1 - ra_n}{1 - r}. \tag{5}$$

If $r = 1$, then Eqs. 4 and 5 cannot be used. However, in that case we have

$$S_n = a_1 + a_1 + \cdots + a_1 = na_1.$$

Example 6

Find the sum of the first 10 terms of the geometric progression 12, 6, 3, ...

Solution Here $a_1 = 12$, $r = \frac{6}{12} = \frac{1}{2}$, and $n = 10$. From Eq. 4,

$$S_{10} = \frac{a_1(1 - r^{10})}{1 - r} = \frac{12[1 - (\frac{1}{2})^{10}]}{1 - \frac{1}{2}}$$
$$= \frac{12[1 - \frac{1}{1024}]}{\frac{1}{2}} = \frac{3069}{128}.$$

Example 7

Find the sum of the series $1 + \frac{1}{3} + (\frac{1}{3})^2 + \cdots + (\frac{1}{3})^5$.

Solution The terms of the series form a geometric progression with $a_1 = 1$ and $r = \frac{1}{3}$. This series is called a *geometric series*. Here $n = 6$ (not 5). From Eq. 4 we have

$$S_6 = \frac{a_1(1 - r^6)}{1 - r} = \frac{1[1 - (\frac{1}{3})^6]}{1 - \frac{1}{3}}$$

$$= \frac{\frac{728}{729}}{\frac{2}{3}} = \frac{364}{243}.$$

Since the last term in the sum is known to be $(\frac{1}{3})^5$, we could have used Eq. 5 to obtain the same result.

Problem Set 20.3

In Problems 1–10, for those sequences that are geometric progressions, find the indicated term.

1. $3, 6, 12, \ldots;$ a_5.
2. $4, 1, \frac{1}{4}, \ldots;$ a_7.
3. $6, -3, \frac{3}{2}, \ldots;$ a_6.
4. $-1, 3, -9, \ldots;$ a_6.
5. $2, 4, 6, \ldots;$ a_5.
6. $\frac{1}{3}, \frac{2}{3}, 1, \ldots;$ a_5.
7. $-4, 2, -1, \ldots;$ a_9.
8. $0.3, 0.03, 0.003, \ldots;$ a_7.
9. $\frac{3}{2}, \frac{9}{4}, \frac{27}{8}, \ldots;$ a_5.
10. $12, -4, \frac{4}{3}, \ldots;$ a_6.

In Problems 11–18, find the indicated sum.

11. $3 + 9 + 27 + \cdots;$ S_6.
12. $1 - \frac{1}{4} + \frac{1}{16} - \cdots;$ S_6.
13. $6 - 12 + 24 - \cdots;$ S_6.
14. $0.1 + 0.02 + 0.004 + \cdots;$ S_5,
15. $0.3 + 0.03 + 0.003 + \cdots;$ S_7.
16. $24 + 12 + 6 + \cdots;$ S_7.
17. $1 + \frac{1}{2} + \frac{1}{4} + \cdots + \frac{1}{128}$.
18. $1 - \frac{1}{2} + \frac{1}{4} - \cdots + \frac{1}{64}$.

19. The first term of a geometric progression is 16. The fourth term is $\frac{1}{4}$. Find r.

20. The first term of a geometric progression is 18 and the fourth term is $\frac{2}{81}$. Find the second term.

21. If a person saves 1¢ the first day, 2¢ the next day, 4¢ the next day, 8¢ the next day, and so on, how much money will the person have at the end of 30 days?

22. Find $\displaystyle\sum_{n=1}^{6} \left(\frac{1}{2}\right)^n$.

In Problems 23–28, find the indicated quantities for the geometric progression that has the given properties.

23. $r = \frac{1}{2}, S_6 = 126;$ a_1, a_6.
24. $a_1 = 1, a_6 = 32;$ r, S_6.
25. $a_1 = \frac{3}{4}, a_n = -96, S_n = -\frac{255}{4};$ r.
26. $a_1 = \frac{1}{2}, a_{10} = 256;$ a_{12}, S_{12}.
27. $r = \frac{1}{3}, S_5 = 121;$ a_1, a_5.
28. $a_6 = 1, a_8 = 9;$ S_5.

29. By means of a pump, air is being removed from a container in such a way that each second, one-tenth of the remaining air in the container is removed. After 5 s, what percentage of air is left? Give your answer to the nearest percentage.

30. A tank full of alcohol is emptied of one-fourth its contents. The tank is then filled with water. This is repeated three more times. What part of the tank is now alcohol?

31. Find the value of an investment of $250 after n years if interest is compounded annually at the rate of 6.5%.

32. Bacteria growing in a culture double their number every day. If there were originally 10,000 bacteria, how many will there be after 8 days?

33. A distant star now has a surface temperature of 10,000°C, and observations indicate that the temperature decreases by 10% every 1000 years. What will be the temperature 4000 years from now?

34. For the star of Problem 33, in how many years will the surface temperature be 7290°C?

20.4 LIMITS OF SEQUENCES

We now consider one of the very fundamental ideas of mathematics—the concept of a limit. The ideas and techniques we shall develop here are useful in both the main topics of calculus, namely, finding derivatives and finding integrals.

We begin by examining rather closely a sequence that conveniently typifies a situation which arises quite naturally in mechanics. Consider a pendulum that is displaced from its equilibrium (rest) position and then released. The pendulum will oscillate back and forth. Let us assume that the length of the first swing was $\frac{1}{2}$ m and that the length of any subsequent swing was exactly one-half the length of the swing that preceded it. If we let a_1 be the length of the first swing, a_2 the length of the second swing, and so on, we have

$$a_1 = \frac{1}{2} = \frac{1}{2^1}$$

$$a_2 = \frac{1}{2}\left(\frac{1}{2}\right) = \frac{1}{2^2}$$

$$a_3 = \frac{1}{2}\left(\frac{1}{2^2}\right) = \frac{1}{2^3}$$

$$a_4 = \frac{1}{2}\left(\frac{1}{2^3}\right) = \frac{1}{2^4}.$$

The pattern continues. For the nth swing of the pendulum,

$$a_n = \frac{1}{2^n}.$$

Thus the sequence whose terms correspond to the lengths of the swings is

$$\left\{\frac{1}{2^n}\right\} = \frac{1}{2^1}, \frac{1}{2^2}, \frac{1}{2^3}, \frac{1}{2^4}, \ldots, \frac{1}{2^n}, \ldots$$

$$= \frac{1}{2}, \frac{1}{4}, \frac{1}{8}, \frac{1}{16}, \ldots, \frac{1}{2^n}, \ldots.$$

Some terms of this sequence are shown on the real number line in Fig. 20.1. Observe that as n gets larger, the terms get closer to zero. Moreover, although $1/2^n$ will never

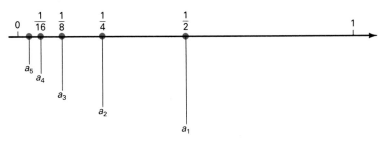

FIGURE 20.1

have a value of zero, for large enough values of n the corresponding terms will be as close to zero as we wish. For example, suppose we wish to find when the length of a swing will be less than $\dfrac{1}{10,000}$ m. Then we must have the inequality

$$\frac{1}{2^n} < \frac{1}{10,000},$$

which is true for $n > 13$ (verify this). That is, beginning with the fourteenth term (the fourteenth swing of the pendulum), each term in the sequence will be less than $\frac{1}{10,000}$ m.

The ideas of the preceding discussion are verbally expressed by saying that as n increases indefinitely, the sequence $\{1/2^n\}$ has zero for a **limit**, or $\{1/2^n\}$ *converges to* zero. Symbolically we write

$$\lim_{n \to \infty} \frac{1}{2^n} = 0. \tag{1}$$

Here the notation $n \to \infty$ means that n is increasing indefinitely through positive integral values. Equation 1 can be read *the limit of the sequence $\{1/2^n\}$ as n increases without bound is equal to zero.* This means that every interval containing zero, no matter how small, contains all the terms of the sequence $\{1/2^n\}$ from some term on.

More generally, to say that

$$\lim_{n \to \infty} a_n = a$$

means that the limit of the sequence $\{a_n\}$ as $n \to \infty$ is the number a. That is, every interval containing a contains all the terms of the sequence $\{a_n\}$ from some term on. For n sufficiently large, a_n is arbitrarily close to a.

Not every sequence has a limit. For example, the terms of the sequence $\{n^2\} = 1, 4, 9, \ldots$ increase without bound as $n \to \infty$, so the sequence has no limit. We denote this situation by writing

$$\lim_{n \to \infty} n^2 = \infty,$$

which can be read *as n increases without bound, the terms of the squence $\{n^2\}$ increase without bound*. The use of the equals sign in this situation does not mean that the limit exists. On the contrary, the symbolism here (∞) is a way of saying specifically that there is no limit and it indicates **why** there is no limit. A sequence that has a finite limit is said to **converge** or to be **convergent**. If a sequence does not converge, it **diverges** or is **divergent**. Thus $\{1/2^n\}$ is a convergent sequence, but $\{n^2\}$ is a divergent sequence. When a sequence converges, its limit must be unique. That is, there can be only one limit.

Example 1

The sequence

$$3, 2, -5, -5, \ldots, -5, \ldots$$

converges to -5, since *every* interval containing -5 must contain all the terms of the sequence from the third term on. For most convergent sequences, however, you may have to ignore many, perhaps a million, of the terms in the sequence before all the remaining terms lie in a given interval if the interval is quite small.

Example 2

a. The terms of the arithmetic sequence $\{-5n\} = -5, -10, -15, \ldots$ decrease without bound, so the sequence diverges; that is, it has no finite limit. Symbolically, we denote this situation by writing

$$\lim_{n \to \infty} (-5n) = -\infty.$$

In fact, because of the common difference d, where $|d| > 0$, *every arithmetic progression is divergent*.

b. The terms of the sequence $\{(-1)^n\} = -1, 1, -1, 1, \ldots$ oscillate between 1 and -1. Thus the sequence has no limit as $n \to \infty$ and hence is divergent.

Example 3

The terms of the sequence

$$\left\{\frac{n+1}{n}\right\} = 2, \frac{3}{2}, \frac{4}{3}, \frac{5}{4}, \frac{6}{5}, \dots$$

appear to be getting closer to 1 as n increases. In fact, for $n = 1000$,

$$a_{1000} = \frac{1001}{1000} = 1 + \frac{1}{1000}.$$

In Example 6 it will be shown that 1 is indeed the limit.

Without going into their proofs, we shall state some theorems on limits and illustrate their use in determining the behavior of various sequences. We begin with the following.

THEOREM 1.

If $|r| < 1$, then $\lim_{n \to \infty} r^n = 0$. If $|r| > 1$, then $\lim_{n \to \infty} r^n$ does not exist and $\{r^n\}$ diverges.

THEOREM 2.

$\lim_{n \to \infty} c = c$, where c is a constant.

THEOREM 3.

$\lim_{n \to \infty} ca_n = c \lim_{n \to \infty} a_n$ if $\{a_n\}$ is convergent.

THEOREM 4.

If each term of a divergent sequence is multiplied by the same nonzero constant, the resulting sequence is also divergent.

Example 4

Determine whether the given sequence converges or diverges. In the case of convergence, find the limit.

a. $\{(-\frac{1}{2})^n\} = -\frac{1}{2}, \frac{1}{4}, -\frac{1}{8}, \dots$

Solution We apply Theorem 1 with $r = -\frac{1}{2}$. Since $|-\frac{1}{2}| < 1$, we have

$$\lim_{n \to \infty} (-\frac{1}{2})^n = 0.$$

The sequence converges to 0.

b. $\{3\} = 3, 3, 3, \ldots$.

Solution   From Theorem 2 with $3 = c$, we have

$$\lim_{n \to \infty} 3 = 3.$$

The sequence converges to 3.

c. $\left\{\dfrac{3}{4^n}\right\}$.

Solution   Note that $3/4^n = 3(\frac{1}{4})^n$. Since $|\frac{1}{4}| < 1$, by Theorem 1 the sequence $\{(\frac{1}{4})^n\}$ converges to 0. Thus, by Theorem 3,

$$\lim_{n \to \infty} \frac{3}{4^n} = 3 \lim_{n \to \infty} \left(\frac{1}{4}\right)^n = 3(0) = 0.$$

The sequence converges to 0.

d. $\{2(\frac{4}{3})^n\}$.

Solution   Because $|\frac{4}{3}| > 1$, by Theorem 1 the sequence $\{(\frac{4}{3})^n\}$ diverges. By Theorem 4, $\{2(\frac{4}{3})^n\}$ also diverges. Note how the terms in the sequence increase without bound as $n \to \infty$:

$$\left\{2\left(\frac{4}{3}\right)^n\right\} = \frac{8}{3}, \frac{32}{9}, \frac{128}{27}, \frac{512}{81}, \ldots.$$

Here are some additional theorems.

THEOREM 5.

If $\{a_n\}$ and $\{b_n\}$ are convergent sequences, then

a. $\displaystyle \lim_{n \to \infty} (a_n \pm b_n) = \lim_{n \to \infty} a_n \pm \lim_{n \to \infty} b_n$,

b. $\displaystyle \lim_{n \to \infty} (a_n b_n) = \left(\lim_{n \to \infty} a_n\right)\left(\lim_{n \to \infty} b_n\right)$,

c. $\displaystyle \lim_{n \to \infty} \frac{a_n}{b_n} = \frac{\displaystyle\lim_{n \to \infty} a_n}{\displaystyle\lim_{n \to \infty} b_n}$ if $b_n \neq 0$ and $\displaystyle \lim_{n \to \infty} b_n \neq 0$.

THEOREM 6.

a. For $a_n > 0$, $\displaystyle \lim_{n \to \infty} a_n = 0$ if and only if $\displaystyle \lim_{n \to \infty} \frac{1}{a_n} = \infty$.

b. For $a_n > 0$, $\displaystyle \lim_{n \to \infty} a_n = \infty$ if and only if $\displaystyle \lim_{n \to \infty} \frac{1}{a_n} = 0$.

Example 5

a. Because $\lim\limits_{n \to \infty} n^3 = \infty$, then by Theorem 6(b), $\lim\limits_{n \to \infty} \dfrac{1}{n^3} = 0$.

b. $\lim\limits_{n \to \infty} \left(2 + \dfrac{1}{n^3} \right) = \lim\limits_{n \to \infty} 2 + \lim\limits_{n \to \infty} \dfrac{1}{n^3}$ [Theorem 5(a)]

$\qquad\qquad\qquad\quad = 2 + 0 = 2$ [Theorem 2 and Example 5a].

Example 6

Find $\lim\limits_{n \to \infty} \dfrac{n + 1}{n}$.

Solution   As $n \to \infty$, the numerator and denominator get arbitrarily large. To describe this we say that the quotient $(n + 1)/n$ has the form ∞/∞. However, we can find the limit by first using some algebra to rewrite $(n + 1)/n$.

$$\lim\limits_{n \to \infty} \frac{n + 1}{n} = \lim\limits_{n \to \infty} \left(\frac{n}{n} + \frac{1}{n} \right)$$

$$= \lim\limits_{n \to \infty} \left(1 + \frac{1}{n} \right)$$

$$= \lim\limits_{n \to \infty} 1 + \lim\limits_{n \to \infty} \frac{1}{n} \qquad \text{[Theorem 5(a)]}$$

$$= 1 + 0 = 1 \qquad \text{[Theorems 2 and 6(b)].}$$

Our result means that as $n \to \infty$, the number $(n + 1)/n$ gets arbitrarily close to 1.

Example 7

Find $\lim\limits_{n \to \infty} \dfrac{2n^2 + 3}{3n^2 + 4n}$.

Solution   As $n \to \infty$, the quotient takes on the form ∞/∞. No algebraic simplification is obvious. A situation like this can be remedied by dividing the numerator and denominator by the greatest power of n that occurs in the denominator (in our case, n^2) and applying Theorem 5. We have

$$\lim_{n \to \infty} \frac{2n^2 + 3}{3n^2 + 4n} = \lim_{n \to \infty} \frac{\dfrac{2n^2 + 3}{n^2}}{\dfrac{3n^2 + 4n}{n^2}}$$

$$= \lim_{n \to \infty} \frac{2 + \dfrac{3}{n^2}}{3 + \dfrac{4}{n}}$$

$$= \frac{\displaystyle\lim_{n \to \infty} \left(2 + \frac{3}{n^2}\right)}{\displaystyle\lim_{n \to \infty} \left(3 + \frac{4}{n}\right)} \qquad \text{[Theorem 5(c)]}$$

$$= \frac{\displaystyle\lim_{n \to \infty} 2 + 3 \lim_{n \to \infty} \frac{1}{n^2}}{\displaystyle\lim_{n \to \infty} 3 + 4 \lim_{n \to \infty} \frac{1}{n}} \qquad \text{[Theorems 5(a) and 3]}$$

$$= \frac{2 + 3(0)}{3 + 4(0)} = \frac{2}{3} \qquad \text{[Theorems 2 and 6(b)].}$$

Example 8

Find $\displaystyle\lim_{n \to \infty} \frac{2n^2}{n^3 + 1}$

Solution   The quotient has the form ∞/∞ as $n \to \infty$. We first divide the numerator and denominator by n^3.

$$\lim_{n \to \infty} \frac{2n^2}{n^3 + 1} = \lim_{n \to \infty} \frac{\dfrac{2n^2}{n^3}}{\dfrac{n^3 + 1}{n^3}} = \lim_{n \to \infty} \frac{\dfrac{2}{n}}{1 + \dfrac{1}{n^3}}$$

$$= \frac{2 \displaystyle\lim_{n \to \infty} \frac{1}{n}}{\displaystyle\lim_{n \to \infty} 1 + \lim_{n \to \infty} \frac{1}{n^3}}$$

$$= \frac{2 \cdot 0}{1 + 0} = \frac{0}{1} = 0.$$

Our approach to the concept of a limit has been intuitive and is in no way rigorous. However, because the limit concept is fundamental in mathematics and lies at the very foundation of higher mathematics, you should have some "feeling" for this notion.

Problem Set 20.4

Find the following limits. In the case of divergence, so state.

1. $\lim\limits_{n \to \infty} (2n)$.

2. $\lim\limits_{n \to \infty} (3n + 4)$.

3. $\lim\limits_{n \to \infty} \left(\dfrac{6}{n}\right)$.

4. $\lim\limits_{n \to \infty} (7 + \frac{1}{3})$.

5. $\lim\limits_{n \to \infty} (3 - \frac{1}{4})$.

6. $\lim\limits_{n \to \infty} \left(\dfrac{-6}{n}\right)$.

7. $\lim\limits_{n \to \infty} (\frac{3}{4})^n$.

8. $\lim\limits_{n \to \infty} (\frac{17}{16})^n$.

9. $\lim\limits_{n \to \infty} [3(\frac{1}{2})^n]$.

10. $\lim\limits_{n \to \infty} \left(\dfrac{n + 1}{2n}\right)$.

11. $\lim\limits_{n \to \infty} \left(\dfrac{3n - 1}{2n}\right)$.

12. $\lim\limits_{n \to \infty} \left(1 + \dfrac{n - 1}{n}\right)$.

13. $\lim\limits_{n \to \infty} \left(\dfrac{n + 3}{4 - n}\right)$.

14. $\lim\limits_{n \to \infty} \left(\dfrac{n^2 - n + 1}{2n^2}\right)$.

15. $\lim\limits_{n \to \infty} \left[\dfrac{1}{5}\left(\dfrac{7}{4}\right)^n\right]$.

16. $\lim\limits_{n \to \infty} \left[8\left(\dfrac{1}{3^n}\right)\right]$.

17. $\lim\limits_{n \to \infty} \dfrac{(100)^n}{(101)^n}$.

18. $\lim\limits_{n \to \infty} \left(\dfrac{3n^2 + 2n + 5}{4n^2}\right)$.

19. $\lim\limits_{n \to \infty} \left(\dfrac{2n^4 - 6n^2 + 5}{n^5}\right)$.

20. $\lim\limits_{n \to \infty} \dfrac{8n^5 - 6n^4 + 3n^3 + 1}{n^6 - 4n^3 + 1}$.

20.5 THE INFINITE GEOMETRIC SERIES

If we are given an infinite sequence, then the indicated sum of its terms

$$a_1 + a_2 + a_3 + \cdots$$

is called an **infinite series** because there are infinitely many terms.

You might at first be alarmed by the notion of an "infinite sum" as just indicated. The word *sum* probably has meaning to you only as far as a finite number of quantities is concerned, and the thought of infinitely many additions may seem awesome. Be assured that we can, in a reasonable way, attach a meaning to such a sum. In fact, it will soon be done, in part, in terms of finite sums. But first, a word about notation.

An infinite series can be represented by the sigma notation

$$\sum_{n=1}^{\infty} a_n = a_1 + a_2 + a_3 + \cdots + a_n + \cdots,$$

where the index n is replaced successively by the integers 1, 2, 3, ... For example,

$$\sum_{n=1}^{\infty} \left(\frac{1}{2}\right)^n = \frac{1}{2} + \left(\frac{1}{2}\right)^2 + \left(\frac{1}{2}\right)^3 + \cdots.$$

If we are given the series $\sum_{n=1}^{\infty} a_n$, then the sum of its first n terms is called the **nth partial sum** of the series and is denoted by S_n:

$$S_1 = a_1$$
$$S_2 = a_1 + a_2 = S_1 + a_2$$
$$S_3 = a_1 + a_2 + a_3 = S_2 + a_3$$
$$\vdots$$
$$S_n = a_1 + a_2 + \cdots + a_n = S_{n-1} + a_n,$$

where S_1 is the first partial sum, S_2 the second partial sum, and so on. Observe that $S_2 = S_1 + a_2$, $S_3 = S_2 + a_3$, ..., $S_n = S_{n-1} + a_n$, and $S_n = \sum_{k=1}^{n} a_k$. The sequence

$$\{S_n\} = S_1, S_2, S_3, \ldots, S_n, \ldots,$$

is called the **sequence of partial sums** of the series.

Example 1

Determine the first four terms of the sequence of partial sums for the series $\sum_{n=1}^{\infty} \frac{1}{n(n+1)}$.

Solution

$$S_1 = \frac{1}{1(1+1)} = \frac{1}{2}$$

$$S_2 = S_1 + \frac{1}{2(2+1)} = \frac{1}{2} + \frac{1}{6} = \frac{2}{3}$$

$$S_3 = S_2 + \frac{1}{3(4)} = \frac{2}{3} + \frac{1}{12} = \frac{3}{4}$$

$$S_4 = S_3 + \frac{1}{4(5)} = \frac{3}{4} + \frac{1}{20} = \frac{4}{5}.$$

Thus the first four terms of $\{S_n\}$ are $\frac{1}{2}, \frac{2}{3}, \frac{3}{4}$, and $\frac{4}{5}$.

If the sequence $\{S_n\}$ of partial sums of the series $\sum_{n=1}^{\infty} a_n$ converges to a finite number L, then L is called the **sum** of the series. That is,

$$\sum_{n=1}^{\infty} a_n = \lim_{n \to \infty} S_n = L.$$

In this case $\sum_{n=1}^{\infty} a_n$ is said to **converge** to L, or to be **convergent**. This means that by adding up a sufficient number of terms of the series, we can approach L as arbitrarily closely as we wish. If $\lim_{n \to \infty} S_n$ does not exist, the series is said to **diverge** or be **divergent**.

We shall now determine the sum of the **infinite geometric series**

$$\sum_{n=1}^{\infty} a_1 r^{n-1} = a_1 + a_1 r + a_1 r^2 + \cdots + a_1 r^{n-1} + \cdots, \qquad \text{where } a_1 \neq 0^*.$$

The nth partial sum, S_n, is

$$S_n = a_1 + a_1 r + a_1 r^2 + \cdots + a_1 r^{n-1},$$

which was previously found to be

$$S_n = \frac{a_1(1 - r^n)}{1 - r}.$$

The limit of S_n as $n \to \infty$ is now considered for the possible values of r.

If $|r| < 1$, then by Theorem 1, $\lim_{n \to \infty} r^n = 0$ and

$$\lim_{n \to \infty} S_n = \lim_{n \to \infty} \frac{a_1(1 - r^n)}{1 - r} = \frac{a_1}{1 - r}.$$

Thus if $|r| < 1$, the geometric series converges to the sum $a_1/(1 - r)$. But if $|r| > 1$, then $\lim_{n \to \infty} r^n$ does not exist, so neither does $\lim_{n \to \infty} S_n$. If $r = 1$, then

$$S_n = a_1 + a_1 + \cdots + a_1 = na_1,$$

which has no limit as $n \to \infty$. If $r = -1$, then

$$S_n = a_1 - a_1 + a_1 - a_1 + \cdots + (\pm a_1).$$

---

* If $a_1 = 0$, then the series is $0 + 0 + \cdots + 0 + \cdots$. We shall not consider this uninteresting case.

This is zero if n is even and is a_1 if n is odd. Hence the series diverges, because a limit of a sequence must be unique. In summary, we have:

The infinite geometric series $\sum_{n=1}^{\infty} a_1 r^{n-1}$ converges if $|r| < 1$ and diverges if $|r| \geq 1$. If the series is convergent, its sum S is given by

$$S = \frac{a_1}{1 - r}.$$ (1)

Example 2

Test the following series for convergence or divergence. In the case of convergence, find the sum.

a. $\sum_{n=1}^{\infty} 8(\frac{1}{2})^n = 4 + 2 + 1 + \frac{1}{2} + \cdots$.

Solution The series is geometric with $a_1 = 4$ and $r = \frac{1}{2}$. Since $|r| < 1$, the series converges and by Eq. 1 the sum S is given by

$$S = \frac{a_1}{1 - r} = \frac{4}{1 - \frac{1}{2}} = \frac{4}{\frac{1}{2}} = 8.$$

b. $6 - 1 + \frac{1}{6} - \frac{1}{36} + \cdots = \sum_{n=1}^{\infty} 6(-\frac{1}{6})^{n-1}$.

Solution The series is geometric with $a_1 = 6$ and $r = -\frac{1}{6}$. Because $|-\frac{1}{6}| < 1$, the series converges and the sum is

$$\frac{a_1}{1 - r} = \frac{6}{1 - (-\frac{1}{6})} = \frac{6}{\frac{7}{6}} = \frac{36}{7}.$$

c. $\sum_{n=1}^{\infty} 4(\frac{5}{3})^n$.

Solution The series is geometric with $r = \frac{5}{3}$. Since $|r| > 1$, the series diverges.

d. $\sum_{n=1}^{\infty} \frac{1}{4^n} = \frac{1}{4} + \frac{1}{16} + \frac{1}{64} + \cdots$.

Solution The series is geometric with $a_1 = \frac{1}{4}$ and $r = \frac{1}{4}$. Since $|r| < 1$, the series converges and the sum is

$$\frac{\frac{1}{4}}{1 - \frac{1}{4}} = \frac{1}{3}.$$

Example 3

The pendulum discussed in Sec. 20.4 had an initial swing of $\frac{1}{2}$ m, and the length of any subsequent swing was one-half the length of the previous swing. How far did the tip of the pendulum move before coming to rest?

Solution We showed that the sequence whose terms give the lengths of the swings is

$$\left\{\frac{1}{2^n}\right\} = \frac{1}{2^1}, \frac{1}{2^2}, \frac{1}{2^3}, \frac{1}{2^4}, \ldots.$$

The corresponding series, which is geometric, is

$$\frac{1}{2} + \frac{1}{4} + \frac{1}{8} + \cdots \frac{1}{2^n} + \cdots.$$

The sum of this series gives the total distance the pendulum tip moves. Here we have $a_1 = \frac{1}{2}$ and $r = \frac{1}{2}$. Thus the sum S is given by

$$S = \frac{\frac{1}{2}}{1 - \frac{1}{2}} = 1 \text{ m}.$$

Example 4

Determine the rational number that corresponds to the repeating decimal $0.\overline{123}$.

Solution The line above the digits 123 is called a **vinculum** and indicates those digits that repeat. Hence

$$0.\overline{123} = 0.123123123\ldots$$

$$= 0.123 + 0.000123 + 0.000000123 + \cdots.$$

Thus the repeating decimal has been expressed as an infinite geometric series with $a_1 = 0.123$ and $r = 0.001$. Therefore, its sum is

$$\frac{0.123}{1 - 0.001} = \frac{0.123}{0.999} = \frac{123}{999} = \frac{41}{333}.$$

That is, $0.\overline{123} = 41/333$.

Problem Set 20.5

In Problems 1–24, find the sum of the series if the sum exists.

1. $\sum\limits_{n=1}^{\infty} (\frac{1}{2})^n.$

2. $\sum\limits_{n=1}^{\infty} (\frac{3}{4})^n.$

3. $\sum\limits_{n=1}^{\infty} (-\frac{2}{3})^n.$

4. $\sum\limits_{n=1}^{\infty} (1.2)^n.$

5. $\sum\limits_{n=1}^{\infty} \left(\frac{7}{6}\right)^n.$

6. $\sum\limits_{n=1}^{\infty} 4\left(\frac{1}{1.1}\right)^n.$

7. $\sum\limits_{k=3}^{\infty} (\frac{3}{5})^{k+2}.$

8. $\sum\limits_{i=5}^{\infty} (-\frac{4}{9})^i.$

9. $\sum\limits_{n=1}^{\infty} 3(-0.2)^n.$

10. $\sum\limits_{n=1}^{\infty} 3(1 - \frac{1}{3})^n.$

11. $\sum\limits_{n=1}^{\infty} 100\left(\frac{1}{4^n}\right).$

12. $\sum\limits_{n=1}^{\infty} \frac{1}{4}(3^n).$

13. $\displaystyle\sum_{n=1}^{2} \left(\tfrac{1}{3}\right)^n.$

14. $\displaystyle\sum_{n=1}^{\infty} \tfrac{9}{4}\left(\tfrac{4}{9}\right)^{n+3}.$

15. $3 + \dfrac{3}{2} + \dfrac{3}{4} + \cdots.$

16. $4 + 1 + \dfrac{1}{4} + \cdots.$

17. $12 + 4 + \dfrac{4}{3} + \cdots.$

18. $\dfrac{1}{1.2} + \dfrac{1}{(1.2)^2} + \dfrac{1}{(1.2)^3} + \cdots.$

19. $-4 + 2 - 1 + \cdots.$

20. $100 - 10 + 1 - 0.1 + \cdots.$

21. $\dfrac{5}{3} + \dfrac{1}{6} + \dfrac{1}{60} + \cdots.$

22. $\dfrac{3}{4} + \dfrac{3}{4^2} + \dfrac{3}{4^3} + \cdots.$

23. $\dfrac{1}{0.1} + \dfrac{1}{(0.1)^2} + \dfrac{1}{(0.1)^3} + \cdots.$

24. $0.02 + 0.002 + 0.0002 + \cdots.$

In Problems **21**–**26**, *determine the rational number that is represented by the given repeating decimal.*

25. $0.\overline{24}.$

26. $0.\overline{42}.$

27. $3.\overline{212}.$

28. $2.0\overline{46}.$

29. $0.021\overline{32}.$

30. $0.15\overline{6}.$

31. When dropped from a height of 4 m, a ball after the first bounce reaches a height of 2 m, after the second bounce a height of 1 m, and so on. What is the total distance traveled by the ball before coming to rest?

32. The tip of a pendulum moves through a distance of 6 cm, after which the distance is constantly decreased on each swing by 10%. Before coming to rest, through what total distance has the tip moved?

33. The first oscillation of a mass suspended on a vertical spring is 20 cm long. If it is observed that the length of each succeeding oscillation decreases by 20%, how far does the mass travel before coming to rest?

34. When a motor is turned off, a flywheel attached to the motor is observed to "coast" to a stop. In the first second it made 190 revolutions, and in each succeeding second it made nine-tenths as many revolutions as the preceding second. How many revolutions did the flywheel make before coming to rest?

35. When a small object is projected up an inclined plane, it is observed to move 10 m in the first second and in any succeeding second it moves four-fifths as far as it did in the preceding second. How far does it travel before coming to rest?

36. The midpoints of the sides of a 10-cm square are joined to form an inscribed square, and this process is continued without end. Find the sum of the areas of all the squares, including the original one.

20.6 THE BINOMIAL THEOREM

In this section we shall develop a formula that gives the series of terms obtained by finding the product or *expansion* of $(a + b)^n$. By using previous rules and direct multiplication, we can find some positive integral powers of the binomial $a + b$.

$$(a + b)^2 = a^2 + 2ab + b^2.$$

$$(a + b)^3 = a^3 + 3a^2b + 3ab^2 + b^3.$$

$$(a + b)^4 = a^4 + 4a^3b + 6a^2b^2 + 4ab^3 + b^4.$$

Looking at our results, we can point out similarities in the expansion of $(a + b)^n$ for $n = 2, 3, 4$.

1. The expansion of $(a + b)^n$ has $n + 1$ terms. For example, in $(a + b)^4$ we have $n = 4$ and the expansion has five terms.
2. The first term is a^n and the last term is b^n.
3. As we move from one term to the next, the exponent for a successively *decreases* by 1 (from n to 1). From the second term on, the exponent for b successively *increases* by 1 (from 1 to n).
4. In each term involving a and b, the sum of the exponents for a and b is n. For example, the second term in the expansion of $(a + b)^4$ contains a^3b^1, and $3 + 1 = 4 = n$.
5. In any term involving b, the exponent for b is one less than the number of the term. For example, the *third* term for $(a + b)^4$ contains b^2, and $2 = 3 - 1$.

We can also find a pattern for the coefficients of the terms in the above expansions of $(a + b)^n$. If the coefficient of any term is multiplied by the exponent for a in that term and then divided by the number of that term, the result is the coefficient of the next term. For example, the first term in the expansion of $(a + b)^4$ is $a^4 = 1 \cdot a^4$. Multiplying the coefficient 1 by the exponent of a (4) and dividing by the number of the term (1), we obtain

$$\frac{1 \cdot 4}{1} = \frac{4}{1},$$

which is the coefficient 4 of the second term. Continuing in this manner, we have

$$(a + b)^4 = a^4 + \frac{4}{1}a^3b + \frac{4}{1} \cdot \frac{3}{2}a^2b^2 + \frac{4}{1} \cdot \frac{3}{2} \cdot \frac{2}{3}ab^3 + b^4 \qquad (1)$$

$$= a^4 + 4a^3b + 6a^2b^2 + 4ab^3 + b^4.$$

In Eq. 1, note that the numerator of the term in which the exponent for b is 2 contains the *two* factors $4 \cdot 3$, and the denominator contains the *two* factors $1 \cdot 2$. Similarly, the numerator of the term in which the exponent for b is 3 contains the *three* factors $4 \cdot 3 \cdot 2$, and the denominator contains the *three* factors $1 \cdot 2 \cdot 3$. Both of these denominators consist of the product of consecutive positive integers and are usually represented by **factorial notation**. If n is a positive integer, then the symbol $n!$, read ***n factorial***, represents the product of the first n positive integers:

$$n! = n(n - 1)(n - 2)(n - 3) \cdots (2)(1).$$

For example,

$$3! = 3 \cdot 2 \cdot 1 = 6$$

$$4! = 4 \cdot 3 \cdot 2 \cdot 1 = 4 \cdot 3! = 4(6) = 24.$$

We define $0!$ to be 1. Using factorial notation, we can express the term involving b^r in the expansion of $(a + b)^n$ as

$$\overbrace{\frac{n(n - 1)(n - 2)\cdots(n - r + 1)}{r!}}^{r \text{ factors}} a^{n-r}b^r .$$

All the patterns that we have observed carry over to the expansion of $(a + b)^n$, where n is *any* positive integer. In summary we have the **binomial theorem**:

BINOMIAL THEOREM

If n is a positive integer, then

$$(a + b)^n = a^n + \frac{n}{1!} a^{n-1}b + \frac{n(n - 1)}{2!} a^{n-2}b^2 + \cdots$$

$$+ \frac{n(n - 1)(n - 2)\cdots(n - r + 1)}{r!} a^{n-r}b^r + \cdots + b^n.$$

Example 1

Use the binomial theorem to expand $(x + 2)^5$.

Solution   We replace a by x, b by 2, and n by 5. The expansion will have six terms.

$$(x + 2)^5 = x^5 + \frac{5}{1!} x^4(2) + \frac{5\cdot 4}{2!} x^3(2)^2 + \frac{5\cdot 4\cdot 3}{3!} x^2(2)^3 + \frac{5\cdot 4\cdot 3\cdot 2}{4!} x(2)^4 + (2)^5.$$

This simplifies to

$$(x + 2)^5 = x^5 + 10x^4 + 40x^3 + 80x^2 + 80x + 32.$$

Example 2

Write the first four terms in the expansion of $(a + b)^{20}$.

Solution   Using the binomial theorem with $n = 20$ gives

$$(a + b)^{20} = a^{20} + \frac{20}{1!} a^{19}b + \frac{20\cdot 19}{2!} a^{18}b^2 + \frac{20\cdot 19\cdot 18}{3!} a^{17}b^3 + \cdots$$

$$= a^{20} + 20a^{19}b + 190a^{18}b^2 + 1140a^{17}b^3 + \cdots.$$

Example 3

Expand $(3x^2 - 1)^4$.

Solution Noting that $(3x^2 - 1)^4 = [3x^2 + (-1)]^4$, we use the binomial theorem with $a = 3x^2$, $b = -1$, and $n = 4$.

$$(3x^2 - 1)^4 = (3x^2)^4 + \frac{4}{1!}(3x^2)^3(-1) + \frac{4 \cdot 3}{2!}(3x^2)^2(-1)^2 + \frac{4 \cdot 3 \cdot 2}{3!}(3x^2)(-1)^3 + (-1)^4$$

$$= 3^4 x^8 + 4(3)^3 x^6(-1) + 6(3)^2 x^4(1) + 4(3)x^2(-1) + 1$$

$$= 81x^8 - 108x^6 + 54x^4 - 12x^2 + 1.$$

Example 4

Find the sixth term in the expansion of $\left(x + \dfrac{2}{y}\right)^{15}$.

Solution Here x plays the role of a, $2/y$ plays the role of b, and $n = 15$. In the sixth term, the exponent for $2/y$ is 5, so the exponent for x is 10. The numerator of the coefficient consists of five decreasing factors beginning with 15, and the denominator is 5! This gives

$$\frac{(15)(14)(13)(12)(11)}{5!} x^{10}\left(\frac{2}{y}\right)^5,$$

which simplifies to

$$\frac{96,096x^{10}}{y^5}.$$

Setting $a = 1$ and $b = x$ in the binomial theorem, we obtain the **binomial series**:

$$(1 + x)^n = 1 + nx + \frac{n(n-1)}{2!}x^2 + \cdots + \frac{n(n-1)\cdots(n-r+1)}{r!}x^r + \cdots,$$

which for $|x| < 1$ can be shown to be a valid equation for **any real number n**. When n is not a positive integer, the series is unending, but nevertheless we can get a reasonable approximation to $(1 + x)^n$ in most cases by considering a few terms only.

Example 5

Write the first four terms of $(1 + x)^{-2}$.

Solution This is the binomial series with $n = -2$.

$$(1 + x)^{-2} = 1 + (-2)x + \frac{(-2)(-3)}{2!}x^2 + \frac{(-2)(-3)(-4)}{3!}x^3 + \cdots$$

$$= 1 - 2x + 3x^2 - 4x^3 + \cdots.$$

Example 6

Approximate $\sqrt{104}$ to three decimal places by using the binomial series.

Solution We can write

$$\sqrt{104} = \sqrt{100 + 4} = \sqrt{100(1 + \tfrac{4}{100})}$$
$$= 10(1 + \tfrac{1}{25})^{1/2}.$$

Because $|\tfrac{1}{25}| < 1$, we can use the binomial series with $x = \tfrac{1}{25}$ and $n = \tfrac{1}{2}$:

$$\sqrt{104} = 10\left[1 + \frac{1}{2}\left(\frac{1}{25}\right) + \frac{\tfrac{1}{2}(-\tfrac{1}{2})}{2!}\left(\frac{1}{25}\right)^2 + \cdots \right]$$
$$= 10\left(1 + \frac{1}{50} - \frac{1}{5000} + \cdots \right)$$
$$= 10(1 + 0.02 - 0.0002 + \cdots)$$
$$\approx 10(1.0198),$$
$$\sqrt{104} \approx 10.198.$$

Considering more terms in this series would not have contributed to the accuracy of the desired approximation. Compare our answer to that obtained with a calculator.

Problem Set 20.6

In Problems 1–12, use the binomial theorem to expand each expression and simplify.

1. $(x + 4)^3$.
2. $(x - 3)^3$.
3. $(y - 2)^4$.
4. $(y + 3)^5$.
5. $(3x + 1)^5$.
6. $(x + h)^6$.
7. $(2z - y)^4$.
8. $(z^2 - 2)^3$.
9. $\left(a - \dfrac{1}{b}\right)^5$.
10. $(x - 2y)^6$.
11. $\left(1 + \dfrac{x}{y^2}\right)^6$.
12. $\left(\dfrac{x}{y} + \dfrac{y}{x}\right)^4$.

In Problems 13–20, find the first three terms in the binomial expansion of each expression and simplify.

13. $(x + 1)^{100}$.
14. $(x - 1)^{45}$.
15. $(2x - 3)^7$.
16. $(x + 2)^8$.
17. $(y^2 - 5x)^{10}$.
18. $(y^3 - 6)^{12}$.
19. $\left(3z^2 + \dfrac{x}{3}\right)^5$.
20. $(a^2 + b^2)^{20}$.

In Problems 21–28, find only the indicated term(s) and simplify.

21. The fourth term of $(x + y)^{15}$.
22. The fifth term of $(\tfrac{1}{2}x - y)^{10}$.
23. The sixth term of $\left(2x - \dfrac{3}{y}\right)^8$.
24. The fourth term of $\left(\dfrac{1}{x^2} - y\right)^7$.

25. The middle term of $(x - 2y)^6$.

26. The middle terms of $\left(\dfrac{1}{x} + \dfrac{1}{y}\right)^5$.

27. The term involving x^6 in $(x^3 - y)^5$.

28. The term involving x^8 in $(2y - 3x^2)^7$.

In Problems 29–32, find the first four terms in the expansion of the given expression and simplify.

29. $(1 + x)^{-3}$.

30. $(1 + x)^{2/3}$.

31. $(1 - y)^{1/2}$.

32. $(1 - x)^{1/4}$.

In Problems 33–40, approximate the given number to three decimal places by using the binomial series.

33. $\sqrt{50}$.

34. $\sqrt{26}$.

35. $\sqrt{61}$.

36. $\sqrt{99}$.

37. $\sqrt[3]{29}$.

38. $\sqrt[3]{66}$.

39. $\sqrt[4]{80}$.

40. $(1.02)^{-4}$.

20.7 REVIEW

Important Terms and Symbols

Section 20.1   Sequence, term of sequence, general term of sequence, a_n, sigma notation, $\sum$, index of summation, upper limit of summation, lower limit of summation.

Section 20.2   Arithmetic progression, common difference (d).

Section 20.3   Geometric progression, common ratio (r).

Section 20.4   Limit of sequence, $\lim\limits_{n \to \infty} a_n = a$, convergent sequence, divergent sequence.

Section 20.5   Infinite series, $\sum\limits_{n=1}^{\infty} a_n$, nth partial sum, sequence of partial sums, sum of infinite series, convergent series, divergent series, infinite geometric series.

Section 20.6   Factorial notation, n factorial $(n!)$, binomial theorem, binomial series.

Formula Summary

Arithmetic Progression

$$a_n = a_1 + (n - 1)d$$

$$S_n = \frac{n}{2}(a_1 + a_n)$$

$$= \frac{n}{2}[2a_1 + (n - 1)d]$$

Geometric Progression

$$a_n = a_1 r^{n-1}$$

$$S_n = \frac{a_1(1 - r^n)}{1 - r} \quad \text{if } r \neq 1$$

$$= na_1 \qquad \text{if } r = 1$$

Infinite Geometric Series

$$S = \frac{a_1}{1 - r} \quad \text{if } |r| < 1$$

Binomial Theorem

$$(a + b)^n = a^n + \frac{n}{1!} a^{n-1}b + \frac{n(n-1)}{2!} a^{n-2}b^2 + \cdots$$

$$+ \frac{n(n-1)(n-2) \cdots (n-r+1)}{r!} a^{n-r}b^r + \cdots + b^n$$

Review Questions

1. An infinite sequence is a function whose domain is the set of _____.

2. The sixth term of the sequence $\left\{ (-1)^{n+1} \dfrac{2n}{n+1} \right\}$ is _____.

3. The sequence $\frac{1}{2}, \frac{2}{4}, \frac{3}{8}, \ldots$ has a general term given by _____.

4. The sequence $-6, 2, 10, \ldots$ is a(n) __(a)__ progression whose __(b)__ is 8.

5. For an arithmetic progression, the nth term is given by the formula __(a)__ and the sum of the first n terms is given by the formula __(b)__.

6. For a geometric progression, the nth term is given by the formula __(a)__ and the sum of the first n terms is given by the formula __(b)__.

7. The sixth term of the series $\sum\limits_{i=1}^{10} (-1)^{i+1} x^{2i}$ is _____.

8. As n increases without bound, the sequence $\{1/n\}$ converges to _____.

9. The limit of any arithmetic progression with difference $d \neq 0$ (does)(does not) exist.

10. $\sum\limits_{n=1}^{\infty} r^n$ converges if _____.

11. The last term in the expansion of $(a + 2b)^{19}$ is _____.

12. True or false: For a sequence to have the number 2 as a limit, all the terms from some point on must be equal to 2. _____

13. The sequence $4, -4, 4, -4, \ldots$ (does)(does not) converge.

14. For what value(s) of a does the sequence $a, -a, a, -a, \ldots$ converge? _____

15. The sum of the geometric series $2 + 1 + \frac{1}{2} + \cdots$ is _____.

16. The value of $4!$ is _____.

17. The number of terms in the expansion of $(4x - 1)^8$ is _____.

18. The geometric progression $1, 1 + r, (1 + r)^2, (1 + r)^3$ has a common ratio of _____.

Answers to Review Questions

1. Positive integers.   2. $-\frac{12}{7}$.   3. $n/2^n$.   4. (a) Arithmetic,   (b) Common difference.
5. (a) $a_n = a_1 + (n - 1)d$,   (b) $S_n = n(a_1 + a_n)/2$.
6. (a) $a_n = a_1 r^{n-1}$,   (b) $S_n = a_1(1 - r^n)/(1 - r)$.   7. $-x^{12}$.   8. 0.   9. Does not.
10. $|r| < 1$.   11. $2^{19}b^{19}$.   12. False (to see this, consider the counterexample $\{2 - 1/n\}$).
13. Does not.   14. $a = 0$.   15. 4.   16. 24.   17. 9.   18. $1 + r$.

Review Problems

*In Problems **1** and **2**, find the tenth term of the given arithmetic progression.*

1. 3, 8, 13, ...

2. 7, 4, 1, ...

*In Problems **3** and **4**, find the sixth term of the given geometric progression.*

3. $8, -2, \frac{1}{2}, \ldots$.

4. 3, 12, 48, ...

*In Problems **5** and **6**, evaluate.*

5. $\displaystyle\sum_{n=1}^{5} (n^2 - 2n)$.

6. $\displaystyle\sum_{n=0}^{4} (-1)^n (2^n - 1)$.

7. Find $1 + \frac{1}{2} + (\frac{1}{2})^2 + \cdots + (\frac{1}{2})^6$.

8. Find $1 + 3 + 5 + \cdots + 33$.

9. How many terms of the sequence $-16, -12, -8, \ldots$ must be added to give a sum of 44?

10. Find the sum of all odd integers between 30 and 60.

11. The twelfth term of an arithmetic progression is -12 and the twenty-third term is 20. Find the sixteenth term.

12. The first term of a geometric progression is 36 and the third term is $\frac{1}{4}$. Find the fifth term.

13. Find the sum $1 + \frac{1}{4} + \frac{1}{16} + \cdots$.

14. Find the sum $1 - \frac{1}{4} + \frac{1}{16} - \cdots$.

15. A ball is released from an initial height of 8 m. After each contact with the floor, the ball rebounds to a height that is three-fourths of the height from which it last fell. What height does the ball reach on the fifth bounce?

16. For the ball in Problem 15, what is the total distance that the ball travels before coming to rest?

*In Problems **17–20**, find the limit, if it exists.*

17. $\displaystyle\lim_{n \to \infty} \frac{2}{n^2}$.

18. $\displaystyle\lim_{n \to \infty} \left(\frac{3}{2}\right)^n$.

19. $\displaystyle\lim_{n \to \infty} \frac{6n^2 + 5n}{1 - 2n^2}$.

20. $\displaystyle\lim_{n \to \infty} \frac{4n^2 + 2n + 5}{n^3 + 4n}$.

In Problems **21–24**, use the binomial theorem to expand each expression.

21. $(x - 4)^4$.

22. $(2x + 1)^5$.

23. $(x^3 + 2y)^3$.

24. $\left(1 - \dfrac{x}{3}\right)^6$.

25. Find the middle term of $(2 - \frac{1}{2}x^2)^{12}$.

26. By using the binomial series, approximate $\sqrt[3]{124}$ to three decimal places.

27. Find $\displaystyle\sum_{k=1}^{\infty} (\tfrac{4}{9})^k$.

28. In the series $1 + \frac{1}{2} + \frac{1}{4} + \cdots$, what is the numerical difference between the nth partial sum and the limit of the nth partial sum?

29. The sum of an infinite geometric series is 6 and the first term is 2. What is the second term?

30. The value of the fifth term in the expansion of $(a + 2)^5$ is 48 for a particular value of a. Find this value.

31. A 12-hour clock strikes once at 1 o'clock, twice at 2 o'clock, and so on. How many strikes will it make in 24 *consecutive* hours?

21

Analytic Geometry

21.1 THE CONIC SECTIONS

In Chapter 8 the properties of straight lines were determined from their algebraic equations. In the following sections we extend the concepts of analytic geometry and concern ourselves with four curves that may be formed by the intersection of a plane with a *right circular cone*.

A **right circular cone** can be thought of as the surface generated by a rotating line that passes through a certain point, called the **vertex** of the cone, and a certain circle (see Fig. 21.1). Any line on the surface of the cone that intersects the vertex is called an **element**, or **generator**, of the cone. The **axis** of the cone is the line through the vertex that makes equal angles with all elements of the cone. The cone extends indefinitely on both sides of its vertex and can be spoken of as a *double right circular cone*. The part of the cone on one side of the vertex is called a **nappe**; the cone has an *upper nappe* and a *lower nappe*.

The **conic sections**, or **conics**, are the *circle*, the *parabola*, the *ellipse*, and the *hyperbola*. They are shown in Fig. 21.2, where the type of curve obtained depends on how the intersecting plane cuts the cone. An **ellipse** occurs when an intersecting plane is not parallel to any generator, as in Fig. 21.2(c). If, in addition, the intersecting plane is perpendicular to the axis of the cone, a **circle** occurs, as in (a). In a sense, a circle can be considered a special case of an ellipse. A **parabola** occurs when the intersecting plane is parallel to an element of the cone, as in (b). The **hyperbola** in (d) occurs when the intersecting plane cuts both nappes.

739

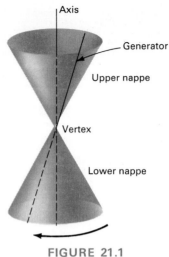

FIGURE 21.1

In comparison to these **regular conics**, certain special cuts in which the intersecting plane passes through the vertex give rise to the **degenerate conics**. If, in the case of Fig. 21.2(a), the intersecting plane also passes through the vertex, the resulting intersection is merely a point. The degenerate case of the hyperbola, namely two intersecting straight lines, occurs when the intersecting plane also contains the axis of the cone, as shown in Fig. 21.3(a). Finally, the parabola degenerates to a straight line if the intersecting plane also passes through the vertex, as shown in Fig. 21.3(b).

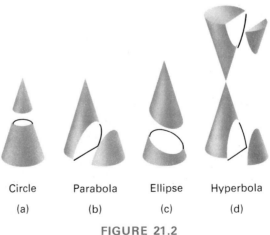

Circle	Parabola	Ellipse	Hyperbola
(a)	(b)	(c)	(d)

FIGURE 21.2

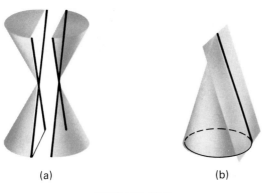

(a)   (b)

FIGURE 21.3

21.2 THE DISTANCE FORMULA

If $P_1(x_1, y_1)$ and $P_2(x_2, y_2)$ are two points in the xy-plane, a formula can be derived for the distance between them—that is, for the length d of the line segment joining the points (see Fig. 21.4). Through P_1 and P_2 we construct horizontal and vertical

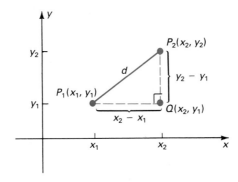

FIGURE 21.4

segments, respectively, which intersect at $Q(x_2, y_1)$. Thus a right triangle P_1QP_2 is formed; its hypotenuse has length d and its sides have lengths $x_2 - x_1$ and $y_2 - y_1$. By the Pythagorean theorem,

$$d^2 = (x_2 - x_1)^2 + (y_2 - y_1)^2.$$

Since d cannot be negative, we obtain the *distance formula*:

> **DISTANCE FORMULA**
>
> $$d = \sqrt{(x_2 - x_1)^2 + (y_2 - y_1)^2}.$$

Because $(x_2 - x_1)^2 = (x_1 - x_2)^2$ and $(y_2 - y_1)^2 = (y_1 - y_2)^2$, the order of the subscripts in the distance formula is immaterial. Thus, given any two points, the distance between these points can be determined by choosing either point as (x_1, y_1) in the formula.

Example 1

Find the distance between the given points.

a. $(5, -2)$ and $(-3, 4)$.

Solution Letting $(5, -2) = (x_1, y_1)$ and $(-3, 4) = (x_2, y_2)$, by the distance formula we have

$$d = \sqrt{(x_2 - x_1)^2 + (y_2 - y_1)^2}$$
$$= \sqrt{(-3 - 5)^2 + [4 - (-2)]^2}$$
$$= \sqrt{(-8)^2 + (6)^2} = \sqrt{64 + 36}$$
$$= \sqrt{100} = 10.$$

If we choose $(-3, 4)$ as (x_1, y_1), we would get the same result.

b. $(3, -6)$ and the origin.

Solution Let $(0, 0) = (x_1, y_1)$ and $(3, -6) = (x_2, y_2)$. Then

$$d = \sqrt{(x_2 - x_1)^2 + (y_2 - y_1)^2}$$
$$= \sqrt{(3 - 0)^2 + (-6 - 0)^2}$$
$$= \sqrt{9 + 36} = \sqrt{45} = 3\sqrt{5}.$$

Problem Set 21.2

Find the distance between the given points.

1. $(2, 3), (5, 7)$.
2. $(4, 5), (12, 11)$.
3. $(0, 5), (2, -2)$.
4. $(1, 3), (1, 4)$.
5. $(-1, -2), (-3, -4)$.
6. $(-4, 4)$, origin.
7. $(2, -3), (-5, -3)$.
8. $(-\frac{3}{2}, \frac{1}{2}), (\frac{1}{2}, \frac{3}{2})$.
9. $(1, -\frac{1}{2})$, origin.
10. $(4, 0), (-1, \sqrt{11})$.
11. $(-5, 0), (0, -12)$.
12. $(0, -2), (-5, -2)$.

21.3 THE CIRCLE

A **circle** is the set of all points in a plane that are at a given distance from a fixed point in the plane.

The fixed point is called the **center**, and the given distance is the **radius** of the circle. In general, suppose that a circle has a radius of r and has its center at (h, k), as in Fig. 21.5. Let (x, y) be any point on the circle. Then its distance from (h, k)

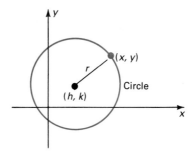

FIGURE 21.5

must be r. Applying the distance formula to (h, k) and (x, y) gives

$$\sqrt{(x - h)^2 + (y - k)^2} = r.$$

Squaring both sides, we have

$$(x - h)^2 + (y - k)^2 = r^2.$$

Any point on the circle must satisfy this equation. Also, it can be shown that all points satisfying the equation lie on the circle. Thus we have the following formula.

$$(x - h)^2 + (y - k)^2 = r^2 \tag{1}$$

is the **standard form** of an equation of the circle with center (h, k) and radius r.

Example 1

Find the standard form of an equation of the circle with the given center and radius.

a. Center $(0, 0)$ and radius $\sqrt{3}$.

   Solution   We use Eq. 1 with $h = 0$, $k = 0$, and $r = \sqrt{3}$.

$$(x - h)^2 + (y - k)^2 = r^2$$
$$(x - 0)^2 + (y - 0)^2 = (\sqrt{3})^2$$
$$x^2 + y^2 = 3.$$

In general,

$$x^2 + y^2 = r^2$$

(2)

is the standard form of an equation of the circle with center at the origin and radius r.

b. Center $(-3, 2)$ and radius 4.

Solution We use Eq. 1 with $h = -3$, $k = 2$, and $r = 4$.

$$(x - h)^2 + (y - k)^2 = r^2$$
$$[x - (-3)]^2 + (y - 2)^2 = 4^2$$
$$(x + 3)^2 + (y - 2)^2 = 16.$$

Example 2

Describe the graph of the given equation.

a. $(x - 1)^2 + (y + 4)^2 = 9$.

Solution This has the form of Eq. 1. By writing this equation as

$$(x - 1)^2 + [y - (-4)]^2 = (3)^2,$$

we see that $h = 1$, $k = -4$, and $r = 3$. Thus the graph is a circle with center $(1, -4)$ and radius 3.

b. $x^2 + y^2 = 5$.

Solution This has the form of Eq. 2 with $r^2 = 5$. Thus $r = \sqrt{5}$. The graph is a circle with center at the origin and radius $\sqrt{5}$.

If we expand the terms in the standard form of a circle, we have

$$(x - h)^2 + (y - k)^2 = r^2$$
$$x^2 - 2hx + h^2 + y^2 - 2ky + k^2 = r^2$$
$$x^2 + y^2 + (-2h)x + (-2k)y + (h^2 + k^2 - r^2) = 0 \qquad \text{[rearranging]}.$$

Because h, k, and r are constants, this equation has the form

$$x^2 + y^2 + Dx + Ey + F = 0,$$

(3)

where D, E, and F are constants. Equation 3 is called the **general form** of an equation of a circle. If an equation cannot be put in this form, its graph is not a circle.

Example 3

Find the general form of an equation of the circle with center $(1, 4)$ and radius 2.

Solution   The standard form is

$$(x - 1)^2 + (y - 4)^2 = 2^2.$$

Expanding gives

$$x^2 - 2x + 1 + y^2 - 8y + 16 = 4$$

$$x^2 + y^2 - 2x - 8y + 13 = 0,$$

which is the general form.

We can determine the center and radius of a circle given in general form by using the method of completing the square to express the circle in standard form. For example, the equation

$$x^2 + y^2 - 6x + 10y + 5 = 0$$

has the general form of Eq. 3. Regrouping gives

$$(x^2 - 6x) + (y^2 + 10y) = -5.$$

Completing the squares in x and y, we have

$$(x^2 - 6x + 9) + (y^2 + 10y + 25) = -5 + 9 + 25,$$

or the standard form

$$(x - 3)^2 + (y + 5)^2 = 29.$$

Thus the graph of the given equation is a circle with center $(3, -5)$ and radius $\sqrt{29}$.

Example 4

Describe the graphs of the following equations.

a. $x^2 + y^2 - y = 0.$

Solution   We complete the square.

$$x^2 + y^2 - y = 0$$

$$x^2 + (y^2 - y) = 0$$

$$x^2 + (y^2 - y + \tfrac{1}{4}) = \tfrac{1}{4} \qquad \text{[completing the square]}$$

$$(x - 0)^2 + (y - \tfrac{1}{2})^2 = (\tfrac{1}{2})^2 \qquad \text{[standard form]}.$$

The graph is a circle with center $(0, \tfrac{1}{2})$ and radius $\tfrac{1}{2}$.

b. $2x^2 + 2y^2 + 8x - 3y + 5 = 0$.

Solution To complete the squares, we first get the coefficients of the x^2- and y^2-terms to be 1. Thus we divide both sides by 2.

$$x^2 + y^2 + 4x - \tfrac{3}{2}y + \tfrac{5}{2} = 0$$

$$(x^2 + 4x) + (y^2 - \tfrac{3}{2}y) = -\tfrac{5}{2} \qquad \text{[regrouping]}$$

$$(x^2 + 4x + 4) + (y^2 - \tfrac{3}{2}y + \tfrac{9}{16}) = -\tfrac{5}{2} + 4 + \tfrac{9}{16} \qquad \text{[completing the squares]}$$

$$(x + 2)^2 + (y - \tfrac{3}{4})^2 = \tfrac{33}{16}.$$

Thus the graph is a circle with center $(-2, \tfrac{3}{4})$ and radius $\sqrt{\tfrac{33}{16}}$ or $\sqrt{33}/4$.

Every circle has an equation of the general form $x^2 + y^2 + Dx + Ey + F = 0$. But an equation of this form does not always have a circle as its graph. The graph could be a point, or there may not be any graph at all. For example, the equation

$$x^2 + y^2 - 2x - 6y + 10 = 0 \qquad (4)$$

may be written

$$(x^2 - 2x + 1) + (y^2 - 6y + 9) = -10 + 1 + 9$$

$$(x - 1)^2 + (y - 3)^2 = 0.$$

This implies a center at $(1, 3)$, but a radius of 0. Thus the graph is the single point $(1, 3)$. Also, if the 10 in Eq. 4 were replaced by 11, then we would have the equation

$$(x - 1)^2 + (y - 3)^2 = -1.$$

This implies that r^2 is -1, a negative number. But, for a circle, r^2 cannot be negative. Thus the equation does not define a circle. In fact, because the left side of the equation is a sum of squares, it can never have a negative value. Therefore the equation has no graph.

Problem Set 21.3

In Problems **1–6**, *find the standard and general forms of an equation of the circle with the given center C and radius r.*

1. $C = (2, 3)$, $r = 6$.
2. $C = (4, -5)$, $r = 2$.
3. $C = (-1, 6)$, $r = 4$.
4. $C = (-2, -3)$, $r = 1$.
5. $C = (0, 0)$, $r = \tfrac{1}{2}$.
6. $C = (3, 0)$, $r = \sqrt{3}$.

In Problems **7–12**, *give the center C and radius r of the circle with the given equation. Also, sketch the circle.*

7. $x^2 + y^2 = 9$
8. $(x - 1)^2 + (y - 2)^2 = 1$.
9. $(x - 3)^2 + (y + 4)^2 = 2$.
10. $(x + 6)^2 + (y + 1)^2 = 3^2$.
11. $(x + 2)^2 + y^2 = 1$.
12. $x^2 + (y - 3)^2 = 16$.

In Problems **13-24**, *describe the graph of the given equation.*

13. $x^2 + y^2 - 2x - 4y - 4 = 0$.

14. $x^2 + y^2 + 4x - 6y + 9 = 0$.

15. $x^2 + y^2 + 6y + 5 = 0$.

16. $x^2 + y^2 - 12x + 27 = 0$.

17. $x^2 + y^2 + 2x - 2y + 3 = 0$.

18. $x^2 + y^2 + 6x - 2y - 15 = 0$.

19. $x^2 + y^2 - 14x + 4y + 38 = 0$.

20. $x^2 + y^2 + 4y - 8x + 21 = 0$.

21. $x^2 + y^2 - 3x + y + \frac{5}{2} = 0$.

22. $9x^2 + 9y^2 - 6x + 18y + 9 = 0$.

23. $2x^2 + 2y^2 - 4x + 7y + 2 = 0$.

24. $16x^2 + 16y^2 + 24x - 48y - 3 = 0$.

Recall that in Chapter 12 we considered nonlinear systems of equations. In Problems **25-28**, *you are given a system of two equations. Use a rough sketch to predict the number of different real solutions of each system.*

25. $\begin{cases} x^2 + y^2 = 4 \\ x^2 - 2x + y^2 - 2y = 2. \end{cases}$

26. $\begin{cases} x^2 - 4x + y^2 = -3 \\ x^2 - 10x + y^2 = -21. \end{cases}$

27. $\begin{cases} x^2 + y^2 = 1 \\ x^2 - 6x + y^2 = -8. \end{cases}$

28. $\begin{cases} x^2 + y^2 = 9 \\ x - y = 1. \end{cases}$

29. Which of the following equations are *not* equations of circles?
   (a) $x^2 + y^2 = 4$.
   (b) $x^2 + 2y^2 = 4$.
   (c) $x^2 - (y - 2)^2 = 4$.
   (d) $x^2 + 2xy + y^2 = 4$.
   (e) $2x^2 + 2y^2 = 4$.
   (f) $2x + 2y = 4$.
   (g) $\dfrac{1}{x^2} + \dfrac{1}{y^2} = \dfrac{1}{4}$.

30. A particle moves in a coordinate plane so that it is always twice as far from $(4, 0)$ as from $(1, 0)$. Determine whether its path is a circle.

31. A racing automobile travels around a circular track at a speed of 52.80 m/s and makes one revolution every 39.25 s. Taking the origin of a coordinate system at the center of the track and approximating π by 3.14, determine an equation of the path of the automobile.

32. When a particle with mass m and charge q enters a magnetic field of induction B with a velocity v at right angles to B, it can be shown that the particle will travel in a circle of radius r, where

$$r = \frac{mv}{qB}.$$

This is one of the basic operating principles of a mass spectrograph and an important consideration in the design of cyclotrons. If a singly charged lithium ion enters a magnetic field of induction $B = 0.4$ webers/m^2 with a speed of 1.17×10^5 m/s, determine an equation of its circular path. For this ion, $q = 1.60 \times 10^{-19}$ C and $m = 1.16 \times 10^{-26}$ kg. (Assume that r is in meters.)

21.4 THE PARABOLA

> A **parabola** is the set of all points in a plane that are equidistant from a given straight line and a given point not on the line.

The given point is called the **focus** and the given line the **directrix**. Let $2p$, where $p > 0$, be the distance from the focus to the directrix. In Fig. 21.6, for convenience we choose the focus at $F(0, p)$ and the directrix having equation $y = -p$.

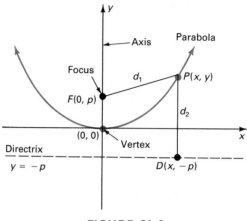

FIGURE 21.6

The line through the focus and perpendicular to the directrix is called the **axis** of the parabola. The axis is a *line of symmetry* in the sense that if a mirror were placed along the axis, then half of the parabola is the mirror image of the other half. The origin lies on the parabola, since it is the midpoint of the segment of the axis that connects the focus and the directrix.

To find an equation of the parabola, we first select an arbitrary point $P(x, y)$ on the parabola. It should be clear that the point of intersection of the directrix and the perpendicular to the directrix from P is $D(x, -p)$, as shown. From the definition of a parabola and the distance formula, we have

$$d_1 = d_2,$$
$$\sqrt{(x - 0)^2 + (y - p)^2} = \sqrt{(x - x)^2 + (y + p)^2}.$$

Squaring both sides yields

$$x^2 + (y - p)^2 = (y + p)^2,$$
$$x^2 + y^2 - 2py + p^2 = y^2 + 2py + p^2.$$

Simplifying gives

$$\boxed{x^2 = 4py.}$$

The coordinates of every point on the parabola satisfy this equation. It can also be shown that any point with coordinates that satisfy $x^2 = 4py$ is a point on the parabola. The equation $x^2 = 4py$ is called the **standard form** of an equation of the parabola with focus at $(0, p)$ and directrix $y = -p$.

The point at which a parabola intersects its axis is called the **vertex** of the parabola. It is the midpoint of the segment of the axis that joins the focus and the directrix. The vertex of the parabola described above is at the origin.

More generally, a parabola with vertex at the origin and a coordinate axis for its axis has four possible orientations, the equations of which can be derived in the manner above. The possibilities are indicated in Fig. 21.7. There is no need for you to

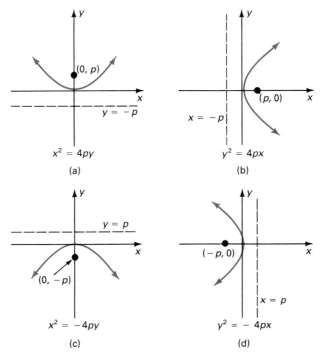

FIGURE 21.7

memorize which type of parabola corresponds to each equation, for the equation itself reveals the orientation of the parabola it represents. Consider, for example, Fig. 21.7(b) and the equation $y^2 = 4px$. Because p is considered positive and y^2 is never negative, it follows that x [or $y^2/(4p)$] is never negative. Thus the parabola opens to the right, as the graph indicates. You are urged to interpret mentally the remaining graphs and equations of Fig. 21.7 in a similar manner. In each case, *p is the distance from the vertex to the focus.* Note that Figs. 21.7(b) and (d) are *not* graphs of functions of x.

Example 1

Find the vertex, focus, and equation of the directrix of the parabola given by $y^2 = -16x$. Sketch the graph.

Solution   This equation has the standard form $y^2 = -4px$, so the vertex of the parabola is at the origin. Because $x = y^2/-16$, x is never positive, so the parabola must open to the left, as shown in Fig. 21.8. Also,

$$4p = 16$$

$$p = 4.$$

Thus the distance from the vertex to the focus is 4, so the focus is at $(-4, 0)$. The equation of the directrix is $x = 4$. To aid you in sketching the graph, we remark that the "*width*" *of a parabola at its focus is 4p.** This means that the parabola $y^2 = -16x$ is 16 units wide along a line perpendicular to its axis and passing through $(-4, 0)$. From this information we plot the points $(-4, 8)$ and $(-4, -8)$. The graph is given in Fig. 21.8.

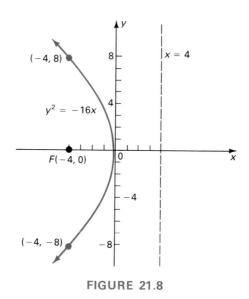

FIGURE 21.8

Example 2

Determine an equation of the parabola with vertex at $V(0, 0)$ and focus at $F(0, -\frac{3}{2})$.

Solution   Refer to Fig. 21.9. From the locations of the focus and vertex, the parabola must open downward and, as a result, y is never positive. Hence, an equation of the parabola has the form $x^2 = -4py$. Because p, the distance from the focus to the vertex, is $\frac{3}{2}$, the required equation is

$$x^2 = -4(\tfrac{3}{2})y$$

$$x^2 = -6y.$$

* The line segment passing through the focus, perpendicular to the axis, and with its ends on the parabola is called the *latus rectum*. Thus the width of the latus rectum is 4p.

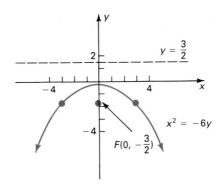

FIGURE 21.9

Consider the parabola with its axis parallel to the x-axis and its vertex at the point $V(h, k)$ as shown in Fig. 21.10, where $2p$, $p > 0$, is the distance from the focus to the directrix. The focus must be at $F(h + p, k)$ and the directrix must be the line $x = h - p$. From the dimensions shown in the diagram, we can deduce that the point of intersection of the directrix and a perpendicular to the directrix from an arbitary point (x, y) on the parabola is $D(h - p, y)$. From the definition of a parabola,

$$d_2 = d_1$$

$$\sqrt{[x - (h + p)]^2 + (y - k)^2} = \sqrt{[x - (h - p)]^2 + (y - y)^2}.$$

Squaring both sides and simplifying yields

$$y^2 - 2ky + k^2 = 4px - 4hp,$$

which can be written in the *standard form*

$$\boxed{(y - k)^2 = 4p(x - h).}$$

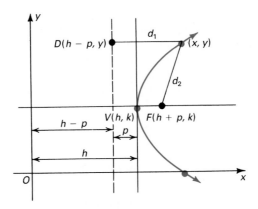

FIGURE 21.10

In a similar manner the standard forms of equations of other parabolas with vertex at (h, k) and axis parallel to a coordinate axis can be derived. The four possibilities are shown in Fig. 21.11.

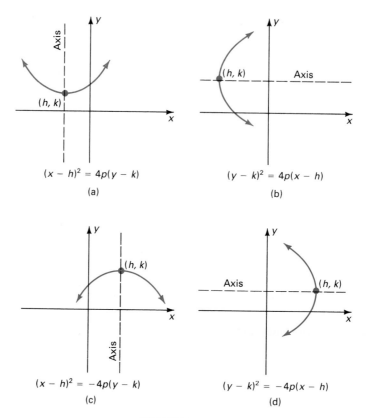

$(x - h)^2 = 4p(y - k)$

(a)

$(y - k)^2 = 4p(x - h)$

(b)

$(x - h)^2 = -4p(y - k)$

(c)

$(y - k)^2 = -4p(x - h)$

(d)

FIGURE 21.11

You should carefully compare the graphs and equations in Figs. 21.7 and 21.11 and observe the obvious patterns. For example, moving (or *translating*) the vertex of the parabola $y^2 = 4px$ from the point $(0, 0)$ to the point (h, k) gives the parabola $(y - k)^2 = 4p(x - h)$. Both parabolas open to the right.

It is left as an exercise for you to expand the standard forms and show that a general form of an equation of a parabola can be written

$$Ax^2 + Dx + Ey + F = 0, \qquad A, E \neq 0 \tag{1}$$

for a parabola with axis parallel to the y-axis, and

$$Cy^2 + Dx + Ey + F = 0, \qquad C, D \neq 0 \tag{2}$$

for a parabola with axis parallel to the x-axis. Conversely, for $A, C, D,$ and E unequal to zero, Eqs. 1 and 2 satisfy the requirements of the locus for a parabola and can be transformed into standard form.

In the case that $E = 0$ in Eq. 1 or $D = 0$ in Eq. 2, three degenerate cases may arise. For example, if $E = 0$ in Eq. 1, then

$$Ax^2 + Dx + F = 0.$$

Let us consider different values of $A, D,$ and F.

1. For $x^2 + 4x + 4 = 0$,

$$(x + 2)(x + 2) = 0$$
$$x = -2.$$

Thus the set of all points satisfying the given equation is the straight line $x = -2$.

2. For $x^2 - 2x - 8 = 0$,

$$(x - 4)(x + 2) = 0$$
$$x = 4 \quad \text{or} \quad x = -2.$$

Thus two distinct parallel straight lines occur. This is the only degenerate case that cannot be illustrated by a conic section.

3. For $x^2 + 4x + 4 = 0$,

$$x^2 + 4x + 4 = -1$$
$$(x + 2)^2 = -1,$$

so no parabola exists.

Example 3

Find the standard form of an equation of the parabola with vertex at $V(-1, 4)$ and focus at $F(-1. 1)$.

Solution   By indicating the data in the plane (Fig. 21.12), we conclude that the parabola must open downward. The equation is of the form $(x - h)^2 = -4p(y - k)$ with $h = -1, k = 4,$ and $p = 4 - 1 = 3$. Thus the equation is

$$(x + 1)^2 = -4(3)(y - 4)$$
$$(x + 1)^2 = -12(y - 4).$$

The graph and directrix are shown in Fig. 21.12. Note that the equation of the directrix is $y = 7$.

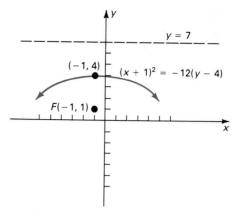

FIGURE 21.12

Example 4

Find the coordinates of the focus and vertex and the equation of the directrix of the parabola

$$y^2 - 8y - 8x + 24 = 0.$$

Solution Rearranging terms and completing the square in y, we have

$$y^2 - 8y + 16 = 8x - 24 + 16$$
$$= 8x - 8,$$
$$(y - 4)^2 = 8(x - 1).$$

Hence, the vertex is the point $(1, 4)$ and the parabola opens to the right. Also, since $4p = 8$, $p = 2$ and the focus lies two units to the right of the vertex at the point $(3, 4)$. A point on the directrix lies two units to the left of the vertex, so the equation of the directrix is $x = -1$.

Example 5

The height s of a ball thrown vertically upward from the ground is given by the equation of motion

$$s = 19.6t - 4.9t^2,$$

where s is in meters and t is elapsed time in seconds. Find the maximum height of the ball.

Solution Note that s is a quadratic function of t. Observe that we can write

$$s = 19.6t - 4.9t^2$$
$$s = -4.9(t^2 - 4t)$$
$$s - 19.6 = -4.9(t^2 - 4t + 4).$$

Thus

$$(t - 2)^2 = -\frac{1}{4.9}(s - 19.6).$$

This is the equation of a parabola, opening downward, with vertex at (2, 19.6), as shown in Fig. 12.13 in Sec. 12.4. Hence the maximum height of the ball is 19.6 m.

Example 5 supplements our discussion of quadratic functions in Sec. 12.4, where it was stated that the graph of a quadratic function is a parabola. It can be shown that if the graph of a quadratic function $y = f(x)$ crosses the x-axis at the points $(x_1, 0)$ and $(x_2, 0)$, then the variable y has its maximum (or minimum) value when

$$x = \frac{x_1 + x_2}{2}. \tag{3}$$

This fact will be used in the following example.

Example 6

Find the maximum value of the quadratic function $y = 20x - x^2$.

Solution   To find the values of x where its graph crosses the x-axis, we set $y = 0$. Then

$$0 = 20x - x^2$$
$$0 = x(20 - x),$$

so

$$x = 0 \quad \text{or} \quad x = 20.$$

By Eq. 3, the maximum value is attained when

$$x = \frac{0 + 20}{2} = 10.$$

Hence the maximum value is

$$y = 20x - x^2$$
$$= 20(10) - (10)^2$$
$$= 100.$$

You should use this technique to verify the result in Example 5.

Problem Set 21.4

In Problems **1–12**, find the coordinates of the vertex V and focus F, an equation of the directrix D, and sketch each parabola.

1. $y^2 = 4x$.
2. $y^2 = -6x$.
3. $x^2 = -8y$.
4. $y^2 = -x$.
5. $x^2 = 2y$.
6. $(x + 2)^2 = 4(y - 7)$.
7. $(y + 2)^2 = \frac{1}{2}x$.
8. $4x^2 = 3(y - 1)$.
9. $(x - 4)^2 = 8(y + 3)$.
10. $(y - 7)^2 = 12(x - 4)$.
11. $(y + 2)^2 = -\frac{1}{4}(x - 1)$.
12. $y = x^2$.

In Problems **13–22**, determine the standard form of an equation of the parabola that has the given properties.

13. Focus $(0, 3)$, directrix $y = -5$.
14. Vertex $(2, 4)$, directrix $y = 6$.
15. Focus $(1, 4)$, vertex $(3, 4)$.
16. Focus $(0, 5)$, directrix $x = -10$.
17. Vertex $(-3, 2)$, directrix $y = 4$.
18. Focus $(-2, -2)$, vertex $(-2, -6)$.
19. Focus $(0, \frac{3}{2})$, directrix $y = -\frac{3}{2}$.
20. Vertex $(3, 1)$, directrix $x = 6$.
21. Focus $(-3, -2)$, vertex $(-4, -2)$.
22. Focus $(0, -4)$, directrix $y = 4$.

In Problems **23–27**, transform the given equation into standard form and determine the coordinates of the focus and vertex.

23. $y^2 - 6y + 4x + 1 = 0$.
24. $2y^2 + 4y - x - 4 = 0$.
25. $3x^2 - 12x - y + 12 = 0$.
26. $x^2 + 3y - 8x + 19 = 0$.
27. $y^2 + 4y - x + 5 = 0$.

In Problems **28–31**, use a rough graph of the given system to predict how many different real solutions exist.

28. $\begin{cases} y^2 = x - 1, \\ y = x^2 - 2x + 1. \end{cases}$
29. $\begin{cases} y = x^2 - 3x, \\ x + y = -4. \end{cases}$

30. $\begin{cases} x = (y - 1)^2, \\ x - y = 2. \end{cases}$
31. $\begin{cases} y^2 = 2x + 1, \\ x^2 + y^2 = 9. \end{cases}$

32. The power P developed in a resistor of resistance R ohms carrying a current of i amperes is given by $P = i^2 R$. If a resistor has a resistance of $10\,\Omega$, sketch a graph of power as a function of current.

33. When an object is thrown straight upward with an initial velocity of 58.8 m/s, its height h, in meters, as a function of time t, in seconds, is given by $h = 58.8t - 4.9t^2$. At what time does the object reach its maximum height and what is that height?

34. The displacement s of an object from a reference point is given by the equation $s = 3t^2 - 24t + 103$, where s is in meters and t is in seconds. What is the minimum displacement of the particle from the reference point?

35. If a light source is placed between the focus and vertex of a parabolic mirror, the rays of light diverge after reflection, whereas if the light source is placed outside the focus, the rays converge after reflection. This is how automobile headlights can give a broad beam of light

(high beams) from one filament and a narrow beam of light (low beams) from a second filament. If the equation of a cross-sectional view of a parabolic mirror is $y^2 = 20x$, where x and y are in centimeters, what may the distance be between the vertex of the mirror and a filament if the light rays are to diverge after reflection from the mirror?

36. When an object of mass $\frac{1}{8}$ kg moves in a straight line on a horizontal surface 4 m above the ground, its energy E, in the absence of rotation, can be given by $E = 4.9 + \frac{1}{16}v^2$, where v is the speed of the object in meters per second, and E is measured in joules. The value of v is taken to be positive for one direction of motion and negative for the opposite direction. Sketch a graph of this energy function for the values of v from $v = -4$ m/s to $v = 4$ m/s.

21.5 THE ELLIPSE

An **ellipse** is the set of all points in a plane such that for each point the sum of its distances from two fixed points is a constant.

The two fixed points in the definition are called the **foci** (the plural of focus) of the ellipse. Let $2c$, where $c > 0$, be the distance between the foci. For convenience we shall locate the foci on the x-axis at points $F_1(c, 0)$ and $F_2(-c, 0)$ (see Fig. 21.13).

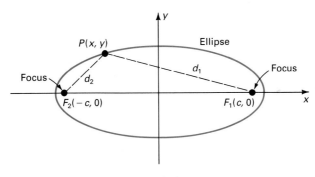

FIGURE 21.13

Furthermore, let the constant sum referred to in the definition be $2a$. To eliminate from our consideration those points on the line segment joining the foci, we must require that $2a > 2c$, or $a > c$. Selecting an arbitrary point $P(x, y)$ on the ellipse and applying the definition, we have

$$d_1 + d_2 = \text{constant}$$
$$\sqrt{(x - c)^2 + (y - 0)^2} + \sqrt{(x + c)^2 + (y - 0)^2} = 2a.$$

Rearranging terms, we have

$$\sqrt{(x - c)^2 + y^2} = 2a - \sqrt{(x + c)^2 + y^2}.$$

Squaring both sides gives

$$x^2 - 2cx + c^2 + y^2 = 4a^2 - 4a\sqrt{(x+c)^2 + y^2} + x^2 + 2cx + c^2 + y^2,$$

which simplifies to

$$a^2 + cx = a\sqrt{(x+c)^2 + y^2}.$$

Squaring both sides, we have

$$a^4 + 2a^2cx + c^2x^2 = a^2(x^2 + 2cx + c^2 + y^2).$$

Rearranging terms and grouping give

$$a^4 - a^2c^2 + c^2x^2 - a^2x^2 - a^2y^2 = 0$$
$$a^2(a^2 - c^2) + x^2(c^2 - a^2) - a^2y^2 = 0.$$

Dividing both sides by $a^2(a^2 - c^2)$ gives

$$1 - \frac{x^2}{a^2} - \frac{y^2}{a^2 - c^2} = 0,$$

which can be written as

$$\frac{x^2}{a^2} + \frac{y^2}{a^2 - c^2} = 1.$$

Because $a > c$, the number $a^2 - c^2$ is positive. If we introduce a new positive number b such that

$$\boxed{a^2 - c^2 = b^2,}$$ (1)

then we can write the preceding equation in the form

$$\boxed{\frac{x^2}{a^2} + \frac{y^2}{b^2} = 1.}$$ (2)

Thus the coordinates of every point on the given ellipse satisfy Eq. 2. Conversely, it can be shown that any point whose coordinates satisfy Eq. 2 is a point on the ellipse. Equation 2 is called the **standard form** of an equation of the ellipse with foci on the x-axis at $(c, 0)$ and $(-c, 0)$, where $a^2 = b^2 + c^2$. The equation $a^2 = b^2 + c^2$ implies that $a^2 > b^2$, so $a > b$.

The relationship between a, b, and c is easily seen from triangle OP_1F_1 in Fig. 21.14. From Eq. 2, if $y = 0$, then $x = \pm a$; thus the x-intercepts are $(\pm a, 0)$. If $x = 0$, then $y = \pm b$; the y-intercepts are $(0, \pm b)$. Segment V_1V_2, which has length $2a$ and passes through the foci, is called the **major axis** and its midpoint is called the **center of**

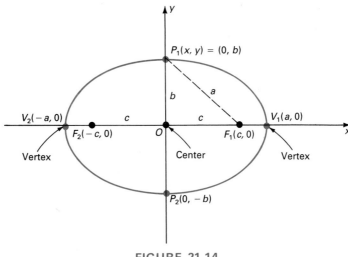

FIGURE 21.14

the ellipse. The ellipse shown has its center at the origin. Segment P_1P_2, which has length $2b$, is called the **minor axis**. We speak of a as the **semimajor axis**; *it is the distance from the center of the ellipse to the end of the major axis.* Similarly, we speak of b as the **semiminor axis**. Since $a > b$, the major axis is longer than the minor axis. The endpoints of the major axis, namely, V_1 and V_2, are called the **vertices** of the ellipse.

For an ellipse having center at the origin and foci on the y-axis [at $(0, c)$ and $(0, -c)$], the standard form is

$$\frac{x^2}{b^2} + \frac{y^2}{a^2} = 1. \tag{3}$$

Here, the major axis lies on the y-axis. The vertices are $(0, \pm a)$. Again, $b^2 = a^2 - c^2$.

In Eqs. 2 and 3, remember that since $a > b$, **the larger denominator is always** a^2. Thus, if the larger denominator is in the x^2-term, the major axis is horizontal. If it is in the y^2-term, the major axis is vertical.

In general, it can be shown that the standard form of an equation of an ellipse with center (h, k) and major axis horizontal is given by

$$\frac{(x - h)^2}{a^2} + \frac{(y - k)^2}{b^2} = 1, \tag{4}$$

and for one where the major axis is vertical, the equation is

$$\frac{(x - h)^2}{b^2} + \frac{(y - k)^2}{a^2} = 1. \tag{5}$$

Example 1

For the ellipse $4x^2 + 9y^2 = 36$, find the center, vertices, foci, and endpoints of the minor axis. Sketch the ellipse.

Solution   To obtain the standard form, we divide both sides by 36:

$$\frac{x^2}{9} + \frac{y^2}{4} = 1.$$

The center is at the origin. Because the larger denominator (9) is under x^2, the major axis lies on the x-axis. Since $a^2 = 9$ and $b^2 = 4$, then $a = 3$ and $b = 2$. Hence, the vertices are $(\pm 3, 0)$ and the endpoints of the minor axis are at $(0, \pm 2)$. From this information we can sketch the graph, as in Fig. 21.15. Also, by rewriting Eq. 1 we can find c:

$$c^2 = a^2 - b^2 = 9 - 4 = 5$$

$$c = \sqrt{5}.$$

Thus the foci are at $(\pm \sqrt{5}, 0)$.

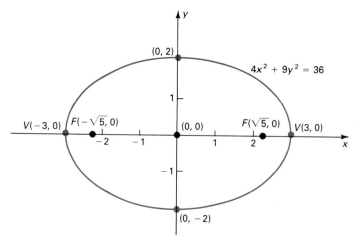

FIGURE 21.15

Example 2

Find an equation of the ellipse with major axis of length eight units, a focus at $(2, 8)$, and center at $(2, 5)$.

Solution   An ellipse with a center at $(2, 5)$ and a focus at $(2, 8)$ must have a vertical major axis. The distance from the center to the given focus is three units. Thus $c = 3$. Also, since the length of the major axis is $2a \, (= 8)$, then $a = 4$. Therefore, by Eq. 1, we have $b^2 = a^2 - c^2 = 16 - 9 = 7$. Thus, because $h = 2$ and $k = 5$, from Eq. 5 the standard form is

$$\frac{(x - 2)^2}{7} + \frac{(y - 5)^2}{16} = 1.$$

The graph is shown in Fig. 21.16.

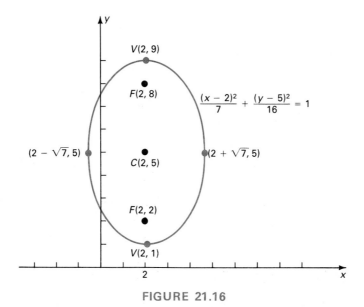

FIGURE 21.16

Example 3

Determine the center, foci, vertices, and endpoints of the minor axis of the ellipse

$$x^2 + 2y^2 + 4x - 4y + 2 = 0.$$

Solution   First we put the equation into standard form. Rearranging and grouping terms, we can write

$$(x^2 + 4x) + 2(y^2 - 2y) = -2.$$

Completing the squares in x and y, we have

$$(x^2 + 4x + 4) + 2(y^2 - 2y + 1) = -2 + 4 + 2.$$

Note that when 1 was added to $y^2 - 2y$ to complete the square in y, it was equivalent to adding 2 to the left side of the equation. Hence 2 had to be added to the right side. This gives

$$(x + 2)^2 + 2(y - 1)^2 = 4.$$

Finally, dividing by 4 gives the standard form.

$$\frac{(x+2)^2}{4} + \frac{(y-1)^2}{2} = 1.$$

Clearly $a^2 = 4$, $b^2 = 2$, and $c^2 = a^2 - b^2 = 2$. Thus $a = 2$, $b = \sqrt{2}$, and $c = \sqrt{2}$. Because $h = -2$ and $k = 1$, the center is at $(-2, 1)$. Also, the major axis is horizontal. Because $c = \sqrt{2}$, the foci are at $(-2 \pm \sqrt{2}, 1)$. Also, because $a = 2$, the vertices are $(-2 \pm 2, 1)$, that is, at $(0, 1)$ and $(-4, 1)$. Lastly, because $b = \sqrt{2}$, the endpoints of the minor axis are at $(-2, 1 \pm \sqrt{2})$.

Problem Set 21.5

In Problems 1–8, find the center C, vertices V, and endpoints E of the minor axis of the given ellipse. Sketch each ellipse.

1. $\dfrac{x^2}{25} + \dfrac{y^2}{16} = 1.$

2. $\dfrac{x^2}{144} + \dfrac{y^2}{169} = 1.$

3. $\dfrac{x^2}{100} + \dfrac{y^2}{144} = 1.$

4. $\dfrac{x^2}{49} + \dfrac{y^2}{4} = 1.$

5. $4x^2 + y^2 = 4.$

6. $16x^2 + 9y^2 = 144.$

7. $\dfrac{(x-2)^2}{9} + \dfrac{(y+3)^2}{4} = 1.$

8. $\dfrac{(x+2)^2}{9} + \dfrac{(y-3)^2}{25} = 1.$

In Problems 9–12, for each ellipse find the center C, vertices V, and endpoints E of the minor axis.

9. $4x^2 + y^2 - 16x = 0.$

10. $2x^2 + y^2 + 8x + 4y + 6 = 0.$

11. $9x^2 + 25y^2 - 54x + 100y = 44.$

12. $x^2 + 2y^2 + 4x - 8y - 6 = 0.$

In Problems 13–21, determine the standard form of an equation of the ellipse with the given properties. Assume the center is at the origin unless otherwise stated.

13. Vertex $(6, 0)$, focus $(5, 0)$.

14. Major axis of length 16, focus $(6, 0)$.

15. Focus $(-8, 1)$, minor axis of length 4, center $(0, 1)$.

16. Focus $(3, 3)$, center on y-axis, vertex $(-5, 3)$.

17. Major axis of length 16 and horizontal, minor axis of length 8.

18. Vertex $(3, 10)$, focus $(3, -6)$, center on x-axis.

19. Vertex $(0, 0)$, center $(0, -8)$, minor axis of length 5.

20. Focus $(-4, -5)$, major axis of length 14, center $(-4, 1)$.

21. Minor axis horizontal and of length 4, focus $(-2, -8)$, center $(-2, -1)$.

22. The arch of a bridge has the shape of one-half an ellipse. The maximum height of the bridge is 50 m and the bridge has a span at water level of 120 m. If the origin of a coordinate system is midway between the ends of the bridge at water level, what is the equation of the ellipse? What is the equation if the origin of the coordinate system is at one end of the bridge at water level?

21.6 THE HYPERBOLA

> A **hyperbola** is the set of all points in a plane such that for each point the difference between its distances from two fixed points, called **foci**, is a positive constant.

Suppose the distance between the two foci is $2c$, where $c > 0$. For convenience we shall locate the foci on the x-axis at points $F_1(c, 0)$ and $F_2(-c, 0)$ (see Fig. 21.17). Let the constant difference referred to in the definition be $2a$, where

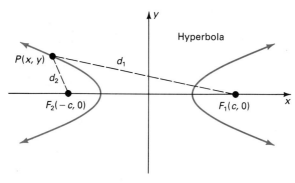

FIGURE 21.17

$a > 0$. Selecting a point $P(x, y)$ on the hyperbola, we have (by definition)

$$d_1 - d_2 = \pm 2a,$$

where the correct sign depends on which of d_1 or d_2 is the larger. Therefore, by the distance formula,

$$\sqrt{(x - c)^2 + (y - 0)^2} - \sqrt{(x + c)^2 + (y - 0)^2} = \pm 2a.$$

Using the same techniques as those used in the preceding section, we obtain

$$c^2 x^2 - a^2 x^2 - a^2 y^2 = a^2 c^2 - a^4,$$

or

$$x^2(c^2 - a^2) - a^2 y^2 = a^2(c^2 - a^2).$$

Dividing both sides by $a^2(c^2 - a^2)$ gives

$$\frac{x^2}{a^2} - \frac{y^2}{c^2 - a^2} = 1. \tag{1}$$

As in the case of the derivation of an equation of an ellipse, it would seem natural to introduce a positive number b such that

$$b^2 = c^2 - a^2.$$ (2)

(Do not confuse this with $b^2 = a^2 - c^2$ for an ellipse.) However, we must be sure that $c^2 - a^2$ is always positive. It is shown in geometry that the difference between any two sides of a triangle is less than the third side. Hence, from Fig. 21.17, for the triangle $F_1 F_2 P$ with $d_1 > d_2$ we have

$$2c > d_1 - d_2,$$

and by definition it follows that

$$2c > 2a, \quad \text{or} \quad c > a.$$

Thus $c^2 > a^2$ and $c^2 - a^2 > 0$. The proof if $d_2 > d_1$ is similar.

Using Eq. 2, from Eq. 1 we obtain the **standard form** of an equation of the hyperbola with foci at $(\pm c, 0)$:

$$\frac{x^2}{a^2} - \frac{y^2}{b^2} = 1,$$ (3)

where $c^2 = a^2 + b^2$.

When $y = 0$, then $x = \pm a$ and hence the hyperbola crosses the x-axis at the points $V_1(a, 0)$ and $V_2(-a, 0)$ (refer to Fig. 21.18). These points, those for which the hyperbola cuts the line through the two foci, are called the **vertices** of the hyperbola. The line segment $V_1 V_2$ that joins the vertices is $2a$ units long and is called the **transverse axis**. The midpoint of the transverse is called the **center** of the hyperbola. In Fig. 21.18 the center is at the origin.

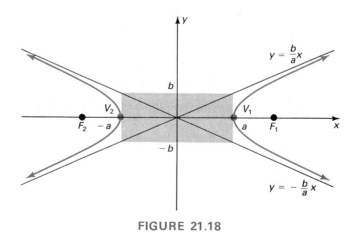

FIGURE 21.18

To determine more precisely the nature of a hyperbola and the geometrical significance of b, we solve Eq. 3 for y:

$$b^2x^2 - a^2y^2 = a^2b^2$$

$$y^2 = \frac{b^2x^2 - a^2b^2}{a^2} = \frac{b^2x^2}{a^2}\left(1 - \frac{a^2}{x^2}\right)$$

$$y = \pm\frac{b}{a}x\sqrt{1 - \frac{a^2}{x^2}}.$$

As x increases or decreases without bound, then the values of a^2/x^2 get closer to zero and the expression under the radical sign approaches a value of 1. We can conclude that y will approach the values $(b/a)x$ and $-(b/a)x$. The straight lines $y = (b/a)x$ and $y = -(b/a)x$ are called **asymptotes** for the hyperbola. They are straight lines that provide a good approximation to the hyperbola when x is far from the origin. These results are indicated in Fig. 21.18.

From the diagram it should be clear that the asymptotes coincide, so to speak, with the diagonals of a rectangle of length $2a$ and width $2b$ and whose vertices are (a, b), $(-a, b)$, $(-a, -b)$, and $(a, -b)$. The line segment on the y-axis joining the points $(0, b)$ and $(0, -b)$ has length $2b$ and is called the **conjugate axis** of the hyperbola. Clearly, the asymptotes provide convenient guide lines for sketching a hyperbola. They are most easily sketched by drawing extended diagonals of the rectangle whose sides pass through the vertices and the endpoints of the conjugate axis. The rectangle and asymptotes are *not* part of the graph. It can be shown that *the equations of the asymptotes of the hyperbola can be found by replacing the 1 in the standard form by zero and solving for y.*

In a similar manner, it can be shown that an equation of a hyperbola with center at the origin, transverse axis along the y-axis and conjugate axis along the x-axis, is

$$\frac{y^2}{a^2} - \frac{x^2}{b^2} = 1. \tag{4}$$

In this case the vertices are located at $V_1(0, a)$ and $V_2(0, -a)$, the foci are at $F_1(0, c)$ and $F_2(0, -c)$, and the lines $y = \pm ax/b$ are asymptotes.

Using the definition, we can show that the standard form of an equation of a hyperbola with center at (h, k) and transverse axis horizontal is given by

$$\frac{(x - h)^2}{a^2} - \frac{(y - k)^2}{b^2} = 1, \tag{5}$$

whereas if the transverse axis is vertical, the equation is

$$\frac{(y - k)^2}{a^2} - \frac{(x - h)^2}{b^2} = 1. \tag{6}$$

Note that a^2 is always associated with the positive term. Again, the equations of the asymptotes can be found by replacing the 1 in the standard form by zero and solving for y.

Finally, a general form of an equation of a hyperbola can be written

$$Ax^2 + Cy^2 + Dx + Ey + F = 0,$$ (7)

where A and C have opposite signs.

Example 1

Discuss and sketch the graph of the hyperbola $\dfrac{y^2}{4} - x^2 = 1$.

Solution From the standard forms of an equation of a hyperbola, a^2 is always associated with the positive term. In this case, $a^2 = 4$ and $b^2 = 1$; that is, $a = 2$, and $b = 1$. Also, $c^2 = a^2 + b^2 = 4 + 1 = 5$, so $c = \sqrt{5}$. Because the equation is of the form of Eq. 4, or, equivalently, the form of Eq. 6 with $h = k = 0$, we deduce that the hyperbola has vertices $V_1(0, 2)$ and $V_2(0, -2)$, foci $F_1(0, \sqrt{5})$ and $F_2(0, -\sqrt{5})$, a vertical transverse axis of length 4, and a horizontal conjugate axis of length 2. We can easily sketch the graph by first locating the vertices and endpoints of the conjugate axis. Then we construct the rectangle whose sides pass through these points. Next, we sketch the asymptotes by drawing extended diagonals of the rectangle. Finally, we draw the hyperbola which passes through the vertices and approaches the asymptotes. The results are shown in Fig. 21.19. Note that the equations of the asymptotes

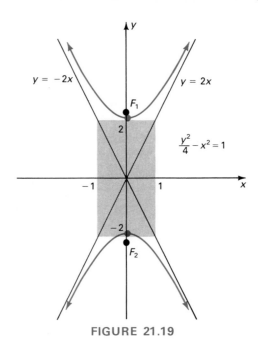

FIGURE 21.19

are $y = 2x$ and $y = -2x$. They are obtained by solving the equation $y^2/(4) - x^2 = 0$ for y.

$$\frac{y^2}{4} = x^2, \qquad y^2 = 4x^2, \qquad y = \pm 2x.$$

Example 2

Discuss and sketch the graph of the hyperbola

$$2x^2 - y^2 - 16x + 4y + 24 = 0.$$

Solution First we put the equation into standard form. The equation can be written

$$(2x^2 - 16x) - (y^2 - 4y) = -24.$$

Completing the squares and simplifying, we have

$$2(x^2 - 8x + 16) - (y^2 - 4y + 4) = -24 + 32 - 4$$

$$2(x - 4)^2 - (y - 2)^2 = 4$$

$$\frac{(x - 4)^2}{2} - \frac{(y - 2)^2}{4} = 1. \tag{8}$$

Equation 8 matches Eq. 5 where $h = 4$ and $k = 2$. Thus the center of the hyperbola is at $(4, 2)$ and the transverse axis is horizontal. Since $a^2 = 2$ and $b^2 = 4$, then $a = \sqrt{2}$, $b = 2$, and $c^2 = 4 + 2$ or $c = \sqrt{6}$. In Fig. 21.20 we locate the center of the hyperbola, the vertices

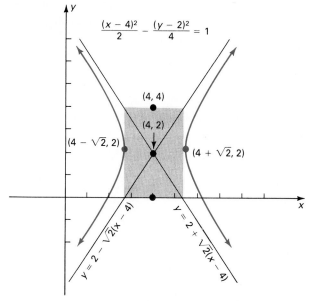

FIGURE 21.20

$(4 \pm \sqrt{2}, 2)$, and the endpoints of the conjugate axis $(4, 2 \pm 2)$. Then the corresponding rectangle is completed and the asymptotes are drawn. The graph is then sketched. As previously mentioned, to find the equations of the asymptotes we set the left side of Eq. 8 equal to zero and solve for y:

$$\frac{(y-2)^2}{4} = \frac{(x-4)^2}{2}$$

$$(y-2)^2 = 2(x-4)^2$$

$$y - 2 = \pm\sqrt{2}(x-4)$$

$$y = 2 \pm \sqrt{2}(x-4).$$

The standard form of an equation of a hyperbola with center at the origin and transverse axis along the x-axis is

$$\frac{x^2}{a^2} - \frac{y^2}{b^2} = 1.$$

If $b = a$, the result $x^2 - y^2 = a^2$ is a hyperbola with mutually perpendicular asymptotes, $y = \pm x$. The corresponding rectangle is, in this case, a square and the curve is called an **equilateral hyperbola**.

We conclude our discussion here by stating that there is one special form of an equation of an equilateral hyperbola. The equation

$$\boldsymbol{xy = c,} \tag{9}$$

where c is a nonzero constant, is an equation of an equilateral hyperbola whose asymptotes are the coordinate axes. The general shapes of the graphs of $xy = c$ for $c > 0$ and $c < 0$ are shown in Figs. 21.21 and 21.22, respectively. If c is positive, the

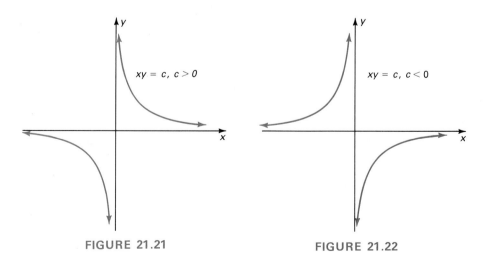

FIGURE 21.21   FIGURE 21.22

foci lie on the line $y = x$, while if c is negative, they lie on the line $y = -x$. The graph of a hyperbola having the form of Eq. 9 can be easily sketched by assuming values for one variable and determining the corresponding values of the other variable.

Problem Set 21.6

In Problems 1–10, find the center C, vertices V, focus F, endpoints E of the conjugate axis, and asymptotes A of each hyperbola. Sketch each hyperbola.

1. $\dfrac{x^2}{16} - \dfrac{y^2}{9} = 1.$

2. $\dfrac{y^2}{25} - \dfrac{x^2}{144} = 1.$

3. $\dfrac{y^2}{36} - x^2 = 1.$

4. $4x^2 - 9y^2 = 36.$

5. $x^2 - y^2 = 4.$

6. $\dfrac{x^2}{16} - \dfrac{(y-2)^2}{16} = 1.$

7. $4(y+3)^2 - 25(x-2)^2 = 100.$

8. $(x+3)^2 - 2y^2 + 8 = 0.$

9. $9x^2 - 36x - 16y^2 - 32y - 124 = 0.$

10. $y^2 - 4x^2 - 10y + 16x - 7 = 0.$

In Problems 11–20, determined the standard form of an equation of the hyperbola satisfying the given conditions. Assume the center is at $(0, 0)$ unless otherwise stated.

11. Focus $(0, 3)$, vertex $(0, 2)$.
12. Transverse axis of length 10, focus $(7, 0)$.
13. Vertex $(4, 0)$, conjugate axis of length 2.
14. Conjugate axis of length 4, focus $(0, 6)$.
15. Center $(-4, 2)$, focus $(-4, 6)$, vertex on x-axis.
16. Center $(-7, 0)$, focus at origin, transverse axis of length 6.
17. Vertex on y-axis, center $(-2, 4)$, conjugate axis of length 3.
18. Vertex at $(4, 0)$, center $(4, 2)$, conjugate axis of length 4.
19. Center on line $y = 4$, vertex $(0, 2)$, focus $(0, 1)$.
20. Vertex $(2, 6)$, focus $(4, 6)$, center on y-axis.

In Problems 21–26, sketch the graph of each hyperbola and state the equations of the asymptotes.

21. $xy = 3.$

22. $xy = -3.$

23. $xy = -5.$

24. $5xy = 6.$

25. $4xy = 1.$

26. $xy = 120.$

27. The speed v of a wave is a function of the frequency f and the wavelength λ, where $v = f\lambda$. For visible light in a vacuum, $v = 3 \times 10^8$ m/s and values of λ range from about 4×10^{-7} to about 7×10^{-7} m. Sketch a graph of frequency versus wavelength for the visible portion of the spectrum.

28. The relationship between the index of refraction of a material, n, the wavelength of light in the material, λ, and the wavelength of light in air, λ_a, is $\lambda_a = n\lambda$. If the wavelength of blue-green light in air is 5000 angstroms, sketch a graph of λ versus n for values of n from 1.5 to 2.5, in increments of 0.1.

29. For an ideal gas at constant temperature, the product of the pressure p and volume v is a constant. A particular sample of such a gas has a pressure of 4 atmospheres and a volume of 5 liters. Sketch a graph of pressure versus volume.

21.7 SUMMARY OF CONIC SECTIONS

It is often important to be able to identify a curve from a brief examination of its equation. Assuming no degenerate cases, from the results of the preceding sections we conclude that the graph of the **general equation of a conic section**

$$Ax^2 + Bxy + Cy^2 + Dx + Ey + F = 0$$

is:

1. A circle if $A = C$, and $B = 0$.
2. A parabola if $A = 0$ or $C = 0$ but not both, and $B = 0$.
3. An ellipse if $A \neq C$ but A and C have the same sign, and $B = 0$.
4. A hyperbola if either
    a. A and C have opposite signs, and $B = 0$, or
    b. $A = C = 0$, and $B \neq 0$.

Example 1

Classify each of the following equations as that of a circle, parabola, ellipse, or hyperbola.

a. $x^2 + y^2 + 3x - 6y - 7 = 0$.

Solution Because the coefficients of the x^2- and y^2-terms are equal ($A = C = 1$), the equation is that of a circle.

b. $2y^2 + x^2 - 4y - 4x - 10 = 0$.

Solution Because the coefficients of the x^2- and y^2-terms are unequal but have the same sign ($A = 1 \neq 2 = C$), the equation is that of an ellipse.

c. $2y^2 + 3y - 4x + 9 = 0$.

Solution As there is a y^2-term but no x^2-term ($A = 0$, $C = 2$), the equation is that of a parabola.

d. $5x^2 - 3y^2 - 5x + 2y + 16 = 0$.

Solution Because the x^2- and y^2-terms are opposite in sign, the equation is that of a hyperbola.

e. $xy = 7$.

Solution Because $A = C = 0$ and $B = 1 \neq 0$, the equation is that of an (equilateral) hyperbola.

Problem Set 21.7

By inspection, classify each of the following equations as a circle, parabola, ellipse, or hyperbola.

1. $3x^2 + 3y^2 + 2x + 5y - 6 = 0$.
2. $3x^2 + 2y^2 + 2x - 7 = 0$.
3. $2y^2 + 3x + 2y + 1 = 0$.
4. $3xy = 18.21$.
5. $x^2 + 3x + 14y - 17 = 0$.
6. $-2x^2 - 2y^2 + 3x - 4y + 17 = 0$.
7. $2x^2 - 3y^2 + 2x + 6 = 0$.
8. $3y^2 - 2x = 4$.
9. $4x^2 + 2y^2 + 3y = 8$.
10. $2x^2 + 3y = 7$.
11. $xy = -3$.
12. $4x^2 + 4y^2 - 6x + 3y + 7 = 0$.
13. $x^2 + 2y^2 + 3 = 2y - y^2$.
14. $4x^2 - 2y^2 - 3x + 4y + 182 = 0$.
15. $x^2 + 5y^2 + x + 17y = 1$.
16. $1.3x^2 - 7.2 = -8.6y^2$.
17. $x^2 + 3x - 4y + 6 = 4$.
18. $3x^2 + 3y^2 - 4 = 0$.
19. $4x^2 - 7y^2 = 16$.
20. $1.2x^2 = 3y + 7.4$.

21.8 PARAMETRIC EQUATIONS

Whenever we graphed an equation in the variables x and y, we obtained points (x, y) by assigning values to one variable and determining corresponding values of the other variable. It is often convenient, however, to express both x and y as functions of a third variable, called a **parameter**.

For example, the equations

$$x = t + 1 \tag{1}$$

$$y = t^2 - 3 \tag{2}$$

define a curve. Here t is the parameter and the pair of equations are called **parametric equations** of the curve.* If $t = 0$, then $x = 1$ and $y = -3$. Thus $(1, -3)$ is a point on the curve. By choosing other values for t, we obtain the table and graph in Fig. 21.23. We connected the points in order of increasing values of t, as shown by the arrows in the graph. Thus the curve is given a directional sense. This is meaningful because the parametric equations could be looked upon as giving the position of a moving particle at time t. Although Fig. 21.23 shows the t-values associated with some points, *the parameter usually does not appear in such a graph at all.*

You may have noticed that the curve in Fig. 21.23 appears to be a parabola. To prove that this is indeed the case, we can find a single equation in x and y by *eliminating the parameter.* Because $t = x - 1$ from Eq. 1, by substituting into Eq. 2 we get the direct relationship between x and y

$$y = (x - 1)^2 - 3$$
$$y = x^2 - 2x - 2, \tag{3}$$

---

* See, for example, Eqs. 1 and 2 in Sec. 16.7, which concern Lissajous figures.

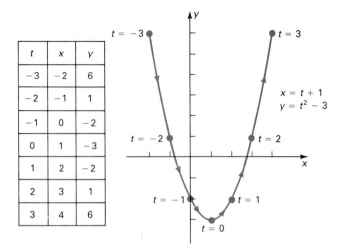

t	x	y
-3	-2	6
-2	-1	1
-1	0	-2
0	1	-3
1	2	-2
2	3	1
3	4	6

which is a familiar form of a parabola. Equation 3 is called a **rectangular form** of the curve. In many cases it is not so simple and sometimes next to impossible to eliminate the parameter. In fact, one of the advantages of parametric equations is that a curve with a complicated equation in x and y may have a very simple parameteric form.

When eliminating the parameter, you must be careful about the domain of the resulting rectangular form, as Example 1 will show.

Example 1

Sketch the graph of

$$x = t^2, \qquad y = t^2$$

and eliminate the parameter.

Solution The graph appears in Fig. 21.24(a). Because $x = t^2 = y$, a rectangular form is $y = x$, whose graph is the straight line in Fig. 21.24(b). Note that the graph in (a) is not the

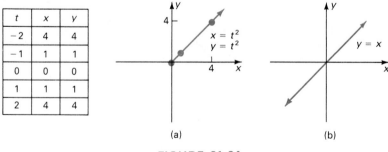

t	x	y
-2	4	4
-1	1	1
0	0	0
1	1	1
2	4	4

(a)   (b)

FIGURE 21.24

complete graph in (b), but only a portion of it. To see why, observe that in the parametric equations, for all values of t we have $x \geq 0$. In (b) we have $-\infty < x < \infty$. That is, we obtain the graph in (a) from the rectangular form $y = x$ by restricting the domain so that $x \geq 0$. The graph in (a) is the correct representation of the parametric equations. The proper rectangular form is $y = x$, *where* $x \geq 0$.

Example 2

Sketch the graph of

$$x = 3 \sin \theta, \qquad y = 4 \cos \theta,$$

and eliminate the parameter.

Solution Here the parameter is θ. Because the sine and cosine functions have period 2π, we need consider θ only in the interval from zero to 2π. We also note that $|x| \leq 3$ and $|y| \leq 4$, because the sine and cosine functions have values between -1 and 1. The graph appears in Fig. 21.25. To eliminate the parameter we write

$$\sin \theta = \frac{x}{3} \quad \text{and} \quad \cos \theta = \frac{y}{4}.$$

From the identity $\sin^2 \theta + \cos^2 \theta = 1$,

$$\left(\frac{x}{3}\right)^2 + \left(\frac{y}{4}\right)^2 = 1$$

$$\frac{x^2}{9} + \frac{y^2}{16} = 1.$$

This is a familiar form of an ellipse.

θ	x	y
0	0	4
$\dfrac{\pi}{4}$	2.1	2.8
$\dfrac{\pi}{2}$	3	0
$\dfrac{3\pi}{4}$	2.1	-2.8
π	0	-4
$\dfrac{5\pi}{4}$	-2.1	-2.8
$\dfrac{3\pi}{2}$	-3	0
$\dfrac{7\pi}{4}$	-2.1	2.8
2π	0	4

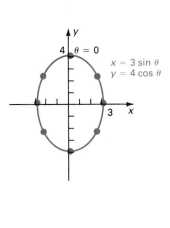

FIGURE 21.25

Example 3

Sketch the graph of

$$x = t^3 - 3t, \qquad y = t^2.$$

Solution   See Fig. 21.26. We include the parameter values $\pm\sqrt{3}$ because they give x a value of zero, since $0 = t(t^2 - 3) = t(t + \sqrt{3})(t - \sqrt{3})$.

t	x	y
-2	-2	4
$-\sqrt{3}$	0	3
-1	2	1
0	0	0
1	-2	1
$\sqrt{3}$	0	3
2	2	4

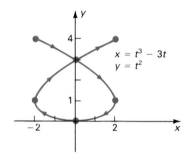

FIGURE 21.26

Example 4

Determine a set of parametric equations for

$$x^3 + y^3 = xy.$$

Solution   Our technique is to let $y = tx$. Then

$$x^3 + t^3 x^3 = x(tx),$$

or

$$x + t^3 x = t$$

$$x = \frac{t}{1 + t^3}.$$

Hence,

$$y = tx$$

$$= \frac{t^2}{1 + t^3}.$$

The parametric equations are $x = \dfrac{t}{1 + t^3}$ and $y = \dfrac{t^2}{1 + t^3}$.

Example 5

In the absence of air resistance, when a projectile with initial velocity v_0 is fired at an angle α with the ground, the coordinates of its position at time t are given by the parametric equations

$$x = (v_0 \cos \alpha)t \tag{4}$$

$$y = (v_0 \sin \alpha)t - \tfrac{1}{2}gt^2, \tag{5}$$

for which the graph is a parabola (Fig. 21.27). Here, g is the constant acceleration due to gravity, h is the maximum height of the projectile, and R is the (horizontal) range. If $v_0 = 20$ m/s, $\alpha = 30°$, and $g = 9.8$ m/s^2, (a) find when the projectile strikes the ground (that is, the time of flight), (b) find the range R, and (c) find the maximum height h.

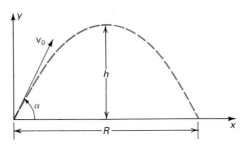

FIGURE 21.27

Solution   Substituting the given data in Eqs. 4 and 5, we obtain

$$x = (20 \cos 30°)t \tag{6}$$

$$y = (20 \sin 30°)t - 4.9t^2. \tag{7}$$

a. When the projectile strikes the ground, then $y = 0$. Thus, from Eq. 7,

$$(20 \sin 30°)t - 4.9t^2 = 0$$

$$t(20 \sin 30° - 4.9t) = 0.$$

Hence either $t = 0$ or $t = (20 \sin 30°)/4.9 = 2.04$. We choose $t = 2.04$ s.

b. The range R is obtained by substituting $t = 2.04$ from Part a into Eq. 6:

$$R = (20 \cos 30°)(2.04) = 35.3 \text{ m}.$$

c. To find h we note that the path of the projectile is a parabola that meets the x-axis when $t = 0$ and $t = 2.04$. From Example 6 of Sec. 21.4 and the discussion immediately preceding it, we conclude that the maximum height is obtained when

$$t = \frac{0 + 2.04}{2} = 1.02 \text{ s}.$$

Thus, from Eq. 7, the maximum height h is given by

$$h = (20 \sin 30°)(1.02) - 4.9(1.02)^2 = 5.10 \text{ m}.$$

Problem Set 21.8

In Problems 1–10, sketch the graph of the curve represented by the given parametric equations. Eliminate the parameter in 1–9.

1. $x = 2t$, $y = t + 1$.

2. $x = t - 3$, $y = 3t + 1$.

3. $x = t$, $y = \dfrac{1}{t}$.

4. $x = t - 1$, $y = t^2 - 2t$.

5. $x = 3 - t$, $y = t - t^2$.

6. $x = \cos t$, $y = 2 \sin t$.

7. $x = 4 \cos t$, $y = 2 \cos t$.

8. $x = \cos 2t$, $y = \cos t$.

9. $x = 2 \cos t - 1$, $y = 2 \sin t - 2$.

10. $x = t^3 - 3t - 2$, $y = t^2 - t - 2$.

In Problems 11–16, find parametric representations for the curves given by the equations in the same manner as in Example 4.

11. $x = y + xy$.

12. $x^2 + y^2 = 9x$.

13. $x^3 + y^3 = 2xy$.

14. $y^2 - 2x^2 = 8y$.

15. $x^2 + 2xy + y = x$.

16. $x^3 - 3xy + y^3 = 0$.

17. By eliminating the parameter, show that a projectile with motion as given by Eqs. 4 and 5 of Example 5 has a parabolic path.

18. A particle moves in the xy-plane such that the coordinates of its position as functions of time t are given by

$$x = r \cos \omega t,$$

$$y = r \sin \omega t,$$

where r and ω are constants. By eliminating the parameter, determine the type of path the particle follows.

19. Sketch the graph of the projectile in Example 5 with the path as given by Eqs. 6 and 7. Choose parameter values of $t = 0, 0.25, 0.50, 0.75$, and so on.

20. Prove that the parametric equations

$$x = a \cos \theta,$$

$$y = b \sin \theta$$

describe an ellipse for $a \neq b$.

21. A projectile is fired from ground level with an initial velocity of 300 m/s at an angle of 40° with the ground (see Example 5). Assume $g = 9.8$ m/s².
    (a) After 3 s, how far has the projectile traveled horizontally and how far vertically?
    (b) Find when the projectile strikes the ground.
    (c) Find the range (to the nearest meter).
    (d) Find the maximum height (to the nearest meter) and the time when it occurs.

22. A body is fired from the ground at an angle of 45° with an initial velocity of 120 m/s. To the nearest meter, find the range of the body (see Example 5). Assume that $g = 9.8$ m/s².

23. The coordinates of the position of a particle at time t are given parametrically by

$$x = 2t, \qquad y = t + 1,$$

where x and y are in meters and t is in seconds. Show that the distance d of the particle from the origin is given by $d = \sqrt{x^2 + y^2}$. Determine at what time(s) t the particle will be 4 m from the origin.

24. The coordinates of the position of a particle (in meters) as functions of time t (in seconds) are given parametrically by

$$x = 2 - t, \qquad y = 3t + 1.$$

For what value(s) of t will the particle be 3 m from the origin? (See Problem 23.)

21.9 REVIEW

Important Terms

Section 21.1	Right circular cone, conic sections, circle, parabola, ellipse, hyperbola, degenerate conics.
Section 21.2	Distance formula.
Section 21.3	Circle, center of circle, radius of circle, standard forms of equation of circle, general form of equation of circle.
Section 21.4	Parabola, focus of parabola, directrix, axis, vertex, standard forms of equation of parabola.
Section 21.5	Ellipse, foci of ellipse, center of ellipse, major axis, minor axis, semimajor axis, semiminor axis, vertices of ellipse, standard forms of equation of ellipse.
Section 21.6	Hyperbola, foci of hyperbola, vertices of hyperbola, center of hyperbola, transverse axis, conjugate axis, asymptotes for hyperbola, standard forms of equation of hyperbola, equilateral hyperbola.
Section 21.7	General equation of conic section.
Section 21.8	Parameter, parametric equations, eliminating the parameter.

Formula Summary

$$\textit{Distance Formula} \quad d = \sqrt{(x_2 - x_1)^2 + (y_2 - y_1)^2}$$

Conic Sections (Standard Forms)

Circle

Center (h, k), radius r:

$$(x - h)^2 + (y - k)^2 = r^2$$

Center (0, 0), radius r:

$$x^2 + y^2 = r^2$$

Parabola

Vertex (h, k), axis $x = h$, distance from vertex to focus $= p > 0$:

$$(x - h)^2 = 4p(y - k) \qquad \text{Opens up}$$
$$(x - h)^2 = -4p(y - k) \qquad \text{Opens down}$$

Vertex (h, k), axis $y = k$, distance from vertex to focus $= p > 0$:

$$(y - k)^2 = 4p(x - h) \qquad \text{Opens to right}$$
$$(y - k)^2 = -4p(x - h) \qquad \text{Opens to left}$$

Ellipse

Center (h, k):

$$\frac{(x - h)^2}{a^2} + \frac{(y - k)^2}{b^2} = 1 \qquad \text{Major axis horizontal}$$

$$\frac{(x - h)^2}{b^2} + \frac{(y - k)^2}{a^2} = 1 \qquad \text{Major axis vertical}$$

Hyperbola

Center (h, k):

$$\frac{(x - h)^2}{a^2} - \frac{(y - k)^2}{b^2} = 1 \qquad \text{Horizontal transverse axis}$$

$$\frac{(y - k)^2}{a^2} - \frac{(x - h)^2}{b^2} = 1 \qquad \text{Vertical transverse axis}$$

Review Questions

1. The set of all points in a plane that are equidistant from a fixed point in the plane is called a(n) _____.
2. The only conic section with asymptotes is the _____.
3. The equation $(x - 2)^2 + (y + 4)^2 = 3$ defines a circle of radius __(a)__ whose center is at __(b)__.
4. The graph of $y^2 = x$ is called a _____.
5. The vertex of the graph of $(y - 2)^2 = 9x$ is at _____.
6. The parabola $x^2 = -4y$ opens___(downward)(to the left)___.

7. The graph of $\dfrac{x^2}{4} - \dfrac{y^2}{9} = 1$ is called a(n) ___(a)___ , and the graph of $\dfrac{x^2}{4} + \dfrac{y^2}{9} = 1$ is called a(n) ___(b)___ .

8. The major axis of $\dfrac{(x+3)^2}{4} + \dfrac{(y-2)^2}{9} = 1$ is ___(horizontal)(vertical)___ .

9. The graph of $xy = -7$ is a(n) _____ .

10. In sketching the graph determined by parametric equations, the parameter ___(does)(does not)___ have to appear in the graph.

11. The graph of a parabola is that of a function of x if the directrix is ___(parallel)(perpendicular)___ to the x-axis.

12. In a plane, the set of all points the sum of whose distances from two fixed points is a constant is called a(n) _____ .

13. In a plane the equation $\dfrac{x^2}{5} + \dfrac{y^2}{5} = 1$ defines a(n) _____ .

Answers to Review Questions

1. Circle.   2. Hyperbola.   3. (a) $\sqrt{3}$, (b) $(2, -4)$.   4. Parabola.   5. $(0, 2)$.
6. Downward.   7. (a) Hyperbola, (b) Ellipse.   8. Vertical.   9. Hyperbola (equilateral).
10. Does not.   11. Parallel.   12. Ellipse.   13. Circle.

Review Problems

*In Problems **1–4**, find the distance between the given points.*

1. $(1, 4), (-3, 2)$.

2. $(-1, -1), (-6, -1)$.

3. $(-8, 2), (0, -4)$.

4. $(-3, -4), (-1, 1)$.

*In Problems **5–8**, find the standard and general forms of an equation of a circle having the given center C and radius r.*

5. $C = (0, 0), r = 5$.

6. $C = (0, -2), r = \sqrt{2}$.

7. $C = (1, -1), r = \frac{1}{2}$.

8. $C = (\frac{1}{2}, \frac{1}{4}), r = 1$.

*In Problems **9–36**, discuss and sketch the graph of each equation.*

9. $x^2 + y^2 = 16$.

10. $(x-4)^2 + (y-3)^2 = 1$.

11. $(x+2)^2 + (y-1)^2 = 7$.

12. $x^2 + (y-1)^2 - 12 = 0$.

13. $9x^2 - 100y^2 = 900$.

14. $3x - 4y^2 = 0$.

15. $36x^2 + y^2 = 36$.

16. $36y^2 - x^2 = 4$.

17. $5x^2 + 2y = 0$.

18. $x^2 + \frac{1}{2}y^2 = 1$.

19. $6x^2 - 1 = -6y^2$.

20. $\frac{1}{49}x^2 - \frac{1}{49}y^2 = 1$.

21. $\dfrac{(x+1)^2}{2} - \dfrac{y^2}{8} = 2$.

22. $(y-6)^2 - (x+2)^2 = 1$.

23. $(y-2)^2 = 12x$.

24. $\frac{1}{2}y - (x-3)^2 = \frac{3}{2}y$.

25. $xy = -8$.

26. $x^2 = \frac{1}{3}y$.

27. $(x+5)^2 + \frac{1}{2}(y-2)^2 = 4$.

28. $x^2 = 36 - (y+2)^2$.

29. $x^2 + y^2 + 5x - 6y + 2 = 0.$

30. $x^2 + y^2 - x - 1 = 0.$

31. $9x^2 + 9y^2 - 18x - 6y + 10 = 0.$

32. $3x^2 + 3y^2 - 6x + 12y + 16 = 0.$

33. $y^2 - 2x - 2y = 4.$

34. $4x^2 + 9y^2 - 16x + 18y = 11.$

35. $2x^2 - 2y^2 + 4x + 10 = 0.$

36. $25x^2 - 2y^2 = -100.$

In Problems **37–39**, *find the standard form of an equation of the given conic.*

37. Parabola: vertex $(2, 1)$ and focus $(2, 4)$.

38. Hyperbola: vertices $(1, 1)$ and $(1, -5)$, and foci $(1, -2 \pm \sqrt{13})$.

39. Ellipse: vertices $(-2, -2)$ and $(-2, 8)$, and foci $(-2, 0)$ and $(-2, 6)$.

40. Sketch the curve and eliminate the parameter:

$$x = 2(2 - t),$$
$$y = t + t^2.$$

41. In the manner of Example 4 in Sec. 21.8, find a parametric representation for the curve given by the equation

$$2x^3 - y^3 = 3xy.$$

The Scientific Calculator

A.1 INTRODUCTION

Many of the numerical calculations required in this text can be performed with the simplest type of calculator available. However, the more complicated evaluations require the sophistication of a *scientific* calculator. In addition to the four basic arithmetic operations of addition, subtraction, multiplication, and division, a scientific calculator can handle squares, square roots, reciprocals, powers and roots, and trigonometric, inverse trigonometric, logarithmic, and exponential functions. Moreover, depending on the particular calculator model, a variety of additional features and capabilities may also be found.

The sequence of operations that allows one to perform a calculation is based, in part, on the type of logic system employed in the design of the calculator. Generally, one of two systems is used. The first is called **algebraic logic** (ALG). Most calculations done with algebraic logic can be entered just as they are stated in a given problem. For this reason the system is very easy to learn. The second logic system is called **reverse Polish notation** (RPN) in honor of Lukasiewicz, a Polish logician (1878–1956). Calculators with this logic are characterized by the absence of an equals key $\boxed{=}$. Although it may not be as easy to learn to use a calculator with this system, two advantages of RPN are the following: (1) intermediate results are displayed as they are calculated, and (2) the use of parentheses is eliminated when you are entering numbers in compound calculations. Furthermore, with RPN a complicated problem can sometimes be solved with fewer keystrokes than with ALG.

The choice of one logic system over the other, as well as choice of calculator model, is simply one of personal preference. Regardless of your choice, however, two points can be made. First, the only way to master the use of your particular calculator is to study the operator's manual that comes with it. Features and techniques of use do vary, and the manual will fully explain the capabilities of your calculator. Second, and most important, you must be aware that the ability to use a calculator does not replace your need to understand the underlying mathematical principles. After all, it is your *understanding* of the mathematics that enables you to solve a problem in the first place! Once a problem is set up, the calculator serves only to simplify the task of performing the numerical calculations.

This appendix is *not* intended to replace your calculator instruction manual. In the sections that follow, it is our purpose simply to illustrate some of the fundamental operations that can be performed with a scientific calculator. In particular, we are concerned with the type of calculations that occur throughout this book. In most numerical examples we give a *representative sequence* of key operations for both algebraic logic and reverse Polish notation. In general, these sequences apply to many calculator models. However, because wide variations in calculator logic do occur, you may find that changes in a particular sequence are necessary when using your own calculator. Although calculator displays of 8 or 10 digits are not unusual in practice, in all that follows *we shall give a rounded display* for our answers.

A.2 DATA ENTRY AND SCIENTIFIC NOTATION

There are slight differences in the techniques for entering and displaying data in the two logic systems. Data entry with RPN logic uses an **enter key**, designated by $\boxed{\text{ENTER}\uparrow}$. For convenience, we shall denote that key by $\boxed{\uparrow}$. In both systems, a **change-sign key**, designated by $\boxed{+/-}$ or $\boxed{\text{CHS}}$, is used to change the sign of the displayed number from positive to negative, or vice versa.

Example 1

Enter the number -63.25.

Solution

ALG: $\boxed{6}\ \boxed{3}\ \boxed{.}\ \boxed{2}\ \boxed{5}\ \boxed{+/-}$ Display: -63.25

RPN: $\boxed{6}\ \boxed{3}\ \boxed{.}\ \boxed{2}\ \boxed{5}\ \boxed{\text{CHS}}\ \boxed{\uparrow}$ Display: -63.25

When only one number is keyed into the calculator, you do not need to use the $\boxed{\uparrow}$ key.

An approximate value of π can be entered directly as $3.1416\ldots$, or you can use the special **pi key**, designated by $\boxed{\pi}$, that is available on all scientific calculators. Pressing $\boxed{\pi}$ immediately enters an approximate value of π and it appears in the display.

The **enter-exponent** (of 10) **key**, or **exponential key**, is designated by $\boxed{\text{EXP}}$, $\boxed{\text{EE}}$, or $\boxed{\text{EEX}}$, and is used to enter either a number in scientific notation or any product, one of whose factors is a power of 10. There are two points to remember! First, the exponent for 10 is entered *after* the exponential key is pressed. Second, for a negative exponent, the $\boxed{+/-}$ key is used *after* the corresponding positive exponent has been keyed in.

Example 2

Enter the number 54.7×10^6.

Solution

ALG: $\boxed{5}$ $\boxed{4}$ $\boxed{.}$ $\boxed{7}$ $\boxed{\text{EE}}$ $\boxed{6}$ Display: 54.7   06

RPN: $\boxed{5}$ $\boxed{4}$ $\boxed{.}$ $\boxed{7}$ $\boxed{\text{EEX}}$ $\boxed{6}$ $\boxed{\uparrow}$ Display: 54700000

If the exponent for 10 had been -6 instead of 6, then the keystroke sequence would remain the same, but the change-sign key would be pressed after the 6 is entered.

With RPN logic, you can avoid displaying a number with a string of zeros (such as in Example 2) by converting the displayed number to scientific notation display. This is done by pressing the **scientific notation key**, designated by $\boxed{\text{SCI}}$, followed by a number key. The number key specifies the number of decimal places to be retained in the display. There will, of course, be a single digit to the left of the decimal point. To change back to a standard decimal display, use the **fixed-decimal key**, designated by $\boxed{\text{FIX}}$, followed by a number key. The number key once again specifies the number of decimal places to be displayed. Some scientific calculators having ALG logic also allow the user to shift back and forth between fixed decimal and scientific notation displays. You should check the instruction manual for your calculator to see if this feature is available and, if so, how it is used.

Example 3

Enter the number -6.81×10^{12}.

Solution

ALG: $\boxed{6}$ $\boxed{.}$ $\boxed{8}$ $\boxed{1}$ $\boxed{+/-}$ $\boxed{\text{EE}}$ $\boxed{1}$ $\boxed{2}$ Display: -6.81 12

RPN: $\boxed{6}$ $\boxed{.}$ $\boxed{8}$ $\boxed{1}$ $\boxed{\text{CHS}}$ $\boxed{\text{EE}}$ $\boxed{1}$ $\boxed{2}$ $\boxed{\uparrow}$ Display: -6.8100000 12

$\boxed{\text{SCI}}$ $\boxed{2}$ Display: -6.81 12

Throughout the rest of this appendix, we shall use a compact notation in which a number in a box represents a keystroke sequence. For example, $\boxed{12.3}$ represents the keystrokes $\boxed{1}\,\boxed{2}\,\boxed{.}\,\boxed{3}$.

A.3 ARITHMETIC OPERATIONS

The four basic arithmetic operations are performed with the use of the four function keys designated by $\boxed{+}$, $\boxed{-}$, $\boxed{\times}$, and $\boxed{\div}$. With RPN logic, the result is displayed immediately after one of the four function keys is pressed; no $\boxed{=}$ key is needed as it is with ALG. In RPN, an operation such as subtraction is executed as soon as the subtraction function key is pressed. The two numbers in the subtraction are essentially positioned or stacked *before* performing the subtraction. The numbers are separated by the use of the $\boxed{\uparrow}$ key.

Example 1

Evaluate $17.2 - 6.9$.

Solution

ALG: $\boxed{17.2}\ \boxed{-}\ \boxed{6.9}\ \boxed{=}$ Display: 10.30

RPN: $\boxed{17.2}\ \boxed{\uparrow}\ \boxed{6.9}\ \boxed{-}$ Display: 10.30

Chain calculations pose unique situations because the way they are handled depends on the particular logic used in the calculator. *You must check the specific instructions in your owner's manual to learn how to use your calculator!* With ALG logic you may be able to use **parentheses keys**, designated by $\boxed{(}$ and $\boxed{)}$, whenever there is doubt in your mind as to how the calculator will treat a given expression.

Example 2

Evaluate $(6.32 + 8.45) \div \pi$.

Solution

ALG: $\boxed{(}\ \boxed{6.32}\ \boxed{+}\ \boxed{8.45}\ \boxed{)}\ \boxed{\div}\ \boxed{\pi}\ \boxed{=}$ Display: 4.70

RPN: $\boxed{6.32}\ \boxed{\uparrow}\ \boxed{8.45}\ \boxed{+}\ \boxed{\pi}\ \boxed{\div}$ Display: 4.70

If the key sequence for ALG logic in Example 2 were performed without keying in the parentheses, the expression evaluated would be $6.32 + (8.45 \div \pi) = 9.01$. This is because of the hierarchy of operations in ALG logic, in which multiplications and divisions are performed before additions and subtractions. There is another way to accomplish the calculation in Example 2. We can use the $\boxed{=}$ key to perform the addition first; in this way the parentheses are not needed at all.

ALG: $\boxed{6.32}$ $\boxed{+}$ $\boxed{8.45}$ $\boxed{=}$ $\boxed{\div}$ $\boxed{\pi}$ $\boxed{=}$ Display: 4.70

Example 3

Evaluate $(6.2 \times 9.0) - (8.0 \div 3.5)$.

Solution

ALG: $\boxed{6.2}$ $\boxed{\times}$ $\boxed{9}$ $\boxed{=}$ $\boxed{-}$ $\boxed{(}$ $\boxed{8}$ $\boxed{\div}$ $\boxed{3.5}$ $\boxed{)}$ $\boxed{=}$ Display: 53.51

RPN: $\boxed{6.2}$ $\boxed{\uparrow}$ $\boxed{9}$ $\boxed{\times}$ $\boxed{8}$ $\boxed{\uparrow}$ $\boxed{3.5}$ $\boxed{\div}$ $\boxed{-}$ Display: 53.51

In the RPN sequence, note that the key operations $\boxed{8}$ $\boxed{\uparrow}$ begin the entry of a new number string; the value of 6.2×9.0 has already been stored. The final keystroke operation, $\boxed{-}$, causes the difference between the stored value of 6.2×9.0 and the value of the last number string $8.0 \div 3.5$ to be displayed.

Example 4

Evaluate $\dfrac{40,000 \times 15.6}{12.6 + 15.7}$.

Solution

ALG: $\boxed{40000}$ $\boxed{\times}$ $\boxed{15.6}$ $\boxed{=}$ $\boxed{\div}$ $\boxed{(}$ $\boxed{12.6}$ $\boxed{+}$ $\boxed{15.7}$ $\boxed{)}$ $\boxed{=}$

Display: 22049.47

RPN: $\boxed{40000}$ $\boxed{\uparrow}$ $\boxed{15.6}$ $\boxed{\times}$ $\boxed{12.6}$ $\boxed{\uparrow}$ $\boxed{15.7}$ $\boxed{+}$ $\boxed{\div}$ Display: 22049.47

Problem Set A.3

Evaluate each expression.

1. $8.735 \div (-8.23)$.
2. 33.65×0.0072.
3. $(8 \times 10^{-6})(62.3)$.
4. $-82.5 \div (5.2 \times 10^{-2})$.
5. $6.23 + (8.2 - 3)$.
6. $0.076 + (4.8 - 7)$.

7. $8\pi - 16.3$.

8. $5\pi - 4.2$.

9. $6.2\pi + [8.3(2)]$.

10. $(6.02 \times 10^{-23})(1.73)$.

11. $26.1 \times 13.2 \times 0.315$.

12. $0.064 \times 7.8 \times 10^{-13} \times \pi$.

13. $\dfrac{6.27 \times 10^{13}}{15.5 \times 8.3}$.

14. $\dfrac{18\pi \times 40,000}{14.9}$.

15. $\dfrac{1}{2}\left(\dfrac{\pi}{3.6}\right)(18.4)$.

16. $\dfrac{6(-3.92)}{0.047}$.

17. $10^4 - [(82.6)(5.3)]$.

18. $\dfrac{76.4}{10^{-2} + 4}$.

19. $\dfrac{5 \times 10^{13}}{26.3 - 18.1}$.

20. $2\pi(3 \times 10^4)(2.6 \times 10^3)$.

21. $21.3 + \dfrac{\pi}{3}$.

22. $\dfrac{4\pi}{3}(8.2 - 16.3)$.

23. $\dfrac{(9 \times 10^9)(8 \times 10^{-6})(5 \times 10^{-6})}{3.0}$.

24. $\dfrac{(9 \times 10^9)(6.2 \times 10^{-6})(-8.4 \times 10^{-6})}{5.1}$.

25. $\dfrac{(18.3\pi)(-7.23)}{13.7 + 6.83}$.

26. $\dfrac{[(1.6 \times 10^{-5}) + (4.2 \times 10^{-5})]\pi}{1100}$.

27. $\dfrac{5\pi + 72.83 - 13}{4.28\pi - 5.17}$.

28. $\dfrac{280,000 \times 0.0000421}{0.006 \times 7,000,000}$.

Answers to Problem Set A.3

1. -1.06.   2. 0.24.   3. 4.98×10^{-4}.   4. -1586.54.   5. 11.43.   6. -2.12.   7. 8.83.
8. 11.51.   9. 36.08.   10. 1.04×10^{-22}.   11. 108.52.   12. 1.57×10^{-13}.   13. 4.87×10^{11}.
14. 1.52×10^5.   15. 8.03.   16. -500.43.   17. 9562.22.   18. 19.05.   19. 6.10×10^{12}.
20. 4.90×10^8.   21. 22.35.   22. -33.93.   23. 0.12.   24. -0.09.   25. -20.25
26. 1.66×10^{-7}.   27. 9.13.   28. 2.81×10^{-4}.

A.4   RECIPROCAL, SQUARE, SQUARE ROOT, AND FACTORIAL

The special function keys described in this section are all one-number function keys. They operate on only *one* number—the number that is displayed by the calculator. This displayed number could be keyed in or it could be the result of a previous calculation. If x is the displayed number, then:

1. The **reciprocal key**, designated by $\boxed{1/x}$, calculates the reciprocal of x for $x \neq 0$. If $x = 0$, an error message is displayed.

2. The **square key**, designated by $\boxed{x^2}$, calculates the square of x.

3. The **square-root key**, designated by $\boxed{\sqrt{x}}$, calculates the square root of x for $x \geq 0$. If $x < 0$, an error message is displayed.

4. The **factorial key**, designated by $\boxed{x!}$ or $\boxed{n!}$, calculates the factorial of a nonnegative integer x, where $x! = x(x - 1)(x - 2)\cdots(2)(1)$ and 0! is defined to be 1. An error message may be displayed if the factorial value exceeds the computational capabilities of the calculator.

The functions above are performed without the use of the $\boxed{=}$ or $\boxed{\uparrow}$ keys, so *the keystroke sequences are generally the same for both ALG and RPN logic.* However, differences in the displays for the two systems may occur.

Example 1

Find the (a) reciprocal, (b) square, and (c) square root of 48.7.

Solution

a. ALG and RPN: $\boxed{48.7}$ $\boxed{1/x}$ Display: 0.0205

b. ALG and RPN: $\boxed{48.7}$ $\boxed{x^2}$ Display: 2371.69

c. ALG and RPN: $\boxed{48.7}$ $\boxed{\sqrt{x}}$ Display: 6.98

Example 2

Evaluate $\dfrac{5\sqrt{2}}{2}$.

Solution

ALG: $\boxed{5}$ $\boxed{\times}$ $\boxed{2}$ $\boxed{\sqrt{x}}$ $\boxed{\div}$ $\boxed{2}$ $\boxed{=}$ Display: 3.54

RPN: $\boxed{5}$ $\boxed{\uparrow}$ $\boxed{2}$ $\boxed{\sqrt{x}}$ $\boxed{\times}$ $\boxed{2}$ $\boxed{\div}$ Display: 3.54

Example 3

Evaluate $3x^2 - 7x$ for $x = 4.2$.

Solution

ALG: $\boxed{3}$ $\boxed{\times}$ $\boxed{4.2}$ $\boxed{x^2}$ $\boxed{-}$ $\boxed{(}$ $\boxed{7}$ $\boxed{\times}$ $\boxed{4.2}$ $\boxed{)}$ $\boxed{=}$ Display: 23.52

RPN: $\boxed{3}$ $\boxed{\uparrow}$ $\boxed{4.2}$ $\boxed{x^2}$ $\boxed{\times}$ $\boxed{7}$ $\boxed{\uparrow}$ $\boxed{4.2}$ $\boxed{\times}$ $\boxed{-}$ Display: 23.52

Example 4

Evaluate $\dfrac{6}{1 + \dfrac{1}{2.8}}$.

Solution

ALG: $\boxed{6}$ $\boxed{\div}$ $\boxed{(}$ $\boxed{1}$ $\boxed{+}$ $\boxed{2.8}$ $\boxed{1/x}$ $\boxed{)}$ $\boxed{=}$ Display: 4.42

RPN: $\boxed{6}$ $\boxed{\uparrow}$ $\boxed{1}$ $\boxed{\uparrow}$ $\boxed{2.8}$ $\boxed{1/x}$ $\boxed{+}$ $\boxed{\div}$ Display: 4.42

Example 5

Find the hypotenuse of a right triangle in which the legs have lengths of 9.2 cm and 18.6 cm.

Solution   Using the Pythagorean theorem, we have

$$c^2 = a^2 + b^2$$
$$= (9.2)^2 + (18.6)^2,$$
$$c = \sqrt{(9.2)^2 + (18.6)^2}.$$

ALG: $\boxed{9.2}$ $\boxed{x^2}$ $\boxed{+}$ $\boxed{18.6}$ $\boxed{x^2}$ $\boxed{=}$ $\boxed{\sqrt{x}}$ Display: 20.75

RPN: $\boxed{9.2}$ $\boxed{x^2}$ $\boxed{18.6}$ $\boxed{x^2}$ $\boxed{+}$ $\boxed{\sqrt{x}}$ Display: 20.75

With RPN note that the intermediate result $(9.2)^2$ is automatically stored. You do not have to press the enter key to store it.

Example 6

Find the surface area of a sphere of radius 1.25 m.

Solution   The surface area A of a sphere of radius r is given by

$$A = 4\pi r^2,$$
$$A = 4\pi(1.25)^2.$$

ALG: $\boxed{4}$ $\boxed{\times}$ $\boxed{\pi}$ $\boxed{\times}$ $\boxed{1.25}$ $\boxed{x^2}$ $\boxed{=}$ Display: 19.63

RPN: $\boxed{4}$ $\boxed{\uparrow}$ $\boxed{\pi}$ $\boxed{\times}$ $\boxed{1.25}$ $\boxed{x^2}$ $\boxed{\times}$ Display: 19.63

Example 7

Find $\dfrac{5!}{4!3!}$.

Solution

ALG: [5] [x!] [÷] [4] [x!] [÷] [3] [x!] [=]　　Display: 0.833

RPN: [5] [x!] [4] [x!] [÷] [3] [x!] [÷]　　　Display: 0.833

Here we used the general fact that $\dfrac{a}{bc} = (a \div b) \div c$.

Problem Set A.4

In Problems 1–32, perform the indicated operations.

1. $\dfrac{1}{0.01683}$.

2. $\dfrac{1}{\sqrt{137.4}}$.

3. $\dfrac{1}{3.2 \times 10^{-5}}$.

4. $5\sqrt{3}$.

5. $\dfrac{6\sqrt{17.2}}{5.1}$.

6. $(5.2)^2 + (6.3)^2$.

7. $(8.3^2 - 4.2)^2$.

8. $\left(\dfrac{1}{2.6 \times 10^{-3}}\right)^2$.

9. $4\pi(3.2)^2$.

10. $\pi(8.7)^2$.

11. $\sqrt{(8.1)^2 + (3.2)^2}$.

12. $\dfrac{(7.45 \times 10^{23})^2}{3\pi}$.

13. $\dfrac{1}{2}(6.23)^2\left(\dfrac{5.2}{3.1}\right)^2$.

14. $(15\pi)^2 + 15\pi^2$.

15. $\sqrt{6.5} - \sqrt{18}$.

16. $5\sqrt{18} - 4.6$.

17. $(3.2 + 5\pi)^2\sqrt{8.2}$.

18. $\dfrac{4 + 5\pi}{\sqrt{182}}$.

19. $\left(\dfrac{2}{\sqrt{5} - \sqrt{3}}\right)^2$.

20. $\left(\dfrac{3.6}{2\sqrt{7} - \sqrt{11}}\right)^2$.

21. $(0.032)\sqrt{(9.6)^2 - (5.2)^2}$.

22. $\left(\dfrac{1}{9\pi \times 16.2}\right)^2$.

23. $(\sqrt{13} - 3.6\pi)^2$.

24. $\dfrac{(6.02)^2 - 13.1}{\sqrt{15.2}}$.

25. $\left(\dfrac{2 + \sqrt{2}}{2 - \sqrt{2}}\right)^2$.

26. $2 + \dfrac{0.2}{4} - \dfrac{(0.2)^2}{64}$.

27. $\sqrt{3! + 5!}$.

28. $\left(\dfrac{4!}{3!2!}\right)^2$.

29. $\dfrac{3 + \sqrt{(-3)^2 - 4(7)(-8)}}{2(7)}$.

30. $\dfrac{-5 - \sqrt{(5)^2 - 4(3)(-4)}}{2(3)}$.

31. $\sqrt{(6.8 - 3.7)^2 + (8.2 - 13.9)^2}$.

32. $(1.63 - 1)\left(\dfrac{1}{3.65} - \dfrac{1}{8.28}\right)$.

33. Evaluate $3(t + 2)^2$ if $t = \frac{1}{8}$.

34. Evaluate $3t^2 - 2t + 1$ if $t = 2.2$.

35. Evaluate $\sqrt{4.7t^2 - t}$ if $t = 4.58$.

A.5   POWERS AND ROOTS

The **power-function key**, designated by $\boxed{y^x}$, is a two-number function key. It raises a positive number y to *any* xth power. For $y < 0$, x must be an integer. The keystroke sequences are slightly different for the two systems of logic. Typical sequences are:

ALG: $\boxed{y}$ $\boxed{y^x}$ $\boxed{x}$ $\boxed{=}$ [The exponent is keyed in *after* the operation key.]

RPN: $\boxed{y}$ $\boxed{\uparrow}$ $\boxed{x}$ $\boxed{y^x}$ [Both numbers are keyed in *before* the operation key. The $\boxed{\uparrow}$ key separates the numbers.]

Example 1

Evaluate 2.6^9.

Solution

ALG: $\boxed{2.6}$ $\boxed{y^x}$ $\boxed{9}$ $\boxed{=}$ Display: 5429.50

RPN: $\boxed{2.6}$ $\boxed{\uparrow}$ $\boxed{9}$ $\boxed{y^x}$ Display: 5429.50

Example 2

Find $3.94^{-1.26}$.

Solution

ALG: $\boxed{3.94}$ $\boxed{y^x}$ $\boxed{1.26}$ $\boxed{+/-}$ $\boxed{=}$ Display: 0.1777

RPN: $\boxed{3.94}$ $\boxed{\uparrow}$ $\boxed{1.26}$ $\boxed{CHS}$ $\boxed{y^x}$ Display: 0.1777

The $\boxed{y^x}$ key can be used to find roots if we use the relation

$$\sqrt[n]{y} = y^{1/n}.$$

The reciprocal key is also useful here.

Example 3

Find $\sqrt[5]{138.7}$.

Solution

$$\sqrt[5]{138.7} = 138.7^{1/5}.$$

ALG: $\boxed{138.7}$ $\boxed{y^x}$ $\boxed{5}$ $\boxed{1/x}$ $\boxed{=}$ Display: 2.682

RPN: $\boxed{138.7}$ $\boxed{\uparrow}$ $\boxed{5}$ $\boxed{1/x}$ $\boxed{y^x}$ Display: 2.682

Some ALG logic calculators may have an **inverse key**, designated by $\boxed{\text{INV}}$. In such cases, roots can be obtained without the use of the reciprocal key. The keystroke sequence $\boxed{y}$ $\boxed{\text{INV}}$ $\boxed{y^x}$ $\boxed{x}$ calculates the xth root of y. Using this feature to redo Example 3, we have:

ALG: $\boxed{138.7}$ $\boxed{\text{INV}}$ $\boxed{y^x}$ $\boxed{5}$ $\boxed{=}$ Display: 2.682

The simplest and most direct method for finding roots is provided on some ALG logic calculators by a special **root key**, designated by $\boxed{\sqrt[x]{y}}$. To redo the problem of Example 3 with such a feature, the sequence is

ALG: $\boxed{138.7}$ $\boxed{\sqrt[x]{y}}$ $\boxed{5}$ $\boxed{=}$ Display: 2.682

In technical work it is often necessary to evaluate the forms 10^x and e^x, where $e = 2.7182\ldots$. Even though these forms could be handled by the use of the power key $\boxed{y^x}$, nearly all scientific calculators have special provisions for handling them. A **natural-antilogarithm key**, or **inverse-logarithm key (base e)**, designated by $\boxed{e^x}$, computes e raised to the xth power, where x is the displayed number. The exponent x may be any number. On some calculators with ALG logic, the natural antilogarithm function is accomplished by the keystroke sequence $\boxed{\text{INV}}$ $\boxed{\text{LN}}$. The *natural-logarithm key* $\boxed{\text{LN}}$ is discussed separately in Sec. A.7.

Similarly, a **common-antilogarithm key**, or **inverse-logarithm key (base 10)**, designated by $\boxed{10^x}$, computes 10 raised to the xth power. Alternatively, this common antilogarithm function might be accomplished by the keystroke sequence $\boxed{\text{INV}}$ $\boxed{\text{LOG}}$. The *common-logarithm key* $\boxed{\text{LOG}}$ is also discussed in Sec. A.7.

Example 4

Evaluate $2.5e^{-1.6}$.

Solution

ALG: | 2.5 | × | 1.6 | +/− | INV | LN | = | Display: 0.5047

RPN: | 2.5 | ↑ | 1.6 | CHS | e^x | × | Display: 0.5047

Example 5

Evaluate $-5.3(10)^{2.7}$.

Solution

ALG: | 5.3 | +/− | × | 2.7 | INV | LOG | = | Display: −2656.29

RPN: | 5.3 | CHS | ↑ | 2.7 | 10^x | × | Display: −2656.29

Problem Set A.5

Evaluate each expression.

1. 3^5.

2. 4^7.

3. 5^{-4}.

4. 8^{-7}.

5. $(-6)^8$.

6. $(-5)^9$.

7. $10^{6.71}$.

8. $10^{-2.3}$.

9. $10^{-0.321}$.

10. e^7.

11. e^{-8}.

12. $e^{5.2}$.

13. $e^{-6.7}$.

14. $e^{\sqrt{3}}$.

15. $10^{\sqrt{6}}$.

16. $(6.32)^{1.74}$.

17. $(2.93)^{-3.4}$.

18. $(-7.6)^4$.

19. $(-8.3)^5$.

20. $(0.47)^{13.2}$.

21. $(6.2 \times 10^{-23})^4$.

22. $(7.93 \times 10^5)^{6.1}$.

23. $\sqrt[5]{13}$.

24. $\sqrt[7]{9}$.

25. $\sqrt[3]{174}$.

26. $\sqrt[3]{(18.3)^2}$.

27. $\sqrt[3]{7.23 \times 10^{19}}$.

28. $\sqrt[4]{8.6 \times 10^{-13}}$.

29. $6(10)^{2\sqrt{3}}$.

30. $\frac{4}{3}\pi(18.7)^3$.

31. $60e^{-1.5}$.

32. $e^{0.63} + e^{-0.63}$.

33. $120(1 - e^{-3.2})$.

34. $\frac{160}{22}(1 - e^{-1.13})$.

35. $\frac{4}{3}\pi[(16.7)^3 - (6.2)^3]$.

36. $(1.6 \times 10^{-19})^4(1.67 \times 10^{27})^2$.

37. $\dfrac{6.27(1 - 1.03^{16})}{1 - 1.03}$.

38. $\dfrac{\sqrt[3]{7.38 \times 10^{10}} + \sqrt[5]{5.28 \times 10^{12}}}{13.3}$.

39. $\dfrac{2.6 \times 10^{-3}}{4\pi(8.85 \times 10^{-12})}\left(\dfrac{1}{7.2 \times 10^{-3}}\right)^{3/2}$.

40. $\pi(3.29 + 6.82)^5 \sqrt[3]{(7.2)^2 + (3.29 - 6.82)^2}$.

A.6 TRIGONOMETRIC AND INVERSE TRIGONOMETRIC FUNCTIONS

All scientific calculators feature special keys for finding values of trigonometric functions. These keys, designated by $\boxed{\text{SIN}}$, $\boxed{\text{COS}}$, and $\boxed{\text{TAN}}$, are used to find the sine, cosine, and tangent, respectively, of the displayed number. When one of these keys is pressed, the calculator interprets the displayed number to be an angle and it determines the value of the appropriate trigonometric function. There may, however, be one necessary preliminary step. *You may have to set your calculator for the proper angular mode of operation.*

Typically, scientific calculators are capable of functioning in up to three different angular modes: degrees, radians, and grads (100 grads = 90°). The angular mode determines how the calculator "reads" the displayed number. For example, when the calculator is in the *degree* mode, it interprets the displayed number to be an angle measured in degrees. Calculators differ in the mechanical method used to set the angular mode. Your calculator may have a slide switch to change modes, it may have individual keys to set each mode, or it may have one key that, with repeated pressings, allows mode changes. In most cases, when a calculator is turned on it is in the degree mode. In all that follows we shall assume that the calculator is set in the appropriate angular mode before a trigonometric function key is used.

Example 1

Evaluate (a) $\sin 52.7°$, (b) $\cos 4\pi/3$, (c) $\tan^2 70°$, and (d) $\sec 110°$.

Solution

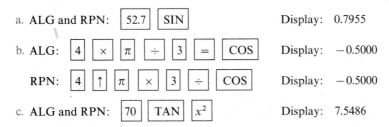

a. ALG and RPN: $\boxed{52.7}$ $\boxed{\text{SIN}}$ Display: 0.7955

b. ALG: $\boxed{4}$ $\boxed{\times}$ $\boxed{\pi}$ $\boxed{\div}$ $\boxed{3}$ $\boxed{=}$ $\boxed{\text{COS}}$ Display: -0.5000

   RPN: $\boxed{4}$ $\boxed{\uparrow}$ $\boxed{\pi}$ $\boxed{\times}$ $\boxed{3}$ $\boxed{\div}$ $\boxed{\text{COS}}$ Display: -0.5000

c. ALG and RPN: $\boxed{70}$ $\boxed{\text{TAN}}$ $\boxed{x^2}$ Display: 7.5486

d. Because sec $110° = 1/(\cos 110°)$, the keystroke sequence is:

ALG and RPN: | 110 | | COS | | 1/x | Display: -2.9238

Cosecants and cotangents of angles can also be found by using the reciprocal relations of Chapter 6.

Example 2

Evaluate $\dfrac{6 \sin 26.44°}{\sin 30°}$.

Solution

ALG: | 6 | | × | | 26.44 | | SIN | | ÷ | | 30 | | SIN | | = | Display: 5.3431

RPN: | 6 | | ↑ | | 26.44 | | SIN | | × | | 30 | | SIN | | ÷ | Display: 5.3431

Example 3

Find the value of c given that

$$c^2 = 10^2 + 40^2 - 2(10)(40) \cos 120°.$$

Solution   We must find the square root of the right side.

ALG: | 10 | | x^2 | | + | | 40 | | x^2 | | − | | (| | 2 | | × | | 10 | | × | | 40 | | × | | 120 | | COS |

|) | | = | | $\sqrt{x}$ | Display: 45.8258

RPN: | 10 | | x^2 | | 40 | | x^2 | | + | | 2 | | ↑ | | 10 | | × | | 40 | | × | | 120 | | COS | | × | | − |

| $\sqrt{x}$ | Display: 45.8258

All scientific calculators are capable of determining an angle θ whose trigonometric value is shown in the display. Typically, this is done by using the **inverse-trigonometric keys** designated | SIN^{-1} |, | COS^{-1} |, and | TAN^{-1} |. With some calculators, the key sequence | INV | | SIN |, | INV | | COS |, or | INV | | TAN | is used instead. The inverse sine function, $\sin^{-1}$, is also called the arcsine function and the symbol $\arcsin x$ may be used instead of $\sin^{-1} x$. Generally, for a displayed trigonometric value x, the corresponding angle θ determined by the calculator will be in the range (in degrees) shown in Table A.1.

TABLE A.1

Function	Range of x	Angle θ
$\sin^{-1}$	$-1 \le x \le 1$	$-90° \le \theta \le 90°$
$\cos^{-1}$	$-1 \le x \le 1$	$0° \le \theta \le 180°$
$\tan^{-1}$	$-\infty < x < \infty$	$-90° < \theta < 90°$

It is important to keep in mind that the angle θ computed by the calculator is measured in degrees, radians, or grads, depending on the angular mode to which the calculator is set. We assume the degree mode is used in the following example.

Example 4

Find an angle B such that

$$\sin B = \frac{6 \sin 75.52°}{8}.$$

That is, find

$$\sin^{-1}\left[\frac{6 \sin 75.52°}{8}\right].$$

Solution

ALG: $\boxed{6}$ $\boxed{\times}$ $\boxed{75.52}$ $\boxed{\text{SIN}}$ $\boxed{\div}$ $\boxed{8}$ $\boxed{=}$ $\boxed{\text{INV}}$ $\boxed{\text{SIN}}$ Display: 46.57

Thus $B = 46.57°$.

RPN: $\boxed{6}$ $\boxed{\uparrow}$ $\boxed{75.52}$ $\boxed{\text{SIN}}$ $\boxed{\times}$ $\boxed{8}$ $\boxed{\div}$ $\boxed{\text{SIN}^{-1}}$ Display: 46.57

Thus $B = 46.57°$.

If the calculator is set to the radian mode just before the inverse trigonometric function key is used in Example 4, the calculator will compute a correct angular value of B in radians, namely, 0.8127. However, if the radian mode is set *before* the 75.52 is entered, the final answer is 0.0912, which is an *incorrect* value for B. In the latter case, the intermediate key sequence $\boxed{75.52}$ $\boxed{\text{SIN}}$ gives the sine of 75.52 *radians*, whereas the problem requires the sine of 75.52 *degrees*.

Problem Set A.6

In Problems 1–22, find the value of the indicated expression. Given your answer rounded to four decimal places.

1. $\sin 56.8°$.

2. $\sin(-108.3°)$.

3. $\sin 2.68$.

4. $\sin\left(-\frac{6\pi}{7}\right)$.

5. $\cos 118°$.

6. $\cos(-113.5°)$.

7. cos 7.25.   8. tan 72.9°.   9. tan 352.1°.

10. tan (−45°).   11. tan 2.83.   12. sec 13.7°.

13. sec 5.83.   14. csc (−68.7°).   15. csc 137°.

16. cot 65°.   17. cot 3.8.   18. cot (−2.2π).

19. $\sin^2 30.6°$.   20. $\cos^2\left(\dfrac{\pi}{7.1}\right)$.   21. $\tan^2 45.7°$.

22. $\sin^2 33° + \cos^2 33°$.

In Problems **23–40,** *find the value of the given expression. Give all answers to two decimal places.*

23. $26.7 \sin 18.5°$.   24. $\dfrac{32.6}{\cos 210°}$.   25. $36.9 \tan 46°$.

26. $18.3 \sin^2\left(\dfrac{\pi}{8}\right)$.   27. $\dfrac{16.3}{\sin^2\left(\dfrac{\pi}{7}\right)}$.   28. $\dfrac{46 \sin 14.1°}{\sin 25°}$.

29. $110 \cos 36.5° + 220 \cos 94.3°$.   30. $28.3 \sin 62.1° + 43.1 \sin 313°$.

31. $\sin^{-1} 0.6231$.   32. $\cos^{-1} 0.8392$.   33. $\text{Arctan } \dfrac{17.6}{-13.2}$.

34. $\tan^{-1} \dfrac{-72.3}{93.4}$.   35. $\text{Arcsin}\left(\dfrac{7 \sin 47.2°}{20.9}\right)$.

36. $\sin^{-1}\left(\dfrac{6.2 \sin 60.3°}{8.4}\right)$.   37. $\cos^{-1}\left[\dfrac{85^2 + 90^2 - 110^2}{2(85)(90)}\right]$.

38. $\sin 32.3° \cos 41.8° + \cos 32.3° \sin 41.8°$.

39. $\dfrac{\tan 83.1° - \tan 22°}{1 + \tan 83.1° \tan 22°}$.   40. $62.4\left(\dfrac{\sin 46.3°}{1 + \cos 46.3°}\right)^2$.

Answers to Problem Set A.6

1. 0.8368.   2. −0.9494.   3. 0.4454.   4. −0.4339.   5. −0.4695.   6. −0.3987.
7. 0.5679.   8. 3.2506.   9. −0.1388.   10. −1.0000.   11. −0.3221.   12. 1.0293.
13. 1.1123.   14. −1.0733.   15. 1.4663.   16. 0.4663.   17. 1.2927.   18. −1.3764.
19. 0.2591.   20. 0.8167.   21. 1.0501.   22. 1.0000.   23. 8.47.   24. −37.64.   25. 38.21.
26. 2.68.   27. 86.58.   28. 26.52.   29. 71.93.   30. −6.51.   31. 38.54°.   32. 32.94°.
33. −53.13°.   34. −37.74°.   35. 14.23°.   36. 39.88°.   37. 77.83°.   38. 0.96.
39. 1.81.   40. 11.41.

A.7   COMMON AND NATURAL LOGARITHMS

Logarithmic function keys, which are available on all scientific calculators, allow you to compute the values of logarithms to base *e* and base 10. The **common-logarithm key**, or **base 10 logarithm key**, designated by $\boxed{\text{LOG}}$, computes the logarithm base 10 of the displayed number. The **natural-logarithm key**, or **base *e* logarithm key**, designated by $\boxed{\text{LN}}$, computes the logarithm base *e* of the displayed number. In each case, the number whose logarithm is to be found must be greater than zero or an error message will appear; the logarithm of a nonpositive number is not defined.

Example 1

Find the (a) common and (b) natural logarithms of 362.7.

Solution

a. ALG and RPN: [362.7] [LOG]   Display: 2.55955

b. ALG and RPN: [362.7] [LN]   Display: 5.89358

Example 2

Evaluate $3.7 \log 8^{2.3}$.

Solution

ALG: [3.7] [×] [( ] [8] [y^x] [2.3] [ )] [LOG] [=]   Display: 7.685

RPN: [3.7] [↑] [8] [↑] [2.3] [y^x] [LOG] [×]   Display: 7.685

Example 3

Evaluate $\sqrt{7}\,e^{\ln(\sin 32.7°)}$.

Solution

ALG: [7] [$\sqrt{x}$] [×] [32.7] [SIN] [LN] [INV] [LN] [=]   Display: 1.4293

RPN: [7] [$\sqrt{x}$] [32.7] [SIN] [LN] [e^x] [×]   Display: 1.4293

Example 4

Evaluate $4 + \dfrac{\log 8}{\log 3}$.

Solution

ALG: [4] [+] [( ] [8] [LOG] [÷] [3] [LOG] [ )] [=]   Display: 5.89279

RPN: [4] [↑] [8] [LOG] [3] [LOG] [÷] [+]   Display: 5.89279

Problem Set A.7

In Problems **1–20**, *evaluate the expressions. Given all answers to five decimal places.*

1. log 4.837.

2. log 0.932.

3. $\log \sqrt{182.4}$.

4. ln 16.47.

5. ln 0.8459.

6. $\ln \sqrt{16.74}$.

7. $\log \left(\dfrac{36.7}{\sqrt{18.3}} \right)$.

8. $\ln (\sqrt{821} + 9.35)$.

9. $\dfrac{\log 16.3}{\log 5.9}$.

10. $7 + \dfrac{\log 9.2}{\log 4.6}$.

11. $\dfrac{4 + \log 18}{3}$.

12. $4 + \dfrac{\log 18}{3}$.

13. $\log (42.3^{8.1})$.

14. $\ln (16.3^{-3.2})$.

15. log sin 52.7°.

16. ln cos 64.3°.

17. $10 \log \dfrac{9.3 \times 10^{-10}}{10^{-12}}$.

18. $\sqrt{8.3} \ 10^{\ln 6.2}$.

19. $5.3 e^{\ln \sin 60°}$.

20. $(5 + \log 13)17.3^{\ln 5.2}$.

Answers to Problem Set A.7

1. 0.68458.   **2.** −0.03058.   **3.** 1.13051.   **4.** 2.80154.   **5.** −0.16735.   **6.** 1.40890.
7. 0.93344.   **8.** 3.63767.   **9.** 1.57253.   **10.** 8.45421.   **11.** 1.75176.   **12.** 4.41842.
13. 13.17336.   **14.** −8.93173.   **15.** −0.09937.   **16.** −0.83550.   **17.** 29.68483.
18. 192.34829.   **19.** 4.58993.   **20.** 672.10449.

Answers to Odd-Numbered Problems

Problem Set 0.2

1. 21.   **3.** 1.   **5.** 20.   **7.** 3.

9. 30.   **11.** 20.   **13.** 0.   **15.** 2.

17. 5.   **19.** 13.   **21.** 2.   **23.** 1.

25. 12.   **27.** 12.   **29.** 11.   **31.** 4.

33. 8, 2.   **35.** 5.   **37.** 4.   **39.** 36.

41. Ten-thousands place.

Problem Set 0.3

1. 8.   **3.** 6.   **5.** $\frac{8}{7}, \frac{7}{7}, \frac{8}{1}$.   **7.** $7\frac{2}{3}$.

9. $3\frac{3}{5}$.   **11.** $1\frac{1}{2}$.   **13.** $3\frac{1}{4}$.   **15.** $\frac{12}{18}$.

17. 20.   **19.** 33.   **21.** 3.   **23.** 3.

25. 15.   **27.** 49.   **29.** $\frac{7}{3}$.   **31.** $\frac{4}{3}$.

33. $\frac{4}{5}$.   **35.** $\frac{11}{24}$.   **37.** $\frac{1}{4}$.   **39.** $\frac{1}{10}$.

41. $\frac{4}{3}$.   **43.** $\frac{9}{2}$.   **45.** 20.   **47.** $\frac{2}{77}$.

49. $\frac{35}{8}$.

Problem Set 0.4

1. 3.   **3.** $\frac{1}{6}$.   **5.** $\frac{12}{13}$.   **7.** $\frac{1}{8}$.

9. 18.   **11.** 20.   **13.** 36.   **15.** 60.

17. $\frac{23}{5}$.   **19.** $\frac{51}{7}$.   **21.** $\frac{19}{12}$.   **23.** $\frac{1}{56}$.

25. $\frac{59}{36}$.   **27.** $\frac{9}{20}$.   **29.** $\frac{19}{30}$.   **31.** $2\frac{11}{12}$.

33. $1\frac{13}{24}$.   **35.** $\frac{17}{6}$.   **37.** $\frac{81}{40}$.

Problem Set 0.5

1. $\frac{5}{3}$.   **3.** $\frac{35}{36}$.   **5.** 0.   **7.** 2.

9. $\frac{10}{27}$.   **11.** $\frac{8}{15}$.   **13.** $\frac{35}{11}$.   **15.** $\frac{27}{10}$.

17. $\frac{11}{6}$.   **19.** $\frac{32}{15}$.   **21.** $\frac{20}{3}$.   **23.** $\frac{1}{6}$.

25. $\frac{27}{4}$.   **27.** $\frac{3}{10}$.   **29.** 20.   **31.** $\frac{9}{2}$.

33. $\frac{9}{175}$.   **35.** $\frac{19}{21}$.   **37.** $\frac{19}{44}$.   **39.** $\frac{119}{135}$.

41. $\frac{10}{27}$.   **43.** $\frac{1}{6}$.   **45.** $\frac{5}{3}$.   **47.** 9.

Problem Set 0.6

1. 135.7416.   **3.** 75.7306.   **5.** 0.0273.   **7.** 0.016.

9. 2.   **11.** 3.   **13.** 5.   **15.** 0.326.

17. 0.00265.   **19.** 984.   **21.** 1.7.   **23.** 0.0002.

25. 79.1.   **27.** 0.0015.   **29.** $\frac{6241}{10,000}$.   **31.** $\frac{3}{500}$.

33. $\frac{12,483}{20,000}$.   **35.** 0.125.   **37.** 0.09375.   **39.** 2.68.

41. 0.6.

Problem Set 0.7

1. 67.78 square centimeters.   **3.** 10.

5. 87.4 centimeters.   **7.** $30°$.

Problem Set 1.1

1. Positive.   **3.** Irrational.   **5.** Set.   **7.** True.

9. False.   **11.** True.   **13.** False.   **15.** False.

17.

19. 4.   **21.** -3.   **23.** 6.   **25.** -12.

27. (a) A constant,   **(b)** A variable.

Problem Set 1.2

1. $4 < 5$.   **3.** $-3 > -5$.   **5.** $0 < x < 1$.   **7.** $x > 0$.

9. $y \geq 4$.   **11.** $4 > 3$.   **13.** Zero, negative.   **15.** $<$.

17. $>$.   **19.** $>$.   **21.** 4.   **23.** $\frac{2}{3}$.

25. 0.14.   **27.** 5.   **29.** -4.   **31.** True.

33. False.   **35. (a)** $40\,\Omega \leq R \leq 60\,\Omega$,   **(b)** $\frac{1}{3} \leq I \leq \frac{1}{2}$.

Problem Set 1.3

1. Commutative law.   **3.** Distributive law.   **5.** Associative law.

7. Commutative law.   **9.** Distributive Law.   **11.** True.

13. False.   **15.** False.   **17.** False.

19. $x + 8$.

21. $12x$.

23. $5xy$.

25. $6 + w + t$.

27. $8 + 4x$.

29. $5z - yz$.

31. $7x - xy$.

33. $xy + xz - xw$.

35. $16y$.

Problem Set 1.4

1. 12.

3. -9.

5. 2.

7. -3.

9. -2.

11. -10.

13. -1.

15. 0.

17. 1.

19. 12.

21. -21.

23. 4.

25. 8.

27. 2.

29. -5.

31. 0.

33. $\frac{6}{7}$.

35. 1.

37. 50.

39. -16.

41. 1.

43. Not defined.

45. 12.

47. 14.

49. 6.

51. 148.

53. -3.

55. 14.

57. 34.

59. $5xy$.

61. x.

63. $6x$.

65. $-24x$.

67. $-4x + 8$.

69. $-\dfrac{x}{yz}$.

71. $\dfrac{x}{yz}$.

73. $15 - (-3)$, $18°C$.

Problem Set 1.5

1. $\dfrac{1}{8}$.

3. $\dfrac{5}{4}$.

5. $\dfrac{x + 1}{x}$.

7. 1.

9. $\dfrac{40}{21}$.

11. $-\dfrac{21}{8}$.

13. $\dfrac{2x}{5y}$.

15. $-\dfrac{6y}{7x}$.

17. $\dfrac{s}{4t}$.

19. $\dfrac{3x}{4}$.

21. $-\dfrac{3xy}{2}$.

23. $-\dfrac{9}{2}$.

25. $\dfrac{y}{x}$.

27. $\dfrac{3}{2p}$.

29. $\dfrac{3xy}{5z}$.

31. $-\dfrac{4}{3}$.

33. $\dfrac{5}{3}$.

35. -3.

37. $\dfrac{y}{14}$.

39. $-6x$.

41. 1.

43. $\dfrac{21}{10}$.

45. $-\dfrac{3}{4}$.

47. $\dfrac{2y}{3x}$.

49. 32.

51. $-\dfrac{4}{3}$.

53. $\dfrac{72}{x}$.

55. $\dfrac{2x}{5y}$.

57. $\dfrac{2y}{xy}$.

59. $\dfrac{18xz}{24yz}$.

61. 0.001824.

63. 316.

65. 0.0257.

67. 2.63.

69. -0.0854.

71. 1.25.

73. 5 diopters.

Problem Set 1.6

1. $\frac{1}{13}$.

3. $\frac{5}{4}$.

5. 8.

7. **(a)** 0.65°C, **(b)** 437.8 cm³.

9. 68°F; 293 K.

11. $\frac{19}{9}$.

13. 478 meters per second.

15. 2% in each case.

17. 1.5 ohms.

Review Problems—Chapter 1

1. Commutative law.   **3.** Associative law.   **5.** Commutative law.
7. Distributive law.   **9.** True.   **11.** True.
13. False.   **15.** False.   **17.** $-\frac{1}{2}$.
19. $xy - 5x$.   **21.** $-10y$.   **23.** -1.
25. -12.   **27.** 1.   **29.** $-20x + 12$.
31. $x - 1$.   **33.** -8.   **35.** $3xz$.
37. 15.   **39.** 5.   **41.** $28x$.
43. $\frac{2}{63}$.   **45.** 12.   **47.** 1.
49. $-12x$.   **51.** $8y - xy$.   **53.** $-\frac{1}{9}$.
55. $-\dfrac{3x}{7}$.   **57.** $-3xy$.   **59.** $\dfrac{5}{9x}$.
61. $-\frac{1}{27}$.   **63. (a)** -6,   **(b)** $-\frac{13}{6}$.
65. (a) 11,   **(b)** 5,   **(c)** 11 **(d)** -5.
67. $-40°$C.

Problem Set 2.1

1. 8.   **3.** -16.   **5.** -16.   **7.** -72.
9. $\frac{1}{3}$.   **11.** $10^6 = 1,000,000$.   **13.** x^{11}.   **15.** y^9.
17. x^7.   **19.** $(x - 2)^8$.   **21.** $\dfrac{x^7}{y^9}$.   **23.** $14x^8$.
25. $-12x^4$.   **27.** x^{16}.   **29.** x^9.   **31.** t^{2n}.
33. x^{29}.   **35.** x^4.   **37.** $\dfrac{1}{x}$.   **39.** $-y^6$.
41. $\dfrac{1}{x^6}$.   **43.** x^{13}.   **45.** x.   **47.** $\dfrac{1}{x^5}$.
49. $a^6 b^6$.   **51.** $16x^4$.   **53.** $16x^{16}y^8$.   **55.** $45y^6$.
57. $\dfrac{a^3}{b^3}$.   **59.** $\dfrac{81}{x^4}$.   **61.** $x^4 y^8$.   **63.** $\dfrac{8y^3}{z^3}$.
65. $\dfrac{4}{9} a^4 b^6 c^{12}$.   **67.** $\dfrac{x^6}{y^{15}}$.   **69.** $\dfrac{x^8 y^{12}}{16 z^{16}}$.   **71.** $-x^{13}$.
73. $16x^8 y^4$.   **75.** $-\dfrac{x^5 y^5}{t^4}$.   **77.** $27x^{10}$.   **79.** 4.
81. $x^{ac} y^{bc}$.   **83.** 31.8.   **85.** 5450.   **87.** 0.747.
89. 81.8.   **91.** 0.127.
93. (a) 18 watts,   **(b)** 8 watts,   **(c)** 0.05 watt.
95. Power is   **(a)** 4 times,   **(b)** 9 times,   **(c)** $\frac{1}{4}$ original value.
97. 7.10.
99. (a) 3.40 cubic meters,   **(b)** a factor of 8.

Problem Set 2.2

1. 1.   **3.** $\dfrac{1}{8}$.   **5.** 27.   **7.** 3.

9. -4.

11. -27.

13. $\dfrac{1}{36}$.

15. $\dfrac{10}{9}$.

17. $\dfrac{25}{4}$.

19. $\dfrac{1}{x^6}$.

21. x^3.

23. $\dfrac{3}{y^4}$.

25. $16x$.

27. $\dfrac{1}{x^5 y^7}$.

29. $\dfrac{2a^2 c^5}{b^4}$.

31. $\dfrac{x^9 z^4}{w^2 y^{12}}$.

33. x.

35. $\dfrac{1}{x^5}$.

37. $\dfrac{8}{x^4}$.

39. $\dfrac{y^{20}}{x^4}$.

41. $\dfrac{2y^4}{x^2}$.

43. $\dfrac{1}{9t^2}$.

45. $\dfrac{x^{15}}{y^{15} z^3}$.

47. t^4.

49. $\dfrac{y^5}{x^8}$.

51. x^3.

53. $\dfrac{y^4}{x^4}$.

55. $\dfrac{5y^2}{8x^2}$.

57. $-xz$.

59. $\dfrac{4x^2 y^{12}}{z^4}$.

61. 0.0189.

63. 14.2.

65. 0.00920.

Problem Set 2.3

1. 6.021×10^{-6}.

3. 1.04×10.

5. 2.62451×10^4.

7. 1.42×10^2.

9. 7.6×10^{-1}.

11. 3.48 or 3.48×10^0.

13. $262{,}000{,}000$.

15. 0.000000000624.

17. 0.2020.

19. $761{,}100$.

21. 5.983×10^{24} kilograms.

23. 6.67×10^{-11}.

25. 2.6×10^2.

27. 6.3×10^{-6}.

29. 4.0×10^6.

31. 2.38×10.

33. 2 newtons.

35. 1.08×10^{21} cubic meters.

37. 2.97×10^{-2} newton.

39. 2.83×10^{-1} ohm.

41. 1.5×10^{-6} farad.

43. 1837.

Problem Set 2.4

1. 6.

3. 2.

5. 7.

7. -3.

9. 4.

11. 2.

13. 0.

15. -5.

17. 2.

19. 0.2.

21. $\dfrac{1}{4}$.

23. -5.

25. 11.

27. $\dfrac{1}{3}$.

29. 5.

31. 8.

33. 0.

35. -1.

37. 0.15.

39. $5\sqrt{2}$.

41. $2\sqrt{3}$.

43. $2\sqrt{2}$.

45. 120.

47. $2\sqrt[4]{3}$.

49. $2\sqrt[5]{2}$.

51. $-5\sqrt[3]{4}$.

53. $\dfrac{\sqrt{14}}{3}$.

55. $\dfrac{\sqrt[3]{10}}{3}$.

57. 5.

59. $-\dfrac{1}{2}$.

61. 4.

63. 4.

65. $\dfrac{3\sqrt{2}}{2}$.

67. $\dfrac{\sqrt{7}}{7}$.

69. $\dfrac{2\sqrt{2}}{3}$.

71. $\dfrac{\sqrt{6}}{2}$.

73. 0.1692.

75. 6.244.

77. 13.

79. (a) 2 meters,

(b) 2.2 centimeters.

81. 3 meters.

83. 0.03 meter.

85. 13 ohms.

87. 3.

89. $\dfrac{3}{2}$.

91. 2.

93. 3070 meters per second.

Problem Set 2.5

1. 5.

3. $\dfrac{1}{9}$.

5. 9.

7. $\dfrac{1}{9}$.

9. 16.

11. 8.

13. -2.

15. 16.

17. $x^{1/2}$.

19. $x^{2/3}$.

21. $x^{3/4}y^{5/4}$.

23. $x^{5/6}y^2$.

25. $x^{9/4}$.

27. $\dfrac{3}{x^{1/2}}$.

29. $(x^2 - 5x)^{2/3}$.

31. x^2.

33. x.

35. x^4.

37. $x^{3/4}$.

39. $3xy$.

41. $x^{3/2}$.

43. y^2.

45. $\dfrac{2}{x^4}$.

47. $\dfrac{8y}{x^6}$.

49. $a^{3/4}b^{3/2}c^{9/4}$.

51. $\dfrac{1}{3x^5}$.

53. $-\dfrac{2}{x^2}$.

55. $\dfrac{x^{1/3}}{y}$.

57. $\dfrac{x^2}{y^2}$.

59. $\dfrac{x^4}{y^2}$.

61. $\dfrac{1}{x^{8/3}}$.

63. $4x^2$.

65. 6×10^{-13} centimeters.

67. $p = 1.75 \times 10^7$ newtons per square meter; $T = 4.99 \times 10^4$ K.

69. 12.2 cubic meters per second.

Review Problems—Chapter 2

In Problems **1–23**, T = true and F = false.

1. F.

3. F.

5. F.

7. F.

9. T.

11. F.

13. F.

15. T.

17. F.

19. T.

21. T.

23. F.

25. 1.

27. $\dfrac{1}{5}$.

29. 9.

31. 10.

33. 8.

35. $\dfrac{1}{4}$.

37. $\dfrac{1}{32}$.

39. x^{13}.

41. $\dfrac{x^{10}}{y^{50}}$.

43. $-32x^5y^{20}$.

45. x^{14}.

47. $-x^5$.

49. $\dfrac{1}{25}$.

51. 3.

53. 0.

55. 13.

57. $\dfrac{1}{9}$.

59. 0.15.

61. $3\sqrt{5}$.

63. $3\sqrt[4]{10}$.

65. $\dfrac{\sqrt{7}}{9}$.　　　**67.** 2.　　　**69.** 6.　　　**71.** $\dfrac{2}{x^4}$.

73. $\dfrac{1}{16t^4}$.　　**75.** $\dfrac{y^6}{x^6}$.　　**77.** $\dfrac{z^2}{x^3y^5}$.　　**79.** $\dfrac{1}{x^2y^2z^2}$.

81. $-27x^{3/2}y^2$.　**83.** $\dfrac{x^8w^8}{y^8}$.　　**85.** $8y^6$.　　**87.** $\dfrac{a^6}{100}$.

89. $2\sqrt{3}$.　　**91.** $\dfrac{2\sqrt{22}}{11}$.　　**93.** 5.64×10^{-5}.　　**95.** 2.8×10^7.

97. (a) 0.064 joule,　**(b)** 0.08 joule,　**(c)** 1.44 joules.
99. It is doubled.

Problem Set 3.1

1. (a) $3x^2$,　**(b)** x^2.　　　**3.** 2, 3, -4.　　　**5.** 2, -2, 1.
7. 4, 1, -2.　　　　　　**9.** 2, $\frac{7}{3}$.　　　　　**11.** a.
13. b, d.　　　　　　　**15.** b, c.　　　　　**17.** b.
19. (a) 1,　**(b)** -4.　**21. (a)** 2,　**(b)** 7.　　**23.** Not a polynomial.
25. (a) 4,　**(b)** $-\frac{2}{3}$.　**27. (a)** 5,　**(b)** -2.　**29. (a)** 0,　**(b)** 56.7.
31. 6.　　　　　　　　　**33.** 8.　　　　　　　**35.** 46.37.

Problem Set 3.2

1. $15x^2$.　　　　　**3.** $-12y$.　　　**5.** $7x - 5$.　　**7.** $-3x^{1/2}$.
9. $\dfrac{2}{x^{1/3}}$.　　　**11.** $40x + 12y$.　**13.** $-14x + 12y$.　**15.** $8y - 5$.
17. $4x - 3y$.　　　**19.** $7a - 8b + c$.　**21.** $2b + c$.　**23.** $5x^2 + 15$.
25. $2xy + 5z - 7$.　**27.** $2x^2 - 9x - 13$.　**29.** $-10 + 4x$.　**31.** $5x + 50$.
33. $-a + 6$.　　　**35.** $29x^2 - 22$.　　**37.** $8a - 11b - 13c$.　**39.** $18x - 24$.
41. $3x - 6 + 6x^2 - 12y - x^3$.　　　**43.** $9 - 100x + 60y$.
45. $-2x - 4$.　　　　　　　　　　**47.** $-(2x^2 - 15x)$.
49. $-(9x^2 + 6x) - 8$.　　　　　　**51.** -2000θ.
53. 1.018 volts.　　　　　　　　　**55.** $x - 2$.

Problem Set 3.3

1. $10xy$.　　　　　**3.** $6x^2y$.　　　**5.** $3a^3b^2$.　　**7.** $-8x^4y^4$.
9. $3xy$.　　　　　**11.** $\dfrac{6y^4}{x^3}$.　　**13.** $a^3b^3c^2$.　**15.** x^3yz^4.
17. $24x^4y^5$.　　　**19.** $90x^{10}$.　　**21.** $a^2b^{21/4}c^{9/4}$.　**23.** $ab^2c^4d^2$.
25. $x^3 - 4x^2 + 7x$.　　　　　　**27.** $-3a^2b + a^3b^2 - a^3b$.
29. $x + 3x^{1/3}$.　　　　　　　　**31.** $-5x^3y + 5xy^3 - 5x^2y^2$.
33. $4x^5y^2 + 8x^4y^4 - 12x^6y^2$.　　**35.** $x^2 + 7x + 10$.
37. $3y^2 - 4y - 4$.　　　　　　　**39.** $9x^2 - 6x + 1$.
41. $16x^2 + 8xy + y^2$.　　　　　**43.** $6x^4y + 6x^3y^2$.
45. $t^3 - 8$.　　　　　　　　　　**47.** $x^4 - 5x^3 - x^2 + 10x - 2$.

49. $x^2 + 2xy + y^2 - 1$.

51. $16x^3 - 4x$.

53. $2xy + y^2$.

55. $6x$.

57. $x^2 + x - 6$.

59. $-15x^2y^2$.

61. $-2x^2 + 3x - 1$.

63. 0.

65. $3.64x^2 + 2.58x - 13.12$.

67. $b + c + 5ab + 5ac$.

69. $r^2 - R^2$.

71. $R_0 + R_0\alpha T - R_0\alpha T_0$.

Problem Set 3.4

1. $\dfrac{b}{2}$.

3. $-\dfrac{2b^2}{a}$.

5. $-c$.

7. $\dfrac{x}{2yz^2}$.

9. $-\dfrac{ac}{b^2}$.

11. $9x^2y$.

13. $\dfrac{x^2}{9y^2}$.

15. $-\dfrac{2y}{7}$.

17. $2x^2 - 3x + 4$.

19. $\dfrac{5}{x} - x + 2$.

21. $2x^2 - 3 + \dfrac{2}{5x}$.

23. $-2 - \dfrac{y}{x}$.

25. $1 + \dfrac{x}{y}$.

27. $\dfrac{3}{y} - x + \dfrac{1}{x^2y^2}$.

29. $-2xy + \dfrac{2y^2}{3x} - \dfrac{7}{3} + \dfrac{4}{3x}$.

31. $-10xy + \dfrac{5y}{2} - \dfrac{1}{y}$.

33. $\dfrac{2}{xy} - 4y^2 - 3xy$.

35. $-2x^6 - \dfrac{6x}{y^2} + \dfrac{1}{y^4}$.

37. $x - 2 + \dfrac{1}{x}$.

39. $\dfrac{xz^2w}{y^3}$.

41. $\dfrac{8x^4y^{15}z^2}{3}$.

43. $\dfrac{4x^8y^{10}}{z^4}$.

45. $x^{1/4} - 3x^{1/12}$.

47. $4y^3$.

49. $2x + 7 + \dfrac{10}{x - 2}$.

51. $1 + \dfrac{1}{x + 2}$.

53. $x - 2 - \dfrac{3}{4x + 1}$.

55. $x^2 + 3x - 2$.

57. $-x^3 + x^2 - 2x + 4 - \dfrac{19}{3x + 5}$.

59. $2x^2 + 1 - \dfrac{2}{4x - 1}$.

61. $x^3 + x^2 - x - 1$.

63. $x + 2 + \dfrac{2x + 1}{x^2 - x + 1}$.

65. $x^3 - x^2y + xy^2 - y^3$.

67. $5x^2 - 13x - 36 + \dfrac{39x + 220}{x^2 - x + 6}$.

69. $1 - \dfrac{T_2}{T_1}; \quad T_1 \neq 0$.

71. $\dfrac{1}{C_1} + \dfrac{1}{C_2} + \dfrac{1}{C_3}$.

73. (a) $2t + 1$, **(b)** 5.

Problem Set 3.5

1. 2500 mm.

3. 8.2×10^{-3} km.

5. 0.15 m.

7. 5 cm.

9. 0.025 m.

11. 6×10^{-6} F.

13. 2.1×10^{-6} μF. **15.** 45 ns. **17.** 6.2×10^{-3} mA.

19. 40,000 g. **21.** 300,000 W. **23.** 200 mW.

25. 0.022 MΩ. **27.** 200 μV. **29.** 13.9 m/s.

31. 6.214×10^{-4} mi. **33.** 8.23 m. **35.** 240 mm^2.

37. 5.1×10^6 cm^3. **39.** 5×10^{-4} m^3. **41.** 25,000 mi/h.

43. 7.5×10^{-6} F. **45.** 331.0 m/s. **47.** 2700 kg/m^3.

49. 9×10^{13} J. **51.** 3.1536×10^9 s.

53. (a) 22.48 m^2,   (b) 54.82 m^3. **55.** 3.8×10^4 L.

57. 3.84×10^{-2} m^2. **59.** 3.94×10^3 torr.

61. \$3.51.

Review Problems—Chapter 3

1. $11x - 2y - 3$. **3.** $-2a + 19b + 4$. **5.** $-8xy + 26$.

7. $9x - 18$. **9.** $3x^2 + 18x - 36$. **11.** $2x^3 y^4 z^7$.

13. $72a^5 b^4$. **15.** $4x^8 y^7$. **17.** $\dfrac{2x^{5/6}}{y^3}$.

19. $2x^{7/4} y^2$. **21.** $x^3 - 2x^2 + 4x$.

23. $-2a^4 b^2 + 2a^3 b^2 - 3a^2 b$. **25.** $x^2 - x - 12$.

27. $x - y$. **29.** $x^2 - 5x + 6$.

31. $x^2 + 4xy + 4y^2$. **33.** $x^3 - 4x^2 + 3x - 12$.

35. $6x^4 - 11x^3 + 3x^2 + 15x - 5$. **37.** $2x^2 - xy + 5x - 3y^2 - 5y + 2$.

39. $x^2 - 12x + 18$. **41.** $\dfrac{ay^2}{x}$.

43. $\dfrac{y^4}{z^2}$. **45.** $-\dfrac{3}{8x}$.

47. $x - 5 + \dfrac{7}{x}$. **49.** $\dfrac{x}{y} - 5y + \dfrac{7}{y}$.

51. $-x - 2xy^3 w^2 + 2x^2 y^2 w$. **53.** $3x^2 + 3x - 1 - \dfrac{2}{2x - 1}$.

55. $x^3 - 2x^2 + 6x - 10$. **57.** $-x^3 + 2x^2 - x + 2 - \dfrac{2}{2x + 1}$.

59. 25 GW. **61.** 25 m/s.

Problem Set 4.1

1. 0. **3.** $\frac{10}{3}$. **5.** None. **7.** Identity.

9. Not an identity.

11. Adding 5 to both sides; equivalence guaranteed.

13. Squaring both sides; equivalence *not* guaranteed.

15. Dividing both sides by x; equivalence *not* guaranteed.

17. Multiplying both sides by x; equivalence *not* guaranteed.

19. Subtracting x from both sides, equivalence guaranteed.

Problem Set 4.2

1. $x = -3.$ **3.** $x = 4.$ **5.** $x = \frac{9}{2}.$ **7.** $x = 24.$

9. $x = 0.$ **11.** $x = -\frac{6}{5}.$ **13.** $x = 2.$ **15.** $x = -14.$

17. $y = 3.$ **19.** $u = \frac{3}{2}.$ **21.** $x = 15.$ **23.** $x = 5.$

25. $x = -\frac{15}{4}.$ **27.** $y = -\frac{15}{4}.$ **29.** $x = \frac{7}{5}.$ **31.** $x = -3.$

33. $x = 2.$ **35.** $y = 11.$ **37.** $z = 2.$ **39.** $x = -2.$

41. $x = 2.$ **43.** $x = \frac{10}{3}.$ **45.** $t = 4.$ **47.** $y = 8.$

49. $x = -\frac{23}{9}.$ **51.** $x = -\frac{1}{4}.$ **53.** $x = -31.$ **55.** $x = -\frac{26}{9}.$

57. $w = \frac{60}{17}.$ **59.** $x = \frac{14}{3}.$ **61.** $z = 3.$ **63.** $x = -\frac{23}{20}.$

65. $z = \frac{1}{13}.$ **67.** $V_2 = \dfrac{P_1 V_1}{P_2}.$ **69.** $R = \dfrac{P}{i^2}.$ **71.** $h = \dfrac{V}{\pi r^2}.$

73. $m = \dfrac{2K}{v^2}.$ **75.** $Q' = \dfrac{Fr^2}{kQ}.$ **77.** $T_2 = \dfrac{VP_2 T_1}{V_0 P_1}.$ **79.** $a = \dfrac{v_0 - v}{t}.$

81. $h = \dfrac{V - 2\pi r^2}{2\pi r}.$ **83.** $t_2 = \dfrac{Q + mct_1 - mL}{mc}.$

85. $E = \dfrac{IR}{1 - e^{-Rt/L}}.$ **87.** $53°C.$

89. 6.7 kg.   **91.** 120 m.   **93.** Yes.   **95.** 40 ft/s.

97. $v^2 = \dfrac{4gh}{3}.$

Problem Set 4.3

1. $x = \frac{8}{7}.$ **3.** $x = \frac{8}{3}.$ **5.** $x = \frac{21}{19}.$ **7.** $x = 1.$

9. $x = \frac{3}{4}.$ **11.** $\frac{17}{9}.$ **13.** 1.   **15.** 7 m, $\frac{35}{3}$ m.

17. $\frac{32}{3}.$ **19.** 24 cm/s.   **21.** 273 cm^3.   **23.** 400.

25. $93.3°C.$ **27.** (a) $90°$, (b) $2°$.   **29.** 259 Hz.   **31.** 543 Hz.

33. $0.05\,\Omega.$

Problem Set 4.4

1. $x + y = 4.$ **3.** $16 = m_1 + 5.$ **5.** $w = x - y - 5.$

7. $4x = y.$ **9.** $r = 2c.$ **11.** $l = 5w - 4.$

13. $m_2 = 0.08m_1.$ **15.** $m_2 = m_1 - 0.08m_1.$ **17.** $x(a + b) = bx + ax.$

19. $2(x + 3) = 5(x - 9).$ **21.** $\dfrac{1}{t_1} + \dfrac{1}{t_2} = \dfrac{1}{T}.$ **23.** $s = vt.$

25. $F = \frac{9}{5}C + 32.$ **27.** $W = mg.$ **29.** 0.25 mL.

31. $(22 - x)°C.$ **33.** $0.72p.$

35. $L = 20 + 5.3W$;   30.6 cm.   **37.** 8 A.

Problem Set 4.5

1. 300.   **3.** 625.   **5.** $4\%.$ **7.** $110\%.$

9. 5.

11. $37\frac{1}{2}$ g of A, $137\frac{1}{2}$ g of B.

13. 112 kg of A, 42 kg of B, 14 kg of C.

15. 65 ft^3 cement, 195 ft^3 sand, 325 ft^3 stone.

17. 18 kL.

19. 420 L of 20% solution, 280 L of 30% solution.

21. 32 mL.   **23.** $7\frac{1}{2}$ km.   **25.** $11\frac{1}{4}$ km.

27. 1500 km.   **29.** 12 min.   **31.** 1027 mi.

33. 3.75 N.   **35.** 5.6 m.   **37.** 421 m.

39. 27°C.   **41.** 12 days, 5.52 m.   **43.** 80 m.

45. 60 cm.   **47.** 500.

Review Problems—Chapter 4

1. $x = \frac{1}{2}$.   **3.** $y = \frac{3}{2}$.   **5.** $x = -\frac{3}{2}$.

7. $z = -\frac{20}{9}$.   **9.** $x = \frac{25}{4}$.   **11.** $u = -\frac{11}{14}$.

13. $x = -32$.   **15.** $x = \frac{37}{21}$.   **17.** $y = \frac{5}{2}$.

19. $Q = \dfrac{EA}{4\pi k}$.   **21.** $C' = \lambda^2(n - 1 - C)$.   **23.** -15.

25. 120.   **27.** 12%.   **29.** 22 ft.

31. 200 mL.   **33.** 18 days.

35. 12 kg of A, 36 kg of B, 60 kg of C.   **37.** $T_0 = \dfrac{l_0 + \alpha l_0 T - l}{\alpha l_0}$.

Problem Set 5.1

1. All real numbers except 0.   **3.** All real numbers.

5. All nonnegative numbers.   **7.** All real numbers.

9. All real numbers.   **11.** All real numbers except -2.

13. All real numbers except $-\frac{5}{2}$.   **15.** 0, 15, -20.

17. 1, 6, $\frac{5}{2}$.   **19.** $7s$, $7(t + 1) = 7t + 7$, $7(7x) = 49x$.

21. 2, $(2v)^2 + 2v = 4v^2 + 2v$, $(x^2)^2 + x^2 = x^4 + x^2$.

23. 12, 12, 12.   **25.** 4, 0, $\dfrac{x^2}{4} + x + 1$.   **27.** 0, $\dfrac{1}{4}, \dfrac{t + 2}{t - 1}$.   **29.** 1, -1, 0, -1.

31. 8, 3, 3, 1.

33. (a) 13.7129,   (b) 27.4258,   (c) 44.7836.

35. 1.59; 5.81; 7.92.

37. y is a function of x; x is a function of y.

39. y is a function of x; x is not a function of y.

41. $P = 4l$.   **43.** (a) $A = \pi r^2$,   (b) $A = \pi d^2/4$.

45. (a) 9.8 m, 9.8 m, (b) no, (c) yes.   **47.** $n = d/12.7$.

49. $V = 4\pi(6 - t)$, where $0 \le t \le 6$.   **51.** $A = 73a^2/4$,

53. (a) 9.81 m/s^2,   (b) 2.8×10^{-3} m/s^2,   (c) no.

55. $\frac{5}{4}$.

Problem Set 5.2

1.

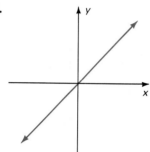

(2, 7)

Q.I

(0, 0)

−1

8 x

$\left(-\dfrac{1}{2}, -2\right)$

−3 (8, −3)

Q.III Q.IV

3.

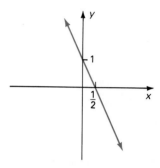

10

12 t

5.

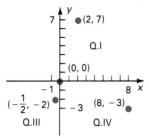

7.

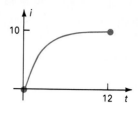

1

$\dfrac{1}{2}$

9.

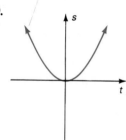

11.

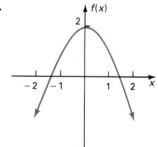

2

−2 −1 1 2

13.

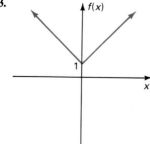

f(x)

1

15.

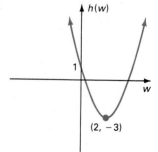

h(w)

1

(2, −3)

17.

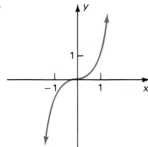

19.

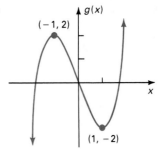

21.

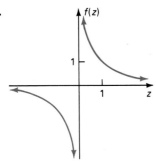

23.

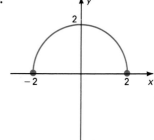

25.

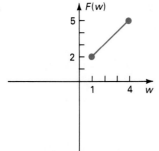

27.

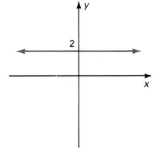

29. Not a function of x.

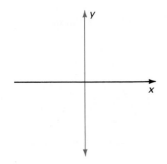

31. Not a function of x.

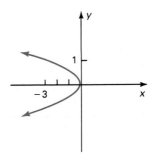

33.

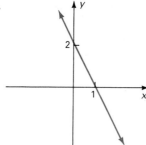

35.

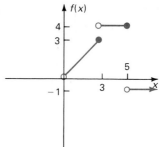

37.

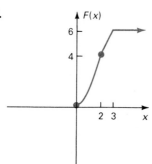

39. (a) 1, 2, 3, 0,   **(b)** all real numbers,   **(c)** all real numbers,   **(d)** -2.

41. (a) 0, -1, -1,   **(b)** all real numbers,   **(c)** all $y \leq 0$.

43.

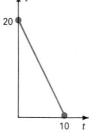

45.

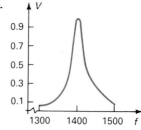

47.

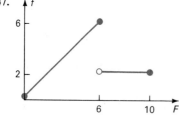

49. t is not a function of V

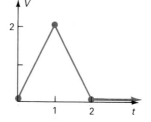

51. $0, -2.$

53.

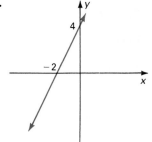

Review Problems—Chapter 5

1. All real numbers.

3. All real numbers except 1 and 2.

5. All real numbers.

7. $7, 46, 62, 3t^2 - 4t + 7.$

9. $0, 3, \sqrt{t}, \sqrt{x^2 - 1}.$

11. $\dfrac{3}{5}, 0, \dfrac{\sqrt{x+4}}{x}, \dfrac{\sqrt{u}}{u-4}.$

13. $-8, 4, 4, -92.$

15. $3 - 7x - 7h.$

17.

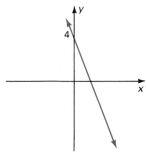

19.

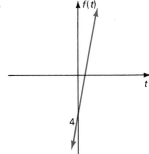

21.

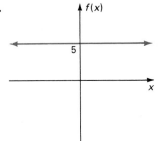

23.

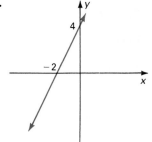

25.

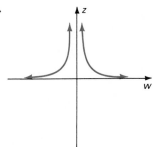

27.

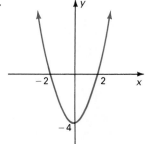

29.

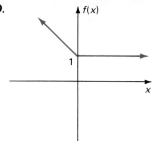

31. $W = 17{,}800 - 1200t$.

Problem Set 6.1

1. $\frac{\pi}{3}$.

3. 135°.

5. 90°.

7. $\frac{\pi}{4}$.

9. $-\frac{11\pi}{6}$.

11. 210°.

13. $-22\frac{1}{2}°$.

15. 4π.

17. 1080°.

19. $\left(\frac{720}{\pi}\right)°$.

21. Second.

23. Fourth.

25. Second.

27. Quadrantal.

29. First.

31. Third,

33. Quadrantal.

35. Fourth.

37. 208°.

39. 50°.

41. 395°, 755°, $-325°$, $-685°$.

43. 581.4°, 941.4°, $-138.6°$, $-498.6°$.

45. 290°, 650°, $-430°$, $-790°$.

47. $\frac{13\pi}{6}, \frac{25\pi}{6}, -\frac{11\pi}{6}, -\frac{23\pi}{6}$.

49. 60°.

51. $\frac{5\pi}{4}$.

53. $\frac{\pi}{2}$.

55. 0.611.

57. 1.470.

59. 135.218°.

61. $-214.401°$.

63. 6.81 km.

65. 14.14 cm.

67. 26.18 cm.

69. 200π m.

71. 69.3 rev/min.

73. 8.7×10^{-4}.

75. 40π, or 125.7.

77. $\left(\frac{108}{\pi}\right)°$, or 34.4°.

79. 40°

Problem Set 6.2

*Answers to Problems **1–13** are in the order sin θ, cos θ, tan θ, cot θ, sec θ, csc θ.*

1. $\frac{3}{5}, \frac{4}{5}, \frac{3}{4}, \frac{4}{3}, \frac{5}{4}, \frac{5}{3}$.

3. $\frac{4}{5}, \frac{3}{5}, \frac{4}{3}, \frac{3}{4}, \frac{5}{3}, \frac{5}{4}$.

5. $\frac{\sqrt{3}}{2}, \frac{1}{2}, \sqrt{3}, \frac{\sqrt{3}}{3}, 2, \frac{2\sqrt{3}}{3}$.

7. $\frac{2}{3}, \frac{\sqrt{5}}{3}, \frac{2\sqrt{5}}{5}, \frac{\sqrt{5}}{2}, \frac{3\sqrt{5}}{5}, \frac{3}{2}$.

9. $\frac{1}{2}, \frac{\sqrt{3}}{2}, \frac{\sqrt{3}}{3}, \sqrt{3}, \frac{2\sqrt{3}}{3}, 2$.

11. $\frac{\sqrt{2}}{2}, \frac{\sqrt{2}}{2}, 1, 1, \sqrt{2}, \sqrt{2}$.

13. $\frac{\sqrt{3}}{3}, \frac{\sqrt{6}}{3}, \frac{\sqrt{2}}{2}, \sqrt{2}, \frac{\sqrt{6}}{2}, \sqrt{3}$.

15. $\sin A = \dfrac{\sqrt{7}}{4}$, $\cos A = \dfrac{3}{4}$, $\tan A = \dfrac{\sqrt{7}}{3}$, $\cot A = \dfrac{3\sqrt{7}}{7}$, $\sec A = \dfrac{4}{3}$, $\csc A = \dfrac{4\sqrt{7}}{7}$;

$\sin B = \dfrac{3}{4}$, $\cos B = \dfrac{\sqrt{7}}{4}$, $\tan B = \dfrac{3\sqrt{7}}{7}$, $\cot B = \dfrac{\sqrt{7}}{3}$, $\sec B = \dfrac{4\sqrt{7}}{7}$, $\csc B = \dfrac{4}{3}$.

17. $\sin \theta = \dfrac{u}{a}$, $\cos \theta = \dfrac{\sqrt{a^2 - u^2}}{a}$, $\tan \theta = \dfrac{u}{\sqrt{a^2 - u^2}}$, $\cot \theta = \dfrac{\sqrt{a^2 - u^2}}{u}$, $\sec \theta = \dfrac{a}{\sqrt{a^2 - u^2}}$,

$\csc \theta = \dfrac{a}{u}$.

19. $\tan \theta = 0.75$, $\sec \theta = 1.25$.

27. $\cos \theta = \dfrac{\sqrt{21}}{5}$, $\tan \theta = \dfrac{2\sqrt{21}}{21}$, $\cot \theta = \dfrac{\sqrt{21}}{2}$, $\sec \theta = \dfrac{5\sqrt{21}}{21}$, $\csc \theta = \dfrac{5}{2}$.

29. $\sin \theta = \dfrac{4\sqrt{17}}{17}$, $\cos \theta = \dfrac{\sqrt{17}}{17}$, $\cot \theta = \dfrac{1}{4}$, $\sec \theta = \sqrt{17}$, $\csc \theta = \dfrac{\sqrt{17}}{4}$.

Problem Set 6.3

1. 0.5299. **3.** 0.9690. **5.** 1.3290. **7.** 4.5483.
9. 1.4169. **11.** 1.8356. **13.** 0.5736. **15.** 0.3988.
17. 0.4142. **19.** 46.6°. **21.** 82.8°. **23.** 31.6°.
25. 0.30. **27.** 1.22. **29.** $\pi/6$. **31.** $\frac{1}{2}$.
33. 1. **35.** 18.4°. **37.** 60°. **39.** $6\sqrt{3}$ V.
41. (a) 163.3 m, **(b)** 153.4 m. **43.** 13.7°.
45. (a) 57.5°, **(b)** 32.5°. **47.** 1.42.

Problem Set 6.4

1. $A = 30°$, $b = 3\sqrt{3}$, $c = 6$. **3.** $B = 45°$, $a = 3\sqrt{2}$, $b = 3\sqrt{2}$.
5. $A = 60°$, $B = 30°$, $a = 4\sqrt{3}$. **7.** $B = 56.5°$, $a = 6.84$, $b = 10.3$.
9. $A = 52.3°$, $B = 37.7°$, $c = 29.6$. **11.** $A = 62.6°$, $a = 47.5$, $c = 53.5$.
13. $A = 65.8°$, $B = 24.2°$, $a = 55.0$. **15.** $B = 77.4°$, $a = 20.3$, $c = 93.0$.
17. $R = 30.3\ \Omega$, $X_L = 19.4\ \Omega$. **19.** $P = 0.85$ W, $P_R = 1.41$ var.
21. 201 m. **23.** 20.3 m. **25.** 5.18 min. **27.** 88.7 m.
29. 42.4 m. **31.** 10.96 m; 33.8°. **33.** 2540 km. **35.** 17.8 m.
37. 2.2 m. **39.** 145 ft, 233 ft.

41. $\dfrac{4\sqrt{3}}{3} = 2.31$ cm. **43.** 275.2 km.

Review Problems—Chapter 6

1. $\dfrac{5\pi}{3}$. **3.** 150°. **5.** $-\dfrac{5\pi}{18}$. **7.** 10°.

9. Third. **11.** First. **13.** 14π. **15.** $\dfrac{3\pi}{2}$.

17. 140°.

19. $\sin \theta = \dfrac{4\sqrt{17}}{17}$, $\cos \theta = \dfrac{\sqrt{17}}{17}$, $\tan \theta = 4$, $\cot \theta = \dfrac{1}{4}$, $\sec \theta = \sqrt{17}$, $\csc \theta = \dfrac{\sqrt{17}}{4}$.

21. $\cos \theta = \dfrac{2\sqrt{6}}{5}$, $\tan \theta = \dfrac{\sqrt{6}}{12}$, $\cot \theta = 2\sqrt{6}$, $\sec \theta = \dfrac{5\sqrt{6}}{12}$, $\csc \theta = 5$.

23. $\dfrac{\sqrt{3}}{2}$.　　　　　　　　　　　　　　　**25.** $\sqrt{2}$.

27. $A = 21.8°$, $B = 68.2°$, $c = 10.77$.　　**29.** $A = 75°$, $b = 1.61$, $c = 6.21$.

31. $B = 44°$, $a = 7.25$, $c = 10.08$.　　　**33.** $B = 57.4°$, $a = 10.78$, $b = 16.85$.

35. 101.3 m.　　　　　　　　　　　　　**37.** 208 mi.

39. 1.81 m, 5.36 m.　　　　　　　　　　**41.** 1.96 mm.

Problem Set 7.1

In Problems **1–5**, answers are in the order: $\sin \theta$, $\cos \theta$, $\tan \theta$, $\cot \theta$, $\sec \theta$, $\csc \theta$.

1. $-\dfrac{\sqrt{2}}{2}$, $-\dfrac{\sqrt{2}}{2}$, 1, 1, $-\sqrt{2}$, $-\sqrt{2}$.

3. $\dfrac{7\sqrt{2}}{10}$, $-\dfrac{\sqrt{2}}{10}$, -7, $-\dfrac{1}{7}$, $-5\sqrt{2}$, $\dfrac{5\sqrt{2}}{7}$.

5. $-\dfrac{\sqrt{3}}{2}$, $\dfrac{1}{2}$, $-\sqrt{3}$, $-\dfrac{\sqrt{3}}{3}$, 2, $-\dfrac{2\sqrt{3}}{3}$.

7. $+$.　　　　**9.** $-$.　　　　**11.** $-$.　　　　**13.** $+$.

15. $-$.　　　　**17.** $+$.　　　　**19.** $-$.　　　　**21.** $+$.

23. $-$.　　　　**25.** $65°$.　　　**27.** $47°$.　　　**29.** $22.6°$.

31. $\dfrac{\pi}{6}$.　　　　**33.** $\dfrac{1}{2}$.　　　**35.** $-\dfrac{1}{2}$.　　　**37.** -1.

39. -1.　　　　**41.** $-\dfrac{2\sqrt{3}}{3}$.　　　**43.** -1.　　　**45.** 1.

47. $-\dfrac{\sqrt{2}}{2}$.　　**49.** $\sqrt{3}$.　　　**51.** $\dfrac{\sqrt{3}}{2}$.　　　**53.** -0.4245.

55. 9.5668.　　**57.** 0.9839.　　**59.** 2.5257.　　**61.** 9.5668.

63. -0.9848.　　**65.** $\dfrac{\sqrt{3}}{3}$, or 0.5774.　　**67.** -0.3327.　　**69.** -0.3420.

71. 0.1577.　　**73.** $135°$, $315°$.　　**75.** $203.0°$, $337.0°$.　　**77.** $60°$, $300°$.

79. $45°$, $135°$.　　**81.** $153.0°$, $207.0°$　　**83.** $40.0°$, $140.0°$.　　**85.** $82.8°$, $262.8°$.

87. $319.8°$　　　**89.** $76.4°$.　　　**91.** $322.0°$.

93. $\cos \theta = -\dfrac{\sqrt{35}}{6}$, $\tan \theta = -\dfrac{\sqrt{35}}{35}$, $\cot \theta = -\sqrt{35}$, $\sec \theta = -\dfrac{6\sqrt{35}}{35}$, $\csc \theta = 6$.

95. $\sin \theta = -\dfrac{\sqrt{33}}{7}$, $\cos \theta = \dfrac{4}{7}$, $\cot \theta = -\dfrac{4\sqrt{33}}{33}$, $\sec \theta = \dfrac{7}{4}$, $\csc \theta = -\dfrac{7\sqrt{33}}{33}$.

97. $\sin \theta = -\dfrac{1}{2}$, $\cos \theta = -\dfrac{\sqrt{3}}{2}$, $\tan \theta = \dfrac{\sqrt{3}}{3}$, $\cot \theta = \sqrt{3}$, $\sec \theta = -\dfrac{2\sqrt{3}}{3}$.

Problem Set 7.2

1. 4.2 km, 45° south of east.
3. $V_x = 122.87$, $V_y = 86.04$.
5. $V_x = 0.53$, $V_y = -10.09$.
7. $V_x = -31.92$, $V_y = -2.23$.
9. $V_x = -38.16$, $V_y = 196.33$.
11. $V_x = 88.17$, $V_y = -121.35$.
13. $V = 8.60$, $\theta = 54.46°$.
15. $V = 6.89$, $\theta = 332.32°$.
17. $V = 5.24$, $\theta = 246.37°$.
19. $V = 3$, $\theta = 180°$.
21. $V_h = 27.14$ m/s, $V_v = 16.96$ m/s.
23. $a_h = 3.83$ m/s^2, $a_v = 3.21$ m/s^2.
25. (a) 28.19 N, (b) 10.26 N.
27. (a) 53.24 N, (b) 37.28 N.

Problem Set 7.3

1. $R = 141.1$, $\theta = 245.1°$.
3. $R = 486.0$, $\theta = 109.4°$.
5. $R = 363.0$, $\theta = 67.5°$.
7. $R = 507.3$, $\theta = 117.2°$.
9. $R = 210.3$, $\theta = 49.5°$.
11. $R = 74.4$ N, $\theta = 66.8°$.
13. 440.0 km.
15. 488.4 km/h, 10.6° north of east.
17. 43.6 km/h, 18.9° south of west.
19. 46.8 km.
21. 8.75 N.
23. 91.8 m/s; 19.3° above horizontal.
25. 5.7° west of south.

Review Problems—Chapter 7

1. $\sin \theta = -\dfrac{6\sqrt{37}}{37}$, $\cos \theta = \dfrac{\sqrt{37}}{37}$, $\tan \theta = -6$, $\cot \theta = -\dfrac{1}{6}$, $\sec \theta = \sqrt{37}$, $\csc \theta = -\dfrac{\sqrt{37}}{6}$.

3. $\sin \theta = -\dfrac{3\sqrt{5}}{7}$, $\cos \theta = -\dfrac{2}{7}$, $\tan \theta = \dfrac{3\sqrt{5}}{2}$, $\cot \theta = \dfrac{2\sqrt{5}}{15}$, $\sec \theta = -\dfrac{7}{2}$, $\csc \theta = -\dfrac{7\sqrt{5}}{15}$.

5. $\tan \theta = -\dfrac{\sqrt{6}}{12}$, $\cot \theta = -2\sqrt{6}$, $\sec \theta = -\dfrac{5\sqrt{6}}{12}$, $\csc \theta = 5$.

7. $\sin \theta = -\dfrac{2\sqrt{10}}{7}$, $\tan \theta = -\dfrac{2\sqrt{10}}{3}$, $\cot \theta = -\dfrac{3\sqrt{10}}{20}$, $\sec \theta = \dfrac{7}{3}$, $\csc \theta = -\dfrac{7\sqrt{10}}{20}$.

9. $-\dfrac{1}{2}$.
11. -1.
13. $\sqrt{2}$.
15. $\dfrac{\sqrt{3}}{3}$.

17. 0.
19. $-\dfrac{2\sqrt{3}}{3}$.

21. $R = 204.4$, $\theta = 15.3°$.
23. (a) 95.3 V, (b) -93.3 V, (c) 87.8 V.
25. $d_x = -200.0$ km, $d_y = -346.4$ km.

Problem Set 8.1

1. 2.
3. $-\frac{8}{13}$.
5. Not defined.
7. 0.
9. 9.
11. 9.8 m/s^2.
13. $\frac{1}{2}$ ohm.
15. $1.2 \times 10^{-5}/°$C.
17. -14 m/s.

Problem Set 8.2

1. $y = 6x - 4$.   **3.** $y = -\frac{1}{5}x - 1$.   **5.** $y = \frac{1}{3}x - 7$.

7. $y = -5x$.   **9.** $y = \frac{1}{2}x + 3$.   **11.** $y = 9x - 23$.

13. $y = 5$.   **15.** $y = x$.   **17.** $y = 2x + 4$.

19. $y = -\frac{1}{2}x - 3$.   **21.** $y = 4$.   **23.** $x = 2$.

25. $y = \frac{1}{2}x + 3$.

27. $y = 2x - 1; m = 2; b = -1$.   **29.** $y = -3x + 2; m = -3; b = 2$.

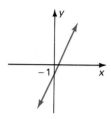 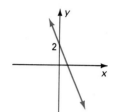

31. $y = 4x; m = 4; b = 0$.   **33.** $y = -\frac{1}{2}x + \frac{3}{2}; m = -\frac{1}{2}; b = \frac{3}{2}$.

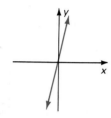 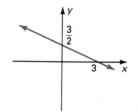

35. $y = 1; m = 0; b = 1$.   **37.**

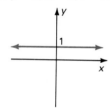 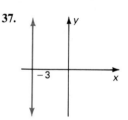

39. $x - y - 3 = 0$.   **41.** $x + 2y - 4 = 0$.   **43.** $4x + 9y - 5 = 0$.

45. $9x - 28y - 3 = 0$.   **47.** $3x - 2y + 24 = 0$.   **49.** 1.

51. -3.   **53.** Yes.

55. **(a)** $s = -\frac{5}{2}t + 70$, **(b)** 10.   **57.** **(a)** $V = \frac{1}{2}i$, **(b)** 5 V.

59. $P = \dfrac{T}{4} + 80$.   **61.** **(a)** Yes, **(b)** 1.8704.

63. **(a)** $v = 2t + 18$; **(b)** No.   **65.** **(a)** $y = \frac{5}{11}x + \frac{600}{11}$, **(b)** 12.

Problem Set 8.3

1. Parallel.   **3.** Parallel.   **5.** Perpendicular.   **7.** Parallel.

9. Neither.   **11.** $y = 4x + 7$.   **13.** $y = 1$.   **15.** $y = -\frac{1}{3}x + 5$.

17. $x = 7$. **19.** $y = -\frac{2}{3}x - \frac{29}{3}$.

21. (a) $y = -\frac{1}{3}x + \frac{1}{6}$, **(b)** $y = 3x - \frac{3}{2}$.

Problem Set 8.4

1. 1.33295. **3.** 1.33089. **5.** 24.9°C. **7.** 35.5°C.

9. 7.670 mm Hg. **11.** 2.4°C. **13.** 8154.3; 0.21. **15.** 24.8.

17. 47.3°C.

Review Problems—Chapter 8

1. $-\frac{1}{3}$. **3.** 0. **5.** $y = -2x + 1$. **7.** $y = \frac{1}{3}x + \frac{11}{3}$.

9. $y = 2$. **11.** $x = 0$. **13.** $y = 3x - 4$. **15.** $y = -\frac{3}{5}x + \frac{13}{5}$.

17. $y = -5x + 7$. **19.** Perpendicular. **21.** Neither. **23.** Parallel.

25. $y = \frac{3}{2}x - 2; 3x - 2y - 4 = 0; \frac{3}{2}$. **27.** $f(x) = -\frac{4}{3}x + \frac{19}{3}$.

29. $s + t - 3 = 0; 0$. **31.** 0.3965; 0.9180.

33. 23.39. **35.** 23.07.

37. 9800 N/m³.

Problem Set 9.1

1. $x = -1, y = 1$. **3.** No solution. **5.** $x = 1, y = 2$.

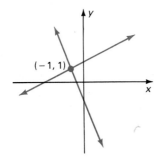

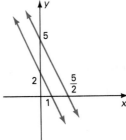

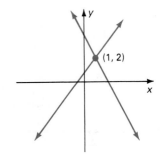

7. The coordinates of any point on the line $y = 6x - 3$.

9. $i_1 = 2.8, i_2 = 0.6$.

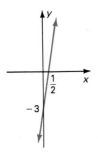

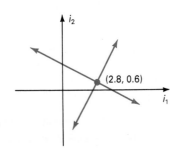

Problem Set 9.2

1. $x = -1, y = 1.$

3. $T_1 = 3, T_2 = 2.$

5. $x = 2, y = -2.$

7. $x = \frac{1}{2}, y = \frac{3}{2}.$

9. $F_1 = 4, F_2 = -5.$

11. $x = 3, y = -1.$

13. $i_1 = 0, i_2 = 18.$

15. The coordinates of any point on the line $2x + 6y = 3.$

17. No solution.

19. $x = 12, y = -12.$

21. $F = 14.7$ N, $N = 49$ N.

23. $i_1 = \frac{13}{7}$ A, $i_2 = -\frac{12}{7}$ A.

25. $v_1 = -28$ m/s, $v_2 = -4$ m/s.

27. $F = 15.0$ N, $N = 40.0$ N.

Problem Set 9.3

1. $x = 4, y = 2, z = 0.$

3. $x = 13, y = 22, z = -1.$

5. $x = \frac{1}{2}, y = \frac{1}{2}, z = \frac{1}{4}.$

7. $x = 0, y = \frac{4}{3}, z = 2.$

9. $x = -10, y = 56, z = -8, w = -98.$

11. $H = 50, T = 50\sqrt{2}, V = 50$ (all in newtons).

13. $i_1 = -2, i_2 = 1, i_3 = -1$ (all in amperes).

Problem Set 9.4

1. 1.

3. 36.

5. $-\frac{25}{12}.$

7. $a - 3b.$

9. $-\frac{2}{7}.$

11. 12.

13. $x = \frac{9}{5}, y = -\frac{2}{5}.$

15. $x = \frac{6}{5}, z = \frac{16}{5}.$

17. $i_1 = 3, i_2 = -5.$

19. $x = \frac{16}{3}, y = \frac{2}{3}.$

21. $x = \frac{7}{16}, y = \frac{13}{8}.$

23. No solution.

25. Since $D = \begin{vmatrix} 1 & 1 \\ 1 & 1 \end{vmatrix} = 0$, Cramer's rule does not apply. But the equations in $\begin{cases} x + y = 2, \\ x + y = -3 \end{cases}$ represent distinct parallel lines and hence no solution exists.

Problem Set 9.5

1. $-16.$

3. 98.

5. $-89.$

7. $x = 4, y = 2, z = 0.$

9. $i_1 = \frac{2}{3}, i_2 = -\frac{28}{15}, i_3 = -\frac{26}{15}.$

11. $x = 1, y = 3, z = 5.$

13. $a = \frac{1}{2}, b = \frac{1}{2}, c = \frac{1}{4}.$

15. $y = 1.$

17. $T_1 = 327.3$ N, $T_2 = 163.6$ N, $a = 1.78$ m/s^2.

Problem Set 9.6

1. 0.

3. 0.

5. 1.

7. 24.

9. $-90.$

Problem Set 9.7

1. 8 m by 5 m.

3. $56.25°$ and $33.75°$.

5. 420 L of 20% solution, 280 L of 30% solution.

7. 3880 L from tank A, 6120 L from tank B.

9. 30 kg of A, 50 kg of B, 20 kg of C.

11. $a = 1, b = -2, c = 0.$

13. 164.5 m.

15. $T_1 = 7.98$ N, $T_2 = 10.26$ N.

17. $T_1 = 493.8$ N, $T_2 = 224.2$ N.

Review Problems—Chapter 9

1. $x = \frac{17}{7}, y = -\frac{8}{7}.$

3. $x = 0, y = 18.$

5. No solution.

7. $x = \frac{1}{2}, y = 1.$

9. The coordinates of any point on the line $2x + 3y = 1.$

11. $x = \frac{17}{20}, y = \frac{31}{20}.$

13. $x = 3, y = 1, z = -2.$

15. $r = 1, s = 3, t = \frac{1}{2}.$

17. 18.

19. $-10.$

21. 3.

23. $-12.$

25. $x = 1, y = 2.$

27. $x = 1, y = -2, z = 1.$

29. 2.5 kg of 20% copper alloy, 12.5 kg of 50% copper alloy.

Problem Set 10.1

1. $x^2 + 8x + 16.$

3. $y^2 + 20y + 100.$

5. $16x^2 + 8x + 1.$

7. $x^2 + x + \frac{1}{4}.$

9. $x^2 - 12x + 36.$

11. $9x^2 - 12x + 4.$

13. $4x^2 - 4xy + y^2.$

15. $9x^2 + 18x + 9.$

17. $4 - 16y + 16y^2.$

19. $x^2 - 9.$

21. $x^2 - 81.$

23. $1 - x^2.$

25. $9x^4 - 25.$

27. $4y^2 - 9x^2.$

29. $36 - x^2.$

31. $x^2 + 11x + 24.$

33. $x^2 + 5x + 4.$

35. $x^2 - x - 2.$

37. $t^2 + 2t - 35.$

39. $x^2 - 5x + 6.$

41. $x^2 - 9x + 20.$

43. $y^2 + y - 6.$

45. $2x^2 + 2x - 12.$

47. $8x^2 - 8x + 2.$

49. $6x^2 - 3x - 3.$

51. $10x^2 - 13x + 4.$

53. $2 + 9t - 35t^2.$

55. $x^2y^4 + 2axy^2 + a^2.$

57. $x^4 - y^4.$

59. $x^2 - 7.$

61. $4x^2 - 4x + 1.$

63. $4x^2 + 24x + 36.$

65. $2xy^2 - 18x.$

67. $a^4b^2 - 4a^2bm^2n + 4m^4n^2.$

69. $x^4 - 16.$

71. 0.

73. $5x^2 - 9x + 11.$

75. $x^3 - 2x^2 - 4x + 8.$

77. $16x^4 - 96x^3 + 144x^2.$

79. $6x + 1.$

81. $x^3 + 6x^2 + 12x + 8.$

83. $8x^3 - 36x^2 + 54x - 27.$

85. $\frac{3}{4}RcZ^2 - \frac{3}{2}RcZ + \frac{3}{4}Rc.$

87. $KE = 2mt^2 + 2mt + \frac{1}{2}m.$

89. $r^2 - R^2.$

Problem Set 10.2

1. $8(x + 1).$

3. $5(2x - y + 5).$

5. $x(5c + 9).$

7. $3x(2y + z).$

9. $x^2(2x - 1).$

11. $x^3y^3(2 + x^2y^2).$

13. $4mx^3(m - 2x).$

15. $3a^2y^3(3a^2 + y^2 - 2ayz).$

17. $(x + 1)(x - 1).$

19. $(x + 1)(x + 3).$

21. $(x - 4)(x - 5).$

23. $(y - 4)(y + 6).$

25. $(y + 6)(y - 6).$

27. $(x + 6)^2.$

29. $(x - 8)(x + 4).$

31. $(y - 5)^2.$

33. $(3x + 1)(x + 2).$

35. $(2y - 1)(y - 3).$

37. $(4x + 1)^2$.

39. $(3 + 2xy)(3 - 2xy)$.

41. $(4y - 1)(y + 2)$.

43. $(2x - 5)(3x + 2)$.

45. $2(x + 3)(x - 1)$.

47. $3x(x + 3)^2$.

49. $4s^2t(2t + 1)(2t - 1)$.

51. $2(2y + 3)(y - 3)$.

53. $2(x + 3)^2(x + 1)(x - 1)$.

55. $2(x + 4)(x + 1)$.

57. $(x^2 + 4)(x + 2)(x - 2)$.

59. $(y^4 + 1)(y^2 + 1)(y + 1)(y - 1)$.

61. $(x^2 + 2)(x + 1)(x - 1)$.

63. $x(x + 1)^2(x - 1)^2$.

65. $2\pi r(r + h)$.

67. $(T_1 - T_2)(c + kT_1 + kT_2)$.

Problem Set 10.3

1. $(1 + y)(x + 4)$.

3. $(y - 2)(x - 4)$.

5. $(2x - 3)(x + 2)(x - 2)$.

7. $(x + y)(x - y)(a + b)$.

9. $(x + 2 + a)(x + 2 - a)$.

11. $(x + 3)(x^2 - 3x + 9)$.

13. $(2y - 3)(4y^2 + 6y + 9)$.

15. $3(2x + y^2)(4x^2 - 2xy^2 + y^4)$.

17. $(a - b)(a^2 + b^2 + 3a + 3b + ab + 3)$.

19. $i = \dfrac{E_2 - E_1}{2R_1 + 3R_2 - 4R_4}$.

21. $x = \dfrac{d - b}{a - c}$.

23. $m = \dfrac{2c}{2gh + v^2}$.

25. $s = \dfrac{7 + at - bt}{a + b}$.

27. $c = \dfrac{Q - mL}{m(t_2 - t_1)}$.

29. $\dfrac{\alpha}{1 + \alpha\beta}$.

Problem Set 10.4

1. $\dfrac{x}{y}$.

3. $\dfrac{a}{bc}$.

5. $-\dfrac{x}{y + z}$.

7. $\dfrac{x + 2}{3x + 5}$.

9. $\dfrac{x + 2}{3}$.

11. 3.

13. $\dfrac{1}{3a}$.

15. $\dfrac{2(2x + 1)}{x - 3}$.

17. $\dfrac{x - 9}{x}$.

19. $\dfrac{3 + m}{4(1 - m)}$.

21. $\dfrac{1}{x + 6}$.

23. $\dfrac{2x + 3}{2x}$.

25. $-\dfrac{t + 5}{t + 3}$.

27. $\dfrac{x - 12}{x - 3}$.

29. $\dfrac{x + 3}{x - 4}$.

31. -1.

33. $\dfrac{x + 7}{7 - x}$.

35. $3 - x$.

37. $\dfrac{1}{2y - x}$.

39. $(a^2 + b^2)(a - b)$.

41. $\dfrac{2x - 1}{3x - 2}$.

43. $3w - 2x + 1$.

45. $\bar{x} = \dfrac{x + 6}{8}$; $\bar{y} = y$.

Problem Set 10.5

1. $\dfrac{7}{xy}$.

3. $\dfrac{4}{x^3}$.

5. $\dfrac{ab^2}{xy^2}$.

7. $-\dfrac{y^2}{(y - 3)(y + 2)}$.

9. $\dfrac{(x - 3)^2}{x^6}$.

11. $-\dfrac{2x - 3}{2x + 3}$.

13. $-(x + y)^2$.

15. $\dfrac{x}{2(x + 3)}$.

17. $\dfrac{(x - 3)^2}{4}$.

19. $\dfrac{x + 3}{x - 2}$.

21. $\dfrac{x + 2}{(x - 3)(x + 1)}$.

23. $\dfrac{x^2 + 4}{x(x - 2)}$.

25. $-\dfrac{(x - 1)^2}{(x + 2)(7 + x)}$.

27. $\dfrac{3xyz^2}{5w}$.

29. $\dfrac{x + 2}{x - 4}$.

31. $4z^2$.

33. $-\dfrac{1}{x(x - y)}$.

35. $\dfrac{6y}{x}$.

37. $\dfrac{2}{9x^2}$.

39. $8x$.

41. $\dfrac{2(c + d)}{c - d}$.

43. $-27x^2$.

45. $\dfrac{x + 3}{x}$.

47. $\dfrac{x - 2}{x - 1}$.

49. $\dfrac{3x - 1}{x + 1}$.

51. $\dfrac{8(x + 2)}{15(x - 2)}$.

53. $\dfrac{FL}{eA}$.

55. It decreases to $\frac{1}{4}$ its original value.

57. $\dfrac{I + 2mr^2}{I}$.

59. $\dfrac{2t + 1}{3t^3}$.

Problem Set 10.6

1. $(x - 4)^5$.

3. $x^2 y^3$.

5. $(x + 3)^2(x - 3)$.

7. $2x(x + 1)$.

9. $\dfrac{x + 5}{x - 3}$.

11. 2.

13. $\dfrac{2x - 1}{x - 1}$.

15. $\dfrac{2y + 3x}{xy}$.

17. $\dfrac{x - 8}{18}$.

19. $\dfrac{3y - 4}{2xy}$.

21. $\dfrac{8x - 21}{(x - 2)(x - 3)}$.

23. $\dfrac{5y^2 - 2x + 3x^2}{x^2 y}$.

25. $\dfrac{5x - 1}{x - 1}$.

27. $\dfrac{x^2 + 2xy - y^2}{(x - y)(x + y)}$.

29. $\dfrac{x^2 + 18x + 9}{2(x - 3)(x + 3)}$.

31. $\dfrac{x + 3}{x + 1}$.

33. $\dfrac{-1}{(x + 1)(x - 1)} = -\dfrac{1}{(x + 1)(x - 1)}$.

35. $\dfrac{x^2 - 2x + 9}{(x + 3)^2(x - 3)}$.

37. $\dfrac{-x^2 - 2x + 1}{(x + 5)(x + 2)(x + 1)}$.

39. $\dfrac{x^2 + 4x - 4}{(x - 2)(x + 2)}$.

41. $\dfrac{2x^2 + x - 1}{x - 1} = \dfrac{(2x - 1)(x + 1)}{x - 1}$.

43. $\dfrac{-x^3 + 3x^2 - x + 3}{x^2(x + 1)(x + 2)}$.

45. $\dfrac{2y^2 - y - 6}{(2y + 1)^2(y + 3)} = \dfrac{(2y + 3)(y - 2)}{(2y + 1)^2(y + 3)}$.

47. $\dfrac{x^2 + y^2 + 4xy}{(x + y)^2(x - y)}$.

49. $\dfrac{9x - 16a - 17}{6}.$

51. $\dfrac{1}{y + 2}.$

53. $\dfrac{x^2 y^2 + 2xy + 1}{y^2}.$

55. $\dfrac{xy}{xy + 1}.$

57. $f = \dfrac{f_0(v_0 U + \epsilon)}{\epsilon}.$

59. $\dfrac{kq_1(x + 2)(x + 3) + kq_2 x(x + 3) + kq_3 x(x + 2)}{x(x + 2)(x + 3)}.$

61. $\dfrac{q_1 r_2 - q_2 r_1}{4\pi\epsilon_0 r_1 r_2}.$

63. $\dfrac{a(R_2 + R_1)(R_2 - R_1)}{kR_1^2 R_2^2}.$

65. $\mathcal{E} = \dfrac{(r_2 + r_1)(\mathcal{E}_1 r_2 + \mathcal{E}_2 r_1)}{r_1^2 r_2^2}.$

Problem Set 10.7

1. $\dfrac{5}{3}.$

3. $\dfrac{1}{x}.$

5. $\dfrac{2x - 3}{x}.$

7. $\dfrac{14}{6x - 1}.$

9. $\dfrac{x(3y - 1)}{y(2x + 1)}.$

11. $\dfrac{x + 3}{2x - 3}.$

13. $x - y.$

15. $\dfrac{x^2 + y^2}{(x + y)(x - y)}.$

17. $\dfrac{3(x + 2)}{x + 3}.$

19. $\dfrac{1}{x}.$

21. $\dfrac{2x + 1}{x^2}.$

23. $\dfrac{y^2 - 2xy + x^2}{x^2 y^2}.$

25. $\dfrac{a(2d + 1)}{2d + 2c + 1}.$

27. $m^2 = \dfrac{m_0^2 c^2}{c^2 - v^2}.$

29. $\dfrac{2av}{2at_r v - v^2 + 2al}.$

31. $k = \dfrac{k_1 k_2 k_3}{k_2 k_3 + k_1 k_3 + k_1 k_2}.$

Problem Set 10.8

1. $x = \frac{1}{4}.$

3. $x = \frac{3}{2}.$

5. $r = \frac{2}{3}.$

7. No solution.

9. No solution.

11. $y = -\frac{1}{2}.$

13. $p = 0.$

15. $x = \frac{10}{7}.$

17. $x = \frac{1}{8}.$

19. $y = 3.$

21. $x = \frac{5}{13}.$

23. No solution.

25. $x = \frac{7}{5}.$

27. No solution.

29. $x = \dfrac{b(4a - 1)}{a(a + 2b)}.$

31. $T_1 = \dfrac{P_1 V_1 T_2}{P_2 V_2}.$

33. $P_2 = \dfrac{V_0 P_1 T_2}{V T_1}.$

35. $q = \dfrac{pf}{p - f}, f = \dfrac{pq}{p + q}.$

37. $R_1 = \dfrac{R_t R_2}{R_2 - R_t}.$

39. $m^2 = \dfrac{p^2}{v^2}.$

41. $R_1 = \dfrac{f(n - 1)R_2}{R_2 - f(n - 1)}.$

43. $149.4 \ \Omega.$

45. $12 \ \Omega.$

47. (a) 500 vib/s,   **(b)** 58.6 ft/s.

49. 13.3 cm.

Review Problems—Chapter 10

1. $x^2 + 12x + 36.$ **3.** $x^2 - 10x + 25.$ **5.** $4x^2 + 16xy + 16y^2.$

7. $x^2 - 64.$ **9.** $9x^2 - 4.$ **11.** $4x^2 - 16y^2.$

13. $x^2 - 2x - 24.$ **15.** $x^2 - 13x + 42.$ **17.** $4x^2 - 14x + 12.$

19. $y^4 - 16.$ **21.** $2x^4 + 2x^3 - 24x^2.$ **23.** $8y - 18.$

25. $16x^3 + 32x^2 - 9x - 18.$ **27.** $2xy^4(3x^2 + 2y^2).$ **29.** $(x - 5)(x - 6).$

31. $(4 + y)(4 - y).$ **33.** $x(x - 8)(x + 7).$ **35.** $(3x - 2)(x + 4).$

37. $2(2x + 5)(2x - 5).$ **39.** $2(z - 4)(z^2 + 4z + 16).$ **41.** $(x^2 + 2)(x + 2)(x - 2)$

43. $2x^3(x - 6)(x - 3)$ **45.** $(x + 4)(2x^2 - 3).$ **47.** $(x + y)(x - y + 1).$

49. $(3z + 2x - 1)(3z - 2x + 1).$ **51.** $\dfrac{6(x - 2)}{x(x - 6)}.$

53. $\dfrac{x - 8}{2x}.$ **55.** $\dfrac{3}{2}.$ **57.** $\dfrac{-x^2 + 3x - 5}{(x - 2)(x - 3)}.$

59. $-3x(x + 1).$ **61.** $\dfrac{3x^2 - 1}{(x - 1)(x + 1)}.$ **63.** $1.$

65. $-2.$ **67.** $\dfrac{x - 2}{x + 2}.$ **69.** $\dfrac{2x}{(x - 1)^2}.$

71. $-\dfrac{3 + x}{(x + 4)(x + 2)}.$ **73.** $\dfrac{x(x + 1)}{x + 2}.$ **75.** $-\dfrac{x + 4}{x + 3}.$

77. $\dfrac{x}{1 + x^2}.$ **79.** $\dfrac{1 - 2x}{x}.$ **81.** $x = -15.$

83. No solution.

85. $C = \dfrac{\lambda^2(n - 1) - C'}{\lambda^2},\ C' = \lambda^2(n - 1 - C).$

87. $B = \dfrac{\lambda D}{2(N - 1)\alpha y - \lambda}.$ **89.** $x = \dfrac{3b - 2a}{a - b}.$

91. (a) Cannot be simplified,   **(b)** $\dfrac{1}{f} - \dfrac{1}{p}.$ **93.** $\dfrac{2\pi^2 me^4}{h^3}\left(\dfrac{1}{n_2} + \dfrac{1}{n_1}\right)\left(\dfrac{1}{n_2} - \dfrac{1}{n_1}\right).$

95. $\dfrac{i^2 L}{2}.$ **97.** $\dfrac{R_1 R_2 R_3}{R_2 R_3 + R_1 R_3 + R_1 R_2}.$

99. $a = \dfrac{bE - P}{EP}.$

Problem Set 11.1

1. $x^2.$ **3.** $2x^4.$ **5.** $3x^8 y^9.$ **7.** $xy^2 z^3.$

9. $\dfrac{x^3}{y^4}.$ **11.** $x^2.$ **13.** $x.$ **15.** $2\sqrt{3}.$

17. $4\sqrt{2}.$ **19.** $2\sqrt[3]{2}.$ **21.** $x^3\sqrt{x}.$ **23.** $2x^2\sqrt[3]{3}.$

25. $x^2\sqrt[4]{xy^2}.$ **27.** $x^2 z\sqrt[3]{yz}.$ **29.** $2ay\sqrt[3]{y^2}.$ **31.** $x^4 y^2 z\sqrt[5]{x^3 z}.$

33. $9yzw^2\sqrt{xz}.$ **35.** $\dfrac{\sqrt{2}}{2}.$ **37.** $\dfrac{\sqrt[3]{50}}{5}.$ **39.** $\dfrac{\sqrt[3]{x^2}}{y}.$

41. $\dfrac{\sqrt{x}}{y^2}.$ **43.** $\dfrac{\sqrt{2xy}}{y}.$ **45.** $\dfrac{\sqrt[3]{2x^2y}}{xy}.$ **47.** $\dfrac{\sqrt[4]{24xy^3z^2}}{2x^2yz}.$

49. $\sqrt[3]{x}.$ **51.** $\sqrt{3}.$ **53.** $2x\sqrt{y}.$ **55.** $\dfrac{\sqrt{xy}}{y}.$

57. $\sqrt[6]{xyz^5}.$ **59.** $x^2\sqrt{xy}.$ **61.** $x^7\sqrt[3]{x^2}.$ **63.** $x^2w^4\sqrt[6]{y^5w}.$

65. $\dfrac{2x\sqrt[4]{x}}{y^2}.$ **67.** $\dfrac{\sqrt{2}}{2}.$ **69.** $\dfrac{\sqrt{xy}}{y^2}.$ **71.** $\sqrt{x}.$

73. $\dfrac{3\sqrt{7}}{7}.$ **75.** $\dfrac{2\sqrt{2x}}{x}.$ **77.** $\dfrac{\sqrt[3]{4}}{2}.$ **79.** $\dfrac{\sqrt[3]{9x^2}}{3x}.$

81. $\dfrac{2\sqrt[5]{x^4y^2z^4}}{3z^2}.$ **83.** $2b\sqrt[4]{8a^3b}.$ **85.** $v = \dfrac{\sqrt{70gh}}{7}.$ **87.** It is halved.

89. $E = \dfrac{\lambda ry\sqrt{r^2 + y^2}}{2\epsilon_0(r_2 + y^2)^2}.$

Problem Set 11.2

1. $3\sqrt[3]{3}.$ **3.** $2x^2\sqrt{2x}.$ **5.** $11\sqrt{3}.$ **7.** $20\sqrt{2}.$

9. $-y\sqrt{x}.$ **11.** $-8\sqrt[3]{2}.$ **13.** $0.$ **15.** $\sqrt[3]{4}.$

17. $-2x\sqrt{2}.$ **19.** $42x\sqrt[3]{3y}.$

Problem Set 11.3

1. $2\sqrt{3}.$ **3.** $18\sqrt{2}.$ **5.** $3\sqrt[3]{12}.$

7. $x\sqrt{6x}.$ **9.** $3.$ **11.** $16x\sqrt[3]{x}.$

13. $2\sqrt{5}.$ **15.** $6\sqrt{2} - 12.$ **17.** $-10 - 2\sqrt{3}.$

19. $-3.$ **21.** $9 + 4\sqrt{5}.$ **23.** $2x + 3\sqrt{x} - 5.$

25. $3xy^3\sqrt{2x}.$ **27.** $31 - 10\sqrt{6}.$ **29.** $46\sqrt{6}.$

31. $2y + 6\sqrt{2y} + 9.$ **33.** $4x^5y^2\sqrt{2y}.$ **35.** $\sqrt[4]{125}.$

37. $x\sqrt[6]{27x}.$ **39.** $3\sqrt[6]{3x^5}.$ **41.** $6x\sqrt[6]{8xy^2}.$

43. $y\sqrt[20]{x^{13}y^2}.$ **45.** $x^2\sqrt[6]{xy^5}.$

Problem Set 11.4

1. $4.$ **3.** $\dfrac{\sqrt{21}}{7}.$ **5.** $\sqrt{6}.$

7. $a\sqrt{2}.$ **9.** $\dfrac{2\sqrt[4]{x^3}}{x}.$ **11.** $\dfrac{\sqrt[3]{12x^2}}{2x}.$

13. $\dfrac{\sqrt[3]{50y}}{5y}.$ **15.** $2 - \sqrt{3}.$ **17.** $-\dfrac{\sqrt{6} + 2\sqrt{3}}{3}.$

19. $-4 - 2\sqrt{6}.$ **21.** $\dfrac{x - \sqrt{5}}{x^2 - 5}.$ **23.** $\dfrac{\sqrt{3}}{3}.$

25. $3 - 2\sqrt{2}$.

27. $\dfrac{5\sqrt{3} - 4\sqrt{2} - 13}{2}$.

29. $\sqrt[4]{6}$.

31. $\dfrac{\sqrt[6]{72}}{2}$.

33. $\sqrt[6]{8x}$.

35. $\dfrac{\sqrt[9]{2y^7}}{y}$.

37. $\sqrt[4]{xy}$.

39. $\dfrac{\sqrt{35}}{5}$.

41. **(a)** $440\sqrt[6]{2}$ vibrations per second, **(b)** $220\sqrt{2}$, 311 vibrations per second.

Problem Set 11.5

1. $x = 27$.

3. $y = \frac{41}{2}$.

5. $x = 4$.

7. $x = -\frac{15}{8}$.

9. $z = 7$.

11. $x = 4$.

13. No solution.

15. $x = 0$.

17. $y = \dfrac{49}{36}$.

19. $g = \dfrac{4\pi^2 L}{T^2}$.

21. 3.9 m.

23. 1.76 m.

25. 67 ft.

Review Problems—Chapter 11

1. $4\sqrt{2}$.

3. $x\sqrt[3]{2}$.

5. $4x^2$.

7. $14\sqrt{2}$.

9. $\sqrt[3]{t^2}$.

11. $\dfrac{\sqrt[4]{24x^2 y}}{2xy}$.

13. $2\sqrt{2}$.

15. $\sqrt{2} - 2\sqrt{3}$.

17. 4.

19. $\dfrac{2\sqrt{7}}{7}$.

21. $\dfrac{3\sqrt[4]{x^3}}{x}$.

23. $3x\sqrt{x}$.

25. x^2.

27. $x\sqrt{3}$.

29. $\dfrac{x\sqrt{y}}{y^2}$.

31. $\dfrac{3\sqrt[3]{x^2 y}}{xy}$.

33. $\dfrac{\sqrt[3]{12x}}{2}$.

35. $\dfrac{\sqrt{6} + 2}{2}$.

37. $x = 10$.

39. $x = 5$.

41. No solution.

43. $x = 10$.

45. $E_{1y} = \dfrac{kq_1\sqrt{35}}{49}$, $E_{2y} = \dfrac{kq_2\sqrt{85}}{289}$.

Problem Set 12.1

1. $x = -2, -1$.

3. $x = 3, -\frac{1}{2}$.

5. $t = 3, 4$.

7. $z = -3, 1$.

9. $x = 6$.

11. $x = 0, 8$.

13. $x = 0, -5$.

15. $t = 0, \frac{7}{3}$.

17. $x = \pm 2$.

19. $x = \pm 5$.

21. $x = \pm\sqrt{6}$.

23. $x = \pm 2\sqrt{3}$.

25. $z = \pm 3$.

27. $x = \frac{1}{3}, -\frac{3}{2}$.

29. $t = \pm\sqrt{15}/2$.

31. $x = \pm\sqrt{7}$.

33. $x = \frac{1}{2}, -4$.

35. $x = 5, -2$.

37. $x = -\frac{1}{2}$.

39. $x = -1$.

41. $t = -5, 1$.

43. $x = 2, 3$.

45. $x = 0, -1$.

47. $x = 4, -2$.

49. $y = -\frac{1}{6}, -\frac{1}{4}$.

51. $x = 7, -1$.

53. $x = -4 \pm 2\sqrt{2}$.

55. $y = \frac{1}{2}, -\frac{3}{2}$.

57. $x = 0, 1, -2$.

59. $x = 2, -1$.

61. $x = 0, 2, -3, 4$.

63. $x = 0, \pm 1$.

65. $x = 0, \pm 8$.

67. $y = 0, -4, -2$.

69. $x = \pm 1, \pm 3$.

71. $x = 0, \pm 1$.

73. $x = \pm 3, \pm 2$.

75. $\pm 2\pi \sqrt{\dfrac{L}{g}}$.

77. $\pm \sqrt{\dfrac{2mgh - mv^2}{I}}$.

79. $t = 10$ s.

81. 4 cm.

83. -4 or 3.

85. 16 cm, 12 cm.

87. 4.5 s.

89. 1 m.

91. $\sqrt{13}$ mm.

Problem Set 12.2

1. $x = -3 \pm \sqrt{10}$.

3. $x = 2 \pm \sqrt{3}$.

5. $y = \dfrac{3}{2} \pm \dfrac{\sqrt{13}}{2}$.

7. $x = -\dfrac{1}{2} \pm \dfrac{\sqrt{17}}{2}$.

9. $x = \dfrac{7}{2} \pm \dfrac{\sqrt{47}}{2}$.

11. $x = -\dfrac{1}{4} \pm \dfrac{\sqrt{17}}{4}$.

13. $x = -1 \pm \sqrt{5}$.

Problem Set 12.3

1. $x = -\dfrac{3}{2} \pm \dfrac{\sqrt{5}}{2}$.

3. $x = 3$.

5. $y = -\dfrac{3}{4} \pm \dfrac{\sqrt{41}}{4}$.

7. $t = -\dfrac{5}{2}$.

9. $x = -1 \pm \dfrac{\sqrt{10}}{5}$.

11. $x = -\dfrac{1}{3} \pm \dfrac{\sqrt{7}}{3}$.

13. $x = \pm 6$.

15. $x = 1, -7$.

17. $z = 0, 2$.

19. $x = -2 \pm \sqrt{2}$.

21. $y = -8$.

23. $x = \dfrac{2}{3} \pm \dfrac{\sqrt{10}}{3}$.

25. $w = \dfrac{1}{5}, 4$.

27. $x = -2 \pm \sqrt{5}$.

29. $x = 0, -\dfrac{4}{5}$.

31. $y = 2 \pm 2\sqrt{2}$.

33. $y = \dfrac{1}{3}$.

35. $s = \dfrac{7}{2} \pm \dfrac{\sqrt{13}}{2}$.

37. $x = \dfrac{3}{2}, -4$.

39. $y = 1, -5$.

41. $z = -1 \pm \sqrt{5}$.

43. $x = \dfrac{1}{2}$.

45. $x = 2 \pm \dfrac{\sqrt{10}}{2}$.

47. $x = -\dfrac{1}{2}, 6$.

49. $x = -10 \pm 4\sqrt{10}$.

51. $x = \dfrac{\sqrt{3}}{4} \pm \dfrac{\sqrt{35}}{4}$.

53. 49; two different real solutions.

55. 0; one real solution.

57. -20; no real solutions.

59. 33; two different real solutions.

61. $x = \dfrac{5y \pm y\sqrt{73}}{6}$.

63. 1.28 s or 2.40 s.

65. 0.91 A.

67. 9 cm³.

69. $m = \dfrac{-D \pm \sqrt{D^2 - 4JS}}{2J}$.

71. $T = 100.1°$.

1. Not quadratic.

3. Quadratic.

5. Not quadratic.

7. Quadratic.

9. (a) $(1, 11)$, (b) Highest.

11. (a) -8, (b) -4 and 2, (c) $(-1, -9)$.

13. Vertex: $(3, -4)$; intercepts: $(1, 0)$, $(5, 0)$, $(0, 5)$.

15. Vertex: $(-\frac{3}{2}, \frac{9}{2})$; intercepts: $(0, 0)$, $(-3, 0)$.

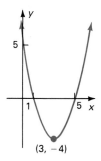

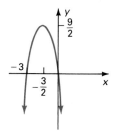

17. Vertex: $(-1, 0)$; intercepts: $(-1, 0)$, $(0, 1)$.

19. Vertex: $(2, -1)$; intercept: $(0, -9)$.

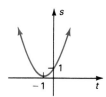

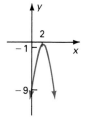

21. Vertex: $(4, -3)$; intercepts: $(4 + \sqrt{3}, 0)$, $(4 - \sqrt{3}, 0)$, $(0, 13)$.

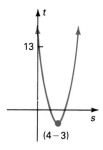

23. Minimum; 24.

25. Maximum; -10.

27. $x = 3$.

29. 50 m by 100 m.

31. (a) $t = 2.50$ s, (b) $s = 8.70$ m.

33. (a) $x = \dfrac{l}{2}$, (b) $M = \dfrac{wl^2}{8}$, (c) $x = 0$, $x = l$.

35. 300 ft by 250 ft.

Problem Set 12.5

1. $x = 3, -6$.

3. $x = -\frac{1}{4}, -\frac{1}{2}$.

5. $x = 6, -2$.

7. $x = 5, -2$.

9. $x = -2$.

11. $x = -1, \frac{13}{10}$.

13. $x = 1, -\frac{18}{5}$.

15. $x = 2, -\frac{4}{5}$.

17. $x = 7$.

19. $z = 4, 8$.

21. $x = 2$.

23. $x = \pm 5$.

25. $x = 0, 4$.

27. $x = 4$.

29. $x = \pm\sqrt{3}, \pm\sqrt{2}$.

31. $x = 2, -\frac{1}{2}$.

33. $x = \pm\sqrt{7/7}, \pm\sqrt{2}/2$.

35. $x = 9$.

37. $x = -4, 1$.

39. $x = \frac{15}{7}, \frac{11}{5}$.

41. $x = \pm 3$.

43. $y = -8, 1$.

45. $6\ \Omega$.

47. 86.8 cm or 33.2 cm.

49. 15 km/h.

51. 23.0 s.

53. 0.316.

55. 1 year and 10 years.

Problem Set 12.6

1. $x = 0, y = 1$; $x = -1, y = 0$.

3. $q = -5, p = -3$; $q = 0, p = 2$.

5. $x = 6, y = -8$.

7. $x = 4, y = 8$; $x = -1, y = 3$.

9. No solution.

11. $x = 3, y = 2$; $x = 3, y = -2$; $x = -3, y = 2$; $x = -3, y = -2$.

13. $x = 2, y = 4$.

15. $p = 0, q = 0$; $p = 1, q = 1$.

17. $w = 3\sqrt{2}, z = 2$; $w = -3\sqrt{2}, z = 2$; $w = \sqrt{15}, z = -1$; $w = -\sqrt{15}, z = -1$.

19. $x = -2, y = -\frac{1}{3}$.

21. 7 by 7 and 3 by 3, or 5 by 5 and 9 by 9 (all in meters).

23. $V_A = \frac{9}{7}$ m/s, $V_B = \frac{30}{7}$ m/s.

25. $3\ \mu$F and $6\ \mu$F, or $6\ \mu$F and $3\ \mu$F.

27. $L = 8$ m, $W = 50$ N.

Review Problems—Chapter 12

1. $x = 5$.

3. $x = 6, -4$.

5. $x = \frac{1}{6}, \frac{3}{2}$.

7. $x = \pm 2\sqrt{3}$.

9. $x = 0, \frac{1}{2}$.

11. $x = 5 \pm 2\sqrt{6}$.

13. $x = -\frac{3}{2} \pm \frac{\sqrt{11}}{2}$.

15. $x = 3 \pm \sqrt{2}$.

17. $x = -\frac{1}{2}$.

19. $x = \frac{1}{2} \pm \frac{\sqrt{11}}{2}$.

21. $x = \pm\frac{3}{4}$.

23. $y = 4, -6$.

25. $z = 2, -10$.

27. $t = \frac{3}{4} \pm \frac{\sqrt{33}}{4}$.

29. $x = -\frac{3}{2} \pm \frac{\sqrt{17}}{2}$.

31. $x = -\frac{5}{4}$.

33. $x = 3$.

35. $x = 4$.

37. No solution.

39. $x = 12$.

41. $x = 64, -27$.

43. $x = -\frac{1}{5}$.

45. $x = -3, y = -4$; $x = 2, y = 1$.

47. $x = -1, y = 4$.

49. Intercepts: $(0, 9)$, $(3, 0)$, $(-3, 0)$;
Vertex: $(0, 9)$.

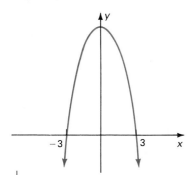

51. Intercepts: $(5, 0)$, $(-1, 0)$, $(0, -5)$;
Vertex: $(2, -9)$.

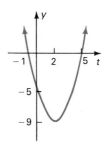

53. -1.

57. (a) 9 s,   **(b)** $t = 3$ s or $t = 6$ s,   **(c)** 4.5 s,   **(d)** 99.23 m.

59. 289 cm^2.

Problem Set 13.1

1. j.   **3.** $-j$.   **5.** 1.   **7.** 1.

9. $9j$.   **11.** $-5j$.   **13.** $4j\sqrt{2}$.   **15.** $\frac{1}{2}j$.

17. $0.3j$.   **19.** $\pi^3 j$.

21. (a) -6,   **(b)** 5,   **(c)** $-6 - 5j$.   **23. (a)** -2,   **(b)** -31,   **(c)** $-2 + 31j$.

25. (a) 0,   **(b)** -3,   **(c)** $3j$.   **27. (a)** 7,   **(b)** $\frac{3}{5}$,   **(c)** $7 - \frac{3}{5}j$.

29. (a) 0,   **(b)** 1,   **(c)** $-j$.   **31. (a)** 7,   **(b)** 0,   **(c)** 7.

33. (a) -2,   **(b)** 0,   **(c)** -2.   **35. (a)** 0,   **(b)** -7,   **(c)** $7j$.

37. $x = 2$, $y = -6$.   **39.** $x = 2$, $y = 16$.

41. $x = -\frac{11}{2}$, $y = -4$.   **43. (a)** True,   **(b)** true,   **(c)** false,   **(d)** true.

45. $x = 2 \pm j$.   **47.** $x = -1 \pm j\sqrt{2}$.

49. $x = 1 \pm j\sqrt{3}$.   **51.** $x = \pm 2j$.

53. $r = -\dfrac{2}{3} \pm \dfrac{j\sqrt{2}}{6}$.   **55.** $r = \dfrac{5}{6} \pm \dfrac{j\sqrt{23}}{6}$.

57. $x = \pm j$.   **59.** $x = \dfrac{1}{2} \pm \dfrac{j\sqrt{15}}{6}$.

61. $R_x = \dfrac{R_2 R_3}{R_1}$, $L_x = R_2 R_3 C_1$.

Problem Set 13.2

1. $-3 - j$.   **3.** $-2 + 3j$.   **5.** $-3 + 5j$.   **7.** $1 + j$.

9. $5 + 5j$.   **11.** $26 + 7j$.   **13.** $16 + 2j$.   **15.** 18.

17. $15 + 6j$.   **19.** $5 + 12j$.   **21.** 29.   **23.** $\dfrac{3}{2} + 2j$.

25. $\dfrac{11}{17} - \dfrac{7}{17}j$.   **27.** $\dfrac{7}{10} - \dfrac{1}{10}j$.   **29.** $\dfrac{2}{17} + \dfrac{8}{17}j$.   **31.** $-\dfrac{3}{2}j$.

33. $2 + 4j$.

35. $\dfrac{7}{61} + \dfrac{45}{61}j$.

37. $6\sqrt{3} + (2 + 4\sqrt{2})j$.

39. $-2\sqrt{10}$.

41. $-38 - 26j$.   **43.** $-16 - 30j$.   **45.** $\dfrac{99}{280} - \dfrac{43}{210}j$.   **47.** $-\dfrac{1}{25} + \dfrac{1}{50}j$.

49. $8 + 6j$.   **51.** $\dfrac{14}{25} - \dfrac{48}{25}j$.   **53.** $-5 - 15j$.   **55.** -1.

57. (a) $\dfrac{7}{5} - \dfrac{1}{5}j\ \Omega$,   (b) 2 V.   **59.** $2 - 7j$.

61. $13 + 8j\ \Omega$.   **63.** $9.02 - 8.24j\ \Omega$.   **65.** $1.48 + 0.23j$.

Problem Set 13.3

1. $4\sqrt{2}(\cos 45° + j \sin 45°)$.

3. $4(\cos 300° + j \sin 300°)$.

5. $5(\cos 90° + j \sin 90°)$.

7. $3\sqrt{2}(\cos 225° + j \sin 225°)$.

9. $\cos 0° + j \sin 0°$.

11. $2(\cos 120° + j \sin 120°)$.

13. $2(\cos 210° + j \sin 210°)$.

15. $5(\cos 270° + j \sin 270°)$.

17. $8.54(\cos 20.6° + j \sin 20.6°)$.

19. $\sqrt{3} + j$.

21. $-3 + 3j\sqrt{3}$.

23. $\sqrt{2} - j\sqrt{2}$.

25. $-3j$.

27. 4.

29. $\dfrac{3\sqrt{3}}{2} - \dfrac{3j}{2}$.

31. $1.932 + 0.518j$.

33. $-0.845 - 1.813j$.

35. A circle of radius 1 with its center at the origin.

37. $a = -3.064,\ b = 2.571$.

39. $-2.719 + 1.268j$.

41. $0.557 - 0.502j$.

43. (a) $6.25\underline{/7.35°}\ \Omega$,   (b) $6.2\ \Omega$,   (c) $0.8\ \Omega$.

45. $51.43\underline{/296.57°}$ V.

47. $3.46 + 10.65j$ V.

49. $42.27°$.

51. -2.

53. $1 - 2j$.

55. $53.5\underline{/56.1°}$.

57. (a) 3.54,   (b) $345.5°$,   (c) $3.54\underline{/345.5°}$.

59. $202.35\underline{/6.92°}$.

61. $133.85\underline{/125.06°}$.

Problem Set 13.4

1. $\sqrt{2}e^{\pi j/4}$.

3. $4e^{5\pi j/6}$.

5. $7e^{3\pi j/2}$.

7. $9.06e^{4.18j}$.

9. $2.8e^{0.25j}$.

11. $3.7e^{2.46j}$.

13. $\cos \dfrac{\pi}{2} + j \sin \dfrac{\pi}{2}$; j.

15. $3\underline{/3\pi/4}$; $\dfrac{-3\sqrt{2}}{2} + \dfrac{3j\sqrt{2}}{2}$.

17. $2\underline{/5\pi/6}$; $-\sqrt{3} + j$.

19. $4\underline{/2.35}$; $-2.81 + 2.85j$.

21. $1(\cos \omega t + j \sin \omega t)$.

Problem Set 13.5

1. $8/60°$. **3.** $6/210°$. **5.** $10/45°$. **7.** $6/225°$.

9. $4/55°$. **11.** $21/71°$. **13.** $\frac{1}{2}/24°$. **15.** $-\sqrt{3} - j$.

17. $2.56 - 0.74j$. **19.** $4.16 + 2.12j$. **21.** $6.59 - 1.48j$. **23.** $5.65 - 4.39j$.

25. $5/340°$. **27.** $6.1 + 3.9j$.

Problem Set 13.6

1. $8(\cos 30° + j \sin 30°), 4\sqrt{3} + 4j$. **3.** $16(\cos 120° + j \sin 120°), -8 + 8j\sqrt{3}$.

5. $\cos 120° + j \sin 120°, -\dfrac{1}{2} + \dfrac{j\sqrt{3}}{2}$.

7. $32(\cos 225° + j \sin 225°), -16\sqrt{2} - 16j\sqrt{2}$.

9. $16(\cos 240° + j \sin 240°), -8 - 8j\sqrt{3}$. **11.** $16(\cos 120° + j \sin 120°), -8 + 8j\sqrt{3}$.

13. $64(\cos 90° + j \sin 90°), 64j$. **15.** $32(\cos 270° + j \sin 270°), -32j$.

17. $1(\cos 150° + j \sin 150°), -\dfrac{\sqrt{3}}{2} + \dfrac{j}{2}$. **19.** $\left(\dfrac{1}{2^{12}}\right)(\cos 0° + j \sin 0°), \dfrac{1}{4096}$.

21. $1, -\dfrac{1}{2} + \dfrac{j\sqrt{3}}{2}, -\dfrac{1}{2} - \dfrac{j\sqrt{3}}{2}$. **23.** $-2 + 2j, 2 - 2j$.

25. $\dfrac{\sqrt{2}}{2} + \dfrac{j\sqrt{2}}{2}, -\dfrac{\sqrt{2}}{2} - \dfrac{j\sqrt{2}}{2}$.

27. $\dfrac{\sqrt{6}}{2} + \dfrac{j\sqrt{2}}{2}, -\dfrac{\sqrt{2}}{2} + \dfrac{j\sqrt{6}}{2}, -\dfrac{\sqrt{6}}{2} - \dfrac{j\sqrt{2}}{2}, \dfrac{\sqrt{2}}{2} - \dfrac{j\sqrt{6}}{2}$.

29. $\sqrt[3]{2}(\cos 50° + j \sin 50°), \sqrt[3]{2}(\cos 110° + j \sin 110°), \sqrt[3]{2}(\cos 170° + j \sin 170°),$
$\sqrt[3]{2}(\cos 230° + j \sin 230°), \sqrt[3]{2}(\cos 290° + j \sin 290°), \sqrt[3]{2}(\cos 350° + j \sin 350°)$.

31. $1, -\dfrac{1}{2} + \dfrac{j\sqrt{3}}{2}, -\dfrac{1}{2} - \dfrac{j\sqrt{3}}{2}$.

33. $\cos 0° + j \sin 0° = 1, \cos 72° + j \sin 72°, \cos 144° + j \sin 144°, \cos 216° + j \sin 216°,$
$\cos 288° + j \sin 288°$.

35. $\sqrt[6]{2}(\cos 15° + j \sin 15°), \sqrt[6]{2}(\cos 135° + j \sin 135°), \sqrt[6]{2}(\cos 255° + j \sin 255°)$.

Review Problems—Chapter 13

1. $20 + 5j$. **3.** $-2 + 12j$. **5.** $-5 + 10j$.

7. 5. **9.** $\frac{7}{5} + \frac{1}{5}j$. **11.** $2 + j\sqrt{3}$.

13. $-5 + 5j$. **15.** $9 - 7j$. **17.** $\frac{14}{5} - \frac{7}{5}j$.

19. $\dfrac{7}{10} + \dfrac{1}{10}j$. **21.** $x = \dfrac{1}{2} \pm \dfrac{3j}{2}$. **23.** $t = \dfrac{3}{4} \pm \dfrac{j\sqrt{15}}{4}$.

25. $8/45°$. **27.** $1/150°$. **29.** $10.6/311.2°$.

31. $3/45°$. **33.** $\dfrac{\sqrt{6}}{2} - \dfrac{j\sqrt{6}}{2}$. **35.** $-1 \div j$.

37. $2.78 + 1.13j$. **39.** $6/90°; 6j$. **41.** $2/225°; -\sqrt{2} - j\sqrt{2}$.

43. $79.626/50°; 51.18 + 61.00j$. **45.** $192/211°; -164.58 - 98.89j$.

47. $\sqrt[5]{2}\,\underline{/45°}$, $\sqrt[5]{2}\,\underline{/117°}$, $\sqrt[5]{2}\,\underline{/189°}$, $\sqrt[5]{2}\,\underline{/261°}$, $\sqrt[5]{2}\,\underline{/333°}$.

49. $5e^{\pi j/2}$.

51. $\sqrt{2}\,e^{3\pi j/4}$.

53. 13.9 A.

55. (a) $1.46 - 0.28j$, (b) $-j\ \Omega$.

Problem Set 14.1

1. $s = kt$.

3. $y = kx^4$.

5. $w = kx^2\sqrt{z}$.

7. 2.

9. $\frac{1}{128}$.

11. (a) $y = 4x$, (b) 24.

13. $\frac{9}{2}$.

15. 96.

17. 2 cm.

19. 256 ft.

21. (a) $W = mg$. (b) 3.34 N.

23. 30 cal.

25. 90 V.

27. 2.3 km/s.

Problem Set 14.2

1. $y = \dfrac{k}{x^3}$.

3. $w = \dfrac{k}{m_1 m_2}$.

5. $w = \dfrac{kx^2}{z}$.

7. $w = \dfrac{kab}{cd}$.

9. 4.

11. 4.

13. (a) $y = \dfrac{36}{x}$, (b) 9.

15. (a) $r = \dfrac{40s}{t^2}$, (b) $\dfrac{160}{81}$.

17. 9.

19. 225.

21. 2250 N; in simplified form, $k = 1$.

23. The result is half the original illumination.

25. 5.73×10^7 m.

27. 6.67×10^{-7} N.

29. $x = \dfrac{12\sqrt{15}}{\sqrt{y}}$.

Review Problems—Chapter 14

1. $\frac{21}{8}$.

3. 27.

5. 1.035×10^8 N/m^2.

7. (a) True, (b) true, (c) false.

9. 32 N.

11. 48,000 cal/s.

Problem Set 15.1

1.

3.

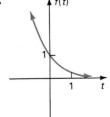

5. 11.0232. **7.** 0.0150. **9.** 81, $\frac{1}{81}$, 3, 469.7632.

11. 12, 6, $\frac{3}{2}$, 0.0355. **13.** 3, $\frac{33}{32}$, $\frac{3}{2}$, 1.0009. **15. (a)** 75 mg. **(b)** 53.3.

17. 0.53 A. **19.** 0.399, 0.242, 0.242.

Problem Set 15.2

1. $\log_4 64 = 3$. **3.** $\log 100{,}000 = 5$. **5.** $2^6 = 64$.

7. $8^{1/3} = 2$. **9.** $\log_6 1 = 0$. **11.** $2^{14} = x$.

13. $\ln 7.3891 = 2$. **15.** $e^{1.0986} = 3$. **17.**

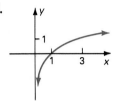

19. 1.9933. **21.** -0.5955. **23.** 2.

25. 3. **27.** $\frac{1}{2}$. **29.** 1. **31.** -2.

33. 0. **35.** -3. **37.** 9. **39.** 125.

41. $\frac{1}{10}$. **43.** e^2. **45.** 2. **47.** 6.

49. 2. **51.** -7. **53.** $\frac{1}{2}$. **55.** $\frac{1}{81}$.

57. 2. **59.** $\frac{5}{3}$. **61.** 0.231. **63.** 16.094.

65. 223.872. **67.** 0.970.

69. -4.1045. **71. (a)** 3.52, **(b)** 1.41×10^{-8}.

73. 24.8 db. **75. (a)** 305.2 mm Hg, **(b)** 5.13 km.

77. 0.01204; 57.57 s. **79. (a)** 0.18145, **(b)** 0.25.

Problem Set 15.3

Since there are different ways to find the values in Problems 1-33, and since the entries in Table 15.1 are only approximations, your answers may differ *slightly* from those given below.

1. 0.6990. **3.** 1.3222. **5.** 1.5441. **7.** 1.3980.

9. 0.3521. **11.** -0.3010. **13.** 4.5155. **15.** -2.7960.

17. 0.1505. **19.** 0.5188. **21.** 0.4471. **23.** -0.2711.

25. 4. **27.** -2. **29.** 2.4771. **31.** 1.0458.

33. -2.2677. **35.** 48. **37.** $\frac{3}{4}$. **39.** 4.

41. -4. **43.** $\frac{9}{2}$. **45.** $-\frac{1}{3}$. **47.** 3.

49. $\log 28$. **51.** $\log_2 \dfrac{x+2}{x+1}$. **53.** $\ln \frac{25}{64}$. **55.** $\log_4 (27\sqrt{2})$.

57. $\log_3 \dfrac{xy}{z}$. **59.** $\log_2 \frac{45}{7}$. **61.** $\ln \dfrac{x^2 y^3}{z^4 w^2}$. **63.** $\log x + \log y$.

65. $\log x - 2 \log z$. **67.** $\frac{1}{2} \log x$.

69. $6(\log x + 2 \log y)$. **71.** $\frac{1}{6}(2 \log x + 3 \log y - 5 \log z)$.

73. $\log x + \log (x + 2) + \log (x - 3)$. **75.** $\frac{1}{2} \log x - \log (x + 2) - 2 \log (x - 3)$.

77. $\frac{1}{2}[2 \log x + 3 \log (x - 3) - \log (x + 2)]$.   **79.** 10.

81. 10 db.   **83. (a)** 3,   **(b)** $2 + M_1$.

Problem Set 15.4

1. 2.0478.   **3.** -0.2058.   **5.** -4.4912.

Problem Set 15.5

1. $x = 1.1402$.   **3.** $x = 4.4022$.   **5.** $t = -3.1699$.   **7.** $t = 0.8518$.

9. $x = 3.5705$.   **11.** $x = 1003$.   **13.** $x = 5$.   **15.** $x = \frac{4}{3}$.

17. $x = \frac{299}{97}$.   **19. (a)** 4634.6 N,   **(b)** 0.24 m.

21. (a) 5×10^{-5} A,   **(b)** 12.88 s.   **23.** $t = 20.48$.

25. 1210.5 cm.

Problem Set 15.6

1. (a) Semilog paper.   **3. (a)** Log paper,   **(b)** $y = \dfrac{600}{x}$.

5. $y = 0.4(3.01)^x$.   **7. (a)** Log paper,   **(b)** $T = 2.0L^{0.5}$.

Review Problems—Chapter 15

1. 5, 13, $\frac{13}{3}$.   **3.** 100, $100e^4 = 5459.8$, $100e^{-3/2} = 22.31$.

5.   **7.** $\log_3 243 = 5$.

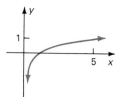

9. $16^{1/4} = 2$.   **11.** $\ln 54.598 = 4$.   **13.** 3.

15. -4.   **17.** -2.   **19.** 2.80265.

21. 16.93551.   **23.** 3.78155.   **25.** -0.45887.

27. 1.55181.   **29.** 3.1101.   **31.** 0.2086.

33. -2.   **35.** $\frac{1}{100}$.   **37.** 9.

39. 3.   **41.** 347.27.   **43.** 0.3958.

45. 1.   **47.** 3.   **49.** 3.

51. $\log \frac{25}{27}$.   **53.** $\ln \dfrac{x^2 y}{z^3}$.   **55.** $\log_2 \dfrac{x^{9/2}}{(x + 1)^3 (x + 2)^4}$.

57. $2 \ln x + \ln y - 3 \ln z$.   **59.** $\frac{1}{3}(\ln x + \ln y + \ln z)$.   **61.** $\frac{1}{2}(\ln y - \ln z) - \ln x$.

63. $2y + \frac{1}{2}x$.   **65.** 1.2619.   **67.** $y = 4(3.5)^x$.

69. 10.0.

Problem Set 16.1

1. $A = 3$, $p = 2\pi$.

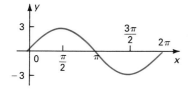

3. $A = 4$, $p = 2\pi$.

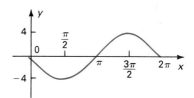

5. $A = 1$, $p = \pi$.

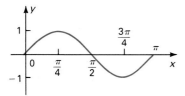

7. $A = 2$, $p = 6\pi$.

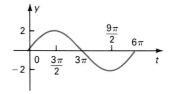

9. $A = 4$, $p = \dfrac{2\pi}{3}$.

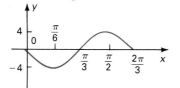

11. $A = 1$, $p = 2\pi$.

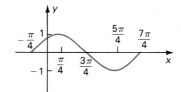

13. $A = 4$, $p = \pi$.

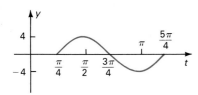

15. $A = 2$, $p = 4\pi$.

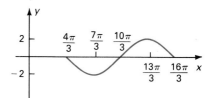

17. $A = 1$, $p = 2$.

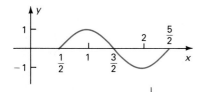

19. Two.

21. (a) 0.72 s, (b) 1.38 Hz.

23.

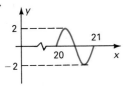

25. (a)

(b) $45°$

Problem Set 16.2

1. $A = \frac{1}{2}$, $p = 2\pi$.

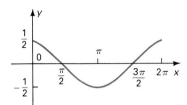

3. $A = 4$, $p = \dfrac{\pi}{2}$.

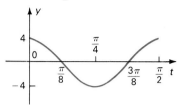

5. $A = 4$, $p = \dfrac{2\pi}{3}$.

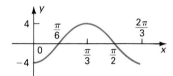

7. $A = 2$, $p = 2\pi$.

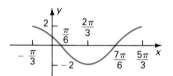

9. $A = 2$, $p = 4\pi$.

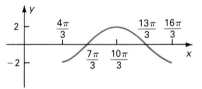

13. y_1 leads y_2 by $\frac{1}{4}$ cycle, or $90°$.

15. $90°$.

Problem Set 16.4

1. $\dfrac{3\pi}{2}, \dfrac{7\pi}{2}$.

3. $0, \pi, 2\pi$.

Problem Set 16.5

1.

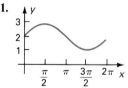

3.

5.

7.

9.

Problem Set 16.6

1. $\dfrac{\pi}{2}$.

3. $\dfrac{\pi}{6}$.

5. 0.

7. $-\dfrac{\pi}{6}$.

9. $\dfrac{\pi}{4}$.

11. $\dfrac{3\pi}{4}$.

13. $\dfrac{1}{3}$.

15. $\dfrac{\sqrt{3}}{2}$.

17. 0.

19. $\dfrac{\sqrt{2}}{2}$.

21. $\dfrac{\pi}{3}$.

Problem Set 16.7

1.

3.

Problem Set 16.8

13. $\left(\dfrac{3}{2}, \dfrac{3\sqrt{3}}{2}\right)$.

15. $(-\sqrt{2}, \sqrt{2})$.

17. $\left(-\dfrac{5\sqrt{3}}{2}, -\dfrac{5}{2}\right)$.

19. $(-\sqrt{2}, \sqrt{2})$.

21. $(-4.68, 1.76)$.

23. $(2, 90°)$.

25. $(2, 300°)$.

27. $(4, 180°)$.

29. $(4, 120°)$.

31. $(6.13, 66.86°)$.

33. $(7.21, 236.31°)$.

35.

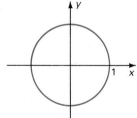

37.

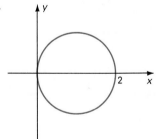

39.

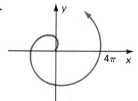

41.

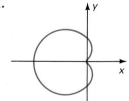

43.

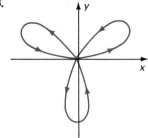

45.

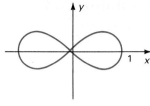

Review Problems—Chapter 16

1. $A = 1$, $p = \dfrac{2\pi}{3}$.

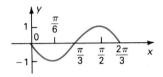

3. $A = 4$, $p = 2\pi$.

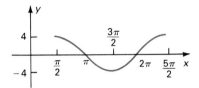

5. $A = 3$, $p = \pi$.

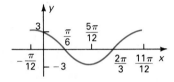

7. $p = \pi$.

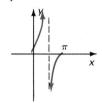

9.

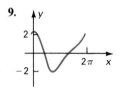

11. $-\dfrac{\pi}{2}$.

13. $\dfrac{\pi}{6}$.

15. $\dfrac{5\pi}{6}$.

17. 0.

19. $-\dfrac{\sqrt{3}}{2}$.

21. 0.8.

23. π.

25. $\left(\dfrac{\sqrt{2}}{2}, -\dfrac{\sqrt{2}}{2}\right)$.

27. $\left(-\dfrac{5\sqrt{3}}{2}, \dfrac{5}{2}\right)$.

29. $(\sqrt{2}, 315°)$.

31. $(4, 180°)$.

33.

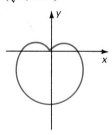

35.

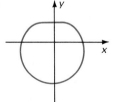

Problem Set 17.2

1. $\dfrac{\sqrt{6}-\sqrt{2}}{4}$.

3. $\dfrac{\sqrt{2}-\sqrt{6}}{4}$.

5. $2-\sqrt{3}$.

7. $\dfrac{\sqrt{2}-\sqrt{6}}{4}$.

9. $\dfrac{-\sqrt{6}-\sqrt{2}}{4}$.

11. $2+\sqrt{3}$.

13. (a) $-\dfrac{7\sqrt{65}}{65}$,   (b) $\dfrac{4\sqrt{65}}{65}$,   (c) $-\dfrac{7}{4}$.   (d) fourth.

15. $-\sin x$.

17. $\sin x$.

19. $\dfrac{1+\tan x}{1-\tan x}$.

21. $\cos 70°$.

31. True.

33. True.

Problem Set 17.3

1. $\dfrac{\sqrt{3}}{2}$.

3. $-\dfrac{1}{2}$.

5. $-\sqrt{3}$.

7. $\dfrac{\sqrt{2-\sqrt{3}}}{2}$.

9. $\dfrac{\sqrt{2+\sqrt{2}}}{2}$.

11. $-\sqrt{2}-1$.

13. $\sin x = \dfrac{4}{5}$, $\cos x = \dfrac{3}{5}$, $\tan x = \dfrac{4}{3}$, $\sin 2x = \dfrac{24}{25}$, $\cos 2x = -\dfrac{7}{25}$, $\tan 2x = -\dfrac{24}{7}$.

15. $\sin x = -\dfrac{1}{3}$, $\cos x = -\dfrac{2\sqrt{2}}{3}$, $\tan x = \dfrac{\sqrt{2}}{4}$, $\sin 2x = \dfrac{4\sqrt{2}}{9}$, $\cos 2x = \dfrac{7}{9}$, $\tan 2x = \dfrac{4\sqrt{2}}{7}$.

17. $\sin x = \dfrac{5}{13}$, $\cos x = \dfrac{12}{13}$, $\tan x = \dfrac{5}{12}$, $\sin \dfrac{x}{2} = \dfrac{\sqrt{26}}{26}$, $\cos \dfrac{x}{2} = \dfrac{5\sqrt{26}}{26}$, $\tan \dfrac{x}{2} = \dfrac{1}{5}$.

19. $\sin x = -\dfrac{3}{5}$, $\cos x = -\dfrac{4}{5}$, $\tan x = \dfrac{3}{4}$, $\sin \dfrac{x}{2} = \dfrac{3\sqrt{10}}{10}$, $\cos \dfrac{x}{2} = -\dfrac{\sqrt{10}}{10}$, $\tan \dfrac{x}{2} = -3$.

Problem Set 17.4

1. $45°, 135°$.

3. $135°, 315°$.

5. $60°, 300°$.

7. $0°, 120°, 240°$.

9. $0°, 180°$.

11. $63.43°, 243.43°$.

13. $38.17°, 141.83°$.

15. $90°, 210°, 330°$.

17. $30°, 60°, 210°, 240°$.

19. $0°, 240°$.

21. $112.5°, 157.5°, 292.5°, 337.5°$.

23. $60°, 90°, 270°, 300°$.

25. $0°, 60°, 180°, 300°$.

27. $30°, 150°, 210°, 330°$.

29. $90°, 210°, 270°, 330°$.

31. $0°, 135°, 180°, 315°$.

Review Problems—Chapter 17

11. $\dfrac{3+4\sqrt{3}}{10}$.

13. $\dfrac{1}{2}$.

15. $\dfrac{1}{2}$.

17. $\dfrac{1}{7}$.

19. $\sin x = \dfrac{15}{17}$, $\cos x = \dfrac{8}{17}$, $\tan x = \dfrac{15}{8}$, $\sin(-x) = -\dfrac{15}{17}$, $\cos(-x) = \dfrac{8}{17}$, $\sin 2x = \dfrac{240}{289}$,

$\cos 2x = -\dfrac{161}{289}$, $\tan 2x = -\dfrac{240}{161}$, $\sin \dfrac{x}{2} = \dfrac{3\sqrt{34}}{34}$, $\cos \dfrac{x}{2} = \dfrac{5\sqrt{34}}{34}$, $\tan \dfrac{x}{2} = \dfrac{3}{5}$.

21. $90°, 270°$.

23. $240°, 300°$.

Problem Set 18.1

1. $C = 31.5°$, $b = 26.19$, $c = 13.83$.
3. $B = 50.47°$, $C = 49.11°$, $c = 7.08$.
5. (a) $B = 26.79°$, $C = 132.75°$, $c = 15.67$,
   (b) $B = 153.21°$, $C = 6.33°$, $c = 2.35$.
7. No triangle.
9. $A = 13.43°$, $B = 27.75°$, $b = 14.28$.
11. $A = 47.6°$, $b = 94.46$, $c = 103.48$.
13. $A = 60°$, $B = 90°$, $a = 8.66$.
15. No triangle.
17. 2479.5 m.
19. 1.2 km.
21. $F = 986.4$ N, $\theta = 70.55°$.
23. 70.8 ft.
25. 25.9 mi/h.

Problem Set 18.2

1. $A = 22.80°$, $B = 129.20°$, $c = 24.23$.
3. $A = 53.83°$, $B = 59.59°$, $C = 66.58°$.
5. $A = 35.89°$, $C = 28.88°$, $b = 22.93$.
7. $A = 77.83°$, $B = 49.06°$, $C = 53.11°$.
9. $A = 81.34°$, $B = 44.62°$, $C = 54.04°$.
11. $r = 11.93$ N, $\theta = 55.6°$.
13. 44.2 km.
15. 24.23 N, 67.2° west of north.
17. 52.41°, 82.10°.
19. 132.29 ft.
21. 37.8°.

Problem Set 18.3

1. 8.21 (units)^2.
3. 32.17 (units)^2.
5. 514.23 (units)^2.
7. 12π cm^2.
9. 36π cm^2.
11. 30π rad/s.
13. 31.8 m.
15. 19.4 rad/s.
17. (a) 40π rad/s, (b) 1120π rad, (c) $\bar{\omega} = 40\pi$ rad/s, $\bar{v} = 80\pi$ cm/s,
    (d) $\bar{\omega} = 40\pi$ rad/s, $\bar{v} = 400\pi$ cm/s.

Review Problems—Chapter 18

1. $A = 97.52°$, $B = 52.48°$, $c = 2.52$.
3. $A = 80°$, $a = 5.91$, $b = 5.64$.
5. $A = 121.86°$, $B = 39.57°$, $C = 18.57°$.
7. $B = 25.66°$, $C = 94.34°$, $c = 23.03$.
9. (a) $B = 13.39°$, $C = 156.61°$, $c = 13.72$,
   (b) $B = 166.61°$, $C = 3.39°$, $c = 2.04$.
11. $\dfrac{3\pi}{2}$.
13. $\dfrac{25\pi}{2}$.
15. 14.48 m, 31.71 m; 22.1 rev.
17. $75\sqrt{3} = 129.9$ (units)^2.
19. 3791 ft.

Problem Set 19.1

1. $x > 4$.
3. $x \le 5$.
5. $x \le -\dfrac{1}{2}$.
7. $s < -\dfrac{2}{5}$.

9. $y > 0$.
11. $x \ge -\dfrac{7}{5}$.
13. $x > -\dfrac{2}{7}$.
15. $\varnothing$.

17. $x < \dfrac{\sqrt{3} - 2}{2}$.

$\dfrac{\sqrt{3} - 2}{2}$

19. $x < 6$.

6

21. $y \le -5$.

-5

23. $-\infty < x < \infty$.

25. $t > \dfrac{17}{9}$.

$\dfrac{17}{9}$

27. $x \ge -\dfrac{14}{3}$.

$-\dfrac{14}{3}$

29. $r > 0$.

0

31. $y < 0$.

0

33. $x \le -2$.

-2

35. $84 < I < 114$.

37.

36

Problem Set 19.2

1. $1 < x < 5$.

3. $x < -1$ or $x > 3$.

5. $-1 < x < 1$.

7. $x < -2$ or $x > 3$.

9. $s \le 0$ or $s \ge 5$.

11. $-3 < x < -2$.

13. $x \le -5$ or $x \ge 4$.

15. $-\frac{3}{2} < z < 4$.

17. $x < -1$ or $x > -1$.

19. $t \le -\frac{3}{2}$ or $t \ge \frac{1}{2}$.

21. $-2 < x < 1$ or $x > 4$.

23. $x < -5$.

25. $y \le -1$ or $0 \le y \le 1$.

27. $x = 0$ or $x \ge 2$.

29. $x < -8$ or $x > 4$.

31. $t \le 0$ or $t > 3$.

33. $x > -2$.

35. $x < -3$ or $-1 < x < 1$.

37. $x < -4$ or $-1 < x \le 1$ or $x \ge 4$.

39. $\frac{1}{4}$ km.

Problem Set 19.3

1. $x = \pm 6$.

3. $x = \pm 6$.

5. $x = -3, 13$.

7. $x = \frac{2}{5}$.

9. $x = \frac{1}{2}, 3$.

11. $-3 < x < 3$.

13. $x > 6$ or $x < -6$.

15. $-1 \le x \le 1$.

17. $x \ge 3$ or $x \le -3$.

19. $-12 < x < 20$.

21. $y \ge 5$ or $y \le -7$.

23. $\frac{4}{3} \le x \le 2$.

25. $-\frac{1}{3} < x < 1$.

27. $t < 0$ or $t > 1$.

29. $x \le 0$ or $x \ge \frac{16}{3}$.

31. The absolute value of any quantity is never negative.

33. (a) $|x - 7| < 3$, **(b)** $|x - 2| < 3$; **(c)** $|x - 7| \le 5$, **(d)** $|x - 7| = 4$, **(e)** $|x + 4| < 2$, **(f)** $|x| < 3$, **(g)** $|x| > 6$, **(h)** $|x - 6| > 4$, **(i)** $|x - 105| < 3$.

35. $|x - 0.01| \le 0.005$.

Problem Set 19.4

1.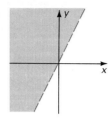

3.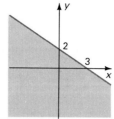

5.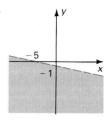

7.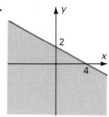

9.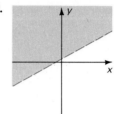

11.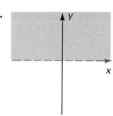

13.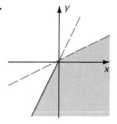

15.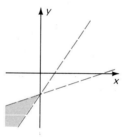

17.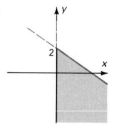

19.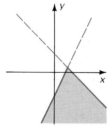

21. No solution.

23.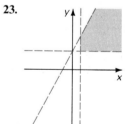

25.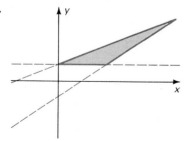

Review Problems—Chapter 19

1. $x < \frac{1}{3}$.

3. $x \le -2$.

5. $t > 1$.

7. $x \ge 40$.

9. $-6 < x < 2$.

11. $y < 0$ or $y > 6$.

13. $x \le -5$ or $x \ge -4$.

15. $-1 < x < \frac{1}{3}$.

17. $-4 < x < 5$ or $x > 9$.

19. $p \le 0$ or $0 \le p \le 8$; more simply, $p \le 8$.

21. $x \le -9$ or $x > -2$.

23. $x < -5$ or $-2 < x < 3$ or $x > 3$.

25. $x = -2, 5$.

27. $x > 2$ or $x < -2$.

29. $0 < x < \frac{1}{2}$.

31. $x \le 0$ or $x \ge 4$.

33. $-2 \le x \le 1$.

35.

37.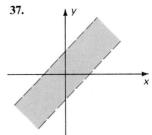

39. No solution.

Problem Set 20.1

1. 3, 6, 9, 12.

3. 2, 6, 12, 20.

5. $0, \frac{1}{2}, \frac{8}{11}, \frac{5}{6}$.

7. x^2, x^4, x^6, x^8.

9. $1, -4, 9, -16$.

11. $1, 0, -1, 0$.

13. $\frac{e}{2}, \frac{e^2}{2}, \frac{e^3}{2}, \frac{e^4}{2}$.

15. n.

17. $3n$.

19. 3^{n-1}.

21. $\frac{(-1)^{n+1}}{n+1}$.

23. 35.

25. 14.

27. 9.

29. $-\frac{3}{16}$.

31. $\frac{7}{4}$.

33. $\sin x + \sin 2x + \sin 3x + \sin 4x$.

Problem Set 20.2

1. 22.

3. -71.

5. Not arithmetic.

7. $\frac{11}{3}$.

9. 4.

11. 110.

13. -360.

15. -108.

17. 620.

19. 135.

21. (a) 44, **(b)** 142.

23. $\frac{32}{15}$.

25. $a_1 = 2, d = 3$.

27. 5050.

29. $a_{16} = 48, S_{16} = 528$.

31. $n = 23, a_n = 36$.

33. 7 cm.

35. $4.65.

37. 110.

39. 3025.

Problem Set 20.3

1. 48.

3. $-\frac{3}{16}$.

5. Not geometric.

7. $-\frac{1}{64}$.

9. $\frac{243}{32}$.

11. 1092.

13. -126.

15. 0.3333333.

17. $\frac{255}{128}$.

19. $\frac{1}{4}$.

21. $10,737,418.23$.

23. $a_1 = 64, a_6 = 2$.

25. -2.

27. $a_1 = 81, a_5 = 1$.

29. 59%.

31. $250(1.065)^n$ dollars.

33. 6561°C.

Problem Set 20.4

1. Div. **3.** 0. **5.** $\frac{11}{4}$. **7.** 0.
9. 0. **11.** $\frac{3}{2}$. **13.** -1. **15.** Div.
17. 0. **19.** 0.

Problem Set 20.5

1. 1. **3.** $-\frac{2}{5}$. **5.** Div. **7.** $\frac{243}{1250}$.
9. $-\frac{1}{2}$. **11.** $\frac{100}{3}$. **13.** $\frac{4}{9}$. **15.** 6.
17. 18. **19.** $-\frac{8}{3}$. **21.** $\frac{50}{27}$. **23.** Div.
25. $\frac{8}{33}$. **27.** $\frac{3209}{999}$. **29.** $\frac{2111}{99,000}$. **31.** 12 m.
33. 100 cm. **35.** 50 m.

Problem Set 20.6

1. $x^3 + 12x^2 + 48x + 64$. **3.** $y^4 - 8y^3 + 24y^2 - 32y + 16$.

5. $243x^5 + 405x^4 + 270x^3 + 90x^2 + 15x + 1$.

7. $16z^4 - 32z^3y + 24z^2y^2 - 8zy^3 + y^4$. **9.** $a^5 - \dfrac{5a^4}{b} + \dfrac{10a^3}{b^2} - \dfrac{10a^2}{b^3} + \dfrac{5a}{b^4} - \dfrac{1}{b^5}$.

11. $1 + \dfrac{6x}{y^2} + \dfrac{15x^2}{y^4} + \dfrac{20x^3}{y^6} + \dfrac{15x^4}{y^8} + \dfrac{6x^5}{y^{10}} + \dfrac{x^6}{y^{12}}$.

13. $x^{100} + 100x^{99} + 4950x^{98}$. **15.** $128x^7 - 1344x^6 + 6048x^5$.

17. $y^{20} - 50xy^{18} + 1125x^2y^{16}$. **19.** $243z^{10} + 135xz^8 + 30x^2z^6$.

21. $455x^{12}y^3$. **23.** $-\dfrac{108,864x^3}{y^5}$.

25. $-160x^3y^3$. **27.** $-10x^6y^3$.

29. $1 - 3x + 6x^2 - 10x^3$. **31.** $1 - \dfrac{y}{2} - \dfrac{y^2}{8} - \dfrac{y^3}{16}$.

33. 7.071. **35.** 7.810. **37.** 3.072. **39.** 2.991.

Review Problems—Chapter 20

1. 48. **3.** $-\frac{1}{128}$. **5.** 25. **7.** $\frac{127}{64}$.
9. 11. **11.** $-\frac{4}{11}$. **13.** $\frac{4}{3}$. **15.** $\frac{243}{128}$ m.
17. 0. **19.** -3.
21. $x^4 - 16x^3 + 96x^2 - 256x + 256$. **23.** $x^9 + 6x^6y + 12x^3y^2 + 8y^3$.
25. $924x^{12}$. **27.** $\frac{4}{5}$.
29. $\frac{4}{3}$. **31.** 156.

Problem Set 21.2

1. 5. **3.** $\sqrt{53}$. **5.** $2\sqrt{2}$. **7.** 7.
9. $\dfrac{\sqrt{5}}{2}$. **11.** 13.

Problem Set 21.3

1. $(x - 2)^2 + (y - 3)^2 = 36$; $x^2 + y^2 - 4x - 6y - 23 = 0$.

3. $(x + 1)^2 + (y - 6)^2 = 16$; $x^2 + y^2 + 2x - 12y + 21 = 0$.

5. $x^2 + y^2 = \frac{1}{4}$; $x^2 + y^2 - \frac{1}{4} = 0$. **7.** $C = (0, 0)$, $r = 3$.

9. $C = (3, -4)$, $r = \sqrt{2}$. **11.** $C = (-2, 0)$, $r = 1$.

13. Circle; $C = (1, 2)$, $r = 3$. **15.** Circle; $C = (0, -3)$, $r = 2$.

17. No graph. **19.** Circle; $C = (7, -2)$, $r = \sqrt{15}$.

21. Point $(\frac{3}{2}, -\frac{1}{2})$. **23.** Circle; $C = (1, -\frac{7}{4})$, $r = \frac{7}{4}$.

25. Two. **27.** None.

29. b, c, d, f, g. **31.** $x^2 + y^2 = 330^2$.

Problem Set 21.4

1. $V(0, 0)$, $F(1, 0)$, $D: x = -1$. **3.** $V(0, 0)$, $F(0, -2)$, $D: y = 2$.

5. $V(0, 0)$, $F(0, \frac{1}{2})$, $D: y = -\frac{1}{2}$. **7.** $V(0, -2)$, $F(\frac{1}{8}, -2)$, $D: x = -\frac{1}{8}$.

9. $V(4, -3)$, $F(4, -1)$, $D: y = -5$. **11.** $V(1, -2)$, $F(\frac{15}{16}, -2)$, $D: x = \frac{17}{16}$.

13. $x^2 = 16(y + 1)$. **15.** $(y - 4)^2 = -8(x - 3)$.

17. $(x + 3)^2 = -8(y - 2)$. **19.** $x^2 = 6y$.

21. $(y + 2)^2 = 4(x + 4)$. **23.** $(y - 3)^2 = -4(x - 2)$, $V(2, 3)$, $F(1, 3)$.

25. $(x - 2)^2 = \frac{1}{3}y$, $V(2, 0)$, $F(2, \frac{1}{12})$. **27.** $(y + 2)^2 = x - 1$, $V(1, -2)$, $F(\frac{5}{4}, -2)$.

29. None. **31.** Two.

33. 6 s; 176.4 m. **35.** Less than 5 cm.

Problem Set 21.5

1. $C(0, 0)$, $V(\pm 5, 0)$, $F(\pm 3, 0)$, $E(0, \pm 4)$.

3. $C(0, 0)$, $V(0, \pm 12)$, $F(0, \pm 2\sqrt{11})$, $E(\pm 10, 0)$.

5. $C(0, 0)$, $V(0, \pm 2)$, $F(0, \pm\sqrt{3})$, $E(\pm 1, 0)$.

7. $C(2, -3)$, $V(2 \pm 3, -3)$, $F(2 \pm \sqrt{5}, -3)$, $E(2, -3 \pm 2)$.

9. $C(2, 0)$, $V(2, \pm 4)$, $E(2 \pm 2, 0)$. **11.** $C(3, -2)$, $V(3 \pm 5, -2)$, $E(3, -2 \pm 3)$.

13. $\dfrac{x^2}{36} + \dfrac{y^2}{11} = 1$. **15.** $\dfrac{x^2}{68} + \dfrac{(y - 1)^2}{4} = 1$.

17. $\dfrac{x^2}{64} + \dfrac{y^2}{16} = 1$. **19.** $\dfrac{x^2}{\frac{25}{4}} + \dfrac{(y + 8)^2}{64} = 1$.

21. $\dfrac{(x + 2)^2}{4} + \dfrac{(y + 1)^2}{53} = 1$.

Problem Set 21.6

1. $C(0, 0)$ $V(\pm 4, 0)$, $F(\pm 5, 0)$, $E(0, \pm 3)$, $A: y = \pm\frac{3}{4}x$.

3. $C(0, 0)$, $V(0, \pm 6)$, $F(0, \pm\sqrt{37})$, $E(\pm 1, 0)$, $A: y = \pm 6x$.

5. $C(0, 0)$, $V(\pm 2, 0)$, $F(\pm 2\sqrt{2}, 0)$, $E(0, \pm 2)$, $A: y = \pm x$.

7. $C(2, -3)$, $V(2, -3\pm5)$, $F(2, -3\pm\sqrt{29})$, $E(2\pm2, -3)$, $A: y = -3 \pm \frac{5}{2}(x-2)$.

9. $C(2, -1)$, $V(2\pm4, -1)$, $F(2\pm5, -1)$, $E(2, -1\pm3)$, $A: y = -1 \pm \frac{3}{4}(x-2)$.

11. $\dfrac{y^2}{4} - \dfrac{x^2}{5} = 1$.   **13.** $\dfrac{x^2}{16} - y^2 = 1$.   **15.** $\dfrac{(y-2)^2}{4} - \dfrac{(x+4)^2}{12} = 1$.

17. $\dfrac{(x+2)^2}{4} - \dfrac{(y-4)^2}{\frac{9}{4}} = 1$.   **19.** $\dfrac{(y-4)^2}{4} - \dfrac{x^2}{5} = 1$.   **21.** $x = 0$, $y = 0$.

23. $x = 0$, $y = 0$.   **25.** $x = 0$, $y = 0$.

27.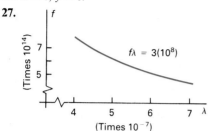

29.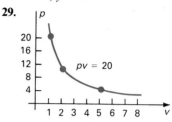

Problem Set 21.7

1. Circle.   **3.** Parabola.   **5.** Parabola.   **7.** Hyperbola.

9. Ellipse.   **11.** Hyperbola.   **13.** Ellipse.   **15.** Ellipse.

17. Parabola.   **19.** Hyperbola.

Problem Set 21.8

1.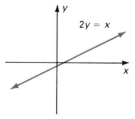

3.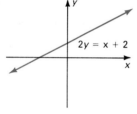

5. $y = -x^2 + 5x - 6$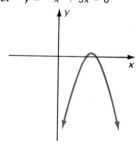

7.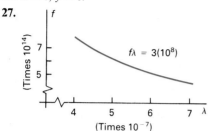

9. $(x+1)^2 + (y+2)^2 = 4$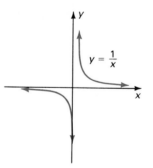

11. $x = \dfrac{1-t}{t}$, $y = 1 - t$.

13. $x = \dfrac{2t}{1 + t^3}, \; y = \dfrac{2t^2}{1 + t^3}.$

15. $x = \dfrac{1 - t}{1 + 2t}, \; y = \dfrac{t(1 - t)}{1 + 2t}.$

21. (a) 689.4 m; 534.4 m, **(b)** 39.35 s, **(c)** 9043 m, **(d)** 1897 m when $t = 19.68$ s.

23. 1.54 s.

Review Problems—Chapter 21

1. $2\sqrt{5}.$ **3.** 10.

5. $x^2 + y^2 = 25$; $x^2 + y^2 - 25 = 0.$

7. $(x - 1)^2 + (y + 1)^2 = \frac{1}{4}$; $x^2 + y^2 - 2x + 2y + \frac{7}{4} = 0.$

9. Circle, $C(0, 0)$, $r = 4.$ **11.** Circle, $C(-2, 1)$, $r = \sqrt{7}.$

13. Hyperbola, $C(0, 0)$, $V(\pm 10, 0)$, $F(\pm\sqrt{109}, 0)$, endpts. of conjugate axis $(0, \pm 3)$, asym. $y = \pm\frac{3}{10}x.$

15. Ellipse, $C(0, 0)$, $V(0, \pm 6)$, $F(0, \pm\sqrt{35})$, endpts. of minor axis $(\pm 1, 0).$

17. Parabola, $V(0, 0)$, $F(0, -\frac{5}{8})$, directrix $y = \frac{5}{8}.$

19. Circle, $C(0, 0)$, $r = 1/\sqrt{6}.$

21. Hyperbola, $C(-1, 0)$, $V(-1 \pm 2, 0)$, $F(-1 \pm 2\sqrt{5}, 0)$, endpts. of conjugate axis $(-1, \pm 4)$, asym. $y = \pm 2(x + 1).$

23. Parabola, $V(0, 2)$, $F(3, 2)$, directrix $x = -3.$

25. Hyperbola, $C(0, 0)$, asym. $x = 0$, $y = 0.$

27. Ellipse, $C(-5, 2)$, $V(-5, 2 \pm 2\sqrt{2})$, $F(-5, 2 \pm 2)$, endpts. of minor axis $(-5 \pm 2, 2).$

29. Circle, $C(-\frac{5}{2}, 3)$, $r = \dfrac{\sqrt{53}}{2}.$ **31.** Point $(1, \frac{1}{3}).$

33. Parabola, $V(-\frac{5}{2}, 1)$, $F(-2, 1)$, directrix $x = -3.$

35. Hyperbola, $C(-1, 0)$, $V(-1, \pm 2)$, $F(-1, \pm 2\sqrt{2})$, endpts. of conjugate axis $(-1 \pm 2, 0).$

37. $(x - 2)^2 = 12(y - 1).$ **39.** $\dfrac{(x + 2)^2}{9} + \dfrac{(y - 3)^2}{25} = 1.$ **41.** $x = \dfrac{3t}{2 - t^3}, \; y = \dfrac{3t^2}{2 - t^3}.$

Index

Note: Pages to appendices are preceded by the appendix letter followed by a colon.

X

x-Axis of coordinate system, 194
x-Intercept, 205, 302, 450
xy-Plane, 194

Y

y-Axis, 194,

Z

Year, light, 136
y-Intercept of line, 299

Zero exponent, 78–83
Zero of function, 187, 189
Zero vector, 270